T0399795

THE ROUTLEDGE HANDBOOK OF COMPARATIVE ECONOMIC SYSTEMS

The Routledge Handbook of Comparative Economic Systems examines the institutional bases of economies, and the different ways in which economic activity can function, be organized and governed. It examines the complexity of this academic and research field, assessing the place of comparative economic studies within economics, paying due attention to future perspectives and presenting critically important questions, analytical methods and relative approaches. This complements the recent revival of the systemic view of economic governance, which was accelerated by the COVID-19 pandemic and likely even more by the renewed East-West clash epitomized by the Russian invasion of Ukraine and the West's reaction to it.

The Handbook is divided into five parts. Each part deals with an issue of relevance for the discipline. The first and second parts look at the subject, content and approach of the discipline and its comparative method. The third part looks at the idiosyncratic nature of different economic systems and their constituent elements. The fourth part considers the outcomes that different economic systems generate and how these outcomes change following the evolution and transformation of economic systems. The last part takes stock and looks ahead at the challenges from a theoretical and applied perspective and the exogenous and endogenous factors promoting the advancement of the discipline, including the interaction between and competition among varied approaches and opposing paradigms.

The Handbook brings together leading international contributors to reflect on the relevant debates and case or country studies, provides a balanced overview of the results achieved and current knowledge, as well as evolving issues and new fields of research. The book provides researchers, students and analysts with a complete, critical and forward-looking presentation and analysis of the content, development, challenges and perspectives of comparative economic studies.

Bruno Dallago is Senior Professor of Economics at the Department of Economics and Management, University of Trento, Italy.

Sara Casagrande is a Post-Doc Research Fellow in Comparative European Studies at the University of Trento, Italy.

THE ROUTLEDGE HANDBOOK OF COMPARATIVE ECONOMIC SYSTEMS

Edited by
Bruno Dallago and Sara Casagrande

Routledge
Taylor & Francis Group

LONDON AND NEW YORK

Designed cover image: Getty Images/101cats

First published 2023
by Routledge
4 Park Square, Milton Park, Abingdon, Oxon OX14 4RN

and by Routledge
605 Third Avenue, New York, NY 10158

Routledge is an imprint of the Taylor & Francis Group, an informa business

British Library Cataloguing-in-Publication Data
A catalogue record for this book is available from the British Library

Library of Congress Cataloging-in-Publication Data
Names: Dallago, Bruno, 1950- editor. | Casagrande, Sara, editor.
Title: The Routledge handbook of comparative economic systems / edited by Bruno Dallago and Sara Casagrande.
Description: 1 Edition. | New York, NY : Routledge, 2023. | Series: Routledge international handbooks | Includes bibliographical references and index.
Identifiers: LCCN 2022028273 (print) | LCCN 2022028274 (ebook) | ISBN 9780367700454 (hardback) | ISBN 9780367700478 (paperback) | ISBN 9781003144366 (ebook)
Subjects: LCSH: Comparative economics. | Economics.
Classification: LCC HB90 .R68 2023 (print) | LCC HB90 (ebook) | DDC 338.9--dc23/eng/20220722
LC record available at https://lccn.loc.gov/2022028273
LC ebook record available at https://lccn.loc.gov/2022028274

ISBN: 978-0-367-70045-4 (hbk)
ISBN: 978-0-367-70047-8 (pbk)
ISBN: 978-1-003-14436-6 (ebk)

DOI: 10.4324/9781003144366

Typeset in Bembo
by KnowledgeWorks Global Ltd.

CONTENTS

LIST OF FIGURES

LIST OF TABLES

LIST OF CHARTS

LIST OF CONTRIBUTORS

Paul Dragos ALIGICA is Professor in the Department of Economic and Administrative Sciences at the University of Bucharest and Senior Research Fellow at Mercatus Center at George Mason University where he teaches in the graduate program of the Economics Department. His academic background includes degrees in economics, sociology and a PhD in political sciences (with a focus on Institutional Theory and Political Economy) at the Workshop in Political Theory and Policy Analysis at Indiana University Bloomington. Aligica's most recent publications are *Comparative Economic Systems* (co-editor with P. Boettke, Edward Elgar International Library of Critical Writings in Economics Series) and *Public Entrepreneurship, Citizenship, and Self-Governance* (Cambridge University Press).

Wladimir ANDREFF is Honorary Professor, University Paris 1 Panthéon-Sorbonne; President of the Scientific Council of the Observatory of the Sports Economy, Ministry for Sports; recipient of the 2019 Chelladurai Award, European Association of Sport Management and Honorary President of the International Association of Sport Economists and of the European Sports Economics Association, former President of the French Economic Association and of the European Association for Comparative Economic Studies. He is author of 17 books, 460 scientific articles and editor of 19 books, published in 18 languages on economic systems, sports economics and international economics including *An Economic Roadmap to the Dark Side of Sport* (Palgrave Macmillan, 2019) and *Comparative Economic Studies in Europe: A Thirty-Year Review* (Palgrave Macmillan, 2021).

Pierfederico ASDRUBALI is Senior Economist at the European Commission and has held positions at the Bank of Italy and at the Italian Presidency of the Council of Ministers. He holds a doctorate in Political Economy from the University of Rome, as well as a PhD in economics from Brown University. He has taught at Brown University, Michigan State University and John Cabot University. His publications have appeared in such journals as the *Journal of Monetary Economics, Quarterly Journal of Economics, Economic Theory* and *Quantitative Economics*. Professor Asdrubali's main interests revolve around the economics of the EU.

Pranab BARDHAN is Distinguished Emeritus Professor of Economics at University of California, Berkeley. He was educated at Presidency College, Kolkata and Cambridge

University, England. He had been at the faculty of MIT, Indian Statistical Institute and Delhi School of Economics before joining Berkeley. He has been Visiting Professor/Fellow at Trinity College, Cambridge, St. Catherine's College, Oxford and London School of Economics. He held the Distinguished Fulbright Siena Chair at the University of Siena, Italy in 2008–2009. He was the BP Centennial Professor at London School of Economics for 2010 and 2011. He is the author of 16 books and editor of 14 other books, and published more than 150 journal articles. More information about him may be found in his website: https://eml.berkeley.edu/~webfac/bardhan/bardhan.htm.

Arielle BEYAERT has been Professor of Econometrics at the University of Murcia, where she currently is an Honorary Collaborating Professor since her recent retirement. She specialized in econometrics at the University of Brussels and the University of Michigan (Ann Arbor). She has devoted all her scientific activity to econometrics, more specifically to nonlinear and non-stationary econometrics, and especially to its applications in the field of international economics and public health. She has been Principal Investigator of several competitive research projects. She has supervised several doctoral theses and has published more than 50 articles in scientific journals of international impact.

Andrea BOLTHO was educated in Italy and at the Universities of London (LSE), Paris and Oxford. From 1966 to 1977, he was at the OECD's Department of Economics and Statistics. In 1973–1974, he was Japan Foundation Fellow at the Research Institute of the Economic Planning Agency, Tokyo. From 1977 to 2007, he was Fellow and Tutor in Economics at Magdalen College, University of Oxford. Since 2008, he has been Emeritus Fellow. At various stages, he was a consultant to the World Bank, the OECD and member of the Academic Council of the IFO Institute, Munich, as well as Visiting Professor at the Collège d'Europe in Bruges (1986–1989) and in various European universities.

Horst BREZINSKI is Professor Emeritus of Technische Universität Bergakademie Freiberg and of Poznan University of Economics and Business. He has held among others Visiting Professorships at the universities of Paris East, Trento, Stockholm School of Economics in Riga. He served as a Dean and as a Vice Rector for studies as well as for international relations in Freiberg. He was the Treasurer of the European Association for Comparative Economic Studies (EACES) from 1992–2011. His research interests have focused in the past on shadow economies in different economic systems, the transition in Central and Eastern Europe as well as on integration in Eastern and Western Europe. At present, his research interests focus on smart specialization and regional development in the Eastern part of Europe.

Sara CASAGRANDE holds a PhD in economics and management from the School of Social Sciences of the University of Trento (Italy), and a master degree in finance. She is a postdoctoral research fellow in Comparative European Studies and member of the research group EIE (Economics and Institutions in Europe). Her research activity includes the European integration process, European institutions and institutional variety and the economic, political and social prospects of the Eurozone. She is the author of journal articles and presentations at conferences. She has published in journals such as *Economic Systems*, *Comparative Economic Studies* and the *Journal of European Economy*.

Alexander CHEPURENKO, Dr. of Economics, is Professor of the School of Sociology of the National Research University Higher School of Economics, Moscow, and Chief

Scientist at the Institute of Sociology of the Russian Academy of Sciences, Moscow. His main areas of research are entrepreneurship, small- and medium-sized business, entrepreneurship education, middle class and comparative analysis of entrepreneurship development in Central and Eastern Europe. In recent writings he is supporting the thesis of a 'backslide transition' and related marginalization of private entrepreneurship in some former USSR republics. He is member of several international and domestic research associations and editorial boards and author or editor of more than 10 monographs and over 150 journal articles.

Misbah Tanveer CHOUDHRY is an Economist, Policy Analyst and Assistant Professor of Business and Economics at Suleman Dawood School of Business (SDSB) at Lahore University of Management Sciences (LUMS). She holds a PhD in economics from the University of Groningen, Groningen, the Netherlands. She has over 15 years of experience in industry and academia. She has remained affiliated with the State Bank of Pakistan, SDSB LUMS, CREESAW and the University of Brunei in various capacities. Her teaching interests lie in the areas of macroeconomics, managerial economics, business strategy and social entrepreneurship. She is extensively engaged in training and consultancy projects for various national and international agencies. Her research work is mainly on the Financial Crisis, economic growth, labor market dynamics and discrimination faced by female and disadvantaged groups in labor markets. Her articles have been published in well-established peer-reviewed journals such as the *International Journal of Manpower, Applied Economics, Economic Systems* and *the European Journal of Development Review*, among others.

László CSABA is Distinguished Professor of International Political Economy at Central European University, Vienna and Corvinus University of Budapest. He is Fellow of the Hungarian Academy of Sciences as well as of Academia Europaea/London. Author of 13 books, 405 articles and chapters in books published in 22 countries, most recently of the chapter 'Illiberal Economic Policies' in: Holmes et al., eds: *Routledge Handbook of Illiberalism*. Abingdon (2022), and the article 'Unorthodoxy in Hungary: An Illiberal Success Story?' *Post-Communist Economies* (vol. 34, no.1, 2022). More on his official website: www.csabal.com.

Donato CUTOLO is Assistant Professor of Entrepreneurship at IE University. He holds a PhD in management from the University of Bologna, and he was a Visiting Scholar at the MIT Sloan School of Management. His research touches upon several areas at the intersection of entrepreneurship, strategic management and economic sociology, focusing on the impacts of digital platforms on society and business and the interaction between these platforms and entrepreneurship. His research has been published in or invited for revisions at the *Journal of Management*, the *Academy of Management Perspectives*, the *Sloan Management Review* and *Advances in Strategic Management*.

Marek DABROWSKI is Non-Resident Fellow at Bruegel, Brussels, Professor at the Higher School of Economics in Moscow, Co-Founder and Fellow at CASE – Center for Social and Economic Research in Warsaw. He was the First Deputy Minister of Finance of Poland (1989–1990), and member of the Monetary Policy Council of the National Bank of Poland (1998–2004). He has also been involved in policy advising and research in several countries of Central and Eastern Europe, former Soviet Union, Middle East and Africa. He was also a Fellow under the 2014–2015 Fellowship Initiative of the European Commission – DG ECFIN and is member of the Academia Europaea.

Bruno DALLAGO, PhD, is Senior Professor of Economics at the Department of Economics and Management, University of Trento, Italy. His research interests include the European Union, comparative economics, the transforming economies of Central and East Europe, SMEs and entrepreneurship, local economic development. He is the author and editor of several scholarly books and journal articles. He is Hengyi Chair at Zhejiang University and was visiting professor at various international universities, president of the European Association for Comparative Economic Studies (1995–1996), consultant to international organizations and a member of various academic and research international advisory boards.

Vilde Lunnan DJUVE is Assistant Professor of Autocratic Politics at the Department of Political Science, University of Oslo. She holds a PhD in political science from Aarhus University, rewarded in 2021. Her work centers on political regime transitions of various kinds, particularly those instigated by regime incumbents, as well as the role of economic, structural and event-based factors such as popular protest in driving those transitions. She has published in the *Comparative Political Studies* journal, as well as outlets such as the APSA Democracy and Autocracy newsletter and the online magazine *Political Violence at a Glance*.

Elodie DOUARIN is Associate Professor in Economics at the School of Slavonic and East European Studies, University College London, UK. Her research focuses on three themes: (i) the non-economic (i.e. in terms of values and beliefs) consequences of economic change, (ii) the importance of values and culture in our understanding of economic outcomes and (iii) a broad reflection on the links between different economics sub-fields or schools of thought, especially transition, institutional and cultural economics. She has recently co-edited the *Palgrave Handbook of Comparative Economics* with Oleh Havrylyshyn.

Brigitte ECKER is Managing Director of WPZ Research and studied business administration at the Johannes Kepler University Linz, where she received her doctorate with distinction in 2003. After several years in the business sector, she joined Joanneum Research – Centre for Economic and Innovation Research in 2004, and the Institute for Advanced Studies in Vienna in 2013 as head of the research group Innovation, Education and Sustainability. In the summer of 2016, she founded WPZ Research, a non-university research institution. Ecker is also a lecturer for Innovation and Technology Management, Research and Science Policy. Her work focuses on RTI policy, higher education research and evaluation.

Gang FAN is Professor of Economics, Peking University PH; President of China Development Institute and Director, National Economic Research Institute. He received his PhD in economics from CASS in 1988. His publications include over 100 academic papers published in Chinese and English journals and 12 books on macroeconomics and economics of development. He is also an advisor to various departments of Chinese Central Government and international organizations such as World Bank and UNDP. He was listed as one of "World's Top 100 Public Intellectuals" jointly by Foreign Policy and Prospect, in 2005 and 2008, consecutively.

James K. GALBRAITH holds the Lloyd M. Bentsen Jr. Chair in Government/Business Relations at the Lyndon B. Johnson School of Public Affairs and a professorship in Government at the University of Texas at Austin. He was Executive Director of the Joint Economic Committee of the United States Congress in the early 1980s, and before that, an economist for the House Banking Committee. He chaired the board of Economists for Peace and Security from 1996 to 2016 and directs the University of Texas Inequality Project. He is a managing editor of *Structural Change and Economic Dynamics.*

José GARCÍA-SOLANES is Emeritus Professor of Economic Analysis at the University of Murcia. He has been a Visiting Professor at the Free University of Brussels and the University of Michigan, and Professor at the University of Valencia, Autonomous University of Madrid, University of Valladolid and University of Murcia. He is a former President of the Spanish Association of International Economics and Finance and evaluator of research projects and Marie Curie grants from the European Commission since 1998. He was awarded the Floridablanca Award for Economics from the Region of Murcia. His main areas of research include macroeconomics, European integration and monetary theory, with numerous published books, handbook chapters and articles in high-impact scientific journals.

H. Stephen GARDNER is Professor of Economics and Director of the McBride Center for International Business at Baylor University where he also served as Chair of the Department of Economics. He has led educational programs in China and Russia and has organized 27 conferences at Baylor and other sites abroad. Gardner holds a BA in economics and Russian studies from the University of Texas at Austin and a PhD in economics from the University of California at Berkeley, is the author/editor of four books and numerous academic articles and serves on the board of the Dallas World Affairs Council.

Claudius GRÄBNER-RADKOWITSCH is Professor of Pluralist Economics at the Europa-University in Flensburg, Germany. He is also Research Associate at the Institute for Comprehensive Analysis of the Economy (Johannes Kepler University Linz, Austria) and Fellow of the ZOE Institute for future-fit economies (Cologne, Germany). In his applied work, he studies international polarization dynamics, mechanisms underlying technological change, as well as the socio-economic implications of economic openness, competition and socio-ecological reforms, both empirically and using agent-based models. His philosophical work focuses on the epistemology of model-based research and the merits and challenges of pluralism in economics.

Paul Roderick GREGORY is a Professor of Economics at the University of Houston, Texas, a Research Fellow at the Hoover Institution and a Research Fellow at the German Institute for Economic Research. He has written about Russia and the Soviet Union.

Jerg GUTMANN is Assistant Professor of Behavioral Law and Economics at the University of Hamburg's Institute of Law and Economics and a CESifo Affiliate. He does research in the fields of political economy, institutional economics and law and economics. His research interests include the measurement of institutions and institutional quality, the use of violence in politics and the effects of culture and religion on the organization of societies.

Kumiko HABA is Professor at Kanagawa University, Professor Emeritus at Aoyama Gakuin University. She received a PhD of International Relations at Tsuda University and was a member of the Science Council of Japan. She is the President of ISA (International Studies Association: in the USA) Asia Pacific (2021–2024), was President of the EUSA Asia Pacific Tokyo Conference (2017) and former Vice President of ISA (2016–2017). She is the Director of the Institute for Global International Relations, Jean Monnet Chair of the European Union. She was a Visiting Scholar at Harvard University, European University Institute, University of Paris, University of London, Hungarian Academy of Science and Visiting Professor at Kyoto University. Her specialty is international politics, comparative politics between EU and Asia, EU and NATO Enlargement to Eastern Europe, Division and Integration of Europe and creating New World Order. She has written 72 books (including editor and co-writer) and more than 230 articles. Recent main books include *100 Years of World Wars and Regional Collaboration* (Springer, 2022), *Brexit and After; Perspectives on European Crises and Reconstruction from Asia and Europe,* (Springer, 2021) and *The Unwinding of the Globalist Dream; EU, Russia and China* (World Scientific, eds. S. Rosefielde, 2017).

William HYNES is Coordinator of New Approaches to Economic Challenges (NAEC) in the OECD Economics Department, which provides a space to question traditional economic ideas and offer new economic narratives. He previously worked as a Senior Advisor to the Secretary General, Senior Economist at NAEC, Advisor in the Sherpa and Global Governance Unit, a policy analyst in the Development Co-operation Directorate and an Economic Affairs Officer at the World Trade Organization. Hynes is an Honorary Professor of University College, London, Associate Fellow and Adjunct Professor in International Economics at the Johns Hopkins University School of Advanced International Studies and has a doctorate from Oxford University.

Miklós ILLÉSSY holds a PhD in management and business administration and is specialized in innovation, social impacts of technological change, organizational changes and in learning organizations. In 2003, he started his career as a Research Associate at the Institute of Sociology of the Hungarian Academy of Sciences. He has been involved in several EU-funded research projects which allowed him to acquire experiences in both qualitative and quantitative international comparative research. Currently, he is a Senior Research Fellow at the Centre for Social Sciences and a Co-Head of the Innovation and Society Research Centre.

Virgil IORDACHE is Director of the Research Center for Ecological Services at the University of Bucharest, where he has been teaching at the Faculty of Biology since 1993. He has degrees in biochemistry, philosophy and a doctorate in ecology. He has specialized in ecotoxicology, institutional analysis and philosophy of sciences. Iordache is the author of numerous books and articles in environmental sciences, philosophy of science and institutional development, and he is the recipient of the Emil Racoviță Award of the Romanian Academy.

Ichiro IWASAKI is Professor at the Institute of Economic Research of Hitotsubashi University, Tokyo, Japan. He received doctoral degree of economics from Hitotsubashi University in 2001. He specializes in corporate finance, comparative economic systems, organizational economics, transition economics and meta-analysis of the economic literature. He is the author of more than 200 scholarly books and journal articles, which have been published, among others, in the *European Journal of Political Economy, International Review of Economics & Finance, Journal of Comparative Economics, Journal of Corporate Finance, Journal of Economic Surveys, Small Business Economics, World Economy* and *World Development.*

Nadia von JACOBI is Assistant Professor at the Department of Economics and Management, University of Trento, and Adjunct Professor for the interdisciplinary PhD Program in Law, Ethics and Economics for Sustainable Development at the University of Milan. Previously, she worked at the University of Oxford and was visiting researcher at UNU-WIDER and Tulane University. Her research focuses on institutional economics, in particular on the role that institutions play for human development, equality and the protection of collective goods. She is interested in the complex mechanics of institutional change, and works with both theory and empirics.

David M. KEMME is Professor and Morris Chair in the Department of Economics at the University of Memphis. He received his BA in mathematics from Miami University and PhD in economics from The Ohio State University, was a Fulbright Scholar in Poland and has received numerous grants for research on economies of Eastern Europe and the CIS. His research interests are in emerging and transition economics, financial crises, modeling and forecasting, and he has published widely on these topics. He is an active member of the European Association of Comparative Economics and serves on the Executive Committee of EACES.

Martin KENNEY is Distinguished Professor of Community and Regional Development at the University of California, Davis and Co-Director of the Berkeley Roundtable on the International Economy. He is an Affiliated Professor with the Instituto di Management at the Scuola Superiore Sant'Anna and a senior advisor at the Research Institute for the Finnish Economy.

Alan KIRMAN obtained his PhD from Princeton and has been Professor of Economics at Johns Hopkins University, the Université Libre de Bruxelles, Warwick University and the European University Institute in Florence, Italy. He was elected a fellow of the Econometric Society and of the European Economic Association and was awarded the Humboldt Prize. He is member of the Institute for Advanced Study in Princeton. He was elected as a foreign member of the Accademia dei Lincei in Rome and is currently the Chief Advisor to the OECD-NAEC Initiative, Directeur d'études at the EHESS Paris and Professor Emeritus of Economics at the University of Aix-Marseille.

Carl Henrik KNUTSEN is Professor of Political Science at the University of Oslo, where he leads the Comparative Institutions and Regimes Research Group, and he is Research Professor at PRIO. His work centers on regime change, autocratic politics and the economic effects of institutions. He is co-PI of the Varieties of Democracy project, and leads several other projects, including an ERC Consolidator Grant on autocratic politics and an assessment of the state of Norwegian democracy. Knutsen has published around 50 journal articles and authored, co-authored, or co-edited seven books.

Masaaki KUBONIWA holds a PhD in economics from Hitotsubashi University, is a Professor Emeritus at Hitotsubashi University and a visiting Professor at National Chengchi University (NCCU) in Taiwan. He has received an honorable doctorate from the Central Economics and Mathematics Institute of Russian Academy of Sciences (CEMI, RAN) in 2003, and a W.W. Leontief Medal in 2004. He authored the book *Russian Economic Development over Three Centuries: New Data and Inferences* (Palgrave Macmillan, 2019).

Clara LATINI has been working as a consultant for a variety of international organizations. She has recently joined the World Bank Group. She has experience with the European Commission, UNSDSN, the New Approaches to Economic Challenges (NAEC) Initiative at the OECD, LSE European Institute and Leibniz IOS Institute. Latini holds an MSc degree in public policy from the London School of Economics and was one of the 100 selected students of the School of Public Policy founded by Enrico Letta. She is a World Economic Forum Global

Shaper, Climate Reality Leader and was selected as a Youth Delegate at the G20 Germany. Latini has been published in *COVID-19: Systemic Risk and Resilience* and soon for the Pontifical Academy of Sciences on Resilience of People and Ecosystems under Climate Stress.

Lailai LI is Associate, Stockholm Environment Institute (SEI). She served as Deputy Director of Stockholm Environment Institute and then retired from China Country Director of World Resources Institute. She is a policy expert on sustainability issues, including poverty and environment, climate change, low-carbon urban transport. Her recent research and volunteering work focus on local governance for sustainability, featuring development and deployment of clean energy and eco-sanitation technologies. She is a sociologist by training, holding PhD in sociology from the University of Pittsburgh.

Justin Yifu LIN is Dean of the Institute of New Structural Economics and Honorary Dean of National School of Development at Peking University. He was Senior Vice President and Chief Economist of the World Bank, 2008–2012. He is the author of more than 30 books including *The Quest for Prosperity, Economic Development and Transition, New Structural Economics, Demystifying the Chinese Economy* and *China's Miracle*. He received a PhD in economics from the University of Chicago in 1986. He is a Corresponding Fellow of the British Academy and a Fellow of the World Academy of Sciences for Advancement of Science in Developing Countries.

Laura LÓPEZ-GÓMEZ holds a PhD in economics, currently works as a lecturer and researcher at the University of Murcia. Her main lines of research are related to institutional quality, economic development and applied econometric techniques. During her pre-doctoral period, she carried out a research stay at the London School of Economics and Political Science. She has published in journals such as *Economic Systems*, the *European Journal of Tourism Research* and *Papeles de Economía Española*, among others.

Davide LUZZATI is a PhD candidate in economics at Sant'Anna School of Advanced Studies in Pisa, Italy. After completing an MSc in statistics at the ETH Zurich, he became interested in the connections between complexity science and economics. After spending time at the École Polytechnique in France and the Weizmann Institute of Science in Israel, he is now focusing his research on how shocks propagate through economic systems, with a particular focus on climate change and natural disasters.

Csaba MAKÓ is Professor at the University of Public Service, Budapest. His research interests include international comparative analysis of the social-economic institutions/regulations of the game-changing technological (digitization, smart automatization, artificial intelligence and algorithmic management) and organizational innovations. Special focus of his research interest related to quality of work, skills formation and employment status. His most recent major project is: 'Democracy at Work through Transparent and Inclusive Algorithmic Management' (INCODING, EU, 2021–2023). His latest publication is 'Automation, Creativity, and the Future of Work in Europe: A Comparison between the Old and New Member States with Special Focus on Hungary', *Intersections. East European Journal of Society and Politics*, 6 (2): 112–129, 2020, DOI: 10.17356/ieejsp.v6i2.625 (with Miklós Illéssy) http://intersections.tk.mta.hu.

Enrico MARELLI studied, taught and carried out research at Bocconi University (Milan, Italy), the London School of Economics (UK) and the University of Pennsylvania (USA). He has been Full Professor of Economic Policy at the Universities of Cagliari, Trieste and Brescia (Italy). He was Executive committee member of the European Association for Comparative Economic Studies (EACES) in 2010–2012; at present, he is Executive Committee Member of the Italian Association for the Study of Comparative Economic Systems (Aissec). He is the author of several books and more than 100 scientific articles in the fields of comparative economics, European economic integration, macroeconomics and economic policies, labor and regional economics.

Satoshi MIZOBATA is a Special Appointed Professor at the Institute of Economic Research of Kyoto University, Kyoto, Japan, and a Council Member of Science Council of Japan. He received doctoral degree of economics from Kyoto University in 1997. He specializes in corporate governance, comparative economics, institutional economics and transition economics. He is the author of more than 200 scholarly books and journal articles, which have been published, among others, in the *Journal of Economics and Business*, *Emerging Markets Finance & Trade*, *Annals of Corporate Governance*, *Annals of Public and Cooperative Economics*, *Post-Communist Economies* and *Economic Systems*.

Martin MYANT is Professor Emeritus at the University of the West of Scotland, UK, and Associate Researcher at the European Trade Union Institute in Brussels where he was formerly head of the research unit on European Economic, Employment and Social Policy. He has been researching the economic and political development and recent history of East-Central Europe for many years with a primary focus on Czechia. His publications include *Transition Economies: Political Economy in Russia, Eastern Europe, and Central Asia* (with Jan Drahokoupil) (Wiley-Blackwell, 2011).

Saeed NOSRATABADI has received a PhD degree in management and business administration from Hungarian University of Agriculture and Life Sciences, Gödöllő, Hungary. Nosratabadi's research interest is mainly on digital transportation. Indeed, the focus of his research is on how the advancements of artificial intelligence models can contribute to the processes of digitalization in the organizations.

Iuldashov NURSULTAN is Research Associate at Nanyang Technological University (NTU), Singapore. Iuldashov scored in the top 1% in the Republican University Entrance Test in the Kyrgyz Republic. He did his undergraduate studies in economics at the American University of Central Asia. He moved to Singapore in 2016 and graduated with a Masters degree in applied economics at NTU, and has been working as a researcher since then. His research interests are in bioethics, economics of economic integration and economics of policy advising. Besides research skills, he also has experience in project management and mentorship at the Economic Growth Centre, NTU. He is a co-author of forthcoming biography of Albert Winsemius, Chief Economic Advisor of Singapore (1961–1983), due to publish in 2022.

Bhavik PARIKH is Associate Professor of Finance at the Gerald Schwartz School of Business at St. Francis Xavier University and a Resident Fellow at the Brian Mulroney Institute of Government. Parikh's research focuses primarily on international finance, tax evasion, emerging markets finance and he has publications in reputed journals such as the *Journal of World Business*, *European Financial Management* and the *International Review of Financial Analysis*. Parikh received his PhD in finance from the University of Memphis, an MS in finance from the Illinois Institute of Technology and his bachelors of electronics and telecommunication engineering from the University of Mumbai.

Paolo PASIMENI is Deputy Chief Economist at the European Commission DG for Internal Market and a Senior Fellow at the Brussels School of Governance. He is an economist, specialized in international macroeconomics. In the past, he has worked as a researcher in Millward Brown, in the Italian Embassy in Cuba and in the Spanish Council for Scientific Research. He holds a PhD and MPhil in applied economics from the University of Seville (Spain) and an MSc in economics from the University of Modena (Italy).

Panagiotis E. PETRAKIS is Professor of Economics Emeritus at the Department of Economics at the National and Kapodistrian University of Athens, Greece, in which he served as Chairman from 2005 to 2009. He is the Chief Scientific Supervisor of the E-Learning Programme of the Center of Continuing Education and Lifelong Learning of the National and Kapodistrian University of Athens. Additionally, he has been a board member in scientific committees in the private and public sectors. He has numerous publications in high-profile international scientific journals and has authored a series of textbooks. His academic interests regard economic development, entrepreneurship, cultural background and human economic behavior.

Richard POMFRET is Professor of Economics Emeritus, University of Adelaide, and Adjunct Professor, Johns Hopkins University SAIS Europe, Bologna. In 1993, he was seconded to the United Nations for a year, advising the Asian republics of the former Soviet Union on macroeconomic policy, and he has acted as consultant to international organizations including the World Bank, Asian Development Bank, OECD and UNDP. His books include *The Age of Equality: The Twentieth Century in Economic Perspective* (Harvard UP, 2011), *The Central Asian Economies in the Twenty-First Century* (Princeton UP, 2019) and *The Economics of European Integration* (Harvard UP, 2021).

Vladimir POPOV is Principal Researcher in the Central Economics and Mathematics Institute of the Russian Academy of Sciences (CEMI RAN); Professor Emeritus at the New Economic School in Moscow; and an adjunct research Professor at the Institute of European and Russian Studies at Carleton University in Ottawa. His recent books include *Mixed Fortunes: An Economic History of China, Russia, and the West* (Oxford University Press, 2014; also published in Chinese); *Mapping the New World Order* (co-edited with Piotr Dutkiewicz) (Edward Elgar, 2018); *Macroeconomic Policies in Countries of the Global South* (co-edited with Anis Chowdhury) (Nova Publishers, 2019); and *When Life Expectancy Is Falling: Mortality Crises in Post-Communist Countries in a Global Context* (Nova Publishers, 2020).

Euston QUAH is Albert Winsemius Chair Professor of Economics and Director of the Economic Growth Centre at Nanyang Technological University (NTU), Singapore. He is also Editor of the *Singapore Economic Review* and President of the Economic Society of Singapore. Quah has published widely in the fields of cost-benefit analysis, environmental economics and law and economics with over 100 peer-reviewed journal articles, periodicals and opinion pieces. In his continuing career as an economic advisor, Quah has been an advisor to many government ministries and statutory boards in Singapore and overseas organizations, including the Asian Development Bank and the World Bank. He is presently serving as a board member of the Competition and Consumer Commission of Singapore, a member of the Social Sciences Research Council of Singapore and a member of the Market Surveillance and Compliance Committee appointed by the Singapore Government. He is a recipient of the Public Administration Medal (Silver) in 2020.

Verena RÉGENT studied sociology and social economics at the Johannes Kepler University Linz and the University of Helsinki. From 2011, she worked in research companies for the acquisition and management of third-party-funded research projects at the interface between social sciences and new technologies. As of 2013, she has been working as University Lecturer for research methods in social sciences. Since 2020, she has been an external expert at the Research Executive Agency of the European Commission. In 2021, she joined WPZ Research as senior researcher. Her work focuses on areas such as higher education research, innovation and knowledge and technology transfer.

Steven ROSEFIELDE is Professor of Economics, University of North Carolina, Chapel Hill. He received his PhD from Harvard University and is a member of the Russian Academy of Natural Sciences (RAEN). His books include: *Democracy and Its Elected Enemies: The West's Paralysis, Crisis and Decline* (Cambridge University Press, 2013); *Inclusive Economic Theory* (with Ralph W. Pfouts) (World Scientific, 2014); *Global Economic Turmoil and the Public Good* (with Quinn Mills) (World Scientific, 2015); *Transformation and Crisis in Central and Eastern Europe: Challenges and Prospects* (with Bruno Dallago) (Routledge, 2016); *The Kremlin Strikes Back: Russia and the West after Crimea's Annexation* (Cambridge University Press, 2016); *The Trump Phenomenon and Future of US Foreign Policy* (with Quinn Mills) (World Scientific, 2016); *Trump's Populist America* (World Scientific, 2017); *China's Market Communism: Challenges, Dilemmas, Solutions* (with Jonathan Leightner) (Routledge, 2017); *The Unwinding of the Globalist Dream: EU, Russia and China* (with Masaaki Kuboniwa, Kumiko Haba and Satoshi Mizobata, eds.) (World Scientific, 2017); *Putin's Russia: Economy, Defence and Military Foreign* (World Scientific, 2020); *Progressive and Populists* (with Quinn Mills) (World Scientific Publishers, 2020) and *Beleaguered Superpower: Biden's America Adrift* (with Quinn Mills) (World Scientific Publishers, 2021).

J. Barkley ROSSER, Jr. was educated at the University of Wisconsin-Madison and has been on the faculty of James Madison University since 1977. Author of over 200 publications, he has served as Editor of the *Journal of Economic Behavior and Organization* and *Review of Behavioral Economics*. With Marina V. Rosser, he is coauthor of *Comparative Economics in a Transforming World Economy*.

Marina V. ROSSER was educated at Moscow State University and served as Senior Researcher at the Institute of World Economy and International Relations, 1984–1989. She was on the faculty of James Madison University, 1977–2019. Author of many articles, she is with J. Barkley Rosser, Jr. coauthor of *Comparative Economics in a Transforming World Economy*.

Miklós ROSTA received his PhD in economics in 2012. Currently, he is the head of the Department of Comparative and Institutional Economics and Director of the Center of Central Asia Research at Corvinus University of Budapest. His main research interests include issues connected to institutional economics and public management studies. He serves as editor in the *Hungarian Economic Review*. His publications appeared in *Public Choice, Administration & Society, International Studies of Management and Organization* and *Society & Economy*. He published a monograph titled *Innovation, Adaptation or Imitation: The New Public Management* in 2012. In 2019, he received a Bolyai research grant from the Hungarian Academy of Science.

Maria SHCHEPELEVA holds a PhD in economics and is Associate Professor at the Department of Theoretical Economics at the National Research University Higher School of Economics (Moscow, Russia). Her research interests comprise FinTech, macrofinance, systemic risk and macroprudential policy and machine learning methods. She has a number of publications in international peer-reviewed outlets, such as *Review of Development Finance, Comparative Economic Studies* and *Annals of Finance*.

Marcello SIGNORELLI is Professor of Economic Policy and elected member of the Presidency Council of the Italian Economic Association. He was elected President of the European Association for Comparative Economic Studies (2010–2012). He organized the first World Congress of Comparative Economics in Rome 2015 and co-organized the second one in St. Petersburg 2017. He has studied, taught and carried out research at the University of Siena (where he graduated in economics and obtained a two-year specialization and a PhD), Columbia University, University of Warwick, UCL, Hitotsubashi University and NRU-HSE. He has published numerous articles in international journals and some books.

Tanja STEIGNER obtained her doctoral degree from the University of South Florida, and she is currently a Professor of Finance in the Accounting, Information Systems & Finance department at Emporia State University. Steigner's research interests focus on mergers and acquisitions, IPOs, tax evasion and cryptocurrencies. Her work has been published in several journals including the *European Financial Management, Financial Review, Journal of World Business, Journal of Financial Research, International Journal of Managerial Finance, American Journal of Business, Quarterly Journal of Finance and Accounting* and *Journal of Applied Financial Economics.*

Mikhail STOLBOV holds a PhD in economics and is Chair of the Department of Applied Economics at Moscow State Institute of International Relations (MGIMO University). His research areas include financial stability and banking, finance-growth nexus, financial innovations, digital economics and finance. Stolbov has published in a number of international peer-reviewed journals, including *Research in International Business and Finance, International Economics, Annals of Finance, Empirical Economics* and *International Economics and Economic Policy.*

Miklós SZANYI is Professor of Economics at Szeged University (Szeged) and Research Adviser at the Institute of World Economics (Budapest). His main research interest has been the microeconomic aspects of transition in East-Central Europe (privatization, foreign direct investments, institutional changes). In the frames of the Varieties of Capitalism literature string, he identified the specific historic social development processes that shaped a unique Central European model of capitalism. His most recent publications interpreted the sudden backsliding of democratic and market institutions in the region based on the values of this model. Szanyi is the author of 12 books and over 100 journal articles.

Vito TANZI was born in Italy and is a citizen of both Italy and the United States. He received his PhD in economics from Harvard in 1967. He has been Professor and Chair of Economics at the American University (1967–1974), Head of the Tax Policy Division (1974–1981) and Director of the Fiscal Affairs Department (1981–2000) at the IMF, President of the International Institute of Public Finance (IIPF) (1990–1994) and Undersecretary for Economy and Finance in the Italian Government (2001–2003). He is the author of 25 books and hundreds of articles in economics journals. An economic effect – the *Tanzi effect* – was named after him.

Vittorio VALLI is Emeritus Professor of Economic Policy at the University of Turin. He taught at the Universities Bocconi, of Padua and Turin and was Visiting Professor at the University of Kyoto, at Seoul National University and at the University of Nice. He was the first President of AISSEC and EACES, the Italian and European Associations for the Study of Comparative Economics. He has published over 100 articles and several books on issues of economic policy, growth and development theory, comparative economic development and labor economics. His most recent book is *The American Economy from Roosevelt to Trump* (Palgrave-Macmillan, 2018).

Stefan VOIGT is Professor at the University of Hamburg and the Director of its Institute of Law & Economics. He is a Fellow with CESifo (Munich). His research focuses on the economic effects of constitutions. More specifically, current research focuses on the economic effects of judicial institutions. Voigt is one of the editors of *Constitutional Political Economy* and a member of various boards including those of *Public Choice* and the *International Review of Law & Economics*. Voigt has consulting experience with both the public and the private sectors.

Hans-Jürgen WAGENER completed his PhD at Munich University. He did research work with Radio Liberty Research, Osteuropa Institut München and the Vienna Institute for International Economic Studies before becoming Professor of Economics at Rijksuniversiteit Groningen, the Netherlands, in 1975. In 1993, he moved to European University Viadrina at Frankfurt (Oder) where he founded the Frankfurt Institute for Transformation Studies. He retired in 2006. His research interests are comparative economics, transformation studies, European integration and the history of economic thinking. His most recent (2021) publication (with Maciej Tymiński and Piotr Koryś): *Sozialistische Ökonomie im Spannungsfeld der Modernisierung. Ein ideengeschichtlicher Vergleich DDR – Polen.*

Friederike WELTER leads the Institut für Mittelstandsforschung, a policy-oriented independent research institute on small business and entrepreneurship since 2013, and holds a Professorship at the University of Siegen. Her main research interests on which she has published widely are contextual entrepreneurship, entrepreneurial behavior, women's entrepreneurship and entrepreneurship policies. She is Senior Editor of *Entrepreneurship Theory and Practice*. For her work on small business and contextual entrepreneurship, she has received several honors, recently as member of the 21st Century Entrepreneurship Research Fellow and the Academia Europaea. The Frankfurter Allgemeine Zeitung regularly lists her among the most influential economists in Germany.

Quentin WODON is Lead Economist at the World Bank. Previously, he managed the Bank's unit on values, faith and development, and served as Lead Poverty Specialist for Africa and Economist/Senior Economist for Latin America. Before that, he taught with tenure at the University of Namur. He also taught at American University and Georgetown University. Trained in business engineering, he first worked in brand management for Procter & Gamble before shifting careers and joining a non-profit working with the extreme poor. He has tried to remain faithful to the cause of serving the less fortunate ever since. He holds four PhDs, served as president of two economics associations and has 500+ publications. His research on education, global health, poverty/inequality and sustainability has been covered by leading news media globally. As part of his volunteer work, he has held multiple positions of leadership with non-profits.

Mirela XHENETI is Senior Lecturer in Entrepreneurship and Small Business at the University of Sussex. Xheneti has a long-standing interest in how institutional change and enterprise policies affect entrepreneurial behavior. This particular interest has led to several recent studies on the informal economy and entrepreneurial behavior among women in developing country contexts and the role of entrepreneurs in supporting the transition to the circular economy. Xheneti's work has appeared in numerous journal articles and book chapters including the *Entrepreneurship and Regional Development Journal*, the *Strategic Entrepreneurship Journal* and *Journal of Business Ethics*. Xheneti serves on the Board of Directors of the European Council for Small Business and Entrepreneurship.

Andrei YAKOVLEV is Senior Researcher at the Institute for Industrial and Market Studies (IIMS) at the National Research University, Higher School of Economics (Moscow, Russia). Since November 2022, he has been Visiting Scholar at the Davis Center for Russian and Eurasian Studies at Harvard University. He was awarded his PhD in economics and statistics at Moscow Lomonosow-University in 1992. His research interests include comparative studies in corporate governance, industrial policy, public procurement and political economy of reforms in economies in transition. In 2015–2019, he was President of Association of Russian Economic Think Tanks (ARETT), and in 2017, he was awarded Yegor Gaigar Memorial Prize in Economics.

PREFACE

The world has changed remarkably since the late 1980s, and the change accelerated with the turn of the century. Changes, for better or for worse, were many and included, among others, transition in former socialist countries, the emergence of formerly undeveloped countries, the diffusion of new technologies, economic and monetary union in the European Union, the International Financial Crisis, COVID-19 pandemic, the rise and apparent demise of globalization, the war in Ukraine. All these and other events significantly and deeply changed the economic landscape around the world.

Economics was often unable so far to grasp the deep meaning of these events and update or rethink appropriately its mainstream. Comparative economic systems produced fine and important analyses and significantly contributed to a better understanding of the different ways in which economies work and led to significant theoretical and methodological progress. Yet the prevailing approach remained primarily geographically circumscribed, as in the case of the studies on transition in Central and Eastern Europe or on China. The microeconomic perspective and quantitative methodologies have dominated the recent development of the discipline. Although this traditional analytic perspective is fine and important, it is time to appreciate that institutional differences matter and even alternative institutional frameworks returned to play a central role and this they do in a coordinated way. Institutions come in bundles and they form networks or systems that are easily recognizable and influence significantly the working of countries and the life of their citizens. Systemic differences and risks returned to the center of the attention also of international military organizations.

Comparative economic systems have again the possibility to acquire a significant role in economics and have confronted with significant challenges and opportunities. It needs to update and change consequently. This sentiment prompted the publisher to propose this Handbook, giving the editors free hand and gratefully providing them with professional and warm support. The editors and the authors of this Handbook share this sentiment.

The comparative approach is potentially more important than ever in this new world in the making. Yet the Handbook has one fundamental message: after years of microspecialization and of geographical concentration, it is time to resume also the interest and reasoning for the economic system as a coordinated network of complementary institutions. This is required by the apparent sliding away of countries with different economic and political systems, the (re)-appearance of systemic challenges and conflicts and the changing geo-economy. Politics and social issues returned forcefully to squeeze the economy. The success of emerging countries with their distinct agendas and challenge to the traditional dominance of Western market economies requires a comparative systemic approach to the causes and factors of changing weights within the global economy. We also witness a growing differentiation within apparently similar economic systems: e.g., the rise of autocratic or illiberal political and economic regimes in competitive market economies and the revival of economic nationalism and isolationism. These developments are jeopardizing the context of globalization and test integration processes including the European one. The world economy is increasingly divided in trade and production blocks. The process of transition has followed divergent routes in different countries, each one showing remarkable static and dynamic consistency and resilience.

Comparative economic systems has an important role to play in analyzing and explaining these processes, building proper theories and devising appropriately tailored policies and institutional reforms. This Handbook aims to provide the Reader and the interested scholar with a broad selection of approaches, topics and perspectives for analytic inspiration and challenges in the years to come, as the Introduction explains.

The Handbook includes 37 chapters divided into five sections along with Conclusions, authored by 68 authors, plus the Introduction by the two editors. The editors aimed to include a broad and varied representation of approaches, issues, geographical provenience, theoretical orientation, age groups to give the reader a grasp of the variety and the potential of the discipline and its advocates.

The gestation of the Handbook witnessed some of the most dramatic events that further increased the relevance of its contribution and message. The Handbook was planned at the beginning of COVID-19 pandemic and it was closed in conjunction with the war in Ukraine and the beginning of a dramatic season of geopolitical tensions with worrying and still unpredictable outcomes. The pandemic brought evidence of the potential and actual significance of major unexpected shocks and obliged authors to use new approaches to working and interacting among them and with the editors. The war made evident, among others, how dangerous are systemic clashes and how important it is to understand and manage systemic differences in advance, when solutions may still have a chance.

Between these two dramatic events, the editors organized two occasions for discussing and presenting the ongoing Handbook. The first occasion was two online panels that the European Association for Comparative Economic Studies (EACES) hosted within its 16th by-annual conference, including members of the Association, some authors and editors of the Handbook. The two panels took place on September 13, 2021. Both events were important for clarifying issues, discussing ideas and finalizing the organization and the message of the Handbook. A conference was organized in Trento (Italy) on October 18–20, 2021 with the participation of nearly all authors. The initial intent of meeting all in person proved soon to be impossible. The pandemic obliged to organize the conference in mixed form with many authors participating online. In spite of the setback, contributions and discussion were high level and lively and quite useful for the outcome of the authoring and editorial efforts. Communication technologies proved their value in supporting our interaction and in overcoming some not-so-obvious problems when direct meeting in one place is possible, such as differences in time zones. One good perception of this "experiment" was to notice how these technologies can have people living in different countries with different features moving close and allowing them to interact freely and proficiently.

The editors are thankful to the publisher for suggesting and offering the precious opportunity to edit and publish the Handbook and for having promptly supported us at every step of the Handbook project. The EACES promptly and effectively supported and hosted the two panels, provided welcome intellectual participation and effectively contributed to the discussion. The Department of Economics and Management of the University of Trento, its Director Prof. Flavio Bazzana and its staff guaranteed a fundamental support to the organization of the conference and the editorial process, provided a relaxed atmosphere and excellent technical devices. The participants, colleagues and students who attended the two EACES panels and the conference in Trento played an important supportive role in the success of both initiatives and for the circulation of the information in the Handbook. We are grateful to the research group EIE (Economics and Institutions in Europe) and its director, Roberto Tamborini at the Department of Economics and Management in Trento, for intellectual challenge and support. We thank all the authors for agreeing to contribute to the Handbook by providing valuable chapters, their participation in the conferences, their cooperative attitude and their self-discipline in complying with the timetable. Last but not least, we are grateful to the referees for their valuable comments and suggestions, the final responsibility for the outcome rests solely with the editors.

Bruno Dallago
Sara Casagrande
(University of Trento)

INTRODUCTION

The Distinct Role and Mission of Comparative Economic Systems

Bruno Dallago and Sara Casagrande

UNIVERSITY OF TRENTO, TRENTO, ITALY

Recent events showed how complex and difficult is to understand, explain, manage and predict the working of economies. Globalization, the transformation of Central-Eastern Europe, the emergence of new economic powers, the International Financial Crisis and the EU sovereign debt crisis, COVID-19 pandemic and – while closing this Handbook – the ongoing crisis spurred by the Russian invasion of Ukraine are just the most visible and analysed events that proved that traditional theories and models are short of suitable explanations and predictions, let alone intervention to modify unsatisfactory trends or avoid potential dangers. Moreover, similar and sometimes internationally coordinated policies had different, even divergent, outcomes in different countries. These observations hold at both macroeconomic and microeconomic levels, with enterprises adapting differently to similar events and reacting to similar policies, and extend to various areas beyond economics, including politics which in turn influence the economy. In spite of analytic progress, abundant supply with sophisticated theories, availability of big data and detailed knowledge, understanding and managing the world appears to be difficult because it is hard to understand and explain the features and processes of a highly complex, interconnected and globalized world. All this requires that the traditional (mainstream) economic view is reconsidered and a more open attitude is taken towards new issues and approaches.

The aim of this introduction is to briefly overview and consider the message of this book on the nature, role and perspectives of comparative economic systems (CES) as an important and promising part of economics and its past, present and future contribution to a better understanding of economic problems. The main goal of the Handbook is to take stock and look at the future of comparative economic systems. The Handbook is organized in five different parts, each one dealing with the main issue of relevance for economics in general and for the discipline in particular. The content and the order of these parts reflect the willingness to take into consideration the most important questions for the discipline, from the most traditional to the most recent ones, and to discuss them from the perspective of the present and future challenges for CES, economic theory and real economies.

The Handbook considers CES's place in the broader context of economic theory, the discipline topics of interest and research, the comparative approaches it utilizes and its readings of the feature and role of the economic system considered as a relevant analytic category. The chapters identify issues, discuss relevant debates and offer a balanced

DOI: 10.4324/9781003144366-1

overview of results achieved and current knowledge. The Handbook considers critically the state of the art of the relevant subject, its importance for the advancement of the field and reflects on the future perspectives of the subject and its relevance for the advancement of the discipline.

In Section I.1, two distinct theoretical views of economics that are important for characterizing different approaches to the comparative analysis of economic systems are considered. In Section I.2, the study of comparative economic systems as presented in Part I of the Handbook is placed against this theoretical background. The following Section I.3 focuses on the comparison between economic systems and, in particular, on the methodological issues and developments connected to the comparative method and presents Part II of the Handbook. Section I.4 presents a brief review of significant positions in the debate on the future of CES and the state of publications. Section I.5 introduces Part III of the Handbook dealing with the microeconomic aspects of CES and the nature of the economic system and its constituent elements, in particular actors, values and interactions in economic systems. Section I.6 deals with the fundamental approaches used in CES and introduces Part IV of the Handbook, which focalizes on the outcomes that different economic systems generate and how these outcomes change following the evolution and transformation of economic systems. Section I.7 introduces the mostly non-economic factors and variables that may be important to consider for understanding the role of different economic systems in the globalized economy. The last Section I.8 introduces Part V of the Handbook and looks ahead by investigating where CES is heading at and its ability to disentangle important challenges for modern economic systems. Section I.9 concludes.

I.1 Managing complexity and economics: Economizing, realism, and the economic system

The lack of interest of economists in the philosophy of science often leads to underestimating the importance of the philosophical postulates underlying the methodologies used within economics. This type of analysis is a precious starting point for understanding how CES can contribute to economics. Since the postwar period and especially in Anglo-Saxon countries, the philosophical horizon of economics was in the neo-positivist tradition. Although neo-positivism has often been used in an inconsistent and contradictory way (Rosemberg 1992), the use of classical physics as a model to be extended to the social sciences, the spread use of mathematical language and the disregard for ethical issues became widespread among economists. Consistent with this philosophical background, instrumentalism imposed itself especially after Friedman's 1953 contribution.

Milton Friedman (1953) presents the main theorization of the strength of an analytic approach disregarding the need for realistic assumptions, an approach that surged to great popularity in recent decades. Friedman stresses that "…the relevant question to ask about the 'assumptions' of a theory is not whether they are descriptively 'realistic', for they never are, but whether they are sufficiently good approximations for the purpose in hand. And this question can be answered only by seeing whether the theory works, which means whether it yields sufficiently accurate predictions" (p. 15). According to this philosophical approach, theories are not true or false but simple instruments that can be adequate or not to solve a problem. Consequently, the realism of assumptions is irrelevant because what matters is the accuracy of predictions. Friedman's instrumentalism shows many affinities with John Dewey's pragmatism: theories are devices whose usefulness depends on their ability to help individuals adapt to the environment and survive. There is no real interest in understanding the nature and working of the real world and, therefore, its economic systems. Therefore, in the economic context, what matters is to develop simplified models capable of providing useful and accurate forecasts.

The appeal of Friedman's explanation lies in its parsimonious approach to complex issues that seem to make the use of analytic and predictive quantitative models apparently possible and useful. Yet Friedman himself stresses another important aspect of his approach: "Positive economics is in principle independent of any particular ethical position or normative judgement. …Its task is to provide a system of generalizations that can be used to make correct predictions about the consequences of any change in circumstances. Its performance is to be judged by the precision, scope, and conformity with experience of the predictions it yields. In short, positive economics is, or can be, an 'objective' science, in precisely the same sense as any of the physical sciences" (p. 4).[1]

Friedman's approach has been criticized among the others by Coase (1982, p. 6), who claimed that "faced with a choice between a theory which predicts well but gives us little insight into how the system works and one which gives us this insight but predicts badly, I would choose the latter, and I am inclined to think that most economists would do the same". Moreover, "no economist could be found who believed in a theory until it had been tested, which would have the paradoxical result that no tests would be carried out" (p. 13). Despite these logical contradictions, Friedman's approach has inherited the charm of the marginalist approach that promises exploiting the advantages of the natural sciences and reaching valid results starting from complex premises and avoiding moral and ethical issues. A difficult goal which, in order to have a semblance of validity, must be based on extreme simplifications of reality. Those simplifications start necessarily from human nature and the characteristics of the economic system.

Implicitly, Friedman restricts the validity of his apparently general method to "the kind of economic system that characterizes Western Nations" (Friedman 1953, pp. 41–42). What is missing in Friedman's method is the explanation of the reasons for the stability of the context, which means that the method lacks an explanation of the existence of the economic system, let alone of what the economic system is and why and how it may play its fundamental role. We are thus left with a partial explanation of the possible range of relevance of positive economics. This issue is not restricted to Friedman's instrumentalist analysis. For example, Paul Samuelson proposed a quite alternative descriptivist approach by emphasizing the importance of empirically grounding the postulates of economics. Despite this, both economists were convinced that the scope of economics is not to explore the deep nature of the economic system but only to provide good previsions (Friedman) or good descriptions of economic phenomena (Samuelson).

This statement suggests a fundamental support to CES: contribute to work out a general theory of the existence, evolution and rationality of different economic systems. This endeavour would concern both the positive and the normative aspects of economics.

In Friedman's view, limited to Western market economies and coherent with methodological individualism, the economic system is not part of the economic domain. That was the time of the dominance of "isms" in CES, largely based on political considerations. Having said that, it is interesting to consider whether CES would be able to satisfy Friedman's objectives by overcoming the limits of his analysis. This means to provide an approach that beyond "any particular ethical position or normative judgement" is able to provide "a system of generalizations that can be used to make correct predictions about the consequences of any change in circumstances". This requires a correct understanding of the features and working of the economic system.

After all, this is the logic of statistical and mathematical models used for simulating the effect of policies and the essence of macroeconomic policies. By the way, this was also the approach of central planning in socialist countries. The distinctive feature of the positive elaboration and normative use of models and policies is the lack in them of an objective scientific nature since they come from or are determined by governmental technical apparatuses, a fact that has much to do with the economic system. It would certainly be interesting to apply CES logic to Friedman's approach to give a more homogenous basis to the generation of different system-specific generalizations to be used to make correct positive and normative predictions. The new comparative economics (NCE) (Dallago and Casagrande 2021, Djankov et al. 2003, Shleifer 2002) offers an interesting albeit controversial attempt in this spirit – although not in the same substance – to use an "objective" method to define economic systems. NCE applies an optimizing approach to the society's choice of its institutions, based on its idiosyncratic institutional possibilities and under the constraint of social losses due to private expropriation (disorder) and to state expropriation (dictatorship).

Although not openly stated in Friedman (1953), indirectly it appears that economics as the science of rationality only applies to the Western world, i.e., to capitalist market economies. In a sense, the role of the study of comparative economic systems justified this latter conclusion. Comparative economic systems in the West dealt mainly with the economic system of "real socialism", i.e., with the Soviet Union and other socialist countries. In this sense, much of CES in the West dealt with what was considered economically irrational and alien, although in socialist countries, the perspective was different as it appears from Valli in this Handbook. This was particularly clear in the debate on the economic calculation in socialism during the 1930s (cf. Wagener in this Handbook). In this debate, the Austrians (von Mises, Hayek) maintained that an economic system that destroyed the market (socialism) could not work because it was irrational: it prevented the formation of competitive market prices and the formation and circulation of dispersed information. Implicitly, the "socialists" (Lange, Lerner) admitted this but maintained that socialism (the public ownership of production means) could work if it imitated the competitive market.

The performance of the Soviet and Central-Eastern European economies (CEEE) was actually impressive, for a time. This showed that an "alien" economic system could improve economic performance, at least in particular circumstances. The same obviously refers to other countries, China being certainly the most prominent among them. An interesting application would also look at variants of the same type of macrosystems, such as the varieties of capitalism (VoC) (Amable 2003, Hall and Soskice 2001; cf. Rosta in this Handbook). The problem with CEEEs' success is that the system had an "abnormal" role for politics; the improvement was not across-the-board (not, e.g. in consumption levels comparable to production) and did not survive its own success. When extensive resources were depleted and the role of political campaigns and non-economic incentives became ineffective, economic performance collapsed. These observations suggest that economic and technical rationality matters, but it is not sufficient since other factors can influence economic performance. In a truly general economic theory and in Friedman's spirit, the relevant question to ask about the assumptions is whether they are sufficiently good approximations in different economic systems. Since when the economic systems are sufficiently different, the condition of obtaining sufficiently accurate predictions does not probably hold, the problem can be solved only through a general theory of the economic system and its role in the economy.

A second important issue with "the consequences of any change in circumstances" concerns the effect of overlooked events (the International Financial Crisis of 2008) and the consequences of unforeseen "black swans" (Taleb 2007), such as the COVID-19 pandemic. Both types of events proved the fragility of Friedmanian economics when systemic and environmental circumstances change abruptly. Simplification is fundamental "to provide a system of generalizations that can be used to make correct predictions", yet it is fundamental to explain how much and how long simplification can go (Brada 2009). A solution to such a dilemma leads to delimiting the sphere of the relevance of any analytic method and economic theory. When the world gets more complex or more unpredictable, alternative analytic solutions must be found to understand, analyse and predict. This is also a dilemma confronting comparative economic systems, together with the question of how, when and in which way CES can contribute to support economics to move to a new paradigm.

In a stimulating and open-minded booklet, Albert O. Hirschman (1982) observed that "societies are in some way predisposed toward oscillations between periods of intense preoccupation with public issues and of almost total concentration on individual improvement and private welfare goals". In a critical early review, political scientist Gianfranco Pasquino (1983) concluded differently: "It seems that Western citizens might move toward a better, more satisfactory integration of their private interests and their public involvement. While a perfect balance might never be reached, the spread of the oscillation will be more limited". Clearly, these two positions offer a significantly different reading of events and long-term trends: although both authors have a dynamic approach, a cyclical pattern prevails in Hirschman's perspective and a relatively smooth integrative process in Pasquino's view. Hirschman's cyclical perspective is connected to his aim of considering human interactions within complex real social systems despite the fact that this complicates economic analysis (Hirschman 1984).

These different views implicitly highlight the central role of the economic system. Hirschman's shifting involvements provide a reasonable explanation to the evolutive pattern and the periodic changes that one can observe within any type of society, due to different combinations of social forces and their interaction with exogenous factors and events. From an CES perspective, one can conclude about a degree of cyclicity of the organization and priorities of societies or – presumably when the interaction overcomes a certain threshold – about systemic change. Yet under less strained circumstances, the economic system has a stabilizing effect. However, when such stabilizing effect weakens or disrupts under the effect of exogenous or endogenous factors, shifting involvements may take over even in a radical form and lead to the establishment or rapid evolution of a different system.

Hirschman's reading complements Taleb's black swan theory, with the important difference that the former is an endogenous theory of a cyclical pattern based on changes in social preferences and choices, while the latter is an explanation of how to properly interpret and take into account unforeseen exogenous shocks. Surely, the endogenous theory of a cyclical pattern would benefit from the insights of a great friend of Taleb, Benoit Mandelbrot, about the possibility of grasping "order" into the apparent and often dramatic "disorder" typical of real systems and financial markets (Mandelbrot and Hudson 2004). In a different but complementary way, Charles Wolf (1993) gives a possible motivation for shifting involvements in that the choice between markets and the government is a choice between imperfect alternatives, each one solving some problems but causing others (cf. also Dallago and Mittone 1996).

In all these cases, Friedman's approach is clearly an unfit general basis for analysis and policy making. The relevant question, then, is how relevant are these events, be they endogenous or exogenous. Are shocks so important and frequent and the nature of the economic system so complex to make the adoption of Friedman's method risky for the stability and performance of a market economy? Is the endogenous accumulation of tensions caused by the consistent use of policies à-la-Friedman important and inevitable? Is instability so relevant to make Friedman's method risky for a correct interpretation of the nature and dynamics of a market economy? The events since the 2008 international crisis apparently suggest that this is the case, evident mistakes in policy making apart. Therefore, it appears that a necessary precondition for using Friedman's analytic method is to verify whether the conditions of the economy are intrinsically stable, thus allowing to proficiently working out a system of generalizations that can be used to make correct predictions. For a scholar in comparative economic systems, this would imply that these generalizations are subject to a consideration of idiosyncratic systemic features that may vary significantly in different countries.

Friedman's analytic method overlooks that economic phenomena are usually not compatible with the logic of invariant knowledge, which may entail both external validity problems and negative exposures to unforeseen and unpredicted shocks, be they endogenous or exogenous. These problems can be better understood by adopting the logic of "possibility trees" or "open-ended results" (Ivarola 2018). This opens the positive problem of the interpretative reliability of the theory in the different cases that may be relevant to an economy and its normative outcomes. If changes in circumstances go beyond the limited frame that Friedman considers, the theory and its normative outcomes may see their predictive strength jeopardized or even falsified. Transition since 1989, the International Financial Crisis of 2008 and the COVID-19 pandemic offer three major recent cases in point, with others (such as climate change and other environmental issues) looming around.

An alternative, realistic approach which highlights the fundamental importance of factors that Friedman disregards is due to institutional and comparative economists, among others. According to Douglas North (1990, 2000, 2005), who represents a perspective important in solving the above economics dilemma, the economy is embedded in a whole range of non-economic variables and processes and the economy itself is made of a wide set of processes and variables with different features and roles. Moreover, "what we really need to know is the interplay between all these features that makes it work" (North 2000, p. 5, cf. also Gutman and Voigt in this Handbook). This takes us quite close to the issue of coordination well known in the tradition of comparative economic systems (Grossman 1967, Kornai 1984, 1990; Wagener in this Handbook) and to the contribution of network analysis in highlighting interconnections within the economy (Pryor 2005a,b, von Jacobi 2018, von Jacobi in this Handbook).

For North, there are three foundations of that interplay: demography, the stock of knowledge and the institutional framework (North 2000, p. 6). It is the interaction among these three foundations that shapes the features of the economy and that determines its outcomes. This clearly exposes an economy to multiple equilibria, which prevents Friedman's generalizations. Coordination is fundamental also at the level of institutions and is embedded in the culture. Indeed, much of this effect descends from "shared mental models" (Denzau and North 1994), i.e., a typically implicit synthetic framework that we construct in our minds to explain how the economy works and which consequently structures our action in the economy. Within such a framework, economic actors "erect an elaborate structure of rules, norms, conventions, and beliefs embodied in constitutions, property rights, and informal constraints that in turn shape economic performance" (North 2000, p. 6). This "scaffolding" is idiosyncratic to each economy, changes very slowly and is an important aspect of the economic system: it "not only constrains the choice set at a moment of time but is the source of path dependence" and "defines the incentive structure of society" (North 2003, p. 2). Incentives, in turn, connect institutions to the real economy. Interestingly, North's ability to identify feedback loops between institutions and beliefs (Hogdson 2017) seems compatible with the feedback loops identified by Hirschman (1970). It is an aspect that seems to confirm their ability to grasp the complex and systemic nature of economies.

In North's view, the economic system – or, better, the broader political economic system – plays a central role in a realistic and elitist view of the society: "The reality of a political economic system is never known to anyone, but humans do construct elaborate beliefs about the nature of that reality: beliefs that are both a positive model of the way the system works and a normative model of how it should work. ...The dominant beliefs, ... over time result in the accretion of an elaborate structure of institutions, both formal rules and informal norms, that together determine economic and political performance". This takes back to Hirschman's shifting involvements: "The path dependence that results typically makes change increments, although the occasional radical and abrupt institutional change suggests that something akin to punctuated equilibrium change in evolutionary biology can occur in economic change as well" (North 2003, p. 4).

North's approach and explanation are at odds with Friedman's: "The pragmatic concern is with the degree to which our beliefs coincide with that reality. ... It is important that we be very self-conscious about the nature of that reality. And even more important is the awareness of just how reality is changing. ... The rationality assumption that has served economists and all the social scientists well for a limited range of issues in microeconomic theory is a devastating shortcoming in dealing with most of the major issues confronting social scientists and policy makers, and it is a major stumbling block to the path of future economic progress" (North 2003, p. 7).

The formal and informal institutions that form the institutional matrix of a political-economic system are fundamental for understanding systemic change since they impose "...severe constraints on the choice of entrepreneurs when they set out to create new or to modify institutions in order to improve their economic or political positions" (North 2003, p. 4). In any case, the critical issue is the change of the institutional matrix, with a caveat: "...when you are trying to improve the performance of an economy, all you can change are the formal rules. In fact you must also change the informal constraints, and you must get enforcement characteristics that will produce the desired results" (North 2003, p. 16; cf. von Jacobi in this Handbook).

North thus offers a broader and more flexible theory than Friedman, a theory that may not lead to clear and univocal answers and policy prescriptions but that can usefully accommodate and explain different situations and occurrences and is powerful for comparative economic systems. North has general validity for a wider variety of circumstances, while Friedman presupposes the stability and invariability of the economic system and looks at the effect of modifications in quantitative variables in a particular economic system.

To summarize the CES perspective and take Friedman and North as the proponents of the two recurrent views in contemporary economics, the following three main conclusions can be proposed. First, Friedman proposes an appealing research method, although this method is short of a general theory of economics. From the perspective of CES, it may perhaps be considered the intellectual origin (but not the direct inspirator) of the NCE and may be useful in analyzing the nature and role of the economic system in economics. Second, North proposes an authoritative – although not uncontroversial – theory of the role of institutions and path dependence and the role of non-economic factors that is much akin to the traditional CES approach. One important difference between North and CES is that the former considers only capitalist market economies, while the latter is open to different kinds of economic systems and thus is more general and enriched with the comparative method. Third, some popular theories, such as the VoC, are similar in their approach to North's in that they consider variants of the capitalist market system and the role of path dependence, but have a prevailing microeconomic focus on different markets, vis-à-vis North's prevailing broad (macroeconomic) approach. Thus, these approaches are important for CES in that they high-light the importance of systemic differences and their resilience and reject the hypothesis of institutional convergence. However, neither approach nor theory answers the fundamental question of the economic interaction among countries with different economic systems, a field in which CES can offer a particularly important contribution.

I.2 Where are comparative economic systems going?

The first part of the Handbook includes theoretical and analytical approaches that analyse the nature of the discipline of comparative economic studies and considers particularly the eco-nomic system. The first part places comparative economic systems in the frame of the discip-line of economics, looks at the subject and content of CES, and its theoretical and analytical approaches aimed to study the economic system. In this part, traditional topics are treated with a perspective aimed to grasp the future of the discipline and its potential contributions to economic theory. In Chapter 1, Hans-Jürgen Wagener offers a comprehensive overview of CES evolution within economic theory. Starting from a detailed reconstruction of the origins of CES, he analyses the concept of the economic system, demonstrating the attempts that have been made to build theoretical frameworks capable of understanding the structure and working of economic systems. His analysis clearly shows the difficulties in identifying objective and comparable concepts allowing for the description and evaluation of economic systems and the analysis of their dynamics. Despite these difficulties, the chapter underlines CES potential contributions for the improvement of the economic discipline thanks to its wide theoretical framework, multidisciplinary approach and empirical and policy orientation. In Chapter 2, Vittorio Valli offers an overview of the main debates and developments of CES after World War II up to now, both in Western and Eastern countries. He also focuses on the application of the comparative method to many important economic problems and discusses the issues related to the use of GDP in comparisons and the importance of considering the method of purchasing power parities. His analysis demonstrates how the discipline has evolved before and after the dissolution of the Soviet Union by underlying how the discip-line has passed from the study of alternative systems to the study of real economies and their constitutive parts and institutions. Valli finally discusses CES ability to disentangle relevant issues such as the unequal distribution of economic power among individuals and countries. Steven Rosefielde, in Chapter 3, offers a theoretical treatment of a key concept for CES: the economic system. He analyses the nature and the historical development of this concept, starting from the classification of economic systems on the basis of Abram Bergson's social welfare function. Then, he describes how this type of classification declined after World War II in favor of the measurement of systems performance. In this regard, Rosefielde discusses the ambiguities connected to the use of GDP in comparisons and the importance of considering nonpecuniary utilities. Finally, he takes stock of the results obtained by CES.

The economic system is a concept strictly interconnected to a systemic and coordinated conception of reality. The awareness of the importance of recovering a systemic dimension in economic analysis has recently grown within CES. Claudius Gräbner-Radkowitsch, in Chapter 4, demonstrates the relevance of this trend by discussing the potential of an evolu-tionary approach to CES. His chapter not only introduces the meta-theoretical foundations of such an approach, but the application to comparative development dynamics in the European Union also underlines the importance of considering the complexity, systemism, and path dependencies in the comparative analysis of economic systems. Consistently with this line of research, Nadia von Jacobi, in Chapter 5, outlines the importance of taking into account the complexity of institutional interconnections for the analysis and comparison of economic systems. Adopting a multidisciplinary perspective, she presents a theoretical and empirical investigation that draws on ecology and symbiosis. Her chapter highlights the potentialities of methodologies such as correlation network analysis for the field of comparative economic systems. These chapters demonstrate how CES is experiencing important developments both from a theoretical and methodological point of view, with a growing interest in a correct interpretation of the systemic features of economies. In this regard, in Chapter 6, Paul Dragos Aligica and Virgil Iordache analyse how CES has faced the problem of a proper conceptualization of resilience. They demonstrate how only recently has CES recognized the importance of this systemic feature in the analysis of economic systems and discuss the great unexplored potential associated with a research agenda centred on the analysis of the role of change, adaptability and resilience in the study of economic systems. In this analysis, they explore the potentials and limits of extending approaches to resilience from other disciplines such as physics or environmental sciences, to the study of economic systems. Richard Pomfret, in Chapter 7, closes the first part of the Handbook with an analysis of the relationship between CES and other economic disciplines and its role in the study of conflicts between economic systems in the 20th century. This last chapter, by investigating future challenges and opportunities for the 21st century, from populist waves to cooperative fraternity, draws some important conclusions about CES research agenda and the development of the discipline.

I.3 The method and role of comparisons

The research and teaching program of comparative economic systems also includes and gives relevance to the comparative method. This is an aspect that – when considered in its deep institutional, historical and other meanings – is missing in mainstream economics, where comparisons are limited to different levels and allocation of economic factors. Comparing different entities is, first of all, an analytic method, yet it also includes the fundamental aspect that differences matter in both quantitative and qualitative and structural sense. This perspective is particularly interesting and important in the case of the European Union, an economic area with a single currency and monetary policy hosting economies that are in different circumstances under various perspectives and considerations but missing a government capable of accommodating ex post the asymmetric effects of policies. These comparisons are quite popular and important among scholars in CES and other fields of specialization. However, these kinds of comparisons require that the economic system – plus the systemic and structural differences among countries – is disregarded. As a consequence, these comparisons are important for highlighting the relation between any change in circumstances and the consequences thereof or the effect of identical policies in different countries (as in the EU following the single monetary policy), although they do not consider whether the change in circumstances (the value of economic variables) may come from systemic features (such as the different sensitivity of outcomes to changes in the economic system in countries with different economic systems).

In the second part of the Handbook, the focus is on the nature and use of the comparative method in comparative economic systems, i.e., the comparison between economic systems or their components, also considering different factors influencing economic performance such as politics or culture. Moreover, it deals with the methodological issues and developments connected to the comparative method. In Chapter 8, H. Stephen Gardner starts conceptualizing the economic system as an interactive set of institutions influenced by culture, political institutions and other environmental variables and analyses criteria for classification such as ownership, coordinating mechanism, incentive systems and objectives. He offers new answers to traditional questions in CES, drawing on recent literature in anthropology, economic history and organizational studies, and suggests that measurements of system performance should take advantage of advances in causal inference and measurements of human well-being. Climate change and pandemic conditions require careful analysis of systemic resiliency. J. Barkley Rosser, Jr. and Marina V. Rosser, in Chapter 9, investigate how CES methods have changed over time, from the comparison of idealized formulations of possible economic systems, the contrast between market systems and planned economies according to economic variables and political factors up to recent developments that focus not only on transition but on cultural and institutional variables. Particularly important is the role of history and the traditional cultural system that can also influence modern and technologically advanced societies. These societies may be classified as new traditional economies and can potentially represent a distinct economic system. In Chapter 10, James K. Galbraith places the focus on the methodological issues related to the comparison of economic inequality for different economic systems. He compares in terms of coverage and value five broad types of inequality datasets with worldwide or major international coverage and independent measurements. These are compared with the Estimated Household Income Inequality (EHII) data set of the University of Texas Inequality Project. Galbraith, after discussing different criteria for comparisons, demonstrates the depth and range of EHII and its broad compatibility with other important datasets. In Chapter 11, Masaaki Kuboniwa introduces a comparative analysis of bilateral trade in value added across Russia and the EU in recent decades. Using Leontief's insight and OECD's intercountry input–output database, he demonstrates how both Russia and EU have benefitted from their bilateral trade. Kuboniwa concludes with important insights about how to obtain data improvements and highlights the importance of peaceful developments in bilateral trade for the growth of countries. The importance of institutions for the understanding and comparison of economic systems comes clearly out in the discussion of these topics. In Chapter 12, Jerg Gutmann and Stefan Voigt discuss issues and challenges in the conceptualization, measurement and comparison of institutions and institutional quality by underlining the connections between CES and institutional economics. They present different definitions and alternative typologies of institutions useful for comparative economic research and emphasize the importance of considering the endogenous nature of many institutions and the role of cultural and geographical factors. Their analysis underlines the importance of distinguishing between formal and informal institutions, an aspect also taken into consideration in Chapter 13, by José García-Solanes, Arielle Beyaert and Laura López-Gómez. They offer an empirical investigation of institutional and economic clusters across the Eurozone. They analyse the links between institutional quality in formal and informal institutions and long-run economic performance by constructing cross-correlograms and identifying different convergence clubs characterized by different convergence processes. Their analysis demonstrates the difficulties of an integration process that involves heterogeneous countries. They find a polarization among European member countries, with some of them apparently locked in traps of low institutional quality and outline incentive-based actions to strengthen institutional convergence in the Eurozone. Coherently with this complex conception of the nature of institutions, Satoshi Mizobata and Ichiro Iwasaki close this second part of the Handbook, in Chapter 14, by demonstrating the importance of quantitative literature review for CES. They present an analytical review of the literature about a relevant traditional CES topic, i.e., the transition from the socialist planned systems in Central and Eastern Europe and post-Soviet countries towards capitalist market economies and focalize in particular on four research areas: the end-of-socialism, the transition strategy, path dependency of transition and corruption in transition economies. These debates permitted economists to gain knowledge about the issues of transition that can represent an important intellectual asset that goes beyond for economic discipline.

I.4 The nature of economic systems

Comparative economic studies started to take notice and adapt progressively to the appearance of new fields and subjects of research, particularly since the disruption of the socialist system in Central and Eastern Europe. They did so by transforming their nature and approach, the topics of interest and reference theories. Overall, CES is less unified as a discipline than it used to be traditionally. It is, above all, less macro and more micro, less analytic and descriptive and more formalized and quantitative, less stretched between mainstream and Marxist theories, more interested in the internal structure and features of varieties of the same system (capitalism) and processes (transformation/transition) and less concerned with grand systems ("isms"). This change strengthened CES' normative significance and potential relevance. However, it is important to note that this change of perspective and priorities weakened CES' ability to develop and update the systemic analytic vision of the economy. As a consequence, our ability to perceive and analyse the causes that could lead to "unforeseen" events (e.g. divergent trajectories of transformation economies, the International Financial Crisis, the pandemic) and to understand and explain the causes of different outcomes of diverse events and policies in dissimilar economic systems was not better than the rest of economics. Our valuable contribution came mostly ex post. With this failure, we lost golden opportunities to revitalize the discipline and increase its relevance in the broader field of economics. It is important to assess why it was so and how to proceed in the search for a new role and contribution of CES.

An interesting debate took place since the unfolding transformation in Central-Eastern Europe, a debate that concerned both the nature and change of economic systems and the achievements in those countries (see Mizobata and Iwasaki in this Handbook). An important component of the debate was about the future of the discipline following the "end of history" (Andreff 2021, Douarin and Havrylyshyn 2021). Different perspectives and ideas were advanced, all sharing the feeling that after 1989 the analytic field was different and things had to change to avoid the risk of scientific irrelevance and academic vanishing or at most be included in the field of country studies. Some authors wrote about a true collapse of the discipline: "The collapse of communism in the late 1980s and early 1990s led to an intellectual stocktaking in the field of comparative political economy and development economics. The older models and empirical estimates seemed to have missed the mark wildly. Economists trained in the traditional manner in these fields saw their human capital investment decline in value more rapidly than they could have ever imagined" (Boettke et al. 2005, p. 288). Writing about the same time, other authors from the field had a more balanced and complex judgement, while others tried to measure the state of the discipline through the approach used by its publications (Murrell 2011).

Hanson (2007) clarified the essence of the problem: earlier, "…we studied the consequences for the functioning of national economies of major differences in the institutional arrangements with which they operated" (p. 1). Since 1989, "The subject has developed, … chiefly in response to real-world changes such as the collapse of communism and the apparent decline of some variants of capitalism, but also in response to changes in adjoining fields of study" (p. 4). Among the latter, Hanson cites institutional economics and the VoC as prominent. On the former side, this change had the important side effect of opening the discipline to the important issue of how economic institutions and economic systems change over time also in a punctuated way. However, on the latter side, some confounding developments are noticed:

"Some work still labelled comparative economics is not what it says on the label; some work under other labels could equally well be called comparative economics" (p. 7). However, a "good deal of work that is currently labelled 'comparative economic studies' is wrongly put in that particular box out of inertia…" (p. 7). These observations lead Hanson to a conclusion that this Handbook deeply shares: "we should try to keep up more with what is going on in these adjoining fields… And we should not become too fixated on 'transition', but recognise that there is a lot of interesting and worthwhile comparison to be done amongst capitalist countries whose institutions can and do vary substantially" (p. 11). This may contribute moving the focus of CES from the comparison of alternative economic systems to the analysis of the nature and role of the economic system. This takes CES to the core of economic theory and to questions that both mainstream theory (Friedman) and institutionalists (North) struggle to answer.

While the debate was unfolding, important changes took place in the role and content of CES as an academic discipline. The consequences of transition and the collapse of the Soviet Union were significant in all Western countries, yet not destructive of the field: referring to the United States, Johnson and Kovzik (2016, p. 24) notice that "the impact of the collapse of the Soviet Union on CES undergraduate courses has been smaller than we would have anticipated". At least in the United States before 1989, CES was among the most popular economics courses at the undergraduate level, and by 1980, 63.1% of US universities offered a course in comparative economic systems (Siegfried and Wilkinson 1982). By mid-2010s, only 20% of universities surveyed by Johnson and Kovzik (2016) offered courses in comparative economic systems annually and an additional 11.8% courses in transitional economies. There was also a decline in the number of textbooks published and their less frequent updating (Foley and Pyle 2003; Kovzik and Johnson 2016; Ross 1995). Moreover, the range of covered issues and the countries considered increased considerably, particularly so for transition countries, and substantial more attention was devoted to the VoC and in particular European countries and the European Union. Probably as a consequence of the broader spectrum of issues and the variety of cases considered, the classification system used tended to become multidimensional (Johnson and Kovzik 2016).

Publications had a different trend. Dallago and Casagrande (2021) examine the number of publications in the EconLit database classified in category P and sub-categories. They find that the total number of publications grew steadily until 2011 and then increased very rapidly, by 45%, between 2012 and 2014. This was due fundamentally to publications on socialist systems (P2 and P3). Since 2015, the number of publications collapsed and was concentrated in the P2 and P3 categories. By 2018, it reached an overall number that was lower than in 2002 and 55% of the 2014 level. However, also the number of publications on capitalist systems in the P1 category decreased considerably: by 2018, it was barely more than one-third of the 2014 level. Also, noteworthy is the fact that academic and scientific associations in the discipline outline their field of interest in different ways and redefine their mission (Dallago and Casagrande 2021, Appendix; cf. also Guo and Lee 2011).

These figures do not necessarily imply that the scientific interest in the field collapsed. Two different occurrences may explain at least part of the drop. First, some scholars in the field choose to attribute their publications to JEL headings other than P (Economic Systems). This is the case of the authors in the NCE (Djankov et al. 2003), but it may be so also for other authors. Second, new research fields that are close to CES or could be easily integrated within it are self-classified under headings other than P. In part, this may be due to the internal organization of category P, which reflects the traditional approach to the discipline amended with ad hoc adjustments to take new important lines of research into consideration.

Johnson and Kovzik (2016, p. 32) are right when they conclude that "As long as methodology, not ideology, is the first priority, the collapse of the Soviet Union does not change anything because the Soviet model was one of many, theoretically possible options". Yet it is just because it is unclear whether alternative economic systems still have a role, and certainly, they do not have a particularly significant role for the time being, that the discipline must take seriously the question of its mission, method and subjects of analysis and teaching. Johnson and Kovzik (2016) propose a two-pronged strategy referring to the teaching and relevance of CES in the undergraduate curriculum. Their proposal refers to teaching in US universities, but the significance may be easily extended also to other countries. The authors propose to change the organization of CES courses and textbooks and better integrate courses in the economics curriculum, particularly by extending the comparative method to economics. This means that courses should be organized not by country but by economic concepts. The course would thus reflect the major characteristics and performance criteria of micro- and macroeconomics, including the efficiency, welfare and growth implications.

The proposal makes sense and is certainly a part of the solution. Yet it concentrates more on the comparative method than on the core issue: the economic system. Indeed, the proposal overlooks what is the major distinctive feature of CES mission and approach: looking also and perhaps primarily at the interaction of the components of an economic system (institutions), the distinct coordination this creates among institutions and economic agents and the way in which complementarities among institutions contribute to the existence and working of distinct economic systems, each with its idiosyncrasies and leading to particular working and performance of the economy. In our view, this is the fundamental mission of CES as an economic discipline that aims at explaining why economic systems are important in both theory and for each country.

I.5 Inside the economic system: Interconnected elements

The third part of the Handbook looks at the nature of the economic system and its constituent elements, in particular actors, values and interactions in economic systems. Verena Régent and Brigitte Ecker's Chapter 15 deals with a comparative analysis of how higher education systems can promote the development of transversal skills required by modern labour markets. Their analysis shows the growing interconnection that exists between the education system and the labour market and retraces the transformation of this relationship over time through a comparison between different European countries. They clearly show how digital skills, soft skills and transformative skills are destined to play an increasingly fundamental role in modern economic systems. Entrepreneurship is an important aspect of economic systems and is a valuable example for investigating the interplay between economic actors, their values and institutions. Friederike Welter and Mirela Xheneti, in Chapter 16, analyse the impact of institutions on entrepreneurship. Institutions set both boundaries and incentives for entrepreneurial activity. Consequently, the nature and pace of development of entrepreneurship are influenced by the interplay between formal and informal institutions. Welter and Xheneti analyse the influence of institutions on incentives and values in different challenging environments and contexts: from transition economies to emerging markets, by paying particular attention to the challenges for female entrepreneurship. The chapter provides a number of pointers for future research into the interplay of institutional contexts and entrepreneurship. The economic implications of gender inequality are considered by Quentin Wodon in Chapter 17. He estimates the global potential cost of gender inequality in terms of losses in human capital wealth (defined as the present value of the future earnings of the current labour force) as opposed to annual losses in income or economic growth. The analysis builds on estimates of the changing wealth of nations. Wodon estimates the cost of gender inequality in earnings globally, regionally and by country income groups. The analysis shows how losses are very large, albeit differ among regions and countries, and tend to increase in absolute value with economic development, given higher earnings in high-income countries. In Chapter 18, Donato Cutolo and Martin Kenney explain how the digitalization process and the emergence of digital platform firms have had a major impact on entrepreneurship and deal with this topic through an analysis of how entrepreneurship needs to be reconceptualized within platform economies. They discuss the risks and consequences associated with the existence of power asymmetries in this new and complex environment. Digitization calls into question the relationships between economic actors, and it can have a relevant impact also on the relationship between firms and workers. In this regard, Csaba Makó, Miklós Illéssy and Saeed Nosratabadi investigate in Chapter 19 whether working practices or strategies exist that allow to improve simultaneously firm's performance and workplace well-being in a context of growing digitalization and innovation. They present a quantitative analysis aimed to verify how different management systems in Europe address this dilemma. They find that employee participation processes can be relevant in this context, an aspect that underlines the importance for CES of analysing the structure and organization of firms and the relationship among its actors. The last two chapters of this part broaden the macroeconomic perspective by analysing the relationship between entrepreneurship, firms and the process of transformation and convergence of the economic systems. In Chapter 20, Wladimir Andreff offers an analysis of multinational companies based in emerging countries and postcommunist transition economies and significantly engaged in investing abroad. Using as a theoretical framework Dunning's investment development path model completed with Matthews's linkage-leverage-learning hypothesis, he observes how these multinationals are growing faster with respect to those based in developed market economies. Andreff discusses the role of the wave of outward foreign direct investment in the development of these emerging countries in the last few decades. A development that, however, has not been uniform in many countries as discussed in the closing Chapter 21 presented by Alexander Chepurenko and Miklós Szanyi. They analyse the outcomes of the transformation processes of former socialist countries of Central and Eastern Europe in the course of the changes, which manifested in these countries in the last few decades. The heterogeneity and/or lack of the systemic character of these changes is the main reason of the divergent outcomes, which are strictly connected to the difference of historical patterns and pathways (cultures, traditions) as well as of the singularity of institutional frameworks established after the collapse of the former system in each of these countries. These results confirm the importance of a systemic (re)vision of the complexity of different economic systems.

I.6 The factors requiring the comparative study of economic systems

The comparative study of economic systems can proceed based on two main approaches: the choice of the comparatist as to what is important and worth comparing and the analysis based on the society's preferences (such as voters, governments, investors, workers). In the former case, the expert chooses a particular perspective – particularly under the influence of a theory or belief – that she/he wants to privilege in order to answer a particular question. Examples are to assess which economic system promotes the fastest growth rate, assures full employment, pursues the highest standard of living for the population, promotes economic development, supports the highest competitiveness of companies and creates the best context for entrepreneurship. The approach can also make use of a complex of variables and related indicators or qualitative features (such as a complex statistical index or a complex of economic and possibly non-economic qualitative variables). Sometimes the comparatist may want to answer a more general, holistic question: which is the best system or the good or best society (Berliner 1999)?

In the latter case, the approach can be similar to the former case, but the starting point is more complex and demanding. It cannot be the preference or the choice of the expert but should take origin from the preferences and choices of society as revealed, for instance, in opinion polls or government's plans and other documents. This approach privileges the consistency of social choices, the cohesion of societies and their economic system and the nature of interrelation of economic, political and social components in the pursuit of socially defined goals.

Both approaches require analytic clarity of what determines the nature and performance of economic systems. This means having a sound analysis of the role of factors, the interrelations existing among them, the role of new factors or events in the general picture. Within this broad picture, it may be wise to choose a subsection of the system to get deeper and more precise answers. Analytical clarity can be reached at an absolute or relative level. In the former case, based on the comparatist's perspective, a sound answer has to be given to the question of which is the best economic system from a particular perspective, *ceteris paribus*, irrespective of the actual possibility for a given system to compete on equal footing with another economic system. A classic example is the comparison of the economic performance of the United States and the Soviet or the Chinese economic systems or some subset of the performance, such as productivity. This approach is useful to answer a particular question, typically significant for normative purposes, but is inevitably reductive as to its contribution to a deeper knowledge of what the economic system is, why different economic systems exist and what their relative advantages and disadvantages are. This approach tends to concentrate on economic factors and disregard other factors (such as politics, society, culture) that are important for economic performance.

In the latter case, the comparison takes into consideration that all other factors are rarely equal when comparing two different economic systems, particularly when they are considered to coincide with the borders of a country or a region and when important factors as the level of development, the endowment of human or physical resources, culture or political and social preferences are different. Clearly, the comparatist's approach can reach more precise results at the price of their heuristic, normative and political weakness. The second approach has the right view of the complexity of comparisons and the nature and role of the economic system and can contribute significantly to a better knowledge of different economic systems and their relation to other non-systemic factors. The price to be paid may be to obtain less clear-cut, more general results. A way of reconciling the two approaches is the comparison of real countries that are very similar under all headings except the economic system or the particular subject of the comparison. Classical cases are the comparison of the two Germanys before unification and of the two Koreas. However, these cases are very limited in number and cannot answer all the important questions that the comparison of different economic systems can give. A logically similar solution, albeit less precise, is to use counterfactual analysis, aiming at assessing what would have happened to a country or economic system in the absence of an intervention or event. In this case, the effect is estimated by comparing counterfactual outcomes, approximated with reference to a comparison group of countries or economic systems, to those observed under the intervention or the event. A typical example is to anticipate the effect of EU membership on a non-member country.

As an approximation of the value of these two different approaches, the fourth part of the Handbook focalizes on the outcomes that different economic systems generate and how these outcomes change following the evolution and transformation of economic systems. Markets, governance, performance and change in economic systems are the keywords of this fourth part. Coherently with the approaches of the previous chapters, the importance of a systemic vision is also emphasized in this part. László Csaba, in Chapter 22, introduces and discusses the importance of systemic governance as a novel concept within CES. He analyses bottom-up and top-down forms of social engineering in different countries with particular attention to the comparison between Western and Eastern countries. His approach demonstrates how the interaction between different economic actors is able to generate spontaneous socioeconomic and political orders and underlines the importance for CES of incorporating this systemic interpretation of social relations for the analysis of economic systems. Andrea Boltho, in Chapter 23, confirms the importance of a systemic perspective also in the analysis of comparative advantage. After a review of traditional and novel approaches in the analysis of comparative advantage, he investigates the systemic determinants of economic specialization and underlines the role of institutions and policies in influencing the pattern of trade and, in particular, in determining the successful performance of some East Asian countries, which have radically changed their export structures. He concludes that at the base of some success stories are interventionist policies centered on import substitution (the cases of Japan and China) or policies based on export promotion (the cases South Korea and Taiwan). In Chapter 24, Pranab Bardhan focalizes on the organizational aspects of governance systems and their impact on the development of countries. He offers a detailed comparison between China and India governance issues. In his analysis, he goes beyond the usual contraposition between authoritarianism and democracy, typical of comparative governance, and underlines the role of political culture, historical development and the complexity of the government organization in shaping a country path of development.

The EU offers a fundamental case study for CES in that it includes and coordinates a group of countries having different traditions, structures, size, informal institutions, political systems, cultures and others. However, they also share some fundamental formal institutions (money, acquis communautaire, justice). The process of European integration thus represents an important topic for CES because it deals with the issue of convergence or divergence among heterogeneous countries that share a common economic and political project. In Chapter 25, Pierfederico Asdrubali and Paolo Pasimeni investigate the sectorial and geographical structure and evolution of the EU Single Market. Through an analysis of trade interdependencies within and outside the Single Market, they illustrate its importance – particularly for the automotive sector and for smaller member states – as well as the challenges it has to face in an increasingly globalized world: from the decrease in the relative weight of the Single Market as a source of final demand to its exposure to global supply chains in strategic sectors. The authors' results pose interesting questions about the possible need to rethink strategic autonomy and economic relations with extra-EU countries that are experiencing faster growth in demand. To fully answer similar questions, it is necessary, however, to better understand the factors behind the complex dynamics within Europe, so as to assess all the strengths and weaknesses of the EU in the context of an increasingly globalized world. In Chapter 26, Miklós Rosta completes these investigations about European countries by analysing whether the transition in Central and Eastern Europe can be considered concluded and whether these transformation processes have generated new VoC. These chapters clearly indicate how many factors influence relationships among countries, and their investigation improves CES understanding of the consequences that economic and non-economic differences in a globalized world have on the economic systems. In the last two chapters, the focus is on two particularly important factors: financial globalization and international tax evasion.

In Chapter 27, Marek Dabrowski analyses the role of globalization in functioning modern economies. In particular, he discusses the impact of the deepening and integration of global financial markets and the role of financial regulation and macroeconomic policy in influencing the trade-off between the micro-and macroeconomic benefits and the costs associated with financial globalization. His analysis demonstrates the irreversibility of the financial integration process which, however, requires greater global policy coordination in order to minimize global shocks, mitigate vulnerability for individual countries and avoid a regulatory race to the bottom. Globalization has various consequences for economic systems that require international collaboration. In Chapter 28, David Kemme, Bhavik Parikh and Tanja Steigner investigate country and system characteristics that are linked to international tax evasion. After a general overview of tax evasion, they focus on the motivation of personal international tax evasion and the characteristics of tax haven countries. According to their analyses, novel characteristics of tax evasion include systemic and cultural characteristics, income inequality, autocracy, sovereign wealth funds and tax morale. Special issues of transition economies are also considered. The determinants and impact of tax evasion are relevant to the study of economic systems, and reducing international tax evasion requires more uniform domestic policies based on international collaboration.

I.7 Different perspectives on the economic systems in the global economy: Independent varieties or structured parts?

The traditional implicit reference of comparative economic studies are countries and their economies or subsets of them, such as firms or the labour market, although some valuable studies also exist at the meso-level such as on regions (Alesina and Giuliano 2015, Andriani and Bruno 2022, Guiso et al. 2006, Tabellini 2010). However, a fundamental question remains open in a globalized economy: are borders and sovereign governments sufficient conditions to justify only secondary attention to international embeddedness, influence, conditionality and interrelations as factors influencing the working and performance of economic systems or is the international context of such importance that the role of national sovereignty is diluted by the dominant international context and its interrelations? (Friedman 2005, Fukuyama 1992).

This question is important for its own sake and because many comparatists are involved in the study of the VoC. According to this increasingly important approach, convergence to one broad system (capitalist market economies) is a fact under the pressure of globalization and transition. However, the dominance of the capitalist system does not mean that national economic systems are institutionally identical. Indeed, different varieties exist and they keep their idiosyncrasies, e.g. in the nature and working of financial and labour markets and enterprises, based on different economic and non-economic factors, including culture, history and geography (Hall and Soskice 2001). However, these idiosyncrasies explain the different adaptations of economies to globalization and to European integration and their different performance, at the level of the entire system or its particular parts. In this perspective, sovereign countries are free to adapt but cannot choose alternatives.

Even more direct is the capitalist world-system approach proposed first by Immanuel Wallerstein (Hopkins and Wallerstein 1982), according to which only one system exists, the capitalist one. All existing countries are part of this system, including former socialist countries before the transition. Yet this system is highly structured, and only formally sovereign countries take part differently in the system. In particular, the dominant countries form the core ("centre") of the system and get the highest economic and political advantages from this. Other countries play a secondary role ("periphery"), suffer from asymmetric exchanges in the world market and see their development largely determined and de facto hindered by the core. The system is thus unique, but the different roles and specializations that countries play in the world system cause their economies and societies to acquire different features and move along different paths. The world system consists consequently of the centre (core) and periphery (and semiperiphery) and their interrelations. The sovereignty of countries in this perspective is limited to the management of the country's particular place and role in the international division of labour.

These different analytic approaches share the understanding that the economic system consists fundamentally of institutions (and occasionally of organizations in which institutions are embedded) that explain the different setup, nature and working of economies. Yet the system itself is under the influence of a set of important factors that define the problems that systems have to solve. The interrelation between the institutional and organizational structure of the system and the factors that influence its existence largely explain the system's performance, depending on the system's ability to adapt, deal with and manage those factors.

Various exogenous and endogenous factors have been and are considered in comparative economic studies. The following ones appear particularly important: the international context and relations, endowments, technology, power relations, competition, incentives, behaviour and preferences (as influenced by culture, ideology, religion, history), policies and reforms. More recently, the importance of major unforeseen events ("black swans"), such as the International Financial Crisis and the COVID-19 pandemic, are also considered as major shocks and sources of systemic risks capable of influencing and changing economic systems (e.g. of causing financial systemic crises and through the effect of these to change the economic system). Lately, the long wave of the ill-conceived and managed demise of the Soviet Union in connection with the crisis over Ukraine may represent a new black swan with significant long-term systemic consequences.

I.8 Agendas for the future of CES

The last part of the Handbook looks ahead by investigating where is CES heading at and its ability to disentangle important challenges for modern economic systems. In this part, the focus is at both the exogenous challenges of sister disciplines and novel theories and the problems to be dealt with, both in theoretical and applied perspectives, and the endogenous factors promoting the possible evolution of the discipline, including the interaction of and competition among the different approaches. In the study of modern economic systems, it now seems out of place to exclude social or political factors because social, political and economic systems coevolve, interact and influence each other. CES is therefore called upon to interact more with other disciplines, and Chapter 29 of Vilde Lunnan Djuve and Carl Henrik Knutsen aims to meet this challenge. In the chapter, they review recent empirical and theoretical literature about how economic performance and different features of economic systems affect political regime stability and change, with special attention to the democratization and autocratization processes. Their study shows the complex interconnections between the economic and political spheres, the important impact of economic features on regime outcomes and underlines the importance of considering the political impact of economic crises. The importance of interdisciplinarity, complexity and systemic vision is also confirmed in this part of the Handbook. In Chapter 30, William Hynes, Alan Kirman, Clara Latini and Davide Luzzati analyse modern socioeconomic systems and the challenges they have to face. They note how modern economies are fragile and vulnerable to political, financial and health crises. This requires to shift attention away from equilibrium, optimality and efficiency and to focus on more prominent properties of social systems and, in particular, on resilience, which is the ability of a system to respond to changes, stressors and turbulences coming from a complex and unstable environment (a topic treated from a theoretical point of view also in Chapter 6). This requires the adoption of an interdisciplinary systemic resilience approach able to build those regulations, safeguards, buffers and policies to better face future shocks. The pandemic is a vivid example of a global shock capable of putting a strain on the socio-economic resilience of modern economic systems. In Chapter 31, Vladimir Popov offers a comparative economic analysis of global health care protection and the costs of underinvestment into the national health care systems. Due to externalities in the health care protection, costs of underinvestment into the national health care system are borne not only by the country in question but by the whole world, so national governments should be held responsible to protect populations from diseases, to provide health care services and to invest efficiently sufficient resources to improve healthy life expectancy. This duty is similar to the obligations in the framework of the responsibility to protect (R2P) concept that requires countries to protect their citizens from human rights violations. From the point of view of ensuring high life expectancy at a given level of per capita income and spending on health care, China is doing better than many other countries, including the United States, which has high per capita income and spends 17% of GDP on health care, but does not provide universal access to health care and lags behind countries with a similar level of economic development in terms of life expectancy (79 years). The coordination of national obligations in the provision of health care services can be a model for tackling other global challenges such as climate change. In Chapter 32, Gang Fan and Lailai Li adopt a comparative perspective for investigating the economics of climate change. There are differences in addressing this challenge in terms of prospects, positions and policies for mitigating carbon emissions between developed and emerging and developing countries. However, global warming, as a global public bad, requires new cooperation between all economic systems. Along with emission trading, carbon taxes and green financing, the great challenge is to develop a shared responsibility for the phenomenon of global warming and mitigate its consequences in order to allow poor countries to follow a healthy development process and guarantee good environmental conditions for future generations. The issues related to future generations are at the core of Chapter 33, presented by Misbah Tanveer Choudhry, Enrico Marelli and Marcello Signorelli. They discuss the impact of the great recession and the pandemic shock on young people with a comparative analysis of labour market dynamics. They discuss the vulnerability of youth labour market performance to macroeconomic shocks, a phenomenon that seems connected to the precariousness of young people often engaged in low-skilled or informal jobs. By identifying and quantifying the implications of these shocks for young generations, they underline the need to promote targeted policy interventions. This topic draws attention to the impact of globalization on the most vulnerable social groups and how national governments can address these challenges. These issues indirectly question the capitalist model of Western economies and its ability to guarantee widespread welfare across age groups. The future of the shape of capitalist economies is not easily predictable. In Chapter 34, Panagiotis E. Petrakis develops four potential scenarios describing alternative futures of capitalist economies. These scenarios are constructed given the risks associated with climate change, pandemics and geopolitical tensions that could transform international economic relationships. Therefore, the growth scenario will not prevail, while the collapse scenario is not examined. The future of Western capitalist societies will be characterized by a transformation scenario outlined by uncertainty and drastic technological changes. During this process, some unstable features will be present but eventually will not prevail. The political economy of these scenarios is influenced by a combination of economic, political and social factors. We can expect the dynamics to be different between developed and developing countries. In Chapter 35, Mikhail Stolbov and Maria Shchepeleva demonstrate how the interaction between financial development, macroprudential policy and economic growth can be different among developing and developed countries. Indeed, while in advanced economies, the link between these variables is clear, in emerging markets such a link is absent and macroprudential policy seems not to have a real impact on financial development. These results underline that the heterogeneity among different economic systems matters and policies should be designed according to the social, cultural, historical and developmental features of countries. These insights should be carefully taken into consideration also when evaluating international projects and relations among countries. In Chapter 36, Euston Quah and Nursultan Iuldashov offer a comparative evaluation of transborder infrastructure projects with a particular focus on the Belt and Road Initiative (BRI). In this study, the historical comparison between the ancient silk road and the contemporary BRI intersects with the socioeconomic implications of an international initiative with strong economic and geopolitical implications, in particular with reference to the redistribution of economic power and possible collaborations between East and West. Many emerging Asian countries and, in particular, China are destined to play a fundamental role in the world economy. The rise of these countries implies a comparison, not only in economic terms but also in terms of values and socio-political models, between East and West. In this regard, Kumiko Haba, in the closing Chapter 37 of the Handbook, claims that, nowadays, we are experiencing a major turning point because the centrality of Europe and the United States as economic and social models may vanish in favour of the emergence of alternative models from East Asia and Southeast Asia. She argues that this passage implies a revision of the values of capitalism threatened by inequalities, economic slowdown and rising populism. According to her analysis, this revision of values should not lead to opposition between different economic models but a new form of cooperation.

I.9 Conclusions: The importance of the evolving domain comparative economic systems

The structure of the Handbook follows a path that, starting from the recognition of the CES potential contributions to the development of the economic discipline, reaffirms the centrality of the economic system as a key concept for economic analysis and the relevance of the comparative approach to understand and master differences, similarities, compatibilities and interactions among countries and their economies and constituents. The economic system is a complex entity defined rationally only to a limited extent and influenced by history, the social and political context. The comparative approach offers different methods to study the interrelationships between different institutions and actors, classify different economic systems and measure and compare their performance. It is therefore clear how much CES can help untangle the challenges that modern economies will have to face: from economic crises to pandemics, from globalization to climate change to new political and military clashes. As will be discussed in depth in the conclusions, CES can bring to economic theory that systemic, complex and interdisciplinary vision that is fundamental to address future challenges.

The complex nature of economic systems, their internal interaction and coordination, and the external factors influencing them explain the possibility of having multiple institutional coordinated solutions ("equilibria"); each one is forming an economic system under the constraint of endowments (including culture, religion, ideology, resources, geography). Several components of the economic system explain why economic systems are different. Among the most often cited and studied such components are the nature, organization and role of the state and of firms; labour relations; the origin, features and control/allocation of capital; property rights; different coordination and regulation of the constituent parts; networks among economic actors.

In a given system and in a particular country, these components have particular and stable features which are strengthened through multiple and continuing interactions. In this sense, we can speak of a locally unique institutional equilibrium, i.e., an economic system that is typical in a given economy or country and that is made of institutions with particular features. In well-working economies, this equilibrium is dynamic and resilient in the sense that it adapts and reacts to changing conditions in the economic (and political, social, domestic and international) context. In an open international economy, when international economic activities and interactions become particularly important (globalization), local unique equilibria interact strongly. A certain degree of structural and, in a more limited way, institutional convergence may follow either spontaneously or promoted and supported by international organizations and powerful countries with the aid of "best practices", such as the Washington Consensus and ideologies. However, since international interaction takes place primarily through production and market exchanges and since institutional factors causing locally unique institutional equilibria tend to be sticky and resilient and significantly based also on informal institutions, institutional convergence is usually limited in its significance and extension and not necessary (e.g. the EU: cf. Casagrande and Dallago 2021).

Comparative economists are well alerted to the limits of systemic convergence. Yet more work is necessary to deeply understand the nature and processes at the basis of these limits. Too many damages came and come from the implementation of policies and reforms based on the conviction that convergence to a supposed best system is inevitable and positive after political obstacles are dismantled (colonization and decolonization, IMF conditionalities, "transition", best practices, EU integration, ungoverned globalization), a conviction akin to Friedman's approach.

We need a better understanding of the origin, change and importance of economic systems. The comparative approach applied to economic systems and their components is a powerful analytic instrument. Yet it is not enough: we also need to go deeply inside the economic system, understand well its nature, structure and dynamics, why it exists and is important, why it is so resilient and difficult to change or foresee the recombination and adaptation of its constituent parts when change is forced and why systemic differences among countries persist, evolve and may even increase or take new forms. We have to better understand whether different countries with different economic systems form a unique world system or whether systemic differences introduce unsurmountable breaks (differences of interest, incompatibilities, conflicts) in the world economy. This certainly requires (also) a broad analysis akin to the classical approach in economics (such as political economy) and due consideration of non-economic factors (also) by means of multidisciplinary analysis. In this way, CES may aim to better explain the present and the evolution of countries and the world economy, thus providing positive and normative analyses with a better and sounder frame, contributing to solving the old debate about the realism of assumptions.

The Handbook does not provide a full and definitive answer to the above questions. Yet it aims at providing ideas, answers and facts that may be useful in stimulating the discipline to move into new directions.

Note

1 Ivarola (2018) criticizes Friedman's analytic method by maintaining that economic phenomena are not compatible with the logic of invariant knowledge, but they can be understood only by adopting the logic of "possibility trees" or "open-ended results". Moreover, the hypothesis of invariant knowledge may entail both external validity problems and negative exposures to a "black swan".

References

Alesina, A. and Giuliano, P. (2015). 'Culture and institutions', *Journal of Economic Literature*, Vol. 53, N. 4, pp. 898–944.

Amable, B. (2003). *The Diversity of Modern Capitalism*, Oxford: Oxford University Press.

Andreff, W. (ed.) (2021). *Comparative Economic Studies in Europe. A Thirty Year Review*, Cham: Palgrave Macmillan.

Andriani, L. and Bruno, R.L. (2022). 'Introduction to the special issue on institutions and culture in economic contexts', *Journal of Institutional Economics*, Vol. 18, N. 1, pp. 1–14.

Berliner, J.S. (1999). *The Economics of the Good Society: The Variety of Economic Arrangements*, Malden, MA and Oxford: Blackwell Publishers.

Boettke, P.J., Coyne, C.J., Leeson, P.T. and Sautet, F. (2005). 'The new comparative political economy', *Review of Austrian Economics*, Vol. 18, Nos. 3–4, pp. 281–304.

Brada, J.C. (2009). 'The new comparative economics versus the old: Less is more but is it enough?' *European Journal of Comparative Economics*, Vol. 6, N. 1, pp. 3–15.

Casagrande, S. and Dallago, B. (2021). 'Benchmarking institutional variety in the Eurozone: an empirical investigation', *Economic Systems*, Vol. 45, N. 1, pp. 1–13 (100838). https://doi.org/10.1016/j.ecosys.2020.100838

Coase, R.H. (1982). "How Should Economists Choose?" *The G. Warren Nutter Lectures in Political Economy*, Washington, DC: American Enterprise Institute.

Dallago, B. and Mittone, L. (eds.) (1996). *Economic Institutions, Markets and Competition. Centralisation and Decentralisation in the Transformation of Economic Systems*, Cheltenham: Edward Elgar.

Dallago, B. and Casagrande, S. (2021). "The 'New Comparative Economics': A Critical Review," in: Elodie Douarin and Oleh Havrylyshyn (eds.), *The Palgrave Handbook of Comparative Economics*, Cham: Palgrave Macmillan, pp. 91–117.

Denzau, A.T. and North, D.C. (1994). 'Shared mental models: ideologies and institutions', *Kyklos*, Vol. 47, N. 1, pp. 3–31.

Djankov, S., Glaeser, E., La Porta, R., Lopez-de-Silanes, F. and Shleifer, A. (2003). 'The new comparative economics', *Journal of Comparative Economics*, Vol. 31, N. 4, pp. 595–619.

Douarin, E. and Havrylyshyn, O. (eds.) (2021). *The Palgrave Handbook of Comparative Economics*, Cham: Palgrave Macmillan.

Foley, M. and Pyle, W. (2003). 'Former socialist economies and the undergraduate curriculum', *Comparative Economic Studies*, Vol. 45, N. 4, pp. 537–553.

Friedman, M. (1953). *Essays in positive economics*, Chicago, IL: University of Chicago Press.

Friedman, T. (2005). *The World Is Flat: A Brief History of the Twenty-First Century*, New York, NY: Farrar, Straus, and Giroux.

Fukuyama, F. (1992). *The End of History and the Last Man*, New York, NY: Free Press.

Grossman, G. (1967). *Economic Systems*, Englewood Cliffs, NJ: Prentice Hall.

Guiso, L., Sapienza, P. and Zingales, L. (2006). 'Does culture affect economic outcomes?', *Journal of Economic Perspectives*, Vol. 20, N. 2, pp. 23–48.

Guo, S. and Lee, J. (2011). 'Keeping up with fashion: recent trends in the subfields of study of doctoral students in economics', *Economics Research Working Paper Series, Paper 20*, http://digitalcommons.fiu.edu/economics_wps/20

Hall, P.A. and Soskice, D. (2001). "An Introduction to Varieties of Capitalism," in: P.A. Hall and D. Soskice (eds.), *Varieties of Capitalism: The Institutional Foundations of Comparative Advantage*, Oxford: Oxford University Press, pp. 1–68.

Hanson, P. (2007). 'The tasks ahead in comparative economic studies: What should we be comparing?' *Japanese Journal of Comparative Economics*, Vol. 44, N. 1, January, pp. 1–14.

Hirschman, A.O. (1970). *Exit, Voice, and Loyalty: Responses to Decline in Firms, Organizations, and States*, Cambridge, MA: Harvard University Press.

Hirschman, A.O. (1982). *Shifting Involvements: Private Interest and Public Action*. Princeton, NJ: Princeton University Press.

Hirschman, A.O. (1984). 'Against parsimony: Three easy ways of complicating some categories of economic discourse', *American Economic Review*, Vol. 74, N. 2, pp. 89–96.

Hogdson, G.M. (2017). 'Introduction to the Douglass C. North memorial issue', *Journal of Institutional Economics*, Vol. 13, N. 1, pp. 1–23.

Hopkins, T.K. and Wallerstein, I.M. (1982). *World-Systems Analysis: Theory and Methodology*, Thousand Oaks, CA: Sage Publications.

Ivarola, L.I. (2018). 'A plea for realistic assumptions in economic modelling', *Theoria: An International Journal for Theory, History and Foundations of Science*, Vol. 33, N. 3, pp. 417–433, https://www.jstor.org/stable/26514393

Johnson, M. and Kovzik, A. (2016). 'Teaching comparative economic systems 25 years after the collapse of the Soviet Union', *International Review of Economics Education*, Vol. 22, pp. 23–33.

Kaasa, A., Vada, M. and Varblane, U. (2014). 'Regional cultural differences within European Countries: Evidence from Multi-country surveys', *Management International Review*, Vol. 54, pp. 825–852.

Kornai, J. (1984). 'Bureaucratic and market coordination', *Osteuropa Wirtschaft*, Vol. 29, N. 4, pp. 306–319.

Kornai, J. (1990). 'The affinity between ownership forms and coordination mechanisms: The common experience of reform in socialist countries', *Journal of Economic Perspectives*, Vol. 4, N. 3, pp. 131–147.

Kovzik, A. and Johnson, M. (2016). 'Comparative economics systems in the undergraduate curriculum: An update', *Journal of Economic Education*, Vol. 47, N. 2, pp. 168–173.

Mandelbrot, B. and Hudson, R.L. (2004). *The (Mis)Behavior of Markets. A Fractal View of Risk, Ruin, and Reward*, New York, NY: Basic Books.

Murrell, P. (2011). 'The way we were: Reflections on the comparative history of comparative economics', *Comparative Economic Studies*, Vol. 53, N. 4, pp. 489–505.

North, D.C. (1990). *Institutions, Institutional Change, and Economic Performance*, New York, NY: Cambridge University Press.

North, D.C. (2000). 'Big-bang transformations of economic systems: An introductory note', *Journal of Institutional and Theoretical Economics/Zeitschrift für die gesamte Staatswissenschaft*, Vol. 156, N. 1, March, pp. 3–8.

North, D.C. (2003). "Understanding the Process of Economic change," *Forum series on the role of institutions in promoting economic growth*, Forum 7, Institutional barriers to economic change: Cases considered, Mercatus Center, George Mason University. (https://mercatus.org/uploadedFiles/Mercatus/Publications/Understanding%20the%20Process%20of%20Economic%20Change.pdf)

North, D.C. (2005). *Understanding the Process of Economic Change*, Princeton, NJ: Princeton University Press.

Pasquino, G. (1983). 'Shifting involvements: Private interest and public action (review)', *SAIS Review*, Vol. 3, N. 1, Winter-Spring 1983, pp. 231–233, DOI: 10.1353/sais.1983.0015

Pryor, F.L. (2005a). 'Market economic systems', *Journal of Comparative Economics*, Vol. 33, N. 1, pp. 25–46.

Pryor, F.L. (2005b). 'National values and economic growth', *American Journal of Economics and Sociology*, Vol. 64, N. 2, pp. 451–483.

Rosemberg, A. (1992). *Economics–Mathematical Politics or Science of Diminishing Returns?* Chicago, IL: University of Chicago Press.

Ross, C.G. (1995). 'The future of the comparative systems course in the undergraduate economics curriculum', *Journal of Economic Education*, Vol. 26, N. 2, pp. 195–200.

Shleifer, A. (December 2002). 'The New Comparative Economics', *NBER Reporter*, Fall, N. 4, pp. 12–15, https://www.nber.org/reporter/fall02/newEconomics.html

Siegfried, J.J. and Walstad, W.B. (2014). 'Undergraduate coursework in economics: A survey perspective', *Journal of Economic Education*, Vol. 45, N. 2, pp. 147–158.

Siegfried, J.J. and Wilkinson, J.T. (1982). 'The economics curriculum in the United States: 1980', *American Economic Review*, Vol. 72, N. 2, pp. 125–138.

Tabellini, G. (2010). 'Culture and institutions: Economic development in the regions of Europe', *Journal of the European Economic Association*, Vol. 8, N. 4, pp. 677–716.

Taleb, N.N. (2007). *The Black Swan: The Impact of the Highly Improbable*, New York, NY: Random House.

von Jacobi, N. (2018). 'Institutional interconnections: Understanding symbiotic relationships', *Journal of Institutional Economics*, Vol. 14, N. 5, pp. 853–876.

Wolf, C. (1993). *Markets or Governments. Choosing between Imperfect Alternatives*, Cambridge, MA: MIT Press.

PART I

Comparative economic studies and the economic system: Theoretical and analytical approaches

1

COMPARATIVE ECONOMIC SYSTEMS AND ECONOMIC THEORY

Hans-Jürgen Wagener

EUROPA-UNIVERSITY VIADRINA FRANKFURT (ODER), GERMANY

Benjamin Ward (1972, 10) once counted comparative economic systems among the slum fields of economics or, even worse, to be in need to use the word "economic" in its customary title. And indeed, *The New Palgrave Dictionary of Economics* does not contain a single reference to the economic system, let alone to the field of comparative economic systems. The closest it gets is mentioning capitalism as a historical formation or a "stage" of social evolution. But "the majority of present-day economists do not use so broad a canvas, concentrating on capitalism as a market system, with the consequence of emphasizing its functional rather than its institutional or constitutive aspects" (Heilbroner 2008, 692). Yet, comparative economics has been a thriving occupation of economists, in times of Cold War perhaps more so than at present, it has its own habitat (e.g. *Journal of Comparative Economics, Comparative Economic Studies, Economic Systems, European Journal of Comparative Economics*), and it has left its traces in the development of economic theory. Among the 20 categories of the *Journal of Economic Literature* classification system, "Economic Systems" has an own slot (P). It will be the task of this contribution to outline the shape and features of the beast and map its home range on the continent of economic science.

1.1 The economic system: A brainchild of Marx and the historical school

Comparative political systems has a long history going back to Aristotle's *Politeia*. Comparative economic systems is a product of the 20th century. The first explicit definition of the economic system is found in Sombart (1925, 14): "the economic process conceived as conceptual unity, which (1) is governed by a particular economic ethos, (2) has a particular order and organization, and (3) applies a particular technology". Sombart obviously refers to Marx's historical materialism describing the mode of production (economic system) as consisting of productive forces (technology), production relations (order and organization), and superstructure (legal and political regulations, culture, economic ethos, among others). At the same time, this first definition comes close to von Bertalanffy's (1968) system-theoretic approach, seeing a system as a heuristic construct of the observer with the aim of reducing complexity.

Adam Smith's *Wealth of Nations* is full of comparative examples over time and space. For the Historical School, as for Marxists, the notion of an economic system, or mode of production,

DOI: 10.4324/9781003144366-3

has been a central object of research shaping the course and the stages of historical development. Neo-classical economics, which superseded these approaches as mainstream, has focused on a different problem: optimization under constraints or allocative efficiency. The economic system was taken as an invariant given and, hence, neglected for a long time. Only in the 1990s this changed dramatically, and it is perhaps not by chance that economic historians, like Douglass North, rediscovered the Marxian-Weberian insights of "history matters", "ideas matter" (Denzau and North 1994, 3), and "institutions matter" (North 1994). This prompts the question: "But Which Ones?" (Bardhan 2005) that must be answered by theoretical analysis and comparative empirics.

The most comprehensive treatment of comparative systems was the Marxist-Leninist political economy. The Stalinist textbook of 1954 (Political Economy 1957) dealt with the precapitalist, the capitalist, and the socialist modes of production. It was circulated in print runs of several millions and obligatory reading for any academic study in the socialist world. Since the background of the approach is a deterministic theory of history with full communism as the end stage, the precapitalist and capitalist modes of production are transitory manifestations of the economic system. In the course of history, they get outmoded. Typical of the textbook, and many others in its wake, is the positive and, hence, critical and dismissive analysis of capitalism and the normative and, hence, idealized description of socialism. Socialist economics, in general, is a theory of the economic system from a comparative point of view (Eckstein 1971a; Wagener 2021). At its core are social ownership and the economic mechanism of central planning held to be superior to private property and the market yielding the firm conviction that socialism will outperform capitalism.

The Marxist approach implies two general insights. Economic systems can be analyzed as models and as case studies (Bornstein 1971, 350–1). The model is an ideal type consisting of elements (technology, institutions, mental models) that the observer, mostly informed by a general theory and empirical evidence, considers characteristic of a particular system (e.g. the competitive market economy). Case studies compare real-world specimens of economic systems. They are historical phenomena, and they are always mixed systems, never reflecting the pure model in a perfect way. This causes difficulties when it comes to evaluating the merits and demerits of economic systems. Some economists, like Ludwig von Mises, have refrained therefore from the empirics of case studies and analyzed the economic system *a priori* purely as a logical outcome of supposedly self-evident assumptions. "Complex phenomena in the production of which various causal chains are interlaced cannot test any theory" (Mises 1949, 31). The result of such reasoning is an unconditional support for capitalism: "no judicious man could hesitate to choose capitalism", and an impossibility theorem for socialism: "Socialism is not a realizable system of society's economic organization because it lacks any method of economic calculation" (Ibid., 676). Thus, Mises's view is a perfect mirror image of the uncompromising Marxist-Leninist conviction of the opposite.

The second Marxian insight is historicity (abhorred by Austrians like Mises and Popper): real-world economic systems are historical phenomena. They have a past influencing their present state (path dependency). And they are determined by their stage of development: pre-industrial, or traditional, societies are distinct from industrial, or modern, societies; technical and organizational progress enables institutional change. The resulting national idiosyncrasies of system design led to a multitude of case studies. In the "Western" textbooks on comparative economic systems, which proliferated mainly in the 1960s and 1970s, models and cases are presented interchangeably. Outstanding examples are Landauer (1964), Bornstein (1965), Grossman (1967), Neuberger and Duffy (1976), Wiles (1977), and Gregory and Stuart (1980). The latter survived the collapse of state socialism (Gregory and Stuart 2004), and new ones were added to the list (Rosefielde 2015; Rosser and Rosser 2017). Evidently, comparative systems had been preferentially a US-American research field and teaching subject. Sputnik 1 (1957) and Gagarin (1961) had shocked the United States and triggered an enhanced political and academic interest in the Soviet Union. Khrushchev's challenge of competition of the two systems was taken up seriously.

These textbooks are basically descriptive. While explaining shortly the theory of competitive markets and central planning, they do not try to develop a general theory of economic systems or institutions. A remarkable exception is Eckstein (1971b). The list of case studies usually included the United States (model capitalism), the Soviet Union (model socialism), Eastern Europe (reform economics), Yugoslavia (the labor managed firm or market socialism), Western Europe (the mixed economy), in particular France (indicative planning) and West Germany (the social market economy), and from the less developed world such as India and China. All these economies were in permanent flux in their institutional development as well as in their performance. Later approaches remembered Max Weber's ([1904] 2002) theory and also highlighted the importance of cultural and religious factors determining the economic system. The Islamic economic system, with its taxing, banking, and financial idiosyncrasies, has attracted special attention (Nienhaus 2010; Visser 2019).

The adjacent fields are institutional and constitutional economics. Their research objects, institutions, and constitutional rules are obviously elements of economic systems. They are approached, however, not historically in a descriptive way. Their analysis uses instead the standard economic model of rational choice under constraints (Voigt 2019, 2020). So, they remedy the often-deplored lack of institutions in the neo-classical mainstream and are a welcome extension of this theory. While institutional economics deals with institutions in general, i.e., the emergence, effect, and change of specific formal and informal rules and, hence, economic choices made within general rules, constitutional economics could be regarded as a subfield of institutional economics analyzing the choice of those general rules. Over the last quarter of a century, both fields have been extremely productive and pushed the limits of economics considerably further.

A second adjacent field is area studies. They specialize in a particular geographic region (Soviet Union, Eastern Europe, Latin America, Asia) and are not confined to the economy. Historically, they were set up to serve the imperial interests of the European colonial powers; they study the politics, economics, law, culture, and languages of a geographical region. Today's most renowned institute, London University's SOAS, was founded in 1916 as School of Oriental Studies, later renamed School of Oriental and African Studies. This name turned politically incorrect. So, only the acronym is used presently, and its field is described as the study of Africa, Asia, and the Middle East, attracting students from all over the world. For comparative economic systems, traditionally focused on the capitalism-socialism dichotomy, Russian and Soviet studies became of special interest. Several of the mentioned textbook authors were also eminent sovietologists: Morris Bornstein, Gregory Grossman, Peter Wiles, Paul Gregory, and Steven Rosefielde. Clearly, area studies are concentrated upon real-world developments in their respective regions and not upon the advancement of abstract economic theory.

1.2 Some theories of economic systems

The traditional neo-classical theory showed little interest in the economic system, as said. There is a simple reason for it: The economic system was considered working itself. In a perfect neo-classical world (costless and perfect information, rational decision-making, no transaction costs), institutions do not matter for allocative efficiency, the central economic problem of this branch of theory. For all possible gains can be realized through agreement and contract in market transactions. By introducing positive transaction costs (Coase 1937) and bounded rationality (Simon 1957), new institutional economics was inaugurated with important repercussions for economic system theory.

Ideally, abstract economic theory was considered valid for any economic system. Vilfredo Pareto ([1906] 1966) demonstrated this explicitly in his *Manuale di economia politica* showing that equilibrium market allocation of resources corresponds *ceteris paribus* exactly to the allocation that a collectivist planner would decree to achieve the optimal use of resources. By implication, equilibrium prices correspond to optimal plan prices. The proof was refined shortly later by Enrico Barone ([1908] 1935). Pareto ([1906] 1966, 364) concluded: "All in all, pure economics does not provide us with a really decisive criterion to choose between a social organization based on private property and a socialist organization". Some 50 years later, the situation had not changed, and Tjalling Koopmans (1957, 147) restated this indifference proposition: "In particular, the economics profession is not ready to speak with anything approaching scientific authority on the economic aspects of the issue of individual versus collective enterprise which divides mankind in our time". Leonid Kantorovich ([1959] 1965), his co-laureate for the 1975 Nobel award, has solved the problem of optimal planning by linear programming where the dual produces "objectively founded valuations" corresponding to general equilibrium prices.

Even if pure economics is indifferent to the theoretical properties of the basic allocation mechanisms, the market or the plan, it does not follow that economists were indifferent to the respective economic systems. Quoting once more Pareto ([1896–1897] 1964, I, 321): "You may imagine beings which are superior in all respects to human beings encountered on earth up to now; then these infinitely knowledgeable, honest, and wise beings may be able with truly superhuman efforts to govern the economic phenomena yielding similar results (utility maximization) as can be reached by the play of free competition". Having to make a choice between superhuman efforts and the free play of market forces, the outcome should be obvious. The knowledge and information problem of central planning became the chief argument of Friedrich von Hayek who concluded in a similar vein: "It is probably evident that the mere assembly of these data is a task beyond human capacity" (Hayek 1935, 211). Oskar Lange (1936, 1937) designed a method to avoid the centralization of all information by institutionalizing Walras' fictional auctioneer setting provisional prices centrally, receiving supply and demand decisions from decentralized firms, and adapting prices accordingly. Eventually, equilibrium is achieved. Apart from theoretical problems, this device solves Hayek's problem only partly since the amount of necessary information transmission is still overwhelming. Lange's device has never been implemented and tested.

In Germany, the comparative analysis of economic systems developed on the basis of Walter Eucken's theory of economic order (*Ordnungsökonomie*). Eucken's approach must be understood against the background of the controversy between the Historical School and the Theoretical School (classical, Austrian, and neo-classical). In Eucken's eyes, both approaches must be combined to understand concrete economic processes. The theoretical starting point is the dichotomy of centrally directed systems and exchange systems. Within these systems, there can be a large variety of different specifications of an order consisting, for instance, of market forms (competitive, oligopolistic, monopolistic), monetary systems (gold standard, credit money, convertibility, exchange control), etc. They lead to ideal morphological systems whose working and effects are targeted by economic theory. The specific economic constitution or order is an individual historical phenomenon. This yields the duality of models and cases, which is the characteristic of the comparative analysis of economic systems.

Eucken's first book (Eucken [1939] 1943) was written under the Nazi rule. This induced him to be rather neutral about the two basic systems. In his second book, published posthumously (Eucken [1952] 1990), he takes a decidedly normative stance about the two systems deduced from efficiency and freedom considerations. The concept of "order" has a double meaning. It is a positive historical fact that can be defective in many respects, and it is an ideal type, historical model, in which proportion and equilibrium prevail. The latter is expressed by Eucken with the medieval term *ordo* creating the very German variety of "ordo-liberalism". In the end, there is only one type of order guaranteeing efficiency and freedom – the competitive order. Its morphological system is described by:

- a functioning price system
- a stable monetary system
- open and free markets
- private property
- freedom of contract
- accountability and
- the predictability of economic policy.

The market system must be complemented by an efficient state since it functions properly only under a regime of the rule of law. To keep the system stable and fair, it needs, in addition, a protective belt of corrective regulations installed by the state:

- monopoly control
- incomes policy
- control of external effects
- readjustment of adverse labor supply behavior (e.g. minimum wages).

This system also had a programmatic function in the transition from central planning of the Nazi and immediate post-war period to the West German social market economy. Its congruity with the so-called Washington consensus (Williamson 1990) of a much later transformation period is obvious.

An alternative approach concentrating on historical forms of an order has been offered since the 1970s by the French regulation school. It was triggered by the crisis marking the end of the *Trente Glorieuses* and fundamental disbelief in the self-healing powers of markets, i.e., neo-classical theory. Its roots can be traced back to Marx's historical materialism putting the institutional matrix or mode of production and its historical development center stage. But unlike Marx, the development is open-ended and not teleological, leading inexorably to communism. And unlike Marx, the neo-classicists, and Eucken, the theory of regulation lacks any normative traits: it considers neither socialist planning nor perfect competition as the most efficient form of order. The only criterion of an actual regulation system is its viability. A system becomes nonviable when external or internal contradictions and crises (or innovations, for that matter) press the agents to revise it.

The main body of research is devoted to capitalism in its manifold historical forms (the best survey is Boyer and Saillard 1995). However, the theory of regulation is also suited for the study of the socialist planned economies (Chavance 1987). The dominant system of regulation is characterized by the economics of shortage (Kornai 1980) and the inability to react adequately to permanent stress and recurrent crises.

By regulation is understood the system of formal and informal institutions that determine and constrain the actual mode of production. Within a given system of regulation, the actual mode of production is reproduced continuously up to the point where major contradictions and crises induce system changes. Capitalism has proven quite resilient in this respect. It is still viable, but it has changed its institutional structure continuously. The basic law of capitalism, according to Marx, is the accumulation of capital. Hence, the regime of accumulation determines the viability of the capitalist mode of production. In the early phase, accumulation is extensive, broadening the capital stock and including more and more workers in the capital-worker nexus. Later, accumulation becomes intensive focusing on the efficiency of the factors of production and innovation. The transition from one phase to the other is a critical turning point of the regime requiring, among others, changes in the financial system and in the capital-labor relationship. Socialist economies, which were subject to a similar trajectory, ran into a final crisis at this turning point.

Within the capitalist context characterized next to accumulation by an exchange economy, the theory of regulation discerns five institutional subsystems or forms determining the functioning of the mode of production:

- The monetary and financial system enabling the exchange of goods, also across borders, and providing credit for accumulation and structural change. Money is not neutral as in the general equilibrium model.
- The labor system which deserves special attention since it substitutes the simple Marxian theory of exploitation. It determines the institutions governing the utilization of wage labor and the living conditions of workers. In the course of time, it underwent several transformations. Capital and labor have naturally opposed interests and, at the same time, are sitting in the same boat. This makes the capital-labor compromise a central feature of the mode of production regulating accumulation and aggregate demand.
- The market forms have been described already by Heinrich von Stackelberg (1934). Regulation theory focusses, however, less on the equilibria, but more on unstable forms of oligopoly considered typical of modern economic systems and on exchange under disequilibrium conditions. This causes difficulties conceiving a satisfactory theory of relative prices.
- The forms of inclusion in the international exchange system: it is the nation state that has been the central object of research, and by force of its sovereignty, it determined the national conditions of international exchange of goods, capital, labor, and ideas. Globalization puts this sovereignty under pressure, and new forms of regulation emerge.
- The forms of governance: while Marxists-Leninists saw the state only as an agent of monopoly capital, the regulation theory is aware of the complex interplay of historical trends, political preferences, and social and economic conflicts which affect state activity. From the minimal state of the 19th century to the modern industrial and welfare state and from liberal democracy to authoritarian dictatorship, actual states exhibit a multiplicity of institutional forms regulating actual economic and social behavior.

The historical world is full of different forms of regulation. The individual regime is in permanent flux adapting to disequilibria, minor and major crises, and contradictions. This process cannot be studied by stationary general equilibrium theory but needs theoretically informed historical and comparative analysis.

The theory of order and the theory of regulation seem to be dealing with similar phenomena. Both lack a satisfactory and consistent body of abstract theory as general equilibrium analysis provides for neoclassical economics. This may be due to the highly complex nature of their object of research. But while ordoliberalism finally leads to the recognition of a natural order to be implemented by a strong state, the theory of regulation remains agnostic about ideal socioeconomic systems. This was reflected in the treatment of the transformation of socialist systems in the 1990s. Ordoliberalists had a clear-cut program of what was to be done (see Eucken's morphology of the competitive system). Regulationists stayed at the sideline, observing what actually was done.

1.3 A conceptual framework to describe and compare economic systems

An economic system may be considered as the totality of structures and processes transforming inputs into outputs. The latter are *desiderata*, the former cause costs. Hence, efficiency, a positive benefit-cost relation, is a central criterion for the evaluation of economic systems, but not the only one. Fairness, stability, freedom and self-expression, health, and education are additional *desiderata* serving equally as criteria. Historical economic systems differ widely with respect to such criteria, which elicits the question: what makes for the difference? Here lies a core motive for comparing economic systems: is it possible to identify factors influencing outcome and to improve an actually existing economic system by way of optimization or benchmarking?

To answer such questions, objective and comparable concepts are needed allowing for the description and evaluation of economic systems. Two major attempts at formulating an appropriate language and nomenclature have been undertaken: Koopmans and Montias (1971), with the extensions of Montias (1976) and Montias and Sturm (1976), and Kornai (1971) who was cognizant of the Koopmans and Montias conference paper of 1968. While Koopmans and Montias aim directly at the comparison of economic systems, Kornai, as the title of his book *Anti-Equilibrium* suggests, intended to set up a system-theoretic alternative to general equilibrium theory. In our context, his conceptual language and the brief mention of comparisons of systems (Kornai 1971, 215–17) are relevant.

Figure 1.1 is a simplified scheme of the economic system (based on Johansen 1977, 55–74). On the left side of the black box, there are the agents: the central authority with the set of its possible policies $\{P_A\}$ and the noncentral agents with their sets of possible decisions (individual policies) $\{P_i; i = 1, ..., N\}$, and the environment $\{E\}$. The agents, as a rule, are not monad-like elements as depicted in Figure 1.1. They usually form organizations such as firms, unions, clubs, communities, etc., creating not only subordination and interdependencies but also ideologies, views, and values. The agents interact within horizontal or vertical structures, markets, and hierarchies (Williamson 1975). $\{E\}$ is a large set of initial factors: technology, initial resources (natural resources, capital stock, population with number, age, health, and skills), initial preferences (in the policy interpretation of the scheme), and noncontrolled external factors. "The system is hardest to define". It "includes all political, social and economic institutions, organizational structure, laws and rules (and the extent of their enforcement and voluntary observance), and all traditions, religious and secular beliefs, attitudes, values, taboos, and the resulting systematic or stochastic behavior patterns" (Koopmans and Montias 1971, 31–2). While the policy interpretation of the scheme sees the environment as the given initial condition including the institutional framework, the system theoretic interpretation differentiates between the natural environment $\{E\}$ and the social-political environment $\{S\}$. It is possible that the natural environment, geography for instance, influences the systemic options as well as the policy options (not depicted in the scheme).

The effective system $\{s\}$ is a subset of $\{S\}$ determined by tradition and constitution. Initially, environment and system are given, but certain elements of E (technology, stocks, e.g.) and

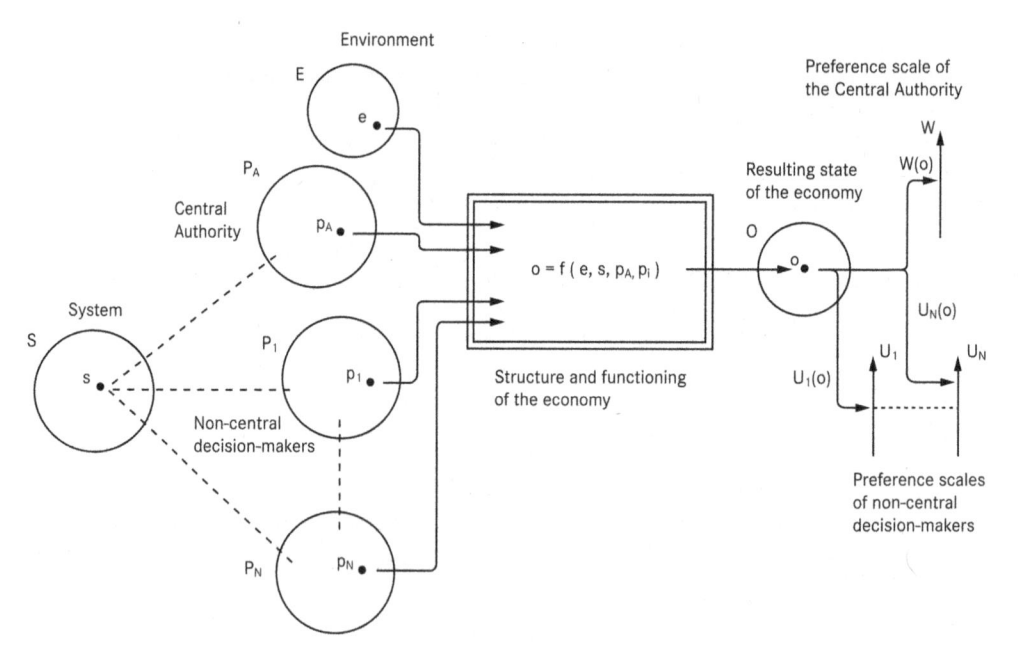

Figure 1.1   A scheme of the economic system.

Source: Johansen (1977, 66), and author's design.

elements of S (institutions) can be altered during the period of observation, while others (values) will change only over a longer period. The agents' perception of the environment is declared as a system characteristic. The dividing line between the system and policies is the time needed to change them: policies are actions within the period of observation; the system is initially given but can be adapted, at least partly, in the course of time (constitutional change).

The sets of possible policy decisions $\{P_A\}$ and $\{P_i\}$ are constrained by the environment $\{e\}$ and the system $\{s\}$, in particular, by technology, organization, and institutional rules and regulations. When $\{P_A\}$ is minimal and the $\{P_i\}$ as large as technically possible, the system is characterized by a minimal state and full *laissez-faire*. When $\{P_A\}$ is maximal and $\{P_i\}$ contains only one element p_i, there reigns full central planning.

The black box

$$o = f(e, p_A, p_i) \tag{1.1}$$

describes the structure and functioning of the economy yielding its outcome, i.e., the state determined by the policies of the agents and their perception or predictions of the given and uncontrolled factors of the environment. The e, p_A, and p_i are vectors of numerical values, as are the o. Such is the policy interpretation of the scheme assuming the system invariant (Johansen 1977, 66–7). The effect of s then must be contained in f.

For the comparison of economic systems, Koopmans and Montias regard s as a variable which yields their "grand relationship":

$$o = f(e, s, p_A, p_j) \tag{1.2}$$

with p_A in P_A (e, s) and p_i in P_i (e, s)

The e_j, s_j, and p_j vary over the j (j = 1, ..., K) economies or economic systems. When it comes to comparing economic systems, the aim is to estimate "the values $f(e_0, s_j, p_{sj})$ of the outcome vectors f for some standardized environment e_0 and for the (s_j, p_{sj}) combinations observed in the economies" (Koopmans and Montias 1971, 37). The outcome of the system hinges essentially on the (s_j, p_{sj}) combinations. This is indeed what policy (actual economic policy and constitutional policy) can do to improve it. But this does not take away the sizeable influence of different elements of the environment. Take, for instance, the Sachs hypothesis: "There is good theoretical and empirical reason to believe that the development process reflects a complex interaction of institutions, policies, and geography" (Sachs 2003, 9). To standardize the environment seems to be a strange idea in this context.

Estimating the "grand relationship" is an extremely demanding task. "The implied assumption is that the laws of physics, chemistry, technology agronomy, human and animal physiology and psychology [...] circumscribe what can be achieved by any given economic organization, in a manner subject in principle to objective inquiry and explicit description" (Koopmans and Montias 1971, 35). This is much too narrow an interpretation of the "grand relationship". For if the system, as said, "includes all political, social and economic institutions, organizational structure, laws and rules (and the extent of their enforcement and voluntary observance), and all traditions, religious and secular beliefs, attitudes, values, taboos, and the resulting systematic or stochastic behavior patterns", the factors determining o will become most diverse, and it is unclear whether they can enter the "grand relationship" with numerical values let alone to allow for first and second derivatives of at least the important outcomes in f.

Obviously, the authors conceive of {O} as the set of possibly produced goods and services and o as the vector of outcomes given predicted values of the uncontrollable factors of the environment, the effective system, and the chosen policies. This, however, is only part of the outcome of the economic process, since simultaneously, it also produces the information (prices e.g.) necessary for the proper working of the economy. This is duly taken into account by Kornai (1971, 39–42), who partitions the economic system into the real sphere describing the material, physical processes, and the control sphere consisting of information and communication elements and their processing.

Such control variables are needed to evaluate the material outcome and to decide about appropriate policies. The outcomes o contain produced goods and services and their prices (including wages, incomes, and rents). The agents must evaluate the o to be able to select rational policies (decisions) before they actually execute their decisions. They do it by way of preference scales or utility functions $U_i(o)$ for the noncentral agents and $W(o)$ for the central agent; the U_i and W (some kind of collective preference function) being elements of the environment or the system. To insert the preferences as externally given is, of course, a bold assumption. If one maintains with Kornai (2008, 191) "individual preferences are largely products of the system itself", the comparison of systems becomes considerably more difficult.

For the decision process taking place in the control sphere, the o are expected outcomes, while for actual production taking place in the real sphere, the o are real outcomes. Both need not be the same. Koopmans and Montias (1971, 36–7) make the crucial assumption that "the policies applied are the best available within the institutional and normative constraints of the system". This boils down to the assumption that the agents know the functioning of the system, i.e., have rational expectations. The attempt to conflate the real and the control spheres by assuming that agents realistically perceive real processes is a heroic fiction. If it is dropped, it must be explained which information agents have and how they form their mental models of reality, which creates new uncertainties in the system.

The individual or collective evaluations allow to aggregate a vector o into a scalar, such that we get an evaluation norm n(o) in the Koopmans and Montias framework like GDP per capita (welfare), the rate of inflation (price stability), or the Gini coefficient (equality):

$$n(o) = f(e, s, p_C, p_i). \tag{1.3}$$

Members of system A will use their preference functions, members of system B theirs, and an outside comparor C his norm. Evidently, $n(o) = f(e, s, p_C, p_i)$ will be different in all three cases. To reduce complexity, Koopmans and Montias introduce a list of *desiderata*, macro norms that can be derived from vector o, such as the level of per capita consumption, growth of per capita consumption, equity in the distribution of living conditions, stability in employment and income, provision of social services and public goods, etc. For the total system, one would need a social welfare function. Famously, Stalin (1952, 45) formulated the basic economic law of socialism: "the securing of the maximum satisfaction of the constantly rising material and cultural requirements of the whole of society" which, according to socialist political economy, differs markedly from the basic economic law of capitalism, profit maximization. However, Marxist-Leninist economists never attempted to specify what such welfare maximization meant *in concreto*. By contrast, Western welfare economics flourished at about the same time with major contributions by scholars holding a stake in comparative systems like Abram Bergson (1938, 1954) and Oskar Lange (1942).

We cannot go into the details of problems and puzzles related to the definition, specification, and measurement of all the variables and relationships connected with the functioning of economic systems. In addition, problems of endogeneity, coevolution, complexity, uncertainty, and subjectivity, e.g., may compound the difficulties. The frameworks of Koopmans and Montias and Kornai are not theories of the economic system but descriptive devices. As such, they can be useful. But it should be clear that even the most simplified description of the economic system and the comparison of different economic systems need the whole body of economics and then will run into problems of empirical verification.

Take the example of the system element rule of law. A standard proposition goes the rule of law will enhance economic welfare. In principle, the proposition can be falsified. The rule of law, however, is a fuzzy concept describing a cluster of individual institutions. Before putting it to an empirical test, its theoretical background must be clarified. The basic idea is that welfare is enhanced by investment, and since the investment decision is by nature linked to risk and uncertainty, the rule of law helps the individual agent to reduce risk and uncertainty about interactions with other agents. If the investment decision is centralized with a central planner, risk and uncertainty exist only for him. The rule of law has no influence upon his decisions and, hence, upon economic welfare. This does not falsify the proposition but qualifies it. And it shows the interdependence of system elements. For the last 50 years, no attempt has been made to estimate the "grand relationship". It does not imply that an objective comparison of economic systems is impossible. The conceptual frameworks of Koopmans and Montias and Kornai clarify the task. As a first step, partial attempts may turn out feasible and fruitful.

Here, we enter the adjacent field of institutional economics. The comparison of economic systems may be called institutional holism aiming at the economic system in its entirety, conspicuously manifested in the exemplary dichotomies (centrally administered vs. exchange economy or capitalism vs. socialism). Such is Kornai's approach, and it remained so even a quarter of a century after the collapse of Soviet-type socialism (Kornai 2016). By contrast, institutional economics pursues a kind of institutional individualism, trying to track the influence of particular institutions upon certain *desiderata*. However, the distinction gets immediately blurred once it is realized that comparative economists want to give policy advice and ascertain not the effect of the total system s on n(o), but δ n(o$_i$)/δ s$_i$, i.e., the effect of a tractable system element upon one *desideratum*: if you improve upon corruption control, you will get higher growth. The institutional economist wants to do the same: "to find out what really drives the results, measures of single institutions are essential" (Voigt 2013, 16). But often, he is confined to identifying only a whole cluster of institutional elements instead of the effective instrument variable.

Let us come back to the rule of law. To test the theoretical hypothesis, the relevant system and outcome variables must be identified and measured. The cumbersome problem of how to measure the variables of the economic system has neither been touched by Koopmans and Montias nor by Kornai. The rule of law is not directly observable, but a cluster of dozens, or more, of individual formal and informal institutions, legal rules and practices, and their acceptance and compliance procedures which may not be distinctly delineated sets. In case these institutions and their implementation are observable and can be expressed numerically (either directly or in the form of an index), one may be able to aggregate them into a wholesale index of the rule of law. Apart of the problem of aggregation weights, "the sum of single components will be of little use because we would not know where to begin looking for the 'actionable indicator'" (Voigt 2019, 123).

It would be rash, however, to dismiss the rule of law as an important system element because its effects seem hard to measure and to omit it from the constitutional design of an efficient system. Both its constitutive features and their import for welfare production can be "understood" in a holistic fashion. The operation Max Weber called "*Verstehen*" or the method of storytelling is useful for comparative economics. "Storytelling is an attempt to give an account of an interrelated set of phenomena in which fact, theory, and values are all mixed together in the telling. Historians of course are the archetypal storytellers" (Ward 1972, 180). After all, it is the story that convinces politicians to become active.

There are other wholesale indices even more broadly composed like the Economic Freedom Index (Voigt 2019, 127–39; Gwartney et al. 2019) which are used extensively in comparative research. The bottom line is that systems and institutions cannot always be decomposed to the level of tractable variables but will contain characteristics of institutional holism.

Difficulties with the measurement of outcomes are no less serious. Let us just briefly mention GDP and national income, which enter a number of *desiderata*. These indicators are generally accepted as objective measures of economic performance, which are only inasmuch as they are constructed by a well-defined and uniform method of national accounting. Presently, the *System of National Accounts (SNA)* is the only "internationally agreed standard set of recommendations on how to compile measures of economic activity in accordance with strict accounting conventions based on economic principles. […] The accounts themselves present in a condensed way a great mass of detailed information, organized according to economic principles and perceptions, about the working of an economy" (European Commission et al. 2009, 1). As long as the Soviet empire existed, a second method was in use: the *Material Product System (MPS)* of the communist countries, which made comparisons across systems very difficult.

"National accounts became the bedrock on which analysis of comparative growth performance was based. It provided a yardstick for assessing the success of policy which had never existed before" (Maddison 2007, 300–1). As a matter of fact, the bedrock is not as solid and immovable as it looks. Since GDP, for instance, is an index of goods and services produced (household production for own use is omitted as well as the state of natural resources like lake Aral), it can be aggregated only by appropriate weights, the prices of these goods and services. Even with perfect prices, price changes over time (development) and price differences across countries (preference disparities) cause the notorious index number problem. If the prices are not nearly scarcity or efficiency prices, they will not fulfill the assumptions of Koopmans and Montias and the resulting index of national income or GDP will not have the usual analytic meaning needed for comparative research. It was widely assumed in the West that Soviet national income statistics suffered from such a deficiency. Abram Bergson (1950a,b, 1961) took great pains to re-estimate the data.

Comparative research has to do with national income or GDP data in national currencies. To make these comparable, purchasing power parities are calculated, an intricate task. So, it must be considered a very bold move when Angus Maddison (2003, 2007) presents historical statistics over a period of 2000 years and across most countries of the world using a uniform set of prices (in the so-called 1990 Geary-Khamis US Dollars). Such a set of data is, of course, a treasure trove for comparative economics and widely used despite critical reservations.

1.4 The dynamics of economic systems

The dichotomous view of economic systems has yielded different hypotheses about their prospective development. Hayek ([1944] 2007) has warned that any deviation from the neoliberal path of virtue will lead onto the slippery road to serfdom. Eucken ([1952] 1990) emphasized the stability of systems and declared mixed orders unstable: "All intermediate solutions (between central administration and competition) are unstable. For they are … systems with a 'tendency to transformation'" (Ibid., 198). It follows from the consistency of the system or the "interdependence of orders" including the economic and the political order (Ibid., 180–4). This hypothesis has been recycled as "affinity of systems" by János Kornai (Mihályi and Szelényi 2021).

By contrast, Jan Tinbergen (1959, 1961) held that economic theory allowed for the construction of a unique optimal regime combining the market and the plan. Since he believed that the socialists and the liberals aim at the same *desiderata*, welfare maximization, and stability, he conjectured the ultimate convergence of economic systems. The problem with this hypothesis is not only the assumption about the *desiderata*. In addition, he left the question unanswered why, to begin with, the two systems got so widely apart if the system managers pursue similar targets and apply the principles of rational choice. Neoclassical abstinence from history may account for this omission.

Economic systems are in permanent flux. They continuously adapt to a dynamic and turbulent environment. It may happen gradually in an evolutionary way. It may also happen in discrete leaps and bounds as in transformation. Theoretical explanations sail under the flag of economic change, systemic change, and institutional change. This is a wide field, and we can only hint at basic aspects of the issue.

As with the concept of the economic system, the analysis of systemic change starts with Marx. In his theory of historical materialism (Marx [1859] 1974), exogenous changes of knowledge (technology) open up new profit opportunities. They may conflict with prevailing production relations (property rights e.g.), which must be adapted to benefit from the new opportunities. This causes further adaptations in the superstructure of legal, political, and social relations, as well as the belief system. Schumpeter ([1908] 1998; [1912] 1934) complements Marxian systemic change by methodological individualism and the figure of the entrepreneur who is the agent of the process. He tries out new commercial combinations, thereby destroying the existing equilibrium, which is restored by imitation on a different level. As a political entrepreneur, he concentrates upon new systemic or institutional combinations. As a scientific entrepreneur, he ventures into new areas of knowledge.

Scholars of new institutionalism like Douglass North have elaborated on this approach. With Marx and Schumpeter, North (2005, 63) holds that "changes in [the] stock of knowledge is the key to the evolution of economies". The source of changed perceptions about the environment may be exogenous (e.g. new competitors), but predominantly it will be endogenous or the result of learning. Learning is based on experiences. "The experiences can be classified into two kinds – those from the physical environment and those of sociocultural linguistic environment" (North 1996, 347) – Kornai's real sphere and control sphere show up again. The real sphere is much more researched than the control sphere. Cognition, the forming of mental models and preferences, information, communication, and risk management – all these are essential for the understanding of the economic process.

As with Marx and Engels for whom the ruling class determined the direction of change, power is the second driver (or retarding force) of change: "the structure of an economic market reflects the beliefs of those in a position to make the rules of the game" (North 2005, 50). This attenuates the implicit optimism of the neoclassical theory of change. For a neoclassicist like Harold Demsetz (1967, 350), a change in the environment, the historical situation, or knowledge creates externalities. The institutional change will take place as long as the expected gains become greater than the cost of internalization. North makes clear that not all alternatives considered profitable will enhance general welfare but may as well redistribute it. Lin (1989) has called welfare enhancing changes induced and welfare redistributing changes imposed resulting from a reshuffle of economic power or reordering of interest groups.

The politico-social concepts of power and class, central to Marxist political economy, are not amenable to purely economic analysis. This fact may have weakened interest in these factors among Western scholars of economic systems. Such interest has been recently revived by Randall Holcombe's (2015, 2018) concept of political capitalism, the "economic and political system in which the economic and political elite cooperate for their mutual benefit" (Holcombe 2015, 41). The model "separates people into two distinct classes: the elites and the masses, or the 1 percent and the 99 percent" (Ibid., 48). Using insights from a public choice theory like lobbying, state capture, and rent seeking, this system comes quite close to Lenin's state-monopoly capitalism. Holcombe missed the chance to subsume "illiberal capitalism" as a result of post-socialist transformation under the heading of political capitalism. It combines market capitalism with political autocracy and prolongs Lenin's primacy of politics. Examples abound in the post-socialist world (Magyar and Madlovics 2020).

Eggertsson (1990, 250) called Demsetz's proposition naïve, since it only gives a motive for change and assumes that it automatically will happen since vested interests in the prevailing regime are not considered. In fact, changes in institutional arrangements are the result of extensive bargaining in the political arena that generates probable winners and losers (Libecap 1989, 21):

"The intensity of political conflict over distribution issues and the likelihood of agreement on institutional change at any time will be influenced by a number of factors including

1.   The size of the aggregated expected gains from institutional change.
2 and 3. The number and heterogeneity of the bargaining parties.
4.   Information problems.
5.   The skewness or concentration of the current and proposed share distribution".

This boils down to the conclusion that "the important role of history complicates the development of a theory to predict the timing, form, and impact of institutional change" (Ibid., 116).

The Johansen-Koopmans-Montias scheme (see Figure 1.1) can be interpreted in a game theoretic setting: the central and individual decision makers must take the decisions of the others into account. and try to strategically optimize their own ones (Johansen 1977, 70–83). A (Nash-)equilibrium exists when none of the agents would like to alter their decision confronted with the decisions of the others. Masahiko Aoki (2001) and Avner Greif (2006) regard institutions as systemic devices to bring about and stabilize possible equilibria. In their institutions-as-an-equilibrium approach, individuals have shared beliefs about the rules of a repeated game. The (Nash)-equilibrium has the nice property that expectations of all players are fulfilled: it is self-sustaining.

Institutions coordinate the beliefs of the agents, which constitute compressed information about the equilibrium or a summary representation of the game: "Agents' strategic choices made on the basis of shared beliefs jointly reproduce the equilibrium state, which in turn reconfirms its summary representation. Thus the institution becomes self-sustaining and information compressed in it becomes taken for granted by the agents. [...] In this way, although endogenously created, an institution becomes objectified" (Aoki 2001, 12). What Aoki and Greif call institution are systemic elements that combine rules or norms and the belief systems or mental models that internalize them and guarantee their implementation.

Institutional change sets in when beliefs deviate from actual conditions (Ibid., 239–44). Once the old beliefs cannot be taken for granted anymore, there arises a cognitive mismatch between what is believed and what is experienced. The cause, as a rule, is exogenous: new knowledge, new markets, external shocks, and political change. This approach remains within the Marx-Schumpeter paradigm. "Endogenous institutional change appears, then, to be a contradiction in terms" (Greif 2006, 241). For why should an agent disturb a given equilibrium which confirms their expectations and which, in turn, is confirmed by their behavior? Indeed, there will be a strong tendency to keep up an existing equilibrium or economic regime. But if it is patently suboptimal and does not live up to expectations, the cognitive mismatch will make itself felt.

Ruling systems exhibit a remarkable tenacity: "Organizations inherited from the past have various capacities that they acquired through their operation: routines, information, and other assets, such as legitimacy; intraorganizational personal relationships and communication codes; information-processing capacities; technological know-how; and human, social, and physical capital" (Ibid., 193). A corruption equilibrium, although visibly suboptimal, is hard to dissolve: why should one play fair when the advantages of fair play materialize only if all behave accordingly? An enterprising system manager intending to alter the situation must convince a critical mass of agents that the game is played with higher payoffs according to different rules. Such difficulties in implementing superior regimes explain, for a great part, the huge differences in the performance of economic and political systems (Putnam 1993). What is needed are "synchronized searches among agents for a redefinition of their respective subjective game models" (Aoki 2001, 241). The history of reform proposals under Soviet-type socialism showcases the difficulties. The system elements are interlocked. Piecemeal reform may turn out ineffective. This insight is common to systems theory. We came across it already in Eucken ([1952] 1990).

Hayek's approach to system change is markedly different from the Marx-Schumpeter paradigm. His is based on Menger (1883) who identified two paths of system development, the pragmatic and the organic. The first is the result of deliberate collective decision-making. The second is "the unreflected result of human activities that are aimed at basically individual intentions (i.e., the unintended outcome of the latter)" (Ibid., 145). The denomination "organic" sounds unfortunate. Although following Menger quite closely, Hayek avoids the term and rather speaks of spontaneous processes. These are the predominant paths in his eyes, while the pragmatic meets with his scathing critique of constructivism which is mainly aimed at socialist planning (Hayek 1978). The reason is a lack of knowledge: "We have never designed our economic system. We were not intelligent enough for that" (Hayek 1979, 164).

Hayek's concept of institution consists of rules and order. Order is the set of rules that govern behavior, and, at the same time, it is the outcome of the behavior, the state of the system which evolves spontaneously like the price system or the system of division of labor. The pragmatic-constructivist theories of system change treat institutions and beliefs separately, the latter intentionally motivating the former. Hayek's evolutionary approach integrates the two: "The mind does not so much make rules as consists of rules of action ... which have come to govern the actions of the individuals because actions in accordance with them have proved more successful than those of competing individuals or groups" (Hayek 1973, 18). This is not far apart from Aoki's and Greif's approach combining conceptually the representation of an equilibrium in the control sphere and the equilibrium in the real sphere together.

The decisive difference is spontaneity. There is no entrepreneur in Hayek, no commercial, no political, no scientific. People have partial knowledge of the existing order. They come more or less at random across new elements and form expectations about them which may turn out correctly or not. Hayek refers to Armen Alchian who held an even more radical view about evolution: "The essential point is that individual motivation and foresight, whilst sufficient, are not necessary" (Alchian [1950] 1977, 27). Innovation, technical and institutional, may be the result of intentional experiments with new combinations, but they can also be the outcome of random factors which the agents may even not be aware of. Intentionality is not necessary for economic progress, and lack of knowledge makes it suspect. Success is adopted by survival, and the agents can be unconcerned about the motives or the random factors behind it. Thus, the economic system becomes "an evolutionary, adopting, competitive system employing a criterion of survival" (Ibid., 31). We are reminded of the French regulationists for whom viability decided about the sustained existence of a set of regulations.

1.5 Is there a new comparative economic system?

While the Marxists had wrongly predicted the imminent breakdown of capitalism, the liberals had not dared to predict the ultimate collapse of socialism. The end of really existing socialism in 1990 came as a surprise and has deprived comparative economic systems of its dominant puzzle, the opposition between individualism and collectivism. This prompted the question of whether the field is in need of a new paradigm or, at least, of a reformulation of the old paradigm. A team of five law and economics scholars boldly presented "The New Comparative Economics" (Djankov et al. 2003). In fact, they preserved the old dichotomy by opposing private and public regulation of economic processes. The key to their approach is the trade-off between disorder and dictatorship: the more private regulation, the more disorder and the more public regulation, the more dictatorship. This corresponds to the Marxist view with respect to individualism and to Hayeks's view with respect to collectivism. Both variables are measured by social cost. In the disorder–dictatorship space, each system is characterized by a line of alternative combinations, the institutional possibility frontier. The curve "is assumed to be convex to the origin. This matches the standard neoclassical assumption that marginal increases in dictatorship produce progressively smaller reductions in disorder" (Ibid., 599). As a matter of fact, there is no such neoclassical theory. The shape of the curve is only an analogy to the indifference curve. It is imaginable that at the left end of the curve a rudimentary form of the rule of law will improve greatly upon the Hobbesian *bellum omnium contra omnes*. And at the opposite end, a transition from authoritarian rule to outright Stalinism can cause a jump in total social cost. But in-between, the curve may as well be a straight line. If its angle is less than 45°, the optimal point is at the left corner, if it is more than 45°, it is at the right corner, and we arrive at the dichotomy of traditional comparative systems. Depending on the inclination of the institutional possibility line, i.e., depending on whether the Marxist or the Hayekian view about the social cost of system arrangements is considered more plausible, the individualistic or the collectivistic corner will rationally be chosen. Mixed systems are suboptimal or, as Eucken had conjectured, will not be stable. A curve convex to the origin produces Tinbergen's optimal regime and his convergence hypothesis. Similar reservations would apply.

This approach raises a host of questions, conceptual, methodological, and empirical. Some pertinent critical remarks can be found in Rosser and Rosser (2008), for instance. The graphical presentation using the example of the property rights regime (see Figure 1.2) suggests the analogy of neoclassical utility theory with indifference curves and budget lines. This is a misunderstanding. Neither is the minimal cost line "a quasi-budget line" (Rosser and Rosser 2008, 31). There is no budget for total social cost to be distributed between disorder and dictatorship. The 45° line is simply the geometric locus of constant total social cost, and its gradient indicates the point on the possibility curve where the marginal decline of the cost of disorder and the marginal increase of the cost of dictatorship are equal, i.e., the point of the minimal total cost. Any gradient deviating from the 45° line, which Rosser and Rosser consider possible, would not allow for cost minimization. Nor is the possibility curve an indifference line. There are no specific institutional preferences in this approach. It is exclusively focused on minimization of total social cost as the only *desideratum*.

But what are the causes that bring about cost minimization? "The strength and the appeal of the new comparative economics is precisely that it is unicausal, emphasizing institutions as the main drivers of differences in economic outcomes, and it has only one criterion, per capita income (or in some cases its growth) by which to judge economic performance" (Brada 2009, 7).

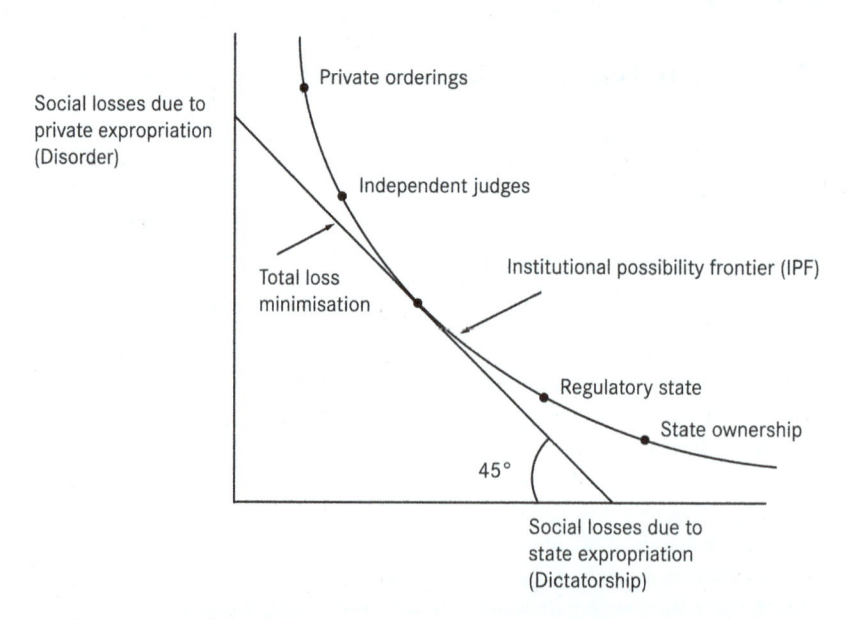

Figure 1.2   The institutional possibility curve.

Source: Djankov et al. (2003, 599).

Institutions matter – ok. But to aggregate the immense multiplicity of institutions, formal and informal, into a single causal factor: civic capital, does not do justice to the complexity of the economic system nor does a single success criterion, GDP per capita.

When society chooses its economic constitution, it is neither constrained by technology and resource capacity, as is the production possibility curve, nor is it constrained by a hard budget line as are the consumer and producer. The institutional possibilities with their social cost characteristics are scattered in the disorder–dictatorship space. What is feasible for a given society depends upon a host of factors, history, tradition, custom, culture, mental models, governance, cognition, etc. Again, by way of analogy with social capital, already a woolly concept, the authors call the whole set "civic capital" – a rather nebulous concept virtually impossible to quantify. Its size determines a frontier beyond which a given society cannot push the efficiency of its systemic choices because of lacking behavioral complementarities. This must be specific for each systemic element, and, thus, it is highly questionable that feasible best choices will be found on a well-shaped possibility frontier.

The idea is not so new after all. Some 50 years earlier, Theo Surányi-Unger (1950) proposed "to apply the apparatus of indifference curves to the problem of how much collectivism and how much 'private enterprise' can or should exist in any given economy [...] an idea which may prove to be a gold mine" (Landauer 1951, 696). However, in his review, Carl Landauer puts his finger on the fundamental problem of the approach: is it necessary to sacrifice a quantity of one "good" (in the case of Djankov et al. (2003) disorder) to obtain more of the other "good" (dictatorship) which yields the analogy of an indifference curve? Do we not "find it possible to introduce more collectivism in a field in which this seems to be useful and at the same time to expand individualism in another field where we can do so with advantage?" (Landauer 1951, 696). Djankov et al. (2003) try to circumvent the problem, as already Landauer (1951, 697) suggested, by applying the device to individual system elements like the property rights regime (see Figure 1.2) and not to the system as a whole. This does not really do away with Landauer's criticism. Take the example of China, where manufacturing and trade are open for private property, while party and state control the commanding (financial) heights with historically unique economic results.

"The New Comparative Economics" did not trigger a noteworthy body of empirical studies. By contrast, the second post-socialist endeavor in comparative economics, the "Varieties of Capitalism" approach (Hall and Soskice 2001), set off an avalanche of new scholarship (Streeck 2010, 24). This is an effort in a firm-centred comparative political economy. While the focus on capitalism in its denomination stresses the departure from the old dichotomous comparative systems, the firm-centred methodology produces an innovative exploration into comparative business systems (Whitley 1999). The parallel with the French regulation school catches the eye.

The guiding hypothesis holds that neither institutional optimization nor increasing international economic integration "will force the institutions and regulatory regimes of diverse nations into convergence on a common model" (Hall and Soskice 2001, vi). The central task of the system is similar everywhere: "firms must develop relationships to resolve coordination problems" (Ibid., 6). But history, tradition, and culture bring about different solutions to this problem which will result in different outcomes of the economic process. In particular, the authors establish specific manifestations of comparative advantage.

The institutional structure is described along five spheres or institutional dimensions:

- Industrial relations,
- vocational training and education,

- corporate governance,
- interfirm relations, and
- coordination problems vis-à-vis their own employees.

In fact, a sixth sphere, financial relations, is mentioned continually, but conceptually it is covered by corporate governance. The focus is on deliberative coordinating institutions at the firm level. Hence, the role of the state remains out of scope. Other studies (for instance, Witt et al. 2018) include more dimensions. Between the institutional spheres or variables, there exist complementarities which cause structural differences and from different structures follow different corporate strategies. This allows identifying clusters of business systems with different coordination devices and strategies.

For a subset of OECD countries, Hall and Soskice have identified two clusters whose ideal types are described as liberal market economies and coordinated market economies. The first relies predominantly on markets and hierarchies to coordinate their activities. The second has recourse also to nonmarket institutions, interfirm networks, corporate organizations, and deliberative institutions. Such institutions are often informal, and their coordinating effort may even be tacit. This makes a high level of social capital a prerequisite for the functioning of the system.

The dichotomy is not essential to the approach. The authors indicate the possibility of a third ideal type within OECD, the Mediterranean countries which are excluded in their study. They may be grouped with coordinated economies. However, the state is playing a prominent role in the interfirm coordination process and, therefore, should also be taken into consideration. The more countries are included, the higher will be the number of identifiable clusters. Witt et al. (2018) analyze the business systems of 61 of the largest economies in the world using a number of statistical methods to identify nine clusters. The problem with such large numbers are the theoretical implications. Witt and his co-authors do not get further than classification. Hall and Soskice establish behavioral characteristics of the two ideal types resulting in differences in outcome, for instance, differences in comparative advantage, in innovative strategies, and in unemployment.

It is widely held that globalization leads to deregulation and thus will level institutional differences. There should be convergence to the liberal market model. This view is opposed by Hall and Soskice (2001, 56–65). They argue that international competitiveness rests not only on (wage-) cost minimization and, hence, on looming capital mobility into low-cost areas. For a good part, it is due to comparative advantage for certain types of goods and services which follows from comparative institutional advantage. Liberal market economies, therefore, have under conditions of globalization a tendency to deregulation. Coordinated market economies with all their nonmarket institutions exhibit a stronger resistance to this trend and still survive.

The "Varieties of Capitalism" approach has aroused critique (a survey in Streeck 2010, 27–34). A first remark addresses the bipolarity which, as we saw, is not essential like in the capitalism–socialism dichotomy. Scholars with a Marxist background see each national economy as an individual manifestation of capitalism (writ large) which "makes their commonality as capitalist political economies and their mutual interrelations more salient" (Ibid., 29). A second issue is the complementarity of institutional arrangements. Besides its empirical validity, a mechanism to bring it about has not been specified. It is conceivable, however, that an evolutionary process will do the job. The third issue of critique, closely related to the functionalism of complementarity, is the economism of the approach. The economic system is analyzed with the focus on the firm, not society or polity. In fact, Hall and Soskice do not deal with capitalism (writ large) but only with business systems in a capitalist setting. Their research agenda does not conform to Marxist political economy: "no room is reserved for political contestation of the socioeconomic order [...] and the possibility of a limited lifespan for one or both of the two main types" (Ibid., 34).

Finally, "Historical and Comparative Institutional Analysis", as proposed by Aoki (2001) and Greif (1998) and already introduced in the previous section, can be seen as a complement to the "Varieties of Capitalism" approach. Its basic feature is the integration of game theory with empirical, historical, and comparative studies. The focus of analysis does not lie on individual institutions but on the complementarities among them also across various spheres of economic activities. "Society's institutions are a complex in which informal, implicit institutional features interrelate with formal, explicit features in creating a coherent whole" (Ibid., 82). The set of relevant rules will not be selected on the basis of empirically confirmed theoretical optimization criteria. They rather emerge by the strategic interactions of the agents and their organizations under the influence of historical aspects, cultural features, beliefs, social and political structures, and cognition. Together with deeply entrenched customs, traditions, and beliefs, the complex complementary structure of the system inhibits immediate reactions to changes in the environment. A conspicuous example has been the persistence of the coordinated market economy in a globalized world. History matters.

The game theory implies two important insights: institutions as equilibria are self-enforcing and multiple equilibria are possible, even highly likely. The first property supports the stability of the system but, at the same time, also explains for the tenacity in the face of suboptimal outcomes. The second feature makes for the coexistence and viability of liberal and coordinated market economies. It also brings about the long-lasting persistence of suboptimal equilibria. It is an empirical fact that societies may live with comparatively less efficient institutional orders unable to adopt "best practice" arrangements. Putnam's (1993) story about Northern and Southern Italy has become a paradigmatic case.

1.6 Conclusion

Comparative economic systems has turned out to be a legitimate member of the research family of economics. Historically, it has contributed to understanding constitutional and performance differences between liberal and collectivist modernization projects. This slice of history has passed away. So, other accomplishments of comparative systems should be pushed to the fore in its future development. Historical and comparative institutional analysis, welfare economics, national accounting and comparative statistics, institutional and mechanism design, systemic change, and transformation research all have benefitted from the comparative systems scholarship. Traditionally, the front line of research was located at the "East" – "West" or capitalism – socialism divide. In a globalized world, the dichotomies have disappeared. A multiplicity of systemic varieties, capitalist and socialist, generated by historical, cultural, natural, and socioeconomic differences, opens up a wide field for a promising scholarship.

What's Wrong with Economics? asked the eminent comparative economist Benjamin Ward (1972) whom we quoted at the beginning of the chapter. In a similar vein, János Kornai (1971) wrote his *Anti-Equilibrium*. Frank Hahn (1973) made the obvious point that criticizing an established paradigm without offering a workable alternative is a futile exercise. However, an individual's critique is mostly better than their positive proposals, as Ward (1972, 239) remarked, since the development of a new paradigm, triggered by individual criticism, is a joint effort of the profession or its younger members. And to this effort, comparative economics can contribute given its broad theoretical basis (Marxism, neo-classicism, historicism), its multidisciplinary approach, and its empirical and policy orientation. Thus, the physicalist neo-classical model has been significantly widened since the early 1970s: "history matters", "ideas matter", and "institutions matter". The economic system is more than a computing machine.

Acknowledgments

Financial support by the German Federal Ministry of Education and Research (registration number 01UJ1806BY) is gratefully acknowledged.

References

Alchian, A. ([1950] 1977). "Uncertainty, Evolution and Economic Theory", in A. Alchian (ed.), *Economic Forces at Work*, Indianapolis, IN: Liberty Fund. pp. 13–35.

Aoki, M. (2001). *Toward a Comparative Institutional Analysis*, Cambridge, MA: MIT Press.

Bardhan, P. (2005). Institutions matter, but which ones? *Economics of Transition* 13: 499–532.

Barone, E. ([1908] 1935). "The Ministry of Production in the Collectivist State", in F.A. von Hayek (ed.), *Collectivist Economic Planning. Critical Studies on the Possibilities of Socialism*, London: Routledge. pp. 245–90.

Bergson, A. (A. Burk). (1938). A reformulation of certain aspects of welfare economics. *Quarterly Journal of Economics* 52: 310–34.

Bergson, A. (1950a). Soviet national income and product in 1937: Part I: National economic accounts in current rubles. *Quarterly Journal of Economics* 64: 208–41.

Bergson, A. (1950b). Soviet national income and product in 1937: Part II: Ruble prices and the valuation problem. *Quarterly Journal of Economics* 64: 408–41.

Bergson, A. (1954). On the concept of social welfare. *Quarterly Journal of Economics* 68: 233–52.

Bergson, A. (1961). *Real National Income of Soviet Russia Since 1928*, Cambridge, MA: Harvard University Press.

Bertalanffy, L.V. (1968). *General Systems Theory: Foundations, Developments, Applications*, New York, NY: Braziller.

Bornstein, M. (1971). "An Integration", in A. Eckstein (ed.), *Comparison of Economic Systems*, Berkeley, CA: University of California Press. pp. 339–55.

Bornstein, M. (ed.) (1965). *Comparative Economic Systems, Models and Cases*, Homewood, IL: Irwin.

Boyer, R. and Saillard, Y. (eds.) (1995). *Théorie de la regulation. L'état des savoirs*, Paris: La Découverte.

Brada, J.C. (2009). The new comparative economics versus the old: less is more but is it enough? *European Journal of Comparative Economics* 6:3–15.

Chavance, B. (ed.) (1987). *Régulation, cycles et crises dans les économies socialistes*, Paris: Éditions de l'EHESS.

Coase, R.H. (1937). The nature of the firm. *Economica* 4:386–405.

Demsetz, H. (1967). Toward a theory of property rights. *American Economic Review* 57:347–59.

Denzau, A.T. and North, D.C. (1994). Shared mental models: ideologies and institutions. *Kyklos* 47:3–31.

Djankov, S. et al. (2003). The new comparative economics. *Journal of Comparative Economics* 31: 595–619.

Eckstein, A. (1971a). "'Eastern' Approaches to a Comparative Evaluation of Economic Systems", in A. Eckstein (ed.), *Comparison of Economic Systems: Theoretical and Methodological Approaches*, Berkeley, CA: University of California Press. pp. 301–35.

Eckstein, A. (ed.) (1971b). *Comparison of Economic Systems: Theoretical and Methodological Approaches*, Berkeley, CA: University of California Press.

Eggertsson, T. (1990). *Economic Behavior and Institutions*, Cambridge, MA: Cambridge University Press.

Eucken, W. ([1939] 1943). *Die Grundlagen der Nationalökonomie*, 3rd ed. Jena: Gustav Fischer.

Eucken, W. ([1952] 1990). *Grundsätze der Wirtschaftspolitik*, Tübingen: Mohr (Siebeck).

European Commission et al. (eds.) (2009). *System of National Accounts 2008*, New York, NY.

Gregory, P.R. and Stuart, R.C. (1980). *Comparative Economic Systems*, Boston, MA: Houghton Mifflin.

Gregory, P.R. and Stuart, R.C. (2004). *Comparing Economic Systems for the Twenty-First Century*, 7th ed. Mason, OH: South Western.

Greif, A. (1998). Historical and comparative institutional analysis. *American Economic Review* 88: 80–4.

Greif, A. (2006). *Institutions and the Path to the Modern Economy: Lessons from Medieval Trade*, Cambridge: Cambridge University Press.

Grossman, G. (1967). *Economic Systems*, Englewood Cliffs, NJ: Prentice Hall.

Gwartney, J. et al. (2019). *Economic Freedom of the World: 2019 Annual Report*, Vancouver: Fraser Institute.

Hahn, F. (1973). The winter of our discontent. *Economica* 40 (159): 322–30.

Hall, P.A. and Soskice, D. (2001). "An Introduction to Varieties of Capitalism", in P.A. Hall and D. Soskice (eds.), *Varieties of Capitalism: The Institutional Foundations of Comparative Advantage*, Oxford: Oxford University Press. pp. 1–68.

Hayek, F.A. ([1944] 2007). "The Road to Serfdom", in B. Caldwell (ed.), *The Collected Works of F.A. Hayek*, Vol. II. Chicago, IL: University of Chicago Press.

Hayek, F.A. (1973). *Law, Legislation and Liberty. Vol. 1. Rules and Order*, London: Routledge.

Hayek, F.A. (1978). "The Errors of Constructivism", in F.A. Hayek (ed.), *New Studies in Philosophy, Politics, Economics and the History of Ideas*, London: Routledge & Kegan Paul. pp. 3–22.

Hayek, F.A. (1979). *Law Legislation and Liberty. Vol. 3. The Political Order of a Free People*, London: Routledge.

Hayek, F.A.V. (1935). "The Present State of the Debate", in F.A. von Hayek (ed.), *Collectivist Economic Planning. Critical Studies on the Possibilities of Socialism*, London: Routledge. pp. 201–243.

Heilbroner, R.L. (2008). "Capitalism", in St. N. Durlauf and L.E. Blume (eds.), *The New Palgrave Dictionary of Economics*, 2nd ed. Vol. I, Basingstoke: Palgrave Macmillan. pp. 688–97.

Holcombe, R.G. (2015). Political capitalism. *Cato Journal* 35: 41–66.

Holcombe, R.G. (2018). *Political Capitalism. How Economic and Political Power Is Made and Maintained*, Cambridge: Cambridge University Press.

Johansen, L. (1977). *Lectures on Macroeconomic Planning. 1. General Aspects*, Amsterdam: North Holland.

Kantorovich, L.V. ([1959] 1965). *The Best Use of Economic Resource*, Oxford: Pergamon.

Koopmans, T.C. (1957). *Three Essays on the State of Economic Science*, New York, NY: McGraw-Hill.

Koopmans, T.C. and Montias, J.M. (1971). "On the Description and Comparison of Economic Systems", in A. Eckstein (ed.), *Comparison of Economic Systems: Theoretical and Methodological Approaches*, Berkeley, CA: University of California Press. pp. 27–78.

Kornai, J. (1971). *Anti-Equilibrium on Economic Systems Theory and the Tasks of Research*, Amsterdam: North Holland.

Kornai, J. (1980). *Economics of Shortage*, 2 Vols, Amsterdam: North Holland.

Kornai, J. (2008). "The System Paradigm", in J. Kornai (ed.), *From Socialism to Capitalism*, Budapest: CEU Press. pp. 183–207.

Kornai, J. (2016). The system paradigm revisited: clarification and additions in the light of experiences in the post-socialist region. *Acta Oeconomica* 66: 547–96.

Landauer, C. (1951). Review of private enterprise and governmental planning – an integration. *American Economic Review* 41: 696–98.

Landauer, C. (1964). *Contemporary Economic Systems: A Comparative Analysis*, Philadelphia, PA: Lippincott.

Lange, O. (1936). On the economic theory of socialism, Part I. *Review of Economic Studies* 4: 53–71.

Lange, O. (1937). On the economic theory of socialism, Part II. *Review of Economic Studies* 4: 123–42.

Lange, O. (1942). The foundations of welfare economics. *Econometrica* 10: 215–28.

Libecap, G.D. (1989). *Contracting for Property Rights*, Cambridge, MA: Cambridge University Press.

Lin, J.Y. (1989). An economic theory of institutional change: induced and imposed change. *Cato Journal* 9: 1–33.

Maddison, A. (2003). *The World Economy: Historical Statistics*, Paris: OECD.

Maddison, A. (2007). *Contours of the World Economy 1-2030: Essays on Macro-Economic History*, Oxford: Oxford University Press.

Magyar, B. and Madlovics, B. (2020). *The Anatomy of Post-Communist Regimes: A Conceptual Framework*, Budapest: Central European University Press.

Marx, K. ([1859] 1974). "Zur Kritik der politischen Ökonomie", in Institut für Marxismus–Leninismus beim ZK der SED (ed.), Marx Engels Werke (MEW), Vol. 13, Berlin: Dietz. pp. 615–42.

Menger, K. (1883). *Untersuchungen über die Methode der Socialwissenschaften und der Politischen Ökonomie insbesondere*, Leipzig: Duncker & Humblot.

Mihályi, P. and Szelényi, I. (2021). Kornai on the affinity of systems: is China today an illiberal capitalist system or a communist dictatorship? *Public Choice* 187: 197–216.

Mises, L.V. (1949). *Human Action. A Treatise on Economics*, New Haven, CT: Yale University Press.

Montias, J.M. (1976). *The Structure of Economic Systems*, New Haven, CT: Yale University Press.

Montias, J.M. and Sturm, P.H. (1976). "Economic Systems and the Concept of Efficiency", in F.L. Altmann, O. Kyn and H.-J. Wagener (eds.), *On the Measurement of Factor Productivities*, Göttingen: Vandenhoek & Ruprecht. pp. 11–32.

Neuberger, E. and Duffy, W. (1976). *Comparative Economic Systems: A Decision-Making Approach*, Boston, MA: Allyn and Bacon.

Nienhaus, V. (2010). Fundamentals of an Islamic economic system compared to the social market economy – a systematic overview. KAS International Reports 2010–11, 75–96. file:///C:/Users/mail/AppData/Local/Temp/Fundamentals%20of%20an%20Islamic%20Economic%20System%20Compared%20to%20the%20Social%20Market%20Economy%20-%20A%20Systematic%20Overview%20(Pdf).pdf (Approached 12-3-2021).

North, D.C. (1994). Institutions Matter. *Economic History* 9411004, University Library of Munich. https://econwpa.ub.uni-muenchen.de/econ-wp/eh/papers/9411/9411004.pdf

North, D.C. (1996). "Epilogue: Economic performance through time", in L.J. Alston, T. Eggertsson, D.C. North (eds.), *Empirical Studies in Institutional Change*, Cambridge, MA: Cambridge University Press. pp. 142–55.

North, D.C. (2005). *Understanding the Process of Economic Change*, Princeton, NJ: Princeton University Press.

Pareto, V. ([1896–7] 1964). "Cours d'économie Politique", in G.H. Bousquet and G. Busino (eds.), *Oevres Complètes*, Vol. I. Genève: Droz.

Pareto, V. ([1906] 1966). "Manuel d'économie politique", in G. Busino (ed.), *Oevres Completes*, Vol. VII. Genève: Droz.

Political economy. (1957). *Political Economy. A Textbook Issued by the Economics Institute of the Academy of Sciences of the U.S.S.R*, London: Lawrence & Wishart. https://www.marxists.org/subject/economy/authors/pe/index.htm

Putnam, R.D. (1993). *Making Democracy Work. Civic Traditions in Modern Italy*, Princeton, NJ: Princeton University Press.

Rosefielde, St. (2015). *Comparative Economic Systems: Culture, Wealth, and Power in the 21st Century*, 3rd ed. Malden, MA: Wiley-Blackwell.

Rosser, J.B. and Rosser, M.V. (2008). A critique of the new comparative economics. *Review of Austrian Economics* 21. https://doi.org/10.1007/s11138-006-0011-z

Rosser, J.B. Jr. and Rosser, M.V. (2017). *Comparative Economics in a Transforming World Economy*, 3rd ed. Cambridge, MA: MIT Press.

Sachs, J. (2003). "Institutions Don't Rule: Direct Effects of Geography on per Capital Income", Working Paper 9490, Cambridge, MA: National Bureau of Economic Research.

Schumpeter, J.A. ([1908] 1998). *Das Wesen und der Hauptinhalt der theoretischen Nationalökonomie*, Berlin: Duncker & Humblot.

Schumpeter, J.A. ([1912] 1934). *The Theory of Economic Development: An Inquiry into Profits, Capital, Credit, Interest, and the Business Cycle*, Cambridge, MA: Harvard University Press.

Simon, H. (1957). *Models of Man*, New York, NY: John Wiley.

Sombart, W. (1925). *Die Ordnung der Wirtschaft*, Berlin: Duncker & Humblot.

Stackelberg, H.V. (1934). *Marktform und Gleichgewicht*, Berlin: Springer.

Stalin, J.W. (1952). *Economic Problems of Socialism in the U.S.S.R*, Moscow: Foreign Languages Publishing House.

Streeck, W. (2010). *E Pluribus Unum? Varieties and Commonalities of Capitalism*, Discussion Paper 10/12. Cologne: Max Planck Institute for the Study of Societies.

Surányi-Unger, T. (1950). *Private Enterprise and Governmental Planning – an Integration*, New York, NY: McGraw-Hill.

Tinbergen, J. (1959). "The Theory of the Optimum Regime", in L.H. Klaassen, L.M. Koyck and H.J. Witteveen (eds.), *J. Tinbergen Selected Papers*, Amsterdam: North Holland. pp. 264–304.

Tinbergen, J. (1961). Do communist and free economies show a converging pattern? *Soviet Studies* 12: 333–41.

Visser, H. (2019). The Islamic economy: its origin, its world view and its claims. *Central European Review of Economics and Management* 3–4: 53–89. file:///C:/Users/mail/AppData/Local/Temp/cerem-v3-i4-765.pdf (Approached 12-3-2021).

Voigt, St. (2013). How (not) to measure institutions. *Journal of Institutional Economics* 9: 1–26.

Voigt, St. (2019). *Institutional Economics. An Introduction*, Cambridge, MA: Cambridge University Press.

Voigt, St. (2020). *Constitutional Economics. A Primer*, Cambridge, MA: Cambridge University Press.

Wagener, H.-J. (2021). "The Political Economy of Socialism Revisited", in W. Andreff (ed.), *Comparative Economic Studies in Europa. A Thirty Year Review*, Cham: Palgrave Macmillan. pp. 13–33.

Ward, B. (1972). *What's Wrong with Economics?* London: Macmillan.

Weber, M. ([2002] 1904). *The Protestant Ethic and the Spirit of Capitalism and Other Writings*, Harmondsworth: Penguin.

Whitley, R. (1999). *Divergent Capitalisms: The Social Structuring and Change of Business Systems*, Oxford: Oxford University Press.

Wiles, P.J.D. (1977). *Economic Institutions Compared*, Oxford: Blackwell.

Williamson, J. (ed.) (1990). *Latin American Adjustment*, Washington, DC: Institute for International Economics.

Williamson, O.E. (1975). *Markets and Hierarchies: Analysis and Antitrust Implications*, New York, NY: Free Press.

Witt, M.A. et al. (2018). Mapping the business systems of 61 major economies: A taxonomy and implications for varieties of capitalism and business systems research. *Socio-Economic Review* 16: 5–38.

2

THE CONTEMPORARY HISTORY OF COMPARATIVE ECONOMIC STUDIES

Vittorio Valli

DEPARTMENT OF ECONOMICS AND STATISTICS "COGNETTI DE MARTIIS", UNIVERSITY OF TURIN, ITALY

2.1 Introduction

Comparative economics has existed since the dawn of time. The application of the comparative method to economic facts or situations was usual in ancient times, though a scholarly discipline has moved the first steps in the 20th century only.

We will mainly restrict our analysis to contemporary years, namely from the end of WWII up to now. Before the beginning of this period, the comparison between two types of capitalist systems, the democratic one and the authoritarian ones of Fascism and Nazism, was also important, while after the war, the basic confrontation between capitalism and socialism became central. Although comparative economic studies have a much larger content, after the war and up to the dissolution of the Soviet Union, strategic and ideological motives induced to concentrate the analysis on the two prevailing comparative economic systems: capitalism and socialism. In the West, the main objects of study were socialism and the socialist countries: Soviet Union, Eastern European countries, Yugoslavia, China and since 1958 Cuba, while in the USSR, Eastern Europe and China, the studies also focused importantly on the main features of capitalism and on the United States, Western Europe and Japan. For example, in the Soviet Union and then in the Russian Federation existed, from 1925 to 1948, the *Institute for World Economy and International Affairs* and since 1956 its successor, *IMEMO* (the *Institute of World Economy and International Relations of the Russian Academy of Sciences*), in 2015 renamed the *Primakov Institute of World Economy and International Relations*. All these institutes reserved great attention to the study of the United States, Canada and Europe (see Cherkasov, 2016). Since 1949 in Poland, there was the *Main School of Planning and Statistics* (from 1991 called again, as it was before WWII, the *Warsaw School of Economics*), which for several years benefited from the contribution of great economists such as Kalecki and Lange and which studied not only various forms of socialism planning and economic development but also important theoretical and empirical aspects of capitalist economies. In Hungary, in most other Eastern European economies and in China, sections of the Academy of Sciences and of several Universities studied the economic, social and political aspects of main capitalist countries.

DOI: 10.4324/9781003144366-4

In the 1990s, the *transition* from socialism to different destinations and the experiences of the European Union and of China, India and several other emerging countries, or poor and submerging ones, was the prevailing object of study of comparative economic experts, together with the study of the varieties of capitalism. However, several other contributions de facto used the comparative method to analyze important economic topics both at macro and micro level in country studies, cross-country analyses, theoretical essays, or various other forms.

In this chapter, we will try to illustrate the comparative method and the *fil rouge* of the comparative analyses made in the field of economics since the end of World War II.

2.2 The comparative method

Knowledge is a complex and tricky process. One of the main instruments of knowledge is the comparative method. We know if somebody is short or tall by comparison, if a country or a person is rich or poor comparing countries or people. Making a comparison between different entities requires simplification and opens the problem of the degree of acceptable simplification. Excessive simplification can hugely distort the analysis and worsen policies. In economics, as well as in other social sciences, we have to do with quantity and quality. Many economists mainly rely on quantitative indicators and often discard qualitative ones. To have good comparisons, it is also essential to have a good instrument of measurement, a good meter. Sometimes economists do not have, or do not use, good meters. Moreover, some quantitative indicators have severe limits.

For example, GDP (gross domestic product) and per capita GDP, which are the most used indicators in many comparative studies and particularly in cross-country analyses, have been severely criticized by great economists such as Nordhaus and Tobin (1972), Stiglitz, Sen and Fitoussi (2009).

The problems of GDP and per capita GDP are numerous. They are not good indicators of the quality of life, and even less of happiness, which is, however, a very difficult concept to define and even more to measure, as the large and growing literature on the economics of happiness has demonstrated. GDP and per capita GDP do not take into account negative externalities, such as the enormous and increasing ones associated with global warming and the pollution of land and water. They do not adequately consider changes in the quality of goods and services due to technological progress and the economic importance of out-of-the market work, such as the precious and incessant work for cooking, shopping, cleaning and the care of children and elder mostly made by women, or the production for self-consumption of agricultural goods. The value attributed to services supplied by the public administration is conjectural: it mainly derives from the wages paid to public servants. Per capita GDP is a statistical average: it does not take into account the existing large inequalities in income and the even larger inequalities in wealth which can greatly influence the quality of life of many individuals and households. The great differences among countries in taxation, public welfare and environmental policies are also very important for the quality of life as well as the functioning of economic institutions, demographic trends, employment opportunities, gender disparities in employment and wages, the inequalities in working time and the relative proportions between good and bad jobs. Since no synthetic indicator can take into account all these aspects, it would be better to use a plurality of indicators as the UNDP *Human Development Index* (2021) and the report by Stiglitz, Sen and Fitoussi (2009) have rightly suggested.

Finally, as it is well known, rates of exchange do not usually correspond to the ratio between purchasing powers of countries, especially if the comparison is made between a rich country and a poor one. Therefore, it is important to compare the levels of GDP and per capita GDP in different countries using the method of purchasing powers. Though the methodologies used for the calculation of purchasing powers are diverse, in this chapter, we will mainly use the estimates made in the seminal works by Angus Maddison regarding the 19th century and the first half of the 20th century and the ones provided by the joint program of World Bank, Eurostat and OECD for recent decades.

The indicators like GDP have serious limits, but also *subjective* indicators, widely used in analyses of economic institutions, have many problems. They are often based upon surveys of statistical samples of the population made in order to analyze various phenomena, such as the perceptions of corruption, happiness, etc. However, perceptions depend very much on the country's historical phase in which the survey is made, on people's expectations and on the possibility of people to have correct and unbiased information about the problems which are objects of the survey. For example, if a country is poor, but the economy is substantially growing, the quality of life of a large part of the population is improving and expectations are good, probably people's perceptions will be more favorable than in a richer country where the economy suffers from an economic crisis and expectations are gloomy.

As we will better see in the next paragraphs, the comparative method is different when applied to the comparison between "ideal types", such as the capitalist and the socialist systems, or between "real economies" or parts of their economic mechanisms. If the comparison is made at the macro-economic level between "real" economies of various countries, the approach can be *horizontal*, substantially based on cross-country analyses, or *vertical*, based on a more complex analysis about differences and similarities of economic, institutional and historical aspects of each country. The first approach is simpler and currently more popular, also because it can profit from vast data sets and the application of sophisticated econometric techniques. Its results are often interesting, but have two important limits. First, cross-country analyses consider, in a certain year or in a certain period of time, countries which are crossing a different historical phase, with different levels of development, different leaders, different socio-political conditions, different phases of evolution of their economic institutions, etc., and it is very difficult to catch all these differences with a few economic indicators, such as per capita GDP, and rough institutional indexes. Second, cross-country analyses do not consider that in each period the economies have complex economic and political interrelations, and these interrelations also tend to change over time according to the different economic, military and political power of each country.

2.3 The concept of system in comparative economics

In comparative economics, the concept of system is mainly used in two ways. It refers to "ideal types", such as socialism and capitalism, and to real countries as "the American economic system" or "China's economic system". A general definition that can embrace both the meanings has been given by Simon Kuznets (1971, p. 251) "a system is a set of institutions (or ideas or activities) united by some regular forms of interaction and interdependence". Sometimes there is a combination of some aspects of both meanings, when, for example, somebody speaks of the "American capitalist economic system" or of "Chinese socialist economic system".

In reality, what is important in order to define an economic system is the strength of the linkages – the interactions and the interdependences – which keep an economy united. Socialism and capitalism are defined by some characteristics that are discussed in Section 2.4. Real countries usually have a long history, which has gradually built a particular identity often based on a common language and sometimes a common religion for the majority of the population, several institutions and common traditional habits and cultural features. As North (1990),

Pejovich (1999) and several other authors have argued, there is a relevant difference between *formal* and *informal institutions*. The former ones (constitutions, statutes, laws and other governmental regulations) can have complex interactions with the latter ones (traditions, customs, religious beliefs, etc.). However, the combination of this historical heritage with socialist or capitalist traits could radically change, but not fully erase, the original characters, deeply rooted in consolidated informal institutions. For example, in the transition years, strong nationalistic drives have re-appeared in former socialist countries, such as Hungary, Poland, Czech Republic, Slovakia, the Russian Federation, the Baltic republics and several other former USSR republics; Slovenia, Croatia, Serbia, Bosnia Herzegovina and other former Yugoslavia states.

2.4 The evolution of comparative economic studies before the dissolution of the Soviet Union

In order to explain in a more detailed way the evolution of comparative economic studies since the mid-1940s, it is important to distinguish between the debate on "ideal-types" and the one regarding the functioning of "real socialism" in the Soviet Union, China or other socialist countries and "real capitalism" in the United States and several other capitalist countries. In various degrees, both aspects are, for example, considered in Borstein (1965), Dobb (1966), Reynolds (1971), Nove and Nuti (1972), Valli (1978, 2020), Dallago (2004), and Andreff (2020).

As regards "ideal-types" of economic systems, capitalism and socialism are usually distinguished according to some basic characteristics (see Chart 2.1).

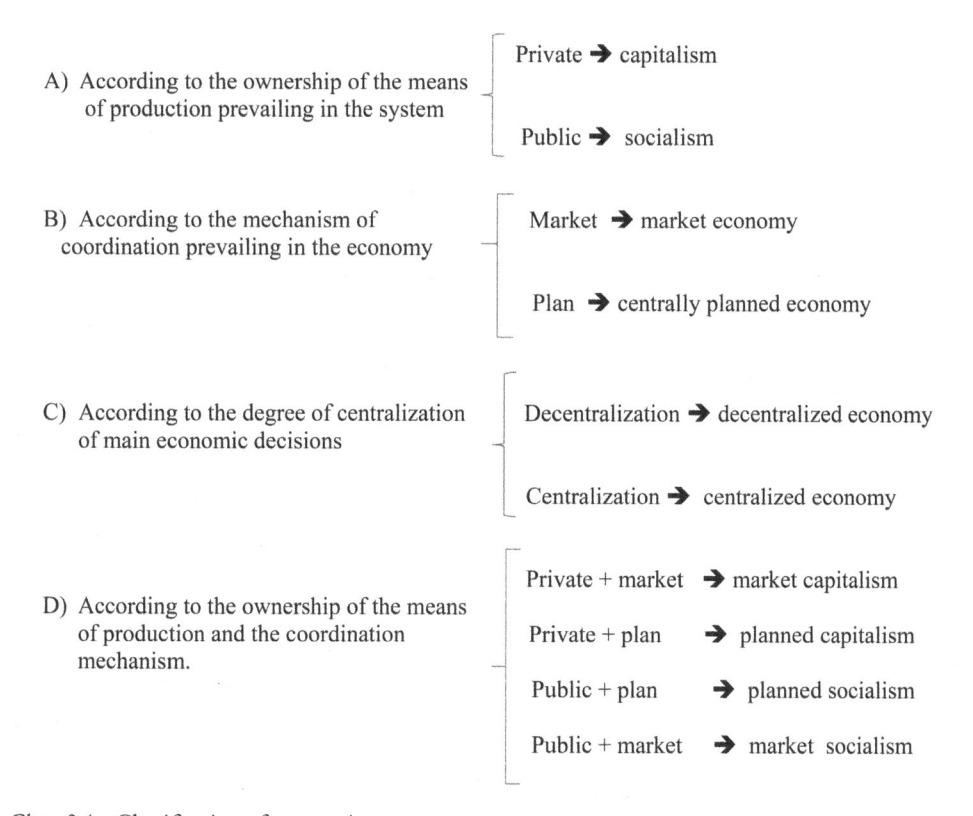

Chart 2.1 Classification of economic systems.

First of all, there is the *ownership of the means of production*: it is mainly public in the socialist system, private in the capitalist one. Second, there is the prevailing *coordination mechanism of the economic system*: the plan in the socialist system, the market in the capitalist one. Third, there is the *degree of centralization of main economic decisions*: they are usually centralized in socialism, decentralized in capitalism. The first character, the ownership of the means of production, is considered as the most relevant one to distinguish between capitalism and socialism.

As point D of Chart 2.1 shows, there might also be complex mixtures of these characteristics. Moreover, in capitalist systems, the term *"mixed economy"* is often used for a country where the property of means of production is mainly private, but there is also a large public sector, with abundant public expenditures and a relevant presence of public enterprises.

In real economies, there can be several combinations of these characteristics in various countries or, in a single country, in different historical phases. For example, after World War II, the Soviet Union had predominantly public means of production (either directly controlled by the State or by cooperatives) and the economic decisions were mainly decided by the central plan and were strongly centralized, while the space for the market and for decentralized economic decisions was very limited.

However, especially in 1965 (Kosygin reform) and in 1987–1988 under Gorbachev's Perestroika (Law on State Enterprise and law on cooperatives), in the Soviet Union, there were important economic reforms. The 1965 reform transformed the system of incentives including profitability and sales but only slightly changed the basic characteristics of the centrally planned economy, while Gorbachev's economic reforms were more radical and contributed to originate the disruption of central planning mechanisms. Less timid than the 1965 Soviet reform, but vastly diversified, albeit partial, reforms had also been introduced in several Eastern European planned economies, in 1949, 1952 and 1965 in Yugoslavia; in 1953–1954 and 1966–1968 in Hungary; in 1964–1968 in East Germany; in 1956–1957 and 1966 in Poland and in 1968–1969 in Romania and Bulgaria. However, up to the fall of the Berlin Wall, with the exception of Yugoslavia, which had chosen a more decentralized self-management approach, the central plan remained at the core of the system, though partially loosened and in a few countries accompanied by a few market activities.

While at the beginning of the 1950s in China, the economic model was, for various aspects, similar to that of the Soviet Union, in today's China, there is a complex combination of public and private ownership of the means of production, of the plan and the market and of centralized and decentralized economic decisions, so that in the book, *The Economic Rise of China and India* (Valli, 2015), we called China's economy as the *economy of the triple mix*. However, the State and the Chinese Communist Party maintain a large control over the functioning of the economy and society through a number of instruments, such as the conservation in strategic sectors of several large state enterprises and of many local TVEs (township and village enterprises); a range of directives of central and local plans; the strict control of most banks, of financial markets, of China's national currency, of the finance of local administrations (cities, towns and provinces); numerous tough interventions on media and internet, on political, religious and ethnic matters and on the choices of private entrepreneurs if contrary to the party's orientations.

Since the 1917 Russian Revolution and the birth of the Soviet Union, for about two decades, the debate was mainly concentrated on the difficult construction of a socialist state and the great differences between the two antagonistic systems: socialism and capitalism. In the Soviet Union, the main issue was the adaptation by Lenin and Stalin of Marx and Engels's ideas to the particular features of a poorly industrialized country crossing a turbulent period. In the West, socialist and communist ideas grew in several countries, though they were harshly contrasted by most governments. In the 1920s and 1930s, there was also an important theoretical debate about the calculus in a socialist planned economy, for some aspects anticipated by Enrico Barone in *Il ministro della produzione nello stato collettivista* (1908). On the basis of a general equilibrium model, Barone concluded that in a collectivist regime production would not be ordered in a way substantially different from that of an individualistic regime. In 1920, Mises instead affirmed that in a socialist economy it was impossible to have a rational economic calculus, mainly because no production factor could be exchanged and so it would be impossible to determine its monetary value. In the 1930s, his paper opened a tense and long debate with the contributions, among others, of (von) Hayek (1935), Lange (1936 and 1937), Lerner (1936), Lange and Taylor (1938), and Dobb (1966). Lange in 1936–1937 replied to Von Mises showing that it was possible to conciliate socialism with economic calculus on the basis of a model of market socialism with perfect competition. Von Hayek admitted the theoretical validity of Lange's model, but stated that it was practically impossible to implement his solution mainly because of the extreme difficulty encountered by officials of the planning agencies in promptly calculating how to modify prices on the basis of the continuously varying differences between supply and demand. However, this kind of debate regards pure and abstract "ideal-type" systems, very different from the functioning of "real" socialist economies. No socialist country has tried and has been able to build a perfect competition system. By the way, also no real capitalist country has perfect competition, since in several important industrial and services sectors, and sometimes also in agriculture, there is the dominant presence of large oligopolistic corporations.

A probably more important theoretical debate, which had relevant consequences also in the post-WWII period, was the one regarding growth and planning models in socialist countries. In 1928 in the Soviet Union, Fel'dman introduced a modified version of Marx's two-sector growth model. While Marx distinguished between the sector producing means of production and the one producing consumption goods, Fel'dman distinguished between sector 1 which includes only the economic activities which expand the productive capacity and sector 2 which includes all the activities which maintain the production at the present level (consumption goods plus reintegration of the existing means of production). He then concluded that in order to obtain a rise in the rate of growth of incomes it was necessary to increase the efficiency of capital, but above all, to invest proportionally more in sector 1 than in sector 2. This meant "industrialization, heavy industry, mechanical industry and electrification"; in other words, a sharp priority is given to heavy industry and capital goods with respect to light industry and consumption goods, including agricultural ones. These priorities were embraced, also for strategic and military reasons, by Stalin since the late 1920s, and were to some extent maintained until the dissolution of the Soviet Union in 1991. This was partly due to the fact that in the post-WWII period it was extremely difficult to maintain a quasi-equilibrium in military and strategic sectors with the United States, which had an economy that was over the double of the one of the Soviet Union in terms of GDP in purchasing powers. For example, in 1952 and in 1973, the Soviet Union had levels of GDP in PPP 33.6% and 42.8% of those of the United States (see Table 2.1). It was so considered necessary by Stalin, and partially also by his successors, to give an absolute priority to strategic and military industries, continuing to compress the production and demand of consumption goods and services for civilian uses. Moreover, while since the 1950s and up to the mid-1970s, the phase of *extensive growth* and the rise in oil and gas prices due to the 1973–1974 great energy crisis had permitted to the Soviet Union to reduce the economic gap vis-à-vis the United States a little, in the following period of *intensive growth* in the USSR, there was a considerable enlargement of the gap. In particular, in the 1980s, the rigidity of the

Table 2.1 Total GDP in PPP in selected countries as % of the United States (1870–2020)

Countries	1870	1913	1952	1973	1990	2020
China	192.9	46.7	18.8	4.7	18.7	117.6
USA	100.0	100.0	100.0	100.0	100.0	100.0
India	137.1	39.5	14.4	11.7	17.6	42.5
Japan	25.8	13.8	12.4	35.6	40.5	25.4
Germany	73.3	45.9	19.4	33.4	25.9	21.3
Russia	85.0	44.9	.....	.....	19.9	19.7
USSR	.....	.....	33.6	42.8	33.2	.....
Brazil	7.1	3.7	6.1	14.8	16.8	15.1
France	73.3	27.9	14.8	20.3	17.2	14.9
UK	101.8	43.4	22.0	19.7	20.0	14.4
Italy	42.5	18.5	11.7	19.5	11.9	11.9

Note: Our elaborations are based on data derived from *Maddison Project Database* (2010) up to 1973 (methods GK up to 1952 and EKS in 1973) and from World Bank (2021a), Eurostat, OECD for the period 1990–2020. The series are not fully comparable. Russia in 1870 and 1913 is the Russian empire, while in 1990 and 2020, it is the Russian Federation. Per capita GDP of the Soviet Union as % of the United States in 1990 is based on GK estimates deriving from Maddison (2007, pp. 104, 342). Germany's data refer to the present borders.

centrally planned system prevailing in the Soviet Union did not permit to create and diffuse innovations in the civilian sector at the same rate as in Western countries, while the price of oil and gas, of which the Soviet Union is an important net exporter, had a heavy fall from 1980 to 1986 and a very small recovery in the following years of the decade. All this heavily contributed to the decline in the growth rate of GDP and productivity in the USSR and also in part to the deep political and social crisis which led to the dissolution of the Soviet Union in 1991.

Table 2.1 also shows the great changes in the world economic equilibria that occurred in the last 150 years and which had important consequences on the trends of comparative economic studies. From the 1870s, to the end of the 19th century, the United States surpassed China, India and the United Kingdom in terms of total GDP in PPP. Some years later, in 1913, the American economy had reached an economic size over double than those of the United Kingdom, China, Germany and the Russian empire. It is true that the UK, France and other countries were the center of powerful colonial empires, but the colonial empires were giants with feet of clay. Their territorial distances; the great language, ethnic, religious and historical differences within the empire; the divide in social status and citizenship between the population of the center and the one of the colonies; the economic center-periphery logic which exacerbated inequalities and, finally, two bloody world wars were all elements which powerfully contributed to the decolonization process and the dissolution of great colonial empires which mainly occurred after the conclusion of WWII. Between 1913 and 1952, many events occurred: two world wars, the Russian revolution, the great depression, the ascent and fall of fascism and Nazism, the birth and permanence of democracies and of several authoritarian regimes in many parts of the world, the beginning of de-colonization, etc. However, the United States succeeded, in spite of the 1929 fall of Wall Street and the succeeding Great Depression, to maintain and even increase its economic leadership. After WWII and the Reconstruction, as regards economic size, roughly measured by total GDP in PPP, only the Soviet Union could rival the United States but at a considerable distance, having a GDP varying between a third and 45% of the US level. Because of its population, larger than the one of the United States, the USSR's per capita GDP as percent of the United States varied between around 28% and 37% in the 1952–90 years, frustrating the expectations of the population, to which Stalin had promised to surpass the level of life of the United States and the other major Western countries in two or three decades. Up to the end of the 1960s, one great advantage of the United States was its higher technological progress in the civilian sector. But a second one was even more important and consisted of the possibility to fully profit in the civilian sector from the advantages of economies of scale and the *Fordist model of development*, a concept that we introduced in Valli (2002, pp. 26–7) and extensively analyzed in Valli (2019) using macroeconomic aspects of Gramsci's Fordism. On the contrary, the Soviet Union had decided to privilege the sectors producing means of production and the military and strategic ones restricting the civilian production of consumption goods. However, since a very large economic size, associated with an adequate level in technology, usually leads to vast economic power, and then, after a certain delay, to a strong military and political power, in the post-WWII period, the United States and the Soviet Union became the two world super powers. Their confrontation led to the *Cold War* and to the almost complete economic and financial separation between the Western bloc, under the influence of the United States, and Eastern Europe, under the influence of the Soviet Union.

This particular geo-political and economic situation was decisive in focusing the attention of a large part of comparative economic studies toward the analysis of the two opposite poles – socialism and capitalism – and toward the dissection of the economies involved in the East–West confrontation. However, many studies also considered *the variants* existing in real socialist and capitalist countries. For example, since 1948–1949, Yugoslavia abandoned the centralized Soviet-type planning model developing a system of workers' self-management in a peculiar form of market socialism. Afterward, Poland in 1956–1957, in 1966 and in the 1970s, Eastern Germany in 1964–1968 and Hungary in 1953–1954 and in 1966–1968 introduced economic reforms, decentralizing part of the economic decisions and introducing a limited space for the market. In 1965, even the Soviet Union introduced timid economic reforms and slightly deeper ones in the second half of the 1980s.

In any case, in terms of per capita GDP in PPP, in the 1952–1990 years, the Soviet Union had never surpassed the 37% of the US level and China the 6%, although China has made, since the economic reforms of 1978, an impressive catching-up outpacing in 2020 the level of the Russian Federation and reaching the 27.1% of the US level (see Table 2.2). However,

Table 2.2 Per capita GDP in PPP as % of the United States in selected countries (1870–2020)

Countries	1870	1913	1952	1973	1990	2020
China	21.7	10.4	5.2	1.1	4.1	27.1
USA	100.0	100.0	100.0	100.0	100.0	100.0
India	21.8	12.7	6.1	4.3	5.0	10.2
Japan	30.0	26.2	22.6	69.4	81.9	66.6
Germany	75.2	68.8	44.1	89.6	81.3	85.3
Russia	38.6	28.0	22.6	.....	33.6	23.9
USSR	.....	.....	28.5	36.3	29.7	.....
Brazil	29.2	15.3	17.0	30.4	28.1	23.5
France	76.7	65.7	53.9	80.8	73.7	72.6
UK	130.5	68.7	68.7	74.2	87.3	85.3
Italy	61.3	48.4	38.7	75.3	77.8	64.4

Source: See note of Table 2.1 and World Bank (2021b) for the years 1990–2020.

in the last three decades, both Russia and China have increased very much their economic and social inequalities, which were much lower than in capitalist countries at the beginning of the 1950s.

2.5 The economics of transition

After the fall of the Berlin Wall and the dissolution of the Soviet Union, the attention of a large part of comparative economic studies switched toward the problem of *transition*. In Russia, Eastern Europe, the Baltic republics and some other former USSR republics, the transition had important political, economic and social aspects. It was in the majority of cases, a transition from an autocracy dominated by the Communist Party to another form of an authoritarian regime or to a full democracy or a guided one. In several countries, there was also the transition from a planned economy to a market or a mixed economy, while from the social point of view, the trends were particularly varied and complex.

In the pre-transition phase, most socialist countries had, for a large part of the population, the security of having a job and a limited salary, a small and modest housing, some education, basic welfare benefits, a relative stability of prices, except in some critical periods of re-alignment of the price system. There were, in general, relatively low economic and social inequalities among the majority of the population, though substantial privileges were conceded to high cadres of the party and other members of the *intelligentsia* or tolerated for exponents of the *second economy,* i.e., the relatively vast informal economy described by Gregory Grossman in 1977. Moreover, the economic conditions of rural population were usually considerably worse with respect to those of the major cities. The basic economic security was, however, accompanied by real wages often stagnant for long periods, extensive weekly hours of work, strict rationing on the supply side, as analyzed in Kornai (1980), and so scarcity, low quality and long queues for many consumption goods, plus an important limitation of freedom in several economic and political activities.

Finally, the 1978–1989 Russian–Afghanistan war had devastating consequences on the economic and political equilibria of the country.

The first years of the transition period were economically ruinous for most Eastern European and former Soviet Union's countries since the old planned system did not function any longer and the new mixed or market economy system did not function yet. Badly conceived privatization programs, crippled state enterprises and a corrupt and disorganized State, lacking the support of dethroned or weaker communist parties with no well-established and credible replacement, did worsen the situation. The level of real GDP fell from 1989 up to 1991–1993 in Poland, Slovenia, Slovakia, Hungary, the Czech Republic, Albania and Uzbekistan, but the loss was completely recovered up to 1999 in the first three countries, and almost fully in the last three countries (see Table 2.3). However, in all the other Eastern European and former USSR countries, the Russian Federation included, the transition crisis was longer and more severe. In several countries, the Russian Federation included, the crisis was deeper and more lasting than the Great Depression of the 1930s in the United States. The fall of real GDP lasted up to the middle or the end of the 1990s, and in several countries, the 1990 GDP level had been fully recovered in terms of real GDP only in the first decade of the 2000s.

In the 1990s, in most countries, the social consequences were devastating, especially for retired persons, women, and younger people, who for many years suffered from lower employment rates, higher unemployment, poorer welfare and, in some cases, very high inflation. Unemployment rose in almost all countries, with the partial exception of Uzbekistan, Turkmenistan, Azerbaijan, Kazakhstan, Kyrgyzstan, Tajikistan, Belarus, Moldova. In the 1990s,

Table 2.3 Selected indicators in Eastern European and former USSR countries in the 1990s

Country	Total real GDP % change 1989–99	Year of minimum real GDP in the 1989–99 period	Index of privatization in 1998 EBRD (1999)	Unemployment rate (%) in 2000
Poland	+22	1991	5	15.0
Slovenia	+5	1992	5	12.0
Slovakia	+1	1993	5	17.9
Hungary	−1	1993	5	8.9
Czech Republic	−5	1993	5	8.8
Albania	−5	1992	3	16.9
Uzbekistan	−6	1995	1	0.6
Belorussia	−19	1995	1	2.1
Estonia	−21	1994	5	7.3
Croatia	−22	1995	3	22.6
Macedonia	−23	1995	3	44.9
Romania	−24	1992	3	10.5
Turkmenistan	−26	1997	3	11.7
Bulgaria	−29	1997	3	17.9
Kyrgyzstan	−34	1995	3	3.1
Lithuania	−37	1994	3	12.6
Kazakhstan	−38	1995	3	3.7
Azerbaijan	−39	1995	1	1.2
Latvia	−40	1995	3	7.8
Armenia	−40	1993	3	9.1
Russian Federation	−42	1998	3	9.6
Yugoslavia	−58	1993	...	26.6
Ukraine	−61	1999	1	4.2
Tajikistan	−67	1996	1	3.0
Moldova	−68	1999	3	1.8
Georgia	−69	1994	3	10.3

Source: See Valli (2002, pp. 97 and 99); UNECE (2001); EBRD (1999); World Bank (2021c).

these countries had scarcely liberalized their economy but had suffered from a severe or very severe depression, with the partial exception of Uzbekistan.

The Gini index for income inequality, which had been very low in pre-transition years, surpassed 30% in some Eastern European and former USSR countries, outpacing in the Russian Federation the level of a capitalist country with a substantially high inequality such as the United States.

Poverty too increased very much and the population decreased in several countries, partly from the consequences of poverty, alcoholism and the worsening of the health system and partly because of local conflicts and large migrations to richer countries.

Focusing the attention on the Russian Federation, Ellman (2000) observed that up to the end of the 1990s the transition crisis led to (a) a rise in the poverty level, (b) a decline in employment, (c) a rise in unemployment, (d) an increase in economic inequalities, (e) a deterioration of collective services and a polarization in their supply, (f) a rise in diseases, (g) the reduction of natality and the rise in mortality and therefore a reduction in population, (h) the strong rise of criminality and corruption and (i) the spread of armed conflicts.

After the 1999 passage from the weak and erratic Yeltsin presidency to Putin's era, the political situation was more stable and the economic recovery was underway. However, the 1990 real GDP level was reached only around 2007; the population continued to fall from

148.4 million people in 1993 to 143.2 million people in 2008, beginning to recover only in the following years. Moreover, the very fragile and corrupt democracy of the first transition years was converted by Putin to a guided democracy with authoritarian traits, including a series of brutal interventions against political opponents. Internal wars, in Chechnya and Dagestan, and external interventions in Crimea and other parts of Ukraine, in Georgia, Syria and Libya, contributed to an increase or smooth down in international tensions. The operations in Eastern Ukraine and the annexation of Crimea led to economic sanctions from the United States and other Western countries but raised domestic nationalistic consensus toward Putin's regime. In the meantime, Russia increased its military strength, partly recovering its international influence, thanks also to its interventions in Syria and Libya and to its huge exports of gas and oil. The brutal invasion of Ukraine in February 2022 and the subsequent Russia-Ukraine war have determined severe consequences in international relations leading also to a decrease of economic growth, a strong increase in inflation and a disruption in trade and investment flows especially in the fields of energy and food.

In several Eastern European and former USSR countries, hasty and often badly designed privatization processes permitted private capitalists close to political power, and sometimes even criminal organizations, to obtain, at low prices, important public assets such as former state enterprises, oil or mining companies, or to control media, construction works, banks and other financial institutions.

International organizations such as IMF and World Bank; the United States, the German and the French governments and the European Union; assertive Western economic consultants such as Jeffrey Sachs and private foundations such as the Open Society Foundations founded by George Soros were rather influential on several Eastern European and Russia's governments in the transition period. They mostly advocated shock therapies and vast privatizations, with diverse and sometimes unsatisfactory results.

Corruption grew and transfers of capital abroad expanded very rapidly, in some cases contributing to depress the value of national currencies and worsen inflationary bursts, as it happened in Russia in the 1990s and in a part of the 2000s.

In the 2000s, the recovery and expansion of Eastern Europe and former USSR countries was vastly differentiated (see Table 2.4) and partly depended on the depth and duration of the transition crisis. The economic expansion was also hindered in most countries by the consequences of the "Great Recession" of 2008–2010 and of the COVID-19 pandemics in 2020–2021. However, in some countries, the phase of expansion was facilitated by catching-up processes, abundant foreign direct investment and the liberalization of external trade; in other ones, such as Azerbaijan, Kazakhstan and the Russian Federation, it was also helped by large oil and gas exports, especially in the years of rising energy prices.

Several Eastern European countries and the Baltic states entered the European Union in 2004 or in the following years. Most former USSR countries, but for the Baltic states, remained under Russian economic and political influence, under the fragile umbrella of the Commonwealth of Independent States (CIS). In some years, Ukraine, Georgia, Azerbaijan and Moldova tried to react to Russia's hegemony, while in 2014, after some previous economic integration steps, Armenia, Belarus, Kazakhstan, Kyrgyzstan signed *the Eurasian Economic Union treaty* with the Russian Federation, with Uzbekistan, Moldova and Cuba as observers. The Union, active since 2015, was declared as a purely economic integration process, but it also had several strategic and political consequences. However, only with Belarus, there has been an attempt to build a real political union with the Russian Federation since 1999, but the present political difficulties of Lukashenko's regime after the contested, and partly fraudulent, 2020 Belarus presidential election, will probably jeopardize the project.

Table 2.4 Indicators in selected Eastern European and former USSR countries in the 2000s

Country	Year in which the country recovered the 1990 real GDP level	GDP in 2019 in constant local currency (2000 = 100)	Real GDP % rate of change 2020/2019	Unemployment rate (%) in 2020
Albania	1999	214.4	−3.3	11.7
Armenia	2004	324.9	−7.6	20.2
Azerbaijan	2004	442.5	−4.3	6.3
Belarus	2003	226.0	−0.9	5.3
Bosnia Herzegovina	....	184.3	−3.0	16.9
Bulgaria	2005	186.0	−4.2	5.7
Croatia (a)	.....	131.8	−8.4	7.2
Czech Republic	1996	169.6	−5.6	2.9
Estonia (a)	.....	196.8	−2.9	6.5
Georgia	2019	278.0	−6.2	12.1
Hungary	1995	160.5	−5.0	4.3
Kazakhstan	2004	319.0	−2.6	6.0
Kyrgyz Republic	2009	225.1	−8.6	7.9
Latvia (a)	......	193.9	−3.6	8.2
Lithuania (a)	......	213.7	−0.9	8.4
Moldova (a)	......	233.8	−6.9	4.7
Montenegro (a)	......	178.3	−15.2	15.9
North Macedonia	2005	166.9	−4.5	18.4
Poland	1994	202.1	−2.7	3.5
Romania	2003	212.8	−3.9	4.8
Russian Federation	2007	187.0	−3.0	5.7
Serbia (a)	......	189.9	−1.0	9.1
Slovakia (a)	......	206.0	−4.8	6.8
Slovenia (a)	.....	155.4	−1.4	5.2
Tajikistan	2013	405.3	+4.5	7.5
Turkmenistan	2005	442.3	.....	4.4
Ukraine (b)	......	151.6	−4.0	9.5
Uzbekistan	2001	342.9	+ 1.6	6.0

Our elaborations.

Sources: World Bank (2021c, 2021d).

Notes: (a) 1990 GDP not available. (b) In 2020, Ukraine had not yet reached the real GDP level of 1990.

2.6 China's diverse transition

China has made a profoundly different transition if compared with most Eastern European and former USSR or former Yugoslavia republics. While the transition in those countries had begun between the end of the 1980s and the beginning of the 1990s, in China, it had started much earlier, with Deng Xiaoping's 1978 economic reforms. Moreover, economic and institutional changes took a longer time, were more gradual than in most Eastern European countries and in Russia and were not accompanied by profound changes in the political and cultural sphere. China only had an economic transition, not a political one, while its society was deeply transformed by economic changes. Since 1978, China's Communist Party has remained firmly in command and has continued to control all main economic, institutional and structural changes. Step by step China has become, as we have already noted, an *economy of the triple mix*. The Asian giant allowed a gradual and growing introduction of the market and so the co-existence of the plan and the market. Moreover, there was a step by step increasing tolerance of small private activities, and then the legal possibility to own means of production, firms and houses, which co-existed with the maintenance of a large network of state firms, state banks and of enterprises controlled by local authorities or cooperatives. Finally, there was a complex mix between centralized economic decisions and decentralized ones operated at a local level or determined by the choices of private firms.

This epochal transformation of the economy has been made in over four decades, and not in a smooth and unilinear way, but by trial and error, several forward and backward steps always made under the strict control of the Communist Party. The political institutions have been only scarcely touched, though a limited, but growing, number of private entrepreneurs has entered the PC (People's Congress) or PPCC (People's Political Consultative Conference). However, if some important private entrepreneur tries to criticize some aspects of the party's line, she/he or her/his firm will soon be subjected to various forms of tough government measures. Harsh armed or judicial and administrative repression means were used in political or ethnic disorders, as in the cases of Tiananmen square (1989) and of recent Hong Kong demonstrations or in Uiguri's or Tibetan zones. Moreover, government's control of media and internet is more and more extensive, so that it is extremely difficult to organize any steady form of political opposition. In this way, the Chinese Communist Party can rely on a solid political leadership, though contrasts between the various factions in the party, or the search for increasing civilian rights in a society and economy which are rapidly changing, or a severe economic crisis, might change the situation in the future.

From 1978 up to 2020, China's average real annual GDP rate of growth (at constant prices in national currency units) was about 9.2%, versus less than 2.5% of the United States and all the major European economies. The extraordinarily rapid expansion of China's economy was due to several factors. First, the passage in agriculture to *the responsibility principle* permitted a rapid increase in labor productivity in the countryside and a large part of the growing rural surplus was destined to finance a massive industrialization process directed not only to heavy and strategic industry but also to the production of civilian consumption goods. Second, *catching-up* processes and *advantages of economic backwardness* (see Gerschenkron, 1962) could widely operate, by means of the passage of millions of workers from agricultural activities, with low productivity, to more productive industrial and tertiary ones, and because of the acquisition of foreign capital and modern technologies, particularly in the special economic zones (SEZ). Third, China could exploit some advantages of the *Fordist model of development*. These advantages were mainly associated with the enormous economies of scale existing in China for the production and sales of electric domestic appliances and associated sectors in the 1980s; for the production and exports of ICT products, ships, chemicals, steel, other industrial goods and services in the 1990s and for the production of automobiles, electric batteries, mobile phones, chips, solar panels, wind turbines, fast trains, internet services, etc. in the 2000s. Fourth, the gradual *trade liberalization*, culminated in the 2001 entry into the WTO, permitted to accelerate the rapid expansion of net exports and so accumulation of an enormous stock of assets in US dollars and other hard currencies, which facilitated the expansion of FDI abroad and then the realization of important infrastructural programs with several other countries, such as the *New Silk Road* (*Belt and Road*) initiative. However, the consequences of the deep Financial Crisis and the *Great Recession* in the Western countries, the trade war with the United States during the Trump administration and the 2020–2021 pandemics crisis contributed to significantly reduce the rate of growth of Chinese exports and real GDP since 2010 and partially re-orient the economy to the domestic market.

The main driving forces behind the extraordinary expansion of China's economy since 1978 were the very high rate of growth of physical investment and of knowledge. The former had increased in the years 1978–2020, three to four times more rapidly than in the United States and the other major industrialized countries. Knowledge is, in general, attained by means of the quantity and quality of basic education, advanced education, research and development efforts, on-the-job training, learning by doing processes and the capacity of rapidly and pervasively spread scientific, technological and organizational innovations in the productive system. At the end of the 1970s, China was backward in all of these fields. In about four decades, if we take the indicators in percentage of total population, the gap has been greatly reduced vis-à-vis the United States and the other major industrialized countries. However, given China's immense population, in 2020, in terms of absolute figures, China had the world highest number of university graduates, of engineers and computers experts, of people engaged in research and development activities, in internet connections, and of people working in sectors of high and medium technological level. As to the quality of studies, OECD-PISA 2018 tests for 15-year-old students also show that for reading, mathematics and sciences Chinese students of few advanced provinces, Macao and Hong Kong had top world performances, though in several internal rural provinces, the level would probably be lower. In any case, though at present in many industrial and service sectors, the technological level of the United States remains consistently higher than in China, in a growing number of economic activities of high and middle technology, such as electric batteries, electric buses, solar panels, ships, some PC components, mobile phones and some internet services, China has reached a competitive advantage over the United States and most other industrialized countries.

The exceptionally rapid industrialization and the tertiary expansion of the Chinese economy have been, however, accompanied by a massive increase in the pollution of air, water and land. For example, since 2006, China has become the top annual emitter of CO_2 in the world, accounting in 2020 for about 227% of the emissions of the United States, the second largest world emitter (Our World in data, 2022). However, in terms of per capita CO_2 annual emissions, China is far below the levels of several oil producing countries, of Mongolia, Saudi Arabia, the United States, Canada, Australia, Russia and a few other industrialized or emerging countries. In 2020, China had per capita CO_2 emissions equal to about 52% of those of the United States, but its percentage tends to constantly rise, also because coal remains China's most important primary source of electric energy. Although China, since the eve of the Beijing 2008 Olympic Games, has started some timid environmental policies, reinforced after the 2015 Paris Agreement on Climate Change, it will probably continue to increase its CO_2 emissions for some years, with the target of reaching a peak in 2030.

The strong industrialization, globalization and the rise of the internet economy, for a long period favoring the coastal zones and the SEZ, the increasing privatization wave, widespread corruption, the pitfalls in the taxation systems and the compression of welfare (almost non-existent for illegal internal migrants in urban areas) have contributed to greatly increase income and wealth inequalities up to the 2008 and to determine a rapidly growing number of private billionaires. Though, after 2008, infrastructural and re-distributive policies and the reduced exports dynamics have contributed to diminish regional and personal income inequalities, China remains a country with large economic and social imbalances, which are in open contrast with its nature as a socialist country.

The original ideals of communism have partly been substituted by the traditional nationalistic goals of *power building*: to become the most powerful country in terms of economic power and then of global military and political power.

2.7 From comparative economic systems to comparative economic studies

The complex and diversified evolution of economic transition in Eastern Europe, former USSR countries and China has confirmed what the fall of the Berlin Wall and the dissolution of the Soviet Union had partly anticipated. The debate on ideal types, such as socialism and capitalism, has almost completely given way to a more articulated debate about the specific characteristics of each "real" economy, in which the national characters are in various proportions combined with capitalist or socialist traits, including the heritage or reactions to long periods of capitalistic or social-democratic or socialist history.

Several contributions have tried to classify different varieties of capitalism. For example, Albert (1991), Berger and Dore (1996), Dore (2000) and Aglietta and Lunghini (2001) introduced or partially used the concepts of the Renan model of capitalism (Germany), Anglo-Saxon capitalism (USA and UK), managerial (Japan), technocratic (France) and family capitalism (Italy). Hall and Soskice (2001) gave a comprehensive assessment of the varieties of capitalism. Several other authors, sociologists and economists have also distinguished between the Nordic or Scandinavian model of capitalism (Denmark, Sweden, Finland and for some aspects Norway) and the Mediterranean one (Greece, Italy, Spain, Portugal). The latter concept was revisited in 2022 in a book edited by Burroni, Pavolini and Regini. The Danish sociologist Esping-Andersen in his influential book *The Three Worlds of Welfare Capitalism* (1990) discussed the relations between welfare and capitalism distinguishing between three types of Welfare State: United States (liberal), Germany (corporatist–statist) and Sweden (social democratic). Although these contributions are useful to analyze important similarities and differences among capitalist countries, they are subject to the great changes that history has determined in political, economic, social institutions and policies in the last few decades. For example, globalization has contributed to bringing closer some aspects of the various economies and raising income and wealth differentials within most Western countries while facilitating the economic expansion of few emerging economies. The periods of crises and economic slowing down have led to reductions in welfare in most capitalist countries. The entry of several Eastern European economies into the European Union has increased the outflow of foreign direct investment from richer to poorer EU countries and the migrations of Eastern European people toward the West. A rich literature on convergence in the European Union has shown that monetary integration without a correct and flexible fiscal integration, an enlarged EU budget and an increasing political integration is insufficient to promote economic convergence and stable growth. Casagrande and Dallago (2021) have analyzed convergence and institutional variety in the European Union using an empirical benchmarking approach. They conclude that "no country can be considered a model for the others" and that "coexistence of different institutional frameworks within the Eurozone is possible, provided that each country improves the operation of its own institutions to make them compatible with the European common goal of monetary and fiscal stability and good national economic performance (growth, employment)" (pp. 1 and 12).

In the last three decades, both at the macroeconomic level and at a sectoral or micro level, the main focus of comparative economics has switched from the study of systems to the study of "real" cases, or problems, or institutions. In particular, the field of comparative economic development has been enriched by a great number of country studies seen in a comparative context, by the direct comparison between two or more countries, by the use of macroeconometric cross-country studies based on large data sets, by the accurate comparative analyses of different institutions, industries, regions, etc. Comparative studies have also been enlarged to developing and emerging economies. The successful cases of rapid and stable growth for a prolonged period, such as it happened in Japan in the 1950–1989 period, South Korea from the 1960 up to now, China since 1978, India from the 1990s to present, have been analyzed in a comparative context in a variety of books and articles.

2.8 The two pyramids of economic power

One problem, however, has been often overlooked by a large part of the comparative economic literature and is associated with the *two pyramids of economic power*. All societies have to co-exist with two pyramids of economic power, one inside the country and the other one at a global level. Within a country, economic power is distributed in unequal proportions, depending on the wealth and the role played by an individual or her/his family in the economic structure. There are a few people at the top of the pyramid, several others at the middle and usually more people at the basis of the pyramid. The second pyramid is at a global level. Giant economies such as the United States and China have more power in economic international relations than middle-size and small economies, also because after a certain delay economic power contributes to determining military and political power. In a comparative analysis it is thus essential to take into account the relative economic power of a country in the world and sometimes also its role played in a regional union, such as the European Union, or in a particular geo-political area. Moreover, since the 1970s, globalization has heavily influenced the two pyramids in most capitalist countries, reducing the powers of politicians and national governments and of local entrepreneurs in the direction of the domestic economies. A growing number of important economic decisions were taken abroad, in the decisional centers of multinationals or of rich invest-ment funds. The power reduction of domestic actors was also inversely associated with the economic size and contractual power of countries where foreign direct investments were located.

Before the crucial transformations of the 1998–1991 years, in the countries belonging to the Soviet bloc, a large part of economic power was reserved to the Soviet Union, while in the transition period, it was mainly transferred to the national governments of Eastern Europe, in increasing measure also to large foreign multinationals investing in these countries, and in part, indirectly, also to the governments of the countries where the strategic control of these corporations is located. A second great impact of economic and financial globalization is the fact that many people at the top of the economic pyramid of a country could greatly increase their relations with people at the top of the economic pyramid of other countries. This has created powerful global interest groups, which can strongly influence global policies, especially if we take into account the fact that eco-nomic power, military power and political power are strictly interrelated. In the bipolar world of the 1950–1989 period, political, military and economic matters were rigidly separated between the Western and the Eastern Bloc, while the present situation is more fluid and differentiated. Next to the two present economic superpowers, the United States and China, there are several regional powers, as India, the European Union, Russia, Brazil, Japan, Indonesia, Iran, Saudi Arabia and Turkey. Even the confrontation between the United States and China does not, for the moment, exclude a great volume of inter-relations in trade, FDI and finance between the two countries, though Trump's admin-istration has tried to halt the globalization drive and contain US imports from China. China's political leaders have tried to extend the country's economic and financial influ-ence in other areas of the world and at the same time to more strictly control the growing economic power of its major private corporations.

2.9 Conclusions

After WWII, comparative economics has been mainly focused on socialism and capitalism and on the "real" functioning of the two superpowers, the United States and the Soviet Union, and their principal allies or vassals. The events and vicissitudes of China's economic ascent in the Maoist period and the country's extraordinarily rapid expansion in the 1978–2020 years have also been the object of a great number of analyses, as well as the economic ascent of India and other important emerging or developing economies.

After the fall of the Berlin Wall, many contributions have studied the varieties of capitalism and socialism and the problems of transition.

In recent decades, many important economic problems have also been treated in a comparative way.

For example, the difficult construction of the European Union, the inclusiveness or exclusiveness of main economic and political institutions and policies, the impact on the economies of democratic or of authoritarian regimes, of freedom, of corruption, of the rule of law, of sustainable or not sustainable policies, have been deeply scrutinized by comparative economic studies.

All these contributions and other ones on sectoral or microeconomic aspects have enriched the discipline, but further progress requires a complex combination of economic, historical and socio-political knowledge. Many cross-country contributions do not take in account the depth of historical and institutional differences in the set of countries they analyze. Several quantitative comparisons are based on poor-quality indicators. We must always keep in mind that history, culture, the environment and social problems matter and that economic power is very unequally distributed among individuals and among countries, and the search for some re-equilibrium is a difficult, but decisive task for the future of mankind.

References

Aglietta, M. and Lunghini, G. (2001). *Sul Capitalismo Contemporaneo*. Torino: Bollati Boringhieri.

Albert, M. (1991). *Capitalism Contre Capitalism*. Paris: Seuil.

Andreff, W. (Ed.) (2020). *Comparative Economic Studies in Europe*. London: Palgrave Macmillan.

Barone, E. (1908). Il Ministro Della Produzione Nello Stato Collettivista, *Giornale Degli Economisti*, 37(2), 267–293, 392–414.

Berger, S. and Dore, R. (Eds.) (1996). *National Diversity and Global Capitalism*. Ithaca-London: Cornell University Press.

Borstein, M. (Ed.) (1965). *Comparative Economic Systems. Models and Cases*. Homewood, IL: Irwin.

Burroni, L., Pavolini, E. and Regini, M. (2022). *Mediterranean Capitalism Revisited: One Model, Different Trajectories*. Ithaca-London: Cornell University Press.

Casagrande, S. and Dallago, B. (2021). Benchmarking Institutional Variety in the Eurozone. An Empirical Investigation, *Economic Systems*, 45, 1–13.

Cherkasov, P. (2016). *IMEMO. History Overview*. Moscow: Ves Mir Publishers.

Dallago, B. (2004). Comparative Economic Systems and the New Comparative Economics, *European Journal of Comparative Economics*, 1 (1), 1–27.

Dobb, M. (1966). *Soviet Economic Development Since 1917*. London: Routledge.

Dore, R. (2000). *Stock Market Capitalism, Welfare Capitalism. Japan and Germany versus the Anglo-Saxons*. Oxford: Oxford University Press.

EBRD. (1999). Transition Report, EBRD, London.

Ellman, M. (2000). The Social Costs and Consequences of the Transformation Process, *Economic Survey of Europe*, 2–3. Geneva: UNECE, pp. 125–140.

Esping-Andersen, G. (1990). *The Three Worlds of Welfare Capitalism*. Princeton, NJ: Princeton University Press.

Fel'dman, G.A. (1928). K Teorii Tempov Narodnogo Dokhoda. *Khoziaistvo*, November and December. English translation (On the Theory of Growth Rates of National Income). In N. Spulber (1964) (Ed.), *Foundations of Soviet Strategy for Economic Growth*. Bloomington, IN: Indiana University Press, pp. 174–202 and pp. 304–331.

Gerschenkron, A. (1962). *Economic Backwardness in Historical Perspective*. Cambridge, MA: Harvard University Press.

Gomulka, A. (2000). Macroeconomic Policies and Achievements in Transition Economies. In *UNECE Economic Survey of Europe*, Geneva, pp. 69–83.

Grossman, G. (1977). The Second Economy in the USSR, *Problems of Communism*, 26 (5), 25–40.

Hall, P.A. and Soskice, D. (2001). *Varieties of Capitalism*. Oxford: Oxford University Press.

(von) Hayek, F.A. (Ed.) (1935). *Collectivist Economic Planning*. London: Routledge & Kegan.

Kornai, J. (1980). *Economics of Shortage*. Amsterdam-London: North Holland.

Kuznets, S. (1971). Notes on Stage of Economic Growth as a System Determinant. In A. Eckstein (Ed.), *Comparison of Economic Systems*. Berkeley, CA: University of California Press.

Lange, O. (1936). On the Economic Theory of Socialism, *Review of Economic Studies*, 4 (1), 53–71.

Lange, O. (1937). On the Economic Theory of Socialism. Part Two, *Review of Economic Studies*, 4(2), 123–142.

Lange, O. and Taylor, F.M. (1938). *On the Economic Theory of Socialism*. Minneapolis, MN: University of Minnesota Press.

Lerner, A.P. (1936). A Note on Socialist Economics, *Review of Economic Studies*, 4(1), 72–76.

Maddison Project Database. (2010). Data retrieved in August 2021 from https://www.rug.nl/ggdc/historicaldevelopment/maddison/releases/maddison-project-database-2020?lang=en

Maddison, A. (2007). *Contours of the World Economy*. Oxford: Oxford University Press.

(von) Mises, L. (1920). *Die Wirtschaftsrechnund in Sozialistichen Gemeinweisen, Archiv fur Sozialwissenschaften und Sozial Politik*. 47, April. English translation in F.A. Von Hayek (1935) (Ed.), *Collectivist Economic Planning*. London: Routledge & Kegan.

Nordhaus, W. and Tobin, J. (1972). *Is Growth Obsolete?* New York, NY: Columbia University Press.

North, D. (1990). *Institutions, Institutional Changes and Economic Performance*. Cambridge: Cambridge University Press.

Nove, A. and Nuti, D.M. (Eds.) (1972). *Socialist Economics*. Harmondsworth: Penguin Books.

OECD. (2021). *2018 Pisa results*. Retrieved in August 2021 from https://www.oecd.org/pisa/publications/pisa-2018-results.htm

Our World in Data. (2022). < https://ourworldindata.org/co$_2$/country/china?country=~CHN#what-are-the-country-s-annual-co$_2$-emissions > retrieved on January 28, 2022.

Pejovich, S. (1999). The Effects of the Interaction of Formal and Informal Institutions on Social Stability and Economic Development, *Journal of Markets & Morality*, 2 (2), 164–181.

Reynolds, L.C. (1971). *The Three Worlds of Economics*. New Haven, CT: Yale University Press.

Stiglitz, J.E., Sen, A. and Fitoussi, J.P. (2009). *Report by the Commission on the Measurement of Economic Performance and Social Progress*. Paris.

UNDP. (2021). *Human Development Report 2021*, retrieved on September 3, 2021 from https://report.hdr.undp.org/

UNECE. (2000). *Economic Survey of Europe*, 2–3, Geneva.

UNECE. (2001). *Economic Survey of Europe*, Geneva: UNECE.

Valli, V. (1978). *Sistemi Economici Capitalisti e Socialisti*. Milano: Unicopli, 1st ed. Milano: CED, 1974, 2nd ed. Unicopli, 1978.

Valli, V. (2002). *L'Europa e l'economia mondiale*. Carocci, Roma.

Valli, V. (2015). *The Economic Rise of China and India*. Torino: Accademia University Press.

Valli, V. (2019). *The American Economy from Roosevelt to Trump*. London: Palgrave Macmillan.

Valli, V. (2020). The Power of Technology in the US and China. In W. Andreff (Ed.), *Comparative Economic Studies in Europe*. London: Palgrave Macmillan, pp. 321–356.

World Bank. (2021a). GDP in PPP. Retrieved August 19, 2021 from https://data.worldbank.org/indicator/NY.GDP.MKTP.PP.KD

World Bank. (2021b). Per capita GDP in PPP. Retrieved August 19, 2021 from https://data.worldbank.org/indicator/NY.GDP.PCAP.PP.KD

World Bank. (2021c). Rate of unemployment (%). Retrieved August 19, 2021 from https://data.worldbank.org/indicator/SL.UEM.TOTL.ZS

World Bank. (2021d). GDP in constant units of local currency. Retrieved August 19, 2021 from https://data.worldbank.org/indicator/NY.GDP.MKTP.KN

3

ECONOMIC SYSTEMS

Nature, Performance, Prospects

Steven Rosefielde

UNC – CHAPEL HILL, CHAPEL HILL, NC, USA

3.1 Introduction

There are 194 self-governing countries. Each government rules its economy. Each creates and/or approves institutions commanding or guiding education, training, employment, property rights, technology, capital, land, finance, commerce, entrepreneurship, and international trade. Each sets rules of conduct for institutions and individuals and fixes boundaries between criminal and legitimate enterprise. Each has the power to tax, subsidize, transfer, mandate, regulate, and determine public policy. Each creates judicial and law enforcement agencies to adjudicate disputes and implement verdicts. Each country has its own culture and political institutions.

The economic system of each country is the ensemble of its purposes, institutions, mechanisms, codes, and norms insofar as they condition and shape rational utilitarian choice.[1] No two systems are identical. Economic systems are necessarily plural because people, governments, and cultures are heterogeneous. Claims to the contrary notwithstanding, there is no such thing as a generic national or global economic system that is best for all nations in a universe where individuals and groups have conflicting desires and some impose their will on others.

The economic performance of each country is partly attributable not only to its prevailing system but also to the diversity of discretionary government policies, cultural preferences, personal tastes, international economic, and politic relations. If policies and cultural preferences cease being discretionary, they become the embedded elements of the system.

Sovereigns (ruling authorities) determine purposes, property rights, design institutions, choose mechanisms, and fix rules of conduct for their systems. Although all systems are unique, they are also divisible into types with shared characteristics.

Many find it illuminating to type systems according to their cultural, social, political, and institutional features. Some stress religion (theocracy versus secularism) or property rights (capitalism versus socialism). Others emphasize governance (democracy versus authoritarianism). Economists tend to spotlight institutions (plans versus markets or subtypes like socialist markets versus capitalist indicative planning).

DOI: 10.4324/9781003144366-5

3.2 Bergson's system function

Abram Bergson was the first theorist to formulate the abstract characteristics and properties of diverse systems rigorously. He devised a social welfare function W, which included an economic sub-function E for this purpose in 1938 (Bergson, 1938, 1954). The W function encompasses all forms of discretionary individual and collective utility seeking (external economies) and the systemic forces constraining unfettered free choice (the system). The E sub-function differs from W solely because it excludes non-commercial activities and relations (leisure), and externalities.[2]

Bergson's W function is as follows:

$$W = W\left(x_1, y_1, a_1^x, b_1^x, a_1^y, b_1^y, \ldots, x_n, y_n, a_n^x, b_n^x, a_n^y, b_n^y, C^x, D^x, C^y, D^y, r, s, t, \ldots\right) \tag{3.1}$$

where C^x and D^x are the amounts of the non-labor factors of production C and D employed in the production unit producing the consumers' good x.

C^y and D^y are the amounts of these factors employed in the production unit producing the consumers' good y.

x_i and y_i are the amounts of x and y consumed by the ith individual and a_1^x, b_1^x, a_1^y, and b_1^y are the amounts of each kind of work performed by him for each production unit during the given period of time.

The symbols $r, s, t, \ldots$ denote elements other than the amounts of commodities, the amounts of work of each type, and the amounts of the non-labor factors in each of the production units, affecting the welfare of the community.[3]

His E sub-function is as follows:

$$E = E\left(x_1, y_1, a_1^x, b_1^x, a_1^y, b_1^y, \ldots, x_n, y_n, a_n^x, b_n^x, a_n^y, b_n^y, C^x, D^x, C^y, D^y\right) \tag{3.2}$$

It is obtained by taking r, s, and t in (3.1) as given.

The "inclusive" function W (Rosefielde and Pfouts, 2014) and sub-function E both implicitly contain sets of systems with distinctive purposes, property rights regimes, institutions, mechanisms, and rules of conduct (the economic system). The invisible fine print includes isoquants (elements of production functions), iso-utility curves (elements of individual and community utility functions), and counterpart micro supply side aspects of property rights, institutions, and codes of conduct.

The E sub-function, assuming the existence of continuous production and utility functions, generates Pareto optional outcomes in the factor, production, distribution, and transfer spaces.[4] Bergson notes that Pareto efficient systems can be capitalist or socialist (Bergson, 1967) and are achievable with both perfect markets and perfect plans (Dorfman, Samuelson and Solow, 1958).[5] The E sub-function determines the potential of efficient Pareto systems. Pareto efficient systems provide a theory normed benchmark for assessing the merit of all imperfectly competitive and anti-competitive E type systems. They exclude r, s, and t variables (non-pecuniary utility generating activities and relations, and externalities disregarded in GDP statistics), although r, s, and t variables can be included on a ceteris paribus basis by assuming for argument sake that they are givens. The assumption is tantamount to switching from E- to a W-type system with r, s, and t parameters.

Bergson recognized that the perfectly competitive market-type Pareto individual utility maximizing system (including democratically determined income transfers), which treats r, s, and t as givens, is not society's only rational choice (Bergson, 1967; Meade, 1993). Sovereigns may prefer alternatives on various grounds. Nonetheless, he ventured the opinion that the Pareto standard provides an attractive and convenient starting point for conversations about "what should be done" (Chernyshevsky, 1863).

The contemporary discipline of comparative economics encompasses all non-Paretian (Gigerenzer and Selten 2002; Harré and Secord, 1973; Kahneman, 2003; Rosefielde and Pfouts, 2014; Rubinstein, 1998; Simon, 1957; Tisdell, 1998) imperfectly competitive, and Pareto ideal systems (capitalist and socialist alike) contained in Bergson's W function and E sub-function. It imitates Isaac Newton's hard science mathematical approach to discovering the universal laws of economic motion, premised on the dubious supposition that human behavior, like gravity, is invariant.[6]

3.3 Bergson's "theory normed" GDP performance standard

World War II deflected Bergson's attention from economic "natural law" and social welfare theory (1938) to the measurement and assessment of system performance.[7] During the war, he served as director of the Russian Analysis Section of the Office of Strategic Studies (OSS) and used his "theory normed" method (adjusted factor costing) to transform Soviet net material product data into comparable Western gross national product and income statistics (Bergson, 1950).[8] He accomplished this by adding imputed rental charges to Marxist labor cost product prices and pioneered the study of sources of Soviet economic growth guided by his E sub-function (Bergson, 1954) and his analysis of the Pareto inefficiency of Soviet economic planning (Bergson, 1964). He compared Soviet GNP, factor productivity, and growth with the American benchmark (Bergson, 1953, 1961, 1963, 1968) and investigated the hypothesis that a low elasticity of factor substitution retarded Soviet economic growth (Bergson, 1979). In doing so, he showed how statistically estimated E sub-functions could be used to quantitatively assess comparative economic performance.

3.4 Ambiguities of GDP success indicators

Bergson's theory normed, quantitative micro and macroeconomic performance method (and versions thereof used by authoritative institutions like the World Bank) is practical, sound and nuanced, but undependable. Economic actors and government statisticians sometimes freely invent, miss adjust, and misleadingly define data (Rosefielde, 2003; Aganbegyan, 1988). The scope of activities that statisticians include in GDP (including defense (Rosefielde, 1987),[9] own-use and criminal activities) may vary significantly among nations. GDP mostly covers goods produced and sold to others and ignores phenomena like income inequality and systemic racism. Moreover, although Bergson acknowledged that some systems prevented individuals from utility maximizing (forced substitution and "value subtracted"),[10] violating the Paretian assumption that goods are worth what people pay for them, he did not adjust Soviet national product statistics for anti-competitive distortions and sundry social aberrations (Rosefielde, 1995; Bergson 1995). Newton's data were less ambiguous.

3.5 Soviet example

The data in Table 3.1 illustrate the difficulty of applying the theory normed method for comparative purposes. Official Soviet comparative GDP statistics indicated that the USSR grew faster than the United States in 1961–1986. Mikhail Gorbachev knew better. He dismissed Goskomstat's

Table 3.1 Comparative national income growth
1961–1986 (average annual growth: percent)

	USSR	USA
1961–86	5.5	3.1
1971–75	4.3	3.4
1981–85	3.6	2.5
1986	4.1	2.5

Source: *Narodnoe khoziaistvo SSSR za 70 Let*, Finansy i
Statistika, Moscow (1987, p. 654).

(State Statistics Committee) figures, convinced that Soviet economic performance was dire
enough to warrant radical economic reform (perestroika) (Gorbachev, 1987; Aganbegyan, 1988).
Had Gorbachev placed his trust in Bergson's assumption that Soviet statistics were "reliable"
(Bergson, 1953), he would have been content to stay the course.

The "unreliability" of Soviet statistics notwithstanding, Bergson's method did prove its
mettle by shedding light on the reality Gorbachev perceived behind the façade of Soviet statistical success. The total factor productivity (TFP) statistics presented in Table 3.2 computed
according to Bergson's method (converting Soviet NMP statistics to the Western GDP
standard) revealed that factor productivity growth 1970–1985 was weak, despite the illusion of
rapid NMP growth officially reported 1961–1986, lending credence to Gorbachev's fear that

Table 3.2 Soviet factor productivity growth 1965–1985 (official industrial output series) percent

	1965–70	1970–75	1975–80	1980–85	1965–85
GNP	6.2	4.3	3.1	2.8	4.1
Combined inputs	3.8	3.8	3.1	2.5	3.3
Workhours	2.0	1.7	1.2	0.7	1.4
Capital	7.4	8.0	6.9	6.3	7.1
TFP	2.4	0.5	0	0.3	0.8

TFP is total factor productivity.

Sources: *Allocation of Resources in the Soviet Union and China – 1985*, Joint Economic Committee of Congress,
March 19, 1986, Table 3.4, p. 80 and Table 3.5, p. 81; Rosefielde, *Economic Foundations of Soviet National Security
Strategy*, unpublished manuscript, 1987, Tables 9.4 and 9.14; Abram Bergson, *Productivity and the Social Systems*,
Harvard University Press, Cambridge, MA, 1978, Appendix Table 3.11, p. 236. *Measures of Soviet Gross National
Product in 1982 Prices*, Joint Economic Committee of Congress, November 1990, Table A-1, pp. 54–57.

Method: The factors are combined, following Bergson, according to the Cobb–Douglas specification (see
Bergson, 1978, pp. 159–60 note 8). The income elasticities (shares) imputed to capital (.328 GNP, .217 industry)
are provided in Bergson (1978, Appendix Table 3.11). Labor is .672 GNP, and .683 industry. Cf. Appendix Table
3.22, p. 245. The factor data are taken from CIA sources: the industrial component of the CIA's GNP is the
official Goskomstat series. TFP growth for aggregate output and industry are computed with the following
function:

$$TFP = \dot{Y} / \left[\alpha \dot{K} + (1 - \alpha) \dot{L} \right] \tag{3.3}$$

where $\dot{Y}$, $\dot{K}$, and $\dot{L}$ are output, capital, and labor growth and α and $(1-\alpha)$ are the output elasticities of these
factors measured in 1955 rubles (GNP) and 1959 rubles (industry). Capital weights are net of depreciation.

planning condemned the USSR to secular stagnation (Birman, 1983; Bergson, 1979, 1989, 1991, 1994; Bergson and Levine, 1983).

3.6 Non-pecuniary sources of utility: Bergson's *r, s, t*

The partial successes of Bergson's theory normed method encouraged many to suppose that his estimates and those of the Central Intelligence Agency (CIA) accurately reflected the comparative merit of the Soviet and American economic systems within a narrow range of uncertainty. Soviet per capita income was roughly half the American benchmark,[11] attributed partly to Russia's relative economic backwardness, but mostly to the anti-competitive ineffi-ciencies of central planning. Those like Bergson, who thought about the issue, found it con-venient to suppose that Soviet non-pecuniary utilities associated with the *r, s,* and *t* were lower than the American benchmark in the same degree.

Were they right? Soviet anti-competitive forces might plausibly have diminished the efficiency of pecuniary (state) and non-pecuniary (non-state) productive activities equally, but the utilitarian cost of the Communist Party's political tyranny was an entirely different matter. Soviet authoritarianism doubtlessly caused the quality of Soviet utilitarian existence to fall far below the 50 percent benchmark set by Bergson's comparative per capita income estimates.

This example spotlights the conceptual importance of *r, s,* and *t* variables (non-pecuniary activities and relations, and externalities). Sovereigns, who choose non-Paretian systems, insofar as they are rational, do so because they believe that the Paretian GDP efficiencies they choose to forgo are more than offset by gains in non-pecuniary *r, s,* and *t* utilities. The proletariat's victory in Lenin's eyes was worth any material sacrifice. Experience subsequently taught Soviet citizens better (Rosefielde, 2015).

People do not live by GDP alone. The quality of their existence depends on a broad array of economic system-dependent, non-commercial activities. Enlightened societies not only provide people with utilities generated by their wages but also additionally utilities produced by congenial conditions of labor, worker solidarity, mutual aid, and coopera-tive communities. These good systems capture external economies and foster self-learning, self-discovery, enterprise, empathy, compassion, virtue, charity, and social harmony while empowering free thought, speech, civil rights, religious liberty, and tolerance. Governments provide some services supporting these objectives including income transfers and social ser-vices (health, housing, transportation, security, and affirmative action) counted in GDP, but the E sub-function excludes the lion share of activities enhancing high-value non-pecuniary utilities.

Good economic systems strive to maximize utility (commercial plus non-commercial) and hence the quality of existence by granting citizens substantial personal freedom and incul-cating values promoting equity and social justice. Bad systems do the opposite. They suppress democracy (authoritarianism), flout human rights (deny equal opportunity and due process), repress personal liberty, regiment, tyrannize, and terrorize society (Solzhenitsyn, 1973). They inculcate values promoting inequity, privilege, and injustice.

Figure 3.1 illustrates the utilitarian benefit that Masahiko Aoki believes Japan enjoys by retaining its non-Paretian communitarian system (Bergson's W function including *r, s, t*) instead of adopting a perfectly competitive Paretian alternative with random non-pecuniary

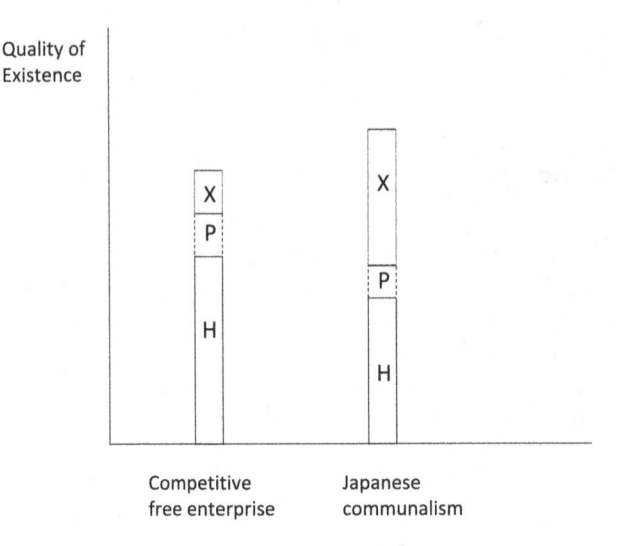

Figure 3.1 Quality of existence.

utilities (Aoki, 2001; Aoki, Gregory and Miyajima, 2007). The utility generated in both variants is the triple summation

$$Q = H + P + X \qquad (3.4)$$

where

1. Q is the quality of national existence (utility).
2. H is household utilities derived from the consumption of private of goods and services produced in the private sector.
3. P is public utilities derived from the consumption of government provided goods and services.
4. X is other utilities generated from unpaid personal self-improvement and relationships (friends, family, community, civic, and political participation and social phenomena like egalitarianism and social justice). Non-commercial utility [$X = u_{aX} + u_{bX}$] measures utility excluded from GDP (because these utilities are derived from unpaid or criminal activities, or difficult to quantify). The subscripts aX and bX refer to utilities experienced by individuals a and b from non-commercial self-services, interpersonal services provided gratis by others, and unpaid spiritual experiences [communing with nature, transcendental, religious, aesthetic, communal, civic, political, social]. Unpaid experiences include self-learning, self-discovery, self-improvement, and self-therapy, gratifying interpersonal relationships (friendship, love, amorous, family, community, social, and political), and communing with the divine, preternatural spirits, and nature, as well as nurture, security, romance, and adventure. Equality, social justice, cooperativeness, amity, harmony, and tranquility are outcomes of constructive non-pecuniary interpersonal behaviors that enhance individual utility without contributing to GDP (H + P). There are two broad types of X utilities (U_{X1}): pleasure generated from unpaid consumption experiences and (U_{X2}) satisfaction derived peripherally from living in congenial political, social, cultural, and natural surroundings.

Aoki contends that the vertical bar measuring the quality of existence (H + P + X) for the Japanese non-Paretian "communalist" system is larger than the perfectly competitive alternative (Rosefielde, 2013), even though anti-competitive aspects of Japan's economy (employment for life, obligatory unpaid overtime work, and profit satisficing) reduce GDP (H + P).

Household and state-generated utilities in Japan are less than they would be under perfect competition due to deadweight inefficiency losses accepted as the price required to obtain countervailing non-pecuniary benefits (Case and Fair, 1999).

The situation however is the reverse for non-pecuniary utilities. The constraints Japanese society place on competition Aoki believes increase non-pecuniary utilities from consensus building, mutual support, and social harmony enough to make Japan's quality of existence under its communalist regime higher than it would be under Paretian perfect competition.

Aoki's reasoning applies to a large set of cases including Thailand's Theravada Buddhist "sufficiency" system and Daniel Markovitz's progressive anti-meritocratic utopia (Markovitz 2020).

3.7 Limits of inclusive utilitarian calculus

Measurement problems obscure the importance of non-pecuniary utilities. Non-commercial experiences are undocumented. They are the result of private experiences individuals and groups have with themselves and among others that are difficult to estimate in monetary terms for a multitude of reasons. Japanese can bear witness to the gratification they derive from communalism, but statisticians cannot reliably calculate its monetary value or quantify and aggregate underlying interpersonal utilities. Likewise, people recognize that democracy, freedom, human rights, social justice, and income equality are beneficial but cannot reach a consensus about their pecuniary worth. Various international institutions including the World Bank, European Union, OECD, and United Nations compile happiness indexes to assess the comparative quality of national existence (taking account of pecuniary and non-pecuniary utilities), but they do not convincingly quantify systems merit.[12] Economists want to calibrate inclusive comparative economic performance unambiguously but cannot overcome the hurdles. Judgments about comparative merit alas must lie mostly in the eyes of the beholder because GDP statistics (E sub-function data) are insufficiently reliable, and social (proxy utility) indicators reflect disputable preferences of those who construct them.

3.8 Coping with imponderables: Pragmatism and social advocacy

According to tradition, although Socrates reportedly said something to the effect that "he knew that he knew nothing" (Bowden, 2005), he qualified this paradox (Socrates' Paradox) by suggesting that people could still make rational choices and successfully navigate their lives by deciphering shadows on the walls of a cave (Allegory of the Cave) (Nettleship, 1955).[13] Economists and others find themselves in the same elusive position regarding the merit of rival national economic systems. They know that they cannot precisely know the inclusive performance of the world's 194 independent national economies with their soft science techniques, but nonetheless many confidently believe that they can discern the essentials by focusing on a few key principles and statistics. Marxist–Leninist–Stalinists contend the state ownership of the means of production, and Communist Party led planning guarantee superior outcomes in the H, P, and X spaces. Proof for them is axiomatic based on the twin assumptions that capitalist motives are vicious and socialist intentions divine. Empirical evidence is subsidiary. If national income statistics confirm their faith, so be it. Otherwise, the only test that matters to Marxist–Leninist–Stalinists is victory over their adversaries.

Contemporary progressives and supporters of open societies make similar claims. Their self-certitude does not make them right (Nance, 2016).

3.9 What we now know through a glass darkly[14]

The soft social science of comparative economic systems is more than 80 years old. What have we learned?

We now know through a glass darkly that

1. The concept of systems is sound, and the performance of the world's 194 systems is imprecisely gaugeable with available standardized data and contemporary quantitative methods.

2. Systems are divisible into types. Most people perceive the alternatives in political economic terms (democracy versus authoritarianism) or ideological caricatures (capitalism versus socialism). Economists debate the merits of markets versus plans and sub-types like market socialism and capitalist "indicative" planning.

3. There are numerous types of socialist economies. Marxist–Leninist–Stalinist plan-command regimes (Soviet Union 1928–1953, Eastern Europe 1947–1991, North Korea 1947–2022) criminalize private property, markets, and entrepreneurship, and feature mandatory state ownership of the means of production, planning, administrative command, state trading, Marxist labor value pricing, and anti-parasite laws.[15] They over-allocated resources to investment and national defense and skimp on consumption. They over-employ labor, ration, and compel consumers to buy what they can (consumer choice) instead of what they want (consumer sovereignty). Marxist–Leninist–Stalinist systems are susceptible to secular stagnation and impose huge deadweight inefficiency losses on society. Open inflation is low (but there is considerable hidden inflation). Finance is prudent. Marxist–Leninist–Stalinist systems are cyclically stable. They despoil the environment and their tyranny diminishes the quality of communist existence.

4. Marxist–Leninist–Xi-ist market communist economies (China 1978–2022, and Vietnam 1991–2022) are state led, top-down Communist Party managed with state freehold ownership of the means of production, for-profit leasing of the state's freehold property, state guided labor, product and commercial markets (including foreign trade), workably competitive wages and prices, and distribution. China has more than a million unpaid concentration camp workers (laogai and laojiao). Marxist–Leninist–Xi-ist communist systems devote substantial resources to defense but are more consumer friendly than command communist regimes. They encourage entrepreneurship and robust international trade, but anti-competitiveness still causes large deadweight inefficiency losses, compounded by tyrannical non-pecuniary dis-utilities. Chinese market communism provides meager social welfare services, shuns affirmative action, and ignores claims for restorative justice. It is indifferent to equal opportunity and contrary to Marxist precepts, is astonishingly inegalitarian. Many question its sustainability (Csaba, 2020).

5. There have been three other Marxist–Leninist national market-communist experiments: Mao Zedong's Great Proletarian Cultural Revolutionary worker self-management model (1966–1976), Pol Pot's Cambodian killing fields variant (1976–1979), and Yugoslav worker managed dividend sharing (1952–1991). All malfunctioned and self-destructed, despite the plaudits of enthusiasts (Wheelwright and McFarlane, 1971).

6. Sovereign leaders of many countries officially describe their systems as socialist: Republic of Cuba, Lao People's Democratic Republic, People's Republic of Bangladesh, Co-operative Republic of Guyana, Republic of India, Federal Democratic Republic of

Nepal, Portuguese Republic, Democratic Socialist Republic of Sri Lanka, and the United Republic of Tanzania. None has been strikingly successful.[16]

7. Most of the world's 194 economies are capitalist systems. There are numerous capitalist types where capitalists (owners of productive assets) profit seek, exert market power, amass wealth, and influence government to anti-competitively augment their income and preserve their privileges. Pure capitalist systems where capitalists rule unopposed are figments of Marxist imagination. Other classes, groups, and individuals always have countervailing economic and political power, and all systems have elements of planning and bureaucratic administration. All are mixed economies. There are several distinct big government capitalist sub-types: liberal–revolutionary progressive welfare states (Biden's America) (Rosefielde and Mills, 2020, 2022), collectivist welfare states (Nordic countries), ordo-liberal regimes (Germany), and authoritarian rent-granting (Russia). All claim to protect the working class, but sentiment in America began shifting toward other vulnerable constituencies during Bill Clinton's presidency. The performance of these sub-types varies considerably. Some are conspicuously more efficient in their private, state, and non-pecuniary activities and enjoy higher quality of existences (Nordic collectivism). High performance is usually, but not always associated with competitiveness and moral integrity. Some nations like Japan with a strong culture of community obligation are able to substitute cooperation and consensus building for competition. Competitive self-reliant, small government capitalist systems (Taiwan and Singapore) have outshined their big government rivals. Authoritarian rent-granting regimes underperform (Russia). No capitalist system is perfectly competitive or perfectly exploitive. All are imperfectly competitive in varying degrees and impose deadweight efficiency losses on their societies.

8. Socialist and capitalist systems are being challenged today by a revolutionary progressive anti-meritocratic tide prioritizing select r, s, and t goals (entitlements, affirmative action, restorative justice) over the material wellbeing of workers and the middle class. Advocates are staunchly anti-capitalist, anti-competitive, anti-growth, and even anti-egalitarian prioritizing need over equity. It will take several decades to judge the performance of neo-progressive systems (Csaba, 2022).

9. Theocracies claim to provide great spiritual benefits, with mixed results in the private and public sectors. Thailand appears to be a major success story, but Iran is sputtering.[17]

10. The economic systems of the world's 194 nations constantly evolve. Reforms and revolutions in the pecuniary and non-pecuniary spheres occasionally cause them to shift from one type (capitalism, socialism, theocracy) and sub-type (liberal welfare states, collectivist welfare states, ordo-liberal regimes, and authoritarian rent granting) to another. Marxist–Leninist–Stalinist systems are robust (exhibiting growth, full employment, price stability), but are prone to secular stagnation, and collapse. Capitalist systems are vulnerable to periodic financial crises, secular stagnation, and black swan revolutions (Taleb, 2007). It is difficult to assess the comparative resiliency of systems because power struggles, often beneath the threshold of perception, constantly jeopardize automatic stabilizers.

11. Prospects for the future depend on a multitude of factors (Kornai, 2010). There is ample scope for constructive institutional reform in all systems, especially reforms that address trade-offs affecting the quality of existence between living standards and r, s, and t non-pecuniary utilities. Entrepreneurship, technological progress, diffusion and transfer have enabled most countries to increase per capita GDP despite diverse disorders and deadweight efficiency losses. They may continue to do so. Finally, cross currents in system priorities may undermine international security, with authoritarian capitalist (Russia) and

communist (China, North Korea) building up their armed forces (Rosefielde and Mills, 2021), while democratic capitalist nations allow their militaries to wither (Rosefielde and Mills, 2020, 2021, 2022).

Notes

1 Economy implies cost saving and utility enhance behavior. If individual choose a rationally or irrationally, then they cannot intentionally economize.
2 The alternative to work is leisure, with the connotation of entertainment. Bergson chose to omit leisure time utilities as distractions from the E sub-function focus on commercially generated activities.
3 Some of the elements r, s, and t, ..., may affect welfare, not only directly, but indirectly through their effect on (say) the amounts of x and y produced with any given amount of resources, e.g., the effects of a change in the weather. On the other hand, it is conceivable that variations in the amounts of commodities, the amounts of work of each type, and the amounts of non-labor factors in each of the production units will also have a direct and indirect effect on welfare, e.g., a sufficient diminution of x_i and y_j may be accompanied by an overturn of the government. But for relatively small changes in these variables, other elements in welfare, I believe, will not be significantly affected. To the extent that this is so a partial analysis is feasible.
4 The continuity assumption is not essential for rational decision-making, but it is an integral aspect of the Paretian perfectly competitive ideal.
5 Robert Dorfman, Paul Samuelson, and Robert Solow, *Linear Programming and Economic Analysis*, New York: McGraw-Hill, 1958. Pareto duality requires a perfect correspondence between the objective functions of both systems. Individual preferences must be the competitive ideal. Soviet planning did not satisfy this requirement. Planner preferences ruled. Bergson understood the distinction.
6 Isaac Newton (1642–1727) invented the calculus in the mid to late 1660s and formulated the theory of universal gravity. His *Philosophiæ Naturalis Principia Mathematica* transformed natural philosophy into modern physical science. Vilfredo Pareto (1812–1882), Paul Samuelson (1915–2009), and others attempted to accomplish the same feat for the economics branch of the soft social sciences.
7 Bergson's norms are "benchmarks" obliquely connected with utility. His W and E sub-function are defined only for activities and utilities. The moral worth of Pareto outcomes is a separate matter.
8 Soviet national income statisticians following Karl Marx treated non-productive services like haircuts as leisure activities and excluded them from GDP. NMP is GDP minus non-productive services.
9 The Soviet defense budget statistic excluded weapons.
10 Value is subtracted when processing reduces a good's utility. The Japanese, for example, only purchased Soviet raw timber because there was no domestic demand for processed Soviet wooden goods.
11 This is the purchasing power parity dollar estimate of Soviet GDP.
12 For example, *World Happiness Report 2020*, March 20, 2020. https://worldhappiness.report/ Happiness is a utilitarian/hedonist concept. Merit subordinates utility to ethical appraisal. Nazis may have been happy in 1939, but this did not make Hitler's economic system meritorious.
13 In saying that I "know" that I do not "know" Socrates is being deliberately "paradoxical". However, it is possible to argue that what he meant was that he was not fully acquainting with the facts. If he were, then he would know that he knows. Plato in the Republic narrates the allegory.
14 1 Corinthians 13:1.
15 The Polish October and Hungarian Revolution of 1956 led to a softening of the Marxist–Leninist–Stalinist paradigm in these countries.
16 This judgment is absolute. Comparison with their non-socialist peers might modify the assessment.
17 Iran's poor economic performance is partly attributable to Western economic sanctions.

References

Aganbegyan, A. (1988). *The Economic Challenge of Perestroika*. Bloomington, IN: Indiana University Press.
Aoki, M. (2001). *Toward a Comparative Institutional Analysis*. Cambridge, MA: MIT Press.
Aoki, M., Jackson, G. and Miyajima, H. (2007). *Corporate Governance in Japan: Institutional Change and Organizational Diversity*. Oxford: Oxford University Press.

Bergson, A. (1938). A Reformulation of Certain Aspects of Welfare Economics. *Quarterly Journal of Economics*, Vol. 52, No. 1, 310–34.

Bergson, A. (1950). Soviet National Income and Product in 1937, Parts I and II. *Quarterly Journal of Economics*, Vol. 64, Nos. 2,3, 208–41, 408–41.

Bergson, A. (editor and contributor) (1953). *Soviet Economic Growth: Conditions and Perspectives*. Evanston, IL: Row, Peterson.

Bergson, A. (1953). Reliability and Usability of Soviet Statistics: A Summary Appraisal. *American Statistician*, Vol. 7, No. 3 (June–July), 13–16.

Bergson, A. (1954). The Concept of Social Welfare. *Quarterly Journal of Economics*, Vol. 68, No. 2 (May), 233–52.

Bergson, A. (1961). *The Real National Income of Soviet Russia Since 1928*. Cambridge, MA: Harvard University Press.

Bergson, A. (1963). The Great Economic Race. *Challenge Magazine*, Vol. 11, No. 6, 4–6.

Bergson, A. (1964). *The Economics of Soviet Planning*. New Haven, CT: Yale University Press.

Bergson, A. (1967). Market Socialism Revisited. *Journal of Political Economy*, Vol. 75, No. 4 (October), 655–73.

Bergson, A. (1968). *Planning and Productivity under Soviet Socialism*. New York, NY: Columbia University Press.

Bergson, A. (1978). *Productivity and the Social System – The USSR and the West*. Cambridge, MA: Harvard University Press.

Bergson, A. (1979). Notes on the Production Function in Soviet Post-war Industrial Growth. *Journal of Comparative Economics*, Vol. 3, No. 2 (June), 116–26.

Bergson, A. (1983). Comparative Productivity: The USSR, Eastern Europe and the West. *American Economic Review*, Vol. 77, No. 3 (June), 342–57.

Bergson, A. (1989). *Planning and Performance in Socialist Economies*. London: Unwin and Hyman.

Bergson, A. (1991). The USSR before the Fall: How Poor and Why? *Journal of Economic Perspectives*, Vol. 5, No. 4, 29–44.

Bergson, A. (1994). The Communist Efficiency Gap: Alternative Measures. *Comparative Economic Studies*, Vol. XXXVI, No. 1, Spring, 1–12.

Bergson, A. (1995). Neoclassical Norms and the Valuation of National Product in the Soviet Union and Its Post-communist Successor States: Comment. *Journal of Comparative Economics*, Vol. 21, No. 3, 390–393.

Bergson, A. and Levine, H. (eds.) (1983). *The Soviet Economy Toward the Year 2000*. London: George Allen & Unwin.

Birman, I. (1983). *Экономика недостач* (Economy of Shortage). New York, NY: Chalidze Publications.

Bowden, H. (2005). *Classical Athens and the Delphic Oracle: Divination and Democracy*. New York: Cambridge University Press.

Case, K. and Fair, R. (1999). *Principles of Economics*. New York, NY: Prentice Hall.

Chernyshevsky, N. (1863). *What is to be Done*. Saint Petersburg.

Csaba, L. (2020). China at the Crossroads. *Acta Oeconomica*, Vol. 70, 5–14.

Csaba, L. (2022). Illiberal Economic Policies, in András Sajó, Renáta Uitz, Stephen Holmes, *Routledge Handbook of Illiberalism*. London: Routledge.

Gigerenzer, G. and Selten, R. (2002). *Bounded Rationality*. Cambridge, MA: MIT Press.

Gorbachev, M. (1987). *Perestroika: New Thinking for Our Country and the World*. New York, NY: Harper Collins.

Harré, R. and Secord, P. (1973). *The Explanation of Social Behavior*. Oxford: Blackwell.

Kahneman, D. (2003). Maps of Bounded Rationality: Psychology for Behavioral Economics. *American Economic Review*, Vol. 93, No. 5, 1449–1475.

Kornai, J. (2010). Innovation and Dynamism: Interaction between Systems and Technical Progress. *Economics of Transition*, Vol. 18, No. 4, 629–670.

Markovitz, D. (2020). *The Meritocracy Trap*. New York, NY: Penguin.

Meade, J. (1993). *Liberty, Equality, and Efficiency*. New York, NY: New York University Press.

Nance, D. (2016). *The Burdens of Proof: Discriminatory Power, Weight of Evidence, and Tenacity of Belief*. New York, NY: Cambridge University Press.

Nettleship, R. (1955). Chapter 4 – The Four Stages of Intelligence. *Lectures on the Republic of Plato*. London: Macmillan & Co.

Rosefielde, S. (1987). *False Science: Underestimating the Soviet Arms Buildup.* Rutgers, NJ: Transaction Press.

Rosefielde, S. (1995). Neoclassical Norms and the Valuation of National Product in the Soviet Union and Its Post-communist Successor States: Comment. *Journal of Comparative Economics*, Vol. 21, No. 3, 375–389.

Rosefielde, S. (2003). The Riddle of Postwar Russian Economic Growth: Statistics Lied and Were Misconstrued. *Europe-Asia Studies*, Vol. 53, No. 3, 469–81.

Rosefielde, S. (2013). *Asian Economic Systems*, Chapter 8. Singapore: World Scientific Publishers.

Rosefielde, S. (2015). Economic Theory of the Second Worst. *Higher School of Economics Journal (HSE)*, Vol. 19, No. 1, 30–44.

Rosefielde, S. (ed.) (2021). *Putin's Russia: Economy, Defense, Policy.* Singapore: World Scientific Publishers.

Rosefielde, S. and Pfouts, R.W. (2014). *Inclusive Economy Theory.* Singapore: World Scientific Publishers.

Rosefielde, S. and Mills, Q. (2020). *Progressive and Populists.* Singapore: World Scientific Publishers.

Rosefielde, S. and Mills, Q. (2021). *Beleaguered Superpower: Biden's America Adrift.* Singapore: World Scientific Publishers.

Rosefielde, S. and Mills, Q. (2022). *America's Future: Biden and the Progressives.* Singapore: World Scientific Publishers.

Rubinstein, A. (1998). *Modeling Bounded Rationality.* Cambridge, MA: MIT Press.

Simon, H. (1957). *Models of Man: Social and Rational – Mathematical Essays on Rational Human Behavior in a Social Setting.* New York, NY: John Wiley & Sons.

Solzhenitsyn, A. (1973). *Gulag Archipelago.* New York: Harper and Row.

Taleb, N. (2007). *The Black Swan: The Impact of the Highly Improbable.* New York, NY: Random House.

Tisdell, C. (1998). *Bounded Rationality and Economic Evolution: A Contribution to Decision Making, Economics, and Management.* Cheltenham: Brookfield.

Wheelwright, E. and McFarlane, B. (1971). *Chinese Road to Socialism: Economics of the Cultural Revolution.* New York, NY: Monthly Review Press.

4

ELEMENTS OF AN EVOLUTIONARY APPROACH TO COMPARATIVE ECONOMIC STUDIES

Complexity, Systemism, and Path-Dependent Development

Claudius Gräbner-Radkowitsch

DEPARTMENT OF PLURALIST ECONOMICS, EUROPA UNIVERSITY FLENSBURG
INSTITUTE FOR THE COMPREHENSIVE ANALYSIS OF THE ECONOMY
JOHANNES KEPLER UNIVERSITY LINZ
ZOE INSTITUTE FOR FUTURE-FIT ECONOMICS, COLOGNE

4.1 Introduction

This chapter describes the central elements of an evolutionary approach to comparative economic studies (EACES). Such an approach is inspired first and foremost by evolutionary economics, one of the most influential 'heterodox' economic research programs that has produced numerous concepts and theories that seem to be natural ingredients to a comparative approach. The evolutionary literature on *National Innovation Systems* (NIS, e.g., Nelson, 1993), the work on *technology gaps* (e.g., Dosi et al., 1990), and *evolutionary growth theory* (e.g., Nelson & Winter, 1982) are early examples of such concepts. As will be argued below, not only has significant progress been made when developing these concepts further, they also align well with concepts that were developed recently in other socio-economic research programs, such as the Post-Keynesian work on *growth models* (Baccaro & Pontusson, 2016), the inter-disciplinary work on *economic complexity* (Hidalgo, 2021), and the critical contributions by *structuralists* and *dependency theorists* (Kvangraven, 2020). In this sense, the main goal of this chapter is to synthesize existing concepts within a consistent framework that is immediately useful for a comparative analysis of economic systems.

Integrating concepts from different research programs and fields is not straightforward, however: every research program (or 'paradigm') comes with its own terminology and meta-theoretical foundation, such as a preferred way to explain empirical phenomena and particular research methods (Gräbner & Strunk, 2020). Thus, whenever one wishes to elaborate on a general approach that encompasses contributions from distinct research programs,

DOI: 10.4324/9781003144366-6

a consistent meta-theoretical framework that explicates all the higher-order assumptions of the approach becomes essential. More precisely, just as any research program, the EACES has, at its core, certain fundamental assumptions as well as certain topical foci. These assumptions do not only determine what kind of theories, concepts, or methods can be successfully integrated into and used within the EACES, but they also provide the analytical vocabulary to distinguish the evolutionary approach discussed here from other approaches to the comparative analysis of economic systems – which is why explicating this core is at utmost essence.

Therefore, the rest of this chapter proceeds as follows: Section 4.2 gives a general overview of the meta-theoretical foundations in terms of ontology and epistemology. This will allow us to distinguish an evolutionary from a non-evolutionary approach and to better understand whether and when such an approach can complement or substitute alternatives. Section 4.3, then, illustrates the approach, in practice, by applying it to recent developments in the European Union. While this is not meant as a self-contained analysis of these developments (which would go way beyond the scope of a handbook chapter), it illustrates how the theoretical concepts can be operationalized and what kind of empirical methods are often useful in applied work. At the end, it provides a non-exhaustive list of topics and concepts that are often handy to consider when applying the EACES in practice (see Table 4.3). Section 4.4 concludes the paper with a short summary and some suggestions for future applications.

4.2 The meta-theoretical core of an evolutionary approach

4.2.1 On the need for a meta-theoretical foundation

Figure 4.1 gives a first indication of why the explication of the meta-theoretical core of a research approach that encompasses distinct paradigms is necessary. What one usually has contact with is merely the tip of the pyramid: concrete models or studies that apply a certain

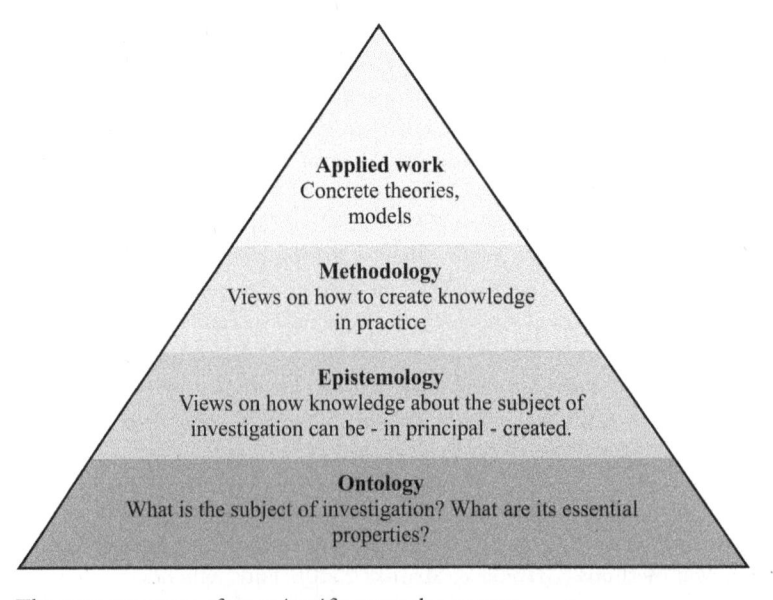

Figure 4.1　The meta-structure of any scientific research program.

approach to a particular phenomenon. This is what the typical journal article is concerned with, and what Thomas Kuhn would consider as "normal science" (Kuhn 2012 [1962]). Yet, in any such application, there are several higher-level assumptions operating in the background. Usually, these are not explicitly discussed in the applied work and refer to what researchers consider to be the *essential properties* of their subject of investigation, i.e., its *ontology*, and the adequate ways to generate knowledge about this subject of investigation, i.e., the *epistemology* of their approach. In economics, for instance, the dominant epistemology is the conviction that any phenomenon should be explained via a model of the phenomenon that features an economic equilibrium and utility-maximizing agents.

Whenever we wish to integrate contributions from distinct paradigms, one has to make sure that they are consistent on the meta-theoretical level, especially with regard to their ontology and epistemology. In the following, the essential aspects of the ontology and epistemology of an EACES will be outlined, both of which are *systemist* by nature. By this we mean that the essential ontological and epistemological features of an evolutionary approach can be linked to the idea of *systemism*, an overall philosophical framework originally developed by Mario Bunge (1996), and already proposed as an umbrella framework for various economic paradigms by Gräbner and Kapeller (2017).[1] In effect, the following exposition not only provides a better idea about the central elements of the EACES but also helps practitioners to see whether it is compatible with their own approach to comparative economic analysis.

4.2.2 *The ontological core: Systems, mechanisms, and evolution*

The basic ontological premise of Bunge's systemism is that everything that exists is either a system or a part of a system. A system as such is "a complex object whose parts [...] are held together by bonds of some kind", whereby these bonds "are logical in the case of a conceptual system, such as a theory; and they are material in the case of a concrete system, such as an atom" (Bunge, 2004, p. 188).[2] More precisely, every system comprises (i) a set of components: its *composition C*, (ii) a set of relations: its *structure S*, (iii) a surrounding within which it exists: its *environment E*, and (iv) a set of *mechanisms M* that operate within the system. Here, a mechanism is "a process (or sequence of states, or pathway) in a concrete system, natural or social" (Bunge, 2004, p. 186). In fact, both Bunge – as most evolutionary economists (see Witt, 2014) – adapts the Darwinian premises that not only something like a 'cause' exists in an ontological sense but also that every event in the world has some cause, which, in principle, can be discovered (e.g., Bunge, 1959, p. 26; Hodgson, 2004, p. 59). These basic premises already provide a useful blueprint that one can use for the description of the essential features of the economic systems that are the main subjects of one's comparative investigation: explicating the most relevant components, relations, and mechanisms, as well as the environments of the systems under investigation, provides for a very neat and transparent summary description for one's comparative study (for more details see Section 4.2.3).

The systemist approach explicitly allows for a *layered ontology*, i.e., systems on different ontological levels – often referred to as the micro, meso, and macro level – that are nested and dependent upon each other. For instance, a firm is a system composed of different components (e.g., workers, owners, customers, etc.). At the same time, however, it is also one part of a larger system, e.g., a particular economic sector, within which it has relations to other components, such as other firms or regulatory institutions.[3] For evolutionary scholars, this layeredness of reality, which is illustrated in Figure 4.2, relates to another fundamental ontological commitment, viz., the relevance of *evolution*. There are two reasons for this: first,

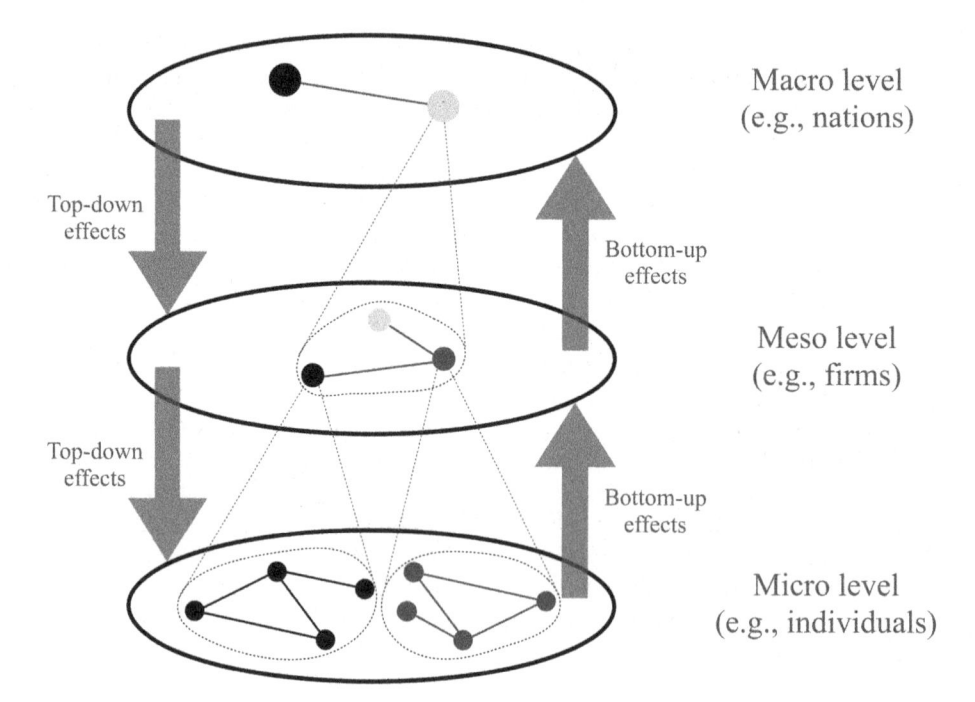

Macro level
(e.g., nations)

Top-down
effects

Bottom-up
effects

Meso level
(e.g., firms)

Top-down
effects

Bottom-up
effects

Micro level
(e.g., individuals)

Figure 4.2 The layered ontology of systemism. Note the pragmatic character of this systematization as a general blueprint to describe the objects one investigates. For a deeper, analytical ontology, which is compatible with this pragmatic approach, see Dopfer and Potts (2004) and Dopfer et al. (2004).

multi-level systems – where each level comprises a system as defined above, and lower-level systems are components of higher-level systems – are particularly likely to evolve in the presence of evolutionary mechanisms. Thus, evolution explains the empirical relevance of such a multi-level approach (see already Simon, 1962). Second, the terminology of micro-meso-macro resembles the analytical system developed by Dopfer et al. (2004), which they derive from what they consider the fundamental ontological core of evolutionary economics, namely, *evolutionary realism* (Dopfer et al., 2004). They argue that the fundamental object of evolutionary analysis is the study of the dynamics of populations of rules, and refer to the level of rule populations as the *meso*, the level of rule users (i.e., agents) as the *micro*, and the level of relations between rule populations as the *macro* level. The processes operating on the meso levels, i.e., the change of generic rules according to a biologically inspired origination-adoption-retention scheme, is where the evolutionary core of evolutionary analysis resides and why any thinking in terms of equilibria is misleading. A more precise discussion of evolutionary realism, however, would go beyond the scope of a single handbook chapter, and excellent introductions are already available (Dopfer & Potts, 2004; Dopfer et al., 2004). Thus, in the following, the focus will be more pragmatic and applied, yet it should be stressed that the micro-meso-macro scheme of Dopfer et al. (2004) rationalizes an important link between the concepts of *systemism* and *evolution*.

An evolutionary analysis usually stresses the joint relevance and mutual interdependence among different levels, i.e., neither level takes precedence over the others. This represents a departure both from radical individualism and holism: not everything on higher levels can be derived from the mechanisms on lower levels (as in a fully individualistic approach). Rather,

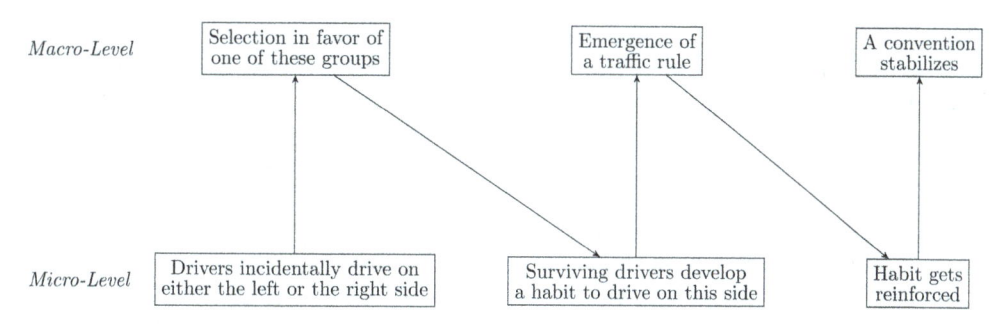

Figure 4.3 Simple example for the relevance of reconstitutive downward effects, as well as upward effects when studying rules.

Source: Gräbner and Kapeller (2017), based on Hodgson and Knudsen (2004).

there is *real novelty* or *emergence* of new phenomena on higher levels, which is why the meso is not merely a derivative of the micro, but a subject of investigation proper. At the same time, higher-level systems cannot be expected to fully transcend their components on lower levels, as it would be the case in a fully holistic approach. Related to this is the focus on *reconstitutive downward effects* (e.g., Hodgson, 2006; see also Elder-Vass, 2012) – the basic idea that there are components of systems that emerge on higher ontological levels because of the interactions among entities on a lower ontological level, yet in a next step impact upon these entities on the lower level and so on. A classic example is that of a social institution: it emerges from the behavior of individuals, yet in a next step, it affects the behavior of the individuals. Of course, this effect might then lead to certain individuals breaking with this institution, or trying to change it, which then again has an impact on the institution as such, culminating in endogenous and persistent dynamics. Hodgson and Knudsen (2004) illustrate this using a model of the emergence and evolution of traffic rules: drivers rather accidentally develop a habit of driving on the left or right side, but from this habit, a self-stabilizing convention develops, which then governs the behavior of drivers in the future (see Figure 4.3).

These circular effects among levels is one reason why evolutionary scholars are often skeptical of the notion of an explanatory *equilibrium* since it is easy to imagine circles of top-down and bottom-up effects that yield constant endogenous dynamics, without ever putting the system at rest. At this point, we will not explore the deeper reasons for why disequilibrium instead of equilibrium is the natural state of reality from an evolutionary perspective (see e.g., Dopfer et al. 2004; Heinrich, 2017). Rather, it should be stressed that the constant evolution of novelty, e.g., in the form of new technologies or institutions, is likely to constantly transform the state of a system such that persistent change is the rule rather than the exception. Consequently, any meaningful investigation should be a dynamic rather than a static one. This brings us to the epistemological implications of the basic ontology introduced so far.

4.2.3 Epistemological features: The CESM model, the principle of evolutionary explanation, and mechanism-based explanations

The ontological commitments introduced in the previous section already have some immediate implications for the epistemology of an EACES: first, when providing a basic description of the objects under study, one should be clear with regard to the four categories that make up the essential properties of any system. Bunge (2004) refers to such description $\mu(\sigma)$ of a system σ as the *CESM model* (where CESM stands for 'Components, Environment, Structure, and

Mechanisms'): $\mu(\sigma) = \langle C(\sigma), E(\sigma), S(\sigma), M(\sigma) \rangle$. Such a general representation comprises an explication of the components $C(\sigma)$, the environment $E(\sigma)$, the structure $S(\sigma)$, and the mechanisms $M(\sigma)$ of a system, which one considers to be essential, and which should, therefore, form the central part of a comparative exercise. The CESM model is a useful device for explicating the vantage point of a comparative analysis and provides a very general blueprint on which two or more economic systems, which are the subjects of a comparative analysis, can be mapped onto to guarantee a transparent study design.

Yet, there are more epistemological features that derive from the ontological commitments mentioned above: first, from the prominent role of mechanisms in the systemist ontology, it follows that explanations must be *mechanism-based* (and, thereby, causal; see Hodgson, 2004; Bunge, 2004; Witt, 2014; Gräbner, 2017).[4] Unfortunately, mechanisms as such are often not observable, so identifying mechanisms must start from conjecturing them and then substantiating one's hypothesis through further analysis. Nevertheless, mechanism-based explanations are feasible and continue to be the ideal in any evolutionary approach. Second, any evolutionary approach must be committed to the *principle of evolutionary explanation* according to which "any behavioral assumption in the social sciences must be capable of causal explanation along (Darwinian) evolutionary lines and be consistent with our understanding of human evolution" (Hodgson, 2004, p. 159). This precludes the use of neat as-if assumptions such as given preferences or utility maximization at the individual level.

This adherence to the ideal of mechanism-based explanations and the principle of evolutionary explanation implies a skepticism against the currently dominant way of explanation in economics, i.e., the commitment to the so-called *optimization-cum-equilibrium modeling approach*. According to this view, a certain phenomenon is explained if one can provide a model of the system in question that features utility-maximizing (i.e., optimizing) agents, as well as an economic equilibrium in which all agents make consistent strategy choices. Both its central ingredients are incompatible with the commitment to the principle of evolutionary explanation as well as the commitment to mechanism-based explanations: First, the use of utility-maximizing agents either contradicts the principle because of ontological reasons – if one really believes that agents maximize utility – or the commitment to mechanism-based explanations – if one only assumes them to behave *as if* they maximized utility since then the true mechanisms would remain unmentioned.

Second, the *a priori* commitment to an equilibrium is incompatible with the commitment to the principle of evolutionary explanation as well as the commitment to mechanism-based explanations since equilibrium models usually do not explicate how the economy reaches a state of equilibrium (in which the equilibrium would be part of the explanandum, not the explanans), but simply use it as an epistemological device, devoid of any underlying mechanism (see also Varoufakis, 2014, Chapter 1).

4.2.4 Summary and methodological implications

It comes as no surprise that the ontological and epistemological elaborations above also have some methodological implications: not all research methods are compatible with the EACES. General equilibrium models, as widely used in economics today, for instance, are incompatible with an EACES because they rely on the optimization-cum-equilibrium approach discussed above. Thus, evolutionary scholars are much more open to the application of simulation-based models, such as agent-based modeling, dynamical systems modeling, and related quantitative methods, but also qualitative case studies. The reason is that these methods have more potential to meet the ontological and epistemological demands of an evolutionary approach.

Section 4.3 exemplifies the application of some quantitative empirical tools that are useful for applications in the spirit of the EACES. A more general overview of modeling approaches is given, for instance, in Heinrich (2017, especially the online Appendix). Given the constant introduction of new methods, however, it is – in the end – the applied researchers who need to judge whether the tools they have in mind are consistent with the meta-theoretical framework introduced above or not.

4.3 An application to comparative development analysis in the European Union

To illustrate how an application of the research program outlined above could look like, this section comprises a short study of the recent developments in European Union from the perspective of an EACES. It is, thus, not meant to comprise a self-contained analysis that provides a complete picture of the said developments, but as an illustration of how the concepts introduced above could be operationalized and applied in practice.[5] Moreover, it is meant to illustrate the usefulness of several empirical methods for a comparative study from an evolutionary view. Each subsection will illustrate one particular method and/or theoretical concept that is suitable to operationalize the meta-theoretical approach delineated in Section 4.2. Table 4.3 at the end of the section summarizes them and provides references for further readings. Note that the focus here will be on quantitative approaches. For examples of the application of more qualitative methods, especially in the context of the NIS approach, see e.g., Dodgson et al. (2008) or Lundvall and Rikap (2022). To replicate the empirical results of this section you may use the code and data provided in Gräbner-Radkowitsch (2022).

The main object of investigation here will be the European Union. In a first step, we will map this object of analysis to the micro-meso-macro scheme introduced above (c.f. Figure 4.2). Within the focus of the present analysis, the Union as a whole represents the macro level, while individual countries correspond to the meso level. The micro level, at this point, will be associated with firms.[6] The main phenomenon of interest is the pattern of socio-economic divergence that is visible at the European level and that is illustrated for the case of income in Figure 4.4.[7] Given the relatively high rates of cumulative growth in the poorer Eastern

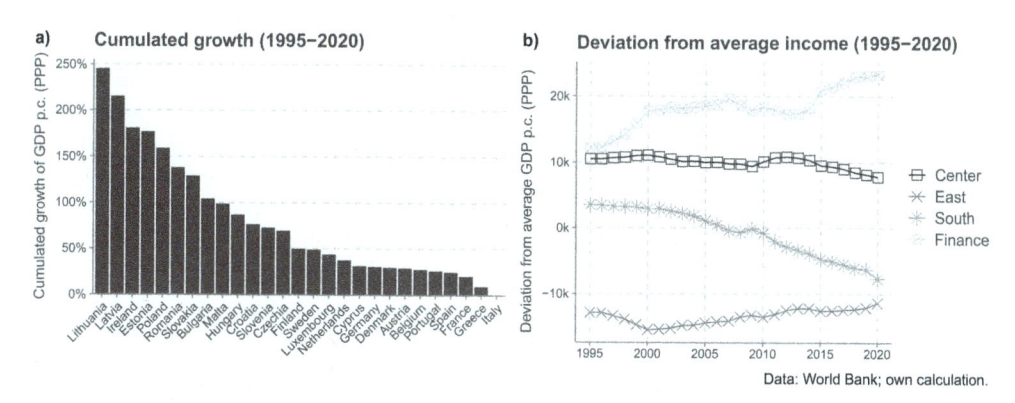

Figure 4.4   Income polarization within the EU. The country groups in panel b are as follows: Center: Austria, Belgium, Denmark, Finland, Germany, Sweden; East: Bulgaria, Croatia, Czech Republic, Estonia, Hungary, Latvia, Lithuania, Poland, Romania, Slovakia, Slovenia; Finance: Cyprus, Ireland, Luxembourg, Malta, Netherlands; South: France, Greece, Italy, Portugal, Spain. They correspond to the development models described in Table 4.2.

European countries since 1995, as shown in Figure 4.4a, this seems surprising. Yet, grouping these countries together to show their absolute levels of income reveals that these rates are far too low to approach the income levels of the Central European countries in a reasonable time frame (Figure 4.4b). At the same time, numerous countries in Southern Europe experienced two basically 'lost decades' and are falling behind the rest of the EU, whereas a small group of 'finance hubs' were able to increase their income relative to the rest considerably. For now, this grouping of the countries will be considered only a pragmatic simplification to aid visualization. As we will discover below, however, this classification of countries can be justified by reference to the underlying development models of these countries (see Table 4.2).

The goal of a comparative study in the spirit of the EACES would be to explain this polarization. In accordance with the meta-theoretical framework outlined in Section 4.2, this means identifying the mechanisms that have brought about these dynamics. The elaborations in Section 4.2 made clear that these mechanisms might operate within the micro, meso, or macro level as defined above, among these levels, or between the levels and the system environment, i.e., the rest of the world economy. As will be elaborated below, it is indeed a distinctively evolutionary finding that mechanisms on different levels are likely to drive the polarization dynamics – a finding with considerable relevance also for applied policy making.

4.3.1 *The distribution of technological capabilities, economic complexity, and growth models*

A central conjecture of evolutionary economics is that the set of *technological capabilities* that a country, region, or firm has accumulated is one important determinant for its economic success (on the concept of capabilities see Aistleitner et al. 2021). Thus, comparing the set of capabilities accumulated within the various member states seems to be a viable first step in approaching the topic of polarization. To do so, however, one would require a measure for this stock of accumulated capabilities that can be consistently applied to different countries – not an easy task. There are several measures proposed in the literature that run under the heading of 'economic complexity'. In all cases, the goal is to quantify the stock of technological capabilities accumulated by the subjects of analysis. Table 4.1 gives an overview of different approaches, which are all meant to measure technological capabilities, but differ in the particular algorithm used to compute complexity, as well as the fundamental data source. This chapter follows the strategy developed by Hidalgo and Hausmann (2009), i.e., it will apply the so-called *method of reflection* to export data, thereby computing the Economic Complexity Index (ECI) for countries and the Product Complexity Index (PCI) for products. For the sake of brevity, we skip the formal exposition of the approach; it can be found in, e.g., Hidalgo (2021), or the Appendix of Gräbner et al. (2020c), on which the following exposition is built.

The idea of the ECI is to infer the stock of capabilities that is present in an economy by looking at the economic activities the firms in this country are able to perform. For reasons

Table 4.1 An overview of selected approaches to compute economic complexity

Data source	Method of computation	Example
Export data	Method of reflections	Hidalgo and Hausmann (2009)
Export data	Fitness algorithm	Tacchella et al. (2013)
Patents	Method of reflections	Balland and Rigby (2017)
Patents	Measure of structural diversity	Broekel (2019)
Input-output table	Method of reflections	Reynolds et al. (2018)

of measurement, the focus is on the activity of producing goods. In other words, a country is assumed to have accumulated a large amount of technological capabilities if its firms are able to produce complex products, i.e., products that *require* a large amount of such capabilities. To break the alleged circularity of computing both the complexity of countries and products, the method proceeds as follows: first, using export data, compute for every country c the *revealed comparative advantage* (RCA) with regard to each product p. A country c is said to have an RCA for a product p, if the share of a product in the export basket of a country is larger than the share of this product in the total exports of the world market. In a next step, one computes the *diversity* of the export baskets of the countries – the number of products a country has an RCA in – and the *ubiquity* of products – the number of countries that are exporting a product with an RCA.

The ECI now seeks to combine two basic intuitions: first, it seems unlikely that very specific skills or materials are required for the production of a product that is ubiquitous. Second, there can be two reasons for why a product can be non-ubiquitous: either it is rare because it is a high-tech product that requires a lot of technological capabilities or it is rare because some ingredients are rare. Computer chips would be an example for rare high-tech products, raw oil for a rare low-tech product. The ECI seeks to distinguish between these two kinds of non-ubiquitous products by referring to the diversity of the countries that export these products. If a rare product is produced by a less-diversified country, i.e., a country that only produces a small fraction of all products, it is unlikely that this product is rare because of the many technological capabilities it requires: if this was the case, the country exporting this product would possess these many technological capabilities and, therefore, export a variety of goods, not only few. It is, thus, more likely that this country possesses a rare raw material that is required to produce this product and that the product is rare simply because its ingredients are rare. At the same time, if a rare product is produced only by well-diversified countries, it is more likely to be rare because it requires a lot of technological capabilities – and only few countries have accumulated this amount of capabilities.

To compute the ECI, one weights the diversity of countries by the ubiquity of the products in the export basket and then the ubiquity of the products by the diversity of the countries that export this good. One continues with this 'reflection' until one reaches an equilibrium and can compute the ECI and PCI (for the technical details, see e.g., Hidalgo, 2021, or the technical Appendix of Gräbner et al. 2020c). The resulting ECI is a measure of the technological capabilities present in a country and the PCI of the amount of capabilities required to produce a product. The prominence of the ECI stems from the fact that it usually correlates strongly with income, and deviations from this correlation are good predictors for future growth rates, indicating that "countries tend to approach the levels of income that correspond to their measured complexity" (Hidalgo & Hausmann, 2009, p. 10574).

If one considers the ECI of European member states, one finds that it not only correlates with their level of income (Figure 4.5a) but also exposes important differences across member states: Central European countries persistently exceed the rest of the Union, while Eastern countries are catching up to them and already surpassed the stagnating countries in Southern Europe and the financial hubs (see Figure 4.5b). These differences in the ECI reflect a more fundamental polarization within the EU, one that becomes visible once we complement the classical, supply-side perspective of economic complexity with a Post-Keynesian demand side perspective, as provided by the concept of a *growth model* (Baccaro & Pontusson, 2016): a growth model is determined by the major sources of aggregate demand, which Baccaro and Pontusson (2016) consider the main stabilizer of aggregate income. Gräbner et al. (2020c) use this concept to delineate two very broad growth models that are of major relevance in the EU: an *export-led*

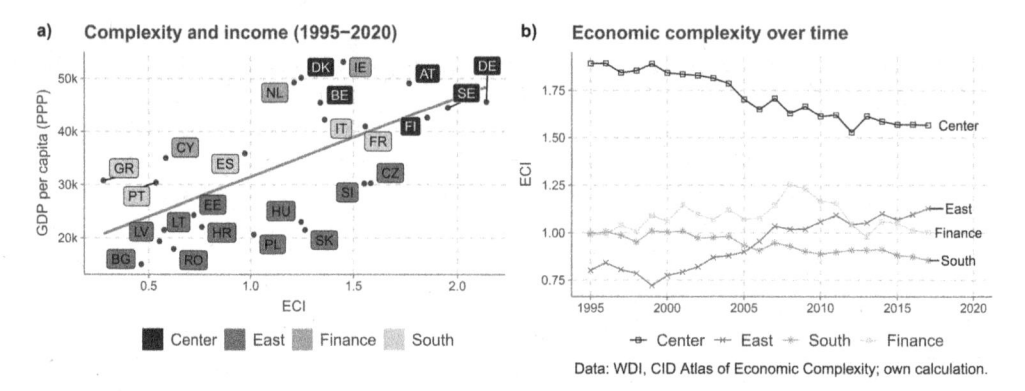

Figure 4.5 The economic complexity of European member states. Panel a is built on mean values over the whole time period, i.e., 1995–2020. Country groups are the same as in Figure 3.1b and correspond to the development models described in Table 4.2, but do not include Luxembourg and Malta because the ECI is not computable for such small countries.

growth model, in which countries stabilize their aggregate demand by selling products to other countries on the world market, and a *debt-led* growth model, where the aggregate demand gets stabilized by the provision of credit to national households. Both models were developed partly as a reaction to the rising domestic inequalities and the resulting decrease in domestic demand (e.g., Atkinson et al. 2011; Kapeller et al., 2019). While the export-led model substitutes domestic demand with exports, the debt-led model stabilizes domestic demand via credit. The problem with the latter approach is that it has been rendered infeasible through the institutional reactions to the Financial Crisis in 2007, which now prevent the relevant actors to incur new debt. In effect, the countries following this model suffered considerable losses in income and have not recovered until today (see Gräbner et al., 2020c, for more details).

This begs the question of why – if the export-led model was superior and did not experience these problems – not all EU countries simply decided to follow such an export-led model? The differences in economic complexity discussed above give the answer: in order to follow an export-led growth model, the firm population of a country needs to be competitive in international markets. In principle, there are two broad sources of competitiveness: low costs on the one and high quality or technological complexity on the other side. For advanced countries, such as basically all members of the EU, the former avenue is, however, difficult to take – at least on a global level: due to social and ecological regulations in the EU, even low-wage countries have difficulty competing with countries such as India, China, or Bangladesh. Thus, it is a widely accepted empirical result that quality or technological complexity is, by far, the most important determinant of firm competitiveness in advanced countries (e.g., Carlin et al., 2001; Sutton, 2012; Dosi et al., 2015).

The accumulation of technological capabilities is, however, a highly path-dependent process (see Aistleitner et al., 2021, for a review on the underlying mechanisms), and specialization patterns, once entered by a particular country, are hard to reverse. Figure 4.6 illustrates the results of this by representing the composition of the export baskets of Germany and Greece since 1995.[8] It is immediately evident that Germany is able to sustain its position as an exporter of rather complex products, such as vehicles, machinery, chemicals, and electronics, while over time, Greece has lost ground even further in these areas. Rather, simple products, particularly minerals (here: especially raw oil), have become more important, reflecting the worrying trend of de-complexification and de-industrialization in Greece.

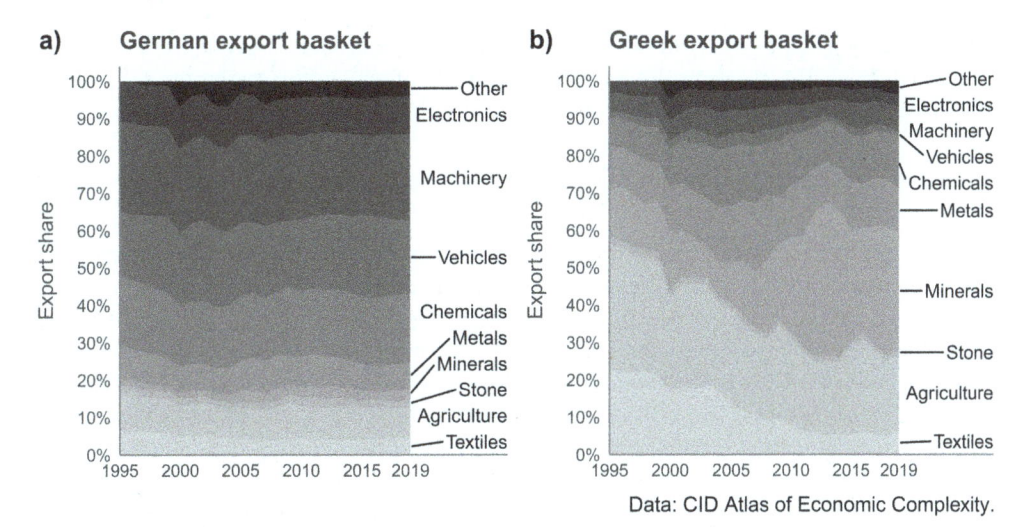

Data: CID Atlas of Economic Complexity.

Figure 4.6 Export baskets of Germany and Greece between 1995 and 2020.

4.3.2 *Technological directedness and path dependency*

To move beyond these illustrative but descriptive examples of Germany and Greece, and to study the path dependency associated with technological change on the meso and macro level via reference to the mechanisms of capability accumulation on the micro level, one may use the indicator of technological directedness developed by Gräbner et al. (2020b): this indicator provides information on the general directedness of technological change, i.e., whether a country is able to expand its stock of technological capabilities or whether it is stagnating or even deteriorating. The general idea is as follows: first, two reference periods must be chosen. In the present case, the period 1995–2005 (pre-Eurozone, pre-Financial Crisis) will be compared against 2010–2020 (post-Eurozone, post-Financial Crisis). Then, the export baskets for each country c during these two periods will be considered and the set of products for which this country was able to increase its exports, P_c^+, determined. We then take the logarithm of the difference in the average product complexity, distinguishing between products that are in P_c^+ and those that are not. In both cases, the observations are weighted according to their share in the export baskets in the ultimate four years, i.e., 2016–2020. This ensures that, in the regressions below, those products that are currently most important for the respective country receive greater weight in determining the directedness of technological change. Specifying $\Phi_{c,i} = 1$ if $i \in P_c^+$ and $\Phi_{c,i} = 0$ if $i \notin P_c^+$ gives rise to the following two regression equations to be estimated with weighted least squares (WLS):

$$\log\left[\sum_{t=2010}^{2020}\phi_{c,i}\pi_{c,i,t} - \sum_{t=1995}^{2005}\phi_{c,i}\pi_{c,i,t}\right] = \beta_c^+ \,\overline{PCI}_{c,i} + u_{c,i} \ \forall i \in P_c^+$$

$$(4.1)$$

$$\log\left[\sum_{t=2010}^{2020}(1-\phi_{c,i})\pi_{c,i,t} - \sum_{t=1995}^{2005}(1-\phi_{c,i})\pi_{c,i,t}\right] = \beta_c^- \,\overline{PCI}_{c,i} + u_{c,i} \ \forall i \notin P_c^+$$

Here, $\pi_{.,c,i,t}$ corresponds to the total value of exports of good i by country c in year t (measured in constant USD) and $PCI_{i,t}$ represents the product complexity of product i in year t. Then,

$\overline{PCI}_{c,i} = \Sigma_t \left\lceil \pi_{.c,i,t} / \Sigma_t \pi_{.c,i,t} \right\rceil$ is the average product complexity over a given time frame. As indicated above, the equations are estimated via WLS, of which the weights $\omega_{c,i}$ are given by the share of the product in the export baskets during the period of 2016–2020:

$$\omega_{c,i} = \frac{\Sigma_t \pi_{.c,i,t}}{\Sigma_i \Sigma_i \pi_{.c,i,t}}, \, t \in \{2016,\dots,2020\} \tag{4.2}$$

In effect, one ends up with two estimates for each country: one, $\hat{\beta}_c^+$, for the relationship between product complexity and product *expansion*, and another, $\hat{\beta}_c^-$, for the relationship between product complexity and product *contraction*. If, for instance, $\hat{\beta}_c^+ > 0$, then the country increases its exports mainly for more complex products, but when $\hat{\beta}_c^+ < 0$, it increases its exports mainly for non-complex products. These estimates are already illustrative, as the example in Figure 4.7 indicates: here, the estimates for the group of expanding products show that while Germany is expanding its exports mainly of more complex products, the exports of more complex products in Greece are deteriorating (i.e., β_{GRE}^+ is negative and β_{DEU}^+ is positive).

To reach the final measure of technological directedness for each country, one then computes a weighted average of the estimates for expanding and contracting products. As weights, one takes the total increases in exports

$$\gamma_c^+ = \sum_{t=2010}^{2020} \phi_{c,i} \pi_{.c,i,t} - \sum_{t=1995}^{2005} \phi_{c,i} \pi_{.c,i,t} \tag{4.3}$$

and the total decreases in exports

$$\gamma_c^- = \sum_{t=1995}^{2005} (1 - \phi_{c,i}) \pi_{.c,i,t} - \sum_{t=2010}^{2020} (1 - \phi_{c,i}) \pi_{.c,i,t}. \tag{4.4}$$

Then, the final indicator can be defined as follows:

$$\theta_c = \frac{\gamma_c^+}{\gamma_c^+ + \gamma_c^-} \hat{\beta}_c^+ - \frac{\gamma_c^-}{\gamma_c^+ + \gamma_c^-} \hat{\beta}_c^- \tag{4.5}$$

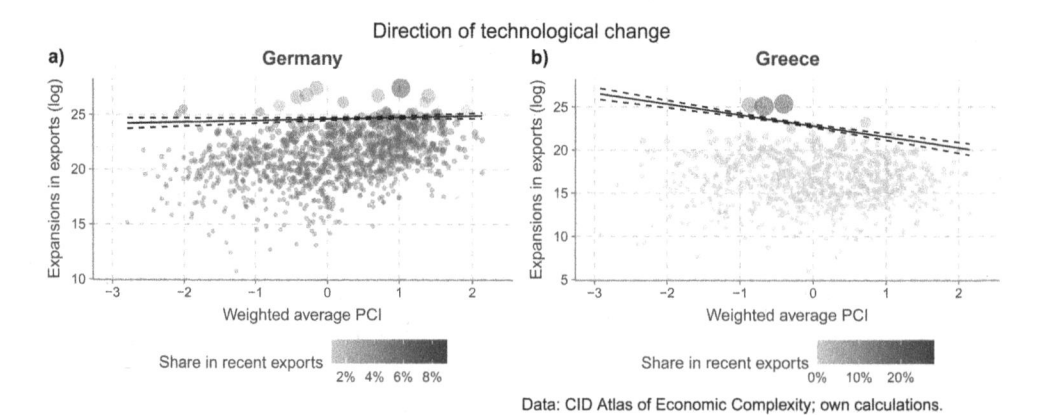

Figure 4.7 The estimated measures for the group of expanding products in Germany and Greece. The slopes of the regression lines correspond to the estimates for β_c^+ as defined above.

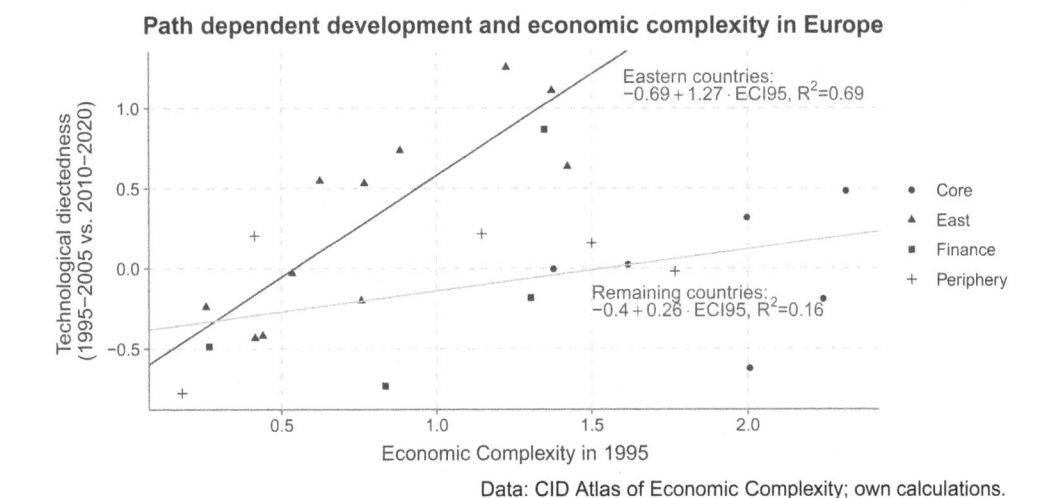

Path dependent development and economic complexity in Europe

Data: CID Atlas of Economic Complexity; own calculations.

Figure 4.8   The path dependence of technological development in Europe. Groups correspond to the development models in Table 4.2.

The resulting indicator θ_c is positive whenever more complex products become relatively more important for country c, i.e., if the direction of technological change is favorable, and negative if simpler products become relatively more relevant and, therefore, the direction of technological change can be said to be detrimental for country c.

This indicator can be used to illustrate the strong path dependence of technological change on the macro level. To this end, one relates the resulting indicator with the initial stock of capabilities in a country, as measured by the ECI at the beginning of the period considered. This is done in Figure 4.8. The strong correlation indicates that the accumulation of technological capabilities is a path-dependent and self-reinforcing process: countries with a higher stock of technological capabilities will have it easier to expand their stock further, while countries with few capabilities have difficulties accumulating more (Hidalgo & Hausmann, 2009). The particularly strong a relationship between Eastern countries illustrates the important role economic complexity is playing in their catching-up strategy, which is mainly built on a growing manufacturing sector. These path dependencies suggest that without exogenous policy intervention, the endogenous polarization among member states is likely to continue.

4.3.3 *Path dependency, development models, and the role of external shocks*

The presence of such path-dependent development patterns, as well as the considerations about different growth models above, begs the question of whether one can delineate a number of different *development models* for the EU, such that countries can be grouped according to the development model they follow. A development model can be understood as a generalization of a growth model and refers to the main driver of socio-economic development in a country. The concept of different development models could also be useful for a comparative analysis since one might begin by delineating different country groups and then focus on a comparative analysis of exemplary cases for each country group. This way, one would be able to reduce the number of meso units one needs to consider significantly. The most immediate taxonomy that is suggested by the literature would classify countries into a set of *core* and a set of *periphery* countries, depending on the growth model they are following, i.e., a debt-led or an export-led model, as discussed above. Such a simple distinction between cores and peripheries, however, seems to be too coarse to make sense of the European polarization more generally: simply dividing the EU into a core and a periphery does not do justice to the heterogeneity of development models in the Union.

Rather, a distinction of four different development models seems to be more appropriate (see Table 4.2 and Figure 4.9 for an overview, as well as Gräbner et al., 2020b for a more extensive discussion): first, there is a group of countries which are mostly located in Central Europe and that are distinguished from the rest by (i) relatively high GDP per capita levels, (ii) firm populations that have accumulated a lot of technological capabilities and that are, therefore, highly competitive on international markets, (iii) a relatively large industrial sector, and (iv) relatively low levels of unemployment. These are countries that build their economic success on the technological superiority of their firms and that are able to follow an export-led growth model as explained above. Usually, these countries also play a politically influential and important role within the EU (and are more likely to establish favorable political framework conditions for their firm populations – the mutual relationship of the micro and meso levels becomes, again, apparent).

The second group is the classical periphery, most of which are located in Southern Europe. While these countries enjoy moderate levels of GDP per capita, their economic outlook is rather sinister: (i) since their firm populations are not nearly as technologically advanced as those of the core countries, their export shares are rather low; (ii) they tend to accumulate significant current account deficits; (iii) in effect, they tend to suffer rather high levels of

Table 4.2 Development models and resulting country groups

Group	Driver of development	Characteristics	Members
Core	Technological superiority on the world market	- High GDP per capita levels - Importance of industrial production - Production of complex products - Relatively low unemployment	Austria, Belgium, Denmark, Finland, Germany, and Sweden
Periphery	Credit (unsustainable)	- Lower export shares - Relatively high public debt - Tend to current account deficits - Relatively high unemployment	Cyprus, France, Greece, Italy, Portugal, and Spain
Catch-Up	Low factor costs, emerging industries	- Relatively low levels of wages and GDP per capita - High degree of foreign ownership - Small service sector - Important manufacturing sector	Bulgaria, Croatia, Czech Republic, Estonia, Hungary, Latvia, Lithuania, Poland, Romania, Slovakia, and Slovenia
Finance	Financial services	- High debt levels of private firms - Important share of finance in terms of gross output - High foreign investment inflows - Large incomes from wealth taxes	Cyprus, Ireland, Luxembourg, Malta, and the Netherlands

Note: The groups are the same as identified by Gräbner et al. (2020b). The group of 'Southern countries' from the previous figures now corresponds to the 'periphery' group, the 'Eastern countries' corresponds to the Catch-up group, and the 'Central European countries' to the 'core'.

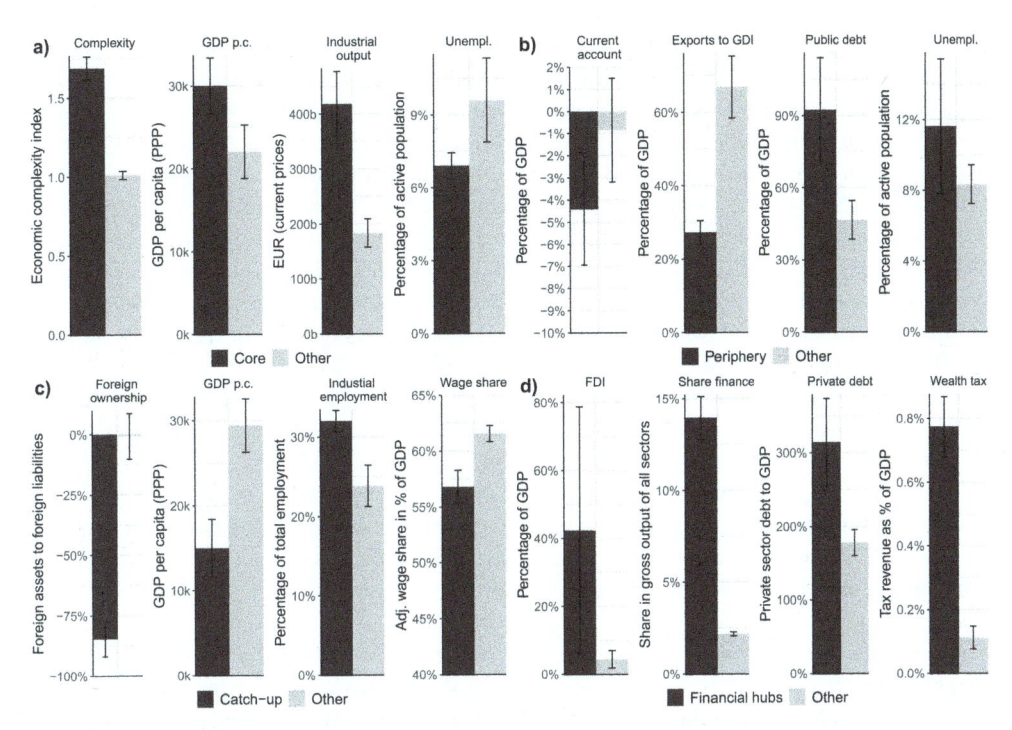

Figure 4.9   The distinctive properties of the countries following different development models; the groups are the same as depicted in Table 4.2, means and variance computed over the time period 2000–2015. (Data taken from Gräbner et al., 2020b; see reproduction material for precise sources.)

unemployment, and (iv), due to their unsustainable debt-led growth model, they tend to have relatively high levels of public debt. These countries suffered from the Eastern enlargement of the Union in the sense that the new members of the EU were able to outperform them, especially via low factor costs, on European markets and substituted them as core suppliers for the complex industries in the core (Gräbner et al. 2020c).

This brings us to the third group, which mostly comprises countries from Eastern Europe. These countries entered the EU only recently, and for many of them, future development is much more contingent than for core and periphery countries. And despite important heterogeneity, all of them are characterized by (i) relatively low factor costs, especially low wages, (ii) currently low levels of GDP per capita, (iii) a relatively small service and large manufacturing sector, which is accumulating technological capabilities rather quickly, and (iv) a high degree of foreign ownership, meaning that many firms are dependent on capital inflows from foreign countries. While some of these Eastern countries show promising catch-up dynamics, it remains to be seen whether they are truly catching up to the richer countries in Central Europe or whether they are converging to the periphery (for a more extensive discussion of the heterogeneity of the Eastern economies, see e.g., Bohle, 2017).

The final country group comprises countries that do not feature any substantial industries but tend to have even higher per capita income levels than the core countries above. This points to the fact that, despite the traditional focus on technology as a driver of development in evolutionary growth theory, there are other ways to become rich. One way, at least under the current institutional framework of the EU and the world economy, is to build a large and de-regulated financial sector and to attract foreign assets through low tax rates and the absence of regulations. Thus, the countries in the EU that follow this strategy are characterized by (i) a large financial sector, both in terms of employment and gross output, (ii) high foreign investment flows, (iii) large incomes from wealth taxes, and (iv) high debt levels of private firms (due to their activities in the financial market). One problem with this development model is that since it is built on the attraction of assets from elsewhere, it often works at the expense of other countries: the Netherlands, for instance, attract US multinationals with very low commercial tax rates, incentivizing these companies to shift their profits into the Netherlands. While this increases tax revenues in the Netherlands by about 2.2 billion USD, the remaining EU member states tend to lose 10 billion in commercial taxes because of this profit shifting (Cobham & Garcia-Bernardo, 2020).[9]

The resulting taxonomy of countries is the same as the one proposed in Gräbner et al. (2020b; for an overview of alternative taxonomies see e.g., Gräbner & Hafele, 2020). It illustrates that while, especially for advanced economies such as those in Europe, the accumulation of technological capabilities is an essential driver of economic development, it is not the only one: the Eastern countries show that, at least in the short run, low factor costs can also be such a driver, and the financial hubs suggest that a focus on finance can also be a source for positive development – albeit at the expense of others.

One important idea underlying this country taxonomy is that it is not only informative regarding the development dynamics of the countries but also regarding how these countries react to external events: it is one central argument in structuralist theory that countries belonging to different structural parts or the global economy, such as the core and the periphery, react differently to the same events, usually to the disadvantages of the peripheries. At least at first sight, this is also true for the present case: Figure 4.10 depicts the impact of the financial crises and the Corona crises on EU member states (for the latter, see also, e.g., Odendahl & Springford, 2020, and Gräbner et al., 2020a), highlighting the lower resilience of some development models.

Some impacts operate in a more subtle way than the ones in Figure 4.10. They also require more advanced techniques to be identified. The example discussed here refers to Gräbner et al. (2020b), who studied the effect of economic integration within the EU on various socioeconomic indicators on the country level, such as GDP, unemployment, debt or the wage share. To this end, the authors proceed as follows: first, they estimate the dynamic effects of European integration on the various indicators using the method of local projections, which

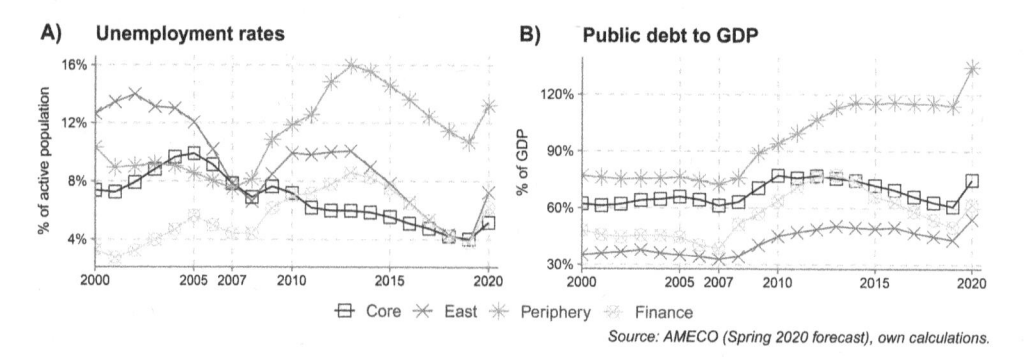

Source: AMECO (Spring 2020 forecast), own calculations.

Figure 4.10   Illustration of the different reactions of distinct development models to the same exogenous shock. The same shocks are more severe and persistent for periphery countries than for the rest. The development models are as in Table 4.2.

comes down to the estimation of a series of linear regression models using the following regression equation:

$$Y_{i,t+k} - Y_{i,t} = \beta^k X_{i,t} + \delta^k Z_{i,t} + \mu_i^k + \eta_t^k + u_{i,t}^k \tag{4.6}$$

in which $Y_{i,t}$ is the dependent variable of interest as observed in time t for country c, $X_{i,t}$ is the central explanatory (or 'shock') variable, $Z_{i,t}$ is a matrix of control variables, μ_i^k and η_t^k are country and time fixed effects, and $u_{i,t}^k$ is the error term. The superscript k denotes the time horizon considered, such that $k = 2$ means to estimate the effect of the shock variable on the dependent variable two time periods after the shock has become effective.

From the series of estimations for different k, one can then derive an impulse response function to quantify the dynamic effect of the shock variable on the dependent variable over time. There is another way to use the results of this model, however: Gräbner et al. (2020b) use the estimates for the fixed effects μ_i^k to cluster the countries using tools from unsupervised machine learning. Since the fixed effects are used to control for country-specific and time-independent effects, grouping countries according to their fixed effects estimates amounts to put countries in the same group whose time-independent properties lead to a similar reaction to an increase in economic integration. Interestingly, the application of different hierarchical clustering algorithms to these fixed effects estimates in Gräbner et al. (2020b) always produces a country grouping that is surprisingly similar to the theoretically derived grouping depicted in Table 4.2 – a striking result that corroborates the delineated development models further (for more details, see Gräbner et al. 2020b). Such an innovative combination of regression and clustering techniques can be useful whenever one suspects that unobservable country characteristics, which one can assume to be stable over the study period, affect the reaction of a country to some external shock. In the present case, the institutions of the countries, especially their national innovation system, seem to be a potential mediator variable that could be driving the results, and which could be subject to a more qualitative and specific comparative analysis.

At this point, however, a word of caution is adequate: while the identification and analysis of different development models and country groups can be very enlightening, it also comes with potential pitfalls. According to Gräbner and Hafele (2020), there are three main challenges that should always be taken into account when using the concept of a development model for comparative analysis: first, the *challenge of dynamics* points to the fact that while the development trajectories of countries are rather stable, there is the possibility that a country switches from one development model into another. Ireland comes immediately to mind when one is looking for an example: while being heavily dependent on the UK until the 1990s, it then transformed into a highly financialized economy that experienced considerable growth rates (for more details on this case, see Regan & Brazys, 2018). The second challenge is the *challenge of ambiguity*. It refers to the fact that some countries are very difficult to classify since they possess properties that one would usually associate with different development models. The most obvious example of this case is France, which is economically part of the European periphery (see also Gräbner et al. 2020b), but because of its size and historical reasons might well count as part of the political core (Gräbner & Hafele, 2020). Finally, the fact that there might be considerable heterogeneity *within* countries gives rise to the *challenge of granularity*: within a country, certain regions play the role of internal peripheries, while others are internal cores. The East/West/North/South divide of Germany or the North-South divide in Spain are examples for this challenge (see also Iammarino et al., 2018).[10] Studying these internal heterogeneities further is an obvious area for future applications of the EACES, given its commitment to the layered ontology of systemism as described in Section 4.2.

Therefore, it is always useful to complement the group-based analysis with a closer look at the individual units. Such an approach should be considered complementary to the analysis of development models since the delineation of the different country groups provides an immediate suggestion on how to select countries to be studied in more depth. The single cases could then be studied qualitatively, e.g., using methods developed in the context of the national innovation systems literature (e.g., Lundvall, 2007), or more quantitatively with tools developed explicitly for comparative case studies, such as the *synthetic control method* discussed at length in Abadie (2021).

4.3.4 Synthesis and further concepts

The previous three subsections were each concerned with a particular aspect of the polarization process in the European Union. In each of the subsections, quantitative empirical methods and theoretical concepts that are useful to operationalize the EACES were introduced. While space constraints prevent a more complete analysis and a more nuanced introduction of the methods, the exposition was hopefully sufficient to illustrate the application of some of the essential elements of the EACES and to show how even a superficial application already points to some interesting avenues for future research.

This section closes by providing a non-exhaustive list of theoretical concepts in Table 4.3. These concepts often play an important role in comparative studies in the spirit of the EACES. Thus, the list should serve researchers as a guidance when conducting a comparative analysis: they might go through the list and test whether each element can help to illuminate the case at hand. Due to space constraints, the single concepts cannot be discussed in the analytical depth they deserve, so references to specialized publications are provided for further reference.

4.4 Summary

This chapter introduced the central elements of an EACES. Since such an approach contains elements from a variety of different research programs, the first part of this chapter outlined its meta-theoretical foundations. Both the ontology and epistemology of this approach are characterized by a systemist view on its objects of investigation. It is firmly rooted in evolutionary theory and stresses the joint relevance of different ontological layers, commonly referred to as micro, meso, and macro, and the mechanisms bridging these levels. Mechanisms also play a central element in the epistemology of the EACES, which is geared to the explication of causal mechanisms driving the dynamics to be explained. The second part of the chapter gave a cursory example of how an application of this approach could look like by studying polarization patterns in the European Union. In this context, several methods that are consistent with the approach were illustrated, and further references to more specialized applications were given. The chapter concluded with a non-exhaustive list of theoretical concepts and topics that are usually valuable to consider within a comparative analysis in the spirit of the EACES. While the chapter necessarily remained cursory in many ways, it hopefully illustrated the potential of the EACES for comparative analyses. The ontological and epistemological guidance it provides, as well as the methods commonly used in the related literature, certainly show much potential to illuminate a number of promising avenues for future research, such as the likely effects of social and ecological transformations as well as adaptations to climate change: in all these (and many more) relevant cases, mechanisms on various ontological levels are important, the mutual dependency of economic and non-economic systems is obvious, and endogenous and nonlinear dynamics are prevalent. The EACES is well prepared to deal with such challenges.

Table 4.3 A non-exhaustive list of theoretical concepts and topical suggestions that often turn out to be insightful when conducting a comparative study in the spirit of the EACES

Concept	Description	Guiding questions	References
Path dependence	In the presence of positive feedback mechanisms, dynamic processes are often non-ergodic and give rise to non-linear dynamics and persistent differences between the objects of the comparative study. Identifying the kind and sources of positive feedback is often an important part of the comparative study.	– What kind of path-dependent process is operating? – Which are the elements competing with each other? What are the quality criteria determining the 'successful' elements? – What are the sources for positive feedback? – Is the process still contingent or is the system already in a state of lock-in?	Dobusch and Kapeller (2013)
Technological capabilities	Capabilities are not only a determinant for economic success at various level, but due to the often path-dependent way capabilities are accumulated; they are also a source of persistent differences in the development paths of different subjects.	– At which level are capabilities accumulated? – Which mechanisms of accumulation are most relevant? – What are barriers to accumulation? How do they differ across subjects?	Aistleitner et al. (2021)
Economic complexity	Economic complexity is one influential and effective way to measure technological capabilities on various ontological levels using different data. Especially interesting are cases where subjects over- or under-perform as compared to what their level of complexity predicts – the explanation is often illuminating.	– How do subjects of analysis differ in terms of their complexity? – What subjects are under- or over-performing with regard to their complexity? Why?	Hidalgo (2021)
Development models	Often the objects of analysis differ regarding the main sources of economic development/success. To explore the questions of whether the resulting models differ in terms of long-term sustainability and whether they are in conflict with each other is often insightful.	– What are the main drivers of development for the different models? – What is the role of the supply and demand side? – Is there a rivalry between the models? – Is there a power asymmetry among the models?	Baccaro and Pontusson (2016), Gräbner et al. (2020c)
Dependency	Whether the objects of the comparative study are independent or dependent on each other is a key element shaping their dynamics. This question also makes visible relations of exploitation and structural dependencies.	– Are there relations of dependency among the subjects of analysis? – Where and when are the origins of this dependency? – Through which mechanism and on which levels do the dependency manifest?	Kvangraven (2020)

Acknowledgements

I want to acknowledge the feedback from the editors of this volume, Sara Casagrande and Bruno Dallago, as well as the extensive and thoughtful comments of Anna Hornykewycz, Katharina Litschauer, and Johanna Rath on earlier versions of this chapter. Their remarks were extremely helpful in improving the work. All the remaining errors are my own. I also want to stress that many of the central ideas of this chapter originated in joint research endeavors with Philipp Heimberger, Jakob Kapeller, and Bernhard Schütz. I am thankful for the opportunity to collaborate with these exceptional scholars and learned a lot from them. Finally, I would like to acknowledge funding by the Austrian Science Fund (FWF) under grant number ZK 60-G27 and for the open access publication, as well as the Oesterreichische Nationalbank (Austrian Central Bank, Anniversary Fund) under project number: 18144.

Notes

1 Systemism must not be conflated with *systems theory*, an influential approach in sociology established mainly through the work of Niklas Luhmann.
2 Systemism is a neat intermediary position between the classical extremes of 'holism' – which focuses social aggregates – and individualism – which focuses on individuals and denies the existence of aggregates, such as social structures altogether.
3 This example illustrates that the terms 'micro', 'meso' and 'macro' do not come with a fixed reference level but are context dependent and need to be explicated. In the example above, for instance, 'micro' might refer to a single firm, 'meso' to a sector', and 'macro' to a nation. But, in another context, 'meso' might be the nation, and macro a supranational entity such as the European Union.
4 This commitment to mechanism-based explanations is complementary to the commitment to *causal explanations*, which are also considered to be an essential feature of evolutionary approaches and directly follow from Darwin's work on evolution (e.g., Hodgson, 2004; Witt, 2014).
5 Such an encompassing analysis would go beyond the scope of a single chapter. This section draws on the insights from a number of earlier works, especially Gräbner and Hafele (2020), Gräbner et al. (2020a, 2020b, 2020c) and Kapeller et al. (2019).
6 As described above, the allocation of the different levels of analysis is pragmatic. One might well introduce an additional level of analysis, e.g., between the micro and the meso level, such as regions. This would help highlighting the polarization patterns that are taking place *within* European member states (see e.g., Iammarino et al., 2018). Such analysis, however, would go beyond the scope of this section, which is mainly meant to illustrate the concepts introduced above.
7 This is not to say that there are not important polarization processes at the individual or regional level in the EU. On these topics, see e.g., Atkinson et al. (2011) or Iammarino et al. (2018).
8 As explained above, data on exported goods is used as a proxy for the goods produced in an economy since data on produced products as such are rarely available. Previous research has shown that exported goods are indeed a good proxy for the latter (e.g., Saltarelli et al., 2020).
9 This practice is one symptom of a detrimental competition among EU member states, a phenomenon that is discussed more completely in, e.g., Kapeller et al. (2019), and often discussed under the labels: *Standortwettbewerb* or *race to the best location*.
10 From a more general perspective, this challenge also applies whenever the overall focus of the analysis is shifted: once the main subject of investigation is not Europe, but the world economy, it might make sense to consider Europe as a meso entity playing the role of a global core region, despite comprising countries such as Greece, which are globally rather part of a core, but locally within Europe part of the periphery.

References

Abadie, A. (2021). Using synthetic controls: feasibility, data requirements, and methodological aspects. *Journal of Economic Literature*, 59 (2), 391–425. https://doi.org/10.1257/jel.20191450

Aistleitner, M., Gräbner, C. and Hornykewycz, A. (2021). Theory and empirics of capability accumulation: implications for macroeconomic modelling. *Research Policy*, 50 (6), 104258. https://doi.org/10.1016/j.respol.2021.104258

Atkinson, A.B., Piketty, T. and Saez, E. (2011). Top incomes in the long run of history. *Journal of Economic Literature*, 49 (1), 3–71. https://doi.org/10.1257/jel.49.1.3

Baccaro, L. and Pontusson, J. (2016). Rethinking comparative political economy. *Politics & Society*, 44 (2), 175–207. https://doi.org/10.1177/0032329216638053

Balland, P.A. and Rigby, D. (2017). The geography of complex knowledge. *Economic Geography*, 93 (1), 1–23. https://doi.org/10.1080/00130095.2016.1205947

Bohle, D. (2017). European integration, capitalist diversity and crises trajectories on Europe's eastern periphery. *New Political Economy*, 33 (1), 1–15. https://doi.org/10.1080/13563467.2017.1370448

Broekel, T. (2019). Using structural diversity to measure the complexity of technologies. *Plos One*, 14 (5), e0216856. https://doi.org/10.1371/journal.pone.0216856

Bunge, M. (1959). *Causality: The Place of the Causal Principle in Modern Science*. Cambridge, MA: Harvard University Press.

Bunge, M. (1996). *Finding Philosophy in Social Science*. New Haven, CT: Yale University Press.

Bunge, M. (2004). How does it work? The search for explanatory mechanisms. *Philosophy of the Social Sciences*, 34 (2), 182–210. https://doi.org/10.1177/0048393103262550

Carlin, W., Glyn, A. and Reenen, J.V. (2001). Export market performance of OECD countries: an empirical examination of the role of cost competitiveness. *Economic Journal*, 111, 128–162. https://doi.org/10.1111/1468-0297.00592

Cobham, A. and Garcia-Bernardo, J. (2020). Time for the EU to close its own tax havens. Tax Justice Network. https://www.taxjustice.net/wp-content/uploads/2020/04/Time-for-the-EU-to-close-its-own-tax-havens_April-2020_Tax-Justice-Network.pdf

Dobusch, L. and Kapeller, J. (2013). Breaking new paths: theory and method in path dependence research. *Schmalenbach Business Review*, 65 (3), 288–311. https://doi.org/10.1007/bf03396859

Dodgson, M., Mathews, J., Kastelle, T. and Hu, M.C. (2008). The evolving nature of Taiwan's national innovation system: the case of biotechnology innovation networks. *Research Policy*, 37 (3), 430–445. https://doi.org/10.1016/j.respol.2007.12.005

Dopfer, K., Foster, J. and Potts, J. (2004). Micro-meso-macro. *Journal of Evolutionary Economics*, 14 (3), 263–279. https://doi.org/10.1007/s00191-004-0193-0

Dopfer, K. and Potts, J. (2004). Evolutionary realism: a new ontology for economics. *Journal of Economic Methodology*, 11 (2), 195–212. https://doi.org/10.1080/1350178041000169412 7

Dosi, G., Grazzi, M. and Moschella, D. (2015). Technology and costs in international competitiveness: from countries and sectors to firms. *Research Policy*, 44 (10), 1795–1814. https://doi.org/10.1016/j.respol.2015.05.012

Dosi, G., Pavitt, K. and Soete, L. (1990). *The Economics of Technical Change and International Trade*. New York, NY: New York University Press.

Elder-Vass, D. (2012). Top-down causation and social structures. *Interface Focus*, 2 (1), 82–90. https://doi.org/10.1098/rsfs.2011.0055

Gräbner, C. (2017). The complementary relationship between institutional and complexity economics: the example of deep mechanismic explanations. *Journal of Economic Issues*, 51 (2), 392–400. https://doi.org/10.1080/00213624.2017.1320915

Gräbner, C. and Hafele, J. (2020). The emergence of core-periphery structures in the European Union: a complexity perspective. *ZOE Discussion Papers, 6*. https://zoe-institut.de/wp-content/uploads/2020/09/zoe-dp6-graebner-hafele-core-periphery.pdf

Gräbner, C., Heimberger, P. and Kapeller, J. (2020a). Pandemic pushes polarisation: the Corona crisis and macroeconomic divergence in the Eurozone. *Journal of Industrial and Business Economics*, 47 (3), 425–438. https://doi.org/10.1007/s40812-020-00163-w

Gräbner, C., Heimberger, P., Kapeller, J. and Schütz, B. (2020b). Structural change in times of increasing openness: assessing path dependency in European economic integration. *Journal of Evolutionary Economics*, 30 (5), 1467–1495. https://doi.org/10.1007/s00191-019-00639-6

Gräbner, C., Heimberger, P. Kapeller, J. and Schütz, B. (2020c). Is the Eurozone disintegrating? Macroeconomic divergence, structural polarisation, trade and fragility. *Cambridge Journal of Economics*, 44 (3), 647–669. https://doi.org/10.1093/cje/bez059

Gräbner, C. and Kapeller, J. (2017). The Micro-Macro Link in Heterodox Economics. In T.H. Jo, L. Chester and C. D'Ippoliti (Eds.), *The Handbook of Heterodox Economics* (pp. 145–159). London, New York, NY: Routledge.

Gräbner, C. and Strunk, B. (2020). Pluralism in economics: its critiques and their lessons. *Journal of Economic Methodology*, 27 (4), 311–329. https://doi.org/10.1080/1350178x.2020.1824076

Gräbner-Radkowitsch, C. (2022). Replication data for: elements of an evolutionary approach to comparative economic studies: complexity, systemism, and path dependent development, *Harvard Dataverse, V2*, UNF:6:vtigZS+M/xhSslIi6jg+YQ == [fileUNF]. https://doi.org/10.7910/DVN/GXKL22

Heinrich, T. (2017). The narrow and broad approaches to evolutionary modeling in economics. *Journal of Economic Issues*, 51 (2), 383–391. https://doi.org/10.1080/00213624.2017.1320912

Hidalgo, C.A. (2021). Economic complexity theory and applications. *Nature Reviews Physics*, 3 (2), 92–113. https://doi.org/10.1038/s42254-020-00275-1

Hidalgo, C. and Hausmann, R. (2009). The building blocks of economic complexity. *Proceedings of the National Academy of Sciences*, 106 (26), 10570–10575. https://doi.org/10.1073/pnas.0900943106

Hodgson, G. (2004). *The Evolution of Institutional Economics*. New York, NY: Routledge.

Hodgson, G. (2006). What are institutions? *Journal of Economic Issues*, 40 (1), 1–25. https://doi.org/10.1080/00213624.2006.11506879

Hodgson, G. and Knudsen, T. (2004). The complex evolution of a simple traffic convention: the functions and implications of habit. *Journal of Economic Behavior and Organization*, 54 (1), 19–47. https://doi.org/10.1016/j.jebo.2003.04.001

Iammarino, S., Rodriguez-Pose, A. and Storper, M. (2018). Regional inequality in Europe: evidence, theory and policy implications. *Journal of Economic Geography*, 19 (2), 273–298. https://doi.org/10.1093/jeg/lby021

Kapeller, J., Gräbner, C. and Heimberger, P. (2019). Economic Polarisation in Europe: Causes and Policy Options. *wiiw Research Report*, 440. https://wiiw.ac.at/economic-polarisation-in-europe-causes-and-options-for-action-dlp-5022.pdf

Kuhn, T. ([1962] 2012). *The Structure of Scientific Revolutions*. Chicago, IL: University of Chicago Press.

Kvangraven, I.H. (2020). Beyond the stereotype: restating the relevance of the dependency research programme. *Development and Change*. https://doi.org/10.1111/dech.12593

Lundvall, B. (2007). National innovation systems – analytical concept and development tool. *Industry & Innovation*, 14 (1), 95–119. https://doi.org/10.1080/13662710601130863

Lundvall, B.-Å. and Rikap, C. (2022). China's catching-up in artificial intelligence seen as a co-evolution of corporate and national innovation systems. *Research Policy*, 51 (1), 104395. https://doi.org/10.1016/j.respol.2021.104395

Nelson, R. and Winter, S. (1982). *An Evolutionary Theory of Economic Change*. Cambridge, MA: Harvard University Press.

Nelson, R.R. (Ed.) (1993). *National Innovation Systems: A Comparative Analysis*. New York, NY: Oxford University Press.

Odendahl, C. and Springford, J. (2020). Three ways COVID-19 will cause economic divergence in Europe, *CER Policy Paper* No. 5/2020. https://www.cer.eu/sites/default/files/pb_econdiv_20.5.20.pdf

Regan, A. and Brazys, S. (2018). Celtic phoenix or leprechaun economics? The politics of an FDI-led growth model in Europe. *New Political Economy*, 23 (2), 223–238. https://doi.org/10.1080/13563467.2017.1370447

Reynolds, C., Agrawal, M., Lee, I., Zhan, C., Li, J., Taylor, P., Mares, T., Morison, J., Angelakis, N. and Roos, G. (2018). A sub-national economic complexity analysis of Australia's states and territories. *Regional Studies*, 52 (5), 715–726. https://doi.org/10.1080/00343404.2017.1283012

Saltarelli, F., Cimini, V., Tacchella, A., Zaccaria, A. and Cristelli, M. (2020). Is export a probe for domestic production? *Frontiers in Physics*, 8, 180. https://doi.org/10.3389/fphy.2020.00180

Simon, H.A. (1962). The architecture of complexity. *Proceedings of the American Philosophical Society*, 106 (6), 467–482.

Sutton, J. (2012). *Competing in Capabilities*. Oxford, UK: Oxford University Press.

Tacchella, A., Cristelli, M., Caldarelli, G., Gabrielli, A. and Pietronero, L. (2013). Economic complexity: Conceptual grounding of a new metrics for global competitiveness. *Journal of Economic Dynamics and Control*, 37 (8), 1683–1691. https://doi.org/10.1016/j.jedc.2013.04.00

Varoufakis, Y. (2014). *Economic Indeterminacy*. New York, NY: Routledge.

Witt, U. (2014). The future of evolutionary economics: why the modalities of explanation matter. *Journal of Institutional Economics*, 10 (4), 645–664. https://doi.org/10.1017/s1744137414000253

5

INSTITUTIONAL INTERCONNECTIONS AND THE PERFORMANCE AND CHANGE OF ECONOMIC SYSTEMS

Nadia von Jacobi

UNIVERSITY OF TRENTO

5.1 Introduction

Any system, whether economic, social or ecological, naturally evokes a notion of complexity: multiple factors and levels interact contemporaneously with each other (Barder, 2012; Beinhocker, 2007; Ramalingam, 2013). Different levels are tied to each other despite them moving and changing at different velocities (Grimm et al., 2005; Holling et al., 1995). When we study institutions and their role within economic systems, we tend to isolate a specific relation – or set of relations – from such an overall system. The risk we run is to underestimate the relevance that the connections we ignore may play. In empirical analysis, such risk is widely acknowledged and addressed by 'treating endogeneity'. Endogeneity refers to the unknown causal directionality of a connection – this is often linked to the presence of other factors that have not been included in the analysis (omitted variable bias).

While instrumental approaches have become mainstream methodological solutions to suspected endogeneity, they only solve parts of the problem (Pande and Udry, 2006; Ray, 2007). Sophisticated econometric analysis may produce reliable and clean results on a specific relation, yet by isolating such relation from its wider context of interconnections, it does not account for multiple contemporaneous effects. It is further not able to give relative weight to the relationship under investigation. We may find a relation to be causal, and significantly so – but is such relation a key driver within an economic system? Or is it part of a broader path of causal relations – or part of a complex constellation in which few relations dominate over others?

These are questions that are inherent in a systemic view on institutions and economic performance (Kuran, 2009; Pryor, 2008). They imply a crucial shift of analysis away from studying single factors, such as growth, inequality, rule of law, financial openness, gender parity – towards a closer inspection of relations – and of the relative positions that such relations assume one versus another.

Envisioning institutions and economic performance as being part of a complex adaptive system (Barder, 2012; Allen and Starr, 1982; O'Neill et al., 1986 in Holling et al. 1995;

   DOI: 10.4324/9781003144366-7

Harford, 2011) has important policy implications, too (Bassanini and Duval, 2009; Dolphin and Nash, 2012; Duit and Galaz, 2008). Any attempt to induce change faces the dense interdependence among structural features: how should change be triggered? Which systemic effects can be expected? Are there leverage points that may provoke change at a greater speed? Which complementary actions do we have to enact simultaneously? Any approach isolating specific relations from the overall system is likely to lead to over-simplifications that may also result in policy mistakes and unintended effects (Bassanini and Duval, 2009; Belloc and Bowles, 2013; Dacin et al., 2002, Hodgson and Stoelhorst, 2014, Langlois, 2016; Thévenon, 2016; Woodruff, 2006 in Voigt, 2013).

While complexity is hard to trace in its entirety (Richardson and Lissack, 2001), this chapter proposes a methodological approach to empirically capture and map multiple interconnections that tie institutional and structural features of an economic system. I depart from the literature on institutional complementarities (Amable, 2000; Aoki, 2001; Boyer, 2004; Hall and Soskice, 2001; Bowles et al., 2003; Pagano and Rossi, 2004; Pagano and Rowthorn, 1994; Pagano and Vatiero, 2015) that have stressed how norms are naturally interdependent with values and other norms. I argue, however, that the economic framework of complements again leads us astray in concentrating on single relations.

Drawing on ecology, and symbiosis in particular (Margulis, 1984; Watkins, 1998), I seek to highlight how a perspective inspired by living organisms is more likely to induce us to investigate multiple relationships at the same time (Grimm et al., 2005; Odum and Barrett, 1971). Furthermore, a perspective inspired by symbiosis is more likely to capture the functional variety we observe when studying formal and informal institutions within an economic system (Gutmann and Voigt, 2020; Voigt, in this volume; Sindzingre, 2006). Functional variety implies that formal and informal institutions may be apt for sound economic performance – or not (Belloc and Bowles, 2013).

Symbiotic relationships can assume different forms, of symmetric (mutualism, competition) or asymmetric kind (commensalism, parasitism). The grounds on which exchange occurs may relate to habitat, service or resource provision (Cain et al., 2011; Jacobi, 2018). Each relation assumes very specific forms and reasons for exchange. Similar patterns have been observed among genes.

In line with such openness to potentially different combinations of values, norms and economic performance, I suggest an exploratory methodological approach – in which the causal directionalities among factors are not defined *ex-ante*. As institutions, social and economic structures are subject to co-evolution, it may be difficult and to some extent arbitrary to define directions of causalities *ex-ante*. Making use of network analysis and recent improvements in abundance of data on institutional and structural factors, this chapter describes a method in which symbiotic relationships among formal and informal institutions – and other socioeconomic structural factors – can be mapped to characterize an economic system (Jacobi, 2018; Jacobi and Amendolagine, 2021).

Such technique enlarges the analytical toolbox of comparison in as much as relations, sub-structures and network properties can be studied to understand the differences in the mechanics that underpin different systems (Martins, 2006). The chapter is structured as follows: Section 5.2 introduces arguments for a systemic approach and why a perspective centred on symbiosis may be promising; Section 5.3 introduces correlation network analysis and how the methodology can be translated to investigate economic systems; Section 5.4 presents emergent findings and weighs limits against potentials for future research in the field.

5.2 Beyond binary relations

Let's depart from the notion that institutions are socially accepted systems of rules (www. winir.org).[1] Why are institutions interconnected at all? They are focal points that lead individuals to prefer certain behaviours over others. The term rule is 'broadly understood as a socially transmitted and customary normative injunction or immanently normative disposition, that in circumstances X do Y' (Hodgson, 2006, p. 3). Norms work in a similar way but tend to 'involve a network of mutual beliefs and involve approval or disapproval' (Tuomela in Hodgson, 2006, p. 5).

The reason why individuals stick to rules and norms is therefore rooted, on the one hand, in the assumption that most others will do the same (Basu, 2018; Tabellini, 2008). This leads to prevalent patterns of behaviour (North, 1990; North et al., 2006) due to fads and informational cascades that occur within social networks (Bikhchandani et al., 1992). On the other hand, rules and norms defend certain values over others – they propose a certain appropriateness of specific behaviours (March and Olsen, 2004). Rules are therefore first interconnected with norms that are not enforced by the state, such as culture, traditions and ethical standards (Voigt, 2018). Such informal rules and norms – if compatible – provide the grounds for the enforcement of formal institutions (Acemoglu and Jackson, 2017; Guiso et al., 2006; Williamson, 2009). Different formal rules – or legally stipulated norms (Hodgson, 2001) – may indeed have emerged from similar value environments. It is therefore quite likely for different institutions to be interconnected with other formal or informal institutions (Alesina and Giuliano, 2015; Belloc and Bowles, 2013; Bisin and Verdier, 2017; Guiso et al., 2006, 2008; North, 1990; Pitlik and Rode, 2017).

In a similar argumentation, institutions are regarded to be composite concepts (Sindzingre, 2006) that combine an element of form with an element of content. While form is potentially measurable, content is likely to be immeasurable, as it enshrines semantic meaning. Such meaning can be different in different places, to different groups, at different moments in time (Sindzingre, 2014). Furthermore, semantic meaning is likely to be tied to other structural factors that affect values, perceptions and collective preferences. Among these, elements such as history (Michalopoulos and Papaioannou, 2013; Naritomi et al., 2012; Tabellini, 2010), geography (Gneezy et al. 2016) and socio-ethnic fractionalization (Alesina and La Ferrara, 2005; Bossert et al., 2011) are all factors that are likely to co-evolve with institutions in as much as they affect cognitive frames and social networks of actors that join, exchange and agree on common rules (Beckert, 2010). Institutions in this sense have been found to enshrine evolutionary aspects, e.g., the evolution of cognitive psychology (Boyer and Petersen, 2012, 2013), which is highly adapted to the specificity of the context.

Viewing institutions as composite (or interconnected) entities makes cross-sectional comparisons that are merely based on their form rather problematic. While a full unpacking of tangible and intangible, semantic and formal elements of institutions is likely to be impossible in quantitative analysis, I propose that the investigation of interconnections is a viable empirical tool to account for a larger part of such crucial components.

5.2.1 Institutional complementarities

A strand of the literature that has advanced thinking on co-evolution of institutions with other factors is one that has tried to put at the forefront of analysis how different rules interlock with each other (Amable, 2000; Aoki, 2001; Boyer, 2004; Bowles et al., 2003; Hall and

Soskice, 2001; Pagano and Rossi, 2004; Pagano and Rowthorn, 1994, Pagano and Vatiero, 2015). Institutional complementarity is present if 'the functional performance of an institution A is conditioned by the presence of another institution B and vice versa' (Höpner, 2005, p. 383). Research in this field has led to important insights within the theory of the firm, innovation studies and an understanding of broader institutional setups, e.g. varieties of capitalism (Hall and Soskice, 2001; Rosta, in this volume; Streeck and Thelen, 2005).

5.2.2 Supermodularity

An interesting extension to complementarities is the concept of supermodularity, which Aoki (2001) introduced building upon Milgrom and Roberts (1990) and Topkis (1978, 2011). Supermodularity conditions are introduced as a framework for games in which the individual choices of economic actors occur in two different institutional domains – and such domains are interdependent. For example, choices within the market are designed as being dependent on another institutional environment, public policy. Aoki outlines that the rules that form endogeneously in one domain can represent exogenous factors for the formation of rules in another domain. In this sense, work on supermodularity paves a road towards the investigation of asymmetries – which are not intuitively present in the study of complementarities.[2] Nevertheless, supermodularity should be regarded as embedded within the institutional complementarities literature.

5.2.3 Symbiosis

While the literature on institutional complementarities helps understanding the deep interdependence between institutions and any other institution or structural factor that co-evolve with them, its roots in microeconomic foundations lead to a tendency to concentrate on single, specific relations (Watkins, 1998). In previous research, I have therefore proposed an analogy to symbiosis, in which institutions and structural factors are studied as if they were living organisms (Jacobi, 2018; Jacobi and Amendolagine, 2021).

Referring to biology and ecology is, of course, not new within institutional economics. Hodgson (2004) traces a very deep track history of how Darwinian thought influenced American Institutionalism, mainly through Veblen, and how evolutionary thinking is re-emerging within institutional research in recent times. Yet, as Watkins (1998) argues, Darwinian thought is itself complementary – or partially functional to neoclassical economic thinking because of its stress on the notion of competition. He suggests that symbiosis theory (Margulis, 1984) may be a more neutral perspective than the predominantly evolutionary thought centred on evolution – which can be broken down into variation, selection and replication/inheritance (Hodgson and Knudsen, 2010; Kingston and Caballero, 2009; Witt, 2014). Symbiosis, of course, enshrines evolutionary processes, often with one organism adapting to another. Yet its key focus rests on two other key aspects of ecology: complexity and interdependence (Jacobi, 2018). In line with such a different focus, symbiosis theory may foster the analysis and comprehension of cooperation – more than that of competition (Watkins, 1998). Yet, to date, economic and institutional analysis that refers to symbiosis is scant.

Battistini and Pagano (2008) extend institutional complementarities to investigate 'selection complementarities' through which they seek to explain how complementary optimization across natural and sexual selection may have led to the extraordinary development of the human brain. Their analogy to biology is centred on epistatic relations or gene interactions within the same organism, which has important commonalities with symbiosis, yet the authors do not explicitly refer to it but focus more on Darwinian evolutionary logic.

Table 5.1 Types of symbiotic relationships: Key features

	Impact of relation on		Type of relation	Correlation coefficient	Economic equivalent	Externalities	
	Factor 1	Factor 2				1 on 2	2 on 1
Neutralism	0	0	Symmetric	Insignificant	–	No	No
Mutualism	+	+	Symmetric	Positive	Complement	Pos	Pos
Commensalism	+	0	Asymmetric	Positive	–	No	Pos
Parasitism	+	–	Asymmetric	(in)Significant	–	Neg	Pos
Competition	–	–	Symmetric	Negative	Substitute	Neg	Neg

Source: Jacobi (2018).

I argue that putting symbiosis theory at centre stage has important advantages for institutional analysis. First, its stress on 'living together of unlike organisms' (De Bary, 1879) frees investigation from the 'functional fallacy' that regards institutions as functional for economic efficiency (Amable, 2016; Jacobi, 2018). Second, symbiosis stresses that each relationship may be highly specific and of mutable nature, warning against oversimplifications in measurement and comparison. Usually, five different types of symbiotic relationships are identified: neutralism, mutualism, commensalism, parasitism and competition (Cain et al., 2011). Third, by envisaging a range of possible relationships, both symmetric and asymmetric interdependencies can be accounted for. Fourth, as no organism lives in isolation with respect to other organisms and its environment (Grimm et al., 2005; Odum and Barrett, 1971; Tomera, 1979), a symbiotic lens on interconnections naturally calls for the investigation of multiple relationships that exist contemporaneously (Jacobi, 2018). Table 5.1 compares symbiotic relationships with the economic concepts of 'complements' and 'substitutes'.

As can be seen in Table 5.1, 'complements' and 'substitutes' correspond to symmetric symbiotic relationships, e.g. mutualism or competition. However, asymmetric interactions in which one organism benefits more than the other from the exchange, either without harming the host (commensalism) or by harming the host (parasitism), cannot properly be expressed through their economic equivalents. Externalities, which usually capture indirect effects, could record asymmetry of interactions by cross-comparing externalities of the two factors studied. In what follows, the methodological approach developed allows mapping symmetric or asymmetric symbiotic relationships among institutional and structural factors – it is here proposed that this may be an exploratory and innovative way to characterize an economic system. Each single symbiotic relationship is placed into a broader map of multiple and simultaneous interdependencies – which jointly form a complex network.

5.3 Which boundaries? The grounds for comparison

Once we embrace a complexity-inspired perspective to study economic systems, some questions need to be addressed before operationalizing the analysis. The first is the natural dilemma where to draw a boundary to a complex system (Grimm et al., 2005; Marinari and Parisi, 2000). Potentially, any factor could be included in the analysis of the system. While data availability may ultimately decide upon which factors can be included or not, the researcher needs to make a careful decision. Any factor included in the system is allowed to form patterns in relation to other factors. There will be factors, however, that are not included in the system but that contribute in defining its boundaries, e.g. the geographical area of reference such as a specific country or province.

Caution needs to be used in the ambition to clearly delimit a complex system (Richardson and Lissack, 2001). While some patterns and features of the system may be robust to slight modification in boundaries, others may not (Marinari and Parisi, 2000; McKelvey, 1997). For comparative purposes, it is however crucial to decide upon some kind of boundary. The elements used to distinguish one system from the other will affect the observations in system structure – and be the grounds for comparison across diverse systems. Still, some care in interpretation is recommendable – remembering that no system (especially an economic, social or political one) exists in isolation but has constant interchanges – and thereby interdependencies – with other systems. Such fluidity of systems should not represent an obstacle to the methodological attempt proposed here. The aim is indeed not to capture the mechanics of every single socio-economic phenomenon but instead to observe and compare emerging patterns in observable relations among a selection of structural factors (Grimm et al., 2005)[3].

By setting specific grounds for the comparison, we must be aware of the potential recommendations that will be derived from such a choice. The methodology proposed makes use of subnational data, which clearly limits the focus on institutional factors, e.g. leaving out constitutions or state functioning. Any attempt for comparison requires data collection efforts that re-create the same pool of variables (factors investigated) for each system. Working at the sub-national level requires considering the relative autonomy, functions and resources that, e.g. provinces or municipalities have – these may be different across different country settings. Despite such differences, the most local level of governance is likely to be comparable in as much as it represents a small-scale reality of democratic exercise in which different values and needs within a society interact and collide.

A key focus of the analysis proposed is the detection of patterns. Patterns are defining characteristics of a system – they are indicators of essential underlying processes (Grimm et al., 2005). Patterns form structures and constellations of relations, such as types of centrality, prevalence of circularity, degree of density (see the next sections, for examples). By comparing structures, constellations, or the relative position of specific factors within the entire system – we seek to explain such differences on the grounds of the system's boundaries.

In this sense, the choice regarding which factors to include in the system and which to exclude also relates to endogeneity and exogeneity. Factors included in the network representing the system are all likely to be endogeneous, whereas factors used for setting the boundaries to the system are momentarily forced into an exogeneous position. While exogeneity may be acceptable in a static analysis, in the long term, many factors are likely to be endogeneous – so Richardson's and Lissack's argument (2001) that all boundaries are artificial should be kept in mind. On the other hand, ignoring boundaries is likely to lead to the pooling of populations that behave differently (cf. Arrow et al., 2000): if the system is set with infinite or too large boundaries, we will only observe average patterns – and any possibility for comparison and for understanding differences in mechanisms between systems will be lost (Grimm et al., 2005). Correlation network analysis can however assist the researcher in identifying factors with greater or inferior exogeneity – the way that the studied factors are placed within the network gives important hints on their degree of endogeneity (see Section 5.5).

In what follows, I use empirical results introduced in Jacobi (2018; 2021) and in Jacobi and Amendolagine (2021) to illustrate the methodology. All variables that appear in computations are measured at the municipality level of Brazil, Germany or Italy (see Table A1 in the annex). For details on Brazilian municipality-level data, see Jacobi (2018) and Jacobi and Amendolagine (2021). For details on German and Italian datasets, see the *LAUDEIT* dataset introduced in Jacobi (2021).

5.4 Correlation network analysis

5.4.1 Networks to grasp multiple interconnections

Although networks may not entirely grasp complexity (Cilliers, 2001), they are the closest representation of complex systems we currently have. Networks are 'stable and recurrent patterns' in some kind of interaction (Ansell, 2006, p. 75). Networks can be multidimensional, multi-level and nonetheless synthesize a set of relations through the structure and patterns that they jointly form (Cranmer et al., 2012). If weighted, networks can properly map flux patterns or, e.g. reflect different velocities at which different levels operate (Grimm et al. 2005; Holling et al., 1995). If directed, networks can summarize important features of mechanics and structure (Fagiolo, 2007). For this reason, a network approach is promising in our attempt to grasp multiple relationships to better understand how specific institutional or economic factors underpin and characterize an economic system. In what follows, I start with the most basic network and then argue for the construction of weighted, directed networks.

Correlation network analysis is a data-reduction technique (Horvath, 2011) that has extensively been used in medical science. Specifically, gene co-expression has been studied through this methodology, leading among others to important insights on how to identify brain cancer and obesity genes or on how atherosclerosis works (Gargalovic et al., 2006; Ghazalpour et al., 2006; Horvath et al., 2006; Lim et al., 2007; Wang et al., 2009 all in Horvath, 2011). In a correlation network, the adjacency matrix 'is constructed on the basis of pairwise correlations between numeric vectors' (Horvath, 2011, p. 91). This means that any gene under investigation becomes a node (or vertex) within the network – the correlation coefficient becomes the edge that binds two nodes, giving weight to their connection. The result is a weighted, undirected network in which it is possible to study centrally located genes and their pathways. In previous work (Jacobi, 2018; Jacobi and Amendolagine, 2021), I have applied such a technique to the investigation of institutional factors. Transferring the object of investigation from genes and their connections, to structural features and their interconnections, I have, e.g. included GDP per capita, different measures of institutional quality, medium size of the enterprise, female labour market participation, dependency rate, etc., and studied which factors locate centrally in such web of connections. Figure 5.1 represents a correlation network computed over institutional and economic factors. Each node represents a municipal feature, whereas edges are statistically significant correlation coefficients. In Figure 5.1, the variable 'income per capita' locates very centrally in the correlation network of Italian municipality features. However, voter turnout at European elections, the share of votes for populist parties and the employment rate also assume a central position in the network.

5.4.2 Thinking in networks

Networks are synthetic representations that can be unpacked by sequentially looking at different layers of results.

5.4.2.1 Relations

First of all, within the web, we may want to focus on relations as a unit of analysis and study their prevalence and characterize such relations as much as possible: which strength do connections have, on average and how is it distributed? Do they tend to bind specific types of factors together? (See Table 5.3 in Section 5.5 as an example.)

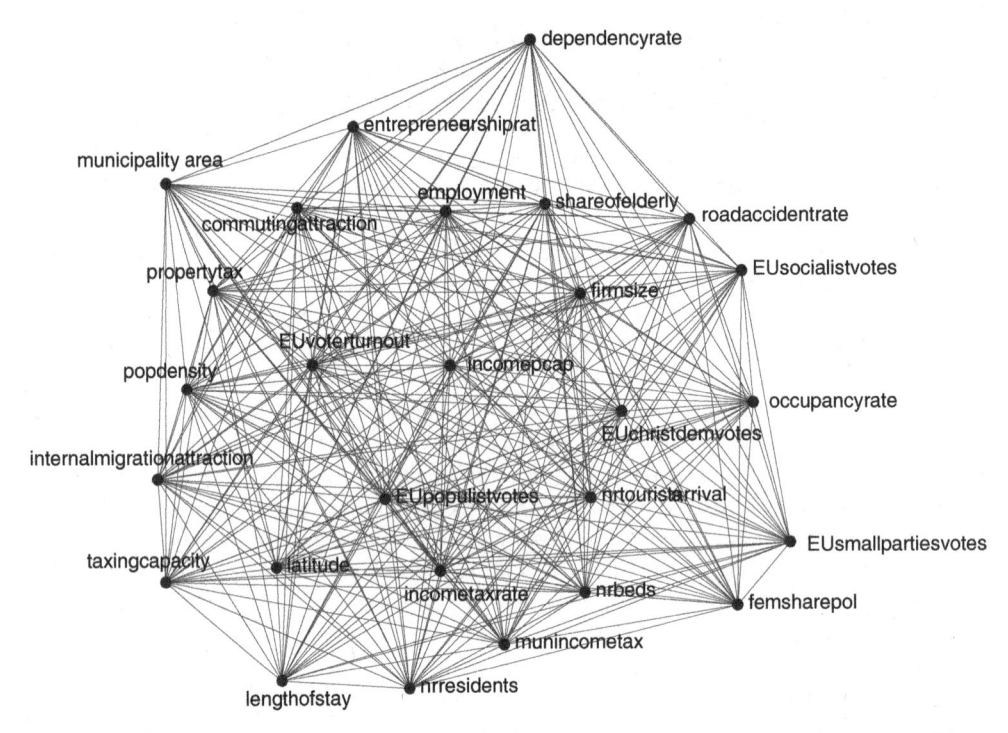

Figure 5.1 Unrestricted correlation network among structural factors measured at the municipality level, Italy.

Source: Elaboration by the author based on German municipality data, LAUDEIT dataset, 2016 – for data details, see Table A1 and Jacobi (2021).

5.4.2.2 Relative position of specific factors

We can next focus on specific factors, or specific nodes in the web and their relative position. For this scope, it is quite straightforward to make use of network statistics (Alatas et al., 2012; Freeman, 1977; Green and Wasserman, 2013; Wasserman and Faust, 1994). Such statistics compute a specific measure of connectedness or centrality of each single node with respect to the overall web. Typical measures are reported in Table 5.2.

5.4.2.3 Network characteristics

The previous two layers of analysis can also be used to acquire information on the system as a whole: when relationships are prevalent, the density of the network is higher. My investigations of institutional interconnections have shown that density slightly tends to rise with degree of economic development, in line with the complexity and development literature (Barder, 2012; Beinhocker, 2007; Ramalingam, 2013). Similarly, any network can be characterized by its average weighted degree centrality, or average betweenness degree centrality, etc. What such measures do is to hint how common very central positions are within the web, yet they are averages so they do not automatically capture, for example, a skewed distribution in terms of centrality among its nodes. Still, comparing systems also means comparing such network characteristics. For example, it can be interesting to observe how networks have very similar characteristics in terms of density and centrality patterns, yet that *different* factors

Table 5.2 Network statistics and their interpretation

Network statistics	Synthetic description	Interpretation in economic systems	References
Unweighted Degree Centrality	Number of ties of the node	Endogeneity, centrality for the system (imprecise)	Alatas et al., 2012
Weighted Degree Centrality	Weighted sum of ties of the node	Endogeneity, centrality for the system (more precise)	Alatas et al., 2012
Closeness Degree Centrality	Sum of shortest paths needed to connect to every other node of the web	Potential for systemic effects as changes diffuse quickly in the web	Bavelas, 1951, Leavitt, 1951 in Freeman, 1977
Betweenness Degree Centrality	Positioned on shortest paths linking other nodes	Channelling, forwarding or mediating indirect effects ('bottlenecks')	Freeman, 1977; Jacobi and Amendolagine, 2021
Eigenvalue Degree Centrality	Recursive measure: number of connections weighted by the importance of neighbouring nodes	Centrality to the system, interdependence	Bonacich, 2007

Source: Elaboration by the author.

position themselves at the more central locations. Figure 5.2 shows two symmetric correlation networks, computed on the same municipal variables collected for Germany (left) and Italy (right).[4] Only edges for which the absolute value of the correlation coefficient is above 0.30 have been included. Both networks present themselves with one largest component, and a smaller component in which only two nodes connect. At a closer look, it is possible to see how different factors locate in different positions in the two networks. For example, latitude has greater centrality in the Italian network than in the German one, as can be seen by the amount of shortest paths that go through the variable 'latitude' in the Italian network. This suggests that variability in this factor is highly connected to other structural factors in Italy.

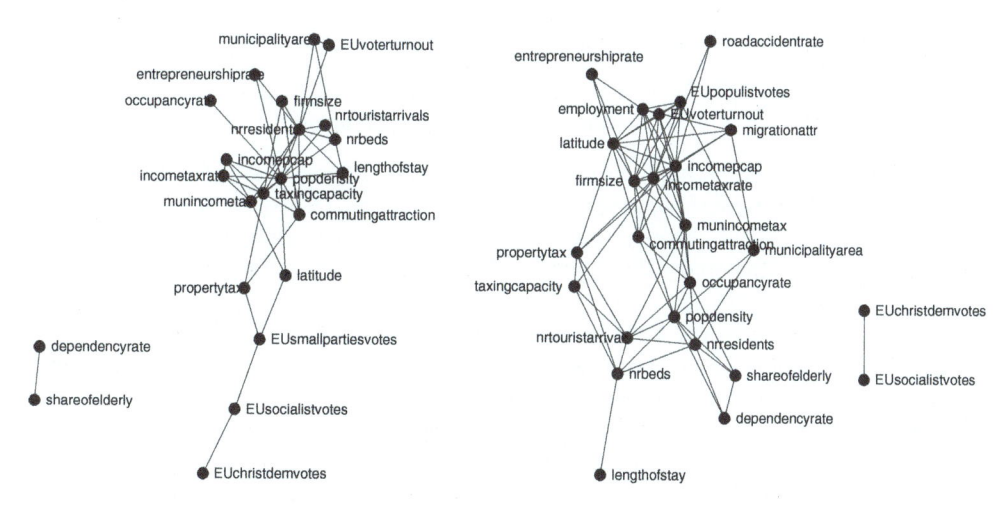

Figure 5.2   Restricted correlation networks among structural factors measured at the municipality level, Germany (left) and Italy (right), correlations >|0.30|.

Source: Elaboration by the author based on LAUDEIT dataset, 2016 – for data details, see Jacobi (2021).

In Germany, latitude appears as a bottleneck that connects most other structural features to European election voting patterns.

5.4.2.4 Paths and motifs

A further layer of investigation can be a specific focus on sub-structures within the overall web. These can be conceived in a linear way, e.g. by following paths that tie two specific nodes. Or they can resemble motifs, such as triangles or more complex constellations that form among a group of nodes.

Looking at paths between nodes can be very insightful (Wright, 1928 in Imbens, 2020). First, a shorter path (not having to pass through many other nodes and their ties) represents a more immediate/potentially stronger relationship. Direct relationships also represent an interesting terrain for policy interventions, as more immediate effects can be expected. Second, multiple paths may tie two different nodes in a network – each 'running through' different connecting nodes (see Figure 5.7 in Section 5.5 as an example). The more paths can be identified, the greater the interdependence between the two nodes, as any modification in an intermediate node is unlikely to drastically change their connection within the web. Yet, the longer the 'shortest path' tying two nodes together, the potentially weaker the connection because of multiple mediating factors.

Apart from paths, motifs can be another object of interest. Motifs broaden our conception of interdependence by abandoning the dyadic view. In triplets, it may not be clear which factor is the starting point, but they allow capturing and mapping the interdependence between three factors (Onnela et al., 2005; Fagiolo, 2007). Triplets depict a tridimensional embedding that gives greater depth to our understanding of a system's structure (see Figure 5.6 in Section 5.4.3.3. as an example).

5.4.3 Key steps for operationalization

In what follows, I summarize what has to be done to implement a correlation network analysis to study economic systems. More detailed information can be found in Jacobi (2018) and its Online Supplementary Material, and in Jacobi and Amendolagine (2021).

5.4.3.1 Which factors at which level?

Of primary concern is the selection of factors to include in the analysis. A minimum of 15 variables should be considered to create a meaningful network. There is no upper limit, but the more factors are included, the more selective will be the interpretation of the results (Grimm et al., 2005). Depending on the choice of boundaries, the level of analysis chosen should grant:

- meaning/relevance for the variable measured
- sufficient amount of observations (preferably at least 200 for symmetric networks, preferably at least 1000 for asymmetric networks)
- sufficient variability (e.g. Constitutions do not vary at the sub-national level)

In my studies implemented in Brazil, Italy and Germany, I have so far opted for the municipality level in as much as it often represents a relevant administrative level in which institutional design and/or implementation takes place. It corresponds to the subsidiarity principle according to which as many services as possible should be delivered at the local level. While representing a challenge in terms of data collection, the municipality level may also more adequately capture differences in terms of informal institutions, e.g. traditions and practices that are complementary to formal institutions. Collecting data at the municipality level may be easy in some contexts and very difficult in others. Certainly, comparisons across systems based on municipality-level data represent a challenge – but are possible, as I describe in Jacobi (2021). To respond to the data requirements of the methodology, national data could only be used in pooled cross-sections. My personal view is that computing a single network of interdependencies across different countries may be more appropriate for other research goals: for institutional analysis, it is likely for too many unobserved confounding factors to be affecting the validity of ties (Imbens, 2020).

5.4.3.2 Data shaping

Once a reasonable pool of data has been collected, data have to be re-shaped (see Jacobi, 2018; Jacobi and Amendolagine, 2021). Statistically, significant correlation coefficients are transformed into a so-called edgelist, which is a typical network dataset in which three variables are included: the names of the two nodes and the weight connecting them. This is obtained by transposing the original dataset in which observations (e.g. municipalities) were organized in rows, and factors measured at the municipality level were organized in columns (Figure 5.3). This means that a correlation matrix is basically at the base of the network. To avoid errors, it is important to properly clean data beforehand to avoid outliers or large amounts of missing values. Log or exponential transformations should also be applied to make each variable's distribution as close to normal as possible.

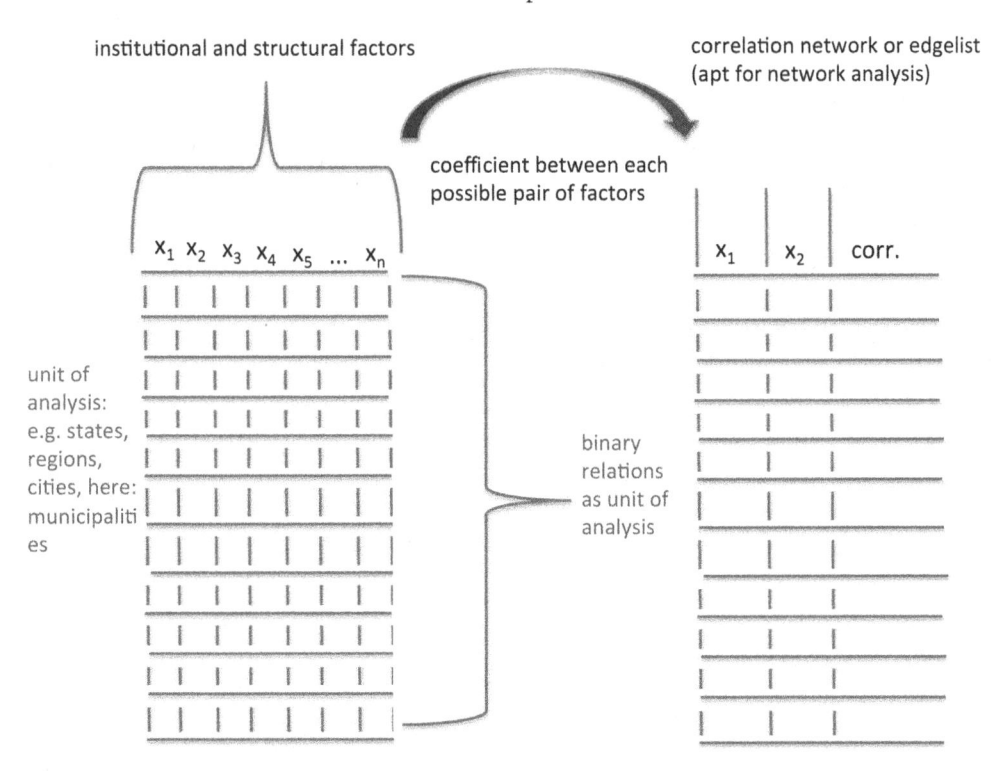

Figure 5.3 Data re-shaping required for correlation network analysis.

Source: Elaboration by the author.

Upon such edgelist, it is possible to compute standard network statistics, such as the degree centrality (C_D) of single nodes:

$$C_D(i) = \sum_{j}^{N} x_{ij} \qquad (5.1)$$

where i is the specific node of interest, and j stands for all other nodes of the network. N is the total amount of nodes included in the network, and x represents the adjacency matrix (Opsahl et al., 2010). In an unweighted network, x_{ij} will be equal to 1 if a link exists between i and j, or will be zero otherwise. In our weighted networks, x_{ij} becomes w_{ij}, where the weight w is the statistically significant correlation coefficient expressing the association between i and j. For an introduction to standard network measures, see Freeman (1977) or Green and Wasserman (2013).

5.4.3.3 Computing a directed weighted network

An extension to standard correlation network analysis makes use of quantile regressions instead of correlations in order to map a complex web of interdependencies (Jacobi, 2018). The aim is to grasp relationships of asymmetric character, as in some symbiotic relationships (see Table 5.1). Instead of computing a correlation coefficient that implies symmetry, I compute two quantile regressions (for five points of the response's distribution, each) in which the dependent and independent variables are switched. In that way, I obtain 10 regression coefficients, which allow tracking how this bivariate regression evolves at higher moments of Y's distribution.

If the relevance in explaining Y of an independent variable X increases at higher moments of Y – but the same is not true when Y and X are swapped, then Y is 'more dependent' on X than vice versa. In line with the framework of symbiosis previously presented, I then derive that Y is a symbiont (Overstreet and Lotz, 2016) and X is a host. A symbiont 'feeds' on a host for its growth. This step has some important implications for the network analysis. The edges that tie nodes are not symmetric any more, but turn into *arcs* or *arrows*. The asymmetry is summarized as follows: any factor serves as a host (starting point of the arc) for a symbiont (head of the arc), which is dependent on the former. Our network then becomes directed, and weighted in as much as a degree of asymmetry is estimated for each arc. Jacobi and Amendolagine (2021) describe a way to derive such asymmetry measure and provide more details on the creation of host–symbiont networks. Figure 5.4 shows a directed weighted network derived from Brazilian municipality level data.[5] Arrows are graduated based on the asymmetry they reflect – the darker the arrow, the stronger the asymmetry. Asymmetry is expressed in percentage point difference when comparing the independent variable's coefficient increase between quantile 20 and quantile 80.[6] As such quantiles are computed in both directions, it is possible to compare the two trends – see Jacobi and Amendolagine (2021) for details.

In Figure 5.4, the many weighted arrows point towards our 'social gathering' measure that records the incidence of community radios, associations and cultural centres – which are bottom-up instances of social-capital enhancing aggregations. 'Socgather' is an informal institutional factor (mid-grey dot) in the web, yet we see it depends on other informal factors (the formality of the economy, the incidence of art groups, the likeliness of missing communication which is computed as ethno-educational fractionalization index across age groups, cf. Bossert et al., 2011) and formal institutional factors (e.g. municipal spending on public goods,

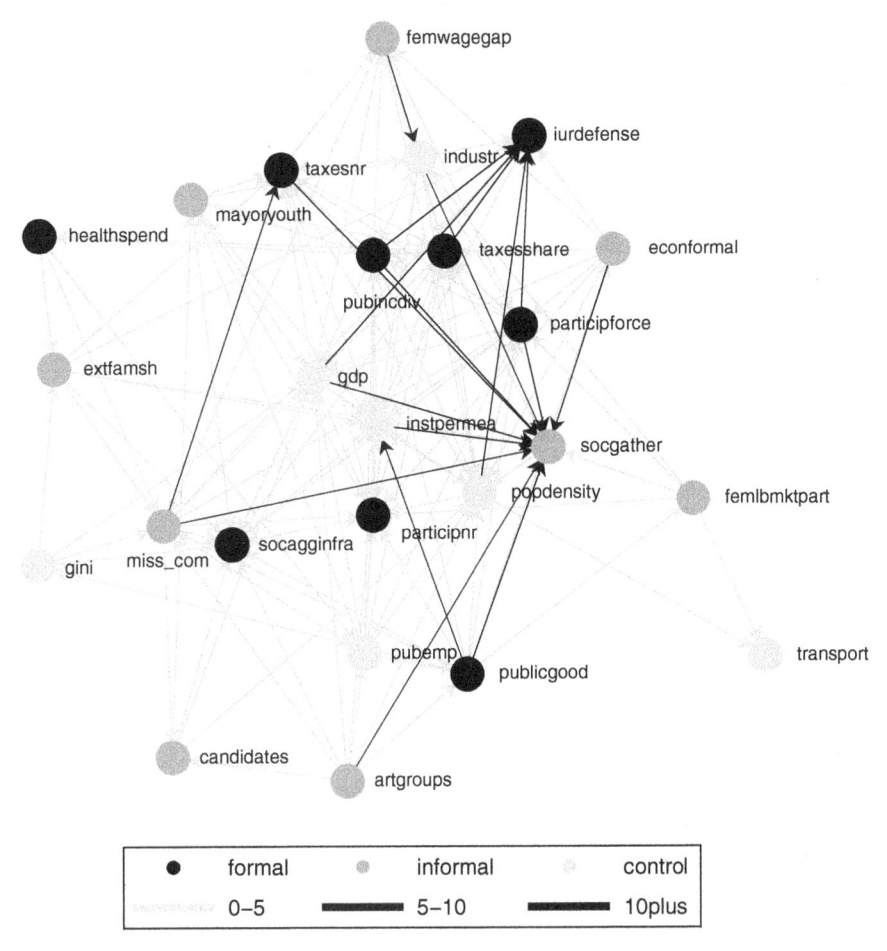

Figure 5.4 Weighted directed network depicting asymmetric symbiotic relationships among structural factors in the South-Eastern macro-region of Brazil.

Source: Elaboration by Jacobi and Amendolagine, unpublished, based on Brazilian municipality data, meso-level dataset, 2010 – for data details, see Table A1 and Jacobi and Amendolagine (2021). Asymmetry in percentage point difference.

the strength of participatory councils – see below – and public income diversification which we use as a proxy for institutional quality). It also appears to depend on control factors we included such as GDP or industrialization.

Weighted, directed networks are slightly more complex to analyze than symmetric ones, but they can be mostly treated along the same lines presented above. Relations can be in focus (see Table 5.3 in Section 5.5), and network statistics can be computed, such as outdegree or indegree centrality (Grund, 2015). Interpretation has of course to be adapted to the directionality of interdependence. For example, high outdegree centrality characterizes a factor that serves as 'host' for many others – and on which many others are dependent upon. High indegree centrality signals greater dependence on multiple other factors.

Figure 5.5 compares two of the most populous Brazilian macro-regions, the North-East (left) and the South-East (right).[7] The weighted directed networks derived from municipality-level data have been restricted to depict only the most asymmetric relationships (equal or

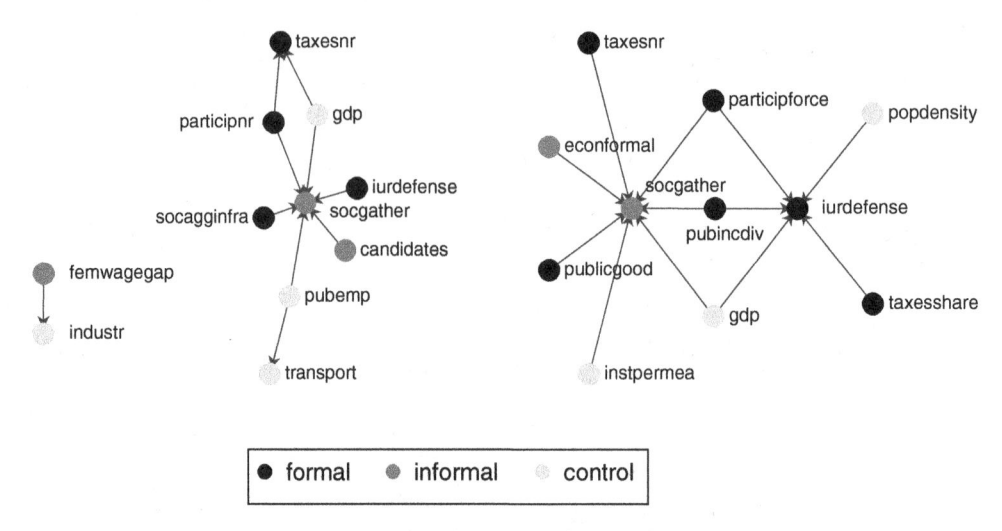

Figure 5.5   Weighted directed networks depicting symbiotic relationships with asymmetry > 10 percentage points, North-Eastern (left) and South-Eastern (right) Brazilian macro-regions compared.

Source: Elaboration by Jacobi and Amendolagine, unpublished, based on Brazilian municipality data, meso-level dataset, 2010 – for data details, see Jacobi and Amendolagine (2021).

above 10 percentage points difference in explanatory power). As above, nodes are coded to reflect formal and informal institutions and a series of control factors.

As can be seen in Figure 5.5, some factors are central in both networks: social gatherings deemed to facilitate the creation of social capital, have high indegree centrality in both networks. Also, in both networks GDP represents a habitat node on which other formal and informal institutions 'feed upon'. The South-Eastern directed network is slightly more dense than the North-Eastern one, in line with their respective development levels.

Participatory councils – a democratic Brazilian institution in which citizens join policy makers in decision-making (Avritzer, 2009; Galletta, 2021) – are present in both networks as 'hosts' providing habitat for other factors. In the North-East, a measure of its number appears, in the South-East a measure of its quality/strength. Taxes are central in both networks, but in the poorer North-East they act as symbiont on other factors, whereas in the more developed South-East taxes serve as a host. In terms of the node categories chosen, we can observe that apart from our measure on informal gatherings, in the North-East, important informal institutions are the female wage gap and the number of candidates voted at municipal elections, which we use as proxy for local democratic attitude. In the South-East, only the degree of formality of the economy enters the restricted network among our potential informal institutional measures.

As with symmetric networks, summary network characteristics can equally be derived, and paths and motifs are similarly computable (Clemente and Grassi, 2018; Fagiolo, 2007; Joyez, 2017; Onnela et al., 2005). The computation of clustering coefficients, for example, captures the tendency of a node to be part of specific motifs (such as a non-frustrated triangle with two outward facing arcs). The computation of clustering coefficients also allows giving greater depth to the study of interdependencies within asymmetric symbiotic networks. For example, while a measure of indegree simply sums up all inward-facing arcs, a measure of inclustering captures the share of closed triplets in which a specific factor receives two inward facing arcs (computed over the total possible closed triplets that node could engage with in the network).

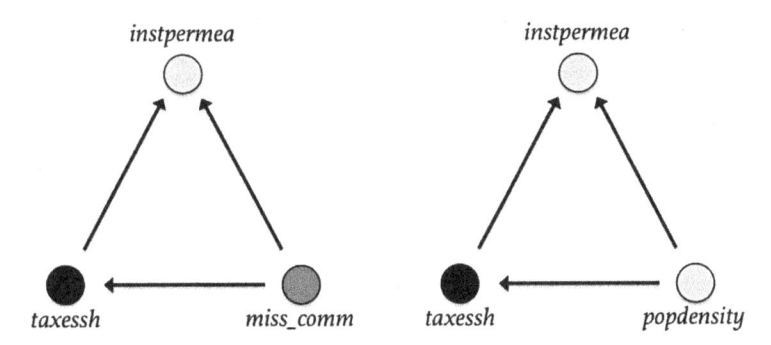

Figure 5.6 Examples of closed triplets found in a weighted directed network: Institutional
permeability, share of taxes, likeliness of missing communication and population density.

Source: Elaboration by Jacobi and Amendolagine, unpublished, based on Brazilian municipality data, meso-
level Dataset, 2010 – for data details, see Table A1 and Jacobi and Amendolagine (2021).

Figure 5.6 shows a close-up of closed triplets that were identified in a weighted
network computed over the entire population of Brazilian municipalities. The triplets depict
some relations held by a measure of 'institutional permeability' – constructed to grasp how
many institutional contacts the single municipality has with other municipalities or hierarchically higher administrative levels.[8] Such measure has high inclustering – hinting multiple
dependence, as can be seen in the two exemplary triplets. In both, institutional permeability
is a symbiont on another factor, through a direct and an indirect channel. In the left panel,
the likeliness of missing communication – is a host for a direct dependency and for an indirect
dependency – that passes through the share of taxes on municipal revenues. In the right panel,
a similar pattern can be observed with population density serving as host.

In the two triplets, the share of taxes will have a high middleman clustering value, whereas
the two host factors assume a high outclustering value (cf. Fagiolo, 2007). Note that within
econometric analysis, the two factors with high outclustering coefficient (miss_comm and
popdensity) would be confounding factors (Imbens, 2020). Closed triplets are of course just
one motif among many possible others (Onnela et al., 2005). Studying paths that tie specific
factors together represents another possibility for analysis, as can be seen in Figure 5.7. Here,
paths have been used to investigate the connections existing between specific factors.

On the left side of Figure 5.7, paths extrapolated from the German weighted directed
networks are depicted, whereas on the right side, the corresponding Italian network has been
used to compute the analogous paths (cf. Figures 5.1 and 5.2 for data). In the upper segment
of the figure, it is possible to see which paths link a formal institutional factor such as property tax to income per capita. In Germany, three paths can be identified; they all pass through
structural factors of geographic or demographic nature, e.g. the municipality area, population
density and a commuters' attraction index (see Jacobi, 2021). In Italy, the same connection
looks different: there are only two paths, and they are longer, implying one passage more.
In Italy, the relationship between property tax collected by the municipality and income per
capita is mediated not only by geographical and structural factors (latitude and the commuters'
attraction index) but also by an economic factor (the employment rate) and by the accident
rate leading to injuries, which we use as a proxy for an attitude not to stick to (traffic) rules.

In the lower segment of the figure, a similar analysis is carried out, but this time linking the
entrepreneurship rate – measured as the incidence of enterprises in the manufacturing sector

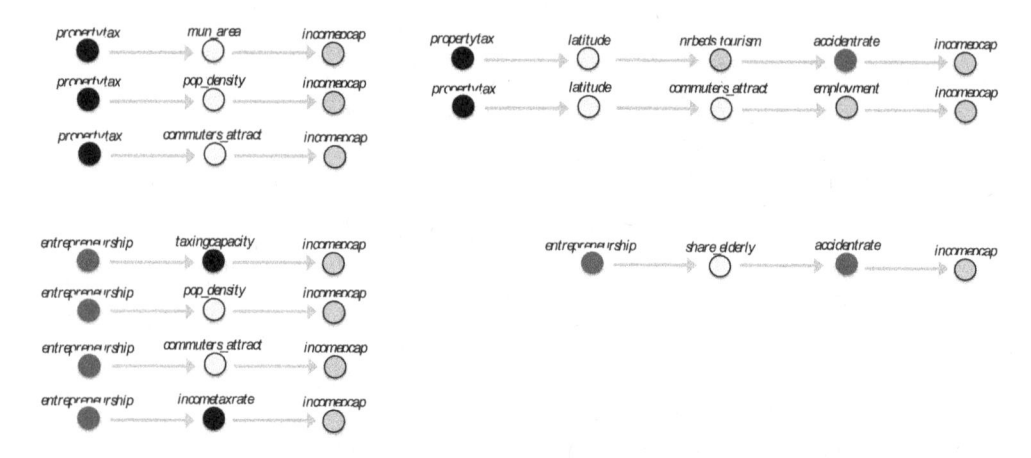

Figure 5.7   Paths extrapolated from weighted directed networks, tying property tax to income per capita, and entrepreneurship rate to income per capita, German (left) and Italian (right) municipality data.

Source: Elaboration by the author based on LAUDEIT dataset, 2016. For data details, see Jacobi (2021).

on the resident population – to income per capita. Again, differences between Germany and Italy can be detected.

In the German network, there are four paths and they are rather short, merely passing through structural features (population density and commuters' attraction) and through two measures of formal institutions, namely the municipal taxing capacity and the income tax rate. In the Italian network, there is only one path linking the two factors, and it is much longer: the ability of the entrepreneurship rate to serve as a 'host' for income per capita is mediated by the share of elderly in the municipal population, and – again – by our proxy for respecting rules reflected in the accident rate.

Figure 5.7 represents just an example of how network analysis can be used to focus on specific problems or relations. Paths are even more fascinating in weighted directed networks, as they are constrained by the directionality given by arcs. In the symbiosis framework, here proposed, directionalities reflect chains of dependencies.

5.5 Emerging insights, limits and potential for future research

The results so far discussed have served as illustrative material to highlight the potential of the methodology proposed here. Empirical investigations have so far been run on Brazilian, German and Italian municipal data. Much more analysis is possible and likely to shed more insights in the future. In what follows, I summarize some key findings that are emerging from the empirical investigations run so far. I also discuss limits and potentials for a future research agenda.

5.5.1 The dependence of formal institutions on informal norms and attitudes

Across different analyses of weighted directed networks run on entire countries or macro-regions, I observed an emerging result that informal institutions have a slightly more frequent tendency to behave as 'hosts', whereas formal institutions tend to be 'symbionts'. Jacobi and Amendolagine (2021) shows the first discussion of this result. Such findings confirm other authors in the argument that informal institutions rule over formal ones (Acemoglu and Jackson, 2017; Belloc and Bowles, 2013; Maseland, 2013; Williamson, 2009) – yet by grounding such mechanics into a framework that accounts for complexity, correlation network analysis seems to mainly acknowledge a point made by Williamson (2000). He argued that culture and tradition change at a much slower speed than formal institutions related to governance. Within complex systems, it has been recognized that slower levels dominate the faster ones (Holling et al., 1995). This tends to explain the prevalent directionality we observe, although co-evolution and reverse causality is also possible. For example, Grosjean (2011) finds that formal institutions may modify informal norms, but only after about 400 years of continuous exposure.

The methodology described here seems to provide insights into how such inter-temporal institutional scales link up with each other. This is likely to provide new important information regarding the performance and (potential) change of economic systems. Which performance indicators (e.g. income per capita or human development) depend on which 'hosts'? And are these hosts subject to fast or slow change? Which social attitudes and informal norms need to be addressed to make policies more effective? These are all questions that can be informed in a more holistic way by studying pathways and structures emerging from the network.

Another interesting aspect I have seen emerging when comparing different networks is that the dependency of formal or informal institutions is more attenuated in contexts that are usually regarded as more advanced in terms of institutional quality or socio-economic progress. Amendolagine and Jacobi (2022) find this when comparing the five Brazilian macro-regions, which range across rather diverse socio-economic development levels. Yet, also in European data such a trend can be observed.

Table 5.3 summarizes host–symbiont relationships so far identified in Germany and Italy. Data limitations determine the amount of informal institutional variables available – which we recall to capture socially accepted systems of rules that are enforced by society itself.

Table 5.3 Host–Symbiont relationships in Germany and Italy, structural factors grouped by category

		Germany		Italy	
		Frequency	*Percent*	*Frequency*	*Percent*
Symbiont (feeding on others)	economic	52	37.41	32	26.02
	informal institution	17	12.23	13	10.57
	formal institution	20	14.39	14	11.38
	demographic	15	10.79	21	17.07
	geographic	15	10.79	15	12.20
	political preference	20	14.39	28	22.76
	total	**139**	**100.00**	**123**	**100.00**
Host (nurturing others)	economic	48	34.53	39	31.71
	informal institution	10	7.19	15	12.20
	formal institution	27	19.42	16	13.01
	demographic	21	15.11	22	17.89
	geographic	15	10.79	27	21.95
	political preference	18	12.95	4	3.25
	total	**139**	**100.00**	**123**	**100.00**

Source: Elaboration by the author on LAUDEIT dataset, 2016. For variable typologies, see Table A1 in the Appendix.

In Table 5.3, three municipal variables proxy informal institutions, namely female political empowerment, voter turnout at European elections and the accident rate leading to injuries (cf. Table A1 in the Appendix). In Italy, these variables jointly engage in 13 asymmetric relations in which they are the symbiont and in 15 relations in which they act as host. In Germany, the same proxies for informal institutions engage in 17 asymmetric relations as symbionts and in 10 as hosts. Informal institutions are more often a host in Italy than in Germany.

An important question to address is whether the directionalities of the symbiotic relationships described imply causalities. In terms of econometric estimation, weighted directed networks estimated through two-way quantile regressions should not strictly be interpreted in causal terms. The bivariate relationships that are estimated at 10 points of the two variables' distributions may, in fact, be tainted by possible statistical noise. While the inclusion of control factors and the restriction to highly significant coefficients is possible, a delicate calibration is necessary. The inclusion of controls in the single bivariate estimations may alter the direct numerical relationship in a non-random fashion. As a network refers to an ontology in which all edges can be interpreted in the same way, I argue that bivariate estimations are preferable to multivariate estimations, despite potential noise.

Weighted directed networks based on two-way quantile regressions capture a numerical relation that can statistically be observed. Instead of strict causalities between single factors, they are likely to capture probabilities for underlying structures (Martins, 2006). The directionalities underpinning such structures could further be used – and tested – in the modelling of network dynamics.

5.5.2 *The relative exogeneity of cultural factors*

Another insight that can be derived from comparative correlation network analysis is that certain factors tend to locate at the margins of the network, whereas others tend to place themselves in its centre. The margins of the network have clearly inferior centrality values in all network statistics, as a marginal position is automatically attributed to those nodes through which fewer shortest paths pass.

In terms of the symbiotic framework proposed, host variables may assume more marginal positions if they do not themselves also engage in other roles as transmitters or symbionts. In more recent attempts, we tried to triangulate culture, informal and formal institutions, where culture is distinguished from informal institutions in as much as it is not strictly tied to regulating interactions but may refer to shared mental models that contribute to one's worldview. I observed that cultural factors tend to locate at more marginal positions in the network. As already mentioned, Williamson (2000) argued for them to be much slower in changing than, e.g. formal institutions. I suggest that a robustness test for deciding upon the boundary of the system could be to check whether the variables used for setting the boundary located at more central or more marginal positions. In particular, where factors are consistently located at marginal positions – they may be more easily used to set the boundaries of the system. For example, in our investigations of Brazilian municipal data, we found that the share of Catholics – which we use as a proxy for culture in line with Inglehart and Baker (2000) – always located at the margin of the network in all five macro-regions, confirming our hypothesis that some cultural factors could be momentarily exogeneized – or excluded from the network – to characterize the boundaries of the system under investigation (see Section 5.3).

5.5.3 Social capital tends to assume the role of the mediator

In recent attempts to unfold the nature and role of informal institutions (Jacobi and Amendolagine, 2021), we discovered that proxies of social capital behave differently with respect to culture and with respect to other informally enforced norms. Social capital can broadly be defined as 'consisting in some aspect of social structure, and in facilitating certain actions of actors within the structure' (Coleman, 1988, p. 98 in Sabatini, 2008, p. 469). Our proxies for social capital in Brazilian municipality data tend to position at the centre of the network (these are: likeliness of missing communication based on educational fractionalization by age and ethnic group, cf. Bossert et al., 2011 and incidence of social capital enhancing gatherings, e.g. community radios, associations and cultural centres). This makes them appear more similar to formal institutions than to informal institutions, at first glance – as informal institutions tend to position at more marginal positions in the network.[9]

Yet, social capital measures stand out, in particular, in terms of a specific clustering behaviour (Fagiolo, 2007), namely they are most often middleman in closed triplets than other factors. Such tendency would confirm the high relevance of social capital for institutional quality and for the performance of economic systems in as much as the middleman – position mediates indirect effects between other factors (Batinti et al., 2019; Sabatini, 2008). Social capital is likely to represent a potential bottleneck factor within an economic system because it serves as a 'facilitator' of institutional effects. We argue that the tendency to treat social capital as analogous to culture or to informal institutions may be misconceived (cf. Jacobi and Amendolagine, 2021). Our complexity patterns suggest that these factors assume a different role within a symbiotic network. We suggest further research in this field.

5.5.4 Listening to different levels

Complexity implies the interaction of different levels, yet the identification of adequate measures at adequate levels is drenched with potential problems. Level–application errors have been mostly analysed in terms of the dangers of disaggregation, famously ever since the recognition of the 'Ecological Fallacy' (Robinson, 1950; Hofstede 1984, 2001), which explains that where the statistical object is a group of people (ecological correlation), the results should not be used to infer about individual behaviour. The reason why aggregate features cannot naturally be applied to the individuals composing the group has to do with *within inequality*. Within our framework of analysis, the ecological fallacy issue can be translated to the problem of disaggregating structural data from the macro to the meso level. By shifting the focus of attention downwards to the municipality level, it is possible to allow for *within inequality* in institutional and economic performance. Disaggregation is already rather common in economic analysis, but less standard in investigations of institutions and their role for economic performance.

A less studied level–application error is 'Individual Difference Fallacy' (Richards et al., 1990), also known as 'Atomistic Fallacy' (Hox, 2002), whereby the aggregation of individual characteristics does not give a correct picture of group characteristics. This is similar to the inherent characteristic of a system – which is more than the sum of its parts. In our case, a measure computed at the municipality level may provide an inadequate picture of sub-groups co-existing within the municipalities.

A fundamental neglect that lies at the heart of the atomistic fallacy is the hypothesis of cross-level equivalence (also known as isomorphism) and the failure to recognize the variety of interactions that may exist between lower-level components and the aggregate measure they constitute. Isomorphism is the assumption that two phenomena are linked with a monotonic function, which implies that the meaning of a concept is identical at the inferior and the superior level. For example, tax collections at the municipality level may have to be interpreted differently if a certain share is forwarded to superior administrative levels. Or certain beliefs proxied at the municipality level may, e.g. be rather different among men and women or across different minorities.

The opposite of isomorphism is non-isomorphism: A famous example of non-isomorphism within the cross-cultural psychology literature is the notion of individualism–collectivism. While these two extremes of a continuum are adequate for characterizing a context, they are inadequate if applied to the individual, as an individual can be idiocentric or allocentric, but hardly collective when on his/her own.

So in choosing levels and measures, great care has to be given to the specific meaning that can be attributed to a specific variable. Also, choosing a specific level for the computation of the network – as, e.g. the municipality – may mean that some measures will be more reliable than others. For example, demographic and social factors may be more accurate when measured at the disaggregated level, whereas parts of the economic system may not properly be captured because they are too interdependent with other municipalities in forming a higher-level entity (e.g. in Italy, the 'sistema locale di lavoro'[10]).

In the future, computational advances are likely to make multi-level networks more interpretable, partially overcoming this delicate calibration of the analysis. The more we include good measures – captured at the correct level, the more we are likely to find new insights. Important is also the inclusion of less studied factors, as they may provide insights on unknown paths and mechanisms. Complexity-embedded results can always be used as a starting point for more in-depth analyses relying on other techniques.

5.6 Concluding remarks

Studying economic systems from the perspective presented here has a series of research implications. As suggested, we may focus on specific typologies of social structures, such as informal versus formal institutions. This distinction can help us identify more sticky parts of the system that are likely to take more time to change. Where a cluster of informal institutions jointly serves as a host for some formal institutions, it may be difficult to alter the formal institutions without jointly targeting (much slower changing) informal elements. Informal institutions – and the constellations they form – in this sense represent some sort of 'attractors' (McKelvey, 1997) in the system, which may lead to resilient behaviour. Yet, comparisons across systems show that formal institutions can mimic the systemic properties of informal institutions – with time and consolidated inclusive political processes (Boranbay and Guerriero, 2019). Multi-level governance therefore should not be seeking to govern diverse systems with the same policies, but should invest in properly fuelling the systems by facilitating information and promoting inclusive participation. Systemic differences then – rooted in slow-changing informal and cultural factors – are likely to continuously shape the patterns that formal institutions – and their interdependencies assume. In this sense, it is of utmost policy relevance to understanding when formal institutions affect cultural factors (Grosjean, 2011; Rosta, in this volume) as prolonged pressure on informal norms and culture may ultimately lead to systemic change.

Appendix

Table A1 List of variables

Variable name	Description	Typology/categorization	Present in figures	Country
artgroups	nr. of artgroups (pcap)	informal	4; 5; 6	BR
candidates	nr of candidates that stood for municipal elections (pcap)	informal	4; 5; 6	BR
commutingattraction	inflow/(inflow+outflow+residents)*100	demographic (control)	1; 2; 7	GER, IT
dependencyrate	((0–14)+(65+))/(15–64)	demographic (control)	1; 2; 7	GER, IT
econformal	indirect taxes/factor GDP	informal	4; 5; 6	BR
employment	% employed on pop 20–64	economic	1; 2; 7	GER, IT
entrepreneurshiprate	nr of firms per 1000 inh.	economic	1; 2; 7	GER, IT
extendfam	living with parents or relatives/total nr of families	informal	4; 5; 6	BR
EUchristdemvotes	% voted for European People's Party member	informal	1; 2; 7	GER, IT
EUpopulistvotes	% voted for Identity and Democracy Group member	informal	1; 2; 7	GER, IT
EUsocialistvotes	% voted for Alliance of Socialists Democrats member	informal	1; 2; 7	GER, IT
EUsmallpartiesvotes	% voted for small parties	informal	1; 2; 7	GER, IT
EUvoterturnout	% of eligible voters who voted at 2014 EU elections	informal	1; 2; 7	GER, IT
femlbmktpart	female labour market participation	informal	4; 5; 6	BR
femsharepol	share of women on elected politicians	informal	4; 5; 6	BR
femwagegap	ratio fem/male average wage	informal	4; 5; 6	BR
firmsize	average size of firm (manufacture)	economic	1; 2; 7	GER, IT
gini	gini index	economic	4; 5; 6	BR
healthspend	p. cap spending on health	formal	4; 5; 6	BR
incomepcap	in 1000s of euros	economic	1; 2; 7	GER, IT
incometaxrate	incometax total/aggregate mun income	formal	1; 2; 7	GER, IT
industr	share of industry in municipal GDP	economic	4; 5; 6	BR
instpermea	nr municipal collaborations across themes	control	4; 5; 6	BR
internalmigration-attraction	(immigrated/(immigrated+emigrated+residents))×100	geographic (control)	1; 2; 7	GER, IT
iurdefense	nr of services provided for juridical defense	formal	4; 5; 6	BR
latitude	north-south position	geographic (control)	1; 2; 7	GER, IT
lengthofstay	average length of stay of tourists	economic (tourism)	1; 2; 7	GER, IT
mayoryouth	inverse of the age of the mayor	informal	4; 5; 6	BR

(Continued)

Table A1 List of variables (*Continued*)

Variable name	Description	Typology/categorization	Present in figures	Country
miss_comm	compounded gaps in illiteracy shares across ethnic-age groups	informal	4; 5; 6	BR
municipality area	area of municipality in ha	geographic (control)	1; 2; 7	GER, IT
nrbeds	nr of beds in accommodation structures per 1000 inh	economic (tourism)	1; 2; 7	GER, IT
nrtouristarrivals	nr of tourist arrivals per 1000 inh	economic (tourism)	1; 2; 7	GER, IT
Occupancyrate	(nrnights/(nrbeds $\times$ 365)) $\times$ 100	economic (tourism)	1; 2; 7	GER, IT
Participforce	average effectiveness of participatory councils	formal	4; 5; 6	BR
Participnr	nr of thematic participatory councils	formal	4; 5; 6	BR
Popdensity	nr. residents/ha	demographic (control)	1; 2; 4; 5; 6; 7	BR, GER, IT
Propertytax	property tax per inhabitant	formal	1; 2; 7	GER, IT
Pubemp	nr. of public employees on tot. workforce	economic	4; 5; 6	BR
Pubincdiv	diversification index of municipality revenue sources	formal	4; 5; 6	BR
Publicgood	share of municipality spending for public goods	formal	4; 5; 6	BR
roadaccidentrate	nr of road accidents with injuries per 1000 inh.	informal	1; 2; 7	GER, IT
Shareofelderly	pop + 65 years/total pop	demographic (control)	1; 2; 7	GER, IT
Taxesshare	share of taxes in total municipal income	formal	4; 5; 6	BR
Taxesnr	nr of taxes collected at the local level	formal	4; 5; 6	BR
Taxingcapacity	total amount of taxes collected (per inh.)	formal	1; 2; 7	GER, IT
Transport	density of transportation services available	geographic (control)	4; 5; 6	BR

Source: Elaboration by the author.

Notes

1 WINIR is the *World Interdisciplinary Network for Institutional Research*.
2 For an extension on this point, see von Jacobi and Amendolagine (2021).
3 Grimm et al. (2005) refer to an optimal degree of complexity, the "Medawar zone", which includes important patterns but does not make interpretation impossible.
4 The LAUDEIT dataset comprises 11092 German municipalities and 7998 Italian municipalities. For more detailed information on comparable German and Italian municipal data, see Jacobi (2021).
5 Empirical results presented on Brazil are computed on 5565 Brazilian municipalities, else said the universe of the Brazilian municipal landscape. The South-East macro-region comprises 1668 municipalities.
6 If any of q20 or q80 were statistically insignificant, we use the min and max among at least three statistically significant estimated coefficients to estimate the trend.
7 The North-East comprises 1794 municipalities.
8 Such measure is derived from municipal budgets, where it is possible to re-construct all in- and out-flows of resources towards other municipalities, the state or the federal union. Flows are grounds for collaboration as a minimum of exchange and communication is necessary to maintain such exchange of resources.
9 Such tendency depends on the specific measure, however. I noticed that measures that tend to capture more sticky informal norms, such as female empowerment, are more marginal than social attitudes that may be more volatile – e.g. political preferences can change much more quickly than rooted views on gender roles.
10 The Local Labour System is a level of analysis that is located at higher level than the municipality (LAU) and at lower level than the province (NUTS3). Unfortunately, it is not automatically comparable to other similar levels in other European contexts.

References

Acemoglu, D. and Jackson, M.O. (2017). Social norms and the enforcement of laws. *Journal of the European Economic Association*, 15(2), pp. 245–295.

Alatas, V., Banerjee, A. G., Chandrasekhar, R., Hanna, R. and Olken, B.A. (2012). Network structure and the aggregation of information: Theory and evidence from Indonesia. Technical report, National Bureau of Economic Research.

Alesina, A. and La Ferrara, E. (2005). Ethnic diversity and economic performance. *Journal of Economic Literature*, 43(3), pp. 762–800.

Alesina, A. and Giuliano, P. (2015). Culture and institutions. *Journal of Economic Literature*, 53(4), pp. 898–944.

Amable, B. (2000). Institutional complementarity and diversity of social systems of innovation and production. *Review of International Political Economy*, 7(4), pp. 645–687.

Amable, B. (2016). Institutional complementarities in the dynamic comparative analysis of capitalism. *Journal of Institutional Economics*, 12(1), pp. 79–103.

Amendolagine, V. and Jacobi, N. von. (2022). Symbiotic relationships among formal and informal institutions: Comparing five Brazilian cultural ecosystems, mimeo.

Ansell, C. (2006). *Network Institutionalism*. Oxford: Oxford University Press, Chapter 5.

Aoki, M. (2001). *Toward a Comparative Institutional Analysis*. MIT Press.

Arrow, H., McGrath, J.E. and Berdahl, J.L. (2000). *Small Groups as Complex Systems: Formation, Coordination, Development, and Adaptation*. Thousand Oaks, CA: Sage Publications.

Avritzer, L. (2009). *Participatory Institutions in Democratic Brazil*. Woodrow Wilson Center Press.

Barder, O. (2012). Development and complexity. *Presentation and podcast made at CGD*. http://www.cgdev.org/doc/CGDPresentations/complexity/player.html

Bassanini, A. and Duval, R. (2009). Unemployment, institutions, and reform complementarities: Re-assessing the aggregate evidence for OECD countries. *Oxford Review of Economic Policy*, 25(1), pp. 40–59.

Basu, K. (2018). Chapter three. The focal point approach to law and economics, *The Republic of Beliefs: A New Approach to Law and Economics*. Princeton, NJ: Princeton University Press, pp. 38–69. https://doi.org/10.1515/9781400889358-004

Batinti, A., Andriani, L. and Filippetti, A. (2019). Local government fiscal policy, social capital and electoral payoff: Evidence across Italian municipalities. *Kyklos*, *72*(4), pp. 503–526.

Battistini, A. and Pagano, U. (2008). Primates' fertilization systems and the evolution of the human brain. *Journal of Bioeconomics*, *10*(1), pp. 1–21.

Beckert, J. (2010). How do fields change? The interrelations of institutions, networks, and cognition in the dynamics of markets. *Organization Studies*, *31*(5), pp. 605–627.

Beinhocker, E.D. (2007). *The Origin of Wealth: The Radical Remaking of Economics and What it Means for Business and Society*. Harvard Business Press.

Belloc, M. and Bowles, S. (2013). The persistence of inferior cultural-institutional conventions. *American Economic Review*, *103*(3), pp. 93–98.

Bikhchandani, S., Hirshleifer, D. and Welch, I. (1992). A theory of fads, fashion, custom, and cultural change as informational cascades. *Journal of Political Economy*, *100*(5), pp. 992–1026.

Bisin, A. and Verdier, T. (2017). On the joint evolution of culture and institutions, Working Paper No. w23375, National Bureau of Economic Research, Cambridge, MA.

Bonacich, P. (2007). Some unique properties of eigenvector centrality. *Social Networks*, *29*(4), pp. 555–564.

Boranbay, S. and Guerriero, C. (2019). Endogenous (in)formal institutions. *Journal of Comparative Economics*, *47*(4), pp. 921–945.

Bossert, W., d'Ambrosio, C. and La Ferrara, E. (2011). A generalized index of fractionalization. *Economica*, *78*(312), pp. 723–750.

Bowles, S., Choi, J.K. and Hopfensitz, A. (2003). The co-evolution of individual behaviors and social institutions. *Journal of Theoretical Biology*, *223*(2), pp. 135–147.

Boyer, P. and Petersen, M.B. (2012). The naturalness of (many) social institutions: Evolved cognition as their foundation. *Journal of Institutional Economics*, *8*(1), pp. 1–25.

Boyer, P. and Petersen, M.B. (2013). Studying institutions in the context of natural selection: Limits or opportunities? *Journal of Institutional Economics*, *9*(2), pp. 187–198.

Boyer, R. (2004). New growth regimes, but still institutional diversity. *Socio-Economic Review*, *2*(1), pp. 1–32.

Cain, M.L., Bowman, W.D. and Hacker, S.D. (2011). *Ecology*. Sunderland: Sinauer Associates.

Cilliers, P. (2001). Boundaries, hierarchies and networks in complex systems. *International Journal of Innovation Management*, *5*(02), pp. 135–147.

Clemente, G.P. and Grassi, R. (2018). Directed clustering in weighted networks: A new perspective. *Chaos, Solitons & Fractals*, *107*, pp. 26–38.

Cranmer, S.J., Desmarais, B.A. and Menninga, E.J. (2012). Complex dependencies in the alliance network. *Conflict Management and Peace Science*, *29*(3), pp. 279–313.

Dacin, T., Goodstein, M. and Richard Scott, J.W. (2002). Institutional theory and institutional change: Introduction to the special research forum. *Academy of Management Journal*, *45*(1), pp. 45–56.

De Bary, A. (1879). *Die Erscheinung der Symbiose*. Strasburg: Verlag von Karl J. Tru übner.

Dolphin, T. and Nash, D. (eds.) (2012). *Complex New World: Translating New Economic Thinking into Public Policy*. London: IPPR – Institute for Public Policy Research.

Duit, A. and Galaz, V. (2008). Governance and complexity – Emerging issues for governance theory. *Governance*, *21*(3), pp. 312–335.

Fagiolo, G. (2007). Clustering in complex directed networks. *Physical Review E*, *76*(2), p. 026107.

Freeman, L.C. (1977). A set of measures of centrality based on betweenness. *Sociometry*, *40*(1), pp. 35–41.

Galletta, S. (2021). Form of government and voters' preferences for public spending. *Journal of Economic Behavior & Organization*, *186*, pp. 548–561.

Gneezy, U., Leibbrandt, A. and List, J.A. (2016). Ode to the sea: Workplace organizations and norms of cooperation. *Economic Journal*, *126*(595), pp. 1856–1883.

Green Jr, H.D. and Wasserman, S. (2013). Network analysis: A definitional guide to important concepts, in T.D. Little (ed.) *The Oxford Handbook of Quantitative Methods in Psychology, Vol. 1*. New York, NY: Oxford University Press.

Grimm, V., Revilla, E., Berger, U., Jeltsch, F., Mooij, W.M., Railsback, S.F., Thulke, H.H., Weiner, J., Wiegand, T. and DeAngelis, D.L. (2005). Pattern-oriented modeling of agent-based complex systems: Lessons from ecology. *Science*, *310*(5750), pp. 987–991.

Grosjean, P. (2011). The weight of history on European cultural integration: A gravity approach. *American Economic Review*, *101*(3), pp. 504–508.

Grund, T. (2015, September). Social network analysis using Stata. In *Proceedings of the United Kingdom Stata Users' Group Meeting*, Stata Users Group.

Guiso, L., Sapienza, P. and Zingales, L. (2006). Does culture affect economic outcomes? *Journal of Economic Perspectives, 20*(2), pp. 23–48.

Guiso, L., Sapienza, P. and Zingales, L. (2008). Social capital as good culture. *Journal of the European Economic Association, 6*(2–3), pp. 295–320.

Gutmann, J. and Voigt, S. (2020). Traditional law in times of the nation state: Why is it so prevalent? *Journal of Institutional Economics, 16*(4), pp. 445–461.

Hall, P.A. and Soskice, D. (2001). An introduction to varieties of capitalism, *Varieties of Capitalism: The Institutional Foundations of Comparative Advantage.* Oxford: OUP, pp. 21–27.

Harford, T. (2011). *Adapt: Why Success Always Starts with Failure.* Farrar: Straus and Giroux.

Hodgson, G.M. (2001). *How Economics Forgot History: The Problem of Historical Specificity in Social Science.* London: Routledge.

Hodgson, G.M. (2004). *The Evolution of Institutional Economics.* Oxfordshire: Routledge.

Hodgson, G.M. (2006). What are institutions? *Journal of Economic Issues, 40*(1), pp. 1–25.

Hodgson, G.M. and Knudsen, T. (2010). *Darwin's Conjecture: The Search for General Principles of Social and Economic Evolution.* Chicago, IL: University of Chicago Press.

Hodgson, G.M. and Stoelhorst, J.W. (2014). Introduction to the special issue on the future of institutional and evolutionary economics. *Journal of Institutional Economics, 10*(4), pp. 513–540.

Hofstede, G. (1984). *Culture's Consequences: International Differences in Work-related Values* (Vol. 5). Newbury Park, CA: Sage Publications.

Hofstede, G. (2001). *Culture's Consequences: Comparing Values, Behaviors, Institutions and Organizations across Nations.* Thousand Oaks, CA: Sage Publications.

Holling, C.S., Gunderson, L. and Light, S. (1995). *Barriers and Bridges to the Renewal of Ecosystems, volume 10.* Columbia University Press.

Höpner, M. (2005). Epilogue to 'Explaining institutional complementarity': What have we learnt? Complementarity, coherence and institutional change. *Socio-Economic Review, 3*(2), pp. 383–387.

Horvath, S. (2011). *Weighted Network Analysis: Applications in Genomics and Systems Biology.* New York, NY: Springer Science & Business Media.

Hox, J.J. (2002). *Multilevel Analysis: Techniques and Applications.* Taylor & Francis.

Imbens, G.W. (2020). Potential outcome and directed acyclic graph approaches to causality: Relevance for empirical practice in economics. *Journal of Economic Literature, 58*(4), pp. 1129–1179.

Inglehart, R. and Baker, W.E. (2000). Modernization, cultural change, and the persistence of traditional values. *American Sociological Review, 65*(1), pp. 19–51.

Jacobi, N.V. (2018). Institutional interconnections: Understanding symbiotic relationships. *Journal of Institutional Economics, 14*(5), pp. 853–876.

Jacobi, N.V. (2021). Comparing institutional textures between Germany and Italy with LAU level data, DEM Working Paper No. 2021/15, Department of Economics and Management, University of Trento, Trento.

Jacobi, N.V. and Amendolagine, V. (2021). What feeds on what? Networks of interdependencies between culture and institutions, DEM Working Paper No. 2021/13, Department of Economics and Management, University of Trento, Trento.

Joyez, C. (2017). NW_WCC: Stata module to calculate Weighted Clustering Coefficients (WCC) in Complex Direct Networks.

Kingston, C. and Caballero, G. (2009). Comparing theories of institutional change. *Journal of Institutional Economics, 5*(2), pp. 151–180.

Kuran, T. (2009). Explaining the economic trajectories of civilizations: The systemic approach. *Journal of Economic Behavior & Organization, 71*(3), pp. 593–605.

Langlois, R.N. (2016). Institutions for getting out of the way. *Journal of Institutional Economics, 12*(1), pp. 53–61.

March, J.G. and Olsen, J.P. (2004). The logic of appropriateness, in R.E. Goodin (ed.) *The Oxford Handbook of Political Science.* Oxford: Oxford University Press.

Margulis, L. (1984). *Early Life.* Boston: Jones and Bartlett Publishers.

Marinari, E. and Parisi, G. (2000). Effects of changing the boundary conditions on the ground state of Ising spin glasses. *Physical Review B, 62*(17), p. 11677.

Martins, N. (2006). Capabilities as causal powers. *Cambridge Journal of Economics, 30*(5), pp. 671–685.

Maseland, R. (2013). Parasitical cultures? The cultural origins of institutions and development. *Journal of Economic Growth, 18*(2), pp. 109–136.

McKelvey, B. (1997). Perspective—Quasi-natural organization science. *Organization Science*, 8(4), pp. 351–380.

Michalopoulos, S. and Papaioannou, E. (2013). Pre-colonial ethnic institutions and contemporary African development. *Econometrica*, 81(1), pp. 113–152.

Milgrom, P. and Roberts, J. (1990). Rationalizability, learning, and equilibrium in games with strategic complementarities. *Econometrica: Journal of the Econometric Society*, 58(6), pp. 1255–1277.

Naritomi, J., Soares, R.R. and Assunção, J.J. (2012). Institutional development and colonial heritage within Brazil. *Journal of Economic History*, 72(2), pp. 393–422.

North, D. (1990). *Institutions, Economic Performance and Institutional Change*. Cambridge: Cambridge University Press.

North, D., Wallis, J.J. and Weingast, B. (2006). A conceptual framework for interpreting recorded human history. NBER Working Paper Series, wp12795.

Odum, E.P. and Barrett, G.W. (1971). *Fundamentals of Ecology*. (Vol. 3, p. 5). Philadelphia, PA: Saunders.

Onnela, J.P., Saramäki, J., Kertész, J. and Kaski, K. (2005). Intensity and coherence of motifs in weighted complex networks. *Physical Review E*, 71(6), p. 065103.

Opsahl, T., Agneessens, F. and Skvoretz, J. (2010). Node centrality in weighted networks: Generalizing degree and shortest paths. *Social Networks*, 32(3), 245–251.

Overstreet, R.M. and Lotz, J.M. (2016). Host–symbiont relationships: Understanding the change from guest to pest, in *The Rasputin Effect: When Commensals and Symbionts Become Parasitic* (pp. 27–64). Cham: Springer.

Pagano, U. and Rossi, M.A. (2004). Incomplete contracts, intellectual property and institutional complementarities. *European Journal of Law and Economics*, 18(1), pp. 55–76.

Pagano, U. and Rowthorn, R. (1994). Ownership, technology and institutional stability. *Structural Change and Economic Dynamics*, 5(2), pp. 221–242.

Pagano, U. and Vatiero, M. (2015). Costly institutions as substitutes: Novelty and limits of the Coasian approach. *Journal of Institutional Economics*, 11(2), pp. 265–281.

Pande, R. and Udry, C. (2006). Institutions and development: a view from below, Economic Growth Center Discussion Paper 928, Yale University, New Haven, CT.

Pitlik, H. and Rode, M. (2017). Individualistic values, institutional trust, and interventionist attitudes. *Journal of Institutional Economics*, 13(3), pp. 575–598.

Pryor, F.L. (2008). System as a causal force. *Journal of Economic Behavior and Organization*, 67, pp. 545–559.

Ramalingam, B. (2013). *Aid on the Edge of Chaos: Rethinking International Cooperation in a Complex World*. Oxford: Oxford University Press.

Ray, D. (2007). Development economics, in L. Blume and S. Durlauf (eds.), *New Palgrave Dictionary of Economics*. London: Palgrave Macmillan.

Richards, J.M., Gottfredson, D.C. and Gottfredson, G.D. (1990). Units of analysis and item statistics for environmental assessment scales. *Current Psychology*, 9(4), pp. 407–413.

Richardson, K.A. and Lissack, M.R. (2001). On the status of boundaries, both natural and organizational: A complex systems perspective. *Emergence*, 3(4), pp. 32–49. DOI: 10.1207/S15327000EM0304_3

Robinson, W.S. (1950). Ecological correlations and the behavior of individuals. *American Sociological Review*, 15, pp. 351–357.

Sabatini, F. (2008). Social capital and the quality of economic development. *Kyklos*, 61(3), pp. 466–499.

Sindzingre, A. (2006). The relevance of the concepts of formality and informality: A theoretical appraisal, in B. Guha-Khasnobis, R. Kanbur and E. Ostrom (eds.), *Linking the Formal and Informal Economy: Concepts and Policies*. Oxford: Oxford University Press.

Sindzingre, A.N. (2014). *Institutions as a Composite Concept: Explaining their Indeterminate Relationships with Paths of Development* (No. hal-01668349).

Streeck, W. and Thelen, K.A. (eds.) (2005). *Beyond Continuity: Institutional Change in Advanced Political Economies*. Oxford: Oxford University Press.

Tabellini, G. (2008). Institutions and culture. *Journal of the European Economic Association*, 6(2–3), pp. 255–294.

Tabellini, G. (2010). Culture and institutions: Economic development in the regions of Europe. *Journal of the European Economic Association*, 8(4), pp. 677–716.

Thévenon, O. (2016). Do 'Institutional complementarities' foster female labour force participation? *Journal of Institutional Economics*, 12(2), pp. 471–497.

Tomera, A.N. (1979). *Understanding Basic Ecological Concepts*. Portland, ME: J. Weston Walch Publishing.

Topkis, D.M. (1978). Minimizing a submodular function on a lattice. *Operations Research*, 26(2), pp. 305–321.

Topkis, D.M. (2011). *Supermodularity and Complementarity*. Princeton, NJ: Princeton University Press.

Voigt, S. (2013). How (not) to measure institutions. *Journal of Institutional Economics*, *9*(1), pp. 1–26.

Voigt, S. (2018). How to measure informal institutions. *Journal of Institutional Economics*, *14*(1), pp. 1–22.

Wasserman, S. and Faust, K. (1994). *Social Network Analysis: Methods and Applications*. Cambridge: Cambridge University Press.

Watkins, J.P. (1998). Towards a reconsideration of social evolution: Symbiosis and its implications for economics. *Journal of Economic Issues*, *32*(1), pp. 87–106.

Williamson, C.R. (2009). Informal institutions rule: Institutional arrangements and economic performance. *Public Choice*, *139*(3), pp. 371–387.

Williamson, O.E. (2000). The new institutional economics: Taking stock, looking ahead. *Journal of Economic Literature*, *38*(3), pp. 595–613.

Witt, U. (2014). The future of evolutionary economics: Why the modalities of explanation matter. *Journal of Institutional Economics*, *10*(4), pp. 645–664.

6

COMPARATIVE ECONOMIC SYSTEMS AND THE ISSUE OF RESILIENCE

Overview of the Classical Literature and Basic Problems of Conceptualization

Paul Dragos Aligica

UNIVERSITY OF BUCHAREST, BUCUREȘTI, ROMANIA
GEORGE MASON UNIVERSITY, FAIRFAX, VA, USA

Virgil Iordache

UNIVERSITY OF BUCHAREST, BUCUREȘTI, ROMANIA

6.1 Introduction

Resilience, broadly defined as "the persistence of a system and its ability to observe change and disturbance and still maintain the same relationships between state variables" (Holling, 1973, 14) due to "the capacity to absorb a disturbance and reorganize (…) while retaining the same function, structure, identity and feedback" (Walker et al., 2004), has had, traditionally, a rather ambiguous and neglected position in the classical Comparative Economic System (CES) literature. This lack of interest is puzzling. After all, as Colander and Kupers (2014, 199) note: "one of the obvious goals of any system is survival. If a system doesn't survive it has little chance of meeting its other goals". What is amazing, they explain, "is that the standard [economics and policy] models do not address survival of the system, or even deal with it. In the standard frame, researchers don't ask what might lead the system to breakdown. Nor do they ask how it can be adjusted to make it less likely to breakdown". Revisiting the CES literature with a view to trace the problem of resilience, broadly defined, confirms Colander and Kupers' assessment: It was only relatively recently that resilience as a systemic feature has hesitatingly become a topic of interest for comparativists.

One of the best ways to place and conceptualize the problem of resilience in the context of CES as a field is to use as a starting point the content of the CES textbooks. The textbooks have always set forth and discussed – sometimes explicitly, at other times implicitly – systemic performance features and criteria. Resilience is one of them. The basic analytic structure, when it comes to examining the performance of an economy – including in terms of resilience –

DOI: 10.4324/9781003144366-8

is that the economy is considered to have as an objective the achievement of a maximal/optimal value of a specific outcome related to performance criteria or norms, subject to constraints coming from various factors. The performance criteria or norms vary – plenty, growth, efficiency, equity, justice, equality, freedom, etc. and, in a sense, dealing with the problem of resilience means to simply add explicitly one more criterion to the list.

The literature (Montias, 1976; Ben-Ner, Montias, and Neuberger, 2013) usually organizes the constrained factors under three categories: (i) The economic system which defines the structure of the economy (Es), (ii) policies that are operationalized within the economic system (Ep) and (iii) environmental factors (Ev), broadly defined, which means that they include technology, resource constraints and, in some cases, geopolitical factors. The objective is to maximize outcomes (O) subject to the three classes of factors. This framework is a generic instrument for the orderly identification of each category of factors and the analysis of their relationship. For instance, when analyzing socialism, we need to disentangle the systemic features from the impact of the environment in which the system is operating. In a similar way, we need to know in what measure an outcome is the result of a policy taken in the system or of the system itself. There is an agreement among the scholars of comparative economics that the ultimate objective of their analysis is "to isolate and measure the impact of the economic system, more precisely the system's rules, customs and regular procedures on basic economic outcomes such as the level and growth of per capita income, the distribution of incomes, stability and national power" (Ben-Ner, Montias, and Neuberger, 2013, 2).

The application of this framework is therefore straightforward: In order to compare systems, we need to pinpoint performance criteria and then operationally deal with each of them in focalized evaluation endeavors. The standard textbook notes at this point a number of ontological-epistemic issues and a number of methodological ones. On the ontological-epistemic side are (a) the plurality of outcomes and norms or criteria that may be applied to assess the outcomes, (b) the existence of trade-offs and tensions between the criteria and (c) the problem of subjectivity and relativism of criteria and norms. Then, three methodological problems derived from those foundational ones are usually introduced. The first is the relativism and contextuality of selecting the performance criteria, as well as that of evaluating them in specific circumstances. The second is the problem of aggregation and its corollary that of assigning weights for aggregation, including the issue whether it is possible or not to create a single index of achievement which could help us to compare systems. Last but not least is the classical technical distinction between the approach based on the ideal model (socialism, capitalism) and the approach based on the reality of a concrete case (USA, USSR) and the injunction that it is important to compare a model with model or case with case. For our purposes, it is important to note that, in the context of our discussion, our focus has to be on only one criterion and not on the overall problem of aggregation of criteria. In our case, the outcome and the criteria of performance related to it is "resilience", broadly defined. However, many of the problems noted remain a challenge in the construction of our specific approach to the definition and assessment of resilience. Our paper will address some of these foundational and methodological themes in its third section.

In the first section, our goal is to see how the resilience criterion has been dealt with in comparative economics literature. The second part will briefly revisit how resilience is conceptualized in other fields and disciplines that may offer a model or benchmark. Analyzing and assessing systemic resilience means an engagement with a phenomenon only rarely and partially evident to the naked eye, for a direct empirical observation. Therefore, the conceptual apparatus – both analytical and normative – brought to the table is in fact decisive in assessing the state of a system's resilience. The third part will overview the most important foundational parameters of thinking about resilience with a view to economic systems.

The paper concludes by synthesizing the basic insights of the overview and by assessing the potential of exploring and mapping the problem of resilience in CES.

6.2 Part 1: Resilience themes in the classical CES literature

Our investigation takes as its starting point what we consider to be a representative sample of the main CES textbooks produced in the second half of the 20th century. The first step in our investigation is to simply go over these textbooks and identify where and how the problem of resilience has been addressed.

6.2.1 The evolution of CES textbooks on performance criteria

Let us start with the very beginnings of the field and with a pioneer of the Western CES literature, whose first edition was published in 1939 and went through nine editions to 1973: W. N. Loucks' *Comparative Economic Systems*. One of the striking features of the volume is the lack of an explicit discussion of the range of criteria to be used in the comparative analysis of economic systems. Consequently, issues related to resilience are not figured out in the text. In this respect, as we will see, the textbook reflects well the dominant views in the field during that period. G. N. Halm's volume *Economic Systems* (1960) was another influential text during the beginning. The book confirms the lack of interest of the authors of the time in an explicit and systematic analysis of the assessment criteria and performance standards. R. H. Blodgett *Comparative Economic Systems* (1944 [1948]), another early textbook, reveals a similar treatment of the performance criteria: Scattered in the text and dealt with mostly in an implicit and indirect manner. The contributions regarding resilience-related themes are mostly indirect and tangent, in most cases addressing just business cycle and macro stability-related issues. Although not presented as a CES textbook, the book edited by Hayek et al., *Collectivist Economic Planning* (1935), was widely used in the 1940s and the 1950s in teaching and research. An overview of the volume which includes texts by F. A. Hayek, N. G. Pierson, L. von Mises, G. Halm and E. Barone reveals that the issue of resilience, under our broad definition, has not been addressed explicitly. However, if we decide that we want to consider the economic calculation debate, a controversy about the feasibility and viability of socialism, as a discussion relevant to the theme of resilience, then the book may be seen as a pioneering contribution in this respect.

An explicit focus on the problem of the criteria of performance and on the complexities and the trade-offs related to that emerged only in the 1960s. In this respect, Gregory Grossman's *Economic Systems* (1974) is a significant contribution and deserves special attention. After the usual caveats regarding the problem of subjectivity in selecting criteria, Grossman notes the fact that "only the dogmatic will insist on applying a single yardstick to measure the performance of all economic systems" (Grossman, 1974, 5–6). He then surveys the criteria he considers to be relevant. He starts with plenty, how much systems produce goods and services (overall and per person), followed by growth which is left a bit sketchy and presented in relationship with development and poverty. Then efficiency is presented in its three forms technical efficiency, static economic efficiency and dynamic efficiency. Finally, he introduces equity, justice and equality, as well as economic freedom under various guises (consumer choice, freedom of choice over jobs, etc.).

In this context, Grossman (1974) addresses what we may consider issues associated with resilience, broadly defined. He dedicates a section to "stability" which he defines as a function of two kinds of closely interrelated phenomena: business cycles and persistent and significant upward or downward movement of prices in general – inflation and deflation. At the same time, he introduces the issue of "security" and it is very important to quote him at this point because he was one of the few who addressed explicitly the issue at that time: "In the more developed countries of today, the individual households economic security is no longer at the mercy of a fickle nature, as it had been until recently". However, "modern man has gained this security at the price of an immeasurably greater dependence on the rest of the society. His insecurity now stems primarily from the unpredictability of social phenomena". Fortunately, in modern societies, he adds, individuals are not "entirely without social protection against unexpected adversity" (Grossman, 1974, 5–6). Grossman goes on to note that "a major type of individual economic insecurity derives from economic instability". But "even in the absence of a depression or inflation and often for no fault of his own, a person may lose his job property or earning power". At that point, one can see how Grossman's take, although promising because of its potential for a broader approach to the issues of resilience, returns to a strict economic, social security, and welfare state interpretation of the problem. In other words, the "security" issue had the potential to open up an approach that goes beyond strict economic security or military security. Yet, it was not pursued in the direction of structural resilience (stability, adaptability). Instead, the focus shifted again to job and income security and the welfare state structures aiming at that.

Grossman's concern with the issue of security is even more notable when seen in conjunction with his rather unique interest in extra-economic criteria in ways which go beyond the standard discussions in other textbooks. Grossman (1974, 11) notes that one does not judge alternative economic systems only by their material aspects. These systems need to satisfy criteria related to ethical, religious and political beliefs. Material success may be looked with suspicion as distorting human values or standing in the way of an idea or good society. In brief, one could detect in Grossman's perspective the elements of an approach able to go beyond the standard economic criteria, and to explore the social forms of organization instrumental in satisfying criteria that are non-economic. One could see here the potential of developing an approach in which the notions of resilience and adaptability might become very relevant. At the same time, Gregory Grossman's perspective, despite its merits, is not following through the potential breakthrough areas implicit in the way he structured his approach to the performance and outcome criteria.

Typical for the mainstream position on systemic features and criteria for the next 20 years was *Comparative Economic Systems* (1974), edited by M. Bornstein. Probably the most influential reader in the field (it went through six editions), it dedicated a methodical treatment of the problem of performance criteria under the label "objectives and instruments of economic policy". The chapter dedicated to the issue identified the following "aims": material welfare, equity, reduction of social tensions, promotion of human values, ethics and religion, protection of persons and properties, external security, political power, international solidarity and personal aims. Under the label of "objectives" were listed: full employment, price stability, improvement in the balance of payments, expansion of production, improvement in the allocation of the factors of production, satisfaction of collective needs – defense, general administration, international affairs, education, public health –, improvement in the distribution of income and wealth, protection and priorities of particular regions and industries, security of supply, improvement in the size or structure of the population, a reduction in working hours. As one can note, it was a large list but one could hardly identify an explicit concern for issues related to resilience. That should not be a surprise as this fact may be connected to the mainstream conception of the economic system. The system is only the aggregation of individual decisions and it is conceptualized most of the time in equilibrium by assumption. Even if the system is subjected to exogenous shocks, it is assumed that it automatically tends to return to an equilibrium position. For such a conception of the economic system, resilience makes no sense and the theories related to endogenous business cycle remain of only marginal concern, if at all.

Three other books written by influential authors in the field illustrate a similar concern for a variety of objectives (aims, criteria, norms) while at the same time are not giving much attention to the problem of stability and resilience. That happened despite the fact that in all three cases the authors were engaging with great care and sophistication in the normative analysis dimension of CES.

J. Berliner (1999) discusses the issue of values at the beginning of his book and then revisits it extensively, by taking the standard performance criteria one by one, in the last chapter. Yet, he is not addressing the problem of resilience other than in the well-known by now a form of the concern with the stability of prices and the business cycle. A relatively similar approach may be identified in John M. Montias' *The Structure of Economic Systems* (1976), a book that is rather ambitious in its technical approach in the attempt to introduce a very precise terminology. Yet, the focus is mostly methodological and not substantive. Again, the issue of resilience is lost in between the lines. Finally, Frederick Pryor's a *Guidebook to the Comparative Study of Economic Systems* (1985), while taking a similar approach to, makes nonetheless an effort to discuss, in the chapter dedicated to economic stability, what he calls "other types of instabilities". The reader would be though disappointed to find out that the section is dedicated to fluctuations in total exports or imports and not to issues related to resilience, broadly defined on the lines of our investigation: "maintenance of system performance either when subjected to external unpredictable perturbations, or when there is uncertainty about the values of internal design parameters" (Carlson and Doyle, 2002; Anderies, Janssen, and Ostrom, 2004).

Out of the set of notable textbooks, Egon Neuberger and William J. Duffy's *Comparative Economic Systems: A Decision-making Approach* (1976) is striking due to the fact that it drops out entirely any distinct discussion of performance criteria, outcomes and systemic performance. The book dully notes that "an economic system is essentially a means towards achieving some fundamental goals of society, such as freedom, egalitarianism, democracy, ecological survival and in material standards for the population" (1976, 2) and that the study of CES focuses on the following questions: What effect does the choice of economic system has on the efficiency with which the economy performs? Second, what is the role of the economic system in economic development and growth? And third what is the relationship between the various economic and political systems and human welfare? The book proceeds by presenting the decision-making approach and the particular way of framing CES analysis endorsed by the authors. The economic system consists of three interrelated components: The decision-making, the information and the motivation structures. The book takes one by one the structures that determine the location of decision-making authorities, the channels through which decision-making authorities channel information and the methods used to motivate each other to achieve their objectives. From time to time, the "outcomes" and the "standards" of performance are mentioned. Yet, there is no explicit or concentrated discussion on themes related to stability, feasibility and resilience.

A. Ben-Ner, J. Montias, and E. Neuberger's *Comparative Economics* (2013 [1994]) is a confirmation of the new trend of abandoning a separated methodical discussion of performance criteria, outcomes and systemic performance. The book is thus defining a shift in the literature which consists of a lack of interest in the wide range of variables usually associated with the assessment of the performance of economic systems. Instead, concepts of efficiency and optimality are assumed and the analysis proceeds on classical assumptions derived from normative welfare economics.

It is only when the peculiar position taken by the authors of the book is introduced that we get an implicit explanation of that lack of interest in issues that we associate with the problem of resilience broadly defined. "It is hardly necessary to stress, they write, that we reject the notion of system integrity at least in its extreme form, according to which the component parts of a system are welded so tightly together that they cannot be separated out or even studied in insulation from each other" (Ben-Ner, Montias, and Neuberger, 2013, 2). Taking such a position undermines the interest in continuity, integrity, functional stability and other features that are systemic and resilience-related. One could theoretically and philosophically speculate regarding the link between this explicit position assumed by the authors and the diminished interest they extend to the problem of resilience, but for our purposes, it is sufficient to note that their book reaffirmed and reinforced past 1989 the comparativists' relative lack of interest in the problem of resilience. Moreover, the book offers the first theoretical justification for that newly regained lack of interest.

That being said, a tendency in the opposite direction may be detected in Paul R. Gregory and Robert C. Stuart, *Comparative Economic Systems* (1999). The book explicitly presents the following criteria to evaluate economic outcomes: economic growth, efficiency, income distribution – fairness; stability – cyclical stability, avoidance of inflation and unemployment, and – interestingly enough – viability of the economic system. For our purposes, the last two, stability and viability of the economic system, are the criteria of interest. Gregory and Stuart (1999, 46) define stability in standard terms as the absence of significant fluctuations in growth rates, the maintenance of acceptable rates of unemployment and the avoidance of excessive inflation. It is a focus on basic standard macro-economic stability issues that may be related to broader resilience issues but which in itself does not account for a straightforward engagement with the problem of resilience and adaptability, on the lines of our approach.

The notable development with the Gregory and Stuart textbook is however an explicit focus on the issue of what they call "the viability of the economic system". The ultimate test of an economic system, they write, is its long-term viability. They note that since the beginning of the Soviet experiment with socialism "there had been little discussion of the long term viability of the planned socialist variant. Rather, discussion had focused on the relative economic performance of planned socialism. Most experts felt that planned socialism, though inefficient, would be able to muddle along, to survive at relatively low levels of efficiency and consumer welfare" (Gregory and Stuart, 1999, 47). Events in the late 80s highlighted the issue of the long-term viability of planned socialism. The rejection of the planned socialist system "cast serious doubts on this economic system's ability to deliver an economic performance strong enough to ensure its continued existence" (Gregory and Stuart, 1999, 47). Gregory and Stuart consider that among the other "basic performance criteria-economic growth, efficiency, income distribution, and stability the long-term viability of the economic system stands out as the dominant test of performance. If an economic system cannot survive, it has clearly proved itself inferior to those systems that can" (Gregory and Stuart, 1999, 47). This interest in the viability of economic systems seems to become the dominant trend, or at least the interest was not stifled by the new comparative economics (Dallago, 2004) and the trends dismissing the systemic view and, by implication, the concerns with systemic integrity and viability.

6.2.2 *The economic calculation debate as a feasibility and resilience issue*

Before moving ahead to further explore the ways of conceptualizing and thinking about resilience, as applied to economic systems, let us briefly take a look at the problem of socialism and the economic calculation debate, seen as a resilience and viability problem. Because if there is a second theme in classical CES, in addition to the concerns with macro-stability and business cycles, which may be interpretable through resilience-focused lenses, then the theme of socialism's feasibility is the most likely candidate. It may be the case that in the standard CES framework, the issues of the possibility and feasibility of socialism are the closest thing one could get in terms of a resilience-relevant perspective. Let us focus now briefly on the economic calculation debate as a resilience discussion.

The classical account, given by Lavoie in 1985, has shown that the debate had several stages and facets. Mises (1990 [1920]) argued that rational economic calculation is theoretically impossible under public ownership. The next stage of the debate was dominated by Hayek et al. (1935) who advanced a series of arguments regarding the concrete computational and informational problems involved in overcoming Mises' arguments via a system of simultaneous equations (Barone, 1908) and/or by developing a decentralized market socialist model using a Walrasian logic (Lange, 1938). Mises demonstrated that, in any complex economy, the socialist planning lacks the knowledge necessary to allocate the resources in rational, efficient ways. Introducing the concept of calculation, Mises pointed out that socialism would lack the necessary tools to appraise and calculate: the existence of a market in the means of production and monetary prices. As such, it will be a dysfunctional system. Hayek had further shown that prices and the market are essential to the dynamic adjustment and the adaptability of the system. The market is an ongoing process of organization, adaptation and adjustment. Framed this way, in the context of a discussion about resilience, it becomes clear why one may consider the economic calculation debate as relevant.

If one adds to all of the above the problem of real-life socialism and of the feasibility of the Eastern Bloc economies as natural experiments in alternative economic systems, one gets even closer to the issue of resilience. The discussion shifts from the theoretical possibility of a system to rationally allocate resources, to a different focus, on the real-life socialism cases in which an experiment to organize the economy on basis different from the market was taking place. Whatever was happening there in terms of structure and organization, it was definitely rather alien to a standard market model based on decentralized allocation of resources and private property. The question was in what measure that system was viable? For how long a system might be able to function on those parameters?

Real-life socialism had demonstrated that the problem of prices might be solved indirectly, by simply using as a reference point the world market prices, based on the pre-existing capitalist system. As Mises pointed out, one should not forget that socialist economies were operating in an environment in which they could resort to economic calculation using the prices established abroad. "Without the aid of these prices their actions would have been aimless and planless. Only because they were able to refer to these foreign prices were they able to calculate, to keep books, and to prepare their much talked about plans" (Mises, 1949, 698–699). Mises's insight was confirmed by the realities of Eastern European economies. The British economist Peter Wiles, visiting Poland, in the 50s, noted that in the day-to-day operation of the socialist economy the "world prices", i.e. capitalist world prices, were used in all intra-[Soviet] bloc trade and as a planning benchmark. Wiles asked the Polish communist planners: "What would you do if there were no capitalist world from which you could obtain all those crucial prices? The Polish planners' notable answer was: 'We'll cross that bridge when we come to it'" (Rothbard, 1991, 74).

The implications are evident. Socialism as a real-life economy and as a system in practice is actually dependent on the functioning of its competitor. At a closer look, this is a stunning conclusion. The problem identified by the calculation debate and the possibility of socialism controversies has become a problem of vulnerability and resilience. If things are approached in that light, the history of the 20th-century socialism becomes a study of the resilience of a system. Once the problem of prices is solved in an *indirect* way, then the study of socialism becomes the study of an experiment of economic organization and the administration of a certain set of economic institutions in particular historical circumstances. What is at stake might not be the efficient allocation of resources based on effective economic calculation but other performance criteria including (and most importantly) those of survival, viability and resilience.

6.2.3 Resilience inside and outside the CES literature

The overview of CES literature brought to the fore mixed results. The problems that we associate today with the theme of resilience were rarely – if ever – made explicit and studied as such. Our survey indicates that resilience, broadly defined, was not a preeminent priority in classical CES studies. Indeed, the issue of stability – defined in macroeconomic terms – was as closest to the theme as one may get by most authors. However, at the same time, one could identify those problems underlying the surface of more familiar CES arguments, themes and debates. If one considers the economic calculation debate and the feasibility of socialism as topics central to CES, then the problem of resilience enters the stage in an indirect but notable way.

Going back to the big picture, one may say that a significant development in the literature during the last 30 years or so has been an increased interest in the issue of what the literature calls "the viability of the economic system". By the 1990s, the issue was becoming more and more salient. Some of that was probably determined by the collapse of the Soviet system and of the illusions regarding the socialist mode of economic organization. Yet, at the same time, one could speculate that other sources were the influence of institutionalism in economics and the rise of environmental economics and of the perspectives built around concepts such as social ecological systems. As we move beyond classical CES to contemporary developments, we note that the problem of resilience (broadly defined to contain both aspects of viability and adaptability) has increasingly become salient for those who maintained an interest in the comparative and alternative economic and governance systems. Moreover, especially after 2001, as the various shocks and crises of the global economic system have demonstrated, the trade-offs between, on the one hand, the optimization of economic systems (that is to say, their organizing and governance aiming at increasing efficiency both static and dynamic), and, on the other hand, the viability, resilience and stability might be in a deep structural tension. It has become increasingly evident that the standard approach to performance criteria and outcomes in CES should include a more acute awareness of the tension between the so called "optimization" approach and the "resilience" approach.

One final observation is in order at this juncture. While the standard, traditional CES literature was not very interested in the issue of resilience, there was nonetheless a parallel intellectual tradition in economic thinking that was focusing on themes that are strongly related to the problem of resilience and was part of the intellectual genealogy of the current concept and interest in this issue. Already in the second part of the 20th century leading economists such as Kenneth Boulding (1966), Nicholas Georgescu-Roegen (1977) and Elinor Ostrom (Ostrom and Janssen, 2004) have made important contributions in terms of reorienting thinking towards issues of sustainability. Out of that, the emergence of environmental economics and of the "steady state economy" perspective has created a robust basis for multiple approaches to the problem of resilience.

This family of approaches was from the very beginning pluralistic in the sense that it focused on multiple performance criteria and systemic objectives. As Herman Daly, one of the most influential figures in this respect noted, such an approach offered expanded economics:

"standard economics confines its attention to the study of how best to allocate given means among given hands. It does not inquire very deeply into the nature of means or the nature of ends" (Daly, 1980, 28). Yet, without a clear conception of the basic means at our disposal – of what in the physical world it is ultimately feasible and resilient "our narrow economics is likely to commit the error of wishful thinking (assuming that just because something is desirable it must also be possible)". Similarly, "unless we inquire into the nature of ends and face the questions of ultimate values, ethics and the ranking of our ends, we are likely to commit the opposite error, that of technical determinism (assuming that just because something is possible it must also be desirable)". Hence, a debate about the relative merits of the steady, stationary or no growth economy and its opposite, the economy in which wealth and population are growing. In this debate, issues of sustainability, stability and resilience become preeminent. The trade-off between, on the one hand, economic efficiency and economic growth-oriented economic system and, on the other hand, the system oriented towards the stability of the stationary state or the sustainability perspective becomes a central issue.

6.3 Part 2: Frameworks for thinking about resilience and economic systems imported from other disciplines

The overview offered by the previous sections has illustrated the fact that thinking about resilience in CES has not been very advanced in the classical literature and why it has, at this point, to mostly rely on concepts, models and approaches developed in other fields (see also Hynes, this volume). Patterns and structures that we associate with resilience phenomena, broadly defined, have been identified by various disciplines, and in many cases, these patterns and models are relevant cross disciplinary. Natural sciences, for instance, offer the most basic and robust such models of conceptualizing and thinking about resilience-related phenomena. This section will provide an overview of some of them. A familiarity with them brings to the fore both the potential and limits of extending these models to economic systems.

Within the large class of natural sciences, two stand out as potential sources of models and insights: physics and environmental sciences. In physics, the term resilience is associated with the study of structural resilience of materials, resilience of networks and resilience of scientific methodology (e.g., resilience of measurements, of computation noise, of model, in the choice of the family of models, of predictions). The structural resilience of material refers to the elastic absorption and release of energy from a material. In a sense, it is the closest phenomenon to our basic intuitions regarding resilience: Between the stress applied to the material (measured as force/area of material) and the response variable strain (measured as change in length resulting from stress relative to the initial length), there are a linear part (*elastic* deformation) and a non-linear part (*plastic* deformation, eventually ending with the fracture of the material). For a linear elastic material, the resilience (measured as unit of energy/unit of volume of material) is defined as the integral of this function from stress zero to the end of the elastic deformation.

The mechanisms explaining resilience are mainly discussed in terms of chemical bounds (metallic, intra-molecular, inter-molecular) and macroscopic structure of the material. This concept of resilience is used in biological and earth and environmental sciences when one is interested in the mechanical properties of objects like molecules, rocks, soil. Topics of interest in biology include understanding the structural resilience of cellular organelles, elastomeric proteins and their combination with other materials for skin replacement or cardiovascular tissues (Aghaei-Ghareh-Bolagh et al., 2016), and soil resilience to compaction in agricultural or civil engineer context (e.g., Venkatesh et al., 2020). While physics offers a clear example of conceptualization of the problem and the oldest and most robust intellectual articulations of the intuitions behind the notion, environmental sciences offer the most socially influential theoretical development of the notion.

In earth and environmental sciences, extra complexity is due to the coupling between abiotic objects and processes. For instance, in ecosystems ecology and systems ecology, consonant with the study of biological communities, there are two relatively independent traditions, one based on linear modeling and one on non-linear modeling of resilience (van Meerbeck et al., 2021). The so called "engineering resilience" is conceptualized with simple dynamical models (linear stability analysis), while the "ecological resilience" is in terms of non-linear dynamic and domains of attraction (attraction basins) (Gunderson, 2000; Grimm and Calabrese, 2011). One research direction about non-linear resilience is qualitative (general patterns of ecosystem dynamic, adaptive capacity and transformability, e.g., the adaptive cycle concept); another one is quantitative (indicators of critical transitions, resulted from time series analysis and spatial patterns analysis of abiotic and biotic variables, Scheffer et al., 2015). There are also attempts to unify two approaches under the umbrella of a more general concept of stability (Meerbeck et al., 2021).

In other earth and environmental sciences (such as geomorphology and hydrology), the approaches to resilience are imported from ecology, either in the "engineering" or in the "ecological" versions. The difference from ecology is that biotic factors are independent variables (driving factors, stressors). They are used to explain the changes of the geomorphic variables, but feedback points are also considered in some cases. For instance, in geomorphology, Philips and Dyke (2016) import the concept of "engineering" resilience, and the associated terms (resistance, recovery, relaxation time), and develop a formalism for hillslope under the stress of storms. Examples from hydrology include groundwater resilience to pollution (attenuation of catastrophic spills, Ma et al., 2015), hydrological resilience of watersheds with different bedrock to wildfire (Spence et al., 2020), resilience of logjams to floods (Wohl and Scamardo, 2020) and the resilience of hydrologic processes occurring in the ecosystem due to climate change (Zhang et al., 2019).

This literature gives a sense of the complexity and variety of phenomena and circumstances to which one should be prepared to apply the notion. That complexity and diversity increases even more when it comes to resilience in human-nature systems. Human-nature systems have an extra complexity compared to earth and environmental objects and processes due to the coupling of ecological objects and processes with social, economic and cultural processes. With that we start to get even closer to the domain of CES. The complexity is simplified by focusing on sub-sets of variables (sectorial approach, by organizations and systems of similar organizations) or by reducing the dimensionality of large-scale objects (discretization in space of the whole system, e.g. cities, regions, countries, under the general term socio-ecological systems).

It is noteworthy that the human factor is increasingly present in this literature. The resilience of human resources is a key element in the success of management (an objective which is informed by knowledge about biological resilience). Formulating the objectives in terms of resilience at the operational level is based not only on the scientific input from biological and environmental science but may involve the local actors, in order to increase acceptance (perspectives on the resilience of water systems, Tepes and Neumann, 2020). At organization scale only, "engineering resilience" (linear) is relevant, but at economic sector level the "ecological resilience") (non-linear, adaptive cycle) can also be taken into consideration (example for agriculture in Ludwig et al., 2018). At a large scale, institutions and collective actions can be incorporated as causes of resilience, for instance, in sociohydrological models of flood resilience (Yu et al., 2017).

The holistic resilience approach can be illustrated by urban resilience to climate-related disasters (resilience based on the adaptive cycle concept including preparedness, absorption, recovery, adaptability and transformability, Tong, 2021), and the resilience of the global production ecosystem (resilience of a network of networks – ecological, technological, social, Nyström et al. 2019). An inventory of mechanisms underpinning such socio-ecological resilience is provided in Cumming and Peterson (2017). The concept of holistic resilience of human-nature systems is useful mainly in the development of public policies and strategic plans. This kind of literature tends to mix the objective aspects of resilience (descriptive science), with the normative ones within the so called "post-normal science".

Summing up our brief overview of these disciplines, we are now in the position to identify the basic and general patterns of thinking about resilience come up as emerging from these relevant literatures. Resilience in physics, biology and environmental sciences describes aspects of the process resulting from a *temporary stressor acting on an entity*. The *entity* can be an *object* (e.g., material, network, biomolecule, cell, tissue, organism, population, soil, river basin, water drainage system, socio-ecological system) or a *process* (e.g., molecular clock, network of cooperation within a species, interaction between species, ecosystem process, natural resource management process). The objects can be static (without change independent of the stressor) or dynamic (changing without stressor at one- or several time scales). The *stressor* is conceptualized in the local ontology of each scientific discipline, for instance as a force, a disease, a removal of species, or as climate change. The stressor is either an *external driving factor* of the entity (most often) or an *internal driving factor* (for instance human action in the holistic socio-ecological approach). The driving factors act most often at the spatial scale of the target entity, but there are cases in biology and environmental sciences when upscaling and downscaling of effects occur (for instance, the effect of a toxic substance will propagate from the scale of cells to that of organisms, and even to ecosystems). The time scale of action is smaller than the lifetime of the target entity and can have various forms (e.g., pulse, ramp, press), durations and frequencies. The *stress* is described as *changes of state* of the entity, with state described in terms of one or more *response variables*. The resilience is explained by *mechanisms* relating the stressor and the changes of state/response variables. Knowledge about mechanisms is useful in order to control/manage the resilience of the target objects and processes with respect to the driving factors and is delivered to the organizations managing the biological and environmental entities.

The analysis of the literature shows that there are five properties relevant for the discussion about resilience in physics, biology and environmental sciences. Definitions of resilience vary between scientific disciplines, and within the same field, but all refer to one or several of these properties: resistance (continuation with unchanged identity), elastic deformation (rebound, restoration of reference identity); plastic deformation with or without loss of functions and extension to new ones (extensibility, reconfiguration, state transition, recovery and extension of functions), adaptability (transformability, evolution with change of identity) and preparedness (intentional). One may expect that once we move to the domain of CES, at least some of them or their features may be relevant either directly or as a model and reference point. We have now a better understanding of how resilience is conceptualized and operationalized in other disciplines. We have a benchmark and a precedent for CES, a field that, we have determined, lacks a systematic engagement with the theme. But let us return now to the main challenge: how to think about resilience when it comes to CES.

6.4 Part 3: Thinking about resilience—Foundational problems

Analyzing and assessing systemic resilience means an engagement with a far from the evident phenomenon. The structures, causes and symptoms of economic resilience are only rarely fully evident to direct empirical observations. In most cases, the empirical verifiable data become available too late in the process. Therefore, the conceptual apparatus – both analytical and normative – brought to the table is in fact decisive in assessing the state of a system's resilience. Hence, the basic categories and structures behind the ways we conceptualize resilience are essential for our operational, analytical and empirical approaches. This section will provide an overview of the most important foundational parameters of thinking about resilience with a view to economic systems.

6.4.1 Basic conceptualization and the dilemma of resilience analysis

A systematic approach to the problem of resilience must start at the level of its basic conceptualization. In this respect, understanding the conceptual topology of thinking about the phenomena we associate with it is the foundation of resilience analysis. Probably the best articulation of this approach has been given by Thorén and Olsson (2018), and as we will see, their approach captures very well the basics we have identified in the previous section. Resilience, they explain, is the ability of a system S to absorb some disturbance D whilst maintaining property I. More specifically, "a system S is resilient if, and only if, when subjected to some disturbance D, I is maintained through the disturbance" (2018, 4). Thorén and Olsson make clear that: (a) I may represent a certain function or structure of a system; (b) I may be seen as standing for the *identity* of the system; if I is maintained, the system is the same; (c) the structure or function in case is not necessarily quantifiable, but may have purely qualitative features; and (d) to specify the I for a given system is to give *persistence criteria* for that system. A concept of resilience can operate with explicit or implicit persistence criteria: "It is rare that persistence criteria are given unambiguously, even when they are explicit" (2018, 4). In brief, Thorén and Olsson have captured thus what seems to be the basic structure of thinking about resilience and have presented it in a simple and concise manner.

Unpacking the gist of this basic structure and developing its analytical implications gives us a deeper and more nuanced understanding of what is implied in any form of resilience analysis – including in CES. For instance, resilience is not a feature or outcome of the system in general but it is always in relationship to a specific disturbance, D. To say that system X is resilient, you have to specify to what more specific disturbance D, it is resilient to. Furthermore, resilience is identifiable through a *specific persistence* criterion, I – a specific property that provides the persistence criterion. Moreover, resilience is something that takes place in a specific context, in specific circumstances. Therefore, one needs to try to specify the relevant conditions in order to determine the resilience – or lack of resilience – in case. To sum up, an economy could not simply be defined as resilient in general. An economy is resilient to particular disturbances, in specific circumstances and in particular aspects. To compare the resilience of two economies means to compare them on similar parameters, regarding similar disturbances and circumstances, as well as similar persistence criteria.

From all of the above, it emerges that at the core of resilience thinking is the interpretive and analytical tension between *persistence* and *transformation*. How do we draw a line between something that could be considered *system persistence* versus something that could be defined as *system change*, or even system *collapse*? This is where the idea of system *adaptability* enters the picture – a concept that links the idea of system *persistence* with the idea of *system change*.

These observations put us in the position to understand the basic analytical and interpretive dilemma of resilience studies. The key question is: How should we establish the criteria for continuity and change, for identity and discontinuity? When and how do we draw the line? Any approach to the problem of resilience is structurally bounded to be confronted with this question. And precisely because of that, any attempt to clarify the standards to be applied in identity, persistence and change creates a dilemma, as there are two ways of approaching this formidable analytical and intellectual challenge.

The first is the objectivist, ontological perspective. In light of this type of approach, we consider that the reality is "out there". An economic system has specific, objectively determinable features which, by their empirical existence in real life, give us the criterion for determining whether or not persistence or change has taken place. For instance, the structure of an industry including its physical location and a particular infrastructure might be considered an objective standard of determining whether or not an industry has been resilient to a specific cataclysmic or disturbance event. This approach obviously requires a strong ontological assumption. It requires a rigid determination of what the system is in objective, empirically determinable ways and what are the facts of its continuity independently of subjective beliefs.

However, there is a second approach which assumes that the facts of continuity are axiologically laden. That there is a strong subjective and relativistic dimension when it comes to determine the identity and the continuity of a system. For instance, what the actors on the ground, those participating in the economic system, think about the continuity of the institutions, structures and operations of a system matters in determining the resilience of the system. Similarly, the values and the normative assumptions held by the evaluators are not objective, neutral and indifferent to the assessment. Once that is recognized, we are now in the position to see the tension between the ontological challenge and axiological challenge in determining the resilience of a system. In what measure could one objectively establish the effects of resilience? In what measure the subjectivity of perceptions and norms is allowed to play a role? Hence, the dilemma of resilience studies.

As Thorén and Olsson (2018, 11) put it, there are several different acceptable ways of describing a system, "even when the systems are strikingly simple". Putting the resilience concept to use, even in very simple, basic cases "rests on a range of idealizations and specifications, all of which are far from obvious". The problem is even more complicated for social and economic systems. The reason is evident: "it is not a question for science to sort out what, ultimately, is central or important about social systems. The danger, to our minds, rests in approaching resilience from the monist perspective even when the pluralist proviso would have been more appropriate. Such an error involves both the introduction of unwarranted ontological claims, and the failure to recognize the values that go into construing the underlying systems" (Thorén and Olsson, 2018, 11).

To sum up, resilience analysis is predicated on this foundational tension generated by the *dilemma of resilience*. Being aware of the unavoidable presence of this dilemma is the first task of all resilience researchers. Classical CES literature has warned us about the foundational difficulties in conceptualization and operationalization of systemic features and performance criteria such as equality, liberty and even efficiency. Resilience is in no way different. In fact, in some respects, it may be posing even more complicated challenges.

6.4.2 Alternative approaches to resilience

Let us take a closer look at several alternative ways of framing the problem of resilience, as these alternative ways have been advanced in the relevant literature. Although the list is not comprehensive, its objective is to capture and outline the basic patterns that have been identified and discussed in the literature, relevant to social systems and social organization.

6.4.2.1 Continuity and identity

We have noted that, one likes it or not, the very notion of resilience hinges on the notions of continuity and identity. The approach to resilience based on the notion of continuity takes as a starting point the idea of a disruption, disturbance that creates a break or an inflection point that challenges and raises questions about the integrity, identity and continuity of the system. "Systems may move in space and inevitably move in time but saltation in either instance constitutes a loss of identity" (Cumming and Collier, 2005, 4). Taking a step further towards analytical applications of the notion requires a double – theoretical and empirical – engagement with this issue. As Cumming and Collier (2005, 3) put it, systems can be considered as a single study unit if they retain their identity. In this respect "the challenge of determining system identity is to establish the natural properties of our study systems that constitute identity conditions over time and space". If that is the case, one could look at the aspect of continuity from three perspectives.

The first is structural. That is to say, to look at the structure of institutional and organizational arrangements in order to determine whether or not the continuity was broken, based on their capabilities to resume their operations within the pre-disturbance structures. One could imagine, for instance, an external shock to an entire industry coming from a dramatic spike in the price of energy or natural resources. The resilience of that industry (and by extension of the economy which is based on that industry) would be defined by the capacity of that industry and economy to resume its operations within the same basic structure of organization, after the shock has been absorbed.

On the other hand, there is the functional perspective which looks at continuity through the lenses of the functions that the institutions and organizations have in an economic system. Continuity in this respect would mean having a system operational after the disturbance, with all its functions resumed, though not necessarily operated through the pre-existing structures. In this scenario or definition of continuity (and by extension of resilience), the capacity of the system to have the functions delivered through alternative means ensures the continuity of the system. The structures, the configurations, are changed, but a certain functionality is restored. A successful shift from a source of energy to another, as a result of a specific disturbance, will demonstrate resilience under this functional definition. The structures of the production of energy are changed, but the functionality is the same throughout the system. As a parenthesis, one should note that the preservation of function is a different criterion from preservation of identity, unless identity is defined purely in terms of function.

The third way of looking at resilience with a view to continuity is through the lenses of adaptation or adaptability. In this light, the system evolves and self-organization (through both structural and functional adjustments) generates a new configuration. From this perspective, the ways of establishing continuity and discontinuity become again a rather complicated thing, as using the structures and functions as criteria becomes rather tricky.

In brief, at a closer look, we see that though apparently straightforward, the approach built around notions of identity and continuity raises as well very profound foundational, philosophical problems. It is a necessary step forward in conceptualizing and making operational the notion of resilience. However, it comes with a profound epistemological, ontological and axiological luggage. The more complex the system, the more profound these philosophical, analytical and methodological problems are. And thus, we reach again to the same conclusion that when it comes to CES, we need to be aware that analyzing the resilience of a system is always a matter of not just empirical data but also of normative and ontological assumptions and frameworks. This conclusion is reinforced by the fragility/antifragility perspective, which offers an alternative way of thinking about the resilience-related phenomenon.

6.4.2.2 *Fragility and antifragility*

Nassim Taleb (2012) outlines a basic taxonomy that distinguishes between engineered systems and complex adaptive systems. Within the category of complex adaptive systems, he further identifies three categories. (a) Fragile systems, systems that do not resist the stress; (b) robust systems, systems that resist stress but only up to a certain point or threshold; and (c) antifragile systems, systems that get better with stress: "Some things benefit from shocks; they thrive and grow when exposed to volatility, randomness, disorder, and stressor ..." (Taleb, 2012, 3). Yet, notes Taleb, "in spite of the ubiquity of the phenomenon, there is no word for the exact opposite of fragile. Let us call it antifragile. Antifragility is beyond resilience or robustness. The resilient resists shocks and stays the same; the antifragile gets better" (Taleb, 2012, 3).

Taleb makes strong claims about these mechanisms, their role in human and social evolution as well as about the systemic properties that they generate. For instance, he claims that Eastern Europe societies and economies have developed resilient features as a result of repeatedly coping with multiple structural shocks and crises over the last 100 years. At the same time, he is skeptical regarding the Western advanced industrial democracies and their capability to withhold crises and shocks. The reason is, obviously, that they did not have the chance to develop resilience features, due to the absence of real structural stressors and shocks, of the nature and scale of those that confronted their Eastern European counterparts.

As articulated by Taleb, antifragility is a fresh way of looking at things. It draws attention to the limits of robustness. When it comes to random events, explains Taleb, "robust" is certainly not good enough. We need the mechanisms "by which the system regenerates itself continuously by using, rather than suffering from, random events, unpredictable shocks, stressors, and volatility" (Taleb, 2012, 8). Two aspects are essential in thinking about antifragility. The first is that antifragility and fragility are degrees on a spectrum and thus have to be understood in relationship to each other as parts of an entangled continuum. The second is that fragile and antifragile are relative, "there is no absolute. You may be more antifragile than your neighbor, but that doesn't make you antifragile" (Taleb, 2012, 8–9).

If this is the case, then antifragility is a common feature of complex systems, and it is necessarily present in any economic system. Traditional problems and themes in CES (the properties of the price system, interventionism, business cycles, etc.) could be reinterpretable in a new light as antifragility-related phenomena. A possible research agenda on these specific lines may be opened in very interesting and constructive directions, as the antifragility angle raises the possibility that economic efficiency and antifragility may be, in many cases, in profound tension in an economic system. Real-life socialism, for instance, may look as a system which is not very efficient but which may develop for certain parameters very resilient antifragility-based features. To sum up, the bottom line is that antifragility may offer an additional and, in many respects, novel way of approaching the problem of CES and its resilience.

6.4.2.3 Connectivity and "Normal Accidents"

One of the most intuitive approaches to resilience and vulnerability is to focus on the interdependence and linkages between the elements of the system. The issue of *connectivity* thus becomes the key to exploring aspects related to resilience. Connections generate and allow exchanges of information, goods, services and capital (Adger, Eakin, and Winkels, 2009). The question is whether, due to an increase in connectivity, a system gets more vulnerable or, on the contrary, it gets more resilient. Is economic connectivity and integration increasing or decreasing the resilience of an economy? Three possibilities are contemplated.

The first is a positive link between connectivity and resilience. The more connected the system is, the more resilient it is. The second looks at the phenomenon from the reversed perspective which draws attention to the increased vulnerability of the system, in light of an increased connectivity. The third alternative is to look at the parabolic form of the relationship. That is to say, the resilience of a system will be highest at intermediate levels of connectivity. To sum up, apparently and intuitively, the relationship between connectivity and resilience seems evident. However, at a closer look, it emerges that simply asserting connectivity or interdependence and then making claims about resilience is not sufficient for resilience analysis. Interdependence or connectivity are not in themselves sufficiently powerful factors to determine unilaterally a predictable variation in the resilience variable (Cumming et al., 2005). Further variables have to be identified, both at the theoretical level and in contextual, applied-level circumstances, in order to be able to make claims about resilience.

The influential work of Chester Perrow (2011) is an example of the connectivity-focused approach to vulnerability and resilience studies. Perrow's units of analysis are mostly at the organizational level and involve a combination of technological and organizational complexity. However, the logic behind his approach has a larger external validity. As such, it functions as a heuristic device helping us to get a better sense of an additional angle on the issue of resilience of complex socio-technological systems, out of which economic systems are an important subclass.

Perrow draws attention to two phenomena that are of major relevance for the vulnerability and resilience of economic systems. The two are *complexity* and *coupling*. Together they help explain the risks involved in complex systems and, more specifically, of a particular category of risk what Perrow calls "normal accidents". The idea is that vulnerabilities in the system may emerge not as a result of human error in design or operation, of an external shock or of an internal malfunction. Instead, the vulnerability and the risk/accident is the result of the normal functioning of the normal structure of the system. The very characteristics of the system become the structural, intrinsic source of accidents. Hence "normal" accidents.

In other words, one could identify situations in which the number of interactions between the parts of the system increases, while at the same time, each element of the system starts to have multiple functions. With that, the interactions become no longer linear but complex, having many branches and feedback loops. This is the complexity dimension. The second major dimension refers to what he calls coupling. Tight coupling means that there is no slack or buffer between two units or components. What happens at the level of one component is directly and almost immediately impacting the other. When these elements are loosely coupled, there is the possibility of buffers and time lags. Therefore, loosely coupled systems have more degrees of freedom in adjusting to shocks and disruptions. Using these conceptual vectors, Perrow creates a typology via a two-by-two matrix having on one axis, the "linear/complex" variable, and, on the other axis, the "lose/tight" variable. His main point is that those systems that combine the feature of complex and tight have characteristics that make them prone to specific kind of vulnerabilities. Interactive complexity and tight coupling induce features increasing the possibility of "normal accident" or a "systemic" accident.

As noted, this analysis has been developed mostly to focus on organizations and especially on organizations that have intricate technological features and components intertwined with their structures. However, there are many lessons and insights that could be derived as regarding economic systems. Probably the most important of them is the idea that properties of the system itself operating in normal, functional ways may generate vulnerabilities and problems of resilience. That generates a more nuanced understanding of the nature of resilience. It looks like the more complex, and the more functionally differentiated, optimized and rationalized a system becomes, the more the possibility of normal accidents increases. A modern, post-industrial, complex technology-based economic system seems to have built in it the possibility of a particular type of accident and a particular type of resilience problem. Again, we see emerging to salience the trade-off between the optimizing system and a resilient system. In other words, it looks like if tight coupling and complexity are intrinsic features of a modern performant economy, then there is a real tension between the efficient economic organization of a system and the resilience of the system (Perrow, 2011).

To sum up, connectivity and interdependence matter. However, it is very difficult to deal with them, given their multifaceted complexity. New tools which increase the capability to deal with issues related to interconnected systems without simplifying to the point of neglecting the interconnectivity factor are needed. Some of these tools have started to emerge and many of them are associated with the field of so called "complexity studies".

6.4.2.4 *The "Complexity Studies" approach*

The complexity approach introduces systemic resilience (seen as the capacity of a system to absorb and adjust to change by learning from it) both as a focus of analytical interest and as an explicit policy goal. Complexity theorists are the most adamant that focusing on efficiency is not enough. In many cases, system-wide efficiency may undermine the resilience of the system. An economy may become more vulnerable due to a structure geared towards producing economic efficiency. As an example, one may take the situation in which financial technology has improved the efficiency of financial services, or the strength and efficiency of particular organizations and institutions, while at the same time, they made the entire banking and financial sector less resilient as a whole to "normal accidents" or external shocks. In a similar way, "just in time" supply chains are an illustration of the trade-off involving efficiency at the expense of resilience. The complexity perspective elaborates on new theoretical grounds, an already familiar theme, arguing that it is necessary to counterbalance the focus on efficiency with a focus on resilience and only then to integrate resilience with efficiency and other specific criteria.

However, it is important to note that complexity studies are introducing a rather different vocabulary and a set of new conceptual and theoretical tools. The field has been bolstered by the developments in computational and analytic technology, which allow the formalization and analysis of multiple and complex relationships and processes able to deal with interconnected systems, without simplifying to the point of neglecting the distinctive features of complex interconnectivity. The tools of complexity science try to capture interconnections beyond the standard linear relationships, equilibria and relatively simple structures of correlation and causation. That is the context in which the themes of "self-organization" and "emergence" have become central to the theoretical apparatus that helps the analysis of the systemic transitions from one state to another and of the dynamics of both stability and change. As Colander and Kupers (2014, 50–52) have explained, central to the approach is to identify the set of rules that govern the dynamics of the evolution of a system and then unlock complexity through focusing on the simpler rules that govern the evolution of the system. Instead of a set of static equations that describe the system, one focuses on these replicator rules and sees how patterns emerge generating complexity. In complexity social science, one searches "not the equations or models defining the existing system, what one searches for are the replicator dynamics of a system in which there is no controller".

The complexity perspective also emphasizes the difference between analysis in linear system terms, in which the concept of equilibrium is central, and analysis in complex system terms, in which the notion of "basins of attraction" replaces the concept of equilibrium. "A basin of attraction is a pattern or an outcome towards which the system evolves even if the initial conditions or replicator dynamics change as long as it begins in the relevant basin" (Colander and Kupers, 2014, 53). Hence, a theoretical backing of the intuition that nonlinear systems have many different possible outcomes is provided. There are multiple basins of attraction and some basins can be deeper than others. When that happens, systems have "lock ins".

The idea of sensitiveness to path or path dependence is central to the new approach. It means that small differences or small changes in the starting point or the replicator dynamics can lead to various different paths as well as to very different outcomes. Minor differences or minor changes may lead to major aggregated or structural differences of patterns. Hence path dependency becomes very important in the structure of analysis of resilience processes. If not general laws or structures of causality but path-dependent processes may lead a system towards the equilibrium or vulnerability, then the analytical focus has to be changed in the direction of identifying critical junctures that lay at the foundation of these various relevant paths to be considered.

Last but not least, the complexity perspective introduces and develops theoretically the idea of tipping point and the associated notions of critical mass (Ball, 2004) and thresholds (Granovetter, 1978). The phenomenon is associated with the notion of sudden change or a system shift from one equilibrium to another or from one basin of attraction to another basin of attraction. In the complexity-perspective path dependency, lock-ins and tipping points have a major role to play in generating structures that might be vulnerable or resilient. The implications for the approaches focused on robustness, stability or resilience are evident. Seen in conjunction, all the concepts outlined so far offer a powerful toolbox for thinking and assessing the resilience of economic systems (Rosser and Rosser, 2018; Holt, Rosser and Colander, 2011).

6.5 Conclusions

The overview of the problem of resilience leads to several conclusions applicable to CES. The most important is of a general nature. Resilience – broadly defined – is a theme only tangentially dealt within the classical CES literature. However, the theme has been increasingly salient in the last decades. That being said, the resilience-centered research agenda continues to be overdue in CES, and there is a huge unexplored potential in the field for the approaches focused on phenomena associated with stability, adaptability and resilience.

There are multiple modes to conceptualizing the phenomenon associated with resilience, and most of them are applicable to the study of economic systems. Yet, all of them are doomed to be confronted by some foundational limits and comparative economic studies researchers have to proceed cognizant of these. The first of them is the dilemma of resilience studies:

How should we establish the criteria for continuity and change, for identity and discontinuity? When and how do we draw the line between something that could be considered *system persistence* versus something that could be defined as *collapse*, when both objective and subjective criteria need to be used in order to establish the standards of identity, persistence and change? That is a dilemma that transcends basic empirical data or normal science procedures and that aspect makes resilience studies extremely difficult.

The second is that of the general trade-offs between efficiency and resilience, a trade-off which emerges as inescapable, irrespective of the way one approaches or conceptualize things. The "efficiency-resilience trade-off" is of paramount importance for CES research and needs to be recognized as such. If a complex system is structured with a view to local efficiency, the risk of systemic failure is higher. Therefore, one needs to consider the systemic trade-off between resilience, on the one hand, and optimizing efficiency on the other. Classical CES literature was driven mainly by neoclassical economics and, even more, by welfare economics assumptions. Efficiency and optimality were a central to its theoretical and analytical architecture. A focus on resilience challenges the entire tradition.

The third is an operational extension of the first two: the problem of measurement. It is correctly argued that there is no proper way to measure resilience. Yet, in a sense, the situation is similar with the cases of other criteria. There is no proper measurement for resilience, but at the same time, there is no proper measure of efficiency. That is to say, "the lack of a proper measurement does not mean that resilience, efficiency or any other goal is unimportant. It just means that we have to accept that our measurements are flawed, and not become too focused on specific measurement" (Colander and Kupers, 2014, 201). That being said, the measurement problem looms large. A comparative approach focused on the issue of resilience needs to confront it, especially as the efficiency-based approach was very successful in building an aggregated assessment apparatus erected on rather solid empirical estimates and proxies.

Last but not least, there is the problem of how does the concept of resilience travel from case to case? This is the twin problem of "conceptual traveling" (the application of concepts to new cases) and "conceptual stretching" (the distortion that occurs when a concept does not fit the new cases). Again, this is not a problem pertaining just to resilience but to any other concept used in comparative studies. As Sartori (1970) has explained, "conceptual traveling" and "conceptual stretching" are at the very foundations of comparative analysis. In addition to that, we should keep in mind that this is not just a theoretical problem, as predictability and contextuality are decisive for the applied, policy-oriented side. Concept traveling is essential for external validity, hence for predictive power. In the end, resilience studies in CES need to contribute to the policy problems and the applied-level dimension. External validity for its key concepts is thus crucial in the practical order of things.

To sum up, all of the above make for a fascinating task ahead for CES scholars. The efforts to develop a resilience-focused research agenda in comparative economic studies are both promising and challenging. Given the remarkable foundational, philosophical, theoretical and analytical dimensions of the task, and given the applied-level empirical and normative implications, such efforts may be, in the end, one of the decisive factors contributing to a revival of CES studies at the beginning at the 21st century.

Acknowledgments

This work was supported by a grant of the Romanian Ministry of Education and Research, CNCS - UEFISCDI, project number PN-III-P4-ID-PCE-2020-1076, within PNCDI III. The authors would like to thank to Bruno Dallago and Sara Casagrande for the comments and suggestions received.

References

Adger, W. N., Eakin, H. and Winkels, A. (2009). "Nested and teleconnected vulnerabilities to environmental change". *Frontiers in Ecology and the Environment* 7(3): 150–157.

Aghaei-Ghareh-Bolagh, B., Mithieux, S. M. and Weiss, A. S. (2016). "Elastic proteins and elastomeric protein alloys". *Current Opinion in Biotechnology* 39: 56–60.

Anderies, J. M., Janssen, M. A. and Ostrom, E. (2004). "A framework to analyze the robustness of social-ecological systems from an institutional perspective". *Ecology and Society* 9(1): 18.

Ball, P. (2004). *Critical Mass: How One Thing Leads to Another.* New York, NY: Farrar, Straus and Giroux (Macmillan).

Barone, E. (1908). *Principi di economia politica.* Roma: Tip. Nazionale di G. Bertero.

Ben-Ner, A., Montias, J. and Neuberger, E. ([1994] 2013). *Comparative Economics.* London: Routledge.

Berliner, J. (1999). *The Economics of the Good Society: The Variety of Economic Arrangements.* Oxford: Blackwell Publishers.

Blodgett, R. H. (1944 [1948]). *Comparative Economic Systems.* New York, NY: Macmillan.

Bornstein, M. (ed.) (1974). *Comparative Economic Systems.* Chicago, IL: Richard D. Irwin.

Boulding, K. E. (1966). "The economics of the coming spaceship Earth" in Jarrett, H. (ed.). *Environmental Quality in a Growing Economy.* Baltimore, MD: Resources for the Future/Johns Hopkins University Press, pp. 3–14.

Carlson, J. M. and Doyle, J. (2002). "Complexity and robustness". *Proceedings of the National Academy of Sciences USA* 99(Suppl 1): 2538–2545.

Colander, D. and Kupers, R. (2014). *Complexity and the Art of Public Policy: Solving Society's Problems from the Bottom Up.* Princeton, NJ: Princeton University Press.

Cumming, G. S. et al. (2005). "An exploratory framework for the empirical measurement of resilience". *Ecosystems* 8(8): 975–987.

Cumming, G. S. and Collier, J. (2005). "Change and identity in complex systems". *Ecology and Society* 10(1): 29.

Cumming, G. S. and Peterson, G. D. (2017). "Unifying research on socio-ecological resilience and collapse". *Trends in Ecology & Evolution* 32: 695–713.

Dallago, B. (2004). "Comparative economic systems and the new comparative economics". *European Journal of Comparative Economics* 1(1): 59.

Daly, H. E. (1980). *Economics, Ecology, Ethics: Essays Toward a Steady-State Economy.* San Francisco, CA: WH Freeman & Co.

Georgescu-Roegen, N. (1977). "The steady state and ecological salvation: A thermodynamic analysis". *BioScience* 27(4): 266–270.

Granovetter, M. (1978). "Threshold models of collective behavior". *American Journal of Sociology* 83(6): 1420–1443.

Gregory, P. R. and Stuart, R. C. (1999). *Comparative Economic Systems.* Boston, MA: Houghton Mifflin.

Grimm, V. and Calabrese, J. M. (2011). "What is resilience? A short introduction" in Deffuant, G. and Gillbert, N. (eds.). *Viability and Resilience of Complex Systems: Concepts Methods and Case Studies from Ecology and Society.* Berlin Heidelberg: Springer-Verlag, pp. 3–15.

Grossman, G. (1974). *Economic Systems.* Englewood Cliffs, NJ: Prentice Hall.

Gunderson, L. H. (2000). "Ecological resilience – in theory and application". *Annual Review of Ecology and Systematics* 31: 425–439.

Halm, G. N. (1960). *Economic Systems: A Comparative Analysis.* Ballwin, MO: Holt, Rinehart and Winston.

Holling, C. S. (1973). "Resilience and stability of ecological systems". *Annual Review of Ecology and Systematics* 4(1): 1–23.

Holt, R. P., Rosser Jr, J. B. and Colander, D. (2011). "The complexity era in economics". *Review of Political Economy* 23(3): 357–369.

Lange, O. R. (1938). *On the Economic Theory of Socialism.* Minneapolis, MN: University of Minnesota Press.

Lavoie, D. (1985). *Rivalry and Central Planning: The Socialist Calculation Debate Reconsidered.* New York, NY: Cambridge University Press.

Ludwig, M., Wilmes, P. and Schrader, S. (2018). "Measuring soil sustainability via soil resilience". *Science of the Total Environment* 626: 1484–1493.

Ma, J., Nossa, C. W. and Alvarez, P. J. J. (2015). "Groundwater ecosystem resilience to organic contaminations: Microbial and geochemical dynamics throughout the 5-year life cycle of a surrogate ethanol blend fuel plume". *Water Research* 80: 119–129.

Montias, J. M. (1976). *The Structure of Economic Systems*. New Haven, CT: Yale University Press.

Neuberger, E. and Duffy, W. J. (1976). *Comparative Economic Systems: A Decision-making Approach*. Boston, MA: Allyn & Bacon.

Nyström, M. et al. (2019). "Anatomy and resilience of the global production ecosystem". *Nature* 575: 98–108.

Ostrom, E. and Janssen, M. A. (2004). "Multi-level governance and resilience of social-ecological systems" in *Globalisation, Poverty and Conflict*. Dordrecht: Springer, pp. 239–259.

Perrow, C. (2011). *Normal Accidents: Living with High Risk Technologies*. Princeton, NJ: Princeton University Press.

Phillips, J. D. and van Dyke, C. (2016). "Principles of geomorphic disturbance and recovery in response to storms". *Earth Surface Processes and Landforms* 41: 971–979.

Pryor, F. L. (1985). *A Guidebook to the Comparative Study of Economic Systems*. Englewood Cliffs, NJ: Prentice Hall.

Rosser Jr, J. B. and Rosser, M. V. (2018). *Comparative Economics in a Transforming World Economy*. Boston, MA: MIT Press.

Rothbard, M. N. (1991). "The end of socialism and the calculation debate revisited". *Review of Austrian Economics* 5(2): 51–76.

Sartori, G. (1970). "Concept misformation in comparative politics". *American Political Science Review* 64(4): 1033–1053.

Scheffer, M. et al. (2015). "Generic indicators of ecological resilience: Inferring the chance of a critical transition". *Annual Review of Ecology, Evolution, and Systematics* 46: 145–167.

Spence, C. et al. (2020). "Hydrological resilience to forest fire in the subarctic Canadian shield". *Hydrological Processes* 34: 4940–4958.

Taleb, N. N. (2012). *Antifragile: Things that Gain from Disorder*. New York, NY: Random House.

Tepes, A. and Neumann, M. B. (2020). "Multiple perspectives of resilience: A holistic approach to resilience assessment using cognitive maps in practitioner engagement". *Water Research* 178: 115780.

Thorén, H. and Olsson, L. (2018). "Is resilience a normative concept?" *Resilience: International Policies, Practices and Discourses* 2(6): 112–128.

Tong, P. (2021). "Characteristics, dimensions and methods of current assessment for urban resilience to climate-related disasters: A systematic review of the literature". *International Journal of Disaster Risk Reduction* 60: 102276.

van Meerbeek, K., Jucker, T. and Svenning, J. C. (2021). "Unifying the concepts of stability and resilience in ecology". *Journal of Ecology* 109: 3114–3132.

Venkatesh, N., Heeralal, M. and Pillai, R. J. (2020). "Resilient and permanent deformation behaviour of clayey subgrade soil subjected to repeated load triaxial tests". *European Journal of Environmental and Civil Engineering* 24: 1414–1429.

von Hayek, F. A., Pierson, N. G., Von Mises, L., Halm, G. and Barone, E. (1935). *Collectivist Economic Planning*. London: Routledge & Kegan Paul.

von Mises, L. (1949). *Human Action*. New Haven, CT: Yale University Press.

von Mises, L. ([1920] 1990). *Economic Calculation in the Socialist Commonwealth*. Auburn, AL: Ludwig Von Mises Institute, Auburn University.

Walker, B. et al. (2004). "Resilience, adaptability and transformability in social–ecological systems". *Ecology and Society* 9(2):5.

Wohl, E. and Scamardo, J. E. (2021). "The resilience of logjams to floods". *Hydrological Processes* 35: e13970.

Yu, D. J., Sangwan, N., Sung, K., Chen, X. and Merwade, V. (2017). "Incorporating institutions and collective action into a sociohydrological model of flood resilience". *Water Resources Research* 53: 1336–1353.

Zhang, Y., Li, W., Sun, G. and King, J. S. (2019). "Coastal wetland resilience to climate variability: A hydrologic perspective". *Journal of Hydrology* 568: 275–284.

7

THE AGE OF EQUALITY AND THE NEW CONFLICTS BETWEEN ECONOMIC SYSTEMS

Richard Pomfret

UNIVERSITY OF ADELAIDE, AUSTRALIA

THE JOHNS HOPKINS UNIVERSITY SAIS EUROPE, BOLOGNA, ITALY

The 20th-century competition between capitalism and central planning was the trigger in the 1950s and 1960s for Western universities to promote research and teaching in comparative economic systems. The academic sub-discipline tended to focus on central planning because the rest of economics covered market economies. The competition between systems was resolved in 1989–1991 with the collapse of central planning in Eastern Europe and the Soviet Union. In the 1990s, the focus of comparative economic studies shifted to the "transition" from central planning, although the precise destination was unclear.[1] By 2000, the transition was essentially over, revealing the many varieties of market-based economies in the formerly planned economies (and in some countries that remained Communist in name).

The situation of comparative economic studies was similar to that of development economics, another sub-branch of economics that emerged and flourished in the second half of the 20th century. Both reflected bifurcations of the world's nations that were important in that period of Cold War and decolonization; Communist versus capitalist economies and developed versus less-developed economies were distinct categories worthy of separate analysis. The chapter's second section discusses the extent to which comparative economic studies and development economics are parts of the major branch of economics that has inquired into the nature and causes of the wealth of nations over the last quarter of a millennium. Although variations in the level of government intervention or in levels of development still exist, the Second and the Third World no longer exist as clearly distinct categories and basing academic sub-disciplines on divisions between planned and market-based economies and between developed and developing economies is no longer tenable.

The future of comparative economic studies will be determined by the evolution of the global economy and the emergence of issues on which international comparisons can increase understanding. Sections 7.3 and 7.4 discuss prospects for the 21st century, arguing for a long-run trend towards cooperative fraternity interspersed with medium-term shocks by populist leaders. Section 7.5 concludes and examines outputs of scholars working in comparative economic studies for indications of the extent to which these developments are represented in current research in comparative economic studies.

DOI: 10.4324/9781003144366-9

7.1 The age of equality

The overarching economic feature of the 20th century was competition between economic systems (Pomfret, 2011). In the 19th century, pre-capitalist systems were overwhelmed by the capacity of capitalist economies to produce more and superior goods for peace and war. A concomitant political development increased liberty and democracy in the dominant capitalist countries. At the same time, inequality between and within different parts of the world increased; by many measures, income and wealth inequality within the leading economies of Europe and areas settled by Europeans peaked in the decade before 1914, and the economic difference between those countries and the rest of the world was stark.[2] Competition between established and emerging European powers culminated in the 1914–1918 War, which marked the end of an era.

The war brought on the Bolshevik Revolution in Russia in October 1917, as well as unsuccessful revolutions in Germany and elsewhere. After the civil war dust settled, the challenge from the Union of Soviet Socialist Republics was whether a centrally planned economy could be as productive as a capitalist market-based economy and could meet targets which included the social equity that capitalism failed to achieve. In the competition between the First-World capitalist countries and the Second-World Communist countries, the success of the USSR in World War II and in achieving many peacetime goals during the post-war decades was attractive to imitators across the Third World in the 1950s and 1960s within the frame of decolonization.

The Cold War competition between economic systems stimulated the emergence of two sub-branches of economics in the capitalist economies; development economics sought to explain why Third World countries were poor and how they could prosper, and comparative economics sought to explain the functioning of the different economic systems in the First World of capitalism and the Second World of centrally planned economies. Arguments for market socialism or a third way between central planning and market-based capitalism failed to gain traction and, despite some theoretical insights, comparative economic studies too often lost its way among the labyrinthine intricacies of Soviet planning mechanisms while failing to identify fatal systemic flaws.

The competition between systems was resolved in 1989–1991 with the collapse of central planning in Eastern Europe and the Soviet Union. Capitalism retained its edge in economic growth driven by technical change. Widely shared prosperity in Western Europe, North America and increasingly in newly industrializing economies of East Asia was in sharp contrast to the economic stagnation in the Soviet Union in the 1970s and 1980s. The capitalism that won the competition with communism was not pre-1914 laissez-faire capitalism but market economies with substantial government intervention to counter market failures and to reduce inequality of opportunity or of economic outcome.

In the 1990s, the focus of comparative economic studies shifted to the "transition" from central planning, although the precise destination was unclear. The sub-discipline flourished as researchers addressed pressing policy issues surrounding the speed of transition and sequencing of reforms. By 2000, the transition was essentially over, revealing the many varieties of market-based economies in the formerly planned economies (and in some countries that remained Communist in name).[3] In the Introduction to his influential textbook *Transition and Economics,* Gérard Roland (2000, xx) emphasized that, while the economic policy debates in transition economies were important for the people in those countries, research on transition could also improve "our understanding of capitalism as an economic system and our understanding of large-scale institutional change".[4]

The varieties of economic systems in formerly centrally planned economies are part of the global range of varieties of capitalism, a concept popularized by Hall and Soskice (2001). An earlier British literature had focused on different roles of government in leading capitalist economies, notably Shonfield (1965) *Modern Capitalism* and Denton et al. (1968) *Economic Planning and Policies in Britain, France and Germany* both of which lauded the role of economic planners in France.[5] However, that literature atrophied as support for indicative planning in market-based economies waned with the neoclassical revival of the 1970s and disappeared in the 1980s when political leaders in Europe and North America adopted stronger pro-market stances. Hall and Soskice (2001) broadened the geographical coverage of modern capitalism and focused on the role of firms with differing national characteristics rather than on the state as the only source of variation across market-based economies.

The transition economies are no longer distinctive as a group, apart from specific elements of their common history as formerly centrally planned economies, and the group characteristics are becoming less distinctive as that common history recedes in time.[6] A fundamental institutional divide is being created between the transition economies of Europe that have joined, or aspire to join, the European Union (EU) since 2004 and the countries of the former Soviet Union that do not have this option.[7]

In the 21st century, the economic systems of the transition economies evolved in response to challenges common to most countries of the world, including the 2007–2009 international crises, the shifting balance of global economic power, the rise of populism and opposition to the top 1%, and the COVID-19 pandemic. Responses to these challenges take place in a global economy that is evolving in response to technological and financial innovations and to the fragmentation of production along global value chains. The global challenges that were not unique to the formerly planned economies raise the questions of whether and how comparative economic studies must change if it is to remain a relevant subject area.

7.2 It is all economics

Comparative economics and development economics followed parallel paths in the late 20th century. The pioneers of development economics in the 1950s were influenced by the Soviet Union's economic success and embraced economic planning, even if not so all-encompassing as Soviet central planning. They emphasized capital formation and were, for the most part, skeptical about international markets. The preferred policy was import-substituting industrialization, and this strategy was adopted in virtually all independent countries of Asia, Africa and Latin America in the 1950s and 1960s. By the 1980s, the strategy's weaknesses were apparent, and an alternative economic strategy of export-oriented manufacturing was proving successful in a handful of countries.

Despite the evidence of the shortcomings of import substitution, switching to an outward-oriented development strategy was difficult. In several Latin American countries, the need for reform was highlighted by the 1982 debt crises. Reform was most thorough in Mexico, which had the external anchors of World Trade Organization (WTO) accession in 1986 and the promise of a free trade agreement with the United States (realized in the 1993 North American Free Trade Agreement, NAFTA). More commonly, with Brazil as the leading example, reforms went through a series of cycles as partial reforms were pushed back and then reactivated only to face pushback again. The simplest explanation is that vested interests that benefited from import substitution were more influential than potential exporters. In sum, institutions and political economy mattered, and static or comparative static economic models that bundled history, institutions, politics, culture, etc., into a *ceteris paribus* assumption were missing fundamental drivers of development.

Researchers on the transition economies were coming to similar conclusions about the importance of history and institutions. After the transitional recession of the early 1990s, the Central and Eastern European countries performed better than the South-east European countries that, in turn, generally outperformed the Soviet successor states in the 1990s.[8] In the former Soviet Union, Kyrgyzstan was a poster boy for the reformist strategies advocated by the International Monetary Fund and the World Bank (the "Washington Consensus"), but its economic performance was disappointing due to the lack of supporting institutions for the new market economy. Neighboring Uzbekistan, pursuing more gradual reforms with more government interventions, experienced a shallower transitional recession and was the first former Soviet republic to regain its 1991 GDP level. Uzbekistan's success was at least partially explained by a more effective public administration that was related to three aspects of the history of Tashkent: capital of the Tsarist Governate of Turkestan, beneficiary of manufacturing facilities transferred from the western USSR at the start of the Great Patriotic War, and host to a large bureaucracy associated with maintenance of the irrigation system on which the Central Asian cotton sector depended.

In the 2000s, both comparative economics and development economics have become more variegated and researchers in both sub-disciplines quote extensively from outside their field. These sources of inspiration are from economic history, institutional economics, and a range of other areas. References back to Adam Smith and Karl Marx or to Barrington Moore's (1966) attempt to understand the social origins of political and economic systems became frequent, as did reference to more recent work by North (1981), Olson (1982), Williamson (1985), and Ostrom (1990).[9] The overarching connecting theme of these authors is concern to address the big economic questions of why some countries or parts of the world become rich while others do not and recognition that the answers go beyond neoclassical economics or reliance on the nation state as the unit of analysis.

The importance of institutions, as broadly defined by North to include difficult to quantify aspects such as honesty or third-party trust, was obvious for poorly governed transition economies mired in widespread corruption and semi-legal activities. Alternative forms of economic organization were also becoming more apparent as the plan versus market dichotomy seemed over simple. Williamson's question, following Coase (1937), of why some things happen in the market while others occur within firms or other organizations is as relevant as Ostrom's question of how people organize themselves to manage resources (challenging Olson's theory of what she called "collective inaction").

These contributions were equally significant for comparative economic studies and for development economics, and major works in the early 21st century were relevant to both fields. In the early 2000s, Acemoglu and Robinson wrote a series of articles, culminating in Acemoglu and Robinson (2006), asking why democracy emerges in some cases and not others and why it has a positive impact on economic growth in some countries and not in others. The comparative study of the post-Columbian Americas by Engerman and Sokoloff (2011) focused on institutions and highlighted the vicious circles of growth-damaging inequality in some countries. The large literatures that both books spawned focused on global evidence of the relationships between democracy or inequality and economic outcomes rather than examining these links in the narrower contexts of formerly centrally planned economies or currently less developed countries.

Neither comparative economics nor development economics has a dominant 21st-century paradigm or methodology, unlike the situation before the 1980s.[10] Both have seen challenges to the previous focus on the nation state as the unit of analysis. Development economists Banerjee, Duflo and Kremer shared the 2019 Nobel Prize in Economic Sciences for their work on microeconomic questions using randomized control trials.[11] Dell won the 2020 John Bates Clark Medal of the American Economic Association for research comparing economies of subnational regions with differing institutional development (Acemoglu, 2021); she has utilized historical and institutional discontinuities in both developing and transition economies. The obvious problem of microeconomic or localized research for comparative economic studies is the degree to which such research can be generalized; is comparison of results from Kerala and Shaanxi, or even smaller units, as valid or as useful as comparing performance of India and China?

Although comparative data on national economies is often more consistent and extensive, some country pairs may be so dissimilar as to invalidate any comparative conclusions, while even similar countries may have differences that undermine analysis of specific sectors. This is related to the question of the counterfactual. For example, in looking at the effect of financial reform followed by boom and bust, I argued in Pomfret (2021a, 113–5) that we can compare similar countries to show the benefits of faster financial reform between 1992 and 2007 (Table 7.1). Of course, each country has unique features and Italy may be a poor counterfactual for a no-financial-reform Spain. An important innovation in techniques is to use synthetic control methods to address the problem of finding comparators, i.e., counterfactual Spain may be better represented by a synthetic country consisting of a weighted average of other countries, with the weights determined by the ability to mimic Spain's pre-treatment experience (Abadie, 2021).[12]

Finally, it is worth mentioning that, in contrast to the growth econometrics of the 1990s that pitched various measures of economic growth as the performance indicator, there seems to be increasing uncertainty about the overall criteria of success. Uzbekistan, the Central Asian success story of the 1990s, clearly fell behind regional rival Kazakhstan between 2000 and 2016. Divergence was driven by the oil boom that favored Kazakhstan, but Uzbekistan's economic performance was hampered by the slow speed of economic reform, i.e., a driver of success in the 1990s became a source of relative failure in the 2000s; Uzbekistan's critics focused on lack of diversification and reliance on remittances from some two million migrant workers in Russia and Kazakhstan – a result of inadequate domestic job creation – as well as on features such as use of child labor in cotton harvesting and torture of political opponents. It was not just about economics.

The Uzbekistan assessment highlights that comparative economic studies has shifted from pre-1989 emphasis on efficient resource allocation to 21st-century emphasis on long-run economic development. Russia illustrates how a long-term perspective may be based on distorted vision of the past or selective choice of points for comparison. Many older Russians draw a negative contrast between the chaos and economic hardship that accompanied the shift to capitalism and democracy by Yeltsin in the 1990s and the economic and political stability of the 1964–1982 Brezhnev era, pointing to the latter's success in improving living standards

Table 7.1 Faster and slower financial reformers, nominal GDP in US dollars: 1992 and 2007

	1992	*2007*	*% Change*		*1992*	*2007*	*% Change*
USA	6,286.8	13,811.2	**119.7**	Germany	2,062.1	3,297.2	**59.9**
UK	1,074.0	2,727.8	**154.0**	France	1,372.8	2,562.3	**86.6**
Spain	612.6	1,429.2	**133.3**	Italy	1,265.8	2,107.5	**66.5**
Ireland	54.3	255.0	**369.6**	Greece	128.4	360.0	**180.4**
OECD	19,764.1	38,219.0	**93.4**	World	24,533.6	54,347.0	**121.5**

Source: Pomfret (2010, 26) based on data from World Bank *World Development Indicators*.

and maintaining domestic and international peace.[13] Focus on the domestic economic chaos and diminution of Russia's global standing in the 1990s ignores the extent to which Yeltsin's reforms provided the underpinning for Russian economic success under Putin, which would be magnified by the fortuitous timing of the 2000–2014 resource boom. The Russian examples illustrate the power of before/after comparisons, which may displace the more appropriate with/without comparison that requires careful analysis of the counterfactual situation.

In sum, although economics in the second half of the 20th century could create sub-disciplines around comparisons between planned and market economies and between developed and developing economies, in the 21st century such divisions are less plausible. Comparisons must be across a wider range of economies or focus on appropriate micro comparisons. The crucial element is to specify a counterfactual.[14] This has long been an issue in economic history and in economics in general and the challenge will be how to do this, perhaps by refining techniques such as randomized control trials at the micro level and synthetic controls at the macro level.

7.3 The age of fraternity

The title of my book *The Age of Equality: The Twentieth Century in Economic Perspective* was based on the French Revolutionary slogan *liberté-égalité-fraternité*, from which I imagined the 19th-century Age of Liberty was followed by concerns in the 20th century about inequality. How is the 21st century shaping up as the Age of Fraternity? Despite many signs of non-fraternal behavior, the existence of global public goods and the need for collective action suggest that fraternity may triumph. This conclusion is reinforced, we must hope, by recognition of the negative consequences of economic nationalism and of war between nuclear-armed great powers.

Turning points based on the arbitrary dating of centuries are simplifications. Many writers and some societies showed concern about equality before the 20th century, and the 20th century included harbingers of international cooperation. Bordo and Schenk (2021) highlight the attempts at international cooperation after 1919, including restoration of the gold standard and formation of the League of Nations, which would be taken up in revised form at Bretton Woods in 1944 and San Francisco in 1945. In 1944–1945, President Roosevelt foresaw enforcement by four policemen – the United States, USSR, UK, and China – but with Communists winning the Chinese civil war and inclusion of France among the permanent members of the Security Council, consensus was rarely possible and veto by one or the other side of the Cold War prevented strong action. UN peacekeeping evolved into separating warring forces in minor theatres rather than enforcing international rules. Moreover, efforts at global decision-making were rarely truly global, especially during the Cold War when the second and third worlds were typically non-participants or minimally fraternal.[15]

The fundamental conflict between national perspectives and anything resembling world government was acknowledged but not resolved. On more technical matters or where cooperation was clearly win-win, agreements were reached and standards agreed upon, although agencies such as the General Agreement on Tariffs and Trade (GATT) or the World Intellectual Property Organization (WIPO) were explicitly intergovernmental rather than representing the global community.[16] On matters of national importance, few countries were willing to give way to the majority. Such differences are almost inevitable, as the literature on the optimal size of nations suggests a trade-off between advantages of size (e.g., in supplying public goods) and benefits of cohesiveness (e.g., to simplify political bargaining) that is likely to lead to national borders reflecting breaks in shared culture or beliefs.

The most striking example of cooperation was the progress from the establishment of the European Coal and Steel Community in 1951 to the EU with a common currency by 1999, although European participation was incomplete and community interest often ran up against divergent national interests or beliefs. The clearest recent evidence of national resistance has been the Brexit referendum in 2016 and the championing of illiberalism by governments in Hungry and Poland. Decision-making has been facilitated by the introduction of qualified majority voting, but courts in Germany and in Hungary have ruled that EU decisions that contravene members' constitutions are illegal; to the extent that constitutions reflect national beliefs, this challenge to EU authority reflects divergences in culture or beliefs.

In the remainder of this section, I will emphasize two positive areas of fraternity in the first quarter of the 21st century: maintaining more or less global free trade and devising new trade rules in response to technological change, and addressing the challenges of climate change.[17] The next section discusses challenges to fraternal globalization from leaders who tap into concerns about globalization and often espouse virulent political and economic nationalism.

International trade has been the handmaiden of global prosperity over the last quarter millennium. Trade always involves winners and losers, but the increased size of the economic pie has tended to triumph in the long run. The 21st century started in the shadow of the November 30, 1999 anti-globalization riots in Seattle, and the Doha Development Round of multilateral trade negotiations has failed to reach a conclusion after two decades of almost fruitless negotiation. The main problem at the WTO is the mixture of a consensus requirement and assertive anti-globalism on the part of emerging economic powers such as India, Brazil, and South Africa. In the face of WTO roadblocks that prevent extending trade rules to new areas, other countries are reaching agreement while recognizing the need for cohesion. On digitalization and e-commerce, for example, consistent rules are being established in mega-regional agreements such as the CPTPP and RCEP or in EU deep agreements. If as seems possible, the UK, United States, and China accede to the CPTPP, its standards and rules will become the global benchmark for facilitating trade.[18]

The most obvious global issue for the 21st century is climate change.[19] Despite some stops and starts along the road to global action, there is widespread agreement on the salience of the issue especially since December 2015 when 196 countries, including all major economies, adopted the legally binding Paris Agreement at the 21st meeting of the Conference of the Parties (COP 21) of the United Nations Framework Convention on Climate Change. Although nations are formulating their commitments slowly and inadequately, there is no doubt that common action is needed to address a public good, and that there is little space for free riding.

7.4 The rocky road of populism

The 20th-century road towards incorporation of measures promoting equality of opportunity and outcome into capitalist economies was rocky, and events in the first half of the 1900s showed little promise of the eventual outcome. Fascism offered an alternative to capitalism or communism, with a charismatic leader uniting workers and capitalists for the national good and often tapping a sense of national injustice. The original fascist regime of Mussolini lasted from 1922 to 1943 and the national socialism of Hitler (1933–1945) was the most destructive. Other populist leaders such as Perón in Argentina (1946–1955) or Phibun in Thailand (1938–1944 and 1948–1957) had differing origins but proposed similar corporatist governance. Fascist regimes lasted longer in Spain (1939–1975) and Portugal (1932–1974), but the economic model was discredited and modified years before the Iberian dictators died. Fascism was often an interlude followed by return to capitalism and liberal democracy, not only in Europe but also in Argentina in 1983, Uruguay in 1985, and Chile in 1990, although the populist interlude could have a lasting impact on their country's political development (e.g. in Argentina and Thailand, the subsequent liberal democracy proved to be unstable). In the long run, fascism was a sideshow to the systemic competition of the 20th century, without the longevity of either communism or capitalism.[20]

In the 21st century, many people consider themselves sidelined by globalization or discount the seriousness or immediacy of climate change, and their support can be marshalled by populist leaders. Although inequality fell after 1914 and welfare-state measures addressed inequalities of opportunity and of outcome in market-based economies, since the 1980s inequality has increased in many countries, driven to some extent by the super-rich top 0.1% many of whom have benefited from globalization. Less well-off groups, especially in declining industries or passed-by towns, blame import competition for economic dislocation, with China an easily identified scapegoat (Autor et al., 2013, 2020). A sense of entitlement can drive the majority to elect a national leader who promises redistributive or national regeneration measures. However, as with fascism, populism is unlikely to be a long-term outcome because of its negative impact on efficiency as economic incentives are undermined.

Examining all populist regimes between 1900 and 2018, Funke et al. (2020) provide evidence of the economic failure of populist regimes after about 15 years.[21] They conclude that despite short-term successes the long-term economic cost of populism is high. After 15 years of a populist government, GDP per capita and household consumption are more than 10% lower than a non-populist counterfactual based on synthetic controls. Over the same time period, they found no decline in income inequality under a populist ruler. Their data support three explanations of poor economic performance and of lasting damage to the economy: rising economic nationalism and protectionism, unsustainable macroeconomic policies, and institutional decay under populist rule.

The easiest polices for a populist leader to deliver are protectionist trade and investment policies and unsustainable macroeconomic policies. In the dataset of Funke et al. (2020), populist regimes increase *ad valorem* import tariffs on average by ten percentage points compared to the non-populist counterfactual. In the short term, the measures benefit import-competing producers while importers of consumer goods are too diffused to see significant price increases or to organize opposition, and potential exporters hurt by the policy may not yet exist. The long-term costs of trade restrictions are well-established and may contribute to the reversion to a liberal market-based economy after the populist episode, as in Spain and Portugal in the 1970s and Argentina under Menem. At the same time, unwinding protectionist tariffs may be tortuous as those benefiting from the tariffs resist reform.[22]

Expansionary macroeconomic policies are also low-hanging fruit in the sense that they are easy to implement and yield short-term benefits. This was a salient feature of Latin American 20th-century populism (Dornbusch and Edwards, 1991). After increasing public expenditure, populist governments typically do not react to rising debt ratios by adjusting the primary fiscal balance, and this non-response leads to accelerating inflation or burgeoning debt. In stable political systems, fiscal policy is constrained to satisfy an inter-temporal budget constraint; despite incentives for governments to spend over the electoral cycle and perhaps have limited concern beyond the next election, formal or informal mechanisms exist to keep debt dynamics off an unsustainable path.

Important among the constraining checks and balances in a liberal democracy are the independence of the judiciary and of the press. Functioning democratic institutions also contribute to long-term growth through innovation, economies of scale, education, and capital accumulation (Acemoglu et al., 2019). Populism erodes these institutional advantages of democracies.

Although adverse economic consequences undermine populist governments and hasten their end in the medium or long term, if the government leaves a large public debt and destroys supporting institutions, the long-term consequences of populism can be significant.

7.5 Conclusions

What is the role of comparative economic studies against this backdrop? The above synthesis suggests that areas for comparative analysis could include differing responses to globalization and towards climate change, as well as cross-country analysis of the economic roots and consequences of populism. A prior assumption will be that institutions matter, but what kind of institutions is important?

Just as the plan versus market debate has withered, so have the democracy versus dictator debate and the distinction between left and right. Recent research has questioned the importance of the individual leader (Easterly and Pennings, 2020) or asked what background is associated with better leadership (Peveri, 2021). Gidron and Mijs (2019) have asked whether economic downturns create an environment in which radical populist parties flourish, concluding that this is the case for the radical left but that support for the radical right is more closely related to longer-term trends such as the impact of immigration. Gethin et al. (2021) find that the left-right political cleavage has been in flux over the last seventy years; the former split between working-class voters on the left and middle-class and upper-class voters on the right has been replaced by a division in which better educated people are on the left and less-educated people and wealthy businesspeople are on the right.

This is a selective handful of articles from the recent literature, which may not capture future trends. From the perspective of research groups in comparative economic studies, regional differences in the evolution of the sub-discipline are striking (see the Appendix). This suggests that the subject area may be broken down into global comparisons that overlap with other sub-disciplines of economics, and regional comparisons in European (Andreff, 2021; Casagrande and Dallago, 2021) or other parts of the world that overlap with area studies.

In sum, it is easy to argue that the discipline of comparative economic studies is in a period of change but harder to identify where that change is heading. A tentative conclusion is that the discipline will be driven by real-world events, notably 21st-century globalization and responding to climate change, which require international cooperation. The challenge will be to explain how responses to these challenges are evolving and under what conditions nationalist opponents to international collaboration gain power.

Notes

1 In this chapter, "comparative economic studies" or CES is synonymous with the subject taught in many universities and associated textbooks. Comparing economic systems has a longer history going back at least to ancient Greece (Brada, 2021).
2 Data in Chancel and Piketty (2021) show increasing global income inequality 1820–1910, both within and between countries. Within-country inequality dropped from 1910 to 1980 while between-country inequality continued to increase. After 1980, within-country inequality rose again while between-country inequality declined.
3 By "essentially over" I mean that the broad nature of the market-based economy had been established in each formerly centrally planned economy. The transition indicators of the European Bank for Reconstruction and Development show large changes during the 1990s but are more stable after 2000. Of course, the process of refining market-based systems continued in the 21st century and, for residents of the countries concerned, the transition remains unfinished business (see chapters by Rosta and by Chepurenko and Szanyi in this volume).

4 Roland also (page xxiv) observes that "In many cases, indeed, research on transition consists simply – and rightly so – in applying existing theories and methods to transition countries, just as they could be applied, say, to Europe or Latin America".

5 This literature provided the intellectual background for Britain's 1965 National Plan for Industrial Modernization and Expansion, which was ignominiously abandoned in 1967.

6 Casagrande and Dallago (2021) identify five sub-varieties of capitalism within the pre-Brexit EU, with the eleven formerly planned economies forming one group. They argue that institutional variety is a strength of the EU as long as each country has high-quality institutions, and they develop an EU benchmark for evaluating institutional quality under seven criteria: efficiency and effectiveness, stability, equity and equality, growth, and development.

7 Asian transition economies could be a third group, although the rejection of Communism and central planning is less clear than in Europe and the former Soviet Union, and the conditions of membership in ASEAN (or the CPTPP or RCEP) are simpler than the EU's *acquis communautaire*.

8 Within the growth econometrics of the time, it was difficult to discriminate between historical, geographical, or initial endowment explanations of this ranking; dummies based on years under Communism, distance from Düsseldorf or number of qualified engineers all worked equally well as explanatory variables (Pomfret, 2002, 90–2).

9 Recognition of the work of Williamson and Ostrom came later in the 2009 Nobel Prize that they shared. North received the Nobel Prize in 1993 for his contribution to economic history; the citation mentioned his emphasis on the role of property rights and institutions to "shed new light on the economic development in Europe and the United States before and in connection with the industrial revolution". Olson died in 1998, probably pre-empting the Nobel Prize that many thought he should have won (66 when he died in 1998, whereas North was 72 when he received the prize).

10 The common fate of CES and development economics was highlighted for me as associate editor of the journal *MOCT/MOST*, an academic journal focused on the economics of transition in Eastern Europe and the former Soviet Union. In the late 1990s, *MOCT/MOST* received many submissions, maintaining a quick turnaround and publishing good quality and topical papers despite a crowded field (e.g. *Journal of Comparative Economics, Comparative Economic Studies, Economic Systems, Economics of Transition*), highlighting the amount of active research in CES. Around 2000, submissions started to decline, and the editors turned to recruiting papers for special issues. As this approach ran out of steam, in 2002 the publisher, Springer, decided to merge *MOST* with a journal called the *Economics of Planning*, whose title reflected the dominant development economics paradigm of the 1960s and was long past its use-by date. The result of the merger was a hybrid journal, renamed *Economic Reconstruction and Change* in 2005, an outcome with little academic purpose driven by the publisher's desire to maintain subscriptions from university libraries rather than discontinue existing journals.

11 The trials have mainly concerned issues related to health and education. The previous Nobel winner associated with development economics, Angus Deaton in 2015, was best known for microeconometric analysis of household survey data, often focused on health or education issues. In recent years, papers at the annual *Life in Kyrgyzstan* conferences overwhelmingly use household survey data to answer questions related to health and education.

12 Campos et al. (2019) have used synthetic controls to compare the impact of EU membership on European countries.

13 The reference point for this rosy view is typically the era before Brezhnev's 1975 heart attack. By contrast, Western observers tend to recall the post-1975 Brezhnev years of economic stagnation and failure in Afghanistan.

14 Another option is comparison to a benchmark, as in the network analysis of cultural traits differences between regions or countries in Nadia von Jacobi's contribution to this volume.

15 For Mazower (2013), the post-1945 story of world governance has been about "governing the world the American way", and the resistance in other nations to American views of the world.

16 The private sector has sometimes established global standards (e.g. for containers), but there is often fear that standards imposed by a large company will be anti-competitive. Even with a small number of suppliers, e.g. the proliferation of low-orbit communication satellites in the 2020s, an international coordinator and regulator will be necessary, and it is unclear whether the UN-affiliated International Telecommunications Union (established in 1865 as the International Telegraph Union) will be up to the task.

17 Reactions to the COVID-19 pandemic were also on balance positive. Despite episodes of blame casting and protectionism, the global collaborative performance in 2020, from sequencing the genome to the rapid development and mass production of vaccines, was unparalleled (Bown and Bollyky, 2021).

18 The Comprehensive and Progressive Agreement for Trans-Pacific Partnership (CPTPP) replaced the Trans-Pacific Partnership in 2017 after President Trump refused to ratify the TPP, which had been largely drafted by the United States. The Regional Comprehensive Economic Partnership (RCEP) signed in November 2020 by the ten ASEAN countries and five regional partners overlaps with the CPTPP; the two agreements have seven signatories in common. EU deep agreement partners include Canada and Japan, both of which are CPTPP partners. In February 2021, the UK lodged a formal application to join the CPTPP. Pomfret (2021b) provides more details.

19 Increased migration from poor to rich countries is also becoming a global issue as refugees and others seek to flee beyond neighboring countries and as ageing populations in high-income countries increase demand-side pressure for additional workers. In the long run, migration is likely to be a source of increased global prosperity and understanding, but in the shorter term it is often a driver of support for populist anti-globalization leaders.

20 At mid-century, both Joseph Schumpeter and his student Paul Samuelson saw populism as the likely successor to 20th-century capitalism, which would be fatally compromised by demands for greater equality. The poorest 51% would vote in a government committed to redistribution policies that undermined capitalism's drivers of economic success. Ocampo (2021) argues that both writers were too greatly influenced by the experience of Argentina, whose specific circumstances they misunderstood.

21 Funke et al. (2020) define populism as a political style that centers on an alleged conflict between "the people" vs. "the elites". This includes all the major fascist regimes. Their conclusions indicate that both left-wing populists, who emphasize distributional and social issues, and right-wing populists, whose rhetoric typically focuses on cultural and religious topics, are equally bad for the economy.

22 A useful counterweight can be an external commitment to trade policy, e.g. accession to the European Union or, in the case of Mexico, joining NAFTA. In the absence of such a counterweight, many South American countries went through a stop-go cycle of liberalization during the "lost decade" of the 1980s as they tried to shed protectionism and other populist policies.

23 The 57 authors were affiliated with institutions in Australia (2), Belgium (1), Canada (1), China (1), Colombia (1), France (7), Germany (2), Hong Kong (6), Spain (1), Sweden (1), Switzerland (2), the UK (6), the United States (26), and Uzbekistan (1).

24 Apart from the subtitle, this session sounds like the most traditionally comparative economic studies session, but the paper titles would have seemed unusual in an ACES session more than a few years earlier: "Persistence through Revolutions", "China versus Europe: Rights, Rule of Law, and Political Stability", "Stratified Spatial Mobility, Local Elites and Economic Growth in China" and "The Rise of Communism in China".

25 The papers from this session were summarized in the *Economist* (Free Exchange section, 23 January 2021) around the theme of when do economic crises lead to political rupture? The crises-rupture link was not automatic but, in the cases of the Nazis' rise to power in Germany, collaboration in France and support for Mussolini in Italy, depended on pre-existing social fault-lines or group networks with historical roots.

26 Two sessions are co-hosted with the Society for Institutional and Organizational Economics (SIOE) and all nine reflect the overlapping interests of the two associations.

References

Abadie, A. (2021). Using Synthetic Controls: Feasibility, Data Requirements, and Methodological Aspects, *Journal of Economic Literature*. 59 (2), 391–425.

Acemoglu, D. (2021). Melissa Dell: Winner of the 2020 Clark Medal, *Journal of Economic Perspectives*. 35 (1), 231–48.

Acemoglu, D. and Robinson, J. (2006). *Economic Origins of Dictatorship and Democracy*. Cambridge: Cambridge University Press.

Acemoglu, D., Suresh, N., Pascual, R. and Robinson, J. (2019). Democracy Does Cause Growth, *Journal of Political Economy*. 127 (1), 47–100.

Andreff, W. (2021). *Comparative Economic Studies in Europe. A Thirty-Year Review. Studies in Economic Transition.* London: Palgrave Macmillan.

Autor, D., Dorn, D. and Hanson, G. (2013). The China Syndrome: Local Labor Market Effects of Import Competition in the United States, *American Economic Review.* 103 (6), 2121–68.

Autor, D., Dorn, D., Hanson, G. and Majlesi, K. (2020). Importing Political Polarization? The Electoral Consequences of Rising Trade Exposure, *American Economic Review.* 110 (10), 3139–83.

Bordo, M. and Schenk, C. (2021). "Unusual, Unstable, Complicated, Unreliable and Temporary": Reinterpreting the Ebb and Flow of Globalization, *NBER Working Paper 29114*, National Bureau of Economic Research, Cambridge, MA.

Bown, C. and Bollyky, T. (2021). How COVID-19 Vaccine Supply Chains emerged in the Midst of a Pandemic, *PIIE Working Paper 21-12*, Peterson Institute for International Economics, Washington, DC.

Brada, J. (2021). A Historiography of Comparative Economics. In E. Douarin and O. Havrylyshyn (Eds.), *The Palgrave Handbook of Comparative Economics* (pp. 19–45). London: Palgrave Macmillan.

Campos, N., Coricelli, F. and Moretti, L. (2019). Institutional Integration and Economic Growth in Europe, *Journal of Monetary Economics.* 103, 88–104.

Casagrande, S. and Dallago, B. (2021). Benchmarking Institutional Variety in the Eurozone: An Empirical Investigation, *Economic Systems.* 45 (1), Article 100838.

Chancel, L. and Piketty, T. (2021). Global Inequality, 1820–2020, *WID Working Paper No. 2021/19* (July 2021 version), World Inequality Lab.

Coase, R. (1937). The Nature of the Firm, *Economica.* 4 (16), 386–405.

Denton, G., Forsyth, M. and MacLennan, M. (1968). *Economic Planning and Policies in Britain, France and Germany.* London: Allen and Unwin.

Dornbusch, R. and Edward, S. (Eds.) (1991). *The Macroeconomics of Populism in Latin America.* Chicago, IL: University of Chicago Press.

Easterly, W. and Pennings, S. (2020). Leader Value Added: Assessing the growth contribution of individual national leaders, *NBER Working Paper 27,153*, National Bureau for Economic Research, Cambridge, MA.

Engerman, S. and Sokoloff, K. (2011). *Economic Development in the America's Since 1500: Endowments and Institutions.* Cambridge: Cambridge University Press.

Funke, M., Schularick, M. and Trebesch, C. (2020). Populist Leaders and the Economy, *ECONtribute Discussion Paper No. 036*, Reinhard Selten Institute, University of Bonn and University of Cologne, Germany.

Gethin, A., Martínez-Toledano, C. and Piketty, T. (2021). Brahmin versus Merchant Right: Changing Political Cleavages in 21 Western Democracies, 1948, *WID Working Paper No. 2021/15*, World Inequality Lab.

Gidron, N. and Mijs, J. (2019). Do Changes in Material Circumstances Drive Support for Populist Radical Parties? Panel Data Evidence from the Netherlands during the Great Recession, 2007-2015, *European Sociological Review.* 35 (5), 637–650.

Hall, P. and Soskice, D. (2001). *Varieties of Capitalism: The Institutional Foundations of Comparative Advantage.* Oxford: Oxford University Press.

Mazower, M. (2013). *Governing the World: The History of an Idea, 1815 to the Present.* New York, NY: Penguin Books.

Moore, B. (1966). *The Social Origins of Dictatorship and Democracy.* Boston, MA: Beacon Press.

North, D. (1981). *Structure and Change in Economic History.* New York, NY: W.W. Norton.

Ocampo, E. (2021). Capitalism, Populism and Democracy: Revisiting Samuelson's Reformulation of Schumpeter, *Documentos de Trabajo Nro. 796*, Universidad del Cema, Buenos Aires.

Olson, M. (1982). *The Rise and Decline of Nations: Economic Growth, Stagflation, and Social Rigidities.* New Haven, CT: Yale University Press.

Ostrom, E. (1990). *Governing the Commons: The Evolution of Institutions for Collective Action.* Cambridge: Cambridge University Press.

Peveri, J. (2021). The Wise, the Politician and the Strongman: National leaders' type and quality of governance, *AMSE Working Paper 2120*, Aix-Marseille School of Economics.

Pomfret, R. (2002). *Constructing a Market Economy: Diverse Paths from Central Planning in Asia and Europe.* Cheltenham: Edward Elgar.

Pomfret, R. (2010). The Financial Sector and the Future of Capitalism, *Economic Systems.* 34 (1), 22–37.

Pomfret, R. (2011). *The Age of Equality: The Twentieth Century in Economic Perspective.* Cambridge, MA: Harvard University Press.

Pomfret, R. (2021a). *The Economic Integration of Europe*. Cambridge, MA: Harvard University Press.

Pomfret, R. (2021b). 'Regionalism' and the Global Trade System, *World Economy*. 44 (9), 2496–2514.

Roland, G. (2000). *Transition and Economics: Politics, Markets, and Firms*. Cambridge, MA: MIT Press.

Shonfield, A. (1965). *Modern Capitalism: The Changing Balance of Public and Private Power*. Oxford: Oxford University Press.

Williamson, O. (1985). *The Economic Institutions of Capitalism: Firms, Markets, Relational Contracting*. New York, NY: Free Press.

Appendix: Regional Divergence in Comparative Economic Studies

In the early 2020s, the evolution of comparative economic studies in Europe and in the rest of the world appears to have diverged. European research in comparative economic studies continues, understandably, to focus on the post-central-planning experience of the countries of Eastern Europe. However, other comparative economic studies researchers appear to have forsaken this geographical area. This Appendix provides some examples of the divergence.

In the collection *Comparative Economic Studies in Europe* edited by Wladimir Andreff (2021) and with contributions by several past officials of the European Association for Comparative Economic Studies, only three of the 19 chapters – two on China and one on e-commerce – do not deal with European issues or post-Communist performance. The titles of over half of the papers at the September 2021 conference of the European Association for Comparative Economic Studies mentioned Eastern Europe or the former Soviet Union, and several other papers focused on the region. The annual best dissertation award went to a thesis on *The Influence of the Washington Consensus Programme on the Transitional Economies of Eastern Europe*.

The Association for Comparative Economic Studies, ACES (US-based but with global membership), organized eight sessions at the American Economic Association 2021 conference in which were presented 27 papers.[23] Two sessions organized around the linking theme of "Thirty Years since the Dissolution of the Soviet Union" inevitably focused on formerly centrally planned economies, but the other six sessions were on (1) China's Economic Growth and Social Development: An Institutional Perspective,[24] (2) The Rise and Fall of Imperial China, (3) Political and Economic Consequences of Norms Unravelling: Evidence from Europe's Darkest Hour,[25] (4) Political Economy in the Information Age, (5) Social Media and Political Economy, and (6) The Real Effects of Public Organization. Apart from the more traditional topics of the former Soviet Union and the Chinese economy, the striking features are the broader reach of institutional studies and the, often long-term, historical perspective. The pattern was even more pronounced in the 2022 ACES program, which had three China-related sessions and six sessions with no regional base; there was not a single paper on the formerly planned economies of Eastern Europe and the Soviet Union, and no author from that region.[26]

PART II

The comparative method: Comparative economics and comparisons of economic systems and economies

8

PRINCIPLES AND METHODS FOR CLASSIFICATION OF ECONOMIC SYSTEMS AND COMPARING THEIR ECONOMIC PERFORMANCE

H. Stephen Gardner

BAYLOR UNIVERSITY, WACO, TX, USA

8.1 Introduction

For millennia, scholars have attempted to design alternative economic and social systems and evaluate their relative performance. Aristotle (c. 350 BCE) claimed that Phaleas of Chalcedon "was the first to affirm that the citizens of a state ought to have equal possessions," but he questioned whether Phaleas's proposal would contribute to social stability. "The nobles," he argued, "will be dissatisfied [not to] receive the honors which they think their due," and the lower classes will gain little satisfaction because "the avarice of mankind is insatiable". Hence, "the beginning of reform is not so much to equalize property as to train the nobler sort of natures not to desire more, and to prevent the lower from getting more; that is to say, they must be kept down, but not ill-treated". Instead of an economic reform, Aristotle called for a system of public education that would attempt to modify cultural norms.

Debate over the design and evaluation of economic and social institutions continues unabated to this day, but in a new and evolving context. Looking backward, we can now draw on the historical experience of globalized capitalism, Soviet-style central planning, Yugoslav and Mondragon producer cooperatives, the microlending revolution, and a wide range of other institutional experiments and innovations. Looking forward, we know that the challenges and opportunities presented by climate change, pandemic diseases, and new technologies (artificial intelligence, robotics, quantum computing, and genomics, to name only a few) will have a major influence on both the design and evaluation of new institutions.

With all of this in mind, we attempt to address the traditional questions of comparative economics in light of historical experience and new challenges and opportunities. We also draw on recent advances in economics and other social sciences that have been insufficiently exploited in the field of comparative economics. These will include innovations in causal inference, economic history and anthropology, organizational studies, and measurements of human well-being, life satisfaction, and systemic resiliency.

DOI: 10.4324/9781003144366-11

We open with our definitions of institutions, economic systems, culture, and the environment, exploring the distinctions and interactions between these conceptions. Next, we will take a new look at the various criteria that have been used for the classification of economic systems and will explore the terminological confusion that has grown only worse over time. Finally, we will survey the issues involved in performance comparisons and consider the new challenges and opportunities presented by climate change, data analytics, and other factors.

8.2 The economic system, culture, politics, and the environment

Drawing on the work of Gregory Grossman (1974) and Douglass North (1991), we define an *economic system* as an interactive (and hopefully complementary) set of institutions that constrain, facilitate, and coordinate the economic behaviors of a society. An *institution* is an organization, practice, convention, or custom that is material and persistent in the life or culture of a society. The most familiar institutions are formal organizations, such as business corporations, labor unions, universities, and government agencies. Equally important, however, are informal organizations and other long-lived practices, conventions, and customs that gain institutional status. These include, for example, systems of monetary exchange, property rights, collective bargaining, racial and gender discrimination, bribery, charitable giving, and taxation. More generally, an institution is any established and generally accepted means of getting things done. We may think of the economic system in any country as a unique collection and network of these institutions.

In their effort to improve economic performance, national leaders will enact economic *policies* and *reforms*. In most cases, a shift in policy can be undertaken without changing the economic system or its underlying institutions. For example, in a country that has a fractional reserve banking system, monetary policy can be implemented by manipulating three *policy instruments*, which are, themselves, economic institutions: open-market operations, central bank lending, and adjustments of reserve requirements of commercial banks. On the other hand, if the current institutional framework seems to be hindering economic and social performance, leaders may support a deeper economic *reform*, typically including a new and different set of policy instruments.

We define the *environment* very broadly to include all of the factors that influence economic performance that are beyond the control of policy makers in the short-to-medium term.[1] For example, annual rainfall has a powerful impact on agricultural performance, but politicians have little *immediate* control over the weather. In a similar way, national leaders cannot *quickly* change the geographic landscape, the endowment of natural resources, the educational level or cultural norms of society, the economic policies or performances of trading partners, or the behavior of military rivals or allies. A person who knows that she will be driving through rough terrain will want to choose an appropriate vehicle for that journey and will modify her driving style to cope with the terrain. In a similar way, we may expect that a society (and especially a democratic one) will select/develop an economic and social system that is adapted to its physical and cultural environment and will follow policies that are required by immediate realities.

The relationships among institutions, policies, and environmental variables are frequently influenced by the time period of analysis. In the long run, most countries have little ability to change their geographic locations or natural resource endowments, but most have policies to improve the health and educational levels of their populations and to avert and mitigate the effects of climate change and foreign conflict. Hence, in the long run, some environmental variables are also policy variables, but, in the short-to-medium term, the natural environment is an uncontrollable reality that requires the adaptation of policies and institutional arrangements.

An important component of the environment in each country is its endowment of *natural resources*. In principle, a country with a rich endowment of resources should have an advantage over countries that are poorly endowed. The United States, for example, has gained enormous benefit from its fertile land, energy resources, temperate climate, and access to the two great oceans. On the other hand, some countries, such as Japan, have been quite successful with relatively poor resource endowments, and others, such as Russia and several countries in Africa and the Middle East, have not performed as well as their resources would suggest. This is not the right place for a full discussion of the so-called *resource curse*, but its existence in some countries and institutional arrangements has been documented quite convincingly by Amin and Djankov (2009), Cabrales and Hauk (2011), and others. We will only note that a deeper analysis of the relationships among the resource base, political and legal institutions, and cultural variable would seem to be fertile ground for specialists in comparative economics who have, thus far, given it relatively little attention. In countries with rich resources, high levels of "power distance," and weak rule of law, it seems that a kleptocratic culture can become deeply embedded in the norms and institutions of society.

8.2.1 The influence of culture

We define the *culture* of a society to include its customary beliefs, values, traditions, behavioral norms, and aesthetic sensibilities that are passed from one generation to another.[2] As North (1990, 1991) has observed, cultural norms are particularly evident in the development of informal institutions, such as the unwritten codes of institutional racism. However, it seems clear that cultural norms are also influential in the establishment of formal organizations, such as venture finance firms and representative governments.

Despite their importance, Alesina and Giuliano (2015) observed that "empirical investigation of the relevance of culture on economic outcomes is fairly new in economics". The same can be said for comparative economic studies. Our review of the indexes of ten textbooks in comparative economics revealed only two (Grossman 1974; Kennett 2004) that included an entry for culture, and the discussions of that concept and its importance were rather brief in both cases.

While they have attracted little attention in economics, cultural variables have been explored more extensively in anthropology, sociology, and political science. Thus, according to the widely used classification devised by Hofstede (2001), the culture of a nation is expressed along six dimensions: "power distance" (acceptance of authority), "individualism versus collectivism," "masculinity versus femininity" (more "feminine" cultures have greater gender equality), "uncertainty avoidance" (versus risk tolerance), "long- versus short-term orientation," and "indulgence versus restraint". Many other dimensions could be added to that list, including, for example, aesthetic creativity, religiosity, and interpersonal trust.

Frederic Pryor (2007) was among the first in our field to formally explore the influence of culture on economic institutions. For a sample of 17 OECD countries, he performed cluster analyses on indicators of culture in the World Values Survey and on institutional characteristics from his own database, finding that the classification of countries according to culture was almost identical to the classification according to institutions. For both cultural norms and institutional characteristics, he identified closely related clusters among Anglo-Saxon, Nordic, Western European, Southern European, and "Other" (which included Japan, alone). Hence, Pryor concluded that cultural norms are highly predictive of institutional characteristics in

OECD countries. Although he surmised that the causal relationship between culture and institutions was bidirectional, his analysis of data from East and West Germany suggested that the economic system has relatively little influence on the cultural system. "Instead," he concluded, "in a democracy, where the economic system is not imposed by force, the cultural characteristics are more likely to determine the economic system, rather than the reverse".

The role of culture has attracted increasing attention in recent years from economic historians and development economists, and, going forward, their methods and findings may have growing importance for comparativists. According to Alesina and Giuliano (2015), the cultural trait that has attracted more attention from economists than any other is *generalized trust*. The importance of this trait, they say, "cannot be overemphasized," and they cite Kenneth Arrow's (1972) observation that "Virtually every commercial transaction has within itself an element of trust, certainly any transaction conducted over a period of time. It can be plausibly argued that much of the economic backwardness in the world can be explained by the lack of mutual confidence". Subsequent research would confirm the importance of trust, supported by rule of law, in the transition from kin-based societies to nation states and in the development of trade, cooperation, and financial markets. Trust, of course, was the title and theme of a volume by Fukuyama (1995).

A remarkable example of the influence of trust on economic institutions and economic development is found in the work of Nunn and Wantchekon (2011). Combining contemporary individual-level survey data with historical data on slave shipments by ethnic group, they find that individuals whose ancestors were heavily raided during the slave trade, hundreds of years ago, are less trusting today. Lingering low levels of individual trust have impeded the development of political, economic, and social institutions, resulting in sustained poverty. "Overall," they conclude, "the findings provide evidence for the importance of internal norms and beliefs in transmitting the impacts of a historical shock, in this case the slave trade. One reason that history matters today is through the evolution of cultural norms".

Another interesting recent line of historical/cultural research comes from Joseph Henrich (2020), an anthropologist, who has revisited an old question – why did industrialization and economic modernity arise first in Western Europe, bypassing the earlier advanced cultures in Asia and northern Africa? His analysis draws particular attention to two innovations in religious culture. First, beginning in the 4th century CE, the Catholic Church began to introduce a series of prohibitions against marriage between close relatives and polygynous marriages. These policies, according to Henrich (p. 167), "sapped the lifeblood from Europe's kin-based institutions, weakened traditional authorities, and eventually dissolved Europe's tribes". People were forced to develop broader networks of marriage and affiliation, opening new opportunities for cooperation in trade and innovation.

Second, in the 16th century CE, Henrich points to the Protestant Reformation, but with a special emphasis on the rapid rise of literacy occasioned by the understanding that all Christians should have access to the Bible. A literate population, of course, has broad significance for the political and economic culture, but Henrich (p. 5) also emphasizes its physiological importance:

> Learning to read forms specialized brain networks that influence our psychology across several different domains, including memory, visual processing, and facial recognition .... The neurological and psychological modifications associated with literacy should be thought of as part of a cultural package that includes practices, beliefs, and institutions ....

8.2.2 *Interdependence of economic and political institutions*

If comparative economists have paid scant attention to cultural variables, we also have failed to fully recognize the interactions between economic and political institutions. We sometimes seem to assume that economic and political institutions are separable and can be analyzed independently. We economists are familiar with the gains that arise from specialization and the division of labor, so we naturally focus on the phenomena and methods that seem most relevant to our discipline. However, if we wish to effectively address the important challenges that confront the planet, we must learn to combine the gains from disciplinary specialization with the added benefits of interdisciplinary cooperation. Albion Small, who organized the first American department of sociology at the University of Chicago, said this in 1910 (Small 1910, p. 38):

> Specialized science, whether physical or social, inevitably passes into a stage of uncorrelated scientific piecework. In this stage of dismemberment, science is as inconclusive through its lack of coherence as it was in an earlier period from its superficiality. That is, it then had breadth without depth, it now has depth without breadth.

In comparative economics, we have built extensive literature on the varieties of capitalism but have taken little account of the growing literature in political science on the varieties and resilience of democracy. That literature is divided between the work of authors who begin with a "minimalist" definition of democracy and those who define it more broadly. The minimalists suggest that democracy requires only for rulers to be selected by competitive elections with broad suffrage (Przeworski 1999, p. 12). That definition recognizes the existence of "illiberal democracies" that have grown in number during recent years, and whose behavior has been discussed by Zakaria (1997) and many others.

On the broader end of the spectrum, the University of Gothenburg Varieties of Democracy Institute considers models "that are far more complex than the mere presence of free and fair elections," distinguishing "between five different principles of democracy: electoral, liberal, participatory, deliberative and egalitarian". Hence, they maintain a database of more than 450 indicators related to democracy, drawn from 202 countries over the period 1789–2018. Their 2021 Liberal Democracy Index (V-Dem 2021) ranks Denmark, Sweden, and Norway as the most democratic countries in the world (the United States ranked 31st), and it finds Eritrea, North Korea, and Yemen to be the world's least democratic (China ranked 174th out of 179).

The relationships between political and democratic institutions are clearly reciprocal. If we consider the influence of economics on politics, the work of Przeworski (1999, 16) and his colleagues suggest that economic performance is the strongest predictor of the durability of democratic rule: "The expected life of democracy in a country with per capita income under $1,000 is about eight years. Between $1,001 and $2,000, an average democracy can expect to endure eighteen years. But above $6,000, democracies last forever".

If we turn to the impact of political and other environmental variables on long-term economic performance, much of the best work has been conducted by Acemoglu, Johnson, and Robinson (2001). In their 2001 article, they found that European colonists adopted very different policies in different locations. In places where Europeans faced high mortality rates, discouraging long-term settlement, they installed extractive institutions. After independence and European departure, new local elites typically maintained those extractive institutions for their own advantage, together with repressing political cultures. According to their estimates, the institutional distortions fully account for low-income levels in Africa and other countries near the equator. In *Why Nations Fail*, Acemoglu and Robinson (2012) extended the historical narrative, arguing that the key for economic development is inclusive (rather than extractive) political and economic institutions. In *The Narrow Corridor* (2019), they focus on striking a healthy balance between a strong civil society and effective, but limited, powers of the state. The state can offer more to its citizens if social institutions also grow in strength. The objective, they say, is to develop the "Shackled Leviathan". In a careful analysis of panel data for 175 countries from 1960 to 2010, Acemoglu, Naidu, Restrepo, and Robinson (2019) found that democratization increased GDP per capita by about 20% in the long run.

The federal or unitary nature of the political system also has clear significance for the structure and performance of economic institutions. For example, Weingast (1995) suggests that an effective federal system can serve as a barrier against excessive centralization of economic power, providing protection for free operation of the market system. It can also provide for more flexible adaptation of economic institutions to local needs and can provide greater scope for systemic and policy experimentation. On the other hand, a noncooperative federal system can sometimes hinder effective policy coordination at the national level, and this can have devastating consequences during times of emergency. During the COVID-19 crisis, the evidence seems to suggest that countries with low levels of cooperation between national and provincial authorities, such as Belgium and the United States, responded poorly to the pandemic, and the more cooperative federal systems in Australia and Germany responded more effectively (Cameron 2021; Pelowski 2021).

8.3 Classification of systems

We can classify economic systems in many different ways. Just as we can classify people according to their height, weight, gender, and age, we can classify economic systems according to a wide range of overlapping criteria. Furthermore, the economic systems of actual countries are never purely capitalist or socialist, market or planned, free or controlled. Real countries have mixed institutional structures that change over time through evolution, reform, and revolution. Cultural norms and other informal institutions tend to change very slowly, but more formal structures, such as systems of taxation, may be adjusted quite suddenly by political leaders.

Scholars in comparative economics, including Koopmans and Montias (1971) and Neuberger and Duffy (1976), have frequently attempted to break free from the grand "isms" – capitalism, socialism, communism, fascism, etc. – because these are value-laden terms from a previous century that may obscure the variety and complexity of modern economic systems. Still, together with the general public, we have found it difficult to cast these terms aside. Here, we will attempt to set them in a broader context and consider their changing shades of meaning.

8.3.1 Classification according to ownership

The most durable classification of economic systems, dating back to Karl Marx and beyond, distinguishes between economies according to the predominant forms of ownership of factories, farms, and other productive assets. Accordingly, *feudalism* is an economic and social system wherein all ownership rights are ultimately held by a queen, king, or other monarch and are delegated down through a hierarchy of princes, dukes, barons, and serfs, subject to their loyalty, payment of tribute, and military and civil service. In a *capitalist* system, the greater part of the means of production is owned outright (not subject to feudal obligations) by private individuals, and in *socialism,* most of the means of production are owned, in some sense, "socially".

Presumably, Marx and others focused on the ownership as their criterion of classification because it tells us something about the power structure of a society. The owner of an asset may have any or all of the following: (1) the right to control how the asset is used; (2) the right to retain income generated by the asset; and (3) the right to transfer ownership of the asset to others. However, even in countries with traditions of free-enterprise capitalism, individual property rights are limited by zoning and inheritance laws, environmental and safety regulations, and other legal and social restrictions. On the other hand, even the most repressive societies usually make some formal or informal allowance for individual ownership.

8.3.1.1 *Varieties of capitalism*

Private/capitalist ownership can take many different forms. A capitalist enterprise may be owned by a sole proprietor, a group of partners, or a network of corporate shareholders who may live in hundreds of countries. In practice, there is little similarity between a sole proprietorship, managed by the owner, and a global corporation, characterized by separation of ownership from control. As Adolf Berle and Gardiner Means (1932, p. 355) observed, "The property owner who invests in a modern corporation so far surrenders his wealth to those in control of the corporation that he has exchanged the position of independent owner for one in which he may become merely recipient of the wages of capital".

We noted above that Pryor's (2007) cluster analysis identified five varieties of capitalism that followed the cultural norms rooted in ethnicity and geography: Anglo-Saxon, Nordic, Western European, Southern European, and "Other" (which included Japan, alone). Similar typologies have been formulated by many other authors, distinguishing among national systems of business organization, governmental intervention, and differences in their markets for labor, capital, and innovation. The Anglo-Saxon labor market, for example, is characterized by a lower level of job security for employed workers, but this has traditionally been thought to yield a higher level of market flexibility and a lower overall rate of unemployment. According to Freeman (2013), that conception of the Anglo-American market was undermined by the experience of the Great Recession.

8.3.1.2 *Varieties and conceptions of socialism*

According to the ownership criterion, a socialist enterprise may be owned by the national government (state socialism), by a local commune, or by a cooperative of producers or consumers. Historically, the leaders of socialist countries often tried to assert that their nation was operating the more genuine form of socialism. Stalin and Khrushchev, for example, claimed that Soviet-style state ownership represented a "higher" form of socialism than Yugoslav worker-managed cooperatives. Tito, together with many Western socialists, countered that the Soviet system was not socialist at all – that it was a system of "state capitalism" – because a small elite, rather than society, had control of the means of production. After Stalin's death, Mao declared that Khrushchev had abandoned the "dictatorship of the proletariat" and was allowing the Soviet Union to slide back into capitalism.

In retrospect, all of these were authoritarian or totalitarian regimes that were unlikely to deliver Marx's (1867) promise of a "society in which the full and free development of every individual forms the ruling principle". In the Soviet-style economies and China (as opposed to Yugoslavia), it would be difficult to argue that society, broadly defined, ever had effective ownership and control of the means of production. So, one could argue that most of the "true" socialist countries have been Western European democracies.

That, in turn, requires us to reconsider the traditional distinction between *democratic socialism* and *social democracy*. On this issue, there has been considerable debate in recent years, and the distinction between the two terms has been fading in popular discourse (in the United States, at least). Traditionally democratic socialists were people who called for nationalization of the "commanding heights of industry" or for extension of cooperative ownership. A social democracy was considered to be a country with an advanced system of social protection, but without any agenda for socialization of property. This distinction is still respected in many European countries, but it is disappearing in the United States where Bernie Sanders, Alexandria Ocasio-Cortez, and many others now declare that they are democratic socialists, although they do not call for socialization of ownership.

This, for example, is the recent manifesto of a group of democratic socialists in Florida (Nissen, McNamee, and Armil, 2021):

> What does "socialism" mean? In simplest terms, it means reversing our unbalanced power relations in both our economy and our political system: political and economic power would be transferred from the few (the 1 percent) to the many (the working class).

> A modern conception of Democratic Socialism must transcend the old view of socialism as strictly government ownership and a 100 percent "planned" economy. Modern socialism will have a use for markets as well as planning – but those markets must be shaped and controlled democratically and not "rigged" for the benefit of the capitalists and their henchmen. By democratizing the economy, modern socialism will do a better job of rewarding people who do useful, beneficial work rather than those who take advantage of the system.

Evidently, this new conception of socialism is gaining traction with young Americans. According to the Gallup Poll, in 1949 a plurality of Americans believed that socialism meant "Government ownership or control," but in 2018, a plurality thought it meant "Equality – equal standing for everybody" (Newport 2018b). Perhaps because they understand the word differently, young and old Americans are split on their support for capitalism and socialism. In 2018, 51% of Americans, aged 18–29, had a positive view of socialism, compared with 30% of those aged 50–64 and 28% of those aged 65 and up (Newport 2018a).

8.3.2 *Classification according to coordinating mechanism*

In any economic system, a large number of decisions must be made each year concerning the production and exchange of commodities and resources. Since millions of people may be involved in making and implementing these decisions, every economic system must employ *coordinating mechanisms* to insure some degree of consistency. Ideally, intended purchases of each commodity should equal intended production, the number of people who enter a given occupation should roughly equal the number of jobs available, and so on. Economic systems are often classified, therefore, according to their predominant coordinating mechanisms.

A *traditional economy* is one in which coordination is maintained through simple perpetuation of a gradually evolving *status quo*. What products will be produced? Those that were produced last year. How will they be produced? Roughly, just as they were produced in the past.

Sons follow their fathers and daughters follow their mothers in a tight web of kinship relations and traditional practices. According to Dalton (1968, p. xvii):

> The lesson of economic anthropology is the unimportance of economic organization in primitive society .... Rather, it is kinship, tribal affiliation, political rule, and religious obligation that control, direct, and are expressed by the economic in primitive societies.
>
> (i.e., where market dependence is absent)

Tradition can predominate as a coordinating mechanism only in relatively stationary societies. In fact, it would be contradictory to speak of a dynamic and growing economy that is coordinated primarily by tradition. Nevertheless, elements and legacies of tradition can be found in any functioning economy. Racial and gender discrimination, for example, have traditionally influenced the patterns of employment in many countries. In the old Soviet Union, economic plans were not prepared in a vacuum; they always built on the results of the previous year. Instead of planning from a blank page, this was known as "planning from the achieved level".

A *market economy* is one in which coordination is predominantly achieved through the free and spontaneous movement of market prices, responding to the forces of supply and demand. However, recent research calls attention to the role of business organization in the market system. In East Asia, for example, the distinctions between economic systems are not centered on market-versus-state dominance, but on the organizational relationships between productive firms. These include, for example, hierarchical *chaebol* structures in South Korea versus a flatter set of firm relationships in Taiwan (Hamilton et al. 2000).

In a *planned economy*, coordination of long-run and/or short-run decisions is attempted by means of a central plan, which is designed to guide the economy toward certain goals or objectives. Given the generality of this definition, a planned economy can take any of the several forms.

Directive planning (or *command planning*), which was employed in the former Soviet Union, China, Eastern Europe, and the US military, is a system whereby the most important long-run *and* short-run decisions are made by a central planning authority and are then passed down to subordinates in the form of instructions, directives, or commands. A directive plan typically includes an annual target for each factory and each important product, and compliance is compulsory. A *centrally planned economy* (CPE) employs directive planning as its predominant coordinating mechanism. Countries that are replacing directive planning with market institutions are commonly known as *transitional economies* (TEs). When we speak collectively about CPEs and TEs, following Marer (1991), we call them *historically planned economies* (HPEs).

Indicative planning, which was employed for many years in France, Japan, and a number of other countries, is a hybrid system that uses the market to coordinate short-run decisions (how many apples to pick this week) in combination with a plan to coordinate long-run decisions (how many apple trees to plant this year). Unlike a directive plan, which must provide detailed instructions to individual producers, an indicative plan typically includes broad goals for entire industries over a long (usually five-year) time horizon. Private companies are not legally required to comply with plan targets, but the government may use fiscal and monetary policy instruments to encourage compliance. Ideally, if it sets goals that are beneficial to all segments of society, an indicative plan should evoke voluntary compliance – it should be a self-fulfilling prophecy.

Quite often, countries that engage in indicative planning also conduct an active *industrial policy* (*IP*). An IP may include several different kinds of programs. First, a list of "winning" and "losing" industries may be formulated, with measures designed to support the former and phase out the latter. For example, the Japanese government supported the development of the steel and auto industries in the 1950s, consumer electronics in the 1960s, computer chips in the 1970s, and "knowledge-intensive" industries in the 1980s. Second, an IP may include measures to strengthen industrial stability and/or competition. Where monopoly power is pervasive, existing companies may be regulated, nationalized, or split into smaller units. Conversely, small companies may be merged into larger units to enhance their financial strength, production efficiency, and competitive position in the world market.

8.3.3 Classification according to incentive systems

Any coordinating mechanism must include a system of incentives to reward socially desirable behavior and discourage inappropriate actions. These are usually divided into three broad classes: coercive, material, and moral incentives.

Coercive incentives, which attempt to modify behavior through actual or threatened force and punishment, played a historic role in ancient Egypt, the American South, Hitler's Germany, Stalin's Soviet Union, and Pinochet's Chile. Slavery was not legally abolished in Mauritania until 1980, and forced labor is still reported in Burma, Cambodia, Haiti, Namibia, Sudan, and several other countries. According to the ILO (2017), 40 million people were victims of modern slavery in 2016. Of those, 25 million were engaged in forced labor and 15 million were held in forced marriage. Women and girls are disproportionately affected by modern slavery, accounting 71% of the total. More than half of the enslaved people are in Asia and the Pacific, but the highest rate of enslavement is in Africa, (7.6 per 1,000 people), followed by Asia and the Pacific (6.1 per 1,000).

Of course, even the most libertarian societies use coercion to raise tax revenues, enforce contracts, and prevent theft, fraud, violence, and other illegal actions. During the COVID-19 pandemic, we have seen that it has been much easier in some cultural systems than in others to enforce mandates for masking, vaccinations, and other containment measures.

Material incentives are those that reward desirable behavior with a claim over material goods, usually through some form of monetary payment. In a competitive market economy, material incentives arise more or less automatically from the operation of the system. If there is a shortage of any product, the resulting increase in its relative price will give producers a material incentive to increase the quantity they supply, and it will give consumers a material incentive to reduce the quantity they demand.

Systems of material incentives become more complicated in the presence of *principal-agent relationships*. Suppose that a "principal," perhaps the owner of a capitalist shoe factory, hires a group of "agents," or employees. What kind of material incentive system should the principal design to elicit the most desirable behavior from the agents at the lowest cost? A system of profit sharing, for example, may encourage the agents to respond more appropriately to market signals, such as an increase in the price of shoes, but it may also be costly (see Sappington 1991).

In an economy coordinated by a directive plan, principal-agent relationships can be even more complex. A material incentive system must be consciously designed and administered to elicit compliance with the plan. Customarily, this involved bonus pay arrangements tied to fulfillment of production targets. However, Soviet-style countries found it difficult to design incentive systems that would simultaneously encourage accurate reporting of economic information to central planners and compliance with both the letter and the intent of the plan.

Moral incentives are designed to elicit desired behaviors by appealing to an emotional cause, such as nationalism, company or personal pride, compassion for the sick and the poor, or the desire for acceptance by one's peers. Moral incentives were employed in "socialist competitions" between factories in the former Soviet Union, in the singing of company songs in Japan, and in the use of slogans, such as "Buy American".

Again, economic systems can be classified according to their dominant incentive systems. Karl Marx predicted that goods would be distributed according to the principle, "to each according to his labor," during the early stages of socialism, whereas the ultimate communist system would be characterized by distribution "to each according to his needs". Early socialism would be based on material incentives, but full communism would shift to moral incentives. Similarly, distinctions may be drawn between *command socialism*, which makes extensive use of coercion; *utopian socialism*, which leans heavily on moral incentives; and *market socialism*, with its stronger reliance on material incentives.

8.3.4 Classification according to objectives

Quite often, the language used in popular culture to describe an economic system is tied most closely to the values and objectives that motivated the adoption of that system. A *free-enterprise economy*, for example, is one in which the protection of individual freedom is a dominant objective. Proponents of free enterprise have always drawn a close connection between economic and political freedoms. According to Milton and Rose Friedman (1979, pp. 2–3):

> Economic freedom is an essential requisite for political freedom. By enabling people to cooperate with one another without coercion or central direction, it reduces the area over which political power is exercised. In addition, by dispersing power, the free market provides an offset to whatever concentration of political power may arise. The concentration of economic and political power in the same hands is a sure recipe for tyranny.

In a *welfare state* or *social democracy*, an equitable distribution of income, full employment, and a sustainable environment are among the leading objectives, and positive governmental action is employed to pursue those objectives. Governmental programs, including countercyclical monetary and fiscal policy, redistribution of income, health and employment insurance, and many other services are supported in the welfare state.

When capitalist ownership is combined with an authoritarian government bent on national economic and military power, the result is a *fascist* system. The relationship between individual rights and the national interest under such a system was described by the Fascist Labor Charter of 1927 (quoted in Sikes 1940, p. 670):

> The Italian Nation is an organism having ends, a life and means superior in power and duration to the single individuals or groups of individuals composing it .... In view of the fact that private organization of production is a function of national concern, the organizer of the enterprise is responsible to the state for the direction given to production.

8.4 Comparisons of system performance

Ultimately, what we really care about is the economic and social performance of our economic system. Given our competitive, nationalistic, and ideological leanings, we inevitably wish to know which economic system is best – capitalist or socialist, American or Chinese, German or Swedish? Here, we briefly consider some of the problems involved in making such comparisons.

8.4.1 Performance indicators

First, of course, there is the problem of selecting performance indicators, measuring them fairly, and assigning weights to them for an aggregative assessment. Historically, performance comparisons were generally based on the height or growth of GDP per capita, despite our knowledge that this was a poor measure of national well-being. Over time, performance comparisons have shifted toward the use of simple synthetic measures, such as the Human Development Index, based on broadly available indicators of health, education, and income. More recently, for a growing number of countries, it has become possible to incorporate survey-based measures of life satisfaction, work-life balance, civic engagement, and other indicators into broader synthetic indexes, such as the OECD Better Life Index. For a full discussion of aggregation issues related to these broader indicators, see Maridal et al. (2018).

Going forward, in light of the COVID-19 pandemic and recent reports from the Intergovernmental Panel on Climate Change, it seems certain that assessments of systemic performance will need to take fuller account of environmental sustainability and the robustness and resilience of our societies to environmental and health crises. Robustness, according to Miroudot (2020), is the ability to maintain operations during a crisis. Resilience, on the other hand, is the ability to recover from a crisis in a reasonable period of time and is addressed more fully in the chapters by Aligica and Hynes in this Handbook.

The FM Global Resilience Index (2021) provides an early attempt at measuring the comparative ability of 130 nations to respond to crises. It includes, for example, measures of exposure to natural disasters, quality of infrastructure, control of corruption, and many other indicators. Currently, by this measure, Denmark, Norway, Luxembourg, and Germany have the highest resiliency rankings; Haiti, Venezuela, Iran, and Chad have the lowest rankings.

Our recent experience with the COVID-19 pandemic also seems consistent with research that has found higher levels of innovation in countries with cultures characterized by individualism, low distance from power, and low aversion to uncertainty (Andrijauskienė and Dumčiuvienė 2017; Chen, Podolski, and Veeraraghavan 2017; Espig, Mazzini, Zimmermann, and de Carvalho 2021). Hence, Anglo-American individualism and risk tolerance evidently supported the creativity that delivered innovative mRNA vaccines in surprisingly short periods of time. Vaccines were also deployed rapidly in China and Russia, but were based on traditional vector technologies, involving the injection of inactivated viruses. All of these vaccines have proved helpful, but the mRNA vaccines seem to provide higher levels of protection and, better still, the newer technology holds promise for deployment against many other diseases, including rabies, influenza, Zika, HIV, and cancer (*Economist* 2021; Gupta 2021).

On the other hand, hyper-individualism, low power distance, and noncooperative federalism in the United States have made it difficult to coordinate and enforce vaccination mandates and mitigation efforts, yielding terrible levels of infection and death (see Brunnermeier 2021; Dubner 2021a,b). With a very different cultural and political system, China has combatted the disease very effectively but has sometimes sacrificed civil liberties, and its lockdowns have disrupted the national economy and global supply chains.

8.4.2 Causal inference

If we wish to know the impact of the economic system on performance, we must first remember that performance is also influenced by a wide range of environmental variables, the skills of policy makers, and cultural norms that are separate from institutional structures. Just as we would not conclude that an automobile is faulty because it is slow when driven by a poor driver in rough terrain, we should not quickly conclude that an economic system is faulty when it performs poorly.

Specialists in comparative economics have also been relatively slow to adopt some of the modern methods of causal inference. In the *Journal of Comparative Economics*, it appears that the first difference-in-differences study was performed by Kluve and Lehmann (1999), only a few years after Card and Krueger published their seminal DiD study on the minimum wage. However, the first regression discontinuity study in *JCE* was Vranken, Macours, Noev, and Swinnen (2011), and the first use of propensity score matching was Bai and Wu (2014).

8.5 Conclusions and the way forward

In his familiar "end of history" essay, Fukuyama (1989) asserted that "the triumph of the West, of the Western *idea*, is evident first of all in the total exhaustion of viable systemic alternatives to Western liberalism" (p. 3). In fairness, he hedged that liberalism would rule the world only "*in the long run*" (p. 4), but, nevertheless argued that fascist nationalism "completely lost its appeal" after World War II (p. 9), that China "can no longer act as a beacon for illiberal forces around the world" (p. 12) and rejected the "assumption that Russia shorn of its expansionist communist ideology should pick up where the czars left off" to rebuild its empire (p. 17).

If Fukuyama's expectations had proved correct, the fields of comparative economics and politics would seem to have little more than historical interest. Instead, we evidently live in a new era of ideological competition *between* and *within* major countries on issues related to liberalism, social tolerance, personal privacy, federalism, environmental protection, global cooperation, and many others. Whereas Deng Xiaoping and his immediate successors made no claim that the Chinese system should be emulated by other countries, Xi Jinping (2017), in his report to the 19th National Party Congress, declared that China now offers "a new option for other countries":

> The Chinese nation ... has stood up, grown rich, and is becoming strong .... The path, the theory, the system, and the culture of socialism with Chinese characteristics have kept developing, blazing a new trail for other developing countries to achieve modernization. It offers a new option for other countries and nations who want to speed up their development while preserving their independence; and it offers Chinese wisdom and a Chinese approach to solving the problems facing mankind.

The field of comparative economic systems had its inception during the rising competition between the Soviet and Western systems, and it seemed to decline when that competition diminished. Today, Elizabeth Economy (2022, p. 217) suggests that the West is engaged in a competition with China "to define the values, norms, and institutions of the 21st century". While that certainly is true, we also are engaged in competitions *within* many of our countries where populist, nationalist, and illiberal movements have gained strength.

The new realms of ideological and systemic competition, paired with the existential challenges of climate change, pandemic disease, and emerging technologies, should generate heightened interest in comparative studies. However, the foregoing analysis suggests that new research should differ from the older literature in many ways:

- The old categories of capitalism and socialism have lost much of their meaning, and comprehensive central planning has nearly disappeared from the face of the earth, so our systems of classification will require substantial revision.
- Economic institutions do not operate in a vacuum. They are embedded in national cultures, political systems, and natural environments that influence their adoption and modify their performance. Going forward, research in comparative economics should be conducted in closer cooperation with specialists in related academic fields.
- We can no longer rely so heavily on aggregate indicators of performance, such as GDP, that disregard environmental sustainability, public health, innovation, and national resilience.
- Comparative economists should take better advantage of modern tools of causal inference.
- Comparative economists have *always* worked for better international communication and understanding. That should continue!

Notes

1 Here, we are loosely following the framework established by Koopmans and Montias (1971), who defined the environment to include resources, initial technology, initial preferences, and external factors. Their definition of resources included natural resources (including climatic conditions), the initial capital stock, and the initial population, including its age, health, skills, and education levels. They made little mention of cultural norms that gain more attention here.
2 For some reason, the definitions of culture offered by economists usually seem to exclude its aesthetic aspect. So, for example, the widely cited definition offered by Guiso, Sapienza, and Zingales (2006) includes only "those customary beliefs and values that ethnic, religious, and social groups transmit fairly unchanged from generation to generation".

References

Acemoglu, D., Johnson, S. and Robinson, J. A. (2001). The colonial origins of comparative development: An empirical investigation. *American economic review*, 91(5), 1369–1401.

Acemoglu, D., Naidu, S., Restrepo, P. and Robinson, J. (2019). Democracy does cause growth. *Journal of political economy*, 127(1), 47–100.

Acemoglu, D. and Robinson, J. (2012). *Why nations fail: The origins of power, prosperity, and poverty*. New York: Crown Business.

Acemoglu, D. and Robinson, J. (2019). *The narrow corridor: States, societies, and the fate of liberty*. New York: Penguin Press.

Alesina, A. and Giuliano, P. (2015). Culture and institutions. *Journal of economic literature*, 53(4), 898–944.

Amin, M. and Djankov, S. (2009). Natural resources and reforms. *World Bank policy research working paper no. 4882*.

Andrijauskienė, M. and Dumčiuvienė, D. (2017). Hofstede's cultural dimensions and national innovation level. *Dubrovnik international economic meeting*, 3(1), 189–205.

Aristotle. (c. 350 BCE). *The politics*, vol. 1. Translated by Jowett, B. Oxford: Clarendon Press. Retrieved August 15, 2021, from https://oll.libertyfund.org/title/jowett-the-politics-vol-1

Arrow, K. J. (1972). Gifts and exchanges. *Philosophy and public affairs*, 1(4), 343–362.

Bai, C. and Wu, B. (2014). Health insurance and consumption: Evidence from China's new cooperative medical scheme. *Journal of comparative economics*, 42, 450–469.

Berle, A. and Means, G. (1932). *The modern corporation and private property*. New York: Macmillan Company.

Brunnermeier, M. (2021). *The resilient society*. Colorado Springs: Endeavor Literary Press.

Cabrales, A. and Hauk, E. (2011). The quality of political institutions and the curse of natural resources. *Economic journal*, 121(551), 58–88.

Cameron, D. (2021). "The relative performance of federal and non-federal countries during the pandemic". In *Federalism and the response to COVID-19: A comparative analysis*, edited by Chattopadhyay, R., Knüpling, F., Chebenova, D., Whittington, L. and Gonzalez, P. London: Routledge India.

Chen, Y., Podolski, E. J. and Veeraraghavan, M. (2017). National culture and corporate innovation. *Pacific Basin finance journal*, 43, 173–187.

Dalton, G. (1968). "Introduction". *Primitive, archaic, and modern economies: Essays of Karl Polanyi*. Garden City: Doubleday.

Dubner, S. (2021a). The U.S. Is Just Different—So Let's Stop Pretending We're Not. *Freakonomics*, 469. Retrieved September 4, 2021, from https://freakonomics.com/podcast/american-culture-1/

Dubner, S. (2021b). The Pros and Cons of America's (Extreme) Individualism. *Freakonomics*, 470. Retrieved September 4, 2021, from https://freakonomics.com/podcast/american-culture-2/

Economist. (2021). Which vaccine is the most effective against the Delta variant? *Economist*. November 17, 2021. Retrieved January 30, 2022, from https://www.economist.com/graphic-detail/2021/11/17/which-vaccine-is-the-most-effective-against-the-delta-variant

Economy, E. (2022). *The world according to China*. Cambridge: Polity Press.

Espig, A., Mazzini, I. T., Zimmermann, C. and de Carvalho, L. C. (2021). National culture and innovation: A multidimensional analysis. *Innovation & management review*. Retrieved January 29, 2022, from https://doi.org/10.1108/INMR-09-2020-0121

FM Global Resilience Index. (2021). Retrieved September 12, 2021, from https://www.fmglobal.com/research-and-resources/tools-and-resources/resilienceindex

Freeman, R. (2013). Failing the test? The flexible U.S. job market in the great recession. *National Bureau of Economic Research, working paper 19587*.

Friedman, M. and Friedman, R. (1979). *Free to choose: A personal statement*. New York: Harcourt Brace Jovanovich.

Fukuyama, F. (1989). The end of history? *National interest*, 16, 3–18.

Fukuyama, F. (1995). *Trust: The social virtues and the creation of prosperity*. New York: Free Press.

Gorodnichenko, Y. and Roland, G. (2017). Culture, institutions, and the wealth of nations. *Review of economics and statistics*, 99(3), 402–416.

Grossman, G. (1974). *Economic systems*, 2nd ed. Englewood Cliffs: Prentice Hall.

Guiso, L., Sapienza, P. and Zingales, L. (2006). Does culture affect economic outcomes? *Journal of economic perspectives*, 20(2), 23–48.

Gupta, S. (2021). The application and future potential of mRNA vaccines. *Yale School of Public Health*. Retrieved January 30, 2022, from https://ysph.yale.edu/news-article/the-application-and-future-potential-of-mrna-vaccines/

Hamilton, G. et al. (2000). Neither states nor markets: The role of economic organization in Asian development. *International sociology*, 15(2), 288–305.

Henrich, J. (2020). *The WEIRDest people in the world: How the West became psychologically peculiar and particularly prosperous*. New York: Farrar, Straus and Giroux.

Hofstede, G. (2001). *Culture's consequences: Comparing values, behaviors, and organizations across nations*. Thousand Oaks, CA: Sage.

ILO. (2017). *Global estimates of modern slavery: Forced labour and forced marriage*. Geneva: International Labour Office.

Kennett, D. (2004). *A new view of comparative economics*, 2nd ed. Mason: Thomason South-Western.

Kluve, J. and Lehmann, H. (1999). Active labor market policies in Poland: Human capital enhancement, stigmatization, or benefit churning? *Journal of comparative economics*, 27, 61–89.

Koopmans, T. and Montias, J. M. (1971). "On the description and comparison of economic systems". In *Comparison of economic systems: Theoretical and methodological approaches*, edited by Eckstein, A. Berkeley: University of California Press, 27–38.

Marer, P. (1991). "Conceptual and practical problems of comparative measurement of economic performance". In *Economic statistics for economies in transition: Eastern Europe in the 1990s*. Washington: U.S. Bureau of Labor Statistics, 5–23.

Maridal, J. H., Palich, L., Morgan, G., Gardner, H. S., McKinney, J. and Bolbocean, C. (2018). Wellbeing indices: A comprehensive inventory of standards and a review of current comparative measures. *Ecological economics*, 149, 1–11.

Marx, K. (1867). *Capital*, vol. 1. Based on the first English edition. Moscow: Progress Publishers. Retrieved September 4, 2021, from https://www.marxists.org/archive/marx/works/1867-c1/

Miroudot, S. (2020). Resilience versus robustness in global value chains: Some policy implications. *VoxEU*. Retrieved August 14, 2021, from https://voxeu.org/article/resilience-versus-robustness-global-value-chains

Neuberger, E. and Duffy, W. (1976). *Comparative economic systems: A decision-making approach*. Boston: Allyn and Bacon.

Newport, F. (2018a). Democrats more positive about socialism than capitalism. *Gallup, Polling matters*. Retrieved August 15, 2021, from https://news.gallup.com/poll/240725/democrats-positive-socialism-capitalism.aspx

Newport, F. (2018b). The meaning of "socialism" to Americans today. *Gallup, Polling matters*. Retrieved August 15, 2021, from https://news.gallup.com/opinion/polling-matters/243362/meaning-socialism-americans-today.aspx

Nissen, B., McNamee, C. and Armil, S. (2021). We are actual Democratic Socialists, and here is what we believe. *Tampa Bay times*. Retrieved August 15, 2021, from https://www.tampabay.com/opinion/2021/04/01/we-are-actual-democratic-socialists-and-here-is-what-we-believe-column/

North, D. (1990). *Institutions, institutional change and economic performance*. Cambridge and New York: Cambridge University Press.

North, D. (1991). Institutions. *Journal of economic perspectives*, 5(1), 97–112.

Nunn, N. and Wantchekon, L. (2011). The slave trade and the origins of mistrust in Africa. *American economic review*, 101(7), 3221–3252.

Pelowski, M. (2021). Did federalism impact the capacity for public health policy response to COVID-19? The case of Germany. Binghamton University citizenship, rights, and cultural belonging working paper series, no. 110.

Pryor, F. L. (2007). Culture and economic systems. *American journal of economics and sociology*, 66(4), 817–855.

Przeworski, A. (1999). "Minimalist conception of democracy: A defense". In *Democracy's value*, edited by Shapiro, I. and Hacker-Cordon, C. Cambridge: Cambridge University Press, 12–17.

Sappington, D. E. M. (1991). Incentives in principal-agent relationships. *Journal of economic perspectives*, 5(2), 45–66.

Sikes, E. (1940). *Contemporary economic systems*. New York: Henry Holt.

Small, A. (1910). *The meaning of social science*. Chicago: University of Chicago Press.

V-Dem. (2021). Democracy report 2021: Autocratization turns viral. University of Gothenburg Varieties of Democracy Institute. Retrieved January 29, 2022, from https://www.v-dem.net/democracy_reports.html

Vranken, L., Macours, K., Noev, N. and Swinnen, J. (2011). Property rights imperfections and asset allocation: Co-ownership in Bulgaria. *Journal of comparative economics*, 39, 159–175.

Weingast, B. (1995). The economic role of political institutions: Market-preserving federalism and economic development. *Journal of law, economics, & organization*, 11(1), 1–31.

Xi, J. (2017). Full text of Xi Jinping's report at 19th CPC National Congress. *China daily*, October 18, 2017. Retrieved January 30, 2022, from http://www.chinadaily.com.cn/china/19thcpcnationalcongress/2017-11/04/content_34115212.htm

Zakaria, F. (1997). The rise of illiberal democracy. *Foreign affairs*, 76(6), 22–43.

9

COMPARING ALTERNATIVE ECONOMIC SYSTEMS

Old and New Approaches

J. Barkley Rosser Jr. and Marina V. Rosser

JAMES MADISON UNIVERSITY, HARRISONBURG, VA, USA

9.1 Introduction

How alternative economic systems have been compared has changed substantially over time. Coming from ancient philosophy and over the centuries, the predecessor of comparative economics was the promulgation of possible ideal societies, utopias. However generally speaking, from Plato's (375 BCE) *Republic* through Sir Thomas More's (1516) *Utopia*, these largely focused on proposed ideal systems, although Plato's dialog does discuss some flaws of existing societies. But these systems largely existed in theoretical isolation. A general problem with all these visions is that they effectively posit an end of history, whereas actually existing economic systems constantly change and evolve, a fact that also holds for economic thought about these matters.

This promulgation of ideal societies accelerated after the French Revolution with the appearance of the utopian socialists, notably St. Simon, Fourier, and Owen, each of whom developed their own versions of such ideal societies, although as with the earlier efforts, not making explicit comparisons with alternatives. Arguably the beginning of comparing economic systems, even if they were all theoretical, came with the work of Marx and Engels, who would comment on forms of socialism competing with their vision, with this specifically involving a critique of the proposals of the utopian socialism visions.

The extension of this would come with the socialist calculation debate, which began at the beginning of there being an actually existing socialist system in what became the USSR. This posed the alternate systems being compared not to be alternative forms of socialism but essentially stylized forms of socialism against idealized forms of capitalism. After World War II as more nations adopted forms of socialist economic systems, the comparisons would increasingly consider the actual operations and performance of the economies of different nations rather than the comparison of idealized versions of these systems. These comparisons would come to recognize varieties of both capitalist and socialist systems developing across the wide array of nations in the world.

The end of the socialist system in the former Soviet bloc led to substantial changes in the comparison of alternative economic systems. While forms of socialism continued to exist in certain nations, the emphasis shifted more to the comparing non-socialist systems. This has

DOI: 10.4324/9781003144366-12

taken the form of further study of varieties of capitalist systems. It has also led to the rise of the new comparative economics in which forms of efficiency and inefficiency in state and private sectors across various mixed economies. It has also seen more emphasis on the influence of cultural and religious systems upon the form of economic systems, as indeed movements urging the increased influence of such elements have spread across many nations.

9.2 The origin of comparing alternative economic systems

As noted already, there has been a long tradition of implicit comparing of alternative economic systems as one figure after another has posed ideal or utopian systems that do not exist and never have in the real world. The implicit comparison is between the ideal utopia and whatever was the existing system that the figure postulating the ideal utopia lived in, with anyone reading or hearing of the ideal utopia when it was initially proposed would presumably understand the implicit comparison. This sort of comparison could continue to be made by later readers of such proposed ideal societies as Plato's Republic who could make the comparison between it and their own societies, even as theirs would differ from that of Plato himself when he wrote.

While Plato's idealized society was not specifically founded on religion, many later such visions were more directly so based and motivated. Reports of sharing of goods among the first follower of Jesus fit into this. A long tradition in Europe of uprisings by peasants and others, such as that led by Munzer in Germany in the early 1500s, drew on the millennarian tradition in Christianity, that the end of the world might be nigh and that a New Jerusalem might be at hand. This motivated people to try to bring these visions of paradise on earth into reality, and such motivations were strong. This manifested itself in a wide-ranging way during the English civil war of the mid-1600s, where multiple factions posed their competing visions of society. Most dramatic was that of the Levellers led by Winstanley who posed a quasi-socialist vision of effectively ending private property in land to be replaced by a system of sharing. The Levellers saw the moment as one of Armageddon and the impending arrival of the Millennium.

It must be noted that while many of these ideas drew on religious prophecies of future paradises, there were some that had some influences coming from real-world examples. The most important one for Europeans after the 1400s was reports of various practices by the Native American Indians. Of course most of those observing them from Europe viewed them as inferior pagans who needed to be converted to Christianity and "civilized" to be proper Europeans through colonization and domination. But some observers saw some of their practices as superior to those of wicked Europe. Probably the first person to be seriously inspired by their example was Sir Thomas More in his *Utopia*.

This idealized example of Native American Indians would continue to influence thinkers even as these discussions became secular during the Enlightenment. A crucial individual in this was Rousseau (1762), who posed an original innocence and perfection of people in simple states of nature where the original social contract would be formed. This vision of an essentially utopian past in simple societies would reappear in the work of Marx and Engels when they posed a period of "primitive communism" in the distant past. Importantly Rousseau's argument would play into the many influences that would lead to the French Revolution, which was arguably driven on dramatically improving society, with some seeing the possibility of an ideal society as the possible ultimate outcome, although the widespread use of the guillotine and the ultimate coming to power of Napoleon disillusioned many who had idealistic hopes about what the revolution would bring.

Which brings us to those thinkers famously labeled "utopian socialists" by Marx and Engels, initially in *The Communist Manifesto* (1848), these figures certainly posing their utopias to the extent they did as alternatives to the existing society that was clearly criticized by the efforts to develop better societies and systems. As it is, while Charles Fourier (1808) and Robert Owen (1813) would propose the formation of new communal communities, with their efforts inspiring up to 140 such efforts in the United States alone, with Brook Farm of the New England transcendentalists inspired by the phalanxes proposed by Fourier and New Harmony in Indiana actually founded by Owen with his sons continuing to live there even as it turned from a communal society to just a conventional town, the father of this group, Henri de Saint-Simon was not what he was thought to be, even though he is one of the most important figures in the history of comparative economics. After all, it is Saint-Simon whom Hayek in his final work, *The Fatal Conceit* (1988), pinpointed as the source of what became the title of that book, the idea that people can be socially engineered to perfection by altering the socio-economic system.

It is a curious thing that Sain-Simon was not really what was claimed of him, being a socialist, although his views changed over time. It was followers of his who were socialists. He fought in the American Revolution with the Marquis de Lafayette and supported the French Revolution when it started, an opponent of feudalism and idleness while supporting science and hard work. He barely survived the Terror of Robespierre, imprisoned in the Palais de Luxembourg. In his "Declaration of Principles" (1817), he declared:

> We believe that government is at least an unnecessary intermediary between those who think about the public interest and those feel it, between political writers and industry. Accordingly, I consider it necessary to find a means of abolishing this useless intermediary. Direct relations should be established between industry and men of letters

In his final work in the year of his death, *Le Nouveau Christianisme* (1825), where he posed a combination of science and religion, he would support some government to help aid the poor and argued for an end to inheritance, while supporting ownership "in common," probably his closest approach to socialism, and this work would inspire followers who clearly did move toward socialist positions, with the very word "socialism" being coined by one of his former followers, Pierre Leroux (1834), with Robert Owen almost immediately picking it up from him in Britain within a year as part of his trade union activism, although Leroux's version also supported a role for religion in it. Despite this, Marx would be an admirer of Leroux. The word "communism" would also be coined in this period by another utopian socialist, Étienne Cabet (1840) who proposed "Icarian" utopian communities and whose writings inspired efforts to start such communities in the United States.

Engels (1880) indeed identified Saint-Simon as the inspiration for the idea of central planning, the charge that Hayek levied against him. But while Marx and Engels clearly saw this planning to be carried out by the state, as in the quote above, for Saint-Simon government was not to be involved. It was not even clear that it was full-blown coordinated planning across firms or sectors, but rather these "direct relations" where the educated and scientific "men of letters" would directly interact with the managers of firms. It is not clear that Saint-Simon supported anything more than what we now think of as "scientific management," while one branch of his followers followed a socialist path, others supported private sector development of infrastructure such as the Suez Canal, and Emperor Napoleon III a great admirer of him. The legacy of Saint-Simon was not only important but also complicated. Arguably it is because of Marx and Engels lumping him with the utopian socialists that most now think of him as a socialist, even if he was barely one in his own lifetime.

Which brings us to Marx and Engels themselves, especially in *The Communist Manifesto* where they labeled these people they criticized as "utopian socialists" even as they took ideas from them. Indeed, this influential work clearly has elements that are utopian even as Marx and Engels denounced such tendencies. They ran through a list of socialisms they found inadequate, including "feudal," "petty bourgeois," "German," "conservative or bourgeois," as well as "critical utopian socialism and communism". Indeed, with that last it must be noted that at this time and for much longer there was no clear distinction between socialism and communism. Many have claimed that when Marx proclaimed "From each according to his ability, to each according to his need" In the *Critique of the Gotha Program* (1875), this was goal of pure communism, while in fact he labeled this "the higher stage of socialism". The distinction between these terms only came into focus in the 20th century.

Of course Marx and Engels mostly avoided declaring how things were to be after the revolution precisely because they viewed such declarations as being "utopian" and unscientific, with scientific socialism being more about studying the historical development of capitalism and its anticipated downfall, although they also criticized for being insufficiently revolutionary. Nevertheless, in *The Communist Manifesto*, they broke down and engaged in precisely that, providing a platform of ten "measures," they considered to be "pretty generally applicable" in "the most advanced countries". This hodge-podge included some items we readily consider to be standard socialist ones such as abolition of property in land, abolition of all right of inheritance (adopted from Saint-Simon clearly), centralization of credit in the hands of the state in monopoly central bank, centralization of the means of communication and transport in the hands of the state, and extension of factories and instruments of production owned by the state (with a nod at being "generally in accordance with a common plan"). None of this was the "withering away of the state" Marx would later call for as part of the higher stage of socialism. This was indeed hard core classic socialism as it would be practiced in many societies later that called themselves socialist or communist.

But then there were items that have come to be adopted by essentially all modern high-income nations. These would include a progressive income tax, free education for all children in public schools, and abolition of child labor, with these last two major ideas strongly advocated by Robert Owen. But then they also had planks that look to be outright utopian, most notably their call for the "combination of agriculture with manufacturing industries, gradual abolition of the distinction between town and country by a more equable distribution of the population over the country," as well as the rather vague "Equal liability of all to labor," although that was associated with dictatorial sounding "Establishment of industrial armies, especially for agriculture". For all their ridicule of the utopian socialists, they both adopted some of their ideas as well as indulging in proposals that lean to being outright utopian themselves. They too joined the movement to proposing utopia in contrast to the existing system they spent most of their time analyzing and criticizing in a supposedly scientific way.

All of this can be viewed as the predecessor of comparative economics as there were no actually existing socialist or communist systems to study and compare with feudal or capitalist ones that did exist, unless one counted the primitive communist systems of earlier societies or possibly those of native or indigenous peoples. So all that was available to compare with the actually existing systems were these various possible utopias, even those that were supposedly inspired by actual practices among such "primitive" indigenous peoples.

9.3 Comparing actually existing capitalism and socialism

That comparative economics moved from being an essentially abstract discussion about various idealized possible utopias to comparing the performance of actually existing economics systems came following the Bolshevik Revolution in Russia of 1917, when a government came to power proclaiming itself to be socialist and committed to moving toward communism, even as no actually existing socialist nation has yet to claim to have achieved true communism, presumably that "higher stage of socialism" proposed by Marx in 1875. Indeed, for the entirety of its existence, the official line of the Communist Party of the Soviet Union was that the system was "in transition" to that ultimate goal of true or pure communism, while lingering in its actually existing state of socialism.

Even so, this more realistic comparative economics still started from an abstract discussion, the famous socialist calculation debate. While indeed in several later writings, Engels had emphasized his and the not fully stated agreement of Marx in supporting some sort of central planning, inspired by the odd case of Saint-Simon, he never spelled out any details of how this was to be done or any specifics of issues or problems that might arise in actually doing this. This discussion came later, although initially still before the Bolshevik Revolution, and so still in a purely theoretical context. Indeed, when Enrico Barone (1908) first seriously discussed the idea of central planning, he did not follow Engels or Marx so directly, but more Walras and Pareto and their conception of an efficient general equilibrium, with Barone posing that it might be possible for a central planner to achieve such an efficient outcome.

It has not always been acknowledged fully that Barone recognized many of the very real problems that would confront real-world central planners in the future, even as he posed this possibly desirable outcome. So he recognized such problems as (1) that the appropriate technical coefficients of production would be inconceivable to know a priori to planning; (2) that to find the appropriate prices would have to be determined through experimental methods, trying various ones to see how they worked out; (3) that determining the plan would probably lead to "an army" of bureaucrats with they being part of a costly "laborious and colossal centralization" that may not still be able to achieve the desired outcome, given how hypothetical "the practical possibility of such a system" was.

While Barone wrote in a theoretical vacuum, by the time the first serious response to him came the Bolshevik Revolution had happened, although its initial failed efforts were probably overly focused on. Thus when von Mises (1920) critiqued Barone, he in the first version of his famous essay cited various odd and failed efforts of the new Bolshevik regime, such as their failed effort to eliminate money, something that indeed Barone had proposed. Of course von Mises's argument went beyond that basically minor point to argue that efficient prices can only be found through free markets in which profit-seeking capitalists are motivated to properly economize. His strong argument would oppose the later arguments by such as Lange (1936) that state-owned system trying to carry out Barone's vision with a market would fail because of the lack of properly motivated profit-seeking capitalists. Essentially Hayek's (1940) arguments regarding information problems were the icing on the cake of this argument, although they would become important in economics more broadly later.

Curiously, this socialist calculation debate remained mostly theoretical and abstract, largely ignoring the actual reality of the world's leading socialist model, the USSR. It went from the NEP of the 1920s, which in many ways looked like what Marx and Engels advocated in their program in *The Communist Manifesto*, which only called for the nationalization of land and what would come to be called "the commanding heights" of the economy, not every small enterprise. A third side of this debate dismissed the concerns over Pareto optimality and market efficiency that occupied Barone and these others who followed him. It drew more on what the actually exiting Soviet Union ended up doing in the 1930s, with Preobrazhensky (1926) arguing that what was needed was to maximize capital investment to the extent possible for rapid economic growth, with Dobb (1933) providing a more detailed defense of this view, arguing that rapid economic growth could overcome the problems of any static inefficiency that might arise from the central planning process. Indeed, for a long time, it looked like this argument had great substance, as the USSR grew more rapidly than did the United States, for quite some time after World War II, certainly well into the 1960s, and even possibly partway into the 1970s before the mounting inefficiencies of its command socialist central planning unequivocally bogged down its growth. And even for some time after that, advocates of this view would continue to praise this perspective, some of them influential Western economists such as Paul Samuelson (Levy and Peart, 2011).

The actual emergence of comparative economics as a recognized sub-discipline in economics came after World War II with the Cold War between the United States and the USSR, with the effort especially to compare these two not only actually existing but also competing economic systems driving much money and effort that eventually led to a full-blown sub-discipline with societies, journals, courses in universities and colleges with textbooks, the full apparatus of a properly recognized sub-discipline of the economics profession. And while it may have lost some of the status in the profession it had during the Cold War, it continues to exist and may even have a revival in a new Cold War between the market capitalist United States and the "socialist market" economy that the People's Republic of China officially describes itself as a nation ruled by a now century-old Communist Party.

9.4 Comparing alternative economic systems in the post-Cold War era

The fall of the Berlin Wall in 1989 and the subsequent end of the COMECON trade group and Warsaw Pact military alliance, coupled with the dissolution of the Soviet Union itself at the end of 1991, brought about the end of the Cold War and a movement away from classic Soviet-style command socialism in most of the states coming out of this seismic set of events. Focus moved to studying the various paths and degrees of transition to some variation of a market capitalist system, although a few, such as Belarus, barely moved at all, while others, such as Estonia, moved fairly rapidly to highly laissez-faire versions of that model and fully joined various Western organizations, from the European Union and even the Eurozone to NATO. In East Asia, Communist parties remained in control in various nations, even as several of them moved more toward market and even semi-capitalist models, such as China and Vietnam, while North Korea remained a holdout with a largely Stalin-style command socialist economic system, even as it de facto allowed for markets in certain sectors, especially agriculture, with Cuba also remaining a holdout, if not as much so as North Korea. But more recently some of the nations in the old Soviet bloc have moved somewhat back toward its model, with Russia renationalizing portions of its energy sector and others also tightening up control by governments in various ways. The old capitalism versus socialism debate has partially reemerged.

Nevertheless, with the end of the Soviet Union, many thought the field of comparative economics might come to an end. Such was stated openly by then Russian Premier Yegor Gaidar in August 1992, in a welcoming address to a conference of the International Economic Association in Moscow when he declared: "Henceforth there we shall not study comparative economic systems but only economic development". The sudden end of the previous paradigm indeed posed a challenge to the sub-discipline. But indeed this led to more nuanced analyses of various alternative systems using various alternative approaches. The field evolved rather than ending.

One such approach derived from the new institutionalist economics of Williamson (2000) and called itself the *new comparative economics* (Djankov et al., 2003). The central concept of this approach is the *institutional possibilities frontier*, which posits a trade-off between social losses due to state predation (dictatorship) versus social losses due to private predation (disorder). Given its particular institutional structure, each society faces its own pattern of trade-offs between these, with their potentially being a social cost-minimizing balance between the public and private sectors. Effectively this becomes a model of a mixed economy. This approach gained considerable attention, along with some questions (Rosser and Rosser, 2008). Some of these questions arose from certain applications made of it to specific issues, one of these involved the theory of *legal origins* by some of the new comparative economists (La Porta et al., 2007) and their advocacy of the superiority of Common Law for minimizing these social costs. This was criticized by Dam (2006) for supposedly oversimplifying the presentation of the legal systems being compared, while Tullock (2005) argued that the Civil Law alternative had at least as many pro-economic growth elements in it as the Common Law, with the generally comparable economic performances of Great Britain and France over time providing evidence for this, these being the leading examples of these competing legal systems.

Following along a similar tack but moving into a somewhat different direction, Acemoglu and Robinson (2012) argued that the most important institutional issues involved had to do with whether an economic system encouraged *inclusive growth* or *extractive growth*, with neither of these necessarily tied more clearly to the balance between the public and private sectors in an economy. Extractive growth is related to the predation idea developed in the new comparative economics approach. Acemoglu and Robinson argued that inclusive growth would be more likely associated with a democratic political system and tend to exhibit both more rapid growth and a more equal distribution of income over time. While it arguably leaves out many important influences, this approach would also attract much attention and become quite influential. However, it has also had its problems, perhaps exemplified by what has happened since their book in Brazil, a case they posed as a model for inclusive growth. Its government would fall in a corruption scandal, with ongoing political instability and an end to the growth that it had been experiencing. Nevertheless it can be argued the approach is still useful in that what happened in Brazil was that a pattern of growth that had appeared to be inclusive turned out to be more extractive than previously understood, with the revelation of this simply shifting it more in that direction, thus leading to many problems, including reduced growth and persistent inequality.

Another approach that has emerged and received much attention, although perhaps more from political scientists than economists, has been labeled *varieties of capitalism*. Implicit in this approach is that indeed capitalism triumphed over socialism at the end of the Cold War, so now all economic systems are basically capitalist. The issue then becomes classifying these varieties of capitalism that societies can become and how they operate (Hall and Soskice, 2001). Perhaps following on the Marxist emphasis on the centrality of the class conflict between workers and capitalists in capitalism, they have tended to focus on the nature of labor-management relations and how labor markets are organized as being a central defining feature of an economic system, while also being open to allowing consideration of other elements as well. This focus leads them to characterize as the most important a contrast between *liberal* capitalist systems and *coordinated* ones. The liberal systems have especially free labor markets with weak unions and little government intervention in their functioning. The coordinated systems stress cooperation among managements, labor unions, and governments, with all of these exercising important roles. Hall and Soskice identify the United States and Great Britain as the prime examples of the liberal system, while Germany is posed as the prime example of the coordinated system, with its *Mitbestimmung (Codetermination)* policies of putting labor union representatives on corporate boards of directors. France is seen as an intermediate case. A criticism of this approach is that it downplays other important aspects of economic systems and also seems to have been largely applied to Europe and Europe-derived economies such as the United States. It also essentially ignores the still-existing socialist systems, although implicitly these are largely in the coordinated category.

While getting less attention than Hall and Soskice and their followers, Pryor (2008) arguably extended their approach to a broader context by introducing a broader set of economic and cultural variables than they did and using cluster analysis to identify groups of economies that seem to be similar to each other over these various variables, which he called "system as a causal force". Unsurprisingly his clusters within Europe resemble to some extent those observed by Hall and Soskice, with them being Anglo-Saxon, Continental, Nordic, and Southern European. However, he was able to expand his approach to a broader global setting. A criticism is that it becomes hard to pinpoint what is really key to identifying a group, given that it is not easy to disentangle how the variables interact in a cluster analysis. Also, some societies end up as isolates, such as Japan, although this may in fact be deeply informative, and indeed while many see similarities between Japan and some other East Asian societies, the Japanese view themselves as quite unique.

This analysis of Pryor has some similarity to the still broader approach of Kuran (2009) who emphasizes total civilizations as the key to defining systems, with culture, economics, and the law especially involved in this categorization. Both of these remind us of the deep importance of the historical roots of economic systems in all parts of the world. Revolutions can happen that massively change a nation's or region's economic system. But deep layers of culture and politics and society persist and reemerge to influence how the new system operates, whether this is the reemergence of Confucian influences within the People's Republic of China or the differing regional economic performances one sees in different parts of Poland depending on whether they were ruled by Russia, Prussia, or Austria during the period of partition there (Grosfeld and Zhuravskaya, 2015), with Grosjean (2011) providing an overview of this idea of the "weight of history".

Which brings us to the idea of the *new traditional economy*, introduced initially by us (Rosser and Rosser, 1996, 1998). Polanyi (1944) introduced the idea of their being three basic systems of allocation: tradition, market, and command. For him, the latter two became the dominant systems in modern, technologically advanced economies, although he saw forms of them existing in earlier, simpler, and less technologically advanced societies. But for tradition, he saw this system as something existing largely in the past, and if in the present then in poor, less developed economies. Whereas allocative decisions arise from markets in market economies and from orders from the state in command economies, in traditional economies, these decisions are strongly driven by what was done in the past, such as a person doing what their parents did for a job, as in European feudalism or the Hindu caste system in rural parts of India. Polanyi argued that traditional economies are embedded in broader cultures, with these often dominated by a religion, as with feudalism being justified by the Roman Catholic Church in medieval Europe, and the caste system justified by the Hindu religion. While Polanyi saw these disappearing in the modern world as economic development proceeds, Rosser and Rosser saw the revival of such systems in modern, technologically advanced societies, at least as movements to re-embed their economies within a traditional cultural system, making them new traditional economies. The first appearance of this movement probably involved the emergence of Islamic economics starting in Pakistan in 1947 with the work of Maududi, who advocated imposing *Shari'a* law codes and having modern economies in Muslim nations obey their principles, such as forbidding interest, or *riba*, and formalizing the charitable system of *zakat*. Arguably the first nation to attempt to have such a system was Iran following its Islamic revolution in 1979, with its leaders proclaiming that their system was a Third Way between the capitalism of the United States and the socialism of the then-existing Soviet Union.

Since the change came in Iran in 1979, many nations have also attempted to impose an Islamic economic system, generally in connection with imposing a Shari'a law code, of which there are several. Even without an entire nation going new traditional, Islamic by adopting such a code and moving to establish and enforce its economic parts, portions of this have appeared in many nations. This has been notably the case for the Islamic banking movement that has arisen during the last half century. Banks that claim to follow the strictures of Islamic law exist now in over 60 nations, including the United States. Islamist movements that advocate imposing such law codes now exist in many predominantly Muslim nations, with them one of the strongest political movements in a substantial number of these nations. These movements vary across nations, both as to which branch of Islam they follow, such as Sunni or Shia, while also varying in the degree of strictness that they advocate, and the methods they pursue to achieve power in their societies.

While Islamic movements have received the most attention, such movements have appeared that follow other religions and have become important in various nations to varying degrees. Among some religions concerns about what constitutes proper or allowed economic behavior have long been concerns officially, with there having been a long succession of papal encyclicals within Roman Catholicism over many centuries that have reflected changing attitudes about various economic matters as the economies in nations have changed. So the Church has gone from advocating essentially feudal systems from the medieval period and such figures as Saint Thomas Aquinas, to advocating corporatist doctrines starting in the late 19th century as the industrial revolution swept across various European and North American nations, to more openly accepting market capitalism while still calling for elements of a welfare state and other limits on a fully laissez-faire economy, such as advocated by such political parties as the Christian Democrats in Germany (Pope Francis, 2013). Weber (1904–1905) argued that the Protestant Ethic played a role in the development of industrial market capitalism, although this may arguably not be a proper example of a new traditional approach. In Israel, ultra-Orthodox groups have advocated imposing laws to obey certain aspects of Jewish law, such as restrictions on activities on Sabbath days. Environmental groups in high-income nations have looked to Buddhism as an inspiration for advocating lower rates of consumption and pollution (Schumacher, 1973, Chap. 4), while some predominantly Buddhist nations having granted much power to Buddhist priestly hierarchies, such as Myanmar (Spiro, 1970).

In India, while the Father of Independence, Mohandas Gandhi developed his own ideas about a proper economic system that drew on some Hindu ideas (Gandhi, 1909; Dasgupta, 1996), and some of his ideas long influenced Indian economic policy, such as protectionism to achieve *swaraj*, or self-sufficiency. However, more recently a movement not all that sympathetic to some of Gandhi's ideas such as supporting tolerance of various religions has appeared that advocates *Hindutva*, or the supremacy of Hinduism in India and the strong enforcement of Hindu laws such as forbidding the killing of cows. Some elements of Gandhian thought are followed by advocates of this view, but others are not (Upadhyaya, 1965; Bokare, 1993). The current government of India officially supports this Hindutva idea, with what it means for economic policy still under development. However, in the case of India, we have the curious situation that it contains both the remnants of an old traditional economic system in the form of the influence of the caste system in much of rural India, while in more technologically advanced urban areas one finds support for an essentially new traditional development of India (Rosser and Rosser, 2005).

Finally in portions of East Asia strongly influenced by Chinese culture, there are movements to increase the influence of Confucian ideas such as harmonious relations, education, and the role of patriarch-led families, although in most of these societies this is more of a cultural movement with influence on economic and social policies rather than full-blown political movements seeking to take control of societies. Nevertheless even in the officially "socialist market," People's Republic of China there is a rising influence of Confucian ideas, in contrast to the Mao period during which these were officially forbidden and suppressed. Many see some of these ideas, such as support for education, as supportive of economic growth, even as in the past Confucianism was seen as not so supportive given attitudes that downgraded the status of merchants. But even in nations that are not openly pro-Confucian observers see influences of Confucianism suggesting new traditional aspects, as in Japan. Perhaps the most curious case is in the two Koreas, in both of which official views are actually anti-Confucian, but many see strong Confucian elements despite the sharp contrast of the market capitalism of South Korea and the command socialism of North Korea, even as they differ over certain elements of Confucian doctrines such as attitudes to merchants or openness to the outside world (Rosser and Rosser, 2016). After all, it has long been claimed that "A Korean is more Confucianist than Confucius himself" (Whigham, 1904).

We note that the new traditional economy is a potentially distinct economic system. It can be debated whether any nation that seems to be pursuing it, such as Iran, has actually achieved it or not. It may be that it cannot be fully achieved, even as the idea of it and the effort to achieve it leads to a system that is some distinctive variant of a mixed capitalist-socialist system.

9.5 Conclusions

We have seen that the development of comparative economics has proceeded through several stages over time. Prior to the coming to power of an avowedly socialist government, led by a Communist Party in 1917 in what had been tsarist Russia, the efforts to compare alternative economic systems were all theoretical. Most of these involved invoking possible utopian systems that might be implemented, with many of these visions inspired at least partly by religious perspectives, whether Saint-Simon's final proposed system that supposedly combined science with Christianity or that of his follower, Leroux, who seems to have coined the very term, "socialism," and who also linked it to a Christian view of the world. Of course, with their anti-religious attitudes and their dismissive application of the term "utopian" to many of their predecessors and their proclamation of their own supposedly strictly scientific and materialistic approach, Marx and Engels seemed to move beyond such ideas. But, in fact, when they actually did make specific proposals about what was supposed to come after the fall of the capitalistic system that they predicted, some of the elements not only drew from those they dismissed, but also in some cases come across as equally utopian, such as their call for the elimination of the distinction between urban and rural areas they made in *The Communist Manifesto*.

This focus on theoretical idealized versions of systems continued for some time after the Bolshevik Revolution, most notably in the socialist calculation debate, which prior to World War II largely eschewed any invocation of actual data on any system, whether that found in the Soviet Union or any of its market capitalist competitors, although this mostly reflected the primitive state of economic data and methods of analysis at the time. It also reflected especially the poor and hotly debated data that was coming out of the Soviet Union, with debates regarding what really did happen in the Soviet economy of the systemically important 1930s even now a matter of substantial study as well as discussion and debate. However, with the arrival of the Cold War after World War II and ongoing improvements in both data collection and econometric methodology, formal comparative economics as a sub-discipline of economics appeared, including with such institutional trappings as societies and journals and courses in colleges and universities. The focus of this sub-discipline became the comparison between the actually existing and competing systems operating in the world's two leading powers that came out of World War II, the market capitalist United States and the command socialist Soviet Union.

Finally, the collapse of the Soviet bloc and the breakup of the Soviet Union itself by the end of 1991 brought about the end of this competition as it had existed, with most of the nations emerging from this turmoil moving in various ways and patterns more in the direction of market capitalism in their economic systems. Some declared this to be the end of the sub-discipline and the emergence of a new one, the economics of transition. But by somewhat more than a decade, this transition process seemed to slow down or end or even reverse to some extent in some locations. It became clear that we still saw a tremendous variety of economic systems around the world worthy of being studied and compared. These comparisons to some extent called for new approaches and categories. So we have seen emphasis on the nature of institutions in the new comparative economics such as legal systems, with demarcation of varieties of capitalist systems, as well as efforts to draw in more elements not strictly tied to economics such as history and culture, with emphasis on clusters of characteristics and civilizations. Among the important elements of this broader approach has been the revival of awareness of the role of religions in societies, with this manifesting itself in new traditional systemic movements drawing on Islam and Hinduism and Confucianism as well as others, seeking to re-embed modern, technologically advanced societies into a socially traditional framework. Ironically this takes the newer approaches to comparative economics somewhat back to its origins in the study of comparing various idealistic utopian systems.

References

Acemoglu, D. and Robinson, J. (2012). *Why Nations Fail: The Origins of Power, Prosperity, and Poverty.* New York: Crown.

Barone, E. (1908). "Il Ministro della Produzione nello Stato Colletivista," *Giornale degli Economisti,* 2, 207–293, 392–414.

Bokare, M.G. (1993). *Hindu Economics: Eternal Economic Order.* New Delhi: Janati Prakashan.

Cabet, É. (1840). *Voyage en Icarie.* Paris: J. Mallel.

Dam, K.W. (2006). *The Law-Growth Nexus: The Rule of Law and Economic Development.* Washington, DC: Brookings Institution.

Dasgupta, A.K. (1996). *Gandhi's Economic Thought.* London: Routledge.

Djankov, S., Glaeser, E., La Porta, R., Lopez-de-Silanes, F. and Shleifer, A. (2003). "The New Comparative Economics," *Journal of Comparative Economics,* 31, 595–619.

Dobb, M. (1933). "Economic Theory and the Problems of a Socialist Economy," *Economic Journal,* 43, 588–598.

Engels, F. (1880). "Socialisme utopique et socialism scientifique," *La Revue Socialiste,* April/May.

Fourier, C. (1808). *Théorie des quatre mouvements et des destinées générales.* Lyon: A. Leipzig.

Francis, His Holy Father. (2013). *Evangeli Gaudium.* Vatican: Libreria Editrice.

Gandhi, M.K. (1909). *Hind Swaraj.* Ahmedabad: Navujvian Publishing House (in Gujarati).

Grosfeld, I. and Zhuravskaya, E. (2015). "Cultural vs. Economic Legacies of Empires: Evidence from the Partition of Poland," *Journal of Comparative Economics,* 43, 55–75.

Grosjean, P. (2011). "The Weight of History on European Cultural Integration: A Gravity Approach," *American Economic Review Papers and Proceedings*, 101, 504–508.

Hall, P.A. and Soskice, D. (2001). "Introduction," in P.A. Hall and D. Soskice, eds. *Varieties of Capitalism: The International Foundations of Comparative Advantage*. Oxford: Oxford University Press, pp. 1–68.

Hayek, F. (1940). "Socialist Calculation: The Competitive Solution," *Economica*, 7, 130–131.

Hayek, F. (1988). *The Fatal Conceit: The Errors of Socialism*. Chicago: University of Chicago Press.

Kuran, T. (2009). "Explaining the Trajectories of Civilization: The Systemic Approach," *Journal of Economic Behavior and Organization*, 71, 593–605.

La Porta, R., Lopez-de-Silanes, F. and Shleifer, A. (2007). "The Economic Consequences of Legal Origins," *Journal of Economic Literature*, 46, 285–372.

Lange, O. (1936). "On the Economic Theory of Socialism," *Review of Economic Studies*, 4, 53–71.

Leroux, P. (1834). "De l'individualisme et du socialisme," *La Revue Encyclopédique*, 1–16.

Levy, D.M. and Peart, S.J. (2011). "Soviet Growth and American Textbooks: An Endogenous Past," *Journal of Economic Behavior and Organization*, 78, 110–125.

Marx, K. (1875). "Kritik der gothauer programms," *Die Neue Zeit*, 1, 1890–1891.

Marx, K. and Engels, F. (1848). *Manifest der Kommunistischen Partei*. London: J.C. Burghard.

Maududi, A.A. (1947). *The Economic Problems of Man and Its Islamic Solution*. London: Islamic Publications.

Mises, L. von. (1920). "Die Wirtschafstrechnung im sozialistischen Gemeinwesen," *Archiv für Sozialwissenschaft um Sozialpolitik*, 47, 86–121.

More, T. (1516). *Utopia*. Leuven: Dirk Martens (in Latin).

Owen, R. (1813). *A New View of Society: Or, Essays in the Formation of Human Character and the Application of the Principle to Practice*. London: Richard and Arthur Taylor.

Plato. (375 BCE). *Republic*. Athens (in Greek).

Polanyi, K. (1944). *The Great Transformation: The Political and Economic Origins of our Time*. Boston: Beacon Press.

Preobrazhensky, Y. (1926). *The New Economics: Experience of the Theoretical Analysis of the Soviet Economy*. Moscow: Izdal'stvo Kommunisticheski akademii (in Russian).

Pryor, F.L. (2008). "System as a Causal Force," *Journal of Economic Behavior and Organization*, 67, 545–559.

Rosser, J.B. Jr. and Rosser, M.V. (1996). *Comparative Economics in a Transforming World Economy*. Chicago: Irwin (2nd edition, 2004, 3rd edition, 2018, Cambridge, MA: MIT Press).

Rosser, J.B. Jr. and Rosser, M.V. (1998). "Islamic and Neo-Confucian Perspectives on the New Traditional Economy," *Eastern Economic Journal*, 24, 495–506.

Rosser, J.B. Jr. and Rosser, M.V. (2005). "The Transition between the Old and New Traditional Economy in India," *Comparative Economic Studies*, 47, 561–578.

Rosser, J.B. Jr. and Rosser, M.V. (2008). "A Critique of the New Comparative Economics," *Review of Austrian Economics*, 21, 81–97.

Rosser, J.B. Jr. and Rosser, M.V. (2016). "The Paradox of the New Traditional Confucian Economies in the Two Koreas," *Comparative Economic Studies*, 58, 119–138.

Rousseau, J.J. (1762). *Du Contract Social, ou Principes du Droit Politique*. Amsterdam: Marc Michel Rev.

Saint-Simon, H. de. (1817). "Déclaration des Principes," *L'Industry*, 2.

Saint-Simon, H. de. (1825). *Le Nouveau Christianisme*. Paris: Bassange Père, A. Sautelet et Cie.

Schumacher, E.F. (1973). *Small Is Beautiful*. New York: Harper & Row.

Spiro, M.E. (1970). *Buddhism and Society: A Great Tradition and its Burmese Vicissitudes*. New York: Harper & Row.

Tullock, G. (2005). "The Case against the Common Law," in F. Parisi and C.K. Rowley, eds. *The Origins of Law and Economics*. Cheltenham: Edward Elgar, pp. 715–734.

Upadhyaya, D. (1965). *Integral Humanism*. Delhi: Navchetan Press.

Weber, M. (1904–05). "Die Protestantische Ethik und der Geist des Kapitalismus," *Archiv für Sozialwissenschaft um Sozialpolitik*, 20, 21.

Whigham, H.J. (1904). *Manchuria and Korea*. London: Ibister.

Williamson, O.E. (2000). "The New Institutionalist Economics: Taking Stock, Looking Ahead," *Journal of Economic Literature*, 38, 595–613.

10
A COMPARISON OF MAJOR WORLD INEQUALITY DATA SETS

James K. Galbraith

LYNDON B. JOHNSON SCHOOL OF PUBLIC AFFAIRS
THE UNIVERSITY OF TEXAS AT AUSTIN, AUSTIN, TX, USA

10.1 The state of world inequality data

Since the landmark publication by the World Bank in 1996 of the Klaus Deininger–Lyn Squire (DS, Deininger and Squire 1996, 1998) data set of world-wide inequality measures, comparative, time-series and panel studies of economic inequality have become a significant field of economic research. But the ambitions of researchers have often run ahead of the quality, consistency and coverage of the data so that many empirical questions remain open to dispute. This situation has in turn spurred new efforts to develop better and more consistent comparative measures of income inequalities.

The data sets now available are of five broad types. There are, first, large bibliographic data sets, of which the preeminent example is the World Income Inequality Database (WIID) of the World Institute for Development Economics Research (WIDER) of the United Nations University (UNU) at Helsinki. WIID is the successor to DS and is a diverse collection of coefficients, chronicling the struggle to measure inequality around the world over the past six decades, with careful documentation as to the concepts and sources of information. But the WIID is not, itself, a data set of comparative measures. It is rather a source, from which such measures may be extracted, according to the preferences and criteria of the researcher.

The opposite approach consists of synthetic measures, represented at a large scale by the Standardized World Income Inequality Database (SWIID) prepared by Frederick Solt at the University of Iowa. SWIID contains some 7000 Gini coefficients each for market and disposable income, covering the world almost comprehensively. But the numbers in the SWIID, while consistent, are not actually measures. They are in many cases imputations, based on relationships across time or between countries, so as to fill in gaps in the statistical record. The imputations are in turn based partly on other data sources, including those examined here.

Original, consistent measures are to be found in two significant data sets: the Luxembourg Income Study (LIS) summary tables and the Statistics on Income and Living Conditions (SILC) data set of the European Union. LIS is based on an intricate process of international harmonization of existing data sets; SILC is based on European surveys. Both are limited in coverage, in the case of LIS because of the demanding preparation required before each number is published, and because the underlying sources are of higher quality in the richer countries. In the case of SILC, the surveys are restricted to European countries.

DOI: 10.4324/9781003144366-13

The fourth type of data set consists of measures supplied to international agencies, mainly (if not exclusively) by the statistical services of their member states. The World Development Indicators (WDI) of the World Bank have achieved wide use as a standard source of world-wide Gini coefficients, in part because of the authority of the Bank and the easy access afforded in the WDI to inequality measures alongside other indicators of economic and social perform-ance. Meanwhile, the OECD has presented a table of inequality measures, concentrated on the OECD member countries, which has also achieved wide recognition for similar reasons.

The final approach to be mentioned here is that of the University of Texas Inequality Project, which in 2005 introduced the Estimated Household Income Inequality (EHII) data set (Galbraith and Kum, 2005). EHII is a panel of estimated Gini coefficients, based on a table of measures and a simple model. The table of measures is called UTIP–UNIDO, consisting of the between-groups components of Theil's T statistics calculated across industrial categories from the Industrial Statistics of the United Nations Industrial Development Organization. UTIP–UNIDO was introduced in 1999 (Galbraith, Lu and Darity, 1999) and was updated as reported in Galbraith *et al.* (2016a). The specific measures reported here may become more remote as time passes, but the underlying techniques will remain as an open invitation to future researchers who may find the alternatives unsatisfactory for the purposes of rigorous comparisons.

The calculations behind EHII are based on a regression that shows the very close relation-ship between inequalities of industrial pay and household income inequalities, as measured in 430 overlapping country-year observations in the original DS data set. Controls specify whether the original DS measure represents inequality of household or persons, of income or expenditure, and whether it is gross or net of tax.[1] Once these are taken into account, the coefficients are very stable and it is possible to use them to produce a large table of estimated Gini coefficients on a consistent gross household income inequality basis, with 4550 observations covering 154 countries from 1963 to 2014.

Thus, although EHII is not a direct measure of income inequality, unlike the SWIID, every observation reported is based on a direct measurement for that country in that year. The advantage of the EHII approach is thus dense coverage without loss of degrees of freedom for statistical purposes. In Galbraith *et al.* (2016a) we show that for at least 40 countries, the EHII measures are mostly plausible as estimates, since they track the movement of other measures well and tend to lie quite close to the (relatively few) direct measures of gross income inequality that exist. However, there are so many different measures of each type of inequality in most countries, with such differences of concept and coverage, that systematic evaluation of data quality against the whole literature is impractical. Comparison to the full literature remains a matter of eyeballs on the page.

The question we take up here follows Galbraith *et al.* (2016b): How does EHII compare to other data sets that each purport – or have been widely taken – to present tables of comparable inequality measures? These are the OECD, the WDI, the SILC and the LIS. We exclude the WIID on the ground that summary measures of its diverse contents are not very meaningful, and we exclude the SWIID because it is based on multiple imputations and derived, in part, from EHII and the other data sets. These exclusions are not meant to imply criticism. The WIID is invaluable as a resource, and the SWIID appears to be largely consistent with EHII so far as we have observed on a case-by-case basis, allowing for the fact that SWIID estimates market and net income inequality, but not gross income inequality. On the other hand, we exclude the World Inequality Database (Piketty *et al.*), which is based on tax measures, and this does imply a critical view, given in detail in Galbraith (2019) and in Galbraith and Halbach (2016).

10.2 Criteria of comparison

There are two criteria that can be deployed to compare data sets of this type. The first is *coverage*. Given the scope of the data set, in terms of countries and years, how many actual observations are to be found and therefore how dense and complete are the measures? This is a relatively straightforward thing to measure, but there are subtleties, including the question of balance across countries and time. Other things equal, a data set that spans a matrix of countries and years in a fairly even way is preferable to one that has an overrepresentation of observations in some countries and a dearth in others.

The second major criterion is *accuracy* – the correspondence of the measures in a data set to the facts on the ground. Here there is a problem: there is *no objective standard* of accuracy in this field. As a matter of principle, we cannot simply compare two Gini coefficients for the same country-year observation, from two different sources, and declare one to be more accurate than another, even if both purport to be measuring the same type of inequality. We can of course rely on the properties of the data set and our confidence in the underlying techniques, or in the authority of the publisher, but these are often subjective and risky judgments, as will be illustrated below. What we can observe is the *consistency* of inequality measures across data sets. Where two data sets compiled by different techniques and from different sources broadly arrive at similar measures, our confidence in the joint accuracy of the two data sets will rise. Where overlapping measures diverge, we should be inclined to caution.

10.3 Standardizing to a common concept

Comparing inequality measures even with matched country-year observations has a major pitfall. Different data sets may measure different inequality concepts. The prevailing data sets from certain sources (the LIS, SILC and OECD data sets are examples) have concentrated on providing measures of net or disposable household income inequality. This measure will differ from gross household income by the extent to which direct taxes have progressive effect. And that will vary substantially from one country to the next, depending on political history, economic system and level of development.

In advanced countries, gross income inequality is substantially higher than disposable income inequality, but by how much? Wang and Caminada (2011) give estimates of fiscal redistribution based on LIS data, but we find that they do not effectively bridge the gap between EHII's gross income inequality and disposable income inequality estimates in other data sets. To free an analysis of differences from bias due to the difference in concepts, we add that mean difference with EHII's gross income concept to all values in the disposable income-based data set; this value is about 6.7 Gini points for LIS, 6.9 Gini points for the OECD and about 7.5 Gini points for the SILC. This is obviously an artificial procedure; it does not prove that gross income inequality exceeds net income inequality by these amounts in any particular case. Still, the striking consistency across data sets of these mean differences in these mostly wealthy countries with similar welfare states – despite differences in the specific country-year observations that are matched with EHII – is a reassuring sign.[2]

The WDI poses yet another set of problems, since it uses a variety of concepts, including both consumption and income measures of inequality, without attempting to standardize them. Differences in consumption and income measures of inequality can be very large. Still, outside the OECD, most estimates of fiscal redistribution (gross to net) are very small, and the mean difference between the WDI as a whole and EHII for some 846 matched observations is only about 1.7 Gini points. This however does not mean that EHII and the WDI are well

Table 10.1 Comparison of coverage across data sources, through 2015

Data set	Total observations	Countries covered	Years covered	Observations through 2008, countries covered by comparison set and EHII	EHII observations matched by countries and years covered, through 2008	EHII observations matched by countries only, 1963–2008
LIS	235	41	1967–2013	206	1319	1415
WDI	1110	149	1978–2013	846	2676	3793
OECD	382	34	1983–2012	286	711	1266
SILC	443	33	1995–2013	288	371	1118
EHII	4550	154	1963–2014	n.a.	n.a.	n.a.

aligned; controlling for regions, mean differences between the WDI and EHII are larger and are reported in Table 10.2.

10.4 Coverage

Table 10.1 presents coverage ratios for the data sets under study. For each data set, we give the following information: total number of countries in the data set; range of years covered; total number of country-year observations. Then we provide the following pairwise comparisons to EHII through 2008: total number of EHII observations in the same range of years for the countries covered; total number of EHII observations for the countries covered, over the full range of years in the EHII data.[3]

EHII has a strong coverage advantage in both the span of countries and depth of time. Only LIS has comparable historical reach, with some observations as far back as 1967, but with a sixth of the observations over a quarter of the countries. Only the WDI has a comparable breadth of countries,[4] but the WDI starts 15 years later and has barely a third of EHII's observations even within the years that it covers. The remaining two data sets are much smaller in time and country coverage, as well as the number of observations.

In all cases, the EHII all-years coverage, going back to 1963, for the countries covered by the other data sources exceeds their own coverage by large factors. In all cases except the SILC, the EHII coverage is much greater even for the period after the other data set begins. The SILC exception arises because SILC begins only in 1995 and extends to 2013, whereas the EHII numbers reported here reach only to 2008; thus, a large fraction of SILC's observations lies outside of EHII's range at the time the table was compiled. In the other cases, the EHII coverage for the same countries and years is on the order of two to six times as dense.

10.5 Comparing data sets

This section summarizes comparisons between EHII and each of the other major data sets. Figure A1.1 gives kernel density estimates for EHII for various regions for selected years.

Table A2.1 summarizes the values for inequality measures in each data set in each country. For the underlying data, presented in detailed tables, refer to Galbraith et al. (2016a,b).

10.5.1 EHII–LIS

The LIS is primarily a database service for researchers in comparative microeconomics. It is not specifically oriented to the production of inequality statistics. However, LIS does produce a table of summary Gini coefficients, carefully adjusted to consistency on various concepts, and these have achieved wide acceptance and use.

The most obvious point is the far greater coverage of EHII. However, it is also clear that the two data sets are highly compatible; they share rankings and also trends to a high degree. Only China appears far out of place in the cross-country rankings, but this could be because China is ranked on its average EHII value, including low values from earlier years, whereas there is only one LIS value for China, from among the peak years in Chinese inequality.

LIS shows higher *relative* values for the United States than EHII – a point of difference likely due to the fact that incomes based on capital values are very important in US data and are not picked up in EHII at all. Since EHII is estimated from pay statistics rather than tax records or income surveys, this suggests that EHII is not based on a model appropriate to capture nonearning sources of income. However, this appears to be a problem very specific to the United States. Apart from the United Kingdom in the OECD comparison below, the same cause does not appear to produce observed discrepancies for other countries. Galbraith *et al.* (2016a) explore this issue in depth.

LIS is lower for Greece than EHII – an unexplained divergence – and has an anomalous one-year discrepancy for France. It has one value for Japan that is considerably lower than the EHII estimate, even after adjusting for the mean degree of fiscal redistribution. Otherwise the two data sets broadly coincide. A notable instance of agreement is the high (singleton) LIS value for India – far out of step with the WDI consumption-based Gini coefficients for that country, but very close to the EHII estimates, with the difference that EHII coverage includes 45 country-year observations for India.

10.5.2 EHII–OECD

With the OECD, again the major difference is in coverage, which is dense in EHII going back to 1963, but very spotty in the OECD's own collection before 2004. Again we adjust for the conceptual difference by shifting the center of the legend for the OECD table by the mean difference for overlapping values, in this case, 6.9 Gini points.

Once this adjustment is made, the two data sets are largely consistent. As does LIS, the OECD shows higher values for the United States than EHII, and also for the United Kingdom, which is the other major economy with large amounts of well-recorded capital asset–based incomes. Korea is one country for which the OECD reports a lower average inequality ranking than EHII; however, OECD data for Korea are all very recent, and the ranking of that country in the EHII data set is influenced by high values earlier on.

10.5.3 EHII–SILC

The SILC is a data set of disposable income inequalities, and therefore the raw Gini values are comprehensively lower than those in EHII or any other data focused on gross household income. Our comparison is therefore again with the SILC values after adjusting the center of the legend, and therefore the break between blue and red, for the mean difference between the two data sets; in this case, the adjustment is 7.5 Gini points.

The advantage of SILC, as noted previously, is excellent coverage over the most recent years. The disadvantage is lack of historical depth and of course the narrow focus on the EU and its near neighbors alone. Discrepancies against EHII within this range of countries appear to be subtle; both data sets show Scandinavia and Eastern Europe to be on the low side, and Southern Europe and especially Turkey to be high.

10.5.4 EHII–WDI

The most challenging comparison is with the WDI inequality measures published by the World Bank. It is not entirely clear what purpose these indicators are intended to serve, since they include a hotchpotch of income and expenditure, and gross and net inequality coefficients. Nevertheless, they are widely cited for comparative purposes and often taken as authoritative.

Unlike LIS, the OECD or SILC, the WDI has global reach, covering 149 countries with 1110 total observations over the years 1978–2013, including 107 observations for 28 countries not covered in EHII (many small island states, Laos, Vietnam, Palestine, DR Congo, Belarus, Turkmenistan, Tajikistan, Uzbekistan and Montenegro), and 178 observations for the years 2009–2013. However, also unlike the three other data sets, the WDI does not offer any consistency in the conceptual basis of its coverage: it includes both expenditure and income inequality measures, and among the income inequality measures, the difference between net and gross is not clearly specified. Therefore it seems to us that an adjustment of the kind made for the other three data sets is not appropriate in this case.

There are 1003 WDI observations for the 147 countries also covered by EHII, not necessarily exactly overlapping in years covered, and 932 observations in the same countries over the span of 1978–2008. EHII has 2676 observations for this period, including observations in 26 countries that have no observations reported in the WDI: Afghanistan, the Bahamas, Barbados, Cuba, Cyprus, Eritrea, the GDR, Hong Kong, Korea, Kuwait, Libya, Luxembourg, Malta, Myanmar, New Zealand, Oman, Portugal, Puerto Rico, Qatar, Singapore, Somalia, Taiwan, Tonga, UAE, Yugoslavia, Zimbabwe. WDI thus overlaps EHII in 121 countries.

To make a comparison, we broke the WDI and EHII down into four large regions: the Americas, Eurasia, Asia, and the Middle East and Africa. This permits us to compare coverage and values in manageable portions. Table 10.2 summarizes the coverage for each region.

A striking aspect of the comparison is the areas of disagreement over inequality values.

For the Americas, the two data sets are in broad agreement, with just a few anomalous values for the WDI in Jamaica and Peru. Both show only a handful of countries in the moderate-to-low inequality range typical of the advanced world; in EHII, these are Cuba, Canada and the United States, with Uruguay, Costa Rica and Nicaragua during the revolutionary period coming in just above. Uniquely, average values for the Americas in WDI are higher than they are in EHII; otherwise EHII measures tend to exceed those in WDI, especially in Asia where WDI incorporates numerous consumption inequality measures.

Table 10.2 EHII and WDI coverage by regions, for countries in EHII

Regions	WDI observations 1978–2013	WDI observations 1978–2008	EHII observations 1978–2008	EHII observations 1963–2008	Number of countries (EHII)	Number of countries (WDI)	Mean difference EHII–WDI
Americas	349	293	518	750	29	25	−6.04
Eurasia	382	323	919	1245	44	39	4.75
Asia and Oceania	107	92	496	692	24	16	5.29
Africa and Middle East	165	138	743	1155	50	41	3.98
Total	1003	932	2676	3842	147	121[a]	1.23

[a] WDI has in addition, 28 countries with 107 total observations that are not covered in EHII; they are excluded above.

For Eurasia, the main area of disagreement is over the inequality values in the countries of the former USSR. In EHII, outside the Baltics, these are all relatively close to each other, and with inequality measures above those for Western Europe, as indicated by their grouping together by rank on the matrix. For the WDI, they are highly diverse, with Ukraine, Moldova and Kazakhstan showing as much more egalitarian than Russia, almost from the start of the separate existence of those countries. In our view, countries with closely related economic structures and histories – such as those of the former USSR – likely shared common inequality characteristics at the outset and even now, although they may diverge as time passes.

For Asia, the most important disagreements are over India and Indonesia, as well as Bangladesh, Nepal, Pakistan and Sri Lanka, which are ranked by the WDI as low-inequality countries – with inequality values below those of Australia, in some cases. This is evidently because of the use of consumption inequality measures for those countries, which tend to run some 20 Gini points below the corresponding income measures. All six countries are ranked as high inequality by EHII, and (as noted above) the EHII measures for India come very close to the singleton income inequality measure for that country recently published by LIS. It seems obvious that even if the expenditure inequality measures are to be taken at face value, they are not comparable with income inequality measures and it is essentially meaningless to include them in the same table.

For Africa and the Middle East, the two sets of measures are discordant. Notably, the EHII value for South Africa is lower than that reported by WDI and also by almost all studies in the survey literature; this appears to be related to the fact that about a third of South African households report zero income in surveys. On the other hand, the cluster of oil producers in the high-inequality range for Africa and the Middle East, from Qatar and Kuwait to Angola, makes sense to us, as do the (relatively) egalitarian measures for Malta, the Seychelles, Algeria, Mauritius, the Gambia, preoccupation Iraq and postrevolutionary Iran. In contrast, the WDI measures for Sub-Saharan Africa do not appear to follow any particular logic of regional or economic structure.

Still, whichever source one chooses, for much of Africa there is very little to go on. On one side, surveys are rare and there is no reason for confidence that they were taken in a consistent manner at different times, let alone across different countries; in fact given the mixture of consumption and income inequality measures in this table, it is clear they were not. On the other side, the industrial sectors of most African countries are small, and so the foundation of the EHII estimate for this region is comparatively weak. We like our model and the fact that it gives results for many countries that track survey measures very well. For Sub-Saharan Africa, however, it may be best to conclude that while inequality is certainly high, and broadly similar to that found elsewhere in developing countries, all precise measures for the region are open to doubt.

The WDI measures, in addition to being sparse, are sometimes volatile within countries over short periods of time. Notable instances of large jumps in Gini scores in adjacent observations over short intervals – usually less than five years – occur for Angola (59 –> 43), Bolivia (42 –> 54), Central African Republic (44 –> 56), Kenya (57 –> 42), Kyrgyzstan (26 –> 53), Paraguay (41 –> 58), Peru (35 –> 56 over one year!), Senegal (54 –> 41), the Seychelles (43 –> 66!) and Venezuela (53 –> 44). Apart from the collapse of communism in the early 1990s, there is a little known basis in the political history of these countries – or almost any country – for such shifts. For these reasons, in our view, the WDI measures of inequality are haphazard. They do not meet the standards set by any of the other comparison data sets, for coverage or comparability.

10.6 Divergences and conclusion

Table 10.3 summarizes the pattern of divergence between EHII and the other major data sets.

As a general conclusion, EHII is highly consistent with LIS, OECD and SILC, notwithstanding the difference in concepts measured, or differences in tax systems and welfare states. However, its coverage and historical depth are far greater. We take the success in tracking the (evidently fairly reliable) inequality measures for rich country disposable income to be a sign of the general power of the relationship between industrial pay inequality and income inequalities, and therefore an indication that the model underlying EHII is widely applicable around the world.

While the reduction in inequality achieved by passing from gross to net income is important in the wealthy countries that predominate in these data sets, differences in that reduction, both across countries and through time, appear to be second order. In poorer countries, the reduction in inequality achieved by tax systems is much smaller, and may be effectively nil, and again the differences in this effect are small. Therefore it appears that in both rich and poor countries, taken as separate groups, differences and changes in gross income inequality are the primary source of differences and changes in inequalities generally. However, for the richer countries, gross income inequality will overstate the degree of inequality actually experienced in household living standards.

EHII is much less consonant with the WDI, which is the only other data set that covers the entire world, even though the mean divergence is small. Rather, a major source of inconsistency appears to be the mishmash of different concepts covered in the WDI, an apparent artifact of the Bank's deference to the reporting preferences and survey histories of its member states. The conclusion we draw is that the WDI inequality coefficients are erratic, and the WDI data set is therefore not a credible source of comparative measures.

The advantages of a consistent panel of reasonably credible income inequality measures, covering all regions of the world over a long period of time, for comparative and global economic research are self-evident. The main patterns revealed by the investigation of such a panel are discussed at length in Galbraith and Choi (2020). A central conclusion here is that to generate such a panel, actual surveys and the associated micro-data are neither necessary

Table 10.3 Summary measures of divergence across data sets

Data set	Years covered	Mean divergence from EHII	Standard deviation of divergence from EHII	Volatility[a] of Gini coefficient across countries	Volatility of EHII Gini across matched countries and years covered
LIS	1967–2008	6.34	4.25	1.87	1.55
OECD	1983–2008	6.88	3.36	1.48	1.61
SILC	1995–2008	7.57	3.75	1.56	0.92
WDI: Americas	1978–2008	−4.82	5.97	3.33	1.85
WDI: Eurasia	1978–2008	6.5	6.57	3.04	2.52
WDI: Asia and Oceania	1978–2008	8.51	9.25	3.08	2.86
WDI: Africa and Middle East	1978–2008	4.34	10.34	4.47	2.3
WDI: All EHII Countries	1978–2008	1.65	8.93	3.53	2.37

[a] Volatility is measured as the mean of country-level standard deviations of Gini coefficients.

nor sufficient. Consistent measures can be estimated from a wide variety of administrative data sets using grouped data that is well maintained over time by established institutions at the national and transnational levels and readily available at trivial cost.

Notes

1 The ratio of manufacturing employment to population is the one other economic variable in the EHII model. Thus EHII is calculated from the estimated coefficients for just two variables, with the controls all set to zero.
2 There are clearly mentioned in these data sets some countries – for instance Turkey and the Baltics – where fiscal redistribution is minor and the mean adjustment is too high, but making a better one would require having reliable calibration specific to the country, for which there is no reliable source.
3 A disadvantage of EHII is that it is not embedded in an ongoing organization and the data may not be updated regularly or at all. The EHII data set may therefore degrade in coverage, relative to the others, over time, and eventually become a proof-of-concept exercise, unless taken up by an appropriate institution. It remains however available for historical work and would be straightforward to update as the records from which it is generated are produced and published by institutions on a regular basis.
4 However, they are not the same countries; the WDI includes 28 countries not covered by EHII, most of them small island states, while omitting an almost equal number of countries that EHII covers.

References

Deininger, K. and Squire, L. (1996). "A New Data Set Measuring Income Inequality". *World Bank Economic Review* 10(3):565–591.

Galbraith, J. (2019). "Sparse, Inconsistent and Unreliable: Tax Records and the World Inequality Report 2018". *Focus, Development and Change*, March, 329–346. https://onlinelibrary.wiley.com/doi/full/10.1111/dech.12475

Galbraith, J. and Choi, J. (June 29, 2020). "Inequality under Globalization: State of Knowledge and Implications for Economics". *Real World Economics Review* 92:84–102. http://www.paecon.net/PAEReview/issue92/whole92.pdf

Galbraith, J., Choi, J., Halbach, B., Malinowska, A. and Zhang, W. (2016b). "A Comparison of Major World Inequality Data Sets: LIS, OECD, EU-SILC, WDI and EHII," in Lorenzo Cappellari, Solomon W. Polachek and Konstantinos Tatsiramos, eds., "Income Inequality Around the World," *Research in Labor Economics*, 44, 2016, pp. 1–48.

Galbraith, J. and Halbach, B. (2016). "A Comparison of Top Income Shares and Global Inequality Datasets," *UTIP Working Paper 73*, August 22, at http://utip.gov.utexas.edu/papers/utip_73.pdf

Galbraith, J., Halbach, B., Malinowska, A., Shams, A. and Zhang, W. (2016a). "The UTIP Global Inequality Data Sets 1963-2008: Updates, Revisions and Quality Checks," in Kaushik Basu, Vivian Hon and Joseph Stiglitz, eds., *Inequality and Growth*, Basingstoke: Palgrave MacMillan. Also published in Joseph E. Stiglitz and Martin Guzman, eds., *Contemporary Issues in Microeconomics*, Basingstoke: Palgrave Macmillan, 2016, pp. 7–39.

Galbraith, J., Jiaqing, L. and Darity, W.A. Jr. (1999). "Measuring the Evolution of Inequality in the Global Economy," *UTIP Working Paper No. 7*, January.

Galbraith, J. and Kum, H. (2005). "Estimating the Inequality of Household Incomes: A Statistical Approach to the Creation of a Dense and Consistent Global Data Set". *Review of Income and Wealth* 51(1):115–143.

Luxembourg Income Study. http://www.lisdatacenter.org/ (Accessed December 19, 2014).

Piketty, T. et al. *The World Top Incomes Database*. http://topincomes.parisschoolofeconomics.eu/ (Accessed December 19, 2014).

Solt, F. *The Standardized World Income Inequality Dataset*. http://myweb.uiowa.edu/fsolt/swiid/swiid.html (Accessed December 19, 2014).

University of Texas Inequality Project. http://utip.lbj.utexas.edu

World Bank. (2007). *World Development Indicators*. Online. http://www.worldbank.org/

Wang, C. and Caminada, K. (2011). "Disentangling Income Inequality and the Redistributive Effect of Social Transfers and Taxes in 36 LIS Countries," *LIS Working Paper No. 567*.

Appendix 1

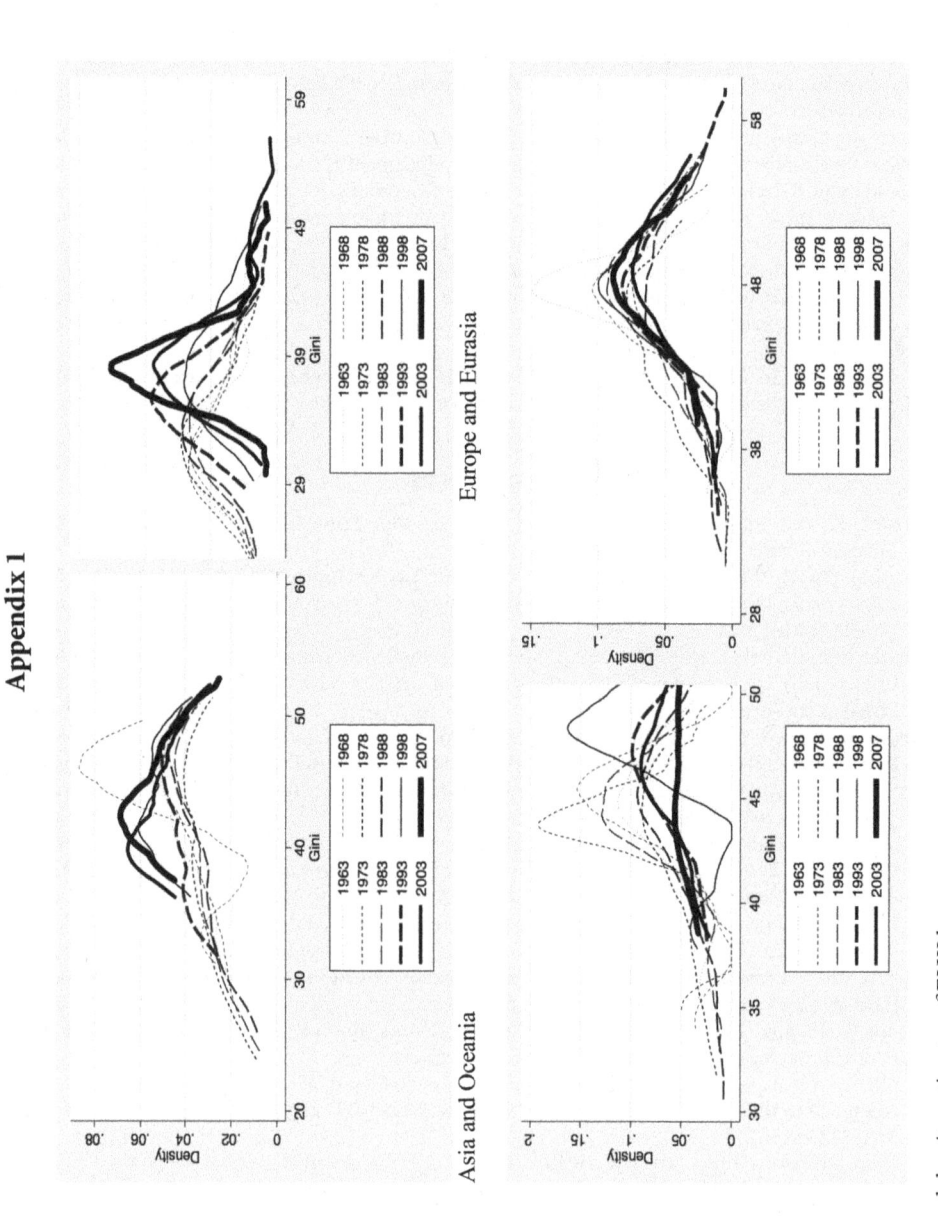

Figure A1.1 Kernel density estimates of EHII by year.

Appendix 2

Table A2.1 Summary of values by country: EHII, WDI, LIS, OECD and SILC

(#Obs refers to years covered; specific years vary; Mean refers to Gini value, adjusted to gross income)

Region	Country	EHII			WDI			LIS			OECD			SILC		
		# Obs	Mean	Std dev	# Obs	Mean	Std dev	# Obs	Mean	Std dev	# Obs	Mean	Std dev	# Obs	Mean	Std dev
Asia and Oceania	Afghanistan	22	40.9	3.9												
	American Samoa															
	Australia	36	33.2	2.2	6	33.1	1.1	8	30.9	1.8	6					
	Bangladesh	27	44.6	2.6	8	30.2	3.2									
	Bhutan				3	41.2	4.9									
	Brunei Darussalam															
	Cambodia	3	51.6	7.9	7	35.8	3.1									
	China	16	35.6	3.5	11	36.3	5.9	1	50.5							
	Fiji	32	44.1	2.9	2	44.8	2.8									
	French Polynesia															
	Guam															
	Hong Kong	36	32.9	8.4												
	India	45	50.0	1.5	6	32.7	1.7	1	49.1							
	Indonesia	36	49.5	1.9	10	31.2	2.5									
	Japan	45	37.2	3.1	1	32.1		1	30.2		6	37.0	1.4			
	Kiribati															
	Korea, Rep.	44	39.8	2.5				1	31.1		7	35.3	0.4			
	Korea, Dem. Rep.															
	Lao PDR				5	33.9	2.4									
	Macao															
	Malaysia	39	41.5	2.5	9	46.4	3.4									

(Continued)

Table A2.1 Summary of values by country: EHII, WDI, LIS, OECD and SILC (*Continued*)

(#Obs refers to years covered; specific years vary; Mean refers to Gini value, adjusted to gross income)

Region	Country	EHII			WDI			LIS			OECD			SILC		
		# Obs	Mean	Std dev	# Obs	Mean	Std dev	# Obs	Mean	Std dev	# Obs	Mean	Std dev	# Obs	Mean	Std dev
	Maldives				2	50.0	17.9									
	Marshall Islands															
	Micronesia, Fed. Sts.				1	61.1										
	Mongolia	17	49.1	2.3	4	33.2	2.6									
	Myanmar (Burma)	10	46.1	3.6												
	Nepal	10	49.3	2.6	4	35.5	6.0									
	New Caledonia															
	New Zealand	33	35.1	3.4							8	36.6	2.5			
	Northern Mariana Islands															
	Pakistan	32	47.6	2.2	9	31.4	1.8									
	Palau															
	Papua New Guinea	25	50.6	1.6	1	50.9										
	Philippines	41	47.4	1.1	10	43.5	1.8									
	Samoa															
	Singapore	46	38.5	3.9												
	Solomon Islands															
	Sri Lanka	26	45.9	2.2	6	36.3	3.7									
	Taiwan	25	31.8	1.6				9	28.9	1.9						
	Thailand	23	46.3	4.2	13	43.1	2.2									
	Timor-Leste				1	30.4										
	Tonga	23	45.9	3.6												
	Tuvalu															
	Vanuatu															
	Vietnam				8	36.5	1.3									

(*Continued*)

Table A2.1 Summary of values by country: EHII, WDI, LIS, OECD and SILC (*Continued*)

(#Obs refers to years covered; specific years vary; Mean refers to Gini value, adjusted to gross income)

Region	Country	EHII			WDI			LIS			OECD			SILC		
		# Obs	Mean	Std dev	# Obs	Mean	Std dev	# Obs	Mean	Std dev	# Obs	Mean	Std dev	# Obs	Mean	Std dev
Eurasia	Albania	19	44.1	7.2	6	30.4	1.3									
	Andorra															
	Armenia	5	53.0	5.0	14	33.7	4.0									
	Austria	44	34.6	1.0	6	29.2	3.1	6	26.3	1.9	8	30.3	0.7	18	26.3	1.4
	Azerbaijan	17	49.5	6.1	7	24.8	9.5									
	Belarus				17	27.3	2.1									
	Belgium	42	35.8	2.5	6	27.4	3.1	6	24.6	2.3	7	34.5	1.1	18	27.4	1.2
	Bosnia and Herzegovina	2	36.2	1.2	3	32.4	2.1									
	Bulgaria	45	31.9	6.0	11	30.2	4.2							14	30.4	4.7
	Channel Islands															
	Croatia	23	37.1	4.2	7	29.1	3.5							11	29.6	1.5
	Cyprus	46	40.2	2.5										11	29.5	1.4
	Czech Republic	44	24.5	3.9	9	25.7	2.4	3	24.2	3.3	11	29.2	1.1	10	25.1	0.4
	Denmark	42	31.3	0.9	7	25.3	1.4	7	23.6	1.3	23	26.8	1.3	15	24.5	2.7
	Estonia	9	34.8	0.4	15	33.3	3.9	4	33.7	2.1	8	35.6	1.5	14	33.5	1.9
	Faeroe Islands															
	Finland	45	32.3	1.2	7	25.7	2.7	7	23.8	2.6	27	29.5	2.8	18	25.1	1.6
	France	30	35.6	1.6	5	33.3	2.9	7	29.6	2.2	16	30.7	1.0	19	28.6	1.3
	GDR	19	22.3	1.6												
	Georgia	11	48.4	1.6	17	40.5	1.2									
	Germany	45	32.9	1.8	9	29.8	1.3	11	26.8	1.3	22	31.4	1.7	16	27.5	2.1
	Greece	41	42.4	1.0	5	34.8	1.4	5	33.2	1.1	11	35.3	1.0	18	33.9	0.8
	Greenland															
	Hungary	43	31.9	5.9	14	27.5	2.4	4	29.6	1.6	15	30.8	1.1	13	26.5	2.4
	Iceland	20	33.0	1.2	3	27.8	1.5	3	25.9	1.6	8	31.3	2.3	10	25.8	2.0
	Ireland	45	36.4	1.1	8	34.6	2.2	8	31.8	1.6	8	34.8	1.3	17	31.2	1.5
	Isle of Man															

(*Continued*)

Table A2.1 Summary of values by country: EHII, WDI, LIS, OECD and SILC (*Continued*)

(#Obs refers to years covered; specific years vary; Mean refers to Gini value, adjusted to gross income)

Region	Country	EHII			WDI			LIS			OECD			SILC		
		# Obs	Mean	Std dev	# Obs	Mean	Std dev	# Obs	Mean	Std dev	# Obs	Mean	Std dev	# Obs	Mean	Std dev
	Italy	40	37.0	1.2	11	34.9	2.0	11	32.6	1.8	9	32.7	1.8	17	31.5	1.2
	Kazakhstan	10	46.2	2.3	12	30.5	2.8									
	Kosovo															
	Kyrgyzstan	13	43.4	3.8	15	34.8	6.4									
	Latvia	16	37.7	2.2	12	32.5	4.1							10	36.1	1.4
	Liechtenstein															
	Lithuania	16	38.8	2.6	14	32.9	3.4							11	34.0	2.1
	Luxembourg	44	32.6	2.4				8	25.6	1.6	11	30.8	1.4	18	27.5	1.3
	Macedonia	20	40.0	4.4	8	38.2	5.0									
	Moldova	17	41.7	4.9	16	34.7	3.9									
	Monaco															
	Montenegro				7	30.0	0.8									
	Netherlands	42	34.3	1.7	8	29.8	1.8	8	25.5	1.5	11	33.0	0.9	18	26.8	1.3
	Norway	44	33.3	1.7	7	26.9	1.8	8	24.0	1.0	8	28.8	1.8	11	24.9	2.3
	Poland	32	32.2	4.7	18	31.8	3.2	7	29.6	2.3	8	32.6	2.6	11	31.7	1.6
	Portugal	39	39.7	2.1							8	37.4	1.7	17	36.1	1.3
	Romania	26	34.6	4.5	17	28.6	1.9	2	28.0	0.1				14	32.6	2.6
	Russia	16	40.2	1.6	13	38.6	5.8	4	38.4	2.6						
	San Marino															
	Serbia				9	30.8	2.1							1	38.0	
	Slovakia	17	36.2	1.6	10	25.8	3.6	5	24.4	3.2	8	29.7	1.5	9	25.4	1.3
	Slovenia	22	31.0	4.0	11	26.8	2.9	5	23.5	1.0	8	25.4	0.4	13	23.1	0.9
	Spain	45	39.5	1.1	7	34.3	1.7	8	32.3	1.7	8	33.9	1.3	19	33.0	1.4
	Sweden	38	28.7	0.9	6	25.3	1.5	8	22.8	2.1	9	28.5	3.5	14	23.6	1.1
	Switzerland	5	32.0	0.3	5	34.4	2.4	5	28.7	1.9	2	29.9	0.7	7	29.8	1.0
	Tajikistan				5	31.8	1.6									
	Turkey	43	45.7	2.3	12	40.5	1.7				7	43.9	2.9	3	45.3	0.6
	Turkmenistan				3	34.2	7.3									

(*Continued*)

208

James K. Galbraith

Table A2.1 Summary of values by country: EHII, WDI, LIS, OECD and SILC (*Continued*)

(#Obs refers to years covered; specific years vary; Mean refers to Gini value, adjusted to gross income)

Region	Country	EHII			WDI			LIS			OECD			SILC		
		# Obs	Mean	Std dev	# Obs	Mean	Std dev	# Obs	Mean	Std dev	# Obs	Mean	Std dev	# Obs	Mean	Std dev
	United Kingdom	41	33.1	3.3	7	37.3	0.8	11	32.1	3.7	16	36.9	1.2	18	32.6	1.4
	Ukraine	17	40.2	2.8	14	28.9	4.1									
	Uzbekistan				4	34.6	8.4									
	Yugoslavia	5	42.2	2.2												
	Algeria	26	39.3	1.4	2	37.8	3.4									
Africa and Middle East	Angola	6	54.0	3.5	2	50.7	11.3									
	Bahrain															
	Benin	7	50.9	1.1	2	41.1	3.5									
	Botswana	21	48.1	2.7	4	60.1	4.4									
	Burkina Faso	10	46.3	2.6	4	45.1	4.7									
	Burundi	17	49.7	2.4	3	36.3	5.2									
	Cabo Verde				2	47.2	4.7									
	Cameroon	28	51.3	4.3	3	42.5	1.9									
	Central African Republic	19	48.1	3.7	3	53.7	9.2									
	Chad				2	41.5	2.5									
	Comoros				1	64.3										
	Congo	14	48.5	2.1	2	43.7	5.1									
	Congo, Dem. Rep.				1	44.4										
	Djibouti				1	40.0										
	Egypt	39	44.5	3.7	5	31.6	1.1									
	Equatorial Guinea															

(*Continued*)

(#Obs refers to years covered; specific years vary; Mean refers to Gini value, adjusted to gross income)

Region	Country	EHII			WDI			LIS			OECD			SILC		
		# Obs	Mean	Std dev	# Obs	Mean	Std dev	# Obs	Mean	Std dev	# Obs	Mean	Std dev	# Obs	Mean	Std dev
	Eritrea	42	46.7	2.2												
	Ethiopia	19	46.6	1.5	5	33.2	4.1									
	Gabon	8	49.8	3.4	1	42.2										
	Gambia	8	42.3	1.4	2	48.8	2.1									
	Ghana	26	48.8	1.1	5	38.6	3.1									
	Guinea				5	41.0	5.1									
	Guinea-Bissau				2	41.7	8.7									
	Iran	42	44.4	4.3	5	43.3	3.3									
	Iraq	27	43.4	3.3	2	29.1	0.7									
	Israel	44	40.3	3.0	8	38.9	2.8	8	34.0	3.1	9	41.8	2.4			
	Ivory Coast	22	47.9	1.3	9	40.1	2.9									
	Jordan	42	48.7	1.5	7	36.4	3.7									
	Kenya	36	49.5	1.7	4	48.4	6.5									
	Kuwait	32	52.4	2.2												
	Lebanon															
	Lesotho	11	50.7	1.7	5	56.6	4.4									
	Liberia	3	50.2	1.4	1	38.2										
	Libyan Arab Jamahiriya	17	45.8	3.5												
	Madagascar	26	45.7	3.3	7	43.0	3.7									
	Malawi	35	50.6	3.6	3	45.5	5.2									
	Mali				4	40.6	7.3									
	Malta	44	34.8	3.0										10	27.7	1.0
	Mauritania				6	42.0	4.5									
	Mauritius	40	40.9	4.3	2	35.8	0.2									
	Morocco	31	49.7	1.6	5	39.9	0.8									
	Mozambique	13	51.4	1.2	3	45.8	1.3									
	Namibia				3	66.5	6.9									

(*Continued*)

Table A2.1 Summary of values by country: EHII, WDI, LIS, OECD and SILC (*Continued*)

(#Obs refers to years covered; specific years vary; Mean refers to Gini value, adjusted to gross income)

Region	Country	EHII			WDI			LIS			OECD			SILC		
		# Obs	Mean	Std dev	# Obs	Mean	Std dev	# Obs	Mean	Std dev	# Obs	Mean	Std dev	# Obs	Mean	Std dev
	Niger				5	37.9	6.0									
	Nigeria	28	45.8	2.6	5	42.6	3.3									
	Oman	15	51.5	1.3												
	Qatar	15	53.1	1.6												
	Rwanda	12	48.8	3.5	4	46.1	11.5									
	Sao Tome and Principe				2	42.3	12.0									
	Saudi Arabia															
	Senegal	29	45.7	4.0	5	43.3	6.1									
	Seychelles	11	36.3	2.4	2	54.3	16.3									
	Sierra Leone				2	37.4	2.9									
	Somalia	12	47.2	1.4												
	South Africa	41	44.3	1.5	6	61.5	4.3	2	59.4							
	South Sudan															
	Sudan	2	48.0	0.1	1	35.3										
	Swaziland	26	50.3	2.5	3	55.2	4.8									
	Syrian Arab Republic	28	46.4	1.7	6	25.3	1.5									
	Tanzania	34	50.1	2.5	4	36.0	2.0									
	Togo	14	49.4	3.4	2	44.1	2.6									
	Tunisia	29	48.3	2.8	6	39.9	2.8									
	UAE	4	46.4	3.1												
	Uganda	19	49.0	1.9	8	43.1	2.6									
	West Bank and Gaza				3	35.7	2.6									
	Yemen	27	48.7	5.7	2	34.7	1.7									
	Zambia	18	47.6	1.7	7	51.5	4.9									
	Zimbabwe	36	45.4	1.7												

(*Continued*)

Table A2.1 Summary of values by country: EHII, WDI, LIS, OECD and SILC (*Continued*)

(#Obs refers to years covered; specific years vary; Mean refers to Gini value, adjusted to gross income)

Region	Country	EHII			WDI			LIS			OECD			SILC		
		# Obs	Mean	Std dev	# Obs	Mean	Std dev	# Obs	Mean	Std dev	# Obs	Mean	Std dev	# Obs	Mean	Std dev
	Antigua and Barbuda															
Americas	Argentina	17	45.7	2.0	23	48.1	3.2									
	Aruba															
	Bahamas	3	50.1	1.2												
	Barbados	28	44.5	1.5												
	Belize	2	47.3	0.6	7	57.6	2.9									
	Bermuda															
	Bolivia	32	48.0	3.2	15	54.2	5.9									
	Brazil	17	48.5	0.7	28	57.8	2.7	3	46.8	1.7						
	Canada	45	36.5	1.6	10	32.7	1.1	12	30.0	1.6	29	34.2	1.5			
	Cayman Islands															
	Chile	44	46.4	2.5	11	54.5	2.1				3	52.0	0.4			
	Colombia	43	45.1	1.1	20	55.8	2.5	3	50.4	2.0						
	Costa Rica	22	42.0	1.2	26	47.3	3.2									
	Cuba	13	32.1	0.9												
	Curacao															
	Dominica															
	Dominican Republic	23	46.7	2.1	18	49.5	1.9									
	Ecuador	45	46.4	2.4	16	52.1	3.5									
	El Salvador	28	45.6	2.0	18	48.8	4.1									
	Grenada															
	Guatemala	26	47.8	3.7	9	55.3	2.8	1	49.0							
	Guyana				2	48.0	5.0									
	Haiti	21	47.0	1.9	1	59.2										
	Honduras	26	44.0	3.1	23	55.7	2.5									
	Jamaica	34	48.6	2.0	8	46.1	10.0									

(*Continued*)

Table A2.1 Summary of values by country: EHII, WDI, LIS, OECD and SILC (*Continued*)

(#Obs refers to years covered; specific years vary; Mean refers to Gini value, adjusted to gross income)

Region	Country	EHII			WDI			LIS			OECD			SILC		
		# Obs	Mean	Std dev	# Obs	Mean	Std dev	# Obs	Mean	Std dev	# Obs	Mean	Std dev	# Obs	Mean	Std dev
	Mexico	31	43.6	1.7	14	49.2	2.1	11	46.3	2.0	7	49.3	2.4			
	Nicaragua	21	41.9	1.6	5	46.4	6.5									
	Panama	40	45.5	2.5	19	54.9	2.9									
	Paraguay	2	44.6	0.2	16	52.4	4.1									
	Peru	21	50.9	3.1	18	48.6	5.2	1	50.2							
	Puerto Rico	12	47.8	1.9												
	Sint Maarten (Dutch part)															
	St. Kitts and Nevis															
	St. Lucia				1	42.6										
	St. Martin (French part)															
	St. Vincent and the Grenadines															
	Suriname	20	46.2	2.2	1	52.9										
	Trinidad and Tobago	26	49.3	2.3	2	41.4	1.6									
	Turks and Caicos Islands															
	United States	42	36.9	1.7	8	39.7	1.7	11	35.2	2.2	30	40.7	1.8			
	Uruguay	32	42.7	3.4	20	44.6	2.2	1	43.9							
	Venezuela	34	43.1	2.5	13	48.0	3.6									
	Virgin Islands															
Total (Type)		3842 Gross income			1110 Mixed			235 Net income			382 Net income			443 Net income		

11

A COMPARATIVE ANALYSIS OF TRADE IN VALUE ADDED ACROSS THE EU AND RUSSIA

Masaaki Kuboniwa

INSTITUTE OF ECONOMIC RESEARCH, HITOTSUBASHI UNIVERSITY, TOKYO, JAPAN

11.1 Introduction

Exports of a country bring about its domestic value added. Usually they also need imports, which induce foreign value added generated in partner countries. This results in trade in value added (TiVA) with global value chains (GVCs) through production sharing. The importance of TiVA and GVCs has been addressed by major international organizations, including the OECD, the WTO, and the World Bank, since around 2010.[1] This chapter provides a comparative analysis of trade in value added across three areas, the EU,[2] Russia, and the rest of the world (ROW). Armed with Leontief's insight and OECD (2021) (ICIO2021), aggregated Russia–EU–ROW input–output tables with 1 sector and 30 sectors are analyzed. Samples cover all years for 1995–2018.[3]

The chapter is structured as follows. Section 11.2 presents essential relationships between changes in the GDPs of Russia and the EU, Russia–EU bilateral trade, and international oil prices. Constructing the simplest Russia–EU–ROW input–output tables, Section 11.3 demonstrates our general accounting framework and defines our measures of trade in value added, including vertical specialization (VS) and value-added exports (VAE), discussing accounting exercises of the decomposition of gross exports into value-added components. Sections 11.4 and 11.5 track trade in value added using the simplest Russia–EU–ROW model with 1-sector and 30-sector versions of ICIO2021 for 1995–2018. Section 11.6 provides concluding remarks, discussing Russian data fraud in ICIO2021.

11.2 Outlook on growth and bilateral trade in Russia and the EU

As is known, the EU (EU28) and Russia with population of about 500 and 140 million, respectively, are the major players in world economics and politics. According to an aggregated version of Russia–EU–ROW model where EU28 is considered a single country, the share of EU28's extra-EU-exports and Russia's exports in the world exports (imports) accounted for 49% and 8%, respectively, in 2018. When we consider intra-EU and intra-ROW trade in addition to extra-EU and extra-ROW trade, the share of EU28's exports and Russia's exports in the world exports were 34% and 2%, respectively, in 2018. Anyway, Russia and the EU play important roles in world trade.

DOI: 10.4324/9781003144366-14

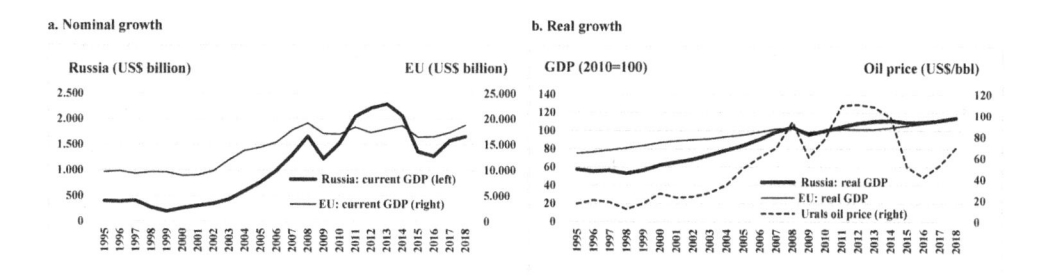

Figure 11.1 GDP growth of Russia and EU.

Sources: ICIO2021, WDI (Jan. 2022), ROSSTAT (www.gks.ru, Jan. 2022), and Reuter.

We briefly look at growth and conventional bilateral trade of Russia and the EU for 1995–2018. Figure 11.1 presents nominal (current US$) and real GDP. Panel (a) of Figure 11.1 shows that the nominal GDP of the EU was averagely about 20 times larger than that of Russia. This ratio included an EU nominal GDP 49 times greater than that of Russia in 1999, due to a great drop in Russia's exchange rate (ruble/US$) after its Financial Crisis, while it was just 12 times greater in 2018. Panel (b) of Figure 11.1 presents the real GDP growth of Russia and the EU (2010 = 100) with Urals oil prices (US$/bbl). The Urals oil price for Russia is closely correlated to the Brent oil price. The average annual growth rates of Russia and the EU were 3% and 1.7%, respectively, for 1995–2018. Russia had a higher growth rate of 7.2% for 1999–2007, thanks to a favorable rise in oil prices, whereas the EU grew only 2.5% in that period. The GDP contracted 7.8% and 4.3% in Russia and the EU, respectively, in 2009 due to the world Financial Crisis with the collapse of the oil price bubble. However, we may witness a co-movement of growth in Russia and the EU. In fact, the correlation coefficient between the two real GDP series was 0.96 for 1995–2018.

Figure 11.2 shows nominal and real bilateral trade in gross terms for 1995–2018. It should be noted that gross exports from Russia (EU) to the EU (Russia) are equal to the gross

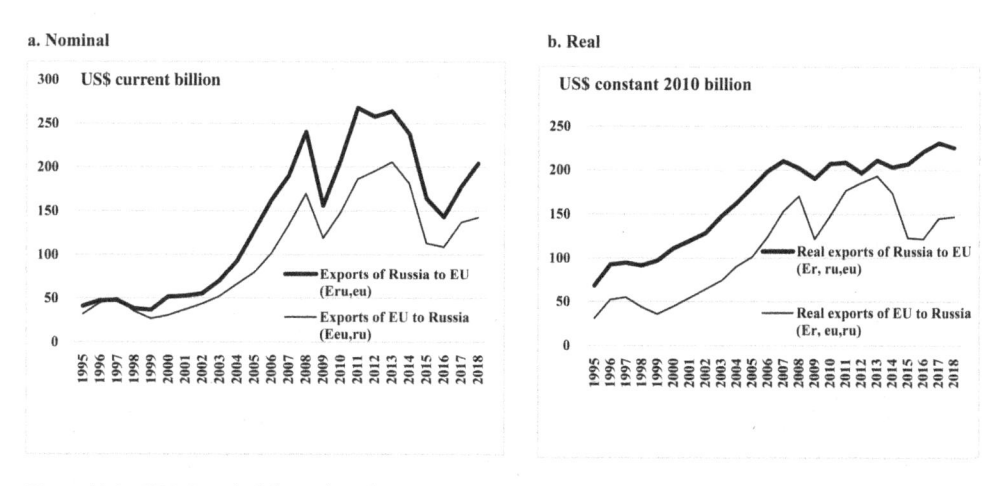

Figure 11.2 EU–Russia bilateral trade.

Sources: ICIO2021 and ROSSTAT website (Jan. 2022).

Note: Real exports of Russia to EU are deflated using Russia's official deflator for its total exports. Real exports of EU to Russia are estimated using Russia's official deflator for its total imports.

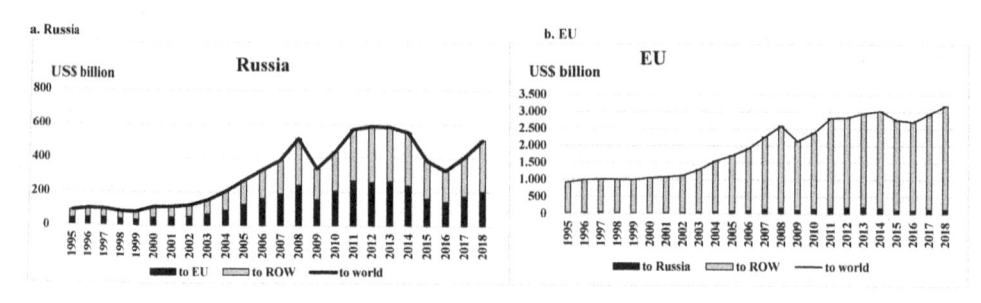

Figure 11.3 Regional distribution of exports in Russia and EU.

Source: ICIO2021.

imports to the EU (Russia) from Russia (EU) in our database framework of inter-country input–output. Russia had chronical surpluses in this bilateral trade balance for every year except 1997. With rises (falls) in oil prices, the nominal surpluses increased (decreased). The average growth rates of nominal exports of Russia and the EU were rather high—7.2% and 6.8%, respectively. Surprisingly, the average growth rate of real exports of EU was 6.2%, larger than that of Russia, at 4.6%. With appreciations in the exchange rate, oil price hikes boosted Russia's imports, including those from the EU, while increases in Russia's export prices were greater than those in its import prices (increases in terms of trade).

Figure 11.3 shows the geographical distribution of exports of Russia and the EU. The EU has absorbed about half of Russia's exports (46% for 1995–2018), whereas Russia has attracted, on average, less than 5% of the EU's total exports for the period.[4] Figure 11.4 demonstrates the dependency of the foreign trade of Russia (EU) on the EU (Russia). Here, dependency is defined by a country (area)'s share of its trade turnover (exports plus imports) in the GDP. Russia's dependency on trade with the EU was very large—ranging between 21% and 30% for 1995–2018 (averagely 23%). It increased from 21% (exports 12%; imports 9%) in 1995 to 30% (17%; 13%) in 1999 and 25% (16%; 10%) in 2005. It decreased to 21% (12%; 9%) in 2009 and remained at the same level of 21% (12%; 9%) in 2018. In contrast, EU's dependency on trade with Russia was rather negligible—ranging between 0.7% and 2.6% (averagely 1.5%). In general, the EU is the most important trade partner for Russia, while Russia is secondary to the EU.

Table 11.1 summarizes basic results of regression among GDP, oil prices, and exports (imports). As was shown in a rigorous manner by Kuboniwa (2012, 2014), Russian GDP and imports have been largely exposed to soaring and plunging oil prices. Here we employ Park's

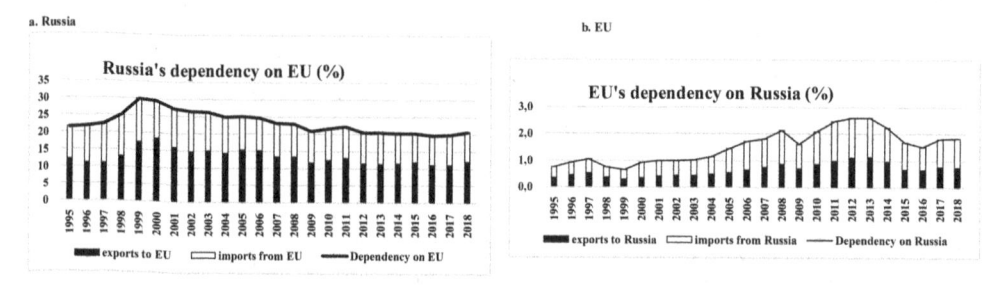

Figure 11.4 Trade dependency in Russia and EU.

Source: ICIO2021.

Table 11.1 Regression 1: GDP growth, oil prices, and exports

Independent variable	Dependent variable						
	Log of real GDPru 1	Log of real GDPeu 2	Log of real GDPeu 3	Log of Eru,eu 4	Log of Eeu,ru 5	Log of real Eru,eu 6	Log of real Eeu,ru 7
Log(oil price)	0.185 *** [6.298]			0.361 *** [15.66]	0.819 *** [7.386]	0.259 *** [5.802]	0.654 *** [8.171]
Log(real Eeu,ru)		0.205 *** [8.144]					
Log(GDPru)			0.406 *** [15.98]				
Constant	3.458 *** [40.07]	3.603 *** [31.29]	2.752 *** [24.72]	1.228 *** [7.606]	1.133 *** [3.476]	3.807 *** [29.49]	1.922 *** [8.167]
Trend	0.024 *** [7.829]			0.021 *** [3.705]	0.017 [1.474]	0.026 *** [4.304]	0.016 * [1.886]
Adj.R^2	0.979	0.704	0.925	0.978	0.921	0.899	0.939

*, **, ***: significance <0.1, 0.05, 0.01. [.]: t-statistics.

canonical cointegration regression (CCR) as an estimator using an adjusted sample from 1996 to 2018. Equation 11.1 of this table demonstrates that Russia's real GDP (*real GDPru*) increases by 1.85% with a fixed effect of a linear trend rate of 2.4% when oil prices (*oil price*) soar by 10%. This trend rate approximately reflects Russia's total factor productivity (TFP) of production function. Equation 11.2 shows the impact of the EU's real exports to Russia (*real Eeu,ru*) on its real GDP (*real GDPeu*). A 1% increase in the EU's exports to Russia (Russia's imports from the EU) leads to 0.2% overall GDP growth of the EU. Equation 11.3 shows a win–win relationship between GDP growth in Russia and the EU. A 1% growth of Russia's GDP results in 0.4% growth of the EU's GDP. Equations 11.4–11.7 suggest strong impacts of oil prices on the bilateral trade in both nominal and real terms.

11.3 Analytical framework

Armed with Leontief's insight, let us proceed to an analysis of trade in value added.

Tables 11.2 and 11.3 present the simplest input–output tables of Russia and the EU (country-based) for 2018, respectively. They are constructed at producer prices that include net taxes on products. Panel (a) of Table 11.1 shows an aggregated version of ICIO2021, while panel (b) presents an aggregated version compiled from the original, official input–output database. Differences between the two panels are rather small. However, focusing on net taxes on products, particularly on exports, they may be seriously different. We wonder whether the OECD made use of Russia's official input–output data in compiling ICIO2021. Unlike other countries, Russia has employed taxes on the exports or export duties of oil and gas instead of corporate income taxes. As taxes on the exports of oil and gas are huge beyond SNA2008's assumption and are essential for the Russian budget, we should be sufficiently cautious regarding the treatment of net taxes on products for Russia.

Table 11.4 demonstrates the simplest version of inter-country input–output tables (internationally based) across Russia, the EU, and the ROW for 2018. Exports and imports are decomposed into intermediate and final demand by country/area.

The theoretical model and concepts follow the generalized framework provided by Kuboniwa (2016). Here we briefly present the simplest one-country input–output model (country based) and 3-country international input–output model using the data of Tables 11.2–11.4. Discussions below can easily be generalized by redefining scalars as matrixes and vectors.

Basic equations for country-based 1-sector input–output analysis are as follows

$$X = AX + f_d + E; M = A_m X + f_m; 1 = 1 \times A + 1 \times A_m + v, \tag{11.1}$$

where

X: domestic output; A: input coefficient ($\underline{X}/X$); fd: domestic final demand; E: exports; M: imports; Am: import coefficient (intermediate imports/X); fm: final demand for imports; v: value-added ratio (V/X); V: value added.

The third equation of Equation 11.1 is a price equation for 1-sector model in monetary terms where the price is always unity. Then, using Leontief inverse (B), "domestic value added ($\underline{DV}$)" directly and indirectly induced by the exports E is, on a country basis,

$$\underline{DV} = v(1-A)^{-1} E = vBE, \; where \; B = (1-A)^{-1}.$$

Production processes involve a consecutive, vertical trading chain generating across many countries, with each country specializing in particular stages of a product's production sequence. The use of imported inputs in producing the exported product, which is a source of

Table 11.2 The simplest input–output table for Russia (country-based): 2018 (producer prices US$ billion)

a. Compiled from OECD ICIO2021

	Country code number	Intermediate demand	Final demand			
		Russia: domestic demand 1	Russia: final demand fd 1	Exports to EU&ROW E 2, 3	Final demand Fd	Output X
Russia: domestic input	1	1,307	1,337	506	1,844	3,151
(Net taxes on products) $\underline{X}$		(94)	(76)	(0.7)	(77)	(171)
Imports from EU&ROW $\underline{M}$	2,3	175	175		175	350
Intermediate input		1,482	1,512	506	2,019	3,501
GDP V		1,669				
Output X		3,151				

b. Compiled from Russia's official input–output data

	Country code number	Intermediate demand	Final demand			
		Russia: domestic demand 1	Russia: final demand fd 1	Exports to EU&ROW E 2, 3	Final demand Fd	Output X
Russia: domestic input $\underline{X}$	1	1,321	1,308	514	1,822	3,143
(Net taxes on products)		(23)	(103)	(51)	(153)	(176)
Imports from EU&ROW $\underline{M}$	2,3	165	184		184	348
Intermediate input		1,486	1,492	514	2,006	3,491
GDP V		1,657				
Output X		3,143				

Sources: Author's compilation using (a) ICIO2021 and (b) ROSSTAT website.

Notes:

1. Russia's domestic input, final demand, GDP, and output include net taxes on products.

2. The Foreign exchange rate is from IMF.

	Case (a)	Case (b)
Input coefficient $A = \underline{X}/X$	0.4149	0.4204
Import coefficient $Am = \underline{M}/X$	0.0554	0.0523
Value-added ratio $v = V/X$	0.5297	0.5273
Leontief inverse $B = (1 - A)^{-1}$	1.7090	1.7253
$\underline{DV} = vBE$	459	468
$\underline{FV} = AmBE$	48	46
$VS = FV/E$	0.095	0.090

Table 11.3 The simplest input–output table for EU (country-based): 2018

| | | Intermediate demand | Final demand | | | |
| | | *(producer prices US$ billion)* | | | | |
	Country code number	*EU* 2	*EU: final demand fd* 2	*Exports to Russia & ROW E* 1, 3	*Final demand* Fd	*Output* X
EU: domestic input $\underline{X}$	2	15,970	17,363	3,184	20,546	36,516
(Net taxes on products)		(890)	(1.107)	(4)	1,110	1,999
Imports from EU&ROW $\underline{M}$	1,3	1,715	1,082		1,082	2,797
Intermediate input		17,684	19,552			37,236
GDP V		18,831				
Output X		36,516				

Source: Author's compilation using ICIO2021.

Notes:
1. EU's domestic input and final demand include net taxes on products.
2. GDP = value added at basic prices + net taxes on products.

Input coefficient A = X/X	0.4373318
Import coefficient $Am = M/X$	0.0469625
Value-added ratio $v = V/X$	0.5157057
Leontief inverse $B = (1 - A)^{-1}$	1.7772463
$DV = vBE$	2,918
$FV = AmBE$	266
$VS = FV/E$	0.083

Table 11.4 The simplest inter-country input–output table for Russia and EU (international base): 2018

(producer prices US$ billion)

| | Country code number | Intermediate demand | | | | Final demand | | | | |
		Russia 1	EU 2	ROW 3	Intermediate demand	Russia F_1 1	EU F_2 2	ROW F_3 3	Final demand Fd	Output Xr
Russia $\underline{X}_{1s}$	1	1,307	161	237	1,705	1,337	43	66	1,446	3,151
EU $\underline{X}_{2s}$	2	76	15,970	1,604	17,650	67	17,358	1,440	18,865	36,515
ROW $\underline{X}_{3s}$	3	98	1,554	64,371	66,023	108	1,044	64,559	65,711	131,734
Intermediate input		1,482	17,684	66,212	85,378					
GDP Vr		1,669	18,831	65,522	86,022					
Output Xr		3,151	36,515	131,734	171,400					

Source: Author's compilation using ICIO2021.

Notes: r, s = 1, 2, 3. 1 = Russia, 2 = EU, 3 = ROW.

Input coefficient matrix $A = (A_{rs}) = (\underline{X}_{rs}/X_s)$

$$A = \begin{pmatrix} 0.4149 & 0.0044 & 0.0018 \\ 0.0242 & 0.4373 & 0.0122 \\ 0.0312 & 0.0425 & 0.4886 \end{pmatrix}$$

Value-added ratio vector $v_r = V_r/X_r$

$$v = (v_r) = (0.5297 \quad 0.5157 \quad 0.4974)$$

Leontief inverse matrix $B = (I - A)^{-1} = (B_{rs})$

$$B = \begin{pmatrix} 1.7099 & 0.0139 & 0.0063 \\ 0.0760 & 1.7811 & 0.0427 \\ 0.1107 & 0.1490 & 1.9595 \end{pmatrix}$$

---

value added produced in foreign countries, is defined as "foreign value added" in Hummels *et al.* (2001). On a country basis, this foreign value added ($\underline{FV}$) is calculated as

$$\underline{FV} = A_m(1-A)^{-1}E = A_m BE.$$

It follows from definitions of $\underline{DV}$ and $\underline{FV}$ that

$$\underline{DV} + \underline{FV} = (v + A_m)BE = (1-A)(1-A)^{-1}E = E.$$

In view of this identity, Hummels *et al.* (2001) proposed a measure of vertical specialization (*VS*) in order to measure the intensity of vertical production sharing in the use of imports: $VS = \underline{FV}/E$. As is shown in Table 11.2, for case a (case b) of Russia, using ICIO2021 (official data), Russia's vertical specialization level was *VSru* = 9.5% (9.0%) in 2018. Table 11.3 demonstrates that the EU's vertical specialization accounted for *VSeu* = 8.3% in 2018. Roughly, the larger an economy is, the smaller its *VS*.

By definition, domestic value added induced by exports directly contributes to GDP growth. Foreign value added implies a country's spillover effects or its dependency on foreign countries. A contemporary significance of foreign value added lies in that it may contribute to the country's GDP through production sharing. We are concerned with both export-led growth and import-led growth through global production sharing.

We introduce the following notations: r, s: indexes of countries/areas (1 = Russia or ru, 2 = EU or eu, 3 = ROW); Xr: country r's output; A_{rs}: intermediate input from country r to produce a unit of a product in country s; Y_r: country r's final demand; and v_r: country r's value-added ratio. Then basic equations for a 3-country/area 1-sector model can be written as

$$X = AX + Y, \ u = uA + v, \tag{11.2}$$

where

$$X = (X_r) = \begin{pmatrix} X_1 \\ X_2 \\ X_3 \end{pmatrix}, \ A = (A_{rs}) = \begin{pmatrix} A_{11} & A_{12} & A_{13} \\ A_{21} & A_{22} & A_{23} \\ A_{31} & A_{23} & A_{33} \end{pmatrix}, \ Y = (Y_r) = \begin{pmatrix} Y_1 \\ Y_2 \\ Y_3 \end{pmatrix}$$

$$u = (1 \ 1 \ 1), \ v = (v_1 \ v_2 \ v_3).$$

The first and second equations of Equation 11.2 are quantity and price equations, respectively, for an international input–output table. A is the international Leontief matrix.

Therefore,

$$X = BY, \ u = vB,$$

where

$$B = (I - A)^{-1} = (B_{rs}) = \begin{pmatrix} B_{11} & B_{12} & B_{13} \\ B_{21} & B_{22} & B_{23} \\ B_{31} & B_{23} & B_{33} \end{pmatrix},$$

$$Y = \begin{pmatrix} Y_1 \\ Y_2 \\ Y_3 \end{pmatrix} = \begin{pmatrix} Y_{11} + Y_{12} + Y_{13} \\ Y_{21} + Y_{22} + Y_{23} \\ Y_{31} + Y_{32} + Y_{33} \end{pmatrix}; \ F_s = \begin{pmatrix} Y_{1s} \\ Y_{2s} \\ Y_{3s} \end{pmatrix}; Y = F_1 + F_2 + F_3,$$

where F_S denotes a final demand vector of destination country s.

Matrix B is the international Leontief inverse. F_s is country s's final demand vector column-wisely sliced by destination.

By virtue of the price equation of Equation 11.2, we have $\Sigma_s v_s B_{sr} = 1$. Let $E_r = \Sigma_{s \neq r} E_{rs}$ be country r's total gross exports. That is to say, $E_1 = E_{12} + E_{13}$, $E_2 = E_{21} + E_{23}$, $E_3 = E_{31} + E_{32.}$ Then, we have the following identities between gross exports and domestic and foreign value added on the international base.

$$E_r = \sum_{s \neq r} E_{rs} = DV_r + FV_r; E_{rs} = DV_{rs} + FV_{rs}.$$

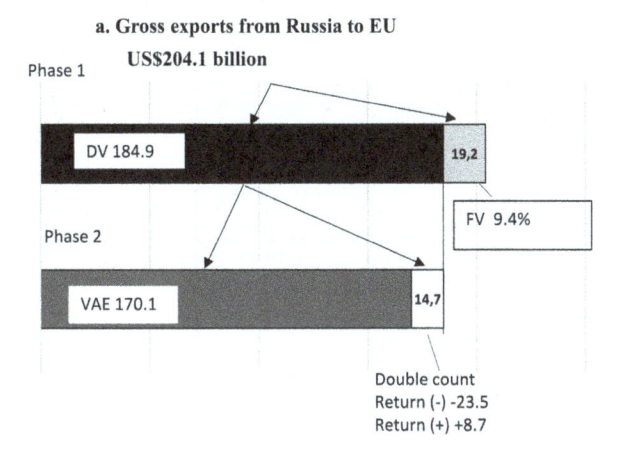

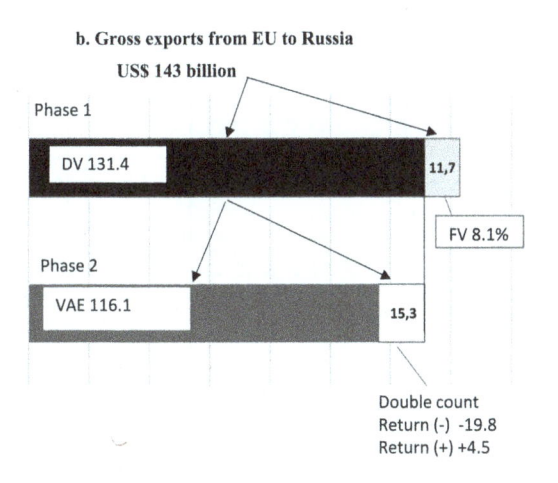

Figure 11.5 Decomposition of gross exports: 2018.

Source: Author's calculation using ICIO2021.

We consider the 2-phase decomposition of gross exports. Figure 11.5 illustrates the decomposition of gross exports in Phase 1 into domestic and foreign value added (*DV* and *FV*), based on Table 11.4. It also displays further the decomposition of domestic value added into value-added exports (*VAE*) and double counts at Phase 2. Table 11.5 summarizes trade in gross and value-added terms across Russia, the EU, and ROW on both a country basis and international basis for 2018. Following the framework of Kuboniwa (2016) and Table 11.4, we track the aggregated trade in value added across the three areas. Discussing numerals based on Table 11.4, we omit the unit of US$ billion in cases with no possibility of misunderstanding.

Phase 1: Decomposition of gross exports into domestic and foreign value added based on Koopman *et al.* (2010–2011, 2014). We define country *r*'s domestic value added (*DVrs*) and foreign value added (*FVrs*), which are induced by gross exports from origin country *r* to destination country *s* (*Ers*), as follows. FV_{rs}^{k} denotes foreign value added induced by gross exports *Ers* from origin/source country *r* to destination country *s*, which is produced by country *k* and returns to home country *k*.

223

Table 11.5 Trade in value added across Russia, EU, and ROW: 2018

		Country base			International base					
								(US$ billion)		
origin r	*destination s*	*Ers*	*DVrs*	*FVrs*	*DVrs*	*FVrs*	*VAErs*	*double count*	*Return (−)*	*Return (+)*
1 Russia	2 EU	204.1	184.8	19.3	184.9	19.2	170.1	−14.7	−23.5	8.7
	3 ROW	302.4	273.7	28.6	273.9	28.5	286.9	13.0	−9.4	22.4
	Subtotal	506.4	458.5	48.0	458.7	47.7	457.0	−1.7	−32.9	31.1
2 EU	1 Russia	143.0	131.1	11.9	131.4	11.7	116.1	−15.3	−19.8	4.5
	3 ROW	3,044.2	2,790.1	254.1	2,796.1	248.1	2,746.2	−49.9	−61.7	11.8
	Subtotal	3,187.2	2,921.2	266.0	2,927.5	259.7	2,862.3	−65.2	−81.5	16.4
3 ROW	1 Russia	206.5	200.9	5.6	201.3	5.2	184.0	−17.3	−27.9	10.6
	2 EU	2,597.3	2,526.3	71.0	2,531.4	65.9	2,306.3	−225.0	−236.3	11.2
	Subtotal	2,803.8	2,727.2	76.6	2,732.7	71.1	2,490.4	−242.3	−264.2	21.8
	Total	6,497.4	6,106.8	390.6	6,118.9	378.6	5,809.6	−309.2	−378.6	69.4

Trade balance		*Gross balance*	*Value-added balance*	*Value added/gross (%)*	*Trade balance*			*Gross balance*	*Value-added balance*	*Value added/ gross (%)*
Russia	with 2 EU	61.0	54.0	88.5	EU		with 1 Russia	−61.0	−54.0	88.5
	with 3 ROW	95.8	102.8	107.3			with 3 ROW	446.9	439.9	98.4
	Total	156.9	156.9	100.0			Total	385.8	385.8	100.0

Sources: Author's estimation using Tables 11.1, 11.2, and 11.3.

Masaaki Kuboniwa

We introduce the following notations for value-added ratios and gross exports with Table 11.4:

$$\hat{V} = diag(v) = \begin{pmatrix} v_1 & 0 & 0 \\ 0 & v_2 & 0 \\ 0 & 0 & v_3 \end{pmatrix} = \begin{pmatrix} 0.5297 & 0 & 0 \\ 0 & 0.5157 & 0 \\ 0 & 0 & 0.4974 \end{pmatrix}$$

$$\hat{E} = \begin{pmatrix} E_{12} & E_{13} & 0 & 0 & 0 & 0 \\ 0 & 0 & E_{21} & E_{23} & 0 & 0 \\ 0 & 0 & 0 & 0 & E_{31} & E_{32} \end{pmatrix} = \begin{pmatrix} 204 & 302 & 0 & 0 & 0 & 0 \\ 0 & 0 & 143 & 3044 & 0 & 0 \\ 0 & 0 & 0 & 0 & 207 & 2597 \end{pmatrix}.$$

Let us constitute $\hat{V}B\hat{E}$.

$$\hat{V}B\hat{E} = \begin{pmatrix} v_1 B_{11} E_{12} & v_1 B_{11} E_{13} & v_1 B_{12} E_{21} & v_1 B_{12} E_{23} & v_1 B_{13} E_{31} & v_1 B_{13} E_{32} \\ v_2 B_{21} E_{12} & v_2 B_{21} E_{13} & v_2 B_{22} E_{21} & v_2 B_{22} E_{23} & v_2 B_{23} E_{31} & v_2 B_{23} E_{32} \\ v_3 B_{31} E_{12} & v_3 B_{31} E_{13} & v_3 B_{32} E_{21} & v_3 B_{32} E_{23} & v_3 B_{33} E_{31} & v_3 B_{33} E_{32} \end{pmatrix}$$

$$= \begin{pmatrix} DV_{12} & DV_{13} & FV_{21}^1 & FV_{23}^1 & FV_{31}^1 & FV_{32}^1 \\ FV_{12}^2 & FV_{13}^2 & DV_{21} & DV_{23} & FV_{31}^2 & FV_{32}^2 \\ FV_{12}^3 & FV_{13}^3 & FV_{21}^3 & FV_{23}^3 & DV_{31} & DV_{32} \end{pmatrix} = \begin{pmatrix} 185 & 274 & 1 & 22 & 1 & 9 \\ 8 & 12 & 131 & 2796 & 5 & 57 \\ 11 & 17 & 11 & 226 & 201 & 2531 \end{pmatrix},$$

$$(11.3)$$

where $DV_{rs} = v_r B_{rr} E_{rs}$, $FV_{rs}^k = v_k B_{kr} E_{rs}$.

Let $FV_{rs} = \Sigma_{k \neq r} FV_{rs}^k$ be foreign value added induced by gross exports from country r to destination s, Ers. Thus, gross exports from origin 1 (Russia) to destination 2 (EU) are decomposed into domestic and foreign value added (DV and FV) as follows:

$$DV_{12} = 185, \quad FV_{12} = FV_{12}^2 + FV_{12}^3 = 8 + 11 = 19, \quad E_{12} = DV_{12} + FV_{12} = 204.$$

Then $VS_{12} = 9.4\%$. As can be easily verified, $VS_{12} = VS_{13} = 9.4\%$. Let country 1's total domestic and foreign value added be $DV_1 = DV_{12} + DV_{13}$, $FV_1 = FV_{12} + FV_{13}$, respectively. Country 1's total gross exports are $E_1 = E_{12} + E_{13}$. We denote country 1's non-bilateral vertical specialization as $VS_1 = FV_1/E_1$. Thus, $VS_1 = 9.4\%$ from Table 11.5. We find that, in the case of a 1-sector model, a country's vertical specialization in its bilateral trade is the same irrespective of the destination partner.

Similarly, gross exports from origin 2 (EU) to destination 1 (Russia) are decomposed into domestic and foreign value added as follows:

$$DV_{21} = 131, \quad FV_{21} = FV_{21}^1 + FV_{21}^3 = 1 + 11 = 12, \quad E_{21} = DV_{21} + FV_{21} = 143,$$

$$VS_{21} = 8.1\%.$$

Also, we have $VS_{21} = VS_{23} = 8.1\%$. We define and denote country 2's total domestic and foreign value added as $DV_2 = DV_{21} + DV_{23}$, $FV_2 = FV_{21} + FV_{23}$, respectively. Country 2's total gross exports are $E_2 = E_{21} + E_{23}$. We define country 2's non-bilateral vertical specialization as $VS_2 = FV_2/E_2$. From Table 11.5, $VS_2 = 8.1\%$.

In the case with a 1-sector model, a country's vertical specialization in its bilateral trade is the same irrespective of the destination partner. We also find negligible differences between results using country and international bases, as shown in Tables 11.2–11.4.

We are now in a position to go further into the next phase (Phase 2) of decomposition of gross exports into value added.

Phase 2: Decomposition of domestic value added into value-added exports and double counts

Definition 1. Johnson and Noguera (2012). Value-added exports, VAE_{rs}, are defined as value added produced in origin country r to provide final demand of destination country s.

$$VAE = \hat{V}_r BF;$$

$$VAE = (VAE_{rs}) = \begin{pmatrix} VAE_{11} & VAE_{12} & VAE_{13} \\ VAE_{21} & VAE_{22} & VAE_{23} \\ VAE_{31} & VAE_{32} & VAE_{33} \end{pmatrix} = \begin{pmatrix} v_1 & 0 & 0 \\ 0 & v_2 & 0 \\ 0 & 0 & v_3 \end{pmatrix} B \begin{pmatrix} F_1 & F_2 & F_3 \end{pmatrix}$$

From Table 11.4, the final demand matrix by destination is written as

$$F = \begin{pmatrix} F_1 & F_2 & F_3 \end{pmatrix} = \begin{pmatrix} 1,337 & 43 & 66 \\ 67 & 17,358 & 1,440 \\ 108 & 1,044 & 64,559 \end{pmatrix}.$$

In view of definition 1, the matrix of value-added exports VAE is

$$\begin{pmatrix} VAE_{11} & VAE_{12} & VAE_{13} \\ VAE_{21} & VAE_{22} & VAE_{23} \\ VAE_{31} & VAE_{32} & VAE_{33} \end{pmatrix} = \hat{V}BF = \begin{pmatrix} 1,212 & 170 & 287 \\ 116 & 15,968 & 2,746 \\ 184 & 2,306 & 63,032 \end{pmatrix}. \tag{11.4}$$

This implies that

$$VAE_{12} = 170;\ VAE_{21} = 116;\ VAE_{13} = 287;\ VAE_{31} = 184;\ VAE_{23} = 2,746;\ VAE_{32} = 2,306.$$

Johnson–Noguera introduced a measure of intensity of production sharing across countries that they call VAX (VAE_{rs} share in gross exports E).

We introduce an alternative definition of value-added exports to trace sources of double counts.

Definition 2. Trefler and Zhu (2010) and Kuboniwa (2016). The number of factors employed worldwide to produce country r's net trade matrix E_{net} is given by

$$\begin{pmatrix} VAE_{12} + VAE_{13} & -VAE_{12} & -VAE_{13} \\ -VAE_{21} & VAE_{21} + VAE_{23} & -VAE_{23} \\ -VAE_{31} & -VAE_{32} & VAE_{31} + VAE_{32} \end{pmatrix} = \hat{V}BE_{net}, \tag{11.5}$$

where

$$\boldsymbol{E}_{net} = \begin{pmatrix} E_{12} + E_{13} & -E_{12} & -E_{13} \\ -E_{21} & E_{21} + E_{23} & -E_{23} \\ -E_{31} & -E_{32} & E_{31} + E_{32} \end{pmatrix}.$$

From Table 11.4, $\boldsymbol{E}_{net}$ is written as

$$\boldsymbol{E}_{net} = \begin{pmatrix} 506 & -204 & -302 \\ -143 & 3{,}187 & -3{,}044 \\ -207 & -2{,}597 & 2{,}804 \end{pmatrix}.$$

In view of definition 2,

$$\hat{\boldsymbol{V}} \boldsymbol{B} \boldsymbol{E}_{net} = \begin{pmatrix} VAE_{12} + VAE_{13} & -VAE_{12} & -VAE_{13} \\ -VAE_{21} & VAE_{21} + VAE_{23} & -VAE_{23} \\ -VAE_{31} & -VAE_{32} & VAE_{31} + VAE_{32} \end{pmatrix} = \begin{pmatrix} 457 & -170 & -287 \\ -116 & 2{,}862 & -2{,}746 \\ -184 & -2{,}306 & 2{,}490 \end{pmatrix}.$$

Thus, we obtain

$VAE_{12} = 170;\ VAE_{21} = 116;\ VAE_{13} = 287;\ VAE_{31} = 184;\ VAE_{23} = 2{,}746;\ VAE_{32} = 2{,}306.$

These results are the same in the case of definition 1. In our definition 2, however, we can specify factors causing differences between domestic value added (DV) and value-added exports (VAE).

$$VAE_{rs} = v_r B_{rr} E_{rs} - v_r B_{rs} E_s + v_r B_{rk} E_{ks}$$
$$= DV_{rs} - \left(FV_{sr}^r + FV_{sk}^r \right) + FV_{ks}^r, \tag{11.6}$$
$$= DV_{rs} - RETURN(-) + RETURN(+),$$

where

$$RETURN(-) = v_r B_{rs} E_s = FV_{sr}^r + FV_{sk}^r,\ RETURN(+) = v_r B_{rk} E_{ks} = FV_{ks}^r.$$

From above and Table 11.4, value-added exports from origin country 1 (Russia) to destination country 2 (EU) account for:

$$VAE_{12} = v_1 B_{11} E_{12} - v_1 B_{12} E_2 + v_1 B_{13} E_{32} = DV_{12} - \left(FV_{21}^1 + FV_{23}^1 \right) + FV_{32}^1 = 170.1,$$

where

$$DV_{12} = 184.9,$$

$$\text{Return}(-) = v_1 B_{12} E_2 = v_1 B_{12} \left(E_{21} + E_{23} \right) = FV_{21}^1 + FV_{23}^1 = 23.5,\ \text{Return}(+) = v_1 B_{13} E_{32} = 8.7.$$

$$VAX_{12} = VAE_{12} / E_{12} = 83.4\%.$$

Similarly, valueadded exports from origin country 2 (EU) to destination country 1 (Russia) are

$$VAE_{21} = v_2 B_{22} E_{21} - v_2 B_{21} E_1 + v_2 B_{23} E_{31} = DV_{21} - \left(FV_{12}^2 + FV_{13}^2\right) + FV_{31}^2 = 116.1,$$

where

$$DV_{21} = 131.4, \text{Return}(-) = FV_{12}^2 + FV_{13}^2 = 19.8, \text{Return}(+) = FV_{31}^2 = 4.5.$$

$$VAX_{21} = VAE_{21}/E_{21} = 81.2\%.$$

As Return(−) > Return(+), we confirm that $VAE_{12} < DV_{12}$ and $VAE_{21} < DV_{21}$. Value-added exports (*VAErs*), however, are not always less than domestic value added (*DVrs*). Here, let us look at value-added exports from origin country 1 (Russia) to destination country 3 (ROW), VAE_{13}.

$$VAE_{13} = v_1 B_{11} E_{13} - v_1 B_{13} E_3 + v_1 B_{12} E_{23} = DV_{13} - \left(FV_{31}^1 + FV_{32}^1\right) + FV_{23}^1 = 286.9,$$

where

$$DV_{13} = 273.9, \text{Return}(-) = FV_{31}^1 + FV_{32}^1 = 9.4, \text{Return}(+) = FV_{23}^1 = 22.4.$$

Hence, $VAE_{13} > DV_{13}$. Foreign value added, FV_{23}^1, which was induced by gross exports from destination country EU to third party country ROW and returned to Russia (produced in Russia), was rather large, while double count as Return(−), which was induced by exports of the third party country ROW and returned to Russia, $FV_{31}^1 + FV_{32}^1$ was rather small. Russia (country 1)'s trade balance with the EU (country 2) in value-added terms in 2018 was $VAE_{12} - VAE_{21} = 170.1 - 116.1 = 54.0$. The Russia–EU balance in gross terms was $E_{12} - E_{21} = 204.1 - 143.0 = 61.0$. Thus, the Russia–EU balance (EU–Russia imbalance) in 2018 was 11.5% smaller when measured in value added (see the lower part of Table 11.5). The Russia–ROW balances in gross and value-added terms were 95.8 and 102.8, respectively, in 2018, where the value-added balance was 7.3% larger than the gross balance. In all, Russia's total balances with the world as measured in gross and value added were both 156.9 in 2018. This is generally true. A country's total trade balance with the world in value-added terms is always equal to that in gross terms. Also, the EU–Russia imbalance was sufficiently compensated by the EU–ROW surplus.

11.4 Tracking trade in value added using the simplest Russia–EU–ROW model with ICIO2021 for 1995–2018

Figure 11.6 shows the decomposition of gross exports of Russia and the EU in Phase 1 in 1995–2018. Figure 11.7 presents Phase 2's decomposition of domestic value added.

Figure 11.8 shows movements of foreign value added (*FV*) and HIY's vertical specialization (*VS*) for Russia and the EU. In this figure, a co-movement of *FV* for Russia and EU can be seen, whereas no co-movement of *VS* is witnessed.

Figure 11.9 demonstrates the dynamics of value-added trade (*VAE*) and Johnson–Noguera's *VAX* for Russia and EU. As in Figure 11.8, a co-movement of *VAE* for Russia and the EU is found, while no co-movement of *VS* is seen.

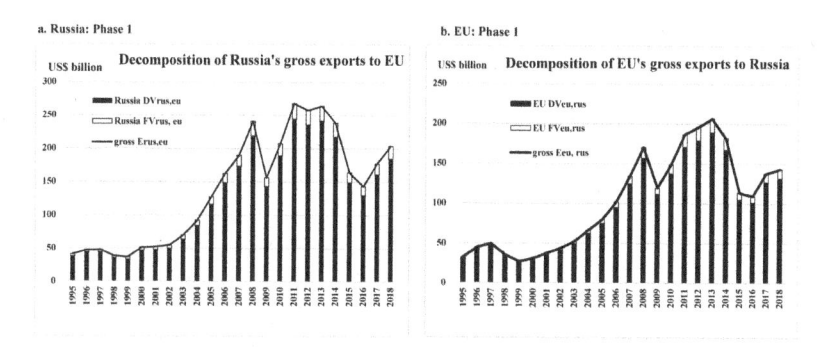

Figure 11.6 Decomposition of gross exports in Russia and EU.

Source: Author's caluculations using ICIO2021.

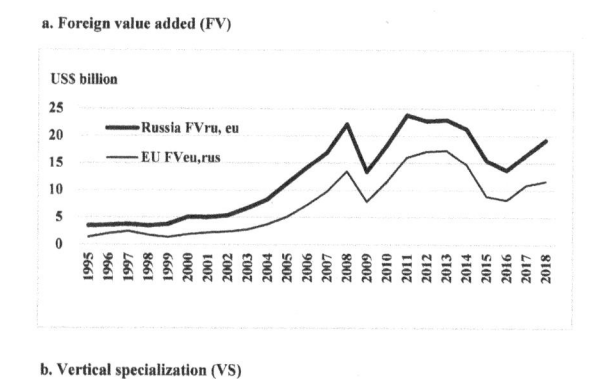

Figure 11.7 Phase 2: Domestic value added (DV) and value-added exports (VAE).

Source: Author's compilation using ICIO2021.

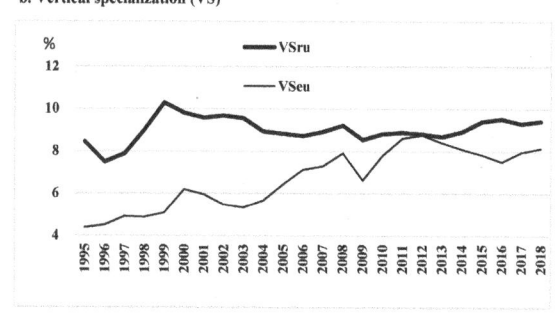

Figure 11.8 Foreign value added (FV) and vertical specialization (VS) in Russia and EU.

Source: Author's compilation using ICIO2021.

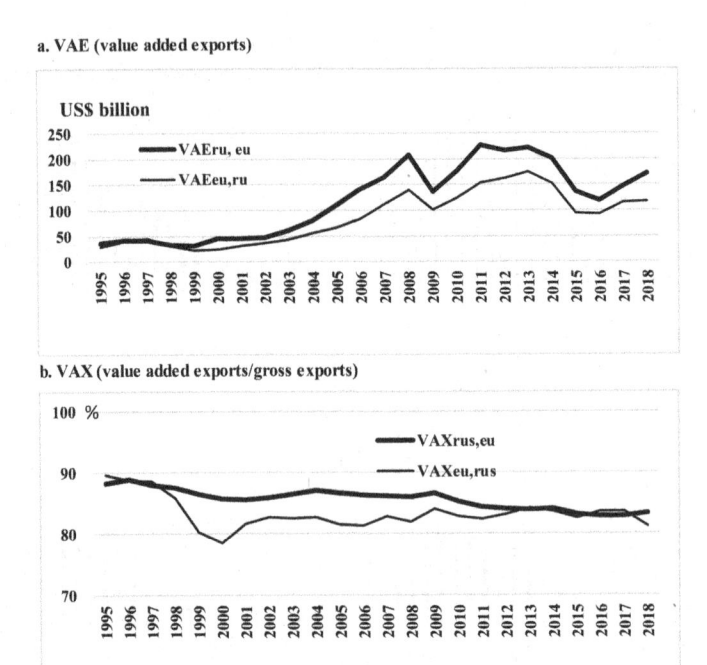

Figure 11.9 Value-added exports and VAX in Russia and EU.

Source: Author's compilation using ICIO2021.

Table 11.6 shows the results of regression 2 concerning growth and exports. Russia's real GDP has strong correlations with gross exports (Eru,eu) and value-added exports ($VAEru,eu$) to EU. As for foreign value added (FV), both $FVru,eu$ and $FVeu,ru$ have strong effects on Russian growth. Regarding vertical specialization measure VS, only Russian-side VS with the help of oil prices has an impact on the country's own growth. The EU's gross and value-added exports with foreign value added have positive effects on a country's own growth, while the goodness of fit shown by adjusted R-squared is rather poor in these relations. Russian foreign value added and vertical specialization have stronger impacts on the EU's growth than on its own growth.

It is noteworthy here to look at the total EU28 and intra-EU varieties of economies as well, using panel data regressions. Figure 11.10 displays the distribution of GDP and vertical specialization ($GDPr, VSr$) of 28 EU members for 2018. The VSs of large economies, including France, are rather low, while those of small ones, including Luxembourg and Malta, are rather high. Figure 11.11 shows changes in vertical specialization measures for the EU3 and the EU4. Panel (a) of the figure demonstrates VSs in the EU3 (three Central European transition countries), where these three economies recorded steady increases until the 2009 crisis, revived, and then stagnated, with the exception of Poland. On the other hand, panel (b) shows VSs in EU's largest 4, the EU4, where, as in the EU3, they showed increases until the 2009 crisis, revived, then decreased again, and further increased, with the exception of France. The French VS stagnated after the revival of the 2009 crisis.

Table 11.7 presents the results of a panel ordinary least square (OLS) regression for the EU28, the EU4, and the EU3 from 1995 to 2018. This table also shows results of the Asia5 and the Asia11 for comparison. Equation 11.1 of Table 11.7 suggests that changes in vertical specialization

Table 11.6 Regression 2: GDP growth and exports

Dependent valuable Independent variable	log(real GDPru)					log(real GDPeu)				
	1	2	3	4	5	6	7	8	9	10
log(oil price)					0.303 *** [10.13]					
log(Eru, eu)	0.205 *** [9.123]									
log(Eeu, ru)						0.161 *** [7.974]				
log(VAEru,eu)		0.203 *** [9.097]								
log(VAEeu,ru)							0.158 *** [7.626]			
log(FVru, eu)			0.231 *** [6.315]						0.157 *** [9.044]	
log(FVeu,ru)				0.164 *** [7.500]				0.127 *** [8.450]		
log(VSru,eu)					1.512 *** [28.96]					
log(VSeu,ru)										0.541 *** [9.030]
c	3.224 *** [37.65]	3.259 *** [39.71]	3.692 *** [69.84]	3.902 *** [151.7]		3.830 *** [42.77]	3.873 *** [44.08]	4.326 *** [154.3]	4.191 *** [101.1]	3.531 *** [31.20]
Trend	0.020 *** [8.182]	0.021 *** [8.704]	0.018 *** [4.525]	0.021 *** [6.966]						
adj.R^2	#RIF!	0.986	0.988	0.970	0.750	0.634	0.604	0.707	0.809	0.814

*, **, ***: significance <0.1, 0.05, 0.01. [.]: t-statistics.

EU's real GDP (real GDPeu) is estimated using WDI (January 2022).

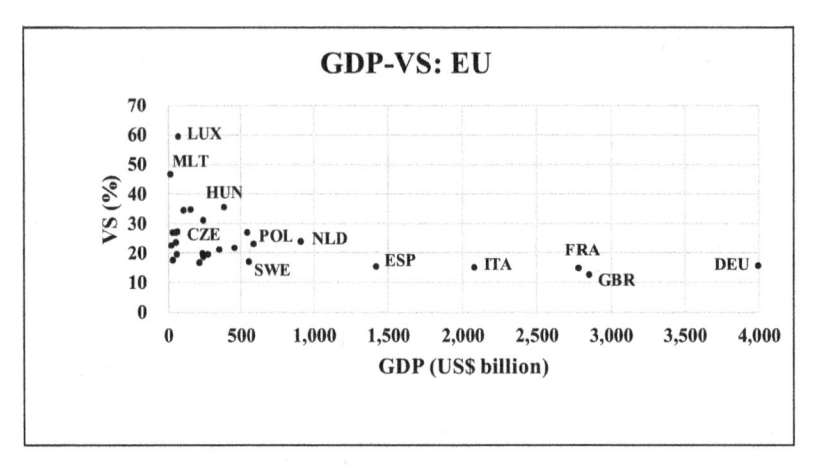

Figure 11.10 GDP and vertical specialization (VS) in member countries of EU: 2018.

Source: Author's estimation using ICIO2021.

have a positive effect on the EU28's growth. Equation 11.2 also demonstrates that vertical specialization has a positive relationship with the EU4's GDP growth. Equation 11.3 shows a positive relationship between changes in the GDP of the EU3 and their vertical specialization in a well-defined manner. A 10% increase of vertical specialization brings about 2% growth of GDP with a fixed effect of annual trend rate of 2.4%. EU3 countries, with highly active intra- and-extra-area trade, appropriately make use of imports or foreign value added for their growth. For the Asia5, which consists of South Korea, Singapore, Taiwan, Thailand, and Vietnam, with increasing foreign trade, a strong positive relationship between their vertical specialization and growth is found. In contrast, Asia11, which includes Malaysia, the Philippines, and Asian giants such as China, Japan, India, and Indonesia in addition to Asia5, demonstrates a negative rela- tionship between changes in vertical specialization and GDP. The Chinese GDP has a strong positive relationship with developments in Taiwanese or Korean vertical specialization, which is beyond the scope of panel regression here. Our regressions suggest a homogeneity within the EU and a heterogeneity within Asia, regarding the relationships between vertical specialization and growth. Further investigation, however, is needed to make a full comparison of Asia and Europe with consideration of more complicated situations.

11.5 Russia–EU–ROW multi-sector input–output analysis

Let us go to an inter-country multi-sector analysis using Kuboniwa (2016) and a 30-sector version of the ICIO2021 at US$ producer prices. This section reports only some results of our computations focusing on manufacturing including machinery because developments of the manufacturing sector, in particular the machinery sector, are major sources of EU growth and are also assumed to be key to the further diversification of the Russian economy.

The left-hand side of Figure 11.12 demonstrates developments in Russia's gross and value- added exports of manufacturing goods to the EU and in foreign value added induced by these exports. It should be noted that the manufacturing sector here includes refined oil. The right- hand side of the figure shows the EU's gross and value-added exports of manufacturing goods to Russia and the foreign value added caused by these exports. Bilateral trade across the EU and Russia had increased in the 2000s until the 2009 crisis then revived but declined with falls in oil prices. Again, with rising oil prices, they increased to some extent in 2017 and 2018.

a. EU3

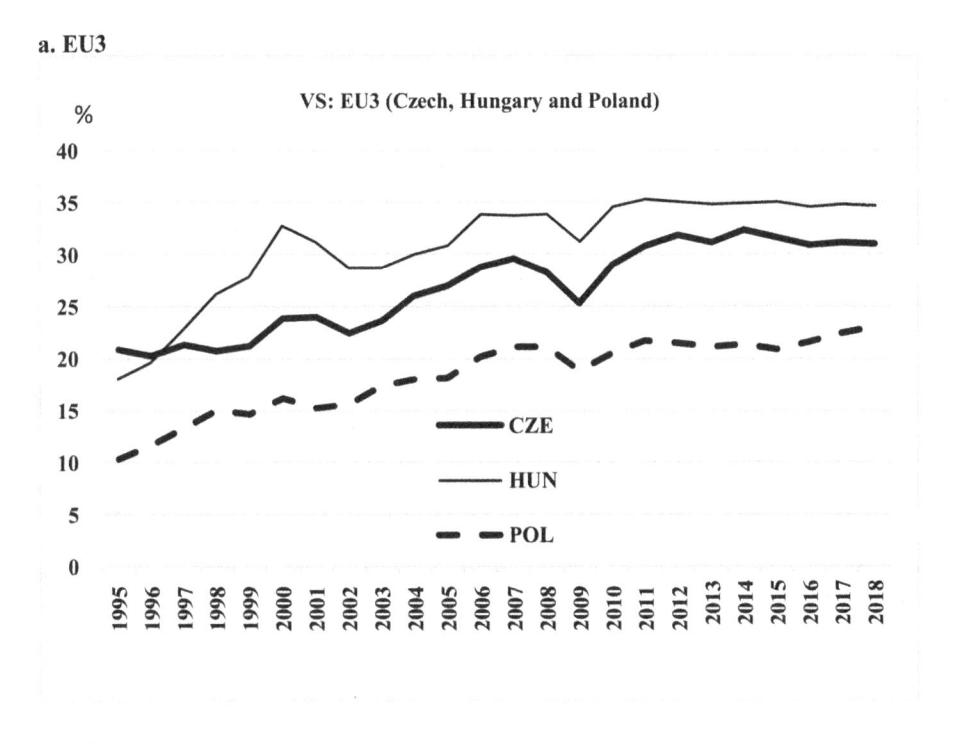

b. EU4

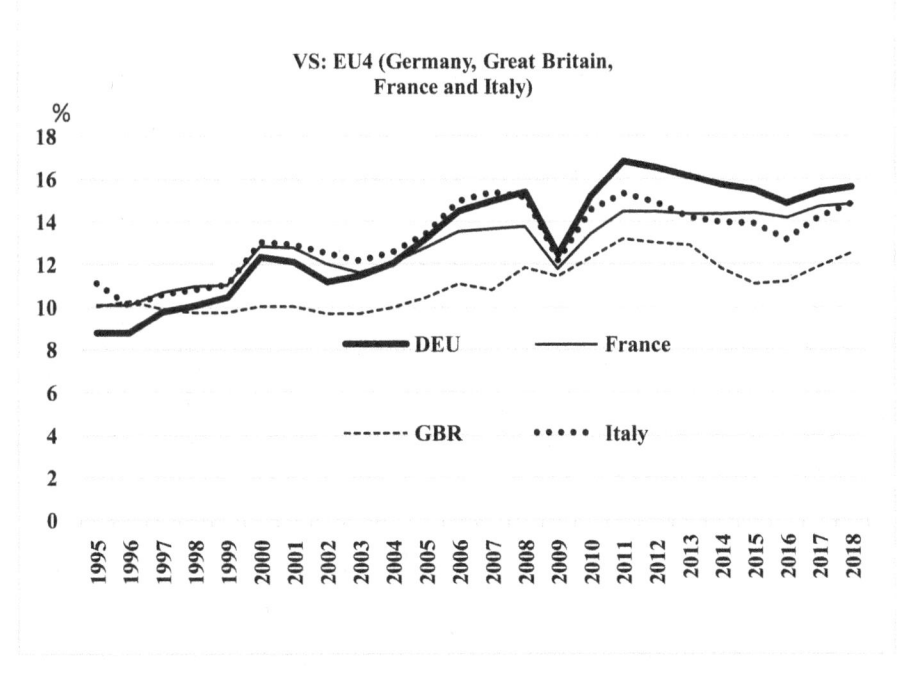

Figure 11.11   GDP and vertical specialization in EU3 and EU4.

Source: Author's compilation using ICIO2021.

Table 11.7 Intermediate demand regression 3: Panel data of GDP growth and vertical specialization (VS)

Independent variable	Dependent variable log(real GDP)				
	EU28 1	EU4 2	EU3 3	Asia5 4	Asia11 5
log(VS)	0.154 ***	0.092 ***	0.203 ***	0.419 ***	−0.039 ***
	[3.196]	[3.083]	[9.510]	[4.823]	[−6.450]
Constant	4.523 ***	4.637 ***	4.506 ***	4.953 ***	3.787 ***
	[50.01]	[67.56]	[61.03]	[45.05]	[243.6]
Trend	0.021 ***	0.011 ***	0.024 ***		0.049 ***
	[20.306]	[15.056]	[5.909]		[82.21]
adj.R^2	0.854	0.755	0.923	0.108	0.810
Observations	672	96	72	120	264

Sources: WDI (January 2022), ICIO2021, and Taiwan Statistics (January 2022).

*, **, ***: significance <0.1, 0.05, 0.01. [.]: White cross section t-statistics.

EU28: EU member countries in 2018.
EU4: Germany, France, United Kingdom, and Italy.
EU3: Czech, Hungary, and Poland.
Asia5: Korea, Singapore, Taiwan, Thailand, and Vietnam.
Asia11: In addition to Asia5, Japan, China, India, Indonesia, Malaysia, and the Philippines.

Figure 11.13 displays movements of vertical specialization of the manufacturing sector associated with the bilateral trade of manufacturing goods between Russia and the EU. The vertical specialization of Russia exceeded that of the EU by more than 2%. The volatility of vertical specialization changes of Russia looks higher than that of the EU. The vertical specialization of Russia associated with its exports to the EU did not show marked increases after 2000. Anyway, in 2016, it reached a peak level of 8.5% due to a larger decline in the denominator of *VS*, namely gross exports. In the period, both gross and value-added exports decreased by 22%, while the foreign value added contracted only by 10%.

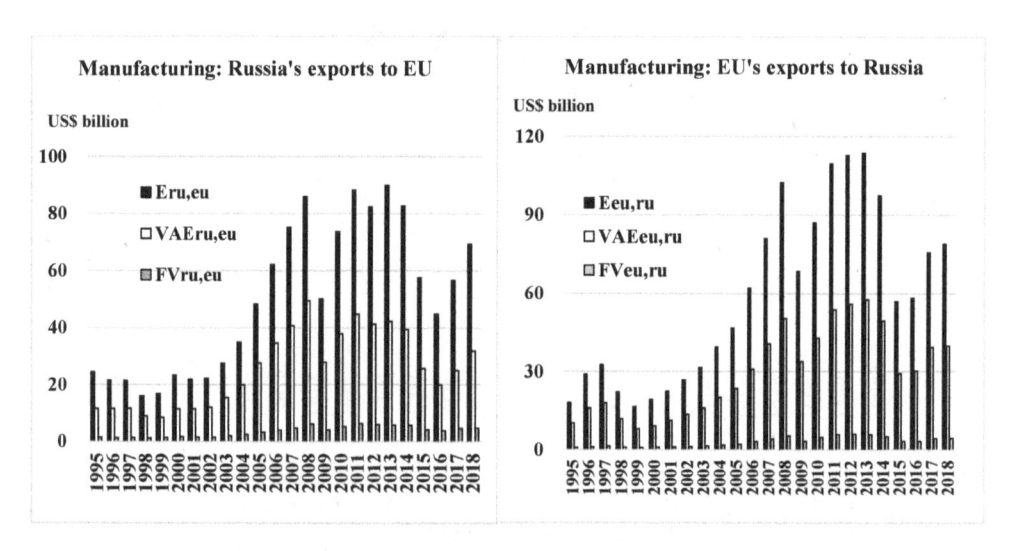

Figure 11.12 Exports of manufacturing from Russia and EU.

Source: Author's compilation using ICIO2021.

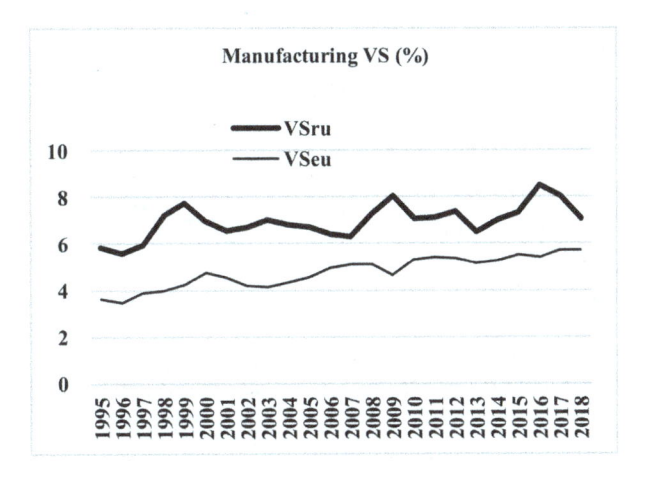

Figure 11.13 Vertical specialization of manufacturing in Russia and EU.

Source: Author's compilation using ICIO2021.

Figure 11.14 shows developments of gross and value-added exports and the associated foreign value added of the machinery sector—which includes electrical equipment, computers, and transportation equipment—in Russia and the EU. Gross exports (value-added exports) of Russia's machinery sector accounted for US$1.3 (0.8) billion in 2001, increased to US$4.2 (3.3) billion in 2008, and then declined to US$2.5 (2.5) billion in 2009. They reached US$5.6 (3.9) billion in 2012 and US$3.8 (2.4) billion in 2018. Russia's machinery exports were, averagely, 35% smaller when measured in value added for 1995–2018. Russia's foreign value added induced by its machinery exports to the EU increased from US$0.5 billion in 2001 to US$2.3 billion in 2008 and declined to US$1.5 billion in 2009. It remained at US$2 billion for 2017–2018. Figure 11.15 suggests that Russia's *VS* of the machinery sector was rather high, averaging 43% for 1995–2018, which was more than ten times higher than that of the EU, 3.8%. This suggests the high intensity of Russia's production sharing for machinery development or its high dependency

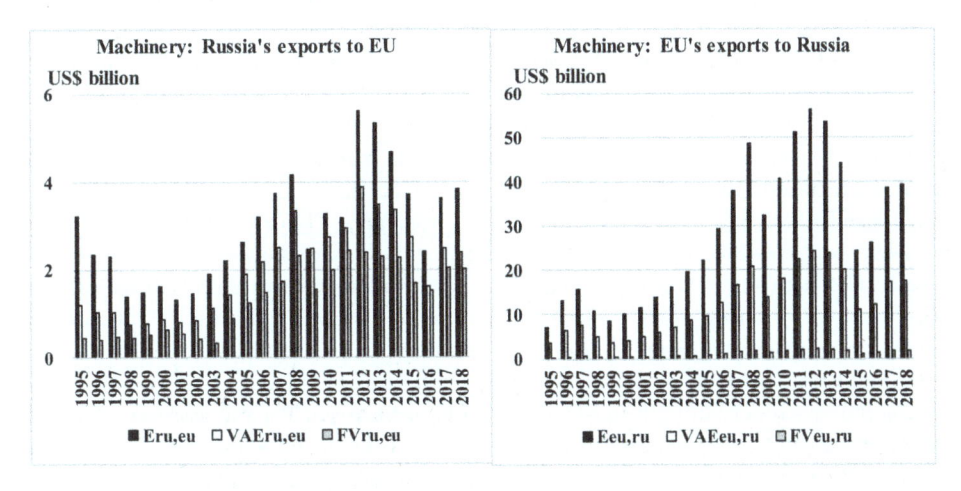

Figure 11.14 Exports of machinery from Russia and EU.

Source: Author's compilation using ICIO2021.

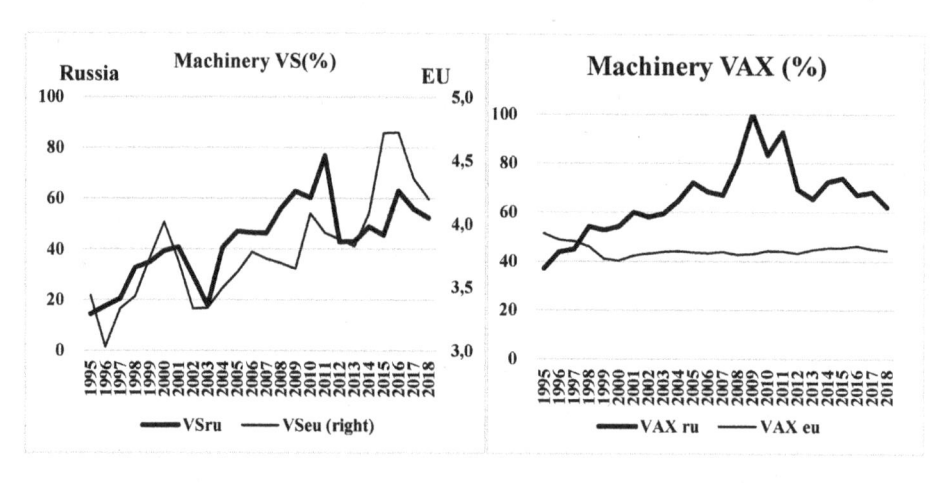

Figure 11.15 Vertical specialization of machinery in Russia and EU.

Source: Author's compilation using ICIO2021.

on foreign countries. Another measure of production sharing may be the ratio of value added to gross exports (Johnson–Noguera's VAX). As for Russia, movements of *VAX* are similar to those of *VS*. The correlation coefficient between the *VS* and *VAX* for Russia is 0.86. In contrast, the EU may rely on EU intra-trade for developments of the machinery sector. Gross exports (value-added exports) of EU's machinery sector to Russia accounted for an average of US$27.9 (12.4) billion for 1995–2018, which was 9.4 (6.2) times larger than Russia's machinery exports to the EU. The EU's machinery exports were an average of 55% smaller when measured in value added. Unlike Russia, there is no correlation between *VAX* and *VS* for the EU.

Table 11.8 demonstrates the results of regression concerning the impact of changes in manufacturing–export-related variables on Russia's overall real growth of manufacturing output (*real manu_ru*). By virtue of Equations 11.1 and 11.2 in this table, it can be stated that the value-added exports of manufacturing from Russia to the EU and from the EU to Russia (both *manu_VAEru,eu* and *manu_VAEeu,ru*) have strongly positive impacts on Russia's manufacturing growth, with a fixed trend rate of more than 3%. Equations 11.3 and 11.4 tell us that the value-added exports of machinery from Russia to the EU and from the EU to Russia (both *machinery_VAEru,eu* and *machinery_VAEeu,ru*) also have strongly positive impacts on Russia's overall manufacturing growth, with a linear trend rate of more than 3%. Equations 11.5 and 11.6 show that manufacturing foreign value added of both Russia and the EU (*manu_FVru,eu* and *manu_FVeu,ru*) have strong impacts on Russian real manufacturing output, with a trend rate of about 3%. As shown by Equations 11.7 and 11.8, this is also true for the machinery foreign value-added effects of Russia and the EU (*machinery_FVru,eu* and *machinery_FVeu,ru*) on Russia's real manufacturing output. Equation 11.9 shows that the vertical specialization of Russian manufacturing (*VSru,eu*) has a positive impact on Russia's real manufacturing growth, with the help of oil prices (*oil price*). Equation 11.10 demonstrates that the vertical specialization of the EU's manufacturing (*manu_VSeu,ru*) has a positive impact on Russia's real manufacturing growth, without the help of oil prices. By virtue of Equations 11.11 and 11.12, the vertical specialization of machinery in both Russia and the EU (*machinery_VSru* and *machinery_VSeu*) has positive effects on Russia's manufacturing. The goodness of fit in Equation 11.11 is rather poor, and the coefficient of Equation 11.12 is greater than that of Equation 11.11. This suggests that the contribution of machinery *VS* of the EU to Russian growth may be larger than that of Russia. Summarizing all regressions in Table 11.8 supports the statement that developments

Table 11.8 Regression 4: Manufacturing growth and exports

Dependent valuable Independent valuable	log(real manu_ru)											
	1	*2*	*3*	*4*	*5*	*6*	*7*	*8*	*9*	*10*	*11*	*12*
log(*manu_VAEru,eu*)	0.166 *** [6.486]											
log(*manu_VAEeu,ru*)		0.111 *** [3.903]										
log(*machinery_VAEru,eu*)			0.158 *** [4.214]									
log(*machinery_VAEeu,ru*)				0.144 ** [2.779]								
log(*manu_FVru, eu*)					0.190 *** [4.946]							
log(*manu_FVeu,ru*)						0.132 *** [3.960]						
log(*machinery_FVru, eu*)							0.144 *** [3.259]					
log(*machinery_FVeu,ru*)								0.144 *** [3.161]				
log(*manu_VSru*)									1.260 ** [2.201]			
log(*manu_VSeu*)										2.134 *** [6.077]		
log(*machinery_VSru*)											0.647 *** [4.250]	
log(*machinery_VSeu*)												2.204 *** [5.900]
log(*oil price*)									0.378 *** [3.429]			
c	3.584 *** [56.81]	3.701 *** [51.68]	4.021 *** [147.2]	3.752 *** [44.79]	3.947 *** [157.7]	3.986 *** [143.0]	4.113 *** [77.98]	4.102 *** [70.52]	6.230 *** [3.834]	11.0 *** [10.2]	5.107 *** [143.0]	11.2 *** [9.796]
Trend	0.032 *** [14.27]	0.035 *** [13.08]	0.031 *** [9.903]	0.032 *** [6.468]	0.027 *** [7.487]	0.032 *** [8.508]	0.029 *** [6.277]	0.032 *** [7.166]				
adj.R^2	0.978	0.947	0.958	0.950	0.973	0.956	0.955	0.952	0.816	0.801	0.450	0.833

*, **, ***: significance <0.1, 0.05, 0.01. [.]: t-statistics.

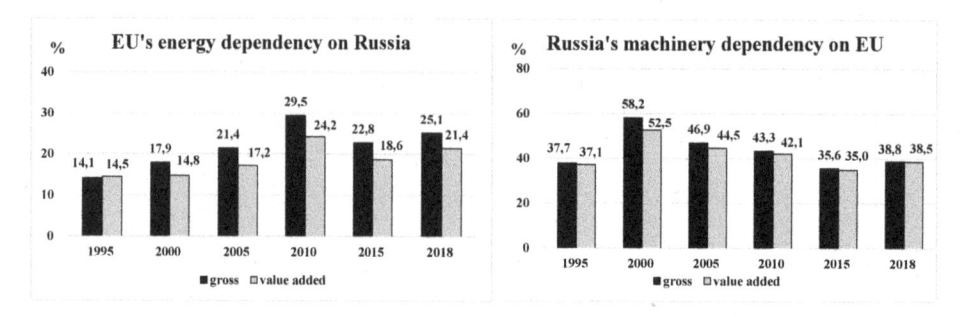

Figure 11.16 Sectoral dependency of EU and Russia.

Source: Author's caluculations using ICIO2021.

Notes: Energy dependency is defined as the share of EU's imports of the mining and refined oil products from Russia in EU's total imports of these products. Machinery dependency means the share of Russia's imports of the computer and electronics, electrical equipment, and transportation equipment in Russia's total imports of these machinery products.

in production sharing of manufacturing, particularly machinery between Russia and the EU, would contribute to the further diversification of the Russian economy.

Here, it is worth mentioning sectoral dependency on Russia or the EU. Figure 11.16 presents close interrelationships between Russia and the EU for energy and machinery for 1995–2018. As was stated, the EU's dependency on Russia looks rather negligible in comparison with Russia's overall dependency on the EU. An exception is the EU's dependency on Russian energy, including crude oil, natural gas, and refined oil. Here, energy dependency is defined as the share of the EU's imports of the mined and refined oil products from Russia of the EU's total imports of these products. Machinery dependency means the share of Russia's imports of the computer and electronics, electrical equipment, and transportation equipment of Russia's total imports of these machinery products. The EU's energy dependency on Russia in gross terms (value-added terms) increased from 14% (15%) in 1995 to 18% (15%) in 2000 and 30% (24%) in 2010. With falls in oil prices, it decreased to 23% (19%) in 2015 and reached 25% (21%) in 2018. On the other hand, Russia's machinery dependency on the EU in gross terms (value-added terms) jumped from 38% (37%) in 1995 to 58% (53%) in 2000 and declined to 43% (42%) in 2010 and 39% (39%) in 2018. Russia's machinery dependency on the EU has been much greater than the EU's energy dependency on Russia. However, it should be noted that the natural gas supply from Russia to the EU is through fixed pipelines based on a bilateral long-term contract. The EU does not have a large selection of energy suppliers, while Russia can substitute other suppliers for the EU for machinery. The EU has made efforts to implement energy-saving technologies with increases in use of renewable resources. Resource-rich Russia is needed to support the EU's efforts. Geographically, the EU is quite near Russia, which makes for lower transportation costs. From this perspective, it is also hard for Russia to substitute other countries for the EU for machinery imports.

11.6 Concluding remarks

We demonstrated that the bilateral trade across Russia and EU positively contributed to GDP growth of the two countries/areas for 1995–2018, making a full use of gross and value-added exports (imports) and foreign value added between Russia and EU. We also found the positive impact of bilateral trade of manufacturing products or machinery products on manufacturing growth in Russia and EU. Both Russia and EU benefitted from the bilateral trade with production sharing. At present, an essential problem is the absolutely low level of Russia's exports of manufacturing goods except for basic metals and refined oil, including machinery. We also suggested that all member countries of EU have a homogeneous relationship between their growth and vertical specialization in contrast to intra-Asia relationships. These results are robust irrespective of EU28 or EU27. Peaceful developments of Russia–EU bilateral trade are essential for further growth of the two areas. EU's transition to decarbonized economy would also force Russia to develop further diversification of its economy with bilateral production share. Any further extension of Russia's invasion into Ukraine without a clear vision of economic growth would destroy past favorable relations between growth and vertical specialization in Russia and EU.

We would like to conclude with remarks on the ICIO data because we wonder whether the ICIO appropriately reflects Russian input–output data for 2011–2018. This also concerns the GDP and gross exports of the mining sector and the refined oil sector, which pay huge taxes on their exports. Following Kuboniwa (2015), we need to reconstruct the ICIO based on critical assessments of the Russian part of ICIO2021. In addition to oil and gas, the military industrial output that accounted for other transportation equipment output or value added in the official statistics should also be revisited. In Russia's official input–output data for 2011–2016, we can identify the military goods industry, as was pointed out by Kuboniwa (2017, 2020). Unlike ICIO2021, the export share of this industry was over 5% in 2015–2016. The military industry exports its products, including weapons, not to the EU but to Asia, the Middle East, or elsewhere. According to our preliminary observations, this industry has not yet involved the EU and other countries in production sharing. Nonetheless, a reconstructed ICIO should also appropriately reflect developments of the military industry. Even though modifications of ICIO2021 would not change the nature of our conclusions in this chapter to a greater extent, we should go to the next step for data improvements.

Notes

1 See the following websites of the OECD, the World Bank, and the WTO.
   - https://www.oecd.org/sti/ind/measuring-trade-in-value added.htm
   - https://www.worldbank.org/en/topic/global-value-chains
   - https://www.wto.org/english/res_e/statis_e/miwi_e/miwi_e.htm
   Foster-McGregor and Stehrer (2013) provided a comprehensive approach to value added content of trade. They failed to develop their theory for bilateral trade, while here we attempt to present a comprehensive exposition of value added content of bilateral trade.
2 Here, the EU refers to the 28 member economies as of 2018 (EU28).
3 ICIO2021 has 45 industrial sectors. It is provided for 66 countries for the years 1995–2018 which include all member countries of EU28 or EU27. Sector correspondence between codes of our 30-sector and ICIO2021 45-sector is shown in the Appendix (Table A.1). Aggregations of ICIO2021 in this chapter were compiled by one of my Japanese colleagues, Professor Yoshisada Shida of Seinan Gakuin University. The author is grateful to his kind efforts.
4 It would be interesting to clarify the role of economic sanctions from 2014 onwards. It is rather difficult to specify sanction effects on GDP growth. IMF (2019) suggested sanctions lowered annual GDP growth rates for 2014–2019 by 0.2 percentage points for 2014–2018. In our estimation, using quarterly data, this negative sanction effect accounted for only 0.14 percentage points for 2014–2019.

References

Foster-McGregor, N. and Stehrer, R. (2013). Value Added Content of Trade: A Comprehensive Approach. *Economics Letters*, 120, 354–357.

Hummels, D., Ishii, J. and Yi, K.-M. (2001). The Nature and Growth of Vertical Specialization in World Trade. *Journal of International Economics*, 54, 75–96.

ICIO2021: OECD (2021). *OECD Inter-Country Input–Output Database* (http://oe.cd/icio).

IMF (2019). *Russian Federation – Article IV Staff Report*, IMF, Washington, DC.

Johnson, R.C. and Noguera, G. (2012). Accounting for Intermediates: Production Sharing and Trade in Value Added. *Journal of International Economics*, 86, 224–236.

Koopman, R., Powers, W., Wang, Z. and Wei, S.-J. (2010–2011). Give Credit Where Credit is Due: Tracing Value added in Global Production Chains. *NBER Working Papers Series. 16426* (September 2010, revised September 2011).

Koopman, R., Wang, Z. and Wei, S. (2014). Tracing Value Added and Double Counting in Gross Exports. *American Economic Review*, 104, 459–494.

Kuboniwa, M. (2012). Diagnosing the 'Russian Disease': Growth and Structure of the Russian Economy. *Comparative Economic Studies*, 54, 121–148.

Kuboniwa, M. (2014). A Comparative Analysis of the Impact of Oil Prices on Oil-rich Emerging Economies in the Pacific Rim. *Journal of Comparative Economics*, 42 (2), 328–339.

Kuboniwa, M. (2015). Russia's Global Value Chain Using Modified World Input–Output Data. *Eastern European Economics*, 53 (4), 277–308.

Kuboniwa, M. (2016). Decomposition of Gross Exports into Value added: an Alternative Accounting System. *CESSA WP 2016-1* (Yokohama National University).

Kuboniwa, M. (2017). Military Industrial Potential, in Rosefielde, S., Kuboniwa, M. et al., eds. *The Unwinding of the Globalist Dream*, World Scientific, Singapore, 141–152.

Kuboniwa, M. (2020). Military Potential Revisited, in Rosefielde, S. ed. *Putin's Russia: Economy, Defence and Foreign Policy*, World Scientific, Singapore, 255–262.

Stöllinger, R., Hanzl-Weiss, D., Leitner, S. and Stehrer, R. (2018). Global and Regional Value Chains: How Important, How Different? WIIW, *Research Report 427*.

Trefler, D. and Zhu, S. (2010). The Structure of Factor Content Predictions. *Journal of International Economics*, 82, 195–207.

Appendix

Table A.1 Sector correspondence

	30-sector code	ICIO2021 45-sector code
1	Agriculture	1, 2
2	Mining	3, 4, 5
3	Food	6
4	Textiles	7
5	Wood	8
6	Paper	9
7	Refined oil	10
8	Chemicals	11, 12
9	Rubber and plastics	13
10	Other non-metallics	14
11	Basic metals	15
12	Fabricated metals	16
13	Computer and electronics	17
14	Electrical, machinery equipment	18, 19
15	Motor vehicles	20
16	Other transport equipment	21
17	Manufacturing nec (not elsewhere classified)	22
18	Electricity and gas supply	23
19	Water supply	24
20	Construction	25
21	Trade	26
22	Transport and communications	27, 28, 29, 31
23	Hotel and restaurant	32
24	Information services	33, 34, 35
25	Finance and insurance	36
26	Real estate and professional services	37, 38
27	Administration	39, 40
28	Education	41
29	Health	42
30	Other services	43, 44, 45

12

CONCEPTUALIZATION AND MEASUREMENT OF INSTITUTIONS

Jerg Gutmann and Stefan Voigt

INSTITUTE OF LAW & ECONOMICS, UNIVERSITY OF HAMBURG
AND CESIFO, MUNICH, GERMANY

Acknowledgements

The authors thank Julian Hambitzer for excellent research assistance. Comments by the editors of this Handbook, Anne van Aaken, Pedro Batista, Niclas Berggren, Mahdi Khesali, Katharina Luckner, Raphael Maesschalck, Hashem Nabas, Evangelia Nissioti, Gabriele Paolini, Pavel Pelikan, Betül Simsek, and Eva van der Zee are gratefully acknowledged.

12.1 Introduction

Economics can be defined as the scientific analysis of decision-making under constraints. Traditional economics has focused on the scarcity of material resources, such as land or water, as the main constraints in economic decisions. Modern economics has not only broadened its scope to analyze decisions in the political and social sphere (e.g., whom to vote for or whether to have children), but it has also recognized that there are important immaterial constraints on human decisions. The economics of information is built on the idea that information is a valuable resource and the costliness of acquiring information has consequences for optimal decision-making.[1] Institutional economics deals with another immaterial constraint, humanly devised rules.[2] These rules, or institutions, have been shown to have dramatic economic, political, and social consequences (see e.g., Acemoglu and Robinson 2012; Greif 2012; North 1990; Persson and Tabellini 2003). Institutional economics works under the assumption that humans can not only operate as individual agents who maximize their own well-being under resource constraints, but they can also collectively define the rules under which interactions take place.

Today, institutional economics is probably the most important branch of comparative economics (Djankov et al. 2003). Institutions govern all interactions in modern economies and the design of institutions is one of the most fundamental and important determinants of economic outcomes. According to Williamson (2010), institutions are embedding not only the continuous process of resource allocation in society, but also governance structures such as firms and contracts, which are used to organize specific economic transactions more efficiently.

DOI: 10.4324/9781003144366-15

In this chapter, we discuss the most fundamental question of institutional economics, i.e., what are institutions? How should we define and classify them? Our discussion in Section 12.2 will show that there is less consensus on this basic question than one might expect. In Section 12.3, we move to a question that is of great relevance to all empirical research on the causes and consequences of institutions: how can and should institutions be measured in quantitative comparative research? Our discussion will demonstrate that both the research question and practical considerations dictate the use of different institutional indicators in different research projects. In Section 12.4, we discuss some key empirical studies on the effects of institutions and how these studies have defined and measured institutions. Section 12.5 ends this chapter with an outlook on future research.

12.2 What are institutions?

Before we propose our own preferred definition of institutions, let us take a look at how institutions have traditionally been defined by researchers in institutional economics. Most of them refer to Nobel Prize winner Douglass North's work to define and categorize institutions. According to North (1990:3), institutions are "humanly devised constraints that shape human interaction". North devotes several pages to explaining what exactly this broad definition refers to, but it is no surprise that North's metaphorical depiction of institutions as "rules of the game" has gained most prominence. After all, it expresses in simple words that institutions are characterized by rules that effectively structure transactions among members of society (i.e., the players of the game). North draws a clear line between institutions and organizations. The latter "consist of specific groups of individuals pursuing a mix of common and individual goals through partially coordinated behavior" (North et al. 2009:15). For North, organizations are players themselves, even if institutions govern cooperation within the organization.

Another Nobel Prize winner, Elinor Ostrom, proposes a definition of institutions that is similar to North's but somewhat more precise. She defines them as "prescriptions that humans use to organize all forms of repetitive and structured interactions" (Ostrom 2005:3; see also Ostrom 1986). Building on these definitions by North and Ostrom, we follow an earlier proposal by Kiwit and Voigt (1995; see also Voigt and Kiwit 1998) and define institutions as commonly known rules that are used to structure recurrent interactions and come with a sanction mechanism. Like the commonly used definitions by North and Ostrom, our preferred definition emphasizes the role of rules, and these rules must be applied systematically, i.e., not arbitrarily. Unlike these definitions, it emphasizes the critical role sanctions play in incentivizing agents to comply with a rule.[3] This is not to say that North and Ostrom did not implicitly expect the rules making up institutions to be enforced, but their definitions did not highlight this aspect. Another caveat of ours concerns North's emphasis that institutions must be humanly devised constraints. Narrowly interpreted, this would mean that institutions can only be created intentionally. We disagree with this narrow interpretation, as rules can emerge spontaneously out of human interaction, without a social planner at the drawing board. Individuals might simply coordinate to drive on one side of the road and once everyone is aware that (pretty much) everyone else is following this rule, it becomes self-enforcing. Nevertheless, we are in agreement with North's emphasis on human design, if it simply intends to separate natural constraints, such as the laws of physics, from constraints that humans create, intentionally or not.

Many authors have proposed definitions of institutions that are quite different from the ones discussed so far. While it is beyond the scope of this chapter to review all of these definitions, we would like to discuss two of them here and explain why we prefer to follow the tradition of North (1990) and Ostrom (1986) in defining institutions. The first definition was proposed by Greif (2012:30): "An institution is a system of rules, beliefs, norms, and organizations that together generate a regularity of (social) behavior". This definition is much broader than the ones presented before. Institutions are not only made up of rules, but also of beliefs and even of organizations. North has rejected both of these elements of Greif's definition. Organizations are problematic, because they are composed of individuals and they themselves are supposed to be constrained by institutions. In our opinion, excluding actors (i.e., organizations) from the definition of institutions was a major contribution by North that has made it much clearer what institutions are and what purpose they serve. Including beliefs in the definition of institutions might be less problematic. Denzau and North (1994) discuss belief structures as a constraint on human decision-making on top of institutions. The main reason why we prefer to keep beliefs separate from institutions is the mode in which they are adopted. Beliefs are the result of learning and individuals are limited in the degree to which they can consciously choose their own beliefs. Rules, in contrast, can be designed and altered by humans and may be deliberately adopted or discarded, at least in principle, with changing circumstances.

The second definition to be contrasted with our preferred definition of institutions is that of Schotter (1981): "A social institution is a regularity in social behavior that is agreed to by all members of society, specifies behavior in specific recurrent situations, and is either self-policed or policed by some external authority". Such delineation is extremely broad, as it includes prices, the use of cash, and many other regularities in behavior. Such an overly broad definition implies that institutions almost matter by definition, because if everything is an institution, then some institutions are bound to have effects. The definition is also problematic because it seems to assume some sort of underlying unanimous consent, but many institutions survive although consent to them is far from unanimous; female genital mutilation is one such example. Finally, in the language of North (1990), behavioral regularities are the (equilibrium) outcome of the game. Defined like this, institutions would be whatever individuals choose to do in strategic interactions. Such a definition demotes institutions from a tool for structuring behavior to merely an observable pattern in behavior.[4]

After explaining how we prefer to define institutions ourselves, we have discussed how competing definitions in the literature deviate from the North and Ostrom tradition of defining institutions as rules of the game. These definitions might refer to either players or even to the outcome of the game as institutions. While definitions cannot be right or wrong, we claim that a definition based on institutions as the rules of the game is more useful than any of the proposed alternatives, as it clearly characterizes institutions and their role in shaping human interaction. Before we move on to discuss the ways in which institutions, as we propose to define them, can be classified further, we take a quick look at how institutions have been defined in academic practice in the leading field journal for institutional economics, the Journal of Institutional Economics (JoIE). We have surveyed all articles published in JoIE in 2020 to determine whether they use the term institutions and, if so, whether and how they define institutions. Among the 59 surveyed articles, 58 refer to institutions, which is not unexpected given the focus of JoIE. Only ten articles (17%) published in JoIE in 2020 explicitly define institutions. Nine of these articles base their definition on North's (1990) conception of institutions as the rules of the game. One article proposes a definition of institutions as equilibria in the spirit of Schotter (1981). Overall, institutions are frequently not defined explicitly, but among the used definitions, North's conception of institutions as rules is clearly dominant. Above, we have recommended a definition that is consistent with those by North

(1990) and Ostrom (1986), but with a stronger emphasis on the mechanism enforcing the rules that make up institutions.

12.2.1 Typologies of institutions

Our discussion of common definitions of institutions has demonstrated how broad a concept institutions are. The rules of the game can come in a myriad of shapes, which is why many authors introduce additional typologies of institutions to clarify what institutions they are actually interested in and where their arguments might not apply. Here, we discuss four such typologies.

The first typology is by far the most popular one and was introduced by Douglass North himself, along with his definition of institutions. He elaborates that institutions can be both "formal constraints – such as rules that human beings devise and […] informal constraints – such as conventions and codes of behavior" (North 1990:4). Unfortunately, this typology led to confusion, because North never clarified what exactly distinguishes "formal" from "informal" institutions. Some authors interpret formal rules as official state laws, others think codification is what matters and informal simply means unwritten. The typology has been interpreted in numerous ways and authors referring to it usually do not clarify how they interpret it.

Due to its ambiguity, we do not consider North's typology very useful, and we are not making further use of it hereafter. Instead, we recommend the use of a typology originally developed by Kiwit and Voigt (1995; see also Voigt 2013, 2019). It distinguishes between "internal" and "external" institutions based on a straightforward criterion and it is illustrated by the rows of the matrix in Figure 12.1. External institutions are enforced by state agents, i.e., where the state threatens to punish those who violate a rule. Internal institutions are not enforced by the state and – since we define institutions as rules with an enforcement mechanism – therefore, they must be enforced by members of society.[5] Within the group of internal institutions, different types can be distinguished according to who threatens to punish offenders. Some rules are self-enforcing (such as driving on a particular side of the road to avoid a collision or using the same vocabulary and grammar as others in order to be understood) and will thus be complied with even in the absence of additional sanction threats (type I).[6] Some rules are enforced simply by individuals' own ethical or religious convictions (e.g., dietary restrictions) and do not require the threat of punishment by other members of

Rule	Enforcement	Origin			
		Deity	Custom	Private actors	State actors
Convention (internal, type I)	Self-enforcing	Convention			
Ethical rule (internal, type II)	Self-imposed sanctions	Ethical rule			
Informal private rule (internal, type III)	Unorganized private sanctions	Religious law	Customary law	Privately created law	
Formal private rule (internal, type IV)	Organized private sanctions				
State law (external)	Organized state sanctions	Hybrid law			State law

Figure 12.1 Typology of institutions.

Note: Typology based on Gutmann and Voigt (2020) and Kiwit and Voigt (1995).

society to generate compliance (type II). In the final two categories of internal institutions, noncompliance with the respective rule is sanctioned by other members of society either spontaneously (e.g., if someone jumps the queue at a bus stop in some countries – type III) or in an organized manner (e.g., by a sports court or private arbitration – type IV).

It should be noted that the same rule can be part of different institutions at the same time. A dietary restriction may, for example, be complied with because of an individual's ethical conviction, while its violation would also be punished by the state or by other members of society. The same applies to our example of driving on one side of the road, which is typically enforced by the state. These can be understood as alternative, but complementary institutions. While the presence of complementary institutions increases the likelihood that the underlying rules are complied with, the opposite holds where the rules that are part of different institutions are in conflict with each other. The fact that institutions, by definition, come with an enforcement mechanism does not imply that institutions will always be complied with, because the expected sanction in case of a rule violation might not be large enough to induce compliance (Becker 1968). To sum up, the typology of "internal" and "external" institutions distinguishes institutions not according to the characteristics of the rule but based on who enforces the rule.

The third typology to be discussed here refers to an aspect of institutions that we have not yet discussed. In Gutmann and Voigt (2020), we propose to distinguish institutions also based on the origin of the rule component. This typology applies to different kinds of laws and, thus, it is not applicable to internal institutions that are self-enforcing or enforced by ethical convictions.[7] In our typology of laws, which is illustrated in Figure 12.1, "state law" refers to institutions that are enforced by the state and the rule component of which was also designed by state actors. Institutions that are enforced by the state without state actors designing the underlying rule are referred to as "hybrid law". One example would be the entrenchment of Sharia law in the constitution (Ahmed and Gouda 2015). Among internal institutions enforced by other members of society, we propose to distinguish three types. Privately created law is based on a rule designed by private actors, such as merchants. If the rule component was supposedly designed by some deity, we speak of "religious law". Where rules are derived from customs that are passed on from generation to generation, we speak of "customary law". We refer to the categories of customary and religious law jointly as "traditional law". This third typology of institutions is based on and extends the second typology of internal and external institutions. One important aspect added by distinguishing the different types of laws is information on how different types of institutions emerge, evolve, and how rigid they are as a consequence. Clearly, traditional law is much more difficult to change than laws that can be willfully altered by private actors or representatives of the state. Of course, also within particular categories, such as state law, the rigidity of institutions can vary significantly. Constitutions, for example, tend to be more difficult to change than regular legislation.[8]

The fourth and final typology we want to discuss here distinguishes institutions based on the kinds of human interactions that are supposed to be governed. Most importantly, it separates political institutions, which constrain collective decision-making and collective action in the political sphere, from economic institutions that regulate exchange among private actors (see e.g., Acemoglu et al. 2005). Although this typology is non-exhaustive and its boundaries are often blurred, it has proven to be useful in many applications. One example for institutions that are difficult to fit into this typology is those constraining the operation of state-owned enterprises.

12.2.2 Institutions and culture

Before we move to the next section and the question how institutions can be measured, we consider it necessary to explain how culture and institutions relate to each other (for a survey, see Alesina and Giuliano 2015). Guiso et al. (2006:23) define culture as "those customary beliefs and values that ethnic, religious, and social groups transmit fairly unchanged from generation to generation". In the same article, Guiso et al. explain that also norms are an element of culture. According to this definition, culture is largely not composed of institutions and most institutions are not culture. However, based on the second and third type of institutions introduced above, we can identify where culture and institutions tend to overlap conceptually. Note the subtle but important distinction we make between culture influencing institutions and culture being institutions. Culture feeds into the rule component of institutions that are classified as traditional law, i.e., those institutions based on customary or religious rules that are enforced by other members of society. Where hybrid law is based on customary or religious norms, it is also closely linked to culture (e.g., the prescription for women in some countries to wear a headscarf or only to take up certain jobs; see Hyland et al. 2020). However, by moving from one society to another, individuals can change the traditional (or hybrid) law they need to comply with, while their culture remains unchanged (e.g., Berggren et al. 2019). The only type of institutions that can be purely culturally determined is rules individuals impose on themselves due to their ethical and religious convictions (type II in Figure 12.1). This category of internal institutions can be argued to largely coincide with aspects of culture. This means that while all institutions, in principle, can be heavily influenced in their design by a prevalent culture, it is only one subcategory of internal institutions that can be considered culture themselves (see also Voigt 2019).

12.3 How can and should we measure institutions?

Having discussed useful definitions and typologies of institutions in the previous section, we now move on to an even more challenging task: the ideal measurement of institutions for quantitative empirical research. The question how institutions should be measured and what indicators of institutions exactly mean is sometimes not taken seriously enough in applied empirical research, which may lead to problems with causal inference or research designs that are inconsistent with the theory to be tested. This section is organized around a number of questions that researchers have to answer, if they want to measure institutions or choose appropriate indicators of institutions for an empirical analysis. (1) What institutions and what aspects of institutions are supposed to be measured? (2) Should institutions be measured individually or in groups? (3) What data sources can be used to measure institutions? To illustrate the involved trade-offs and challenges, we draw on examples from the field of constitutional economics (see Voigt 2020 for background material).

Any attempt at measuring institutions should start by asking what exactly is supposed to be measured. Let's assume we are interested in measuring judicial independence, which can be considered an institution, a bundle of institutions or a result of institutions. In a first step, we would clarify what we mean by judicial independence. Here, we define judicial independence as the existence of a rule according to which judges must be able to decide cases without interference by the members of other government branches. This has important implications, as this definition would, for example, not include judges' decisions being influenced via bribery. Given that the theoretical concept we are interested in is an external institution, we have to ask ourselves if we want to measure judicial independence as it is prescribed by the law (*de jure*) or if we want to measure whether judges are independent in practice (*de facto*). Surprisingly, this decision makes a big difference, as *de jure* and *de facto* indicators of judicial independence are uncorrelated (Feld and Voigt 2003; Voigt et al. 2015). Another important question that follows from our definition of institutions is whether we are interested in measuring the rule component of the institution, its enforcement mechanism or both. Voigt and Gutmann (2013), for example, demonstrate that *de jure* constitutional property rights are only conducive to economic growth if they are enforced by a *de facto* independent judiciary. Property rights serve as the rule component of the institution and the independence of the judiciary is used as a proxy for how likely it is that the executive gets sanctioned for violating these constitutional rights.

Another important question concerns whether individual institutions are supposed to be measured or rather bundles of institutions. Voigt (2013) has suggested that empirical research should move from measuring broad aggregates of institutions, such as democracy, property rights, or the rule of law, towards individual institutions. The latter are actionable, i.e., if we know that a particular institution leads to desirable outcomes, policy makers may try to implement them. Robinson (2013) and Shirley (2013) generally agree with the desirability of studying individual institutions rather than bundles, but both of them have also voiced important concerns about focusing on measuring individual institutions. Shirley's argument is that in spite of improved measurement of institutions, cross-country growth regressions will not generate many new insights. One way to read Shirley's comment is that there are far more institutions in the world than there are jurisdictions, making it impossible to link them individually to economic or other outcomes. It may already be challenging to disentangle the effects of different bundles of institutions due to insufficient degrees of freedom, although some studies are trying to do exactly that (Acemoglu and Johnson 2005; Gutmann and Voigt 2019).

Robinson's (2013) concerns have a different focus. He provides powerful arguments for why one might actually be interested in studying bundles of institutions – rather than doing it out of necessity. Bundles are more easily comparable than individual institutions that might exist only once or a few times in their specific design. Of course, one does not have to bundle institutions in order to compare institutions to each other that are not perfectly identical, but bundling is one way to address the problem. Moreover, if some institutions are only implemented in a particular bundle, one cannot attribute outcomes to only one part of that bundle anyway. Finally, there might be important complementarities between institutions within a bundle that would be difficult to model. In other words, the effect of one institution might depend on the presence of others that are part of the same bundle. This final argument leads us back to Shirley's (2013) concern about a general lack of degrees of freedom in comparative research on institutions.

Overall, measuring and studying individual institutions rather than bundles of institutions is desirable, but often not feasible. Researchers need to take pragmatic decisions in dealing with the involved trade-offs. Discussing in detail how single institutions can be bundled into aggregate indicators is beyond the scope of this chapter. Statistical approaches range from simple weighted or unweighted averages of individual institutional indicators over factor or principal component analysis to unobserved component models, Bayesian factor analysis or Bayesian structural models. Gutmann and Voigt (2018), for example, create a rule of law indicator and multiple sub-indicators for the main dimensions of the rule of law from dozens of indicators provided by the World Justice Project. Gutmann et al. (2022) develop indicators of governments' compliance with constitutional rights for individual rights categories and across rights categories, based on data from the Comparative Constitutions Project (Elkins et al. 2009) and the Varieties of Democracy project. Both datasets are constructed using simple statistical techniques, such as factor analysis or averaging. The World Bank's Worldwide Governance Indicators and Fariss' human rights scores are examples of datasets constructed using more advanced statistical algorithms (Fariss 2019; Kaufmann et al. 2011).

Our third question concerns the data sources from which we can draw information on institutions. If we are trying to measure external institutions, we might want to collect information from legal text. Elkins et al. (2009), for example, have coded all written national constitutions in the world based on their English translation. Others have coded data from subconstitutional legislation concerning specific legal issues (see e.g., Powell et al. 2021). The advantage of such data is that it is objective and rather simple to obtain. However, data derived from constitutions and legislation only provide information on *de jure* institutions. As we have argued above, *de jure* and *de facto* information can differ significantly (see e.g., Chilton and Versteeg 2020; Feld and Voigt 2003; Law and Versteeg 2013; Voigt et al. 2015).

If we are not only interested in the law in the books but hope to measure how the law constrains behavior in practice, we need to think of data sources other than legal text. One option would be to utilize information from government reports and statistics or from court judgments. Obviously, such information will be more easily available and reliable in some countries than in others. If governments are effective and transparent enough, data from government sources can provide a sound picture of the *de facto* institutions in these countries. However, in most countries this is not a realistic assumption (see e.g., Qian and Yanagizawa 2009). Therefore, *de facto* institutions are typically measured based on information from other, independent sources. It can come from citizens, NGOs, the media, or country experts. The primary techniques used in practice are interviews of citizens or experts or the coding of reports and data provided by NGOs or media outlets. All of these have been criticized for different reasons. Media coverage might not be unbiased (Enke 2020), NGOs have an agenda that might have to be taken into account, citizens might not understand complicated language or questions, and so-called country experts might lack information on what is actually happening on the ground. These are just some examples for potential concerns that the users and producers of indicators measuring institutions need to weigh carefully. One important question across all these data sources is how objective the data is, because subjective data can be subject to various biases (Gutmann et al. 2020). Yet, in some applications, subjective data might be what we are interested in using. Decisions of economic actors, for example, will be based on their subjective evaluation of the quality of institutions, rather than on their objective quality. In most applications, having objective data at hand will be desirable.

So far, we have asked which data sources could be used to measure external institutions. Measuring internal institutions poses somewhat different problems. First of all, most internal institutions are not codified and the *de jure–de facto* dichotomy, thus, is not very useful with respect to internal institutions. Like in the case of *de facto* external institutions, it is natural to ask citizens about the rule and the sanction component of internal institutions, as it is members of society who enforce the institution. Media, NGOs, and country experts can only serve as secondary sources of information. As an alternative to surveying citizens to learn about the relevant internal institutions in a society, experiments are becoming increasingly important. Their advantage is that the produced data does not reflect mere claims about rules and their enforcement, but it can be observed what rules experimental subjects follow and how willingly they sanction rule breakers (Cohn et al. 2019; Falk et al. 2018; Gächter and Schulz 2016; Voigt 2018).

Independent of the three questions we have asked here, those producing their own datasets of institutional indicators should follow some good research practices. Original data should be stored, and it should be clear how it has been obtained. Manipulation (e.g., imputation or deletion) and coding of variables should be thoroughly documented and justified. Data should be stored in standardized formats and sufficient documentation should be provided to understand how data points were generated and how the data can be interpreted. Researchers should publish their data and documentation when studies using their data are published or they should at least be prepared to provide data and documentation on request to researchers interested in replicating analyses underlying the published research.

12.4 The effects of institutions: What do we know?

In this section, we briefly discuss some empirical evidence on the relationship between institutions and economic development. Acemoglu et al. (2005) and Voigt (2019, 2020) contain broader surveys of the relevant literature.

In their seminal contribution to the literature on institutions and growth, Acemoglu et al. (2001) provide compelling evidence that historically determined institutions are responsible for large differences in countries' income levels today. Acemoglu et al. argue that Europeans adopted very different colonization strategies across colonies. Where Europeans faced high mortality rates, it was unattractive to settle and colonizers were likely to set up extractive institutions. In contrast, locations with low settler mortality rates attracted settlements, which were organized under more inclusive institutions. Acemoglu et al. show that historical settler mortality rates are associated with the quality of contemporary institutions and income levels. Exploiting these differences in settler mortality rates as an instrumental variable for current institutions, Acemoglu et al. estimate large effects of institutions on income per capita.

Some economists believe that geography – and not institutions – is the single most important determinant of economic growth. Easterly and Levine (2003) show that if one accounts for the effects of geography that are mediated via institutions, direct effects of geography are only of secondary importance. Rodrik et al. (2004) run a "horse race" between three competing explanations, namely geography, institutions, and international trade. Rodrik et al.'s study is broader than that by Easterly and Levine because it takes international trade explicitly into account, but the main results are very similar. Rodrik et al. find that institutions are crucial for economic development. Geography is important in the sense that it influences institutions. The direct effect of geography on growth again appears to be less relevant.

We have already referred to the contribution of Acemoglu and Johnson (2005) above. They propose to separate ("unbundle") the growth effect of property rights institutions from that of contracting institutions. Secure private property rights primarily imply protection from government intervention, whereas contracting institutions allow people to enter into contracts with each other. Both property rights institutions and contracting institutions fulfill important functions, but sidestepping the government with regard to property rights institutions is much more difficult than concluding enforceable contracts in the absence of reliable contracting institutions. Based on this argument, Acemoglu and Johnson (2005) expect the security of private property rights to be more important for economic growth than contracting institutions. This hypothesis is corroborated by their empirical analysis.

A bundle of institutions whose relationship to economic prosperity has attracted particular attention is democracy. Lipset (1959) famously formulated the hypothesis that democracy was created and consolidated by a broad process of modernization. Acemoglu et al. (2008, 2009) provide empirical evidence that rejects this hypothesis by including country- and year-fixed effects in panel data estimations. Their results have been questioned by some economists (see, for example, Gundlach and Paldam 2009). Others have highlighted that the average null effect estimated by Acemoglu et al. (2008, 2009) hides significant effect heterogeneity between former colonies and non-colonies (Cervellati et al. 2014). Regarding the inverse effect of democracy on growth, Acemoglu et al. (2019) exploit exogenous spatial waves of democratization to identify a causal effect of democracy on GDP per capita. Colagrossi et al. (2020) confirm in a meta-analysis that democracy has a positive effect on economic growth beyond the reach of publication bias, although it is weaker than that of human capital.

The studies we have discussed so far are concerned with the growth effects of external institutions. Next, we consider the potential relevance of internal institutions for development.

Putnam (1993) argues that the *de facto* quality of Italy's local institutions can be explained by the local development of its civil society. La Porta et al. (1997) ask whether these results are generalizable beyond the case of Italy. They find that generalized trust has a significant effect on the economy. La Porta et al. are not the only ones who find that trust has important economic effects. Guiso et al. (2006) show that trust is associated with a higher likelihood of becoming a successful entrepreneur. Being perceived as trustworthy facilitates the conclusion of contracts. Higher levels of trust are also associated with lower levels of corruption (Uslaner 2002; Bjørnskov 2010) and stronger economic performance (Knack and Keefer 1997; Zak and Knack 2001).

However, there is an institutionalist school that argues that trust is determined by the institutional environment. In other words, trust might not be exogenous. In contrast, the culturalist school argues that people learn a basic sense of trust early in life and at least the core of trust is stable over time. Emigrants from low-trust regions in Southern Italy, for example, carry their mistrust with them (Guiso et al. 2009). Berggren and Bjørnskov (2011) find, similarly, that differences in trust levels between US states today are directly related to the country of origin of the families who immigrated to a particular state. This suggests that it is possible to treat trust as exogenous.

Inspired by Putnam's (1993) analysis, Tabellini (2010) asks whether stable components of culture can explain differences in the economic development of regions that share formally identical external institutions. This implies that culture would be an important determinant of how external institutions are implemented. Tabellini expands on Putnam's study by analyzing 69 regions in eight different countries (the United Kingdom, the Netherlands, Belgium, France, Spain, Portugal, Italy, and Germany). Tabellini uses survey answers to measure four different aspects of culture: trust, respect for others, individual self-determination, and obedience. The first two traits are assumed to increase not only the number of welfare-enhancing transactions, but also the voluntary participation in the provision of public goods. The latter traits are assumed to make entrepreneurial behavior more likely. Arguably, the first two traits capture social capital and the latter ones something akin to "confidence in the individual".

Tabellini shows that there is a strong correlation between culture and economic development, but that is insufficient to prove that culture determines economic development. To address this problem, Tabellini argues that historical institutions have shaped culture, which in turn affected economic development. He proposes two instrumental variables, namely the literacy rate in the second half of the 19th century and the quality of political institutions between 1600 and 1850. The quality of political institutions is measured by the degree to which the executive was constrained. To exclude the possibility that it was economic development in 1850 that determined culture, Tabellini controls for economic development at that time. He finds that across European regions, culture is significantly associated with differences in productivity levels and economic growth.

12.5 Outlook

Undeniably, the New Institutional Economics has been highly successful in demonstrating the importance of institutions for all human decision-making, even if there is a discussion about the use of inadequate indicators of institutions in some empirical studies (see Glaeser et al. 2004 for criticism and Robinson 2013 for an opposing view). Here, we have attempted to give an overview of the most important and promising definitions and typologies of institutions that have been proposed. Having a clear idea of the central concept of interest in a study is, of course, a necessary condition for taking the next step and deciding how to measure it in a way that makes different data points comparable to each other.

Studies measuring the effects of external institutions are much more common than studies on the effects of internal institutions. An important reason for this imbalance could be that data on external institutions are more readily available. Yet, failed attempts of colonizers, imperial powers, modernizers, and even philanthropists to restructure entire societies according to their imagination should have made the far-reaching importance of internal institutions clear to everyone. If the rules that are part of external and internal institutions formulate conflicting prescriptions, i.e., behaving in accordance with one implies violating the other, this should have far-reaching consequences for transaction costs and economic development. Additional studies on the effects of conflicting institutions are an important desideratum. Internal institutions and their effects can be studied, but appropriate indicators need to be identified first (Voigt 2018 discusses some measurement strategies).

Beyond definitions and measurement, we have surveyed some of the known effects of institutions. Since institutions themselves are endogenous, at least in the long run, understanding their determinants could help us understand to what extent and how they can be improved and how conflicts between different (types of) institutions can be avoided. Identifying the factors that determine internal institutions is challenging. Most internal institutions are not created by design. They evolve over time typically without single individuals shaping this process. The determinants of personality traits and shared norms in a society have been studied by disciplines such as comparative cultural psychology or ethnology. Only recently have economists begun to evaluate some of their hypotheses with the tools used in economics. Here is a very incomplete overview of aspects that have been analyzed:

- The prevailing subsistence mode in a society may affect cooperation levels. Differences in cooperation norms have, e.g., been identified between rice farmers who rely on fields that are either rainfed or irrigation-managed (Tsusaka et al. 2015).
- Pathogens can make physical contact with strangers a question of life or death. Norms making a very clear distinction between in-group and out-group may be a consequence of the presence of pathogens. Fincher et al. (2008) show a strong statistical association between pathogen prevalence and various measures of collectivism, i.e., preference of the in-group over the out-group.
- "Big Gods", i.e., Gods with the capacity to always monitor everyone's behavior and the power to sanction misbehaving individuals, can save monitoring costs. If most members of a society believe in such gods, there might be less need for organized or external rule enforcement to generate rule compliance. These societies may therefore grow larger, which facilitates a division of labor and, hence, economic development (Norenzayan 2013).
- Widespread belief in witchcraft may be conducive to mistrust because people are afraid of being accused of being a witch. Gershman (2016) shows that belief in witchcraft is not only associated with lower levels of trust but also with lower levels of charitable giving.

These are just a few examples for how geography and religion can lead to the emergence and evolution of internal institutions. Integrating these findings more systematically into institutional economics promises to be a fruitful endeavor.

Notes

1 See Stiglitz (2002). To make sure that employees work hard while not being monitored, an employer might, e.g., pay them a bonus based on their measurable performance.
2 Below, we discuss this characterization of institutions critically and we propose what we consider to be a more useful definition.
3 According to this definition, private contracts are not institutions, as their contents are not commonly known, whereas contract law is made up of institutions. Hence, contracts, not unlike organizations, are based on institutions without being institutions themselves. This illustrates that while there are important overlaps between Institutional Economics and Law & Economics, the latter is not strictly a subcategory of the former.

Recent literature in Law & Economics discusses the substitutability of rewards and sanctions in law enforcement (e.g., Aidt et al. 2021; Mungan 2021; Van Aaken and Simsek 2021). Our definition of institutions, however, does not allow for rules that are enforced via promised rewards, because this turns rule compliance into a simple economic transaction. Hilbe and Sigmund (2010) use evolutionary game theory to show that societies evolve towards using punishment rather than rewards to enforce compliance, although rewards might be superior in a low-cooperation environment.
4 Below, we explain that the one subtype of institutions for which Schotter's definition appears appropriate to us are self-enforcing institutions.
5 Hodgson (2006) has argued that North's typology of formal and informal institutions can also be interpreted as being based on whether or not the rules are enforced by a court. However, that is not how it is commonly understood. Otherwise, our preferred typology would only be a refinement of North's typology.
6 This is the only type of institution, which is also consistent with Schotter's (1981) definition of institutions as behavioral regularities.
7 Thus, we define law here as institutions that are enforced by someone else than the individual who is supposed to follow the rule. Furthermore, our definition of law is broad as it is not limited to rules that are designed, codified, or enforced by representatives of the state.
8 Williamson (2010) discusses the rigidity of institutions based on North's typology of formal and informal institutions, which, as we have explained above, has its drawbacks. Roland (2004) distinguishes fast-moving from slow-moving institutions without drawing on North's typology.

References

Acemoglu, D. and Johnson, S. (2005). Unbundling institutions. *Journal of Political Economy* 113(5): 949–995.

Acemoglu, D., Johnson, S. and Robinson, J. A. (2001). The colonial origins of comparative development: An empirical investigation. *American Economic Review* 91(5):1369–1401.

Acemoglu, D., Johnson, S. and Robinson, J. A. (2005). Institutions as the fundamental cause of long-run growth. In: Philippe Aghion and Steven N. Durlauf (eds.), *Handbook of economic growth*, Volume 1A, Amsterdam et al.: North-Holland, pp. 385–472.

Acemoglu, D., Johnson, S., Robinson, J. A. and Yared, P. (2008). Income and democracy. *American Economic Review* 98(3):808–842.

Acemoglu, D., Johnson, S., Robinson, J. A. and Yared, P. (2009). Reevaluating the modernization hypothesis. *Journal of Monetary Economics* 56(8):1043–1058.

Acemoglu, D., Naidu, S., Restrepo, P. and Robinson, J. A. (2019). Democracy does cause growth. *Journal of Political Economy* 127(1):47–100.

Acemoglu, D. and Robinson, J. A. (2012). *Why nations fail: The origins of power, prosperity, and poverty.* New York: Crown Publishers.

Ahmed, D. I. and Gouda, M. (2015). Measuring constitutional Islamization: Insights from the Islamic constitutions index. *Hastings International and Comparative Law Review* 38(1):1–76.

Aidt, T. S., Albornoz, F. and Hauk, E. (2021). Foreign influence and domestic policy. *Journal of Economic Literature* 59(2):426–487.

Alesina, A. and Giuliano, P. (2015). Culture and institutions. *Journal of Economic Literature* 53(4): 898–944.

Becker, G. S. (1968). Crime and punishment: An economic approach. *Journal of Political Economy* 76(2): 169–217.

Berggren, N. and Bjørnskov, C. (2011). Is the importance of religion in daily life related to social trust? Cross-country and cross-state comparisons. *Journal of Economic Behavior and Organization* 80(3):459–480.

Berggren, N., Ljunge, M. and Nilsson, T. (2019). Roots of tolerance among second-generation immigrants. *Journal of Institutional Economics* 15(6):999–1016.

Bjørnskov, C. (2010). How does social trust lead to better governance? An attempt to separate electoral and bureaucratic mechanisms. *Public Choice* 144(1/2):323–346.

Cervellati, M., Jung, F., Sunde, U. and Vischer, T. (2014). Income and democracy: Comment. *American Economic Review* 104(2):707–719.

Chilton, A. and Versteeg, M. (2020). *How constitutional rights matter*. New York: Oxford University Press.

Cohn, A., Maréchal, M. A., Tannenbaum, D. and Zünd, C. L. (2019). Civic honesty around the globe. *Science* 365(6448):70–73.

Colagrossi, M., Rossignoli, D. and Maggioni, M. A. (2020). Does democracy cause growth? A meta-analysis (of 2000 regressions). *European Journal of Political Economy* 61:101824.

Denzau, A. T. and North, D. C. (1994). Shared mental models: Ideologies and institutions. *Kyklos* 47(1):3–31.

Djankov, S., Glaeser, E., La Porta, R., Lopez-de-Silanes, F. and Shleifer, A. (2003). The new comparative economics. *Journal of Comparative Economics* 31(4):595–619.

Easterly, W. and Levine, R. (2003). Tropics, germs, and crops: How endowments influence economic development. *Journal of Monetary Economics* 50(1):3–39.

Elkins, Z., Ginsburg, T. and Melton, J. (2009). *The endurance of national constitutions*. Cambridge: Cambridge University Press.

Enke, B. (2020). What you see is all there is. *Quarterly Journal of Economics* 135(3):1363–1398.

Falk, A., Becker, A., Dohmen, T., Enke, B., Huffman, D. and Sunde, U. (2018). Global evidence on economic preferences. *Quarterly Journal of Economics* 133(4):1645–1692.

Fariss, C. J. (2019). Yes, human rights practices are improving over time. *American Political Science Review* 113(3):868–881.

Feld, L. P. and Voigt, S. (2003). Economic growth and judicial independence: Cross-country evidence using a new set of indicators. *European Journal of Political Economy* 19(3):497–527.

Fincher, C. L., Thornhill, R., Murray, D. R. and Schaller, M. (2008). Pathogen prevalence predicts human cross-cultural variability in individualism/collectivism. *Proceedings of the Royal Society B* 275(1640):1279–1285.

Gächter, S. and Schulz, J. F. (2016). Intrinsic honesty and the prevalence of rule violations across societies. *Nature* 531:496–499.

Gershman, B. (2016). Witchcraft beliefs and the erosion of social capital: Evidence from Sub-Saharan Africa and beyond. *Journal of Development Economics* 120:182–208.

Glaeser, E. L., La Porta, R., Lopez-de-Silanes, F. and Shleifer, A. (2004). Do institutions cause growth? *Journal of Economic Growth* 9(3):271–303.

Greif, A. (2012). *Institutions and the path to the modern economy: Lessons from medieval trade*. Cambridge: Cambridge University Press.

Guiso, L., Sapienza, P. and Zingales, L. (2006). Does culture affect economic outcomes? *Journal of Economic Perspectives* 20(2):23–48.

Guiso, L., Sapienza, P. and Zingales, L. (2009). Cultural biases in economic exchange? *Quarterly Journal of Economics* 124(3):1095–1131.

Gundlach, E. and Paldam, M. (2009). A farewell to critical junctures: Sorting out long-run causality of income and democracy. *European Journal of Political Economy* 25(3):340–354.

Gutmann, J., Metelska-Szaniawska, K. and Voigt, S. (2022). *The comparative constitutional compliance database*. ILE Working Paper 57, University of Hamburg.

Gutmann, J., Padovano, F. and Voigt, S. (2020). Perception vs. experience: Explaining differences in corruption measures using microdata. *European Journal of Political Economy* 65:101925.

Gutmann, J. and Voigt, S. (2018). The rule of law: Measurement and deep roots. *European Journal of Political Economy* 54:68–82.

Gutmann, J. and Voigt, S. (2019). The independence of prosecutors and government accountability. *Supreme Court Economic Review* 27:1–19.

Gutmann, J. and Voigt, S. (2020). Traditional law in times of the nation state: Why is it so prevalent? *Journal of Institutional Economics* 16(4):445–461.

Hilbe, C. and Sigmund, K. (2010). Incentives and opportunism: From the carrot to the stick. *Proceedings of the Royal Society B* 277(1693):2427–2433.

Hodgson, G. M. (2006). What are institutions? *Journal of Economic Issues* 40(1):1–25.

Hyland, M., Djankov, S. and Koujianou Goldberg, P. (2020). Gendered laws and women in the workforce. *American Economic Review: Insights* 2(4):475–490.

Kaufmann, D., Kray, A. and Mastruzzi, M. (2011). The worldwide governance indicators: Methodology and analytical issues. *Hague Journal on the Rule of Law* 3(2):220–246.

Kiwit, D. and Voigt, S. (1995). Überlegungen zum institutionellen Wandel unter Berücksichtigung des Verhältnisses interner und externer Institutionen. *ORDO: Jahrbuch für die Ordnung von Wirtschaft und Gesellschaft* 46:117–148.

Knack, S. and Keefer, P. (1997). Does social capital have an economic payoff? A cross-country investigation. *Quarterly Journal of Economics* 112(4):1251–1288.

La Porta, R., Lopez-de-Silanes, F., Shleifer, A. and Vishny, R. W. (1997). Trust in large organizations. *American Economic Review: Papers and Proceedings* 87(2):333–338.

Law, D. S. and Versteeg, M. (2013). Sham constitutions. *California Law Review* 101(4):863–952.

Lipset, S. M. (1959). Some social requisites of democracy: Economic development and political legitimacy. *American Political Science Review* 53(1):69–105.

Mungan, M. C. (2021). Rewards versus imprisonment. *American Law and Economics Review* 23(2):432–480.

Norenzayan, A. (2013). *Big gods: How religion transformed cooperation and conflict.* Princeton: Princeton University Press.

North, D. C. (1990). *Institutions, institutional change and economic performance.* Cambridge: Cambridge University Press.

North, D. C., Wallis, J. J. and Weingast, B. R. (2009). *Violence and social orders: A conceptual framework for interpreting recorded human history.* Cambridge: Cambridge University Press.

Ostrom, E. (1986). An agenda for the study of institutions. *Public Choice* 48(1):3–25.

Ostrom, E. (2005). *Understanding institutional diversity.* Princeton: Princeton University Press.

Persson, T. and Tabellini, G. (2003). *The economic effects of constitutions.* Cambridge: MIT Press.

Powell, E. J., McDowell, S. C., O'Brien, R. and Oksasoglu, J. (2021). Islam-based legal language and state governance: Democracy, strength of the judiciary and human rights. *Constitutional Political Economy* 32(3):376–412.

Putnam, R. D. (1993). *Making democracy work: Civic traditions in modern Italy.* Princeton: Princeton University Press.

Qian, N. and Yanagizawa, D. (2009). The strategic determinants of U.S. human rights reporting: Evidence from the Cold War. *Journal of the European Economic Association* 7(2/3):446–457.

Robinson, J. A. (2013). Measuring institutions in the Trobriand Islands: A comment on Voigt's paper. *Journal of Institutional Economics* 9(1):27–29.

Rodrik, D., Subramanian, A. and Trebbi, F. (2004). Institutions rule: The primacy of institutions over geography and integration in economic development. *Journal of Economic Growth* 9(2):131–165.

Roland, G. (2004). Understanding institutional change: Fast-moving and slow-moving institutions. *Studies in Comparative International Development* 38(4):109–131.

Schotter, A. (1981). *The economic theory of social institutions.* Cambridge: Cambridge University Press.

Shirley, M. M. (2013). Measuring institutions: How to be precise though vague. *Journal of Institutional Economics* 9(1):31–33.

Stiglitz, J. E. (2002). Information and the change in the paradigm in economics. *American Economic Review* 92(3):460–501.

Tabellini, G. (2010). Culture and institutions: Economic development in the regions of Europe. *Journal of the European Economic Association* 8(4):677–716.

Tsusaka, T. W., Kajisaa, K., Pede, V. O. and Aoyagi, K. (2015). Neighborhood effects and social behavior: The case of irrigated and rainfed farmers in Bohol, the Philippines. *Journal of Economic Behavior & Organization* 118:227–246.

Uslaner, E. M. (2002). *The moral foundations of trust*. Cambridge: Cambridge University Press.

Van Aaken, A. and Simsek, B. (2021). Rewarding in international law. *American Journal of International Law* 115(2):195–241.

Voigt, S. (2013). How (not) to measure institutions. *Journal of Institutional Economics* 9(1):1–26.

Voigt, S. (2018). How to measure informal institutions. *Journal of Institutional Economics* 14(1):1–22.

Voigt, S. (2019). *Institutional economics: An introduction*. Cambridge: Cambridge University Press.

Voigt, S. (2020). *Constitutional economics: A primer*. Cambridge: Cambridge University Press.

Voigt, S. and Gutmann, J. (2013). Turning cheap talk into economic growth: On the relationship between property rights and judicial independence. *Journal of Comparative Economics* 41(1):66–73.

Voigt, S., Gutmann, J. and Feld, L. P. (2015). Economic growth and judicial independence, a dozen years on: Cross-country evidence using an updated Set of indicators. *European Journal of Political Economy* 38:197–211.

Voigt, S. and Kiwit, D. (1998). The role and evolution of beliefs, habits, moral norms, and institutions. In: Herbert Giersch (ed.), *The merits of markets: Critical issues of the open society*, Berlin et al.: Springer, pp. 83–108.

Williamson, O. E. (2010). The new institutional economics: Taking stock, looking ahead. *Journal of Economic Literature* 38(3):595–613.

Zak, P. J. and Knack, S. (2001). Trust and growth. *Economic Journal* 111(470):295–321.

13

CONVERGENCE IN FORMAL AND INFORMAL INSTITUTIONS AND LONG-RUN ECONOMIC PERFORMANCE IN THE EURO AREA

José García-Solanes

DEPARTMENT OF ECONOMIC ANALYSIS, CAMPUS DE ESPINARDO,
UNIVERSITY OF MURCIA, MURCIA, SPAIN

Arielle Beyaert and Laura López-Gómez

DEPARTMENT OF QUANTITATIVE ECONOMICS, CAMPUS DE ESPINARDO,
UNIVERSITY OF MURCIA, MURCIA, SPAIN

13.1 Introduction

The progress toward European monetary integration in the first half of the 1990s was based on the analysis of the benefits and costs of adopting a common currency – synthesized in the Delors Report (Committee for the Study of Economic and Monetary Union, 1988) and in Emerson et al. (1992) – ignoring the criteria of the optimum currency areas (OCA) theory.[1] The OCA's endogeneity thesis, pioneered by Frankel and Rose (1998), gave a boost to this strategy by establishing that the adoption of a common currency would lead member countries to comply with the OCA criteria over time (ex-post). It was argued that the governance of the Eurozone and the need for its economies to be more flexible and adaptable should spur the necessary structural reforms and promote convergence in per capita income and welfare, which are the main goals of the Maastricht Treaty (1992). The most enthusiastic defenders of an early monetary unification claimed that EMU would also promote convergence in institutional aspects such as social conventions, property rights, labor regulations, non-tariff barriers and even political union in the long term.

But this view was not unanimous and other researchers highlighted the negative aspects of a rapid EMU. The view that seemed to prevail is the cautious one, arguing that the EMU increases the likelihood of gradual reforms (Mongelli, 2008, p. 40). After 22 years of EMU, the effects of the common currency should already be observed not only on short-term aspects, such as cyclical synchronization, but also on the convergence of both per capita income and in national institutions. Our analysis goes in that direction, performing two types of analysis. In a first step, we examine the convergence in two composite indicators of institutional quality, one referred to the formal institutions and another to informal ones, within the Eurozone since the adoption of the single currency. We use two composite indices derived from the Worldwide Governance Indicators and apply to them the methodology of Phillips and Sul (2007, 2009). In a second step, we analyze the links between institutional quality and long-run economic performance constructing cross correlograms between institutional quality and potential GDP per capita, both in level and growth rate.

In synthesis, we find that there is no institutional convergence in the Eurozone as a whole, but two clubs with different convergence processes are detected for each indicator. For both indicators, the group of countries converging to higher quality levels (Club 1) is in the north and west of the euro area (EA), whereas the club with poorer institutional quality (Club 2) is in the east and south of EMU. In informal institutions, Club 2 is made of Spain, Italy, Malta, Cyprus, Slovenia and Slovakia. The members of Club 2 in formal institutions are the aforementioned countries minus Italy plus Belgium, France, Portugal and Latvia. A common feature of Clubs 1 and 2 is that their convergence processes – toward different long-term levels – are very slow. We also find that in all cases, except for informal institutions in Club 2, improvements in the institutional quality are associated with increases in the potential GDP per capita with some evidence of potential GDP convergence. We also get certain evidence that, in this association, institutional quality anticipates the level of potential GDP.

The rest of the chapter is organized as follows. Section 13.2 reviews the literature on institutional convergence in the EA; Section 13.3 performs the empirical analysis; Section 13.4 derives the main policy prescriptions; and, finally, Section 13.5 summarizes the concluding remarks.

13.2 Brief review of the literature on institutional quality convergence among European countries

The convergence of per capita income is an economic integration objective clearly settled in both the Delors Report (1988) and the Maastricht Treaty (1992). It is an essential requirement to share the benefits of monetary unification to all European citizens and to strengthen economic and social cohesion within the EA, as established in the Single European Act (Article 130a). However, convergence in per capita income is a necessary though not sufficient condition for countries to achieve long-lasting levels of well-being and prosperity. As Díaz del Hoyo et al. (2017) point out, good functioning of the institutions is a prerequisite for income convergence to be achieved on solid and durable foundations.

There is abundant empirical evidence that the quality of institutions is the main driver of long-term economic growth, and that other factors considered in the growth theory such as geography, human capital and technological change impact on development only through their effects on institutions. See, for instance, Rodrik et al. (2004), Hall and Jones (1999), Easterly and Levine (2002) and Acemoglu et al. (2014).

The relevance of institutions in explaining cross-country differences in growth and long-run GDP per capita is also theoretically demonstrated in recent models of endogenous growth. Altman (2009) and Zhao et al. (2020) are two good examples. Hence, it is relevant to find out whether the institutional quality of groups of countries converges toward similar levels in the long term. In the following lines, we briefly review the still not abundant literature on institutional convergence in the countries of the EU and/or the Eurozone.

Schönfelder and Wagner (2016) analyze the extent to which the European integration process brings the institutional development of 33 European countries closer together.

They perform System Generalized Method of Moments (GMM) estimations using the World Bank's Worldwide Governance Indicators and data from the period 1996 to 2012 and find that the prospect of being part of the EU contributed to raising institutional quality in most indicators. However, neither the fact of being part of the EA nor the preparation to enter it influenced the institutional development of the countries; furthermore, it seems that the adoption of the euro has had a negative influence on the control of corruption in the EA member countries.

Arestis et al. (2018) calculate indices of institutional inequality of the Eurozone countries by estimating Gini coefficients. Using the Global Competitiveness Index developed by the World Economic Forum for the period 2007–2017, they obtain that the main sources of institutional inequality lie in the indicators of ethics and corruption, government influences on court decisions, and the deficient protection of property rights.

Schönfelder and Wagner (2019) examine whether institutional convergence occurs throughout the European integration process, applying descriptive statistics analysis and σ- and β-convergence tests, for various groups of European countries. They used three sets of institutional development indicators: the Worldwide Governance Indicators (WGI), the product market regulation indicator of the OECD and the business regulation indicator of the World Bank. These authors detect β-convergence in the three types of indicators for the broad group of countries formed by the EU and its aspirants and candidates, but a lack of σ- and β-convergence within the Eurozone in terms of World Governance.

Beyaert et al. (2019) apply stochastic convergence tests to six groups of variables from the International Country Risk Guide (ICRG) for the period 1986–2018. They find that there is no convergence in any of the variables and for none of the groups or subgroups of European countries considered. Furthermore, they perform distributional dynamics analysis which reveals that, since the introduction of the euro, neither the countries of the periphery (Greece, Italy, Spain, Portugal, Ireland, Malta and Cyprus) nor the Eastern European countries of the Eurozone (Estonia, Latvia, Lithuania, Slovakia and Slovenia) have followed a process of "catching up" with respect to the three countries with the best institutional quality in the EA.

Pérez-Moreno et al. (2020) investigate the institutional convergence in the Eurozone during the years of the Great Recession (2008–2014) and the subsequent years (2014–2017), to assess how the business-cycle phases affect institutional convergence. They used indicators included in the Global Competitiveness Index developed by the World Economic Forum as representatives of the business world. Their results indicate that institutional divergence prevails in the Eurozone in the aftermath of the Global Financial Crisis, with stronger intensity than in other groups of countries. Moreover, the Eurozone countries most negatively affected are those traditionally considered as the periphery of the Eurozone.

Very recently, some researchers have been examining the possibility that institutional convergence is configured in terms of convergence clubs, based on the idea that institutional dynamics can have multiple equilibria in the long run, as in the theory of economic growth. Under this assumption, the convergence tests should detect several clubs. And since institutional quality is a fundamental determinant of the level of long-term per capita income, the countries in the sample would tend to very different levels of per capita income and well-being in the long run. A flourishing strand of the literature has applied the log-t convergence test developed by Phillips and Sul (2007, 2009) and improved by Von Lyncker and Thoennessen (2017). This test is particularly useful to detect convergence clubs since, apart from taking into account the possible common factor representing the long-term trend within a group, it also includes idiosyncratic effects of group members in the short term, which are not taken into account in cross-sectional tests as for example in the traditional σ- and β-convergence analysis.

As far as we know, Kar et al. (2019) are the first authors who applied Phillips and Sul's (2007, 2009) tests to detect institutional convergence clubs. They use a sample of 117 countries with different degrees of development and the institutional indicators of the ICRG. With data from the period 1985–2015, they show that many developing countries are caught in very low-level institutional traps and cannot converge toward the levels of the more advanced countries. They perform a similar analysis to detect clubs in per capita income and conduct bivariate probit regressions to show that institutional traps are significant determinants of per capita income traps. Performing a very similar analysis to Kar et al. (2019) and using the "Marketization Index" as a measure of institutional quality, Glawe and Wagner (2019) obtained results similar to Kar et al. (2019) but limited to the provinces of China.

Glawe and Wagner (2021a) investigate the formation of institutional clusters within the European Union applying Phillips and Sul's (2007, 2009) log-t test based on four WGI indicators – and their average – for the period 2002–2018. They detect four clubs converging to different steady states, which follow a clear geographical pattern. The countries with the best institutions are in the northern and western parts of the EU, while those with the worst institutional performance are ex-communist countries in Central Europe, with the exception of Poland and the Czech Republic, and some old EU members situated in the south such as Italy and Greece. The authors also discover heterogeneity in the speed of convergence within the different clusters and differences in the transition paths between clubs. García Solanes et al. (2021) applied the same technique coupled with kernel distributional analysis to the countries of the Eurozone and distinguishing between formal and informal institutions. They detected several convergence clubs with geographical patterns similar to Glawe and Wagner (2021a).

Using a different and interesting approach, Casagrande and Dallago (2021) analyze to what extent the institutions of each EU country are far from the European benchmark that they build based on 15 pillars that incorporate the economic, political and social dimensions and deduce the criteria and sub-pillars that each country must improve in order to approach the shared benchmark.

In the following section, we analyze the institutional convergence in the EA and the link between the configuration of convergence clusters and the long-run economic conditions of the member countries.

13.3 Clusters in institutional quality within the euro area

13.3.1 Institutional convergence clubs

In this section we apply Phillips and Sul's (2007, 2009) log-t test improved by Von Lyncker and Thoennessen (2017) (henceforth PSLT) to identify convergence clubs within the Eurozone focusing on two synthetic indicators of institutional quality extracted from the six Worldwide Governance Indicators of the World Bank. We extend part of our previous work in García Solanes et al. (2021) with a more complete analysis of both the convergence tests and the convergence dynamics of each country within each club. With respect to the Glawe and Wagner (2021a) work, in addition to extending the time sample with one year, our analysis presents the following differences. First, we focus on the EA rather than the EU because our primary interest is finding out implications for the stability of the Eurozone and the future of the single currency; second, we perform a separate analysis for formal institutions, on the one hand, and informal institutions on the other, on the basis that, as explained below, they have a very different nature and give rise to distinct economic implications.

The PSLT methodology uses panel data of the institutional indicator of interest to which it applies various algorithms to detect groups of countries whose institutions converge to each other. To this end, it models the behavior of the countries in both the long and short term and analyzes whether the heterogeneity of the countries in the group with respect to the possible long-term common component disappears over time. The procedure is used to detect global or absolute convergence among all the members of the panel if it exists, or to identify possible convergence clubs and groups of divergent countries. In the Appendix of this chapter, we offer a synthesis of this methodology.

In this section, it is sufficient to indicate that the crucial element of the analysis is made up of a Student's t-statistic, robust to autocorrelation and heteroscedasticity, called the "log-t statistic", associated with the contrast of the nullity of the coefficient "q" of the explanatory variable "logarithm of time" (log (t)) in a simple regression in which the explained variable is a concrete transformation – justified in detail by Phillips and Sul (2007) – of the variables under study. In our case, these variables are several indicators of institutional quality of the Eurozone countries. We examine the convergence of those indicators one at a time. Institutional convergence between the countries of a group referring to a given indicator is rejected at 5% if the log-t test applied to the data of this group takes a value lower than −1.65. It is also important to bear in mind that the estimated value, $\hat{q}$, of q also provides the estimation of the rate of decay, $\hat{b}$, related to the speed of convergence of the variables toward the common long-term component. The relationship between both parameters is $\hat{q} = 2\hat{b}$ (see the Appendix for details). To understand the results commented below, it is also important to know that the methodology estimates a relative distance of each country of the group under study with respect to the group mean. Let us denote this distance as h_{it}, where i stands for country, and t is the time period (see Equation A.2 of the Appendix). The time series of h_{it} for country i, is called the relative transition path of country i, toward the group mean.

Once convergence clubs are detected, to better understand their characteristics it is interesting not only to examine the relative transition path of each country within its club (i.e. the time series of h_{it}), but it is also interesting to examine the *average* relative transition path of each club with respect to the *whole* Eurozone. The average relative transition path is the equivalent of h_{it} but at the level of a given club with respect to the whole Eurozone, i.e. i refers now to club i within the Eurozone, instead of to country i within its club. This average relative path is therefore computed taking, for each t, the cross-section average data of all the countries of club i and comparing it to the cross-section average data of all countries of the Eurozone.

We apply the PSLT methodology to two composite indices of the six Worldwide Governance Indicators elaborated by Kaufmann et al. (2010).[2] We consider justified and necessary to differentiate between formal and informal institutional variables, given that the natures of one and the other are very different: following North (1990), formal institutions refer to legal and judicial frameworks and the implementation of government policies and tend to change abruptly. On the contrary, informal institutions are linked to the culture, habits and behaviors of the agents, and they tend to change continuously but at a slow pace.

OECD (2008) provides guidelines to construct composite indicators. Since we use institutional variables that are normalized and measured with the same units, and there is no indication about the relative importance of the variables within each group, we construct the composite indicators as simple averages of the individual components. So, the first composite index is the average of three formal institutional variables: political stability, rule of law and regulatory quality. The second one is a compounded average of three informal institutions indicators: voice and accountability, government effectiveness and control of corruption. The two composite indices are built with the available data for the years after the implementation of the euro: 2002–2019.

Table 13.1 Formal institutions composite index: Convergence clubs

	Countries	Estimated coefficient $\hat{q}$	Log-t statistic	Stand. error	p-value	Estimated rate of decay b
	Whole Eurozone group	−1.083	−6.178	0.175	0.000 Divergence	−
Club 1	Finland, Luxembourg, the Netherlands, Estonia, Austria, Germany, Ireland and Lithuania	−0.099	−0.41	0.241		−0.049 Nonsignificant
Club 2	Belgium, Malta, Portugal, Latvia, Slovenia, Spain, France, Cyprus and Slovakia	−0.175	−0.751	0.232		−0.088 Nonsignificant
Divergents	Greece and Italy					

Table 13.1 shows the clubs that have been obtained for the *formal* institutional quality indicators.

According to the results of Table 13.1, the composite indices of the Eurozone countries corresponding to the quality of their formal institutions do not converge to each other in the Eurozone taken as a whole (first row of Table 13.1). However, two convergence clubs are detected. Club 1 is made of Finland, Luxembourg, the Netherlands, Austria, Germany, Ireland, Estonia and Lithuania. In this first convergence cluster, the estimated value $\hat{q}$ of q is negative, which might be strange since it would give rise to a negative value of the rate of decay; however, given its associated standard error, $\hat{q}$ does not significantly differ from zero, so that the estimated rate of decay does not significantly differ from zero either. This implies that the convergence speed in this group is extremely slow (see the Appendix for more details). Club 2 is made of Belgium, Malta, Portugal, Latvia, Slovenia, Spain, France, Cyprus and Slovakia. The same situation is occurring here: the rate of decay does not significantly differ from zero, so that this group also constitutes a club of very slow convergence. It must be kept in mind that these two groups of countries constitute two different convergence groups even if, within each group, the convergence is slow. It is noteworthy that the Financial Crisis does not seem to have had an impact on these convergence processes. Two countries diverge from all the remaining ones and these are Greece and Italy.

As far as convergence dynamics is concerned, Figure 13.1 shows the relative transition paths of each club with respect to the Eurozone average. Two messages emerge from this figure. First, on average the countries of Club 1 exhibit a better institutional performance than those of Club 2 (note that the average relative level of Club 1 is above 1.2 on the whole period, whereas Club 2 does not reach the level of 0.9). Second, in Club 1, the situation improved till around 2014 and worsened afterwards, whereas in the worst positioned Club 2, the situation hardly changed over the whole period.

Figures 13.2 and 13.3 provide information about what happens within each club. Remember that Club 1 is made of core countries of the Eurozone plus Ireland, Estonia and Lithuania. Figure 13.2 helps understanding the composition of this cluster: the core countries of the EA occupy the higher positions (they are all of them above 1, except Germany that is close to 1 from below) and these countries as a whole slightly worsen their performance overtime. On the opposite, Estonia and Lithuania started in a much worse relative

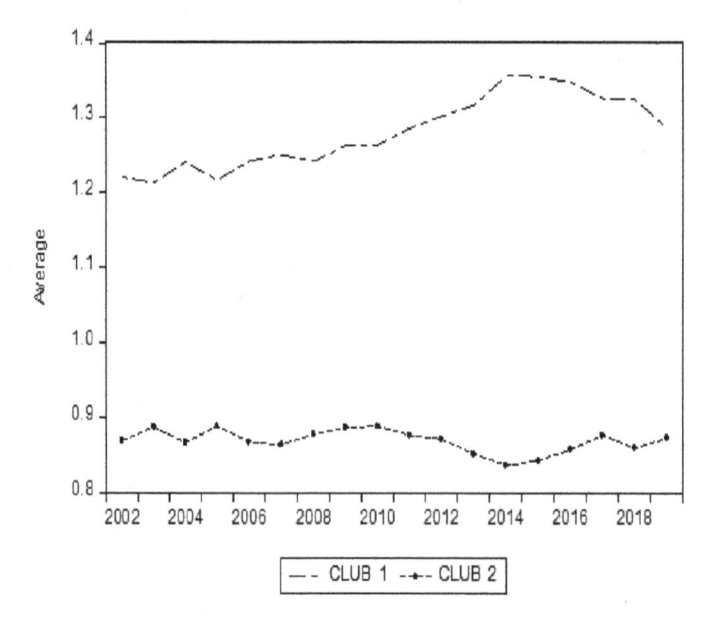

Figure 13.1 Formal institutions: Relative transition paths of each club with respect to the Eurozone average.

position at the beginning of the period (around 0.7 or below) but steadily improved their situation overtime, so that overall, all the countries of this club ended up closer to each other at the end of the period.

With respect to Club 2, Figure 13.3 informs about some more volatility in these countries, although the overall tendency is to have the best positioned countries slightly worsening their position, whereas the worst positioned ones improving theirs.

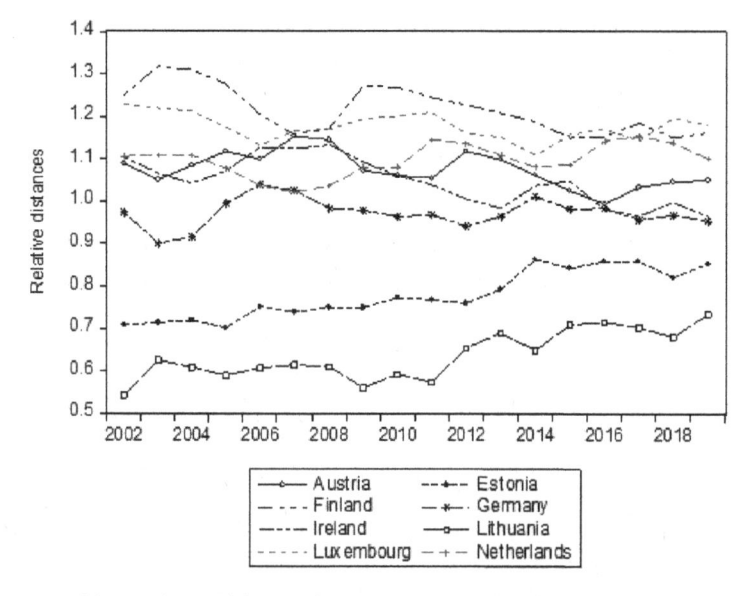

Figure 13.2 Formal institutions, Club 1: Relative transition paths of each country of the club with respect to the club average.

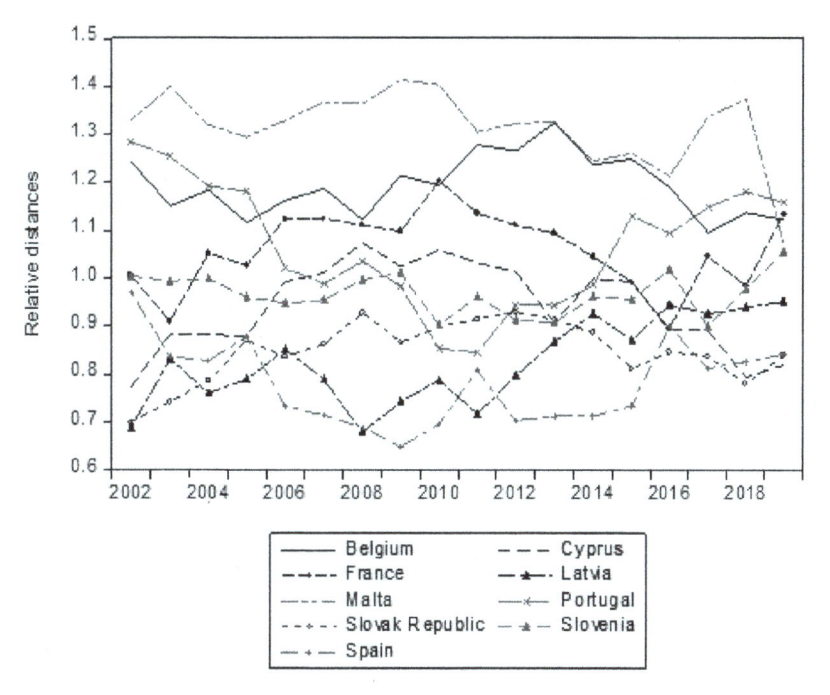

Figure 13.3 Formal institutions, Club 2: Relative transition paths of each country of the club with respect to the club average.

As far as the *informal* composite index is concerned, the results are presented in Table 13.2: no convergence is detected for the Eurozone as a whole, although two convergence clubs are identified, as is the case with the formal institutions index. However, the convergence clubs are distinct. The first cluster includes the eight components of Club 1 in formal institutions plus Belgium, France and Latvia. This corresponds to an enlarged core of the Eurozone plus the three small Baltic European countries. Note that the estimated rate of decay is not signifi-cantly different from zero, which means that the countries of this group, although showing a

Table 13.2 Informal institutions composite index: Convergence clubs

	Countries	Estimated coefficient $\hat{q}$	Log-t statistic	Stand. error	p-value	Estimated rate of decay b
	Whole Eurozone group	−1.013	−6.804	0.149	0.000 Divergence	−
Club 1	Finland, the Netherlands, Luxembourg, Germany, Lithuania, Austria, Belgium, Ireland, France, Estonia and Latvia	−0.165	−0.954	0.173		−0.083 Nonsignificant
Club 2	Slovenia, Malta, Cyprus, Spain, Slovakia and Italy	−0.396	−1.616	0.245		−0.198 Nonsignificant
Divergents	Greece and Portugal					

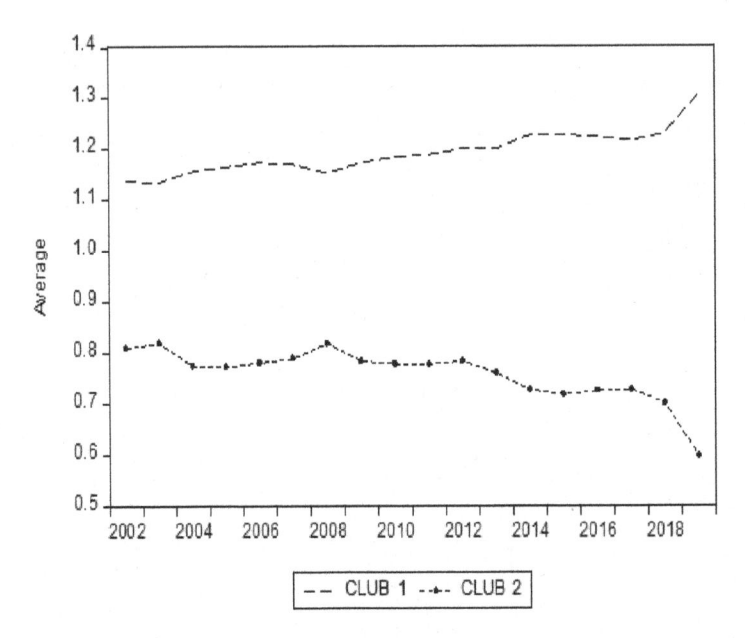

Figure 13.4 Informal institutions: Relative transition paths of each club with respect to the Eurozone average.

convergence process and a homogeneity different form the other euro countries, do converge very slowly to each other in informal institutions. The second cluster is made of Spain, Italy, Slovenia, Slovakia, Malta and Cyprus, which all belong to the so-called periphery. Their convergence process is also very slow since the rate of decay is again nonsignificant. Finally, Greece again and in this case, Portugal diverges from the rest of countries.

Concerning the relative transition paths, Figure 13.4 indicates that the two clubs are distant form each other, but less than in the case of formal institutions. And in contrast with what happened with the formal institutions, the situation of informal institutions has improved overtime in Club 1, whereas it worsened in Club 2. In other words, the countries of Club 2 have converged toward a worse situation and the two clubs are becoming increasingly distant form each other.

As for the situation of each country within each club, Figure 13.5, referred to Club 1 members, reveals a pattern very similar to that of Club 1 countries in formal institutions: the core countries form a sub-group within this club with a better institutional situation, which nonetheless is slightly worsening over time; a second group is formed by Latvia, Lithuania and Estonia, which are much worse positioned but following an improving trend almost continuously over time. As a result, at the end of the period, all countries are closer to each other than at the beginning and they end up with a better overall position as commented before in Figure 13.4.

In Club 2 (Figure 13.6), again two subgroups can be identified: one formed by Italy and the Slovak Republic that are both below the club average all along the period, and the rest of countries with a better institutional quality but that is worsening over time, especially in the case of Spain and Cyprus at the beginning of the period and Malta at the end of the period. So overall, all these countries get closer to each other, but they evolve on average to a worse position as reflected and commented in Figure 13.4.

The results of our analysis allow us to highlight, as a summary, the following points. First, consistent with Glawe and Wagner (2021a), there is a clear institutional polarization in the

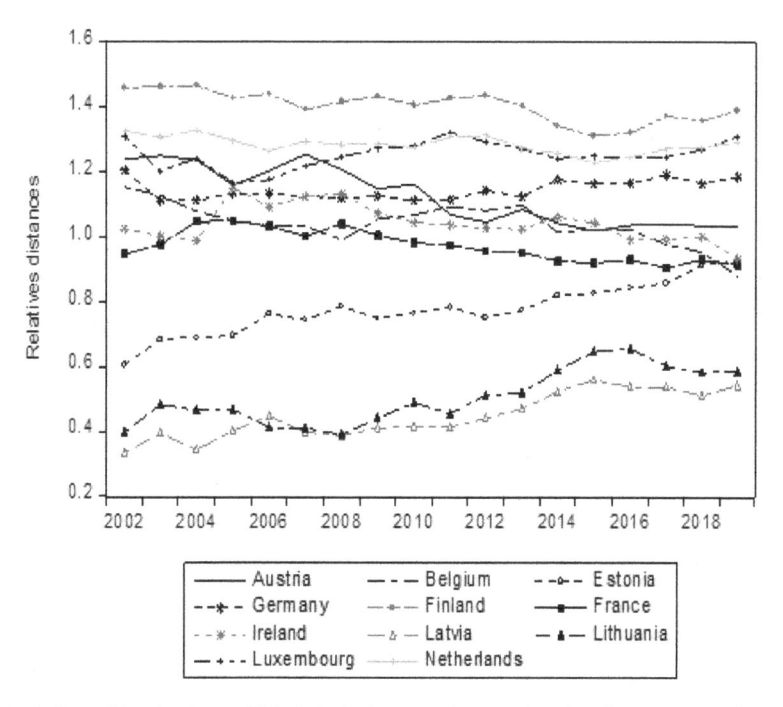

Figure 13.5   Informal institutions, Club 1: Relative transition paths of each country of the club with respect to the club average.

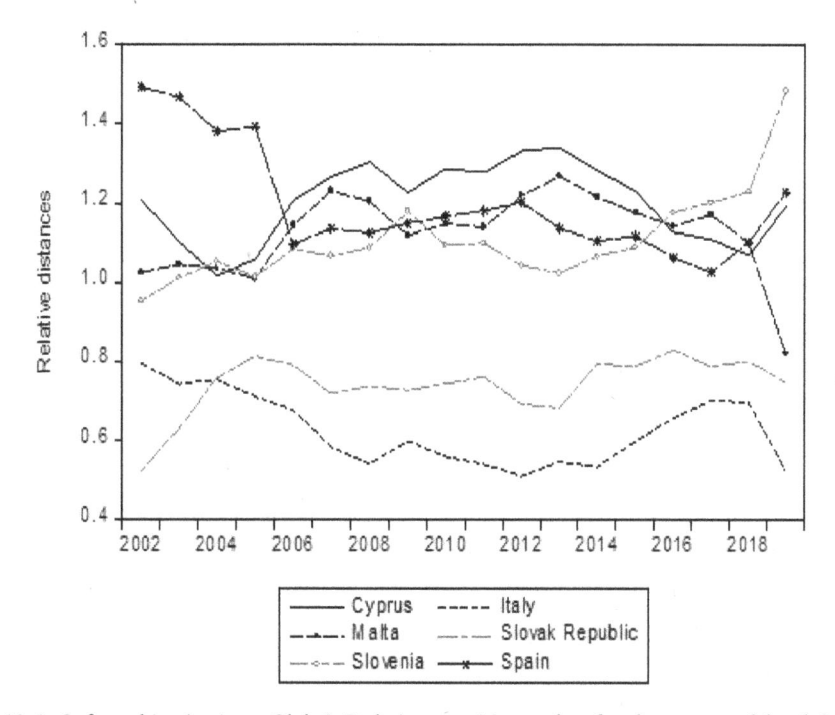

Figure 13.6   Informal institutions, Club 2: Relative transition paths of each country of the club with respect to the club average.

EA for the two types of institutions analyzed here, with geographical features that mark the differentiation: on the one hand, a group of countries in the north and west of the area with relatively high-quality institutions and, on the other hand, another set of economies from the east and south of the area. Second, what should create concern is that the gap between the two groups tends to widen, something that is very evident when we look at the dynamics of the two composite quality indicators. These results are in line with the findings of other works reviewed in Section 13.2 of this chapter. Third, our results reveal that polarization is accompanied by different levels of long-term institutional equilibrium shared by several countries, as reflected by the detection of convergence clubs. Fourth, the convergence speeds within each convergence club are very low.

Our analysis also allows us to detect the existence of countries that are caught in traps of very low institutional quality, from which they will not be able to escape if they do not adopt very drastic measures. The criterion is to see which countries have stabilized institutional levels below the average for the entire EA without converging to the other countries. In terms of formal institutions, the trapped countries are Italy and Greece, and in informal institutions Greece and Portugal.

It seems clear, then, that Club 2 countries need to improve both their formal and informal institutions. As far formal institutions is concerned, using the results of the meticulous study of Casagrande and Dallago (2021) on the scores achieved by EU countries on a wide range of institutional pillars and sub-pillars, the countries of this club should improve confidence in institutions in general (government, judicial system etc.), which may require reforming those institutions. Regarding their informal institutions, Club 2 members need to further develop the confidence in the state's ability to maintain public order and to strengthen cultural development. These authors also highlight the need for institutional actions in the economic sphere to improve the investment environment and increase efficiency, effectiveness and equity. In particular, post-communist countries need to develop their financial infrastructure much more.

In the next section, we explore the possible relationships between institutional quality and long-term economic performance, which will help us to uncover the economic implications for member countries of pertaining to a given institutional convergence club.

13.3.2 Relationships between institutional quality and long-term economic results

Since, according to the theoretical and empirical evidence in the literature, institutions influence long-term economic results, the next step of our analysis will center on *potential* GDP per capita, and its rate of variation, as representatives of long-term economic performance, and its connections with institutional quality. For this purpose, we build cross correlograms between institutional quality – both formal and informal – and potential GDP per capita, both in level and growth rate, within each institutional cluster.

The cross correlogram between two time series is a useful statistical tool to examine the estimated cross-correlations over time between the two series, especially to detect whether one can be considered a leading indicator for the other or not. If we denote by $X(t)$ the value of the first variable at period t and by $Y(t)$ the value of the other variable at that same period, then the graph of the cross correlogram between the two variables will provide the visual representation of the estimated correlation between $X(t)$ and $Y(t-1)$, $Y(t-2)$, ..., $Y(t-k)$, as well as the correlation between $X(t)$ and $Y(t+1)$, $Y(t+2)$, ..., $Y(t+k)$. In other words, it provides correlation at lags -1, -2, ..., $-k$ and at leads 1, 2, ..., k. The "leads" correlations and the "lags" correlations are not identical since $corr(X(t), Y(t - k)) \neq corr(X(t), Y(t + k))$. In fact, if the estimated cross-correlations for leads are significant and those for lags are not, X can be considered as a leading indicator for Y. And vice versa, if the estimated cross-correlations for lags are significant and those for leads are not, Y can be considered as a leading indicator for X. If the correlations are significant both for leads and lags, this means that there exists a bidirectional correlation between the two; but the way in which the lead correlations differ from the lag correlations may be informative about the most probable leading indicator of one variable for the other.

In this case, we present the cross correlogram between the composite institutional indicators as the X variable and the per capita potential output as the Y variable, as well as between the institutional indicators and the per capita potential output growth rate.[3] We study these cross-correlations by convergence club.

All the cross correlograms are represented in Figures 13.7a–13.10b. In these figures, the gray columns refer to the lead correlations between the institutional indicator at t and potential output (in level or in growth rate, depending on the graph) at $t+i$, whereas the black columns refer to the lag correlations between the institutional indicator at t and potential output (in level and in growth rate) at $t-i$. In these graphs, the interval between the two horizontal dashed lines indicates the 95% confidence band, so that any estimated cross-correlation column that falls entirely inside this band is not significantly different from zero, whereas all those that end outside this band reflect a significant cross-correlation.

Starting with the convergence Club 1 in formal institutions, made of the core countries (except the Netherlands that diverge) and Ireland, Lithuania and Estonia, Figure 13.7a, referring to the cross correlogram between the levels of the institutional indicator and of the per capita potential GDP, reveals several interesting facts. The first one is that the cross-correlation is positive, both for leads and lags, which means that the better the institution quality the higher the potential output over time and vice-versa. The second one is that this correlation is more intense in the first leads and lags, starting at values well above 0.5 that only gradually decrease to zero over more than 15 years. The correlations are significant up to lead 15 and to lag 13. So, the relation is intense and long lasting. The third fact is less obvious but interesting to note, since it will be observed in almost all cases: the cross-correlations at leads are slightly higher than the cross-correlations at lags, which means that the institutional indicator seems to be more a leading indicator for potential output than the other way around.

Considering now the cross-correlations between the institutional indicator and the growth rate leads and lags of the per capita potential output, the results are presented in Figure 13.7b. The cross-correlations are now lower and negative, and also slowly decaying till around lag 11 and lead 9. So, the higher the quality of institutions, the lower the increase in potential output, and vice-versa. This fact, together with what we have detected in Figure 13.7a, is a reflection of the convergence process that we have detected and commented earlier in Club 1: here the convergence is mainly due to the fact that lower institutional countries (with lower potential output too) converge toward the best positioned ones – in per capita potential GDP – whose situation is rather stable over the period and convergence in their potential outputs is also detected.

As far as Club 2 is concerned, the cross correlograms are presented in Figure 13.8a and b. In the first one, some characteristics are similar to those detected for Club 1: positive and slowly decaying cross-correlations between the formal institutions' indicator and the leads and lags of per capita potential output. However, these positive values are drastically smaller: they are well below 0.5 from the beginning. But on the other hand, the characteristic of the

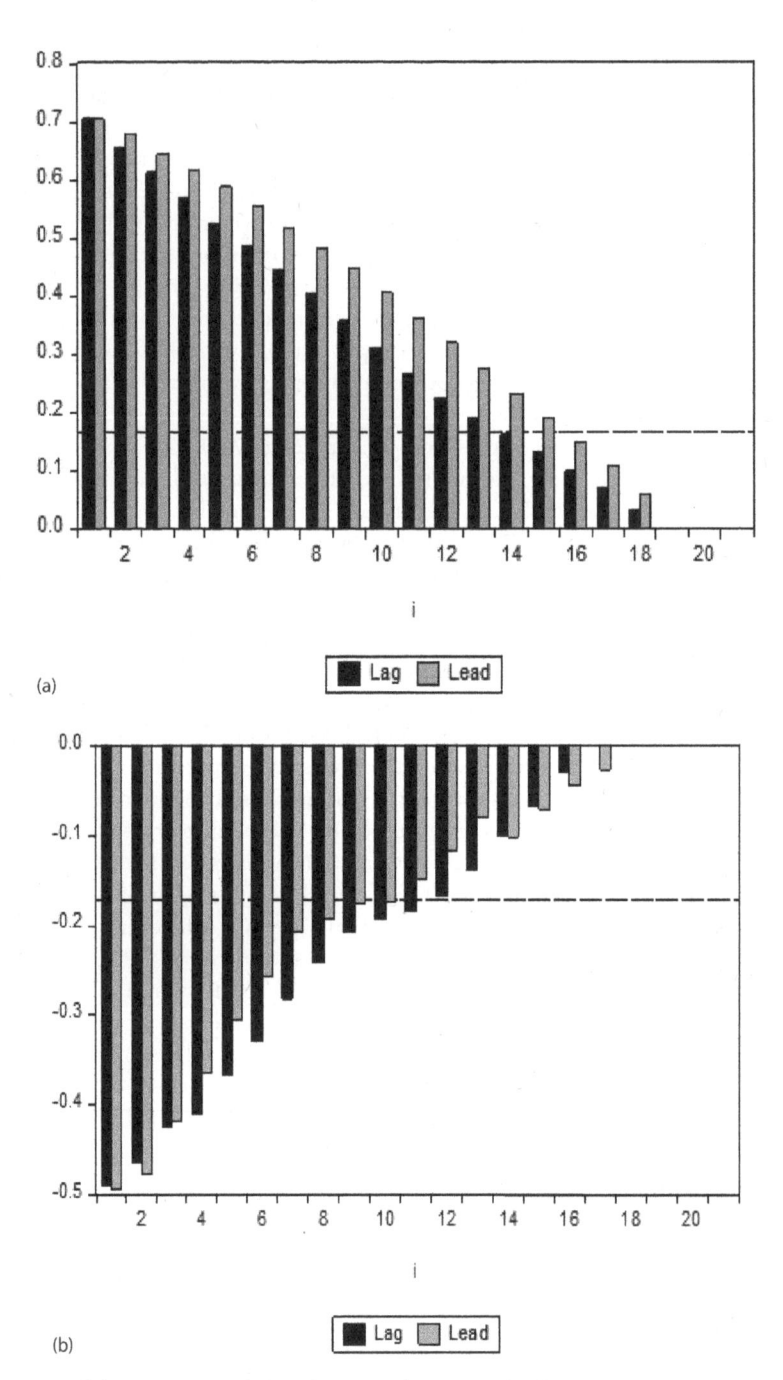

Figure 13.7 (a) Club 1, cross-correlations between the composite formal institutions index at t and the level of potential GDP per capita i periods before (lag, at $t - i$) and i periods ahead (lead, at $t + i$). (b) Club 1, cross-correlations between the composite formal institutions index at t and the growth rate of potential GDP per capita i periods before (lag, at $t - i$) and i periods ahead (lead, at $t + i$).

Sources: Own calculations. Data from the WGI of the World Bank, AMECO and World Development Indicators of the World Bank.

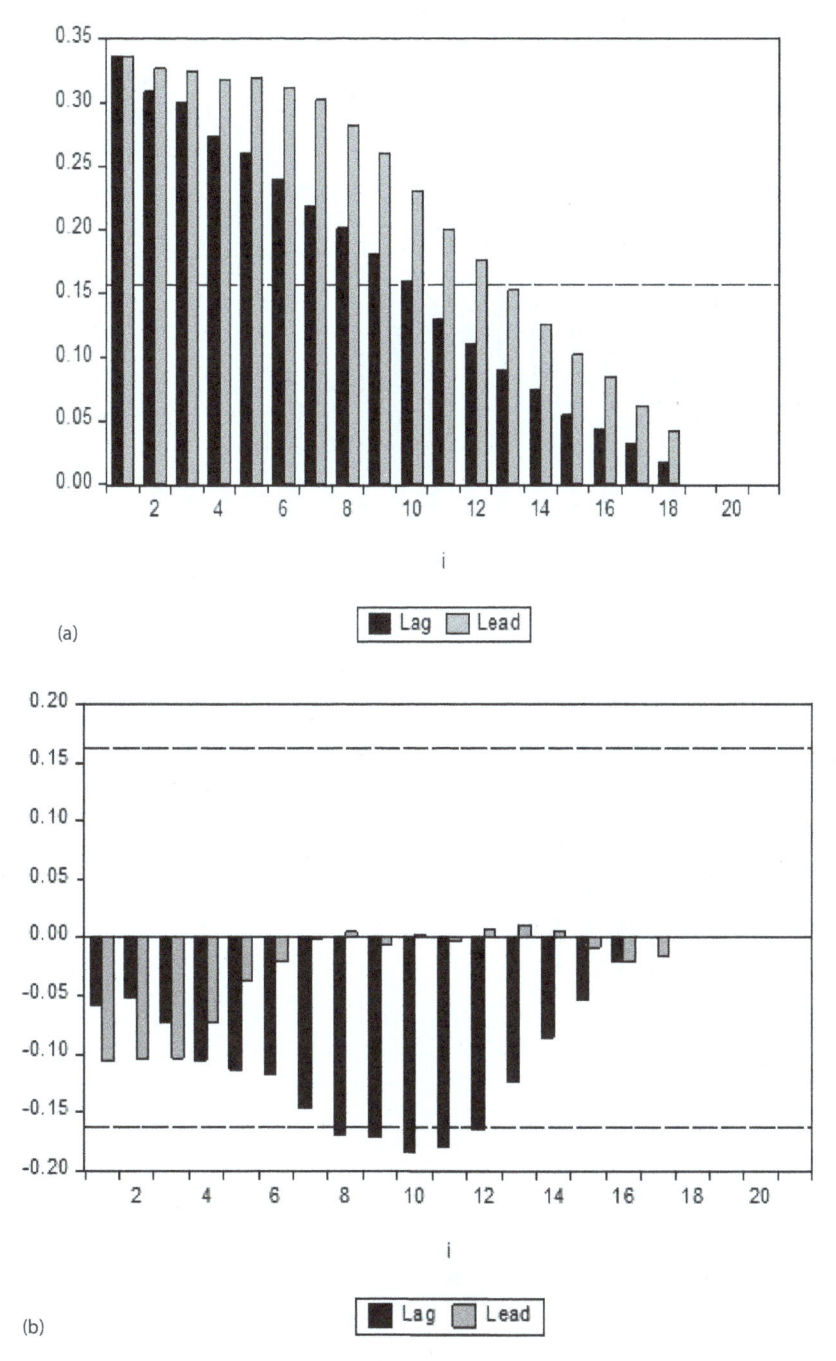

Figure 13.8   (a) Club 2, cross-correlations between the composite formal institutions index at t and the level of potential GDP per capita i periods before (lag, at $t - i$) and i periods ahead (lead, at $t + i$). (b) Club 2, cross-correlations between the composite formal institutions index at t and the growth rate of potential GDP per capita i periods before (lag, at $t - i$) and i periods ahead (lead, at $t + i$).

Sources: Own calculations. Data from the WGI of the World Bank, AMECO and World Development Indicators of the World Bank.

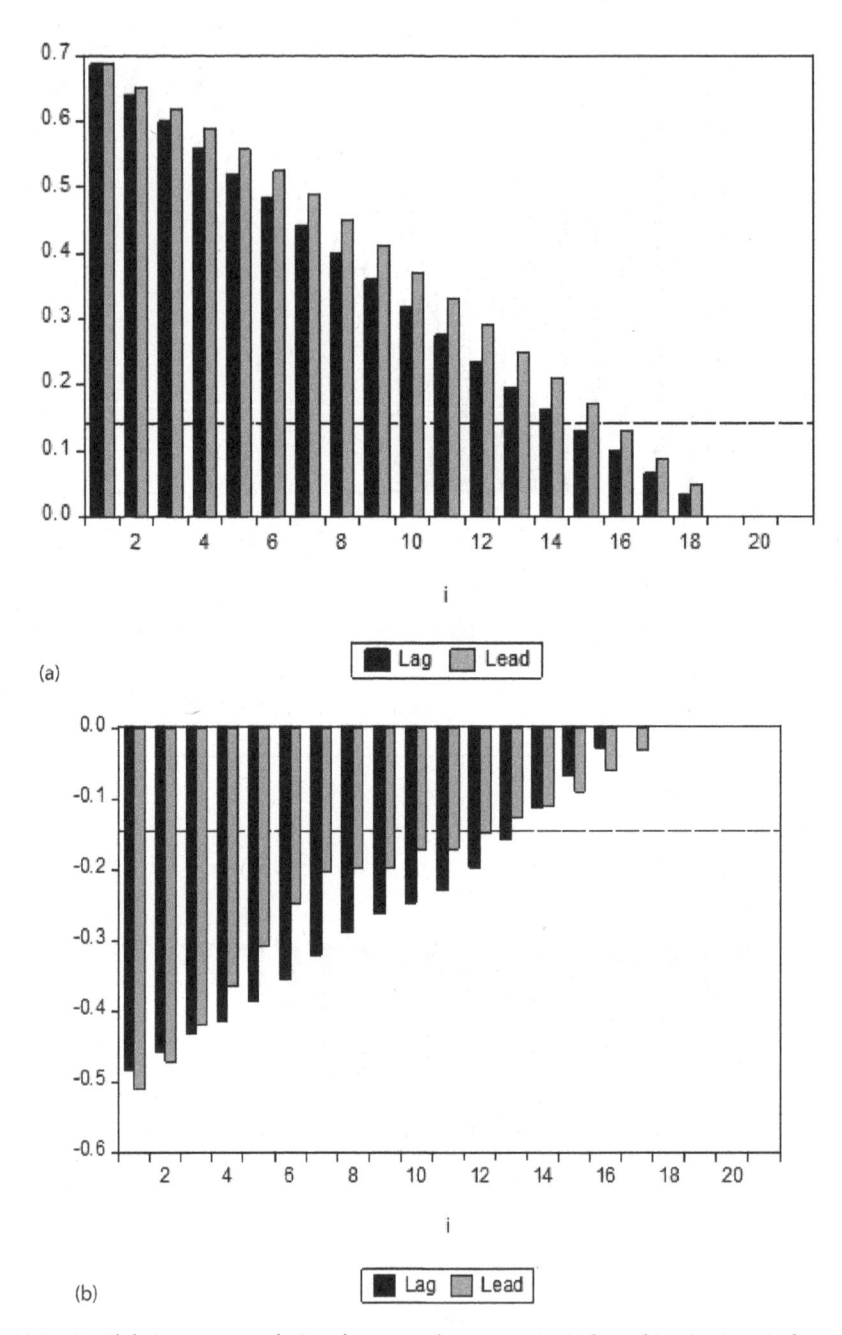

Figure 13.9 (a) Club 1, cross-correlations between the composite informal institutions index at t and the level of potential GDP per capita i periods before (lag, at $t - i$) and i periods ahead (lead, at $t + i$). (b) Club 1, cross-correlations between the composite informal institutions index at t and the growth rate of potential GDP per capita i periods before (lag, at $t - i$) and i periods ahead (lead, at $t + i$).

Sources: Own calculations. Data from the WGI of the World Bank, AMECO and World Development Indicators of the World Bank.

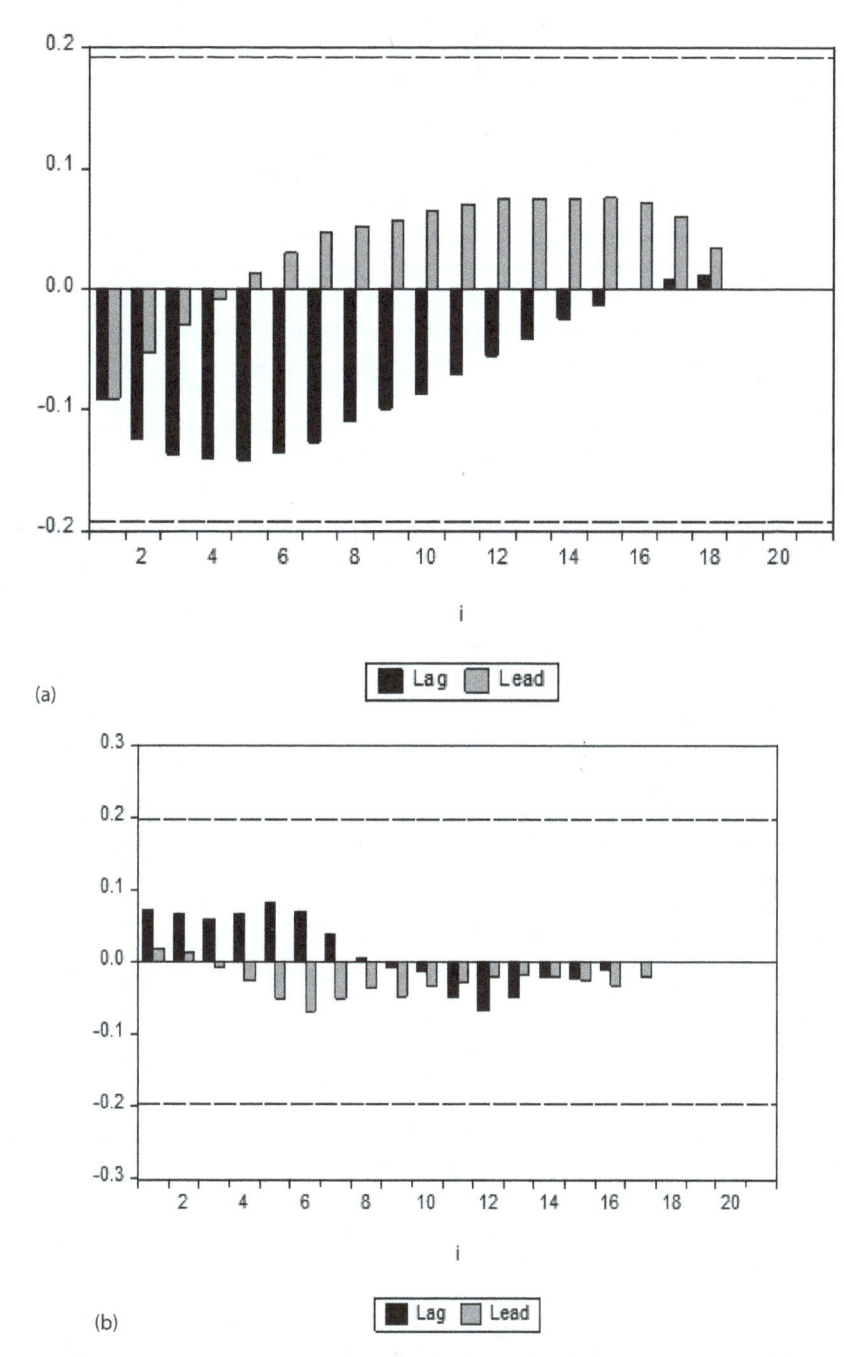

Figure 13.10 (a) Club 2, cross-correlations between the composite informal institutions index at *t* and the level of potential GDP per capita *i* periods before (lag, at *t − i*) and *i* periods ahead (lead, at *t + i*). (b) Club 2, cross-correlations between the composite informal institutions index at *t* and the growth rate of potential GDP per capita *i* periods before (lag, at *t − i*) and *i* periods ahead (lead, at *t + i*).

Sources: Own calculations. Data from the WGI of the World Bank, AMECO and World Development Indicators of the World Bank.

institutional variable being a better leading indicator of the future potential output than the other way around is stronger, both in terms of absolute difference between the leads and lags cross-correlation and in terms of relative difference with respect to the order of magnitude of these cross-correlations. So, it seems that in Club 2, made of countries with, in general, a lower potential output and lower quality of institutions than most countries of Club 1, improvements in institutional quality might be more specifically helpful for a better welfare in the future than the other way around. In Figure 13.8b, the cross-correlations between the institutional indicator and the rate of growth of the potential output are again negative, although they are small and globally nonsignificant, with some concrete exceptions for the lag cross-correlations. This gives some support to the idea that the institutional convergence, which defines this club, is not as much associated with economic convergence in the long run as in Club 1.

Let us now examine the case of the *informal* institutions' indicator. Concerning Club 1, what Figure 13.9a and b indicates is fundamentally similar to what occurs with the corresponding Club 1 of the formal institutions' indicator: strong and slowly decaying cross-correlations between the indicator and the leads and lags of the level of potential output, with symptoms that the institutional indicator is more of a leading indicator of the potential output than the other way around; significantly negative and slowly decaying cross-correlations when the rate of growth of the potential output is concerned, reflecting therefore the convergence process in potential GDP of worse positioned countries toward better positioned ones.

However, in terms of informal institutions and as far as Club 2 is concerned, the cross-correlations differ drastically from all preceding cases. As shown in Figures 13.10a and 13.10b none of the cross-correlations in this case are significantly different from zero, neither for the lags nor for the leads. According to this, in this convergence club, there is a total disconnection between the quality of informal institutions and the potential output at past or future values. One possible explanation is that the period is too short to unravel the effect of informal institutional quality on long-term economic performance in this group of countries, so that informal institutions mainly affect short-term economic behavior.

The heterogeneity in both institutions and economic performance has important policy implications for the design and future prospects of EMU, which we analyze in the following section.

13.4 Policy implications

Our results show that within the EA, there are two levels of (very slow) convergence in each indicator of institutional quality – formal and informal – which may be associated with different long-term equilibria in potential GDP per capita. This diversity of long-term equilibria for the variables involved, and its likely consequences for the sustainability and survival of the Eurozone, has given rise to two theoretical positions as far as economic policies in the EU and EA are concerned.

On the one hand, some scholars, such as Glawe and Wagner (2021b), suggest that heterogeneity in institutions within the EU is a danger because it implies diversity of national preferences concerning institutional and economic models, which accentuates the economic imbalances between the core (mainly Club 1) and the periphery (mainly Club 2) of the EU, and the EA. In their opinion, the situation is aggravated by the unanimity rule that hinders agreements at the community level, and by the possibility of bail out that discourages reforms within each country. The solution proposed by these authors is a multi-speed Europe with two main groups: a group of countries willing to undertake the necessary reforms, composed approximately by the countries of the core (grossly Club 1), and other group of states that wish to remain in the EU/EA but progressing more slowly. It is important to bear in mind that, under this reasoning, the institutional and economic benchmark for the two groups of countries is the model prevailing in Club 1.

However, as argued by Casagrande and Dallago (2021), this convergence toward a single liberal economic model may not happen and it is not sure it can be desirable. As these authors argue, countries can achieve similar economic results in terms of sustainability, efficiency and stability based on their own and diverse institutional frameworks. They build a European reference framework (European benchmark) and apply a score methodology to measure the distance of each country to the frontier in a multitude of institutional pillars and sub-pillars. Note that this approach proposes a shared and measurable reference, drawn from the objectives expressed in the European Treaties, instead of an economic and institutional model specific of a country or group of countries.

Our results and possible prescriptions are in line with the coexistence of idiosyncratic institutions highlighted by Casagrande and Dallago (2021). In this work, we show that in the EA there are two institutional clubs in each of the two composite indicators we have studied, and from this, we deduce that the countries on the periphery of the EA (Club 2) should strive to improve the quality of their institutions, without necessarily adapting their economic and institutional frameworks to particular models of other countries. Improving their idiosyncratic institutions while, at the same time, applying reforms to increase their potential GDP is a way for these countries to overcome the limits of Club 2 and become part of a superior, and in the future potentially single, European club within the EA. The countries of Club 1 also need to undertake institutional reforms to approach the shared European benchmark. Our analysis indicates that, in countries of Club 2, the institutional improvement efforts must be particularly intense in institutions of an informal nature.

13.5 Concluding remarks

In this work, we have investigated the convergence in institutional quality among the countries of the EA, and the extent to which the characteristics of this convergence process interact with the achievement of similar levels of potential output per capita in the long run. We have used two composite institutional indicators, one for formal institutions and another for informal ones, both derived from the six Worldwide Governance Indicators elaborated by the World Bank for the years after the creation of the euro.

Applying the methodology of Phillips and Sul (2007, 2009), we find that there is no global institutional convergence – in none of the composite indicators – in the EA as a whole. We detect, instead, two convergence clubs for each composite indicator, characterized by a very low convergence speed and geographical polarization: countries with better quality institutions (Club 1) are located in the north and west of the EA, whereas the lower quality ones (Club 2) are found in the east and south of EMU. Moreover, some countries seem caught in traps of low institutional quality, since they are diverging more and more from the rest of the members of the Eurozone. The situation is especially worrying for Greece and Italy in formal institutions, and for Greece and Portugal in the case of informal institutions. These results indicate that the countries of the EA have not taken advantage of their euro adoption to improve their institutions and bring them closer to shared European standards.

Interestingly, within each club, national improvements in the institutional quality are associated with increases in the potential GDP per capita following a process of potential GDP convergence. This regularity occurs in Club 1 for each institutional indicator, and to a lesser extent in Club 2 for formal institutional quality, but not for informal institutions. We also detect that when association between potential GDP and institutional quality takes place, there is some evidence that the latter anticipates the former. The main implication is that the members of Club 2 have to make significant efforts to improve the quality of their institutions, while implementing reforms conducive to higher potential GDP, as a way to raise the level of their long-term economic and societal well-being. It is true that this also requires a change of EU institutions and policies, since the present ones create asymmetric effects to the disadvantage of Club 2 countries, as argued, for instance, by Dallago (2016). If successful, these efforts would contribute to create a unique club in the euro zone with a higher level of GDP per capita, which is one of the main objectives of the European treaties. Efforts are even more pressing and justified in the case of informal institutions.

The efforts required by the members of Club 2 do not mean that the core countries (Club 1) do not have duties to do at the institutional level. Although they are part of a superior club, their institutions have many aspects to improve that should be borne in mind. Even with an aggregate analysis like ours, we have shown that in formal institutions the situation of this club worsened after 2015. We also saw that although in informal institutions the position of the club has been improving, several individual and important countries of this club worsened. Descending to the details, Casagrande and Dallago (2021) find notable deficiencies in social development and social efficiency in the northern countries, with deteriorating trajectories after 2007, in addition to low level of solidarity and self-destructing tendencies.

Although corrective actions are to be done mainly at the level of each country, it is also appropriate to design European incentive-based mechanisms. For instance, one proposal by Papaioannou (2016) and Beyaert et al. (2019) is that part of the European funds, established in regular European budgets, be conditional on the implementation of well-defined institutional reforms in the countries with lower institutional performance. The countries of Club 1 must also correct their institutional deficiencies, and the European institutions improve the symmetry in the macroeconomic adjustments that until now have harmed the peripheral countries of the Eurozone. Well-defined incentives designed at the European level are, indeed, necessary to reach and enhance the overall institutional, economic and therefore societal well-being that will guarantee a cohesive Europe.

Notes

1 Mongelli (2008) provides a comprehensive analysis of the properties of the OCA theory and the relationships of this theory with the monetary integration process in Europe.

2 The content of each institutional variable, as described by the World Bank is as follows:

Political stability and absence of violence/terrorism: Political stability and absence of violence/terrorism measure perceptions of the likelihood of political instability and/or politically motivated violence, including terrorism.

Rule of law: Reflects perceptions of the extent to which agents have confidence in and abide by the rules of society, and in particular the quality of contract enforcement, property rights, the police and the courts, as well as the likelihood of crime and violence.

Regulatory quality: Reflects perceptions of the ability of the government to formulate and implement sound policies and regulations that permit and promote private sector development.

Voice and accountability: Reflect perceptions of the extent to which a country's citizens are able to participate in selecting their government, as well as freedom of expression, freedom of association and a free media.

Government effectiveness: Reflects perceptions of the quality of public services, the quality of the civil service and the degree of its independence from political pressures, the quality of policy formulation and implementation and the credibility of the government's commitment to such policies.

Control of corruption: Reflects perceptions of the extent to which public power is exercised for private gain, including both petty and grand forms of corruption, as well as "capture" of the state by elites and private interests.

3 Potential GDP comes from: AMECO (https://ec.europa.eu/info/business-economy-euro/ indicators-statistics/economic-databases/macro-economic-database-ameco/ameco-database_en). Potential GDP per capita has been obtained by dividing potential GDP by total population of the corresponding country obtained from the World Development Indicators of the World Bank.

References

Acemoglu, D., Gallego, F. A. and Robinson, J. A. (2014). Institutions, human capital, and development. *Annual Review of Economics*, 6(1), 875–912.

Altman, M. (2009). A behavioral-institutional model of endogenous growth and induced technical change. *Journal of Economic Issues*, 43(3), 685–714.

Arestis, P., Bárcena-Martín, E. and Pérez-Moreno, S. (2018). Differences in institutional quality across euro area countries: Which factors contribute most to inequality? *Panoeconomicus*, 65(3), 363–379.

Beyaert, A., García-Solanes, J. and López-Gómez, L. (2019). Do institutions of the euro area converge? *Economic Systems*, 43(3), 1–18.

Casagrande, S. and Dallago, B. (2021). Benchmarking institutional variety in the Eurozone: An empirical investigation. *Economic Systems*, 45(2021), 100838.

Committee for the Study of Economic and Monetary Union. (1988). Rapport on economic and monetary union in the European Community, European Commission.

Dallago, B. (2016). *One Currency, Two Europe*. Singapore: World Scientific Publishing Co.

Díaz del Hoyo, J.L., Dorrucci, E., Heinz, F.F. and Muzicarova, S. (2017). Real convergence in the euro area: A long-term perspective, European Central Bank, Occasional Paper Series, no. 203/ December.

Easterly, W. and Levine, R. (2002). It's not factor accumulation: Stylized facts and growth models. *Central Bank of Chile working paper*, (6), 61–114.

Emerson, M., Gros, D., Italianer, A., Pisani-Ferry, J. and Reichenbach, H. (1992). *One Market, One Money: An Evaluation of the Potential Benefits and Costs of Forming an Economic and Monetary Union*. Oxford: Oxford University Press.

Frankel, J.A. and Rose, A.K. (1998). The endogeneity of the optimum currency area criteria. *Economic Journal*, 108(449), 1009–1025.

García Solanes, J., Beyaert, A. and López-Gómez, L. (2021). Clubes de convergencia institucional en la zona del euro. *Papeles de Economía Española*, 168, 48–63.

Glawe, L. and Wagner, H. (2019). The deep determinants of economic development in China—A provincial perspective. *Journal of the Asia Pacific Economy*, 24(4), 484–514.

Glawe, L. and Wagner, H. (2021a). Convergence, divergence, or multiple steady states? New evidence on the institutional development within the European Union. *Journal of Comparative Economics*, 49(3), 860–884.

Glawe, L. and Wagner, H. (2021b). Divergence tendencies in the European integration process: A danger for the sustainability of the E(M)U? *Journal of Risk Financial Management*, 14(3), 104. Available at https://doi.org/103390/jrfm14030104.

Hall, R.E. and Jones, C.I. (1999). Why do some countries produce so much more output per worker than others? *Quarterly Journal of Economics*, 114(1), 83–116.

Kar, S., Roy, A. and Sen, K. (2019). The double trap: Institutions and economic development. *Economic Modelling*, 76, 243–259.

Kaufmann, D., Kraay, A. and Mastruzzi, M. (2010). The worldwide governance indicators: Methodology and analytical issues. *World Bank policy research working paper* (5430).

Mongelli, F.P. (2008). European economic and monetary integration and the optimum currency area theory, *European Economy*, Economic Papers 302/February.

North, D.C. (1990). *Institutions, Institutional Change and Economic Performance*. 28th ed. Cambridge: Cambridge University Press.

OECD. (2008). *Handbook on Constructing Composite Indicators. Methodology and User Guide*. http:// composite-indicators.jrc.ec.europa.eu.

Papaioannou, E. (2016). Needed: A European Institutional Union. *Vox, CEPR's Policy Portal*, 12 February, 1–11.

Pérez-Moreno, S., Bárcena-Martín, E. and Ritzen, J. (2020). Institutional quality in the Euro area countries: Any evidence of convergence? *Journal of Contemporary European Studies*, 28(3), 387–402.

Phillips, P.C. and Sul, D. (2007). Transition modeling and econometric convergence tests. *Econometrica*, 75(6), 1771–1855.

Phillips, P.C. and Sul, D. (2009). Economic transition and growth. *Journal of Applied Econometrics*, 24(7), 1153–1185.

Rodrik, D., Subramanian, A. and Trebbi, F. (2004). Institutions rule: The primacy of institutions over geography and integration in economic development. *Journal of Economic Growth*, 9(2), 131–165.

Schönfelder, N. and Wagner, H. (2016). Impact of European integration on institutional development. *Journal of Economic Integration*, 31(3), 472–530.

Schönfelder, N. and Wagner, H. (2019). Institutional convergence in Europe. *Economics: The Open-Access, Open-Assessment E-Journal*, 13(2019–3), 1–23.

Von Lyncker, K. and Thoennessen, R. (2017). Regional club convergence in the EU: Evidence from a panel data analysis. *Empirical Economics*, 52(2), 525–553.

Zhao, L., Yujing, C. and Tianruo, G. (2020). Economic growth with endogenous economic institutions. *Macroeconomic Dynamics*, 24(4), 920–934.

Appendix: log-*t* convergence tests

The starting model of the procedure is the one-factor factorial model for the variable X_{it} under study, which in our case is a specific indicator of institutional quality of country i $(i = 1,..., N)$ at time o t $(t = 1,..., T)$:

$$X_{it} = \alpha_i \mu_t + \varepsilon_{it}:$$

where α_i is the idiosyncratic systematic component, specific to country i and capturing short-term behavior, while μ_t is the factor common to all countries and captures long-term behavior; ε_{it} is the error term. In this model, α_i measures the idiosyncratic distance between the common factor and the systematic part of X_{it}. The model thus aims to capture the evolution of the individual indicator X_{it} with respect to the common factor via its two idiosyncratic elements: the systematic element α_i and the random element ε_{it}.

To make it suitable for convergence analysis, Phillips and Sul (2007) extend this model in two directions. On the one hand, they allow the idiosyncratic systematic element to evolve over time, so that α_i becomes α_{it}. On the other hand, they attach to this element a random component so that it absorbs the error ε_{it}. In this way, the model is open to the possibility that the distance of country i to the common factor will reduce and adopt a convergence behavior toward the common factor over time.

With these modifications, the initial model transforms into the following one:

$$X_{it} = \alpha_{it}\mu_t + \varepsilon_{it} = \left(\alpha_{it} + \frac{\varepsilon_{it}}{\mu_t} \right)\mu_t = \beta_{it}\mu_t \tag{A.1}$$

According to model (A.1), the term β_{it} would give us the random and time-varying distance of country i from the common factor. Therefore, if β_{it} tends over time to the same constant for all the countries in the panel, i.e. $\forall i$, we would say that these countries converge. The model, however, contains more unknowns than data in the panel, since neither β_{it} nor μ_t are observable. To circumvent this obstacle, Phillips and Sul (2007) propose to use what they call the "relative transition path" reflected in the evolution over time of the "relative transition coefficient" defined as follows:

$$h_{it} = \frac{X_{it}}{N^{-1}\Sigma_{i=1}^{N} X_{it}} = \frac{\beta_{it}}{N^{-1}\Sigma_{i=1}^{N} \beta_{it}} \qquad (A.2)$$

Each h_{it} provides the relative distance of each country from a common mean. Thus, convergence of countries to their common mean is detected if $h_{it} \to 1$ for all i. Alternatively, if there is convergence, the "cross-section" variance of these h_{it}, H_t, decreases over time:

$$H_t = \frac{1}{N} \sum_{i=1}^{N} (h_{it} - 1)^2 \to 0, \; t \to \infty \qquad (A.3)$$

However, the fact that the cross-section variance decreases over time does not in itself imply that there is global convergence between the N countries. It could indeed be the case that this variance decreases because there are two or more subgroups of countries that converge with each other (two or more convergence clubs), without the two subgroups moving closer together over time (global divergence).

To design an operational procedure to test for convergence to take into account the possible existence of convergence subgroups, it is necessary to assume a specific structure for the loading coefficients β_{it}. Phillips and Sul (2007) opt for the semi-parametric specification of the following decay model:

$$\beta_{it} = \beta_i + \frac{\sigma_i \epsilon_{it}}{L(t) t^b} \qquad (A.4)$$

where β_i is the value that β_{it} would reach in the long run, σ_i is an idiosyncratic scaling parameter and $L(t)$ is a slow function of time t as, for example, the logarithmic function log (t). Finally, b is the rate at which panel heterogeneity decays. Not that the value that b takes has an implication on the type of convergence process. It is obvious that $b < 0$ implies the absence of convergence, whereas $b > 0$ implies convergence, and the larger the b, the higher the speed of convergence. More concretely, $b \geq 1$ implies absolute convergence (convergence in level), whereas $b < 1$ can be interpreted as conditional convergence or convergence in growth rates. By the same token, $b = 0$ is also compatible with convergence but would reflect a slow convergence process that would occur only at the speed of $1/L(t)$.

In this framework, the null hypothesis for detecting convergence will therefore be:

$$H_0 : \beta_i = \beta \; \forall \; i \text{ and } b \geq 0$$

The alternative hypothesis can take on of two forms:

$$H_A : \begin{array}{l} 1. \; \beta_i \neq \beta \; \forall \; i \; or \; b < 0 \\ 2. \; \beta_i \neq \beta \text{ for some } i, \text{ and } b \geq 0 \end{array}$$

If we cannot reject the null hypothesis, there is global convergence for all panel members. If the one accepted is alternative hypothesis 1, we would detect absolute divergence and if, on the contrary, the one accepted is alternative hypothesis 2 then we would detect the existence of convergence clubs. The concrete value of b in each club would inform us about the speed and type of convergence.

Phillips and Sul (2007) show in detail that Equations (A.1)–(A.4) lead to the following regression model, which allows us to test for convergence in an operational way:

$$\left[\log(H_1/H_t) - 2\log\big(\log(t+1)\big)\right] = \hat{p} + \hat{q}\log(t) + \hat{u}_t \qquad (A.5)$$

$$\text{for } t = [rT], [rT]+1,\ldots, T$$

where the fitted coefficient of log(t) is $\hat{q} = 2\hat{b}$, where $\hat{b}$ is the estimated value of the decay parameter in (A.4). Note that this estimate starts at $t = [rT]$, i.e. the integer part of rT, $0 < r < 1$. The authors recommend using $r = 0.3$, which is the value we employ. Equation (A.5) is called the "*log(t) regression model*" because it is the function we use in the estimation.

The procedure consists of contrasting in (A.5) $H_0 : b \geq 0$, using for this purpose the t-statistic – robust to heteroscedasticity and autocorrelation – of the coefficient $\hat{q}$ in a left one-sided test. In other words, we calculate the $t_{\hat{q}}$ statistic obtained with a heteroskedasticity- and autocorrelation-consistent (HAC) estimate of the standard deviation of $\hat{q}$, which is called the "*log-t statistic*" and if $t_{\hat{q}} < -1.65$ then the null hypothesis of convergence is rejected at the 5% significance level. On the opposite, if it is not rejected, we conclude that there is overall convergence among all group members at the same 5% level.

If we cannot accept the null hypothesis of absolute convergence, it is necessary to detect whether convergence clubs exist. For this purpose, we use a clustering algorithm developed by Phillips and Sul (2007, 2009), which consists of four stages.

Stage 1: the countries are or.dered in decreasing order of the value of X_{it}, $t = T$, i.e. according to the value of the countries' indicator at the last date of the sample.

Stage 2: the first convergence club with the highest statistical evidence of convergence is sought. To identify it, the first two countries from the list of stage 1 are selected and checked to see if they converge with each other. If so, the country in third position is added to the convergence testing, and if so, this country is added to the group. We proceed in this way until we arrive at an extended subgroup for which convergence is rejected. Then the values of the values of the *log-t* statistics of all the convergent subgroups are compared to identify the first convergence club, or "central convergence club", as the subgroup with the highest *log-t* statistic. If the first two countries fail the convergence test, country 1 is eliminated from the group and the process just described is repeated by starting it with the country initially situated in second position.

Stage 3: the remaining countries are added one at a time to the central club and the *log-t* test is computed on the enlarged group made of the central club and the country under study, and all countries for which the $t_{\hat{q}}$ of the enlarged group is greater than a certain c are pooled in a subgroup. Then if a *log-test* applied on the central convergence club combined with the subgroup provides a value for $t_{\hat{q}} > -1.65$, all units of the subgroup are added to the central convergence club. If not, the critical value c is increased, and the procedure is repeated.

Stage 4: in this last stage, a group is formed with the countries that have been left out of the central club and we apply the *log-t* test to check whether they form another club; if it cannot be concluded that these countries form a second convergence club, then stages 1–3 are repeated to determine whether there are subgroups of convergence clubs within this group. If no subgroup is detected or some country is left out of the detected subgroups, we conclude that these countries left outside the convergence clubs diverge.

Once this process has been carried out and different convergence clubs have been detected, a merging process is carried out, because the number of convergence clubs detected in stages 1–4 depends on the value of c and a high value of c generates the possibility of over-estimating the number of convergence clubs. So, it is necessary to detect whether subgroups can be merged into new larger clubs; and once this is done and new larger convergence clubs have been identified, the group of countries initially detected as divergent might not diverge anymore with respect to the new clubs. So, a double set of corrections has to be carried out. For that purpose, we use the methodology developed by Von Lyncker and Thoennessen (2017) that consists of two algorithms. The first one is the club merging algorithm: if P convergence clubs have been initially identified, there exist (P-1) groups of adjacent clubs and a *log-t* test is applied on each. For a given group of adjacent clubs, its *log-t* test is compared to the critical value of -1.65 and to the value of the *log-t* test of the following group of adjacent clubs, to decide whether to merge or not this group into a new larger convergence club (see Von Lyncker and Thoennessen, 2017, p. 532 for details). The second algorithm is the merging algorithm for diverging countries. First of all, a *log t*-test is applied to all diverging countries in block and if the test is significant, the diverging countries form now their own convergence club and the algorithm stops. If not, a *log-t* test is applied to each diverging country combined with each convergence club at a time; if the highest value of the resulting $t_{\hat{q}}$ statistics of all the possible combinations is greater than -1.65, then the corresponding diverging country is added to the corresponding convergence club; as a result, the number of diverging countries is reduced by one and the merging algorithm of diverging countries is initiated again. The algorithm stops when there is no combination of convergence club-diverging countries with a $t_{\hat{q}}$ statistics greater than -1.65 and all countries left are truly diverging countries (see Von Lyncker and Thoennessen, 2017, p. 533 for more details).

As a final comment, it is worthwhile keeping in mind how to interpret the estimated value of q in case convergence is detected in our empirical analysis. Given that $\hat{q} = 2\hat{b}$, where $\hat{b}$ is the estimated value of the decay parameter in (A.4), and given the interpretation of the value of b as described below in Equation (A.4), we may say that:

- if $\hat{q}$ is significantly above 2, absolute convergence is detected between the converging units
- if $\hat{q}$ is significantly above 0 but not significantly above 2, conditional convergence is detected between the converging units
- if $\hat{q}$ is not significantly different from 0 but convergence is nevertheless detected by the log-*t* test, this convergence is very slow.

14
COMPARATIVE ECONOMIC STUDIES OF TRANSITION

Four Lessons from Analytical Reviews of the Literature

Satoshi Mizobata

INSTITUTE OF ECONOMIC RESEARCH, KYOTO UNIVERSITY, KYOTO, JAPAN

Ichiro Iwasaki

INSTITUTE OF ECONOMIC RESEARCH, HITOTSUBASHI UNIVERSITY, TOKYO, JAPAN

14.1 Introduction

Whether the starting point of the collapse of socialism should be November 1989, when the citizens of the united Germany demolished the Berlin Wall, or December 1991, when Mikhail Gorbachev resigned as president of the Soviet Union, is a matter for historians. Whichever date is adopted, the fact remains that the systemic transformation from the socialist planned economy to a capitalist market-oriented economy in Central and Eastern Europe (CEE) and the former Soviet Union (FSU) countries has been ongoing for a sufficiently long time for analysis. Throughout the past 30 years, economists around the world have investigated the reform experiences of the former socialist countries with great enthusiasm. The accumulation of research generated by these academic activities has had such an impact that it has led to the establishment of a new research field of so-called transition economics.

Today, transition economics has reached maturity. The topics covered by this study field are not limited to comparative economic systems, but include macroeconomics, microeconomics, international economics, public economics, labor economics, financial economics, industrial organization, development economics, and environmental economics. At the same time, however, some areas are quite unique to transition economics, and it is also true that research on these areas forms the core of this study domain.

In this chapter, we will digest the results of our quantitative reviews of the literature, focusing on four research objectives that have gained particular momentum in the field of transition economics, including: (1) the end-of-socialism debate; (2) the transition strategy debate; (3) the debate of path dependency of transition; and (4) the debate of corruption in transition economies. Then, we will discuss the policy implications of these four controversies as main lessons from the transition economics.

DOI: 10.4324/9781003144366-17

This chapter is organized as follows: In Section 14.2, we examine researchers' consideration of the factors that led to the failure of socialism. In Section 14.3, we show the overall structure of the transition strategy debate, in which researchers heatedly argued what kind of reform paths to adopt in order to create a market economy in CEE and FSU countries. In Section 14.4, we present the views of researchers who have discussed the degree of path dependence of the transition to a market economy. In Section 14.5, we show how researchers discuss the *pros* and *cons* of corruption in transition economies. And finally, in Section 14.6, we briefly discuss four lessons learned from the study of transition economies as concluding remarks.

14.2 Why did socialism fail?

To understand the process of systemic transformation from the socialist planned economy to a capitalist market economy, it is necessary to understand the starting point and/or initial conditions. There is no doubt that the answer to the question, "Why did socialism fail?", captures an important part, though not all, of it. Therefore, in this section, we will address this question.

To obtain a solution to this issue, Uegaki et al. (2018) adopted a political economy approach. This is because there is currently no way to find a study that squarely opposes the purely economic arguments of Ludwig von Mises and Friedrich Hayek, who proved that socialism (or communism) is impossible to manage economically, and there exists a firm consensus in the academic community that the so-called socialist calculation debate has already been settled (Boettke, 2001). Nevertheless, it is still of great significance for us to question why socialism failed at that time, whether there was any difference in the triggers of the failure between Russia and Eastern Europe, and what the specific aspects of the failure were, if the factors of the socialist failure were supposed to be layered from the essential to the circumstantial. In order to examine these aspects, we had to consider factors other than pure economic ones. Therefore, we attempted to examine the responses of researchers to the question as to why socialism failed through an analytical review of the related literature.

As a first step, referring to the monographs of leading scholars, we summarized the major factors of socialist failure according to the following eight themes: The first is "International Environment/Cold War/Militarization" that argues that the Soviet Union and Eastern Europe overexpanded their militaries during the Cold War, which became a burden on the economy and promoted its collapse. The second is the "Federalism/Ethnicity Problem" that touches on a narrative that various difficulties, including ethnic problems, were forced into a fabricated federal system, and the system finally collapsed as the contradictions erupted. The third is "Policy Failure" that includes an argument that, even if we basically accept the Mises-Hayek theory of the impossibility of a socialist economy, we still have to look carefully at the factors of policymaking to discover why the system failed at that time. The fourth is "Decline in the Marginal Productivity of the System". It acknowledges that the socialist system had great potential for promoting the industrialization of developing countries, but that the effect fades with the country's economic development, and, consequently, the advantages of socialism have been largely lost.

The fifth theme is "Lack of Innovation and Entrepreneurship" that argues that the socialist system did not promote innovation and did not foster entrepreneurship, thus making it unavoidable that the productive capacity of the national economy would stagnate in socialist countries, leading to their defeat in the global competition with capitalist countries. The sixth is "Political System," referring to the dictatorship of the Communist Party and the repression of liberty and freedom of the population by the secret police (and in some cases, detention and imprisonment) under it. The seventh is "Dysfunction of the Planned System/Soft Budget Constraints and Shortage/Monopoly of Property Rights" that is based on the Mises-Hayek theory of the impossibility of socialism, but the scope of the discussion is not limited to this. The eighth and final factor is "Priority on Heavy Industry/Stagnation of Living Standards/ Lack of Incentives". This argument contains two different features: The first is that the socialist system, for various reasons, inevitably inclined toward heavy industry; as a result, the supply of consumer goods to the population was virtually neglected, which led to a decline in people's willingness to work, which, in turn, resulted in a collapse of the socialist economy. The second is that, in socialist societies with restrictions on civil liberties, the authority forces the people to accept these restrictions, while at the same time, there was an implicit "social contract" between the two sides to guarantee a minimum standard of living, to include free medical care and full employment. However, under the international conditions of the diversification of consumption and informatization, citizens in socialist countries became greatly dissatisfied with their minimal lives under strong restrictions, and this movement caused social conflicts and chaos that led to the collapse of socialism.

Keeping the above arguments in mind, we next selected a total of 274 articles as the basic literature of the end-of-socialism debate from research works published between 1989 and 2017. Figure 14.1 shows the frequency distribution of these 274 articles by year of publication. As shown in the figure, the number of publications has been gradually decreasing over the years, but it is worth noting that researchers' attention to the issue of the end of socialism had not waned, even in 2017. Figure 14.2 summarizes our survey results of the basic literature on whether each of the eight major factors of socialist failure argued above is mentioned, and if so, how many factors are supported or rejected. In this regard, it should be noted that papers that do not mention any failure factors account for 29%, or 80 studies of the basic literature.

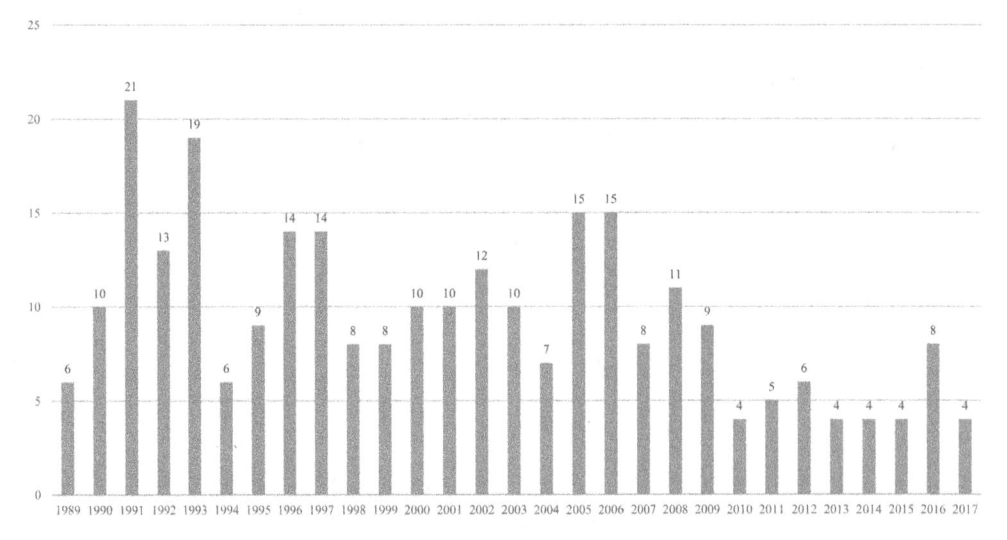

Figure 14.1 Frequency distribution of publication years of the basic literature of the end-of-socialism debate.

Source: Uegaki et al. (2018, Figure 1.2, p. 43).

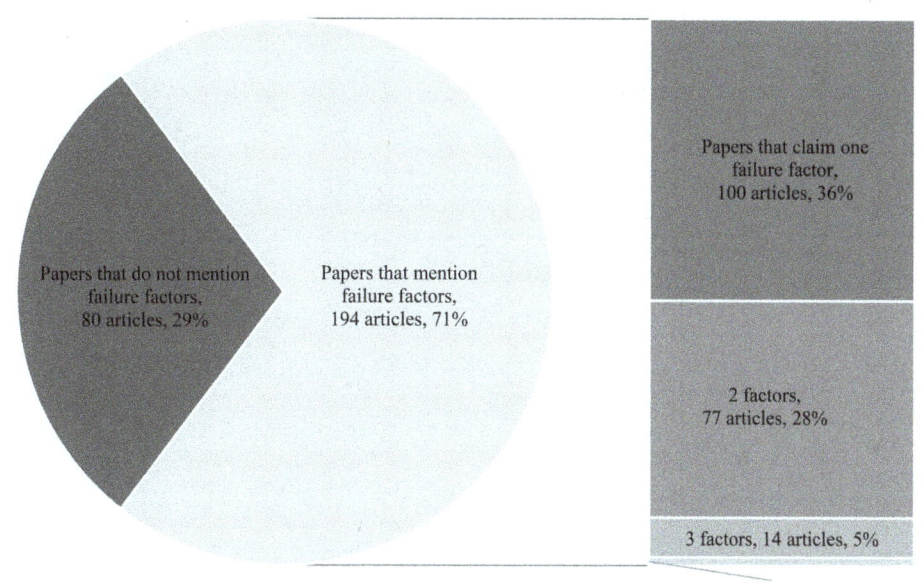

Figure 14.2   Breakdown of the basic literature by number of claims for socialist failure factors.

Source: Uegaki et al. (2018, Figure 1.3, p. 43).

This does not mean that these 80 publications discuss factors other than the above eight elements. Rather, they argue nothing about the causes of socialist failure.

Figure 14.3 shows the breakdown of factors of socialist failure asserted by the authors of the remaining 194 papers. The total does not add up to 194 because a single paper may mention more than one factor, as indicated in the right band graph of Figure 14.2. As Figure 14.3 shows, the seventh factor of "Dysfunction of the Planned System/Soft Budget Constraints and Shortage/Monopoly of Property Rights" is claimed as the main cause of the collapse of socialism by the largest number of references (108 of 194), followed by the third factor of "Policy Failure". However, the character of these two arguments is quite different, because the former is rooted in the nature of the socialist economic system and argues that the system was doomed to fail sooner or later, while the latter implies that the socialist economic system might have survived longer if appropriate policies had been instituted. This dichotomy can be applied to other factors as well. In other words, the fifth, sixth, and eighth factors share the same characteristics of the seventh factor, while the first, second, and fourth factors have characteristics resembling the third factor. Therefore, we named the former "the inevitability theory" of socialist failure and the latter "the repentance theory," and then, we tried to characterize the overall tendencies of the 194 papers. More specifically, the number of inevitable and repentance factors mentioned by a particular article is called the "intensiveness of inevitability" and the "intensiveness of repentance," respectively. In addition to these two indices, we defined the "degree of repentance" of each article as the index calculated by the following formula:

Degree of repentance
 = intensiveness of repentance (number of repentance factors mentioned)
  − intensiveness of inevitability (number of inevitable factors mentioned)

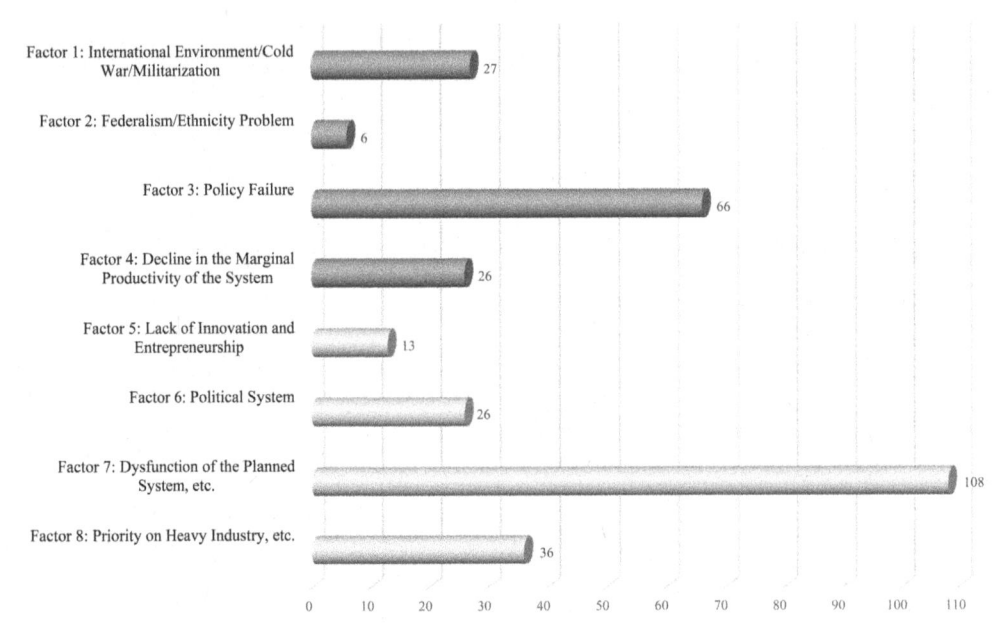

Figure 14.3 Number of publications by factor of socialist failure.

Source: Uegaki et al. (2018, Figure 1.4, p. 44).

Note: One hundred ninety-four papers that mention socialist failure factors are covered.

For instance, if a paper claims that the first, fourth, sixth, and seventh factors caused the collapse of the socialist economy, then the repentance degree of the paper would be 1, and the inevitability degree would be 3, resulting in a degree of repentance of −2. Figure 14.4 shows the results of classifying the 194 articles using this method. It is clear from the results based on the degree of repentance that the broad theoretical economic belief that socialism was doomed to fail influenced many researchers to assume that socialism would inevitably collapse. These findings imply that, as pointed out above, the so-called socialist calculation debate may have been settled in purely economic terms, but not in political economy terms.

Further, we examined the relationship between the debate attitude of each paper shown in Figure 14.4 and the literature attributes, consisting of the analytical angle, author attribute, and publication media attribute by cross tables and multivariate regression analysis. Here, we mention the following three points that represent particularly interesting results obtained from these statistical and econometrical analyses. First, there is a high probability that literature that actively and extensively argues for the factors of socialist failure is written by researchers who have a theoretical interest in the political situation in socialist countries and the state of socialist economies. Second, differences in the regions and major subjects of research are likely to have a significant effect on the decision-making process of researchers as to which of the prevailing theories of the causes of socialist failure to advocate. It is noteworthy from this perspective that studies that chose China and Russia/Soviet Union as their target country tend to emphasize the repentance theory of socialist failure, while the literature that chose Eastern Europe as its target region has a high probability of asserting the inevitability theory. Third, despite the qualitative differences in the indicators of repentance and inevitability, the distinction among China, Russia/Soviet Union, and Eastern Europe as target areas has a decisive influence on these indicators.

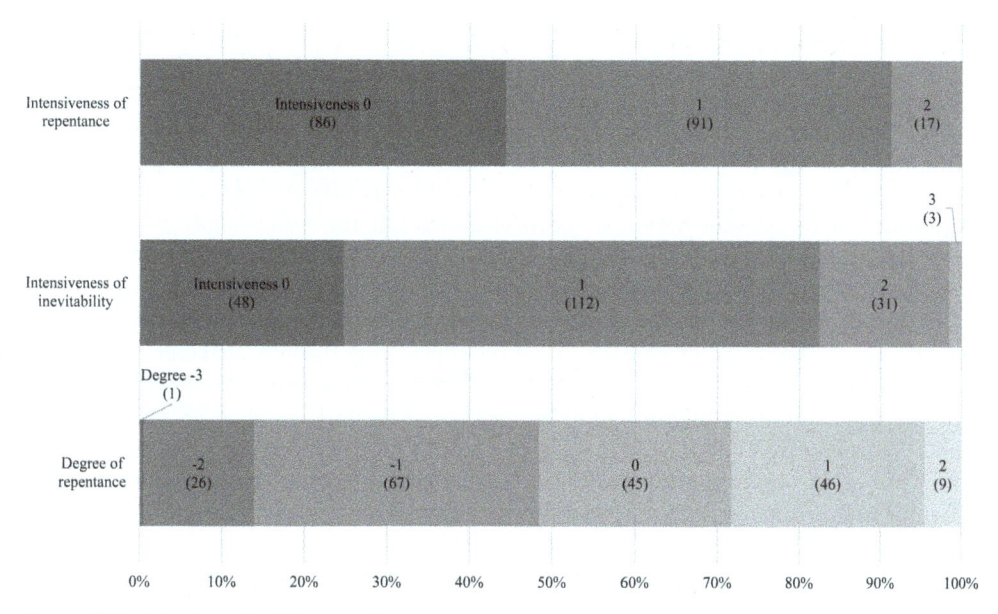

Figure 14.4 Number of publications by intensiveness of inevitability, intensiveness of repentance, and degree of repentance.

Source: Uegaki et al. (2018, Figure 1.5, p. 45).

This figure classifies 194 papers that mention socialist failure factors in terms of the intensiveness of inevitability and the intensiveness and degree of repentance defined in the text. The number of relevant publications is in parentheses.

The above findings should not be interpreted to imply that because the literature on Russia and the Soviet Union tends to argue for the repentance theory, while the literature on Eastern Europe tends to argue for the inevitability theory, this directly reflects the history and reality of socialist failure in each region. In other words, it should not be concluded that the socialist system in Russia and the Soviet Union collapsed due to some accidental factors, while in Eastern Europe it collapsed due to factors inherent in the system. We stress, in this regard, that the process of socialist failure in Russia and the Soviet Union was much more complicated than that in Eastern Europe. Therefore, it is possible that researchers who study Russia and the Soviet Union are forced to pay more attention to various coincidental factors, and, as a result, they tend to develop arguments that simply do not agree with the inevitability theory. Nevertheless, more insights are required to grasp the relationship between the historical facts and the attitude of researchers about the causes of socialist failure. The debate still contains serious research issues that need to be explored in depth.

14.3 Radicalism or gradualism: Which is supported as a transition strategy?

Of all the controversies in economics, few have been as hotly contested as the "transition strategy debate" over what kind of reform track CEE and FSU countries should adopt toward the creation of a capitalist market economy. The transition strategy debate in the late 1980s and early 1990s was very heated indeed because the debate was about deciding the road map; hence, the argument regarding this subject involved the supremacy of theoretical schools and many leading economists and spread beyond the boundaries of the academic world. A dozen years later, transition economics was established as a major study area of modern economics.

The pioneering transition strategy debate has been one of the most important subjects in this research field.

The transition strategy debate has developed as an argument between two conflicting reform philosophies, radicalism, and gradualism. Here, *radicalism* denotes a policy philosophy that demands prompt and parallel implementations of the reform packages advocated by the Washington Consensus. It is also called *shock therapy* or *the big-bang approach*, reflecting the content of its relevant policy recommendations. On the other hand, *gradualism* is a collective term antithetical to radicalism; thus, the reform measures recommended by its advocates are extremely varied. As compared to radicalists, gradualists show a certain congruity in their debate attitude toward a transition strategy, approving a milder policy implementation process in terms of time speed and/or emphasizing theoretical and practical needs to promote structural reforms in a reasonable policy sequence. Some researchers point out that, among transition economies, some nations have followed a unique reform track that cannot be categorized either as radicalism or gradualism; some skeptics even question the *raison d'etre* of the transition strategy debate itself. However, they are in a minority, and it is indisputable that the overwhelming majority of people who have participated in the debate so far have stated their opinions, focusing on the validity and relevance of the two contrasting reform philosophies. Therefore, Iwasaki and Suzuki (2016, 2020) attempted to conduct an analytical review of the existing literature in order to clarify whether researchers really give more support to radicalism or gradualism.

Figure 14.5 shows our search results of the literature published during the 28 years from 1989 to 2016 using EconLit, an electronic academic literature database. In the figure, "searched literature" refers to the research works found by the mechanical search, while "basic literature" denotes the collection of papers selected for analytical review. As shown in the figure, the debate on transition strategy had become substantially active immediately after the breakdown of the Soviet Union in late 1991; it also had gathered remarkable momentum in 1994, five years after the fall of the Berlin Wall; in 1996, five years after the downfall of the Soviet

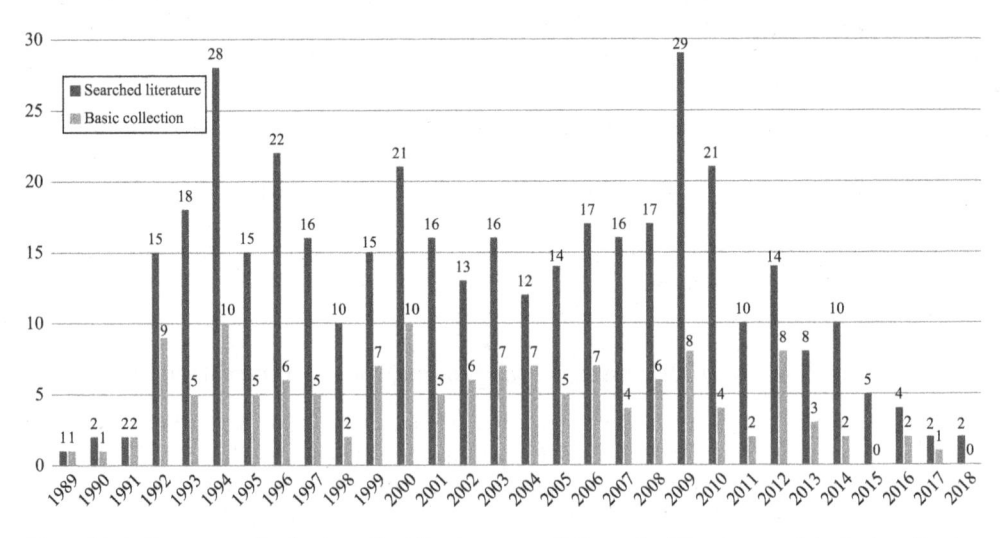

Figure 14.5 Frequency distribution of publication years of all searched literature and the basic collection of the transition strategy debate.

Source: Iwasaki and Suzuki (2020, Figure 2.1, p. 28).

Union; in 2000, the end of the century; and in the two years between 2009 and 2010, which marked the 20th anniversary of the demise of the Communist Bloc and the international crisis. This suggests that the transition strategy debate was strongly inspired by the exit of the Soviet Union from world history and that researchers have continually revived their interest in this issue at each historical milestone.

Next, we boldly classified the debate attitudes of each paper of the basic literature from the following three perspectives: time speed, policy sequence, and institution. The overall structure of the transition strategy debate that emerged from this classification process is illustrated as a tree diagram in Figure 14.6. In this figure, *radicalism* denotes a group of researchers who share the idea that big bang and speedy implementations of policy packages are indispensable for establishing a market economy in the former socialist economies. The underlying logic of this idea is that economic transitions must be carried forward as quickly as possible and, consequently, a single round of expeditious execution of necessary reform measures is essential. Despite the consistency of its policy recommendations, however, the radicalists can be divided into two research groups. One is the *universal radicalism* group that maintains that the best option for the CEE and FSU countries should be radicalism, irrespective of differences in the degree of perfection in the planned system and other historical preconditions. The second is the *conditional radicalism* group that affirms that implementing a transition strategy based on radicalism is a better option than gradualism as long as a series of initial conditions antecedent to reforms, such as the government's adequate policy capability and the citizens' sufficient understanding and tolerance of capitalism, is minimally met.

Meanwhile, *gradualism* advocates have a unified voice against the radicalists in criticizing radicalism's "speed-before-quality," "haphazard," and "unrealistic" approach. Moreover,

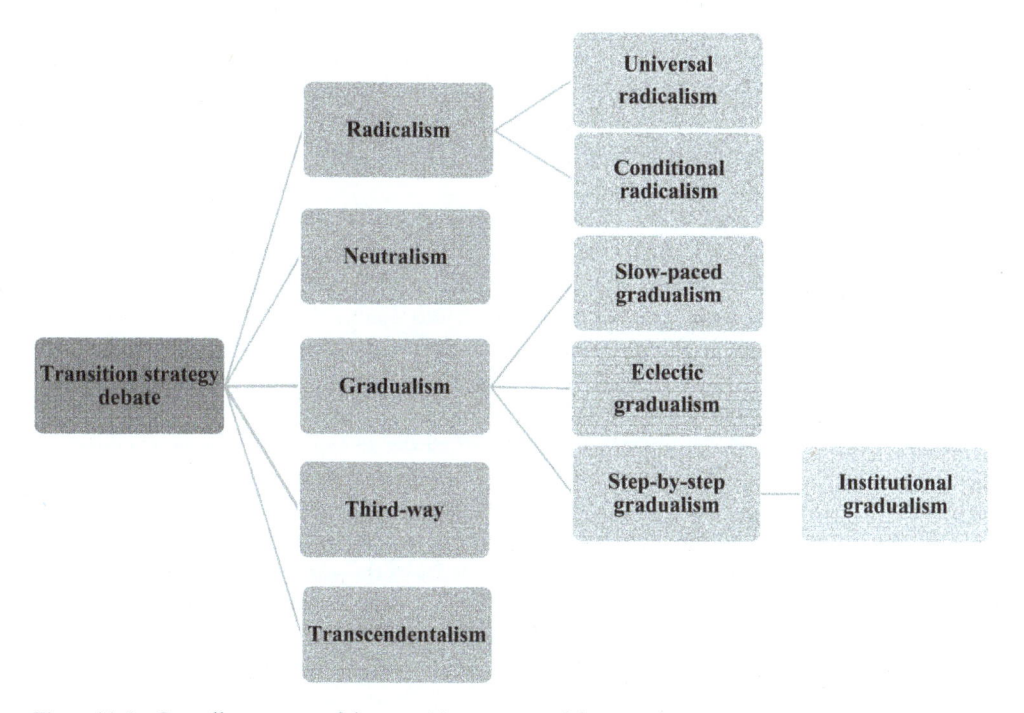

Figure 14.6   Overall structure of the transition strategy debate.

Source: Iwasaki and Suzuki (2020, Figure 2.3, p. 35).

gradualists contend that radicalism is highly likely to be associated with socially intolerable negative side effects. When it comes to basic reasons for justifying the gradualist approach, however, gradualists have a more varied rationale in comparison with their radicalist counterparts. In fact, among gradualists, there is a *slow-paced gradualism* group, which asserts that the transition to a market economy should be carried forward over time so that any social downfall can be avoided, in light of the necessity of effectively controlling the side effects of structural reforms. In contrast to the debate attitude of the slow-paced gradualism group, some researchers particularly emphasize the importance of policy sequence in order to successfully carry out structural reforms that might drastically change a given economic system, while at the same time avoiding excessive social confusion. They form the *step-by-step gradualism* group. In addition to these advocates of step-by-step transition strategy, the gradualists also embrace advocates of *institutional gradualism*, who stress that the establishment of institutions that constitute the foundation of the market economy and democracy, such as property rights and the rule of law, should become the top priority in order to advance the transformation. Moreover, the gradualists comprise another mass of researchers who regard the assertions of both slow-paced and step-by-step gradualism as equally important justification for denouncing radicalism. We call them the *eclectic gradualism* group.

Further, there is another research group that takes the side of neither the radicalists nor the gradualists. The essence of their argument is that radicalism and gradualism are not intrinsically paradoxical to each other, but rather are alternative options; therefore, neither of the two can always be superior to the other theoretically and practically. Based on this notion, they further maintain that, in the real world, policymakers may well choose either gradualism or radicalism as their basic transition strategy on a case-by-case basis, depending on the relevant country's actual conditions; in some cases, a mixture of both, or switching between the two at different stages, would even be possible. Their debate attitude can be described as *neutralism* because they remain in the framework of the radicalism-versus-gradualism debate while, at the same time, keeping at arm's length from both the radicalists and the gradualists. Neutralists have something in common with the conditional radicalism group; however, they should be clearly distinguished in the sense that their debate stance is more thoroughly neutral than is that of conditional radicalism.

Not all researchers who have discussed transition stay within the radicalism-versus-gradualism framework. For instance, several researchers have claimed that some transition countries have carried out a third reform track that cannot be classified as either radicalism or gradualism. Moreover, other researchers have serious doubts about the significance of the transition strategy debate itself. These research groups can be respectively called *third-way thinkers* and *transcendentalists*. These two heterodox research groups are a very small minority, and, hence, our analytical review focused on the major three factions.

In accordance with this determination, we classified the 140 studies of the basic collection based on their respective debate attitudes. Figure 14.7 summarizes the results. As shown in panel (a) of this figure, the gradualists leave both the radicalists and the neutralists far behind in terms of the number of their publications. In fact, 97 research works are classified as gradualism-advocating literature, accounting for 69.3% of the entire basic collection. In this sense, gradualism is the majority view.[1] Meanwhile, 30 studies espouse the radicalist view, accounting for 21.4% of the total. As panel (b) of Figure 14.7 shows, 27 of these 30 studies were written by researchers who firmly believe in the universality of radicalism. This fact reflects the monolithic nature of the radicalists. The remaining 13 studies are products of researchers who expressed their neutral position in the debate; however, the neutralists have not published even half the number of studies by radicalists. In this way, the conflict between the radicalists

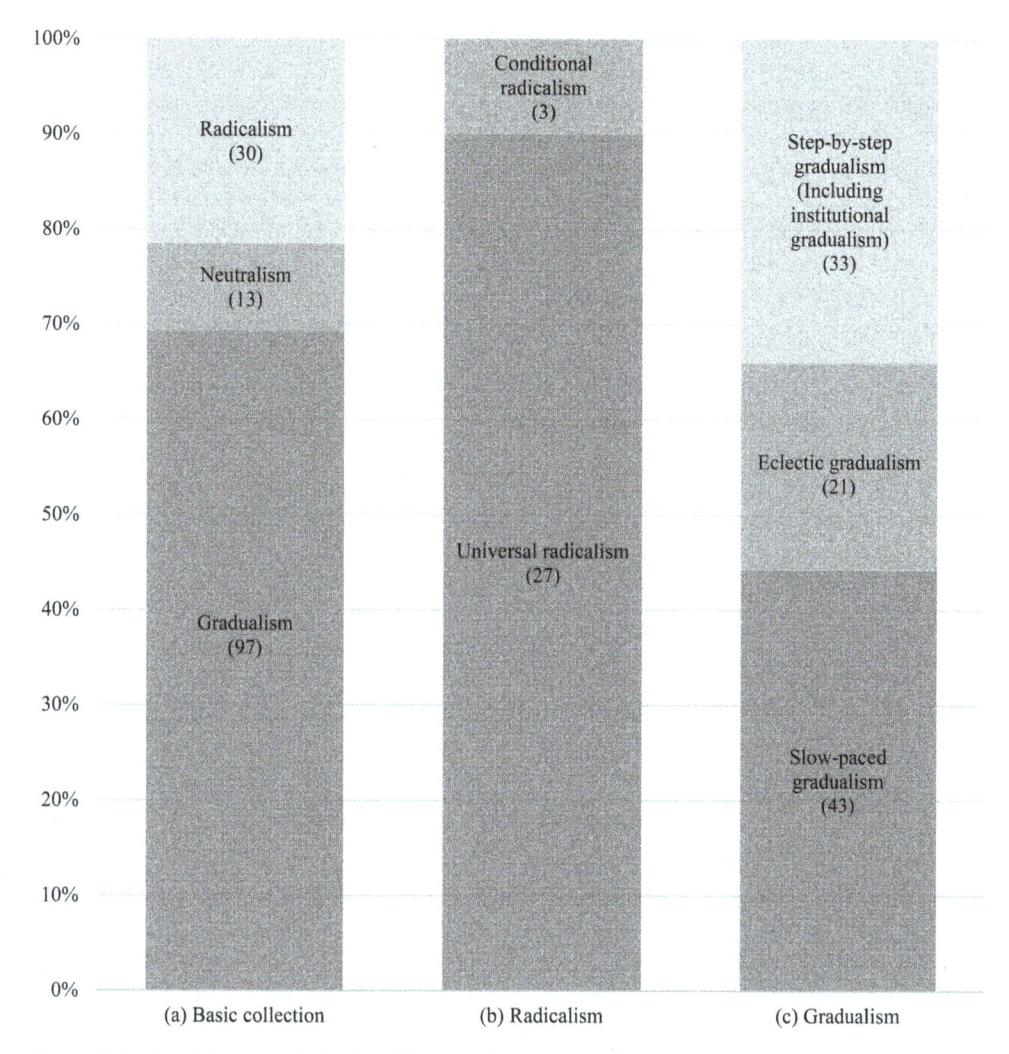

Figure 14.7 Breakdown of the basic collection of the transition strategy debate by debate attitude.

Source: Iwasaki and Suzuki (2020, Figure 2.4, p. 36).

Note: Numbers in parentheses are those of the relevant literature.

and the gradualists is obvious. Panel (c) of Figure 14.7 exhibits the subclassifications of the gradualists. According to this panel, the slow-paced gradualism group published 43 of the 97 studies, or 44.3% of the total studies created by the gradualists. Meanwhile, the step-by-step gradualism group and the eclectic gradualism group published 33 studies (34.0% of the total) and 21 studies (21.6%), respectively, suggesting that the power balance is almost even among the three research groups. Moreover, 18 studies belong to the institutional gradualism group that places the most emphasis on the importance of institution building, accounting for more than half (54.5%) of the total studies by the step-by-step gradualism group. These findings demonstrate that the debate attitude of the gradualists is varied, and no particular view overwhelms the others. This is in clear contrast to the radicalists, who demonstrate a consistent view about their policy recommendation for economic transition.

As the next step, as attempted in the previous section, we have examined the relationship between the debate attitude and publication attributes in the basic literature through a cross-tabulation analysis and regression estimation of a qualitative choice model. These quantitative analyses revealed interesting findings for deeper understanding of the transition strategy debate, that is, authorship attributes—including affiliated institutions, their locations, research experiences, and gender—as well as influence on the academic world are closely related both to the degree of radicalism and the degree to which policy sequence is stressed among gradualists. It also becomes clear that studies that discuss a desirable mode of the transition strategy in line with a specific country or a policy area tend to express much clearer debate attitudes, as compared with general policy discussions. In addition, it is also proven that empirical examination is more frequently carried out to back up radicalism. In other words, the author profiles, research subjects, and methodologies are a major source of the diversified arguments regarding theoretical orientation and transition strategies during the last quarter century.

Our answer to the question of whether researchers expressed more support for radicalism or gradualism is gradualism. However, if we are asked whether we would strongly recommend gradualism to countries attempting to transition to a market economy, the answer is NO. This is because the analytical framework of "radicalism versus gradualism," while a very effective means of fostering interesting issues as a device for academic debate, was, unfortunately, ineffective as a prescription for the difficulties faced by CEE and FSU countries in reality. In the process of responding to suggestions from the heterodox third-way thinkers and severe criticism from the transcendentalists, the transition strategy debate has room to develop into a more useful framework for policy recommendations.

14.4 Is the transition path dependent?

The capitalist economies formed in CEE and FSU countries are based on very different rules of the game and institutions different from those of socialism, so that the view on transition implies a break in the historical development. The result of the formation of capitalism is not so simple. The market economies that have actually been formed contain institutions that can be described as legacies of the past, and they can be seen to reflect the historical development path of each country. In this case, transition implies continuity and evolution, not rupture. Market economy transitions do not exist in isolation from history.

Mizobata and Horie (2019) focused on the concept of path dependency, which helps us to understand the consequences of transition, i.e., the institutional changes that have occurred during the transition process. The authors look at the diverse implications encompassed by path dependency on the basis of the following understanding: "a process where contingent events or decisions result in institutions being established that tend to persist over long periods of time and constrain the range of options available to actors in the future, including those that may be more efficient or effective in the long run" (Campbell, 2010, p. 90). In the path-dependency view, history is seen as a process that constrains people's behavior in the long term.

Only when the consequences of a transition are called into question can it be considered whether the transition is path dependent. Hence, the question, "is the transition path dependent," becomes more important over time. Where path dependence is accepted, post-transition societies rely on the varieties-of-capitalism view, but where they converge with the institutions of developed markets, path dependence is not sufficiently supported.

To deal with the challenges noted above, we next selected a total of 122 articles as the basic literature of the path-dependency approach on the transition economies from research works published between 1989 and 2012. The articles were written by 191 authors. Among the basic literature, we identified 107 studies that had directly used path dependency and related concepts. Based on these studies, the authors further identified base reference literature from wherever path dependency was mentioned in these studies. That brought the number of cited literature items to 439.[2]

The distribution of the basic literature citations by year of publication (Figure 14.8) reveals that considerably fewer studies were published in the 1990s. Far more papers drew on the path-dependency concept in the 2000s than in the 1990s, and this fact is not confined to transition economics, as evidenced by another literature survey about organization theory in general (Vergne and Durand, 2010). This tendency can also be observed in the literature retrieved from the EconLit database by only using the keywords "path dependency" (the correlation coefficient is 0.64). Therefore, it is not abnormal that fewer papers drew on the path-dependency concept in the 1990s than in the 2000s in fields related to transition economics. More papers were published in the 2000s, with the peak being in 2006–2007, which suggests that researchers have focused not on the initial stage of the transition but on the diversified transition results. Within the list of basic literature, 103 papers can be classified on the basis of specific regions and periods, and, in terms of regions, all transition economy countries were covered, including China. In relative terms, early analyses are inclined to focus on the CEE regions in keeping with the rate of transition, although this does not mean specialization in any particular region (Figure 14.9). Symbolically, two main works during the 1990s, i.e., Stark (1996) and Hausner et al. (1993), paid attention to Hungary (industrial organizations) and Poland (regional development), respectively. The periods subject to analyses range over the entire structural transformation period, but to be more exact, they concentrate on the 1990s, and there is a rapid reduction in studies covering subsequent periods. It can be said that empirical analyses on the subject phenomenon during the 1990s had not yet blossomed

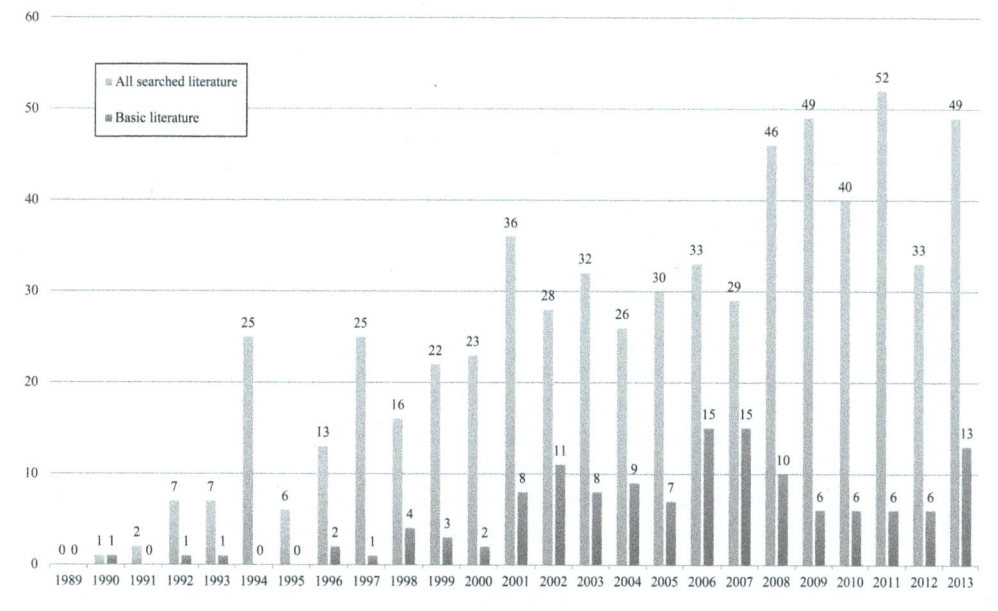

Figure 14.8 Frequency distribution of publication years of all searched literature and the basic literature of path dependency in transition economies.

Source: Mizobata and Horie (2019, Figure 2, p. 6).

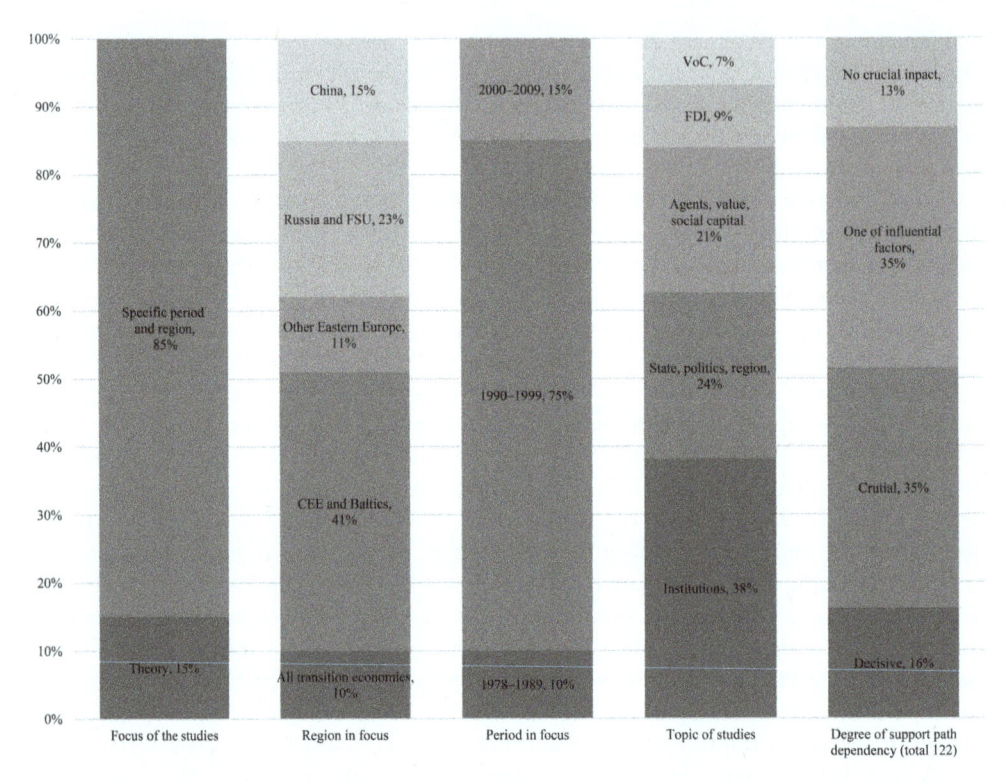

Figure 14.9 Basic literature characteristics and the degree of support for path dependency.

Source: Mizobata and Horie (2019, Figure 3, p. 7).

within this same decade since the course of events could only be discussed from a short-term perspective; thus, in-depth studies did not fully emerge until the 2000s, when the results of the transition and the degree of its completion became obvious enough to be discussed.

The transition results are not necessarily restricted by these initial conditions. "A simple version of path dependence that emphasized the 'lock-in' effect of initial conditions does not seem to be present in the reform outcomes in the cases at hand" (Frye, 2010, pp. 251–252). To put it plainly, path dependency is not seen as a trigger for crucial institutional formation. Frye (2010) even argued that "there is some evidence that countries with bad initial conditions can catch up to countries with good initial conditions over time" (p. 252). Zakaria (2013) also completely rejected the path-dependent view and insisted that the rules of the socialist system disappeared. On the other hand, some studies have argued that the very path dependency strongly impacts strategies for institutional selection, with Hausner et al. (1995) as a representative example. "Post-socialist trajectories are heavily dependent on a dense and complex institutional such that the (often invisible) remnants of previous economic and political orders still shape expectations and patterns of conduct" (ibid., p. 4). Instead of the determinism or the doctrine of necessity, Hausner et al. (1995) regarded "strategic selection" as the core concept of path dependency.

With regard to transitional economy theory, no scholar has ever completely denied historical impacts in his/her discussion. Hence, the authors set the following two evaluation standards for any discussion of path dependency: One is the Frye–Zakaria standard that does not recognize any initial condition as a critical trigger in the transition results and policy selections and, thus, denies any function of path dependency; the other is the Hausner standard that considers path dependency as decisively regulating strategic selections. Based on these evaluation standards, the degree of support has been divided into four degrees of impact whose distribution shows that many papers consider path dependency as being decisively or critically influencing, which is logical, given the nature of the basic literature. However, the distribution that includes many modest evaluations as well indicates that the evaluation of path dependency varies within transition economics. Path dependency cannot be overestimated, considering that the economic agents themselves have changed. Nevertheless, as long as institution building is emphasized in transition economies, there are no studies that completely deny the impact of path dependency. In fact, as shown in Figure 14.9, 87% of the basic literature considers path dependency to be a factor influencing the outcomes and strategies of market economy transitions, and around half of the literature considers it important. Hence, the evolutionary approach, which argues for a strong effect of path dependence, appears to be dominant.[3]

The empirical analysis of the influence of path dependence (Mizobata and Horie, 2019, p. 29, Table 4) then reveals the following five points:

First, when other conditions remain the same, the earlier the publication year of the study in question, the more conservative its evaluation of path dependency. Studies that argue against its impact have appeared largely since 2006, and this corresponds to the period when institutions began to show a tendency toward convergence in the wake of the EU's expansion into CEE and when transitional countries entered their period of economic growth. According to views arguing against this impact (16 studies), political factors and external factors such as multinational enterprises and the EU have indeed worked very well, not to mention the policies. "Powerful external forces ... the overwhelming influence of IFIs, TNCs, and the EU on the emerging new order" (Bohle and Greskovits,2012, p. 55) could not be ignored, especially in the small European countries. The number of papers on path dependency has increased in tandem with the rise in the number of opponents of the path-dependency concept who have stressed external factors as well as politics.

Second, researchers who belong to institutions located in CEE and FSU countries have a higher probability of publishing studies that do not recognize any significant effect. The lack of emphasis on path dependency by authors located in transition countries is a surprising result. This seems to reflect the heterogeneity seen from the outside and the longing for global standards seen by insiders. On the other hand, a unique development path has been formed in China (Zhang and Sun, 2012), and yet path dependency has not necessarily occupied a decisive place in Asia due to the view regarding the flying geese model of development, the presence of strong states, and the presence of multinational enterprises, and other factors.

Third, as compared to empirical research, theoretical research consists of more studies that do not stress path dependency.

Fourth, differences in study themes have a great impact on the path-dependency effect. In fact, studies that focused on "formal institutions," "informal institutions," or "region and local identity" as their study themes have an obviously stronger tendency to stress the significance of path dependency in the process toward a market economy. This is attributed not only to the fact that institutions after the transition have not converged to Western-type ones, but also to the fact that mutually adverse markets have been constructed both among transitional countries and among regions within transitional countries. Moreover, there is another approach in which path dependency is supposed to be an explanatory factor for the mutation of a formed market. Stark (1996) and Stark and Bruszt (1998) can be considered prime examples of this and have thus had a substantial impact on later studies.

Fifth, as far as citations are concerned, before 1979, the literature emphasizes the old institutional school, while in the 1980s it concentrates on North (1990) and David (2001). Authors who seek a theoretical rationale in studies on evolutionary economics by Bernard Chavance and Geoffrey Hodgson or studies on social network theory by Mark Granovetter are more likely to highly estimate the significance of the path-dependency effect. Meanwhile, authors who draw on the path-dependency theory in technological changes, as represented by Paul A. David, or comparative politics, as represented by Kathleen Thelen, are more likely to downplay the path-dependency effect. David Stark's papers and works have had an overwhelming impact. Among the selected studies, 37 (the actual number on the basis of excluding duplications), which account for more than one third of the entire selected literature citations, have cited Stark's studies, including his joint writings. The citation of any of Stark's papers itself has not led to either strong support for path dependency or criticism against it.

The transition to a market economy had a strong sense of rupture, and research focusing on economic policy was central to the theory of transition economies. However, as a result of the formation of various market economies and the increasing emphasis on history, particularly the impact of socialist legacies, the presence of path dependency has become increasingly important in the work of Stark (1992). Institutional research also became a tailwind for the acceptance of path-dependency theory. Hence, years after transition, path dependency remains an important issue in the debate regarding the role of institutions in transition economies, including both formal and informal institutions; however, with the passage of time, generational change is likely to bring questions about path dependency. "History (past) matters," but "present also matters". Thus, it seems that path dependency and related analytical concepts have been refined as a way of looking at institutional formation and change in the time-constrained study of transition economies.

14.5 Is corruption a lubricant for transition?

Corruption is an ambiguous, broad-ranging concept. The process of securing private gains in connection with official duties can only be described as corruption, as in a case of deviating from legal frameworks and systems, including rent-seeking, and "privatizing" state power (Offe, 2004, p. 79). Other views of corruption, as extensions of this definition, include a "misuse of public office for private gain" (Treisman, 2007, p. 360) or, as advocated by the private think-tank Transparency International,[4] "the abuse of entrusted power for private gain". The widely used International Corruption Perceptions Index relies on this last definition. Politically speaking, corruption is an impediment to democracy and the rule of law; economically, it decreases national wealth, distorts fair market structures and competition, destroys social structures through the loss of people's trust, and worsens the environment through deficiencies in environmental legal and regulatory systems (Transparency International; Rose-Ackerman and Palifka, 2016).

Under the transition, while corruption did exist as a legacy of the bureaucratic socialist economic system, at the same time, it has taken a new form as corruption of the market's moral code. That is, corruption during the transition of systems appears as both a legacy and a collateral development of the transition itself. Furthermore, even if corruption causes both political and economic losses, "under specific conditions"—when, in the process of nation-building (e.g., during the transition of systems), building market systems on top of the legacy of a socialist economic system that had conformed excessively to the bureaucracy— "corruption even improves economic outcomes" (Rose-Ackerman and Palifka, 2016, p. 32).

This is because corruption makes it possible to reduce transaction costs by avoiding excessive bureaucratic systems. This is a hypothesis that corruption is a form of greasing the wheels.

From an early stage, the studies of corruption in transition economies have focused mainly on macro and micro studies. Macro studies have used an approach that considers macroeconomic performance during the 1990s to have been underestimated and argues that unofficial economic sectors, including corruption, need to be assessed properly. Micro research has advanced in a more broad-ranging and complex manner, since phenomena equivalent to the selling off of state property appeared in the process of privatizing ownership and management—which should be seen as the star policy of the transition of systems—and as the transition of systems was accompanied by a lack of transparency in reorganizing the bureaucratic structures responsible for approving and authorizing building in the new state. For this reason, the study of corruption also served as proof that research on the transition of systems was developing in an interdisciplinary manner, encompassing not only economics but also other fields, such as political science and sociology.[5]

Following Treisman (2000; 2007), Suzuki and Mizobata (2020) also proposed theoretical hypotheses, mainly from the aspects of causes, effects, and culture and values, based on the assumptions of research on corruption and rent seeking under the transition of systems—that causes and effects are correlated with each other and that each is characterized by internal connections between cause and effect factors. We raise the fourteen hypotheses on causative factors, on effect factors, and on culture and values.

To objectively test the above hypotheses, Suzuki and Mizobata (2020) investigated a total 559 articles as the basic collection of corruption research from research works published from 1995 to 2017. As seen in Figure 14.10, while there is some variation in the number of works by publication year, a trend toward an exponential increase can be observed.

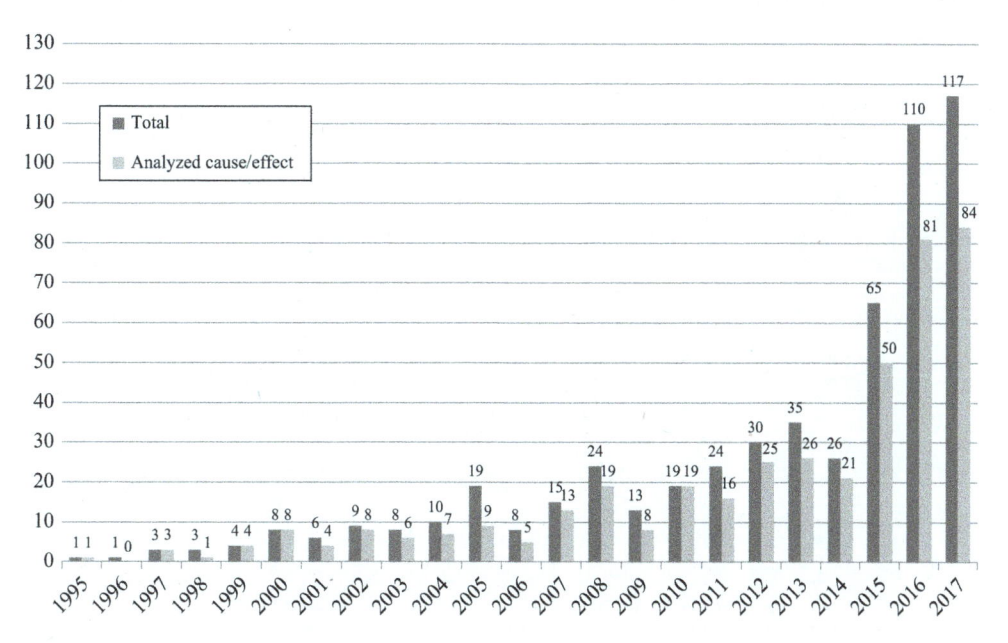

Figure 14.10   Frequency distribution of publication years of the basic collection of corruption in transition economies.

Source: Suzuki and Mizobata (2020, Figure 5.2, p. 155).

With regard to the research content, Figure 14.11 presents an outline of the basic collection by attributes of authorship and publication media. In total, the authors of the 559 works in the basic collection numbered 1109, of whom 328 were affiliated with research institutions in North America, 136 in the United Kingdom, and 164 in western Continental Europe, while 154 were affiliated with research institutions in CEE countries, 59 in FSU countries, and 185 in other countries. As such, about two-thirds of researchers were from countries other than former socialist states. At the same time, totaling the number of works in the basic collection in five-year intervals shows that few works were published during the 1990s, but the number has skyrocketed over the years. Although one factor behind this increase might

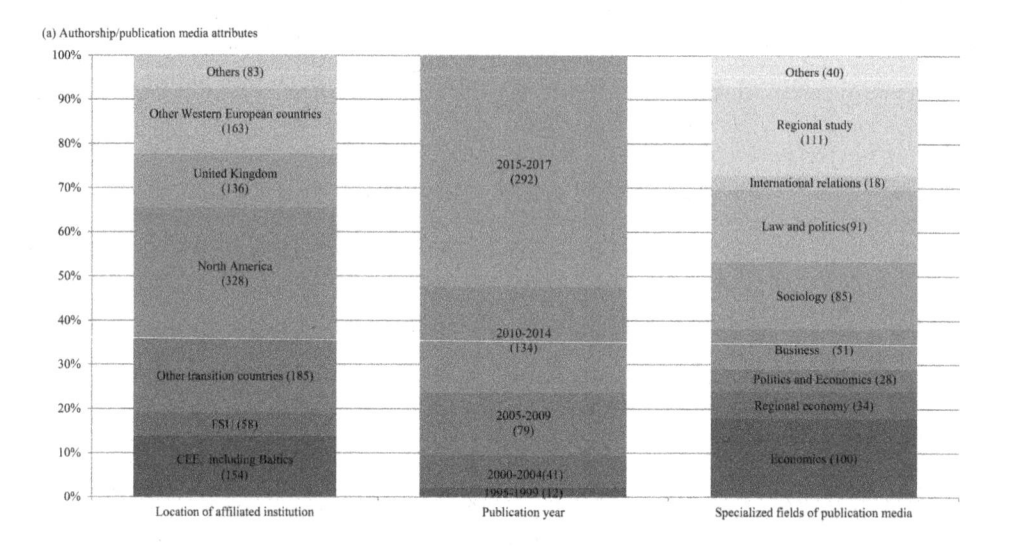

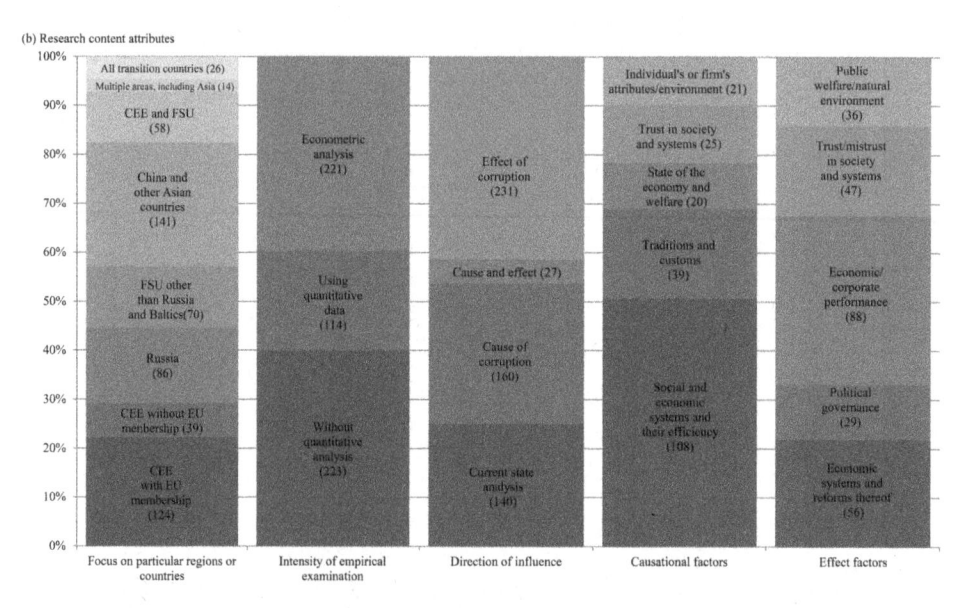

Figure 14.11   Breakdown of the basic collection of corruption research by literature attribute.

Source: Suzuki and Mizobata (2020, Figure 5.3, p. 156).

be the availability of the objective index from Transparency International, mentioned above, as an effective index for research use, it also is affected by factors such as an increase in the number of social surveys and the manifestation of actual large-scale corruption. The results of hypothesis testing and the main relevant works of the literature are as follows:

H1: Corruption is rarer under an efficient social and economic system. Researchers of transition economies do not dispute the argument that factors such as the quality and consistency of the design of social and economic systems govern levels of corruption.

H2: Corruption is rarer under conditions of democracy and political stability. Clearly there is strong support for the hypothesis that, in general, democracy and political stability have restraining effects on corruption.

H3: Corruption is rarer in developed economies or where wages are high. Overall, more studies supported than rejected this hypothesis; however, some show that, when viewed over the short term, there were different aspects of the relationship between wealth realization and the restraint of corruption, and the nonlinear relationship between the two may need to be further considered.

H4: Corruption is more common in resource-rich nations. As compared to the other hypotheses, relatively few studies argued that the presence of natural resources itself was a decisive factor affecting corruption, but no studies rejected this hypothesis.

H5: The privatization of ownership increases the likelihood of corruption. A look at the studies over time shows that, while those published during the 1990s tended to support the hypothesis, there has been increasing advocacy for the effects of privatization of ownership on restraining corruption. It can be inferred that progress toward private ownership and the spread of corruption are, objectively and over a longer term, more likely to lead to finding a negative correlation; there also is a need to pay close attention to conditions and environments.

H6: Liberalization reduces the likelihood of corruption. Overall, there is a struggle between those who support this hypothesis and those who reject it. However, research on the former Soviet Union and China shows a strong tendency for seeing liberalization as inducing corruption, and analyses of Central and Eastern Europe and multiple regions show a tendency to conclude that liberalization restrains corruption.

H7: Corruption hinders economic growth. The overwhelming majority of studies supported this hypothesis. There is a kind of consensus, at least among researchers studying the economies of CEE and the FSU, that corruption is harmful to an economy.

H8: Corruption expands the informal sector. A small majority supported this hypothesis. While none of the studies that rejected it were of the view that corruption restrains the informal economy, they mainly argued that corruption was not a primary factor or that it had no particular influence.

H9: Corruption increases economic disparity and reduces the level of public welfare. The only study that rejected this hypothesis was that of Hung et al. (2017), which pointed out the possibility that corruption could increase returns in corporate units. However, the vast majority supported the hypothesis.

H10: Corruption worsens governance. The overwhelming majority of studies supported this hypothesis. Overall, it is widely recognized that corruption hinders governance, while other results may be demonstrated in extremely specific cases in which corruption deeply permeates society.

H11: Corruption hinders transitional reforms. Because the relationship described in this hypothesis is considered a natural state of affairs, few of the studies reviewed in this paper addressed this theme head on.

H12: The degree of the permeation of communism is connected to corruption. No strong opinion was identified in the basic collection opposing the hypothesis that the vestiges of the former era served as a hotbed for corruption.

H13: Religion and culture are connected to corruption. No views could be found that rejected this hypothesis. In contrary, the vast majority of studies supported it.

H14: Public distrust of society and systems is interrelated with corruption. The vast majority identified a relationship between corruption and distrust in society and systems. Thus, these arguments suggest that corruption and the public's trust in society are two sides of the same coin, showing just how important the social capital of mutual trust among individuals and groups can be.

A diverse range of points at issue are involved in corruption in transition economies, reflecting the complex interrelationships between corruption and delayed or distorted improvements in various social, economic, and cultural aspects of transitioning societies. In light of these circumstances, this paper posited hypotheses regarding the main points at issue in research on corruption in transition economies, based on a basic collection of 559 works, testing each hypothesis by the degree to which the literature supported it.

A number of considerations must be noted when interpreting these results since, generally speaking, it is hard to imagine ethical or social support for corruption as a form of misusing a public position for personal gain or to imagine advocating for policies that would support corruption, regardless of the political system, as shown by the systematic review conducted in this paper. There is unlikely to be an argument against the statement that the dominant view is a rejection of corruption, both socially and economically. On further reflection, however, while the most important central point of this chapter was to verify the degree of support for the greasing-the-wheels hypothesis—assuming conditions in which the markets of transition economies are not functioning fully and democratic political systems have not yet taken root, while the psychological legacy of dependency on and fear of the state remains from the previous socialist history, and the level of performance of their duties by the public officials who manage the apparatus of the state is low, then corruption may be tolerated as the second-best solution—for the most part, the basic collection does not support this hypothesis. However, what has been identified is the presence of an interrelationship in which efficient and transparent social, political, and economic systems reduce corruption, and a low level of corruption increases the quality of these systems.

There are three layers of corruption: pre-transition corruption, corruption in the transition process, and post-transition corruption. Discrepancies in the scale of corruption among transition economies still remain, depending on their cultures, histories, values, and systems. As a result, even if we reject the greasing-the-wheels hypothesis for transition economies as a whole, studies that support it, even if few in number, can be confirmed regarding Russia. The continuing differences between the FSU on one hand and CEE and the Baltic states on the other are grounded in the scale of differences in the systems they have developed, in addition to the size of the legacies (debts) they have inherited.

14.6 Concluding remarks: Four lessons from the transition literature

We have digested the results of our analytical reviews of the transition literature on socialist failure, transition strategies, path dependency of economic transition, and corruption, which are form the core study areas of the transition economics. In the anthology of Iwasaki (2020), in addition to these four research objectives, we and other contributors have also examined issues related to the economic crisis and recovery, enterprise privatization, poverty, the socialist legacy of human resource management, international trade, foreign direct investment as well as environmental reforms in transition economies. These articles also provide a full account of the scholarly works published over the past three decades. Those who are interested in the contents of this chapter are strongly encouraged to refer to these works.

In lieu of a conclusion, let us provide a somewhat transcendental discussion of the lessons drawn from our examination of the four academic debates mentioned above. The first is that socialism failed for a variety of reasons, but its own dysfunctionality was the greatest reason. It is often pointed out that countries are destroyed more by internal failures than by external attacks, and it is an indisputable fact that the socialism established in Eastern Europe and Eurasia also failed mainly because of the internal dysfunctionality of the socio-economic systems.

The second lesson is that although the voices of the radicalists were loud, the majority of economists still favored gradualism. In the early 1990s, the radicalists, who loudly advocated for the implementation of the Washington Consensus, had a huge presence and were thought to be on par with or even ahead of the gradualists. However, in reality, the transformation of an economic system is not an overnight project. This is a belief shared by the overwhelming majority of economists.

The third lesson is that marketization is a path-dependent process, which implies the diversity of capitalist economies. The passage of time, however, imposes new conditions on the market economy, such as generational change, digitalization, and innovation, and in the context of globalization, external conditions also change significantly. Therefore, market economy policies must reflect both the past and the present in a balanced way.

The fourth and last lesson, which may be common sense, is that corruption cannot work effectively as a lubricant in an economic system and in a market economy. When market institutions become ineffective and governments lose credibility, the quality of both markets and governments deteriorates, and economic welfare declines. However, as the experience of developed countries has shown, the above common sense does not take hold so easily in societies because the policies of transition, such as liberalization and privatization, run the risk of amplifying corruption and because the culture, history, values, and pre-transition economic institutions run the risk of preserving corruption.

Looking back over the three decades of transition to a market economy, we observe diversity in the economic systems of the post-communist region; this diversity is also closely linked to fluctuations/great changes in the global economy. The specificity of the region's capitalist economies, however, is not at the source of the above lessons. The four lessons drawn by transition economics apply to the world economy as a whole, and to modern economics itself. Economics does not lead to a functioning market economy through traditional formulaic prescriptions but by questioning its theoretical foundations in the face of new phenomena of market transition.

Acknowledgments

This chapter presents a research outcome financially supported by the Ministry of Education, Culture, Sports, Science and Technology of Japan (KAKENHI Grant Nos. 23243032 and 20H01489). We thank Bruno Dallago and Sara Casagrande, the editors of the book, for their helpful comments on the earlier version of this paper, Eriko Yoshida for her research assistance, and Tammy Bicket and Akira Ishida for their editorial assistance. We also would like to express our sincere gratitude to Norio Horie, Fumikazu Sugiura, Taku Suzuki, and Akira Uegaki for their consent in reprinting and citing some of the co-authored papers in this chapter.

Notes

1 Without duplication, the number of all authors in the basic collection is 163. Among them are 159 authors whose articles are all classified in a single category; these include 37 radicals (23.3%), 19 neutralists (11.9%), and 103 gradualists (64.8%). Therefore, we can also confirm the predominance of gradualists based on the number of authors in each category.

2 Mizobata and Horie (2019) additionally examined literature from 2013 to 2015 (second investigation). For the second investigation, we extracted 126 studies from EconLit's database, and 113 papers were analyzed. The basic literature was 40 studies. The authors' conclusion does not change, given the additional literature.

3 This trend can be observed in the second investigation. Among 40 base-extracted literature, authors find no impact in 15%, one factor in 27.5%, significant impact in 35%, and decisive impact in 22.5%.

4 Headquartered in Berlin and with 100 branch offices worldwide, Transparency International is a large-scale international NGO that aims to solve corruption issues around the world. Its website is: https://www.transparency.org/.

5 Although research on corruption during the transition of systems began at the same time as the transitions themselves, only since 2000 has the topic of corruption secured its status within transition research. Initially, publication by the NGO Transparency International of its Corruption Perceptions Index served as the major impetus behind the shift from research inclined toward case studies to empirical research; this is related to the fact that this index began to be used in analysis as an indicator of the degrees of market maturity and transition to a market economy. Distinguishing features of research on corruption include the facts that research has been led by an international organization rather than a specific individual, that research has advanced since the 2000s, and that the number of quantitative studies increased with the use of the above index in research. This integrated indicator of corruption, developed in 1995, rated 180 countries in 2018 on a scale of 0 (the highest degree of concern about corruption) to 100 (the lowest). It was calculated based on 13 reports from 12 international agencies regarding concern about corruption among businesspeople and national experts over the most recent two years. The global average score is 43, with Denmark scoring the highest, at 88, and Somalia the lowest, at 10.

References

Boettke, P. J. (2001). *Calculation and Coordination: Essays on Socialism and Transitional Political Economy*, Routledge: New York.

Bohle, D. and Greskovits, B. (2012). *Capitalist Diversity on Europe's Periphery*, Cornell University Press: Ithaca and London.

Campbell, J. (2010). "Institutional Reproduction and Change," In: Morgan, Glenn, John Campbell, Colin Crouch, Ove Kaj Pedersen and Richard Whitley eds., *The Oxford Handbook of Comparative Institutional Analysis*, Oxford University Press: New York.

David, P. (2001). "Path Dependence, Its Critics and the Quest for Historical Economics," In: Garrouste, Pierre and Stavros Ioannides eds., *Evolution and Path Dependence in Economic Ideas*, Edward Elgar: Cheltenham, pp. 15–40.

Frye, T. (2010). *Building States and Markets After Communism*, Cambridge University Press: New York.

Hausner, J., Jessop, B. and Nielsen, K. (eds.) (1993). *Institutional Frameworks of Market Economies: Scandinavian and Eastern European Perspectives*, Avebury Ashgate: Aldershot.

Hausner, J., Jessop, B. and Nielsen, K. (eds.) (1995). *Strategic Choice and Path-Dependency in Post-Socialism: Institutional Dynamics in the Transformation Process*, Edward Elgar: Aldershot.

Hung, C.-H. D., Jiang, Y., Liu, F. H., Tu, H. and Wang, S. (2017). "Bank Political Connections and Performance in China," *Journal of Financial Stability*, 32, pp. 57–69.

Iwasaki, I. (ed.) (2020). *The Economics of Transition: Developing and Reforming Emerging Economies*, Routledge: Abingdon and New York.

Iwasaki, I. and Suzuki, T. (2016). "Radicalism versus Gradualism: An Analytical Survey of the Transition Strategy Debate," *Journal of Economic Surveys*, 30(4), pp. 807–834.

Iwasaki, I. and Suzuki, T. (2020). "Transition Strategy Debate: Radicalism versus Gradualism," In: Iwasaki, Ichiro, ed., *The Economics of Transition: Developing and Reforming Emerging Economies*, Routledge: Abingdon and New York, pp. 25–66.

Mizobata, S. and Horie, N. (2019). *Path-Dependency of Economic Transition: An Analytical Review*, KIER Discussion Paper No. 1014, Kyoto Institute of Economic Research, Kyoto University: Kyoto.

North, D. C. (1990). *Institutions, Institutional Change and Economic Performance*, Cambridge University Press: Cambridge.

Offe, C. (2004). "Political Corruption: Conceptual and Practical Issues," In: Kornai, Janos and Susan Rose-Ackerman eds., *Building a Trustworthy State in Post-Socialist Transition*, Palgrave Macmillan: New York, pp. 77–99.

Rose-Ackerman, S. and Palifka, B. J. (2016). *Corruption and Government: Causes, Consequences, and Reform*, Second edition, Cambridge University Press: Cambridge, UK.

Stark, D. (1992). "Path Dependence and Privatization Strategies in East Central Europe," *East European Politics and Societies*, 6(1), pp. 17–54.

Stark, D. (1996). "Recombinant Property in East European Capitalism," *American Journal of Sociology*, 101(4), pp. 993–1027.

Stark, D. and Bruszt, L. (1998). *Postsocialist Pathways: Transforming Politics and Property in East Central Europe*, Cambridge University Press: Cambridge.

Suzuki, T. and Mizobata, S. (2020). "Social Confusion and Corruption: Investigating the Causes and Effects of a Breakdown of Ethics," In: Iwasaki, Ichiro ed., *The Economics of Transition: Developing and Reforming Emerging Economies*, Routledge: Abingdon and New York, pp. 145–178.

Treisman, D. (2000). "The Causes of Corruption: A Cross-National Study," *Journal of Public Economics*, 6, pp. 399–457.

Treisman, D. (2007). "The Causes of Corruption: A Cross-National Study," In: Berglof, Erik and Gérard Roland eds., *The Economics of Transition: The Fifth Nobel Symposium in Economics*, Palgrave Macmillan: New York, pp. 251–271.

Uegaki, A., Sugiura, F. and Iwasaki, I. (2018). "Why Socialism Failed: Approaching from Political Economy," In: Iwasaki, Ichiro ed., *Lectures on Comparative Economics: Theory and Empirics of Marketization*, Nippon Hyoron Sha: Tokyo, pp. 31–65. (In Japanese).

Vergne, J.-P. and Durand, R. (2010). "The Missing Link between the Theory and Empirics of Path Dependence," *Journal of Management Studies*, 47(4), pp. 736–759.

Zakaria, P. (2013). "Is Corruption an Enemy of Civil Society? The Case of Central and Eastern Europe," *International Political Science Review*, 34(4), pp. 351–371.

Zhang, W. and Sun, F. (2012). "Resurrection Through Adaptation: The Dynamics of China's "Comcapitalism" Model," *Journal of Comparative Asian Development*, 11(2), pp. 349–378.

PART III

Actors, values and interactions in economic systems

15

TRANSVERSAL SKILLS IN HIGHER EDUCATION CURRICULA

Empirical Evidence from Austria, Ireland and Portugal

Verena Régent and Brigitte Ecker

WPZ RESEARCH, VIENNA, AUSTRIA

15.1 Introduction

The labor market has been seeing rapid changes in the recent past, particularly driven by the green and digital transformation and accelerated through the COVID-19 pandemic. Jobs with routine tasks are increasingly substituted by automation – this is true for both manual (e.g. operating, controlling or equipping machines) and cognitive routine tasks (e.g. calculating, accounting, correcting, measuring; Kuba, 2017; Wedenig et al., 2017). But also jobs with non-routine activities are subject to changes when it comes to job design and work structure (Tegtmeier, 2021). A recent study shows that, while only 1% of currently existing occupations are "fully automatable" and 60% of currently existing occupations have 30% of tasks automatable based on current technology, almost all jobs we know nowadays are expected to change in their nature and will be increasingly focused on tasks that require more technological, social and emotional skills (Dondi et al., 2021).

Appropriate action is required from educational systems in order to keep citizens abreast of labor market changes. This chapter is focusing on higher education (HE) institutions (HEIs) and their efforts and challenges to release HE graduates who are demanded on the labor market. The aspect of graduates' employability has been rising in importance to HEIs since the 1980s, when a public understanding of HEIs' roles in their respective regions as well as their societal and economic responsibility emerged, and was picked up by HEIs as their "third mission" (e.g. Etzkowitz & Leydesdorff, 2000). Meanwhile, it has become international consensus that HEIs are responsible to (1) ensure the labor market relevance of their educational offerings, and (2) equip their graduates with skills beyond the domain-specific competences in their study discipline: In the *European Education Area*, HEIs are supposed to focus on the aspect of *skill development* (European Commission, 2020); the recent joint initiative from the European Commission and the OECD *Labor Market Relevance and Outcomes of Higher Education* (LMRO) is striving to reflect labor market developments in HE by means of systemic and

DOI: 10.4324/9781003144366-19

institutional approaches. The study at hand will provide a concise overview of this transformation of HE systems and the rise of the notion of graduates' "job readiness" (e.g. Liu et al., 2021) as a new paradigm for HEIs.

At the same time, it must be acknowledged that ensuring labor market relevance of their educational offering is a challenging undertaking for HEIs. On the very top, it requires access to relevant information sources (e.g. employers, chambers, associations) as well as certain flexibility in curricula development. As Burk and Hetze (2020) illustrate, e.g., for the German HE system, many HEIs not only face financial, technical, administrative or legal burdens, but also lacking staff qualification. Another particular challenge lies in recognizing present demands while, at the same time, anticipating future labor market needs. Given that students are educated for a future labor market, this requires sensitivity and a sense of proportion when it comes to adaptations in the curricula. Finally, the legitimate question for the very purpose of HE arises, and particularly how useful the dependence of HE on the (future) labor market is at all (Wheelahan and Moodie, 2021).

The study at hand is focusing on the role of "transversal skills" as efficient tool for HEIs to enhance graduate employability regardless of the study field and provides comparative empirical evidence for Austria, Ireland and Portugal through curriculum analyses. The rest of the chapter is structured as follows: In Section 15.2, the transformation of HE systems toward graduate employability will be illustrated, elaborating on current trends in HE systems and the role of transversal skills. Section 15.3 will outline the methodology of the empirical investigation, Section 15.4 provides country profiles of the three sample countries. Section 15.5 serves to present the results of the empirical analysis, Section 15.6 provides a conclusion and discussion.

15.2 Transformation of higher education systems

Graduate employability has not always been of major concern in HE systems. HEIs used to be seen as places that equip students with academic and occupational skills necessary to be part of a pertinent academic community, much rather than to provide a service for employers or train students for succeeding in the workplace. For example, students were educated to form and proclaim their own ideas, but less so to be collaborative thinkers, problem solvers or communicators (MacDermott & Ortiz, 2017; Tewari & Sharma, 2016). Still in 1998, Oblinger and Verville stated: "The work world has changed enormously, and higher education has not".

In the late 1990s and early 2000s, however, public understanding as well as HEIs' self-perception on the societal role of HE has been on the change. The term of HEIs' "third mission" was coined by Etzkowitz and Leydesdorff in 2000, referring to HEIs additional tasks and purposes next to the "traditional missions" of teaching and research (Etzkowitz & Leydesdorff, 2000). With this notion, HEIs increasingly opened up to their non-academic environment and focused on their (regional) social and economic contribution (Berghäuser & Hölschel, 2020; Henke et al., 2016). Part of this notion is the care for their graduates when it comes to labor market compatibility, as well as their cooperation with potential future employers.

It was not without external, particularly political and financial pressures that HEIs have incorporated the notions of third mission and graduate employability into their agendas. They have been confronted with a more challenging environment due to reasons such as internationalization in research and education, extended competition with an increasing and more varied number of organizations for funding, faculty and students, harmonization pressures of national university systems (e.g. Bologna process), but also an increased demand for transparency and accountability of (research) results (Dziminska et al., 2018). With a specific view to graduate employability, the Bologna declaration from 1999 mentioned "employability based on HE" as concrete goal of the Bologna process (EHEA, 1999), followed by the EHEA (*European Higher Education Area*) ministerial conference in 2015, stating that: "Fostering the employability of graduates throughout their working lives in rapidly changing labour markets [...] is a major goal of the EHEA" (EHEA, 2015). More generally through all levels of education, education providers are supposed to focus on the aspect of *skill development* (European Commission, 2020) in the *European Education Area*. In this light, the implementation of the notion of graduate employability can partially be seen as HEIs' response to a changing environment (aligned with the idea of institutionalist isomorphism; DiMaggio & Powell, 1983; Kitagawa et al., 2016), and a stronger interdependence with that environment.

In line with this changing self-perception among HEIs, also public understanding and expectations have shifted toward the idea that it is HEIs' responsibility to ensure labor market compatibility. On the one hand, (higher) education has been identified as powerful tool to fight unemployment and precariousness of employment (Pardo-Garcia & Barac, 2020). As such, expectations have risen that HEIs respond to volatile labor market needs and the "variable structure of abilities required by employers" (O'Reilly et al., 2015), and also to mitigate skills and qualification mismatches.

While the expectations are high, there is no consensus in the academic literature, nor among practitioners how to render graduates "employable", "job ready" or "career ready". Authors like Moreland (2006) refer to skills such as to be autonomous, able to adapt to innovations, to work in groups, take responsibilities, have attitudes in favor of maintaining and renewing their skills and be reflexive. Brundier et al. (2021), Laguna-Sánchez et al. (2019) or Barth et al. (2007) see the need to implement key competences in sustainability as cross-cutting matters in HE curricula to foster graduate employability. At the same time, evidence from pertinent research (e.g. Ayoubi et al., 2017; Sarfraz et al., 2018; Singh et al., 2017) suggests that the concept of job-readiness also varies across cultures and economies. In particular, significant differences can be found between emerging and developed economies, as well as between high turnover labor markets (e.g. United States) and more stable labor markets (e.g. EU countries and Japan). In the latter, for example, a greater extent of employees' commitment, dedication and loyalty are required, because employees in these countries use to stay in their jobs for a longer period of time. In contrast, employees in high turnover labor markets are required to have a more entrepreneurial and global mindset as well as greater flexibility (Sarfraz et al., 2018).

There is little pertinent research on whether, how and which of these employability skills are implemented in HEIs' educational offerings. Due to the lack of a common academic and practical definition, implicitly, it is upon each individual HEI to follow labor market developments and integrate what they consider necessary (and feasible within their financial, legal and administrative possibilities) to enhance their graduates' employability in the frame of their educational offerings.

15.2.1 *Trends in higher educational offerings*

When observing the development of educational offerings at HEIs with a view to graduate employability in the past decade, a global trend is that multi-disciplinarity and interdisciplinarity have become increasingly widespread (see e.g. May Lee & Yuan, 2018). Most notably, this concerns the integration of modules on (generic) digital skills through a variety of different study programs other than Informatics. Depending on the HEI and the specific study programs, these span from basic software and internet user skills up to (basic) programing skills (LMRO, 2021). Next to the rising prominence of digital skills, an increasing need for interdisciplinarity can also be detected for graduates of science, technology, engineering and mathematics (STEM)-disciplines (Manzini, 2021; OECD, 2011; Shuman et al., 2005). In particular, STEM-graduates face the increasing relevance of non-traditional competences. Manzini (2021) describes not only soft and "professional" skills such as team working, leadership, communication, intercultural skills and flexibility, but also the requirement of understanding the impact of technical solutions in a global, economic, environmental and societal context. Also Graham (2018) refers to the need for a "social education" for STEM graduates; Klaassen et al. (2019) point to the close linkage between scientific-technical competences to contextual characteristics (economic, social, political, cultural) and to the main societal challenges. In addition, Marina et al. (2019) find increased emphasis on foreign language proficiency in STEM study programs.

The trend of interdisciplinarity poses fundamental challenges and trade-offs to the design of education programs. For example, Manzini (2021) sees tensions between providing the desirable level of vertical specialization, multi- and interdisciplinarity as well as horizontal competences within an already challenging and intense undergraduate and graduate STEM education. Therefore, the question arises how to implement the desired interdisciplinarity apart from simply adding contents. There is agreement in the pertinent literature that conveying additional non-traditional skills also requires non-conventional teaching methods, such as "embedded teaching" (incorporating teaching strategies into everyday activities or routines) or "situated teaching" (connecting students with actual social problems through experiential and reflective practice or problem-based learning; Doyle et al., 2019; Van den Beemt et al., 2020).

In terms of curriculum design, there are different ways to integrate non-traditional, cross-disciplinary and employability skills in the educational offering. In particular, two wide-spread options can be observed: On the one hand, there is the trend of implementing (mostly optional) extension programs or extension curricula for giving graduates the possibility to upskill in certain fields, disciplines or competences (see e.g. de Gusmão, 2022). On the other hand, it can be observed that optional or mandatory course modules comprising non-traditional or cross-curricular employability skills are integrated into the curricula (Menz, 2020); oftentimes, they are offered for more than one study program and thus can present an efficient way for HEIs to embed said skills into their offerings.

15.2.2 *Transversal skills as key competences*

Observing trends in HE systems and surveying employer needs, researchers have increasingly tried to elicit which precise skills are supposed to enhance HE graduate employability in recent years. For example, a recent study of *McKinsey Global Institute* focuses on the question of skills that enhance HE graduate employability (Dondi et al., 2021) and described a total of 56 "Distinct Elements of Talent" (DELTA) which they categorized as cognitive, interpersonal, self-leadership and digital skills. In their surveys, the authors found a significantly increased chance of being employed for respondents with higher DELTA proficiencies.

More central to the study at hand is the notion of "future skills", a term that was coined in 2018 by the German association *Stifterverband* and updated in 2021 in a collaborative study with *McKinsey & Company*. They can be defined as "skills and attitudes whose relevance (according to employers) will grow in the professional life of the future" (Burk & Hetze, 2020). Importantly, the authors distinguish between (1) skills that are required in a broad range of employees as new working modes are emerging and (2) specialist technical skills, which are increasingly demanded on the labor market but only required in specialized occupations. The latter primarily concern highly specialized digital skills such as data science, hardware/web development or robotics. Future skills relevant for a broad range of employees involve "classical soft skills" such as the ability to adapt, problem-solving attitude or entrepreneurial thinking, "generic digital skills" like data literacy, software skills or digital learning, and "transformative skills", which are non-digital key competences essential to tackle current societal challenges coming from the climate crisis or the COVID-19 pandemic (Suessenbach et al., 2021).

The model of future skills is illustrated in Figure 15.1, indicating that the skills relevant to a broad range of employees/HE graduates can be considered "transversal skills", a term coined by the OECD in 2019 and emphasizing both the cross-disciplinarity and generic nature of skills, as well as an efficiency when it comes to implementing these skills in HEI's educational offerings, e.g. by creating synergies within and/or across curricula. In its *Learning Compass 2030*, the OECD (2019) defined transversal skills as skills that are "especially valued by employers" and that "(…) can be transferred across different contexts (…) with the potential to reduce curriculum overload and encourage deeper understanding over time as it is inter-related with different topics or subjects". By applying this definition to Suessenbach et al. (2021)'s taxonomy of generic digital and non-digital future skills required in a broad range of employees regardless of their specialization, a total of 15 skill sub-categories can be extracted (see Table 15.1).

The study at hand uses this taxonomy as basis for its curriculum analysis in Austria, Ireland and Portugal. So far, the empirical evidence of the prevalence of transversal skills in curricula throughout HE systems is weak. There are studies focusing on individual study programs or individual skill categories via curriculum analyses, but there is hardly any evidence on the macro-level; if so, then it is rather generated by surveying HEI-representatives, as done by Burk and Hetze (2020) for the German HE sector and the category of generic digital skills. Their findings suggest that around 72% of German HEIs have implemented new educational offerings

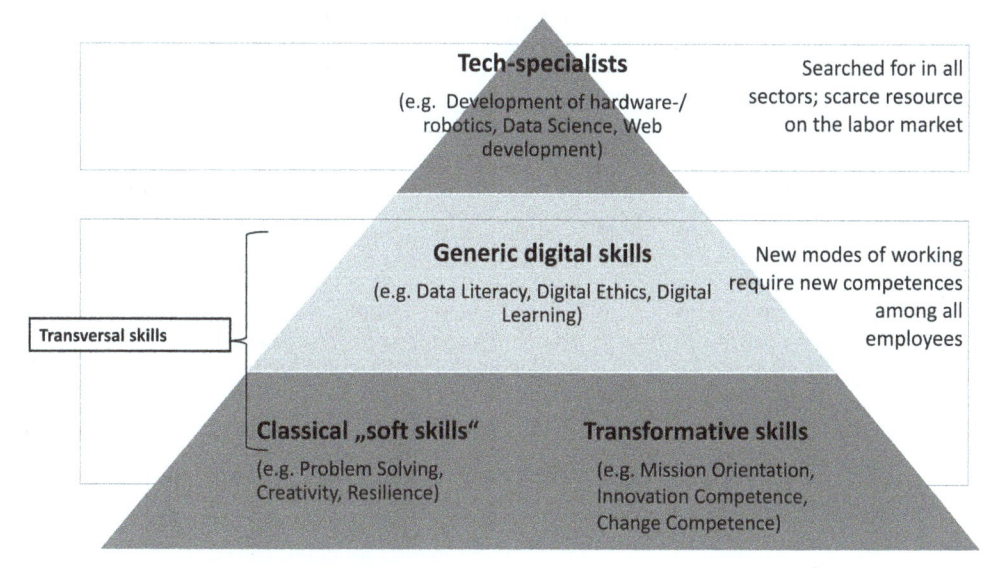

Figure 15.1 Future skills and transversal skills.

Source: Adapted from Suessenbach et al. (2021, p. 5).

Table 15.1 List of transversal skills: Their categories, sub-categories and description

Category	Sub-category	Description
Generic digital skills	Digital literacy	Maintaining basic digital abilities, e.g. careful use of own personal digital data, understanding of basic security rules on the internet, use of mainstream software
	Digital ethics	Critically questioning digital information and effects of one's own digital activities, ethical decision-making
	Digital collaboration	Use of online channels for efficient interaction, collaboration and communication with others; effective and efficient collaboration independent of physical proximity; appropriate etiquette and appearance in digital communication
	Digital learning	Understanding and embedding of digital information; judgment of information from different digital sources; extension of knowledge in selected fields; using learning software
	Agile working	User-oriented, responsible and iterative collaboration in teams by using agile working methods
Classical soft skills	Problem-solving	Solving concrete tasks independently by using own ability to judge and a structured approach
	Creativity	Developing original ideas for improvement (e.g. for existing processes) or ideas for innovation (e.g. for new products)
	Entrepreneurial thinking	Independent acting and working based on self-initiative; high self-efficacy; responsibility for results and processes (ownership)
	Intercultural communication	Goal-oriented and nuanced communication between diverse groups; foreign language skills; competence and sensibility to address a message to its listeners
	Resilience	Achievement in difficult situations and against constraints without permanent impairment; focused and responsible delivery of tasks; recognizing and addressing risks early; ability to adapt; sovereignty against technological and societal changes
Transformative skills	Ability to judge	Reflexion of societal challenges (ecological, social, democratic goals, UN Sustainable Development Goals, sustainable economy, energy literacy); judgment of scientific findings and media reporting
	Innovation competence	Generating innovation (products, services, processes, activities) in professional or private context in order to contribute to mitigate societal challenges and secure independence; questioning status quo and implementing new ideas
	Mission orientation	Development of a mission; creating mission narratives; ability to inspire, convince and move people
	Change competence	Development of strategies for implementing goals for change; understanding for dynamics of groups, institutions, networks and systems; acceptance of sustainable and cultural changes
	Dialog and conflict competence	Overcoming disciplinary and functional limitations; balancing tension and solving dilemmas; understanding for contradictory perspectives and dealing with ambiguities; courage for public debate and sharing one's opinion

Source: Adapted from Suessenbach et al. (2021, p. 6).

for conveying generic digital skills; however, most of these offerings are optional, and among all participating public universities, none indicated to have a compulsory module for all disciplines (and 17.2% compulsory modules for at least one study program). Similarly, precise evidence from HEI surveys or systematic curricula analyses for other countries cannot be found.

15.3 Methodology

The study at hand aims at filling this gap by systematically analyzing whether and how transversal skills are conveyed at public universities in three different European countries, which are Austria, Ireland and Portugal. The three countries were selected into this comparative case study design in order to provide for a heterogenous case study sample. The purpose behind the heterogeneous sampling strategy lies in establishing how HEIs embedded in different systemic conditions approach the question of conveying transversal skills to their graduates. Next to major differences in the economic systems, labor markets and levels of development in the three selected countries, they also differ in terms of their HE systems and with regard to how these affect labor market performance. In the following section, country profiles will illustrate a more detailed analysis of the differences among the three selected countries with regard to parameters relevant for the question of HE skill development and graduate employability.

Data from the three countries was gathered through a curriculum-analysis from public, non-specialized universities. In order to enhance comparability, only universities with more than 10,000 students were included into the sample. With this selection criterion, 6 of 7 Austrian public and non-specialized universities, 7 of 7 Irish and 6 of 13 Portuguese universities were considered,[1] which led to comparable median sizes in terms of students (Austria [AT]: 24,000, Portugal [PT]: 23,000, Ireland [IE]: 18,500). With the exceptions of the University of Vienna (90,000 students) and the University of Lisbon (50,000 students), the remaining universities in the sample count between 12,000 and 31,000 students. The sample universities offer between 19 and 131 Bachelor programs each that were considered (see Table 15.2).

Table 15.2 Sample of public universities: Their number of students and number of investigated BA programs

Austria	University of Vienna	90,000	56
Austria	University of Graz	30,500	60
Austria	University of Innsbruck	27,000	41
Austria	Johannes Kepler University Linz (JKU)	21,000	25
Austria	University of Salzburg	16,000	31
Austria	University of Klagenfurt	12,000	19
Portugal	University of Lisbon	50,000	74
Portugal	University of Porto	31,000	46
Portugal	University of Coimbra	26,000	45
Portugal	NOVA University of Lisbon	20,000	42
Portugal	University of Minho	19,600	49
Portugal	University of Aveiro	14,000	45
Ireland	University College Dublin	33,000	131
Ireland	University College Cork	20,000	125
Ireland	National University of Ireland, Galway	19,000	68
Ireland	Dublin City University	18,500	85
Ireland	Trinity College Dublin	17,500	108
Ireland	University of Limerick	17,000	72
Ireland	Maynooth University	14,000	121

Source: Authors' illustration.

The curriculum analysis was focused on the entire set of Bachelor programs at each of the sample universities. In total, 1,243 Bachelor programs were investigated. The level of Bachelor programs was selected because they represent the first and foundational study cycle that is attended by the largest share of students at a given university. Due to the Bologna process, the Bachelor programs are (1) comparable in structure and program design, and they share a similar total amount of *European Credit Transfer and Accumulation System* (ECTS)-credits for all disciplines throughout all Bologna countries, and (2) supposed to foster practice-orientation and employability, which makes them particularly relevant for the study at hand.

For each Bachelor program, the curriculum was screened for the presence of transversal skills according to the definition mentioned above. While this approach cannot pay attention to differences in the students' conditions or levels of experience that they already have, it is very well suitable to generate evidence on the content-wise integration of transversal skills on a macro-didactic level in the three countries.

The curriculum analysis followed a qualitative deductive coding strategy, which queries the empirical material according to a pre-defined coding scheme (see e.g. Flick, 2002; Früh, 2017). The taxonomy of transversal skills presented in Table 15.1 was used as coding scheme, and the corresponding descriptions (which can also be understood as learning objectives) as coding manual. The investigation followed a three-steps procedure: (1) The title and description of the study program were screened; (2) the title and description of the respective module were screened and compared to the code scheme and coding manual; (3) if the course/module exceeded five ECTS credits[2] and matched a code description, it was assigned the respective code and category, but only if it was not identified as specialized skill of a particular study program. This aspect was controlled for by a comparison with the title and description of the respective study program (e.g. in the curriculum of Informatics, none of the modules representing the category "generic digital skills" was considered. In contrast, a course or module of "generic digital skills" in a Bachelor program such as Business Administration or History was considered).

There are some limitations inherent to the approach: First, the level of analysis within the curricula was the module titles and descriptions. Clearly, they differed among the countries, universities and study programs in scope and information value. Moreover, when applying the analysis scheme to the empirical material, theoretical considerations play a role, but much is left to the researchers' interpretation – an aspect that is inherent to all qualitative research approaches. Finally, it must be noted that each module was coded with one primary code (and very few with a second or a third code, in the rare cases that several transversal skills were conveyed in the frame of one and the same module). In the run of the analysis, only the primary code was considered. An example from the analysis grid can be found in Table 15.3.

The herewith collected data was analyzed quantitatively in terms of frequency analyses and summary statistics. This particular type of a mixed methods approach was selected because of the complexity of the collected data as well as the aim for comparison between the three countries. Analyzing qualitative information quantitatively is a relatively seldom, though established research practice that is suitable to explore complex relationships emerging from qualitative data (see e.g. Fakis et al., 2014).

Table 15.3 Examples from analysis grid

Study program (university)	ECTS	Module title	Module description	Mandatory	Skill category	Skill sub-category
International Business Administration (JKU Linz)	6	Introduction to Software Development with Python	• Knowledge of foundations of programing concepts and paradigms • Ability to use different programing environments • Knowledge regarding syntax of python, data structures (data types, variables, operators, strings, lists, dictionaries) and control structures (case differentiation, clauses, switches and loops), standard I/O, functions and exception handling, file system, important libraries for data analysis	Yes	Generic digital skills	Digital literacy
Pharmaceutical and Industrial Chemistry (University of Limerick)	6	Process trouble shooting	• Methodologies used in the analysis of practical processing problems, techniques used in the solution of practical processing problems, process data gathering and critical thinking skills, troubleshooting methodologies and techniques in practical processing scenarios, skills in the solution of complex, open-ended problems, use of finite volume software to predict the flow field and concentration patterns to a selected engineering problem, use of interpersonal communication skills in the assessment and resolution of management issues associated with industrial process problems	No	Classical soft skills	Problem-solving

Source: Authors' illustration.

15.4 Characteristics of the sample countries' higher education sectors and economies

In order to justify the selection of the sample countries Austria, Ireland and Portugal, and to frame the contexts necessary for interpreting the results of the curriculum analysis, relevant indicators in the three countries will be compared in the present section. In principle, the selection of the three countries fulfills the criteria of a heterogenous purposive sampling strategy: Even though all three countries are comparable in terms of the number of inhabitants (IE: 5.01 Mio., AT: 8.93 Mio., PT: 10.3 Mio.), they have different preconditions with regard to criteria that are relevant to this study, in particular in their HE sectors as well as their economies. Most obviously, they differ dramatically when it comes to their GDP/capita, which is clearly below the EU average in Portugal (23,284 compared to an EU average of approx. 33,000; values of 2019), while clearly above EU average in Austria (50,121 in 2019) and almost 1.5 times higher than the EU average in Ireland (80,778 in 2019). Also in 2020, the first year touched by the COVID-19 pandemic, the Irish GDP/capita remained more than twice as high than the European average; the Austrian GDP/capita was 24% higher and the Portuguese 23% lower than the EU average (Eurostat, 2021a).

Also the share and composition of HE graduates varies in the three countries concerned. The highest share of individuals with a HE degree in the total population can be found in Ireland with a total of 47.3%. Thereof, the large majority is holding a Bachelors degree as the highest degree attained (27.6%), Masters degrees are less widespread (11.6%). The share of academics in the population is less elevated in Austria and Portugal. In Austria, only 33.8% of the population hold a HE degree, the majority resulting from short-term tertiary education (15.5%) which, however, also comprises certificates of secondary schools offering vocational training (*Berufsbildende Höhere Schulen*), which can be considered an Austrian peculiarity. In contrast to Ireland, the Bachelors degree as highest degree attained is less widespread (4.3%) than the Masters degree (12.8%). Considering the ratio of Bachelor and Masters degrees, Portugal has a similar pattern as Austria with 7% Bachelor and 18.3% Masters degrees. Considering the total share of individuals with a HE degree in the population, Portugal ranges clearly below the EU average with 26.2% (OECD, 2020) as can be viewed in Figure 15.2.

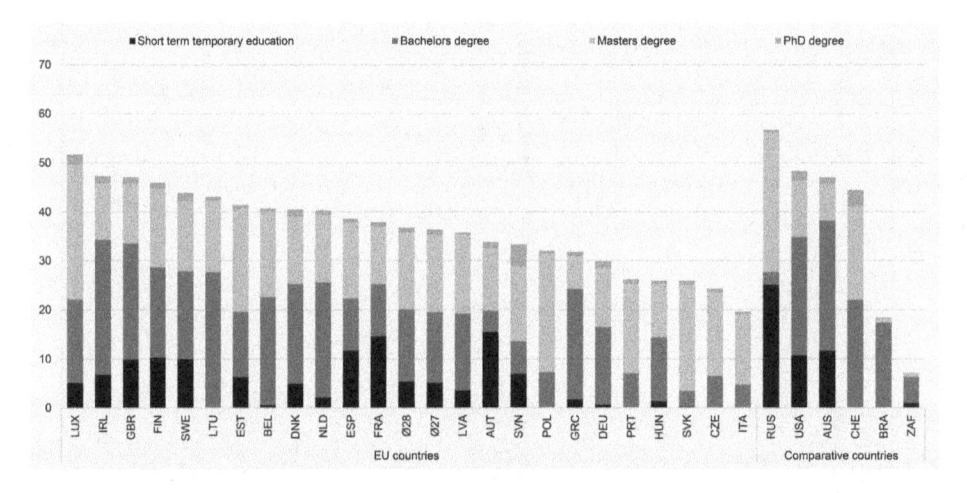

Figure 15.2 Share of the population with higher education degrees.

Source: OECD (2020).

15.4.1 *Differences in the national higher education systems*

Most notably, the three countries' HE systems differ with regards the role of the public versus the private HE sector. Austria's HE system has traditionally been relying on public funding to a much higher extent than in the two other countries. Looking at government expenditure per student in tertiary education expressed as percentage of GDP per capita in 2015, the Austrian government spent 36% of its GDP/capita per student in tertiary education, the Portuguese government close to 27%, the Irish government 19% (Roser & Ortiz-Ospina, 2019). When comparing the inflation-adjusted change in public funding to universities from 2008 to 2019, Austria is among the top investors with a plus of 20% and more, while Irish and Portuguese HEIs faced declines of 20% or more throughout the same period (Bennetot Pruvot et al., 2021).

In the most recent publication of their "annual public funding observatory", Bennetot Pruvot et al. (2021) set public funding trends in relation to student enrolment and economic growth between 2008 and 2019. They show that in Austria, increases in public HEI funding fell out higher than both student number growth and economic growth throughout the observed period. Oppositely, in Ireland, funding decreased despite student number growth and economic growth. In contrast, Portuguese public funding increased higher than economic growth, but lower than student number growth. As a consequence, the three countries also face differences in their annual public expenditure on HEIs per student (AT: 11,365, IE: 7,716, PT: 4,710 € per student in full-time equivalents, values for 2015, see Eurostat, 2021b).

The different roles of the public versus the private HE sector are also expressed in the number of students enrolled at private and public HEIs. In autumn term 2020/21, a total 245,663 students were enrolled in Irish HEIs, which is an increase of 4.3% in comparison to the previous year and a rise of 17.5% through the past six years (HEA, 2021). Thereof, close to 38% of students were enrolled in the private sector, which makes the largest proportion in all the three observed countries (PT: 18.64%; Statistics Portugal, 2021; AT: 4.3%, Statistik Austria, 2021). Austria counted a total of 387,775 enrolled students in autumn term 2020/21, a plus of 3.11% compared to the previous year. Through the last six years, the number of students enrolled in Austria has remained relatively stable. Compared to the Irish growth in student numbers since 2014, Austria registered a growth of moderate 3% (Statistik Austria, 2021). In Portugal, a total of 411,995 students were enrolled in tertiary education in autumn term 2020/21, which is an increase of close to 4% compared to the year before, and an increase of close to 14% throughout the past six years (Statistics Portugal, 2021).

Significant differences between the three countries can also be found when it comes to the allocation mechanisms of public funding. While performance agreements determine the

Table 15.4 Development of public funding of HEIs in relation to student enrolment and economic growth between 2008 and 2019

Country	Public funding student enrolment	Public funding and economic growth
Austria	Funding increase higher than student number growth	Funding higher than economic growth
Portugal	Funding increase lower than student number growth	Funding higher than economic growth
Ireland	Funding decrease despite student number growth	Funding decrease despite economic growth

Source: Bennetot Pruvot et al. (2019).

allocation of public funding to Austrian universities primarily, they play a secondary role in Portugal and Ireland. In Portugal, the primary mechanism for allocating public funding to universities is input related (with indicators such as the number of BA/MA/doctoral students and staff; ECTS, degrees and external funding obtained). In Ireland, the input-oriented mechanisms dominate for teaching-related funding, while for research-related funding, output-oriented mechanisms are decisive (based on indicators such as obtained research contracts) (Dallago, 2020).

Further differences can be found in details of the structures of degrees, while overall, the three countries implemented reform processes to comply with the requirements of European harmonization according to the *Bologna strategy* and therefore introduced aspects such as the *European Credit Transfer System* in study cycles, mobility mechanisms or diploma supplements in the early 2000s. Moreover, in all three countries, different HEI types exist that comprise public and private universities/colleges with a more general, research-oriented and scientific education on the one hand, and institutions with a focus on applied research and development on the other (IE: "Institutes of Technology", AT: "Universities of applied sciences", PT: "Polytechnics"). Moreover, in Austria and Ireland, there are specialized pedagogic institutions for teacher education (IE: "Colleges of Education", AT: "Pedagogic HEIs"). In Portugal, teachers' education is embedded in regular universities.

According to the *Bologna strategy*, in each of the observed countries study programs are offered by study cycle, all of which comprise Bachelors, Masters and PhD degrees. The Irish HE system distinguishes between "undergraduate" programs (Bachelors) and "postgraduate" programs (Diploma, Masters or PhD). In Austria and Portugal, the Masters program is much rather referred to as "graduate program", and only programs addressed to students with completed Masters degrees are considered "postgraduate". It can be assumed that this difference in perception of a Masters degree, in Austria and Portugal as essential component to become a "graduate", in Ireland an extra cycle to become a "post-graduate", is part of the reason why Masters degrees are more widespread in Austria and Portugal as highest educational attainment than a Bachelors degree. In Austria, for example, Bachelor graduates use to have difficulties in finding qualified employment, since they continue to be considered closer to a upper secondary school graduate than to a "fully educated" academic (LMRO, 2021). Also in Portugal, a relatively large share of tertiary students pursue a Masters degree, either through long first degrees (*mestrado integrado*) or following a Bachelors degree (*mestrado*). In 2017, about 33% of all tertiary students in Portugal were enrolled on Masters level, which is more than double than the OECD average of 16% (OECD, 2020).

15.4.2 *(Higher) education, the labor market and job mismatches*

The three observed countries also differ with a view to how well (higher) education graduates are integrated into the labor market. Unsurprisingly, general unemployment rates among HE graduates are relatively low in all the three countries. In comparison, Austria has constantly had the lowest unemployment rate among HE graduates since 2008 (around 3%), while the Irish and Portuguese rates have seen their highs (Portugal in 2010 with more than 10%, Ireland in 2016 with more than 16%) but declined in 2017 and remained below (Ireland) or just above (Portugal) 5% until 2020 (see Figure 15.3; OECD, 2021). Considering employment of young HE graduates (within one to two years after their graduation, see Figure 15.4), the Portuguese employment rate has been clearly below that of the two other countries between 2004 and 2020 (Eurostat, 2021), while the Austrian rate has been on the rise as of 2005 and remained stable on a relatively high level. The Irish rate has seen a low with the outbreak of

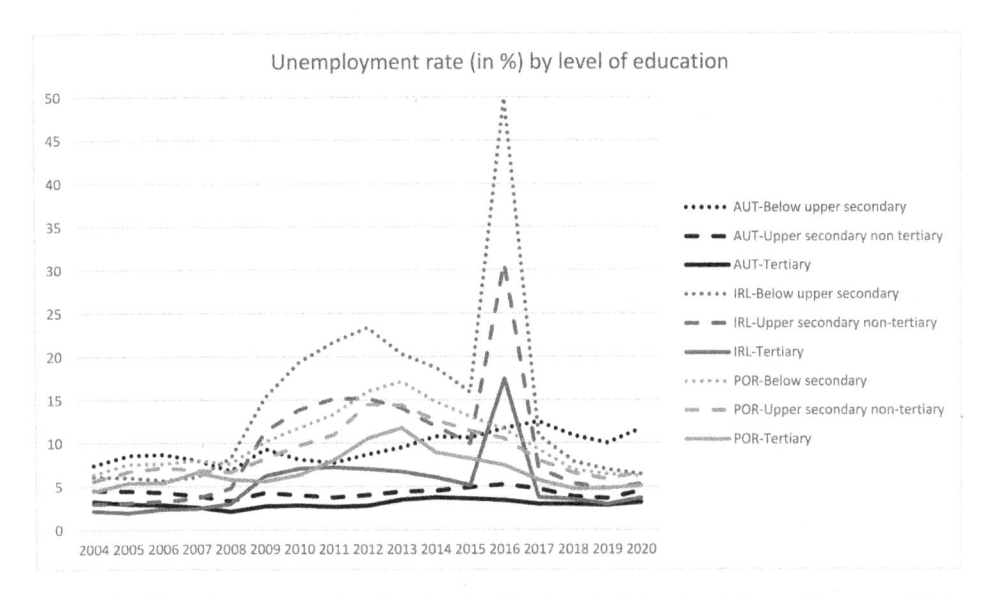

Figure 15.3   Unemployment rate by education level in Austria, Ireland and Portugal between 2004 and 2020.

Source: Authors' illustration, based on data from Eurostat (2021c).

the financial and economic crisis in 2008 and only came back to a level of 85% as of 2017 (Eurostat, 2021c).

Another important indicator is that of job mismatch, which reflects the extent of how well the conveyed skills in a (higher) education system match the skills demanded on the labor market. Here, vertical and horizontal job mismatches can be distinguished. According to data from Eurostat (2021), vertical job mismatch refers to the discrepancies between educational

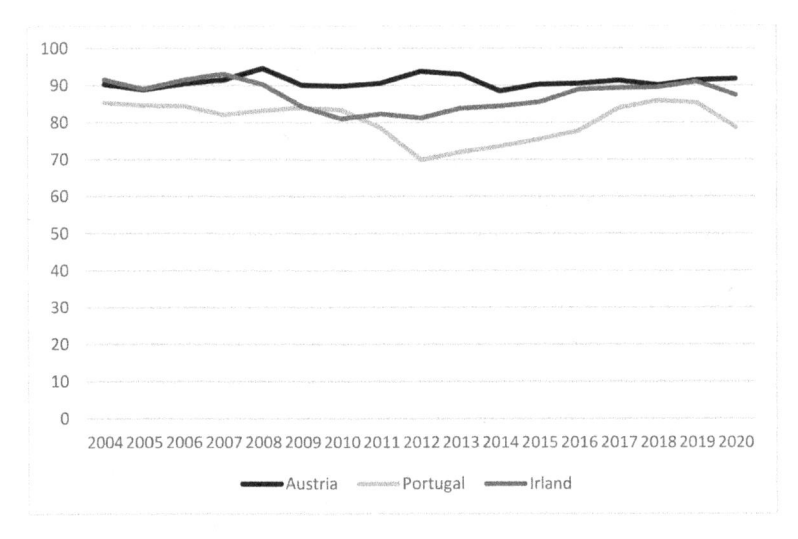

Figure 15.4   Employment rate among young higher education graduates (1–3 years after graduation) in Austria, Portugal and Ireland.

Source: Authors' illustration, based on data from Eurostat (2021c).

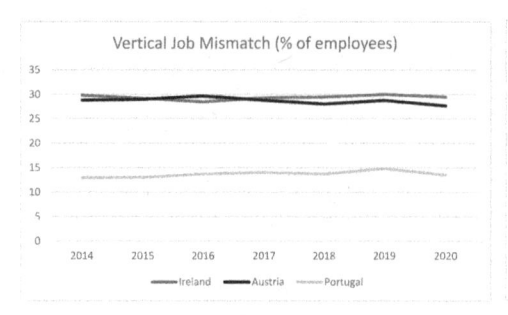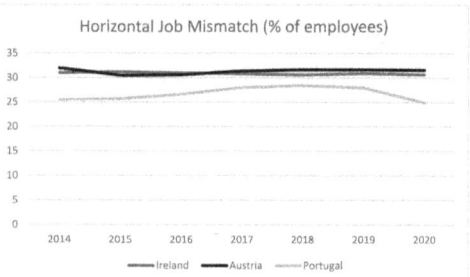

Figure 15.5   Vertical and horizontal job mismatch in percent of employees for Ireland, Austria and Portugal: 2014–2020.

Source: Authors' illustration, based on data from Eurostat (2021).

attainment levels and occupations. That is, if the mismatch is high in an economy, many employees hold occupations below their educational attainment level – they are overqualified. In contrast, horizontal job mismatch expresses misalignments between the education field of the highest level of education attained and occupations. If horizontal mismatch is high in an economy, many employees hold occupations that might match their educational attainment levels, but not their educational discipline. Figure 15.5 compares the extent of vertical and horizontal job mismatch of employees in Austria, Ireland and Portugal (Eurostat, 2021d).

As can be viewed in figure 15.5, Ireland and Austria have been facing relatively high levels of vertical and horizontal job mismatch between 2014 and 2020. For Ireland, the share of employees who are formally overqualified for their occupations was moving around 30% in the period observed. Austria's share of overqualified personnel has slightly decreased since 2016 and was at around 27% in 2020. Similarly, Austria and Ireland face a high share of horizontal job mismatch of around 30% (Ireland) or slightly above (Austria). In Portugal, in contrast, vertical mismatch remained below 15% through the observed period, while the horizontal mismatch was higher but stagnating as of 2018. In 2020, Portuguese employees facing a horizontal job mismatch made up 25% of all employees, thus less than in the other two countries. The different levels of job mismatch in the three countries are not surprising, given the different nature of their economies and labor markets. For example, higher shares of temporary contracts increase both vertical and horizontal mismatch (because employers and workers are less selective), while higher long-term unemployment particularly decreases overqualification (because less-able workers are kept out of employment; Croce and Ghignoni, 2012). The differences might also be due to the different extent of job polarization in the three countries (Goos & Manning, 2007), i.e. the trend of growing shares of high- and low-skill jobs at the expense of medium-skill jobs, which often leads to overqualification. Job polarization uses to be particularly high in countries that adopt the technical progress rapidly and replace manual and cognitive routine tasks by technology (Sparreboom & Tarvid, 2016). This also affects HE graduates, since a (small) proportion of them (e.g. in Austria 25%, see Wedenig et al., 2017) uses to perform cognitive, and, to a lesser extent, manual routine tasks.

15.5 Results from the curriculum analysis

The following section will present results from the curriculum analyses in the three countries. Even though the analysis aimed at revealing differences and communalities on the level of national HE systems, a certain diversity was also found within the national systems, which will be presented in the first part of this section, while the second part aims at comparing at national level. The third part is dedicated to analyzing the found (sub-)categories of transversal skills.

15.5.1 Diversity within national HE systems

The curriculum analysis showed that all of the observed universities have transversal skills embedded in their educational offerings, and all of them offer transversal skill modules at least in selected Bachelor programs. Some universities offer additional optional extension programs also comprising transversal skill modules. One essential finding is that most universities that do so offer less transversal skill modules within their Bachelor curricula. One example is the University of Vienna with a total of 155 "extension curricula" of 15–30 ECTS which are "compulsory optional subjects", meaning that Bachelor students must attend one or several of these modules but are free to select which ones. At the same time, less than a third of the University of Vienna's Bachelor programs have transversal skill modules anchored directly within the curricula. Similar findings were made for the Universities of Graz and Innsbruck in Austria, and the Universities of Porto and Minho in Portugal. At Irish universities, many Bachelor curricula foresee (compulsory) optional electives. In the case of University College Dublin, for example, a substantial number of its compulsory electives can be categorized as transversal skill modules, while less than 15% of its Bachelor programs have transversal skill modules explicitly embedded in their curricula. In contrast, one university that goes against this tendency is the Alpen Adria University Klagenfurt, which offers (purely optional) extension curricula that can be categorized as transversal skill modules; at the same time, 100% of its Bachelor programs contain explicit transversal skill modules. In the run of the analysis, extension curricula or other elective modules were disregarded, unless they were explicitly anchored within a particular Bachelor program; thus, the herewith presented results do not reflect any additional, extracurricular modules.

When it comes to the number of transversal skill modules in the curricula, there is also great heterogeneity within the observed countries – particularly among the Irish universities – that are only partly linked to university size and the number of the offered Bachelor programs (see Table 15.5). To a great extent, they show how universities design their curricula differently. For example, when it comes to foreign language courses which were sub-categorised "intercultural communication skills" in study programs other than language studies, some universities explicitly list each available language and each level of proficiency explicitly in their curricula, others only use a generic placeholder such as "Foreign Language I". Thus, in the said sub-category, there are major differences between the universities, e.g. 65 modules at University College Cork (thereof 63 language courses) versus 0 modules at Dublin City University.

Further differences can be seen when it comes to the allocation of ECTS, which differs greatly between, and partly within, the three countries (as outlined below; see Table 15.5). While the Portuguese universities have similar mean ECTS values allocated to their transversal skill modules (standard deviation of 0.29 ECTS), the Austrian and Irish mean values differ more strongly (standard deviations of 2.5 and 2.8 ECTS, respectively). In Austria, the Universities of Linz and Innsbruck have relatively low ECTS values (means of around 8.5), while the University of Graz has a mean of more than 15 ECTS. In Ireland, the University of Limerick has a mean value of 6 ECTS for transversal skill modules, while Trinity College Dublin has a mean that is more than twice as high with 14.3 ECTS. At Dublin City University, the majority of modules have either 5 or 10 ECTS. As mentioned above, modules valuing

Table 15.5 General overview of universities and countries

University	ECTS of transversal skill modules							
	Share of programs with transversal skills modules (in %)	Number of transversal skill modules	Min	Max	Mean	Median	Number of mandatory transversal skills modules	Share of mandatory modules (in %)
University of Lisbon	36.49	79	6	7	6.01	6	14	17.72
University of Porto	4.35	5	6	6	6	6	5	100
University of Coimbra	51.11	64	6	12	6.09	6	19	29.69
NOVA University of Lisbon	64.29	18	6	7.5	6.08	6	14	77.78
University of Minho	16.33	9	6	10	6.69	6	3	33.33
University of Aveiro	72.41	99	6	12	6.35	6	73	73.74
Average Portugal	**40.83**	**46**	**6**	**9.08**	**6.2**	**6**	**21.33**	**55.38**
University of Vienna	30.91	23	7	15	11.3	10	10	43.48
Johannes Kepler University of Linz	68	30	6	24	8.68	6	21	70
University of Graz	16.67	19	6	24	15.1	13.5	11	57.89
University of Innsbruck	21.95	18	7.5	14	8.31	7.5	9	50
Paris Lodron University of Salzburg	41.94	16	6	21	11.4	12	16	100
Alpen Adria University of Klagenfurt	100	43	6	36	12.7	12	7	16.28
Average Austria	**46.58**	**24.83**	**6.4**	**22.3**	**11.3**	**10.17**	**12.33**	**56.28**
University College Dublin	14.5	64	10	15	11.9	10	3	4.69
University College Cork	21.6	89	10	30	10.3	10	17	19.1
National University of Ireland, Galway	20.59	64	10	15	12.5	12.5	0	0
Dublin City University	10.34	10	10	10	10	10	2	20
Trinity College Dublin	6.48	7	10	20	14.3	10	4	57.14
University of Limerick	27.78	39	6	6	6	6	15	38.46
Maynooth University	16.53	214	7.5	15	7.78	7.5	0	0
Average Ireland	**17.22**	**70.5**	**8.9**	**16**	**10.6**	**9.33**	**6.33**	**22.45**

Source: Authors' illustration.

5 ECTS were not counted in the analysis, even if content wise, they would have matched the definition underlying this study. In parts, the observed discrepancies are due to qualitative differences in design of the modules and their workload (see below) which are not reflected in the assigned (sub-)categories. That said, the findings are in line with well-known and persisting difficulties in harmonizing credit allocation across universities and, even more so, across Europe (see e.g. Veiga et al., 2019).

Finally, there is a certain heterogeneity in the universities' focus of transversal skill modules, which is particularly pronounced in Ireland and Portugal (see Table 15.7). For the three skill categories, Austrian universities show the greatest uniformity. Particularly when it comes to the category of generic digital skills, the standard deviation for the number of modules offered at Austrian universities is less than 2.5 (in contrast: 13.3 in Portugal and 20.5 in Ireland). The greatest heterogeneity within the Irish sector can be found in the category of classical soft skills with a standard deviation of 37.6, which is partly due to the different handling of language modules in Irish curricula as indicated above. In contrast, the number of offered transversal skill modules in the category of classical soft skills shows considerably more homogeneity in Austria (standard deviation of 3.3) and Portugal (6.7). In the category of transformative skills, Portuguese universities have a highly varying offering (standard deviation of 19.1), similar to Irish universities (19.8). It is also the category in which Austrian universities show their highest heterogeneity (5.9).

15.5.2 Findings on a national level

In spite of the above-mentioned heterogeneity across universities, some important findings could be elicited on national level. As can be seen in Table 15.5, among the three countries, Austrian universities hold the biggest share of Bachelor programs that offer transversal skill modules explicitly within their curricula (close to 47%), followed by Portugal with close to 41%. In contrast in Ireland, only slightly above 17% of the programs offer transversal skill modules. Coherently, the five universities with the largest share of programs offering transversal skills exclusively comprise Austrian and Portuguese universities with shares between 51.1% (University of Coimbra) and 100% (Alpen Adria University of Klagenfurt), while the five universities with the lowest shares comprise three Irish universities and range between 4.35% (University of Porto) and slightly above 16% (University Minho; see Table 15.6).

Table 15.6 Universities with the highest (above) and the lowest (below) share of programs offering transversal skill modules

Alpen Adria University of Klagenfurt	100
University of Aveiro	72.41
Johannes Kepler University of Linz	68
NOVA University of Lisbon	64.29
University of Coimbra	51.11
University of Porto	4.35
Trinity College Dublin	6.48
Dublin City University	10.34
University College Dublin	14.5
University of Minho	16.33

Source: Authors' illustration.

As outlined above, it was found that the allocation of ECTS to transversal skill modules varies strongly between the observed universities; they do so even more between the three countries. In Portugal, the considered transversal skill modules have a mean of 6.2 ECTS, while in Austria it is almost twice as high with 11.3 ECTS. Ireland ranges in between with 10.2 ECTS. Major differences between the countries were also found when it comes to the question whether the transversal skill modules are mandatory in the respective curriculum. Here again, Austrian universities have the highest mean share of mandatory modules with 56.3%, closely followed by Portugal with 55.4%. In Ireland, on average only 22.5% of the modules are mandatory (see Table 15.5).

The analysis also revealed differences with a view to study fields in which transversal skill modules are offered. For analyzing this aspect, the study programs were categorized on the basis of the OECD's "List of Fields of Science and Technology" (2007). Adaptations to the classification were made in order to better reflect the observed universities' division in faculties. Interdisciplinary programs were categorized according to the respective university's own assignation of the subject to a faculty.[3] Figure 15.6 shows the number of transversal skill modules offered per study field per university and per country, as well as the share of all modules per field and per country. For Portugal, the large majority with close to 40% of all transversal skill modules are offered in programs belonging to engineering and technical sciences, followed by the natural (including agricultural and health) sciences with over 26%. The other study fields hold a considerably smaller share of transversal skill modules, particularly the legal sciences in which slightly more than 1% of all transversal skill modules are offered.

In contrast, both in Austria and Ireland, the highest shares of transversal skill modules can be found in the fields of social and economic sciences (AT: 30%; IE: close to 25%), followed by the Arts, Humanities and Educational sciences (AT: close to 27%; IE: close to 24%). It is noticeable that in Austria and Ireland, as in Portugal, the legal sciences hold the smallest share

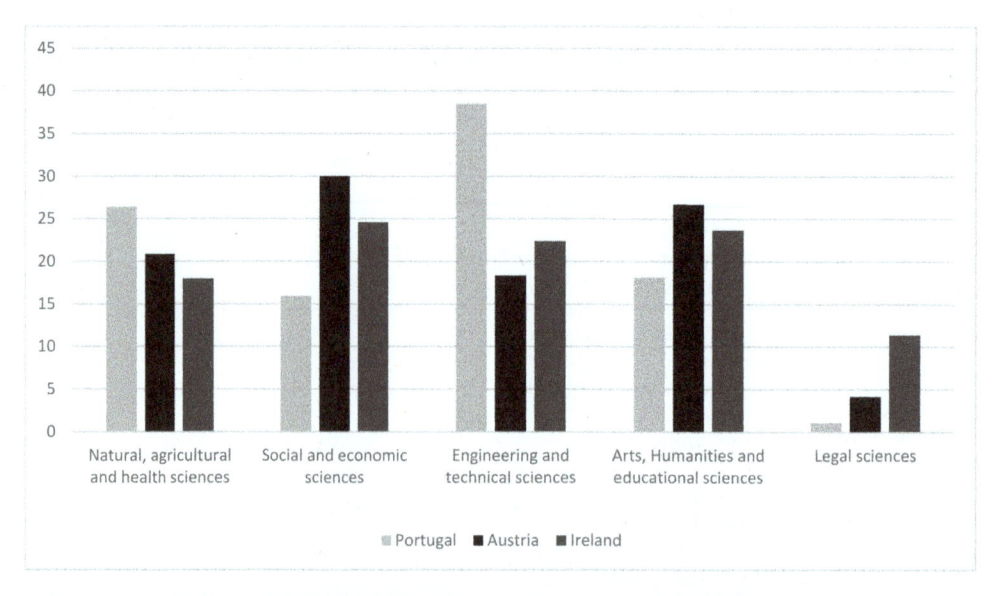

Figure 15.6 Share of all transversal skill modules per study field per country.

Source: Authors' illustration.

of transversal skill modules[4]; however, the gap to the other study fields is less pronounced in Austria with more than 4% and even less so in Ireland with more than 11%.

15.5.3 Representation of skill (sub-)categories

Data was also analyzed along the three different transversal skill categories and their 15 sub-categories as they were represented at the three countries' observed universities. With the exceptions of the sub-categories "agile working" and "digital collaboration", both belonging to the category generic digital skills, all sub-categories were found in the investigated curricula, even though in diverging frequency (see Figure 15.7).

While the sub-categories "digital learning" and "resilience" only have two mentions each, the most frequent sub-categories represented in the Bachelor curricula of all the three countries are "intercultural communication" (267 mentions), "ability to judge" (216) and "digital literacy" (206). The sub-category "intercultural communication" is particularly strongly represented in Irish curricula, which take 80% of all mentions. In contrast, "ability to judge" is almost evenly represented in all three countries. For "digital literacy", Portugal takes close to 50% of all mentions. Looking at the total of Portuguese transversal skill modules, "digital literacy" is the sub-category that is most strongly represented and takes more than 37% of all sub-categories represented at Portuguese universities. This is markedly more than in the remaining countries (Austria: 26%, Ireland: 15%).

Table 15.7 compares the number of represented sub-categories, the number of modules and mean ECTS values per module on the level of categories. Classical soft skills is the category with most sub-categories represented in the curricula of all the three countries, with average

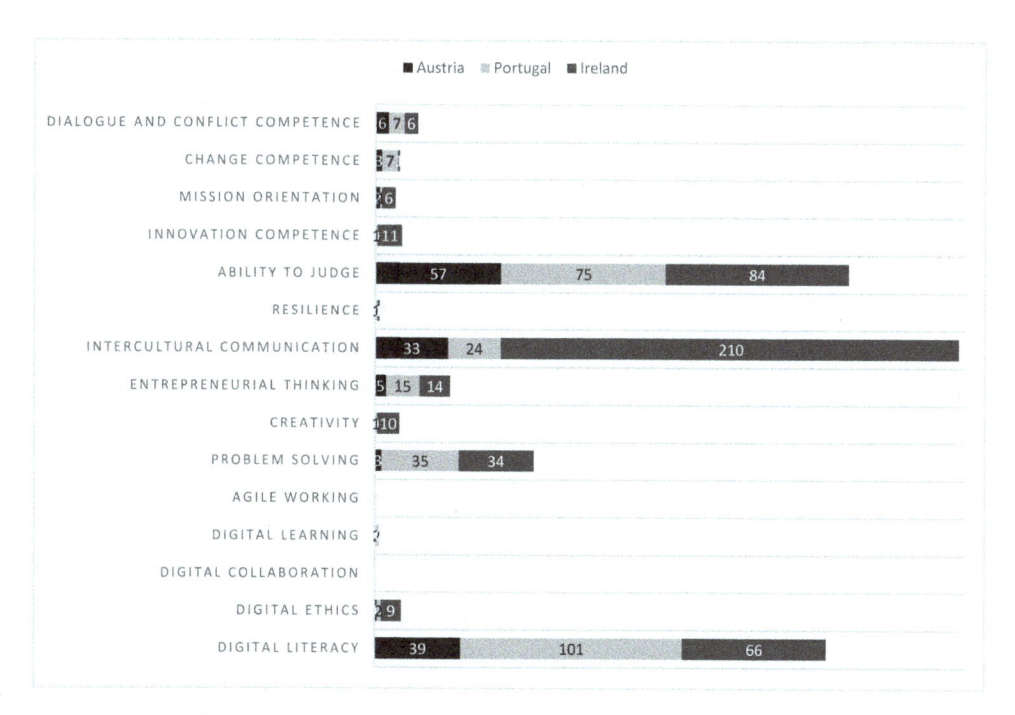

Figure 15.7 Number of transversal skill modules per sub-category per country (absolute numbers).
Source: Authors' illustration.

Table 15.7 Indicators for the three categories per university and per country

	Generic digital skills			Classical soft skills			Transformative skills		
	Number of sub-categories	Number of modules	Average ECTS	Number of sub-categories	Number of modules	Average ECTS	Number of sub-categories	Number of modules	Average ECTS
University of Lisbon	1	35	6	3	5	6	3	39	6
University of Porto	2	2	6	2	2	6	1	1	6
University of Coimbra	2	11	6.34	4	17	6	3	36	6
NOVA University of Lisbon	1	14	6.12	2	2	6	2	2	6
University of Minho	2	3	7.75	1	1	6	2	5	6
University of Aveiro	1	40	6.92	3	49	6.31	3	10	6
Average PT	**1.5**	**17.5**	**6.52**	**2.5**	**12.67**	**6.05**	**2.33**	**15.5**	**6**
University of Vienna	1	9	10.44	3	4	9.75	2	10	10.56
Johannes Kepler University of Linz	1	9	10.29	1	7	6.57	4	13	8.71
University of Graz	1	7	14.5	1	4	13.5	1	8	13.88
University of Innsbruck	1	3	7.5	3	6	9.92	3	9	7.78
Paris Lodron University of Salzburg	2	4	11	2	7	11	2	5	12.5
Alpen Adria University of Klagenfurt	1	8	12.43	2	13	11.14	2	22	12.55
Average AT	**1.17**	**6.67**	**11.03**	**2**	**6.83**	**10.31**	**2.33**	**11.17**	**11**
University College Dublin	2	15	10	1	20	14.25	3	29	11.94
University College Cork	2	5	10	3	67	16.67	2	17	10
National University of IE, Galway	0	0	–	2	61	11.25	1	1	10
Dublin City University	1	1	10	1	6	10	1	3	10
Trinity College Dublin	0	0	–	2	2	10	2	5	15
University of Limerick	2	7	6	4	25	6	3	7	6
Maynooth University	1	57	7.5	3	104	7.77	3	56	7.52
Average IE	**1.14**	**12.14**	**8.70**	**2.29**	**40.71**	**10.85**	**2.14**	**16.86**	**10.07**

Source: Authors' illustration.

values between 2 (Austria) and 2.5 (Portugal) sub-categories per university. In terms of the number of modules, the category classical soft skills is most strongly represented in Ireland with a mean value of close to 41 modules per university. As outlined above, this is partly due to the way language courses are indicated in many Irish curricula. In total, almost 60% of all transversal skills modules in Irish curricula fall into the classical soft skills category. Its relative importance in Irish curricula is also expressed in terms of average ECTS values: The Irish value of 10.85 ECTS per classical soft skill-module is relatively high, both compared to the two other countries' values for the same category and to the Irish values for the remaining two categories. In contrast, in Austria and Portugal, the category of classical soft skills has the lowest average ECTS value throughout all three categories.

The lowest number of sub-categories could be found in the category of generic digital skills, with mean values ranging from 1.14 (Ireland) to 1.5 (Portugal) sub-categories per university. This emphasizes the leading role that Portugal takes in the category of generic digital skills among the three countries: As Table 15.7 shows, also with a view to the number of generic digital skill modules, Portuguese universities have the highest mean value with 17.5 modules per university. This is almost twice as high than in Austria (6.67) and 30% higher than in Ireland (12.14). Also, the Portuguese mean ECTS value of 6.52 is relatively high in that category, given that Portugal has been found in this study as a country with relatively moderate ECTS allocation for transversal skill modules: It is higher than the Portuguese mean value through all transversal skill modules (6.2) and comes close to the Irish mean value in the generic digital skill category (8.70, while the Irish mean through all transversal skill categories is as high as 10.2 ECTS). These findings substantiate the evidence of Portugal's particularly strong focus on conveying digital skills in the frame of their curricula.

In the category of transformative skills, the coverage of sub-categories is comparable in the three countries (between an average of 2.14 [IE] and 2.33 [AT, PT] per university). For the case of Austria, the transformative skills category is the one with the highest number of modules (almost twice as high as in the remaining two categories). The sub-category "ability to judge" takes more than 38% of all transversal skills modules in Austrian study programs (in contrast only 27.6% in Portugal and 18.4% in Ireland). This suggests a relatively high importance of the transformative skills category in Austrian curricula compared to the other two countries.

15.6 Conclusion and discussion

Focusing on the notion of HE graduate employability and leaning on Suessenbach et al. (2021)'s future skills, this chapter introduced the concept of transversal skills and investigated whether and how transversal skills were embedded in Bachelor programs of Austria, Ireland and Portugal. A total of 1,243 curricula from public universities in the three countries were investigated via a curriculum analysis in order to elicit communalities and differences on the level of national HE systems. One essential finding was, however, that a certain heterogeneity exists within the national systems, which can only partly be explained by the universities' autonomy. In particular, inconsistencies in the allocation of ECTS were detected when comparing mean ECTS values allocated to transversal skill modules of the same category. Also when comparing the national systems, major differences in the ECTS allocation were found. This is in line with previous findings on continuing inconsistencies in ECTS allocation, as e.g. stressed in Veiga et al. (2019).

Further differences between the three HE systems were found with a view to how well represented transversal skills are in the Bachelor programs, and whether or not they are mandatory. In Austria and Portugal, almost half of all Bachelor curricula offer transversal skill modules, and in both countries more than half of these modules are mandatory. In contrast, in Ireland both values circulate around 20%. Moreover, the three countries show a different concentration of transversal skill modules on the level of study fields: In Portugal, most modules are offered in engineering, technical and natural sciences, while the focus in Austria and Ireland is on social and economic sciences as well as the humanities.

On the level of categories and sub-categories of transversal skills, there is strong evidence for a clear focus of Portuguese universities on generic digital skills, particularly digital literacy. The general digital skills category is substantially more represented in Portugal than any of the other categories and is also clearly more pronounced than in the two comparative countries. In contrast, Irish universities show a stronger focus on the classical soft skill category, while Austrian universities have higher scores in the category of transformative skills. Further research is necessary to bring these results in relationship with other parameters in the countries' HE systems and their labor markets for HE graduates. In particular, the focus on generic digital skills throughout all disciplines in Portugal can be investigated with a view to their relatively low prevalence of job mismatch, since a digitally literate workforce may be able to better handle technological progress (following up on Sparreboom and Tarvid, 2016).

There are limitations to this study inherent to the applied methodology as outlined in Section 15.3. In addition to these, it must be noted that analyzing qualitative differences within the found sub categories in the curricula was not an objective of this study, nor questioning the suitability of Suessenbach et al. (2021)'s skill taxonomy in its empirical application. In both regards, further research is necessary. For example, the digital literacy sub-category covers a wide range of skills from the use of spreadsheet software up to basic programing in the curricula. More detailed investigations are necessarily to gain more profound knowledge on the different nature of skills that are conveyed within a transversal skill (sub-)category.

Acknowledgments

The research discussed in this chapter was assisted by Bernhard Würfel and Mara Kritzinger.

Notes

1 For the case of Austria, there are 22 public universities, thereof 15 specialised universities (medical, technical, business, arts). From the remaining seven non-specialised universities, one was excluded from the sample because it has less than 10,000 students. In Ireland, there is a total of 7 non-specialised public universities that were all included into the sample. For Portugal, there are 13 public universities that fulfill the above-mentioned criteria, out of which the 6 public universities with more than 10.000 students were considered.

2 This limitation was set in order to exclude "micro-courses".

3 For example, the study program of "Business Informatics" was counted to the Social and Economic Sciences at those universities where it is offered from the Faculty of Social and Economic Sciences; the study program "Business Law" was counted to the Legal studies at those universities where it is offered from the Faculty of Law. Further adaptations to OECD (2007): Agricultural and Health Sciences were counted to the Natural Sciences; Arts, Humanities and Educational Sciences were bundled as one category; Legal sciences were separated from Social and Economic Sciences.

4 It must be noted that Legal Sciences is the smallest study field considered in this study. According to OECD (2007), it is supposed to be counted to the Social and Economic Sciences. For the purposes of this study, it was used as separate category to better reflect the observed universities' division in faculties (those offering legal studies have a separate Faculty of Law).

References

Ayoubi, R.M., Alzarif, K. and Khalifa, B. (2017). The employability skills of business graduates in Syria. *Education + Training, 59*(1), 61–75.

Barth, M., Godemann, J., Rieckmann, M. and Stoltenberg, U. (2007). Developing key competencies for sustainable development in higher education. *International Journal of Sustainability in Higher Education, 8*(4), 416–430.

Bennetot Pruvot, E., Estermann, T. and Stoyanova, H. (2021). European University Association. *Public Funding Observatory Report 2020/2021 Part 2.* https://eua.eu/downloads/publications/eua%20pfo%20part%202%20report.pdf

Berghäuser, H. and Hölschel, M. (2020). Reinventing the third mission of higher education in Germany: Political frameworks and universities' reactions. *Tertiary Education and Management, 26,* 57–76. https://doi.org/10.1007/s11233-019-09030-3

Brundier, K., Barth, M., Cebrián, G., Cohen, M., Diaz, L., Doucette-Remington, S. and Zint, M. (2021). Key competencies in sustainability in higher education—Toward an agreed-upon reference framework. *Sustainability Science, 16*(1), 13–29.

Burk, M. and Hetze, P. (2020). Hochschul-Barometer. Lage und Entwicklung der Hochschulen aus Sicht ihrer Leitungen, Ausgabe 2020.

Croce, G. and Ghignoni, E. (2012). Demand and supply of skilled labour and overeducation in Europe: A country-level analysis. *Comparative Economic Studies, 54*(2), 413–439. doi:10.1057/ces.2012.12

Dallago, B. (2020). European higher education: Challenges and achievement, in: Andreff W. (ed.). *European Comparative Economic Studies: Thirty Years After. In Honour of Horst Brezinski,* Palgrave MacMillan, pp. 111–147.

de Gusmão, C.M.G. (2022). Digital competencies and transformation in higher education: Upskilling with extension actions. *Training Engineering Students for Modern Technological Advancement.* Hershey, PA: IGI Global, pp. 313–328.

DiMaggio, P.J. and Powell, W.W. (1983). The iron cage revisited: Institutional isomorphism and collective rationality in organisational fields. *American Sociological, 48,* 147–160. https://doi.org/10.2307/2095101

Dondi, M., Klier, J., Panier, F. and Schubert, J. (2021). *Defining the Skills Citizens Will Need in the Future World of Work. Public & Social Sector Practice.* McKinsey & Company. https://www.mckinsey.com/industries/public-and-social-sector/our-insights/defining-the-skills-citizens-will-need-in-the-future-world-of-work

Doyle, A., Gumaelius, L.B., Pears, A.N. and Seery, N. (2019). Theorizing the role of engineering for society: Technological activity in context? In 2019 ASEE Annual Conference & Exposition. ASEE.

Dziminska, M., Fijalkowska, J. and Sulkowski, L. (2018). Trust-based quality culture conceptual model for higher education institutions, in: Sustainability 2018, 10, 2599. doi: 10.3390/su10082599

EHEA. (1999). European Higher Education Area and Bologna Process. http://www.ehea.info/

EHEA. (2015). European Higher Education Area and Bologna Process. http://www.ehea.info/

Etzkowitz, H. and Leydesdorff, L. (2000). The dynamics of innovation: From national systems and "mode 2" to a triple Helix of university-industry-government relations. *Research Policy, 29,* 109–123.

European Commission. (2020). COM (2020/625 final).

Eurostat. (2021a). GDP per capita, consumption per capita and price level indices. *Eurostat Statistics Explained.* https://ec.europa.eu/eurostat/statistics-explained/index.php?title=GDP_per_capita,_consumption_per_capita_and_price_level_indices

Eurostat. (2021b). Annual expenditure on educational institutions per pupil/student based on FTE, by education level and programme orientation. https://ec.europa.eu/eurostat/databrowser/view/educ_uoe_fini04/default/table?lang=en

Eurostat. (2021c). Database Employment and unemployment. https://ec.europa.eu/eurostat/web/lfs/data/database

Eurostat. (2021d). Experimental statistics – skills. https://ec.europa.eu/eurostat/web/experimental-statistics/skills

Fakis, A., Hilliam, R., Stoneley, H. and Townend, M. (2014). Quantitative analysis of qualitative information from interviews: A systematic literature review. *Journal of Mixed Methods Research, 8*(2), 139–161.

Flick, U. (2002). *Qualitative Sozialforschung.* Hamburg: Rohwolt.

Früh, W. (2017). *Inhaltsanalyse. Theorie und Praxis.* 9. Auflage. Konstanz/München: UVK Verlagsgesellschaft mbH.

Goos, M. and Manning, A. (2007). Lousy and lovely jobs: The rising polarization of work in Britain. *Review of Economics and Statistics, 89*(1), 118–133. doi:10.1162/rest.89.1.118

Graham, R. (2018). *Global State of the Art in Engineering Education.* Boston, MA: MIT.

HEA. (2021). Higher Education Authority Ireland. Key Facts and Figures 2020/21. https://hea.ie/2021/10/11/higher-education-key-facts-and-figures-2020-2021/

Henke, J., Pasternack, P. and Schmid, S. (2016). Third mission von hochschulen. Eine definition. *Das Hochschulwesen, 64*(1/2), 16–22.

Kitagawa, F., Barrioluengo, M.S. and Uyarra, E. (2016). Third mission as institutional strategies: Between isomorphic forces and heterogeneous pathways. *Science and Public Policy, 43/6*, 736–750.

Klaassen, R., van Dijk, M., Hoope, R. and Kamp, A. (2019). *Engineer of the Future – Envisioning Higher Engineering Education in 2035.* Delft, The Netherlands: TU Delft.

Kuba, S. (2017). *Arbeitsmarkteffekte der Digitalisierung.* AK Policy Paper. Arbeiterkammer Wien.

Laguna-Sánchez, P., Abad, P., de la Fuente-Cabrero, C. and Calero, R. (2019). A university training programme for acquiring entrepreneurial and transversal employability skills, a students' assessment. *Sustainability, 12*(3), 796.

Liu, O.L., Ling, G. and Fishtein, D. (2021). Charting the skills for the future: Perspectives from employers and higher education institutions. *Chinese/English Journal of Education Measurement and Evaluation, 2*(2), 24–32.

LMRO. (2021). Labour Market Relevance and Outcomes of Higher Education. https://www.oecd.org/education/higher-education-policy/ (Unpublished)

MacDermott, C. and Ortiz, L. (2017). Beyond the business communication course: A historical perspective of the where, why, and how of soft skills development and job readiness for business graduates. *IUP Journal of Soft Skills, 11*(2), 7–24.

Manzini, R. (2021). Teaching and learning transversal competences in management engineering, in: Proceedings of the 14th EPIEM Conference 2021, pp. 17–23. https://www.tugraz.at/fileadmin/user_upload/Institute/BWL/Home/Startseite_Topics/20210601_Proceedings_of_the_14th_EPIEM_Conference_V_1.0_Final_Published.pdf

Marina, O., Yakusheva, I. and Demchenkova, O. (2019). Examining undergraduate students' and in-service graduates' perceptions of their professionally oriented foreign language needs. *Journal of Language and Education, 5*(1). https://doi.org/10.17323/2411-7390-2019-5-1-63-84

May Lee, R. and Yuan, Y. (2018). Innovation education in China: Preparing attitudes, approaches, and intellectual environments for life in the automation economy, in: Gleason N. W. (ed.). *Higher Education in the Ear of the Fourth Industrial Revolution.* Singapore: Palgrave MacMillan, pp. 93–120.

Menz, M. (2020). Integrating academic skills and employability-revisiting the learning journal. *Journal of Perspectives in Applied Academic Practice, 8*(1), 115–120.

Moreland, N. (2006). Entrepreneurship and Higher Education: An Employability Perspective. *Learning and employability*, Series One; The Higher Education Academy: York, UK. https://www.quality-researchinternational.com/esecttools/esectpubs/morelandentrpreneur.pdf

O'Reilly, J., Eichhorst, W., Gábos, A., Hadjivassiliou, K., Lain, D., Leschke, J. and Russell, H. (2015). *Five Characteristics of Youth Unemployment in Europe: Flexibility, Education, Migration, Family Legacies, and EU Policy.* Thousand Oaks, CA: Sage Open, p. 5.

Oblinger, D. and Verville, A.L. (1998). *What Business Wants from Higher Education.* Phoenix, AZ: Oryx Press.

OECD. (2007). List of fields of Science and Technology. https://www.oecd.org/science/inno/38235147.pdf

OECD. (2011). Skills for innovation and research. http://www.oecd.org/sti/inno/skillsforinnovation-andresearch.htm

OECD. (2019). OECD Future of Education and skills 2030. OECD Learning Compass 2030. A series of concept notes. https://www.oecd.org/education/2030-project/contact/OECD_Learning_Compass_2030_Concept_Note_Series.pdf

OECD. (2020). Education at a Glance 2020: OECD Indicators. OECD Publishing, Paris. https://www.oecd.org/education/educationat-a-glance-19991487.htm/?refcode=20190209ig

OECD. (2021). Education at a Glance 2021: OECD Indicators. OECD Publishing, Paris. https://data.oecd.org/emp/employment-by-education-level.htm#indicator-chart

Pardo-Garcia, C. and Barac, M. (2020). Promoting employability in higher education: A case study on boosting entrepreneurship skills. *Sustainability, 12*(10), 4004. https://doi.org/10.3390/su12104004

Roser, M. and Ortiz-Ospina, E. (2019). Tertiary education. Our world in data. UR: https://ourworldindata.org/tertiary-education

Sarfraz, I., Rajendran, D., Hewege, C. and Mohan, M.D. (2018). An exploration of global employability skills: A systematic research review. *International Journal of Work Organisation and Emotion*, *9*(1), 63–88.

Shuman, L.J., Besterfield-Sacre, M. and McGourty, J. (2005). The ABET "professional skills"—Can they be taught? Can they be assessed? *Journal of Engineering Education*, *94*(1), 41–55.

Singh, R., Chawla, G., Agarwal, S. and Desai, A. (2017). Employability and innovation: Development of a scale. *International Journal of Innovation Science*, *9*(1), 20–37.

Sparreboom, T. and Tarvid, A. (2016). Imbalanced job polarization and skills mismatch in Europe. *Journal for Labour Market Research*, *49*(1), 15–42.

Statistics Portugal. (2021). Students enroled in tertiary education. https://www.ine.pt/xportal/xmain?xpid=INE&xpgid=ine_base_dados&bdpagenumber=1&bdnivelgeo=00&atributoordenar=null&atributoordem=null&contexto=bd&bdtemas=1112&bdfreetext=Word(s)%20to%20find&bdind_por_pagina=15&xlang=en

Statistik Austria. (2021). Studierende, belegte Studien. http://www.statistik.at/web_de/statistiken/menschen_und_gesellschaft/bildung/hochschulen/studierende_belegte_studien/index.html

Suessenbach, F., Winde, M., Klier, J. and Kirchherr, J. (2021). *Future skills 2021. 21 Kompetenzen für eine Welt im Wandel*. Diskussionspapier Nr. 3. Essen: Stifterverband.

Tegtmeier, P. (2021). *Informationsbezogene Tätigkeiten im digitalen Wandel. Arbeitsmerkmale und Technologieeinsatz*. Baua: Preprint, DOI: 10.21934/baua:preprint20210115

Tewari, R. and Sharma, E. (2016). An investigation into the expectations of the recruiters and the preparedness of the management graduates for effective on job performance", *IUP Journal of Soft Skills*, *10*(1), 14–23.

Van den Beemt, A., MacLeod, M., Van der Veen, J., Van de Ven, A., Van Baalen, S., Klaassen, R. and Boon, M. (2020). Interdisciplinary engineering education: A review of vision, teaching, and support. *Journal of Engineering Education*, *109*(3), 508–555.

Veiga, A., Magalhães, A. and Amaral, A. (2019). Disentangling policy convergence within the European higher education area. *European Educational Research Journal*, *18*(1), 3–18.

Wedenig, P., Zenz, D., Niederl, A. et al. (2017). Digitalisierung der Arbeitswelt am Beispiel Kärnten. Endbericht.

Wheelahan, L. and Moodie, G. (2021). Analysing micro-credentials in higher education: A Bernsteinian analysis. *Journal of Curriculum Studies*, *53*(2), 212–228.

16

INCENTIVES, VALUES, AND THE CREATION OF OPPORTUNITIES FOR ACTION AND INTERACTION

Friederike Welter

INSTITUT FÜR MITTELSTANDSFORSCHUNG (IFM) BONN AND
UNIVERSITY OF SIEGEN, SIEGEN, GERMANY

Mirela Xheneti

UNIVERSITY OF SUSSEX, UK

16.1 Introduction

The role institutional frameworks play in shaping economic action is undisputed. Entrepreneurial action as one form of economic action is highly embedded in its institutional context and, to some extent, determined by society's institutional order, especially with regards to entrepreneurs' choices about effort allocation (Baumol and Strom, 2007). Baumol's work (1990) was amongst the first to acknowledge that institutions provide incentive structures that guide individual action and determine whether these actions will be directed towards entrepreneurship or other forms of occupations. Most famously, Baumol was concerned with the quality of entrepreneurship, arguing that institutional incentive structures direct entrepreneurial action towards different uses, distinguishing between productive, unproductive and destructive activities as defined by the economic value they provide for society. Institutions therefore affect not only the existence of entrepreneurship but also the type or nature of society's resource allocation (Baumol, 1990).

Following Baumol's work, there has been extensive research in entrepreneurship looking at how different sets of institutions affect entrepreneurial action (Stenholm et al., 2013). Most of this research distinguishes between formal and informal institutions and attempts to understand how they, individually or simultaneously, impact different rates and quality of entrepreneurship across countries. A smaller body of literature has looked at how the interplay of formal and informal institutions and, most importantly, the nature of incentives and values such interplay provides for individual entrepreneurs influence forms of entrepreneurial action. In this chapter, using insights from institutional theory, we explore this interplay not only through looking at the experience of different countries at different stages of institutional development but also through the lens of values imbued in different sets of institutions that guide entrepreneurial action towards other than commercial activities to include environmental and social ones. In order to achieve our aims, the chapter is structured as follows:

DOI: 10.4324/9781003144366-20

First, we conduct a review of the literature on institutions and entrepreneurship, followed by a focus on those incentives and values that guide entrepreneurial activity. Second, we clearly link this discussion to the interplay of various institutions and their impact on entrepreneurial behavior emphasizing how institutional voids provide opportunities for entrepreneurial agency. Throughout the chapter, we place the theoretical discussion into context by using several illustrative examples from work in unstable or complex institutional contexts. We conclude with a number of implications for both theory and practice.

16.2 Institutions and entrepreneurial action

Following North (1990), most literature defines institutions as the set of rules, norms and values that are designed to offer structure and stability to human action and interaction (also see Gutmann and Voigt, in this Handbook). North (1990) distinguishes between formal rules – constitutions, legal arrangements and property rights – and informal rules – values, social norms and traditions codes of conduct that define what societies consider as acceptable or appropriate. It is an established fact by now that institutions restrict and enable entrepreneurial actions, thus influencing the nature and pace of the development of entrepreneurship (Welter and Smallbone, 2011). In their enabling function, institutions contribute to opportunities for entrepreneurial action, by reducing transaction costs and uncertainties connected to entrepreneurship, while in their restrictive function, they add to the costs of doing business and can negatively affect returns from entrepreneurship.

16.2.1 How formal institutions influence entrepreneurial action

Much research has studied the impact of formal institutions on entrepreneurship. Formal institutions refer to those laws and rules, which directly impact the costs of starting, growing or closing a business, such as regulations for market entry and exit and commercial law. For example, bankruptcy laws that are entrepreneur friendly and do not excessively punish business failure also lower entry barriers to entrepreneurship and, in turn, seem to encourage more start-ups and higher risk-taking (for a more detailed discussion and related studies, see the extensive literature review by Lee et al., 2021). Formal institutions also include those rules and policies influencing the desirability and feasibility of entrepreneurship. Examples are property rights and the constitution, welfare policies, labor market and tax policies and education policies, which contribute to individual skills and knowledge about entrepreneurship, as well as the general legal framework. For example, legal regulations create possible entrepreneurial opportunities where they allow private (business) ownership and make provisions for enterprises to legally exist as has been the case in former centrally planned economies, during their initial stage of transformation towards market economies (Smallbone and Welter, 2009). Beyond these countries, property rights have less of an influence on business entry, but they are fundamental for business growth (Estrin et al., 2013), for example, when restricting the spatial expansion of businesses. Legal regulations also contribute to entrepreneurial action when indirectly fostering new business fields as is the case with regulations on climate change, for example.

In general, formal institutions are difficult to evaluate in their impact on entrepreneurial actions. For labor market institutions, for example, research has shown contradictory effects. Some studies confirm a detrimental influence of rigid labor market institutions on nascent and early-stage entrepreneurship (van Stel et al., 2007) and in the motivations (necessity/ opportunity or high growth/low growth entrepreneurship) (e.g., Bosma, 2009 cited in

Fu et al., 2018) because they increase the costs of doing business. Other research finds a positive, but indirect influence of flexible labor market regulations on high-growth entrepreneurship (e.g., Baughn et al., 2010; Henrekson et al., 2010). Yet other studies also show a more indirect impact of non-business policies. High-growth entrepreneurship, for example, is influenced positively through policies that facilitate access to human and financial capital (Bowen and De Clercq, 2008): Educational policies do not only create awareness for entrepreneurship as a career option; they provide skills and alertness, thus influencing opportunity recognition and exploitation, but they may also impact on later business development by providing individuals with more confidence in their capability to grow a business. Moreover, formal institutions are gendered, influencing women and men entrepreneurs differently. For example, in cases of a deficient rule of law, Hampel-Milagrosa (2010) suggests one-stop agencies for women entrepreneurs to prevent bribery and extortion through government officials. Estrin and Mickiewicz (2011) show the impact of social policies, in this case, maternity leave provisions, on the general likelihood of women's entrepreneurship but, interestingly, found no significant impact on those women wishing to start high-potential businesses. Government policies fostering women's entrepreneurship may also have unintended negative consequences for those staying "behind" in wage employment, as they lose their peers and negotiation power, thus widening the gender pay gap (Castellaneta et al., 2020).

Recent research suggests that it is not single formal institutions as such that impact entrepreneurship, but rather institutional bundles that differ across countries, thus drawing our attention to institutional diversity and the interplay of different formal institutions as a key influence for entrepreneurial action (e.g., Dilli, 2021; Elert et al., 2019; Herrmann, 2019). Using the concept of varieties of capitalism which explains different forms of capitalism through country-specific institutional settings, Dilli et al. (2018) show how complementary bundles of entrepreneurship-relevant institutions foster varieties in entrepreneurial outcomes: So-called liberal market economies with flexible formal institutions (notably the Anglo-Saxon countries) foster Schumpeterian entrepreneurship, while more regulated economies such as in Continental Europe support more incrementally innovative forms of entrepreneurship, and countries with restrictive institutions such as to be found in emerging economies favor low-tech entrepreneurship.

This also emphasizes the role of government as a key player in designing, implementing and enforcing formal institutions. In this regard, some research studies the quality of the formal institutional frame, contributing another facet of the more indirect effects of formal institutions on entrepreneurship. For example, while lighter regulation burdens can be linked to higher rates of high-aspiration entrepreneurial entries, the rule of law moderates these institutional effects such that regulation only significantly impacts high aspiration entrepreneurial entries where the rule of law is strong (Levie and Autio, 2011). If the rule of law is missing or deficient, this allows for arbitrary and discretionary actions by administration and corruption (Aidis et al., 2010), thus increasing the costs and uncertainty for any entrepreneurial actions unless potential entrepreneurs are well connected and able to influence such decisions in their favor.

16.2.2 *How informal institutions influence entrepreneurial action*

Informal institutions are deeply embedded within a society and only change over long times because they are part of the habitual behavior of individuals (North, 1990; Williamson, 2000). Informal institutions include societal norms and other non-written rules, together with our shared and culturally learned understanding of these rules that regulate our behavior and general attitudes. Societal norms indirectly impact general attitudes towards entrepreneurship, as they suggest what a society deems desirable and acceptable, thus influencing the desirability of and preferences towards entrepreneurship, but also fear of failure. Societal norms also directly influence entrepreneurial action because they result in non-written standards for accepted and tolerated business behavior such as fair business practices. Based on a comprehensive review of 25 years of institutional entrepreneurship studies, Urbano et al. (2019, p. 38) conclude that "informal institutions are more relevant for explaining entrepreneurial activity and its economic consequences".

Of high importance is the value a society generally puts onto entrepreneurship (Davidsson and Wiklund, 1997; Valdez and Richardson, 2013), as a sign for tolerating and fostering entrepreneurial activities and also allowing for potential role models. The Global Entrepreneurship Monitor has provided ample evidence on the variations around the world in relation to whether or not a career as an entrepreneur is valued in society (www.gem. org). Generally, cultures that are socially supportive, not only positively influence the level and quality of entrepreneurship as well as entrepreneurial self-efficacy but also the existence of entrepreneurial opportunities (Stephan and Uhlaner, 2010). Where societies are not supportive of entrepreneurship, and levels of societal desirability of pursuing entrepreneurship as a career choice are low, this actually contributes to higher levels of internationalization of early-stage businesses, whereby individuals compensate for the uncertainty in home markets (Muralidharan and Pathak, 2018).

Research on women's entrepreneurship emphasizes the indirect link between a society that values women's participation in labor markets and their increased participation in entrepreneurship (Pathak et al., 2013). Gendered labor-market institutions such as female business leadership, wage inequality and public expenditure on childcare have been shown to influence women's decision to start a business indirectly through their effect on societal perceptions (Elam and Terjesen, 2010). Where society mainly attributes house-bound and family-oriented responsibilities to women, this may negatively impact their entrepreneurial actions because such informal institutions restrict the opportunities for women wishing to enter entrepreneurship and grow their businesses. Women's entrepreneurship also has been discussed as one means of balancing family and work. However, for women, family obligations may also come at a too high price (e.g., forfeiture of wage employment), leaving entry into entrepreneurship as one last resort to work and take care of family responsibilities, but possibly leading to lower income and lower status entrepreneurship (Cliff, 1998; Thébaud, 2016).

Following in the wake of Max Weber's seminal study on the protestant ethics of capitalism, entrepreneurship research has also studied the role religions can play for entrepreneurial action and for entrepreneurial opportunities to emerge (e.g., Audretsch et al., 2007; Drakopoulou Dodd and Gotsis, 2007) – in fact, there is renewed interest in this theme currently (e.g., Block et al., 2020; Rietveld and Hoogendoorn, 2022; Smith et al., 2019; Smith et al., 2021). Dana (2010) identifies several links between religions and entrepreneurship. First, religions influence the value placed on entrepreneurship differently (e.g., Islam supports a work ethic conducive to entrepreneurship). Second, they influence the nature of entrepreneurship by only allowing entry into specific professions in which entrepreneurs could prosper as there was no or little competition. Third, religious rules provide opportunities for entrepreneurship (e.g., producing and selling halal or kosher food). Finally, religions may also hamper entrepreneurial actions, even if indirectly. In many parts of Central Asia, for example, the transition towards market economies went hand in hand with a resurge of patriarchal societal attitudes and religious values, restricting women, especially if young and unmarried, to the family home. This fostered low-threshold and low-income businesses with little potential for business development and growth, although it assisted some of those women entrepreneurs in emancipating themselves and, over time, changing community attitudes towards working women (Welter and Smallbone, 2008).

16.2.3 How values influence entrepreneurial action

When it comes to values and the mechanisms through which they influence entrepreneurship, research has emphasized the role of culture as an informal institution, looking at how individual and societal values encourage different forms of entrepreneurial action. This research stemmed from dissatisfaction with the inability of economic-based explanations to account for the different entrepreneurial rates between countries at similar levels of economic and formal institutional development (e.g., Liñán and Fernandez-Serrano, 2014). Culture can be broadly defined as "the set of values and beliefs people have about how the world (both nature and society) works as well as the norms of behavior derived from that set of values" (Roland, 2020; p. 1). In a recent review of the literature on culture and entrepreneurship, Stephan (2020) shows that work in this area has focused on two main perspectives: culture as expressed through the values that individuals hold and culture as shared values and norms that are transmitted across generations. Schwartz (2006) who has contributed theories of values both at the individual and national levels distinguishes clearly between the values held at the individual level as deriving from biological and psychological needs and those at the cultural level that have at their core the needs of societies for survival over time. While both perspectives have been used, several scholars suggest that the second perspective holds more explanatory power because it measures what individuals in a society consider as typical behaviors, also recognizing that individual values might not be the best predictors of behavior (Hechavarría and Brieger, 2022; Stephan and Uhlaner, 2010).

Nevertheless, much of what we currently know about the link between culture and entrepreneurship is based on theories of individual values such as the work of Hofstede (2001), Schwartz (1992) and Inglehart (1997). For example, Hayton et al. (2002) following Hofstede's work consider entrepreneurial cultures to embody the values of individualism, masculinity and low uncertainty avoidance and power distance. Similarly, Morales et al. (2019) using Schwartz' theory of values posit that commercial entrepreneurs exhibit values such as the need for control, autonomy, variety and novelty that make life challenging. They strive for achievement and social recognition. Non-commercial entrepreneurs, on the other hand, place emphasis on values such as benevolence and universalism that imply a concern for the welfare of others and that of the planet. Several other studies in various contexts have assessed this empirically, showing how these pro-social values are given more priority to by social entrepreneurs (e.g., Bargsted et al., 2013; Ruskin, 2016).

Another stream of research focuses on Ingleheart's (1997) theory of post-materialism linking self-expression to entrepreneurship and, most importantly, noting how it differs for different types of entrepreneurship with a focus on social and environmental entrepreneurship for post-materialistic societies, where the emphasis is not on survival and material goods but non-material values such as self-expression. These studies see the link between entrepreneurship and culture as related, amongst other things, to the social legitimacy of entrepreneurship in a society or its desirability (Stephan, 2020). Hechavarria and Brieger (2022) suggest that culture informs the entrepreneurial behavior of men and women differently because each uses cultural practices and repertoires in different ways. This relationship is particularly strong for social entrepreneurship.

Liñán and Fernandez-Serrano (2014) test the relationship between values and entrepreneurial rates in different European Union countries using the theory of cultural values of Schwartz (2006) that groups national cultures along three bipolar dimensions: *Mastery versus harmony values* reflect the difference between societies where individuals are encouraged to take charge and initiate change and those where they harmoniously fit the existing structures. *Autonomy versus embeddedness* reflects the view of individuals as autonomous entities in a society. *Egalitarianism versus hierarchy* reflects whether societies consider individuals as equal or whether there is a hierarchical and unequal distribution of power and resources (Stephan, 2020; p. 125). The authors find that different from the stereotype of European societies being based on values of mastery, egalitarianism and autonomy, there is variation between countries which affects the levels of entrepreneurship observed. They cluster countries in four groups, each with different sets of national values and rates/types of entrepreneurship: English-speaking countries are characterized by high levels of mastery, autonomy and egalitarianism and have the highest levels of entrepreneurship; Central and Eastern European countries are mainly characterized by embeddedness, hierarchy and harmony and have relatively high levels of entrepreneurship albeit of the necessity nature; North European countries are high in autonomy but also very strong in egalitarianism and harmony and as such have the lowest level of entrepreneurship; and Mediterranean countries are characterized by egalitarianism and harmony and really low levels of autonomy that lead to a higher incidence of necessity entrepreneurship.

Research in this area is increasing with attempts being made to show how different levels of analysis – individual, firm and cultural levels – interact in order to understand the conditions under which entrepreneurial action occurs. This body of literature, however, does not try to establish whether certain national cultural values have particular links to the way individual entrepreneurs interact with formal institutions. Such interaction is very important, as we discuss in the section below.

16.3 The interplay of institutions and entrepreneurial action

16.3.1 How institutions interact and impact entrepreneurial action

Although a large body of work aims to understand the effect of formal or informal institutions on entrepreneurship, it is their interaction that plays a more crucial role in patterns of entrepreneurial action (Welter and Smallbone, 2011). Williams and Vorley (2017) conceptualize this interaction as either complementary/aligned, when informal institutions support or accommodate formal institutions, thus contributing to an effective formal frame for entrepreneurial action, or substitutive, when informal institutions compete with and substitute for formal institutions, thus remedying a deficient formal frame for entrepreneurial action. Research has suggested that when regulatory (or formal) institutions are considered as unfair or inefficient informal institutions such as values and beliefs of particular groups in a society guide individual behavior (Welter and Xheneti, 2015). This interplay between formal and informal institutions and entrepreneurship, however, is complex and often difficult to disentangle in practice, as explained by a number of mixed and sometimes outright contradictory empirical results, for example, regarding the impact of business failure institutions on entrepreneurial actions (Lee et al., 2021).

Value and beliefs about gender roles are a good example that can illustrate how choices women make in relation to entrepreneurial activity are determined to a large extent by the interaction of formal and informal institutions. According to Welter et al. (2014), societal expectations of gender roles and role-adequate behavior influence formal institutions such as laws allowing for women to enter the labor market, and they in turn are influenced by formal institutions like welfare, tax and family policies. For Denmark, Neergaard and Thrane (2011) demonstrate that legal institutions that favor gender equality in public life and on the labor market still perpetuate gender imbalances at home, forcing women to take on the double burden of entrepreneurship and family care. Thébaud (2015) shows the differential impact of institutional arrangements on the nature and extent of women's entrepreneurship. She suggests that women are less likely to use entrepreneurship as last resort, if formal institutions support women in balancing work with family obligations (e.g., paid leave, subsidized childcare, part-time employment regulations). Her empirical findings for 24 countries show that supportive family policies reduce the odds of women in early-stage and established business ownership, but there are smaller gender gaps related to business size, growth aspirations and innovation propensity. Thus, where the institutional interplay results in work-family conflicts, women are more likely to select entrepreneurship as option, but with fewer growth orientations. Xie et al. (2021) suggest that beneficial institutional arrangements differ for women's entrepreneurship as such and for growth-oriented women's entrepreneurship: For the former, entrepreneurial cognitions are decisive; for the latter, the overall entrepreneurial culture – indicating the importance of informal institutions.

Institutional misalignments with major impacts on entrepreneurial actions have been extensively studied for former socialist countries (e.g., Manolova et al., 2008; Peng and Heath, 1996; Vorley and Williams, 2016). Welter and Smallbone (2011, p. 110) recount a typical example of an entrepreneur who started a minibus service in Moldova. In her case, a deficient legal frame allowed for arbitrary official actions and fostered corruption, with such rule-breaking behavior known to both sides from Soviet times: "It took her several months to register her business and obtain licenses. For each document she brought, clerks asked for payment or presents, sometimes having established fixed sums per document. Once up and running, she needed to continue bribing the police, the State Traffic Inspectorate and pay to her 'roof,' which is a Mafia-like structure offering protection to her business. The day before the interview, her driver had been stopped four times, each time paying a 'fine' to four different officials from the State Traffic Inspectorate".

Institutional misalignment often arises out of path dependency. The socialist period "trained" people to rely heavily on social contacts and networks in making daily life possible and also forced them to circumvent or even break existing rules, if required. During transition times, such learnt behaviors helped entrepreneurs to cope with deficient formal institutions. For example, entrepreneurs ensured access to financial resources through semi-legal or illegal shuttle trading across borders in a context where banks initially were not familiar with financing new and small firms (Smallbone and Welter, 2001). Such entrepreneurial actions, however, contradict formal institutions, as they "(...) bear little resemblance to the legitimate courses of action stipulated by the formal rules" (Nee, 1998, p. 86). While helpful and viable actions during the early stages of transition, at least in the short run, they also prevent business development in the long run and may result in suboptimal resource allocation at a macro level.

The interaction of formal and informal institutions and their effects on entrepreneurial action is not only complex but also subject to change over time. In the short term, institutional misalignments mainly appear to have a negative impact on entrepreneurial actions. Where entrepreneurs and other actors recur to path-dependent actions, this is generally seen as perpetuating existing informal institutions that however are in conflict with current formal institutional arrangements, thus preventing institutional change. However, institutions do not simply have a linear or unidirectional effect on entrepreneurial activities at various stages, but entrepreneurship also contributes to changing institutional arrangements. Where individuals draw on trusted and learned behaviors, this can contribute to needed institutional adjustments and change, over time. Moreover, newer research points to a differential impact of such legacies between former socialist countries (Williams and Vorley, 2017): Path-dependent entrepreneurial actions are much more common in former Soviet countries, while entrepreneurship in post-conflict countries (in this case the Kosovo) is characterized by more path-breaking behavior.

Institutional misalignment and the associated competing demands for individuals and organizations have also been researched in the case of social and sustainable entrepreneurs who often need to balance the commercial and social goals of their organizations. An increasing body of literature recognizes that the institutional context of such entrepreneurial activities is very important in understanding the complexities they face (e.g., Muñoz and Kibler, 2016). In pursuing such entrepreneurial action, these actors face a conflict between personal and local values and local or wider societal issues (Cherrier et al., 2018). O'Neil and Ucbasaran (2016) show very powerfully how environmental entrepreneurs felt dissonance between their values and those of the audiences they were trying to gain legitimacy from, ending up having to tone down their own beliefs and accommodating those of their audiences in order to ensure the survival of their ventures. This illustrates the extent to which formal institutions, social norms and cultural values can act as barriers to entrepreneurial action trying to enact social change (see also Dorado and Ventresca, 2013).

Taken together, this evidence also draws attention to the interplay between historical informal institutions, the current institutional contexts and entrepreneurship. For example, historical and place-bound knowledge trajectories together with entrepreneurial traditions have been found to positively impact today's innovative business activities (Del Monte and Pennacchio, 2020; Fritsch and Wyrwich, 2018), while early industrialization has been shown to have long-term – negative or positive – imprinting effects on today's entrepreneurship. For Great Britain, Huggins et al. (2021) demonstrate the cognitive lock-in and change-averse effects on local cultures in regions that previously had been dominated by large-scale industries. Aparicio et al. (2020) suggest that in parts of Colombia, gold mining traditions originating from the 16th century, partly explain entrepreneurship today. In Germany, historically high levels of regional entrepreneurship impact positively on today's entrepreneurial personalities in the same regions because an early entrepreneurship tradition resulted in place-based role models, which were transmitted between generations (Fritsch et al., 2019). Such entrepreneurial traditions even appear to survive disruptive political shocks as has been studied for Kaliningrad, formerly Soviet, now a Russian enclave (Fritsch et al., 2019). Such empirical evidence demonstrates the importance of historical traditions for today's entrepreneurship.

16.3.2 How entrepreneurs use institutions and values to identify and exploit opportunities

Where institutional contexts are deficient, this not only hinders entrepreneurial action but also generates entrepreneurial opportunities. Two mechanisms are of importance here: Institutional misalignments result in so-called institutional holes or institutional voids that entrepreneurs can explore and entrepreneurs experience, interpret and perceive institutions and institutional arrangements differently. One entrepreneur may see institutional misalignments as opportunities she could offer business solutions to, while another may perceive deficient institutions as a barrier to her activities. For example, Kwapisz (2019) draws attention to the impact of actual and of perceived formal institutions on entrepreneurship. In her study, only 6% of entrepreneurs perceived government bureaucracy as a major barrier to their activities (and of these, only 54% check those regulations), and only 1% stated such regulations as a reason to quit their entrepreneurial activities. So far, however, the individually differing mental construction of institutions by entrepreneurs and the role this plays for opportunity creation have received little attention. Thapa et al. (2021), in a study of the formalization of business activities run by women entrepreneurs in the context of Nepal, show that entrepreneurs do indeed subjectively internalize institutions and argue for an approach that emphasizes the situated social interactions in explaining individuals' meaning making. They suggest that such a focus helps to capture the heterogeneity of experiences in the informal economy, the nature of choices (or lack of) amongst different groups of the population such as women, and how they inform subjective assessments of formalization that are contextually embedded in complex socio-cultural settings underpinned by a range of different and perhaps competing values and norms (Thapa Karki et al., 2020; p. 17).

More research has looked at the role of institutional voids, often defined as the inability of existing (formal) institutions to support efficient and effective market transactions. As a result, a large body of literature has focused on how informal institutions make up for these deficiencies not acknowledging that informal institutions themselves, including norms, values and beliefs, are often not able to support efficient transactions that might contribute to productive market activities (Webb et al., 2020). Both types of voids, despite their seemingly negative influences on entrepreneurial actions, also provide opportunities for entrepreneurial agency towards changing institutional contexts. Here, a more recent strand of research is studying the resourcefulness of entrepreneurs, exploring the manifold ways entrepreneurs make use of institutions to identify, create and exploit opportunities. Baker and Welter (2020) understand these entrepreneurial actions as entrepreneurs "doing context", that is, entrepreneurs are enacting and constructing the contexts they inhabit through interaction. They consider it as an incremental process of entrepreneurs using various skills, resources or strategies in responding to their context that shape both context and who they are and what they do.

Several studies have explored the historical contexts of entrepreneurial opportunities and actions. During Soviet times, for example, individuals used state property and resources for private entrepreneurial activities that were semi- or illegal but often tolerated (Dallago, 1990). They were also quick to identify opportunities for barter, buying whatever was available and exchanging later on, sold garden surplus on informal markets or on the streets and – illegally – traded across borders as soon as international holiday travels were allowed within the Soviet Bloc in the early 1970s (Morawska, 1999). Today's cross-border shuttle trading could be seen as a continuation of the Soviet "repair society" that fostered resourcefulness in its people (Gerasimova and Chuikina, 2009), allowing them to quickly identify opportunities for entrepreneurship. Related studies on cross-border entrepreneurship show entrepreneurs creatively re-using informal institutions like their shared cultural and historical backgrounds on both sides of a national border, to circumvent and exploit unfavorable border institutions to their personal advantage (e.g., Cassidy and Polese, 2011; Fadahunsi and Rosa, 2002; Polese and Rodgers, 2011). Welter et al. (2018) find that entrepreneurial actions in border contexts are characterized by both continuity and change. The former reflects the sociocultural commonalities and common knowledge of "how things worked" in the past allowing cross-border entrepreneurs to rely on tangible and intangible resources evolving from hardship times and intergenerational solidarity. Change, on the other hand, reflected how some individuals also learned to embrace and respond to the challenges of their unstable border contexts. In a similar vein, Korsgaard et al. (2021) illustrate how entrepreneurs interact with their contexts by looking at the role the spatial context plays in the efforts of entrepreneurs to mobilize resources. Both Welter et al. (2018) and Korsgaard et al. (2021) provide powerful accounts of how individual entrepreneurs draw very widely from their resource-constrained environments for enabling their entrepreneurial action.

Entrepreneurs have also been shown to strategically use institutional voids to ensure market participation and initiate change in their communities. For example, Welter et al. (2018) observed that those who were involved in informal cross-border activities found legitimacy for their law-breaking activities in the expectations of close-knit communities for entrepreneurial action that benefits the whole local community rather than the individual alone. This was exemplified in the case of offering local communities affordable products, jobs or more generally maintaining good neighborly and social relations. Other research has studied the nature of opportunities offered by institutional change and the strategies that entrepreneurs or other social actors develop in response to institutional change and voids. Mair and Marti (2009), for instance, discuss how social entrepreneurs address institutional voids impeding market participation in rural Bangladesh. Bjerregaard and Lauring (2012) look at the ways entrepreneurs work with multiple or contradictory institutional logics in bringing about institutional change in Malawi. In case of India, Cherrier et al. (2018) show that social entrepreneurs do not see the coexistence of overlapping and contradictory institutions as constraints but rather as resources for developing innovative and creative responses that can transform their social value propositions. As importantly, the study also finds that these entrepreneurs' actions are both shaped by and are shaping their context by showing how social value creation is not a fixed process but one that changes overtime as entrepreneurs engage with the complexities of their environment. Sydow et al. (2021) explore how entrepreneurs in Kenya work around both formal and informal institutional voids. They identified two main workaround strategies – hybridization of goals and orchestration of business relationships – to delineate how in such contexts entrepreneurs need to change the nature of their goals to include those aiming to solve social issues in their environment and need to forge different types of business relationship to avoid the different uncertainties they face. They see both practices as fulfilling the bigger goal of supporting the development of an institutional scaffolding that would pave the way for the creation of new institutions.

Many of the studies referenced in this section acknowledge the role of entrepreneurs as institutional change agents (Welter and Smallbone, 2015). Entrepreneurial action does not only change institutions over time and creates economic outcomes at the business and economy level, but it also contributes to leveling social inequalities and the emancipation of marginalized groups. For example, research on women's entrepreneurship has been quite influential in highlighting social value creation. By providing evidence on the diverse motives, goals and outcomes of women's entrepreneurship (Jennings and Brush, 2013), this literature has conceptualized entrepreneurship as social change (Calás et al., 2009) and emancipation (Rindova et al., 2009). Similarly, research on informal types of entrepreneurial activities has shown that individuals, households or even whole communities nurture family and social relations through their engagement in different entrepreneurial activities, thus emphasizing the subjective, temporal and contextual nature of value creation (Welter and Xheneti, 2015).

16.4 Outlook

We conclude our review with a brief outlook towards future research on the interplay of institutions, values and entrepreneurial actions in different contexts. To summarize our findings: Most research on institutions presented in this chapter considers them as having a homogenous effect on individual entrepreneurs within a country. This neglects the fact that institutions are experienced, enacted and interpreted differently by individuals along their social position, prompting the need for more micro-level research that explores these issues in more depth. Much research also tends to consider institutions as operating in the same way across a country, not acknowledging the various socio-spatial characteristics of various localities. Despite some recent acknowledgment of this by Webb et al. (2020), most research does not sufficiently engage with the rich institutional arenas of local contexts and the ways they interact with agents to produce distinct sets of resources and entrepreneurial opportunities (Xheneti et al., 2019).

Recently, entrepreneurship research generally has started to emphasize the enactment and construction of contexts through narratives, language and imagery (see the review of related work in Welter, 2019), and on the role the materiality of places and artefacts (Muñoz and Kimmitt, 2019) or urban planning and architectural designs have for contexts to be perceived as entrepreneurial, thus fostering or hindering entrepreneurship (Welter and Baker, 2021). These themes can also be applied to the interplay of institutions and entrepreneurial actions. Research questions could involve, for example: In which ways do the language and the imagery entrepreneurs and others use to enact institutions contribute to creating entrepreneurial opportunities? Do language and narratives (both at the individual and at society level) perpetuate or support institutional change, in turn restricting or fostering entrepreneurial action? Also, the increasing and encompassing digitization of our economies and societies poses interesting challenges for research on institutions and entrepreneurial action: Do informal institutions become more fluid and change easily, nowadays? Or do informal institutions keep their stickiness and only change over long time? Finally, entrepreneurship research on individual and societal values guiding entrepreneurial action and that on the importance of variances of capitalism to explain differences in the nature and extent of entrepreneurship could be integrated, providing new insights into the interplay of institutions and entrepreneurial action from a multi-level perspective.

There is also a need to adapt the methods we use when studying the interaction of institutions and entrepreneurship. Given the dynamic and complex nature of such interaction, longitudinal methods seem to be more attuned to capturing the processual, temporal, and non-linear nature of entrepreneurial choices in particular socio-cultural and spatial contexts. Moreover, the narrative, visual and linguistic turn in entrepreneurship studies also provides access to novel methods to study this topic.

References

Aidis, R., Estrin, S. and Mickiewicz, T. (2010). Size Matters: Entrepreneurial Entry and Government. *Small Business Economics*, 39(1), 119–139. doi: 10.1007/s11187-010-9299-y

Aparicio, S., Muñoz-Mora, J. C. and Urbano, D. (2020). A Historical Perspective on Institutions and Entrepreneurship in a Developing Country. *Academy of Management Proceedings*, 2020(1), 17535. doi: 10.5465/AMBPP.2020.17535abstract

Audretsch, D. B., Bönte, W. and Tamvada, J. P. (2007). Religion and Entrepreneurship. *Jena economic research paper, no 2007-075*. Jena: Max Planck Institute.

Baker, T. and Welter, F. (2020). *Contextualizing entrepreneurship theory*. London: Routledge.

Bargsted, M., Picon, M., Salazar, A. and Rojas, Y. (2013). Psychosocial Characterization of Social Entrepreneurs: A Comparative Study. *Journal of Social Entrepreneurship*, 4(3), 331–346.

Baughn, C., Sugheir, J. S. and Neupert, K. (2010). Labor Flexibility and the Prevalence of High-Growth Entrepreneurial Activity. *Journal of Small Business and Entrepreneurship*, 23(1), 1–15. doi: 10.1080/08276331.2010.10593470

Baumol, W. J. (1990). Entrepreneurship: Productive, Unproductive, and Destructive. *Journal of Political Economy*, 98(5), 893–921. doi: www.jstor.org/stable/2937617

Baumol, W. J. and Strom, R. J. (2007). Entrepreneurship and Economic Growth. *Strategic Entrepreneurship Journal*, 1(3–4), 233–237. doi: 10.1002/sej.26

Bjerregaard, T. and Lauring, J. (2012). Entrepreneurship as Institutional Change: Strategies of Bridging Institutional Contradictions. *European Management Review*, 9(1), 31–43. doi: 10.1111/j.1740-4762.2012.01026.x

Block, J., Fisch, C. and Rehan, F. (2020). Religion and Entrepreneurship: A Map of the Field and a Bibliometric Analysis. *Management Review Quarterly*, 70(4), 591–627.

Bowen, H. P. and De Clercq, D. (2008). Institutional Context and the Allocation of Entrepreneurial Effort. *Journal of International Business Studies*, 39(4), 747–767. doi: 10.1057/palgrave.jibs.8400343

Calás, M. B., Smircich, L. and Bourne, K. A. (2009). Extending the Boundaries: Reframing "Entrepreneurship as Social Change" through Feminist Perspectives. *Academy of Management Review*, 34(3), 552–569.

Cassidy, K. and Polese, A. (2011). Performing the Cross-Border Economies of Post-Socialism. *International Journal of Sociology and Social Policy*, 31(11/12), 632–647. doi: 10.1108/01443331111177841

Castellaneta, F., Conti, R. and Kacperczyk, A. (2020). The (Un) Intended Consequences of Institutions Lowering Barriers to Entrepreneurship: The Impact on Female Workers. *Strategic Management Journal*, 41(7), 1274–1304. doi: 10.1002/smj.3133

Cherrier, H., Goswami, P. and Ray, S. (2018). Social Entrepreneurship: Creating Value in the Context of Institutional Complexity. *Journal of Business Research*, 86, 245–258.

Cliff, J. E. (1998). Does One Size Fit All? Exploring the Relationship between Attitudes Towards Growth, Gender, and Business Size. *Journal of Business Venturing*, 13(6), 523–542. doi: 10.1016/s0883-9026(97)00071-2

Dallago, B. (1990). *The irregular economy: The "underground" economy and the "black" labour market*. Aldershot and Brookfield: Gower.

Dana, L. P. (2010). Introduction: Religion as an Explanatory Variable for Entrepreneurship. In L. P. Dana (Ed.), *Entrepreneurship and religion* (pp. 1–24). Cheltenham: Edward Elgar.

Davidsson, P. and Wiklund, J. (1997). Values, Beliefs and Regional Variations in New Firm Formation Rates. *Journal of Economic Psychology*, 18(2–3), 179–199. doi: 10.1016/S0167-4870(97)00004-4

Del Monte, A. and Pennacchio, L. (2020). Historical Roots of Regional Entrepreneurship: The Role of Knowledge and Creativity. *Small Business Economics*, 55, 1–22. doi: 10.1007/s11187-019-00139-8

Dilli, S. (2021). The Diversity of Labor Market Institutions and Entrepreneurship. *Socio-Economic Review*, 19(2), 511–552. doi: 10.1093/ser/mwz027

Dilli, S., Elert, N. and Herrmann, A. M. (2018). Varieties of Entrepreneurship: Exploring the Institutional Foundations of Different Entrepreneurship Types Through 'Varieties-of-Capitalism' Arguments. *Small Business Economics*, 51(2), 293–320. doi: 10.1007/s11187-018-0002-z

Dorado, S. and Ventresca, M. J. (2013). Crescive Entrepreneurship in Complex Social Problems: Institutional Conditions for Entrepreneurial Engagement. *Journal of Business Venturing*, 28(1), 69–82. doi: 10.1016/j.jbusvent.2012.02.002

Drakopoulou Dodd, S. and Gotsis, G. (2007). The Interrelationships between Entrepreneurship and Religion. *International Journal of Entrepreneurship and Innovation*, 8(2), 93–104. doi: 10.5367/000000007780808066

Elam, A. and Terjesen, S. (2010). Gendered Institutions and Cross-National Patterns of Business Creation for Men and Women. *European Journal of Development Research*, 22, 331–348. doi: 10.1057/ejdr.2010.19

Elert, N., Henrekson, M. and Sanders, M. (Eds.). (2019). *The entrepreneurial society: A reform strategy for the European Union*. Berlin: Springer Nature.

Estrin, S., Korosteleva, J. and Mickiewicz, T. (2013). Which Institutions Encourage Entrepreneurial Growth Aspirations? *Journal of Business Venturing*, 28(4), 564–580. doi: 10.1016/j.jbusvent.2012.05.001

Estrin, S. and Mickiewicz, T. (2011). Institutions and Female Entrepreneurship. *Small Business Economics*, 37(4), 397–415. doi: 10.1007/s11187-011-9373-0

Fadahunsi, A. and Rosa, P. (2002). Entrepreneurship and Illegality: Insights from the Nigerian Cross-border Trade. *Journal of Business Venturing*, 17(5), 397–429. doi: 10.1016/S0883-9026(01)00073-8

Fritsch, M., Obschonka, M. and Wyrwich, M. (2019). Historical Roots of Entrepreneurship-facilitating Culture and Innovation Activity: An Analysis for German Regions. *Regional Studies*, 53(9), 1296–1307. doi: 10.1080/00343404.2019.1580357

Fritsch, M., Sorgner, A., Wyrwich, M. and Zazdravnykh, E. (2019). Historical Shocks and Persistence of Economic Activity: Evidence on Self-Employment from a Unique Natural Experiment. *Regional Studies*, 53(6), 790–802. doi: 10.1080/00343404.2018.1492112

Fritsch, M. and Wyrwich, M. (2018). Regional Knowledge, Entrepreneurial Culture, and Innovative Start-Ups Over Time and Space—An Empirical Investigation. *Small Business Economics*, 51(2), 337–353. doi: 10.1007/s11187-018-0016-6

Fu, K., Larsson, A.-S. and Wennberg, K. (2018). Habitual Entrepreneurs in the Making: How Labour Market Rigidity and Employment Affects Entrepreneurial Re-Entry. *Small Business Economic*, 51, 465–482. doi.org/10.1007/s11187-018-0011-y

Gerasimova, E. and Chuikina, S. I. (2009). The Repair Society. *Russian Studies in History*, 48(1), 58–74. doi: 10.2753/RSH1061-1983480104

Hampel-Milagrosa, A. (2010). Identifying and Addressing Gender Issues in Doing Business. *European Journal of Development Research*, 22(3), 349–362. doi: 10.1057/ejdr.2010.12

Hayton, J. C., George, G. and Zahra, S. A. (2002). National Culture and Entrepreneurship: A Review of Behavioral Research. *Entrepreneurship Theory and Practice*, 26(4), 33–52.

Hechavarría, D. M. and Brieger, S. A. (2022). Practice Rather Than Preach: Cultural Practices and Female Social Entrepreneurship. *Small Business Economics*, 58, 1131–1151. doi: 10.1007/s11187-020-00437-6

Henrekson, M., Johansson, D. and Stenkula, M. (2010). Taxation, Labor Market Policy and High-Impact Entrepreneurship. *Journal of Industry, Competition and Trade*, 10(3–4), 275–296. doi: 10.1007/s10842-010-0081-2

Herrmann, A. M. (2019). A Plea for Varieties of Entrepreneurship. *Small Business Economics*, 52(2), 331–343. doi: 10.1007/s11187-018-0093-6

Hofstede, G. (2001). *Culture's consequences: Comparing values, behaviors, institutions and organizations across nations*. Thousand Oaks, CA; London; New Delhi: Sage Publications.

Huggins, R., Stuetzer, M., Obschonka, M. and Thompson, P. (2021). Historical Industrialisation, Path Dependence and Contemporary Culture: The Lasting Imprint of Economic Heritage on Local Communities. *Journal of Economic Geography*, 21(6), 841–867. doi: 10.1093/jeg/lbab010

Inglehart, R. (1997). *Modernization and postmodernization in 43 societies*. Princeton, NJ: Princeton University Press.

Jennings, J. E. and Brush, C. G. (2013). Research on Women Entrepreneurs: Challenges to (and from) the Broader Entrepreneurship Literature? *Academy of Management Annals*, 7(1), 663–715. doi: 10.1080/19416520.2013.782190

Korsgaard, S., Müller, S. and Welter, F. (2021). It's Right Nearby: How Entrepreneurs Use Spatial Bricolage to Overcome Resource Constraints. *Entrepreneurship & Regional Development*, 33(1–2), 147–173.

Kwapisz, A. (2019). Do Government and Legal Barriers Impede Entrepreneurship in the US? An Exploratory Study of Perceived vs. Actual Barriers. *Journal of Business Venturing Insights*, 11, e00114. doi: 10.1016/j.jbvi.2019.e00114

Lee, C. K., Wiklund, J., Amezcua, A., Bae, T. J. and Palubinskas, A. (2022). Business Failure and Institutions in Entrepreneurship: A Systematic Review and Research Agenda. *Small Business Economics*, 58, 1997–2023. doi: 10.1007/s11187-021-00495-4

Levie, J. and Autio, E. (2011). Regulatory Burden, Rule of Law, and Entry of Strategic Entrepreneurs: An International Panel Study. *Journal of Management Studies*, 48(6), 1392–1419. doi: 10.1111/j.1467-6486.2010.01006.x

Liñán, F. and Fernandez-Serrano, J. (2014). National Culture, Entrepreneurship and Economic Development: Different Patterns Across the European Union. *Small Business Economics*, 42(4), 685–701.

Mair, J. and Marti, I. (2009). Entrepreneurship in and Around Institutional Voids: A Case Study from Bangladesh. *Journal of Business Venturing*, 24(5), 419–435. doi: 10.1016/j.jbusvent.2008.04.006

Manolova, T. S., Eunni, R. V. and Gyoshev, B. S. (2008). Institutional Environments for Entrepreneurship: Evidence from Emerging Economies in Eastern Europe. *Entrepreneurship Theory and Practice*, 32(1), 203–218. doi: 10.1111/j.1540-6520.2007.00222.x

Morales, C., Holtschlag, C., Masuda, A. D. and Marquina, P. (2019). In Which Cultural Contexts do Individual Values Explain Entrepreneurship? An Integrative Values Framework Using Schwartz's Theories. *International Small Business Journal-Researching Entrepreneurship*, 37(3), 241–267. doi: 10.1177/0266242618811890

Morawska, E. (1999). The Malleable Homo Sovieticus: Transnational Entrepreneurs in Post-communist East Central Europe. *Communist and Post-Communist Studies*, 32(4), 359–378. doi: 10.1016/s0967-067x(99)00022-7

Muñoz, P. and Kibler, E. (2016). Institutional Complexity and Social Entrepreneurship: A Fuzzy-set Approach. *Journal of Business Research*, 69(4), 1314–1318.

Muñoz, P. and Kimmitt, J. (2019). Rural Entrepreneurship in Place: An Integrated Framework. *Entrepreneurship & Regional Development*, 31(9–10), 842–873. doi: 10.1080/08985626.2019.1609593

Muralidharan, E. and Pathak, S. (2018). Sustainability, Transformational Leadership, and Social Entrepreneurship. *Sustainability*, 10(2). doi: 10.3390/su10020567

Nee, V. (1998). Norms and Networks in Economic and Organizational Performance. *American Economic Review*, 88(2), 85–89.

Neergaard, H. and Thrane, C. (2011). The Nordic Welfare Model: Barrier or Facilitator of Women's Entrepreneurship in Denmark? *International Journal of Gender and Entrepreneurship*, 3(2), 88–104. doi: 10.1108/17566261111140189

North, D. C. (1990). *Institutions, institutional change, and economic performance*. Cambridge: Cambridge University Press.

O'Neil, I. and Ucbasaran, D. (2016). Balancing "What Matters to Me" with "What Matters to Them": Exploring the Legitimation Process of Environmental Entrepreneurs. *Journal of Business Venturing*, 31(2), 133–152.

Pathak, S., Goltz, S. and Mari, W. B. (2013). Influences of Gendered Institutions on Women's Entry into Entrepreneurship. *International Journal of Entrepreneurial Behaviour & Research*, 19(5), 478–502. doi: 10.1108/IJEBR-09-2011-0115

Peng, M. W. and Heath, P. S. (1996). The Growth of the Firm in Planned Economies in Transition: Institutions, Organizations, and Strategic Choice. *Academy of Management Journal*, 21(2), 492–528. doi: 10.5465/amr.1996.9605060220

Polese, A. and Rodgers, P. (2011). Surviving Post-Socialism: The Role of Informal Economic Practices. *International Journal of Sociology and Social Policy*, 31(11/12), 612–618. doi: 10.1108/01443331111177896

Rietveld, C. A. and Hoogendoorn, B. (2022). The Mediating Role of Values in the Relationship between Religion and Entrepreneurship. *Small Business Economics*, 58, 1309–1335. doi: 10.1007/s11187-021-00454-z

Rindova, V., Barry, D. and Ketchen Jr, D. J. (2009). Entrepreneuring as Emancipation. *Academy of Management Review*, 34(3), 477–491.

Roland, G. (2020). Culture, Institutions, and Development. In J. M. Baland, F. Bourguignon, J. P. Platteau and T. Verdier (Eds.), *The handbook of economic development and institutions* (pp. 414–448). Princeton, NJ: Princeton University Press.

Ruskin, J., Seymour, R. G. and Webster, C. M. (2016). Why Create Value for Others? An Exploration of Social Entrepreneurial Motives. *Journal of Small Business Management*, 54(4), 1015–1037.

Schwartz, S. (2006). A Theory of Cultural Value Orientations: Explication and Applications. *Comparative Sociology*, 5(2–3), 137–182.

Schwartz, S. H. (1992). Universals in the Content and Structure of Values: Theoretical Advances and Empirical Tests in 20 Countries. *Advances in Experimental Social Psychology*, 25, 1–65.

Smallbone, D. and Welter, F. (2001). The Distinctiveness of Entrepreneurship in Transition Economies. *Small Business Economics*, 16(4), 249–262. doi: 10.1023/A:1011159216578

Smallbone, D. and Welter, F. (2009). *Entrepreneurship and small business development in post-socialist economies*. London: Routledge.

Smith, B. R., Conger, M. J., McMullen, J. S. and Neubert, M. J. (2019). Why Believe? The Promise of Research on the Role of Religion in Entrepreneurial Action. *Journal of Business Venturing Insights*, 11, e00119. doi: 10.1016/j.jbvi.2019.e00119

Smith, B. R., McMullen, J. S. and Cardon, M. S. (2021). Toward a Theological Turn in Entrepreneurship: How Religion Could Enable Transformative Research in Our Field. *Journal of Business Venturing*, 36(5), 106139.

Stenholm, P., Acs, Z. J. and Wuebker, R. (2013). Exploring Country-Level Institutional Arrangements on the Rate and Type of Entrepreneurial Activity. *Journal of Business Venturing*, 28(1), 176–193. doi: 10.1016/j.jbusvent.2011.11.002

Stephan, U. (2020). Culture and Entrepreneurship: A Cross-Cultural Perspective. In M. M. Gielniek, M. S. Cardon and M. Frese (Eds.), *The psychology of entrepreneurship* (pp. 118–144). New York and London: Routlege.

Stephan, U. and Uhlaner, L. M. (2010). Performance-based vs Socially Supportive Culture: A Cross-national Study of Descriptive Norms and Entrepreneurship. *Journal of International Business Studies*, 41(8), 1347–1364.

Sydow, A., Cannatelli, B. L., Giudici, A. and Molteni, M. (2022). Entrepreneurial Workaround Practices in Severe Institutional Voids: Evidence from Kenya. *Entrepreneurship Theory and Practice*, 46(2), 331–367. doi: 10.1177/1042258720929891

Thapa Karki, S., Xheneti, M. and Madden, A. (2021). To Formalize or Not to Formalize: Women Entrepreneurs' Sensemaking of Business Registration in the Context of Nepal. *Journal of Business Ethics*, 173, 687–708. doi: 10.1007/s10551-020-04541-1

Thébaud, S. (2015). Business as Plan B: Institutional Foundations of Gender Inequality in Entrepreneurship across 24 Industrialized Countries. *Administrative Science Quarterly*, 60(4), 671–711. doi: 10.1177/0001839215591627

Thébaud, S. (2016). Passing up the Job: The Role of Gendered Organizations and Families in the Entrepreneurial Career Process. *Entrepreneurship Theory and Practice*, 40(2), 269–287. doi: 10.1111/etap.12222

Urbano, D., Aparicio, S. and Audretsch, D. B. (2019). Twenty-five Years of Research on Institutions, Entrepreneurship, and Economic Growth: What Has Been Learned? *Small Business Economics*, 53(1), 21–49. doi: 10.1007/s11187-018-0038-0

Valdez, M. E. and Richardson, J. (2013). Institutional Determinants of Macro-Level Entrepreneurship. *Entrepreneurship Theory and Practice*, 37(5), 1149–1175. doi: 10.1111/etap.12000

van Stel, A., Storey, D. and Thurik, A. (2007). The Effect of Business Regulations on Nascent and Young Business Entrepreneurship. *Small Business Economics*, 28(2), 171–186. doi: 10.1007/s11187-006-9014-1

Vorley, T. and Williams, N. (2016). Between Petty Corruption and Criminal Extortion: How Entrepreneurs in Bulgaria and Romania Operate within a Devil's Circle. *International Small Business Journal*, 34(6), 797–817. doi: 10.1177/0266242615590464

Webb, J. W., Khoury, T. A. and Hitt, M. A. (2020). The Influence of Formal and Informal Institutional Voids on Entrepreneurship. *Entrepreneurship Theory and Practice*, 44(3), 504–526. doi: 10.1177/1042258719830310

Welter, F. (2019). The Power of Words and Images – Towards Talking About and Seeing Entrepreneurship and Innovation Differently. In D. B. Audretsch, E. Lehmann and A. N. Link (Eds.), *A research agenda for entrepreneurship and innovation* (pp. 179–196). Cheltenham and Northampton, MA: Edward Elgar.

Welter, F. and Baker, T. (2021). Moving Contexts onto New Roads – Clues from Other Disciplines. *Entrepreneurship Theory and Practice*, 45(5), 1154–1175. doi: 10.1177/1042258720930996

Welter, F., Brush, C. and De Bruin, A. (2014). The Gendering of Entrepreneurship Context. *Working paper 1/14*. Bonn: IfM Bonn.

Welter, F. and Smallbone, D. (2008). Women's Entrepreneurship from an Institutional Perspective: The Case of Uzbekistan. *International Entrepreneurship and Management Journal* (4), 505–520. doi: 10.1007/s11365-008-0087-y

Welter, F. and Smallbone, D. (2011). Institutional Perspectives on Entrepreneurial Behavior in Challenging Environments. *Journal of Small Business Management*, 49(1), 107–125. doi: 10.1111/j.1540-627X.2010.00317.x

Welter, F. and Smallbone, D. (2015). Creative Forces for Entrepreneurship: The Role of Institutional Change Agents. *Working paper 1/15*. Bonn: IfM Bonn.

Welter, F. and Xheneti, M. (2015). Value for Whom? Exploring the Value of Informal Entrepreneurial Activities in Post-Socialist Contexts. In G. McElwee and R. Smith (Eds.), *Exploring criminal and illegal enterprise: New perspectives on research, policy and practice* (pp. 253–275). Bingley: Emerald.

Welter, F., Xheneti, M. and Smallbone, D. (2018). Entrepreneurial Resourcefulness in Unstable Institutional Contexts: The Example of European Union Borderlands. *Strategic Entrepreneurship Journal*, 12(1), 23–53. doi: 10.1002/sej.1274

Williams, N. and Vorley, T. (2017). Fostering Productive Entrepreneurship in Post-conflict Economies: The Importance of Institutional Alignment. *Entrepreneurship & Regional Development*, 29(5–6), 444–466.

Williamson, O. E. (2000). The New Institutional Economics: Taking Stock, Looking Ahead. *Journal of Economic Literature*, 38(3), 595–613. doi: 10.1257/jel.38.3.595

Xheneti, M., Madden, A. and Thapa Karki, S. (2019). Value of Formalization for Women Entrepreneurs in Developing Contexts: A Review and Research Agenda. *International Journal of Management Reviews*, 21(1), 3–23.

Xie, Z., Wang, X., Xie, L., Dun, S. and Li, J. (2021). Institutional Context and Female Entrepreneurship: A Country-Based Comparison Using fsQCA. *Journal of Business Research*, 132, 470–480. doi: 10.1016/j.jbusres.2021.04.045

Website: www.gem.org

17

WHAT IS THE POTENTIAL COST OF GENDER INEQUALITY IN LOST EARNINGS?

Global Estimates Based on the Changing Wealth of Nations

Quentin Wodon[1]

THE WORLD BANK, WASHINGTON, DC, USA

17.1 Introduction

Researchers looking at the impact of gender inequality on development have typically focused on annual measures of income or growth in income (e.g. Elborgh-Woytek et al., 2013; Cuberes and Teigner, 2015; McKinsey Global Institute, 2015). These analyses focus on the potential losses in gross domestic product (GDP) from inequality between women and men in labor markets. For example, in a pioneer study for a large number of countries, the McKinsey Global Institute (2015) reports potential gains in GDP from gender equality of up to $28 trillion or 26 percent of GDP by 2025 under a full-potential scenario as compared to a 'business-as-usual' scenario without gender equality. The McKinsey Global Institute study also considers a best-in-region scenario in which all countries would match the rate of improvement of the best-performing country in their region. This would add $12 trillion in annual GDP by 2025.

This focus on income is natural since GDP is the standard measure according to which the economic performance of countries is measured today. Yet GDP growth could be considered as a relatively short-term measure of performance, which may be misleading about the health of an economy because it does not reflect whether a country is investing in the assets base that will sustain its long-term growth. For example, a country could deplete its natural capital base or fail to invest in its people and still be able to generate high rates of GDP growth in the short or medium run, although probably not in the long run.

In this paper, I rely on a different approach to measure the losses in earnings that result from gender inequality or, equivalently, the gains associated with gender equality in labor markets. Instead of measuring losses from inequality as annual flows (the GDP approach), I focus on losses in human capital (the wealth approach). This is done by measuring lifetime losses in earnings. More precisely, human capital wealth is defined as the present value of the future earnings of today's labor force, considering individuals aged 15 and above.

DOI: 10.4324/9781003144366-21

At least three arguments justify using a wealth (stock) approach as opposed to a GDP (flow) approach to measure losses in earnings due to gender inequality. First, using a flow approach does not reveal the full magnitude of the losses in earnings faced by women throughout their working life. Estimates of losses from gender inequality in labor markets based on human capital wealth are substantially larger than those based on GDP simply because wealth is larger than GDP. The full magnitude of the losses from gender inequality appears only when considering human capital wealth or women's earnings over their lifetime.

Second, a flow approach tends to emphasize losses for individuals at the peak of their earnings since they account for a larger share of the labor earnings in GDP. Again, it seems more appropriate to look at individuals' lifetime earnings to better reflect expected losses from gender inequality. This should give a higher weight to younger individuals than is the case with the flow approach.

Third, and most fundamentally, a wealth approach is forward-looking as it emphasizes sustainability. As already mentioned, countries' economic development has traditionally been assessed through GDP per capita, a measure of the income produced by a nation in a given year. Similarly, economic performance has been traditionally assessed through growth in GDP per capita. This is perhaps why most studies of the impact of gender inequality on earnings have focused on GDP. But with which resources is GDP produced? GDP, or more precisely the consumption component of GDP, is essentially the annual return or income that a country reaps from its wealth, the assets base that it uses for production.

Wealth consists of natural capital such as agricultural land, forest, oil, gas and minerals, to give a few examples. It also consists of produced capital – think about infrastructure, machinery, factories, or buildings. Finally, wealth consists of human capital, such as a well-educated and productive labor force. These three categories – produced, natural, and human capital – are considered the three main components of the changing wealth of nations, which together with net foreign assets provide the assets base that countries rely on to produce GDP capita from year to year.

Given the advantages of wealth accounting over annual earnings measures to measure losses in earnings due to gender inequality, I rely in this paper on research recently completed by the World Bank on the Changing Wealth of Nations study (Lange et al., 2018). Building on two previous reports (World Bank, 2006 and 2011), the Changing Wealth of Nations 2018 study covers the period 1995 to 2014. It includes not only estimates of produced capital and natural capital, as did previous reports, but also estimates of human capital following the approach suggested by Jorgensen and Fraumeni (1992a,b).[2] The estimations of human capital are based on household survey data. They represent a significant improvement over past estimates where total wealth included a large unexplained residual called 'intangible capital'. This residual, it turns out, consists for the most part of human capital. By measuring the shares of human capital wealth associated with men and women at the country level, the methodology enables me to estimate lifetime earnings losses due to gender inequality.

The paper is structured as follows. The next section presents the methodology for the estimations. The following section presents the key results. A brief conclusion follows.

17.2 Methodology and data

As noted in Hamilton et al. (2018), two basic approaches can be used to measure human capital wealth (see Lieu and Fraumeni, 2020 for an introduction to the literature on human capital measurement). The first approach relies on measures of investment – typically with a focus on public spending for education. This is the approach used when computing Adjusted Net Saving at the World Bank, treating public sector expenditure on education as an investment. Unfortunately, these measures are only loosely connected to the value of the human capital created. Analysis of the relationship between investments by countries in education and the performance of education systems often shows that the links are not very strong – spending better is often more important than spending more.

The second approach looks instead at the valuation of the outcomes of investments in human development and not investments per se. This is the approach used here. Following Jorgensen and Fraumeni (1992a,b), human capital wealth is defined as the discounted value of future earnings for a country's labor force. While the approach is simple conceptually, several steps must be undertaken for the estimations. In practice, the estimates account for the likelihood that various types of individuals will be working, and how much they are expected to earn when working. By 'various types' of individuals, I mean individuals categorized by age, sex, and level of education. Essentially, household surveys are used to construct a dataset that captures (1) the probability that individuals are working depending on their age, sex, and years of education and (2) their likely earnings when working, again, by age, sex, and years of schooling. This is done separately for men and women and results in estimates of human capital wealth by gender. Typically, women earn significantly less than men.

Estimates of the likelihood of working for individuals are based on observed values in household and labor force surveys. Estimates of expected earnings are based on Mincerian wage regressions (see the Appendix for a more technical description). The regressions are used to compute expected earnings throughout individuals' working life, considering their sex, education level, and assumed experience (computed based on age and the number of years of education completed). Expected earnings are computed for all individuals in the surveys from age 15 to age 65, noting that some individuals may go to school beyond age 15. The analysis also considers the life expectancy of the labor force. In countries with high life expectancy, workers are expected to work until age 65, but in other countries, they may not be able to. For simplicity, when estimating the present value of future earnings, the same discount factor for future earnings is applied to all countries.

The household surveys used for the computation of the earnings profiles – as well as the probability of working – are nationally representative and part of the World Bank's I2D2 database. The surveys are, in most cases, of good quality, but they may still generate estimates that are not consistent with either the system of national accounts or population data for the countries. Therefore, two adjustments are made. First, to ensure consistency of the earnings profiles from the surveys with published data from national accounts, earnings estimates from the surveys are adjusted to reflect the share of labor earnings (including both the employed and the self-employed) in GDP as available in the Penn World Tables. Second and separately, the estimations also rely on two variables obtained from data compiled by the United Nations Population Division: (1) population data by age and sex (so that the data in the household surveys can be better calibrated) and (2) mortality rates by age and gender (so that the expected years of work can be adjusted, accounting for the fact that some workers will die before age 65). Again, as in Hamilton et al. (2018, see also on the link with growth models Nayihouba and Wodon, 2018), I adjust data from the surveys to population estimates from the United Nations to ensure that estimates are adequate. For individuals in the 15-to-24 age group, the probability of remaining in school is also considered.

Given the estimation of human capital wealth based on Mincerian wage regressions, the measure accounts not only for the number of years of schooling completed by workers but also for the earning gains associated with schooling (which implicitly factors in the quality of learning in school), whether individuals work (labor force participation), and for how many years they work (accounting for health conditions through life expectancy).

Estimations of human capital wealth are done separately for men and women. This means that once I have estimates of human capital wealth by gender, I can estimate losses in human capital wealth due to gender inequality in a very simple way. If I denote a country's human capital wealth as measured from the expected future earnings of women and men as HC_M and HC_W, respectively, and the adult population of men and women by POP_M and POP_W, the earnings per adult men and women can be defined as $hc_M = HC_M/POP_M$ and $hc_W = HC_W/POP_W$. Under gender equality, interpreted as ensuring that adult men and women have the same future expected earnings, human capital for women would increase from hc_W to hc_M. Therefore, the loss in human capital wealth from gender inequality is measured as $(hc_M - hc_W) \times POP_W$.[3]

The estimation of the losses in human capital wealth due to gender inequality provided in this paper simply assumes that women could work and earn as much as men. The estimation does not consider the potential effects on men of rising earnings and hours worked for women. I do not account for the fact that men's earnings may decrease if women become better educated and have access to the same employment opportunities as men (for example, resulting from reductions in occupational segregation). I also assume that women can allocate more time to labor market work without a negative impact on men's working hours, therefore not considering the possibility of men having to allocate more time to household chores or unpaid care. Women tend to do most of the domestic work, especially in developing countries. As women work more hours in paid employment, they may have less time for unpaid domestic work, which could affect the number of hours that men may be able to spend in paid employment, depending on options for elderly, child, or other care services available to households. Many other effects could be at work as women catch up with men in earnings. Here, for simplicity, I only compute how much more human capital countries would gain if women had the same lifetime earnings profile as men without any decrease in men's earnings.

In that sense, the estimate could be considered an upper bound of the losses from gender inequality because I do not factor in the potential general equilibrium impact of higher work and earnings for women on men or the labor market more generally. However, the estimation could also be a lower bound of the losses. Indeed, higher earnings for women could lead to more economic activity with positive multiplier effects on the economy and, thereby, wages. Furthermore, if systems for the provision of care to family members were expanded, a substantial share of the time now allocated to unpaid care could become paid care work. The literature also suggests that as countries develop and women join the labor market or work longer hours, this may primarily reduce free time and time spent on domestic chores. Overall, especially through multiplier effects, unleashing women's earnings potential could generate even larger earnings and human capital gains for both men and women than suggested in this paper. The analysis also does not account for intergenerational benefits from unleashing women's earnings potential through better education, health, and employment opportunities for their children. In any case, all estimates should only be considered as orders of magnitude.

The analysis covers 141 countries. In a handful of cases, estimates of labor earnings by gender obtained from household surveys seemed to be off by a wide margin. In those few cases, interpolations or imputations were used instead. For countries from the Gulf Cooperation Council (Bahrain, Kuwait, Oman, Qatar, Saudi Arabia, and the United Arab Emirates), because no household survey data were publicly available, estimates of human capital per capita were based instead on a simple estimation taking into account the countries' GDP per capita and education level,[4] and gender shares were based on published data from other

Table 17.1 Number of countries included in the analysis by region and income group

Aggregate group	Low income	Lower-middle income	Upper-middle income	High-income non-OECD	High-income OECD	Total
East Asia & Pacific	1	6	4	1	3	15
Europe & Central Asia		6	10	4	23	43
Latin America & Caribbean	1	6	12	3	1	23
Middle East & North Africa		5	4	7		16
North America					2	2
South Asia	1	4	1			6
Sub-Saharan Africa	21	10	5			36
Total	**24**	**37**	**36**	**15**	**29**	**141**

Source: Author, based on Lange et al. (2018).

sources. While all estimates should be considered only as orders of magnitude since they rely on a range of assumptions, this is especially the case for estimates for these countries.

Estimates are provided by five-year intervals for the period from 1995 to 2014. Countries are classified by geographic region and income group. For the income group classification, per capita gross national income (GNI) is used to assign a country to an income group. The classification of countries may change over time as their GNI changes from year to year. For example, 52 countries were classified as low income in 1995, but only 28 were so classified in 2014. I use the country classifications for 2014 for the 141 countries in the dataset, resulting in the distribution of countries by income group and region shown in Table 17.1.

Before presenting the results of the analysis, an additional clarification may be worth making. First, there are structural differences in earnings between sectors. Women are more present in certain sectors of the economy than others. This is often referred to as occupational segregation, in which discrimination plays a role, but other factors may be at work too. This is one of the reasons why there is gender inequality in earnings, and it is accounted for in the methodology since overall earnings for men and women are compared, with part of the difference due to occupational segregation. The fact that women are often paid less for the same work performance (a clear phenomenon of discrimination) or that they may work fewer hours than men is also included in the analysis since again, from household surveys, the aggregate earnings profiles of men and women are constructed, taking these differences also into account. All these factors, as well as a range of others (including in many countries lower educational attainment for women in comparison to men), are implicitly taken into account in the overall estimates of the cost of gender inequality in earnings.

17.3 Results

17.3.1 Estimates of losses due to gender inequality in earnings

Before presenting results on losses in wealth due to gender inequality, this section presents baseline estimates of human capital and total wealth from Lange et al. (2018). Table 17.2 provides global estimates in absolute value and per capita terms. The analysis is based on data for 141 countries accounting for 95 percent of the world's population. All estimates are in constant US dollars of 2014. As mentioned earlier, total wealth includes natural capital, produced capital, human capital, and net foreign assets.

Global wealth stood at $1,143 trillion in 2014. This represented an increase in real terms of 66 percent over 20 years (average annual growth rate of 2.6 percent per year). Human capital

Table 17.2 Baseline estimates of global wealth: 1995–2014

	1995	2000	2005	2010	2014
	Total wealth, Trillions, constant 2014 $				
Total wealth	689.9	790.9	889.1	1,024.7	1,143.2
Produced capital	164.8	187.9	226.9	269.0	303.5
Natural capital	52.5	54.2	70.0	97.2	107.4
Human capital	475.6	552.7	595.4	661.1	736.9
Net foreign assets	−2.9	−3.9	−3.3	−2.6	−4.6
Population (billions)	5.35	5.73	6.09	6.47	6.78
	Per capita wealth, constant 2014 $				
Total wealth	128,929	138,064	145,891	158,363	168,580
Produced capital	30,793	32,801	37,237	41,570	44,760
Natural capital	9,803	9,463	11,487	15,019	15,841
Human capital	88,874	96,478	97,707	102,170	108,654
Net foreign assets	−540	−678	−539	−395	−676
	Share of total wealth				
Total wealth	100%	100%	100%	100%	100%
Produced capital	24%	24%	26%	26%	27%
Natural capital	8%	7%	8%	9%	9%
Human capital	69%	70%	67%	65%	64%
Net foreign assets	0%	0%	0%	0%	0%

Source: Author, based on Lange et al. (2018).

wealth reached $737 trillion in 2014, an increase of 55 percent since 1995 (average annual growth rate of 2.2 percent). Globally, human capital accounts for more than two-thirds of total wealth, versus just under one-tenth for natural capital and about a quarter of produced capital. In per capita terms, total wealth stood at $168,580 per person in 2014 versus $128,929 in 1995. Human capital wealth stood at $108,654 per person in 2014 versus $88,874 in 1995. As will be shown in subsequent sections of this paper, inequality in human capital and total wealth between countries is high. In high-income OECD countries, total wealth per capita is above $700,000 and human capital wealth is close to $500,000 per person. This is more than 90 times the levels in low-income countries where human capital wealth is at $5,564 per person.

At the global level, the dynamics of human capital wealth accumulation are driven by shifts in OECD and upper-middle-income countries simply because those countries account for 87 percent of global wealth (65 percent for the OECD alone). The proportions are even larger for human capital wealth. In these countries, the share of human capital wealth in total wealth has fallen slightly in recent years in part because labor earnings as a share of GDP have declined in OECD countries due to technological change, stagnating wages, and in some countries, a reduction in the share of the population in the labor force due to ageing.

By contrast, for low-income and lower-middle-income countries, the share of human capital wealth in total wealth is increasing. Many of these countries are experiencing a demographic transition and are reaping the benefits of the demographic dividend as population growth rates slow, and the population is becoming better educated. While substantial progress has been achieved to close gender gaps in educational attainment at the primary level, the returns to education are often larger at higher levels of schooling. At those levels, gender gaps in educational attainment remain, especially in low-income countries. Furthermore, as countries achieve higher levels of economic development, human capital wealth dominates.

At lower levels of economic development, natural capital continues to account for a larger share of wealth.

Table 17.3 provides estimates of the shares of human capital wealth for women today globally and the losses in human capital wealth due to gender inequality. Globally, in 2014, women accounted for 38 percent of human capital wealth versus 62 percent for men. These are also essentially the proportions observed for upper-middle and high-income OECD countries, which account for the bulk of human capital wealth. In low-income and lower-middle-income countries, women account for only a third or less of human capital wealth. In those countries, gender inequality thus generates in proportional terms a larger loss in human capital wealth, and thereby in total wealth, as will be discussed further below.

How large are the potential losses in wealth resulting from gender inequality globally? As shown in Table 17.3, women's human capital could increase from $283.6 trillion to $453.2 trillion with gender equality. This represents a potential loss in a global wealth of $160.2 trillion. The estimated increase in human capital wealth from the base is 21.7 percent in 2014, and for total wealth (including natural and produced capital as well as net foreign assets), the increase in wealth is estimated at 14.0 percent. On a per capita basis (including not only the adult population but also children), gender inequality could lead to a loss in wealth of $23,620 per person. These potential losses are clearly large. They underscore the benefits that could be reaped globally from achieving gender equality.

Over time, the estimate of the total wealth lost due to gender inequality increased from $123.2 trillion in 1995 to $160.2 trillion in 2014, which is about twice the value of global GDP. This increase comes from population growth, as well as higher standards of living. But other factors that affect human capital wealth at the country and regional level also play a role, including factors that affect the share of labor earnings in GDP over time.

As a share of baseline wealth, losses from gender inequality tend to be slightly lower in 2014 than in 1995. This is in part because there is a (slow) movement towards more equality in many

Table 17.3 Global losses in wealth from gender inequality: 1995–2014

	1995	2000	2005	2010	2014
	Global wealth, Trillions, constant 2014 $				
Baseline gender shares of human capital					
Men's share of human capital	63%	63%	62%	61%	62%
Women's share of human capital	37%	37%	38%	39%	38%
Human capital wealth by gender					
Human capital, men	301.2	349.1	371.6	405.5	453.2
Human capital, women	174.4	203.6	223.8	255.6	283.6
Loss from gender inequality					
Counterfactual human capital, women	297.6	344.5	366.4	398.4	443.8
Increase in human capital	123.2	140.9	142.6	142.8	160.2
Loss as a share of baseline human capital	25.9%	25.5%	24.0%	21.6%	21.7%
Loss as a share of baseline total wealth	17.9%	17.8%	16.0%	13.9%	14.0%
	Per capita wealth, constant 2014 $				
Baseline global wealth					
Human capital per capita, men	56,290	60,940	60,980	62,672	66,832
Human capital per capita, women	32,584	35,538	36,727	39,498	41,823
Loss from gender inequality					
Loss in human capital per capita	23,030	24,603	23,391	22,068	23,620

Source: Author.

countries over time, which makes the losses smaller. But in addition, human capital in high-income countries has been declining slightly in recent years due among others to ageing and a reduction in the share of labor income in GDP. This in turn contributes to a small reduction of the losses from gender inequality over time as a share of the baseline wealth estimates.

17.3.2 Comparison with previous studies

How do the results compare to previous studies? Comparisons can be made for both the estimates of (i) gender shares in earnings which are key for the estimation of the losses from gender inequality and (ii) the magnitude of the losses associated with gender inequality.

Previous studies have focused on gender shares in GDP, while I estimate gender shares in the human capital wealth. Still, given that both approaches are based on earnings data, they should generate similar gender shares. This is indeed the case. The gender shares of GDP reported by the McKinsey Global Institute (2015) are similar to ours. The same conclusion is reached when comparing globally the estimates of women's share of human capital wealth to estimates of women's contribution to GDP from the World Economic Forum's Gender Gap Report (2017). Broadly, there is alignment at least at the global and regional levels.[5]

My estimate of women's share of human capital wealth at 38 percent globally in 2014 is close to McKinsey's estimate of women's contribution to GDP at 37 percent. Gender shares are broadly similar at the regional level as well. For East Asia and the Pacific, women's share of human capital wealth is 35 percent, while McKinsey reports women's contributions to GDP of 41 percent for China and 34 percent for the rest of the region. In Europe and Central Asia, women's share of human capital is at 39 percent in this study, versus 38 percent for their share in GDP in Western Europe and 41 percent for Eastern and Central Europe in the McKinsey study. In Latin America and the Caribbean, the share for women is at 44 percent versus 33 percent for McKinsey. In the Middle East and North Africa, the estimate is at 27 percent versus 18 percent for McKinsey. The shares for North America are virtually the same at 41 percent and 40 percent. In South Asia, the share is at 19 percent versus 17 percent for India and 24 percent for other countries in the McKinsey study. Finally, for Sub-Saharan Africa, I have the same share for women at 39 percent.

What about the magnitude of the estimated losses? As mentioned in the introduction, the McKinsey Global Institute (2015) study reports potential gains in GDP from a 'full potential' scenario of $28 trillion or 26 percent of GDP in 2025 versus a 'business-as-usual' scenario without gender equality. I report losses in human capital wealth from gender inequality of $160 trillion or 14 percent of the baseline estimate of global wealth. The estimate is larger in absolute value simply because wealth is larger than GDP. In 2014, global wealth was estimated at $1,143 trillion for the 141 countries included in the analysis, while global GDP for those countries is estimated at $75 trillion.[6] Wealth is thus 15 times larger than GDP. But in proportionate terms, the estimate is more conservative. This paper suggests a loss of 14 percent of baseline wealth, which is smaller than the loss of 26 percent of GDP suggested in the McKinsey Global Institute study.

Various factors could account for the difference in proportional impacts between this paper and the McKinsey study. Probably the largest factor at work is the fact that the estimates of losses from gender inequality based on human capital wealth in this paper account for the labor share in GDP. In the McKinsey study, GDP appears to be fully allocated to men and women using the following identity: GDP = (working-age population) × (labor-force participation rate) × (employment rate) × (full-time equivalent rate) × (labor productivity per full-time equivalent employed). When relying on human capital wealth estimates, I scale my estimates to the labor share in GDP. It turns out that labor earnings account for just over half of GDP in most countries. This apparent difference in methodology could lead my estimates of losses in percentage terms to be at about half those suggested by the McKinsey study, which is the case. Still, as mentioned earlier, this type of estimate is only meant to give orders of magnitude of the potential losses from gender inequality as opposed to precise values. Clearly, estimates from both this paper and the McKinsey study suggest that losses from gender inequality in earnings are large, whether one relies on a GDP or a wealth approach to measure them.

17.3.3 Estimates of losses by region

The losses in human capital wealth from gender inequality differ between regions and between countries classified by broad income groups. Table 17.4 provides the estimates for overall losses in human capital wealth and wealth per capita for seven regions: East Asia and the Pacific, Europe and Central Asia, Latin America and the Caribbean, the Middle East and North Africa, North America, South Asia, and finally Sub-Saharan Africa.

Table 17.4 Losses from gender inequality by region: 1995–2014

	1995 ($ 2014)	2000 ($ 2014)	2005 ($ 2014)	2010 ($ 2014)	2014 ($ 2014)
East Asia & Pacific					
Loss in human capital ($ trillions)	34.2	35.8	37.7	42.1	49.9
Loss in human capital per capita ($)	18,627	18,450	18,663	20,130	23,253
% loss in total wealth	24.5%	22.1%	20.8%	17.1%	16.6%
Europe & Central Asia					
Loss in human capital ($ trillions)	32.4	36.3	37.2	38.8	41.6
Loss in human capital per capita ($)	39,892	44,511	45,045	46,261	48,884
% loss in total wealth	14.3%	14.8%	13.7%	13.0%	13.3%
Latin America & Caribbean					
Loss in human capital ($ trillions)	7.3	5.9	6.5	6.7	6.7
Loss in human capital per capita ($)	15,500	11,558	11,945	11,468	10,940
% loss in total wealth	14.3%	10.5%	10.2%	8.8%	7.9%
Middle East & North Africa					
Loss in human capital ($ trillions)	1.6	2.1	2.4	2.7	3.1
Loss in human capital per capita ($)	9,275	11,261	11,220	11,150	11,757
% loss in total wealth	10.2%	11.8%	9.9%	7.7%	7.4%
North America					
Loss in human capital ($ trillions)	43.4	55.1	51.3	43.3	47.2
Loss in human capital per capita ($)	146,791	175,923	156,600	126,052	133,299
% loss in total wealth	18.8%	19.5%	16.3%	13.3%	13.5%
South Asia					
Loss in human capital ($ trillions)	3.3	4.6	6.5	7.4	9.1
Loss in human capital per capita ($)	2,664	3,383	4,374	4,613	5,405
% loss in total wealth	28.8%	32.2%	35.0%	29.4%	29.4%
Sub-Saharan Africa					
Loss in human capital ($ trillions)	1.1	1.1	1.0	1.9	2.5
Loss in human capital per capita ($)	2,016	1,927	1,435	2,480	2,914
% loss in total wealth	7.6%	8.8%	6.3%	9.8%	11.4%

Source: Author.

Consider the estimates for 2014. The largest total losses in wealth from gender inequality are observed for East Asia and the Pacific, North America, and Europe and Central Asia, in each case at between $40 trillion and $50 trillion. This is because many of the countries in these regions are high-income or upper-middle-income, and thereby they concentrate much of the world's human capital wealth. In per capita terms as well, the losses are larger in those regions. But the losses in other regions are substantial too, including in comparison to current levels of development. For example, in South Asia, the losses from gender inequality are estimated at $9.1 trillion. In Sub-Saharan Africa, the losses are at $2.5 trillion. This is the smallest estimate across regions. However, as a share of initial wealth, the losses from gender inequality in Sub-Saharan Africa represent 11.4 percent of the base regional wealth, which is larger than the loss in Latin America and the Caribbean and especially the Middle East and North Africa in part because of high levels of natural capital from sub-soil assets (especially oil) in that region. The loss in total wealth from the base of gender inequality is the highest in South Asia because this is also the region with the lowest initial share of women in human capital.

17.3.4 Estimates of losses by income groups

Losses from gender inequality also differ between countries ranked by income groups, defined according to the World Bank classification (low income, lower-middle income, upper-middle income, and high income). In this section, I differentiate between high-income OECD and other high-income countries. The latter group includes several oil-producing countries from the Middle East. Table 17.5 provides the estimates for these five income groups.

Table 17.5 Losses from gender inequality by income group: 1995–2014

	1995 ($ 2014)	2000 ($ 2014)	2005 ($ 2014)	2010 ($ 2014)	2014 ($ 2014)
Low-income countries					
Loss in human capital ($ trillions)	0.4	0.5	0.6	0.8	1.1
Loss in human capital per capita ($)	1,335	1,406	1,415	1,675	2,052
% loss in total wealth from base	11.5%	13.5%	13.8%	14.2%	15.1%
Lower-middle-income countries					
Loss in human capital ($ trillions)	6.8	7.6	9.4	11.0	13.5
Loss in human capital per capita ($)	3,407	3,472	3,958	4,275	4,967
% loss in total wealth from base	19.2%	20.7%	20.4%	18.1%	19.1%
Upper-middle-income countries					
Loss in human capital ($ trillions)	11.2	11.3	16.1	20.9	26.5
Loss in human capital per capita ($)	6,032	5,764	7,872	9,800	12,067
% loss in total wealth from base	11.8%	10.0%	11.9%	10.4%	10.7%
High-income non-OECD					
Loss in human capital ($ trillions)	2.7	3.6	3.8	4.7	5.4
Loss in human capital per capita ($)	10,637	14,047	14,378	17,021	18,672
% loss in total wealth from base	6.5%	8.6%	7.4%	7.1%	7.0%
High-income OECD					
Loss in human capital ($ trillions)	102.2	117.9	112.6	105.4	113.7
Loss in human capital per capita ($)	108,593	121,735	112,859	102,567	108,631
% loss in total wealth from base	19.8%	19.8%	17.3%	15.2%	15.3%

Source: Author.

Consider again the estimates for 2014. In absolute terms, the largest total losses in wealth are observed for high-income OECD countries and upper-middle-income countries (which include China). Together these two groups of countries experience a loss of $140.2 trillion in human capital wealth due to gender inequality. The other countries together lose $20 trillion in human capital wealth. But again, in percentage terms from the base, the picture is different. Low-income countries lose 15.1 percent of their base level of wealth (including all types of capital) under gender inequality, which is slightly larger than the loss for the world, at 14.0 percent, as shown in Table 17.3. Note also that losses from gender inequality are lower in proportional terms from the base in high-income non-OECD countries, in part because many of these countries have substantial oil reserves and thereby higher levels of natural capital in their baseline wealth. Absolute losses in human capital wealth from gender inequality are (much) higher in high-income than in low-income countries simply because the levels of wealth on which losses are applied are higher in high-income countries.

17.4 Conclusion

The objective of this paper was to demonstrate that the economic cost of gender inequality in earnings is high. The analysis was conducted using new measures of human capital wealth to account for lifetime losses. Losses in human capital due to gender inequality are estimated at $160 trillion globally in 2014. On a per capita basis, gender inequality generates losses in wealth of $23,620 per person. By contrast, gender equality would raise the (changing) wealth of nations by 14.0 percent globally. The losses differ between regions and income groups since levels of human capital wealth also differ.

To increase women's earnings and human capital wealth, investments throughout the life cycle are needed, starting with early childhood development and learning in schools, and continuing with improved job opportunities in adulthood. In the labor market specifically, as noted in World Bank (2012), and as discussed in more details in Wodon and de la Brière (2018) and Wodon et al. (2020), successful interventions can be implemented to address time use constraints, facilitate access to productive assets, and solve market and institutional failures that penalize women. Interventions however need to be tailored in terms of age (young women face specific barriers and opportunities), poverty (very poor women need more than a single intervention) and type of participation (considering wage workers, entrepreneurs, and farmers). But smart delivery and implementation can lead to positive impacts. Addressing constraints often requires incentives and nudges, but what is also needed is to take on women's subordinate position in the family and the traditional division of labor for household chores and care in many contexts.

Notes

1 This chapter builds on a broader study on the cost of gender inequality globally funded by the Canadian Government, the Children's Investment Fund Foundation, and the Global Partnership for Education. The chapter builds on work at the World Bank on the Changing Wealth of Nations, with special thanks to Glenn-Marie Lange. The author is grateful to Benedicte de la Briere as well as Sameera Al Tuwaijri, Luis Benveniste, Niklas Buehren, Caren Grown, and Oni Lusk-Stover for very valuable comments. The findings, interpretations, and conclusions expressed in this chapter are only those of the author and should not be attributed to the World Bank, its affiliated organizations, members of its Board of Executive Directors or the countries they represent.

2 In October 2021, the World Bank (2021) published an update of the changing wealth of nations study with very similar findings in terms of the role played by human capital wealth. The estimates in this paper are however based on the 2018 data release.

3 In very rare cases when hc_W is larger than hc_M, I could raise hc_M to the level of hc_W, but for standardization, I instead adjust hc_W downwards. These rare cases do not make any meaningful difference to the overall results however.

4 The estimations of human capital result from a log-log regression with as explanatory variables GDP per capita and the average numbers of years of education in the sample of countries used for estimation.

5 As to whether one set of approaches is better than another at the country level to estimate women's shares of GDP or human capital wealth, this is a question that needs to be investigated further. The results may vary from one country to another depending on the quality of the underlying data. But for broad aggregates as reported here, the underlying shares are fairly similar.

6 My estimation includes a larger set of countries than included in the McKinsey Global Institute study, although this does not make a very large difference for estimates of global losses given that most of the wealth, especially human capital wealth, remains concentrated in upper-middle-income and high-income countries and the fact that these countries are also included for the most part in other studies including that by the McKinsey Global Institute.

References

Cuberes, D. and Teignier, M. (2015). How Costly Are Labor Gender Gaps? Estimates for the Balkans and Turkey. *World Bank Policy Research Working Paper 7319*. Washington, DC: The World Bank.

Elborgh-Woytek, K., Newiak, M., Kochhar, K., Fabrizio, S., Kpodar, K., Wingender, P., Clements, B. and Schwartz, G. (2013). Women, Work and the Economy: Macroeconomic Gains from Gender Equity. *IMF Staff Discussion Note*. Washington, DC: International Monetary Fund.

Hamilton, K., Wodon, Q., Barrot, D. and Yedan, A. (2018). Human Capital and the Wealth of Nations: Global Estimates and Trends, in G.M. Lange, Q. Wodon and K. Carey (eds.). *The Changing Wealth of Nations 2018: Sustainability into the 21st Century*. Washington, DC: The World Bank.

Jorgensen, D.W. and Fraumeni, B.M. (1992a). The Output of Education Sector, in Z. Griliches (ed.). *Output Measurement in the Service Sectors*. Chicago, IL: University of Chicago Press.

Jorgensen, D.W. and Fraumeni, B.M. (1992b). Investment in Education and US Economic Growth. *Scandinavian Journal of Economics*, 94(Supplement): 51–70.

Lange, G.M., Wodon, Q. and Carey, K. (2018). *The Changing Wealth of Nations 2018: Sustainability into the 21st Century*. Washington, DC: The World Bank.

Liu, G. and Fraumeni, B.M. (2020). *A Brief Introduction to Human Capital Measures*. NBER Working Paper Series No. 27561. Cambridge, MA: National Bureau of Economic Research. http://www.nber.org/papers/w27561

McKinsey Global Institute. (2015). *The Power of Parity: How Advancing Women's Equality Can Add $12 Trillion to Global Growth*. London: McKinsey Global Institute.

Nayihouba, A. and Wodon, Q. (2018). Gains in Human Capital Wealth: What Growth Models Tell Us, in G.M. Lange, Q. Wodon and K. Carey (eds.). *The Changing Wealth of Nations 2018: Sustainability into the 21st Century*. Washington, DC: The World Bank.

Wodon, Q. and de la Brière, B. (2018). Unrealized Potential: The High Cost of Gender Inequality in Earnings. *The Cost of Gender Inequality Notes Series*. Washington, DC: The World Bank.

Wodon, Q., de la Brière, B., Malé, C., Montenegro, C., Nguyen, H. and Onagoruwa, A. (2020). *How Large Is the Gender Dividend? Measuring Selected Impacts and Costs of Gender Inequality*. Washington, DC: The World Bank.

World Bank. (2006). *Where Is the Wealth of Nations? Measuring Capital for the 21st Century*. Washington, DC: The World Bank.

World Bank. (2011). *The Changing Wealth of Nations? Measuring Sustainable Development in the New Millennium*. Washington, DC: The World Bank.

World Bank. (2012). *World Development Report 2012: Gender Equality and Development*. Washington, DC: The World Bank.

World Bank. (2021). *The Changing Wealth of Nations 2021: Managing Assets for the Future*. Washington, DC: The World Bank.

World Economic Forum. (2017). *The Global Gender Gap Report 2017*. Geneva: The World Economic Forum.

Appendix: Methodology for Estimating Human Capital Wealth

The approach used for measuring human capital is outlined in Hamilton et al. (2018) as well as Lange et al. (2018). The measures of human capital wealth rely on estimations conducted with household surveys, with calibration of the results based on the share of labor earnings in GDP in the national accounts. The first step in the analysis consists in estimating earnings regressions. Denote an individual's age by a (from age 15 to 64) and years of schooling by e (from 0 to 24). Years of experience are approximated as $x = \max(0, a - e - 6)$. Mincerian Wage regressions are estimated as

$$\ln(y_i) = \alpha + \beta_1 e_i + \beta_2 x_i + \beta_3 x_i^2 + \varepsilon_i$$

On the basis of these regressions, a matrix of expected earnings is constructed. Each cell in the matrix accounts for wages earned by the population of age a and education level e. If n_{ae} is the number of workers of age a and years of schooling e, each cell in the matrix is defined as

$$H_{ae} = n_{ae} \exp\left(\beta_1 e + (\beta_2 + \beta_3 x_{ae}) x_{ae}\right)$$

Total expected earnings from the survey are estimated as $= \Sigma_a \Sigma_e H_{ae}$. For consistency with the National Accounts, all cells in the matrix of expected earnings from the survey are scaled up or down by the ratio of labor earnings in the National Accounts W to labor earnings in the survey. This generates a set of wages by age group and education level $w_{ae} = (W/T) H_{ae}$. The data are disaggregated by sex as well as the type of employment.

For notation purposes, I consider only the disaggregation into self-employed workers and wage earners here. w_{ae}^m denotes a sell in the remuneration matrix for employed workers, and w_{ae}^s the corresponding cell in the matrix for the self-employed. Similarly, the number of workers of both groups is denoted by n_{ae}^m and n_{ae}^s and the population of age a and education level e by pop_{ae}. Probabilities of being in employed or self-employment are estimated as $p_{ae}^m = n_{ae}^m / pop_{ae}$ and $p_{ae}^s = n_{ae}^s / pop_{ae}$.

Two additional parameters are used in the estimations. First, since estimates are provided for the adult population ages 15–64, I compute a probability, denoted by r_{ae}^{e+1}, that a person of age a and education e will undertake an extra year of education (and thereby not work during that year). Second, I compute age cohort survival rates from life tables, denoted as $v_{a,a+1}$.

Total human capital is calculated as the discounted value of lifetime earnings of two population subgroups, those aged 25–65 (assumed to have finished schooling), and those aged 15–24 who have some probability of still being in school. Denote the discount factor by d. For an individual with age a and education e randomly drawn from the sub-population aged 25–65, the discounted lifetime income h_{ae} is estimated based on the following recursion:

$$h_{ae} = p_{ae}^m w_{ae}^m + p_{ae}^s w_{ae}^s + d * v_{a,a+1} * h_{a+1,e}$$

This expression states that the lifetime income of a representative individual aged 25–65 is the sum of two parts: current labor income taking into account the probabilities of being either employed or self-employed, plus lifetime income in the next year, adjusted by a discount factor and the corresponding survival rate.

For an individual aged between 15 and 24, the expression is slightly more complex in order to allow for the possibility of continuing one's education. In the next year, the individual must choose between two courses of action: the first is to continue their work (holding the same education level as before) and earn income of $d * v_{a,a+1} * h_{a+1,e}$ with the probability $\left(1 - r_{ae_-}^{e+1}\right)$; the second is to undertake one more year of education and (after finishing) to receive income as $d * v_{a,a+1} * h_{a+1,e+1}$, with the probability of r_{ae}^{e+1}. In each case, a proportion $v_{a,a+1}$ is assumed to survive. The recursive relationship is therefore:

$$h_{ae} = p_{ae}^m w_{ae}^m + p_{ae}^s w_{ae}^s + \left(1 - r_{ae}^{e+1}\right) * d * v_{a,a+1} * h_{a+1,e} + r_{ae}^{e+1} * d * v_{a,a+1} * h_{a+1,e+1}$$

Because data on earnings are available in the surveys by sex, human capital can be estimated separately for men and women and used to compute the cost of gender inequality in earnings at the level of countries, regions, or globally.

18
ENTREPRENEURSHIP IN THE PLATFORM ECONOMY
Power Asymmetries and Risk

Donato Cutolo

IE UNIVERSITY, MADRID, SPAIN

Martin Kenney

UNIVERSITY OF CALIFORNIA, DAVIS, CA, USA

"The court (platform) maintains its power by remaining secretive about its operations. And since it is accountable to no one except itself, it does not have to make its actions public".

"Since the court (platform) is a closed system that operates on its own rules, and since the court's (platform's) power is so absolute, it is effective at rebuffing any effort from outsiders (complementors) – including ambitious defendants (complementors) – to penetrate its mysteries".

(Apologies to Franz Kafka)

18.1 Introduction

Globally, an ever-greater number of business sectors are being integrated into the platform economy (Kenney & Zysman 2016; Kenney et al., 2021), even as these businesses face a Kafkaesque relationship with their particular platforms. The inequity in these relationships is apparent. And yet, scholars such as Brynjolfsson and McAfee (2014) hail the opportunities that platforms create for entrepreneurs. Researchers studying platforms have emphasized the importance of platform complementors in providing variety and innovation to generate a platform's "ecosystem" (Boudreau & Lakhani, 2009; Parker et al., 2016), though they ignore the inequality inherent in the relationship. While recognizing the tremendous new business opportunities created by online platforms, we differ from many others in arguing that enterprises dependent upon a platform are not independent, in the traditional sense, but, rather, are "platform-dependent" as discussed by Cutolo and Kenney (2021). Building on this concept, we explore the profound impact that the "platform economy" (Kenney & Zysman, 2016, 2019) has upon the enormous number and variety of entrepreneurs (Aldrich & Ruef, 2018).

DOI: 10.4324/9781003144366-22

The economic centrality of platforms heralds a new reality for entrepreneurs (Cutolo et al., 2021). Digital platforms such as Amazon, eBay, Etsy, Google search and advertising, Instagram, and YouTube make it easier than ever for entrepreneurs to build a business and generate income. Yet, for entrepreneurs building businesses on the platform—that is, the "complementors"—any misstep, many of which can be identified by the all-seeing algorithms, can lead to summary judgment followed by Kafkaesque adjudication. In 2021, both entrepreneurs and existing businesses navigate a world in which customers want to make their purchases online, so an online presence is necessary. As a result, participation in a platform's ecosystem has become vital for their existence and growth (Kenney & Zysman, 2016; Parker et al., 2016).

The broad shift in business-to-consumer activity online has led to a fundamental alteration in power, to the point that the digital platforms intermediating economy activity have transformed the market. As a result, the economy is being (re)structured by platform firms. Even firms that are not directly selling through a digital platform are affected by online services such as Google search and ranking algorithms, to the point that for many firms, not appearing in Google search results is tantamount to nonexistence. The importance of being discovered and well ranked on Google's search results has resulted in the business of search engine optimization. In large measure, the study of the impacts of platforms has concentrated on labor platforms, such as Uber (e.g., Berg & Johnston, 2019; Cramer & Krueger, 2016) or Upwork (Popiel, 2017), crowdfunding (Sorenson et al., 2016), and retail (Khan, 2016). Despite its transformative impact, the implications on entrepreneurs have been studied less (for a few exceptions, see Autio et al., 2018; Cutolo & Kenney, 2021; Nambisan, 2017; Sussan & Acs, 2017). Whereas studies have been conducted regarding the impact of digital platforms on entrepreneurs and the entrepreneurial process, most have been laudatory or have not considered the implications for businesses that have become dependent upon the platform.

The entrepreneurial process, which is already characterized by high risk, is both eased and made more precarious by being dependent upon a platform. The precarity is increased as the venture is vulnerable to unilateral, often irresistible, and difficult to appeal decisions made by platform owners. Platform-based entrepreneurs face not only risk that is incalculable as the platform has godlike powers ranging from complete visibility into the dependent entrepreneur's business to an ability to unilaterally change the terms of participation, up to suspension and removal from the platform, which results in a loss of any and all equity that the entrepreneur has created (Zuboff, 2019). As a result, those dependent upon a platform suffer not only the normal risks and anxiety that come with building a firm but a new type of risk due to their dependence upon the platform. To understand this precarity, it is necessary to understand the pitfalls of using the "ecosystem" metaphor to describe the economic space created for complementors.

The paper begins by defining platforms and discussing their role in entrepreneurship. We then critique the ecosystem metaphor as problematic, though, for lack of a better term, we continue to use "ecosystem" and "complementors". We then describe the resources that the platform provides to members of its ecosystem. This is followed by an introduction of the concept of Platform Dependence introduced by Cutolo and Kenney (2021) with a description of the powers that the platform owner wields over complementors, arguing that entrepreneurship in such an environment is fundamentally different than previous concepts of entrepreneurship. The discussion and conclusion explore the implications of our results for understanding entrepreneurship today.

18.2 Entrepreneurs and platforms

Platforms have been defined in a variety of ways (Baldwin & Woodward, 2009; Parker et al., 2016; Evans et al., 2006). We adopt Gawer's (2014, p. 1240) definition "that platforms are evolving organizations or meta-organizations that: (1) federate and coordinate constitutive agents who can innovate and compete; (2) create value by generating and harnessing economies of scope in supply or/and in demand side of the markets; and (3) entail a modular technological architecture composed of a core and a periphery". Our discussion is confined to online software platforms because they have powerful generative potential—that is, they enable the creation of new output, structure, or behavior, often without direct input from the system originator (Zittrain, 2008). This is accomplished by the provision to platform users of various social and technical boundary resources (Ghazawneh & Henfridsson, 2013) that attract complementors to join and thereby constitute its ecosystem (Jacobides et al., 2018). Although it is true that complementors join a platform's ecosystem for various reasons (Boudreau & Jeppesen, 2015; Jeppesen & Frederiksen, 2006), the contributors of interest to us are those who do so with entrepreneurial intent.

Digital platforms facilitate and simultaneously shape the emergence of novel entrepreneurial opportunities. When conceptualizing the emergence of entrepreneurial opportunity, it is important to consider the role of contextual elements or enablers such as "single, distinct, external circumstances, which—by affecting supply, demand, costs, prices or payoff structures—can play an essential role in eliciting and/or enabling a variety of venture development attempts" (Davidsson, 2015, p. 684). Although contextual elements operate at the environmental level and can be actor independent, particular actors often influence or even have a central role as external enablers (Davidsson, 2015). By orchestrating entire ecosystems of value creation and exchange (Nambisan, 2017) and by providing resources for various stages of the entrepreneurial process (von Briel, Davidsson, & Recker, 2018), digital platforms not only are external enablers but also open new spaces where entrepreneurs can create new firms.[1] Effectively, they become the context for entrepreneurial activity (Cutolo & Vang, 2021).

Platform-based entrepreneurs are mundane retail or service businesses (Barley, Bechky, & Milliken, 2017). They have a great variety: opening a knitwear shop on Etsy, eBay, or Amazon, creating a YouTube channel, writing apps, creating a reselling business on Amazon, and starting a business based on Google advertisement referrals are only some of the types of businesses that can be established on a digital platform (Haefliger, Jäger, & Von Krogh, 2010; Keinan et al., 2015; Kim, 2018). The enormous population of platform-based entrepreneurs has received far less attention, as scholars have focused on the platforms. This relative lack of attention is noteworthy considering the sheer number of these entrepreneurs (Table 18.1 shows the number of entrepreneurs operating on the major platforms).

Entrepreneurship research tends to focus on extraordinary firms often are described as *gazelles* and *unicorns*, rather than studying the far more common ordinary entrepreneurs, which digital platforms are spawning in the millions (Aldrich & Ruef, 2018). The dearth of research on entrepreneurs on digital platforms is even more problematic considering that essentially all entrepreneurship today is predicated upon operating in a platform-defined context (Autio et al., 2014). In 2021, Amazon and other digital platforms are where consumers learn about and search for goods and services (Kaziukenas, 2021). The growing centrality of platforms is evidenced by the need for even the most powerful established brands to consider whether a presence on Amazon is necessary. For example, Nike had resisted selling through Amazon in part out of fear of undercutting their existing vendors, but in 2018, Nike capitulated and opened a small Amazon shop (Galloway, 2018; Kelley, 2018)—only to close it two years later.

Table 18.1 Largest transaction platforms and estimated revenue of ecosystem complementors

Platform	Date established	Description or major activity	Revenue 2020/2021	Number of entrepreneurs 2020/2021	Source
Apple iOS/App Store	2008	Marketplace	$85.1 billion	2.2 million apps	https://www.statista.com/statistics/296226/annual-apple-app-store-revenue/ https://www.statista.com/statistics/276623/number-of-apps-available-in-leading-app-stores/#:~:text=Number%20of%20apps%20available%20in%20leading%20app%20stores%202021&text=As%20of%20the%20first%20quarter,million%20available%20apps%20for%20iOS
Amazon[a]	1995	Marketplace	$80.5 billion	6 million	https://www.statista.com/statistics/259782/third-party-seller-share-of-amazon-platform/#:~:text=Amazon%20seller%20revenues&text=In%202020%2C%20the%20e%2Dcommerce,percent%20over%20the%20previous%20year https://www.marketplacepulse.com/articles/amazon-reaches-six-million-third-party-sellers
Google Play	2008	Marketplace	$48 billion	3.48 million apps	https://www.statista.com/statistics/444476/google-play-annual-revenue/ https://www.statista.com/statistics/276623/number-of-apps-available-in-leading-app-stores/#:~:text=Number%20of%20apps%20available%20in%20leading%20app%20stores%202021&text=As%20of%20the%20first%20quarter,million%20available%20apps%20for%20iOS
eBay	1995	Marketplace	$10.3 billion	19 million globally	https://expandedramblings.com/index.php/ebay-stats/ https://investors.ebayinc.com/financial-information/annual-reports/default.aspx (2020 Annual Report)
YouTube	2005	Video sharing	$19.8 billion	394,000 fulltime creators, 37 million channels	https://www.businessofapps.com/data/youtube-statistics/ https://blog.youtube/inside-youtube/youtubes-creative-economy-small-businesses-big-impact/
Etsy	2005	Marketplace	$1.7 billion	4.4 million active merchants	https://investors.etsy.com/press-releases/press-release-details/2021/Etsy-Inc.-Reports-Fourth-Quarter-and-Full-Year-2020-Financial-Results/default.aspx
Shopify	2004	Software for online sales	$2.9 billion	1.7 million merchants	https://news.shopify.com/shopify-announces-fourth-quarter-and-full-year-2020-financial-results
Instagram	2010	Video Sharing social media	N/A	200 million business accounts	https://business.instagram.com/getting-started?ref=igb_carousel

[a] Amazon Marketplace third-party revenue.

To appreciate the impact of the platform economy, it is important to explore how entrepreneurial activity changes when operating through a platform ecosystem. In the next section, we unpack the unusual characteristics of platform ecosystems when they are compared to other environments referred to as ecosystems.

18.3 The platform ecosystem and complementor metaphor: Concealing dependency

The literature nearly always postulates that the complementors and platform owners in these ecosystems share similar objectives in relation to the value proposition to customers (Jacobides et al., 2018; Nambisan & Baron, 2013). For example, Wareham et al. (2014, p. 1198) refer to complementors as "autonomous actors, act as entrepreneurs, invoking the speed of market mechanisms while focusing their own portfolio of domain expertise, sector knowledge, and relational capital to create locally relevant solutions".

This comforting collaborative image in which platform owners and autonomous complementors "depend on each other and share a common fate" (Tiwana et al., 2010, p. 52) promises a flat power structure between the actors that allows successful platform owners to have "hundreds if not thousands of partners [that] also participate in platform-based 'ecosystem' innovation" (Gawer & Cusumano, 2014, p. 417). These authors never reflect upon what "partnership" or symbiosis means in markets controlled by a platform that has the power to determine the rules of engagement or to unilaterally punish or even expropriate its partners.

Some have recognized that platform owners are able to "impose rules and constraints, create inducements and otherwise shape behaviors" (Boudreau & Hagiu, 2009, p. 3). More succinctly, as Nambisan and Baron (2013, p. 1073) observe, the other ecosystem actors must "surrender part of their autonomy and independence" to align their businesses with the desires of the platform leader (Tavalaei & Cennamo, 2018). Alignment may include the platform owners absorbing the businesses of their complementors (Gawer & Cusumano, 2002; Gawer & Henderson, 2007; Zhu & Liu, 2018). Decisions to absorb or eliminate their complementors' businesses are portrayed as a mechanism to defend the ecosystem, which aimed at exercising better quality control (Zhu & Sun, 2018) or at stimulating innovation with a better customer experience (Gawer & Cusumano, 2002). In contrast to these benign interpretations, Zhu and Liu (2018) show that Amazon's entry into market segments created by independent merchants is aimed at its most successful complementors.

Because platform owners can impose rules, boundaries, and directions, complementors bear the risks of entrepreneurship while lacking the freedom and security typical of an independent business (Nambisan & Baron, 2013). Scholars studying digital platforms have mostly embraced an ownership perspective to look at the strategies and the dynamics put in place to generate and maintain value in the ecosystem (Gawer & Cusumano, 2002; Gawer & Henderson, 2007; Boudreau, 2010); hence, the issues faced by complementors are underinvestigated (Tavalaei & Cennamo, 2018). The effect of these power dynamics on the myriad small complementary businesses is explored only in passing.

We have indicated that the "ecosystem" metaphor is problematic, and yet it is not entirely incorrect. Recognition is growing among scholars that more research should be devoted to the members of business ecosystems (Kapoor & Agrawal, 2017). Platforms provide their ecosystem members with significant resources, which we discuss in the next section, and, paradoxically, it is these resources that give the asymmetric power to the platform owner who has an omniscient view and the ability to unilaterally expel any complementor or customer, and change the rules that govern the actions of platform-based entrepreneurs.

18.4 Entrepreneurs, complementors, and resources

Enrolling in a platform ecosystem as a complementor through acceptance of the terms and conditions means acceptance not only of the current goals and general value proposition of the platform owner but also any changes in these that might occur in the future (Nambisan & Baron, 2013). To be successful, there is a fundamental contradiction faced by every platform as an intermediary—it requires complementors and consumers to populate its ecosystems. Therefore, platforms provide significant incentives to both sides, consumers and producers, to join their ecosystem. All things being equal, the higher the number of actors offering complementary products on the platform, the more robust the platform is and the higher the total value created in its ecosystem (Gawer & Cusumano, 2014). Of course, as Boudreau (2012) finds, there may be a limit to the number of complementors able to join a platform ecosystem. To attract entrepreneurs, platform owners must provide access, opportunities, resources, and even subsidies because the provision of tools lowering the costs of connecting to the platform and accessing customers encourages platform adoption. In the economics literature, these resources are considered subsidies (Boudreau & Hagiu, 2009). In this section, we enumerate the most salient resources used to attract complementors.

18.4.1 Customer access

The fundamental benefit of using a platform for those providing goods or services, whether it be advertisers paying for advertising, or Etsy sellers, or Uber drivers, is customer access. This refers to the platform's ability to match customers and buyers. In size, these markets range from global (online sales) to extremely local (locating a Lyft driver). As Table 18.1 shows, the differences in scale can be enormous. Whether a market or an advertising-supported platform, the purpose is to reduce discovery and transaction costs, creating a technological infrastructure that makes discovery of this enormous mass of sellers possible, thereby creating new spaces for entrepreneurs.

18.4.2 Access to resources

New ventures require a variety of resources, including capital, skilled workers, networks, and customers, to overcome the liability of newness (Stinchcombe, 1965). To attract participants, platforms provide a remarkable array of resources, including interfaces, templates, manuals, and other technical support, either gratis or at low cost. Platforms must offer such resources, even at a loss, to lower entry barriers (Nambisan, 2017; Nambisan, Siegel, & Kenney, 2018). In Table 18.2, the variety of resources offered by Etsy is listed and described.

The scale of investment in these resources to lower entry barriers and facilitate complementors business can be enormous, as it includes engineering for APIs and data analysis, marketing and sales information, training, and other resources. Platforms such as YouTube have permanent facilities (YouTube spaces) in key cities globally. These investments are meant to attract platform-based entrepreneurs by creating sunk costs and locking them in.

18.4.3 Platform legitimacy

The anonymity of online transactions between parties means that there is little intrinsic trust between parties as they do not know each other and their transactions are unlikely to be repeated (Jøsang et al., 2007). Platforms have developed a number of features meant to

Table 18.2 Selected resources provided to entrepreneurs by Etsy (2022)

Services	Free or paid	Type of service	Description
Application programming interfaces (APIs)	Free	Auxiliary resources	Etsy APIs allow the creation of apps to manage listings, analyze sales history and feedback, control shop appearance, and access certain customer information. In 2019, 70 APIs were available on the website
Etsy Handbook	Free	Training	Educational resources, such as articles, webinars, and posts that teach sellers how to start, manage, and scale their Etsy businesses. They focus on taxes, shipping, and marketing, with updates every week
Etsy Craft Entrepreneurship	Free	Training	Educational program for underserved communities
Etsy Payment	Paid	Auxiliary resources	Dedicated system provided by Etsy to streamline payments for sellers and buyers
Etsy Training Videos	Paid	Training	Online videos to improve sales
Etsy Forums	Free	Community building	Advice, discussion of changes, etc.
Etsy Stats	Free	Site analytics	Information on traffic, listings, and customers

mitigate this primordial condition, which makes transactions possible. Effectively, the platform is the guarantor that the transaction will not result in fraud by either side. This legitimacy is created by a number of mechanisms for ensuring sufficient satisfaction to ensure repeat usage (Grabner-Kraeuter, 2002). The first and most widely recognized feature for increasing trust is a seller and buyer ranking and commenting systems that provide ex ante information for previous parties to a transaction (Forman et al., 2008).[2] Further, these ranking and comment systems provide an automatic form of monitoring and disciplining errant transaction parties (Bucher, 2012; Scott & Orlikowski, 2012).

The second platform feature that increases legitimacy is the employment of both algorithmic and human curation to identify dishonest or undesirable participants. These curators can ban or remove products such as counterfeits or those violating copyrights or posting offensive material on YouTube.[3] Such curation validates that the entrepreneurs in the ecosystem are legitimate and can be trusted. Without such curation, the platform would be likely to lose users and in extreme situations could collapse completely.

18.4.4 Low entry barriers

Costs of entry have long been understood as an entry barrier for entrepreneurs (Amit, Muller, & Cockburn, 1995). In the case of digital platforms, entry barriers are often very low. For example, new entrants can begin with part-time activities, and many YouTubers began in their bedroom or dorm room, some YouTubers have outsourced fulfillment to either Amazon or independent vendors (McGinnis 2019), and eBay sellers began by selling miscellaneous items from their home or garage. In all of these cases, for some, these amateur activities evolved into full-time professional businesses (Demetry, 2017; Kim, 2018).

The success of a digital platform is predicated upon attracting users and complementors. It does this by lowering entry barriers and reducing risk, and, when successful, these resources can foster ecosystems within which these entrepreneurs operate as the platforms' complementors (Eckhardt, Ciuchta, & Carpenter, 2018; Nambisan et al., 2018). The eased entrance into the ecosystem has the contradictory effect over time of creating a lock-in effect due to the asset-specific nature of the investment and the lack of portability of the cumulative investment by the complementor in terms of reputation, transaction history, and repeat customers. The next section explores the features of a platform that transforms entrepreneurial activity from an assertion of independence to a state of dependence.

18.5 Mechanisms for creating platform dependence

Entrepreneurs establishing their business on a platform operate in fundamentally different context from traditional entrepreneurs that establish firms in the physical world (Cutolo & Kenney, 2021). To attract entrepreneurs, the conditions for engagement must be attractive—so attractive that often the platform must initially subsidize complementors in an effort to tip the market and achieve lock-in. This is particularly the case when the entrepreneurs must make significant asset-specific investments, which become a sunk cost that integrates the entrepreneur into the platform's ecosystem. The greater the investment is (often it is cumulative), the greater is the dependence on the platform. Ceteris paribus, the more successful entrepreneurs are on a platform, the more dependent they are.

Platform owners act as private regulators who are expected to reduce negative externalities created by complementors in order to maximize the value for the system as a whole (Boudreau & Hagiu, 2009; Evans, 2012). The profit of the platform owner and the value of the ecosystem are directly linked, and insufficient control over opportunistic behaviors by "complementors" may degrade the ecosystem and even result in the platform's failure (Täuscher & Kietzmann, 2017). Platforms thus are strongly incentivized to perform their regulatory role, and they can rely on a large set of enforcement instruments, including exclusion (Strahilovetz, 2006).

All entrepreneurs face challenges; those that build a business on a platform face unique risks that emanate from the platform. In a recent study, Wen and Zhu (2018, p. 16) found that app developers responded to Google's threat of market entry and subsequent competition with their app by undertaking "no entry deterrence behavior, such as price reduction and additional innovation ... because of the platform owner's power, its entry is unlikely to be deterred". This response suggests that they understood that resistance was futile.

18.5.1 Platform as panopticon

The platform owner has an encompassing view of the activities of other ecosystem participants (Boudreau & Lakhani, 2009). It is important to note that the platform's perspective is not complete in that it can be gamed or spoofed in many ways. The term "asymmetric information access" underappreciates this power (Shapiro & Varian, 1998). In platform markets, the owner rations the specific information to the various sides—of course, the information provision is optimized to benefit the platform owner.

Platform power is illustrated by the case of Amazon, where a former Amazon employee stated that Amazon retained "the most valuable data for itself; provides less valuable data to marketplace sellers". The employee continued that the "most valuable info Amazon doesn't share is info about which people have searched for a particular product in the past". This allows Amazon to "target their private label products with perfect precision" (Capitol Forum, 2018).

Platform-based entrepreneurs only have the knowledge about its customer that the platform provides. The ability to observe all activities on the platform while providing only curated data to the complementors (and customers) ensures the platform owner maximum leverage.

18.5.2 Entry into the dependent entrepreneur's business

As the intermediary, the platform not only brokers relationships, it can also direct traffic. This centrality enables the platform to identify vendors or market segments that are particularly lucrative. This market "intelligence" facilitates the identification of opportunities and facilitates the introduction of a competitive product, the establishment of a "tax" to appropriate surpluses or even the acquisition of the complementor. For example, after recognizing the potential for the browser to be a new killer application, Microsoft destroyed the new entrant, Netscape, and its business model, by introducing Internet Explorer which was bundled into the operating system (Yoffie & Cusumano, 1998). In effect, Microsoft redesigned the Windows operating system platform to absorb functions developed by its ecosystem member, Netscape (Eisenmann, Parker, & Van Alstyne, 2011).

A platform owner may not always be successful in absorbing the functions of complementors. To illustrate, Intuit was the target of acquisition by Microsoft that the Department of Justice blocked on antitrust grounds. After the attempt failed, Intuit remained the market leader in consumer accounting software (Newman, 1997).

Compared to the PC era where platforms like Microsoft dominated the scene, online digital platforms have far greater visibility into their ecosystems. For example, Amazon can identify independent third-party vendors whose products sell well in its marketplace, examine the product, and decide whether the profit margins are attractive (Zhu & Liu, 2018). It can then enter the market with its 136 private label brands and 373 exclusive brands (TJI, 2019). This process was described by a former employee:

> Let's say Amazon wants to get into folders. I would find all of the ASINs [Amazon Standard Identification Number] that are being sold on the website now. I'd pull up the history. I'd look at the volumes, price points. Regardless of whether it was sold wholesale or third party, I'd pull it all together. I'd look and see what's the hottest product. What's the hottest variation in color? We'd have these folders in these colors at this price point, and we'd go off and make it ourselves.
>
> (Capitol Forum, 2018, p. 3)

Online platforms can survey activities on their platform, research the opportunity, and then decide whether it is economically viable to introduce a competitive product. Here, the innovator or firm providing the best product can have their profits competed away, and they have no recourse.

18.5.3 Input control

As the ecosystem curators, platform owners must manage their complementors—a necessity to prevent the platform ecosystem from becoming dysfunctional (Thies, Wessel, & Benlian, 2018; Jacobides et al., 2018). Input control ensures that complementors abide by the terms and conditions for participation (Tiwana 2015, 2014). Although this is not the typical principal-agent problem, it has similarities. Input control is a vexing issue for platform-based entrepreneurs because they must invest prior to the product (often digital) being accepted for sale/distribution. Because the platform may change acceptance criteria at any time and without warning, a platform-based business model is precarious. For example, recent decisions by Google, YouTube, and Facebook to demonetize, ban, or demote various websites are based upon policy changes in regarding what content is acceptable. Because platform-organized markets are largely winner-take-all, the platform-based entrepreneurs' products often cannot be easily shifted to another platform or channel.

18.5.4 Changing the terms of participation

For rational actors, the market entry decision is made on the basis of a cost-benefit analysis, based upon an understanding of market rules. In an offline business, the most salient terms are leases, supplier, customer, and competitor relationships and government regulation. To participate on a platform, users must agree to the terms and conditions for participation. Regardless of the service provided by the platform, the key clause in these contracts is that all other clauses can be changed unilaterally at the discretion of the platform owner. The terms have two components: first, "hard" components that are the core of the platform, i.e., the software or algorithms, the software development kits (SDKs) and APIs. These literally frame what can be done. Second, "soft" components, such as rules, principles of community, etc., that determine, for example, what can be sold or said on the platform. Both the hard and soft platform "rules" can be changed at will. To illustrate, the template determines, for example, the number of pictures that can be used on an eBay listing or the method of communicating between buyer and seller. In contrast, a "soft" change could be a decision to ban or demonetize a certain point of view. An illustration of this is YouTube's decision to demonetize various channels—our point is not whether the content should be sanctioned—the point is that it could be.

Product price and profit margins are existential decisions for any business. For platform-based entrepreneurs, core issues such as the share of revenue accruing to the platform and the complementor are invariably set solely at the platform owner's discretion. To illustrate, in fall 2018, eBay unilaterally announced an increase in its commission fees in books, DVDS, and movies categories to 12% while removing the fee discount that eBay Store owners enjoyed (Steiner, 2018), thereby unilaterally affecting profit margins. Even prices can be determined. For self-published books in the Kindle marketplace priced from $2.99 to $9.99, Amazon pays the author 70% of the retail download price, but only 35% for those priced above or below this range. In this respect, Amazon arbitrarily forced its complementors to accept its preferences.

The terms of participation are of critical importance as they speak directly to entrepreneurial independence. Entrepreneurs conducting business through their own website are not vulnerable to the abrupt changes in their business context that are the conditions for platform-based entrepreneurs. Put differently, terms of participation require platform-based entrepreneurs to surrender many of the attributes of being an entrepreneur.

18.5.5 Platform access

Although exclusions can be for undesirable behavior (Evans, 2012), they can just as easily be "distorted away from pure value creation in the ecosystem towards actions that lead to higher platform profit" (Boudreau & Hagiu, 2009, p. 8). The literature suggests that platform owners should be a neutral or, at least, a trusted party. However, this need not be the case. To illustrate, in return for Apple agreeing to sell on Amazon, the quid pro quo was that the unauthorized independent Apple resellers had their listings removed (Kelley, 2018). In this case, Amazon sacrificed the independents in return for the Apple account, thereby violating the assumption of neutrality. Effectively, mechanisms necessary to protect the ecosystem can be used to pursue other goals that advantage the platform. The power of exclusion poses a threat to platform-based entrepreneurs, and such decisions can occur without warning.

18.5.6 Customer relationships

The most fundamental relationship in capitalism is between a vendor and their customer. It is fundamental to learn what the customers' needs are. However, in platform-organized markets, the platform is the intermediary through which a transaction is consummated. It is vitally important for the platform to keep platform-based entrepreneurs estranged from its customer, if they were in direct contact, they would have little need for an intermediary. Platform-based entrepreneurs depend upon the platform to maintain the connection, and, if the entrepreneur loses platform access, then the customer access is also lost. To illustrate, YouTubers actively cultivate their community by interacting with their fans to build their followers. When YouTube blocks creators, they immediately lose access to their fan base and have no way of contacting them to move them to a new platform.

The separation of providers from customers is normal for most platforms. For example, in 2019, Apple launched Apple News+, a magazine and newspaper subscription service on which publishers could provide their content to Apple, which would then aggregate and provide it to Apple users for a $10 per month fee, of which Apple would retain 50%. As with many other platform services, this one separates the producer from their customers (Sloane, 2019). Once established, this separation would be difficult to reverse. Separation from one's customers gives "ownership" of customers to the platform.

After which the platform can unilaterally set the conditions for customer engagement.

18.5.7 Ranking systems as a control mechanism

Ranking systems are essential features of many platforms because they function as mechanisms to foster trust, identify better vendors, and direct aiding discovery and reducing transaction uncertainty (Jøsang et al., 2007; Tadelis, 2016). Not surprisingly, ceteris paribus, users are more likely to select a higher-ranked item—whether in search results or a ranking system (Ghose et al., 2014). Further, they directly influence customer preferences, as Luca (2011) found that a one-star increase in a Yelp rating led to a 5–9 percent increase in a restaurant's revenue and visibility. Effectively, the ranking systems are meant to and do shape behavior (Scott & Orlikowski, 2012). For platform-based entrepreneurs, the ranking systems are both vital for discovery and success, and perilous as they can change suddenly and are nearly impossible to contest (Taylor, 2019).[4]

The algorithms and the data used to generate the rankings are invariably hidden. For the platform owner, there is little incentive to provide any transparency. The standard reason is that revealing the algorithms could open them to manipulation and opportunistic behavior. As a result, platform-based entrepreneurs can only speculate on what behavior will satisfy the algorithm. Psychologically, the platform-based entrepreneurship is embedded in a system, not only of risk, but more seriously, profound uncertainty. Moreover, algorithmically generated results are often accepted as objective and not the result of human programming. The status of the results as objective deflects the questions regarding the potential for bias or self-serving in the rankings. This can conceal the platform's agenda, as the algorithms can be engineered to provide results that are beneficial to the firm's goals while appearing to be objective.

As a result, the ranking system and the changes in it can appear to be capricious (Scott & Orlikowski, 2012). To illustrate, the scores that determine rankings are often driven in part by monetary considerations provided to the ranker by the organization being ranked. These nonorganic ranking systems include, for example, a weight for whether the ranked organization advertises with the platform can generate extra income beyond the normal sales fees that a platform might charge.[5]

Ranking systems and the reviews so critical to their effectiveness are critical for the operation of platforms, since they provide a low-cost, trust creation, monitoring, and conformity-enforcing mechanism. The knowledge that advertising on the platform can impact the ranking and thus product placement on the website places great pressure on platform-based entrepreneurs to invest in advertising regardless of whether it provides actual benefits. Moreover, if advertising on the platform affects ranking and thus sales, then platform-based entrepreneurs that are competitors will bid until their profits are driven to their lowest acceptable profit margins.

18.5.8 *Delisting*

Platforms are private marketplaces and thus access and delisting are solely at the discretion of the owner. And, as such, participation can be terminated for any activities deemed to violate the current terms and conditions that can be altered unilaterally without prior notice. For platform-based entrepreneurs, the decision has immediate financial repercussions. Delisting can be triggered by user complaints or by the algorithms that monitor the platform. The platform need not provide any information so the victim can understand the reasons for suspension or its reversal. While most platforms have appeal mechanisms, these may take time—despite the fact that platform-based entrepreneurs may no longer receive any income. Appeal is complicated by the cryptic information regarding the reasons for suspension compounded by the unclear criteria for adjudicating the appeal. Moreover, even in the case of successful appeals, platform-based entrepreneurs do not return to the status quo ante, as competitors will have displaced them in the rankings. In fact, the infractions reported to the platform may actually be the product of unethical competitor behavior (Luca & Zervas, 2016; Woollacott, 2017). Recognizing this possibility, Amazon charges its vendors a retainer fee of between $1,600 and $5,000 per month for the ability to call an Amazon employee to understand and appeal Amazon's unilateral actions (Del Rey, 2020). Effectively, the possibility of delisting means that platform-based entrepreneurs' entire business is at risk of destruction at any moment and they are charged for the ability to speak to someone to rectify the situation.

18.5.9 *Concluding thoughts*

For entrepreneurs, platforms have a contradictory character. First and particularly initially, platforms offer platform-based entrepreneurs many resources. In return, platforms benefit from their innovations and entrepreneurial effort, which attract users, and often the platforms share in the income produced. As these platforms and ecosystems grow and mature, the importance of the individual complementor decreases. Platform owners are running a business, so they seek to increase revenues and profits. A platform "ecosystem" complementors experience the commensality in ways that are more akin to the serfs being part of an ecosystem operated by the feudal lord—in contrast, to a natural ecosystem.

18.6 Discussion and conclusion

Research on entrepreneurial dynamics in platform ecosystems has concentrated on the ease of entry, market access, and other such technical conditions. The power of platforms as central intermediaries and their ability to "tax" various sides appear to be true not only in the West but also in quite different political economies such as China, though there may be quite different institutional configurations, such as the Chinese predilection to platform business groups (Jia & Kenney, 2020). Remarkably, only recently has the unequal power relationship between the platform owner and the ecosystem complementors been considered by academic scholars. Normally, when the relationship between owners and complementors is discussed, it is in terms of commensalism or mutual benefit. Clearly, the platform owner as the provider of tools and ecosystem curator is necessary and deserves compensation. But the power asymmetries are so stark that complementors are best understood as dependent entrepreneurs whose very existence depends upon the platform.

Consider again entrepreneurs in the pre-internet platform era. Certainly, Microsoft could destroy ecosystem complementors, as Netscape discovered to its peril. However, for a variety of reasons, including enforcement of US antitrust laws, Microsoft was limited in its use of platform dominance in the PC industry to enter the business of its various complementor firms. There can be little doubt that governments can enforce existing laws on antitrust and create new laws and even regulatory agencies to redress the balance between the platforms and the increasingly large swathes of society affected by them (Cioffi et al., 2022). Today, an ever-greater variety of economic activities are being organized by platforms. In retailing, the production of music, news commentary, or software, the provision of rides or accommodations, and all sorts of other products and services, both entrepreneurs and existing businesses are being integrated into platform ecosystems. Platforms provide the entrepreneurs with various boundary resources to ease their market entry, access to customers, and legitimacy. In return, entrepreneurs' businesses are vulnerable in ways that they were not in the offline world. Entrepreneurs whose business is dependent upon a platform face a level of precarity now that is far greater than during the preplatform era. Platform-based businesses are entirely exposed to the platform owner's panoptic gaze.

Entrepreneurship and building a business have always been fraught with risk. However, the willingness to bear this risk has been coupled with the belief that success is based on one's own efforts—a world in which most capable entrepreneurs can build a sustainable business (Sarasvathy, 2008). Dependence upon a platform challenges such assumptions, as this risk extends to the basic tools for doing business, as platform owners can control access to customers, prices, profit margins, and thereby survival of the business.

Awareness of the encompassing power of these platforms is growing, as is the precarity of entrepreneurs who depend upon these systems. To illustrate, a business that is not discoverable through a Google search can effectively be said to not exist. This demonstrates that current discussions of regulating platforms still have not grasped the dynamics of the new business environment, in which platforms have acquired godlike powers to banish errant complementors from the garden, can see all activities within their realm, separate parties to a transaction, and unilaterally change the conditions for any and all users—either in very granular fashion or comprehensively.

Governments have gradually gained awareness that these platforms are using their godlike powers in their own interests and against the business dependent upon them (see, for example, Cioffi et al., 2022). In response to the growing number of grievances against unfair treatment, policy makers have been increasingly concerned with the appropriateness of current policy frameworks to promote a sustainable and healthy environment for platforms' entrepreneurs. For example, the Indian government recently required Amazon and the Walmart-owned Flipkart to choose between being online retailers and sales platforms because they could not both have their own inventory and be online marketplaces. And the European Commission is fast-tracking the Digital Markets and Digital Services Acts. Finally, the Chinese government has moved remarkably rapidly to regulate its platform firms (McKnight et al., 2021).

Conceptualizing entrepreneurs in a platform economy as a dependent is particularly useful when we consider that an increasing number of scholars have proposed that entrepreneurship is an effective response to the evolution of work to be more contingent, fluid, and uncertain (Barley et al., 2017; Brynjolfsson & McAfee, 2014). What we have shown is that the platform's provision of resources to entrepreneurs is a poisoned chalice because it also locks in the entrepreneur. Therefore, what is the meaning of entrepreneurship in a platform ecosystem? Under these circumstances, how can platform-based entrepreneurs enact the "emancipatory potential of entrepreneurship" (Rindova et al., 2009)? To what extent do entrepreneurs understand this dependency when developing their business on a platform and how does this awareness influence their actions? Finally, what are entrepreneurs' degrees of freedom in developing their business when the platform can identify those creating Schumpeterian rents and act to appropriate them?

Notes

1 Joseph Schumpeter theorized that new technologies or other market changes could open new economics spaces to be occupied by entrepreneurs who construct new business models capable of exploiting the opportunities.
2 In China, which suffers from even greater distrust of strangers, Alibaba implemented an escrow system in which the buyer would place the money in escrow with Alibaba and only release it when the transaction was satisfactorily completed (Yu and Shen, 2015).
3 We are not arguing that these systems are flawless, only that they exist and provide some reassurance regarding the bona fides of the product.
4 Many of the ranking systems are based on anonymous customer reviews. One problem is that the reviewers are not vetted and competitors can give their rivals bad reviews and rankings as a competitive strategy.
5 For a description of this in the case of Expedia, see Maher (2016).

References

Aldrich, H.E. and Ruef, M. (2018). Unicorns, gazelles, and other distractions on the way to understanding real entrepreneurship in the United States. *Academy of Management Perspectives, 32*(4), 458–472.

Amit, R., Muller, E. and Cockburn, I. (1995). Opportunity costs and entrepreneurial activity. *Journal of Business Venturing, 10*(2), 95–106.

Apple, Inc. (2019). Addressing Spotify's claims. Retrieved from https://www.apple.com/newsroom/2019/03/addressing-spotifys-claims/

Autio, E., Kenney, M., Mustar, P., Siegel, D. and Wright, M. (2014). Entrepreneurial innovation: The importance of context. *Research Policy, 43*(7), 1097–1108.

Autio, E., Nambisan, S., Thomas, L.D. and Wright, M. (2018). Digital affordances, spatial affordances, and the genesis of entrepreneurial ecosystems. *Strategic Entrepreneurship Journal, 12*(1), 72–95.

Baldwin, C.Y. and Woodard, C.J. (2009). The architecture of platforms: A unified view. In Gawer, A. (Ed.), *Platforms, Markets and Innovation* (pp. 19–44). Cheltenham: Edward Elgar.

Barley, S.R., Bechky, B.A. and Milliken, F.J. (2017). The changing nature of work: Careers, identities, and work lives in the 21st century. *Academy of Management Discoveries, 3*(2), 111–115.

Berg, J. and Johnston, H. (2019). Too good to be true? A comment on Hall and Krueger's analysis of the labor market for Uber's driver-partners. *ILR Review, 72*(1), 39–68.

Boudreau, K. (2010). Open platform strategies and innovation: Granting access vs. devolving control. *Management Science, 56*(10), 1849–1872.

Boudreau, K.J. (2012). Let a thousand flowers bloom? An early look at large numbers of software app developers and patterns of innovation. *Organization Science, 23*(5), 1409–1427.

Boudreau, K.J. and Hagiu, A. (2009). Platform rules: Multi-sided platforms as regulators. In Gawer, A. (Ed.), *Platforms, Markets and Innovation* (pp. 163–191). Cheltenham: Edward Elgar.

Boudreau, K.J. and Jeppesen, L.B. (2015). Unpaid crowd complementors: The platform network effect mirage. *Strategic Management Journal, 36*(12), 1761–1777.

Boudreau, K. and Lakhani, K. (2009). How to manage outside innovation. *MIT Sloan Management Review, 50*(4), 69–76.

Brynjolfsson, E. and McAfee, A. (2014). *The Second Machine Age: Work, Progress, and Prosperity in a Time of Brilliant Technologies.* New York, NY: W.W. Norton.

Bucher, T. (2012). Want to be on the top? Algorithmic power and the threat of invisibility on Facebook. *New Media & Society, 14*(7), 1164–1180.

Capitol Forum. (2018). Amazon: EC investigation to focus on whether Amazon uses data to develop and favor private label products. *Capitol Forum, 6*(393), 1–4. https://thecapitolforum.com/wpcontent/uploads/2018/11/Amazon-2018.11.05.pdf

Cioffi, J., Kenney, M. and Zysman, J. (2022). Platform power and regulatory politics: Polanyi for the 21st Century. *New Political Economy, 27*(5), 1–17.

Cramer, J. and Krueger, A.B. (2016). Disruptive change in the taxi business: The case of Uber. *American Economic Review, 106*(5), 177–82.

Cutolo, D. and Kenney, M. (2021). Platform-dependent entrepreneurs: Power asymmetries, risks, and strategies in the platform economy. *Academy of Management Perspectives, 35*(4), 584–605.

Cutolo, D. and Vang, J. (2021). Digital platforms. In L.-P. Dana (Ed.), *World Encyclopedia of Entrepreneurship* (pp. 93–104). Cheltenham, England: Edward Elgar Publishing.

Cutolo, D., Hargadon, A.B. and Kenney, M. (2021). Competing on platforms: Recognizing and navigating the risks. *MIT Sloan Management Review, 62*(3), 22–30.

Davidsson, P. (2015). Entrepreneurial opportunities and the entrepreneurship nexus: A reconceptualization. *Journal of Business Venturing, 30*(5), 674–695.

Del Rey, J. (2020). Amazon has created fertile ground for bribery schemes, sellers say. *Recode* (October 26) https://www.vox.com/recode/2020/10/26/21534740/amazon-seller-support-suspensions-bribery-indictment

Demetry, D. (2017). Pop-up to professional: Emerging entrepreneurial identity and evolving vocabularies of motive. *Academy of Management Discoveries, 3*(2), 187–207.

Eckhardt, J.T., Ciuchta, M.P. and Carpenter, M. (2018). Open innovation, information, and entrepreneurship within platform ecosystems. *Strategic Entrepreneurship Journal, 12*(3), 369–391.

Eisenmann, T., Parker, G. and Van Alstyne, M. (2011). Platform envelopment. *Strategic Management Journal, 32*(12), 1270–1285.

Etsy. (2022). Retrieved from https://Etsy.com

Evans, D.S. (2012). Governing bad behavior by users of multi-sided platforms. *Berkeley Technology Law Journal, 27,* 1201–1250.

Evans, D.S., Hagiu, A. and Schmalensee, R. (2006). *Invisible Engines: How Software Platforms Drive Innovation and Transform Industries.* Cambridge, MA: MIT Press.

Forman, C., Ghose, A. and Wiesenfeld, B. (2008). Examining the relationship between reviews and sales: The role of reviewer identity disclosure in electronic markets. *Information Systems Research, 19*(3), 291–313.

Galloway, R. (2018, April 30). Nike X Amazon: To partner, or not to partner. *Digital Innovation and Transformation.* Retrieved from https://digit.hbs.org/submission/nike-x-amazon-to-partner-or-not-to-partner/

Gawer, A. (2014). Bridging differing perspectives on technological platforms: Toward an integrative framework. *Research Policy, 43*(7), 1239–1249.

Gawer, A. and Cusumano, M.A. (2002). *Platform Leadership: How Intel, Microsoft, and Cisco Drive Industry Innovation.* Boston, MA: Harvard Business School Press.

Gawer, A. and Cusumano, M.A. (2014). Industry platforms and ecosystem innovation: Platforms and innovation. *Journal of Product Innovation Management, 31*(3), 417–433.

Gawer, A. and Henderson, R. (2007). Platform owner entry and innovation in complementary markets: Evidence from Intel. *Journal of Economics & Management Strategy, 16*(1), 1–34.

Ghazawneh, A. and Henfridsson, O. (2013). Balancing platform control and external contribution in third-party development: The boundary resources model. *Information Systems Journal*, *23*(2), 173–192.

Ghose, A., Ipeirotis, P.G. and Li, B. (2014). Examining the impact of ranking on consumer behavior and search engine revenue. *Management Science*, *60*(7), 1632–1654.

Grabner-Kraeuter, S. (2002). The role of consumers' trust in online-shopping. *Journal of Business Ethics*, *39*(1–2), 43–50.

Haefliger, S., Jäger, P. and Von Krogh, G. (2010). Under the radar: Industry entry by user entrepreneurs. *Research Policy*, *39*(9), 1198–1213.

Jacobides, M.G., Cennamo, C. and Gawer, A. (2018). Towards a theory of ecosystems. *Strategic Management Journal*, *39*(8), 2255–2276.

Jeppesen, L.B. and Frederiksen, L. (2006). Why do users contribute to firm-hosted user communities? The case of computer-controlled music instruments. *Organization Science*, *17*(1), 45–63.

Jia, K. and Kenney, M. (2020). The Chinese platform business group: An alternative to the Silicon Valley model? *Journal of Chinese Governance*, *7*(21), 1–23.

Jøsang, A., Ismail, R. and Boyd, C. (2007). A survey of trust and reputation systems for online service provision. *Decision Support Systems*, *43*(2), 618–644.

Kapoor, R. and Agarwal, S. (2017). Sustaining superior performance in business ecosystems: Evidence from application software developers in the iOS and Android smartphone ecosystems. *Organization Science*, *28*(3), 531–551.

Kaziukenas, J. (2021, November 9). Amazon Is the Default Search Engine. Marketplace Pulse. Retrieved from https://www.marketplacepulse.com/articles/amazon-is-the-default-search-engine

Keinan, A., Maslauskaite, K., Crener, S. and Dessain, V. (2015). The blond salad. Harvard Business School Case 515-074. Retrieved from https://hbr.org/product/The-Blonde-Salad/an/515074-PDF-ENG/

Kenney, M. and Zysman, J. (2016). The rise of the platform economy. *Issues in Science and Technology*, *32*(3), 61–69.

Kenney, M. and Zysman, J. (2019). Work and value creation in the platform economy. In Kovalainen, A. and Vallas, S. (Eds.), *Research in the Sociology of Work*. Bingley, United Kingdom: Emerald Insight.

Kenney, M., Bearson, D. and Zysman, J. (2021). The Platform Economy matures: Exploring and measuring pervasiveness and power. *Socio-Economic Review* (forthcoming).

Khan, L.M. (2016). Amazon's antitrust paradox. *Yale Law Journal*, *126*, 710–805.

Kim, H. (2018). Knitting community: Human and social capital in the transition to entrepreneurship. Working paper. Graduate School of Business, Stanford University (accessed April 27, 2019) https://www.gsb.stanford.edu/sites/gsb/files/jmp_hyejun-kim.pdf

Luca, M. (2011). Reviews, reputation, and revenue: The case of Yelp.com. Working Paper 12–016, Harvard Business School, Boston.

Luca, M. and Zervas, G. (2016). Fake it till you make it: Reputation, competition, and Yelp review fraud. *Management Science*, *62*(12), 3412–3427.

Maher, M. (Senior vice president, Global Partner Group, Expedia, Inc.). (2016). Understanding the science behind Expedia's Marketplace. https://discover.expediapartnercentral.com/2016/12/27/understanding-the-science-behind-expediasmarketplace/+&cd=1&hl=en&ct=clnk&gl=us

McKnight, S., Kenney, M. and Breznitz, D. (2021). Platformizing the Economy? Building and Regulating Chinese Digital Platforms (July 21). https://papers.ssrn.com/sol3/papers.cfm?abstract_id=3885190

Nambisan, S. (2017). Digital entrepreneurship: Toward a digital technology perspective of entrepreneurship. *Entrepreneurship Theory and Practice*, *41*(6), 1029–1055.

Nambisan, S. and Baron, R.A. (2013). Entrepreneurship in innovation ecosystems: Entrepreneurs' self–regulatory processes and their implications for new venture success. *Entrepreneurship Theory and Practice*, *37*(5), 1071–1097.

Nambisan, S., Siegel, D. and Kenney, M. (2018). On open innovation, platforms, and entrepreneurship. *Strategic Entrepreneurship Journal*, *12*(3), 354–368.

Newman, N. (1997). From Microsoft Word to Microsoft World: How Microsoft is building a global monopoly. A NetAction White Paper, http://www.netaction.org/msoft/world/MSWord2World.html

Parker, G., Van Alstyne, M. and Choudary, S.P. (2016). *Platform Revolution: How Networked Markets Are Transforming the Economy and How to Make Them Work for You*. New York, NY: W.W. Norton.

Popiel, P. (2017). "Boundaryless" in the creative economy: Assessing freelancing on Upwork. *Critical Studies in Media Communication, 34*(3), 220–233.

Rindova, V., Barry, D. and Ketchen, D. (2009). Entrepreneuring as emancipation. *Academy of Management Review, 34*(3), 477–491.

Sarasvathy, S.D. (2008). *New Horizons in Entrepreneurship. Effectuation: Elements of Entrepreneurial Expertise.* Northampton, MA: Edward Elgar.

Scott, S.V. and Orlikowski, W.J. (2012). Reconfiguring relations of accountability: Materialization of social media in the travel sector. *Accounting, Organizations and Society, 37*(1), 26–40.

Shapiro, C. and Varian, H.R. (1998). *Information Rules: A Strategic Guide to the Network Economy.* Boston, MA: Harvard Business Press.

Sloane, G. (2019, February 12). Publishers weigh in on Apple's terms in new subscription service. *AdAge*. Retrieved from https://adage.com/article/digital/greedy-apple-half-publishing-subscriptionsales/316619/

Sorenson, O., Assenova, V., Li, G.C., Boada, J. and Fleming, L. (2016). Expand innovation finance via crowdfunding. *Science, 354*(6319), 1526–1528.

Steiner, I. (2018, August 7). Fall update: eBay raises fees as it makes more demands on sellers. Ecommerce Bytes Blog. Retrieved from https://www.ecommercebytes.com/C/blog/blog.pl?/pl/2018/8/1533654011.html

Stinchcombe, A. (1965). Social structure and organizations. In March, J.G. (Ed.), *Handbook of Organizations* (pp. 142–193). Chicago, IL: Rand-McNally.

Strahilovetz, L. (2006). Information asymmetries and the rights to exclude. *Michigan Law Review, 104*(8), 1834–1898.

Sussan, F. and Acs, Z.J. (2017). The digital entrepreneurial ecosystem. *Small Business Economics, 49*(1), 55–73.

Tadelis, S. (2016). Reputation and feedback systems in online platform markets. *Annual Review of Economics, 8*(1), 321–340.

Täuscher, K. and Kietzmann, J. (2017). Learning from failures in the sharing economy. *MIS Quarterly Executive, 16*(4), 253–264.

Tavalaei, M.M. and Cennamo, C. (2018). In search of status: Exploring niche players' strategies in entrepreneurial ecosystems. *Academy of Management Proceedings, 2018* (1), 10822.

Taylor, J. (2019). 'Google's power is extraordinary': businesses turn to the courts over bad reviews. Guardian (June 9) https://www.theguardian.com/technology/2019/jul/10/googles-power-isextraordinary-businesses-turn-to-the-courts-over-bad-reviews

Thies, F., Wessel, M. and Benlian, A. (2018). Network effects on crowdfunding platforms: Exploring the implications of relaxing input control. *Information Systems Journal, 28*(6), 1239–1262.

Tiwana, A. (2014). *Platform Ecosystems: Aligning Architecture, Governance, and Strategy.* Waltham, MA: Morgan Kaufmann.

Tiwana, A. (2015). Evolutionary competition in platform ecosystems. *Information Systems Research, 26*(2), 266–281.

Tiwana, A., Konsynski, B. and Bush, A.A. (2010). Platform evolution: Coevolution of platform architecture, governance, and environmental dynamics. *Information Systems Research, 21*(4), 675–687.

TJI. (2019, February 12). TJI Amazon brand database. Retrieved from https://this.just.in/amazon-branddatabase/

von Briel, F., Davidsson, P. and Recker, J. (2018). Digital technologies as external enablers of new venture creation in the IT hardware sector. *Entrepreneurship Theory and Practice, 42*(1), 47–69.

Wareham, J., Fox, P.B. and Giner, J.L. (2014). Technology ecosystem governance. *Organization Science, 25*(4), 1195–1215.

Wen, W. and Zhu, F. (2018). Threat of platform-owner entry and complementor responses: Evidence from the mobile app market. NET Institute Working Paper No. 16-10. Retrieved from https://ssrn.com/abstract=2848533/

Woollacott, E. (2017, September 9). Amazon's fake review problem is now worse than ever, study suggests. *Forbes*. Retrieved from https://www.forbes.com

Yoffie, D.B. and Cusumano, M.A. (1998). *Competing on Internet Time: Lessons from Netscape and Its Battle with Microsoft.* New York, NY: Simon & Schuster.

Yu, Y. and Shen, M. (2015). Consumer protection as the 'open sesame' that allows Alibaba to crush the forty thieves. *Journal of Antitrust Enforcement, 3*(suppl_1), i228–i241.

Zhu, F. and Liu, Q. (2018). Competing with complementors: An empirical look at Amazon.com. *Strategic Management Journal, 39*(10), 2618–2642.

Zhu, F. and Sun, S. (2018). JD: Envisioning the future of retail. Harvard Business School Case 618–051, May.

Zittrain, J. (2008). *The Future of the Internet and How to Stop It*. New Haven, CT: Yale University Press.

Zuboff, S. (2019). *The Age of Surveillance Capitalism*. New York, NY: Blackstone.

19

IS IT POSSIBLE TO IMPROVE SIMULTANEOUSLY FIRM PERFORMANCE AND WORKPLACE WELL-BEING?[1]

Small and Medium-Sized Enterprises in European Comparison

Csaba Makó

INSTITUTE OF INFORMATION SOCIETY, UNIVERSITY OF PUBLIC SERVICE, BUDAPEST, HUNGARY

Miklós Illéssy

INSTITUTE OF SOCIOLOGY, CENTRE FOR SOCIAL SCIENCES, HUNGARY

Saeed Nosratabadi

CENTRE FOR SOCIAL SCIENCES, BUDAPEST, HUNGARY

19.1 Introduction

The dilemma of workplace well-being and firm performance in organizations has been an issue that organizations have always tried to balance (Cotton & Hart, 2003; Dall'Ora et al., 2016; Lamb & Kwok, 2016). Different schools of thought govern the management of organizations, and these schools offer different solutions to cope with this challenge. European countries are generally divided into seven categories in terms of institutional settings: Nordic countries (including Denmark, Finland, and Sweden), Continental countries (including Austria, Belgium, France, Netherland, Luxembourg, and Germany), Mediterranean countries (Greece, Italy, Portugal, and Spain), Anglo-Saxon countries (including Ireland and United Kingdom), and post-socialist countries,[2] or in other words, post-socialist counties, which they are divided into three categories: North Eastern Europe (including Estonia, Latvia, and Lithuania), Central Eastern Europe (including Czech Republic, Poland, Hungary, Slovakia, Slovenia, Croatia), and South Eastern Europe

DOI: 10.4324/9781003144366-23

(including Bulgaria and Romania). The context of the company managerial system of each of these countries has unique characteristics composed – among others – by the patterns of industrial relations system (IRS), vocational training and education system, welfare and governance systems (Hall & Sockice, 2001; Sapir, 2006; Eurofound, 2013; Gallie, 2018; Makó & Illéssy, 2020; Makó et al., 2021).

On the other hand, there is no evidence-based and generally accepted consensus among the labor process experts on what types of working practices/strategies ensure both high performance in the firms and high quality of workplace well-being. Therefore, the current study intends to overcome this knowledge deficiency by investigating how different managerial systems deal the dilemma of workplace well-being and firm performance. This study, inspired by European Company Survey (ECS) 2019 conceptual framework, first analyzes how external environment factors such as innovation, digitalization, and product market strategy affect intra-organization characteristics such as (Eurofound and Cedefop, 2020):

1. Work organization: autonomy and complexity in work (task structure)
2. Skills use practice (skills requirements/skills match and skills formation)
3. Employee voice (development of the direct and indirect representative participation)

In addition, the main purpose of this study is to examine which of these organizational characteristics affect the performance of companies and workplace well-being and whether it is possible that both variables, namely company performance and workplace well-being, improve at the same time? In other words, the output of the quantitative analysis of this study will show in which institutional setting (or which socio-economic system) in Europe this balance between workplace well-being and firm performance has been established and what factors have the greatest impact.

Figure 19.1 represents the conceptual framework which is analyzed in this study.

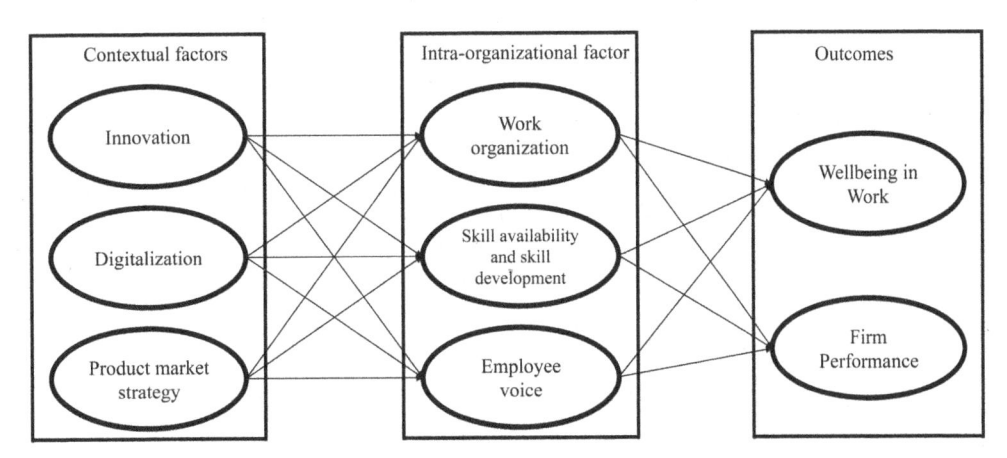

Figure 19.1 The study's model for examining the factors affecting firm performance and workplace well-being.

Source: Authors' own construction based on European Company Survey 2019 conceptual framework (Eurofound and Cedefop, 2020:7).

Figure 19.1 represents the conceptual model that is tested in this study. This model is inspired by the proposed ECS 2019 conceptual framework. Since the main purpose of this study is to study in which European country groups organizations have been able to be both profitable (i.e., have increased firm performance) and that have been able to improve workplace well-being at the same time. In the proposed ECS 2019 conceptual model, workplace well-being and firm performance are considered two outputs resulting from interactions between intra-organizational and environmental factors. In this model work organization, skill availability and skill development, and employee voices are intra-organization variables that their impact on organizational performance as well as workplace well-being are examined. On the other hand, the impact of external environment factors such as innovation, digitalization, and product market strategy on all the intra-organizational factors is also examined. For a deconstruction of these factors into variables and survey questions, please refer to Annex 19.1.

19.2 Methodology and data collection

In order to analyze the performance of existing systems of thought in Europe in the field of organizational management, European countries are first divided into seven groups based on the similarity of the socio-economic system, which are: (1) Nordic countries, (2) Continental countries, (3) Mediterranean countries, (4) Anglo-Saxon countries, (5) North Eastern European countries, (6) Central Eastern European countries, and (7) South Eastern European countries.

The statistical analysis carried out in a sample of 21,869 human resource (HR) managers in the EU-27 countries and in the United Kingdom, using ECS 2019 dataset. Beside HR managers, the survey originally covered employees' representatives in the firms where interest represent bodies were present and were eager to fill the questionnaire. Due to the extremely low response rate in some countries, the data collected from 3,073 employee representatives was dropped from the data-set analysis. This may result in an asymmetric, management-oriented outcome of our analysis.

Simultaneous study of the perspective of employees (or their representatives) and the perspective of managers would provide a more realistic view of the phenomena under study. Because such an approach would reduce discrimination and prejudice in assessing the conditions of each of the model variables. Employee perspectives could provide important contributions to evaluating variables such as employee voice, skills use practice, and even the degree of digitalization penetration and innovation of organizations.

In addition, the ECS dealt with exclusively small, medium, and large companies: 83% of companies participating in the ECS 2019 belong into the category of the small firms, 15% are medium-sized firms, and only 2% belong into the large firm sector. This is not by chance as the overwhelming majority of the European firms is composed by micro firms (93.3%); however, the rest is divided by following the above proportion, that is, 5.7% of all firms are small companies, 0.9% is medium sized firms, and only a tiny minority (0.2%) represents the large enterprises (Muller et al., 2021:9).

The data in this database is presented by countries, so to analyze the data based on schools of thought, European countries were divided into seven clusters, and data related to all organizations studied in all countries of a cluster was considered the representative of that cluster. For example, the first cluster, called Nordic countries, includes Denmark, Finland, and Sweden, data from all participating organizations of the three countries considered one cluster.

In the same way, all these seven groups of countries were analyzed. In order to quantitatively analyze the data, structural equation modeling (SEM) methods were used using SmartPLS 3.0. Because in SEM, the ability to analyze, at the same time, direct and indirect and systematic relationships between variables is possible (Ringle et al., 2015). SEM makes it possible to study the causal relationships between the variables of a model simultaneously. In SEM, the relationships between the main variables of the model are called structural models, and two main criteria are used to evaluate the structural model. The first criterion is that the path coefficients between the two variables whose causal relationships have been tested are significant. If the P-value corresponds to a path coefficient is less than 0.05, that path coefficient is significant at least at the 95% confidence interval. The second criterion is the coefficient of determination (R^2), which indicates how much of the change in the dependent variable is determined by the independent variables/s (Ringle et al., 2015). It should be noted that to analyze the ECS 2019 dataset using structural equations, the data must first be cured. This curation took place in two stages of aligning the unit of measurement and adapting the data for SmartPLS 3.0. In comparison to the statistical tool of the latent cluster analysis used in the ECS 2019 data-set analysis by the Eurofound and Cedefop, our data analysis examined the causal relationships between model variables in different country clusters in Europe. In other words, in the latent class analysis in the Eurofound report (2019), all the companies studied were classified based on their performance on a variable (e.g., digitalization). However, in this study, the effect of variables on each other was analyzed. In this approach, first the effect of external environment factors on the organizational characteristics was investigated and then the effect of organizational characteristics on outputs, which are firm performance and workplace well-being, was statistically tested using SEM.

19.3 Results and discussion

The data analysis output is summarized in Tables 19.1 and 19.2. In Table 19.1, each of the relationships can be compared in four country clusters: Nordic Countries, Continental Countries, Mediterranean Countries, and Anglo-Saxon Countries. The results imply the existence of a negative and significant relationship between digitalization and employee voice and digitalization and 'skills availability and skills development' in all four areas (although the relationship between digitalization and employee voice in Mediterranean countries is not significant). This means that digitalization has a negative impact on employee voice, and the more digitalization is implemented in organizations, the less chance employees have of expressing their needs. The negative impact of digitalization on 'skills availability and skills development' means that in organizations where jobs are more digitized, jobs require new skills that do not match the current skills of employees, and on the other hand, the current programs of these organizations are not enough to improve skills.

On the other hand, the results of the test of the impact of digitalization on the work organization show that the loading factor of the relationship between these two variables is positive and at a level of confidence of at least 95% is significant for all four country clusters. This means that the available evidence shows that digitalization facilitates outsourcing and has increased employee empowerment, but by examining the impact of the work organization on firm performance, it can be seen that this variable has a negative and significant effect on firm performance. In other words, digitalization not only has an inverse relationship with employee voice and 'skills availability and skills development', but it also has an inverse and indirect impact (i.e., through the work organization) on firm performance.

Table 19.1 Statistical analysis of the relationships between variables for companies in EU–15 countries: Nordic countries, Continental countries, Mediterranean countries, Anglo-Saxon countries

	Path coefficient			
Propositions	Nordic countries	Continental countries	Mediterranean countries	Anglo-Saxon countries
Digitalization -> Employee voice	−0.175***	−0.169***	−0.233	−0.201**
Digitalization -> Skills availability and skills development	−0.139***	−0.126***	−0.063**	−0.15***
Digitalization -> Work organization	0.173***	0.137***	0.088***	0.082*
Innovation -> Employee voice	−0.068**	−0.11***	−0.052	−0.107*
Innovation -> Skills availability and skills development	−0.027	−0.044**	−0.041	−0.031
Innovation -> Work organization	0.255***	0.232***	0.259***	0.312***
Product market strategy -> Employee voice	0.098**	0.129***	0.114	0.19*
Product market strategy -> Skills availability and skills development	0.116***	0.126***	0.13***	0.069
Product market strategy -> Work organization	−0.043	−0.05**	−0.075*	−0.044
Work organization -> Workplace well-being	0.028	−0.031	−0.029	0.027
Work organization -> Firm performance	−0.095***	−0.113***	−0.103***	−0.161***
Skills availability and skills development -> Workplace well-being	−0.043	0.043	0.008	−0.034
Skills availability and skills development -> Firm performance	0.087***	0.076***	0.108***	0.065
Employee voice -> Workplace well-being	−0.123	0.156	0.176	0.174*
Employee voice -> Firm performance	0.017	0.079***	0.018	0.075*

* All the loading factors are significant at the 95% confidence level.
** All the loading factors are significant at the 99% confidence level.
*** All the loading factors are significant at the 99.9% confidence level.

The results show that the work organization variable has a negative and significant effect on the performance of companies in all clusters of countries because the loading factor of this relationship is negative and at a confidence level of 99.9% is significant. This means that outsourcing and increasing employee authority reduces the performance of companies. The empirical findings also disclose that there is no evidence to confirm the impact of 'skills availability and skills development' on firm performance and even on workplace well-being in any of the clusters of countries.

Table 19.2 Statistical analysis of the relationships between variables for companies in the post-socialist countries: North Eastern European, Central Eastern European and South Eastern European countries

Propositions	Path coefficient		
	North Eastern European countries	Central Eastern European countries	South Eastern European countries
Digitalization -> Employee voice	−0.228***	0.162	−0.167*
Digitalization -> Skills availability and skills development	−0.152***	−0.052	−0.05
Digitalization -> Work organization	0.085*	0.106***	0.077*
Innovation -> Employee voice	−0.058	0.038	−0.093***
Innovation -> Skills availability and skills development	−0.029	−0.056**	−0.088*
Innovation -> Work organization	0.278***	0.261***	0.28***
Product market strategy -> Employee voice	0.12***	−0.092	0.175***
Product market strategy -> Skills availability and skills development	0.183***	0.138***	0.111**
Product market strategy -> Work organization	−0.065*	−0.067**	−0.003
Work organization -> Workplace well-being	−0.017	0.079	−0.02
Work organization -> Firm performance	−0.061*	−0.132***	−0.092***
Skills availability and skills development -> Workplace well-being	−0.015	−0.019	−0.087
Skills availability and skills development -> Firm performance	0.104***	0.093***	0.029
Employee voice -> Workplace well-being	0.179	0.195	0.296***
Employee voice -> Firm performance	0.108***	−0.045	0.162***

* All the loading factors are significant at the 95% confidence level.
** All the loading factors are significant at the 99% confidence level.
*** All the loading factors are significant at the 99.9% confidence level.

It is also revealed that the innovation also had a negative and significant effect on employee voice in the three clusters of Nordic Countries, Continental Countries, and Anglo-Saxon Countries. In other words, the higher the level of innovation in these three groups of countries, the lower the direct/indirect employee participation. The loading factor of the impact of innovation on 'skills availability and skills development' for Continental countries is also negative and is significant at the 99% confidence level. This means that in the organizations studied in this cluster, high innovation has reduced the degree of compatibility of available skills and skills required for the job. On the other hand, available training programs do not meet the needs of the jobs, because the requirements are changed by innovation. The innovation variable, like digitalization, has a positive and significant effect on the work organization in all four clusters of countries. This illustrates that innovations have increased employee autonomy and facilitated outsourcing in organizations.

The loading factors of the impact of product market strategy on the employee voice for the Nordic, Continental, and Anglo-Saxon countries are positive and significant, and also the loading factors of the product market strategy and 'skills availability and skills development' for the Nordic, Continental, and Mediterranean countries are positive and significant. On the other hand, the loading factors of the impact of the product market strategy on the work organization for the Continental and Mediterranean countries are negative and significant. These findings indicate that the type of strategy that organizations take to market their products can affect their intra-organizational characteristics.

Among the country clusters, it is only in the Anglo-Saxon countries cluster that both the workplace well-being and the firm performance increase simultaneously and only under the influence of the employee voice. In other words, the employee voice variable acts like a link that has been able to simultaneously improve workplace well-being and firm performance in the Anglo-Saxon countries. Because the loading factor corresponding to employee voice and workplace well-being and employee voice and firm performance is statistically significant at the coefficient level of 95%.

Comparison of the results of the four EU-15 countries clusters with the post-socialist countries of the EU confirms the relationships between the variables. For example, Table 19.2 confirms the negative and significant impact of digitalization on employee voice as well as 'skills ability and skills development'. Table 19.2 shows the loading factors and their significance level for the relationships between the variables among the three country clusters of Northeastern European countries, Central Eastern European countries, and Southeastern European countries. The results show that digitalization has reduced direct/indirect employee participation in Northeastern and Southeastern European countries. On the other hand, empirical evidence indicates that digitalization has a significant negative impact on 'skills ability and skills development' in Northeastern European countries. Among post-socialist countries, innovation has also had a negative impact on employee voice (in Southeastern European countries) as well as 'skills ability and skills development' (in Central Eastern European and Southeastern European countries). According to the findings presented in Table 19.2, innovation, in the post-socialist countries, has also improved the work organization. In other words, innovation facilitates outsourcing as well as increasing employee autonomy in the organization. Significance of the effects of product market strategy path coefficients on intra-organizational characteristics can also be seen in Table 19.2, where product market strategy has a positive significant effect on employee voice (in North Eastern and South Eastern European countries) and 'skills ability and skills development' (in all three cluster countries); and it has a negative and significant effect on the work organization (in North Eastern and Central Eastern European countries).

The results also articulate that work organization has no effect on workplace well-being but has a negative and significant effect on the performance of companies in all three country clusters. On the other hand, the existence of a positive and significant effect of 'skills ability and skills development' on the firm performance (in North Eastern and Central Eastern European countries) indicates that the more employees' skills match their tasks, and the more chances employees have to use training programs related to their job descriptions, the higher firm performance.

Among the post-socialist countries, the South Eastern European countries are the only region where the workplace well-being and the performance of companies have increased at the same time, of course, this increase has taken place in the shadow of the increase in the employee voice. In other words, the employee voice is the gateway to simultaneously improve workplace well-being and firm performance in Southeastern European countries. Of course, the results show that the employees' voice has a positive and significant effect on the performance of companies in the North Eastern Europe. This finding shows that in Eastern countries, employee participation (either direct or through their representative) has ultimately increased the performance and profitability of organizations, but for some reason (which may be the conditions governing the management of organizations in this country group) this participation of employees has not resulted in workplace well-being.

19.4 Conclusion

The riddle of workplace well-being and firm performance has posed many challenges to the management of organizations. In this study, we aimed to investigate whether different firm strategies (or different institutional settings) have been able to provide a solution to address this dilemma. The results of quantitative analysis show that this is a serious challenge in five groups of countries (including Nordic countries, Continental countries, Mediterranean countries, Northeastern European countries, and Central Eastern European countries), but two groups of countries, namely the Anglo-Saxon countries and South Eastern European countries, have been able to simultaneously improve the workplace well-being and firm performance, but two groups of countries, namely the Anglo-Saxon countries and South Eastern European countries, have been able to simultaneously improve the well-being of employees and firm performance. A careful examination of this finding showed that the organizations studied in these two countries were the only ones in which, first, the firm performance and the employee well-being were achieved in practice, and second, these conditions took place only by increasing employee participation, whether their direct participation or participation through their representatives. Only Ireland from the Anglo-Saxon countries, and Bulgarian, from the countries of South East Europe, organizations were able to achieve this through the employee voice factor. Explaining these results from both economic and social-cultural perspective would be a rather difficult exercise relying exclusively on the present quantitative data analysis. It would be necessary to complete this statistical analysis with the national case studies to understand the filtering roles of the national institutional settings (e.g., the labor relations system, education and welfare system, management culture, economic structure). This could be an important future research agenda. However, it is worth noting that in the latest quantitative analysis of the European IRSs, both Bulgaria and Ireland are belonging into the cluster of the 'voluntarist associational governance' – together with Cyprus, the Czech Republic, Latvia, Lithuania, Malta, and Romania. This cluster is characterized by the weak formal structure of representation and participation right and '... employee representative bodies are voluntary' (even where these are mandated by law, and there are no legal sanctions for non-observance) (Eurofound, 2018:37). In addition, the Bulgarian labor market is shaped by a lack of the skilled workforce, and the strong labor market position of the skilled labor forces the management to 'care' more carefully with their demand (Kirov, 2021a, 2021b). In other words, in these countries, the focus on improving employee participation processes, both directly and through the representative, increases the overall performance of the organization and provides workplace well-being. In addition, the findings of this study disclose that in most of the countries under study, digitizing jobs and being pioneers in innovation create new requirements for tasks that do not match the current skills of employees. On the other hand, the training programs of organizations are not appropriate enough to align the level of needs of employees with the skills required for the job. In addition, this study revealed that outsourcing and increasing the employee autonomy reduces the firm performance. These findings recommend managers when they are digitizing activities, they should come up with more careful planning and pay special attention to employees' voices to improve workplace well-being.

Notes

1 Project no. TKP2021-NKTA-51 has been implemented with the support provided by the Ministry of Innovation and Technology of Hungary from the National Research, Development and Innovation Fund, financed under the TKP2021-NKTA funding scheme.
2 During the data analysis, we focus only on the post-socialist countries and drop from the analysis Malta and Cyprus.

References

Cotton, P. and Hart, P. M. (2003). Occupational Well-being and Performance: A Review of Organisational Health Research. *Australian Psychologist*, Vol. 38, No. 2, pp. 118–127.

Dall'Ora, C., Ball, J., Recio-Saucedo, A. and Griffiths, P. (2016). Characteristics of Shift Work and Their Impact on Employee Performance and Well-being: A Literature Review. *International Journal of Nursing Studies*, Vol. 57, pp. 12–27.

Eurofound. (2013). *Work Organisation and Employee Involvement in Europe*, Luxemburg: Publications Office of the European Union, p. 84.

Eurofound. (2018). *Measuring Varieties of Industrial Relations in Europe: A Quantitative Analysis*, Luxemburg: Publications Office of the European Union, p. 62.

Eurofound and Cedefop. (2020). *European Company Survey 2019: Workplace practices unlocking employee potential*. Retrieved from Luxembourg.

Gallie, D. (January 2018). *Quality of Work and Innovative Capacity: Implications for Social Equality*, Paris: QuInnE H-2020 EU Project Meeting, p. 30.

Hall, P. A. and Sockice, D. (2001). *Varieties of Capitalism: The Institutional Foundations of Corporative Advantage*, Oxford: Oxford University Press, p. 540.

Kirov, V. N. (2021a). Interview on the interpretation of the Bulgarian location in the 'voluntarist associational governance' cluster in the European of Industrial Relations Systems, 17th December, 2021.

Kirov, V. N. (2021b). *Flexibility and Insecurity – Sociological Analysis of Work and Employment in Bulgaria: 1989 – 2019*, Dissertation of "Doctor of Science" – Professional Arena 3.1. Sociology, Anthropology and Cultural Sciences, Scientific Specialty "Sociology", Sofia: Bulgarian Academy of Sciences (BAS), p. 321.

Lamb, S. and Kwok, K. C. (2016). A Longitudinal Investigation of Work Environment Stressors on the Performance and Well-being of Office Workers. *Applied Ergonomics*, Vol. 52, pp. 104–111.

Makó, C. and Illéssy, M. (2020). Automation, Creativity, and the Future of Work in Europe: A Comparison between the Old and New Member States with a Special Focus on Hungary. *Intersections: East European Journal of Society and Politics*, Vol. 6, No. 2, pp. 112–129.

Makó, C. S., Illéssy, M., Heidrich, B., Chandler, N. and Nostratabadi, S. (2021). Open Innovation and Learning Capabilities: An International Comparison of SMEs, Budapest: Budapest Business School (unpublished manuscript), p. 20.

Muller, P., Devnani, S., Ladher, R., Cannings, J., Murphy, E., Robin, N., Ramos Illam, S., Aranda, F., Gorgels, S., Priem, M., Scmid, S., Bohn, N. U., Lefebre, V. and Frizis, I. (2021). Annual Report on European SMEs 2020/2021, Digitisation of SMEs – SME Performance Reviewed 2020/2021, Brussels: European Commission, p. 185.

Ringle, C., Da Silva, D. and Bido, D. (2015). Structural equation modeling with the SmartPLS.

Sapir, A. (2006). Globalization and the Reform of European Social Models. *Journal of Common Market Studies, JCMS*, Vol. 44, No. 2, pp. 369–390.

Annex 19.1 Deconstruction of the factors used in the analysis to variables and survey questions

Factors	Question codes	Questions
Collaboration and outsourcing	actprod_4	Is this establishment engaged in the production of goods, assembly of parts or delivery of services?
	actdede_5	Is this establishment engaged in the design or development of new products or services?
Job complexity and autonomy	teamex_16	A team is a group of people working together with a shared responsibility for the execution of allocated tasks. Team members can come from the same unit or from different units across the establishment. Do you have any teams fitting this definition in this establishment?
	teasin_17_1	With regard to the employees doing teamwork, do most of them work in a single team or do most of them work in more than one team?
	tauton_18_1	Please think about the tasks to be performed by these teams. Who usually decides how the tasks are distributed within the team?
	supchek_26	Different establishments use different approaches to manage the way employees carry out their tasks. Which of these two statements best describes the general approach to management at this establishment? Please think about the approach that is used the most by managers.
	compprobs_d_29	For how many employees in this establishment does their job include finding solutions to unfamiliar problems they are confronted with? Your best estimate is good enough.
	comorg_d_30	For how many employees in this establishment does their job include independently organizing their own time and scheduling their own tasks? Your best estimate is good enough.
	pcwkmach_d_31	For how many employees at this establishment is the pace of work determined by machines or computers? Your best estimate is good enough.
Skills requirements and skills match	skillsmatch_d_32_1	What percentage of employees have the skills that are about right to do the job?
	overskill_d_32_2	What percentage of employees have a higher level of skills than is needed in their job?
	underskill_d_32_3	What percentage of employees have a lower level of skills than is needed in their job?
	skillch_33	How quickly do the knowledge and skills needed from the employees in this establishment change?
Training and skill development	contr_d_34	How many employees in this establishment are in jobs that require continuous training? Your best estimate is good enough.
	learnnoneed_d_35	How many employees in this establishment are in jobs that offer limited opportunities to learn new things? Your best estimate is good enough.
	training_36_1	What are the most important ways through which employees in this establishment can become more skilled at their jobs?

(Continued)

Annex 19.1 Deconstruction of the factors used in the analysis to variables and survey questions (Continued)

Factors	Question codes	Questions
	piadtrain_37	In 2018, how many employees in this establishment participated in training sessions on the establishment premises or at other locations during paid working time? Your best estimate is good enough.
	onjob_d_38	In 2018, how many employees in this establishment have received on-the-job training or other forms of direct instruction in the workplace from more experienced colleagues? Your best estimate is good enough.
	trainatall_39	Since the beginning of 2016, has this establishment provided any training to any of its employees?
	wpsupp_40	Workload and work schedules can prevent the participation of employees in training activities. Which of the following statements best describes what happens in practice at this establishment?
	trski_41_1	How important is 'Ensuring that employees have the skills they need to do their current job' for providing training to employees in this establishment?
	trflex_41_2	How important is 'Allowing employees to acquire skills they need to do other jobs than their current job. For instance, to allow for job rotation or career advancement. ' for providing training to employees in this establishment?
	trinn_41_3	How important is 'Increasing the capacity of employees to articulate ideas about improvements to the establishment' for providing training to employees in this establishment?
	trmot_41_4	How important is 'Improving employee morale' for providing training to employees in this establishment?
Indirect employee participation	emporg_47	Is the company to which this establishment belongs a member of any employers' organization which participates in the negotiation of collective agreements?
	canat_48_1	Are the wages of any employees in this establishment set by a collective agreement negotiated at the national or cross-sectoral level?
	casec_48_2	Are the wages of any employees in this establishment set by a collective agreement negotiated at the sectoral level?
	careg_48_3	Are the wages of any employees in this establishment set by a collective agreement at the regional level?
	cacom_48_4	Are the wages of any employees in this establishment set by a collective agreement negotiated at the establishment or company level?
	caocc_48_5	Are the wages of any employees in this establishment set by a collective agreement negotiated on behalf of employees with a specific occupation?

(Continued)

Annex 19.1 Deconstruction of the factors used in the analysis to variables and survey questions *(Continued)*

Factors	Question codes	Questions
	caoth_48_6	Are the wages of any employees in this establishment set by another type of collective agreement?
	mmerconfirm_v4_1	Does Trade union representation exist in this establishment?
	mmerconfirm_v4_2	Does Works council exist in this establishment?
	mmerconfirm_v4_3	Does Public sector equivalent of works council exist in this establishment?
	mmerconfirm_v4_4	Does Non-union staff representation exist in this establishment?
	mmerconfirm_v4_5	Does Non-union staff representative exist in this establishment?
	mmerconfirm_v4_6	Does Other country-specific bodies exist in this establishment?
	mmerconfirm_v4_7	Does Other country-specific individuals exist in this establishment?
	mmerconfirm_v4_8	Does There is no official employee representation exist in this establishment?
	mmerconfirm_v4_9	Does Trade union representative/shop steward exist in this establishment?
	eratt_50	How would you describe the general attitude of the employee representation at this establishment? The term establishment' refers to the local site at which you work.
	indir_51_1	Management prefers to consult with the employee representation.
	indir_51_2	Management prefers to consult with employees directly.
	indir_51_3	Management prefers to consult with the employee representation and with employees directly.
	ertrus_52	In your opinion, to what extent does management at this establishment trust the employee representation?
Direct employee participation	regmee_53_1	Meetings between employees and their immediate manager used to involve employees in this establishment in how work is organized?
	staffme_53_2	Meetings open to all employees at the establishment used to involve employees in this establishment in how work is organized?
	dissinf_53_3	Dissemination of information through newsletters, website, notice boards, email, etc. used to involve employees in this establishment in how work is organized?
	somedi_53_4	Discussions with employees through social media or in online discussion boards used to involve employees in this establishment in how work is organized?
	eidelay_55	In your opinion, to what extent does involving employees cause delays in the implementation of changes?

(Continued)

Annex 19.1 Deconstruction of the factors used in the analysis to variables and survey questions
(Continued)

Factors	Question codes	Questions
	eicomp_56	In your opinion, to what extent does involving employees in work organization changes give the establishment a competitive advantage?
	mmepinorg_57_1	To what extent have employees directly influenced management decisions in the organization and efficiency of work processes?
	mmepindism_57_2	To what extent have employees directly influenced management decisions in dismissals?
	mmepintrain_57_3	To what extent have employees directly influenced management decisions in training and skill development?
	mmepintime_57_4	To what extent have employees directly influenced management decisions in working time arrangements?
	mmepinpay_57_5	To what extent have employees directly influenced management decisions in payment schemes?
	mmerinorg_58_1	To what extent has the employee representation influenced management decisions in the organization and efficiency of work processes?
	mmerindism_58_2	To what extent has the employee representation influenced management decisions in dismissals?
	mmerintrain_58_3	To what extent has the employee representation influenced management decisions in training and skill development?
	mmerintime_58_4	To what extent has the employee representation influenced management decisions in working time arrangements?
	mmerinpay_58_5	To what extent has the employee representation influenced management decisions in payment schemes?
Innovation	innoprod_9	Since the beginning of 2016, has this establishment introduced any new or significantly changed products or services?
	innoproc_10	Since the beginning of 2016, has this establishment introduced any new or significantly changed processes either for producing goods or supplying services?
	innomark_11	Since the beginning of 2016, has this establishment introduced any new or significantly changed marketing methods?
Digitalization	ictcomp_d_19	How many employees in this establishment use personal computers or laptops to carry out their daily tasks?
	ictapp_20	Since the beginning of 2016, did this establishment purchase any software that was specifically developed or customized to meet the needs of the establishment?
	ictrob_21	Robots are programable machines that are capable of carrying out a complex series of actions automatically, which may include the interaction with people. Does this establishment use robots?

(Continued)

Annex 19.1 Deconstruction of the factors used in the analysis to variables and survey questions *(Continued)*

Factors	Question codes	Questions
	itprodimp_22	Does this establishment use data analytics to improve the processes of production or service delivery?
	itperfmon_23	Does this establishment use data analytics to monitor employee performance?
	itperfmonuse_24	Since the beginning of 2016, how would you say the use of data analytics in this establishment has changed?
Product market strategy	pmstratlp_65_1	How important is 'offering products or services at lower prices than the competition' for the competitive success of this establishment?
	pmstratbq_65_2	How important is 'offering products or services that are of better quality than those offered by the competition' for the competitive success of this establishment?
	pmstartcust_65_3	How important is 'customising products or services to meet specific customer requirements' for the competitive success of this establishment?
	pmstratnps_65_4	How important is 'regularly developing products, services or processes that are new to the market' for the competitive success of this establishment?
Firm Performance	prodvol_68	Since the beginning of 2016, how has the amount of goods or services produced by this establishment changed?
	profit_69	In 2018, did this establishment make a profit?
	profplan_70	Did this establishment expect to make a profit in 2018?
	chempfut_71	In the next three years, how do you expect the total number of employees in this establishment to change?
Employee well-being	sickleave_59	Do you think the level of sickness leave in this establishment is too high?
	lowmot_60	Overall, how motivated do you think employees in this establishment are?
	retainemp_62	How difficult is it for this establishment to retain employees?
	qwprel_63	How would you describe the relations between management and employees in this establishment in general?

20

MULTINATIONAL COMPANIES BASED IN THE NEW WAVE EMERGING COUNTRIES AND POST-COMMUNIST TRANSITION ECONOMIES

Wladimir Andreff

UNIVERSITE DE PARIS 1 PANTHEON-SORBONNE, FRANCE

If defined as a company having settled production plants in more than one country, the very first multinational companies (MNCs) emerged by the mid-19th century (Wilkins, 1970). Then, a first boom in their outward foreign direct investment (OFDI) was observed from 1875 to 1895 and again in the 1920s; this so-called internationalisation of capital stepped back during the economic crisis in the 1930s and World War II, and started booming again since the late 1950s (Andreff, 1976). Most OFDI waves were flowing out from Western European, North American, and then Japanese most developed domestic economies that were coined the "Triad" in the 1970s. No one developing country was a significant participant in these OFDI booms. Russia started investing abroad in the last two decades of the 19th century, though after 1932, Soviet enterprises were practically prohibited from operating foreign subsidiaries, but a few (Andreff, 2017a); a similar regulation was extended to other centrally planned economies with a Communist political regime after 1945.

Since the 1970s, new MNCs based in the Third World started investing abroad, on the brink of a stage of capitalism globalisation characterised in developed countries by "global multinationals" (Andreff, 1996). In the early 21st century, the most dynamic OFDI growth was no longer witnessed to flow from Triad home economies. The first new countries where significant OFDI started spreading from are the biggest emerging countries, the so-called BRICS – Brazil, Russia, India, China, and South Africa. Such investment abroad is related to economic development in these countries, which are no longer underdeveloped or developing economies; instead, they are emerging as new (or in close future) fully fledged developed economies. The strategy and significance of these newcomers in OFDI business is well-known today (Andreff, 2014, 2016a; Sauvant, 2008).

DOI: 10.4324/9781003144366-24

A less-known evolution is that a number of other emerging countries are on the same tracks as the BRICS (Brazil, Russia, India, China, South Africa), with regard to OFDI, namely during the early 21st century: in this chapter, they have coined the New Wave Emerging Countries (NWECs). On the other hand, after the collapse of the former Soviet system and a few years of transitional recession, firms based in Post-Communist Transition Economies (PCTEs) started investing significantly abroad since the mid-1990s (Andreff, 2003). Except Russia, all PCTEs are smaller domestic economies than the NWEC ones and, consequently, smaller investors abroad, but they are newcomers to the OFDI business either. Again, this new spread of OFDI is related to economic development since the transition is a bifurcation from a former centrally planned extensive development path toward a market-oriented more intensive economic development. Therefore, it makes sense comparing MNCs based in the NWECs with those based in PCTEs, and this is what the present chapter is all about.

First, the two country subsamples are precisely delineated (Section 20.1). A relevant theoretical framework for analysing OFDI in a comparative approach to economic development, *i.e.* Dunning's investment development path (IDP) model completed with Matthews's linkage-leverage-learning (LLL) hypothesis, is briefly reminded (Section 20.2). MNCs based in the NWECs and PCTEs are compared within a historical perspective (Section 20.3), then with their OFDI growth paces and features (Section 20.4). Section 20.5 compares the results of econometric testing of the same IDP model with OFDI data pertaining to the NWECs and PCTEs, before concluding.

20.1 Two country samples

A sample of 13 NWECs has been gathered through a data selection process over a threshold reached by a country in terms of OFDI (Andreff, 2016a). First, significant investors abroad were defined, in 2014, as all those countries holding at least a $1 billion OFDI stock abroad according to UNCTAD (2015) data published in the *World Investment Report*. With such criterion, 91 countries in the world were kept in the database. Then, the database was cleaned from obviously non-emerging countries starting with 30 developed market economies, defined as having over $20,000 GNI (gross national income) per capita in 2014, which were dropped. Among the 61 remaining countries, there were the five BRICS. They were left aside since they are quite specific due to their huge (geographical, economic, and population) size – therefore, they were not to be included in the NWEC group. Moreover, their OFDI has already been studied in above-mentioned references.

PCTEs also must be cleaned off the sample of 56 remaining countries. These transition economies are not yet fully fledged market economies. Though they are not former underdeveloped or developing countries either, owing to the former centrally planned development policy; rather than being underindustrialised, they had reached an intermediary level of economic development (though distorted in favour of heavy industries) and had closed their economy to inward and outward FDI for decades. Seventeen PCTEs were significant foreign investors in 2014, including Russia (already accounted for with the BRICS), 16 of which were dropped. The sample of potential newly emerging economies came down to 40. Some countries kept in the sample have their economic development and consequently their inward FDI and OFDI very much dependent on rent-extracting activities based on crude products such as oil and gas or raw materials exploitation. Due to this specific endowment in natural resources, Algeria, Angola, Congo DR, Costa Rica, Gabon, Iraq, Kuwait, Libya, Morocco, Oman, Peru, Qatar, Saudi Arabia, Togo, United Arab Emirates, Venezuela, and Zambia, i.e. 17 countries were skipped out from a potential NWEC sample.

Table 20.1 The sample of 13 New Wave Emerging Countries in 2014

Rank	Country	OFDI stock In 2014[a]	Population Million	GDP $bn 2014	GNI/ Capita	Geographic. size[b]
1	Malaysia	135.7	29.9	338	11,120	329
2	Mexico	131.2	125.4	1295	9,870	1,944
3	Chile	89.7	17.8	258	14,910	744
4	Thailand	65.8	67.7	405	5,780	511
5	Colombia	43.1	47.8	378	7,970	1,110
6	Turkey	40.1	75.9	798	10,830	770
7	Argentina	35.9	43.0	538	13,480	2,737
8	Philippines	35.6	99.1	285	3,500	298
9	Indonesia	24.1	254.5	889	3,630	1,812
10	Nigeria	10.3	177.5	569	2,970	911
11	Egypt	6.8	89.6	287	3,050	995
12	Iran	4.1	78.1	425	7,120	1,629
13	Pakistan	1.7	185.0	244	1,400	771

Sources: World Bank and UNCTAD.

[a] In $ billion.
[b] In thousand square kilometres.

GDP: Gross domestic product.
GNI: Gross national income.

Among the 23 remaining countries, some are not actually major investors abroad because they are basically hubs or platforms for round-tripping and trans-shipping OFDI used by other domestic economies to invest abroad. Usually, they are tax havens, free trade zones or tax-friendly countries: therefore, Lebanon, Bahrain, Trinidad & Tobago, Cook Islands, Liberia, Panama, Bahamas, Barbados, Macao, and Mauritius were not kept in the NWEC sample.

Once these 10 countries were subtracted, the subsample of NWECs was left with the 13 following countries ranked according to their OFDI stock in 2014: Malaysia, Mexico, Chile, Thailand, Colombia, Turkey, Argentina, the Philippines, Indonesia, Nigeria, Egypt, Iran, and Pakistan (Table 20.1). These 13 NWECs can compare to the BRICS in that they are big countries both in terms of population and GDP, located in wide national geographical territories, and they have enjoyed swift economic development in the past two decades; this has been statistically tested (Andreff 2017b).

During the 1980s, 14 countries were centrally planned economies with a Communist political regime since the so-called socialist-orientated developing countries[1] (Andreff, 1989) were not considered as Communist centrally planned economies. After the break-up of the Soviet Union, Czechoslovakia, and Yugoslavia and German reunification, the world economy was left with 33 PCTEs. North Korea and Cuba are not yet clearly "post"-Communist, and in China, even with an emerging market economy, the country is still ruled by a Communist Party in power; these three countries are not taken on board with the PCTEs. Regarding Kosovo, Mongolia, Tajikistan, Turkmenistan, and Uzbekistan, knowledge is rather scarce about their OFDI because their investment abroad is nearly non-existent, below $10 million an OFDI stock in 2014, according to UNCTAD data, while Vietnamese OFDI emerged only recently, in 2014. Since Russia is a PCTE and a significant economic neighbour and partner for nearly all other PCTEs, it is retained in the sample, even though it is often classified as one of the BRICS otherwise.

Keeping Russia and Vietnam, the PCTE subsample comprises 26 countries (Table 20.2). Now, applying the threshold used for delineating the NWEC subsample – a $1 billion OFDI

Table 20.2 The sample of post-communist transition economies in 2014

Rank	Country	OFDI stock in 2014[a]	Population Million	GDP $bn 2014	GNI/ Capita	Geographic size[b]
1	Russia	431.9	144.7	2,064	13,795	17125
2	Poland	54.9	38.1	545	13,789	313
3	Hungary	39.6	9.8	140	13,715	93
4	Kazakhstan	27.2	17.3	221	11,488	2725
5	Czech Republic	19.0	10.6	208	18,300	79
6	Azerbaijan	11.2	9.5	170	7,688	87
7	Ukraine	9.7	45.1	134	2,926	604
8	Vietnam	7.5	91.7	186	1,934	331
9	Estonia	6.3	1.3	27	19,765	4
10	Slovenia	6.2	2.1	50	23,929	20
11	Croatia	5.4	4.3	58	13,194	57
12	Slovakia	3.0	5.4	101	18,360	49
13	Serbia	2.8	8.9	44	5,948	88
14	Lithuania	2.7	3.0	49	16,137	65
15	Bulgaria	2.2	7.2	57	7,783	111
16	Georgia	1.5	3.7	18	4,311	70
17	Latvia	1.2	2.0	31	15,477	65
18	Romania	0.7	20.0	200	9,865	238
19	Belarus	0.6	9.4	79	8,105	208
20	Kyrgyzstan	0.4	5.8	7	1,239	199
21	Montenegro	0.4	0.6	5	7,418	14
22	Albania	0.2	2.9	13	4,609	29
23	Armenia	0.2	2.9	12	4,172	30
24	Bosnia-Herzegovina	0.2	3.5	19	5,365	51
25	Moldova	0.2	3.0	8	2,578	34
26	Macedonia	0.1	2.1	11	5,366	25

Sources: World Bank and UNCTAD.

[a] In $ billion.
[b] In thousand square kilometres.
GDP: Gross domestic product.
GNI: Gross national income.

stock in 2014 –, one should drop the nine last-ranked PCTEs in Table 20.2. However, considering that PCTEs are latecomers in the OFDI business even compared with the NWECs (Section 20.3) on the one hand and, on the other hand, that being much smaller economies (GDP, population, territory) than the NWECs they must not have OFDI of comparable magnitude; all the 26 countries are kept in the PCTE subsample. In fact, the selection criterion has moved down to $100 million an OFDI stock (Macedonia) for PCTEs in 2014 instead of $1 billion for NWECs.

Now, it is to be noticed that earlier than 2014, for some years, the following 11 countries exhibited no OFDI stock at all: Armenia, Belarus, Bosnia-Herzegovina, Georgia, Kazakhstan, Kyrgyzstan, Macedonia, Moldova, Montenegro, Serbia, and Vietnam. Eventually, the operational subsample, namely used for econometric testing (Section 20.5), contains only 15 countries (Andreff & Andreff, 2017). Therefore, the size of the PCTE subsample is comparable to the NWEC's one.

Looking at Tables 20.1 and 20.2, the empirical evidence is that NWECs are quite bigger countries than PCTEs in terms of population: Mexico, Indonesia, Nigeria, and Pakistan can compare to, or are bigger than Russia, and the Philippines and Egypt are in the same range as

Vietnam. The smallest NWEC, Chile, has a population 14 times bigger than Estonia's (and 30 times bigger than Montenegro's). Except Russia, the largest national geographical territory on the earth, only Kazakhstan can compare to Argentina and Mexico; the geographically smallest NWEC, the Philippines, is 75 times larger than Estonia (and 21 times Montenegro's size).

The level of economic development, approximated by GNI per capita in 2014, is much more scattered across PCTEs where Slovenia (roughly $24,000) is more developed than Western developed market economies such as Greece and Portugal, while Kyrgyzstan ($1,239) is less developed than the least developed NWEC (Pakistan, $1,400). Among the NWECs, all countries' GNI per capita, except Pakistan's, are concentrated between roughly $15,000 (Chile) and about $3,000 (Egypt, Nigeria). Therefore, it is not surprising that OFDI stock is more scattered across PCTEs (4,300 times bigger in Russia than in Macedonia) than across NWECs (80 times bigger in Malaysia than in Pakistan). The last observation suggests a potential relationship between OFDI and economic development, which is retained in the theoretical framework.

20.2 The theoretical framework: IDP model and LLL hypothesis

The analysis of FDI and its determinants often distinguishes pull factors from push factors (Andreff, 2016b). Pull factors attract and drive FDI into a given country, otherwise coined host country's factors of attractiveness to FDI (Andreff, 1999). They differentiate host countries. Push factors usually are referred to home country-specific variables. They basically are drivers for a home country substituting investment abroad for domestic investment; they explain why investment is pushed outwards beyond domestic borders. Push factors such as domestic market size (GDP or population) and level of economic development (GNI per capita) underlie the IDP model elaborated by Dunning (1981) and Dunning & Narula (1998), while the home country technological level has been tested as a driver pushing investment abroad as well (Andreff, 2003).

The IDP model relates different stages of inward FDI and OFDI to successive stages of a home country's economic development. In the first stage, a country hosts very little inward FDI and does not invest at all abroad. In the second stage, it becomes attractive to inward FDI and achieves its very first OFDI, being a net FDI importer. In the third stage, due to its new technological competences and low unit labour cost, the country attracts very significant inward FDI and its MNCs start investing substantially abroad, though the country remains a net FDI importer. In the fourth stage, a country – now a fully fledged developed economy – invests more OFDI than it receives inward FDI; its FDI balance becomes positive. In the fifth – which is the last – stage, the now post-industrial country roughly reaches a balance between its inward and outward FDI.

The economic literature about OFDI from the NWECs is rare, even rarer if one sticks only to push factors' analyses. Such factors have been used to explain OFDI from Malaysia (Goh & Wong, 2011; Masron & Shahbudin, 2010; Saad et al., 2014; Teo et al., 2015), from Thailand (Cheewatrakoolpong & Boonprakaikawe, 2015), from the Philippines (Bano & Tabbada, 2015), from Turkey (Anil, et al., 2011; Kayam & Hisarciklilar, 2009), and for OFDI from both emerging and transition economies (Kayam, 2009). The literature on OFDI from the PCTEs is dominated by approaches of pull factors as main determinants, given the small size of their home markets, except Russia. However, the idea that domestic push economic factors determine OFDI can be found for OFDI from Poland (Gorynia et al., 2010; Götz, 2013), from Lithuania (Casas & Dambrauskaitė, 2011; Mockaitis et al., 2006), and from all the PCTEs (Andreff, 2003; Andreff & Andreff, 2017).

Another theoretical underpinning of OFDI from Asian emerging countries is the LLL hypothesis suggested by Mathews (2002) to explain the expansion of "Dragon Multinational Enterprises". This hypothesis stresses that emerging countries' MNCs are keen to establish links, including alliances and joint ventures with incumbent MNCs, to leverage resources, and to learn from these incumbents. Thus, latecomers acquire and absorb foreign resources and improve their competitive position through multinational growth. They enter outsourcing networks. They can leverage resources from other firms' strengths, namely via technology licensing contracts, imitation, and reverse engineering (Mathews, 2006).

Matthews LLL hypothesis has been used in few articles (Banga, 2007) looking at domestic determinants of OFDI from Asian developing countries, and it is of interest to extend this approach to all the sampled NWECs, and to test whether the same hypothesis may be relevant for the PCTE subsample. It was noticed that inward FDI in PCTEs significantly contributed to industrial restructuring (Andreff, 2007) and to domestic firms' favouring internationalisation toward export markets (Puig-Gomez, 2014). Inward FDI must have facilitated further OFDI from PCTEs in tune with the LLL hypothesis.

Rugraff (2010) noted that the participation of indirect investors – foreign-owned MNCs – in OFDI from PCTEs is directly linked to the magnitude of inward FDI flows, in the case of Central Eastern European countries (CEECs), which is an important dimension of the LLL hypothesis since some elements of their ownership advantages will spill over to local firms, helping them to progressively internationalise. The presence of foreign owners (inward FDI) is used as an explanatory factor of OFDI from Poland (Gorynia et al., 2014; Wasowska, 2013), and from nine CEECs (Damijan et al., 2014). Kuzel (2017) showed that subsidiaries of the world's largest MNCs located in Poland have well-established local business partners and have built vertical linkages with domestic firms. Such linkages create favourable conditions for the exchange of information, solutions, and business experience and the diffusion of knowledge and skills and sharing technical information and know-how. This corresponds to both the third IDP phase, as Kuzel stresses it, and a process in tune with the LLL hypothesis.

20.3 Two different OFDI development schemes in past economic history

The starting point in the development of NWEC-based MNCs dates back to the 1970s, primarily for some Latin American front runners. For most NWEC-based MNCs, their first investment abroad is traced back to the 1980s; and to the 1990s for Iranian MNCs. A UN report (ONU, 1978) had pointed at 170 foreign subsidiaries of Latin America-based MNCs (called *multilatinas*), basically from Argentina, Chile, Colombia, and Mexico, established in other Latin American countries in the 1970s.[2] The same report assessed OFDI stocks from Indonesia, the Philippines, and Hong Kong in other South-East Asian countries to be up to $1.5 billion in 1976.

A UN (1988) report had listed $3.6 million FDI outflows from Colombia and $1.2 million from the Philippines in 1975; in 1980, FDI outflows were reaching $105 million from Colombia, $43 million from Chile, $6.5 million from Egypt, and $2.6 million from Thailand, while Argentina was already divesting $110 million previously invested in Latin American countries. OFDI in the services industry was also witnessed from Argentina, Chile, Colombia, and the Philippines. In 1980, OFDI stock was up to $13 million from Thailand, $31 million from Pakistan, $39 million from Egypt, $42 million from Chile, $137 million from Colombia, $171 million from the Philippines, and $414 million from Malaysia (UNCTAD, 1994). Indeed, the first wave of OFDI from Argentina dates back to 1900–1930;

Table 20.3 OFDI stock from the NWECs: 1985–1999 ($million)

NWECs	1985	1990	1992	1993	1994	1995	1996	1997	1998	1999	N[a]
Argentina	6,079	6,105	n.a.	n.a.	n.a.	10696	n.a.	7,616	18,184	19,277	3.2
Chile	102	178	713	1,144	2,027	2,815	3,848	5,928	8,860	13,515	132.5
Colombia	301	402	476	476	868	1,028	1,220	1,866	2,381	2,397	8
Egypt	59	131	229	223	254	365	370	499	584	630	10.6
Indonesia	49	25	n.a.	83	96	701	1,295	2,073	2,117	2,189	44.7
Iran	0	0	0	0	0	77	80	138	154	184	2.4[b]
Malaysia	749	2,283	n.a.	4,516	6,328	8,903	10,809	12,725	15,240	16,880	22.5
Mexico	533	575	n.a.	1,039	2,084	4,132	n.a.	5,278	5,825	6,625	12.4
Nigeria	5,334	9,652	n.a.	n.a.	11,197	11,186	11,893	11,516	11,164	11,256	2.1
Pakistan	127	282	n.a.	264	258	266	274	239	244	468	3.7
Philippines	171	154	154	128	155	1,209	1,091	1,527	1,698	1,858	10.9
Thailand	14	398	701	933	1,426	2,173	n.a.	1,951	1,978	2,346	167.6
Turkey	161	154	246	260	344	268	371	622	996	1,641	10.2

Sources: UNCTAD, World Investment Reports.

N = OFDI.

[a] 1999 divided by OFDI 1985.
[b] 1999/1995.

after a post-war collapse, Argentine OFDI had started up growing again earlier than 1965 with acceleration in 1969–1980 (Katz & Kosacoff, 1984).

OFDI from most NWECs started increasing significantly in the 1990s (Table 20.3). Five front runners, Argentina, Colombia, Malaysia, Mexico, and Nigeria, had already invested abroad over $300 million in 1985. Then, the growth of their OFDI stock was below average among the NWECs from 1985 to 1999. Three fast growers or catching-up countries, in terms of OFDI, were Chile, Indonesia, and Thailand with the highest OFDI stock growth rates. Egypt, Pakistan, the Philippines, and Turkey were slower movers, though with a small amount of OFDI in 1985 and a slower OFDI growth rate than the catchers-up. Iran is a latecomer with its first OFDI appearing in the UN data only in 1995.

In its early stage, OFDI from the NWECs did not evolve on a smooth path at a regular pace. NWECs' direct investment abroad was punctuated by a series of economic crises that temporarily halted or sharply slowed down FDI outflows. Such was the case of the 1982 debt crisis that affected the four sampled Latin American NWECs. The South-Eastern Asian crisis triggered by the collapse of the Thai baht in 1997 hindered OFDI from Thailand, Indonesia, Malaysia, and the Philippines. Other NWECs suffered from different crises, an oil doom in Nigeria, a balance of payment crises and an earthquake in Turkey, an eight-year war with Iraq in Iran, and decades of war and social instability in Pakistan. The aforementioned crises had been followed in all the NWECs by stabilisation and adjustment policies, liberalisation, deregulation, and privatisation that offered new substantial incentives to inward and then outward FDI. Finally, in the 2000s, NWECs' OFDI surged up at a pace that compares to BRICS' OFDI.

Russian enterprises began to invest in China, Persia, and Mongolia in the late 19th century (Bulatov, 2001). In 1914, the current value of Russian OFDI stock reached $3.8 billion (Wilkins, 1990). During the interwar period, the USSR withdrew its OFDI, except for some trading subsidiaries in Afghanistan, Iran, Mongolia, and Turkey to sustain foreign trade. Some Soviet companies invested in the West, such as the Russian Wood Agency in London (1923), Anglo-Soviet Shipping in London (1923), Amtorg in New York (1924), Moscow Narodny Bank in London, and Eurobank in Paris (Andreff, 2017a). In the wake of Brezhnev's economic reforms, central foreign trade organizations were allowed to invest abroad from the USSR and other CMEA (Council of Mutual Economic Assistance) countries. The overall amount of OFDI from these countries was slightly over $1 billion, that is, 0.3% of worldwide OFDI stock in 1978 (Andreff, 1987). Various estimates of OFDI from CMEA countries were published, the last one for 1990 in a United Nations study (UNTCMD, 1992): out of Eastern Europe's OFDI stock amounting to $1,226 million, $699 million were held by Soviet enterprises in industrial subsidiaries and $13 million by Soviet banks.

The USSR reopened the door to joint ventures with foreign partners by a 1987 decree, followed by another decree (1989) and a law (1991) that definitely allowed inward FDI without restriction. This legislation, kept by the Russian Federation, was a preliminary condition for foreign countries to accept OFDI from Russian firms. The same process emerged in CEECs with an earlier opening to inward FDI in Yugoslavia (1967), Romania (1971), Hungary (1972), Poland (1976), and all other CMEA countries between 1986 and 1992. In a sense, this was a launch pad for their coming OFDI.

From 1990 to 1993, due to CMEA disintegration, the break-up of the former Soviet Union and transitional recession, OFDI from this area was reduced to practically nothing. In the early years of the transition process, the expansion of PCTE firms abroad was often interpreted as a capital runaway, if not an exodus, toward more friendly and stable, less risky foreign investment climates than in home countries. Then, OFDI from PCTEs actually started spreading abroad after 1993 (Andreff, 2002). From 1994 to 2000, among the PCTEs, the biggest OFDI stock was held by MNCs based in Russia and then in Hungary, Poland, Croatia, the Czech Republic, and Slovenia (Table 20.4); more detailed data is given in Andreff (2003).

Therefore, OFDI development is a rather long-term – historical – process in both the NWECs and PCTEs, but it has not been a smooth and stable development. From time to time, it was interrupted or slowed down by exogenous factors (crises) in the NWECs, followed by a booming recovery, whereas in the PCTEs, OFDI was practically stopped and forbidden during Soviet times. After such a long break, since 1993–1994, firms investing abroad from the PCTEs are to be considered as newcomers (and latecomers) even when compared with the NWEC-based MNCs.

Table 20.4 OFDI from the PCTEs: 1994–2000 ($million)

Home country	1994	1995	1998	1999	2000	2000 flow
CEECs of which	**664**	**2,167**	**4,359**	**4,689**	**5,516**	**964**
Czech Republic	206	345	804	698	784	118
Estonia	12	68	198	272	429	157
Hungary	115	383	1,101	1,565	2,012	532
Poland	223	539	1,165	1,365	1,491	126
Slovenia	n.a.	504	563	607	655	48
CIS of which	**394**	**3,138**	**7,978**	**9,583**	**12,914**	**3,330**
Kazakhstan	n.a.	n.a.	10	14	18	4
Russia	386	3,015	7,377	8,586	11,637	3,050
Ukraine	8	97	98	105	106	1
Uzbekistan	n.a.	n.a.	282	264	321	57
Balkans of which	**36**	**1,268**	**1,668**	**1,751**	**1,834**	**83**
Albania	36	48	69	76	82	6
Croatia	n.a.	703	992	1,024	1,052	28
Total	**1,094**	**6,573**	**14,005**	**16,023**	**20,264**	**4,377**

Sources: UNCTAD, World Investment Reports.

20.4 OFDI growth paces, features, and strategies

In the 21st century, the variation of OFDI stock went on being unstable and differentiated across countries in the two NWEC and PCTE subsamples (Tables 20.5 and 20.6). In 2000, no one of the 39 countries was yet a big investor abroad. The leaders were Argentina, Chile, Malaysia, and Russia with over $10 billion an OFDI stock held abroad; their followers were Mexico, Nigeria, and Colombia. Except Russia, all the PCTEs were still small investors; only Hungary and Poland could compare with some NWECs in this respect.

Then, OFDI was actually booming in the two country subsamples during 2000–2007 (see the N1 multiplier in Tables 20.5 & 20.6). The fastest OFDI growth was witnessed in those countries that started investing significantly abroad such as Kazakhstan, Ukraine, or Lithuania, followed by countries that consolidated their position as significant foreign investors: Indonesia, Mexico, Turkey, Azerbaijan, the Czech Republic, Estonia, Hungary, Poland, and Slovenia.

The impact of the economic crisis that burst out in 2008 was different in the two country subsamples and within each subsample. Looking at multipliers N2 and N3, it is striking that OFDI growth had swiftly accelerated during the crisis from four NWECs, Thailand, the Philippines, Colombia, and, to some extent, Chile, so that in 2019 the three leaders in OFDI are no longer Argentina, Chile, and Malaysia, as in 2000, but rather Mexico, Thailand, and Chile. In these countries, OFDI seems to have been resilient to the financial and economic crisis impact, thus resembling Chinese OFDI (Andreff, 2016c). OFDI growth pace was more than reasonably high in times of crisis in Egypt, Indonesia, and Turkey, while it remained slower from Argentina and Pakistan. In Iran, Malaysia and Nigeria, OFDI was affected by the crisis since its stock decreased from 2014 to 2019. With the three latter exceptions, overall, OFDI flowing from NWECs kept a rather high momentum when muddling through the crisis, higher than the one from PTCEs.

Russia alone represents between 60% and 80% of overall OFDI stock from PCTEs, depending on the year. With the Financial Crisis and Great Recession in 2008, its booming OFDI trend changed dramatically. Russia's OFDI stock grew much more slowly from 2008 to 2014, and it even decreased between 2014 and 2019.[3] The future of Russian OFDI in the West is bleak and shadowed with uncertainty. Despite this reverse trend, in 2019, Russia remains

Table 20.5 OFDI stock from NWECs: 2000–2019 ($billion)

NWECs	2000	2007	2014	2015	2016	2017	2018	2019	N1[a]	N2[b]	N3[c]
Argentina	20.2	26.9	35.9	37.3	38.8	40.9	42.3	43.5	1.33	1.33	1.21
Chile	18,3	32,5	89,7	87.4	110.1	124.3	119.3	131.6	1.78	2.76	1.47
Colombia	3,8	10,4	43,1	47.3	51.8	55.5	60.6	63.8	2.74	4.14	1.48
Egypt	0,6	1,8	6,8	7.7	7.2	7.4	7.8	8.2	3.00	3.78	1.21
Indonesia	2,3	21,4	24,1	30.2	58.9	65.9	72.3	78.8	9.30	1.13	3.27
Iran	0,4	1,5	4,1	2.5	3.7	3.7	3.9	4.0	3.75	2.73	0.98
Malaysia	15,9	58,2	135,7	136.9	126.9	128.5	118.9	118.6	3.66	2.33	0.87
Mexico	8,6	44,7	131,2	151.9	148.6	180.1	152.5	230.4	5.20	2.94	1.76
Nigeria	4,1	5,5	10,3	11.7	13.0	14.3	15.7	8.9	1.34	1.87	0.86
Pakistan	0,5	1	1,7	1.7	2.1	1.9	1.9	1.9	2.00	1.70	1.12
Philippines	1,9	5,6	35,6	41.1	45.4	47.8	51.9	52.6	0.92	6.36	1.48
Thailand	2,4	7	65,8	68.1	85.6	107.3	121.4	137.4	2.92	9.40	2.09
Turkey	2,5	12,2	40,1	44.7	38.0	41.4	49.9	47.8	4.88	3.29	1.19

Source: UNCTAD (2020).

[a] N1 = 2007/2000.
[b] N2 = 2014/2007.
[c] N3 = 2019/2014.

Table 20.6 OFDI stock from PCTEs: 2000–2019 ($billion)

PTCEs	2000	2007	2014	2015	2016	2017	2018	2019	N1[a]	N2[b]	N3[c]
Albania	0.08	0.02	0.2	0.3	0.4	0.5	0.6	0.7	0.25	10.00	3.50
Armenia	0.03	0.01	0.2	0.3	0.6	0.6	0.6	0.5	0.33	20.00	2.50
Azerbaijan	0.7	4.7	11.2	15.4	17.9	22.1	23.7	26.1	6.71	2.38	2.33
Belarus	0.01	0.04	0.6	0.7	0.7	0.8	0.9	1.4	4.00	15.00	2.33
Bosnia-Herzeg.	0.04	0.02	0.2	0.3	0.3	0.5	0.5	0.5	0.50	10.00	2.50
Bulgaria	0.09	0.6	2.2	3.1	2.1	2.8	2.7	2.8	6.67	3.67	1.27
Croatia	1.1	3.5	5.4	5.5	5.0	6.1	6.6	1.1	3.18	1.54	0.20
Czech Republic	0.8	6.7	19.0	18.5	18.6	23.7	34.8	45.4	8.38	2.84	2.39
Estonia	0.4	5.9	6.3	6.1	6.5	7.7	8.0	10.1	14.7	1.07	1.60
Georgia	0.06	0.08	1,5	1.7	1.9	2.4	2.6	2.9	1.33	18.75	1.93
Hungary	2.0	18.3	39,6	38.5	25.0	28.6	29.0	33.7	9.15	2.16	0.85
Kazakhstan	0.02	2.2	27.2	23.9	20.7	20.5	16.7	15.6	110.0	12.36	0.57
Kyrgyzstan	0	0.02	0.4	0	0	0	0.01	0.01	∞	2.00	0.03
Latvia	0.2	0.8	1.2	1.2	1.4	1.8	2.0	1.8	4.00	1.50	1.50
Lithuania	0.03	1.6	2.7	2.2	2.4	3.4	4.2	4.7	53.3	1.69	1.74
Macedonia	0.01	0.04	0.1	0.1	0.1	0.1	0.1	0.1	4.00	2.50	0
Moldova	0.02	0.04	0.2	0.2	0.2	0.2	0.3	0.3	2.00	5.00	1.50
Montenegro	0	0.2	0.4	0.4	0.2	0.2	0.3	0.2	∞	2.00	0.50
Poland	1.5	19.6	54.9	27.8	24.8	31.0	28.5	24.8	13.1	2.80	0.45
Romania	0.1	0.9	0.7	0.6	0.9	0.9	0.7	1.3	9.00	0.78	1.86
Russia	11.6	255.2	431.9	252.0	335.8	382.3	344.1	386.6	22.00	1.69	0.90
Serbia	0	0	2.8	2.9	3.0	3.6	3.8	4.1	0	∞	1.46
Slovakia	0.3	1.6	3.0	2.6	2.7	3.4	3.7	4.7	5.33	1.88	1.57
Slovenia	0.7	6.1	6.2	5.5	5.7	6.9	8.1	7.0	8.71	1.02	1.13
Ukraine	0.1	6.1	9.7	9.6	7.5	7.5	7.4	8.0	61.00	1.59	0.82
Vietnam	0	0	7.5	8.6	10.0	10.5	10.7	11.1	0	∞	1.48

Source: UNCTAD (2020).

[a] N1 = 2007/2000.
[b] N2 = 2014/2007.
[c] N3 = 2019/2014.

the biggest foreign investor among the 39 sampled countries, ahead of Mexico and Thailand. The next most important foreign investor among the PCTEs is the Czech Republic in 2019, close to the amount of Argentina's OFDI and ahead of four NWECs (Egypt, Iran, Nigeria, Pakistan).

Indeed, the crisis shock on OFDI was quite different across PCTEs. The most affected, with a decrease in their OFDI stock between 2014 and 2019, were Croatia, Poland, Kazakhstan, Ukraine, and Hungary and, between 2007 and 2014, Romania. The best performers in terms of OFDI during the crisis were the Czech Republic, Azerbaijan, Bulgaria, and some starting latecomers (Albania, Armenia, Belarus, Bosnia, and Georgia). Each PCTE muddled through the crisis on its own path at its own pace, and consequently, the crisis impact on OFDI is highly scattered in magnitude and variety. After the crisis, just like before the crisis, PCTEs remain minor investors abroad – except Russia – compared to most NWECs.

In line with the IDP model, countries may be classified in the first, second, and third stages of economic and OFDI development according to the fact that they are meeting pre-defined thresholds for their OFDI/GDP and outward/inward ratios. A country moves from one IDP stage to the next when it breaks through some representative threshold. On the OFDI side of IDP, it is sometimes assumed that an OFDI/GDP ratio higher than 5% and an OFDI stock/inward FDI stock ratio higher than 25% are two hypothetical qualifiers for the third stage of IDP model (Andreff, 2003), which is supposed to characterise emerging market economies.

Table 20.7 Comparative features of OFDI from the NWECs and PCTEs

NWECs	Outward FDI stock/GDP		Outward/inward FDI stock		PCTEs	Outward FDI stock/GDP		Outward/inward FDI stock	
	2000	2014	2000	2014		2000	2015	2000	2015
Argentina	7.3	6.7	29.9	31.5	Albania	2.7	2.6	20.0	6.3
Chile	15.7	34.8	40.0	43.2	Azerbaijan	9.4	2.9	11.1	69.4
Colombia	3.8	11.4	33.9	30.4	Bulgaria	0.8	6.3	2.9	7.4
Egypt	0.7	2.3	3.0	7.7	Croatia	4.1	11.3	18.4	20.8
Indonesia	1.6	2.7	9.2	9.5	Czech Rep.	1.1	10.2	3.3	16.4
Iran	1.3	1.0	15.4	9.5	Estonia	5.1	26.9	10.7	32.3
Malaysia	20.8	40.1	30.2	101.4	Hungary	4.4	31.9	10.6	41.8
Mexico	1.9	10.1	7.1	38.8	Latvia	2.5	4.4	9.5	8.3
Nigeria	8.5	1.8	17.2	11.9	Lithuania	0	5.3	0	15.3
Pakistan	0.9	0.7	7.2	5.5	Poland	0.6	5.9	2.7	13.0
Philippines	2.1	12.5	13.8	62.3	Romania	0.3	0.3	1.6	0.9
Thailand	2.0	16.3	7.8	33.0	**Russia**	**4.8**	**19.0**	**64.6**	**97.5**
Turkey	1.8	5.0	13.3	23.8	Slovakia	1.4	3.0	8.2	5.4
					Slovenia	4.0	12.9	27.6	46.6
					Ukraine	0.6	10.6	5.3	15.5
					Vietnam	0	0.6	0	1.3

Sources: Calculated from UNCTAD and World Bank data.

Looking at Table 20.7 with this reference in mind, in 2000, only Argentina, Chile and Malaysia, and nearly Russia, had reached the third stage of the IDP model, thus qualifying for being considered as emerging economies from the standpoint of their OFDI development. Now, in 2014/15, five other NWECs have joined the third stage, Colombia, Mexico, the Philippines, Thailand, and nearly Turkey. Among PCTEs, Estonia, Hungary, and Slovenia have joined Russia in the emerging country group, while Russia is on the brink of reaching a 100% outward/inward FDI ratio beyond which a country is considered, in the IDP model, as a developed economy (from the OFDI standpoint). Unfortunately, due to the slowdown of Russian OFDI in the past recent years, Russia's outward/inward FDI ratio dropped down to 83.3% in 2019.

Data about strategies of the NWEC-based MNCs are extremely scattered in the literature. The primary motive driving their OFDI is the search for new markets or the preservation of existing ones (market-seeking strategy). Asian NWEC-based MNCs are slightly less focused on market-seeking than *multilatinas* (Latin American MNCs).

Russian MNCs often developed a market-seeking OFDI in their traditional markets such as the CIS and CEECs; it is also the rationale for Russian OFDI in Western markets, where Russian products face tough competition. Since other PCTEs have small domestic markets, their MNCs have definitely adopted a market-seeking strategy.

Other OFDI strategies can be found in the two country subsamples though they are less widespread. Efficiency-seeking OFDI is found in Argentine, Chilean, Hungarian, Malaysian, Polish, Slovene, and Thai companies.

A resource-seeking strategy, sometimes attempting to take over their most needed suppliers abroad by means of M&As, is adopted by Russian MNCs that invest abroad in the mining, oil, and gas industries, in particular in CIS countries; some Azeri, Hungarian, Kazakh, and Slovene MNCs also invest for securing resources abroad.

Finally, asset seeking in view to acquiring foreign (mainly Western) technology and R&D intensive units has pushed forward cross-border M&As launched by Hungarian, Mexican, Polish, and Russian firms.

With regard to the geographical distribution of OFDI from the NWECs and PCTEs, they have a nearly similar profile (Andreff, 2017a,b). From available data, it appears that NWEC-based MNCs primarily invest in neighbouring countries, close to their home country, in countries where they have some familiarity through trade, ethnic, and cultural ties. The second privileged area for their OFDI is located in developed market economies.

Available data suggests some similarity in the geographical distribution of PCTEs' OFDI stock, in two privileged areas: neighbouring PCTEs and developed market economies, namely in EU countries. Except Russia, and to a lesser extent Hungary, they do not invest much in more distant emerging and developing countries. In contrast, Russia's and Ukraine's OFDI are more concentrated on tax havens, including a significant proportion of round-tripping investment.

When it comes to the industrial distribution of NWEC and PCTE OFDI, the paucity of very scattered data is even worse. Overall, OFDI from the NWECs is highly concentrated in the services sector though the share of the manufacturing industry is rather significant. MNCs from PCTEs invest abroad, first in the services industry, then in the manufacturing industry, and a minor share of OFDI flows into the primary sector (oil, gas, raw materials). Among the few exceptions to this scheme, regarding OFDI in services, a more significant share has been invested abroad in finance and banking from the Czech Republic and Estonia. The weight of the manufacturing industry and then the primary sector in OFDI is comparatively high in Russia.

20.5 Comparative results of econometric testing

In view of verifying whether the determinants of NWEC and PCTE OFDI are in tune with Dunning's IDP model and Matthews' LLL hypothesis, and in line with a previous modelling (Andreff, 2003), an econometric model has been estimated, taking on board for explaining each home country i's outward foreign direct investment stock in year t ($OFDI_{i,t}$) over the 2000–2015 period of time, the following variables:

$$OFDI_{i,t} = a.GDP/capita_{i,t} + b.\ SIZE_{i,t} + c.g_{i,t} + d.TECH_{i,t} + e.\ Xhightec_{i,t} + f.\ INFDI_{i,t-k} + u_i$$

with the explanatory variables standing for:

$GDP/capita_{i,t}$: gross domestic product per inhabitant in home country i in year t used as a proxy for the country's level of economic development;

$SIZE_{i,t}$: domestic market size[4] of home country i in year t (either gross domestic product $GDP_{i,t}$ or population $POP_{i,t}$ can be used as a proxy for domestic economic size);

$g_{i,t}$: the annual index of GDP growth in home country i in year t;

$TECH_{i,t}$: technological level in home country i in year t; under the constraint of available data, the proxy for this variable is:

$Patent_{i,t}$: the number of technological patents registered in home country i in year t in the NWECs subsample, and

$SCIENT_{i,t}$: the number of scientists working in home country i in year t in the PCTEs subsample;

$Xhightec_{i,t}$: the share of high-technology exported products in overall export[5] of home country i in year t;

$INFDI_{i,t-k}$: inward foreign direct investment stock hosted in home country i in year $t-k$.

Data on outward and inward FDI stock are taken from UNCTAD, while statistics for GDP (in PPP $), population, GDP per inhabitant, GDP growth rate, the number of patents, the number of scientists, and the share of high-tech export in overall export have been collected from the World Bank database for the same 16 years in the 11 NWECs and 15 operational PCTEs. Those readers interested in detailed data collection and econometric technicalities – first an OLS estimation, then using a panel data with testing fixed and random effects – are referred to Andreff and Andreff (2017) and Andreff (2017b).

The major results of econometric testing (Appendix 20.1 for the NWECs and Appendix 20.2 for the PCTEs) confirm the relevance of a Dunning-Matthews theoretical framework.

The level of economic development (GDP/capita) is a significant push factor that determines OFDI. The higher an NWEC's level of economic development, the more it invests abroad, absolutely in tune with Dunning's IDP model. The same relationship holds, though with lower coefficients, for the PCTE subsample when using an OLS regression. With panel data testing, the relationship weakens and turns out to be negative some years because a part of the IDP model's explanation is captured by the LLL effect triggered by previous inward FDI. Investment of PCTE-based MNCs is pushed outwards by an increasing level of domestic economic development on the one hand and, on the other hand, by cooperation and competition with foreign (Western) MNCs established in their domestic market.

In both subsamples (NWECs and PCTEs), the economic size is a significant explanatory variable of OFDI. When it comes to the NWECs, a negative sign relating OFDI to GDP confirms Kayam's (2009) results. The negative sign for the coefficient of this variable means that the smaller an NWEC, *i.e.* the smaller its domestic market size, the more its firms substitute OFDI for domestic investment in a small home market. This indirectly verifies a substitution effect between OFDI and local investment in NWEC-based MNCs' strategies. Since the same relationship can be taken for granted in the case of PCTEs whose domestic markets (except Russia's) are much smaller than the NWECs' ones, the domestic economic size is approximated by population that markedly differentiates across PCTEs. The relationship is significant but positive, which can be interpreted as the bigger a PCTE domestic economy (such as Poland), the bigger is its firms' capacity to invest abroad.

GDP growth rate boosts OFDI in both samples; fast-growing home economies are more likely to invest abroad. MNCs from fast-growing NWEC and PCTE home countries are likely to invest more abroad than MNCs from NWECs and PCTEs with slower growth. However, the relationship is not significant when inward FDI is lagged by three years in the NWEC subsample and when it is lagged by one year in the PCTE subsample. This suggests that both GDP growth rate and inward FDI (see below) determine OFDI, but it takes a different span of time for this triangular relationship to be plainly at work (and for the LLL effect to strongly interfere with Dunning's IDP).

Technological variables are explanatory of NWECs' and PCTEs' OFDI though with a negative sign whatever the proxy adopted for technological level ($SCIENT_{i,t}$ or $Patent_{i,t}$). OFDI is higher when the number of scientists or registered patents in the home economy is lower. NWEC-based and PCTE-based MNCs do not benefit from a domestic technological gap to invest abroad because only few of them, in few industries, are on the global technological frontier. The observed results rather suggest that they invest abroad in view of seeking technological assets (absent in the home country and missing to the domestic scientists), while they are using less sophisticated technologies than the brand new ones (based on the last patents registered) and probably technologies more adapted to the economic environment of their neighbouring emerging and developing countries. Such a result is in line with analyses that stress the role of strategic asset seeking, especially for firms that face ownership disadvantages and wish to leverage them with knowledge acquired from abroad. This strategy has appeared in the car industry, for instance, in the Geely-Volvo case (Balcet & Ruet, 2011), while at the macroeconomic level, it has seriously jeopardised the standard foreign trade and investment theory (Andreff & Balcet, 2013). This evidence is a springboard for further research.

With regard to the share of high-tech products in overall exports, it is a determinant of OFDI only when this ratio is over 25% (below this share, the coefficient is not significant) in the NWECs. It is only when NWECs reach a high enough domestic technological level that this provides a comparative advantage on which their local firms can rely for investing abroad in addition to their high-tech exports (a complementary relationship between OFDI and high-tech export). But this relationship is not significant below 25% of high-tech products in total exports. Then, the interpretation goes as follows. There is a technological gap between NWEC-based MNCs and their competitors based in the most technologically advanced economies; they suffer from a negative technological gap that hinders their OFDI instead of benefitting from a positive gap, which usually triggers OFDI. Firms are not yet capable of exploiting their technologies through investing abroad, although they can export (a few) high-tech products of good quality.

A similar analysis pertains to PCTE-based MNCs, which suffer from a negative technological gap compared with companies based in the most technologically advanced economies but, owing to lower domestic production costs, they are used to specialise in exporting lower specifications and differentiated quality products. However, OFDI can substitute this kind of high-tech exports (see the negative sign of the coefficient, Appendix 20.2). Contrary to NWEC-based MNCs, there is a substitution effect between OFDI and high-tech exports from PCTEs.

Finally, a strong and significant relationship between OFDI and lagged inward FDI suggests that a process similar to Mathews' LLL hypothesis must be at work. The coefficient for this relationship increases with the time lag when one goes from inward FDI one year before up to three years before. It takes time for LLL relationships to materialise and thus for previous inward FDI to strengthen as a determinant of OFDI. In the case of PCTEs, this confirms Gorynia et al. (2014) and Davidkov and Yordanova's (2015) conjectures. The econometric evidence means that NWEC-based and PCTE-based MNCs greatly benefit from their local relationships with (Western) foreign investors who previously invested in their home domestic economies. The value of coefficients relating PCTEs' OFDI to their previous inward FDI is higher than in the NWECs' case; the LLL effect surprisingly shows up as being stronger in PCTE-based MNCs than in NWEC-based MNCs even though the latter are looking more like dragon multinationals for which Matthews has conceptualised the LLL hypothesis.

Overall, the level of economic development and home market size are major determinants of NWECs and PCTEs' OFDI. The home country's technological level also plays a role in the process, either as a constraint pushing investment abroad in view of acquiring technological assets that are missing in the home country or as a factor of specialisation in lower quality (and cost) high-tech exports that may be completed (NWECs) or substituted (PCTEs) by OFDI. Opening the home country to inward FDI and (Western) foreign MNCs has been a rocket pad for its further OFDI and expansion of its own MNCs. PCTEs seem to stick to a similar scheme of OFDI as the one of NWECs; their companies taking a stake in relationships (linkage, leverage, learning) with foreign investors in their domestic economy for expanding their investment abroad. This may lead NWECs and PCTEs to consolidate their position in the third stage of the IDP model in the years to come.

20.6 Conclusion

During the past decade or so, the number of studies about OFDI from emerging and transition economies has quickly increased. However, very few studies have compared OFDI in all transition economies, and practically no one has compared OFDI across the NWECs since this country sample has been defined only recently. The present chapter is a first attempt at comparing OFDI from transition economies and from the NWECs. A number of similarities have been exhibited as well as some subsample specificities, or time lags, between respectively NWEC-based and PCTE-based MNCs. The next step in this new avenue for further research should be to systematically compare OFDI in the two country subsamples retained in this chapter with better-known OFDI undertaken by BRICS-based companies.

Notes

1 Afghanistan, Algeria, Angola, Benin, Burma, Congo, Ethiopia, Guinea, Iraq, Madagascar, Mozambique, Nicaragua, South Yemen, Syria, and Tanzania at that time.
2 Argentine investors began cross-border production in the first half of the 20th century and were still dominating the geography of Southern American FDI in 1970; now, they account for a much smaller share.
3 Adding to the crisis impact, Western sanctions and Russian counter-embargo must have affected Russian OFDI downwards. Ruble depreciation since 2014 is also a hindrance to OFDI by Russian-based MNCs.
4 The market size can be taken as either the population (POP is taken on board for the PCTEs) or GDP (retained in the case of NWECs, all with big populations).
5 $Xhightec_{i,t}$ is treated as a dummy variable. Each year a country falls in a class 1 if its ratio x of high-tech export to overall export is between 0% and 5% ($0 < x \leq 5\%$); it falls in class 2 if the ratio is between 5% and 25% ($5\% < x \leq 25\%$); and it falls in class 3 if the ratio is higher than 25% ($x > 25\%$). Class 1 is taken as the reference in econometric testing.

References

Andreff, M. and Andreff, W. (2017). Multinational companies from transition economies and their outward foreign direct investment. *Russian Journal of Economics (Voprosy Ekonomiki)*, *3*(4), 445–74.

Andreff, W. (1976). *Profits et structures du capitalisme mondial*. Paris: Calmann-Lévy.

Andreff, W. (1987). *Les multinationales*, Repères 54. Paris: La Découverte.

Andreff, W. (1989). Testing the Soviet-type industrialisation model in socialist-orientated developing countries. In S. Gomulka, Y.C. Ha and C.O. Kim (Eds.). *Economic Reforms in the Socialist World* (pp. 183–99), London: Macmillan.

Andreff, W. (1996). *Les multinationales globales*. Repères 187. Paris: La Découverte.

Andreff, W. (1999). The global strategy of multinational corporations and their assessment of Eastern European and C.I.S. countries. In V. Tikhomirov (Ed.). *Anatomy of the 1998 Russian Crisis* (pp. 9–53), Melbourne: Contemporary Europe Research Centre, The University of Melbourne.

Andreff, W. (2002). The new multinational corporations from transition countries. *Economic Systems*, *25*(4), 371–79.

Andreff, W. (2003). The newly emerging TNCs from economies in transition: A comparison with Third World outward FDI. *Transnational Corporations*, *12*(2), 73–118.

Andreff, W. (2007). Transition through different corporate governance structures in postsocialist economies. Which convergence? In H. Overbeek, B. van Apeldoorn and A. Nölke (Eds.). *The Transnational Politics of Corporate Governance Regulation* (pp. 155–76), Abingdon: Routledge.

Andreff, W. (2014). Outward foreign direct investment by Brazilian and Indian multinational companies: Comparison with Russian-Chinese multinationals. In S. Balashova and V. Matyushok (Eds.). *The Trajectory of Growth and Structural Transformation of the World Economy Amid International Instability* (pp. 252–97), Moscow: Peoples' Friendship University of Russia, Moscow.

Andreff, W. (2016a). Sampling emerging economies from the standpoint of their outward foreign direct investment. *Emerging Economies*, 4, 15–19 (Osservatorio sulle economie emergent – Torino).

Andreff, W. (2016b). Outward foreign direct investment from BRIC countries: Comparing strategies of Brazilian, Russian, Indian and Chinese multinational companies. *European Journal of Comparative Economics*, 12(2), 79–131.

Andreff, W. (2016c). Maturing strategies of Russian multinational companies: Comparison with Chinese multinationals. In D. Dyker (Ed.). The World Scientific Reference on Globalisation in Eurasia and the Pacific Rim: Investment, Innovation, Energy, Migration and Development (*Foreign Investment* (Vol. 1, pp. 77–120)), London: Imperial College Press/World Scientific.

Andreff, W. (2017a). Maturing strategies of Russian multinational companies: A historical perspective. In K. Liuhto, S. Sutyrin and J.-M. F. Blanchard (Eds.). *The Russian Economy and Foreign Direct Investment* (pp. 25–42), Abingdon: Routledge.

Andreff, W. (2017b). New-wave emerging multinational companies: The determinants of their outward foreign direct investment. *Chinese Business Review*, 16(2), 55–81.

Andreff, W. and Balcet, G. (2013). Emerging countries' multinational companies investing in developed countries: At odds with the HOS paradigm? *European Journal of Comparative Economics*, 10(1), 3–26.

Anil, I., Cakir, O., Canel, C. and Porterfield, R. (2011). A comparison of inward and outward foreign direct investment determinants in Turkey. *International Journal of Business and Social Science*, 20(2), 141–55.

Balcet, G. and Ruet, J. (2011). From joint ventures to national champions or global players? Alliances and technological catching-up in Chinese and Indian automotive industries. *European Review of Industrial Economics and Policy* [online serial], 3.

Banga, R. (2007). Drivers of outward foreign direct investment from Asian developing countries. UNCTAD-India, pp. 195–215.

Bano, S. and Tabbada, J. (2015). Foreign direct investment outflows: Asian developing countries. *Journal of Economic Integration*, 30(2), 359–98.

Bulatov, A. S. (2001). Russian direct investment abroad: History, motives, finance, control and planning. *Economics of Planning*, 34(3), 179–94.

Casas, R. and Dambrauskaitė, V. (2011). Impact of external business environment factors on internationalization of Lithuanian born global companies. *Ekonomika*, 90(3), 120–35.

Cheewatrakoolpong, K. and Boonprakaikawe, J. (2015). Factors influencing outward FDI: A case study of Thailand in comparison with Singapore and Malaysia. *Southeast Asian Journal of Economics*, 3(2), 123–41.

Damijan, J., Kostevc, C. and Rojec, M. (2014). Outward FDI and company performance in CEECs. *CESIS Electronic Working Paper Series*, No. 381.

Davidkov, T. and Yordanova, D. (2015). Enhancing SME internationalization in a transition economy: The role of internal factors. *International Journal of Latest Trends in Finance & Economic Sciences*, 5(3), 945–56.

Dunning, J. H. (1981). Explaining the international direct investment position of countries: Towards a dynamic or development approach. *Weltwirtschaftliches Archiv*, 119, 30–64.

Dunning, J. H. and Narula, R. (1998). The investment development path revisited: Some emerging issues. In J. H. Dunning and R. Narula (Eds.). *Foreign Direct Investment and Governments. Catalysts for Economic Restructuring* (pp. 1–41), London: Routledge.

Goh, S. K. and Wong, K. N. (2011). Malaysia's outward FDI: The effects of host market size and home government policy. *Journal of Policy Modeling*, 33(3), 497–510.

Gorynia, M., Nowak, J. and Wolniak, R. (2010). Foreign direct investment of Central and Eastern European countries, and the investment development path revisited. *Eastern Journal of European Studies*, 1(2), 21–36.

Gorynia, M., Nowak, J., Trapczynski, P. and Wolniak, R. (2014). Internationalization of Polish firms via foreign direct investment: A multiple-case study approach. In M. A. Marinov and S. T. Marinova (Eds.). *Successes and Challenges of Emerging Economy Multinationals* (pp. 184–216), London: Palgrave Macmillan.

Götz, M. (2013). Exploring foreign direct investment from Poland using grounded theory method. *Oeconomica Copernicana*, 3(4), 73–96.

Katz, J. and Kosacoff, B. (1984). Les multinationales de l'Argentine. In S. Lall (Ed.). *Les multinationales originaires du Tiers Monde* (pp. 179–269), Paris: Presses Universitaires de France.

Kayam, S. S. (2009). *Home Market Determinants of FDI Outflows from Developing and Transition Economies.* Eskisehir: Anadolu International Conference in Economics, June 17–19.

Kayam, S. S. and Hisarciklilar, M. (2009). Determinants of Turkish FDI abroad. *Topics in Middle Eastern and North African Economies,* 11.

Kuzel, M. (2017). The investment development path: Evidence from Poland and other countries of the Visegrad group. *Journal of East-West Business, 23*(1), 1–40.

Masron, T. A. and Shahbudin, A. (2010). Push factors of outward FDI: Evidence from Malaysia and Thailand. *Journal of Business & Policy Research, 5*(1), 54–68.

Mathews, J. A. (2002). *Dragon Multinationals: Toward a New Model for Global Growth.* New York, NY: Oxford University Press.

Mathews, J. A. (2006). Dragon multinationals: New players in 21st century globalisation. *Asia Pacific Journal of Management, 23*(5), 5–27.

Mockaitis, A. I., Vaiginiené, E. and Giedraitis, V. (2006). The internationalization efforts of Lithuanian manufacturing firms – Strategy or luck? *Research in International Business and Finance, 20*(1), 111–26.

ONU. (1978). *Les sociétés transnationales dans le développement mondial: un réexamen.* New York, NY: Nations Unies.

Puig-Gomez, A. (2014). Foreign direct investment and industrial policy: A comparison of results for the cases of Slovenia and Hungary. *International Journal of Business and Social Science, 5*(8), 73–9.

Rugraff, E. (2010). Strengths and weaknesses of the outward FDI paths of the Central European countries. *Post-Communist Economies, 22*(1), 1–17.

Saad, R. M., Noor, A. H. M. and Nor, A. H. S. M. (2014). Developing countries' outward investment: Push factors for Malaysia. *Procedia—Social and Behavioral Sciences, 130,* 237–46.

Sauvant, K. P. (2008). (Ed.). *The Rise of Transnational Corporations from Emerging Markets: Threat or Opportunity?* Cheltenham: Edward Elgar.

Teo, Y. N., Tham, S. Y. and Kam, A. J. Y. (2015). Re-examining the determinants of Malaysia's outward FDI. *Pertanika Journal of Social Sciences & Humanities, 23*(S), 173–88.

UN. (1988). *Transnational Corporations in World Development: Trends and Prospects.* New York, NY: United Nations.

UNCTAD. (1994). *World Investment Report: Transnational Corporations, Employment and the Workplace.* Geneva: United Nations.

UNCTAD. (2020). *World Investment Report: International Production Beyond the Pandemic.* New York, NY and Geneva: United Nations (and previous issues).

UNTCMD. (1992). *The East-West Business Directory 1991/1992* (Sales No. E.92.II.A.20). New York, NY: United Nations, Transnational Corporations and Management Division.

Wasowska, A. (2013). Ownership structure and the internationalization process of publicly-listed companies in Poland. *Management and Business Administration. Central Europe, 22*(3), 82–97.

Wilkins, M. (1970). *The Emergence of Multinational Enterprise.* Cambridge, MA: Harvard University Press.

Wilkins, M. (1990). Investissement étranger et financement de la croissance américaine (XIXe siècle-début du XXe). *Revue d'Economie Financière, 14*(2), 67–79.

Appendices

Appendix 20.1 The determinants of outward foreign direct investment from New Wave Emerging Countries

Dependent variables	OLS			Panel data					
				Fixed effects			Random effects		
	H1: LLL t–1	H2: LLL t–2	H3: LLL t–3	H1: LLL t–1	H2: LLL t–2	H3: LLL t–3	H1: LLL t–1	H2: LLL t–2	H3: LLL t–3
GDP	−0.195**	−0.182***	−0.202***	−0.522***	−0.431***	−0.436***	−0.291***	−0.237**	−0.250***
GDP per capita	3.013***	3.092***	3.199***	5.321***	5.332***	5.452***	3.829***	3.955***	4.108***
GDP growth rate	76.258*	101.058**	52.9998	74.692*	97.075**	45.256	72.215*	96.278**	44.230
C2 X high tech	4.023	3.568	3.469	−3.271	−2.997	−3.589	1.444	1.212	0.831
C3 X high tech	9.478***	9.213***	8.829***	−4.755	−3.457	−4.709	2.719	3.208	2.585
Patent	−0.286***	−0.315***	−0.293***	−0.242**	−0.295***	−0.293***	−0.265**	−0.311***	−0.303***
INFDI t–1	0.255***			0.262***			0.269***		
INFDI t–2		0.282***			0.272***			0.283***	
INFDI t–3			0.310***			0.306***			0.315***
Constant	−102.357**	−128.864***	−78.925**	−108.755**	−133.905***	−80.506**	−101.918**	−128.757***	−75.349*
σ u				15.165	13.969	13.732	8.814	8.663	8.240
σ e				14.052	13.719	13.236	14.052	13.719	13.236
σ				0.538	0.509	0.518	0.282	0.285	0.279

σ u is the standard deviation of the country-level random effects.

σ e is the standard deviation of the pure error term.

σ is the proportionate contribution to the total variance by the panel-level variance component.

*** Significant at a 1% threshold.

** At 5%.

* At 10%.

Appendix 20.2 The determinants of outward foreign direct investment from Post-Communist Transition Economies

Dependent variables	OLS			Panel data					
				Fixed effects			*Random effects*		
	H1: LLL t–1	H2: LLL t–2	H3: LLL t–3	H1: LLL t–1	H2: LLL t–2	H3: LLL t–3	H1: LLL t–1	H2: LLL t–2	H3: LLL t–3
GDP per capita	1.268***	1.676***	1.852***	−0.786	−0.115	0.248	−0.168	0.507	0.699
GDP growth rate	0.465	0.966**	0.909**	0.087	0.704**	0.676**	0.124	0.724**	0.649*
POP	1.424***	1.521***	1.666***	−5.885*	10.522***	−13.304***	1.208***	1.301***	1.530***
SCIENT	−5.330***	−5.028***	−5.325***	−4.123***	−3.686***	−5.504***	−4.617***	−4.141***	−4.972***
X high tech	−0.789**	−0.921***	−1.014***	−1.419**	−1.947***	−1.661***	−1.118**	−1.542***	−1.590***
INFDI t–1	0.799***			0.799***			0.826***		
INFDI t–2		0.838***			0.798***			0.847***	
INFDI t–3			0.952***			0.945***			0.981***
Constant	−20.902***	−26.128***	−27.075***	147.94**	241.02***	302.93***	−4.378	−10.196	−10.736
σ u				258.62	433.13	550.24	15.088	15.645	16.464
σ e				22.767	24.452	22.523	22.767	24.452	22.523
σ				0.992	0.997	0.998	0.305	0.290	0.348

σ u is the standard deviation of the country-level random effects.

σ e is the standard deviation of the pure error term.

σ is the proportionate contribution to the total variance by the panel-level variance component.

*** Significant at a 1% threshold.

** At 5%.

* At 10%.

21

PARALLEL PROCESSES AND DIVERGENT OUTCOMES

The Transformation of the Economies of Former Socialist Countries

Alexander Chepurenko

SCHOOL OF SOCIOLOGY, NATIONAL RESEARCH UNIVERSITY
HIGHER SCHOOL OF ECONOMICS, MOSCOW

FEDERAL CENTER OF THEORETICAL AND APPLIED SOCIOLOGY OF
THE RUSSIAN ACADEMY OF SCIENCES, MOSCOW

Miklós Szanyi

FACULTY OF ECONOMICS AND BUSINESS ADMINISTRATION,
UNIVERSITY OF SZEGED, SZEGED

KRTK INSTITUTE OF WORLD ECONOMICS, BUDAPEST, HUNGARY

All happy families are alike, each unhappy family is unhappy in its own way.

Leo Tolstoy, *Anna Karenina*

21.1 Introduction

The collapse of Socialism in several countries in the eastern part of Europe in the late 1980s and beginning of the 1990s raised many hopes and fostered the idea of a more or less uniform and easy transition toward the Western model of market and democracy.

After the economic and political collapse of the Soviet bloc, US-led international advisory institutions continued exporting the then-still-successful neoliberal agenda to the region in the form of the SLIP (stabilization – liberalization – institutional reforms – privatization) recommendations. The first phase of the systemic changes in Central and Eastern Europe (CEE) was designed according to the logic of this program. The transformation started with a serious economic decline in all transition economies (Kornai, 1994). The main reason for the crisis was the fundamental change in the environment. Public demand contracted to a small fragment of previous levels due to fiscal problems and the drop in demand for military equipment. Protected export markets of the Soviet bloc were liberalized and became competitive. Consequently, the GDP dropped, unemployment increased and the state budget ran huge deficits.

 DOI: 10.4324/9781003144366-25

The most urgent policy task was, therefore, the stabilization of the economy, mainly through austerity measures, followed by the stepwise introduction of the market economic institutions and competition through the liberalization of the markets, including imports. Former state-owned enterprises, SOE, should become subject of the privatization. All these measures meant a huge workload not only for governments but also for companies. Firms also had to make adjustment steps, establishing themselves almost from scratch.

However, already in the middle of the 1990s, it became clear that the development would be neither quick nor direct and uniform. The Central European and Baltic countries followed the general principles of the Washington Consensus (Williamson 1989), which, at that time, played the role of a tuning fork of strategies of the capitalist transition of these countries in a more accurate way and achieved visible success in order to enable a perspective of the EU accession. Meanwhile, Southeast European countries and the remnants of the former USSR were less consistent and speedy. The main reasons of these differences at that time were connected with different models and the tempo of privatization and institution building, chosen by the governments of former Socialist countries, i.e. shock therapy vs. gradual reforms, under the influence of several internal circumstances (Heybey and Murrell, 1999; Kolodko, 2000; Roland, 2000; Denizer et al., 2001).

The countries, which seemed to be more successful, especially those that formed the Visegrad group in 1991, could count on a quick European Union accession. Other, mostly SEE countries' accession became problematic because of serious institutional weaknesses that should be first corrected to receive this permission. It also became clear that the Commonwealth of Independent States (CIS) and some nonaligned former Soviet republics would never become part of the big Europe due to geopolitical reasons. Thus, the concept of a "transition" of the complete former Eastern bloc, toward a Western-styled capitalism, lost its relevance.

After the crisis of 2008–2009, it became evident that, even in the new EU member states, different economic and political developments manifested. The ECE economies slowed down and exhibited growth rates analogous to the low rates prevailing in the "old" EU countries. The formulation of the new integration pattern produced a high structural unemployment and increasing inequality. These effects again reduced the popularity of market economic transition and European integration and fostered populist parties in several new EU member states.

Even more problematic trends occurred in some Balkan and CIS countries, where corruption and political entrepreneurship played a much more important role due to the weakness of the civil society and opposition, as well as ethnic conflicts, raised serious crises and shaped the negative conditions for the establishment of a market economy (Falcetti et al., 2003). Especially, some former Soviet republics were either stuck in the very initial stage of reforms or in the establishment of mixed models of economy, with a strong role of the state and embedded nepotism (Jones Luong, 2002). Moreover, in the two biggest countries of the former Soviet Union, Russia and Ukraine, "crony capitalism" (Haber, 2002) flourished, known from the modern history of Asia and Latin America.

Thus, at least in the first decade of the 21st century, the applicability of the normative paradigm of a "systemic transition", based on the idea of import and adaptation of Western institutions, has been questioned. Instead, alternative economic and social models have evolved, reflecting the intrinsic characteristics of the economies and societies. The search for alternative theories was complicated and is still not finished.

The chapter is structured as follows. In the next part, we describe the state of the art in the literature on socio-economic aspects of systemic change in the CEE. The third, fourth and fifth parts are devoted to the analysis of the related processes in the East and Central Europe (ECE), the Balkans and the three former USSR republics, Russia, Ukraine and Belorussia, respectively. The final part contains some concluding remarks.

21.2 State of literature on the reasons of different trajectories of Post-Socialist economic development in Central and Eastern Europe (CEE)

The literature on the diversity of Post-Socialist development in Europe is discussing three related questions. First, whether the development of the Post-Socialist economies goes in the same or different directions. These sorts of considerations usually led toward a typology of Post-Socialist trajectories. Second, what are the reasons or main sets of factors behind the diversity of the groups of economies and societies? Third, what is the impact of these factors on economic and social development? How do they divert countries from the originally envisaged development path and what are the dynamics of these processes?

At the very beginning, the processes of systemic changes in these countries were viewed mostly as an import of Western institutions, based on the "Washington Consensus" and its SLIP model (stabilization – liberalization – institutions' building – privatization of SOEs) and "modernization through integration" with the EU, quite similar to the "modernization through internationalization" in some countries of Latin America (Przeworski et al., 1995). It was expected that the developmental model would be the same and would follow the strategic concepts of a quick and radical systemic transition designed by international financial organizations. The main question was: how to move from the planned economy to market economies, should it be achieved quickly as a "big bang" or through gradualist reforms? (Podkaminer, 2013, p.11). Any divergence from the common and uniform way of systemic transition was seen as temporary tension that can be surmounted.

In spite, such a view was much too simplistic, its focus on the emergence of new economic institutions, which should adequately support the market economy and its actors during the process of systemic changes, was a challenge in helping to elaborate new theoretical interpretations of the systemic change, using concepts of the new institutionalism, public choice, evolutionary and behavioral economics (Kornai, 1990, 2000; Lavigne, 1995; Roland, 2000; Aslund, 2002). But close to the end of the first decade of the "transition", it became evident that the outcomes of the market reforms differed very much by country and were far from the initial hopes of the quick establishment of a sustainable market economy and democratic political order; the concept of a "transition" began to lose its authority (Carothers, 2002). It seemed that the processes in the region should be viewed as an open-ended transformation of the former system, with all the constraints inherited, rather than as a lineal transition toward a single given predetermined goal.

Thus, at the beginning of the 2000s, the variety of capitalism (VoC, see Hall and Soskice, 2001; Amable, 2003) approach replaced the "transition" paradigm and was used to explain the realms in the CEE (Mendelski, 2010; Bluhm, 2010). The VoC theory initially was developed to explain the Western realms with its two main types of contemporary capitalism, the liberal market economy (LME) and the coordinated market economy (CME). Accordingly, the systemic changes in the CEE region were no longer considered, in terms of establishing any homogeneous "Eastern European capitalism" (Stark 1996), and the applications of the VoC theory to the CEE countries went soon beyond the LME vs. CME typology. In search of reasons of peculiarities of the economic development of these countries, several new concepts were proposed in the literature (King and Szelenyi, 2005; Lane and Myant, 2007; Nölke and Vliegenthart, 2009; Bohle and Greskovits, 2012; Schneider and Paunescu, 2012; Bluhm et al., 2014; Farkas, 2016).

After the economic crisis of 2008–2009, the development of some Post-Socialist economies, including the CEE countries, became even more problematic. Mainly, the new explanations sought to derive the specific features of several Post-Socialist economies and societies from the analysis of different historical trajectories of the development. Path dependence concept (North, 1990), and the idea of the Polanyian pendulum (Polányi, 1944; Nölke and May, 2019), featured this approach. The lack of substantial convergence during the process of transition and the causes and consequences of the subordinate place in the international division of labor was emphasized characterizing the CEE countries "dependent market economies" (DMEs) or "semi-periphery economies" (Nölke and Vliegenthart, 2009).

According to the "path dependence" approach, former Socialist economies' development was predetermined by the historic traditions of three former empires – the Austrian (ECE), the Ottoman (SEE) and the Russian (CIS and former Soviet republics except Baltic states). The DME concept or "semi-periphery economy" means that Post-Socialist economies were subordinated to the rules of neoliberal globalization, by the power of MNCs and the financial support coming from international donors. They became critically dependent on these external tools of economic development and less able to develop based on the intrinsic drivers and actors (small entrepreneurship, household behavior, etc.). Szanyi (2019a) argued that this kind of dependence on regional political and economic powers is observed throughout the modern history of CEE. Based on Ferenc Jánossy's "trend lines of economic development" concept, Szanyi and Szabó (2020) stated that the historic path dependence fixed the potential growth trajectories for the various Post-Socialist countries. Changes in the slope of the trend lines (that is long-term adjustment of the development trajectory) happened rarely and only occasionally offering the catching up opportunities to a few countries.

However, all these concepts focused mainly on ECE and partly on Baltic States; they did not say much about the development outside of the region, in the CIS or Balkan States, where processes called "backslide transition" happened in an even more open way (Cianetti et al., 2018).

An empirically based approach, to disclose the specifics of some trends in CEE, was elaborated by Baltowski, Kozarzewski and Mickiewicz (2020), who attempted to contribute to the conceptualization of "state capitalism". They fixed six basic features of state capitalism as follows: "(1) politicization of SOEs: the government and political elite use the state-controlled enterprise sector as a source of rents; (2) politicization of SOEs à rebours: the state-controlled enterprise sector (their staff, executives and affiliated trade unions, among others) is the main rent-seeker itself; (3) cronyism: the main beneficiaries of state capitalism are private agents from outside the public sector; (4) oligarchy (a consolidated form of cronyism): very powerful private agents have a very significant influence on economic policy; (5) economic populism (clientelism): a patronage system where the political elite transfers goods to clients in chosen social groups expecting their political support in return; (6) economic nationalism: the state exerts an impact on the economy the declared objective of which is to enhance, in the long run, the state's political capacity, military power or international importance. The state itself may be treated here as the major beneficiary" (Papko and Kozarzewski, 2020, p. 9–10).

State capitalism, or according to some other authors, the "state-permeated capitalism" (Nölke and May, 2019) was used to explain developments in very different Post-Socialist countries (Szanyi, 2019b), starting with the EU members Hungary and Poland, up to dictatorships (like Belarus or Turkmenia) and autocracies (like Russia, Azerbaijan or Kazakhstan).

In parallel, Kornai (2016) provided a conceptual description of the varieties of transition in Post-Socialist countries making the basic distinction based on three primary and six secondary characteristics of property ownership and the mechanisms of economic coordination as well as some important consequences (ibidem, p. 553). The revision of the concept expanded the dichotomy and introduced a third "hybrid" paradigm: autocracy and patronage (ibidem, p. 565). However, autocracy was interpreted mainly as a variation of the political system, being an important but not exclusive element of the system. Therefore, the original primary and secondary characteristics of the two basic paradigms (capitalism and socialism) may remain applicable regardless of the political systems (democracy, autocracy and dictatorship). In this sense, Milanovic (2019) is using the term "political capitalism".

A similar but more comprehensive concept was developed by Magyar and Madlovics (2020), based on the assumption that the key difference between them consists in the level of separation of the three different spheres of social action – politics, economy and communal activities. "Proceeding from the West towards the East, it can be observed that this separation of the spheres of social action has either not been realized or only rudimentarily" (Magyar and Madlovics, 2020, p. 9). Thus, they are providing the three basic and three "intermediate types" of CEE socio-economic systems. The three basic types are the liberal democracy, communist dictatorship and patronal autocracy, and the three intermediate types are the conservative autocracy, market-exploiting dictatorship and patronal democracy. This typology is also reflecting the CIS and other Post-Soviet countries, and China and Asian Socialist regimes as well. However, being a normative construct, it does not enable us to trace the economic dynamics and to discover the reasons of the different tempo of economic development across the Post-Socialist countries.

There are some methodological questions that hamper the progress of comparative Post-Socialist economy research.

First, the "path dependence" explanations look desperate because, when the trajectories of these countries are completely predetermined by the historic past, any activities of political entrepreneurs to establish new institutions, maintaining the norms and rules of a market economy, should be viewed as doomed forever. As Djankov and Hauck (2016) suggested, there is strong empirical evidence on the correlation of transition performance and imperial affiliation, as well as religion in this Post-Socialist region.

Second, some streams of literature raise doubts about whether capitalism is a prospective destination point of the developments at last in some former Socialist countries ("backslide transition" or some of the ideal types of Post-Socialist regimes), "we are trapped in the analytical language that gained dominance in the 1990s. Although the transition paradigm has been consensually rejected, we kept the terminological framework of Western-type polities and have continued to use the language of liberal democracy to describe post-communist systems" (Magyar and Madlovics, 2020, p. 3).

Third, the question about the nexus between the common features and the specifics of each region or its economy in the larger CEE area is discussed.

Fourth, there is no evidence of any interplay of the reasons and factors between the inter-regional versus intra-regional diversity of the socio-economic development models of the CEE countries.

21.3 East-Central Europe (ECE) in the 1990s–2010s

The main question of the systemic change process in ECE now is: why has the envisaged development of LME stalled, and in some sense, rolled back, even in the most advanced Post-Socialist economies? The argument that the fundamental concept of the LME is in crisis after 2008–2009 can only partially explain the decline of liberal concept in ECE countries, some local circumstances contributed to the demise of the LME principle there.

The analysis will separate the two periods of pro-market economic policy in the ECE countries.

21.3.1 Phase one: ECE liberal transition

During the 1980s, economic and military dominance of the United States posed impossible development tasks for the Soviet bloc that could not be met. Their catching-up attempts overburdened the economy and produced serious imbalances, especially in the structure of GDP spending. Private consumption declined and serious supply shortages emerged. Additionally, quick technological change and the oil price shocks of the 1970s posed such adjustment challenges that the system of central planning could not meet. Though some small open economies, with more intensive trade and some investment links to the West: Hungary, Poland and Yugoslavia, experimented with partial reforms, aimed at improving the incentives of firms and individuals, and introducing in controlled ways, some elements of the market economy. Yet, the reforms could not fundamentally alter the central planning system, mainly because the most important segments of the economy remained untouched.

After the beginning of systemic changes, however, the ECE governments followed different tactics in their transition policies to keep the countries afloat. The Czech and Slovak governments, for example, depreciated the currency by 60 percent, in order to improve the price competitiveness of the economic agents and increase import prices. This should have provided SOEs with the necessary leeway to take adjustment measures, and manage privatization. The Polish government decided for shock therapy, a quick liberalization of the economy that reinforced companies' adjustment more effectively. Hungary followed a more gradualist policy introducing liberalization measures less quickly and concentrating efforts on foreign investors' attraction into the privatization process.

Variations in the speed and sequencing of the SLIP were the main feature of the "transitology" phase of research (see Roland, 2000). More lasting consequences were bound mainly to the privatization process. The Czech and Slovak did not face large debt burden, hence did not feel forced to sell state property immediately in order to generate budget revenue. Instead, they used the privatization for establishing a proprietor middle class. Privatization was started by the voucher privatization scheme. It was then applied with modifications also by the Russian authorities. This meant distributing vouchers among the citizens for free, which would later be used for obtaining real corporate shares. To ensure the success of the program, the Czech government accommodated the market shocks of liberalization. In the end, most citizens sold their vouchers to state-owned investment funds and did not become proprietors. Instead, the state property was transferred to another type of state property that did not produce more effective owners' control and improvement in corporate activities (Mertlik, 1995). In Slovakia, much of the distributed ownership rights were collected in the hands of the cronies of the Meciar government, thus giving way to a form of insider privatization. The socio-economic results of the voucher privatization in Slovakia, as well as the institutional traps which occurred, were similar in Russia.

The Hungarian privatization preferred the sales method to master the inherited heavy foreign debt burden. Since domestic capital accumulation was very weak, and high level of foreign debt also had to be managed, the lion's share of the SOEs was sold to foreign investors. This led to another kind of institutional trap, namely, producing the DME model (Nölke and Vliegenthart, 2009).

In the case of Poland, a more balanced, transparent and slower privatization process was carried out, which allowed the transfer of state property to domestic owners in competitive ways. The rationale of this choice can be found in the relatively bad economic and political performance of the country during the 1970s and 1980s, culminating in the introduction of the martial law (1980) and the emergence of the Solidarity movement. Solidarity functioned originally as a kind of trade union. Yet, intensive conflicts with the government soon changed it to a political movement that orchestrated later also the transition process. This political heritage required the new Polish governments to seek for a consensus in privatization matters. Therefore, the first comprehensive privatization law was passed only in 1996.

As a consequence of all the SLIP measures, by the end of the 1990s, in the ECE countries, the systemic transformation was by and large finished. Their economies became dominantly privately owned and deeply integrated into the global economy. The integration through FDI also happened in countries that did not favor foreign firms in the privatization process. Essentially, they all became exposed to the global economy and could not develop their own global players competitive in size, and technological level (Szanyi, 2020). This "asymmetric interdependence" amplified critical voices of the transition process after the 2008–2009 crisis in the ECE countries.

21.3.2 Phase two: "Illiberal counter-revolution"

The "illiberal counter-revolution"[1] was led by the nationalistic political and economic elite that did not feel favored in the liberal phase of the economic and political changes (Szanyi, 2017; Magyar and Madlovics, 2020). Global companies usually offered better jobs, higher incomes and they contributed to the budget revenues substantially, despite the fiscal incentives that they received or the usage of transfer pricing to allocate revenues and profit repatriation (Szanyi, 2017). It is mainly the less competitive local business elite that forms an alliance with populist political forces, which fuels the social rejection of the FDI-based development. The new populist political agenda is anti-globalist, anti-EU and anti-democratic (authoritarian).

The rather abrupt change in the political orientation of many ECE countries toward populism (Douarin and Mickiewicz, 2017; Dumas, 2018; Rodrik, 2018) is thus mainly the result of the changing power relations within the national elites. The "comprador elite" (Drahokoupil, 2008), which was ruling during the first stage of the systemic changes, lost influence when the neoliberal agenda was shaken. Another important factor of the change was political: the ECE countries became members of the European Union in 2004, but the anchoring role of the EU gradually lost power after the accession. The third factor was the dissatisfaction of the people with the slow convergence process to other EU member countries. It is very telling that the name of the governing Czech populist party recalls this dissatisfaction: ANO means the "Action of Dissatisfied Citizens".

The populist political parties in the ECE region are pragmatic and less radical when political action is considered. For example, the Hungarian government vehemently opposes the influence of global business on the ground, like their profit repatriation. Yet, selected MNCs continue to receive the same generous fiscal incentives that they used to, from the very beginning of the transition process (Szanyi, 2017). The high-level performance of global business helps keeping the macroeconomic performance rather sound in the region. The other major external source of macroeconomic stability is sizeable cash transfer from the EU.

While ECE governments readily use EU transfers they do not like and hotly debate effective EU control over transfers from the structural funds. These contribute to 2–4 percent of GDP, thus, without them, the ECE economies' growth would stall. Yet, all countries, but especially Poland and Hungary after their illiberal turn, are frequently charged with fraud in the usage of the EU money becoming an additional source of the governing political elite's rent and, thus, strengthening the populist regimes. Nevertheless, the political and economic stability of the ECE region did not change for the worse, under the populist governments, after the EU accession.

As a consequence of the systemic change in the ECE region, a new European division of labor evolved. Core Europe (EU-15) hosts the headquarters of global businesses conducting much of the upper and lower ends of the value chain. Product design, branding, sales promotion, production planning, resource allocation, etc. are activities that usually provide high added value and are the domain of the old EU economies. The ECE region serves as a workshop for the multinational companies. Their activity in the region is concentrated mainly around the production, with a comparatively lower level of value added. Analysts state that this kind of division of labor is stable and the ECE countries entered the "low value capture trap" (Szalavetz, 2017). This means that a multinational firms' local activity does not contribute to more sophisticated, better yielding activities. In the longer run, this could lead to a kind of the middle-income trap.

Concluding, we would point out some factors of closeness of the developmental models of the ECE countries: first, the relatively high level of GDP per capita and well-being, as compared with other Post-Socialist economies (most of the Balkans and CIS) at the initial stage; second, the small internal markets of the ECE, therefore FDI played a very significant role during the first stage of liberalization and privatization; third, the intensive adjustment of the formal institutions to EU rules and a rapid accession to the EU; fourth, the absence of dramatic external shocks (like the war in the former Yugoslavia or the Chechen war in Russia, or the war in the east of Ukraine, etc.); fifth, a common past (most ECE countries belonged to the Austrian empire) and a relatively short period of Socialism.

The variance occurred due to different strategies of the systemic change (shock reforms vs. gradualism), influenced by differences in the initial economic and political conditions. Consequently, different institutional frameworks were established and different structures of powerful interest groups evolved. This latter fact led to the manifestation of country-specific approaches to the role of the FDI (especially in the banking system) and of EU structural funds, the models of the social policy, etc., in ECE countries.

21.4 Balkans and beneath

Traditionally, the East Balkans consisted of Romania, Bulgaria and Greece, while the West Balkans of Yugoslavia and Albania. From the viewpoint of the systemic change, the East and West Balkans should be separated, although they share a lot of common historic and cultural heritage. Their religion and former imperial affiliation (Turkish Empire) was the same, except Croatia and Slovenia. Yet, another important feature, the multiethnic population, was also common. These countries were also rather slow with systemic changes. At least, many analysts state that, during the 1990s, with the exception of Slovenia, no real change in political power occurred in the region, including Romania or Bulgaria led by the ex-Communist Party or its leader (Appel and Orenstein, 2018). This delay in the political transformation, caused by the lack of an influential contra elite, was, perhaps, the most important reason for delays in economic transformation and the slow evolution of market economic institutions. Changes accelerated only after the ending of the Yugoslav war in 1999; the final defeat of the communist regime in 2000, and after the effective negotiations about the EU membership of Romania and Bulgaria in the early 2000s.

21.4.1 Phase one: Civil wars and ethnic conflicts

At the time the ECE countries started changing their political and economic systems, at the beginning of the 1990s, the Balkan countries were involved in huge political and ethnic conflicts.

The dissolution of former Yugoslavia occurred in a very bloody war among, principally, all nationalities of the multiethnic country, except Slovenia. In the first phase, Slovenia and Croatia achieved independence, yet Croatia did not stop the armed conflict with the local Serbian minority until they were expelled from the country's territory in 1995. Slovenia managed, from the very beginning, to start a gradualist transition toward a social-democratic model of a market economy partly with elements of the former Yugoslav self-governance model.

The status of other parts of former Yugoslavia was normalized much later. The countries involved in the war were left out of political and economic integration process with the EU that the Visegrád countries enjoyed. During the first stage, they suffered massively from war, and a total deconstruction of the civil economy; informal and illegal economies, corruption and tax evasion flourished, and the wellbeing of citizens declined rapidly. Under such circumstances, any contingent economic changes were impossible.

The situation was different in the East Balkans. The survival of incumbent Communist Party leaders at the highest levels of the administration led to half-hearted reforms, which did not produce effective institutions (Krastev, 2002). Corruption and crime remained widespread and uncontrolled, which then also thwarted the membership negotiations with the EU (Appel and Orenstein, 2018).

Before the EU accession of Bulgaria, Romania and Croatia, in the second half of the 2000s, changes in these countries were rather slow. They maintained, wherever possible, big business in state ownership, in order to stabilize the economy during the dangerous times of the social and ethnic conflicts (Bitzenis, 2003). Surviving paternalism served as a continuous hotbed of corruption (Hellman et al., 2000; Innes, 2013). Small business development was the main engine of economic growth in agriculture and tourism (in the case of Croatia); however, large segments of this bottom-up small entrepreneurship were informal or even illegal ("unproductive and even destructive entrepreneurship", in terms of Baumol, 1990; see Sauka and Welter, 2007). Later, big business was either transferred to the possession of political cronies (mainly in Bulgaria) or privatized to foreign investors (Romania). In all countries, macroeconomic stabilization had been a primary issue since the wars; corruption and social tensions consumed a lot of state revenue, in the form of high subsidies and unsuccessful tax collection. The situation improved in the 2000s, when trust in the Balkan countries started to evolve after the troubled 1990s. Then, most countries successfully restored macroeconomic stability (Pop-Eleches, 2009). Nevertheless, austerity measures weakened the fragile position of governments (Schimmelfenning and Sedelmeier, 2005), and the generous aids and loans that helped the ECE countries' stabilization were not readily available for the Balkan countries because being conditional on institutional changes (fighting crime and corruption) and other political requirements (Barlemann et al., 2002; Bitzenis, 2003).

In the case of Serbia, the situation was even worse. Yet, Slobodan Milosevic's regime in Serbia was overthrown by the massive NATO air raids that caused tremendous material damage to the otherwise also rather weak Serbian economy. In the case of Bosnia, the political situation was stabilized through massive international subsidies and the repatriated incomes of immigrant workers. However, the shadow economy's share is rather high in all Balkan countries (Williams and Bezeredi, 2020), which causes the governments to be financially relatively weak.

21.4.2 *Phase two: Consolidation*

The violent breakup of the former Yugoslavia and sluggish political transformation of Bulgaria and Romania thwarted institutional changes and economic modernization. EU membership of Romania and Bulgaria was made conditional on tackling corruption and crime (Wedel, 2001; Innes, 2013). The development was reinforced by international institutions and the European Union; yet, the Romanian and Bulgarian governments tried to avoid, or water down, the impacts of the newly established market institutions (Schimmelfenning and Sedelmeier, 2005; Racovita, 2011; Appel and Orenstein, 2018). The process is still monitored by EU institutions. The World Bank governance indicators show permanently low indices for Romania and Bulgaria.

Underdevelopment and institutional weaknesses continued to block the inflow of capital even after the EU accession. The EU transfers were slow to penetrate, due to the lack of competitive projects of the two Balkan countries. FDIs, the main vehicles of economic progress and modernization in the ECE region, were also fairly weak. The Balkans missed investments during the 1990s and afterward and could not provide such strong incentives that would have redirected already established investments. Generally, the market became saturated, FDI slowed down during the 2000s. Few new investments were carried out in Romania and lately, also in Serbia, in manufacturing. Investments in retail trade and the financial sector, that is consumer market-bound activities, took the lion's share of FDI stock (UNCTAD, 2018).

Most of the former Yugoslav republics started neoliberal reforms only at the second stage, after the end of the civil wars. Thus, the conditions for establishing a new economic order were much worse than in neighboring countries: declined and partly demolished industry, a very low level of wellbeing of population, an embedded illegal economy and corruption. Slow economic development caused massive emigration from the Balkan countries to Western Europe (Krastev, 2002). After the accession round was completed and also labor markets liberalized in core Europe (EU-15), an avalanche of migration occurred, mainly from the Balkans and also from Poland and more recently, from Hungary. The migration is a clear indicator of the modest success of economic and political change: the contrast in living standards to the EU did not change much since the systemic change had started. The remittances of guest workers back to their home countries had become an important macro-economic stabilizer in all Balkan countries (Krastev, 2002). Its importance is also growing in Hungary.

In contrast to the ECE, Balkan integration in the European labor division system is even lower. They serve as a pool of unskilled labor, supplying core of Europe's service industry, construction and agriculture. Thus, they also serve as a buffer of labor, taking up the shocks in core Europe's economy. This unfavorable situation can only be changed if local capital accumulation accelerates and economic and political framework conditions improve.

The common features of the systemic change in the Balkan region relate to, first, a lower level of economic development and wellbeing of population compared with the ECE region (except Slovenia); second, multiple shocks of the wars in the 1990s; third, the common past (mostly belonging to the Ottoman empire, except some former Yugoslav republics), and the large role of informal institutions and norms; fourth, a much more limited impact of the EU and international finance organizations on the process of systemic changes. These historic determinants played primary role leaving relatively minor importance to differences of the socialist era that were present between East Balkans (Bulgaria and Romania) and West Balkans (Yugoslavia).

Despite these similarities, there are also differences within the Balkan countries. Contrary to most of the former Yugoslav republics, where the economies and population were devastated by the wars, Slovenia, Bulgaria and Romania could start systemic changes earlier, even if these reforms were gradual and, in the cases of Bulgaria and Romania, inconsistent.

21.5 Russia, Ukraine and Belarus

Russia, Belarus and Ukraine started basing on similar economic (close to 70 years of dominance of planned economy, absence of private entrepreneurship), political (Communist Party as the single actor of the electoral process) and mental (a bizarre mix of Orthodox and Marxist–Leninist norms and values) preconditions, like in most of the former Yugoslav republics. Additionally, there were similar features, such as a relatively low level of the wellbeing of the population compared with the state of their economies, the dominant role of heavy industry, the same historical heritage (cultural norms, etc.), the prevalence of the Russian language in economic and everyday routines; the strong influence of former "red directors" on the design and implementation of the initial reforms; the low impact of FDI on economic restructuring, etc.

The nature and number of initial problems in these countries were far more substantial than in ECE (Dabrowski and Antczak, 1995). They spent a much longer time under the Soviet regime of planned economy, had no experience with partial market reforms (contrary to Hungary in the 1960s–1970s, or Poland in late 1980s) and no influential opposition.

In spite of many commonalities, the three analyzed countries also experienced some differences. Contrary to Russia, Ukraine and Belarus never had experience of a national state and governance. Differently to Ukraine, and especially Belarus, Russia faced huge difficulties with the status of the regions (oblasts vs. national republic). In contrast to Ukraine (coal mines) and Belarus (potash fertilizers), Russia had much larger amounts of natural resources (oil, gas, etc.) to be sold on international markets, which even led to the singled experience within the CEE region, namely the growing flow of FDI from Russia since the mid of the 1990s. Lastly, because during the Soviet time, most ambitious researchers, experts and statesmen either moved to Russia from other Soviet republics by themselves or were recruited by Communist Party or federal authorities. The quality of national elites was different in Russia, on the one side, and Belarus and Ukraine, on the other.

All three countries passed through different stages of their systemic change, which not coincided by time or by nature. To simplify, we divided their trajectories in two main periods: the first steps after the divorce of the USSR republics (ca. till the end of the 1990s), and the second stage of the stepwise diverging trajectories (mostly, since the beginning of the 2000s).

21.5.1 Shock reforms vs. back and forth (the 1990s)

21.5.1.1 Russia: Shock reforms and the political defeat of the reformers

The program of reforms, proposed by Prime Minister Yegor Gaidar, was based on the SLIP ideas, however, proceeded in a different sequence. The liberalization was started before the stabilization, and the privatization was launched in parallel with the establishment of new institutions. Moreover, under the pressure of the influential lobby of "red directors", in 1992–1993, the Government expanded the money supply and credits at explosive rates, but it soon led to very high inflation and to a deterioration in the exchange rate of the ruble and to the buildup of inter-enterprise arrears. To support continued production under these circumstances, the SOEs relied on loans from other enterprises or on barter deals.

In late 1992, deteriorating economic conditions and a sharp conflict with the parliament led President Yeltsin to dismiss Yegor Gaidar. The new government of Viktor Chernomyrdin considered macroeconomic stabilization as a primary goal; already in 1993, the annual inflation rate was around 1,000 percent, an improvement compared with more than 2,500 percent in 1992, but still very high.

In 1994, Chernomyrdin presented a set of moderate reforms to continue the macroeconomic stabilization. The key measure of the economic restructuring program, in the first half of the 1990s, was voucher privatization, formally similar to the Czech and Slovak model but conducted under different socio-economic and political conditions, which started under Gaidar in late 1992. Voucher holders could become shareholders, or sell the vouchers, or invest them in private voucher funds. By the end of June 1994, the voucher privatization program's first phase was finished. Ownership of 70 percent of Russia's large- and medium-sized SOE and of more than 90 percent of small enterprises was transferred to private owners, mostly the former directors.

The next phase of the privatization was started, aiming to sell state-held shares for cash, mostly by virtue of the loans-for-shares belonging to commercial banks affiliated with a few nouveau-riches. It provided the government with cash, based on the collateral of enterprise shares that banks presumably would be able to sell later. Due to the big public debt, the state was unable to pay back the credits; therefore, most of the biggest state enterprises that took part in the loans-for-shares deal were taken over by a few industrial-financial groups, which formed the economic basis of the new Russian oligarchy (see Gaidar, 1996; Guriev and Megginson, 2007).

Under such circumstances, first institutional traps (Polterovich, 2007) occurred, i.e. situations when a reformer, while correctly denoting the goals, used means which might be perceived by the population as not legitimate. This led to a stepwise deviation of the vector of reforms from the initially proclaimed goals.

The first institutional trap was generated in the course of the privatization. Aimed to enable a fast development of the private economy, the voucher privatization in Russia led, de facto, to a transfer of most SOEs primarily to insiders ("red directors") and partly to newly established voucher funds, it failed to open the access to the formerly state-owned assets for bottom-up growing businesses but rather has distorted the emerging business environment (Hellman and Schankerman, 2000; Guriev and Megginson, 2007) due to a fading of general competition (Glaeser et al., 2003; Sonin, 2003). While trying to foster the development of market actors and institutions, the reformers opened the door to a growing rent-seeking and the emergence of the "phony capitalism" (Yavlinsky, 1998), undermining the positions of the radical reformers and liberal ideas in Russia.

21.5.1.2 Ukraine: Failed attempts to start reforming the economy

Ukraine gained independence in 1991. Due to the transformational recession (Kornai, 1994), the inflation had reached prohibitive levels; output was shrinking fast; little or no progress had been made on privatization; monetary and budgetary discipline were nonexistent and foreign debts were accumulating fast (Dabrowski, 1994; Havrylyshyn et al., 1994; Ishaq, 1997; Grigoriev et al., 2017). Only in 1995, a systemic attempt to start economic reforms was made, and the first Constitution of Ukraine was adopted in 1996. At the end of 1996, the new government submitted to parliament a new program of economic reforms, including further deregulation of economic activity, tax reduction for enterprises and cutting of tax allowances, in order to secure budget revenue.

Economic reform, however, did not progress; the land and agricultural reform was blocked by the agrarian lobby in the Ukrainian Rada. The continued conflict between the different branches of the political system, mostly between the Rada and the President; various interests of very powerful oligarch groups made a more consistent and quick progress impossible (Ishaq, 1997).

There were some institutional traps that occurred during the first years of Post-Soviet existence of Ukraine and prevented a sustainable development of economic reforms there. First, the attempt to provide regions with more mandatory functions under a weak central government soon led to a formation of mighty regional groups of interests, consisting of political entrepreneurs, "red directors" and new businessmen, foremost in Kyiv, Dnipro and Donetsk, but also in Kharkov and Odessa, which soon transmitted their economic competition into a political rivalry, using third countries as external allies. The second institutional trap resulted from the desire to achieve economic independence; to do so, Ukraine, since the 1990s, steadily decreased trade with most former Soviet republics. But it created immense problems for the Ukrainian steel, mining and engineering enterprises, with outdated technologies and marketing strategies, which were unsustainable with international markets. Thus, a decision taken by non-economic considerations enforced the economic decline in the country.

In general, close to the end of the 1990s, Ukraine continued to fail in its attempts to start systemic changes in the economy.

21.5.1.3 Belarus: On the way toward a "state capitalism"?

In Belarus, a contingent process of establishing a market economy never started (Havrylyshyn, 2007; Korosteleva, 2007; Rovdo, 2009; Papko and Kozarzewski, 2020). The government never fully liberalized prices or the exchange rate; privatization was slow and very selective, it did not include large enterprises which remained state owned, but some institutional changes did take place in the management of them in terms of corporatization. In 1994, under a deep economic recession, the first presidential elections were won by Aleksandr Lukashenko. He soon dismantled the separation of powers and consolidated control over the state in his hands. In 1996, Belarusian authorities took control of the biggest commercial banks and reintroduced tight price controls. Privatization was stopped in 1995, when Lukashenko's decree canceled the results of the first voucher auction.

State authorities succeeded with the process of taking control over the economic system by the end of 1996, when the government adopted "Main directions of social and economic development for the years 1996–2000". It formulated some macro-economic targets, including the GDP growth rate, an increase in industrial and agricultural output, lowering the inflation rate, unemployment and the national currency exchange rate. Enterprises were obliged to meet targets concerning output growth, exports and wage growth. This program was based on the absence of hard budget constraints in the operation of SOEs and banks.

As the Belarusian authorities proclaimed the goal to establish a common state with Russia, such a policy guaranteed several favorable economic conditions from Russia, for many years, especially cheap oil and gas from Russia to Belarusian state enterprises.

Belarus tried to postpone the inevitable economic changes. One of the most important reasons was the absence of an own tradition of stateness, and the related weakness of the traditions of governance, especially regarding monetary policy. However, sustaining a semi-Socialist economy, Belarus was, from the very beginning, locked in several institutional traps. The most important of them were the "debt trap" (under soft financial constraints for SOEs, old debts are financed by the issuing of new ones), the "social burden trap" (the Belarusian state has, over three decades, spent much of its resources in social services, as a welfare state) and the "resource curse trap" (some key manufacturing branches of the Belarusian economy were based on preferential access to subsidized delivery of Russian oil and gas) (Rudy, 2020).

With regard to the 1990s, the economic model of Belarus could be labeled as a "rent based state capitalism" (Baltowski et al., 2020; Papko and Kozarzewski, 2020).

21.5.2 Diverging paths: The end of the 1990s and the first decades of the 21st century

21.5.2.1 The Russian way from "phony capitalism" to patronal autocracy

In Russia, after the Financial Crisis of 1998, GDP growth soon averaged 6.7 percent annually. Two factors pushed the economy forward in the first decade after the crisis: a depreciation of the ruble in September 1998, and rising oil prices since 1999.

This rapid GDP growth and tax revenues allowed the establishment of a Stabilization Fund to pay off government debts; inflation diminished to single-digit numbers in 2006.

Oil and gas, as well as other natural resources, became the most important items in the economy of Russia. But due to these circumstances, the institutional trap of the "rent curse" was revealed (Auty and Furlonge, 2019).

Additionally, due to the fast economic growth in 2000–2007, the public sector grew. Secure jobs, with a limited working day, stable, growing salary and several additional bonuses became more and more attractive for the population. As a consequence, the third institutional "trap of middle income" occurred. The incentives to launch one's own business or even to change from the state to the private sector diminished.

An increase in direct state interventions into the economy was manifested in 2003. It took two forms, the formation of state holding companies in some sectors, designated by the state as "strategically important", and the displacement of foreign capital from strategic enterprises. The increase in Russian state involvement in the economy was a sign of changing the ideology, from supporting the market economy to a modernization approach (Ferdinand, 2007).

During the crisis of 2008–2009, the state used its financial resources, not only to support the "fat cats", but also to drastically increase the general dominance of the state in the economy, primarily in the form of a public-private partnership in huge strategic projects, increasing of procurement by state institutions, state and semi-state owned firms, etc. Thus, during 2010–2020, Russia turned to establish the "administrative regime" (Sakwa, 2010), or "patronal autocracy" (Magyar and Madlovics, 2020).

21.5.2.2 Ukraine: From aborted reforms to a restart

Due to the weakness of presidential power, its steady conflicts with the Rada and corruption, the economic growth in Ukraine has been slow over the first two decades of its independence. The short-term economic rise, during 2003–2007, was based on the growth of exports to Russia and was characterized by a sharp increase of external debt. However, after the 2008–2009 crisis, the economy did not recover.

Ukraine's model of economic development, over the 1990s, beginning of 2000s, was rather simple: the oligarchs received their rent from a few large industries and competed for power and control over regional and national budgets, while most households suffered, and many of them received their incomes from relatives, who worked in Russia or in the EU countries. Ukraine's economic fallacy was caused by massive deindustrialization, the share of added value of industrial production and the exports reduced. However, some large enterprises in the east of the country (especially in metallurgy), until recently, remained competitive.

Citizens were constantly frustrated with the economic situation and expressed their dissatisfaction frequently. The first serious sign of a direct intervention of ordinary people in the political clashes was the "Orange Revolution" of 2004, but the restart of economic reforms was half-hearted and accompanied by rivalry among the reformist parties and leaders representing different regional clans of Ukrainian oligarchs. Later, it was interrupted by the victory of Victor Yanukovych, who became president in 2010.

The presidency of Yanukovych followed a period of global recession; corruption persisted during his tenure, as well as conflicts between different groups of oligarchs. The protracted slowdown and decline of the wellbeing of the Ukrainian population have resulted in open socio-political turmoil of Kiev's Maidan in 2014.

Recovering, under the conditions of an armed conflict in Donbass, and loss of the Crimea in 2014, would require from President Zelensky, a standard austerity policies and structural reforms to maintain macroeconomic stability, reduce inflation, interest rates and public debt (World Bank, 2019).

In the recent years, after a 4 percent decline in 2020, the partial recovery in the manufacturing sector and services elevated the GDP growth in the second half of 2021; however, on a sequential basis, the economy contracted by 0.8 percent in that second quarter compared with the same period of 2020. After steadily accelerating over the past year, the annual inflation remained at 10.2 percent level in August 2021. Fostering the sustainability of reforms, thus, remains the key precondition of the economic recovery.

21.5.2.3 Belarus: Becoming a market-exploiting dictatorship?

In Belarus, during the past two decades, GDP growth was higher than the average in Ukraine and Russia (Adarov et al., 2016) but accompanied by high inflation, budget deficit and currency crises. The core of the Belarusian economic model throughout this period was a combination of rents, extorted from Russia, in exchange for political concessions and soft budget constraints on the SOEs, complemented by an administrative control of the economy.

However, some new tendencies appeared after the economic crisis in 2015: the successive reduction of subsidies to SOEs and deregulation; the growing role of private enterprises, especially in the new sectors (IT, etc.); the growing concentration of the new private sector, due to the top-down corporatization of SOEs and establishing of large private firms (Papko and Kozarzewski, 2020). But the annual economic growth in the country, after 2015, remains on the level of a bit more than 1 percent.

Besides, according to Rudy (2020), there are several institutional traps, limiting the sustainability of the Belarusian economic model; in addition to the "debt trap", the "social burden trap" and the "resource curse trap", which occurred already in the 1990s, there were the "middle-income trap" (rising salaries as part of the social contract no longer led to country-fast development, as measured by GDP per capita); the "conflict neighbors trap" (as tensions between Ukraine and Russia were steadily growing) and the "trap of the forceful pressure" (occurring when the excessive control agencies' pressure slowdowns the activity of the economic agents).

The established Belarusian economic model cannot be explained on the basis of the VoC theory (Korosteleva, 2007), nor of the "state capitalism". Rather, it can be defined as a "dictatorship using market economy" (Kornai, 2016).

* * *

Overall, the reasons for the divergence of the systemic changes, Russia, Ukraine and Belarus showed over 30 years (1990–2020) the different modes of the systemic change: (a) the different quality of the initial strategies and the amount and quality of the support of these strategies by the economic and political elites; (b) differing traditions of the own stateness; (c) different kinds of institutional traps, which accompanied the systemic changes.

At the time when this volume was already under printing, the military operation of Russia in Ukraine happened. It has not only caused death of many people and damage to the economies of both countries but changed substantially the developmental trends there and in the whole global economy. It seems that three scenarios are possible; whether one of these scenarios or a mix of it will be realized is a question of a nearest future:

- Russia and Belarus would make the backslide transition in a more quick tempo further on their own, while Ukraine could gain its sovereignty over the biggest part of the country, and the market-oriented development could become even more quick and sustainable due to a massive institutional and financial support by the EU and international organizations;
- Ukraine would become part of the system of mobilization and state dominance in the economy, economic and political sanctions would isolate the economies of the three countries for a longer period, a revival of a commando economy of scarcity would become highly likely;
- The shock of sanctions and international boycott for the economies of Russia and Belarus would be so deep that the political regimes there might become threatened; however, the future trajectories of economic and political developments there seem now to be unpredictable.

Anyway, these developments will have a serious impact also on the economic developments and modification of socio-economic models in the whole CEE region, and on the dynamics of the whole global economy and its future trends.

21.6 General conclusions

There are no doubts that all CEE regions and countries have showed some similarities during the last 30 years of systemic changes.

However, the ECE, Balkan and CIS countries also showed different performance and outcomes after this systemic transformation. There is a broad bundle of socio-economic models, from dictatorships using market institutions to liberal economies, which appeared in these countries. The reasons for such differences are related, in the literature, predominantly to the historical preconditions and the situation at the inception stage. In this chapter, some other possible explanations of this growing diversity, including those which occurred during the systemic changes, were identified and are summarized in Table 21.1.

Some other reasons that could have influenced the divergent paths of socio-economic changes in CEE but which remain less discussed are worth mentioning here. For instance, the interplay between some global trends of socio-economic development and the systemic change in the CEE. There were already some explanations in the literature that if the systemic change would happen earlier, in the 1970s, it could proceed faster and with more evident socio-economic outcomes, at least in the ECE (Podkaminer, 2013). It seems that the idea of the unfavorable impact of the current declining general trend of the global economic development on the systemic change of Post-Socialist CEE economies needs to be proven, based on the Kondratieff theory of long cycles of economic development (Rennstich, 2002; Grinin and Korotayev, 2015).

The systemic changes in this large region of Europe will remain one of the most important areas of comparative economic studies in Europe also in future, because the variety of socio-economic models in Europe has grown significantly; moreover, the processes of divergent developments in the CEE seem to have different stages and seem to be far from the consolidation.

Table 21.1 Factors of the similarity and diversity of socio-economic models in CEE

	ECE	Balkans		Former USSR (Russia, Ukraine, Belarus)	
Preconditions at the beginning of the systemic changes:					
Historic past	Former Austrian empire	Partly former Ottoman empire, partly former Austrian empire		Former Russian empire, predominance of the Russian language	
Level of economic development at the beginning	GDP per capita higher than in other former Socialist economies	GDP per capita lower than in ECE, but higher than in former USSR		GDP per capita higher than in other former USSR countries	
Size and homogeneity	Small economies, spatial homogeneity (except Poland)	Civil and ethnic wars in some republics of the former Yugoslavia	Peaceful conditions (Bulgaria, Romania, Slovenia and Croatia)	Large economies, spatial heterogeneity (except Belarus)	
Economic model before the beginning of the systemic change	Marginal private sector under Socialism	"Market socialism" in former Yugoslavia	Planned economy in Eastern Balkans over 40 years	Common past: Planned economy over 70 years	
Sources of the new elites	Influential opposition under the Socialist period forming the new elite	Nationalist (new + old) elites in former Yugoslavia	Mimicry of old elites, rise of new elites	Absence of influential national contra-elites under the Socialist period	Schism of elites (Ukraine)
Impact of the FDI from established market economies	Massive inflow of FDI	Low FDI inflow		"Too big to be eaten", very low FDI impact on the processes of economic change	
General influence of the EU	Strong influence of the EU	New (weak) independent states, moderate influence of the EU	Old states captured by former communists, moderate influence of the EU	New stateness, new rules and order in establishment, limited influence of the EU and international organizations	
	New national currencies or Euro (Slovenia, Slovakia, Balitc states)	Old national currencies (Hungary, Czech Republic, Poland)	New currencies (former Yugoslavia), DM as a parallel currency	Old established national currencies, DM as a parallel currency	Russian ruble until 1993, then own currencies

Institutional traps during the systemic change: privatization outcomes and crony capitalism; frustration and resentment in the population consciousness

Note

1 The term was introduced to political science with pejorative tune by Fareed Zakaria: "Democratically elected regimes… are routinely ignoring constitutional limits on their power and depriving their citizens of basic rights and freedoms. ….we see the rise of a disturbing phenomenon in international life – illiberal democracy" (Zakaria, 1997, p. 22).

References

Adarov, A., Bornukova, K., Havlik, P., Hunya, G., Kruk, D. and Pindyuk, O. (2016). The Belarus Economy: The Challenges of Stalled Reforms. In: R. Dobrinsky (Ed.), *The Vienna Institute for International Economic Studies*, Research Report 413. Vienna.

Amable, B. (2003). *The Diversity of Modern Capitalism*. London: Oxford University Press.

Appel, H. and Orenstein, M. (2018). *From Triumph to Crisis: Neoliberal Economic Reform in Postcommunist Countries*. New York: Cambridge University Press.

Aslund, A. (2002). *Building Capitalism. The Transformation of the Former Soviet Bloc*. New York: Cambridge University Press.

Auty, R.M. and Furlonge, H.I. (2019). *The Rent Curse. Natural Resources, Policy Choice, and Economic Development*. Oxford and New York: Oxford University Press.

Baltowski, M., Kozarzewski, P. and Mickiewicz, T. (2020). State Capitalism with Populist Characteristics: Poland and Hungary. In: M. Wright, G. Wood, A. Cuervo-Cazurra, P. Sun, I. Okhmatovskiy and A. Grosman (Eds.), *Oxford Handbook on State Capitalism and the Firm* (pp. 731–760). Oxford: Oxford University Press.

Barlemann, M., Hristov, K. and Nenovsky, N. (2002). *Lending of Last Resort: Moral Hazard and Twin Crises: Lessons from the Bulgarian Financial Crisis 1996/1997*. Mimeo: University of Michigan.

Baumol, W. (1990). Entrepreneurship: Productive, unproductive, and destructive. *Journal of Political Economy*, 98(5/1), 893–921.

Bitzenis, A. (2003). What was behind the delay in the Bulgarian privatization process? *Emerging Markets Finance and Trade*, 39(5), 58–82.

Bluhm, K. (2010). Theories of capitalism put to the test: Introduction to a debate on Central and Eastern Europe. *Historical Social Research/Historische Sozialforschung*, 35(2), 197–217.

Bluhm, K., Martens, B. and Trappmann, V. (2014). Introduction. In: K. Bluhm, B. Martens and V. Trappmann (Eds.). *Business Leaders and New Varieties of Capitalism in Post-Communist Europe*. London and New York: Routledge.

Bohle, D. and Greskovits, B. (2012). *Capitalist Diversity on Europe's Periphery. Cornell Studies in Political Economy*. Ithaca – London: Cornell University Press.

Carothers, T. (2002). The end of the transition paradigm. *Journal of Democracy*, 13(1), 5–21.

Cianetti, L., Dawson, J. and Hanley, S. (2018). Rethinking "democratic backsliding" in Central and Eastern Europe – looking beyond Hungary and Poland. *East European Politics*, 34(3), 243–256.

Dabrowski, M. (1994). The Ukrainian way to hyperinflation. *Communist Economies and Economic Transformation*, 6(2), 115–137.

Dabrowski, M. and Antczak, R. (1995). Economic Transition in Russia, the Ukraine and Belarus in Comparative Perspective, CASE – Center for Social and Economic Research, Warsaw, Studies and Analyses, No. 47, July.

Denizer, C., Gelb, A., De Melo, M. and Tenev, S. (2001). Circumstance and choice: The role of initial conditions and policies in transition economies. *World Bank Economic Review*, 15(1), 1–31.

Djankov, S. and Hauck, O. (2016). *The Divergent Post-Communist Paths to Democracy and Economic Freedom*. Washington, DC: Peterson Institute for International Economics, Working Paper No. 10.

Douarin, E. and Mickiewicz, T. (2017). *Economics of Institutional Change: Central and Eastern Europe Revisited*. Cham: Springer.

Drahokoupil, J. (2008). Who won the contest for a new property class: Structural transformation of elites in the Visegrád Four region. *Journal for East European Management Studies*, 13(4), 360–377.

Dumas, C. (2018). *Populism and Economics*. London: Profile Books.

Falcetti, E., Sanfey, P. and Taci, A. (2003). Bridging the gaps? Private sector development, capital flows and the investment climate in South-Eastern Europe, Working Paper No. 80, European Bank for Reconstruction and Development.

Farkas, B. (2016). *Models of Capitalism in the European Union. Post-Crisis Perspective.* London: Palgrave Macmillan.

Ferdinand, P. (2007). Russia and China: Converging responses to globalization. *International Affairs*, 83(4), 655–680.

Gaidar, E. (1996). How the nomenklatura "privatized" its own power. *Russian Politics & Law*, 34(1), 26–37.

Glaeser, E., Scheinkman, J. and Shleifer, A. (2003). The injustice of inequality. *Journal of Monetary Economics*, 50(1), 199–222.

Grigoriev, L., Buryak, E. and Golyashev, A. (2017). The transition of Ukraine's economy. *Russian Social Science Review*, 58(2–3), 262–289.

Grinin, L.E. and Korotayev, A.V. (2015). *Great Divergence and Great Convergence. A Global Perspective.* New York: Springer.

Guriev, S. and Megginson, W. (2007). Privatization: What have we learned? Annual World Bank Conference on Development Economics - Regional 2007: Beyond Transition. P. 249–296.

Haber, S. (2002). The political economy of crony capitalism. In: S. Haber (Ed.), *Crony Capitalism and Economic Growth in Latin America: Theory and Evidence* (pp. x–xxi). Stanford: Hoover Institute.

Hall, P.A. and Soskice, D. (2001). An introduction. In: P.A. Hall and D. Soskice (Eds.), *Varieties of Capitalism. The Institutional Foundations of Comparative Advantage* (pp. 1–68). Oxford: Oxford University Press.

Havrylyshyn, O. (2007). *Fifteen Years of Transformation in the Post-communist World. Rapid Reformers Outperformed Gradualists,* Washington, DC: Cato Institute.

Havrylyshyn, O., Miller, M. and Perraudin, W. (1994). Deficits, inflation and the political economy of Ukraine. *Economic Policy*, 9(19), 353–401.

Hellman, J. and Schankerman, M. (2000). Intervention, corruption and capture: the nexus between enterprises and the state. *Economics of Transition*, 8(3), 545–576.

Hellman, J.S., Jones, G. and Kaufmann, D. (2000). Seize the State, Seize the Day: State Capture: Corruption, and Influence in Transition. Policy Research Working Paper No. 2444, World Bank, Washington, DC.

Heybey, B. and Murrell, P. (1999). The relationship between economic growth and the speed of liberalization during transition. *Journal of Policy Reform*, 3(2), 121–137.

Innes, A. (2013). The political economy of state capture in Central Europe. *Journal of Common Market Studies*, 52(1), 88–104.

Ishaq, M. (1997). The Ukrainian economy and the process of reform. *Communist Economies and Economic Transformation*, 9(4), 501–517.

Jones Luong, P. (2002). *Institutional Change and Political Continuity in Post-Soviet Central Asia: Power, Perceptions, and Pacts.* Cambridge: Cambridge University Press.

King, L. and Szelenyi, I. (2005). Post-communist economic systems. In: N.J. Smelser, R. Swedberg (Eds.), *The Handbook of Economic Sociology* (pp. 205–232). Princeton, NJ: Princeton University Press.

Kolodko, G.W. (2000). *From Shock to Therapy. Political Economy of Postsocialist Transformation.* Oxford – New York: Oxford University Press.

Kornai, J. (1990). *The Road to a Free Economy. Shifting from a Socialist System: The Example of Hungary.* New York: W.W. Norton.

Kornai, J. (1994). Transformational recession: The main causes. *Journal of Comparative Economics*, 19(1), 39–63.

Kornai, J. (2000). Ten years after the road to a free economy: The Author's self-evaluation. In: *Annual World Bank Conference on Development Economics* (pp. 49–66). Washington, DC: The World Bank.

Kornai, J. (2016). The system paradigm revisited: Clarification and additions in the light of experiences in the post-socialist region. *Acta Oeconomica*, 66(4), 547–596.

Korosteleva, J. (2007). Belarus: Heading towards state capitalism? In D. Lane and M. Myant (Eds.), *Varieties of Capitalism in Post-Communist Countries* (pp. 221–238). New York: Palgrave Macmillan.

Krastev, I. (2002). The Balkans: Democracy without choices. *Journal of Democracy*, 13(3), 39–53.

Lane, D. and Myant, M. (2007). *Varieties of Capitalism in Post-Communist Countries.* London – New York: Palgrave Macmillan.

Lavigne, M. (1995). *The Economics of Transition. From Socialist Economy to Market Economy.* Basingstoke: Macmillan.

Magyar, B. and Madlovics, B. (2020). *The Anatomy of Post-Communist Regimes: A Conceptual Framework.* Budapest – New York: CEU Press.

Mendelski, M. (2010). The varieties of capitalism approach goes east: institutional complementarities and law enforcement during post-communist transition. In: A. Krause and V. Trappman (Eds.), *What Capitalism? Socio-Economic Change in Central Eastern Europe* (pp. 8–44). Jena: Universitaet Jena.

Mertlik, P. (1995). Czech privatization: from public ownership to public ownership in five years? *Prague Economic Papers*, 4(4), 321–336.

Milanovic, B. (2019). *Capitalism, Alone: The Future of the System that Rules the World*. Cambridge, MA: Harvard University Press/Belknap Press.

Nölke, A. and May, C. (2019). Liberal versus organised capitalism: A historical–comparative perspective. In: T. Gerőcs and M. Szanyi (Eds.), *Market Liberalism and Economic Patriotism in the Capitalist World System* (pp. 21–42). London – New York: Palgrave Macmillan.

Nölke, A. and Vliegenthart, A. (2009). Enlarging the varieties of capitalism: the emergence of dependent market economies in East Central Europe. *World Politics*, 61(4), 670–702.

North, D.C. (1990). *Institutions, Institutional Change and Economic Performance*. Cambridge: Cambridge University Press.

Papko, A. and Kozarzewski, P. (2020). The evolution of Belarusian public sector: From command economy to state capitalism? CASE – Center for Social and Economic Research, Warsaw, Studies and Analyses, No. 136, July.

Podkaminer, L. (2013). *Development Patterns of Central and East European Countries* (in the course of transition and following EU accession). Wien: Verein Wiener Inst. für Internat. Wirtschaftsvergleiche (WIIW).

Polányi, K. (1944). *The Great Transformation*. Boston, MA: Beacon Press.

Polterovich, V. (2007). Institutional Trap. In *New Palgrave Dictionary of Economics*, 2008, https://ssrn.com/abstract=1751839

Pop-Eleches, G. (2009). *From Economic Crisis to Reform: IMF Programs in Latin America and Eastern Europe*. Princeton, NJ: Princeton University Press.

Przeworski, A., Bardhan, P.K., Kolarska-Bobińska, L., Pereira, L.C.B., Wiatr, J.J. and Bruszt, L. (1995). *Sustainable democracy*. Cambridge, MA: Cambridge University Press.

Racovita, M. (2011). Europaization and effective democracy in Romania and Bulgaria. *Romanian Journal of Political Sciences*, 11(1), 28–49.

Rennstich, J.K. (2002). The new economy, the leadership long cycle and the nineteenth K-wave. *Review of International Political Economy*, 9(1), 150–182.

Rodrik, D. (2018). Populism and the economics of globalization. *Journal of International Business Policy*, 1(1–2), 12–33.

Roland, G. (2000). *Transition and Economics. Politics, Markets and Firms*. Cambridge, MA: MIT Press.

Rovdo, V. (2009). *Sravnitelnaya politologiya, chast' 3* [Comparative political science. Vol. 3], Vilnius: European Humanities University.

Rudy, K. (2020). State capitalism in Belarus: Behind economic anemia. In: A. Rozanov, A. Barannikov, O. Belyaeva and V. Smirnov (Eds.), *Public Sector Crisis Management*. Intechopen. https://www.intechopen.com/books/public-sector-crisis-management/state-capitalism-in-belarus-behind-economic-anemia

Sakwa, R. (2010). The dual state in Russia. *Post-Soviet Affairs*, 26(3), 185–206.

Sauka, A. and Welter, F. (2007). Productive, unproductive and destructive entrepreneurship in an advanced transition setting: the example of Latvian small enterprises. In: R. Aidis and F. Welter (Eds.), *Empirical Entrepreneurship in Europe* (pp. 87–111). Cheltenham: Edward Elgar.

Schimmelfenning, F. and Sedelmeier, U. (2005). Introduction: Conceptualizing the Europeanization of Central and Eastern Europe. In: F. Schimmelfenning and U. Sedelmeier (Eds.), *The Europeanization of Central and Eastern Europe* (pp. I–XII). Ithaca, NY: Cornell University Press.

Schneider, M.S. and Paunescu, M. (2012). Changing varieties of capitalism and revealed comparative advantages from 1990 to 2005: A test of the Hall and Soskice claims. *Socio-Economic Review*, 10(4), 731–753.

Sonin, K. (2003). Why the rich may favor poor protection of property rights? *Journal of Comparative Economics*, 31(4), 715–731.

Stark, D. (1996). Recombinant property in East European capitalism. *American Journal of Sociology*, 101(4), 993–1027.

Szalavetz, A. (2017). Upgrading and value capture in global value chains in Hungary: More complex than what the smile curve suggests. In: B. Szent-Iványi (Ed.), *Foreign Direct Investment in Central and Eastern Europe* (pp. 127–150). New York: Palgrave Macmillan.

Szanyi, M. (2017). Impacts of the crisis on the FDI-led development model in Hungary: Emergence of economic patriotism or shift from the competition state to patronage. In: P. Havlik and I. Iwasaki (Eds.), *Economics of European Crises and Emerging Markets* (pp. 149–170). Cham: Springer.

Szanyi, M. (2019a). The Balkan model and the balkanization of East Central Europe. IWE Working Paper, No. 258.

Szanyi, M. (2019b). Introduction: The revival of the state. In: M. Szanyi (Ed.), *Seeking the Best Master: State Ownership in the Varieties of Capitalism* (pp. 1–12). Budapest: CEU Press.

Szanyi, M. (2020). Changing trends of foreign direct investments in East Central Europe. In: A. Szunomár (Ed.), *Emerging-market Multinational Enterprises in East Central Europe* (pp. 21–47). London – New York: Palgrave Macmillan.

Szanyi, M. and Szabó, G. (2020). Defining the long-term development trends of countries in East-Central Europe in the context of political cycles, *International Journal of Public Administration.* Retrieved July 3, 2021, from https://www.tandfonline.com/doi/abs/10.1080/01900692.2020.1749850

UNCTAD. (2018). *World Investment Report.* Geneva.

Wedel, J.R. (2001). Clans, cliques and captured states: rethinking 'transition' in Central and Eastern Europe and the former Soviet Union. Helsinki, *WIDER Discussion Paper* No. 58.

Williams, C.C. and Bezeredi, S. (2020). Evaluating the impacts on firm productivity of informal sector competitors: Results of a business survey in South-Eastern Europe. *International Journal of Entrepreneurship and Small Business*, 41(4), 524–524.

Williamson, J. (1989). What Washington means by policy reform. In: J. Williamson (Ed.), *Latin American Readjustment: How Much has Happened*. Washington, DC: Peterson Institute for International Economics.

World Bank. (2019). *Ukraine Economic Update, November 19*. Retrieved July 3, 2021, from https://pubdocs.worldbank.org/en/100071574084094307/Ukraine-economic-update-Fall-2019-en.pdf

Yavlinsky, G. (1998). Russia's phony Capitalism. *Foreign Affairs*, 77(3), 67–79.

Zakaria, F. (1997). The rise of illiberal democracy. *Foreign Affairs*, 76(6), 22–43.

PART IV

Markets, governance, performance and change of economic systems

22

SYSTEMIC GOVERNANCE[1]

László Csaba

CENTRAL EUROPEAN UNIVERSITY AND CORVINUS
UNIVERSITY OF BUDAPEST

The mainstream view of macroeconomics, as represented by authoritative volumes (Burda and Wyplosz, 2017; Blanchard and Summers, 2019), tends to treat fundamental changes of the macro-system to be outside the scope of macroeconomic theory and policy-making proper. This approach has cemented itself despite the momentous changes not only in Central and Eastern Europe, but also in China, Russia, and many other parts of the globe. Macroeconomics is the art of balancing between fiscal and monetary legs, and macroeconomic theory is about the combination of factors and ways of interpreting equilibria. Macroeconomics and policies based on it are about inflation and (full) employment, fiscal and monetary aggregates, exchange rates, trade, and the interaction among these. *Institution building is outside the scope of its attention,* at least for two reasons.

First, modern macroeconomics, ever since Samuelson, has not really been concerned about this issue (though in the past 15–20 years accepting that 'institutions matter' has become a platitude for most of the literature). Second, and related to the former, institution building is seen as an exceptional, one-time endeavor, which needs case-by-case consideration and adaptation to changing local conditions. As such, political economy of reforms, i.e., the art of implementing economic insights on the ground, under often hostile or ignorant political environment is seen as an area for political science and public administration, thus falling outside the scope of economic analysis. This holds also for the academic interpretation of the root causes of success and failure, be that of China's rise or Central European democratic backsliding, two issues on which libraries have been produced, and not only in the past decade.

True, that transition studies constituted a bold attempt to integrate those broader insights into economic investigation. However, even the boldest and broadest attempts (Merkel, Kollmorgen and Wagener, 2019; Kolodko, 2021) remained compartmentalized. Analyses are confined to time and space, major claims are context specific, with limited if any transferability to other cases or situations, let alone different time periods. This is exactly the opposite to how mainstream economics has evolved, with its emphasis on formal presentation, being the basic criterion for good academic quality. A mere glimpse into the recent output of top ten academic journals of RECEP rankings may suffice to those who yet need being convinced.

The present chapter is an attempt to offer an interpretative framework in which changes in economic systems may be understood and explained through a single analytical perspective. In so doing, we follow the secular trend in mainstream macroeconomics where macro-claims must be rooted in micro-insights, as expounded recently in Galbács (2020). For our subject, this requires reliance on management sciences if we address issues in real-world economic systems.

 DOI: 10.4324/9781003144366-27

Therefore, macro for us is never the same as aggregated micro-insights. All the less so, as the horizontal and vertical interactions between the two and the environment may and often does produce outcomes that would not follow from a simple adding up. Thus, *the systemic view diverges from the dominant trend in theory.*

While in macroeconomics the agency is usually the administration, or the central government, in management sciences it has become customary to include horizontal elements and intertwining into the analytical frame, both from the incentive and information processing perspectives. Thus, in the latter, we tend to talk mostly of *governance, rather than administration,* which stresses the hierarchical subordination among the various layers of management. Since comparative economics has long been studying the power of the ruled,[2] even over those making the plan or policy decisions, it is a legitimate extension if we apply this insight to the macroeconomic level. Systemic governance is thus the complexity of constructivist, man-made rules and the outcomes shaped by spontaneous reactions of firms, individuals, and local and foreign players in a multimillion actor game. Bagenholm et al. (2021) provided an exhaustive account of the dimensions and considerations of how this approach is being applied to assess the quality of real-world governments across the globe.

Our basic research question is the interface between human deliberations and spontaneous outcomes. The paradox, first highlighted in detail by Ludwig von Mises (1940 [1963]) would be put today in the form of the role of system design, i.e., various forms of constructivist deliberations, in shaping outcomes in different societies. Explaining *why some of the solutions do work under one setting and fail in a different one* has long been a topic of inquiry within comparative economic studies. But even in broader, global context, as Ilene Grabel (2017) demonstrated, international financial organizations, including the once infamously rigid and dogmatic IMF (International Monetary Fund), which used to be conventionally criticized for its one-size-fits-all approach, adopted a line where context specificity rules over doctrinal chastity or academic coherence. We may join her in seeing this as a forward-looking development.

In the following, *we shall counter-pose the experience of Central Europe,* with the preeminence of top-down or reverse planning approach to introducing Western type of social market economy, *with East Asia.* The latter region is best exemplified by China, with their a-theoretical, experimental approach, where a series of small steps have been following one another. Rather than adhering to a secret master plan, 'all options are kept open' when deciding over the next major step. We investigate when and which strategy is more fruitful and why so.

22.1 Central Europe: The laboratory for social constructivism

With the collapse of the external and later the internal Soviet Empire, the newly emancipated nations of Central Europe have emerged as fertile ground for natural experiments of 'returning to Europe', namely by establishing parliamentary democracies and social market economies of the West European type. According to the consensus view, documented in a series of books, the first decade was spent on bringing about the foundations of market and democracy. The second decade was spent on accession to the European Union (EU) and taking over incrementally its *acquis Communautaire.* The third decade by a corrective, called usually as 'illiberal democracy'. Despite the traditional differences by the country, dating back to their formation, Visegrád countries can and should be subsumed under a single model of development. Their commonalities prevail over much deeper differences from post-Soviet and post-Yugoslav states as well as from the Baltics.

This third phase was characterized not only by managing the two crises, the Great Recession of 2008–2009 and the COVID pandemic in 2020–2021, but also by the emergence of a new state-led model. While the Baltic States qualify as an outlier, being addicted to the neoliberal model, the Visegrád Countries and Croatia have changed their previous FDI-driven modernization strategies. Some analysts (Blum and Varga, 2021) baptized it as a conservative developmental state, highlighting the focus on workfare, picking winners and activist industrial policies, market protectionism, and governmental differentiation across economic subjects by size, nationality, and closeness to the governing party, all reminiscent of the practices of East Asian Tigers in the 1970s and 1980s.

It remains a subject of academic and policy controversy if, and to what degree, this characterization holds or is a caricature of actual state of affairs (as explained in Csaba, 2021). From our perspective, the evolution of the third decade is certainly deeper going and more profound, more lasting in all planes of analysis, than the ad hoc assessment of calling it a simple derailment would have it.

What we could observe has been *a prime case of how the concept of systemic governance works under real-world conditions.* None of the governments of the region has ever declared their distinctness from the EU standards, including the European Fiscal and Banking Union and its institutions, including the Single Supervisory Mechanism and the Single Resolution Mechanism. The European Stability Mechanism and the Next Generation Fund constitute further giant steps toward supranational decision-making, while these do not require – as frequently misinterpreted – the convergence of domestic economic models (more on this in Casagrande and Dallago, 2021).

What counts from our angle is that Central European countries have gradually moved toward a profoundly statist model not to meet the formal and informal criteria of the 'ever closer European Union'. On the contrary, joining the single currency would have required more rules-based fiscal and monetary arrangements, less interventionism, and weakening the developmental statist ambitions by the local governments.

If we take those ambitions, including the priority of growth promotion and sovereigntist aspirations, going way beyond the economic sphere, the mechanism of change becomes easy to follow. The governments advocated a not-so hidden agenda of state-led development, with a focus on picking winners, of retaking back control over a previously extremely transnationalized banking sector (Önder and Özerlimi, 2016) and energy economy, as well as trade and communication. As the Hungarian governing party formulated back in 2010, their ascent to power was meant to be 'more than a change of guard in government, though less of a regime change'. This formulation has proven to be a precise one.

Systemic governance in this case has not relied on projects elaborated with the involvement of international financial institutions and independent academic expert, as was the case in the 1990s. Much of the policy change has been improvised in reactions to the challenges of the day, should they have come from the EU, the global capital markets, or local politics. But overall, the changes *in toto* resulted *in much more than ad hoc adjustments,* or corrections of previous economic and political imbalances.

It would be difficult, or even in vain, to search for an overall plan of actual changes, implemented in Poland, Hungary, Slovakia, and Czechia. Analysts strongly disagree about how to assess the outcome. János Kornai (2016) spoke of a hybrid regime, Mihályi and Szelényi (2020) of a prebendal, rent-seeking state, while Magyar and Madlovics (2020) of a mafia state, where the intertwining between the party-state and the economy replicates the intimate relationships observed in South Italy and China. What all of them agree is the focus on spontaneous, ad hoc decisions, taken at the highest level, with economic consequences being though relevant, but by no means overwhelming. The personal enrichment component is demonstrable but remains insufficient for an exhaustive explanation of outcomes. The latter do reflect the broad priorities of the power holders, but owing to the horizontal aspects, feedbacks of various sorts, *they are a long way from replicating something of a carbon copy of any elaborate master plan, let alone financial calculation, or growth strategy on par with East Asia.*

Which were the empirically observable methods of changing the neoliberal model into a quasi-developmentalist-statist one? The answer is far from being simple, as *certain measures* – like nationalization or privatization, supporting monopolies or creating competition – *could serve diametrically opposite objectives,* depending on the context of the country and time.

In his broad empirical overview, Szanyi (2019a) highlights the growing *étatisme*, connections to the ruling party, ad hoc interventions, and securing monopoly positions for those favored, while crowding out non-supported foreigners and private ventures not belonging to the oligarchy among the most frequent arrangements. One of the more recent examples includes the takeover of the market for cafeteria provision, previously held by foreign companies. The dispute settlement forum of the World Bank obliged the Hungarian state to pay no less than 100 mn euros in compensation for the confiscation of foreign interests, only to be passed over to the hands of local providers.

Yet another new method cited by our sources includes nationalization, as a temporary measure. In several cases, though not exclusively in the financial sector, *establishments have been taken over by the state only for a transitory period.* Often supported by lavish injections of capital and/or debt reliefs, these ventures tended to be sold later to private owners, known to be the benefactors of the governing party.

Yet another frequently used method is to declare *an investment to be of national economic relevance. If that is the case, at the end of the day, no rules should be followed.* These rules may include considerations of competition policy, of state aid (controlled by the EU), of transparency, of accountability, or the requirement of equal treatment of market players before the courts.

Open favoritism as ongoing governmental policy in various well-known ways can thus be justified, and *no remedy for losses can be found,* either at national or international fora. The World Bank ruling cited above is thus to be taken as an exception, rather than the rule. If for no other reason, owing to the cost, the time-consuming nature, the complexity, and the regular foreign presence required for these fora to be efficacious, most players give up rather than enter a hopeless contest against those in power.

Given the growing intertwining among market and state agents, it is often *difficult to disentangle, which is the dog and which of them is the tail.* This division of roles may be changing over time, while the administration retains the right of initiative. For this reason, the top-down nature of the game is clear according to the literature we cited. Patronage, rent-seeking, regulatory capture, and the like are well-known terms to denote *various forms of political capitalism* from Latin America to East Asia.

What is straightforward from the empirical studies (Győrffy, 2021) is that the Baltics, committing themselves to 'neoliberalism', i.e., open markets and delineation of public and private spheres of the economy, have been faring better than the Central Europeans who have opted for a local edition of the conservative developmental state model. The analysis above lists a variety of scores in which the comparison works in favor of the former periphery of the Soviet Empire.

This includes not only the qualification for the single currency, which acts as a cushion against global economic disturbances, but also the qualitative indicators, as the share of IT intensive output of production, the upgrading of exports to higher echelons of the value chain, and not least results of student competences (as reflected in PISA scores), which is a forward indicator of future high-quality output. *In their case, systemic governance aimed at sustaining and deepening the free market arrangements* that emerged from the ruins of the Soviet Empire, not least owing to the total rejection of the Communist heritage as alien and backward looking.

No other post-socialist country could make such an open and final break with its Communist past, than the Baltics.

In this success story, foreign investment and foreign participation in local economic upgrading have been instrumental (cf empirics and its interpretation in the monographs of Gevorkyan, 2018 and Kolodko, 2021). This is the other side of the same coin, namely of the bottom-up component that helped to render Baltic nationalism a forward-looking force. In so doing, this helped to overcome the failures that have been inevitable in creating markets. Reviving traditions dating back to the Hanseatic League, sustaining intimate relationship to other Scandinavian countries, being active and constructive participants in both NATO and the EU *allowed the interaction of micro- and macro-processes that yielded a favorable self-reinforcing process over the past three decades.*

Even this fragmentary overview allows us to prove *both in Central Europe and in the Baltic States the process of transformation has been of top-down nature.* Changing priorities in Central Europe and, in contrast, sticking to the public choices of the early 1990s in the Baltics explain to a large degree the economic choices and, in turn, the divergent outcomes. Social constructivism did work in both country groups, though the outcomes reflect not only the diverging nature of the choices of those in power. Societal feedback was secured via regular elections, and lively investigative journalism, the use of social media by the government, as well as national and EU level court activism. This allowed for a fair degree of policy continuity in Slovakia and Czechia, and major discontinuities in Poland and Hungary.

22.2 China: The prime example of pragmatic bottom-up incrementalism

Being aware of the broad international academic and policy controversy over Chinese development, we cannot even aspire for presenting a concise picture of the developments in the Middle Kingdom. In the present section, we adopt a model-like approach, where China figures as a case for bottom-up forms of systemic governance dominating governmental projects, and social constructivism in general. By the time of writing, the country possesses with the largest GDP (Gross Domestic Product) globally in absolute terms, when measured in purchasing power parity, it is the largest exporting power of the globe, having overtaken Germany and the United States, is a major capital exporter and a defining power in terms of applying artificial intelligence in a number of areas.[3] Thus, China is a country under Communist rule; still, it is a far cry from the industrial museum, what the Soviet Empire used to be.

The controversy in recent years revolved about the nature of growing Chinese ambitions. Namely if and to what degree the Belt and Road Initiative and many other forms of active influencing, from capital investments in Africa to establishing large university campuses in Europe, extending the web of Confucius Institutes, and providing financial and military assistance without open political conditionality all trigger academic debates, which we shall ignore in this place. The listed developments are meant to illustrate the dynamic nature of Chinese developments and its being very unlike anything we know about the Soviet Union and Russia.

Our subject is just one dimension of Chinese development, namely the *nature of governance, which has yielded these staggering outcomes.* Chinese strategy is known to be the opposite to that of Central Europe. At the highest level of abstraction, *it is lack of the constructivist element,* especially of a preconceived end stage, which is perplexing. In turn, the *de-emphasis of institutional factors, especially of building formal institutions,* which have been the backbone of transition strategy in Central Europe, which is peculiar.

Xu (2015) has gone the farthest in underscoring the role of informal institutions in shaping the outcomes. Many other authors highlight the role of *cultural traditions and the role of the diaspora,* especially in the United States and Canada, which mold the actual, often undocumented workings of the Chinese business model, and not only in FDI-dominated areas. In short, *horizontal coordination mechanisms have been at least as relevant as the traditionally emphasized vertical ones.*

This observation does not mean the neglect of top-down policies or the disregard for the political ramifications of economic decentralization. In a country of China's size, it is unsurprising to observe the sustaining of decentral management by a small, though active central state. The limits to spontaneous change, including setting the barriers to how far economic change may trigger political democratization, have been clearly set by the Communist Party, at least since the Tienanmen Square events of June 1989.

Unlike in Central Europe, *the track of political and economic changes has been kept separate.* Likewise, while supporting experimentation with a broad range of property forms, truly private ventures tended to be kept small, or medium size at maximum, not exceeding 22–25 per cent of total national asset value. By advocating non-state property forms, Chinese policymakers mean, in most of the cases, cooperatives, municipally owned enterprises, or various forms of corporatization, as well as joint ventures (as opposed to full foreign ownership via acquisitions and FDI).

The process *of economic change and partial liberalization has thus proceeded under governmental control.* As Gang Fang et al. (2019) explain, this was an enlightened absolutist approach, where much of the detail has been left to local managers. Meanwhile control both over macroeconomic and political processes has remained in the hands of Communist Party leadership. Growth has been fueled primarily by high factor inputs, including a 41–49 per cent rate of fixed capital formation as a share in GDP and ensuring full employment. Furthermore, as the above cited article explains, the *classical Domar effect*, i.e., impacts of restructuring employment in favor of higher productivity industries played a pivotal role.

In this process, *a particular Chinese feature emerged, reliance on trial and error.* Explicating this practice in detail and illustrating it with several empirical cases, Wendy Leutert (2021) talks about institutional innovation through iteration, which *allows for finding out the best fit without relying on a detailed master plan.* The usual way of applying this insight is that an innovation is practiced only in one or some province(s). If successful, the solution is spread nationwide, or in a growing number of provinces. As Chinese provinces are huge, both in terms of territory and population, often comparable to European states, this incrementalism allows for the coexistence of competing solutions. This – together with cultural and institutional peculiarities, expounded by P. Bardhan in this Handbook – may be a major explanation why experimenting worked in China, while the same approach failed miserably in Russia.

The room for, and the practice of, experimentation with competing options is also the case in some less centralized federal states such as Switzerland or Brazil. But the Chinese practice of experimental testing is unique in the long history of policy reforms, and so is the bottom-up approach. The successful model of the 1980s was first tested as an experiment by later Premier Zhao Ziyang when he managed Sichuan Province and later extended to the entire country. While experimentation was anything but unknown in the Soviet Union, their fate was usually marginalization. No wonder, in a vertically organized centralized state, the alien body is likely to evaporate. By contrast, the decentralized organization of China followed experimental solutions, including the Special Economic Zones, to flourish, without impeding the traditionalist practices of the neighboring regions.

It is understood that modern growth theory would forecast severe limitations to the sustainability of such a growth model eventually. Authoritative Chinese analysts talk about the need for supply-side reforms (Fan Cai, 2020, chapters 13 and 14) that allow the country to move on a path, where total factor productivity growth rather than factor inputs decide over the rate of growth. This is the way to cope with the problem of aging and environmental challenges. Financial intermediation can no longer be unilaterally subordinate to investment decisions taken by the center through bureaucratic bargains. *This insight is certainly a call for changing the vertical axis in systemic governance,* else the limitations of purely horizontal innovations are likely to come to the fore.

One of the many paradoxes of Chinese economic development has been the huge territorial and vertical inequality. In terms of regions, the backward West is – figuratively – home of the Middle Ages, while seashore cities, especially in the Special Economic Zones, exhibit a vibrant life, resembling American or Japanese counterparts. The per capita income difference may be as much as 13–15 times, as between Albania and Liechtenstein, still within one single polity (unlike the European countries in the comparison). In terms of Gini coefficient, the cited World Bank source estimate is 38.6, which is comparable to figures of Burundi, Indonesia, or Morocco. The trouble is that the named countries do not have egalitarian communism as an officially declared ruling ideology, nor do they possess the historic legacy of communitarianism.

The centralization tendency under the first decade of the Xi Presidency since 2012 has diminished the size of inequality (cf below), while the composition of the ruling stratum seems to have been changed. This happened in part due to political purges, in part due to market processes, most conspicuously illustrated by the collapse of the second-largest developer company of China, Evergrande in December 2021.

Under this angle, it is noteworthy that recent empirical analysis of Kanbur et al. (2021) has found the growth of inequalities peaking and even diminishing in the past decade. This may be due to the growing centralization of income policies, the introduction of partially state-run and partially corporate financed pension system as well as the growing central administration of prices. *In short, both vertical and horizontal aspects of systemic governance have come to play.* And diminishing inequality under more centralization has been one of the traditional laws of traditional comparative economics.

In the final assessment (at least for this section), we may come to the following conclusion. The centralized, but experimenting and innovative, Chinese system allowed the country to grow if it was a low level of development. The current per capita GDP at market prices is put to 11,819 US dollars, whereby the country is only number 61 from among the 160 countries ranked by the IMF in 2021.[4] This is in line with the received wisdom about the temporary uses of centralized management for resource mobilization and thus being adequate for the take-off period. But this may well be followed by the much-theorized middle-income trap. If the government is unwilling or unable to implement those far-reaching institutional reforms, which favor innovation and bottom-up endogenous growth, deceleration of growth is not just conceivable but even likely.

While China remained the only major country with positive growth in 2020 despite COVID, growth recovered to previous levels in 2021. But this is likely to be a one-time game, as the long-term trend is one of decline. The peak year of modern Chinese GDP growth was at 14 pc back in 2007, halving to 7.8 pc by 2012, further slowing to 7 pc in 2015, 5.95 pc in 2019, 2.4 pc in 2020 – that was world championship in the COVID year – and recovering at a robust rate of 8.1 pc in 2021 (preliminary), slowing down to 5.1 pc only in 2022 (World Bank Group: China Economic Update, 22 Dec. 2021), *which fits in the longer-term trend.* Once we consider that China tended to grow with a fixed capital formation ratio of 49 pc of GDP, currently down to 40 pc, and allocative efficiency being low, *the Domar and Solow inspired insights about the inevitability of secular slowdown seem to hold.* The alternative – as the Chinese analysts cited above – would be to radicalize market reforms, which does not seem to be the agenda of the Xi Presidency.

Furthermore, China has come to a crossroad (Csaba, 2020), not least due to the ongoing and even strengthening political centralization. The return of statism has long been demonstrable in the economy (Lardy, 2019). Reinforcing the Maoist principles and practices, including surveillance of dissidents and suppression of political disagreements on grounds of 'deviation from the Party line', seems to have been long forgotten or assigned to history books have been revived, according to Zhen (2020) and sources cited above and below. But reality is complex: *systemic governance reflects the empirically tested reality that economic and political decision-making may though be divorced, but only for a limited amount of time.* In the longer run, coherence emerges since the same person is unlikely to act from 8 to 16 hours as a bureaucrat, a Party loyalist, and start thinking in unconventional, innovative fashions from 16 to 24 hours. He who expects order in one dimension is unlikely to revolutionize technology and trade through his second self.

As I tried to elaborate in the article above, we do not yet have enough insights to tell if the game is over, and traditionalists are back on track. Many observers (Schuman, 2021) claim so. What we can venture is the conclusion that a strategy of continuous, even gradual, modernization and catching up with Singapore (59,500 US dollars) or Hong Kong (37,190 US dollars) in terms of per capita income would certainly require additional efforts in the direction of marketization and related regulation, which ensures the civilized outcomes of the business interplay. Evergrande may well have been the latest warning.

22.3 Systemic governance: A specific vehicle of comparative studies

Having conducted a schematic exercise in comparative economic studies, we have attempted to show how the concept of systemic governance may be helpful – in understanding real-world phenomena. This ambition has traditionally been a main driver of inquiries in the social sciences, though it has become gradually fading from the increasingly formal modern economics. It is coherence and the maths one uses which is the arbiter of decent quality research. No less of an authority than former chief economist of the World Bank, the 2018 Nobel winner Paul Romer (2015), reminded us of the dangers that the perfunctory use of mathematics often covers 'politics masquerade as science', while neglecting the tight, substantive, and logical interrelationships, which should be the backbone of the academic argument.

Our concept is not liable to formal testing. Still, as we hope to have illustrated, it may be helpful in comprehending real-world phenomena, not explained sufficiently by ruling approaches. This is how such old-fashioned concepts as trustworthiness and personal integrity, solidity, or even fundamental uncertainty have returned to economic analyses, especially following the Great Recession.

As the insightful analysis of Grzegorz Kolodko (2020) indicates, the rise of China could not have been predicted on the grounds of previously available theories. Neither neoclassical approaches, where the combination of factors is everything, nor historically informed, old institutionalism would have predicted the breakthrough in what he terms the move from the Third World to the First World. In so doing, the truly intriguing aspect is that of technological change. Players like Huawei or Lenovo would have been unthinkable in the Soviet Union, and comparative economics of the classical brand had convincing explanations, why so. Still, by highlighting the interaction of factors, mostly specific to China and its history, not least the considerable freedom allowed to entrepreneurs to experiment and imitate foreign solutions, sustaining intimate relationship to the diaspora, not least via FDI and cultural community, have produced miracles. Parts of China have long been integrated in the global system, as the COVID testified, while others, as Uiguria or Tibet, have an exceptionally long way to it.

But similarly, intriguing is the experience of backsliding in Central Europe. As the countries have been exposed to the common rules and increasingly supranational arrangements of the European Fiscal and Banking Union, the European Court of Justice, and not least of the European Central Bank and an ever more activist Commission, the regress into more statist options has been a surprise. If it happens under the banner of inter-governmentalism, *étatisme* is not something to be rejected out of hand. At the end of the day, it is Prime Ministers who sit on the Council, which has the final say on everything of relevance. This follows from the Treaties, even if some recent practices of promoting national champions are obviously out of line with the spirit and sometimes even the letter of European regulations.

As the analytical narratives we cited in the first section all agree, individual mishaps, individual errors, or slippages may well be attributed to coincidental factors. However, the genuinely interesting and worrying element is the multiplication of mistakes, all pointing in the same direction. This is what János Kornai (2021) in his last book calls repeatedly an autocracy, where people are not killed or imprisoned for their dissenting views, as in Belarus or North Korea, but they may lose their jobs, access to publicity, or forced to sell their property at bargain prices, when an 'irresistable' offer emerges.

A telling example of how *the traditional meaning of privatization versus nationalization may change* can be taken from the banking sector. Here re-imposing national majority ownership counts as a basic strategy for the Fidesz government in the entire 2010–2022 period. The most illustrious among the many similar cases has been that of the Hungarian Foreign Trade Bank, MKB. This institution had been privatized to the Bayerische Landeszentralbank, not least to ensure capital backing at a crisis that may erupt on global markets. Surprisingly to many, it was the mother company, the Bavarian parastatal that got into trouble in 2009, due to their involvement on the American subprime market, while MKB was still faring well. As one of the conditions for recovery from German public money, the regulator prescribed that the BLZ sells off all its affiliations abroad, since these qualify as risky.

The MKB controlling much of the finances of the top echelons of business and politics was finally bought in 2015 by a group of private persons, led by Imre Balogh, by that time CEO (currently deputy CEO) of MKB and former Deputy Governor of the National Bank. The gentleman received a multibillion low-cost credit to purchase the bank. The institution needed recapitalization, which happened in several tranches. Finally, in 2020, the bank was sold to Lőrinc Mészáros, who is a close friend of the PM. The bank was merged with two others, Budapest Bank, bought from GE Capital in 2017, and Takarékbank, a conglomerate of rural savings' cooperatives. The thus emerging Hungarian Bank Holding is comparable in asset size to the previously market-dominant OTP.

It is difficult to explain to anyone familiar with bank economics, what is the logic of merging three banks with entirely different clientele, different cultures, and different managements/histories. Besides the top management, everything seems to have remained intact. In sum, no feedback from the market. Alas, until spring 2022, not even a common stamp or a common logo of the conglomerate was created, which suggests a formal merger, following a political and power logic. The relative efficiency, and especially the improvement in the performance of the constituent banks, is yet to be established, but is not over the all-out recovery of financial intermediation in general.

State property has amassed a completely new meaning between the two crises in the global economy (Szanyi, 2019b). And so had state regulation, over and above the classical role of the custodian of public interest against private monopolies and political arbitrariness, as the classical book of Eucken (1940 [1992]) would have suggested. But if we follow the reading of Robert Wade (2018) it is still a very distinct creature from the East Asian practices, where private property and co-decision of business and political elites have been the rule. By contrast, the literature and empires we cited all indicate a model where political power is the independent and business power the dependent variable.

Rochlitz and associates (2020) rightly termed the above as business capture, by reverting the more classical concept of state capture, when – as in Latin America – business groups dominate public offices. But this has evolved under the Putin era into institutionalized and centralized corruption, where the subordination of business interest is even more explicit.

The literature is divided on what to think of this strange interlude. Voszka (2021) for one argues that this is a trend observable also in the West positively triggered by the Great Recession, particularly in countries like Spain, Italy, and France; thus, it is not to be singled out as a peculiar feature of post-communist change. By contrast, many of our sources cited above, especially Magyar and Madlovics (2020) and Szelényi and Mihályi (2020) underscore the sociopolitical content and consequences of this institutional change, driving all countries concerned farther away from any form of liberal market economy, irrespective of historical preliminaries or geographical location. In the latter reading, Putinism is not a perversion but a central model of modern political capitalism. Self-enrichment, as opposed to any interpretation of a public purpose, has been prevailing, as a formative element.

Here we have another example, where *foreign and domestic, political, and economic, personal, and market considerations all coexist*. None of the previously available theories, either of political science or of finance, would have been helpful in explaining what could be observed. *Systemic governance is the clue.* No macro- or micro-theory on its own could replace this interdisciplinary concept and toolkit of analysis.

The concept is useful if *we are to explain in positive terms what the illiberal state and the authoritarian model of the economy mean in Central Europe,* without replacing previous, established concepts, complementing those. The statist turns, which are by no means restricted to the post-communist world, have revived the age-old debate if civilized market economy and parliamentary democracy are mutually supportive, or presuppose one another eventually, or by contrast, this claim is doctrinaire and made obsolete by history. The original suggestion goes back to the founding father of the German social market economy, Walter Eucken (1940 [1992]) who famously argued, on the ground of empirical and philosophical considerations, that *the two orders are inherently intertwined.* Therefore, eventually, no dictatorship can coexist with a market economy, and no democratic system survives the lack of a market economy.

The case of market socialism, i.e., a democratic superstructure based on a centrally managed economy and public property, has been shown to be unfeasible both in theory and on the ground (Kornai, 1993; Kornai, 2007).

While not preempting the chapters on China in this volume, we may recall that Chinese authors regularly speak of a socialist market economy, where *the use of market forces remains constrained and instrumental to serving* and reflected in major *policy objectives set by the Communist Party.* Therefore, investment decisions continue to be made centrally, rather than following signals of a thin and segmented capital market (Lin, 2012 and Zhang, 2014, two authors not yet accounting for the further centralization that occurred since their publication).

The other option is more complex. With the global revival of statism governmental management of economic affairs has spread throughout the country and the sector. We have cited above the debate if it is triggered by hyper-globalization or by political regression to authoritarian populism. The collection of papers edited by Szanyi (2019b) gives a broad overview of how and why appreciating *the role of public management of economic affairs has been gaining momentum and has become part of good manners also in advanced economies.* Powerful interpretations of the developmental state (Wade, 2018) also argue in favor of combining statism with dynamic economic growth. This is plausible, but not our reading of events.

What we have seen is more interventionism without more public property and central management. In East Asia, while the model is a long way from the original Washington Consensus, it is based on the role of private business and open foreign relations, including finances. In Western Europe and the United States, we see classical big government more along the traditional tax and spend manner, or of selective protectionism, including R&D support and market oversight, not a general trend to populist-authoritarian rule, as was feared under the Trump era. By contrast, reverting market reforms in Russia and China, but also in Poland and Hungary, in a different quality, have entailed limitations on the previous 'neoliberal' political arrangement.

Relying on the concept of systemic governance, we may be less surprised. This concept provides *the micro- and meso-economic foundation for understanding what we see in the macro. Overall — though not in the short run — Eucken was right.*

22.4 Preliminary wrap-up

In this chapter, we introduced a novel concept in comparative economic studies, systemic governance. Building on established approaches in management, we made some productive steps. First, a micro-based approach to macroeconomics was introduced, which does not neglect but incorporates the institutional dimension in explaining various varieties of capitalism. Second, we provided justification for multidisciplinary approaches. Third, in parallel to financial economics, we advocated the use of qualitative approaches in understanding real-world phenomena. Fourth, we provided schematic analyses of top-down and bottom-up cases of social engineering. Finally, we attempted to integrate our insights in previously available knowledge.

This intellectual journey may prove the usefulness of comparative economic studies approach to understanding real-world phenomena. While being just one of the many competing and conceivable options, we hope to have contributed to clarifying what is the future and what are the analytical and policy uses of this field of inquiry.

Notes

1 Useful comments of the editors, as well as of D. Győrffy and G.W. Kolodko are appreciated with the usual caveats.
2 Iván Szelényi (2016) reminds us of the fact, that the insight about the *Macht des Beherrschten* goes back to the writings of Max Weber, as a fourth type of power. This insight, no matter how foundational for modern thinking, has been forgotten more than once.
3 For long term standardized and comparable data cf: databank.worldbank.org, accessed on 12 June 2021.
4 IMF: *World Economic Outlook,* April, 2021 (retrieved on 11 June 2021).

References

Bagenholm, A. et al. eds. (2021). *The Oxford Handbook of the Quality of Government.* Oxford and New York: Oxford University Press.
Blanchard, O. and Summers, L. eds. (2019). *Evolution or Revolution? The State of Macroeconomic Policies.* Cambridge, MA and London: MIT Press.
Blum, K. and Varga, M. (2021). Conservative developmental statism. In: Pickel, A., Blum, K. and Varga, M. eds: *Handbook of Economic Nationalism.* Cheltenham: Edward Elgar (in print, text accessed via ResearchGate, 21 May).

Burda, M. and Wyplosz, C. (2017). *Macroeconomics: A European Text*, 7th edition. Oxford and New York: Oxford University Press.

Cai, F. (2020). *Demographic Perspective of China's Economic Development*. Abingdon: Routledge.

Casagrande, S. and Dallago, B. (2021). Benchmarking institutional variety in the Eurozone: an empirical investigation. *Economic Systems*, vol. 45, no. 1, article no. 100 838 (retrieved from Elsevier website, 20 May).

Csaba, L. (2020). China at the crossroads. *Acta Oeconomica*, vol. 70, special issue no. 1, pp. 3–14.

Csaba, L. (2021). Institutions and change: new horizons for economic theory. In: Gerőcs, T. and Ricz, J. eds: *The Post-Crisis Developmental State*. Houndmills: Palgrave, pp. 13–31.

Eucken, W. (1940 [1992]). *The Foundations of Economics: History and Theory in the Analysis of Economic Reality*. Heidelberg: Springer Verlag.

Fang, G., Ma, G. and Wang, X. (2019). Institutional reform and economic growth in China: a 40-year progress report toward marketization. *Acta Oeconomica*, vol. 69, special issue no. 1, pp. 7–20.

Galbács, P. (2020). *The Friedman–Lucas Controversy in Macroeconomics: A Structuralist Approach*. London: Academic Press.

Gevorkyan, A. (2018). *Transition Economies: Transformation, Development and Societies in Central-Eastern Europe and the Former Soviet Union*. Abingdon: Routledge.

Grabel, I. (2017). *When Things Don't Fall Apart: Global Financial Governance and Developmental Finance in an Age of Privatization*. Cambridge, MA and London: MIT Press.

Győrffy, D. (2021). The middle-income trap in Central and Eastern Europe. *Comparative European Politics*, vol. 20, no. 1, pp. 90–113.

Kanbur, R., Wang, Y. and Zhang, X. (2021). The great Chinese inequality turnaround. *Journal of Comparative Economics*, vol. 49, no. 2, pp. 467–482.

Kolodko, G.W. (2020). *China and the Future of Globalization: The Political Economy of China's Rise*. London: I.B. Tauris.

Kolodko, G.W. (2021). *The Quest for Development Success: Bridging Theoretical Reasoning with Economic Practice*. Lanham, MD: Lexington Books.

Kornai, J. (1993). Market socialism revisited. In: Bardhan, P. and Romer, J. eds: *Market Socialism: The Current Debate*. Oxford and New York: Oxford University Press, pp. 42–68.

Kornai, J. (2007). *From Socialism to Capitalism*. Budapest and New York: CEU Press.

Kornai, J. (2016). The system paradigm revisited. *Acta Oeconomica*, vol. 66, no. 4, pp. 547–596.

Kornai, J. (2021). *Töprengések (Reflections)*. Budapest: HVG-Orac.

Lardy, N. (2019). *The State Strikes Back: The End of Economic Reform in China?* Washington, DC: Peterson Institute of International Economics Press.

Leutert, W. (2021). Innovation through iteration: policy feedback loops in China's economic reform. *World Development*, vol. 138, February, article no. 105 173.

Lin, J.L. (2012). *Demystifying the Chinese Economy*. Cambridge and New York: Cambridge University Press.

Magyar, B. and Madlovics, B. (2020). *The Anatomy of Post-communist Regimes. A Conceptual Framework*. Budapest and New York: CEU Press.

Merkel, W., Kollmorgen, R. and Wagener, H.J. eds. (2019). *The Handbook of Political, Social and Economic Transformation*. Oxford and New York: Oxford University Press.

Önder, Z. and Özildirim, S. (2016). Foreign banks, financial crises, and macroeconomic fluctuations. *Economics of Transition and Institutional Change*, vol. 24, no. 3, pp. 447–469.

Rochlitz, M., Kazun, A. and Yakovlev, A. (2020). Property rights in Russia after 2009: from business capture to centralized corruption? *Post-Soviet Affairs*, vol. 36, nos. 5–6, pp. 434–450.

Romer, P. (2015). Mathiness in the theory of economic growth. *American Economic Review*, vol. 105, no. 5, pp. 89–93.

Schuman, M. (2021). The undoing of China's economic miracle. *The Atlantic*, vol. 163, no. 1, online edition, accessed on 9 June.

Szanyi, M. ed. (2019b). *Seeking the Best Master: State Ownership in the Varieties of Capitalism*. Budapest and New York: CEU Press.

Szanyi, M. (2019a). The emergence of patronage and changing forms of rent seeking in Central and Eastern Europe. *Post-Communist Economies*, vol. 34, no. 1, pp. 122–141.

Szelényi, I. (2016). Weber's theory of domination and post-communist capitalisms. *Theory and Society*, vol. 45, no. 1, pp. 1–24.

Szelényi, I. and Mihályi, P. (2020). *Varieties of Post-Communist Capitalism: A Comparative Analysis of Eastern Europe, Russia, and China*. Leiden: Brill.

von Mises, L. (1940 [1963]). *Human Action: A Treatise on Economics,* 3rd, revised edition. Chicago, IL: Contemporary Books.

Voszka, É. (2021). The dynamics of state ownership: the decisive role of crises. *Acta Oeconomica*, vol. 71, no. 2, pp. 235–257.

Wade, R. (2018). The developmental state: dead or alive? *Development and Change*, vol. 49, no. 2, pp. 518–541.

Xu, G.-D. (2015). The institutional foundations of China's unbalanced economy. *Europe-Asia Studies*, vol. 67, no. 1, pp. 1351–1370.

Zhang, W.-Y. (2014). *The Logic of the Market: An Insider's View of Chinese Economic Reform.* Washington, DC: CATO Institute.

Zhen, J. (2020). Artificial intelligence and China's authoritarian rule. *International Affairs*, vol. 96, no. 6, pp. 1441–1459.

23

INSTITUTIONAL AND POLICY DETERMINANTS OF ECONOMIC SPECIALIZATION*

Andrea Boltho

MAGDALEN COLLEGE, UNIVERSITY OF OXFORD, OXFORD, UK

23.1 Introduction

This volume is primarily concerned with comparative studies of different economic systems. Inevitably, therefore, it privileges the study of institutions. This chapter looks at what determines countries' international trade specialization, i.e., their comparative advantage. The apparent overlap with institutions would seem relatively thin. Most theories and most comparative evidence suggest that a country's comparative advantage is primarily determined by purely economic forces such as technology, factor endowments, tastes (in turn a function of income), etc. Institutions and economic systems are not absent, but, traditionally, they have not loomed large as factors influencing trade patterns.

Section 23.2 briefly looks at what are considered to be the standard explanations for why countries specialize in the production and export of particular goods covering in turn the Ricardian approach (which privileges international differences in technology), the neo-classical Heckscher–Ohlin model (which gives pride of place to countries' differing factor endowments) and more modern approaches that look at what is called intra-industry trade (and stress the role played by differing tastes and incomes, as well as by scale economies and imperfect competition, in forging trade patterns). Section 23.3 turns to two more recent strands in the literature which have introduced the role of institutions. One has emphasized specific institutional features (e.g., the legal characteristics of countries, their regulation, and their financial structures) which can confer comparative advantage to sectors dependent on such institutions; another one has looked, more broadly, at different varieties of capitalism as sources for different patterns of specialization.

Section 23.4 shifts from what is basically a static approach to a dynamic one, by looking at what has caused the often deep and rapid transformations in countries' industrial structures and export composition across time and at the possible role of institutions in this process.

*The author is grateful to Wendy Carlin, Vijay Joshi and the editors of this volume for numerous helpful comments. The chapter was written between the spring and the winter of 2021, a period during which the author had no access to any public library. This meant that a number of relevant books and historical statistical sources could not be consulted. The resulting text inevitably reflects this.

While most institutions change only slowly and are thus unlikely to have strong effects on dynamic comparative advantage, economic policies, be they of the import-substitution or of the export promotion variety, can, by contrast, have such effects. Economic history suggests that there are instances in which policies did succeed in altering a country's comparative advantage and thus creating successful infant (and, eventually, mature) industries. A brief Conclusions section briefly concludes.

Throughout, the accent will be on the manufacturing sector. The time period covered stretches over a century (though most of the empirical findings in the literature pertain to the period following World War II, or even only to the period 1980–2020). The country coverage is limited to the industrialized countries of Western Europe, North America and the Far East (including, therefore, some emerging economies such as South Korea, Taiwan or China, but not the bulk of the developing world).

23.2 What determines comparative advantage?

Since Ricardo's path-breaking work on comparative advantage (Ricardo, 1817),[1] economists have tried to explain why different countries specialize in the production of different goods. The literature on the subject is vast and clearly no monocausal explanation has been found. This section will, very briefly, recapitulate the major traditional views that have been expounded.

Ricardo himself stressed differences in labor productivity, arising in turn from different climatic conditions or different production technologies. This clearly shed light on what were the main trade flows of the early 19th century. Climatic conditions were an obvious explanation for trade in many primary agricultural products, exported by overseas colonies to Europe. Similarly, different technological endowments explained the exports of manufactures from Europe to the developing economies in the rest of the world. Since then, studies stressing the importance of labor productivity have found often strong correlations with particular export patterns (e.g., MacDougall, 1951 and 1952). However persuasive such findings are, they do not necessarily fully vindicate an explanation stressing solely different technologies if only because superior labor productivity in one country may be due not so much to a more efficient production function specific to that country but, possibly, to a greater endowment of capital per worker.

It is this possibility that led to the establishment of an alternative theory which rejected the idea that technology and production functions differed across the world and put in its place differences in the relative endowments of factors of production, primarily labor and capital. The so-called Heckscher–Ohlin model (from the names of its two principal progenitors) has become the most widely (though not universally) accepted view of what determines trade flows: namely factor intensities. Countries that are relatively labor abundant will export goods that are relatively intensive in the use of labor and vice-versa for relatively capital abundant countries. Simplicity, parsimoniousness and compatibility with the neo-classical model have made of this approach the workhorse of international trade theory. And an abundant literature has found that factor intensities can, indeed, throw a good deal of light on trade patterns (e.g., Davis and Weinstein, 2001).

Two empirical findings, however, have cast some doubt on the generality of the approach. The first was the so-called Leontief paradox that argued, on the basis of empirical evidence, that the country with the largest capital endowment in the world, the US, rather than exporting capital-intensive goods was, in 1947, importing relatively capital-intensive goods (Leontief, 1953). Numerous explanations have been put forward to explain this apparent anomaly, of which by far the most persuasive has been the addition of a third factor of production namely human capital (which was then, and still is, relatively abundant in the United States). Adding human capital to physical capital and to unskilled labor did away with the paradox and paved the way for numerous other studies which showed trade patterns fitting the now modified Heckscher–Ohlin theorem (e.g., Balassa 1979 and 1986; Romalis, 2004).

The second attack on this theorem came from a different and more recent finding: the discovery that from the late 1950s onward, a growing volume of trade took place between countries with very similar technologies and very similar factor endowments (within Western Europe in particular, but also between other advanced countries) and consisted of very similar products (Grubel and Lloyd, 1975). A tentative OECD estimate[2] suggested that for most member countries of the Organization 60–80 per cent of trade in manufactures, over the years 1997–2008, was of an intra-industry nature, going from a low of 50 per cent for Japan to a high of 90 per cent for Belgium (OECD, 2010).

This finding clearly went against both the Ricardian and the Heckscher–Ohlin approaches which stressed trade of very different products and between very different countries, be this in their technological prowess or in their factor endowment. Of the many explanations put forward for the existence of such intra-industry trade, two probably stand out, both of which break with the neo-classical tradition. One allows for imperfect competition and scale economies within countries, the other for differences across countries in tastes and in the demand for variety that comes with relatively high incomes (Greenway and Milner, 1987).

The difference in tastes hypothesis (Linder, 1961) assumes that countries will specialize in products favored by domestic consumers, with high-income countries producing high-quality goods and finding niche markets for them abroad. Cheaper varieties of the same good will be produced in lower income countries and some will be sold in the high-income ones (a possible example could be Volvo and Fiat cars, both of which are consumed, if in different proportions, in Sweden and Italy). And the imperfect competition assumption allows both Volvo and Fiat to achieve scale economies in production, strengthening their competitive advantages.

A further strand of the literature looks at changes through time in comparative advantage by stressing technological leads and lags and the so-called product cycle. The Heckscher–Ohlin model assumes technology to be the same all over the world and does not allow, therefore, for localized bursts of technological innovation. Since these, however, do occur in different parts of the world and at different times, a country may reap a quasi-monopoly for either a new product or a new process (Posner, 1961). This advantage may be only temporary as imitation of the new technology spreads across the world, or it could become semi-permanent if the initial innovation spurs further innovations allowing the country to reap dynamic economies of scale. Alternatively, it could even lead to a reversal of trade flows as in the product cycle theory (Vernon, 1966). In this approach, a labor-saving innovation takes place initially in a country with high labor costs. The Posnerian quasi-monopoly advantage that this innovation confers may, however, be eroded not by imitation abroad but by the outward direct investment of firms located in the innovating country. As products get standardized through time, lowering unit costs becomes increasingly important and production of the good in question may be transferred to a more labor abundant country. The cycle closes when the latter country starts exporting the product back to the original innovating country.

It should be noted that in all these various approaches, the major ultimate forces determining comparative advantage are also those that determine longer term growth in standard economic theory: capital accumulation, labor force growth and technological progress. This view, however, has been increasingly put into question in more recent years by scholars who stress the role of institutions in shaping both long-run growth and patterns of trade (Acemoglu *et al.*, 2005; Nunn and Trefler, 2014).

23.3 Do institutions matter for comparative advantage?[3]

Commerce and manufactures can seldom flourish long in any state which does not enjoy a regular administration of justice, in which the people do not feel themselves secure in the possession of their property, in which the faith of contracts is not supported by law, and in which the authority of the state is not supposed to be regularly employed in enforcing the payment of debts from all those who are able to pay. Commerce and manufactures, in short, can seldom flourish in any state in which there is not a certain degree of confidence in the justice of government.

Adam Smith cited in Rodrik *et al.* (2004, p. 131)

As this quote from the father of political economy suggests, institutions and policies are hugely important. Their smooth functioning is implicit in the various traditional approaches to comparative advantage briefly surveyed in the previous section and is clearly necessary for the pursuit of international trade. Indeed, it can be argued that it is institutions that are behind the endowments that traditional theory focuses on, be these Ricardo's technology or human capital accumulation: "19th century English comparative advantage in advanced manufacturing goods can be traced back in no small part to its institutions, institutions that promoted innovation and commercial enterprise" (Nunn and Trefler, 2014, p. 263).[4] This and the next section will look at whether their smooth functioning is uniform across the world.

It was clearly not uniform when central planning prevailed in many East European countries (and elsewhere). The abundant literature on differing economic systems at the time, however, had little to say on what determined the comparative advantage of the centrally planned economies. These traded, of course, but the composition of their trade usually reflected decisions based on very imperfect indicators of comparative costs, imperfect because of the absence in all these countries of a proper pricing mechanism reflecting relative scarcities. Trade with the capitalist world before the fall of the Berlin Wall in 1989 was limited, with Eastern Europe and the Soviet Union selling principally primary products (e.g., coal from Poland or oil, timber, minerals and furs from the Soviet Union) and importing machinery from West Germany, France or Italy. Within the Eastern trading area (Comecon), some trade relations reflected pre-World War II specializations with East Germany and Czechoslovakia, for instance, concentrating on exports of machinery. Though Comecon attempted to plan some production and trade flows across the member countries, not much happened since the institution had little or no supra-national authority. Exports often just reflected a crude factor endowment approach though, paradoxically, a mid-1960s Russian study suggested that Soviet exports were more capital-intensive than Soviet imports – a Leontief paradox in reverse (Boltho, 1971).[5] The institutional differences between East and West were huge; their impact on trade was, arguably, very limited.

Institutional factors may well be more important in shedding light on the trade patterns of today's market economies, even if their institutions do not differ as much as those of the centrally planned economies did at the time. An increasing body of research has in recent years looked at some of the possible influences that institutions may have on a country's exports specialization.[6] The starting point for much of this work has been the realization that in the many sectors in which there are no spot markets for inputs, production must rely on complex inter-relationships between firms which require either trust or binding legal agreements. In such instances, mechanisms to ensure contract enforcement are crucial. Countries which have better legal institutions, security of property rights and efficient courts make it easier for firms to specialize in more complex products that require relation-specific investment (and/or a large number of inputs), such as aircraft production, electrical and electronic machinery or other sophisticated manufactures (Nunn, 2007). Northern advanced countries have, on the whole, better judicial institutions than their Southern developing counterparts and their specialization in such technologically advanced products may thus reflect not only high levels of human capital or R&D expenditure, but also their institutional advantage. Empirical evidence confirms some of these findings (Berkowitz *et al.*, 2006; Levchenko, 2007; Costinot, 2009). Indeed, it has been argued that "contract enforcement explains more of the global pattern of trade than countries' endowments of physical capital and skilled labor combined" (Nunn, 2007, p. 594), a remarkable finding given the near unanimity, in earlier writings, on the finding that human and physical capital are the major determinants of a country's comparative advantage.

A further institutional feature that can throw light on countries' export structures is the development of their financial markets: "Industrial sectors that are relatively more in need of external finance develop disproportionately faster in countries with more-developed financial markets" (Rajan and Zingales, 1998, p. 559). In other words, the larger and more efficient such markets are, the more outside finance is available for firms and this, in turn, provides an advantage in producing and exporting manufactured goods that, in particular, exploit scale economies (Beck, 2002 and 2003). Similarly, it has been found that financially advanced economies export more in sectors intensive in outside finance. These are found primarily in advanced manufacturing activities, such as professional and scientific equipment or electrical machinery (Manova, 2013). It has even been claimed that: "differences in financial systems are more important determinants of the pattern of specialization between OECD countries than differences in human capital" (Svaleryd and Vlachos, 2005, p. 135), with the financial system seen as a "factor of production". This is another startling proposition, comparable to the one mentioned above about the importance of contract enforcement.

A study attempting to quantify all these various strands of institutional influences on comparative advantage (including those coming from the labor market, for which see more below) confirms their overall importance relative to the more traditional Heckscher–Ohlin forces (Chor, 2010). These matter of course, with both human and physical capital having sizeable effects on comparative advantage. The interactions between relation-specific investment or input complexity and the quality of a country's legal system take, however, pride of place. Indeed, legal institutions seem to matter more for explaining trade flows than even physical distance (*ibid.*).

The literature surveyed so far has mainly looked at institutions that show marked differences between advanced and developing economies. The rule of law, relative judicial efficiency, established property rights, protection of investors or well-developed financial markets are all features that figure much more prominently in the OECD countries than in, for instance, Latin America, South Asia or Sub-Saharan Africa. And these features help specialization in complex manufacturing production and/or in advanced technological products which, in turn, favor economic growth. The inevitable conclusion is "to those who have shall be given".

It is unlikely that this state of affairs will change rapidly. Much of the literature surveyed so far argues that it is particular institutions that generated comparative advantage in complex sectors and this, in turn, fostered development. The assumption is that causality goes from institutions to development and that developing countries should therefore copy what are basically Anglo-American institutions which "often favor the rich over the poor, capital over labor and finance capital over industrial capital" (Chang, 2011, p. 473). Yet, many of the richer countries' institutions evolved incrementally over long periods of time or were acquired only after rapid economic development had already taken place. Causality is, perhaps, not as simple as much of the literature suggests.

A different strand of the literature looks instead at very broad institutional differences within the advanced countries themselves (Hall and Soskice, 2001). This relatively recent and very general approach, rooted in corporate behavior, also puts forward an institutional view of comparative advantage. Contrary to the literature seen so far, which would broadly advocate a convergence of national institutions toward "best practice" models, this approach, which goes under the name of "varieties of capitalism", argues that different institutional infrastructures can prosper in different countries. The approach is very interesting; for the time being, however, it lacks firm empirical support as far as comparative advantage is concerned.[7]

Hall and Soskice distinguish between two main forms of modern capitalism: liberal market economies and coordinated market economies. In the former group, made up of countries such as the US, the UK, Canada or Ireland, "firms coordinate their activities primarily via … competitive market arrangements" (Hall and Soskice, 2001, p. 8). These economies are characterized by rapid innovation, flexible labor markets with great freedom for managers to hire and fire, dependence on stock markets, etc. In the latter group, in which figure Japan, Germany, the Netherlands, Switzerland and others, "firms depend more heavily on non-market relationships to coordinate their endeavors" (*ibid.*, p. 8). Much greater reliance is here put, for instance, on so-called patient capital provided by a financial system, centered on universal banks, that closely cooperates with firms and accepts employment protection and non-market coordination in industrial relations. Clearly, such a system requires institutions that provide sharing of information, monitor behavior and, potentially, sanction defections. Culture, informal rules and history also shape outcomes.[8]

This approach is then used to formulate a theory of "comparative institutional advantage" which argues that corporate strategies will differ across different countries. This, in turn, will lead them to specialize in producing different goods which rely on different institutional supports, particularly so in the case of innovations. Thus, liberal market economies will have an advantage in radical innovations which require rapid changes and risk taking, easy access to venture finance and/or flexibility in hiring and firing (e.g., biotechnology, semiconductors or complex systems such as telecommunications). Conversely, coordinated market economies can better support incremental innovation, with the workforce itself, secure in its employment, ensuring high quality and contributing to product or process changes in areas such as mechanical engineering, consumer durables or machine tools. Indeed, data from the European Patent Office classifying products by whether their technological progress is innovative or incremental, show a startling picture, with Germany and the US, for instance, having almost opposite specialization patterns in patent activity (*ibid.*, pp. 42–43). This finding lends strength to a view that stresses that such very broad institutional differences have an impact on comparative advantage.

In the same vein are approaches that look more specifically at institutional differences within labor markets in the advanced economies. It has thus been argued that countries with relatively rigid labor markets (i.e., countries that would fit with the Hall–Soskice classification of coordinated market economies) specialize in products with low demand volatility, which can often be found at later stages of the product cycle and in which sudden declines in demand, and hence expensive redundancies, are less likely. The opposite happens in countries with more flexible labor markets and relatively low firing costs. These tend to specialize in "young" and often high-tech goods which exhibit more volatile demand and employment patterns (Saint-Paul, 1997; Cuñat and Melitz, 2012).

As Hall and Soskice (2001) argue, their country classifications are not immutable. Institutional features can change from one decade to the next, and so can specialization patterns. This was shown to be the case, for instance, for Italy and Japan between the 1950s and the 1990s (Boltho, 2001). At the outset, the two countries exported very similar commodities,[9] usually low-tech and with relatively low-income elasticities of demand on world markets (e.g., clothing and various semi-manufactures). Four decades later that picture had changed. Italy's exports were still concentrated in semi-manufactures and consumer goods (if of a much higher quality than in the 1950s), but Japan's now consisted overwhelmingly of machinery, transport equipment and precision instruments.[10] Two major explanations were put forward for these very divergent developments: greater "long-termism" in Japanese than in Italian firms and, more tentatively, a more successful industrial policy in Japan than in Italy. The latter argument points to another, if less direct, way in which institutions can affect comparative advantage, namely the role of economic policies.

23.4 Can policy affect comparative advantage?

This issue has been hotly debated for decades, if not for a century or two, and no agreed view has yet been found. Broad and impressionistic historical evidence would suggest that policies favoring particular sectors can create successful infant industries. The early industrialization of Europe was, almost certainly, crucially helped by import-substitution vis-à-vis the more advanced products exported by Asia. France's and Italy's silk industries, for instance, copied China's technology already in the late Middle Ages (de Zwart and van Zanden, 2018). Protectionism may or may not have played a role in this. Where it definitely played a crucial role was in the development of Europe's textile industry in the 18th century. Thus, Britain's cotton production, which was at the heart of the country's industrial revolution, took off initially when cotton imports from India were first hit by duties from 1701 onward and later by an outright ban in 1721 (O'Brien *et al.*, 1991). France and Spain similarly banned cotton and silk imports from Asia at the turn of the 18th century (Berg, 2003). France also intervened to protect its porcelain manufacturer at Sèvres and heavy duties were imposed on imports of Far Eastern ceramics in England (*ibid.*). America's 19th century industrialization may also have been helped by the protectionism that the young Republic introduced already early in the century and then greatly strengthened after the Civil War. That this helped the US manufacturing sector remains disputed (Taussig, 1910; Cohen and DeLong, 2016; Irwin, 2017), but more general evidence for a number of advanced countries suggests that in the 19th century at least, protectionism and growth were strongly correlated with each other and this correlation may well have had some causal links (Bairoch, 1972; O'Rourke, 2000; Clemens and Williamson, 2004).

Protectionism, understandably, came in for widespread condemnation following its wholesale adoption at the time of the Great Depression. The post-World War II settlement thus strived to promote free trade through multilateralism, the establishment of GATT and, in the European context, the creation of the Common Market and its subsequent developments. These policies turned out to be extremely successful and, partly in the light of this success, the encouragement to infant industries that many developing countries have been pursuing since the 1950s has come in for increasing criticism by the academic literature, often for good reasons. The theoretical case against such policies has been eloquently made (e.g., Baldwin 1969; Corden, 1974) and there is ample empirical evidence showing that more often than not they were unsuccessful (e.g., Kruger and Tuncer, 1982; Bell *et al.*, 1984; Pack and Saggi, 2006; for a more nuanced view see Bardhan, 2016).

Yet, there are also counterarguments starting with J.S. Mill's 1848 case for infant industry protection being welfare enhancing (Irwin, 1991).[11] Tariffs, in this argument, allow a fledging industry with much potential for "learning by doing" in a young or developing economy to achieve scale economies and, eventually, become competitive on world markets. The argument has been shown to be theoretically sound (e.g., Redding, 1999),[12] but usually encounters two major objections. The first one relates to the very real danger of lobbying for tariffs by vested interests engaged in rent-seeking activities. The second one relates to the information needed by the policy maker to judge whether protection is justified. This is vast, encompassing, *inter alia*, knowledge about present and future productivity growth in the chosen sector, both at home and abroad, and under both free trade and protection! (see also Pack and Saggi, (2006) for an even longer list). Decisions will, inevitably, involve elusive estimates of private and social risks and costs as well as value judgments and expressions of faith (Grubel, 1966).

These would seem to be insurmountable objections. Yet, the experience of some East Asian countries suggests that, perhaps, they were not as insurmountable as all that. Japan, South Korea, Taiwan and China have all, if in different ways, promoted industrialization at home in the post-World War II period, including providing various forms of help and protection to specific sectors. Most observers would consider them among the most successful economies in the world. Some preconditions were, of course, favorable. Japan, South Korea (henceforth: Korea) and Taiwan had a high level of human capital already at the outset (Temple, 1997), relatively equal income distribution and relatively good institutions. Taking total years of schooling as a rough indicator, Japan in 1950 was second only to the US and Canada among the major countries, while Korea and Taiwan were at levels comparable to those of the major economies of Western Europe. All were way ahead of, for instance, Brazil, Mexico, Turkey, let alone India (Barro and Lee, 2013). Income distribution was relatively equal by international standards and the bureaucracy almost certainly more competent and probably less corrupt than in most other developing economies and thus better able to withstand lobbying efforts (Boltho and Weber, 2009).

Three of these four countries lacked natural resources and had, therefore, to privilege manufacturing which, in the 1950s and 1960s, in a world still beset by protectionism especially vis-à-vis Asia, was a risky bet. Thus Japan, already in the 1950s, inspired by the writings of an inter-war economist on the "flying geese"[13] pattern of imports, production and exports through time (Akamatsu, 1961, originally published in 1937) engaged in widespread protection of its domestic manufacturing producers. The car industry was emblematic (Genther, 1990). A whole panoply of instruments was used by the Ministry of International Trade and Industry to protect the industry and while mistakes were made (e.g., in trying to foster a "people's car") (*ibid.*), the sector's overall growth was remarkable, with international competitiveness achieved, at least in the parts industry, already by the mid-1960s (Adachi *et al.*, 1983). More generally, Japan extended protection to many of its industries over the half century that followed World War II and its comparative advantage changed dramatically, as was mentioned in Section 23.3. As has persuasively been argued, import protection was instrumental in generating export promotion (Krugman, 1994). One crucial ingredient in this success story was a high degree of domestic competition, with rival *keiretsu* firms pursuing growth and market share maximization policies (protection against outsiders, in other words, but ruthless competition within the country). And the authorities contributed to this by sharing out imported technologies among rival firms. This reinforced competitive pressures, in contrast to a policy that would have handed out foreign technology to one or two companies favored because of their lobbying activities or even corrupt practices.

The stress on competition was not lost in the other three East Asian countries, but the emphasis differed. Japan could pursue policies of import-substitution because its size allowed several firms in each sheltered sector to achieve the required scale economies. Korea and Taiwan were (and are) too small for such a policy to be viable. Korea protected domestic industry against imports but was not successful in the years 1955–1965 (Westphal, 1978). The country thus turned to export promotion. This was achieved by granting subsidies to the larger *chaebols* on condition that they fulfill stringent export targets on world markets (Amsden, 1989). The competition, in other words, was with foreign not domestic producers and the targets were limited to selected sectors (Westphal, 1981). The emblematic industries in this instance were steel, shipbuilding and, more recently, electronics, none of which seemed promising ex-ante in a small and very poor country.[14]

Taiwan was almost certainly less interventionist than Japan or Korea (let alone China). Yet Taiwan too helped its industry directly, through large public investments, and indirectly via preferential treatment in public purchases, generous tax concessions and depreciation allowances as well as through interest rate subsidies (Rodrik, 1995). Foreign direct investment was also controlled so as to protect domestic firms from potential take-over activities, if in less draconian fashion than in Japan and Korea (Wade, 2004). And competition was ensured by the presence of a large network of small- and medium-sized firms.

China's development over the last four decades has, of course, been very different. State intervention was, and still is, much, much greater than in the three other countries. And state intervention in many forms (and, in particular, in the form of subsidized credit) helped exports successes by state-owned firms in heavy industry and, more recently, in high-tech sectors. Yet competition has also been greatly encouraged, by allowing, for instance, a good deal of regional experimentation (Bardhan, 2016; see also Bardhan's Chapter 24 in this volume). And it is fierce in the very dynamic private sector. State-owned enterprises have been more protected, but many have been forced to either merge or close down. Interestingly, China seems to have followed Japanese practices by establishing oligopolistic competition among some major players in, for instance, oil or telecoms (Naughton, 2008). The opening of the economy to foreign trade has also raised competitive pressures. As was said, referring to this opening: "Reform has pushed China's economy towards extraordinarily high levels of competition" (Brandt and Rawski, 2008, p. 14).

That comparative advantage changed in these four countries over time is illustrated by Figures 23.1 and 23.2. Figure 23.1 shows the share in world exports of manufactures of the four East Asian countries and of the United States, Germany and the UK over a century. The pre-World War II data (Federico and Tena-Junguito, 2019) as well as the statistics going from 1950 to 1980 are more tentative than the post-1980 WTO data. As they stand, the figures show how from minimal shares in 1950 or 1970 or 1980 (depending on country), East Asia made very significant inroads in manufacturing world trade in the 20 or 30 following years.

This impression is reinforced by Figure 23.2, which shows (even more) tentative estimates of revealed comparative advantage indices for the capital-intensive and high-tech products which the East Asian countries selected for promotion: the Standard International Trade Classification (SITC) 7 category, which encompasses machinery and transport equipment.[15] The picture shown is startling: almost vertical and almost parallel soaring lines at three different points in time. In 1955, Japan's index stood at 0.4, the same value as the index for Korea and Taiwan in 1973 and for China in 1993.[16] By 2020, the indices for Japan and Korea plus Taiwan stood above 1.30, China's above 1.

Japan, Korea, Taiwan and China actively promoted their manufacturing sectors and, within them, helped particular industries. Japan, Korea, Taiwan and China scored remarkable successes on the world market for manufactures and for some of their favored industries. Are these two features related? Correlation, of course, is no proof of causation and views on this issue differ markedly. At one end of the spectrum are authors who see governments as having successfully influenced the course of events (e.g., Boltho, 1985; Amsden, 1989; Vestal, 1993;

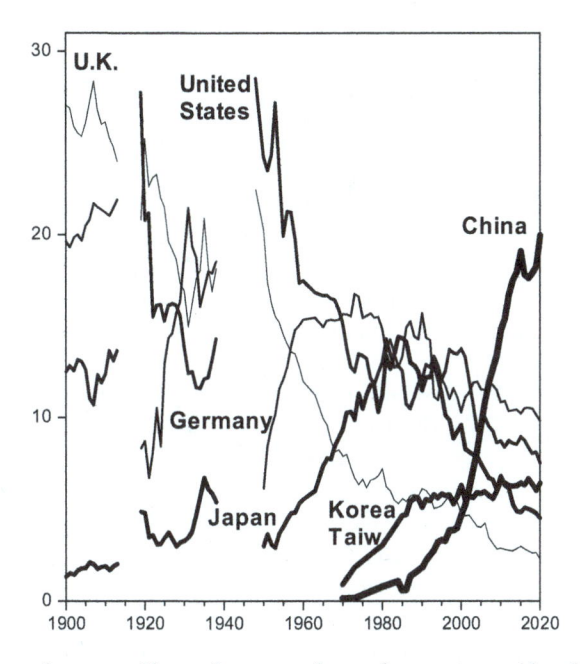

Figure 23.1 Export performance. Share of exports of manufactures in world trade in manufactures.

Sources: Batchelor et al. (1980); Federico and Tena-Junguito (2019); GATT, Annual Reports; OECD, Foreign Trade Statistics; UN, International Trade Statistics, 1900–1960; WTO, Statistics on Merchandise Trade.

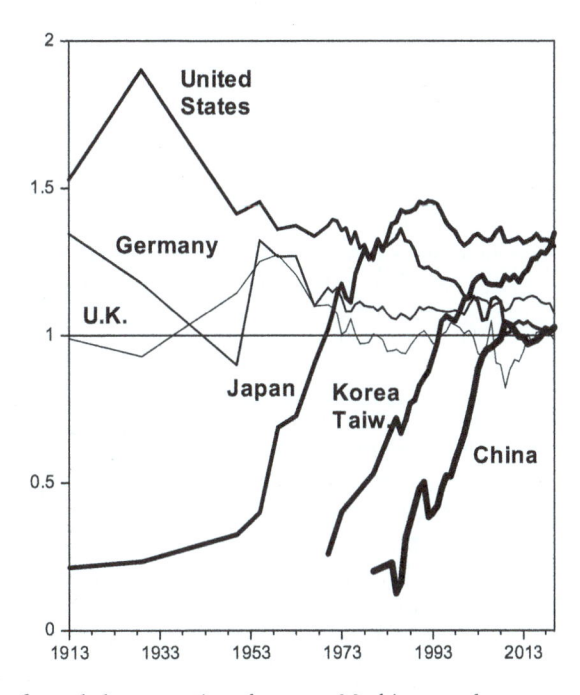

Figure 23.2 Indices of revealed comparative advantage. Machinery and transport equipment (SITC 7).

Sources: Batchelor et al. (1980); Maizels (1970); OECD, Foreign Trade Statistics; UN Comtrade Database; WTO, Stats. on Merchandise Trade.

Rodrik, 1995; Wade, 2004; and, especially, Cherif and Hasanov, 2019). At the opposite end are scholars who belittle the role of policy (e.g., Little, 1979; Calder, 1993; Little *et al.*, 1994; Beason and Weinstein, 1996; Pack and Saggi, 2006), with others taking an intermediate, if somewhat skeptical, position (e.g., World Bank, 1993; Noland and Pack, 2003).

On balance, the view that what happened was the happy outcome of market forces discovering the "natural" comparative advantage of these economies seems far-fetched. Few would have said that Japan in the 1950s had an obvious opportunity in car production. The Bank of Japan, for instance, was very skeptical of this and favored the light industry that most outside observers also thought appropriate for Japan at the time (Genther, 1990). Nor would many have thought that polyethylene or consumer electronics, for instance, would have been similar success stories.

The World Bank in 1960 was scathing about the prospects of a steel industry in Korea (Redding, 1999). Yet, in 1973, the Korean government created and then greatly helped a new steel company (Posco). By 1985, Posco had become one of the world's lowest cost producers (*ibid.*). Similarly, the government played an important direct and indirect role in the extremely rapid growth of the country's very successful shipbuilding industry (Lee, 1990).[17] The amazing achievement of Taiwan's semi-conductor manufacturing company (TSMC), today one of the world's largest producer of advanced chips, resulted in no small part from the government's initial choice in 1974 of semi-conductors as a key industry in receipt of significant R&D funding and, later, of the direct injection of capital into the firm's creation in 1987 (National Research Council, 2003). And the incentives are continuing.[18]

As for China, it has relentlessly encouraged its high-tech industries through direct subsidies, preferential buying schemes, tax concessions, etc.[19] A particularly successful (pre-WTO accession) policy was that of trading access to the buoyant Chinese market in exchange for technology. One striking example of this (high-speed railway equipment) saw two major foreign companies, Kawasaki and Siemens, share their knowledge with China's main state-owned rolling-stock manufacturer, CSR (Robinson, 2010). CRRC, CSR's successor company, has now eclipsed its former Japanese, German and other Western competitors.

Some may dismiss these examples as anecdotal evidence, others may point to the mistakes that the policymakers committed. There is no doubt that mistakes were made, yet overall many, though by no means all, observers will probably conclude that even these were bearable and that interventionist policies were broadly successful. Consumers no doubt suffered losses when protection raised prices but, to paraphrase Tobin's famous quip (Tobin, 1977): "It takes a heap of Haberger triangles to fill years of above average growth".

23.5 Conclusions

Many factors determine a country's comparative advantage. Until quite recently there was almost universal agreement that factor endowments, especially those of human and physical capital, were the most important determinants. Tastes and technology, in so far as they differed across countries, were, at times, also considered as possible causes of international trade flows. Institutions and policies that this chapter has argued are also important determinants, were either almost ignored, as in the case of institutions, or, when it came to policies that were considered unorthodox, were seen as deeply flawed attempts at interference with natural (and optimal) market forces.

The role of institutions has become more prominent in recent years. Numerous studies have shown that institutions (in, for instance, the legal area, the financial system or the labor market) can play an important role in helping countries achieve a comparative advantage in, usually, relatively elaborate or high-tech products. The more complex the product, the more important is the quality of the country's legal framework (Kowalski, 2011). And this conclusion has been reinforced by the more encompassing "varieties of capitalism" literature. This has introduced novel and very interesting sub-divisions of the advanced market economies into various types which, despite often highly similar factor endowments, trade rather dissimilar commodities (unlike intra-industry exchanges) in part because of differing governance structures in their capital and labor markets.

The chapter has also explored an additional dimension by arguing that interventionist policies, if pursued consistently and over a prolonged period of time, could also be considered as a form of institution. The accent in this case has been put on several East Asian countries which, much more than other advanced economies, have, in the post-war period, systematically favored specific parts of their manufacturing sectors, usually characterized by relatively high-income elasticities of demand on world markets. The unfashionable conclusion reached was that many of these efforts did, indeed, succeed (and in China's case are still succeeding) in generating successful exporting sectors and higher growth rates than might otherwise have been expected in the absence of deliberate government efforts. It is also readily admitted, however, that these examples may not easily be transplanted into other developing countries which lack some of the institutional and social preconditions that characterize East Asia.

That institutions matter in economics is an obvious self-evident truth. That they matter in the area of international trade is, perhaps, less self-evident. The material covered in the previous pages suggests that here too their role is clearly very important.

Notes

1 Path-breaking in more than one way. As Paul Samuelson said of it, it is one of the few propositions in economics that is both true and non-trivial: *"That this idea is logically true need not be argued before a mathematician; that it is not trivial is attested by the thousands of important and intelligent men who have never been able to grasp the doctrine for themselves or to believe it after it was explained to them"* (as quoted in OECD, 2011, p. 32).

2 Tentative because "… measurement crucially depends on the level of disaggregation chosen for the analysis" (OECD, 2010, p. 210).

3 A very comprehensive and far more detailed survey of much that is covered in this section can be found in Nunn and Trefler (2014).

4 The quality of institutions is also likely to influence the volume of trade. Better institutional quality may well raise trust and reduce uncertainty and hence transaction costs. This in turn would boost international trade and may explain why institutionally similar economies (such as the OECD member countries) trade disproportionately more with each other (de Groot *et al.*, 2004).

5 The paradox may not have been that paradoxical after all if, as seems to be the case, raw material extraction is very capital-intensive. The bulk of Soviet exports at the time consisted of commodities.

6 Going back in time, historical research has, for instance, shown that institutions were crucial for the resurgence of trade in the Middle Ages. Be it in the Mediterranean in the 11th century or across Western Europe in the 13th or 14th centuries, coalition of merchants or merchant guilds and the Hansa League developed effective collective action and credible enforcement mechanisms which facilitated trade expansion (Greif, 1993; Greif *et al.*, 1994).

7 An early and partially successful attempt at finding empirical support for the role of institutions (in this instance, corporate ownership concentration) in promoting export performance in the industrialized countries can be found in Carlin *et al.* (2001).

8 Allowance is also made for a possible third category, called Mediterranean (e.g., Italy, Spain and Turkey) marked by a past agrarian history and large state intervention. Countries in this group tend to share coordinated market characteristics in the financial field and liberal market characteristics in labor relations. Subsequent work has also added a fourth category encompassing the countries of Eastern Europe which combine some of the features of the Mediterranean and of the coordinated market economies (Dilli *et al.*, 2018).

9 As measured by a positive and statistically significant rank correlation of their revealed comparative advantage indices for manufacturing products in 1955. These indices measure the ratio between a country's share of world exports in a particular product and its share of total world exports.

10 By 1995, the positive and significant 1955 rank correlation between Italian and Japanese indices of revealed comparative advantage had turned into an equally significant negative correlation.

11 Protection can also be welfare enhancing if it improves a (large) country's terms of trade or, in the case of a successful strategic trade policy, if it shifts rents from foreigners to domestic producers (Brander, 1986; Krugman, 1987). In neither case, however, is the aim that of changing a country's comparative advantage, unlike the infant industry argument.

12 Indeed, a successful policy can be shown to be welfare enhancing for both the protecting country and for the rest of the world (Redding, 1999).

13 Akamatsu coined this term because the shape of the output, export and import curves he had plotted reminded him of the inverse V pattern of wild geese flying in partly overlapping formations.

14 In as late as 1960, GDP per capita, in purchasing power parities, was lower in Korea than in Sub-Saharan Africa. By 2019, it was 13 times higher (Conference Board, 2020).

15 The data shown in Figures 23.1 and 23.2 come from a variety of sources from both economic historians and from several international organizations (GATT, OECD, UN, WTO). The series were linked to each other but there is clearly no certainty that all the links that were established are reliable. Hence, both charts convey an impression of broad trends but cannot really provide accurate figures for the years preceding 1980.

16 Korea and Taiwan have been bundled together to make Figures 23.1 and 23.2 more readable; the evolution through time of the two countries' revealed comparative advantage indices for SITC 7 are, in any case, quite similar.

17 Infant industries, it has often been argued, remain infants forever. Korea's shipbuilding industry may have achieved maturity within only a few years after its inception (Bell *et al.*, 1984).

18 Taiwan's government apparently still covers nearly 50 per cent of the land and construction costs of the country's semi-conductor industry. As a result, total costs for a producer are lowered by perhaps 25–30 per cent (The White House, 2021).

19 The depth and breadth of China's help to, for instance, its semi-conductor industry are illustrated in OECD (2019).

References

Acemoglu, D., Johnson, S. and Robinson, J.A. (2005). Institutions as the Fundamental Cause of Long-run Growth. In P. Aghion and S. Durlauf (Eds.), *Handbook of Economic Growth*, Vol. 1A. London: North Holland.

Adachi, F., Ono, K. and Odaka, K. (1983). Ancillary Firm Development in the Japanese Automobile Industry. In K. Odaka (Ed.), *Motor Vehicle Industry in Asia*. Singapore: Singapore University Press.

Akamatsu, K. (1961). A Theory of Unbalanced Growth in the World Economy. *Weltwirtschaftliches Archiv*, 86 (2), 196–217.

Amsden, A. (1989). *Asia' Next Giant: South Korea and Late Industrialization*. New York, NY: Oxford University Press.

Bairoch, P. (1972). Free Trade and European Economic Development in the 19th Century. *European Economic Review*, 3 (3), 211–245.

Balassa, B. (1979). The Changing Pattern of Comparative Advantage in Manufactured Goods. *Review of Economics and Statistics*, 61 (2), 259–266.

Balassa, B. (1986). Comparative Advantage in Manufactured Goods: A Reappraisal. *Review of Economics and Statistics*, 68 (2), 315–319.

Baldwin, R.E. (1969). The Case against Infant-Industry Tariff Protection. *Journal of Political Economy*, 77 (3), 295–305.

Bardhan, P. (2016). State and Development: The Need for a Reappraisal of the Current Literature. *Journal of Economic Literature*, 54 (3), 862–892.

Barro, R.J. and Lee, J.W. (2013). A New Data Set of Educational Attainment in the World, 1950–2010. *Journal of Development Economics*, 104, 184–198.

Batchelor, R.A., Major, R.L. and Morgan, A.D. (1980). *Industrialisation and the Basis for Trade*. Cambridge: Cambridge University Press.

Beason, R. and Weinstein, D.E. (1996). Growth, Economies of Scale and Targeting in Japan (1955–1990). *Review of Economics and Statistics*, 78 (2), 286–295.

Beck, T. (2002). Financial Development and International Trade: Is There a Link? *Journal of International Economics*, 57 (1), 107–131.

Beck, T. (2003). Financial Dependence and International Trade. *Review of International Economics*, 11 (2), 296–316.

Bell, M., Ross-Larson, B. and Westphal, L.E. (1984). Assessing the Performance of Infant Industries. *Journal of Development Economics*, 16 (1–2), 101–128.

Berg, M. (2003). Asian Luxuries and the Making of the European Consumer Revolution. In M. Berg and E. Eger (Eds.), *Luxury in the Eighteenth Century*. Basingstoke, UK: Palgrave.

Berkowitz, D., Moenius, J. and Pistor, K. (2006). Trade, Law, and Product Complexity. *Review of Economics and Statistics*, 88 (2), 363–373.

Boltho, A. (1971). *Foreign Trade Criteria in Socialist Economies*. Cambridge: Cambridge University Press.

Boltho, A. (1985). Was Japan's Industrial Policy Successful? *Cambridge Journal of Economics*, 9 (2), 187–201.

Boltho, A. (2001). Foreign Trade Performance: From Early Similarities to Present Diversity. In A. Boltho, A. Vercelli and H. Yoshikawa (Eds.), *Comparing Economic Systems: Italy and Japan*. Basingstoke, UK: Palgrave.

Boltho, A. and Weber, M. (2009). Did China Follow the East Asian Development Model? *European Journal of Comparative Economics*, 6 (2), 267–286.

Brander, J.A. (1986). Rationales for Strategic Trade and Industrial Policy. In P.R. Krugman (Ed.), *Strategic Trade Policy and the New International Economics*. Cambridge, MA: MIT Press.

Brandt, L. and Rawski, T.G. (2008). China's Great Economic Transformation. In L. Brandt and T.G. Rawski (Eds.), *China's Great Economic Transformation*. New York, NY: Cambridge University Press.

Calder, K.E. (1993). *Strategic Capitalism – Private Business and Public Purpose in Japanese Industrial Finance*. Princeton, NJ: Princeton University Press.

Carlin, W., Glyn, A. and Van Reenen, J. (2001). Export Market Performance of OECD Countries: An Empirical Examination of the Role of Cost Competitiveness. *Economic Journal*, 111 (468), 128–162.

Chang, H.-J. (2011). Institutions and Economic Development: Theory, Policy and History. *Journal of Institutional Economics*, 7 (4), 473–498.

Cherif, R. and Hasanov, F. (2019). The Return of the Policy That Shall Not Be Named: Principles of Industrial Policy. *IMF Working Paper*, WP 19/74, March.

Chor, D. (2010). Unpacking Sources of Comparative Advantage: A Quantitative Approach. *Journal of International Economics*, 82 (2), 152–167.

Clemens, M.A. and Williamson, J.G. (2004). Why Did the Tariff-Growth Correlation Change after 1950? *Journal of Economic Growth*, 9 (1), 5–46.

Cohen, S. and DeLong, J.B. (2016). *Concrete Economics: The Hamilton Approach to Economic Growth and Policy*. Boston, MA: Harvard Business Review Press.

Conference Board. (2020). *Total Economy Database*, April 2020, www.conference-board.org/data/economydatabase.

Corden, W.M. (1974). *Trade Policy and Economic Welfare*. Oxford: Oxford University Press.

Costinot, A. (2009). On the Origins of Comparative Advantage. *Journal of International Economics*, 77 (2), 255–264.

Cuñat, A. and Melitz, M.J. (2012). Volatility, Labor Market Flexibility and the Pattern of Comparative Advantage. *Journal of the European Economic Association*, 10 (2), 225–254.

Davis, D.R. and Weinstein, D.E. (2001). An Account of Global Factor Trade. *American Economic Review*, 91 (5), 1423–1453.

de Groot, H.L.F., Linders, G.-J., Rietveld, P. and Subramanian, U. (2004). The Institutional Determinants of Bilateral Trade Patterns. *Kyklos*, 57 (1), 103–124.

de Zwart, P. and van Zanden, J.L. (2018). *The Origins of Globalization*. Cambridge: Cambridge University Press.

Dilli, S., Elert, N. and Herrmann, A.M. (2018). Varieties of Entrepreneurship: Exploring the Institutional Foundations of Different Entrepreneurship Types through 'Varieties-of-Capitalism' Arguments. *Small Business Economics*, 51 (2), 293–320.

Federico, G. and Tena-Junguito, A. (2019). World Trade, 1800-1938: A New Synthesis. *Revista de Historia Económica – Journal of Iberian and Latin America Economic History*, 37 (1), 9–41.

Genther, P.A. (1990). *A History of Japan's Government-Business Relationship: The Passenger Car Industry*. Ann Arbor, MI: University of Michigan Press.

Greenway, D. and Milner, C. (1987). Intra-Industry Trade: Current Perspectives and Unresolved Issues. *Weltwirtschaftliches Archiv*, 123 (1), 39–57.

Greif, A. (1993). Contract Enforceability and Economic Institutions in Early Trade: The Maghribi Traders' Coalition. *American Economic Review*, 83 (3), 525–548.

Greif, A., Milgrom, P. and Weingast, B.R. (1994). Coordination, Commitment, and Enforcement: The Case of the Merchant Guild. *Journal of Political Economy*, 102 (4), 745–776.

Grubel, H.G. (1966). The Anatomy of Classical and Modern Infant Industry Arguments. *Weltwirtschaftliches Archiv*, 97 (2), 325–342.

Grubel, H.G. and Lloyd, P.J. (1975). *Intra-Industry Trade*. London and Basingstoke: MacMillan.

Hall, P.A. and Soskice, D. (2001). An Introduction to Varieties of Capitalism. In P.A. Hall and D. Soskice (Eds.), *Varieties of Capitalism: The Institutional Foundations of Comparative Advantage*. Oxford: Oxford University Press.

Irwin, D.A. (1991). Challenges to Free Trade. *Journal of Economic Perspectives*, 5 (2), 201–208.

Irwin, D.A. (2017). *Clashing over Commerce: A History of US Trade Policy*. Chicago, IL: University of Chicago Press.

Kowalski, P. (2011). Comparative Advantage and Trade Performance: Policy Implications. *OECD Trade Policy Papers*, No. 121.

Kruger, A.O. and Tuncer, B. (1982). An Empirical Test of the Infant Industry Argument. *American Economic Review*, 72 (5), 1142–1152.

Krugman, P.R. (1987). Is Free Trade Passé? *Journal of Economic Perspectives*, 1 (2), 131–144.

Krugman, P.R. (1994). Import Protection as Export Promotion: International Competition in the Presence of Oligopoly and Economies of Scale. In H. Kierzkowski (Ed.), *Monopolistic Competition and International Trade*. Oxford: Oxford University Press.

Lee, T.-W. (1990). Korean Shipping Policy: The Role of Government. *Marine Policy*, 14 (5), 421–437.

Leontief, W. (1953). Domestic Production and Foreign Trade: The American Position Re-Examined. *Proceedings of the American Philosophical Society*, 97 (4), 332–349.

Levchenko, A.A. (2007). Institutional Quality and International Trade. *Review of Economic Studies*, 74 (3), 791–819.

Linder, S.B. (1961). *An Essay on Trade and Transformation*. London: John Wiley.

Little, I.M.D. (1979). An Economic Renaissance. In W. Galenson (Ed.), *Economic Growth and Structural Change in Taiwan*. Ithaca, NY: Cornell University Press.

Little, I.M.D., Lipsey, R.G. and Togan, S. (1994). Trade and Industrialisation Revisited. *Pakistan Development Review*, 33 (4), 359–389.

MacDougall, G.D.A. (1951). British and American Exports: A Study Suggested by the Theory of Comparative Costs. Part I. *Economic Journal*, 61 (224), 697–724.

MacDougall, G.D.A. (1952). British and American Exports: A Study Suggested by the Theory of Comparative Costs. Part II. *Economic Journal*, 62 (247), 487–521.

Maizels, A. (1970). *Growth and Trade*. Cambridge: Cambridge University Press.

Manova, K. (2013). Credit Constraints, Heterogeneous Firms, and International Trade. *Review of Economic Studies*, 80 (2), 711–744.

National Research Council. (2003). *Securing the Future: Regional and National Programs to Support the Semiconductor Industry*. Washington, DC: The National Academies Press.

Naughton, B. (2008). A Political Economy of China's Economic Transition. In L. Brandt and T.G. Rawski (Eds.), *China's Great Economic Transformation*. New York, NY: Cambridge University Press.

Noland, M. and Pack, H. (2003). *Industrial Policy in an Era of Industrialization: Lessons from Asia*. Washington, DC: Institute for International Economics.

Nunn, N. (2007). Relationship-Specificity, Incomplete Contracts, and the Pattern of Trade. *Quarterly Journal of Economics*, 122 (2), 569–600.

Nunn, N. and Trefler, D. (2014). Domestic Institutions as a Source of Comparative Advantage. In G. Gopinath, E. Helpman and K. Rogoff (Eds.), *Handbook of International Economics*, Vol. 4. Amsterdam: Elsevier.

O'Brien, P.K., Griffiths, T. and Hunt, W. (1991). Political Components of the Industrial Revolution: Parliament and the English Cotton Textile Industry, 1660-1774. *Economic History Review*, 44 (3), 395–423.

O'Rourke, K.H. (2000). Tariffs and Growth in the Late 19th Century. *Economic Journal*, 100 (463), 456–83.

OECD. (2010). *Measuring Globalisation: OECD Economic Globalisation Indicators*. Paris: OECD.

OECD. (2011). Comparative Advantage: Doing What You Do Best. *OECD Observer*, No. 286, 32.

OECD. (2019). *Measuring Distortions in International Markets: The Semiconductor Value Chain*. Paris: OECD.

Pack, H. and Saggi, K. (2006). Is There a Case for Industrial Policy? A Critical Survey. *World Bank Research Observer*, 21 (2), 267–297.

Posner, M.V. (1961). International Trade and Technical Change. *Oxford Economic Papers*, 13 (3), 323–341.

Rajan, R.G. and Zingales, L. (1998). Financial Dependence and Growth. *American Economic Review*, 88 (3), 559–586.

Redding, S. (1999). Dynamic Comparative Advantage and the Welfare Effects of Trade. *Oxford Economic Papers*, 51 (1), 15–39.

Ricardo, D. (1817). *On the Principles of Political Economy and Taxation*. Reprinted, Harmondsworth, UK: Penguin, 1971.

Robinson, M. (2010). China's New Industrial Revolution. *BBC News* (1.8.2010).

Rodrik, D. (1995). Getting Intervention Right: How South Korea and Taiwan Grew Rich. *Economic Policy*, 10 (20), 53–107.

Rodrik, D., Subramanian, A. and Trebbi, F. (2004). Institutions Rule: The Primacy of Institutions over Geography and Integration in Economic Development. *Journal of Economic Growth*, 9 (2), 131–165.

Romalis, J. (2004). Factor Proportions and the Structure of Commodity Trade. *American Economic Review*, 94 (1), 67–97.

Saint-Paul, G. (1997). Is Labour Rigidity Harming Europe's Competitiveness? The Effect of Job Protection on the Pattern of Trade and Welfare. *European Economic Review*, 41 (3–5), 499–506.

Svaleryd, H. and Vlachos, J. (2005). Financial Markets, the Pattern of Industrial Specialization and Comparative Advantage: Evidence from OECD Countries. *European Economic Review*, 49 (1), 113–144.

Taussig, F.W. (1910). *The Tariff History of the United States* (5th ed.). Reprinted, Auburn, AL: Ludwig von Mises Institute, 2010.

Temple, J. (1997). St. Adam and the Dragons: Neo-Classical Economics and the East Asian Miracle. *Oxford Development Studies*, 25 (3), 279–300.

Tobin, J. (1977). How Dead is Keynes? *Economic Inquiry*, 15 (4), 459–468.

Vernon, R. (1966). International Trade and International Investment in the Product Cycle. *Quarterly Journal of Economics*, 80 (2), 190–207.

Vestal, J.E. (1993). *Planning for Change: Industrial Policy and Japanese Economic Development, 1945–1990*. Oxford: Clarendon Press.

Wade, R. (2004). *Governing the Market* (2nd ed.). Princeton, NJ: Princeton University Press.

Westphal, L.E. (1978). The Republic of Korea's Experience with Export-led Industrial Development. *World Development*, 6 (3), 347–382.

Westphal, L.E. (1981). Empirical Justification for Infant Industry Protection. *World Bank Staff Working Paper*, No. 445.

White House, The. (2021). *Building Resilient Supply Chains, Revitalizing American Manufacturing, and Fostering Broad-based Growth*. Washington, DC: A Report by the White House.

World Bank. (1993). *The East Asian Miracle*. New York, NY: Oxford University Press.

24

GOVERNANCE ISSUES IN DEVELOPMENT

A China–India Comparative Study

Pranab Bardhan

UNIVERSITY OF CALIFORNIA, BERKELEY

24.1 Introduction

In the arena of comparative economic systems, the China–India comparison is an obvious one. These two largest countries in the world, with ancient civilizations, mainly agrarian economies over many centuries, quite poor at the time of Liberation/Independence, adopted different political systems, started economic reform about the same time in the early 1980s, and then enjoyed high growth over the last three decades. From about 1990 onward, the Chinese economic growth rate has been much faster, and the economic-structural change in China has been much more impressive. But this chapter is not on comparative performance as such,[1] but on comparative governance underlying that performance.

Even on comparative governance, the usual discussion in much of the literature in terms of authoritarianism and democracy is highly simplistic. It is arguable that some of the differences have less to do with generic regime types, more with the complexities of the internal organization of government and the historically evolved political culture in the two countries. As briefly discussed in Bardhan (2013), authoritarianism is neither necessary nor sufficient for some of the distinctive features of Chinese governance, both positive and negative—and their roots actually go long back in history—just as some of the recently observed dysfunctionality of governance in the United States or India is not inherent in their democratic process.

In this chapter, I shall focus particularly on the Chinese governance system, as it is less well-known to most readers, but at each main section, I shall draw comparison with the corresponding governance features in India. I shall concentrate on the following three general aspects of Chinese governance, from the point of view of economic development:

1. Internal Organization of Government
2. Abuse of Governance and Corruption
3. Decentralized Structures and Practices

DOI: 10.4324/9781003144366-29

24.2 Internal organization of government

24.2.1 Political meritocracy

It is often pointed out that unlike in most authoritarian countries, China has a political meritocracy. China's dramatic economic success has now convinced even some Western scholars—see for example the book by Bell (2015)—not to speak of the members of the Chinese elite, that in terms of performance Chinese political meritocracy can achieve as well as (or even better than) a multiparty democracy: an issue of special urgency at a time when there is widespread shakiness of confidence in liberal democracy.

Not merely are officials in China selected on the basis of an examination system that goes way back in imperial history, their career promotion depends on how well the local economy performs. This works better than in, for example, democratic India's top administrative system, where promotion is based more on seniority than on performance, even though recruitment is on the basis of civil service examinations.

An immediate question that arises is: in the political system, who defines what is 'meritorious' and what is not?

It is possible that what may look like meritorious performance to the Chinese Party elite and its Central Organization Department *Zhongzubu* may not be considered so by many others in the general population, particularly in a large country with inevitable diversities and conflicts of objectives—not to speak of the outlying regions where performance by centrally appointed provincial leaders considered meritorious by the Party may not be judged so by many in the ethnic groups like Tibetans or Uighurs.

In general, how do we know what people consider meritorious without institutions of downward accountability?

One of the distinctive features of democracy is that the criteria of meritorious performance arise out of open public discussion. Thus, how much of a political leadership's performance is meritorious may include considerations of pluralism and inclusiveness in the decision process itself. Democratic performance emphasizes the process as much as outcome. In this process, citizens in a democracy are not treated as children: what is good for them is not decided by a patrimonial leadership, as is the case much too often in China (or Singapore). This is valid even when the latter leadership is very wise and benevolent.

Also, in a democracy, the performance criteria are much more multi-faceted reflecting the pluralist agenda—it is uncommon to reward an official mainly on the basis of the growth rate of the local economy—and, thus, the incentives get diluted and are less effective. A similar dilution is happening in China now when other criteria (like environmental goals) enter performance evaluation.

24.2.2 Performance vs. loyalty

The general understanding in China is that career concerns of top officials act as a key determinant of economic growth at the local level, particularly the county and prefecture levels. And job rotation of officials at that level provides useful on-the-job training at diverse localities. Of course such performance incentives sometimes also generate plenty of side income or rent-earning opportunities (for example, from sales of local government land and mining rights), which, while helping local revenue and local development, are also used to enable private illicit income for officials.

What about the large numbers of the rank and file of public employees, who mostly remain in one place and for whom career incentives through promotion are not that relevant? They used to help themselves to all kinds of supplemental compensations, perks, and benefits making up for low salaries. In other authoritarian countries, such systems of supplemental compensation sometimes degenerate into local loot and plunder—the proverbial extreme case is that of Zaire under Mobutu, where soldiers and bureaucrats were not paid but left to fend for themselves (this tradition largely continues in the Democratic Republic of Congo even today). It is likely that in China this system for the low-level officials was constrained from being excessive by the career concerns of the top local leaders.

But a less well-known factor about Chinese promotion system is that as one climbs up the political ladder, to the provincial levels and beyond, performance factor seems to diminish in importance in career prospects, and the factor of political connections assumes significance—this is suggested, for example, by Landry, Lu and Duan (2017) from an analysis of a comprehensive dataset of political appointments at the provincial, prefectural and county levels. They find that the link between economic performance—in terms of GDP and revenue growth—and promotion is the strongest for county officials, significant for municipal officials, and insignificant for provincial officials. Similarly, from a comprehensive biographical database of all provincial leaders from 1978 until 2012 and an analysis of their promotion patterns, Su, He and Tao (2016) find no evidence supporting the claim that competence has played much of a role in the central personnel decisions. Instead, links with the Politburo members or family connection with senior Party leaders are more important.

There are also quid pro quo transactions. Using data for over a million land transactions during 2004–2016 Chen and Kung (2018) have shown

1. that provincial Party secretaries in selling local government land gave firms linked with Politburo members nearly 60% price discounts compared to others (an even more substantial discount to the firms of members of the top Standing Committee of the Politburo); and
2. in return such discount-givers were estimated to be 23% more likely to be promoted to positions of national leadership (in general the larger the discount the higher was the chance of promotion).

The recent crackdowns have somewhat reduced the chances for such promotions.

In any case, such a general system of promotion has at least one important implication compared to other countries: since performance incentives operate at least at the lower levels, higher-level leaders, even when they are selected on the basis of their loyalty to the current leadership at the top, are likely to have some measure of field-tested competence and experience.

This balance of performance and loyalty over an official's career path leads to a major advantage that China enjoys in the quality of its bureaucracy, compared to many other countries (including, say, the United States or India), not to speak of many authoritarian countries where loyalty rules over minimum competence.

Of course, this also means that competent officials who are not sufficiently well-connected to the top current leadership in China may reach a 'glass ceiling'. Some of them may then turn to alternative ways of earning rewards (including some corrupt ways). These corrupt ways have now been substantially curbed in the recent anti-corruption campaigns. There is even some evidence that high-performers connected to previous top leaderships were particularly likely to be investigated, although the campaigns have gone much beyond merely penalizing rival power groups.

In India, meritocratically recruited bureaucrats are manipulatively transferred. The threat of transfer to unattractive departments or locations acts to ensure loyalty to their political masters. The lure of postretirement plum jobs for ex-bureaucrats assigned by political leaders also works to keep the former pliant. This often means that junior officers under-invest in acquiring expertise, and one hears about corrupt deals between Indian politicians and bureaucrats in the process of 'transfers and postings'. There are also stories about vertical corrupt transactions in buying and selling of positions in the Chinese bureaucracy, some of which have been revealed in the recent anti-corruption campaigns—from the data one finds vertical correlation between corruption indictments at higher and lower levels across provinces. In India, such corruption may be somewhat more subject to public scrutiny by media, social movements, and investigative agencies, which are usually more open and intense than in China (although the misuse of the agencies by top leadership against political opponents has been rising in India).

In the UK, such manipulative transfers are less common. The system in the United States, on the other hand, is characterized by high turnover of senior civil servants (long before firing by twitter under a recent President).

The political-bureaucratic distinction particularly at higher levels is, of course, blurred in China, as the Party is supreme. But even in Western democracies, the political control over senior appointments and promotions in public service has increased over time. Even in the UK, the insulation of career civil service has declined somewhat, and this insulation has always been much weaker in the United States than in the UK (or Denmark or New Zealand).

The issue of political control pertains not just to the civil service but also to the various regulatory bodies that any complex economy requires—like the entities that regulate public utilities (e.g. electricity, civil aviation, and telecommunication) and apex bodies regulating monetary or environmental policy or financial markets. Decisions in such regulatory bodies need special expertise and some insulation from the day-to-day political pressures and some independence from political interference. Such independence is often completely lacking in the Chinese system—commitment to independence even when earnestly announced by the political leadership is not ultimately credible.

But even in democracies, the balance between autonomous experts and the need for periodic public review of their decisions to ensure accountability has been difficult to achieve. In India, there are very few genuinely independent regulatory bodies (even apart from the problem of their capture by generalist Indian Administrative Service officers). Even the semi-independence of the Reserve Bank of India, the central bank, has been under some stress.

24.2.3 *Organizational capacity to foster technological innovations*

In terms of the governance capacity to foster technological innovations, China has advanced much more than most developing countries (including India), particularly in terms of R&D as percentage of GDP (though public R&D support often neglects small and medium enterprises), restructuring and upgrading of elite universities, and measures of progress in science and technology. Even in agriculture, much greater success with hybrid rice in China than in India has been attributed to much larger public sector investment in China in research, diffusion of technology, and seed production.

China, of course, has been very successful in the 'catching-up' process of industrial development, of learning and imitating off-the-shelf technology (sometimes making foreign partners in joint ventures part with their technology as a condition of access to its large market). In some day-to-day applications and enhancement of existing internet-based technology (mobile payment, e-commerce, transport, etc.), China is now more advanced than the United States. China, in general, has been successful in what is called 'second generation innovations' using established technologies to find new products and processes, much less so in cutting-edge novel technology. But even in the latter, China is advancing, and the major technological race with the West is currently in 'deep tech' areas like artificial intelligence, quantum computing, chip-making, and biotechnology.

But in any future advances beyond the existing technological frontier, China has a major advantage and a major disadvantage. The advantage follows from the large size of the population and of the domestic market. Innovations (like those involving artificial intelligence and machine learning) that thrive on economies of scale, network externalities, and big data feedback loops will find hospitable ground in China.

The disadvantage for China follows from the lack of an open system that could encourage free spirit, critical thinking, challenging of incumbent organizations and methods, and diversity rather than conformity—these are necessary ingredients of many types of creative innovations. The current system of state promotion and guidance of globally successful large private technological enterprises is worth examining from this point of view. On the one hand, the state wants them to be 'national champions', on the other hand, it does not want them to be internationally too prominent or financially too successful—in particular, autonomously powerful enough to be outside the ambit of its control, supervision, and surveillance. Will an autonomously successful firm be considered too 'independent' for the comfort of the Party? This was most recently evident in the way the Chinese government clamped down on the companies of one of its most successful entrepreneurs, Jack Ma, after he gave a speech in October 2020, where he has been perceived by the top leadership to be (mildly) critical of some of the practices of state banks and regulators. The government dramatically stopped the IPO offering (which would have been the world's largest such offering) of the fintech company, Ant, and initiated an anti-trust probe of Alibaba, the e-commerce giant. All this in spite of the fact that these companies are central to China's online economy and Mr. Ma is a member of the Party. Since then other successful 'platform' companies (like Tencent and Didi) and education technology companies have faced regulatory wrath. This has caused a great deal of uncertainty and problems of investor confidence for private technology developers (particularly in the area of consumer services).

While all this may be about the political price of too much success, there are also questions on the side of failures. For example, will the Chinese state allow the full forces of 'creative destruction' that Schumpeter associated with innovations? In 2017, the total no. of annual insolvency cases was smaller in China than even Romania, not to speak of the advanced industrial countries. More recently, some local companies in sectors like coal and property development have been allowed to default in the bond market, but whether large companies like the property giant Evergrande or groups controlled particularly by the central government will be allowed to face collapse (as opposed to soft landing) is yet to be seen.

Are today's successful incumbent firms (private or public) 'too big to fail', or in the case of clusters, 'too many to fail'? Will the all-powerful Party consider a major commercial failure or a prolonged stock market slump as a sign of lack of public confidence in it? Will it allow the development of independent legal institutions that are essential for an increasingly complex economy?

Much also depends on the nature of future innovations. Some innovations are of the 'disruptive' kind that challenges incumbent firms (which the US private innovators in collaboration with venture capitalists are good at and a politically connected large entrenched organization usually is not). Other innovations are of the steady 'incremental' kind that adds up to significant gains (the Japanese call it kaizen), in which some large organizations in Germany, Japan, and South Korea have excelled. It is likely that the Chinese system is more conducive to this incremental kind of innovations.

24.2.4 *Upward vs. downward accountability*

Even though at the top level between the provincial and the central leadership in China, there is some degree of reciprocal accountability (as provincial officials constitute about half of the Central Committee of the Party that elects Politburo members), it is probably correct to say that the Chinese system is by and large one of upward accountability.

Downward accountability provides more political legitimacy to democratic governments, but such accountability, as we have indicated before, can sometimes degenerate into pandering to short-run interests and pressure groups, particularly at election time. Short-run cyclical official behavior before the Party Congress is not unknown in China, but in general, it is much easier for leaders to take long-run decisions under the Chinese governance system.

But a severe flaw of the upwardly accountable Chinese system is that mistakes in such top-level decisions or outright abuses of power (in collaboration with crony business interests) take longer to detect and to correct (as the flow of information upward is tortuous or choked and the tendency to cover up is often too strong). The recent abolition of term limits for the President and the decline of the collective leadership that Deng Xiaoping had put in place will make this problem more acute.

In multiparty democracies like India, the open adversarial relation between the government and opposition parties and the free media usually uncovers the mistakes and abuses much sooner, and corrections are prompted by public protests, agitations, and, ultimately, electoral sanctions. This also means that the information problem that even well-meaning bureaucrats in the Chinese system face is less severe in multiparty democracies—of course, in China, unlike in many authoritarian countries, the information problem is partly relieved through decentralization (more on this later).

Apart from mistakes and information problems upward accountability systems also face difficulty in inspiring bottom-up energies and spontaneous creativity.

In India, in the last few years, the regime has overcentralized most decisions in the Prime Minister's Office and tried to suppress the media and other channels of scrutiny and criticism and so is displaying some of the problems associated with insufficient downward accountability.

24.2.5 *Systemic stability*

One concern about the Chinese governance system is around the mechanism through which a system that can go off-equilibrium on account of various kinds of political or economic shocks is restored to equilibrium. In the face of a crisis, the Chinese state often tends to overreact, suppress information, and act heavy-handedly, thereby sometimes magnifying the dimensions of the crisis. (Even in the initial fumbling over the outbreak of the COVID-19 pandemic in Wuhan—the same thing happened during the SARS outbreak—the lower-level officials had an incentive to suppress bad news.) This systemic feature also generates low tolerance for short-run economic volatility and the rush to reckless fiscal policies that exacerbate the staggering problems of capital misallocation that China faces. The institutional mechanisms for structural reform have now become particularly weaker, as the resolution of internal governance conflicts is now more dependent on personalized channels.

There also remains the larger institutional issue that China has faced throughout history: how to institutionally guarantee the rule of a 'good emperor', as opposed to a 'bad emperor', or that of a good emperor not turning bad. The recent disruption in the conventions of collective leadership and the acceleration of the cult of personality in leadership can only worsen this problem.

As the economy becomes more complex and social relations become more convoluted and intense, the absence of transparent and accountable processes and the attempts by a 'control-freak' leadership to force lockstep conformity and discipline will generate acute tension, conflicts, and informational inefficiency.

In India, despite all the recent ominous signs of a democracy sliding into a form of a majoritarian overreach, it is probably still correct to say that the system structurally remains somewhat more resilient than in China. In both countries (more in China than in India) nationalist glory and the cult of personality of the top leader are becoming a convenient cover for any lapse in performance.

24.3 Abuse of governance and corruption

Over the last quarter century, there has been a tight, often collusive, relationship between business and politicians in China. This is evident from (a) frequent interchanging of positions between executives in public sector companies and the Party's Central Committee; (b) some of China's richest private businessmen are members of the National People's Congress (China's Parliament) and the People's Political Consultative Conference, an important advisory body)—there are even accounts of large 'donations' made before such businessmen are selected for these bodies in China; and (c) the number of influential Party members who can be described as plutocrats—the wealth data from Hurun Reports suggest that the average net worth of the richest 70 members of the National People's Congress in China is several times that for the richest 70 members of the US Congress or the Indian Lok Sabha (lower house of Parliament).

All this is apart from the influence of the top political families ('princelings') who have long been in lucrative monopoly contracts with the state or paid with stakes in business projects facilitated by them—some juicy recent anecdotes on this are narrated in the recent book by Shum (2021). The ownership of many private companies is so murky and intertwined with the public-sector companies that it is often difficult to keep track of the boundaries of the business-politics nexus. There have also been cases of successful private companies 'persuaded' to invest billions of dollars' worth in backing state-owned companies. In general, there has been an excessive growth in luxury properties that enriched both the political and business elites.

The recent crackdowns on corruption may have reduced some egregious cases of malfeasance and conspicuous consumption, but members of what is called the 'red aristocracy', as long as they belong to the loyalist political factions, have been largely shielded. In any case, the over-centralization of power and increased nontransparency of political control have left the essential institutional channels of patronage and corruption intact and may have in some cases substituted one set of crony capitalists by another. Meanwhile by making top bureaucrats nervous about arbitrary punishment from above, it has discouraged them from taking risky or bold decisions leading to what is called 'lazy governance' in China.

The business-politician nexus is, of course, quite common in India. Of the current ruling party Members of Parliament in India about half are businessmen, the corresponding percentage for MP's of all parties taken together is about a quarter. The businessmen bring their own money for election campaigns and other political expenditure, and company donations to party funds for election are large, and now, under the anonymous election bond system, openly nontransparent. In recent years, there have been many stories about two giant business houses receiving regulatory favors from the government and wallowing in crony capitalism have enriched themselves disproportionately.

Both countries have similar patterns of rampant influence-peddling, policy manipulation, politically connected firms getting favors in government contracts, loans from public banks and access to prize real estate, monopoly mining rights, etc. China being more involved in massive construction and infrastructure activities, which are usually 'rent-thick', there is more scope for corruption, as seems to be suggested by both anecdotal and empirical evidence. Fisman and Wang (2014) detected corruption in state asset sales by comparing the prices of publicly traded assets to those of nonpublicly traded assets.

Even to take an example from a different area, like public health: drug prices are usually much higher in China than in India, even though the single-payer system in Chinese healthcare should have given the government more bargaining advantage vis-a-vis the drug companies. People attribute this to the more entrenched kickback system between drug companies and doctors, hospitals, and officials in China.

It is likely that the business–politician collusion in governance is somewhat more subject to public scrutiny in India than in China, and the courts are somewhat more independent in India (though clogged and corrupt, particularly at the lower levels). The scrutiny of collusive behavior by Indian media is now under some shadow with the concentration of its business ownership.

Also, we have noted that the relation with the all-powerful Party is somewhat precarious for the Chinese business tycoons, as political disloyalty or even suspected 'independence' is punished more harshly than in India. Indian politicians may be a bit more dependent on businessmen, particularly in view of election funding.

24.4 Decentralized structures and practices

A very distinctive feature of the Chinese governance system is that Chinese political centralization (in the imperial authority in the past and in that of the Party in recent decades) has been historically tempered by a unique blending of political centralization with economic and administrative decentralization. Xu (2011) has described the system as 'regionally decentralized authoritarianism', in contrast with most authoritarian systems that are highly centralized.

India in some sense is the obverse—combining political decentralization (regional power groupings have been quite strong at least until the middle of the last decade) with economic centralization (with the regions dependent on central finance, the vertical fiscal imbalance is quite severe).

China has much better modes of management of infrastructure financing and construction at the local level. For example, urban infrastructure there is constructed, operated, and maintained by separate companies set up by the city government, whereas in India, the municipal government itself does it through its own departments. The latter are financially strapped, as they do not have much taxation power and are perpetually dependent on the state government for funds. In general, even after the centralizing reforms since 1994, the fiscal system is much more decentralized in China, where sub-provincial levels of government tend to spend more than half of total government budgetary expenditure, compared to about 3% in India (this is not including the large off-budget revenue-raising and expenditure of local governments in China). The much worse performance of sub-provincial local bodies in India in the last-mile delivery of public services and facilities is partly attributable to this (even though Chinese local governments have also much larger responsibility for infrastructure-building and public services). In India, the emphasis has been more on fiscal transfers to local governments than on local tax autonomy. In China, in municipal finance central government transfers declined over time to insignificance, and there is more dependence on domestic loans and extra-budgetary revenues like land transfer fees.

In both China and in India, decentralization tends to accentuate regional inequality, though in India, the constitutional body of the Finance Commission tends to partially compensate for this by allocating redistributive transfers to poorer regions.

In comparison with India and other developing countries, the Chinese local government is much more involved in local business development, not just in public services delivery. A few years back when the private automaker, Zhejiang Geely Holding Group, bought up the Swedish car company Volvo in a widely publicized move, much of the money was actually provided by the local municipal government—something unthinkable in India. Jurisdictional competition for mobile resources and business and regional competition in growth rates influencing career promotion of officials have usually played a much more important role in Chinese local development.

But in recent years, the pace of experimentation and trial-and-error pilot projects in local areas, which characterized the early reform period, has slowed down. The current regime's more centralized and personal loyalty-based leadership has made experimentation even more difficult.

A growing literature in decentralization all over the world has pointed to the problem of capture of local governments by the elite (including officials and intermediaries) and the frequent diversion of benefits and resources to non-target groups.[2]

In India, there is plenty of evidence of landed interests undermining decentralized welfare programs for the poor, apart from state political administration and legislators hampering devolution of power to the municipalities and village councils. China's more egalitarian land use rights distribution after de-collectivization may have prevented the rise of a landed oligarchy that has often captured local governments in parts of rural India.

However, in recent decades, Chinese decentralization has not been able to avoid the problem of serious local elite capture. Chinese local business in collusion with local officials has been at the root of problems of arbitrary land acquisition, toxic pollution, and violation of safety standards in food and in work for factories and mines. Such collusion is much more rampant in China than, say, in India, primarily because China has fewer checks from below on abuse of power.

On safety standards, for example, Chinese coalmine death rates are reported to be 15 times higher than that in India (the death rates even per unit of coal output is much higher). On the basis of provincial-level panel data on key state coal mines in China from 1995 to 2005, Jia and Nie (2015) provided evidence that decentralization makes collusion between official regulators and firms more likely (in the Chinese media such collusion is called *guan-mei goujie*) and is correlated with increases in coal mine fatality rates. This is also consistent with the general finding of Fisman and Wang (2015) that politically connected firms in China have higher rates of workplace fatalities, based on firm-level data collected from different industries between 2008 and 2011. There is also suggestive evidence in the Jia and Nie paper that media exposure can act as a deterrent against collusion.

There are also fewer checks on debt-fueled overinvestment and excess capacity in local government-controlled or politically connected firms (currently a source of major macro-economic problems in China). China's central leadership is now trying to rein in the mounting debt problem of local governments and their dependence on the shadow banking system.

This completes our brief assessment of the strengths and weaknesses of the Chinese governance system in comparison with that in India. Our major purpose has been to show that some of the positive features of the Chinese system (like career incentives for officials to promote local development, or decentralized structure of management of infrastructure building and local business development) do not necessarily depend on the authoritarian system—they can very well be adopted, with proper reforms of organization and incentives, in a democratic country. Even the general ability of the Chinese top leadership to quickly coordinate and mobilize the state machinery is not a feature of authoritarianism—note its absence in many authoritarian countries in Africa, Asia, or Latin America, and its vibrant presence in democratic Japan, South Korea, or Taiwan, not to speak of Scandinavia.

On the other hand, some of the major problems in Chinese governance arising from the lack of downward accountability, choking of information flows delaying course correction in case of serious mistakes in decisions, lack of public scrutiny of corrupt collusion between officials and businessmen, and a systemic tendency in the face of a crisis to overreact, suppress information, and act heavy-handedly, thereby making the system less resilient—these are all ugly features of authoritarianism that one should seriously take into account, even if one cares mainly about performance of a system and not the intrinsic value of democratic freedom. One hopes that a consideration of these factors will help India and other developing countries in resisting the allure of authoritarian capitalism that China is pushing as an alternative model.

Notes

1 For a general analysis of comparative performance up to the end of the first decade of this century, see Bardhan (2013).
2 See for an overview, Bardhan (2002).

References

Bardhan, P. (2002). "Decentralization of Governance and Development," *Journal of Economic Perspectives*, 16, no. 4: 185–205.

Bardhan, P. (2013). *Awakening Giants, Feet of Clay: Assessing the Economic Rise of China and India.* Princeton, NJ: Princeton University Press.

Bell, D. (2015). *The China Model: Political Meritocracy and the Limits of Democracy.* Princeton, NJ: Princeton University Press.

Chen, T. and Kung, J. K. (2018). "Busting the 'Princelings': The Campaign against Corruption in China's Primary Land Market," *Quarterly Journal of Economics*, 134, no. 1: 185–226.

Fisman, R. and Wang, Y. (2014). "Corruption in Chinese Privatizations," NBER Working Paper No. 20090.

Fisman, R. and Wang, Y. (2015). "The Mortality Costs of Political Connections," *Review of Economic Studies*, 82: 1346–82.

Jia, R. and Nie, H. (2015). "Decentralization, Collusion, and Coalmine," *Review of Economics and Statistics*, 99: 105–18.

Landry, P. F., Lu, X. and Duan, H. (2017). "Does Performance Matter? Evaluating Political Selection Along the Chinese Administrative Ladder," *Comparative Political Studies*, 51, no. 8: 1074–1105.

Shum, D. (2021). *Red Roulette: An Insider's Story of Wealth, Power, Corruption, and Vengeance in Today's China.* New York, NY: Scribner.

Su, F., He, M. and Tao, R. (August 2016). "Meritocracy and Patronage in State Building: Evidence from Provincial Leaders in China," Renmin University, Beijing.

Xu, C. (2011). "The Fundamental Institutions of China's Reforms and Development," *Journal of Economic Literature*, 49, no. 4: 1076–1151.

25

TRADE INTERDEPENDENCIES IN THE EU SINGLE MARKET

Pierfederico Asdrubali

JOHN CABOT UNIVERSITY, ROME, ITALY

Paolo Pasimeni

BSOG – VRIJE UNIVERSITEIT BRUSSEL, BRUSSELS, BELGIUM

25.1 Introduction

The process of European integration pivots on the progressive establishment of a common area where the elimination of barriers to the free movement of goods, services, people and capital across Member States leads to the creation of the Single Market.

The Single Market refers to the EU[1] as one territory and aims at ensuring the free circulation of people, goods, services and capital by removing borders and regulatory obstacles to free movement across this territory. Its current dimension is comparable to the US market in terms of GDP; it includes 500 million consumers, and 22 million businesses, and represents one of the major assets for the EU. From a political point of view, it represents a powerful lever because granting access to one of the richest markets of the world endows the EU with considerable negotiating power in the relations with third countries and multinational corporations. However, despite being at the origin a fundamentally macroeconomic project, the Single Market structure has seldom been assessed from a macroeconomic perspective (Jones, 1983; Mariniello et al., 2015, for a review).

The relevance of the Single Market has traditionally been studied at microeconomic level, by exploring how the removal of barriers improves efficiency in the allocation of factors and benefits consumers. The classical analysis by Viner (1950) pioneered the so-called static effects of trade integration (trade creation, trade diversion, etc.) while Balassa (1961) introduced the dynamic effects (scale economies, external economies, etc.). An equally large literature has dealt with the microeconomic aspects of factor mobility (allocation efficiency, wage/interest convergence, etc.). An illustration of the relevance of the microeconomic approach to the European Single Market can be found in accounts like Sapir (1992), Dahlberg (2015), and Wolfmayr et al. (2019).

The progressive construction of the Single Market aims at providing a number of macroeconomic benefits, compared to segregated national markets. On the supply side, it provides richer and more diversified sources of funding, lower transaction costs, a more dynamic business environment, the critical mass to achieve economies of scale and a better allocation of factors of production. On the demand side, it grants a larger reserve of domestic

DOI: 10.4324/9781003144366-30

demand to the businesses that have access to it, therefore shielding them from negative cyclical developments in the rest of the world. By improving the efficient allocation of factors and taking advantage of the large domestic demand, the Single Market therefore fulfils important macroeconomic functions.

This chapter studies the trade interdependencies in the EU Single Market, along with their effects on the structure and composition of aggregate supply and demand; then it analyses the long-term evolution of these trade interdependencies, in light of the underlying integration dynamics of the Single Market. We take the view that all four components of the Single Market – free circulation of goods, services, capital and people – affect trade patterns, to a greater or lesser extent. As an obvious example, increased mobility of people and capital can alter the profile of comparative advantages, favour the attainment of scale economies, facilitate links with specific partner countries, etc.

The chapter uses the OECD Trade in Value Added ("TiVA") dataset[2] to investigate both sector-specific and country-specific features of trade integration, by disentangling the multiple interconnections among sectors and countries. The production of goods and services is not only directed to final demand; on the contrary, in an interconnected economy, with specialisation patterns driving trade and production, an increasing share of production is directed to intermediate goods and services, which serve as inputs for other sectors and countries. We consider those interconnections, both upstream ("backward linkages") and downstream in value chains ("forward linkages"), to define the structure of the EU Single Market. We show how this structure has evolved over time and how of its reliance on the EU with respect to the rest of the world has changed.

The next section discusses the macroeconomic relevance of the Single Market, while Section 25.3 describes its structure. Section 25.4 explains the sectoral interdependences and Section 25.5 the sectoral relevance of the Single Market, in comparison with the rest of the world. Section 25.6 shows the interdependences across countries, and Section 25.7 measures the relevance of the Single Market for each Member State. Section 25.8 then documents how such interdependences and relevance have changed over time, and Section 25.9 finally concludes.

25.2 The macroeconomic relevance of the Single Market

Removing tariff and non-tariff barriers to trade, fostering cross-border capital flows, and supporting people's mobility across countries were all key decisions to launch the Single Market project; however, such a profound transformation of the European economies was inevitably bound to spill over to other areas and policies. The optimal mix of macroeconomic policies could no longer be determined by each country independently, given the growing interdependencies brought about by increased factor mobility and trade.

It is in this context that the project of the Economic and Monetary Union (EMU) was launched, leading to the establishment of a single currency and a common monetary policy, managed by the European Central Bank. At the same time, the need for consistent fiscal and structural policies across countries arose, leading to subsequent attempts to better coordinate policies that remained entrusted to national governments, in an unprecedented decoupling with monetary policy (Goodhart, 1998).

The rationale underpinning the creation of EMU related to the need to facilitate the smooth functioning of the forthcoming Single Market (Emerson et al., 1992).[3] Almost 30 years later, the development of the monetary union and its incomplete architecture call for a better functioning Single Market to facilitate the functioning of the EMU (Juncker et al., 2015).

If 30 years ago the move towards the EMU was justified by the challenges posed by the Single Market, today the efforts to make the EMU more resilient to macroeconomic fluctuations and fully sustainable over time highlight the need for a Single Market where factors, goods and services circulate smoothly. The interdependence between the two projects is increasingly manifest.

An integrated and well-functioning common market, where goods, services, workers and capital are more mobile, can provide a degree of macroeconomic stabilisation through the private sector to partly compensate the missing stabilisation function, that in complete economic and monetary unions operates also through a common fiscal instrument. This means that in a flexible Single Market in the event of large shocks factors can be reallocated more easily and prices be more flexible, thereby increasing the resilience of the monetary union. Having a large market at their disposal, moreover, shields domestic companies from global downturns, providing them with the access to a large reserve of aggregate demand. This is precisely one of the key advantages of a set of countries establishing a common market among them, that allows individual countries to reap the benefits of a large market even without merging all into a single jurisdiction (Alesina and Spolaore, 2005).

The debate about the future of EMU is strictly linked to this notion of the availability of market mechanisms for macroeconomic stabilisation; for the time being the key source of macroeconomic stabilisation for the EMU comes from the Single Market. Market mechanisms can play a stabilizing role through improved mobility of factors (Mundell, 1973; Eichengreen, 1992).[4] There is indeed evidence that in the United States, for instance, they provide a great degree of stabilization (Nikolov, 2016), which is nevertheless supported by public mechanisms for stabilization, such as the federal budget (Nikolov and Pasimeni, 2019). The experience of the Great Recession proved that the amount of risk sharing provided by markets remains generally inadequate (Berger et al., 2018) and that in complete federal states there is always a public channel providing macroeconomic stabilization through a common fiscal capacity.

Nevertheless, there is surprisingly little analysis about the contribution of the Single Market to the sustainability of the monetary union. In order to bridge this gap, this chapter analyses the evolution of trade interdependence within the Single Market, first in terms of structure of the market, by looking at the interlinkages among countries and sectors, and then by studying the long-term evolution of these interdependencies.

In order to draw a meaningful picture of the role of the Single Market in facilitating integration, it is necessary to compare its evolution to a realistic counterfactual, which is not the level of integration *before* the Single Market, but rather the level of integration that EU countries have achieved with the rest of the world *during* the same period. We do so by comparing integration among countries *within* the Single Market with the integration of EU countries with the rest of the world, *outside* the Single Market.

25.3 The sectoral and geographical structure of the Single Market

25.3.1 EU sectors

The EU economy, as other advanced economies, is based mainly on services, as they represent about 70% of total output; nevertheless, the EU maintains a strong industrial base and, as an aggregate, is the second largest manufacturer of the world, after China and before the United States. Wholesale and retail trade and general business services are the largest sectors, followed by real estate and construction. In terms of manufacturing, chemicals (including pharmaceuticals), non-metallic mineral products, food and transport equipment (including motor vehicles), are the most relevant ones (Chart 25.1).

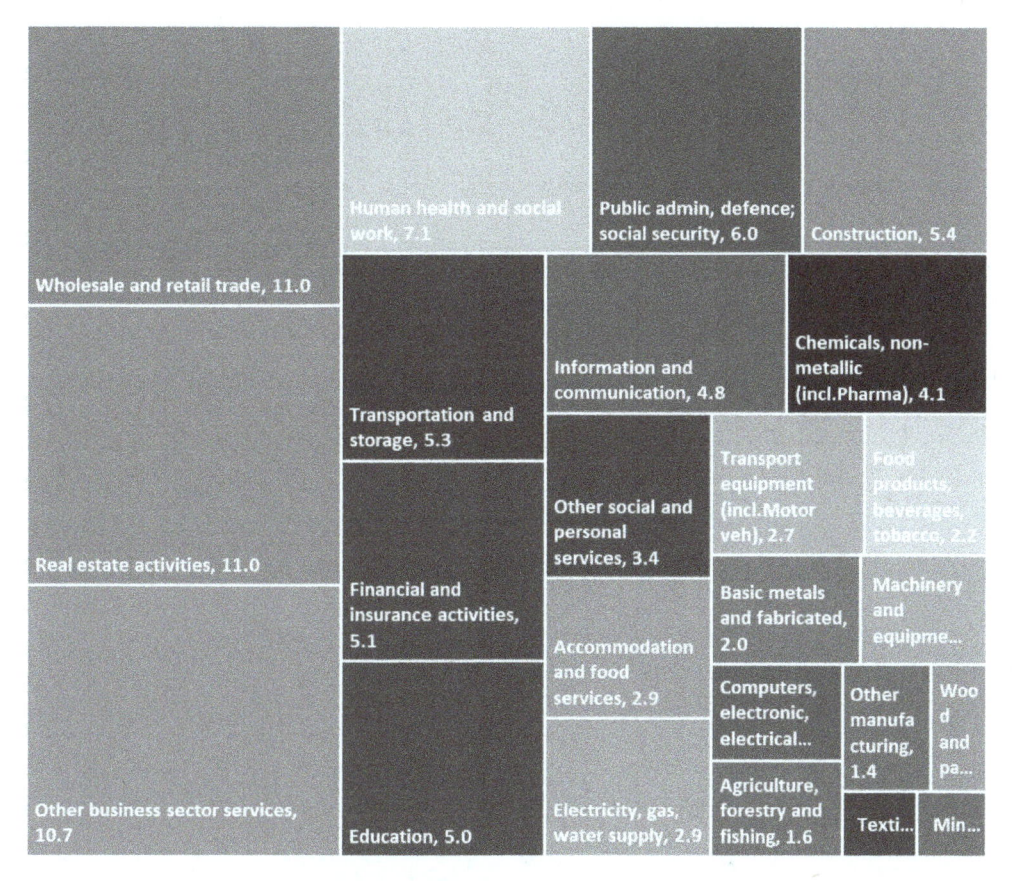

Chart 25.1   Sectoral shares of total value added in the EU.

Source: Authors' elaborations, based on OECD data.

Note: The indicator measures the share of each sector in the economy (total value added).

This structural composition of the European economy has been essentially stable over time, as the relative importance of sectors has not changed considerably. However, in the decade between 2005 and 2015, some sectors, such as construction and telecommunications, have seen a noticeable reduction in their share of value added, to the benefit of information technology and other business services, health and social work and, among manufacturing sectors, of the production of motor vehicles, the shares of which have increased (Chart 25.2).

Such sectoral shifts, although limited, are consistent with a structural change in the economic model of the EU, and of the euro area in particular, from a higher reliance on non-tradeable towards more tradeable sectors and external demand, that occurred after the Great Recession.

25.3.2 EU countries

Germany is the largest economy of the EU, accounting for one fifth of total GDP, followed by the UK, France, Italy and Spain, as the other major ones (Chart 25.3). Like the sectoral shares, also the country shares have been rather stable over time, with few but remarkable exceptions: Poland, on the positive side, and Italy, on the negative side, are the ones that have seen their

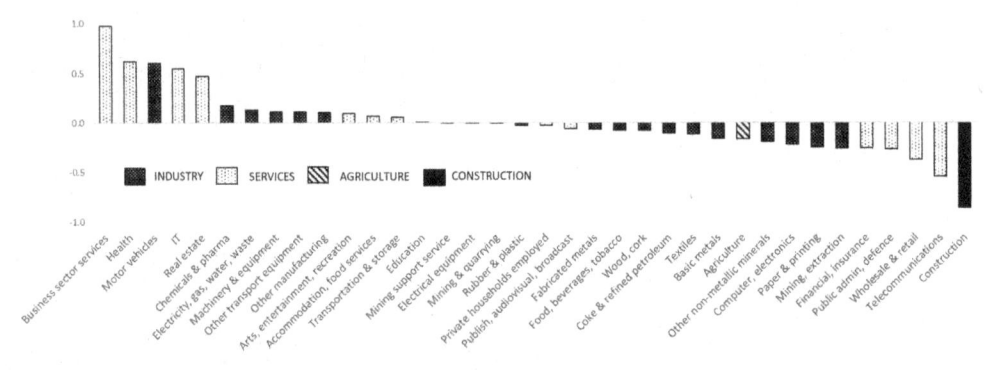

Chart 25.2 Change in the sectoral shares of output (EU: 2005–2015).

Source: Authors' elaborations, based on OECD data.

Note: The indicator measures changes in the share of each sector in the economy (total value added) between 2005 and 2015.

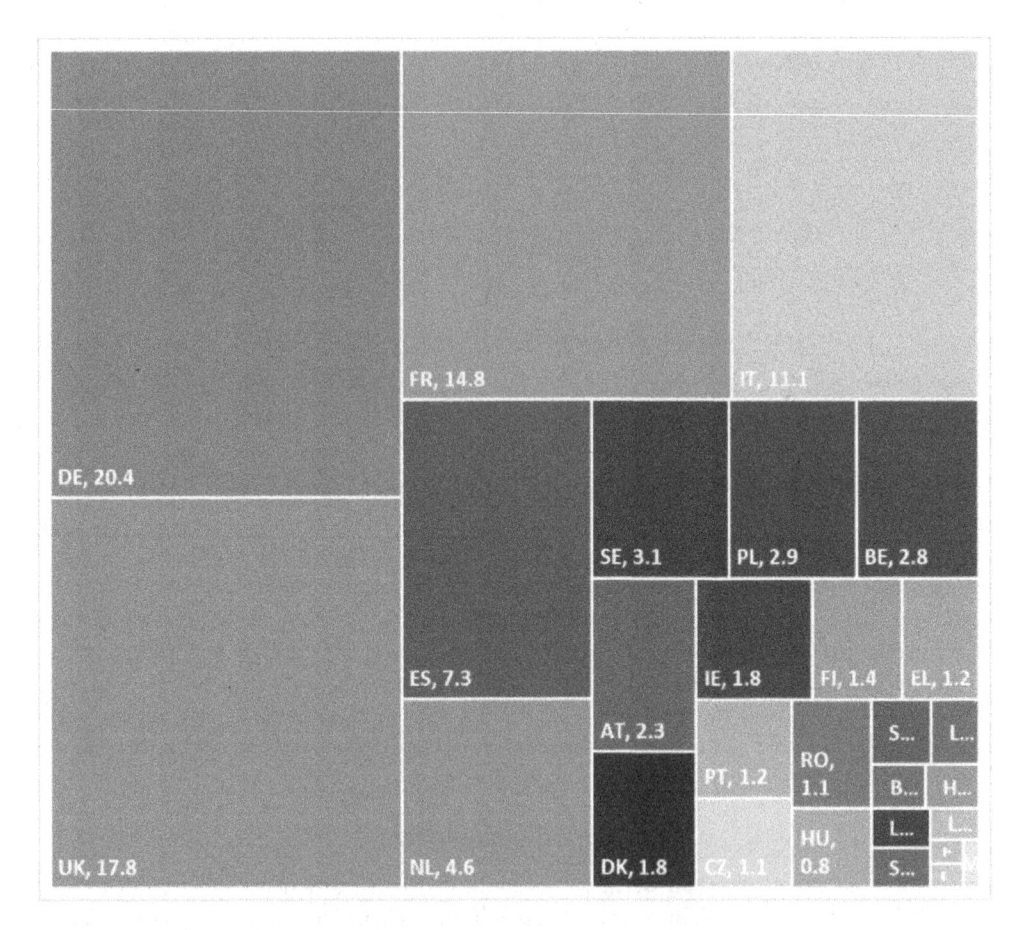

Chart 25.3 Country shares of EU GDP.

Source: Eurostat.

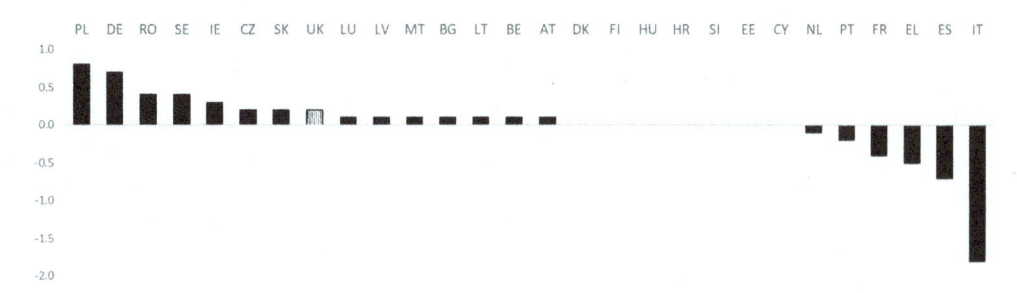

Chart 25.4   Change in the country shares of GDP (EU: 2005–2015).

Source: Authors' elaborations, based on Eurostat data.

Note: The indicator measures changes in the share of each country in the EU GDP between 2005 and 2015.

shares change considerably. Countries that joined the EU in 2004 or afterwards have generally improved their positions, pointing to a positive catching up process (Chart 25.4).

25.4 Interdependences among sectors

Beyond the relative size of sectors, the structural composition of the Single Market can also be analysed by taking into account the interdependences among them. In other words, it is possible to trace the backward and forward linkages between EU sectors in terms of both supply and demand. When we look at the supply side, we take into account the backward linkages that shape supply chains for each sector. When we look at the demand side, we take into account the forward linkages that contribute to the final demand for each sector. The interdependence among sectors is key to understand how a shock to production or to demand in one sector can propagate to the rest of the economy, affecting the others. We call it "vertical" interdependence, to distinguish it from the cross-country links, that we study afterwards.

25.4.1 Vertical supply chains

The concept of vertical supply chains helps us assess how each sector contributes to the other's value added, through the provision of intermediate products or services used in the production by another sector. We measure this contribution through the share of value added in each sector originating from intermediates produced by other sectors. We use data about trade in value added to get a precise illustration of the imports of intermediates used in production.

In a first approximation, we observe that the service sectors are much more "autonomous" than industry or agriculture, as 91% of service value added is independent of the other two macro-sectors. Services are also an important source of inputs for agriculture and industry, as they contribute to almost one third of their value added, while the opposite is not true. This confirms the characteristics of the EU economy as mainly a "service economy".

In order to properly understand the EU sectoral interdependences, however, we should take a more precise look at specific sectors, and at their bilateral interlinkages. For this reason, we replicate the analysis with a greater level of detail, by studying pairwise relations between the 36 sectors accounting for the total output in the economy. To this end, we build a matrix of sectoral interdependence in terms of value added (Chart 25.5).

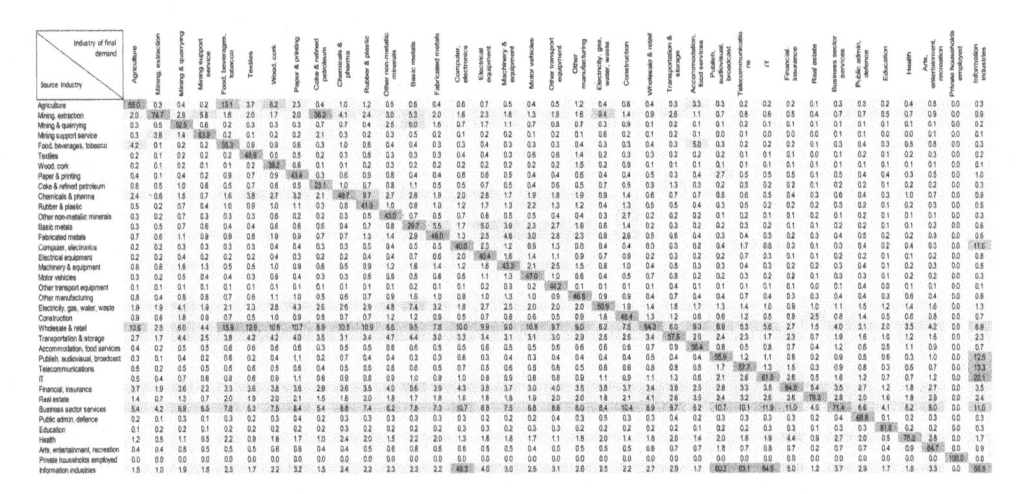

Chart 25.5 Sectoral interdependence in the EU: Supply value chains.

Source: Authors' elaborations, based on OECD TiVA data.

Note: The indicator measures the % share in the value added of each column sector generated by each row sector's supply of intermediate inputs; columns represent the dependence of each sector on the others, and sum to 100 (except for "information industries", which is an aggregate); rows represent the contribution by each sector to the others.

General business services and wholesale and retail services, on top of being the largest in terms of output, are also the most important ones in terms of contribution to other sectors' value added. They are, in other words, key hubs in the economy, as they generate a relevant share of value added produced in other sectors. Mining and quarrying are also a key source of value, but their contribution to the economy is less widespread, as it concentrates mainly in chemicals and non-metallics and in electricity, gas and water supply. Financial services, as expected, are a relevant source of value for almost all sectors. In terms of dependence, the food sector, wood and paper industry, machinery and chemicals are highly reliant on inputs originating from other sectors (notably mining and quarrying are very important for chemicals), as more than half of their value added originates from intermediates coming from other sectors. Typical services, such as education, health and real estate activities, instead, are quite "independent", as almost 80% of their value added is originated within the same sector.

25.4.2 Vertical demand flows

The interdependences among sectors can also be seen from the demand side perspective. To this end, we perform a similar analysis by measuring, for a given sector, how much the other sectors represent in terms of final demand, measured by the share of value added purchased by the downstream sectors. This gives an idea of the forward linkages across sectors.

Manufacturing sectors tend to rely more on final demand by services sectors than the other way around. The chart shows the very important role played by construction as a source of final demand for many manufacturing sectors. Food, beverages and tobacco are, as one would expect, crucial in absorbing agricultural production, as coke and refined petroleum are for mining and quarrying, and the production of machinery and equipment and of motor vehicles is for basic and fabricated metals. Among the services sectors, it is interesting to observe that general business services are often directed to construction, to wholesale and retail trade, to public administration and to transportation and storage (Chart 25.6).

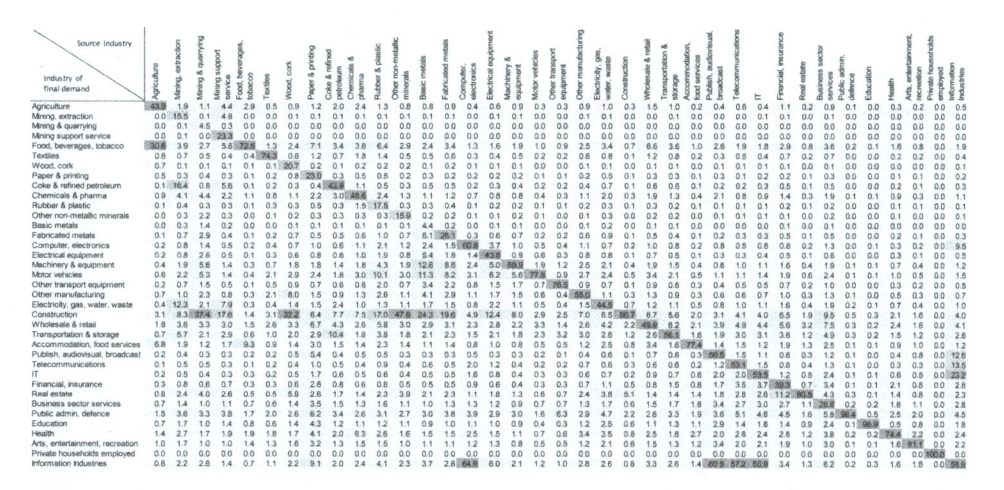

Chart 25.6 Sectoral interconnectedness in the EU: Final demand value.

Source: Authors' elaborations, based on OECD TiVA data.

Note: The indicator measures the % share of value added of each column sector generated by each row sector's final demand; columns represent the dependence of each sector on the demand of the others, and sum to 100 (except for "information industries", which is an aggregate); rows represent the demand absorbed by each sector.

25.5 The sectoral relevance of the Single Market

After looking at the interlinkages across sectors within the Single Market, we analyse how much the Single Market is relevant for each sector. We do so on both the supply side and the demand side, by measuring the share of value added created in supply chains within the Single Market and the share of final demand that for each sector can be attributed to the Single Market.

25.5.1 Sectoral exposure to international value chains and markets

We analyse the geographical exposure of each sector to imports of intermediates used in the production and to foreign markets as sources of final demand. Among the three macro-sectors of the economy, industry and agriculture have a large exposure to international value chains, while services, being less tradeable, are much more reliant on domestic sources of intermediate inputs. Industry is also widely exposed to foreign markets as more than half of its production is exported, while for agriculture almost 60% of production is consumed within national borders. Services, as expected, are less tradeable and for more than 3/4 directed to domestic demand.

By studying the exposure to international markets and to international supply chains, in comparison with the relevance of the domestic markets for both supply and demand, we can better understand how sectors work in practice, and how internationally integrated or autonomous they are. The sectoral detail confirms that manufacturing sectors are much more open to international trade, while services rely more on domestic value chains and demand, within national borders (Chart 25.7).

As one would expect, most of the value chains develop within national borders; however, manufacturing in the EU relies for about 23% of its value added on intermediate products originated outside the EU and for almost 29% on cross-border value chains within the Single Market. Among the key sub-sectors, "Textile", "Coke and refined petrol" and "Computers and electronics" are the ones most exposed to extra-EU sources of inputs, while "Motor

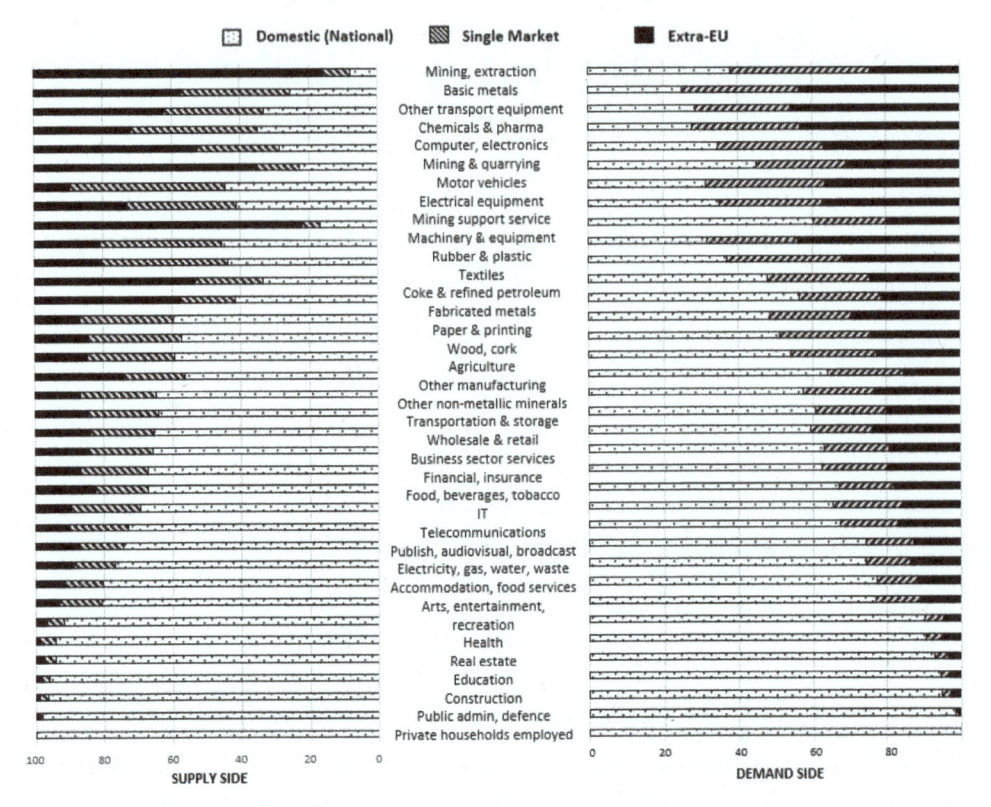

Chart 25.7 Geographical exposure of sectors: Supply chains and final demand.

Source: Authors' elaborations, based on OECD TiVA data.

Note: For each sector, the indicator measures: On the supply side (left), the share of value added produced using domestic inputs within each Member State, and the share of value added which depends on intermediate inputs generated abroad, with the distinction between the EU Single Market and extra-EU countries; on the demand side (right), the share of final demand absorbed domestically within each Member State, and the share which is absorbed by exports, with the distinction between the EU Single Market and extra-EU markets.

vehicles" is the most integrated sector within the Single Market, therefore relying to a great extent on intra-EU value chains. Finally, the "Pharmaceutical" sector is highly exposed along both dimensions, of intra-EU and extra-EU value chains.

On the demand side, the EU manufacturing sector is even more reliant on extra-EU markets, where one third of its final production is sold; only 42% is absorbed by domestic demand within each Member State, and another 25% by cross-border trade within the Single Market. Chemical and pharmaceutical products, motor vehicles and transport equipment, machinery and basic metals are typical sectors for which exports, within and outside the Single Market, represent the largest share of final demand.

25.5.2 *The relevance of the Single Market*

By comparing the exposure of each sector to supply chains developed within the Single Market and to cross-border final demand within the Single Market (i.e. exports from one Member State to the other), we can determine the relevance of the Single Market for each sector and also whether the Single Market is primarily a source of intermediates for production or a source of demand for a given sector (Chart 25.8).

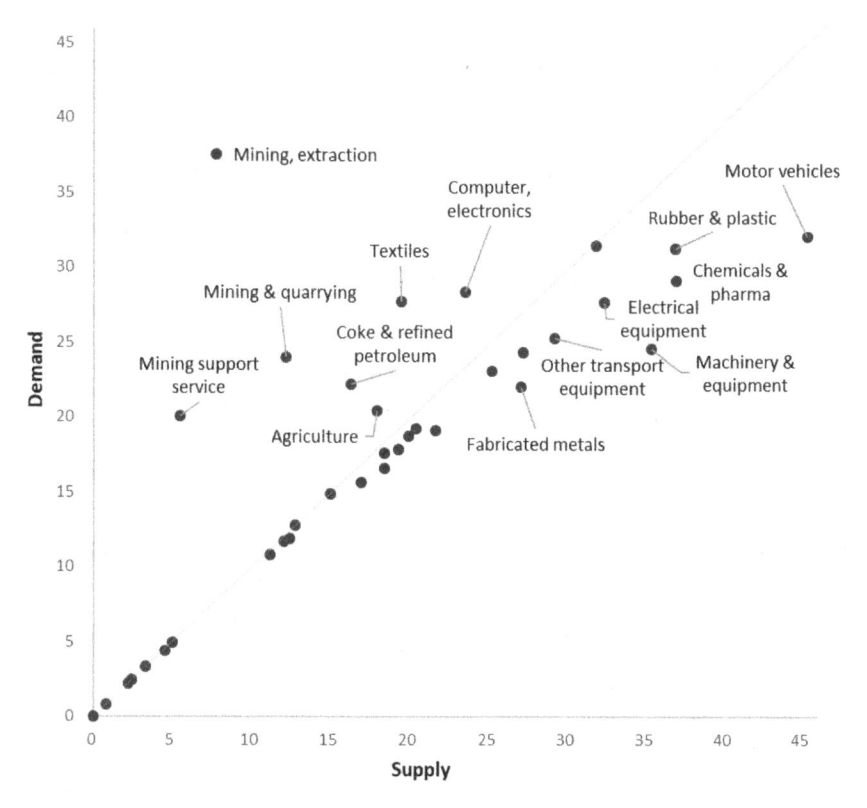

Chart 25.8   The relevance of the Single Market: Supply chains and final demand.

Source: Authors' elaborations, based on OECD data.

Note: On the horizontal axis, the indicator measures for each sector the share of value added that depends on intermediate inputs generated by cross-country supply chains within the Single Market; on the vertical axis, the indicator measures for each sector the share of final demand absorbed by exports within the Single Market.

As already noticed, manufacturing sectors tend to be more reliant on foreign inputs and demand, and, in fact, we find them towards the top-right of the chart, where the share of value added and the share of final demand generated by the Single Market are higher. The second observation is that we find most of the sectors along the 45° line, which means that the Single Market is for them as important on the supply side as it is on the demand side. However, we find a few of them off the line, and this offers interesting insights about these sectors.

For sectors such as motor vehicles and transport equipment, or for chemical and pharmaceutical products, for rubber, plastics and metals, the Single Market is more relevant as a source of key intermediates, than for being a large reservoir of demand. In the case of the production of motor vehicles, for instance, the extended supply chains built within the Single Market across different Member States contribute to almost half of the total value added generated by this sector.

On the other side, the whole mining industry (including extraction, quarrying, support services, refining, etc.) finds in the Single Market an important source of demand rather than intermediate inputs. This is consistent with the fact that the EU has a scarce endowment of raw materials and is instead a large importer of such goods. Similarly, but to a lower extent, for textile and for computers and electronics, the EU is more relevant as a market for final products rather than as a source of inputs.

25.5.3 Dependence on extra-EU supply and demand

By the same token, by comparing the exposure of each sector to supply chains and export markets outside the EU, we can determine the extra-EU dependence of each EU sector. When looking at extra-EU exposure, again we find that manufacturing sectors are the most exposed, which confirms their more tradeable nature. For instance, the EU is highly dependent on extra-EU supply and demand for basic metals. The dependence on extra-EU is low for service sectors and is similar along the two dimensions of demand and supply (Chart 25.9).

The sectors for which such dependence is higher display remarkable differences along the two dimensions (they tend to depart from the 45° line) and, therefore, represent interesting cases. On one side, the EU production of computers and electronics, textiles and coke and refined petroleum is highly exposed to extra-EU supply chains, which provide key intermediates; in these sectors, the share of value added originating from such extra-EU supply chains is close to half of the total value produced. On the other side, for the automotive sector, for the production of machinery, and for chemical and pharmaceutical products, the extra-EU world is very important as it represents a sizeable export market that absorbs almost half of the EU production.

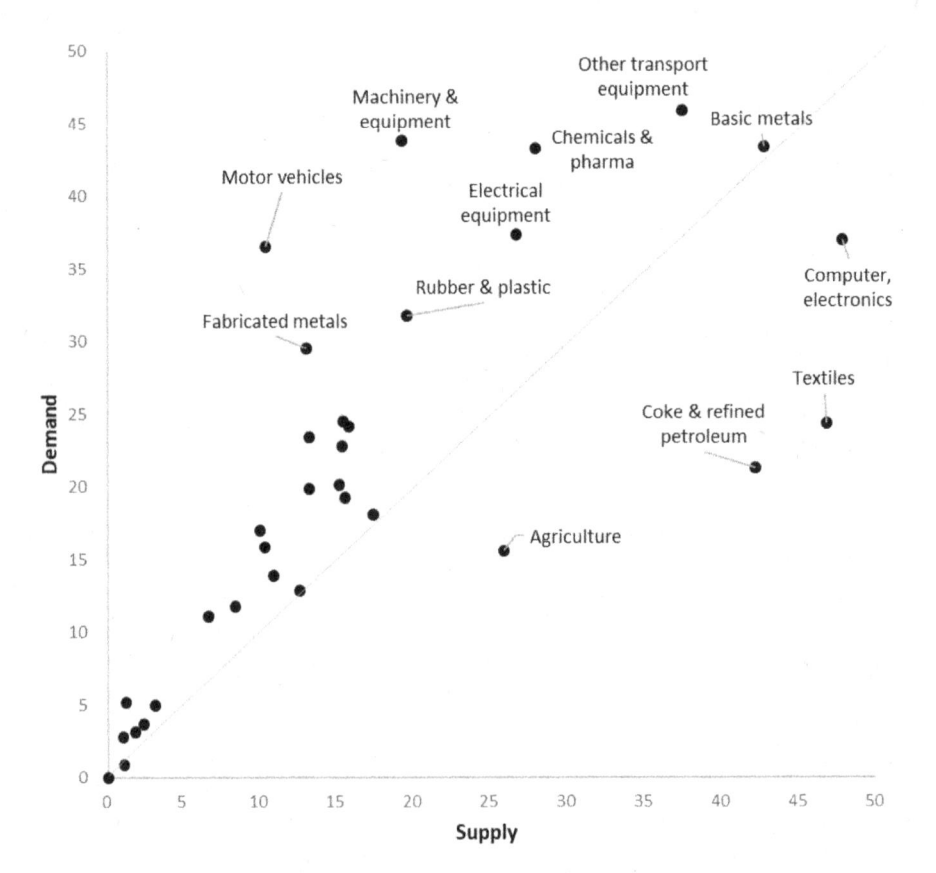

Chart 25.9 The dependence on extra-EU supply and demand.

Source: Authors' elaborations, based on OECD data.

Note: On the horizontal axis, the indicator measures for each sector the share of value added that depends on intermediate inputs generated by extra-EU supply chains; on the vertical axis, the indicator measures for each sector the share of final demand absorbed by exports to the rest of the world, outside the Single Market.

The two dimensions of dependence, on extra-EU supply chains and export markets, have important implications for the policy decisions about the so-called strategic autonomy of the EU. For those cases in which the EU is highly dependent on intermediate inputs crucial for production, ensuring an adequate and diversified supply of those inputs (e.g., through reshoring) will be of the essence. For the other cases, instead, in which the EU is highly dependent on extra-EU demand, a careful trade policy, coupled with adequate stimulus of domestic demand, would be crucial.

25.6 Interdependence among countries

In order to study the interdependence among Member States within the Single Market, we apply to the country-level the same methodology used for the analysis of sectors. On the supply side, we determine how much value added in the total production of one Member State originates from intermediates produced in other countries. On the demand side, we measure how much the demand generated by other countries contributes to absorbing the production of a given Member State. The combination of these two flows illustrates the cross-country bilateral links operating within the Single Market.

25.6.1 Cross-country supply chains

Cross-country supply chains operate within the Single Market as production becomes more integrated. Each country generates part of its value added relying on inputs produced domestically, within its borders, part by using intermediates coming from other EU countries, and part with inputs originating outside the EU. The next chart shows, along the diagonal, the share of total value added that each country produces domestically, in the columns the share of value added of each country that is due to inputs coming from other EU Member States, and in the last row the share that is due to inputs from the rest of the world (Chart 25.10).

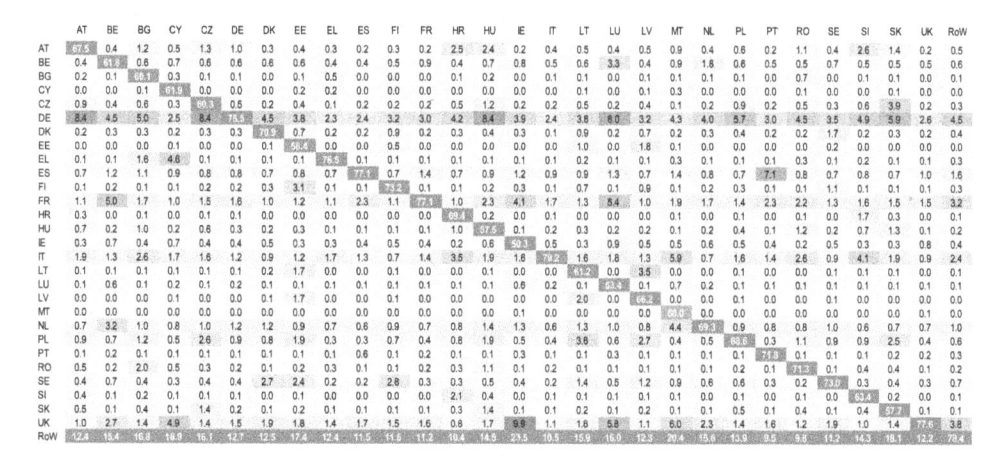

Chart 25.10 Cross-country interdependence in the EU: Value added.

Source: Authors' elaborations, based on OECD data.

Note: The indicator measures the % share in value added of intermediate inputs used in each country and generated in other EU countries and in the rest of the world (extra EU); columns represent the dependence of each country on the others, and sum to 100; rows represent the contribution by country to the other's value added.

As one would expect, larger economies produce a bigger share of value added within their national borders, while smaller ones are more dependent on foreign sources. Italy is the country most reliant on domestic production, with almost 80% of the value of its output generated internally, followed by the UK and other major EU economies (France, Spain and Germany). Among smaller economies, Greece, Finland and Sweden have a particularly low level of foreign dependence, while Malta, Ireland and Luxembourg are the most dependent on foreign sources; the former two, in particular, exhibit a very large exposure to extra-EU countries (last row).

Germany is clearly the main partner country in terms of contribution to value added produced by other EU Member States, followed by Italy and France. The UK is also an important source of value added for other EU countries, to the same level as Italy and France; its contribution is concentrated on the financial sector and consequently its relevance higher for those countries whose financial sector is particularly relevant.

Beyond the broad importance of the largest economies, the heat map in Chart 25.10 also highlights the relevance of geographical proximity, i.e. the interdependence among the Baltic States and in the Iberian Peninsula. In terms of dependence, the single most important bilateral relation is between Ireland and the UK: about 10% of total value added produced by Ireland originates from the UK, and this has obvious relevance in the context of Brexit. Similarly relevant, although arguably less problematic, is the dependence of Austria, Czech Republic, Hungary and Luxembourg on German inputs. By removing artificial barriers to the movement of goods, services, people and capital, the Single Market has facilitated the development of country interdependencies based on (political) economic grounds, as brought out, for example, by gravity equation estimations (see Wolfmayr et al., 2019).

25.6.2 Cross-country demand flows

Being the largest common market of the world in terms of income, the EU Single Market represents a great source of demand for its members, and for the trade partners around the world that have access to it. EU countries, like most advanced countries around the world, generally sell most of their production within their borders but are also great exporters, trading extensively among them and with the rest of the world. The following heat map shows along the diagonal, the share of final demand that each country satisfies domestically, in the columns the share of final demand of each country that is due to exports to other EU Member States, and in the last row the share that is due to exports to the rest of the world (Chart 25.11).

Larger countries have larger domestic markets, which can of course absorb a larger share of their production; the UK, France, Italy and Spain absorb more than three quarters of their production domestically. There are, however, some exceptions to this general rule: smaller economies, such as Greece or Finland, show similar shares of domestic demand, while the largest economy of the EU, Germany, relies on domestic demand less than its size would suggest; this is consistent with the export-led growth model adopted by this country, reflected in its large current account surplus. Luxembourg, Ireland and Malta, on the other side, rely on exports more than they rely on domestic demand, due to their small size and to the specific nature of their economies.

Germany remains, nevertheless, the most important export market for the other EU countries, followed by France and the UK, whose size is smaller, but whose domestic demand is more buoyant than the German one. It is also apparent the frequent strong link created by geographical proximity between a larger and a smaller economy, whereby the first becomes a

	AT	BE	BG	CY	CZ	DE	DK	EE	EL	ES	FI	FR	HR	HU	IE	IT	LT	LU	LV	MT	NL	PL	PT	RO	SE	SI	SK	UK
AT	64.8	0.3	1.2	0.4	1.6	0.9	0.2	0.4	0.2	0.2	0.2	0.2	2.3	2.2	0.4	0.4	0.7	0.7	0.4	1.4	0.3	0.7	0.2	1.1	0.3	3.1	2.1	0.1
BE	0.4	61.1	0.7	0.4	1.0	0.6	0.4	0.5	0.3	0.4	0.4	0.9	0.4	0.7	1.0	0.3	0.8	4.3	0.4	1.9	0.8	0.5	0.6	0.8	0.5	0.6	0.6	0.4
BG	0.2	0.1	60.7	0.2	0.2	0.1	0.1	0.1	0.4	0.0	0.0	0.0	0.1	0.4	0.1	0.1	0.1	0.1	0.1	0.2	0.1	0.1	0.0	0.5	0.0	0.2	0.2	0.0
CY	0.0	0.0	0.1	62.0	0.0	0.0	0.0	0.1	0.5	0.0	0.0	0.0	0.0	0.0	0.0	0.0	0.0	0.0	0.0	0.0	0.0	0.0	0.0	0.1	0.0	0.0	0.0	0.0
CZ	0.8	0.2	0.4	0.2	86.4	0.4	0.2	0.2	0.1	0.1	0.1	0.1	0.4	0.9	0.3	0.2	0.2	0.3	0.2	0.2	0.2	1.0	0.1	0.3	0.2	0.5	2.8	0.1
DE	7.8	3.9	3.5	2.0	8.3	69.6	3.1	2.8	1.8	2.1	2.0	2.1	5.3	7.3	4.2	2.0	3.5	8.7	2.3	5.6	4.7	6.1	2.1	3.3	2.2	5.1	6.4	1.6
DK	0.2	0.4	0.2	0.2	0.3	0.4	66.3	1.2	0.2	0.2	0.3	0.1	0.2	0.3	0.4	0.1	1.2	0.4	1.2	0.3	0.4	0.4	0.2	0.1	1.5	0.3	0.3	0.2
EE	0.0	0.0	0.0	0.2	0.0	0.0	0.2	55.7	0.0	0.0	0.9	0.0	0.0	0.0	0.1	0.0	1.3	0.0	0.9	0.0	0.0	0.0	0.0	0.0	0.1	0.0	0.0	0.0
EL	0.1	0.2	2.2	1.5	0.1	0.1	0.1	0.1	78.3	0.1	0.1	0.1	0.1	0.2	0.2	0.2	0.1	0.2	0.1	0.2	0.2	0.1	0.1	0.3	0.1	0.2	0.1	0.1
ES	0.6	1.0	0.9	0.2	1.2	0.8	0.6	0.3	0.3	75.7	0.5	1.1	0.6	1.4	1.6	0.8	0.8	1.9	0.4	0.8	0.9	0.8	3.9	0.7	0.5	0.7	1.1	0.7
FI	0.2	0.2	0.1	0.2	0.3	0.2	0.7	5.7	0.1	0.1	74.0	0.1	0.1	0.2	0.4	0.1	0.6	0.3	0.8	0.1	0.3	0.3	0.1	0.1	1.3	0.1	0.2	0.1
FR	1.5	4.9	1.8	0.7	2.5	2.2	1.2	1.2	0.9	2.9	1.0	78.0	1.0	2.3	3.3	1.9	1.9	5.9	0.9	2.1	2.2	2.1	2.8	2.6	1.5	2.1	2.8	1.4
HR	0.3	0.0	0.1	0.0	0.1	0.1	0.0	0.0	0.0	0.0	0.0	0.0	68.5	0.4	0.0	0.1	0.0	0.1	0.0	0.1	0.0	0.0	0.1	0.0	2.3	0.2	0.0	0.0
HU	0.7	0.2	0.3	0.2	0.7	0.3	0.1	0.1	0.1	0.0	0.1	0.1	0.5	52.6	0.2	0.1	0.0	0.2	0.1	0.2	0.4	0.1	0.7	0.1	1.1	1.7	0.1	0.1
IE	0.1	0.4	0.2	0.1	0.3	0.2	0.2	0.2	0.1	0.2	0.3	0.4	0.1	0.2	35.4	0.2	0.1	2.2	0.1	1.6	0.4	0.2	0.3	0.1	0.2	0.1	0.1	0.7
IT	1.9	1.8	2.4	0.7	1.7	1.3	0.8	0.6	1.3	1.3	0.6	1.3	2.6	2.3	2.8	77.1	1.2	4.7	0.7	1.9	1.4	1.5	0.9	2.4	0.8	4.8	2.2	0.7
LT	0.0	0.1	0.1	0.3	0.1	0.0	0.1	1.8	0.0	0.0	0.1	0.0	0.0	0.1	0.0	0.0	61.8	0.0	3.1	0.1	0.1	0.3	0.0	0.0	0.1	0.1	0.1	0.0
LU	0.0	0.3	0.0	0.0	0.0	0.1	0.0	0.0	0.0	0.0	0.0	0.1	0.0	0.0	0.1	0.0	0.0	34.3	0.0	0.0	0.0	0.0	0.0	0.0	0.0	0.1	0.0	0.1
LV	0.0	0.0	0.0	0.1	0.1	0.0	0.1	2.1	0.0	0.0	0.1	0.0	0.0	0.0	0.0	0.0	2.3	0.0	66.0	0.0	0.0	0.2	0.0	0.0	0.1	0.0	0.0	0.0
MT	0.0	0.0	0.0	0.1	0.0	0.0	0.0	0.0	0.0	0.0	0.0	0.0	0.0	0.0	0.0	0.0	0.0	0.0	0.0	45.3	0.1	0.0	0.0	0.0	0.0	0.0	0.0	0.0
NL	0.7	2.8	0.7	0.4	0.8	0.8	0.7	0.7	0.3	0.5	0.6	0.5	0.5	0.9	1.4	0.3	0.7	2.7	0.6	0.4	65.1	0.8	0.5	0.6	0.9	0.6	0.7	0.8
PL	0.8	0.6	0.7	0.7	2.2	0.8	0.6	0.6	0.2	0.3	0.5	0.3	0.7	1.3	0.7	0.4	1.6	0.7	0.8	0.3	0.5	66.8	0.2	0.5	0.6	1.0	2.4	0.2
PT	0.1	0.2	0.1	0.0	0.2	0.2	0.1	0.1	0.1	1.1	0.1	0.2	0.1	0.2	0.3	0.1	0.1	0.3	0.1	0.2	0.2	0.1	71.7	0.1	0.1	0.1	0.1	0.1
RO	0.5	0.2	2.5	0.4	0.5	0.2	0.1	0.1	0.3	0.1	0.1	0.2	0.8	1.1	0.2	0.1	0.2	0.4	0.1	0.2	0.4	0.4	0.1	72.0	0.1	0.6	0.7	0.1
SE	0.4	0.7	0.4	0.6	0.6	0.5	2.7	3.5	0.3	0.3	2.2	0.3	0.3	0.6	0.7	0.2	1.4	1.0	1.6	0.8	0.6	0.9	0.3	0.3	69.5	0.4	0.5	0.3
SI	0.3	0.0	0.1	0.0	0.1	0.1	0.0	0.0	0.0	0.0	0.0	0.0	1.4	0.2	0.0	0.1	0.0	0.1	0.0	0.0	0.0	0.1	0.0	0.1	0.0	57.4	0.2	0.0
SK	0.3	0.1	0.2	0.2	1.8	0.2	0.1	0.1	0.0	0.1	0.0	0.1	0.5	0.9	0.1	0.1	0.1	0.1	0.1	0.1	0.1	0.5	0.1	0.2	0.1	0.4	86.1	0.0
UK	1.4	3.3	1.7	3.3	2.5	2.2	2.0	1.6	1.7	2.4	1.2	1.9	0.9	2.4	8.1	1.4	2.2	5.5	2.0	15.0	2.9	2.3	2.6	1.3	1.9	1.3	2.2	79.1
RoW	15.9	16.9	18.6	24.4	16.3	17.6	19.4	20.0	12.5	11.6	15.2	12.1	12.9	20.0	38.0	13.5	17.3	24.9	16.5	23.0	17.0	13.0	13.2	11.9	17.1	16.8	16.0	13.2

Chart 25.11   Cross-country interdependence in the EU: Final demand.

Source: Authors' elaborations, based on OECD data.

Note: The indicator measures the % share of final demand for the value added produced by each column country that is absorbed by exports to each row EU country and in the rest of the world (extra EU); columns represent total final demand for each country and sum to 100; rows indicate how much each country represents in terms of final demand for the others.

key export market for the second; this is typically the case of France for Belgium, of Finland for Estonia, of Italy for Slovenia and of Spain for Portugal. The UK is disproportionately important as export market for Ireland, but for Malta as well. Germany, instead, has become a sort of hub for many neighbouring countries, as it is an extremely relevant market for Luxembourg, Czech Republic, Austria, Hungary, Slovakia and Poland.

25.7 The relevance of the Single Market for the EU Member States

The maps of cross-country interlinkages have shown the degree of interdependence within the Single Market; now we analyse how relevant the Single Market is for each Member State. We look again at both the supply and the demand side: we measure the share of value added created in supply chains within the Single Market and the share of production by each country that is absorbed by the others. We distinguish between the domestic market (within the national borders of each Member State), the imports from and exports both to other EU Member States and to the rest of the world.

25.7.1 Country exposure to international value chains and markets

First, we look at the geographical exposure of each country to imports of intermediates used in the production and to foreign markets as sources of final demand. The largest Member States can of course benefit from a relatively larger domestic market, for both supply chains and final demand, so that their international exposure is lower than for smaller countries. Germany, nevertheless, shows a lower reliance on its domestic market, for both demand and supply, than its size and status of largest EU economy would suggest; on the other side, Greece and Finland are instead more inward-oriented than their relatively small sizes would suggest (Chart 25.12).

When we look at the specific reliance of each Member State on the Single Market, we find no big differences along the two dimensions of supply and demand: higher reliance on the

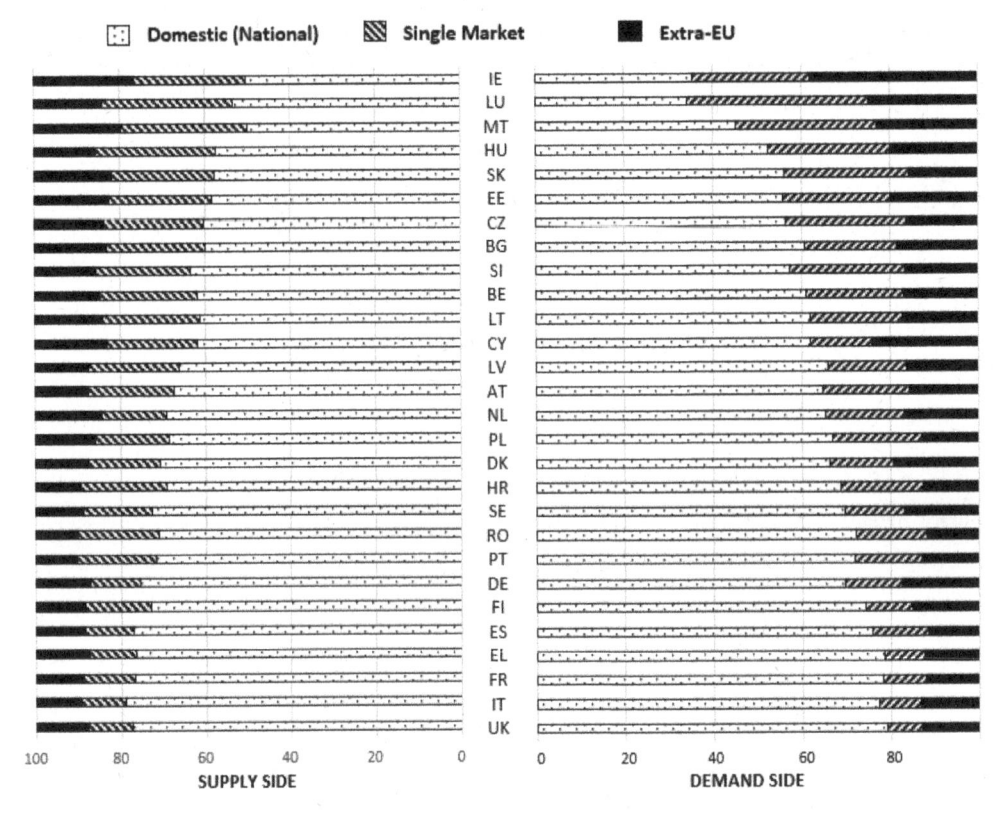

Chart 25.12 Geographical exposure of EU countries: Supply chains and final demand.

Source: Authors' elaborations, based on OECD data.

Note: For each Member State, the indicator measures, on the supply side (left), the share of value added produced domestically and the share of value added which depends on intermediate inputs generated abroad, with the distinction between the EU Single Market and extra-EU countries; on the demand side (right), the share of final demand absorbed domestically and the share which is absorbed by exports, with the distinction between the EU Single Market and extra-EU markets.

Single Market for the supply chains is generally associated with higher reliance on it also as a source of final demand. Almost all Member States, in fact, lay along the 45° degree line in the following chart; the only outlier is Luxembourg, the specific economic model of which based on financial services makes it more interested in the Single Market as a source of demand rather than supply (Chart 25.13).

Luxembourg, nevertheless, is the country for which the Single Market is most relevant, when taking into account both dimensions of supply and demand; interestingly, on the opposite side, the UK is the country for which the Single Market is least relevant, followed by Italy and Greece.

There is often a debate about the relation between the (direct and indirect) benefits of belonging to the EU Single Market and the contributions paid by each Member State to the EU Budget; such a debate neglects many other relevant benefits of the EU integration and other kinds of non-financial contributions that Member States make to the EU. Nevertheless, for purely illustrative purposes, it seems useful in this analysis to look at the correlation between a simple index of reliance on the Single Market and the net financial position of each Member State vis-à-vis the EU Budget.

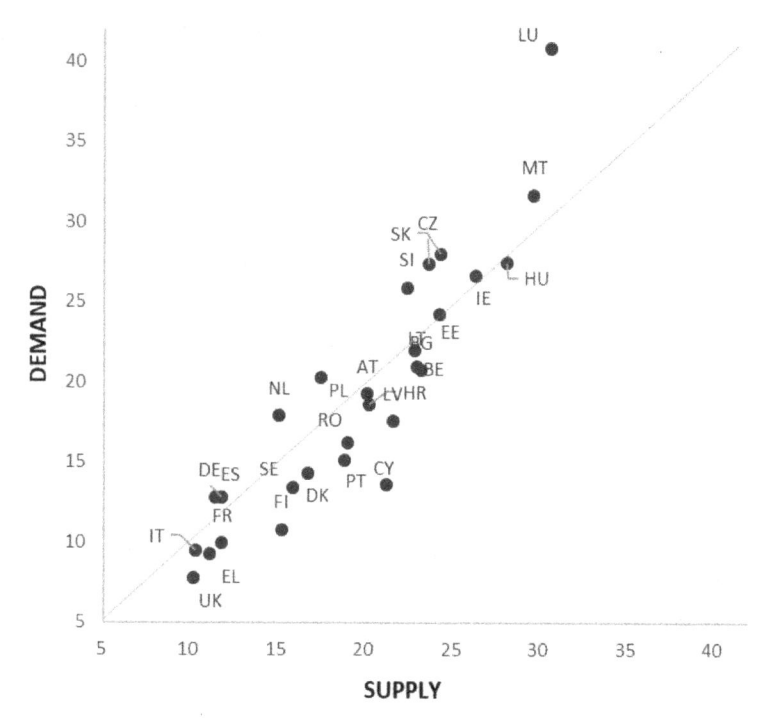

Chart 25.13 The relevance of the Single Market for EU Member States: Supply chains and final demand.

Source: Authors' elaborations, based on OECD data.

Note: On the horizontal axis, the indicator measures for each country the share of value added that depends on intermediate inputs generated by cross-country supply chains within the Single Market; on the vertical axis, the indicator measures for each country the share of final demand absorbed by exports within the Single Market.

The degree of reliance on the Single Market is measured as the average between the share of value added due to cross-country supply chains within the Single Market and the share of final demand coming from other EU countries to capture both dimensions. The net financial position vis-à-vis the EU Budget is measured as the average operating budget balance as a share of GDP over the latest five years for which data are available[5].

Abstracting from all other contributions to and benefits from the process of European integration (which should, however, remain relevant for a proper and comprehensive assessment of costs and benefits of the EU Budget[6]), in this illustrative exercise higher reliance on the Single Market should correspond – all else equal – to worse net balance vis-à-vis the budget, i.e. to higher net contributions. Countries closer to the top-right corner in Chart 25.14 are those better off when considering both criteria, while those closer to the bottom-left corner are those worse off.

In the top right extreme, we find Hungary, as the country with the best net balance vis-à-vis the EU budget and the third most benefitting from the Single Market; on the other side, closer to the bottom left corner, we find the UK, as the country least reliant on the Single Market and one of the main net contributors to the budget. The net payers all share a very similar financial balance vis-à-vis the budget, comprised between −0.2% and −0.4% of Gross National Income, as such balance is *de facto* capped by several correction mechanisms; however, they differ more in terms of reliance on the Single Market as a source of supply and demand: Belgium is the net payer that benefits the most, followed by Austria, the Netherlands,

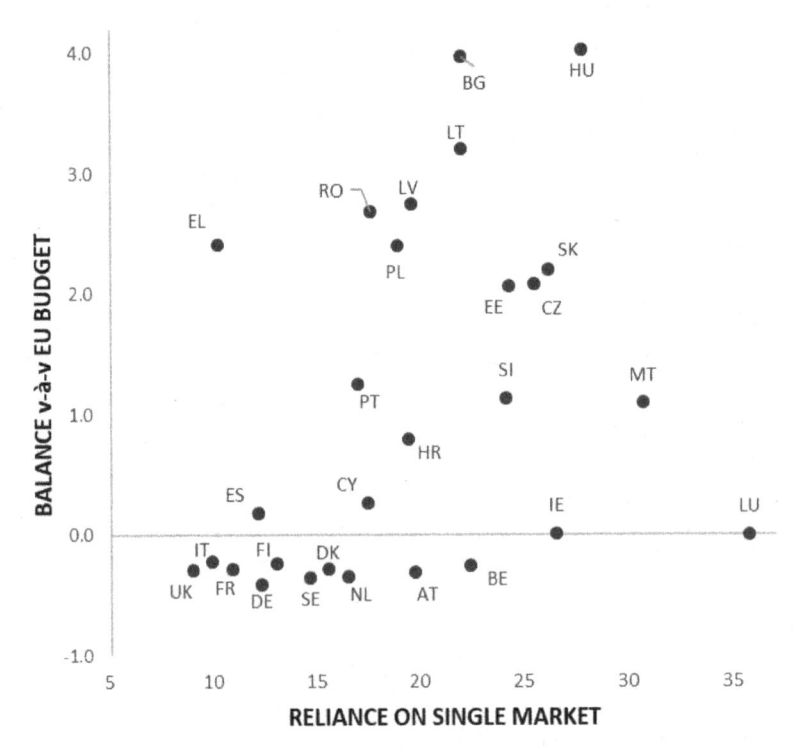

Chart 25.14 Benefits from the Single Market and contribution to the EU budget.

Source: Authors' elaborations, based on DG BUDGET and OECD data.

Note: On the horizontal axis, the indicator measures for each country the average between the share of total value added due to cross-country supply chains within the Single Market and the share of final demand coming from other EU countries; on the vertical axis, the indicator measures the operating budget balance of each Member State with the EU Budget, as a share of its Gross National Income, averaged over five years (2015–2019).

Denmark, Sweden and Finland. Of the largest Member States, Germany benefits more than France, followed by Italy, and, finally, as mentioned, the UK.

Central and Eastern European countries seem to be relying more on the Single Market than their other partner countries, which may be due to their geographical proximity, as well as to their integration in value chains of the main industrial country, i.e. Germany. Many of the countries that are relying more on the Single Market are also those who have joined most recently the EU.

25.7.2 Country dependence on extra-EU supply and demand

If the Single Market is generally equally relevant as a source of intermediates for production and of final demand, for most EU countries, trade with the rest of the world tends to be instead more relevant as a source of demand. When we look at the specific exposure of each Member State to extra-EU value chains and final demand, we find that for the vast majority of them the second aspect is more relevant. In general, EU countries are more dependent on the rest of the world as an export market than as a source of intermediates for production (Chart 25.15).

This result is consistent with the overall large and increasing trade surplus of the EU, and of the euro area in particular, which signals that the whole region pursues an export-led growth model. Such a growth model might explain the relatively larger importance of manufacturing

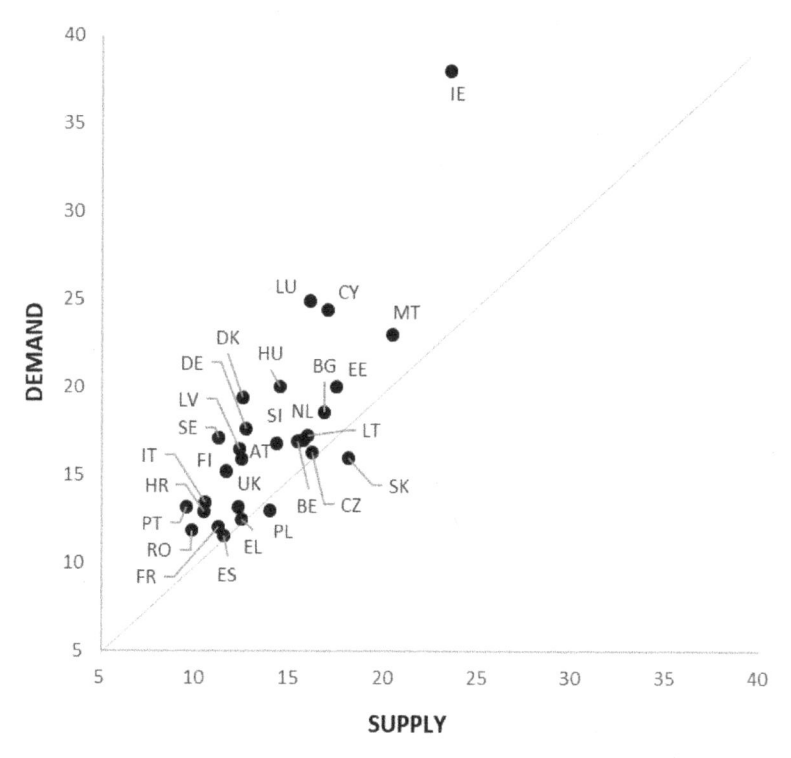

Chart 25.15 The dependence of EU Member States on extra-EU supply and demand.

Source: Authors' elaborations, based on OECD data.

Note: On the horizontal axis, the indicator measures for each country the share of value added that depends on intermediate inputs generated by extra-EU supply chains; on the vertical axis, the indicator measures for each country the share of final demand absorbed by exports to the rest of the world, outside the Single Market.

and of other tradeable sectors (for instance tourism) but is less consistent with the relative position of the EU as a high-income region in the world.

25.8 Changes in the structural characteristics of the EU economy

We look now at changes over time in the structural characteristics of the EU economy in terms of reliance on domestic markets, on the Single Market and on the rest of the world, along the two dimensions of supply and demand. We take the two extremes of the time series available in the OECD TiVA dataset, i.e. 2005 and 2015, and look at the changes that occurred during that decade (Chart 25.16).

25.8.1 General EU trends

First, we observe that the largest part of the EU economic activity remains of course domestic, as the share of inputs for production and of final demand of the domestic market is of a higher order of magnitude compared with foreign markets (top right box). Nevertheless, the reliance of EU countries on domestic markets has decreased over the decade considered, in particular on the demand side; this means that in 2015, the share of total production absorbed by the domestic market was considerably lower than in 2005. This is consistent with the move towards an export-led growth model, implying higher reliance on foreign sources of demand.

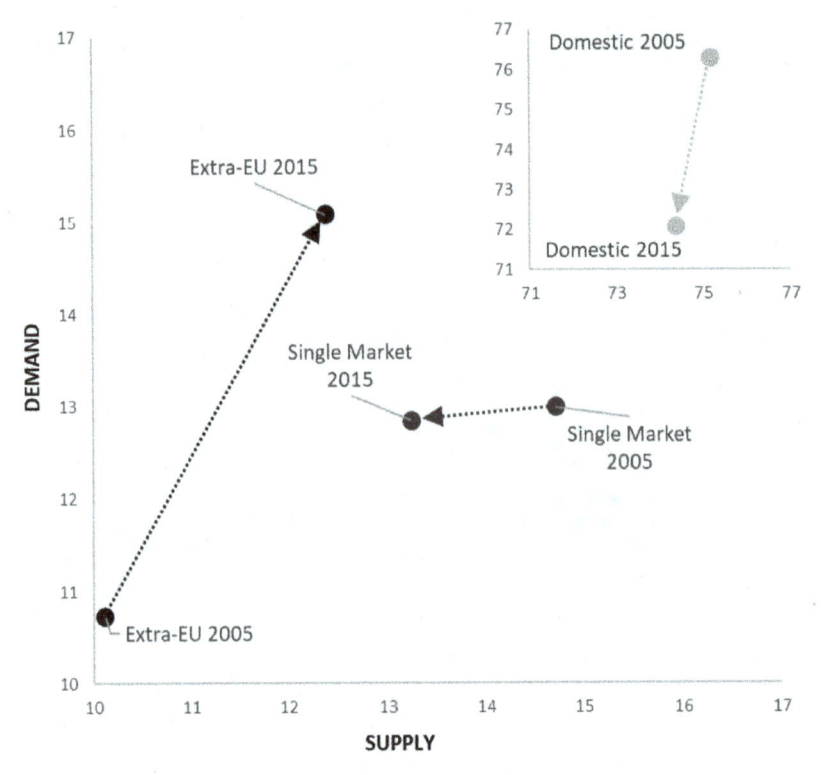

Chart 25.16   Change in the structural characteristics of the EU economy (2005–2015).

Source: Authors' elaborations, based on OECD data.

Note: The horizontal axis measures the share of value added that originates within national borders (domestic), from cross-border supply chains within the Single Market, and from extra-EU value chains; the vertical axis measures the shares of final demand that is due to national markets (domestic), to cross-border trade within the Single Market, and to extra-EU markets.

Second, outside national borders, the Single Market remains more important than the rest of the world in terms of supply chains, although the difference has drastically reduced. In other words, while in 2005 almost 15% of total value added produced in the EU was due to inputs proceeding from cross-border trade within the Single Market and only 10% was due to inputs proceeding from the rest of the world, ten years later the two shares are almost similar.

Third, the biggest change during the decade considered occurred on the demand side: EU countries in 2015 rely more on extra-EU markets as a source of final demand than on the Single Market, while in 2005 the opposite was true. This is due to the important increase in the share of extra-EU markets in final demand, compensating the decrease in the share of domestic national markets, while the share of the Single Market remained almost constant.

To sum up, the analysis of temporal shifts in the relative importance of domestic, EU and extra-EU markets, on both the supply and the demand side, points to a relative although small decline of the importance of the Single Market and to a higher orientation of EU countries towards the rest of the world, in particular as a source of final demand. The macroeconomic policies oriented towards regaining competitiveness after the Great Financial Crisis may have contributed to this outcome. In particular, the need for several countries in the euro area to regain competitiveness by containing unit labour costs and the simultaneous consensus pushing towards restrictive fiscal policies have contributed to a lower growth of domestic demand in the Single Market, and, in particular, in the euro area. Against this background, it is not surprising then that the Single Market has decreased its relative importance with respect to the rest of the world as a source of final demand.

25.8.2 Sector-specific and country-specific trends

The analysis of sector-specific and of country-specific dynamics can help disentangle the specific drivers of the general trends observed at EU level; in particular, we want to understand which sectors and which countries have changed their relative dependence on the Single Market in comparison with extra-EU markets. To this end, we compare the relative reliance on intra-EU and extra-EU supply and demand, for each country and for each sector of the economy.

For most sectors, supply chains within the Single Market have decreased their relative importance, to the benefit of extra-EU ones. In particular, textiles is the sector, whose reliance on extra-EU supply chains has increased the most, a trend consistent with the predominant role acquired in the world by China in this sector, over the period considered. On the other side, motor vehicles, despite being the most integrated sector in supply chains within the Single Market, is the one for which such reliance has decreased the most (Chart 25.17).

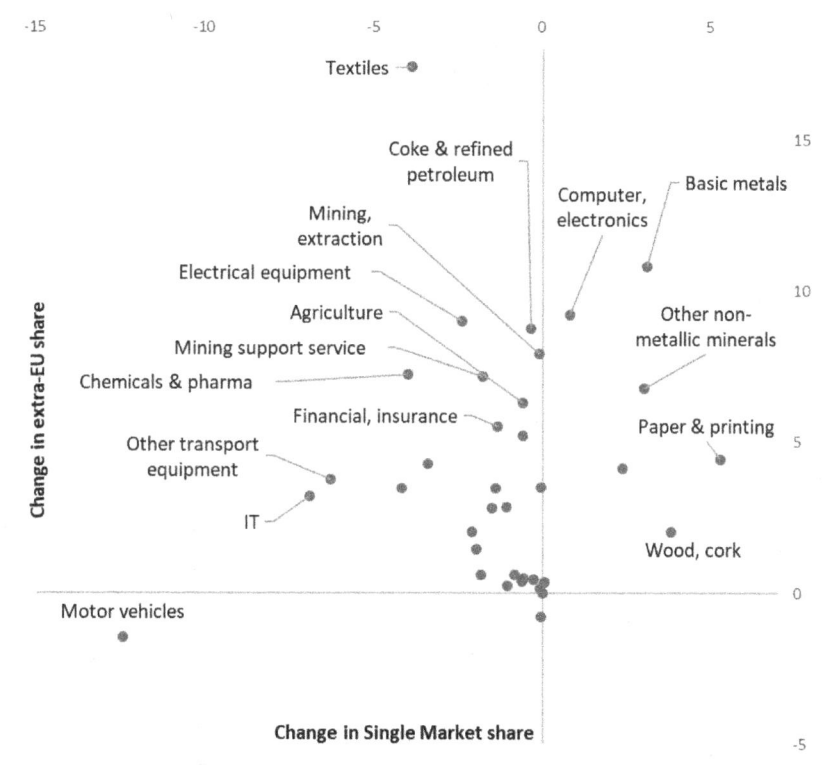

Chart 25.17 Change in the relative importance of the Single Market for international supply chains (Sectors: 2005–2015).

Source: Authors' elaborations, based on OECD data.

Note: The horizontal axis measures for each sector the change between 2005 and 2015 in the share of value added that originates from cross-border supply chains within the Single Market; the vertical axis measures the change over the same period in the share of value added that instead originates from extra-EU supply chains.

A number of sectors, such as computer and electronics, basic metals and other non-metallic minerals and paper and printing, have moved markedly towards greater integration in global value chains, both within and outside the Single Market. There seems to be no sector for which integration in extra-EU supply chains has decreased and within the Single Market has increased, during the decade considered.

When we look at the relative shares in final demand, we also find that all sectors increased their reliance on extra-EU markets. The automotive sectors, chemicals and pharmaceuticals, machinery and electrical equipment in particular increased their exposure to extra-EU export markets by more than 10% over the decade considered. Most of them in parallel decreased their relative reliance on the Single Market as a source of final demand. Key exception to this trend is the mining industry, for which the Single Market has become a more important source of demand (Chart 25.18).

We then move on to study the change in the relative importance of the Single Market for each Member State, relative to the rest of the world. We perform the same analysis as in the case of sectors, along the two dimensions of supply and demand.

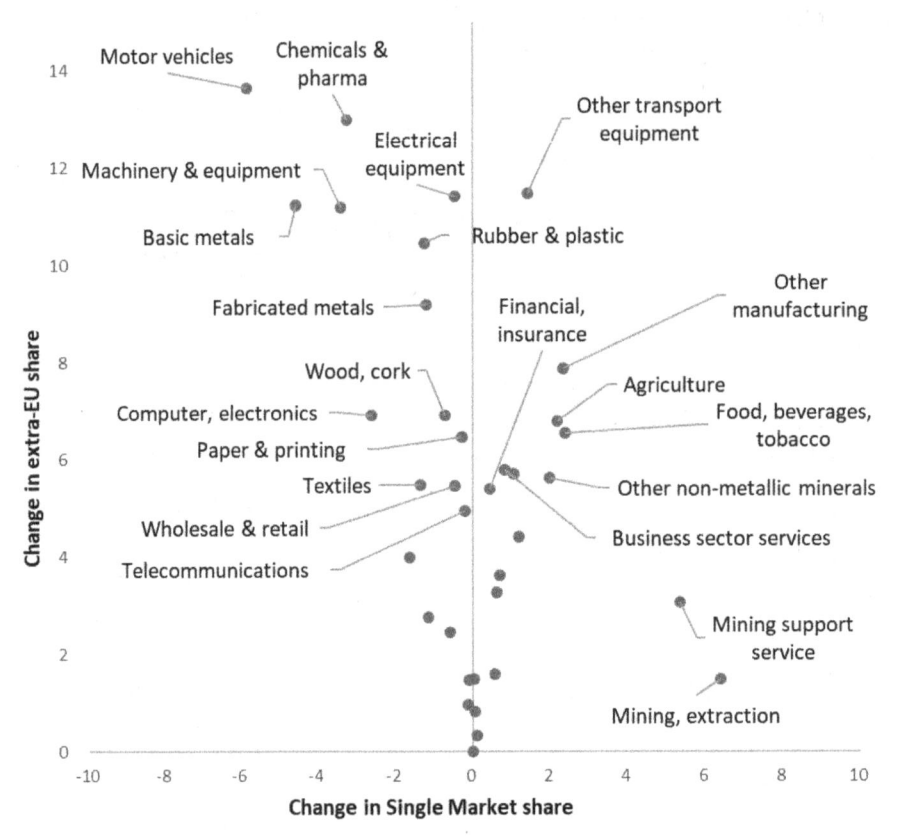

Chart 25.18   Change in the relative importance of the Single Market for final demand (Sectors: 2005–2015).

Source: Authors' elaborations, based on OECD data.

Note: The horizontal axis measures for each sector the change between 2005 and 2015 in the share of final demand that is absorbed by exports within the Single Market; the vertical axis measures the change over the same period in the shares of final demand that is instead absorbed by exports to the rest of the world.

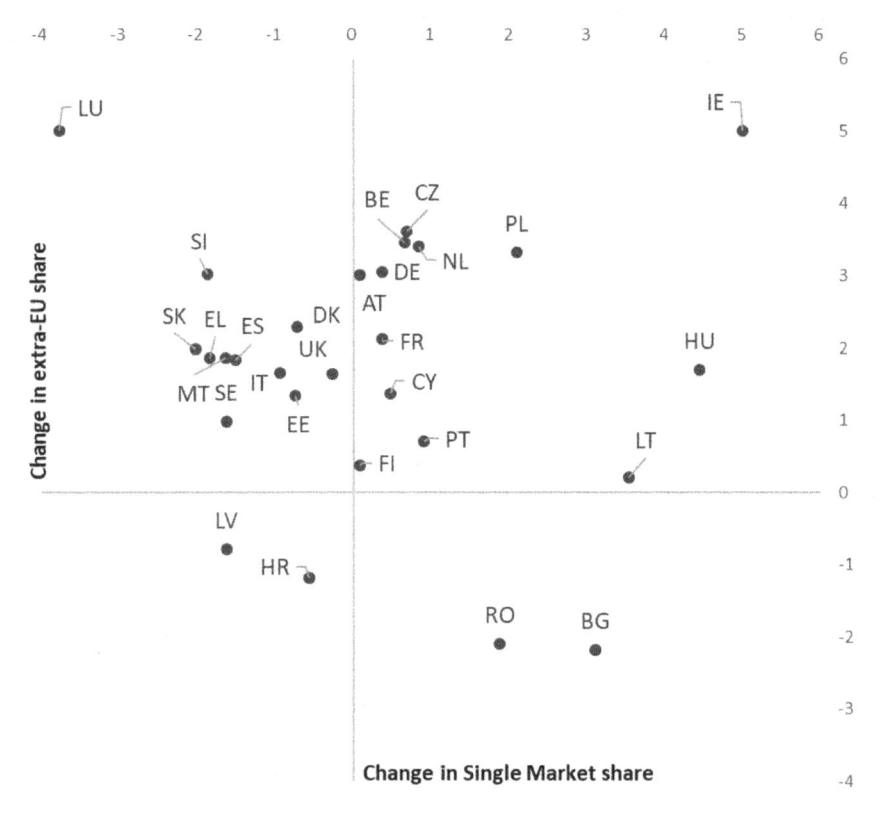

Chart 25.19   Change in the relative importance of the Single Market for international supply chains (Member States: 2005–2015).

Source: Authors' elaborations, based on OECD data.

Note: The horizontal axis measures for each Member State the change between 2005 and 2015 in the share of value added that originates from cross-border supply chains within the Single Market; the vertical axis measures the change over the same period in the share of value added that instead originates from extra-EU supply chains.

Extra-EU supply chains have become more relevant over the period considered for all EU countries, with the exception of Romania, Bulgaria, Croatia and Luxembourg; for the former two, moreover, the relative importance of the Single Market has increased. The Single Market as an important source of supply chains has also significantly increased its relevance for Ireland, Hungary, Lithuania and Poland, and to a lower extent for other Member States (on the top right quadrant) for which the reliance on extra-EU supply chains has also increased (Chart 25.19).

The trend towards a higher importance of extra-EU supply chains compared with intra-EU ones, previously observed, is driven by countries such as Luxembourg, Italy, the UK, Spain, Slovenia, Slovakia, Greece, Malta, Sweden, Denmark and Estonia.

On the other side, the general trend towards higher reliance on extra-EU countries as export markets and key sources of demand is common to each and every Member State. What differentiates them is the change in the relative importance of the Single Market as a source of final demand: for almost half of them it has become more relevant, for half less so; in this latter group, we find the largest EU countries: Germany, France, Italy and the UK (Chart 25.20).

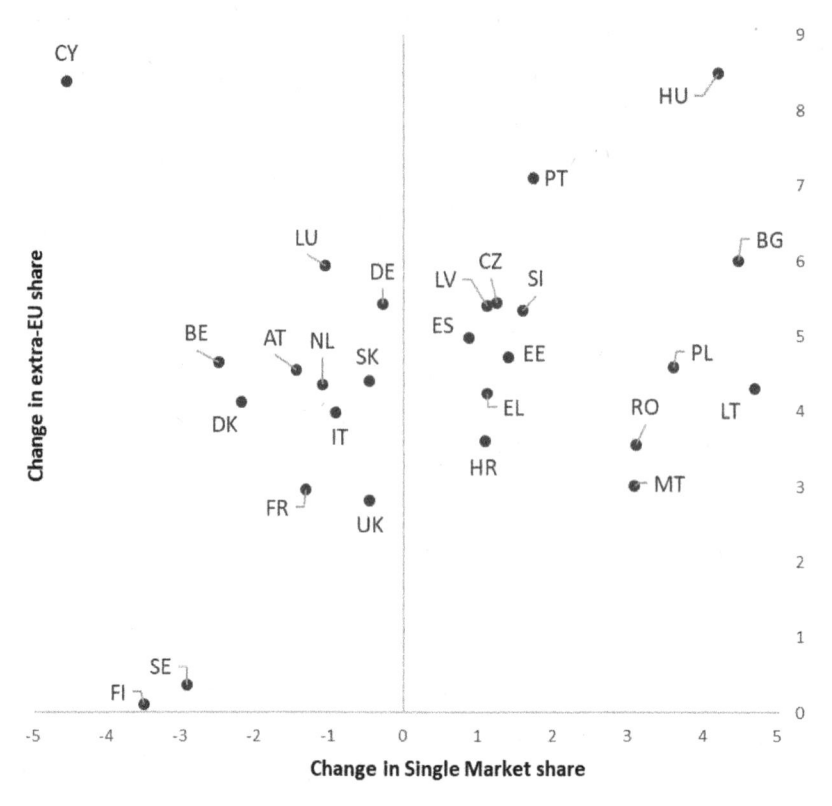

Chart 25.20 Change in the relative importance of the Single Market for final demand (Member States: 2005–2015).

Source: Authors' elaborations, based on OECD data.

Note: The horizontal axis measures for each Member State the change between 2005 and 2015 in the share of final demand that is absorbed by exports within the Single Market; the vertical axis measures the change over the same period in the shares of final demand that is instead absorbed by exports to the rest of the world; Ireland is out of scale, as its reliance on extra-EU final demand has increased by 15% over the decade considered.

25.9 Conclusion

The analysis presented in this chapter provides an overview of the structural features of the Single Market, in terms of sectoral composition, interconnectedness across sectors and countries, exposure to international value chains, both within the Single Market and with the rest of the world, and their evolution over time.

Services produce the largest share of value added in the EU, as in most advanced economies; the EU remains, nevertheless, the second largest manufacturer of the world. In terms of sectoral interconnectedness, service sectors tend to be more "autonomous" than industry or agriculture, in the sense that most of their value added is produced within the same sector and not so much due to inputs by other sectors. General business services and wholesale and retail services are key contributors to the rest of the economy, as they generate a relevant share of value added produced in other sectors. Looking at the demand side, then, manufacturing sectors rely more on final demand by service sectors than the other way around; it is also worth underlining the very important role played by construction as a source of final demand for many other manufacturing sectors, thus for the whole economy.

Service sectors rely more than industry or agriculture on domestic markets, both in terms of supply and of demand. The Single Market is particularly relevant for some industrial sectors: motor vehicles and the whole automotive supply chain is the most integrated in the Single Market. On the opposite side, the mining industry (including extraction, quarrying, support services, and refining) finds in the Single Market an important source of demand rather than of intermediate inputs; this is consistent with the fact that the EU has a low endowment of raw materials and is instead a large importer of such inputs. This situation is reflected then in the opposite exposure to extra-EU supply chains and final demand: the automotive industry relies greatly on exports to extra-EU markets as a source of final demand, while the mining industry is heavily dependent on inputs coming from extra-EU supply chains.

This has different implications for the policy decisions about the so-called strategic autonomy: for those sectors in which the EU is highly dependent on foreign demand, a careful trade policy, coupled with adequate stimulus of domestic demand, is crucial; for those sectors in which the EU is highly dependent on inputs for production, instead, reshoring and ensuring adequate and diversified supply of those inputs will be of the essence.

At country level, the largest economies are of course less dependent on foreign inputs and demand than the others. Germany is the main partner country for the rest of the EU, although more in terms of source of production inputs than as a source of final demand. The analysis also shows the importance of geographical proximity in explaining strong bilateral links or clustering of countries – for instance in the Iberian Peninsula, among the Baltic States, between France and Belgium, and the UK and Ireland. Ireland, in particular, is disproportionately dependent on the UK both as a source of inputs and final demand, and this has obvious relevance in the context of Brexit. Germany, instead, has become a sort of hub for many neighbouring countries that strongly depend on it: Austria, Luxembourg, the Czech Republic, Hungary, Slovakia and Poland.

Smaller EU countries also tend to rely more on the Single Market, given the relatively smaller size of their domestic economy. If we compare such reliance on the Single Market, along both dimensions of supply and demand, with the net contribution of each Member State to the EU budget, we find Hungary on one extreme, as the country with the most positive net balance vis-à-vis the EU budget and the third most benefitting country from the Single Market, and the UK on the opposite side, as the one least reliant on the Single Market and one of the net contributors to the EU budget. Within the group of net payers, Belgium emerges as benefitting the most from the Single Market, followed by Austria, the Netherlands, Denmark, Sweden and Finland; among the largest Member States, Germany benefits more than France, followed by Italy, and finally, as mentioned, the UK.

Over time, the absolute volume of trade carried out among countries within the Single Market has of course increased, in parallel with an overall global trend. However, if we consider the relative importance of the Single Market for EU countries with respect to the same trends of trade integration taking place for each of them with the rest of the world, we find that such *relative* importance of the Single Market has decreased in the decade between 2005 and 2015. This applies in particular to the demand side: while the share of total value added produced in the EU due to inputs proceeding from cross-border trade within the Single Market remains almost constant (though slightly decreasing), the share of final demand due to exports towards extra-EU markets is now larger than the one due to exports within the Single Market.

For most of the sectors, supply chains within the Single Market have decreased their relative importance, to the benefit of extra-EU ones; this is particularly visible for textiles and motor vehicles. During the decade considered, there seems to be no sector where supply chain integration has decreased with the extra-EU and increased within the Single Market. The same applies to the demand side, as all sectors increased their reliance on extra-EU markets and most of them in parallel decreased their relative reliance on the Single Market as a source of final demand.

The analysis has shown that the Single Market has indeed constituted a powerful lever for trade integration in the EU. Its relevance remains on average higher than that of the rest of the world as a source of intermediate production inputs, for almost all Member States. Nevertheless, it is not immune to broad macroeconomic policy actions. Indeed, the strong policy shift towards measures to regain competitiveness through internal devaluation in the euro area has probably reduced the Single Market's potential as a source of demand for the Member States. It is no coincidence, in fact, that in those same years, the rest of the world has become a more important source of final demand for EU countries.

This descriptive analysis of trends taking place in the EU Single Market opens relevant questions for further research, to understand the factors behind them. What can mitigate the EU exposure to global supply chains in strategic sectors? How should the strategic autonomy be considered, when designing domestic economic policies and trade policies? These questions are today at the core of EU policy and, whatever the answers, they imply a more strategic role of the Single Market.

Acknowledgements

The information and views set out in this article are those of the authors and cannot be attributed to the institutions to which they belong.

Notes

1 For the purpose of this work, given that the analysis is based on data preceding the withdrawal of the UK from the EU, the EU is considered here as including 28 Member States.
2 For a description of the 2005 edition of the dataset, see Brezillon et al. (2010).
3 The economic rationale for the creation of EMU was also based on the so-called impossible trinity of free capital flows, fixed exchange rates and independent monetary policy. The trilemma was applied to the European monetary system by Padoa-Schioppa (1982), who spoke of an impossible quartet (the fourth element being free trade), and was popularised by Krugman (1987, 1999).
4 Mundell (1973) and Eichengreen (1992) had suggested that a monetary union among countries keeping their fiscal autonomy could potentially compensate for the lack of a common fiscal capacity through the so-called private insurance channel, brought forward by financial integration.
5 Given the high volatility of the operating budget balance of some Member States, due to the effective payment of some large envelopes, it is important to smooth this volatility with a five-year average.
6 Indeed, the overall net benefits of the EU budget go beyond the Single Market, to encompass economic-union-level policies, like monetary policy and macroeconomic coordination.

References

Alesina, A. and Spolaore, E. (2005). *The Size of Nations*. Cambridge, MA: MIT Press. January.
Balassa, B. (1961). *The Theory of Economic Integration*. London: Allen and Unwin.
Berger, H., Dell'Ariccia, G. and Obstfeld, M. (2018). "Revisiting the Economic Case for Fiscal Union in the Euro Area". IMF Departmental Paper No. 18/03. Washington, DC.
Brezillon, J., Guichard, S. and Turner, D. (2010). "Trade Linkages in the OECD Trade System". OECD Economics Department Working Papers No. 811, ECO/WKP(2010)67, 27 October.
Dahlberg, E. (2015). *Economic Effects of the European Single Market. Review of the Empirical Literature.* Stockholm, Sweden: The National Board of Trade.

Eichengreen, B. (1992). *Should the Maastricht Treaty Be Saved?* Princeton, NJ: Princeton University.

Emerson, M., Gros, D., Italianer, A., Pisani-Ferry, J. and Reichenbach, H. (1992). *One Market, One Money: An Evaluation of the Potential Benefits and Costs of Forming an Economic and Monetary Union.* New York, NY: Oxford University Press.

Goodhart, C.A. (1998). The two concepts of money: implications for the analysis of optimal currency areas. *European Journal of Political Economy* 14(3): 407–432.

Jones, A.J. (1983). "Withdrawal from a Customs Union: A Macroeconomic Analysis," In A.M. El-Agraa (ed.), *Britain within the European Community: The Way Forward.* Basingstoke: Macmillan, pp. 75–87.

Juncker, J.-C., Tusk, D., Dijsselbloem, J., Draghi, M. and Schulz, M. (2015). *Completing Europe's Economic and Monetary Union (The Five Presidents' Report).* European Commission, February.

Krugman, P. (1987). "Economic integration in Europe: Conceptual issues," In T. Padoa Schioppa (ed.), *Efficiency, Stability and Equity: A Strategy for the Evolution of the Economic System of the European Community.* Oxford: Oxford University Press.

Krugman, P. (1999). O Canada – a neglected nation gets its Nobel. *Slate,* October 10.

Mariniello, M., Sapir, A. and Terzi, A. (2015). *The Long Road towards the European Single Market.* Bruegel Working Paper 2015/01, March.

Mundell, R. (1973). "Uncommon Arguments for Common Currencies," In H. G. Johnson and A. K. Swoboda (eds.), *The Economies of Common Currencies.* London: Allen & Unwin.

Nikolov, P. (2016). Cross-border risk sharing after asymmetric shocks: Evidence from the euro area and the United States. *Quarterly Report on the Euro Area* 15(2): 173–196.

Nikolov, P. and Pasimeni, P. (2019). *Fiscal Stabilization in the United States: Lessons for Monetary Unions.* Levy Economics Institute of Bard College Working Paper, 2019(926), 1–34.

Padoa-Schioppa, T. (1982). "Capital Mobility: Why is the Treaty Not Implemented?" *Bancaria.* Reprinted in T. Padoa-Schioppa (1994), *The Road to Monetary Union in Europe.* Oxford: Clarendon Press.

Sapir, A. (1992). Regional Integration in Europe, *Economic Papers* n. 94, September.

Viner, J. (1950). *The Customs Union Issue.* New York: Carnegie Endowment for International Peace.

Wolfmayr, Y., Friesenbichler, K., Oberhofer, H., Pfaffermayr, M., Siedschlag, I., Di Ubaldo, M., Tong Koecklin, M. and Yan, W. (2019). *The Performance of the Single Market for Goods after 25 Years.* Final report for the European Commission, Luxembourg, July.

26

VARIETIES OF CAPITALISM IN CENTRAL AND EASTERN EUROPE

A Ferry Boat Region

Miklós Rosta[*]

After their transition, Central and Eastern European (CEE) countries became liberal democracies and capitalist systems, but not without great effort. Twenty years since their regime changes, several of the countries in this region have undergone substantial transformation, but stable political and economic systems have failed to emerge. In this chapter, I explore why this is the case. Drawing on institutional economics and comparative economic theories, I introduce a new typology of Varieties of Capitalism (VoC) for the CEE region. History and path dependency are also decisive in Central and Eastern Europe: the countries of the region possess a dualistic value system; their informal institutions are characterized by both Western and Eastern values. Western values are linked to the enlightenment and contain elements of substantive democracy, while Eastern values are the opposite. After the regime changes, Western values became dominant in the region, influenced by the European Union and a rejection of the Soviet past. Even if the transition from communism to capitalism satisfies the indicators laid out by János Kornai, this type of capitalism did not stabilize. The determinant factor is whether the capitalist system is democratic or non-democratic. Within these two main types, the coordination mechanism distinguishes the capitalist sub-types. In democratic systems, creative coordination is dominant, whereas in non-democratic systems, destructive coordination is.

26.1 Introduction

More than thirty years after the fall of the Berlin Wall, examining the results of the transition of the post-socialist countries is an important and necessary duty of economists and political scientists. In doing so, we can acquire valuable knowledge regarding radical system change both in the economic and political spheres. The divergent paths that these countries took

[*] Miklós Rosta, Associate Professor at Corvinus University of Budapest, miklos.rosta@uni-corvinus.hu. The author thanks Sara Casagrande, Bruno Dallago, and Randall G. Holcombe for their useful suggestions. The author gratefully acknowledges the financial support of the János Bolyai Research Scholarship of the Hungarian Academy of Sciences (BO/00782/19/9).

DOI: 10.4324/9781003144366-31

are well known and were analyzed in depth by Chepurenko and Szanyi (in this Handbook). Although scholars have scrutinized the process of transition and the economic systems after regime change (Åslund, 2018a; Havrylyshyn, 2013; Stiglitz, 2002; Svejnar, 2002), and there are some typologies of CEE economic systems in the Varieties of Capitalism (VoC) literature (Bohle & Greskovits, 2012; Farkas, 2011; Nölke & Vliegenthart, 2009), there is no comprehensive typology which would explain why and how economic and political systems transformed after the Financial Crisis of 2007/2008 (Åslund, 2018b; Győrffy, 2022) and following the rise of populism and illiberal ideas (Hanley & Vachudova, 2018; Kornai, 2015; Toplišek, 2020). The original VoC typologies (Amable, 2003; Hall & Soskice, 2001) cannot be applied to CEE countries due to the different historical paths they took, and because of the empirical relevance of the typologies before the Financial Crisis diminished significantly.

In this chapter, an analytical framework is proposed for describing the economic systems of Central and Eastern Europe based on the theories of institutional economics. The next section outlines the literature of VoC with a specific focus on Central and Eastern Europe. Then the framework of institutional analysis of transition is presented. Finally, the framework is integrated with the VoC literature. The conclusion returns to the research question and summarizes the findings.

26.2 Varieties of capitalism in Central and Eastern Europe

In the diverse literature on market economies, VoC is an important and widespread approach for describing various economic systems, especially Western ones. Hall and Soskice (2001) undertake an analysis of advanced Western capitalist systems with a fundamental focus on corporations as the most important actors. Their work has made a significant contribution to the development of comparative economics by adding institutional factors to the macro-economic approach to the economics of organizations and by using them to explain the diversity of capitalist economic systems. The authors differentiate liberal market economies (LMEs) and coordinated market economies (CMEs). The main difference between them lies in the mode of coordination, which determines the economic areas in which firms will be successful (advanced manufacturing – CMEs vs. innovation – LMEs). A stable economic system with a competitive advantage is built on a set of complementary and consistent institutional complementarities, but more than one institutional complementarity is possible, i.e. economic growth can be achieved with different institutional frameworks. The assumption is that the different institutional bundles cannot be assembled in a voluntaristic way, but that there is a strong interaction between them, the consistency of which, if disrupted, becomes sub-optimal. This is what they call institutional complementarities, i.e. certain institutional solutions will only be effective in enhancing economic growth in combination with other solutions (Hall & Gingerich, 2009; Jacobi, in this Handbook). These institutional bundles make different coordination mechanisms stronger in different market economies. The questions are why different societies choose different institutional bundles, who chooses these institutions, and what causes the choice to be consistent or not (Amable, 2016). The transition countries of Central and Eastern Europe have pursued different strategies to move away from a Soviet-style planned economy to an economic system that gives them a stable competitive economic advantage and allows them to catch up with the level of development and prosperity of Western European countries.

Many have analyzed and attempted to incorporate the search for a way forward in Central and Eastern European (CEE) countries into the literature. By analyzing the capitalist economic systems of the CEE countries, and the new EU member states, Farkas (2011) found that these countries form a distinct group in the VoC literature. The main features of these countries are their relative lack of capital, weak civil society, and the strong influence of the European Union and other international organizations. Nölke and Vliegenthart (2009) introduced the model of dependent market economies, which are characterized by the lack of innovation, and by hierarchical coordination. These economies depend on the headquarters of transnational corporations, which control their subsidiaries by hierarchical coordination. The institutional structure of dependent market economies also provides a stable comparative advantage in the market for industrial assembly and semi-standardized industrial production. These market economies are heavily dependent on the headquarters of transnational corporations that have invested significant working capital in the country. Drahokoupil and Myant (2015), in their analysis of transition economies, highlighted and typified the international integration of these economies. Five different regimes were distinguished: foreign direct investment (FDI) based (Central and Eastern-European countries), peripheral market economies (Baltic countries), an order state (Belarus), oligarchic/client-based economies (Russia and CIS countries) and aid/remittance-based regimes (Armenia, Kyrgyzstan, Tajikistan, Uzbekistan, Albania, Moldova, and Bosnia-Herzegovina). These systems differ significantly in the amount of inward FDI and the role of the state in the functioning of the economy. Feldmann (2019) analyzed the capitalist systems of emerging economies by summarizing three books (Bohle & Greskovits, 2012; Schneider, 2013; Walter & Zhang, 2012). Based on these volumes, the VoC literature defines at three levels: firm-centered, governance-centered, and state-centered approaches. While Schneider (2013), just like Hall and Soskice (2001), applies the firm-centered approach to Latin American countries, Walter and Zhang (2012) used the governance-centered approach to analyze countries in East and South Asia. Bohle and Greskovits (2012) used the state-centered approach to examine the economic systems of the countries of East-Central Europe.

Whichever approach is chosen, the prerequisite for constructing a new VoC typology is to be able to point to an institutional bundle that is consistent and defines the dominant coordination mechanism of an economy, which can be used to gain a comparative advantage over other types of economic systems. An inconsistent institutional bundle will not be stable and thus will not serve the competitiveness and growth of the economy. Thus, the main question in the VoC literature is how to construct consistent institutional bundles and how different bundles would contribute to the development of the economy. Bohle and Greskovits (2012) depart from Polányi's idea of the perennial conflict between economic efficiency, social cohesion, and political legitimacy. Their analysis is thus macro-level, based on the close interconnection of political and economic systems and institutions. For them, examining institutional bundles means examining not only economic institutions but also political institutions, i.e. economic institutions must not only fit together, but they must also be in synergy with political institutions to achieve economic growth. Consequently, the state and the elite are of paramount importance to them, and their decisions are fundamental to the strategy along which countries formulate their institutional arrangements. If the elite's choices are decisive, the question arises as to whether their choices are aimed at increasing social welfare or maximizing their own utility and how to ensure the stability of the institutional environment in which they are operating (Holcombe, 2018). The authors identify three economic systems in the East Central European region: neoliberal capitalist, embedded neoliberal capitalist, and neocorporatist capitalist. The neoliberal economic system is exemplified by the Baltic states (Estonia, Latvia, and Lithuania), Bulgaria and Romania, the embedded neoliberal by the Visegrad countries (Czech Republic, Poland, Hungary, and Slovakia), and the neocorporatist system by Slovenia. The authors take an empirical approach to the countries of the region, starting with their regime changes, finding that the Soviet legacy is not deterministic but leaves room for public policy innovation that has had a significant impact on the development path of these countries. While uncertainty and unpredictability are fundamental features of innovation, the authors identify two factors that were employed by the makers of public policy – local elites – in ensuring a stable capitalist transition in the region. One is nationalism – not to be confused with xenophobia – and the other is the greater use of the welfare net and compensation for the losers in the transition. The Baltic states used nation-building and nationalism to take a radical neoliberal economic turn. Rejection of the Soviet past and fear of Russian interference also reinforced nationalism, while at the same time making the population accept the power of change. The Visegrad countries also adopted neoliberal economic policies but compensated the losers more strongly. Slovenia relied more on the involvement of trade unions in economic decision-making and did not apply many elements of neoliberal economic policy. The authors conclude that neoliberal economic policies, which were mainstream during the period of regime change, played a dominant role in the transformation of the economic systems in the region.

In this chapter, Bohle and Greskovits' (2012) approach is the most relevant, as it considers political systems and economic systems together. Hall and Soskice's (2001) original theory, which focuses on enterprises, is inappropriate for analyzing and typifying economic systems in transition countries, if only because autonomous corporate actors independent of the state were not a meaningful force during the transition period, so the direction of the transition was determined by the state and thus by the shapers of the political system. Just like Bohle and Greskovits (2012), I understand regime change as a strategy, a series of public policy decisions taken from a starting position (one-party communist dictatorship, state ownership, and bureaucratic coordination) towards a strategic goal (multiparty system, capitalist system based on private property and market coordination) accepted by the elite. However, the framework outlined in the next section goes beyond their model. In my framework, I pay particular attention to the relationships and interactions between the different layers of institutions, which are crucial to the economic system that emerges in a country. Examining institutions starts from the theory of institutional stickiness (Boettke et al., 2015).

26.3 A framework for analyzing transition as an institutional change of economic systems

Transition is a strategy for implementing institutional change to put a society in a better economic and social position. The question raised by the literature on transition and VoC is the following: how can we create a strategy which will help us to successfully implement such a comprehensive social transformation which will result in an economic system with a stable comparative advantage? My proposition is that transition can be only successful and sustainable if the fundamental policy interventions which modify formal institutions such as ownership structures, coordination mechanisms, sectoral regulations, etc., stick to the informal institutions of a given society. This is a necessary condition; however, it is not sufficient for a successful transition. This is in line with the literature, including the seminal work of Boettke et al. (2008, pp. 332–333) in which they utilize the regression theorem which states that "the stickiness, and therefore likely success, of any proposed institutional change is a function of that institution's status in relationship to indigenous agents in the previous time period".

Boettke et al. (2015, p. 124) define institutional stickiness as "the ability or inability of new institutional arrangements to take hold where they are transplanted...". Their framework suggests that institutions created spontaneously by endogenous actors (Indigenously Introduced

Endogenous Institutions – IENs) are the stickiest ones. These institutions are imbued with the beliefs, customs, and values of the society. Boettke et al. (2015) look at informal institutions as a homogeneous set of norms, habits, and traditions. Those institutions which are introduced top-down by endogenous actors (for example by the government) are called Indigenously Introduced Exogenous Institutions (IEX). These institutions are less sticky than IENs. Nevertheless, they still align with the values, customs, and beliefs of the given society, since the authority which introduces them is an endogenous actor (part of that society), so it understands these factors well and is able to craft them in such a way that they will be consistent with them. The least sticky institutions are those which are introduced by exogenous actors in a top-down manner. These are the Foreign-Introduced Exogenous Institutions (FEX), such as recommendations from the IMF or the regulations of the European Union (Linden, 2002). It is worth noting that these FEX institutions could stick as well, but the likelihood is much lower than it would be with IEXs or even IENs. What makes institutions sticky? The glue is the Mētis, which is the local knowledge of how members of the society interact with each other and live together successfully. This knowledge comes from the history of the given society and is passed down the generations. Mētis "represents a wide array of practical skills and acquired intelligence in responding to a constantly changing natural and human environment" (Scott, 1998, p. 313). The local knowledge cannot be learnt but can be acquired by participating in the activities of the society. Mētis "includes skills, culture, norms, and conventions, which are shaped by the experiences of the individual" (Boettke et al., 2015, p. 129). To understand the skills, norms, and conventions – the collective tacit knowledge – an outsider has to participate in activities in that society because such knowledge is not easy to learn from texts alone.

Boettke et al. (2015) is a useful starting point; however, a more complex framework can be created for analyzing the transition process and the economic systems in Central and Eastern Europe.

As described above, in developing the theoretical framework for this chapter, particular attention has been paid to the study of the relationships and interactions between different layers of institutions. The starting point was the theoretical frameworks of Bohle and Greskovits (2012) and Boettke et al. (2015). The institutional shell within which public policy innovations

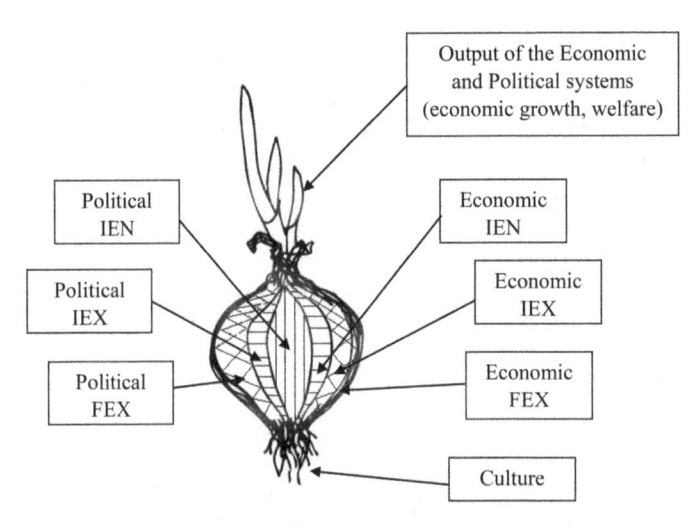

Figure 26.1 Institutional onion.

Source: Author's compilation based on Boettke et al. (2008, p. 344).

have emerged during the transition period consists of three layers: the informal institutions spontaneously followed and accepted by members of society (IEN), the formal institutions prescribed by the political leaders (elites) of society and enforced by the state (IEX), and the institutions created from outside by the international community, whether through policy recommendations or binding international treaties (FEX). There is a close interaction between the three layers of the institutional matrix, but the formal institutions designated by the elite have a special role to play, since it is the part of the institutional shell where social change is taking place: state ownership is giving way to private ownership, bureaucratic coordination to market coordination. However, the analysis of formal institutions alone is not sufficient for understanding social change and explaining its processes. The interactions between the three levels of institutions together explain the mode of transformation, the strategy of trans-formation, and the extent to which the emerging economic system will be stable and generate comparative advantage. The institutional bundle is built like an onion, with different levels of complex institutional bundles (Figure 26.1).

The institutional shell, like the layers of an onion, is tightly packed and forms a single unit. Each layer is itself made up of diverse political and economic institutions, which are inter-dependent. The different parts of the institutional matrix must be consistent – i.e. each part must be free of internal contradictions – and coherent – i.e. each part must fit together – to form an independent economic and political system that is stable and capable of providing the country with a competitive advantage in some area. Stability and "stickiness" between institutional layers are provided by the mētis. It is the mētis that enables members of society to understand, apply, and maintain institutions. The mētis not only holds the strata together but also reduces friction between them and reduces transaction costs in interactions between members of society.

There have been many studies to distinguish between formal and informal institutions (Helmke & Levitsky, 2004; Hodgson, 2006; Lauth, 2015; North, 1990; C. R. Williamson, 2009) and the boundaries between culture and informal institutions (Alesina & Giuliano, 2015; Lauth, 2015). The distinction between culture, informal institutions (IEN), formal institutions (IEX), and foreign-introduced institutions (FEX) is summarized in Table 26.1.

Table 26.1 Culture and types of institutions

Categories	Culture	Institutions		
		IEN	IEX	FEX
Modus of change	Spontaneous	Spontaneous	Planned	Planned
Codification	No codification	No codification	Codified	Codified
Evolution (constructed and imposed)	Endogenous/ bottom-up manner	Endogenous/ bottom-up manner	Exogenous/ top-down manner	Exogenous/ top-down manner
Relationship between actors	Horizontal	Horizontal	Vertical	Vertical
Enforcement	No direct enforcement	Enforced by society	Enforced by state	Enforced by an external actor
Individual action	No intention to determine individual action	Determine individual action	Determine individual action	Not necessarily determine individual action
Time horizon of change	long	long	short	short

Source: Author's compilation based on Boettke et al. (2015) and Lauth (2015).

North's (1990, pp. 3–6) definition is a good starting point, namely that "[i]nstitutions are the rule of the game in a society or, more formally, are the humanly devised constraints that shape human interaction. In consequence they structure incentives in human exchange, whether political, social, or economic […] Institutions include any form of constraint that human beings devise to shape human interaction. Are institutions formal or informal? They can be either […]. The major role of institutions in a society is to reduce uncertainty by establishing a stable (but not necessarily efficient) structure to human interaction".

While the literature is consistent in defining the distinction between informal and formal institutions (Williamson, 2009), the boundaries between culture and informal institutions are much harder to draw (Alesina & Giuliano, 2015; Lauth, 2015). Informal institutions can be seen as part of culture; the violation of which is sanctioned by society and thus limits individual action. Culture contains many values and traditions that are not sanctioned and therefore do not constrain behavior in the interaction between individuals (Lauth, 2015). These non-sanctioned values and traditions are, however, channeled into informal institutions and stabilize their functioning.

VoC and the literature on the economics of transformation focus predominantly on formal institutions (IEX) and examine the relationship between these institutions, noting that they should be mutually reinforcing (Hall & Gingerich, 2009). This middle layer of formal institutions is neither static nor necessarily intentionally planned (Amable, 2016). Polanyi's (1957) approach which sees the capitalist system as an economic system genetically charged with conflict (see Bohle & Greskovits, 2012), fits in well with the analysis of the formal institutional bundle (IEX). Indeed, the distribution of wealth between different social groups is based on formal institutional bundles (IEX), which are the most likely to provide the different actors in society with the opportunity to modify the distribution according to their own needs. In the case of informal institutions and institutions determined by external actors, the different groups in society have much less opportunity to do so. It also follows that changing formal institutions (IEX) becomes the real battleground for different groups in society for modifying the economic system in ways that benefit them. A number of works have addressed this issue (Amable, 2016; Bohle & Greskovits, 2012; Holcombe, 2018; Stiglitz, 2012), which have shown that formal institutions (IEX) provide the elite in society with the opportunity to maintain the status quo and thus influence the allocation of resources in ways that secure their status in the long term. These works draw attention to an important social problem that formal institutions are instruments of vertical power in the hands of elites, but they do not shed light on how past decisions limit the possibilities to change these institutions. Formal institutions can be changed within strict limits. Informal institutions link formal institutions to past decisions and the long-term development of society, which are imposed by society itself. Institutions created by external actors embody the limits imposed by external actors on a given society, which are enforced by external actors through various means (e.g. IMF loans, EU soft law, hard law).

The first constraint can be captured by the notion of institutional path dependence, while the second, external constraint can be related to the theory of gravity. Levi (1997, p. 28 cited by Pierson 2000, p. 252) explains that "[p]ath dependence has to mean, if it is to mean anything, that once a country or region has started down a track, the costs of reversal are very high. There will be other choice points, but the entrenchments of certain institutional arrangements obstruct an easy reversal of the initial choice. Perhaps the better metaphor is a tree, rather than a path. From the same trunk, there are many different branches and smaller branches. Although it is possible to turn around or to clamber from one to the other – and essential if the chosen branch dies – the branch on which a climber begins is the one she tends to follow". Path dependency is one of the basic features of the institutional bundle. The interdependence of institutional layers leads to stability by reducing uncertainty and increasing returns to society. As North (1990, p. 95) states, "[i]n short, the interdependent web of an institutional matrix produces massive increasing returns". The path dependence, which ceteris paribus does indeed produce increasing returns, may, however, in the case of a change in the external environment, hamper the adaptation of the economic and political system to the change, which may put the actors of the economic system at a competitive disadvantage.

While the path dependency theory points out how the informal institutions and the culture limit the opportunities of the elites to modify the formal institutions[1], the gravity theory[2] highlights how external actors narrow the field for public policy innovation. Larger countries have a gravitational pull, attracting their smaller neighbors (Shleifer & Treisman, 2014, p. 101; Sonin, 2013, p. 7). The interaction is two-sided, even if the larger one has a stronger influence on the smaller one. Nevertheless, there is a counter-effect as well: larger neighbors who have significantly different institutions, or are associated with aggression, may have a "push effect" (e.g. Russia on Poland or on the Baltic states). In the CEE region, larger neighbors who should be considered include the Russian Empire (Russia/Soviet Union) with its Eastern Orthodox religion, Prussia (Germany) and the Habsburg Empire (Austria) with Catholicism, and even the Ottoman Empire (Turkey) with Islam. If we analyze all the post-socialist countries, then the Chinese Empire (China) and the Mongol Empire are also influential players with their mix of Confucianism and Buddhism[3]. Since the transition, the European Union has clearly had the strongest gravitational pull on CEE countries, and it can be seen as an anchor for liberal democracy and capitalism in the region (Campos, 2021; Epstein & Jacoby, 2014). Of course, countries are not planets; they have their own societies, and these societies' culture are shaped by their history, for which the Baltic states provide clear evidence; however, without the European Union, they would not have been able to shift away from Russia[4]. As Shleifer and Treisman (2014, p. 93) state, "the countries of Central Europe have become more European; those of Central Asia, more Asian", or Sonin (2013, p. 7) phrases it, "neighbors matter a lot".

If we look at Central and Eastern European countries from a broader perspective, their institutional shells and institutional layers are heterogeneous. This rooted in the history of the region. These countries were occupied by Western and Eastern empires many times over hundreds of years. Their institutional settings were modified several times and adapted to each occupier's institutional systems. Western and Eastern empires introduced and enforced their own institutions in CEE countries, so these foreign institutions (FEX) modified the local IEX and IEN institutional layers. The modification of these layers took hundreds of years, and they were stabilized by force. FEX institutions have a rather small impact on IEX because it is the least stickiest part of the institutional shell (Boettke et al., 2015); however, if this continues over a longer period, it modifies the IEX and even the IEN institutions. Without adaptation to the FEX institutions imposed by the foreign powers, CEE societies would not have had the chance to survive. That is the reason why we cannot speak of homogeneous institutional bundles in CEE, and this is the reason why CEE countries' economic and political systems are much more fragile than countries in the West or the East. As an example, Hungary was part of the Ottoman Empire for 150 years, part of the Habsburg Empire and other Western Empires for over 320 years, and influenced by the Soviet Union for more than 50 years, so it is no surprise that the Hungarian soul is so clearly divided between Western and Eastern values (Balogh, 2020; Keller, 2010; Korkut, 2017; Rac, 2014). As Endre Ady, one of the most famous Hungarian poets, wrote: "Ferry country, Ferry country, Ferry country: even in his ablest dreams he has sailed between two shores: from East to West but preferring to go back" (Ady, 1905)[5]. The same is true of Poland and the countries of the West Balkans.

It is important to note that neither Eastern nor Western values are superior to the other; nevertheless, they are competing and exclude each other (Rac, 2014). Western values are connected to enlightenment and liberalism, to human rights, civil rights, political rights, pluralism, and to accepting the market as the dominant coordination mechanism in the economy based on Weberian instrumental rationality[6] (Weber, 1978). Eastern values deny liberal values. They are state-centric, anti-pluralist, and based more on authority, with an acceptance of hierarchical coordination as a dominant coordination mechanism. As Keller (2010, p. 38) points out, "…Hungary is located somewhere on the borderline of the Western and Eastern values structure. Otherwise, this statement is not only a values-structure characteristic one, since previous works – mostly historical – also called the attention to the fact that Hungarian history simultaneously bears the characteristic features of Western and Eastern social development". These values are the core elements of the informal institutions (IEN layer of the institutional onion). It follows that the informal institutions of the countries of the region are full of tensions due to these conflicting values. Informal institutions do not complement but repel each other, which make it difficult to establish stable political and economic systems based on institutional complementarities as the VoC literature suggests. These values are in constant competition for dominance in the heart of the institutional shell. Competition becomes visible and tangible at the level of formal institutions, where groups in a society with different values compete for a dominant position and try to stabilize their position. History has so far shown that neither group is able to gain the upper hand over the other in the long term, so the region oscillates between Eastern and Western values. Heterogeneity and tensions in informal institutions also make the system of formal institutions unstable, as institutional cohesion is weak. In turn, unstable formal institutions lead to unstable economic and political institutions. Stability can be ensured mainly by external forces (historically the Habsburg Empire in the West or the Russian and Ottoman Empires in the East).

As Figure 26.2 shows, the three layers of the institutional onion can only be analyzed simultaneously and that institutional complementarity (Hall & Gingerich, 2009) characterizes each of them simultaneously. To further complicate the analysis, institutional complementarity applies not only to economic institutions but also to political institutions. The interdependence between the three layers and in each layer between political and economic institutional

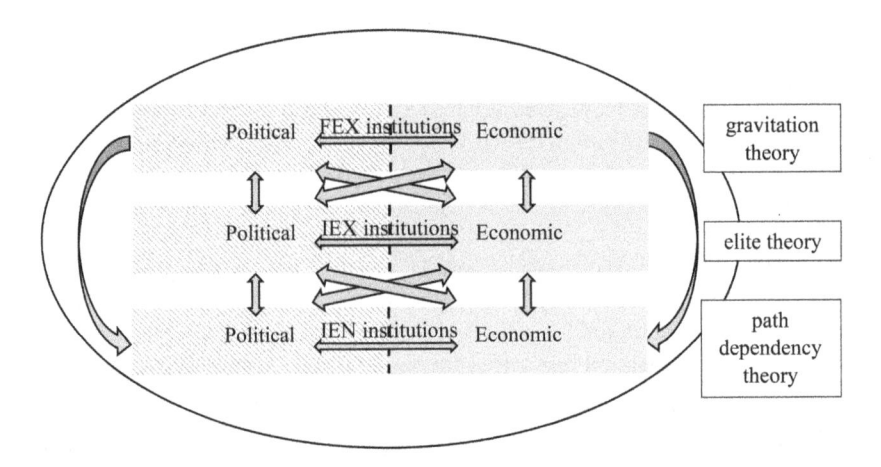

Figure 26.2 Institutional complexity.

Source: Author's compilation.

bundles makes the institutional setting extremely complex. Examining the interaction between these two types of institutions is crucial for economic and political systems. In the past, many economists have argued for the primacy of economic institutions, while modern political economy essentially advocates the primacy of political institutions (Acemoglu & Robinson, 2012). In the case of the Central and Eastern European countries, whose societies operated under almost total state control under the communist regime, autonomous economic actors were notably absent[7]. The historical past of these societies also predisposes economic actors to a dependent relationship with the state and the political elite that embodied it. Dependent capitalism, as defined by Nölke, in CEE does not only imply dependence on external actors (the center of multinational corporations) but also dependence of economic actors on the political elite. Political institutions exert considerable influence on economic institutions. That is the reason why political actors have a superior position vis-á-vis economic actors in the region. For a successful economic policy, decision-makers need to understand the complexity of the institutional onion. The theories presented here – institutional stickiness, path dependency, elite theory, and gravitation theory – are useful tools for analyzing the complex institutional system and institutional change.

It is this complex institutional environment shown in Figure 26.2 that provides political actors the space to implement their own ideas by drawing on certain parts of the heterogeneous institutional structure of society[8]. *Informal institutions and the notion of path dependency associated with them play a prominent role in the development of individual societies.* Nevertheless, their impact is not deterministic, since the culture and informal institutions of individual societies are dualistic, and this value competition is opening up the space for a range of policy innovations and a competition of the elites.

The competition of elites can be analyzed by the elite theory (Best & Higley, 2018; Holcombe, 2018). After 2007/08, it was observed in many CEE countries that the elites could utilize the duality of the informal institutions (based on Eastern vs. Western values) and try to establish a predatory system based on one of the sides (predation is closer to Eastern-type values[9]) and suppress those actors who followed other values (Western-type values) (regarding illiberal systems in CEE, see: (Bluhm & Varga, 2020; Csaba, 2021; Hanley & Vachudova, 2018; Kapidžić, 2020; Kornai, 2016). In such systems, the most important public policy tasks were to enlarge those parts of the society which followed the Eastern-type values underpinning formal institutions (IEX), to disconnect from those externally introduced institutions (FEX) which tried to support the other values (Western), or to try to connect with those which supported Eastern-type values. If those parts of the society which followed the Eastern-type values became a stable majority, then the system would become sustainable (see Wintrobe, 2018).

The comprehensive institutional change – modifying each level of the institutional onion – is always caused by external and internal shocks, which can be triggered by both IEX and FEX institutions[10]. These shocks can modify the status between the two sides of the informal institutions and turn the society to the other side (from the domination of Eastern values to Western values or vice versa). For example, after Hungary's transition in 1989, the Western value system became dominant as society rejected Soviet-style rule[11]. This change was supported by the EU and the IMF (FEX) (Linden, 2002). In addition, the regime-changing elite of 1989 also adopted a Western approach and established formal institutions such as a constitution and checks and balances (IEX). The Western approach was steadily weakened, but two shocks caused the IEN to turn around and the Eastern approach to become dominant: the 2007/2008 global economic crisis (an external shock) and a controversial speech given by Ferenc Gyurcsány, Prime Minister of Hungary, in Balatonőszöd in 2006, and the wave of protests that followed[12].

According to our model, the types of economic systems and their main characteristics, which are essentially determined by formal institutions, are jointly influenced by informal and externally imposed institutions. As described above, the relationship is non-deterministic, with formal institutions being the choice of political elites and their innovative solutions creating the economic systems we observe. These public policy innovations may themselves feed back into informal institutions, even if the causal chain clearly leads from informal institutions to formal institutions. In my view, economic systems are primarily determined by political institutions, through the political system (Acemoglu et al., 2005; Acemoglu & Robinson, 2008). Although capitalist systems can operate under liberal democracies, hybrid systems, and dictatorships, the characteristics of the economic order are fundamentally influenced by the political system. The variation between different types of systems is also influenced by informal institutions – their homogeneity – and externally imposed institutions and their durability (Acemoglu & Robinson, 2022).

Based on the institutional framework described above, a new typology of economic and political systems can be presented.

26.4 Varieties of capitalism in Central and Eastern Europe: A framework

There are three conditions for creating a typology of economic systems in VoC literature (Nölke & Vliegenthart, 2009, p. 676): "(1) the existence of an alternative overall economic coordination mechanism closely related to (2) a relatively stable set of institutions based on marked institutional complementarities, that leads to (3) a set of specific comparative advantages (in relationship to CME and LME) and a superior economic performance over comparable, but less pure, socioeconomic systems".

The typology outlined in Figure 26.3 assumes that to establish a comprehensive typology of economic systems in CEE, it is not enough to analyze formal institutions (e.g. forms of government-employer-employee interaction, trade union regulation, banking, R&D) (Bohle & Greskovits, 2012; Farkas, 2011) or externally imposed institutions (e.g. proposals based on the Washington Consensus supported by the IMF, EU, and directives from large multinational companies' headquarters to their subsidiaries in the region) (Jacoby, 2001; Linden, 2002; Nölke & Vliegenthart, 2009). A comprehensive typology should examine all three layers of the institutional onion and the interactions between them. In addition, the examination of political institutions is paramount because the degree of political freedom is a fundamental determinant of the functioning of capitalism (see Magyar & Madlovics, 2020). In countries with limited substantive democracy[13], that is with less Western values (liberal values, see Rhoden, (2015))[14], the autonomy of economic actors is reduced, and dependence on state and political actors increases. Hence, the primary decision point is whether CEE countries will follow the path of democratic or non-democratic capitalism in their transformation[15]. The decision is strongly influenced by the extent to which informal institutions – traditions, norms, and values – are linked to core liberal values: civil rights, political right, and horizontal accountability. Democratic capitalism is strongly rooted in the acceptance of these Western values by a society, while non-democratic capitalism emerges where a society follows Eastern values.

However, the stability of systems in the Central and Eastern European region is not a given because these societies' value systems are not unified as a result of historical influences but are composed of conflicting values that compete with each other. Political elites can reinforce different aspects of a society's value system by sending signals (Balogh, 2020) to the citizens related to one or the other value system (Eastern or Western values), which is either helped or hindered by externally imposed institutions. After the regime change in Central and Eastern

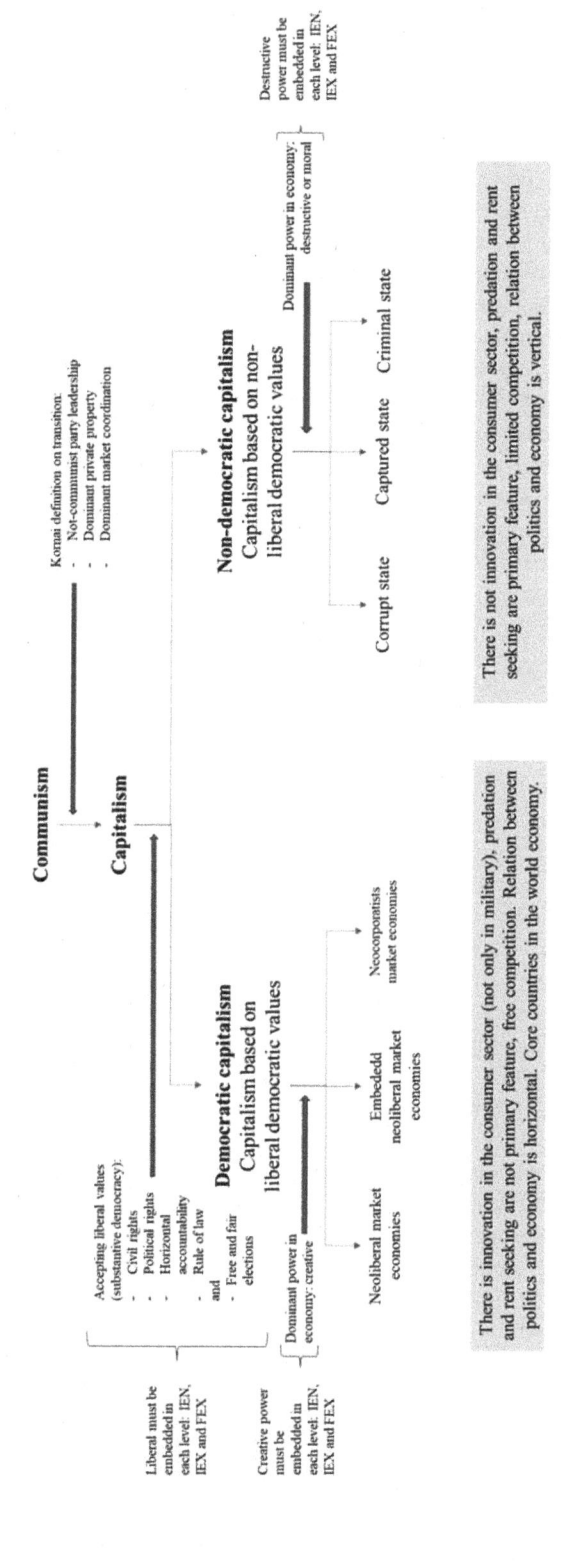

Figure 26.3 Varieties of capitalism in Central and Eastern Europe: A framework.

Source: Author's compilation, based on Boettke et al. (2015); Bohle and Greskovits (2012); Kornai (1999); Magyar and Madlovics (2020); Vahabi (2004).

Europe, elites stood for democratic capitalist systems, but the crisis of 2007/08 shifted first the political and then the economic systems in most of the countries towards non-democratic systems[16]. It should be stressed that it is not procedural democracy that matters but the extent to which the idea of freedom is implemented (Rhoden, 2015). Hungary has led the way in the move towards non-democratic capitalism (Kornai, 2015, 2016; Mihályi & Szelényi, 2020; Scheiring, 2021), but the other countries in the region (Poland, Czech Republic, Croatia, Slovenia, Slovakia) are also clearly following suit (Hanley & Vachudova, 2018; Kapidžić, 2020; Przybylski, 2018). Societies with dualistic value systems have unstable economic and political systems. As long as the informal institutions are open to both types (democratic and non-democratic capitalist systems), their stability is always in question and can only be ensured by external institutions or with coercion.

Within the two main types, democratic and non-democratic capitalist systems, the coordination and hence the relation to property determines the type of capitalist subsystem. Vahabi's (2004, p. 3) creative, destructive, and moral-ideology divisions support the model presented here. "Creative power is a type of economic power, which is based on the institution of property. It refers to the ability to create (produce, exchange) value (use and exchange value) in all its material and immaterial forms which embrace both organizational and technical capabilities [...] Destructive power is the power to destroy use or exchange values. It can also be used to protect property rights and thus, it is the basis of law and sovereignty. It includes not only coercive and threat power but also non-violent forms of pressure such as strikes and boycotts. [...] The third type of power, moral and ideological power, can be defined as the power to form and influence opinions, beliefs and the meaning of sacredness".

All three coordinating mechanisms are well developed in the literature (see Commons, 1970; Galbraith, 1983; Russell, 2004). Creative (economic) power is a type of horizontal coordination, while destructive and moral-ideology power is vertical coordination between actors. Destructive power is strongly connected to the sovereign state which has the right to use coercion, while political parties, churches, and even schools use moral-ideology power to convince other actors to follow their will. As Vahabi (2004, p. 19) formulate, "the separation of destructive and creative power primarily occurred during capitalism, while in precapitalist societies as well as in the Soviet bloc, such separation did not exist". All the three coordination types are present in each system, but the proportions vary considerably between the different types of system. Creative (economic) coordination in democratic market economies is present in significantly higher proportions in each type than in non-democratic types. For the sub-types, Bohle and Greskovits' (2012) typology (neoliberal, embedded neoliberal, and neocorporatist capitalist) fits well because they focus on both political and economic institutions in a democratic environment.

For non-democratic market economies, destructive coordination is present in much higher proportion than in democratic market economies. The decisive presence of destructive coordination in an economic system modifies the incentive system of the economic actors (Baumol, 1990; Choi & Storr, 2019). Rent seeking (Åslund, 1999; Mihályi & Szelényi, 2019) and predation becomes a dominant feature of these capitalist systems. In post-communist states, Magyar and Madlovics (2020) analyzed in these types of capitalist systems in detail. They identified three types of state: 1) the corrupt state, 2) the captured state, and 3) the criminal state. The corrupt state "is a state where corruption influences the implementation of the law" (Magyar & Madlovics, 2020, p. 102). Rent-seeking activities permeate all levels of the state, although separately managed. Even in this type of system, key liberal values are damaged. In a captured state system, not only is there corruption in the implementation of the law but also in its creation – the process – as well. A captured state is "a corrupt state where corruption influences

Varieties of Capitalism in Central and Eastern Europe

the content of laws and rules as well. On this level, corruption vertically reaches even the higher layers of governance and, rather than manifesting in only occasional transactions, it shows signs of a regular nature with more or less permanent chains of corrupt vassalage. Furthermore, although state capture on this level is partial in the sense that the instruments of public authority are not fully appropriated by corrupt actors, corruption becomes a structural element of the system" (Magyar & Madlovics, 2020, p. 102). The criminal state is the system where predation and rent seeking are the most dominant features. A "[c]riminal state is a captured state where corruption is centralized and monopolized by the ruling elite. On this level, the instruments of public authority are fully appropriated by the hierarchy of corrupt actors, usually a political enterprise gaining constitutional powers (for full appropriation requires disabling legal checks and corrupting a multitude of state institutions on the national level). Thus, corruption becomes, in a criminal state, a constituting element of the system" (Magyar & Madlovics, 2020, p. 103).

Coordination and the relationship of economic agents to property are linked back to political institutions: where political freedom is not guaranteed; it is not possible to have the kind of market coordination that is characteristic of democratic capitalist systems. Market coordination and the self-limiting attitude of the state ensure the possibility of competition between economic actors. Political and economic freedom go hand in hand and form a coherent whole. This freedom ensures that democratic capitalist systems are more innovative, that actors earn income in a value-added way, and that corruption and rent-seeking are not the primary features of the systems. The above characterization helps to make the two systems comparable but does not characterize them comprehensively. Democratic capitalist systems also have many significant problems, e.g. significant material inequalities. They also share the main characteristics of non-democratic systems but to a substantially lesser extent: corruption, the relationship between the state and market actors is opaque and, as a consequence, formal institutions in these systems often favor the elite. However, corruption, rent seeking, predation, and the use of destructive coordination are not primary systemic features, while in non-democratic systems, these are systemic ones (Rock, 2009; Treisman, 2007). The differences are not quantitative but structural/institutional.

The switch between types within the two broad categories can be achieved by changing the economic institutions (coordination and ownership), but the switch between democratic and non-democratic capitalism requires a change in the political institutions and thus in the functioning of the political system.

Although the present typology is specifically designed for Central and Eastern European countries, the theoretical framework can be applied to other regions of the world.

26.5 Summary

This chapter presents an analytical framework for analyzing economic systems in Central and Eastern Europe. The starting point is that the institutional bundle is multilayered and that the interdependent relationships between these layers need to be examined in addition to the institutional bundle that makes up each layer. The study of formal institutions alone is not sufficient for a comprehensive analysis of economic systems, so attention is drawn to the fact that the development of a region cannot be understood without examining informal and external institutions. The analysis of the interaction between political and economic institutions at each institutional level is crucial, given that the type of economic system is primarily determined by political institutions. Without basic freedoms – i.e. substantive democracy – a different market economic system can operate than when freedoms

are guaranteed. The primary systemic aspect of the typology proposed is thus the state of substantive democracy, while the secondary aspect is coordination and the closely related property rights. The transition between democratic and non-democratic market economies (and vice versa) requires changes in the political system and political institutions. Since the Central and Eastern European countries possess a dualistic value system (Western and Eastern values), there is an opportunity for the elite to shift between different types of capitalism. The transition between the two major types of systems is driven by external and/or internal shocks that change which part of the value system is dominant. The chapter also provides policy implications for the political forces that want to lead their countries towards Western democracies and democratic market economies: without a deep understanding of informal institutions and without strengthening the social acceptance of the Western values (substantive democracy), they will not be able to keep and lead the CEE states' economies towards democratic market economies.

Notes

1 For a broader framework on culture, institutions, and social equilibria, see Acemoglu and Robinson (2021).
2 Gravitation theory is mostly used in trade and FDI flow literature (Carstensen & Toubal, 2004). theory is mostly used in trade and FDI flow literature (Carstensen & Toubal, 2004).
3 Religions are an important part of culture, many times used by proxies. The countries listed represent different cultural traits.
4 Baltic states are culturally closer to CEE and to Western Europe than to Russia; however, Russia is a direct neighbor. To understand the Baltic – EU relationship, see Whitefield et al. (2006).
5 The poem in Hungarian: "Komp-ország, Komp-ország, Komp-ország: legképességesebb álmaiban is csak mászkált két part között: Kelettől Nyugatig, de szívesebben vissza" (Ady, 1905). Endre Ady is one of the most famous Hungarian poets, see https://www.britannica.com/biography/Endre-Ady.
6 "[I]nstrumental rational (zweckrational), that is, determined by expectations as to the behavior of objects in the environment and of human beings; these expectations are used as 'conditions' or 'means' for the attainment of the actor's own rationally pursued and calculate ends [...] Action is instrumentally rational (zweckrational) when the end, the means, and the secondary results are all rationally taken into account and weighed" (Weber, 1978, pp. 24 and 26).
7 Destroying market forces was never fully successful in the communist system, considering the second economy, see Grossman (1977).
8 I focus on political actors because political actors have the power to modify the IEX institutions, both economic and political ones. Economic actors do have an influence on political actors, but only political actors can implement changes in IEX institutions.
9 As Holcombe (2020, p. 289) states: "[p]rior to the Enlightenment, when citizens viewed themselves as subjects of the state, the duty of the state's subjects was to carry out their rulers' mandates. The widespread acceptance of Enlightenment ideas greatly curtailed the power of the state because citizens came to view the state as the servant of the people rather than the other way around. The Enlightenment's ideology provided a foundation for citizens to resist their predatory governments". The ideas of the enlightenment are strongly connected to Western values.
10 Gradual institutional change is possible; however, it would only modify informal institutions over a very long time, see Williamson (2000).
11 As Balogh (2020, p. 2) states, "Yet in most cases the 'Eastern option' would stretch no further than Russia (Suslov, 2012), and importantly, it would over the past three decades remain marginal vis-á-vis the Western orientation".
12 Ferenc Gyurcsány was the prime minister of Hungary between 2004 and 2009. He led a coalition government of social democrats (MSZP) and liberals (SZDSZ). On May 26, 2006, he made a speech in Balatonőszöd in which he admitted that the government had made mistakes and lied. He said: "[...] There is not much choice. That's because we fucked up. Not a little, a lot. In Europe, no country has ever done such a stupid thing as we have done. It can be explained. Obviously, we've lied through the last one and a half or two years. It was quite clear that what we were saying was

not true. [...] And in the meantime, we did nothing for four years. Nothing. You can't name any significant government action that we can be proud of, beyond bringing the government back from the shit end of the term. Nothing". The speech shocked Hungarian society. In many cities, mass demonstrations started, one becoming violent in Budapest. This famous speech was a trigger; dissatisfaction with the government's policies was already widespread.

13 Substantive democracy means that democracy is based not only on the procedure (fair elections) but there is a shared value system that stands behind it. Elections are a critical part of the definition of democracy with a focus on how we elect our political leaders, while substantive elements are also critical parts of the definition with a focus on how we are governed and how we can participate in the political processes. To be clear: having elections is a necessary but not sufficient condition of substantive democracy.

14 Liberal values (political rights, civil rights, horizontal accountability) are at the core of substantive democracy. They are accepted by all actors (conservative, social democrats, greens, etc.) who support liberal democracy as a political system and democratic capitalism. Social democrats may choose a coordinated market economy, while liberals may support a liberal market economy; both are committed to a democratic economic system, only different sub-types.

15 Mihályi & Szelényi (2020, p. 171) distinguish between liberal and illiberal capitalism. Liberal capitalisms are based on rule of law, separation of power, free media, and fair and free elections, while illiberal capitalism weakens separation of power and strengthens the executive branch.

16 Scheiring (2021, p. 268) states that national capitalists revolt against the liberal order and support the capitalism with "authoritarian characteristics" because they are better off in such an accumulative state. Accumulative state "is an authoritarian political solution to manage the internal contradictions of dependent development, institutionalized as a compromise between transnational capital, national capital and the nationalist faction of the political class, designed to help each wing of power bloc to accumulate capital" (Scheiring, 2021, p. 270). Political elite before 2010 did not pay attention to the national economic interest and the polarization of the national economic elite.

References

Acemoglu, D. and Robinson, J. (2012). *Why nations fail: The origins of power, prosperity and poverty.* New York: Crown.

Acemoglu, D. and Robinson, J. (2022). Non-Modernization: Power–Culture Trajectories and the Dynamics of Political Institutions. *Annual Review of Political Science, 25*(1), first-online. https://doi.org/10.1146/annurev-polisci-051120-103913

Acemoglu, D. and Robinson, J. A. (2008). Persistence of Power, Elites, and Institutions. *American Economic Review, 98*(1), 267–293. https://doi.org/10.1257/aer.98.1.267

Acemoglu, D. and Robinson, J. A. (2021). *Culture, institutions and social equilibria: A framework* (Working Paper 28832). National Bureau of Economic Research. http://www.nber.org/papers/w28832

Acemoglu, D., Johnson, S. and Robinson, J. A. (2005). Institutions as a fundamental cause of long-run growth. In P. Aghion and S. N. Durlauf (Eds.), *Handbook of economic growth* (Vol. 1, pp. 385–472). Elsevier. https://doi.org/10.1016/S1574-0684(05)01006-3

Ady, E. (1905). *Ismeretlen Korvin-Kódex margójára ['To the Margins of an Unknown Corvin Codex'].* https://www.arcanum.com/en/online-kiadvanyok/AdyProza-ady-prozaja-1/7-kotet-5265/cikkek-tanulmanyok-1905-oktober-11906-junius-14-5266/8-ismeretlen-korvin-kodex-margojara-52BD/

Alesina, A. and Giuliano, P. (2015). Culture and Institutions. *Journal of Economic Literature, 53*(4), 898–944. https://doi.org/10.1257/jel.53.4.898

Amable, B. (2003). *The diversity of modern capitalism.* Oxford: Oxford University Press.

Amable, B. (2016). Institutional Complementarities in the Dynamic Comparative Analysis of Capitalism. *Journal of Institutional Economics, 12*(1), 79–103. https://doi.org/10.1017/S1744137415000211

Åslund, A. (1999). The end of rent-seeking: The end of postcommunist transformation. In A. N. Brown (Ed.), *When is transition over?* (pp. 51–68). Kalamazoo, MI: W.E. Upjohn Institute for Employment Research.

Åslund, A. (2018a). Ten Lessons from a Quarter of a Century of Post-communist Economic Transformation. *Economics of Transition, 26*(4), 851–862.

Åslund, A. (2018b). What Happened to the Economic Convergence of Central and Eastern Europe After the Global Financial Crisis? *Comparative Economic Studies, 60*(2), 254–270. https://doi.org/10.1057/s41294-018-0060-x

Balogh, P. (2020). Clashing Geopolitical Self-images? The Strange Co-existence of Christian Bulwark and Eurasianism (Turanism) in Hungary. *Eurasian Geography and Economics*, 1–27. https://doi.org/10.1080/15387216.2020.1779772

Baumol, W. J. (1990). Entrepreneurship: Productive, Unproductive, and Destructive. *Journal of Political Economy*, *98*(5), 893–921.

Best, H. and Higley, J. (Eds.). (2018). *The Palgrave handbook of political elites*. London: Palgrave Macmillan.

Bluhm, K. and Varga, M. (2020). Conservative Developmental Statism in East Central Europe and Russia. *New Political Economy*, *25*(4), 642–659. https://doi.org/10.1080/13563467.2019.1639146

Boettke, P. J., Coyne, C. J. and Leeson, P. T. (2008). Institutional Stickiness and the New Development Economics. *American Journal of Economics and Sociology*, *67*(2), 331–358. https://doi.org/10.1111/j.1536-7150.2008.00573.x

Boettke, P. J., Coyne, C. J. and Leeson, P. T. (2015). Institutional stickiness and the new development economics. In L. E. Grube and V. H. Storr (Eds.), *Culture and economic action*. Cheltenham, UK: Edward Elgar Publishing. https://www.elgaronline.com/view/edcoll/9780857931726/9780857931726.00011.xml

Bohle, D. and Greskovits, B. (2012). *Capitalist diversity on Europe's periphery*. Ithaca, NY: Cornell University Press.

Campos, N. F. (2021). The EU anchor thesis: Transition from socialism, institutional vacuum and membership in the European Union. In E. Douarin and O. Havrylyshyn (Eds.), *The Palgrave handbook of comparative economics* (pp. 353–368). Cham: Palgrave Macmillan.

Carstensen, K. and Toubal, F. (2004). Foreign Direct Investment in Central and Eastern European Countries: A Dynamic Panel Analysis. *Journal of Comparative Economics*, *32*(1), 3–22. https://doi.org/10.1016/j.jce.2003.11.001

Choi, S. G. and Storr, V. H. (2019). A Culture of Rent Seeking. *Public Choice*, *181*(1), 101–126. https://doi.org/10.1007/s11127-018-0557-x

Commons, J. R. (1970). *The economics of collective action*. Madison: University of Wisconsin Press.

Csaba, L. (2021). Illiberal economic policies. In *Routledge handbook of illiberalism*. New York, NY: Routledge.

Drahokoupil, J. and Myant, M. (2015). Putting comparative capitalisms research in its place: Varieties of capitalism in transition economies. In M. Ebenau, I. Bruff and C. May (Eds.), *New directions in comparative capitalisms research: Critical and global perspectives* (pp. 155–171). Basingstoke, Hampshire: Palgrave Macmillan UK. https://doi.org/10.1057/9781137444615_10

Epstein, R. A. and Jacoby, W. (2014). Eastern Enlargement Ten Years On: Transcending the East–West Divide? *JCMS: Journal of Common Market Studies*, *52*(1), 1–16. https://doi.org/10.1111/jcms.12089

Farkas, B. (2011). The Central and Eastern European Model of Capitalism. *Post-Communist Economies*, *23*(1), 15–34. https://doi.org/10.1080/14631377.2011.546972

Feldmann, M. (2019). Global Varieties of Capitalism. *World Politics*, *71*(1), 162–196.

Galbraith, J. K. (1983). *The anatomy of power*. Boston, MA: Houghton Mifflin.

Grossman, G. (1977). The Second Economy of the USSR. *Problems of Communism*, *26*, 25.

Győrffy, D. (2022). The Middle-income Trap in Central and Eastern Europe in the 2010s: Institutions and Divergent Growth Models. *Comparative European Politics*, *20*(1), 90–113. https://doi.org/10.1057/s41295-021-00264-3

Hall, P. A. and Gingerich, D. W. (2009). Varieties of Capitalism and Institutional Complementarities in the Political Economy: An Empirical Analysis. *British Journal of Political Science*, *39*(3), 449–482.

Hall, P. A. and Soskice, D. (2001). *Varieties of capitalism: The institutional foundations of comparative advantage*. Oxford: Oxford University Press.

Hanley, S. and Vachudova, M. A. (2018). Understanding the Illiberal Turn: Democratic Backsliding in the Czech Republic. *East European Politics*, *34*(3), 276–296.

Havrylyshyn, O. (2013). Is the transition over? A definition and some measurements. In *Handbook of the economics and political economy of transition* (pp. 87–102). London: Routledge.

Helmke, G. and Levitsky, S. (2004). Informal Institutions and Comparative Politics: A Research Agenda. *Perspectives on Politics*, *2*(4), 725–740. https://doi.org/10.1017/S1537592704040472

Hodgson, G. M. (2006). What Are Institutions? *Journal of Economic Issues*, *40*(1), 1–25.

Holcombe, R. G. (2018). *Political capitalism: How economic and political power is made and maintained*. Cambridge, UK: Cambridge University Press; Cambridge Core. https://doi.org/10.1017/9781108637251

Holcombe, R. G. (2020). Progressive Democracy: The Ideology of the Modern Predatory State. *Public Choice*, *182*(3), 287–301. https://doi.org/10.1007/s11127-019-00637-z

Jacoby, W. (2001). Tutors and Pupils: International Organizations, Central European Elites, and Western Models. *Governance, 14*(2), 169–200. https://doi.org/10.1111/0952-1895.00157

Kapidžić, D. (2020). The Rise of Illiberal Politics in Southeast Europe. *Southeast European and Black Sea Studies, 20*(1), 1–17. https://doi.org/10.1080/14683857.2020.1709701

Keller, T. (2010). Hungary on the World Values Map. *Review of Sociology, 20*(1), 27–51.

Korkut, U. (2017). Resentment and Reorganization: Anti-Western Discourse and the Making of Eurasianism in Hungary. *Acta Slavica Iaponica, 38*, 71–90.

Kornai, J. (1999). Reforming the welfare state in postsocialist economies. In A. N. Brown (Ed.), *When is transition over?* (pp. 99–113). Kalamazoo, MI: W.E. Upjohn Institute for Employment Research.

Kornai, J. (2015). Hungary's U-turn: Retreating from Democracy. *Journal of Democracy, 26*(3), 34–48.

Kornai, J. (2016). The System Paradigm Revisited: Clarification and Additions in the Light of Experiences in the Post-socialist Region. *Acta Oeconomica, 66*(4), 547–596.

Lauth, H. J. (2015). Formal and informal institutions. In J. Gandhi and R. Ruiz-Rufino (Eds.), *Routledge handbook of comparative political institutions* (pp. 56–69). London: Routledge.

Levi, M. (1997). A model, a method, and a map: Rational choice in comparative and historical analysis. In M. I. Lichbach and A. S. Zuckerman (Eds.), *Comparative politics: Rationality, culture, and structure* (pp. 19–41). Cambridge: Cambridge University Press.

Linden, R. H. (Ed.). (2002). *Norms and nannies: The impact of international organizations on the central and east European states.* Lanham, MD: Rowman & Littlefield.

Magyar, B. and Madlovics, B. (2020). *The anatomy of post-communist regimes: A conceptual framework.* Budapest: Central European University Press.

Mihályi, P. and Szelényi, I. (2019). The place of rent-seeking and corruption in varieties of capitalism models. In T. Gerőcs and M. Szanyi (Eds.), *Market liberalism and economic patriotism in the capitalist World-system* (pp. 67–97). Cham: Springer International Publishing. https://doi.org/10.1007/978-3-030-05186-0_5

Mihályi, P. and Szelényi, I. (2020). The Two Forms of Modern Capitalism: Liberal and Illiberal States: A Criticism of the Varieties of Capitalism Paradigm. *Comparative Sociology, 19*(2), 155–175. https://doi.org/10.1163/15691330-BJA10006

Nölke, A. and Vliegenthart, A. (2009). Enlarging the Varieties of Capitalism: The Emergence of Dependent Market Economies in East Central Europe. *World Politics, 61*(4), 670–702. https://doi.org/10.1017/S0043887109990098

North, D. C. (1990). *Institutions, institutional change and economic performance.* Cambridge: Cambridge University Press. https://doi.org/10.1017/CBO9780511808678

Polanyi, K. (1957). *The great transformation. The political and economic origins of our time.* Boston, MA: Beacon Press.

Przybylski, W. (2018). Explaining Eastern Europe: Can Poland's Backsliding Be Stopped? *Journal of Democracy, 29*(3), 52–64. https://doi.org/10.1353/jod.2018.0044

Rac, K. (2014). East and West in Modern Hungarian Politics. *Hungarian Cultural Studies, 7*, 198–213.

Rhoden, T. F. (2015). The Liberal in Liberal Democracy. *Democratization, 22*(3), 560–578. https://doi.org/10.1080/13510347.2013.851672

Rock, M. T. (2009). Corruption and Democracy. *Journal of Development Studies, 45*(1), 55–75. https://doi.org/10.1080/00220380802468579

Russell, B. (2004). *Power, a new social analysis.* London: Routledge.

Scheiring, G. (2021). Dependent Development and Authoritarian State Capitalism: Democratic Backsliding and the Rise of the Accumulative State in Hungary. *Geoforum, 124*, 267–278. https://doi.org/10.1016/j.geoforum.2019.08.011

Schneider, B. R. (2013). *Hierarchical capitalism in Latin America.* Cambridge: Cambridge University Press.

Scott, J. C. (1998). *Seeing like a state. How certain schemes to improve the human condition have failed.* New Haven, CT: Yale University Press.

Shleifer, A. and Treisman, D. (2014). Normal Countries: The East 25 Years After Communism. *Foreign Affairs, 93*, 92.

Sonin, K. (2013). The End of Economic Transition. *Economics of Transition and Institutional Change, 21*(1), 1–10. https://doi.org/10.1111/ecot.12006

Stiglitz, J. E. (2002). *Globalization and its discontents* (Vol. 500). New York, NY: WW Norton & Company.

Stiglitz, J. E. (2012). *The price of inequality. How today's divided society endangers our future.* New York, NY: WW Norton & Company. https://wwnorton.com/books/the-price-of-inequality/

Svejnar, J. (2002). Transition Economies: Performance and Challenges. *Journal of Economic Perspectives*, *16*(1), 3–28. https://doi.org/10.1257/0895330027058

Toplišek, A. (2020). The Political Economy of Populist Rule in Post-Crisis Europe: Hungary and Poland. *New Political Economy*, *25*(3), 388–403. https://doi.org/10.1080/13563467.2019.1598960

Treisman, D. (2007). What Have We Learned About the Causes of Corruption from Ten Years of Cross-National Empirical Research? *Annual Review of Political Science*, *10*(1), 211–244. https://doi.org/10.1146/annurev.polisci.10.081205.095418

Vahabi, M. (2004). *The political economy of destructive power*. Cheltenham, UK: Edward Elgar Publishing.

Walter, A. and Zhang, X. (2012). *East Asian capitalism: Diversity, continuity, and change*. Oxford: Oxford University Press.

Weber, M. (1978). *Economy and society: An outline of interpretive sociology*. Berkeley, CA: University of California Press.

Whitefield, S., Rohrschneider, R. and Alisauskiene, R. (2006). Support for the European Union in the Baltic States. In R. Rohrschneider and S. Whitefield (Eds.), *Public opinion, party competition, and the European Union in post-communist Europe* (pp. 187–202). New York, NY: Palgrave Macmillan US. https://doi.org/10.1007/978-1-137-11500-3_10

Williamson, C. R. (2009). Informal Institutions Rule: Institutional Arrangements and Economic Performance. *Public Choice*, *139*(3), 371–387. https://doi.org/10.1007/s11127-009-9399-x

Williamson, O. E. (2000). The New Institutional Economics: Taking Stock, Looking Ahead. *Journal of Economic Literature*, *38*(3), 595–613. https://doi.org/10.1257/jel.38.3.595

Wintrobe, R. (2018). An Economic Theory of a Hybrid (Competitive Authoritarian or Illiberal) Regime. *Public Choice*, *177*(3–4), 217–233.

27

FINANCIAL GLOBALIZATION, FINANCIAL REGULATION, AND MACROECONOMIC POLICY[1]

Marek Dabrowski

BRUEGEL IN BRUSSELS, BRUSSELS, BELGIUM

HIGHER SCHOOL OF ECONOMICS IN MOSCOW, MOSCOW, RUSSIA

CASE – CENTER FOR SOCIAL AND ECONOMIC RESEARCH IN WARSAW, WARSZAWA, POLAND

27.1 Financial globalization and forces behind it

There is no single definition of financial globalization as there is no single definition of globalization.[2] For this analysis, we will use the one offered by Prasad et al. (2003), who define financial globalization as '...*rising global linkages through cross-border financial flows.*' This definition is simple and clear enough to capture the analyzed phenomenon's essence. On the other hand, according to the same authors, '*financial integration refers to an individual country's linkages to international capital markets.*' Both concepts are closely interrelated and can be used interchangeably in practice (Prasad et al., 2003).

In its contemporary reincarnation, financial globalization is a relatively young phenomenon. Although economic historians (see e.g., Bordo et al., 1999; O'Rourke and Williamson, 2000; Morys et al., 2008) distinguish another period of globalization, including the financial one (between 1870 and 1914), it was brutally interrupted by WWI. As a result, most of the 20th century (in particular, from the Great Depression in the early 1930s until the 1970s) was characterized by trade protectionism and capital movement restrictions not only in what in the jargon of the International Monetary Fund (IMF) is called emerging-market and developing economies (EMDEs) but also in most advanced economies (AEs).[3]

It is also worth remembering that the pre-WWI globalization was limited to then AEs (most of today's EMDEs remained in colonial dependence, and they benefited from this process only marginally and often in a distorted form) and was technically less sophisticated due to less developed means of global communication (in practice, the telegraph was the only technical channel of rapid information transmission and conducting financial transactions and, therefore, of financial market arbitrage). As a result, the specter of financial market products traded internationally was also smaller compared to the contemporary era.

The gradual change to dominant post-WWII financial market fragmentation along national borders started in the 1980s in AEs and a decade later – in EMDEs.[4] Greater integration of

DOI: 10.4324/9781003144366-32

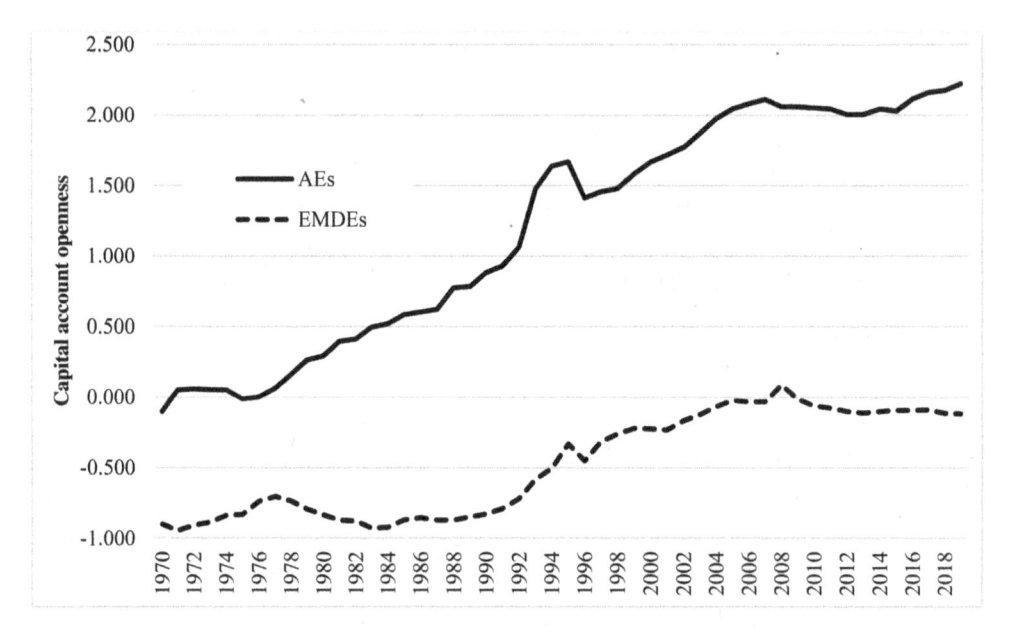

Figure 27.1   The Chinn-Ito Capital Account Openness Index (KAOPEN): 1970–2018.

Source: Chinn and Ito (2006); Ito and Chinn (2020); http://web.pdx.edu/~ito/Chinn-Ito_website.htm; http://web.pdx.edu/~ito/Chinn-Ito_website.htm and author's own calculation.

Notes: The Chinn-Ito Capital Account Openness Index is based on the information taken from the IMF's Annual Report on Exchange Arrangements and Exchange Restrictions (AREAER). The degree of current and capital account control is normalized within the scale of −1.92 (minimum openness) and 2.33 (maximum openness). Data represent simple averages of indexes of respective groups of countries. The entire sample amounts to 182 countries.

financial markets has been the result of advancing current and capital account liberalization across the world (Figure 27.1), the deregulation of the banking sector and other financial markets segments (through the elimination of various forms of financial repression), the international expansion of large banks and non-bank financial institutions between AEs and to EMDEs, the privatization of banks and other financial institutions, and finally the rapid progress in information and communication technologies (ICT) and financial innovations (facilitated, in turn, by a combination of legal innovations and new ICT tools). All these factors have eliminated institutional, legal, and technical barriers to unrestricted capital movement, especially private financial flows, across the globe, substantially reduced transaction costs, and helped to integrate national financial markets into a single global market.

Figure 27.2 shows a dynamic of cross-border net nominal flows of direct and portfolio investments (in current US$) for two major groups of countries (according to the IMF WEO classification): AEs and EMDEs for four decades (between 1980 and 2020).[5] The data for EMDEs is available from 1997 only. The main message from this graph is that substantial flows in AEs started in the 1990s and EMDEs – a decade later. The culmination of nominal global flows came in the 2000s. Smaller but still substantial capital flows characterized the 2010s. It resulted from disruption in financial intermediation, recession (especially in AEs), and higher uncertainty caused by the Global Financial Crisis (GFC) of 2007–2009. In addition, the new post-crisis macro- and microprudential regulations increased the costs of financial intermediation and investment financing (Dabrowski, 2021).

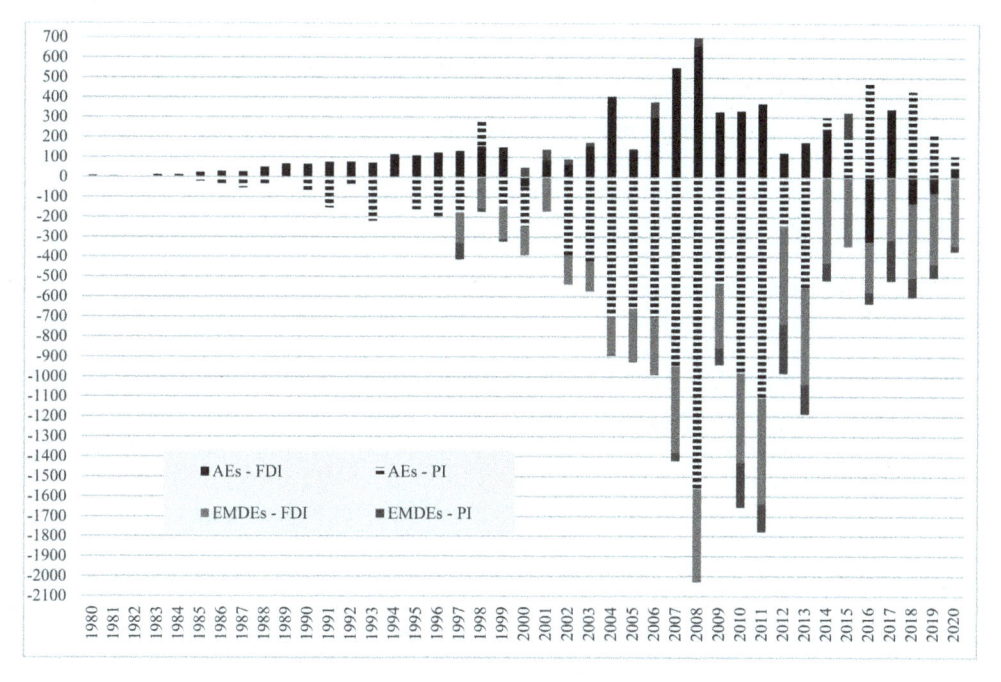

Figure 27.2 Cross-border net direct and portfolio investment flows in US$ billion, world total: 1980–2020 (BoP statistics).

Source: World Economic Outlook database, April 2021.

Note: Positive value means net capital outflow, negative value – net capital inflow.

The dynamics of nominal capital flows (Figure 27.2) broadly correspond with the dynamics of the financial liberalization process (Figure 27.1). The period of rapid liberalization (the 1980s and 1990s in AEs, and 1990s and early 2000s in EMDEs) led, with some time lag, to a rapid expansion of cross-border capital flows. After the GFC, stagnation in further liberalization, or even its partial reversal in EMDEs, caused a diminishing of these flows.

Another conclusion coming from the analysis of Figure 27.2 relates to the direction of capital flows. EMDEs were net recipients of direct investment during the analyzed period, while AEs were net exporters of this investment in most recorded years. Net portfolio flows seemed to play a less significant role in EMDEs, while they were more critical in AEs. Interestingly, these flows changed direction: since 2014, AEs became a net exporter of portfolio investment. Perhaps it was a result of record-low interest rates in most AEs.

27.2 Micro- and macroeconomic benefits and costs of financial globalization

In the microeconomic sphere, an unrestricted capital movement helps allocate savings across national borders, spending them for the most productive purposes. On the one hand, it increases the rate of return for saving owners. On the other, it decreases the costs of investment financing. It also deepens national financial markets and makes them more competitive, reducing costs and improving the quality of financial intermediation. It is essential in small and medium-sized economies outside major financial centers. In the case of EMDEs, it helps accelerate the process of financial sector development and its maturing.

Cross-border financial flows play an essential auxiliary role in supporting trade flows, both in goods and services, by providing less expensive trade financing and the broader specter of financial instruments tailored to the needs of specific sectors and types of transactions. The role played by international financial flows was best illustrated by the immediate consequences of the GFC in 2008 when severe disruption in financial intermediation (including its cross-border component) led to a temporary collapse in the world's trade volume in goods and services by 10.4% as compared to 2007. In 2009, it rebounded by 12.7%.[6]

There are also other less direct positive effects of unrestricted capital movement. For example, it stimulates flows of innovations, know-how, and best management practices (this applies, in the first instance, to direct investment but not only). It creates pressure for business-friendly regulations and policies (see Section 27.7).

However, there are also socially more challenging microeconomic effects of unrestricted capital flows. They increase competitive pressure on local enterprises and accelerate structural changes. While it can help increasing total factor productivity, it can also cause failure of local firms and unemployment.

Globalization, particularly a financial one, is often blamed for increasing income inequality on a national level, especially in AEs. It happens, among others, due to the so-called de-location effect, that is, optimization of global value chains by moving various components of the production and distribution processes from AEs to EMDEs. It leads to job losses and downward pressure on wages and salaries of low- and medium-skilled employees in AEs. On the other hand, there is an expansion of high-skilled and high-paid (but limited in number) jobs in management, research and development, product design and marketing, finance, and other business-related services in AEs, which benefits better-off elites (Milanovic, 2016; Stiglitz, 2016; Sachs, 2017).

The available body of empirical research (e.g., Jaumotte et al., 2008; Lang and Mendes Tavares, 2018) finds the positive impact of foreign direct investment (FDI) on national income inequalities. It suggests a trade-off between decreasing global inequalities and increasing national inequalities, especially in AEs, thanks to globalization, including unrestricted capital movement (Dabrowski, 2018).

In the macroeconomic sphere, an unrestricted capital movement increases the pool of available savings (above the gross national saving rate) and, respectively, sources of investment financing in recipient countries. Consequently, it may be an essential vehicle of growth acceleration and income-per-capita convergence between lower- and higher-income countries (Maskin, 2015), contributing to decreasing global income inequalities, that is, between citizens of the world (see Wolf, 2005).

Financial globalization also allows for intertemporal consumption smoothing and international risk sharing (Prasad et al., 2003; Asdrubali and Kim, 2008). However, if poorly managed, such smoothing may lead to excessive fiscal and current-account imbalances and excessive fiscal and external debt (see Section 27.6).

The most considerable risk of financial globalization is related to the volatility of capital flows (see Figure 27.2). As a result, it exposes national economies to external shocks more frequently than in the case of closed capital accounts.

There has been an extensive debate on factors that determine the vulnerability of individual economies, which are open to capital flows, to external shocks. Prudent economic policies and mature institutions can increase resilience to such shocks (Prasad et al., 2003). It has been demonstrated, among others, by the varied reaction of emerging-market economies to the most recent COVID-19-related crisis (Dabrowski and Dominguez-Jimenez, 2020). Those economies, which represented more robust macroeconomic and institutional fundamentals and enjoyed solid market reputation (several economies of East and South-East Asia and Central and Eastern Europe), experienced a milder shock and had a larger room of macroeconomic maneuver than those which entered the crisis with substantial disequilibria and the troubled history of previous turmoil. Among the latter, Argentina and Lebanon, which defaulted on their public debt, and Turkey recorded a considerable devaluation of their currencies and high inflation.

However, it is worth remembering that financial globalization is not the only and very often the main factor causing an external vulnerability. Trade and migration-related links (labor remittances) in the contemporary global economy are strong enough to facilitate the transmission of external shocks. Let us mention, for example, periodic episodes of a sudden decline in oil and other commodity prices, which deteriorate the terms of trade of commodity exporters.[7]

Apart from volatility of global capital flows and increased exposure to external shocks, financial globalization creates several challenges to national macroeconomic policies, limiting its maneuver room. They are related, among others, to (i) balance-of-payment (BoP) management (see Sections 27.3 and 27.4), (ii) monetary policy (see Section 27.5), and fiscal policy (see Section 27.6). Overall, financial globalization decreases the room for discretionary policy measures and puts disciplining pressure on these policies, which will be further discussed in Section 27.7. It is also why politicians on a national level, especially those representing populist and nationalistic programs, dislike globalization.

27.3 Balance-of-payment management

Financial globalization has changed the conditions and the logic of BoP management.

The 'traditional' approach to BoP analysis was based on the realities of largely closed (or only partly open) economies with a limited role in cross-border private capital flows and the ability of national governments to influence the saving and investment decisions of domestic economic agents. Such an analysis usually started from domestic competitiveness factors; in the first instance, labor unit costs denominated in foreign currency. These factors determined the trade and current account balance. Capital account transactions had to counterbalance the current account.

If a country ran a current account deficit, it needed, for example, foreign credit (private or official), FDI, or other kinds of capital inflow to finance that deficit. If it ran a current account surplus, this surplus had to be absorbed in the form of capital account transactions with the opposite sign, through various forms of capital exports/outflows or increasing official reserves (which is also a form of capital export).

If the current account balance was considered unsustainable, policy adjustment was needed, given difficulties in counterbalancing capital account transactions. The adjustment might be implemented through the instruments of exchange rate policy (devaluation or revaluation of domestic currency), trade policy, monetary and fiscal policies (which determined the level of domestic absorption), and others.

Summing up, in a world of restricted capital mobility, the current account balance determines capital account flows. In a world of free capital mobility, however, reverse causality dominates. In a small open economy, net capital flows (at least their private component) have a largely exogenous character. The current account balance must adapt to changes in the capital account (through changes in real exchange rates).

Figure 27.3 illustrates the mirror character of changes in net direct and portfolio investment and current account balances in Latin America and the Caribbean, a relatively

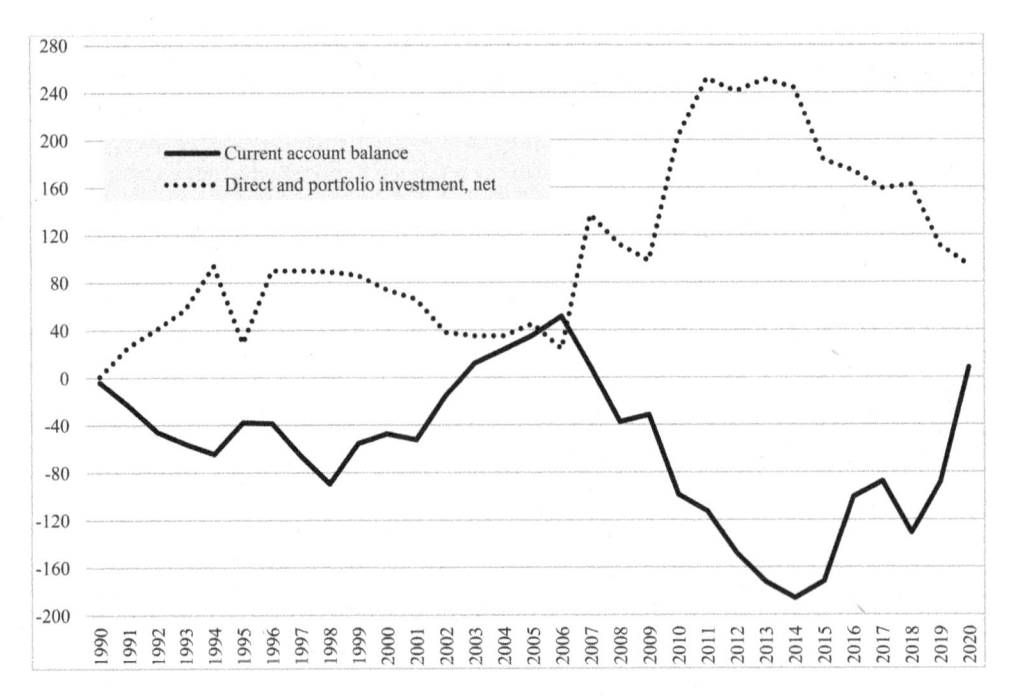

Figure 27.3 Net direct and portfolio investment and current account balance in Latin American and Caribbean countries: 1990–2020 (in US$ billion).

Source: IMF World Economic Outlook, April 2021.

homogeneous emerging-market region (in terms of the direction of capital flows) dominated by economies with largely open capital accounts. Its experience since the 1990s confirms the phenomenon of limited control of national macroeconomic policy over current account balances and real exchange rates in a world of unrestricted capital movement. Even if a country's monetary authority controls its nominal exchange rate through a currency peg or managed float, the real exchange rate adjusts to the BoP equilibrium through inflation differentials.

Living in a world of largely unrestricted capital movement also requires a new attitude to current account imbalances. The 'traditional' analytical framework for the BoP mentioned above was based on the explicit or implicit assumption that today's current account deficit must be compensated by future current account surpluses (a current account must be balanced at least over the long term). It was related to another implicit (not clearly articulated and not consistently well recognized) assumption that capital ownership residency has a fixed character (see Dabrowski, 2006). It means that capital invested in country A, financed by savings from country B, will 'belong' to the latter, including its right to repatriate factor income (interest or dividend) and – eventually – the invested capital stock. Such assumptions might be justified in a world of restricted capital movement, which, in turn, was reflected in the empirical phenomenon of the 'home country bias' in investing gross national saving as described by Feldstein and Horioka (1980).

Following the 'traditional' analytical framework, each kind of net capital inflows (including FDI) leads to the accumulation of a country's external liabilities, which (1) cannot grow indefinitely, (2) must be repaid at some point, (3) and that the higher they are, the more vulnerable the country's external position is. Consequently, various numerical criteria (for example, a current account deficit exceeding 4 or 5% of GDP – see Summers, 1996) were applied both by international financial institutions and private investors in the late 1990s and early 2000s to identify countries considered as potential candidates for a BoP crisis.

It often led to paradoxical conclusions when countries considered by international investors as business-friendly, and therefore attracting large amounts of private investment (and consequently running high current account deficits) were assessed as conducing unsustainable policies and 'overheated.' On the contrary, countries characterized by a poor business climate which were not able to attract net private capital inflows or even suffered from net capital outflows (of both residents and non-residents) recorded either balanced or positive current accounts and were considered as macroeconomically 'healthy' under the '5% doctrine.'

All the above-discussed shortcomings of the 'traditional' BoP analytical framework call for its substantial revision.

First, in a world of largely unrestricted capital movements, sources of capital do not often have a country of origin, given the transnational character of major corporations, financial institutions, and investment funds, even if they invest on behalf of residents of concrete countries. In addition, with the free movement of people, physical persons (particularly wealthy ones) may change their country of residence (domicile), moving together with their accumulated savings.

Second, private investors seek the highest rate of return in their investment/reinvestment decisions, regardless of their country of residence. Each rate of return consists of two major components: (1) a country-related component reflecting a country's investment climate and (2) a project-related component.

Third, there is not necessarily a diminishing rate of return with respect to a country-related component. It means that country A may offer a higher rate of return than country B for similar projects for an extended period due to a better investment climate.

However, if the investment climate deteriorates (or investors fear such deterioration) and the expected rate of return in country A becomes lower than that of country B, the direction of capital movement may change. Such change will affect not only non-residents but also residents.

In our new framework, country A (capital importer) is not immunized from the danger of capital outflows. Still, such a danger originates from changes in the country-related component of the expected rate of return (comparing to other countries) rather than from the non-resident origin of the invested capital.

Some countries can generate a systematically higher national saving rate than others above their own investment needs for various historical, demographic, institutional, and other reasons. Unrestricted capital movement and the global financial market enable moving this excess saving to countries/locations where they can be invested in the most efficient way to benefit both savers and investors (see Section 27.2).

However, one cannot say that current account imbalances have become irrelevant. As long as country A has its currency and sovereign monetary and fiscal policies, at some point, its current account deficit may start to be considered by investors as too high and its liabilities in foreign currency unsustainable. It may cause its exchange rate risk premium (devaluation risk) to increase and its expected rate of return to decrease. These developments may trigger a sudden outflow of capital (both resident and non-resident) and a BoP/currency crisis. Thus, the current account balance and, more generally, the balance of payments must remain a subject of interest and concern of national economic policies.

27.4 Controlling the size, direction, and structure of capital flows

Suppose the BoP and current account balances still matter. How may national governments influence the size and direction of capital flows, the critical exogenous factor determining a country's external position, and its room of maneuver in monetary, fiscal, and regulatory policy spheres (see Sections 27.5–27.7)? Below we will analyze the specter of available policy instruments and their limitations.

Capital controls such as a ban on specific transactions, license requirements to conduct them, and the taxation of capital flows (explicit or implicit, for example, unremunerated reserve requirements) are formally unavailable for members and advanced candidates of the European Union (EU) because such controls violate the *acquis communitaire* (one of the four single market fundamental freedoms). The non-EU countries which belong to the Organization for Economic Cooperation and Development (OECD) are also constrained by the OECD Code of Liberalization of Capital Movements, although in a less rigorous way than in the case of the EU *acquis* (see OECD, 2012).

However, countries that are not constrained by international treaties and other formal obligations and have tried capital controls have found those tools problematic. Individual instruments may have some but rather a temporary impact on the structure and maturity of capital flows (see Baba and Kokenyne, 2011). Suppose a country has already reached an advanced degree of its economic openness and financial sector sophistication. In that case, capital movement restrictions could be quite easily circumvented through current account transactions, those capital account transactions which remained open, off-shore markets, and various kinds of derivatives.

Thus, despite having many advocates (see e.g., Rodrik, 2009; Gallagher, 2012), the ultimate effect of capital controls is problematic, especially in countries that try to go back from capital account openness to a more restrictive regime. They will contribute to various kinds of market distortions (Kose et al., 2010; Forbes, 2005) and decrease capital flows' transparency rather than help to impact their size, direction, and structure. Besides, the idea of selective capital control is based on the controversial assumption that there are 'good' (for example, FDI) and 'bad' (short-term portfolio investment) flows. The latter is often called 'speculative' and considered damaging.

In reality, portfolio investments are often complementary to FDI (one of the forms of corporate financing) and 'speculation' is a primary mechanism of market arbitrage, clearing, and integration with the global market. Furthermore, if a financial market is sufficiently deep, sophisticated, and liquid, the differences between long- and short-term and direct and portfolio investment become blurred.

The effectiveness of monetary policy in terms of its influence on the size, direction, and structure of private capital flows is somewhat limited and depends on the monetary policy regime. There is no impact under a hard peg because there is no sovereign monetary policy at all. A flexible exchange rate allows for some accommodation of volatility in capital flows through either nominal appreciation or depreciation of a national currency and associated exchange rate risk premiums or adjustments of the central bank's interest rates. However, if the exogenous changes in private capital flows are strong enough, a country's tolerance of exchange rate fluctuation can reach economic and political limits (see Section 27.5). In addition, in some circumstances, both capital inflows and outflows may become self-accelerating under flexible exchange rates (speculation for currency appreciation or depreciation).

Adjusting interest rates in response to fluctuations in capital flows involves the risk of damaging domestic macroeconomic conditions with negative consequences for the real sector:

exchange rate cuts may cause the economy to overheat, whereas a radical increase of interest rates to stop capital outflow may trigger a downturn.

Hybrid monetary regimes, which target both exchange rate and interest rate/monetary aggregates, may try to sterilize both capital inflows and outflows. However, sterilization of capital inflows is usually costly and ineffective in the long term as it creates a one-way bet for the market players. In turn, sterilizing capital outflows may easily lead to a meltdown of international reserves and trigger a speculative attack against the country's currency (see Section 27.5).

Fiscal policy may impact the current account as it influences net national saving (a fiscal deficit decreases net national saving and a fiscal surplus increases it). However, one should take into account the offsetting effects in terms of net private financial flows. For example, fiscal contraction, widely considered one of the measures to diminish current account imbalances, may not necessarily bring the expected results due to 'crowding-in' effects (Rostowski, 2001). Investors usually perceive successful fiscal adjustment as decreasing country risk (increasing the expected return rate). It boasts private capital inflows, thus leading to higher account deficits.

Fiscal policy may also have some microeconomic impact through various kinds of fiscal incentives and disincentives. For example, in some countries which experienced housing markets booms and busts in the 2000s and 2010s, special tax incentives artificially stimulated housing investments. However, in most cases, such incentives or disincentives influence the structure of capital flows rather than their total volume.

The same relates to the micro-prudential regulation of financial institutions. They may have a benefit of their own by increasing the robustness and resilience of a financial sector. However, their impact on capital flows may concern their structure rather than the overall volume.

Finally, macroprudential regulation may have some impact on both the volume and structure of capital flows. However, it depends on the practical operationalization of this concept: what kind of financial flows and variables will be monitored, by whom and according to which criteria, and what kind of preventive and corrective instruments can be adopted (see Borio, 2018). In some countries, it serves as a new label for the old practices of capital control.[8]

The above analysis confirms our earlier view on the limited potential of national policies in small open economies to regulate BoP, current account balances, and the real exchange rate in a world of unrestricted capital movement (see Section 27.3). It means that prudent macroeconomic (especially fiscal) and regulatory policies at the national level may increase a country's financial safety and ability to withstand various exogenous BoP shocks but do not guarantee its complete immunity against external turbulence and BoP crisis.

27.5 Capital mobility and monetary policy

Monetary policy is another area dramatically affected by financial globalization. The first lesson learned by several EMDEs and some AEs in the 1990s[9] was the impossibility to control both exchange rate and money supply (interest rates) in the world of unrestricted capital movement. It refers to the 'impossible trinity' (see e.g., Frankel, 1999) or the 'macroeconomic trilemma' (see e.g., Obstfeld et al., 2004). According to this principle, a country must give up one of the following three goals: exchange rate stability, monetary independence, or financial market integration (see Figure 27.4); it cannot have all three simultaneously.

However, even under a freely floating exchange rate and inflation targeting, the room for maneuver of national monetary policy in a small open economy is limited and determined by political and economic tolerance of exchange rate fluctuations (Rey, 2013). 'Leaning against

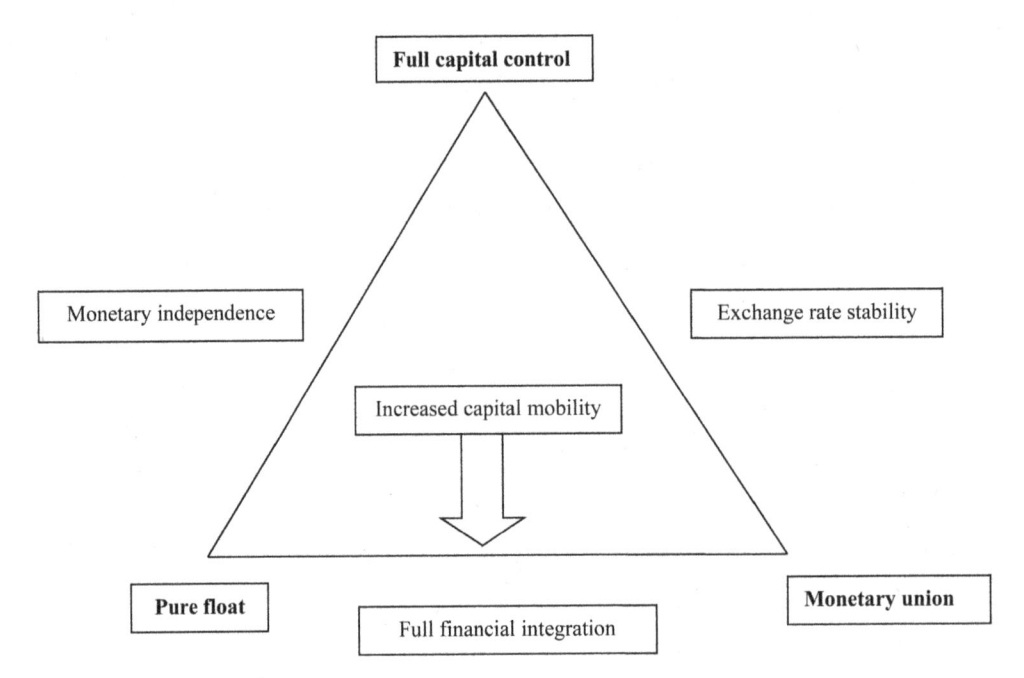

Figure 27.4 The impossible trinity.

Source: Frankel (1999).

the winds' of international financial markets usually leads to either appreciation or depreciation of a domestic currency. Excessive appreciation deteriorates the competitiveness of domestic producers. In contrast, excessive depreciation may have adverse pass-through effects on inflation and increase the domestic currency value of foreign currency-denominated liabilities. It may trigger a flight from the domestic currency, especially in countries with fresh memories of high inflation/hyperinflation, insufficiently credible national monetary policy, and high actual dollarization or euroization. For these reasons, the central bank's interest rate decisions must consider international financial market trends and not deviate too much from them.

On the other hand, changes in interest rates on international financial markets are determined by the monetary policy decisions of central banks of major AEs, in particular, the US Federal Reserve Board (Fed). The global integration of financial markets and the role of the US dollar as the number one international reserve and transaction currency lead to a situation when the Fed's monetary policy decisions have an economic impact far beyond its legal jurisdiction (see Ghosh et al., 2012). To a lesser extent, this also relates to the Euro.

Monetary policy decisions in major AEs put other central banks, including those in EMDEs, uncomfortable. Because of their limited ability to 'lean against the wind' (see above), they must follow the decisions of leading players even if macroeconomic conditions in their own countries differ substantially. Very often, what is perceived by central banks of smaller countries as external shocks (increase in commodity prices or sudden changes in country risk perception) is a by-product of the monetary decisions of major central banks.

Solving this conflict would require broadening the Fed's actual mandate and goal function. The same applies to other central banks that issue international reserve currencies. They should focus more on international spillovers of their monetary policy decisions (see Ostry et al., 2012 on source-country policies). It is not a matter of policy altruism but a well-recognized interest of their economies. In many instances, negative externalities will come back, like a boomerang, to a given monetary authority, even if it happens with a time lag. They may have a form of higher commodity prices, financial bubbles, and BoP crises in other economies but affect the home country's financial sector, etc.

A cross-border competition between individual currencies is a crucial determinant of the relative strength of respective central banks and their impact on the international monetary system.[10] Regardless of whether they are residents or non-residents in a given jurisdiction, owners of money balances can move them freely across borders seeking the highest rate of return. It contradicts many textbook models of monetary policy, which assume, explicitly or implicitly, the central bank's monopoly on money emission, i.e., using only domestic currency by economic agents. The reality, however, is far from this assumption. Economic agents retain at least some freedom of choice of means of payments and storing their financial wealth. Foreign currencies, especially the US dollar and Euro, play a dominant role in such a menu even when national law requires the use of domestic currency for some transactions, for example, paying wages and salaries, taxes, or selling goods and services on the domestic market.

Currency substitution is not a new phenomenon. Historically, it was always present in cases of war, high inflation or hyperinflation, inconvertibility of the national currency, etc., even if holding foreign currencies was legally banned and the subject of criminal prosecution (think about the experience of former communist countries). However, financial globalization and liberalization of the financial industry have increased economic agents' access to various foreign currency-denominated assets and decreased transaction costs of currency substitution.

As a result, one can distinguish between two categories of monetary jurisdictions: 'core' and 'periphery.' The first one refers to global transaction currencies – US dollar, Euro, Japanese yen, British pound, and Swiss franc. Perhaps the Chinese yuan can also join this group at some point, but as for now, it does not play a role of a global currency and is not fully convertible. All other currencies belong to the periphery because they play only local, i.e., national role, but they face competition from global currencies.

The group of peripheral currencies is not homogeneous. Individual currencies differ in terms of credibility record and stability and, therefore, resilience to various shocks. For example, this group includes currencies of some AEs (Canada, Australia, New Zealand, Nordic countries, Korea, Singapore), which, although they do not play a global role, are not challenged by currency substitution for credibility reasons (some of those countries record high level of dollarization for transaction reasons or because they host international financial centers).

On the other hand, most of the central banks in EMDEs face credibility challenges due to past currency and public debt crises, high inflation or hyperinflation episodes, shallowness and fragility of their financial sectors, and political instability. It is the main factor limiting their room of maneuver and the possibility to resort to unconventional monetary policy measures such as asset purchasing programs (Dabrowski and Dominguez-Jimenez, 2020).

It has been seen during both GFC and COVID-19 crises when the demand for core currencies increased (causing their appreciation and deflationary pressure). At the same time, the demand for many peripheral currencies decreased, leading to the opposite effects such as currency depreciation and inflationary pressures.

As shown in Figure 27.5, the income velocity of broad money (by definition, inversely related to the demand for broad money) decreased since 2007 in core currency areas, except the United Kingdom. The increasing demand for broad money has come partly from the outside (i.e., from non-residents), given the increasing global role of core currencies and the tendency towards currency substitution in peripheral currency areas during periods of prolonged financial turmoil.

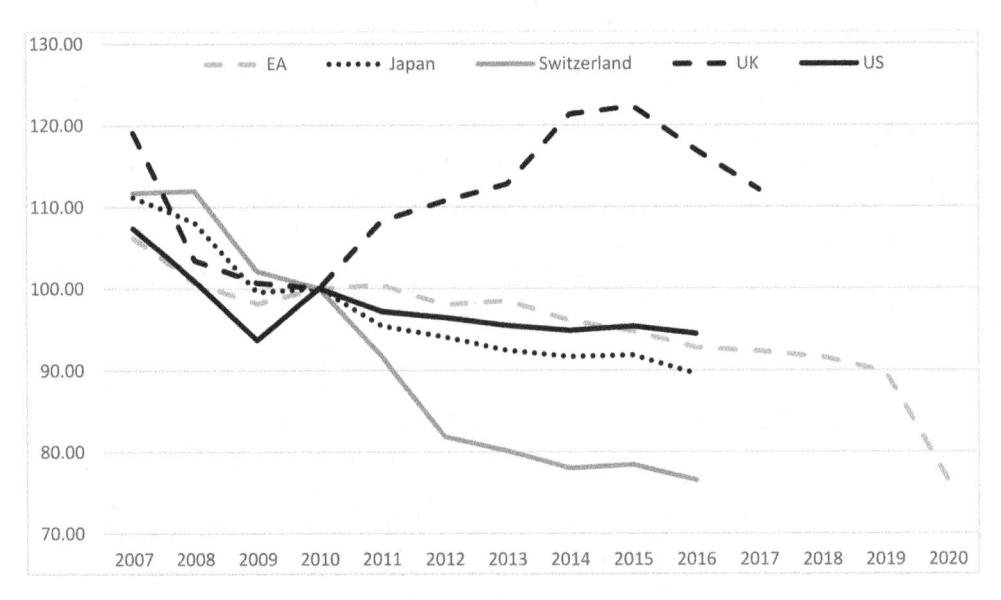

Figure 27.5   Income velocity of broad money (V) in core currency areas, 2007–2020 (nominal GDP/broad money), 2010 = 100.

Source: IMF International Financial Statistics (www.data.imf.org).

27.6 Financial globalization and fiscal policy

Financial globalization allows most governments to borrow from international markets. Furthermore, domestic borrowing is also less expensive and more competitive, thanks to integrating national financial markets with the global market. In extreme circumstances, the necessity to borrow from abroad may originate from an absence of non-inflationary domestic sources, resulting from either the poor development of the financial market or a lack of residents' confidence in the future creditworthiness of the government. In the second case, it is also difficult to borrow from external commercial sources. International financial institutions, such as the IMF or the World Bank, are the only available sources.

As a result of external borrowing, short-term fiscal constraints may become relaxed, allowing for more intertemporal consumption smoothing (see Section 27.2), more public investment, or just postponing some politically unpopular fiscal adjustment decisions. However, the increased room for fiscal policy maneuver can also 'demobilize' the government and weaken fiscal discipline, leading to a cumulation of excessive public debt. Given the volatile character of global financial flows (see Section 27.1), it can make public debt management more vulnerable to global financial market sentiments changes.

Financial globalization also gives the government a choice of currency in which they want to borrow.[11] Borrowing in foreign currency can be particularly attractive in countries with a recent history of high inflation or hyperinflation. Borrowing in the national currency is either impossible or very expensive (due to the high yields required by creditors). The situation in which economic agents (in both the government and the private sector) cannot borrow in their national currency has been termed 'original sin' by Hausmann (2001).

In less extreme cases (i.e., in the absence of a strong mistrust in the national currency), borrowing in a foreign currency may look attractive, at least in the short term, due to lower interest rates. International markets with financial instruments denominated in global currencies

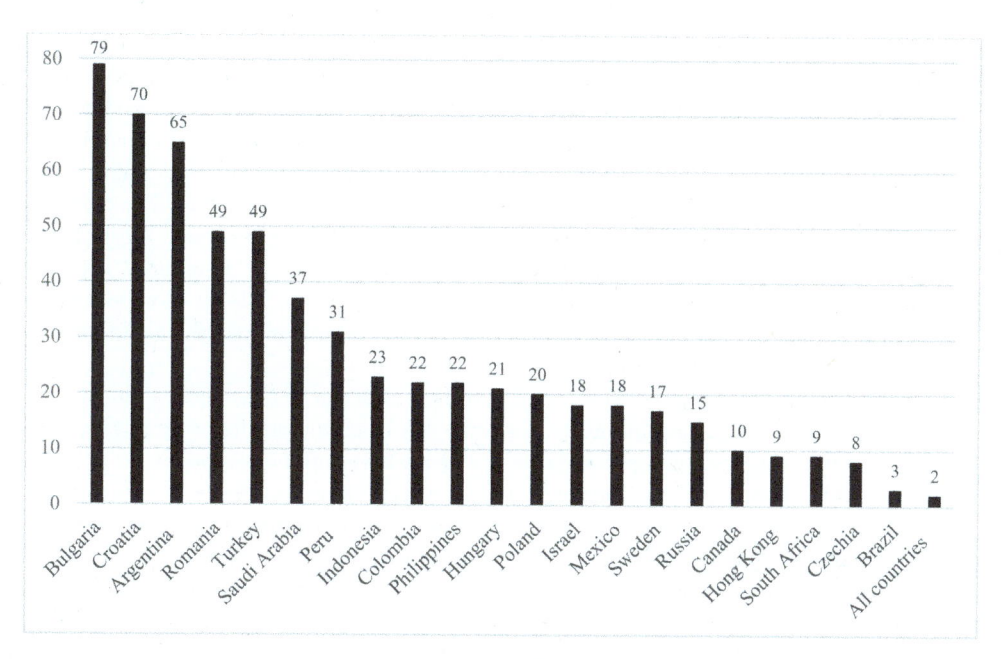

Figure 27.6   Share of foreign currency-denominated debt in total general government long-term debt (above 1-year maturity), in %, end of 2020.

Source: Bogdanova et al. (2021), Table C4, p. 24.

are also deeper and more liquid than the domestic market of any EMDE using its currency (even with the participation of non-residents). As a result, it is possible to borrow internationally in larger amounts and more cheaply.

However, borrowing in a foreign currency creates unhedged liabilities. When a national currency depreciates, the total public debt denominated in the national currency (and its relation to GDP) increases automatically.

While Bogdanova et al. (2021) show a systematically declining share of foreign currency-denominated debt in total general government gross debt since 2000 (which perhaps may be attributed to the development of financial markets and the progress towards macroeconomic stabilization achieved by many EMDEs), it must be put against the trend of rapidly growing size of gross debt (in absolute figures and relation to GDP), the tendency, which started well before the COVID-19 crisis (Kose et al., 2021). Furthermore, there is a group of countries where the share of foreign currency-denominated debt remains high (Figure 27.6). It includes countries with currencies pegged to Euro, planning to join the Euro area soon (Bulgaria and Croatia), and countries that have experienced macroeconomic and financial credibility problems for several decades (Argentina and Turkey).

27.7 Regulatory competition, global policy coordination, and policy sovereignty

Unrestricted cross-border capital movement allows economic agents to search for jurisdictions with more business-friendly regulations (see Section 27.3), maximizing their return rates. They look for lower and simpler taxation, transparent tax and customs administration, little or no corruption, adequate protection of property rights and contract enforcement, national treatment of foreign investors, simple financial regulations, competent public administration, fewer bureaucratic barriers (the so-called 'red' tape), macroeconomic, financial and political stability, policy predictability, etc. It leads to regulatory competition between jurisdictions, putting disciplining pressure on national and subnational legislation, taxation, political attitude to business (especially a foreign one), and various administrative practices. The numerous international surveys and ratings such as the World Bank's Doing Business, World Bank's Worldwide Governance Indicators, Heritage Foundation Index of Economic Freedom, Transparency International Corruption Perception Index, or the Global Competitiveness Index of the World Economic Forum serve as analytical tools to compare the quality of governance in individual jurisdictions.

Overall, cross-country regulatory and policy competition can be considered a positive phenomenon but only to a certain point. It creates the risk of regulatory free riding (race to the bottom) and the temptation to open regulatory and tax havens if it goes too far.

In the world economy, there are pretty many such jurisdictions,[12] in most cases – small countries. The EU regularly publishes the list of '...of non-cooperative jurisdictions for tax purposes,'[13] but this is only the tip of the iceberg, that is, the list of extreme cases of non-transparency and non-cooperation. Some countries resort to tax dumping practices even within the EU, especially in corporate taxation, either by offering lower tax rates or concluding individual tax deals with large corporations (Keuschnigg et al., 2016).

The international regulatory and policy cooperation should eliminate the existing loopholes and 'race to the bottom' and set the best regulatory standards for national governments. However, this is easier to say than do. There are at least three kinds of obstacles. The first one has a theoretical or conceptual character: balancing regulatory competition and harmonization properly. The second is to agree on a concrete harmonization standard, which depends on an individual country's legal and political tradition. The third relates to the diversified interests of respective countries, often masked by reference to its sovereignty and unwillingness to compromise it.

There are policy and regulatory areas in which more considerable progress has been accomplished. First, it concerns financial sector regulation, both globally and within the EU, especially after the GFC. However, there is little tax policy cooperation and harmonization other than the limited exchange of information about taxpayers and some pressure on tax havens. The attempts to harmonize, at least partly, principles of corporate income taxation within the EU have not brought visible progress yet (Valero, 2020). The agreement reached at the G7 summit in June 2021 on introducing a global minimum corporate tax rate of at least 15% (Rappeport, 2021) regardless of the location of company headquarters may limit harmful tax competition. Still, its full implementation worldwide may take many years.

Global coordination of monetary policies is even more problematic and remains relatively limited. Hypothetically, it could help decrease the one-way dependence of smaller central banks regarding core players. However, this is not likely to happen, at least not soon, for at least two reasons.

The first one has an institutional character and has to do with the differences in the legal mandates of individual central banks, some of them being exclusively responsible for price stability (European Central Bank [ECB]); others also obliged to promote maximum employment goals and moderate long-term interest rates (the Fed) and specific guarantees of their independence anchored in national legal systems.

Second, even if the institutional obstacles were overcome, global monetary policy coordination would face a shortage of macroeconomic theory providing conceptual and analytical tools for such coordination. For the time being, there is no conceptual clarity on how to define and measure global money supply or global liquidity (see Chen et al., 2012 for an attempt to estimate global liquidity), which factors and mechanisms determine changes in global money supply (however defined), what is the role of cross-country money multipliers under various exchange rate regimes, etc. All the theoretical models of monetary policy (like the Taylor rule) analyze its determinants, tools, and consequences within a single national economy. There is no global monetary model, or there are not even sufficient external spillovers in national models.

Attempts of global macroeconomic policy coordination undertaken so far within the Multilateral Consultation framework of the IMF (see IMF, 2007) and the Group of Twenty (G-20) (see G20, 2012, paragraph 7) have focused mainly on current account imbalances and their reduction through greater nominal exchange rate flexibility.

However, it is worth admitting that in the extraordinary circumstances (GFC in 2008–2009, COVID-19 crisis in 2020–2021), core central banks coordinated their anti-crisis measures and offered other central banks liquidity support in the form of currency swaps (Fed, ECB) and repo lines (ECB in 2020–2021). On top of that, monetary expansion in core currency areas helped EMDEs overcome the effects of an adverse shock (massive capital outflows) caused by the COVID-19-related financial panics in February and March 2020 (Kalemli-Ozcan, 2020).

27.8 Conclusions

Financial globalization seems irreversible under the current circumstances despite periodic financial crises and other shocks (such as the COVID-19 pandemic). It creates a necessity to adjust economic theory and policy at both the national and global levels to unrestricted capital movements rather than the reinvention of capital controls and the isolation of individual countries from the turbulences of international markets. It is a task for academia, market analysts, policymakers, and international institutions.

Financial globalization offers numerous benefits but makes national economies more vulnerable to external shocks and dependent on global business and financial cycles (see Section 27.3). Even the best-designed national policy mix in a small open economy cannot guarantee complete immunity from external shocks triggered by policy decisions of other countries, especially the most prominent players. However, the limited room for decision-making at the country level (due to constraints imposed by international markets) should encourage national policymakers to seek greater international cooperation and coordination in micro and macroeconomic policies.

It is a formidable task and a long way to go but worth a try. It requires overcoming political constraints, building new legal and institutional frameworks, and developing a theoretical background and analytical tools for global coordination/decision-making. Smaller countries have an obvious incentive to participate in such an effort: they have already lost a substantial part of their sovereignty in macroeconomic management. However, the big players should also understand and accept the advantages of a collaborative approach and share their policy-making power: even the largest economies are not isolated from the rest of the world.

Suppose their authorities are concentrated too much on narrow domestic agendas. In that case, they risk exporting problems and distortions to others (beggar-thy-neighbor policies) with the probability that the external damage will affect them sooner or later. The decision of President Nixon's administration to abandon a gold parity of the US dollar in August 1971 (see Garten, 2021) can serve as one of the most prominent historical examples of such unilateral action. It led to dismantling of the Bretton Woods system of fixed but adjustable pegs, turbulences in the global economy in the 1970s, trade, financial, and political tensions in relations with the closest US allies (Western Europe and Japan); all of them negatively affected the US economy.

The role of an economic superpower, including the issuance of a global reserve currency, does not only come with extra privileges. It also comes with responsibilities.

To help policymakers strengthen international coordination of economic policies, the economic and other social science disciplines should develop respective theoretical models of a global economy based on a better understanding of global interlinks and spillovers and cross-country comparative research of various economic systems and policies.

Notes

1 In this chapter, I partly borrow from my previous analyses – see Dabrowski (2013, 2017, and 2018).
2 See e.g., https://www.piie.com/microsites/globalization/what-is-globalization for discussion of this concept. Following Wolf (2005, p. 14), we define economic globalization as '*the integration of economic activity across borders, through markets.*'
3 See the IMF World Economic Outlook (IMF WEO) country grouping https://www.imf.org/en/Publications/WEO/weo-database/2020/April/select-country-group.
4 Trade liberalization process was launched immediately after the WWII with conclusion of the General Agreement on Tariffs and Trade (GATT) in 1947, but it was limited to trade in goods between then AEs and progressed rather slowly – see https://www.wto.org/english/news_e/news17_e/gen_30oct17_e.htm.
5 See also Batini and Durand (2020) for a similar picture.
6 See https://www.imf.org/en/Publications/WEO/weo-database/2021/April/weo-report?a=1&c=001,110,200,&s=TRADEPCH,&sy=2007&ey=2010&ssm=0&scsm=1&scc=0&ssd=1&ssc=0&sic=0&sort=country&ds=.&br=1.
7 Volatility of oil and some other commodity prices can be reduced or deepened by actions of producers' cartels such as the Organization of the Petroleum Exporting Countries (OPEC) or governments who manage strategic reserves.
8 See IMF (2012, Box 2) on the differences between capital flow management instruments and macroprudential measures and their potential overlaps.
9 Think about a series of speculative attacks against the European Exchange-Rate Mechanism ERM in 1992–1993 – see Buiter et al. (1998).
10 Potentially private virtual (digital) currencies such as the Bitcoin can join this competition. However, such a scenario is unlikely to happen soon due to continuous technical shortcomings of existing private currencies and regulatory restrictions on their use (Prasad, 2021).
11 The classification of borrowing sources based on residence is not identical with the currency of borrowing. In the world of unrestricted capital movement, non-residents can purchase government securities and lend to the government in its national currency, and residents can finance public debt denominated in a foreign currency.
12 See Zucman (2015) for the historical analysis of tax havens and attempt to estimate the scale of tax avoidance caused by their existence.
13 See https://www.consilium.europa.eu/en/policies/eu-list-of-non-cooperative-jurisdictions/ for the one adopted on February 22, 2021.

References

Asdrubali, P. and Kim, S. (2008). Incomplete Intertemporal Consumption Smoothing and Incomplete Risk Sharing, *Journal of Money, Credit and Banking*, Vol. 40, Issue 7, pp. 1521–1531. https://doi.org/10.1111/j.1538-4616.2008.00170.x
Baba, C. and Kokenyne, A. (2011). Effectiveness of capital controls in selected emerging markets in the 2000s, *IMF Working Paper*, WP/11/281, December, https://www.imf.org/-/media/Websites/IMF/imported-full-text-pdf/external/pubs/ft/wp/2011/_wp11281.ashx

Batini, N. and Durand, L. (2020). Analysis and Advice on Capital Account Developments: Flows, Restrictions and Policy Toolkits, *IEO Background Paper*, BP20-02/02, Independent Evaluation Office of the International Monetary Fund, August 18, https://ieo.imf.org/-/media/IEO/Files/evaluations/completed/09-30-2020-imf-advice-on-capital-flows/cfm-bp03-analysis-and-advice-on-capital-account-developments-flows-restrictions-and-policy-toolki.ashx

Bogdanova, B., Chan, T., Micic, K. and von Peter, G. (2021). Enhancing the BIS government bond statistics, *BIS Quarterly Review*, Bank for International Settlements, June, pp. 15–24, https://www.bis.org/publ/qtrpdf/r_qt2106.pdf

Bordo, M.D., Eichengreen, B. and Irvin, D.A. (1999). Is Globalization Today Really Different than Globalization a Hundred Years Ago? *NBER Working Paper*, No. 7195, June, https://www.nber.org/system/files/working_papers/w7195/w7195.pdf

Borio, C. (2018). Macroprudential frameworks: experience, prospects and a way forward, Speech by Mr. Claudio Borio, Head of the Monetary and Economic Department of the BIS, on the occasion of the Bank's Annual General Meeting, Basel, June 24, 2018, https://www.bis.org/speeches/sp180624a.pdf

Buiter, W.H., Corsetti, G.M. and Pesenti, P.A. (1998). Interpreting the ERM Crisis: Country-Specific and Systemic Issues, *Princeton Studies in International Finance*, No. 84, March, International Economics Section, Department of Economics Princeton University, https://econpapers.repec.org/RePEc:fth:prinfi:84

Chen, S., Liu, P., Maechler, A., Marsh, C., Saksonovs, S. and Shin, H.S. (2012). Exploring the dynamics of global liquidity, *IMF Working Paper*, WP/12/246, http://www.imf.org/external/pubs/ft/wp/2012/wp12246.pdf

Chinn, M.D. and Ito, H. (2006). What Matters for Financial Development? Capital Controls, Institutions, and Interactions, *Journal of Development Economics*, Vol. 81, Issue 1, October, pp. 163–192. http://web.pdx.edu/~ito/w11370.pdf

Dabrowski, M. (2006). Rethinking Balance-of-Payments Constraints in a Globalized World, *CASE Network Studies and Analyses*, No. 330, http://www.case-research.eu/sites/default/files/publications/11517190_sa330_0.pdf

Dabrowski, M. (2013). Managing Capital Flows in a Globalized Economy, in Nowotny, E., Mooslechner, P. and Ritzberger-Gruenwald, D. (eds.). *A New Model for Balanced Growth and Convergence. Achieving Economic Sustainability in CESEE Countries*, Cheltenham and Northampton, MA: Edward Elgar.

Dabrowski, M. (2017). *Fiscal Sustainability Challenges*, Beau Bassin: LAP Lambert Academic Publishing, https://www.morebooks.de/store/gb/book/fiscal-sustainability-challenges/isbn/978-3-330-06656-4?currency=EUR

Dabrowski, M. (2018). Examining Interrelation between Global and National Income Inequalities, *Russian Journal of Economics*, Vol. 4, Issue 3, pp. 266–284. https://rujec.org/article/30170/download/pdf/

Dabrowski, M. (2021). Thinking Beyond the Pandemic: Monetary Policy Challenges in the Medium- to Long-Term, briefing paper prepared for the European Parliament's Committee on Economic and Monetary Affairs (Monetary Dialogue March 2021), March 4, PE 658.221, http://www.europarl.europa.eu/cmsdata/230556/CASE_formatted.pdf

Dabrowski, M. and Dominguez-Jimenez, M. (2020). Emerging market central banks and quantitative easing- high-risk advice, *Bruegel blog*, August 26, https://www.bruegel.org/2020/08/emerging-market-central-banks-and-quantitative-easing-high-risk-advice/

Feldstein, M. and Horioka, C. (1980). Domestic Saving and International Capital Flows, *Economic Journal*, Vol. 90, pp. 314–329, June.

Forbes, K.J. (2005). The Microeconomic Evidence on Capital Controls: No Free Lunch, *NBER Working Paper*, No. 11372, May, https://www.nber.org/system/files/working_papers/w11372/w11372.pdf

Frankel, J.A. (1999). No Single Currency Regime is Right for All Countries or at All Times, NBER Working Paper, No. 7338, September, https://www.nber.org/system/files/working_papers/w7338/w7338.pdf

G20. (2012). Communiqué of Ministers of Finance and Central Bank Governors of the G20, Mexico City, November, 4-5, http://www.g20mexico.org/index.php/en/press-releases/537-final-communique

Gallagher, K.P. (2012). Regaining Control? Capital Controls and the Global Financial Crisis, in Grant, W. and Wilson, G.K. (eds.). *The Consequences of the Global Financial Crisis: The Rhetoric of Reform and Regulation*, Oxford: Oxford University Press, https://oxford.universitypressscholarship.com/view/10.1093/acprof:oso/9780199641987.001.0001/acprof-9780199641987-chapter-7

Garten, J.E. (2021). *Three Days at Camp David: How a Secret Meeting in 1971 Transformed the Global Economy*, New York, NY: Harper Collins.

Ghosh, A.R., Kim, J.I., Qureshi, M.S. and Zalduendo, J. (2012). Surges, *IMF Working Paper*, WP/12/22, January, https://www.imf.org/external/pubs/ft/wp/2012/wp1222.pdf

Hausmann, R. (2001). The Polish road to the Euro: An envious Latin American view, paper prepared for the Conference on 'The Polish Way to the Euro' organized by the National Bank of Poland, October 22–23.

IMF. (2007). Staff Report on the multilateral consultation on global imbalances with China, the euro area, Japan, Saudi Arabia, and the United States, June 29, http://www.imf.org/external/np/pp/2007/eng/062907.pdf

IMF. (2012). The liberalization and management of capital flows: An institutional view, *IMF Policy Paper*, November 14, http://www.imf.org/external/np/pp/eng/2012/111412.pdf

Ito, H. and Chinn, M. (2020). Notes on The Chinn-Ito Financial Openness Index 2018 Update, July 12, http://web.pdx.edu/~ito/Readme_kaopen2018.pdf

Jaumotte, F., Lall, S. and Papageorgiou, C. (2008). Rising Income Inequality: Technology, or Trade and Financial Globalization? *IMF Working Papers*, WP/08/185, July, http://www.imf.org/~/media/websites/imf/imported-full-text-pdf/external/pubs/ft/wp/2008/_wp08185.ashx

Kalemli-Ozcan, S. (2020). Emerging Market Capital Flows under COVID: What to Expect Given What We Know, *Special Series on COVID-19*, The International Monetary Fund, September 16, https://www.imf.org/-/media/Files/Publications/COVID19-special-notes/en-special-series-on-COVID-19-emerging-market-capital-flows-under-COVID.ashx

Keuschnigg, C., Loretz, S. and Winner, H. (2016). Tax Competition and Tax Coordination in the European Union, in Badinger, H. and Nitsch, V. (eds.). *Routledge Handbook of the Economics of European Integration*, London and New York, NY: Routledge.

Kose, M.A., Nagle, P., Ohnsorge, F. and Sugawara, N. (2021). *Global Waves of Debt: Causes and Consequences*, Washington, DC: World Bank, https://openknowledge.worldbank.org/handle/10986/32809

Kose, M.A., Prasad, E., Rogoff, K. and Wei, S.-J. (2010). Financial Globalization and Economic Policies, in Rodrik, D. and Rosenzweig, M. (eds.). *Handbook of Development Economics*, Elsevier, Vol. 5, Chapter 65, pp. 4283–4359, https://doi.org/10.1016/B978-0-444-52944-2.00003-3

Lang, V.L. and Mendes Tavares, M. (2018). The Distribution of Gains from Globalization, *IMF Working Paper*, WP/18/54, March, http://www.imf.org/~/media/Files/Publications/WP/2018/wp1854.ashx

Maskin, E. (2015). Why Haven't Global Markets Reduced Inequality in Emerging Economies? *World Bank Economic Review*, Vol. 29, Supplement, pp. S48–S52. https://scholar.harvard.edu/files/maskin/files/world_bank_econ_rev-2015-maskin-s48-52.pdf

Milanovic, B. (2016). *Global Inequality: A New Approach for the Age of Globalization*, Cambridge, MA: Harvard University Press.

Morys, M., Daudin, G. and O'Rourke, K.H. (2008). Globalization 1870-1914, *Economics Series Working Papers*, No. 395, May, University of Oxford, Department of Economics, https://ideas.repec.org/p/oxf/wpaper/395.html#download

O'Rourke, K.H. and Williamson, J.G. (2000). When Did Globalization Begin? *NBER Working Paper*, No. 7632, April, https://www.nber.org/system/files/working_papers/w7632/w7632.pdf

Obstfeld, M., Shambaugh, J.C. and Taylor, A.M. (2004). The Trilemma in History: Tradeoffs among Exchange Rates, Monetary Policies, and Capital Mobility, *NBER Working Paper*, No. 10396, March, https://www.nber.org/system/files/working_papers/w10396/w10396.pdf

OECD. (2012). *OECD Code of Liberalization of Capital Movements*, http://www.oecd.org/daf/internationalinvestment/investmentpolicy/39664826.pdf

Ostry, J., Ghosh, A.R. and Korinek, A. (2012). Multilateral Aspects of Managing the Capital Account, *IMF Staff Discussion Note*, SDN/12/10, September 7, https://www.imf.org/-/media/Websites/IMF/imported-full-text-pdf/external/pubs/ft/sdn/2012/_sdn1210.ashx

Prasad, E.S. (2021). Five myths about cryptocurrency, *Brookings Opinions*, May 24, https://www.brookings.edu/opinions/five-myths-about-cryptocurrency/?

Prasad, E.S., Rogoff, K., Wei, S.-J. and Kose, M.A. (2003). Effects of Financial Globalization on Developing Countries: Some Empirical Evidence, *IMF Occasional Paper*, No. 220, https://www.imf.org/external/pubs/nft/op/220/index.htm

Rappeport, A. (2021). Finance Leaders Reach Global Tax Deal Aimed at Ending Profit Shifting, *New York Times*, June 11, https://www.nytimes.com/2021/06/05/us/politics/g7-global-minimum-tax.html

Rey, H. (2013). Dilemma Not Trilemma: The Global Financial Cycle and Monetary Policy Independence, http://www.helenerey.eu/AjaxRequestHandler.ashx?Function=GetSecuredDOC& DOCUrl=App_Data/helenerey_eu/Published-Papers_en-GB/_Documents_2015-16/ 147802013_67186463733_jacksonholedraftweb.pdf

Rodrik, D. (2009). The IMF Needs Fresh Thinking on Capital Controls, *Project Syndicate*, November 11, http://www.project-syndicate.org/commentary/the-imf-needs-fresh-thinking-on-capital-controls

Rostowski, J. (2001). The Approach to EU and EMU Membership: The Implication for Macro-economic Policy in the Applicant Countries, in Dabrowski, M. and Rostowski, J. (eds.). *The Eastern Enlargement of the EU*, Boston/Dordrecht/London: Kluwer Academic Publishers.

Sachs, J.D. (2017). America, we still have a jobs problem, CNN.com, July 7, http://edition.cnn. com/2017/07/07/opinions/americas-jobs-problem-sachs/index.html

Stiglitz, J. (2016). Globalization and its new discontents, *Project Syndicate*, August 5, https://www.project-syndicate.org/commentary/globalization-new-discontents-by-joseph-e–stiglitz–2016-08

Summers, L.H. (1996). Commentary, in Hausmann, R. and Rojas-Suarez, L. (eds.). *Volatile Capital Flows*, Washington, DC: Inter-American Development Bank.

Valero, J. (2020). Finance ministers to discuss fiscal dumping inside the EU at Berlin meeting, *EURACTIV.com*, September 8, https://www.euractiv.com/section/economy-jobs/news/finance-ministers-to-discuss-fiscal-dumping-inside-the-eu-at-berlin-meeting/

Wolf, M. (2005). Why Globalization Works, *Yale Nota Bene*, New Haven, CT, and London: Yale University Press.

Zucman, G. (2015). *The Hidden Wealth of Nations: The Scourge of Tax Havens*, Chicago, IL, and London: University of Chicago Press.

28

INTERNATIONAL TAX EVASION

Sources, Paths, and Destinations

David M. Kemme

FOGELMAN COLLEGE OF BUSINESS AND ECONOMICS,
UNIVERSITY OF MEMPHIS, MEMPHIS, TENNESSEE, USA

Bhavik Parikh

GERALD SCHWARTZ SCHOOL OF BUSINESS, ST. FRANCIS XAVIER UNIVERSITY,
ANTIGONISH, NOVA SCOTIA, CANADA

Tanja Steigner

SCHOOL OF BUSINESS, EMPORIA STATE UNIVERSITY, EMPORIA, KANSAS, USA

28.1 Introduction

Personal tax evasion via international offshore financial centers has garnered worldwide attention. One prime example is the publication of the *Panama Papers* (leaked internal files from the Panamanian law firm Mossack Fonseca) in 2016 by the International Consortium of Investigative Journalists (ICIJ). These files contained information on approximately 215,000 offshore entities connected to individuals in more than 200 countries and territories.[1] After the leak, governments have recouped around $1.36 billion in unpaid taxes, fines, and penalties. The impact of this leak can still be felt all over the world. Recently, the U.S. Securities and Exchange Commission charged several Canadians for violating anti-fraud provisions of the U.S. Security Act.[2]

In the fall of 2021, the ICIJ, which now consists of more than 600 journalists in 117 countries, leaked close to 12 million documents that demonstrate that even after the *Panama Papers* exposure, the use of offshore havens has not slowed down. On the contrary, the *Pandora Papers* disclose 14 offshore service providers involved in setting up companies in tax havens, more than 300 politicians who use such offshore companies, the location of other beneficiaries of these companies, and U.S. states that allow trusts as a tax shelter vehicle.[3,4]

While there has been much recent public attention, international tax evasion has been the focus of government tax authorities and multilateral organizations for several decades. The OECD has had an ongoing program of research and policy guidance since the early 2000s, and at the 2009 London Summit, it took the lead against tax evasion, bank secrecy, and tax havens, as well as tax avoidance by corporations.[5]

The evasion of domestic taxes by individuals is not uncommon but varies significantly across countries. For individuals of financial means and sophistication, international evasion methods have become ever more attractive. This review focuses primarily on personal rather than corporate tax evasion. Still, we briefly discuss corporate motivations and behavior, but only to the extent that tax evasion strategies by corporations are similar to those by individuals, and the motivations serve as a foundation for the examination of personal tax evasion. In doing so, we identify motives and methods for international tax evasion. Next, we define what tax havens are and discuss country as well as systemic characteristics and policies that influence international tax evasion. Further, we also examine the economic impact and policies, such as tax amnesties, to prevent evasion.

The following section provides an overview of the differences between tax avoidance and tax evasion for personal and corporate taxpayers. In Section 28.3, we focus on motivations for tax evasion, and in Section 28.4, we focus on the characteristics of tax havens. We then describe the characteristics of economies that are the predominant source of international portfolio flows associated with tax evasion. For example, these include macroeconomic factors and transportation costs; personal factors, such as tax morale, wealth, and tax rates; and systemic characteristics, such as autocracy, income inequality, and sovereign wealth funds (SWFs).

28.2 Tax avoidance (planning) vs. tax evasion: General overview

The methods, magnitudes, and determinants of corporate and personal tax evasion are quite different. Corporate tax avoidance is often closely related to evasion, and both have similar determinants. We discuss corporate tax avoidance, corporate tax evasion, and personal tax evasion below for a general overview of the topic.

28.2.1 Corporate tax avoidance

Tax avoidance, commonly called tax planning, is the legal strategy of taking advantage of the tax law to minimize taxes owed. Graham (2003) provides an excellent review of the impact of taxes on domestic and multinational corporations (MNCs). He explores the apparent paradox that corporations do not pursue tax benefits as aggressively as potential benefits would suggest. Desai and Dharmapala (2006) conclude that managers who receive more incentive compensation tend to engage less in tax sheltering. A related study finds that tax avoidance schemes have no impact on firm value in general. However, the firm value increases when well-governed firms with little opportunity for rent diversion engage in tax avoidance (Desai and Dharmapala, 2009). Various incentives, capabilities, and opportunities to avoid paying corporate taxes result in different levels of long-term effective tax rates. Dyreng *et al.* (2008) report that one-quarter of their U.S. sample firms paid less than a 20% effective tax rate over ten years. In comparison, the average effective tax rate was 30%, and the nominal tax rate during the 1995–2004 sample period was 35%. Compared to U.S. firms, European firms have experienced a declining difference between the nominal and effective tax rates due to tax avoidance (Thomsen and Watrin, 2018). Additional studies reveal that tax avoidance via tax shelters is positively related to the firm's information technology capabilities (Hamilton and Stekelberg, 2016), level of institutional ownership (Khan *et al.*, 2016), and lack of brand name capital (Austin and Wilson, 2017).

28.2.2 Corporate tax evasion

While tax avoidance or tax planning efforts that minimize tax liabilities are perfectly legal activities, tax evasion is not. Individuals and companies evade taxes by not reporting certain income from labor or capital (Sandmo, 2005).[6] When owners pay managers to engage in tax evasion schemes, they must compensate managers *ex-ante* for their efforts to minimize detection risk and the associated monetary penalties to the managers.

The additional incentive pay is necessary because the courts will not enforce any contract that promises extra compensation for penalties after illegal activities are detected (Chen and Chu, 2005). Hanlon *et al.* (2007) confirm that tax-evading firms offer their executives higher bonuses and more stock options. Joulfaian (2000) shows that managers tend to have a specific predisposition to act in that capacity. Evaluating a random sample of 11,528 U.S. corporate income tax returns filed in 1987, he finds that managers of tax-evading firms are three times more likely to understate their own personal taxes than managers of non-evading firms. As far as penalties are concerned, they are more effective in deterring tax evasion when they target the tax manager instead of the shareholders (Crocker and Slemrod, 2005).

Specific firm characteristics seem to make corporate tax evasion more likely. For example, larger firms, multinational firms, and privately held firms (Hanlon *et al.*, 2007) and U.S. corporations with owners from countries that are considered to be highly corrupt tend to engage more in tax evasion (DeBacker *et al.*, 2015). "Tax-dodging" by such large MNCs has led the European Commission to consider new proposals such as complete financial disclosure of multinationals to all European countries.[7]

Kourdoumpalou (2016) examines the relationship between corporate governance practices and tax evasion for Greek publicly listed companies. The tax gap is used as the measurement of tax evasion. His results point out that tax evasion is lower for companies whose chairman of the board is also one of the part owners of the company. Furthermore, the percentage of the stock held by the owner, the family members, and the board members all lead to a lower association with tax evasion.

Jansky and Prats (2015) examine the role of tax havens from the perspective of Indian MNCs. Looking at the financial and ownership data of 1,500 MNCs, they find that MNCs with links to tax havens report lower profits and pay lower taxes than MNCs without such ties. Thus, profit-shifting strategies can significantly reduce the government's tax revenues, which seriously undermines efforts to tackle socio-economic issues in India. In addition, the current transfer pricing regulation might not be effective in tackling tax evasion caused by the profit-shifting behavior of MNCs (Jansky and Prats, 2015).

Country characteristics further increase the likelihood of tax evasion behavior. For example, Tsakumis *et al.* (2007) use Hofstede's (1980) cultural index scores and find that a country's cultural profile also plays a role in tax evasion.[8] Specifically, they found that countries with high uncertainty avoidance and power distance and low individualism and masculinity are linked to more significant tax evasion.[9] Richardson (2006), using data from 47 countries, combines culture and other institutional variables to study their impact on tax evasion. He finds that countries with a higher level of uncertainty avoidance and lower level of individualism, legal enforcement, trust in government, and religiosity indicate a higher level of tax evasion.

Khlif *et al.* (2016) examine the relationship between the level of sustainability and tax evasion for 65 developed and developing countries. They also test whether corruption can moderate the relationship between sustainability and tax evasion. Their results show that the level of tax evasion is negatively associated with the level of sustainability and the quality of the infrastructure for countries with low corruption. On the other hand, countries with high corruption have an insignificant relationship between tax evasion and sustainability. Individuals in countries with low corruption tend to accept and trust their government and comply with the tax rules.

There are countries where tax evasion is more prevalent due to the size of their shadow economy.[10] Cobham (2005) estimates that most evaded taxes come from the shadow economy, followed equally by corporate misconduct and individuals with offshore asset holdings.

The size of the shadow economy varies widely, even in developed economies. For example, IMF (2021) reports the European Union average of 22.9%, emerging market economies 33.6%, and the CIS countries 40.8% in 2019. The estimated average "tax gap" for the EU-28 was 10.7% in 2014, or an average of about 51.9 billion USD per country (Raczkowski (2015)). These estimates are trending upward from earlier studies. Russia is a country with reportedly high corruption (Levin and Satarov, 2000) and a shadow economy of 44% of GDP in 2013 (Fakhrutdinova *et al.*, 2015). Yet, their new flat tax system of 2001 has reduced tax evasion, most significantly from individuals who benefited the most from lower tax rates (Gorodnichenko *et al.*, 2009).

Thus, factors such as cultural profile, the predisposition of managers, size of the shadow economy, corporate governance, corruption, and potential corporate misconduct have been identified as determinants of corporate domestic tax evasion. We will return to country characteristics concerning personal tax evasion in Section 28.5.

In the recent past, incriminating documents have been leaked that made international headlines. Most notably, the 2021 *Pandora Papers* revealed 130 billionaires with hidden offshore accounts, including "[a]mbassadors, mayors and ministers, presidential advisers, generals, and a central bank governor" (Shiel, 2021). *Bahama Leaks* shared data from about 175,888 shell corporations and trusts in the Bahamas in 2016. *Offshore Leaks* provided 2.5 million documents covering 130,000 offshore accounts and pointing to tax avoidance and/or evasion via trusts in 2013. Further, the *Paradise Papers* leaked offshore investment information in 2017 that included high-profile companies such as AIG, members of royal families, and politicians.

One of the most famous tax evasion scandals was uncovered with the *Panama Papers*, exposing shell corporation schemes by the Panamanian law firm Mossack Fonseca in 2016.

O'Donovan *et al.* (2019) discuss three primary reasons to create offshore shell corporations. First, firms may use these offshore vehicles to finance bribes to win contracts tendered by corrupt government officials. Second, firms may use offshore shell corporations to avoid or evade taxes to create firm value. Lastly, managers might find it easier to extract resources for their personal gain in poorly governed firms using these offshore financial corporations.

28.2.3 *Personal tax evasion*

We now turn to tax evasion on the personal level. The decision to evade is often described as a portfolio optimization problem (Auerbach and King, 1983), where, based on the classic frameworks of Becker (1968) and Allingham and Sandmo (1972), one weighs the benefits of tax evasion against the risk of detection and its associated consequences.[11] There are two main avenues for tax evasion by individuals: underreporting/omitting income and over-reporting costs in general and concealing assets and capital income by placement in offshore shell corporations in tax havens.

Focusing on the underreporting of earned income, Clotfelter (1983) finds a positive relationship between marginal tax rates and underreporting. Friedland *et al.* (1978) further report that the probability of underreporting increases for unmarried individuals. The amount of underreporting increases with the tax rate for male taxpayers and married individuals, while it decreases with the taxpayer's age. Benedek and Lelkes (2011) review tax records of 230,000 taxpayers in Hungary and conclude that the self-employed evade more taxes than employees, and high-income taxpayers evade proportionally more. This behavior diminishes the progressive nature of the tax system. Likewise, tax evasion via underreporting in Greece reduces the principle of progressivity of the income tax system, with an increase in income inequality and poverty (Matsaganis and Flevotomou, 2010). The evasion by Swiss taxpayers further increases with inflation and decreases when taxpayers have more direct control of public budgets (Pommerehne and Weck-Hannemann, 1996). But who precisely underreports their earnings/income? Alstadsæter *et al.* (2019, Figure 7) show that in Scandinavian countries, taxpayers in the 0–99.5th percentile of total wealth distribution evade an average of 6% of their owed taxes via underreporting earned income, as determined by random audits. However, the wealthiest 0.01% of the taxpayers evade 30% of owed taxes via sophisticated offshore evasion (as determined by leaks).

Scandinavian countries are, of course, not alone in evading taxes by holding assets in tax havens. Alstadsæter *et al.* (2018, Figure 5) show that Scandinavian countries and the U.S. actually hold less of household wealth offshore relative to their GDP than the world average of 9.8%, while most other European countries (including the U.K.), Russia, Saudi Arabia, and the UAE are among the countries with the most extensive household wealth holdings offshore relative to their GDP. If unreported, these assets represent tax evasion due to the omission of capital income. Gravelle (2009) expects lost revenue to the IRS based on an expected USD 1.5 trillion of offshore wealth to range between USD 33–50 billion, with global losses equal to USD 255 billion. Similarly, Zucman (2017) estimates that the top elite households hold a combined wealth of $8.7 trillion offshore via tax shelters. Although the amount of offshore wealth held in tax havens has been increasing, the number of individuals holding the wealth has decreased, and only the wealthiest of the wealthy are able to bypass stricter rules and safely shelter assets in shell corporations, trusts, foundations, and holdings (Zucman, 2014). Johannesen and Zucman (2014) focus on tax evasion using bank deposits in a tax haven. They conclude that evaders will transfer their assets into countries that do not have tax exchange agreements with their home country if their current tax haven location signs such an agreement. Kemme *et al.* (2017, 2020) also examine tax evasion of the wealthy via shell corporations and illustrate how these schemes are designed.

To summarize, underreporting of income taxes is prevalent at almost all income levels; however, international evasion of taxes via tax havens is unique to the financial elite (Kemme *et al.*, 2020).

28.3 Motivations for personal tax evasion

The U.S. Government Accountability Office announced a $458 billion annual gross tax gap between 2008 and 2010. After late payment and penalties, the IRS estimated a remaining annual net tax gap of $406 billion for the same time period. This is the amount that U.S. tax authorities are unable to collect (US GAO, 2019). These amounts are growing and have recently been a significant topic of discussion by the U.S. Congress. Among the most widely discussed motivations to evade taxes is the magnitude of personal wealth, country tax rates, the likelihood of discovery and its consequence, personal level of tax morale, and trust in public institutions (Christensen, 2011). Each of these motivations is discussed below.

28.3.1 Personal wealth

Of course, the more wealth an individual accumulates over time, the larger the annual tax obligation on the income produced becomes. Hence, it makes sense that the incentive of *preserving* one's wealth is more pronounced in wealthier individuals. A conservative estimate is that about 8% of global wealth is stored in offshore accounts, much more than officially reported to worldwide tax authorities (Zucman, 2014). As a result, the wealthiest 0.01% seemingly evade approximately 25% of taxes on income produced by their wealth by keeping unreported assets offshore; in Norway, the top 0.1% of households keep 50% of their wealth overseas (Alstadsæter *et al.*, 2019). The U.S. accounts for 20.4% of global offshore wealth, valued at $2.2 trillion, with an estimated loss of tax revenues (to U.S. tax authorities) equal to $40.1 billion per year (Tax Justice Network, 2020).

28.3.2 Tax rates

Another logical conclusion is that all else equal, tax evasion is more prevalent in countries with high tax burdens. Bernasconi *et al.* (2014) present a theoretical framework of tax evasion, followed by a laboratory experiment, concluding that tax evasion increases with increasing tax rates. Chiarini *et al.* (2013) also link tax rates to evasion using Italian time-series data. Similarly, Hanlon *et al.* (2015) show this for the U.S. and Kemme *et al.* (2017) for a large sample of countries, both examining roundtripping of assets via tax havens. Fisman and Wei (2004) examine the effect of tax rates on tax evasion in China. Their results imply that a one percentage point increase in tax rates is associated with a 3% increase in tax evasion. They also indicate that when China receives imports from Hong Kong, Chinese companies underreport the value of imports and mislabel higher tax products as lower tax products. According to OECD data, countries that have the highest statutory net personal tax rate on dividend income include Ireland (51%), Korea (43.95%), Denmark (42%), Canada (39.34%), U.K. (38.10%), France (34%), Chile (33.33%), Norway (31.68%), Belgium, (30%), Sweden (30%), and the U.S. (28.91%).[12] Of these countries, three contribute most to total global offshore wealth: U.S. (20.4%), U.K. (12.2%), and Ireland (5.6%) (Tax Justice Network, 2020).[13] Hence, not all residents of countries with high tax rates send their wealth offshore with equal passion.

28.3.3 Likelihood of discovery

Pommerehne and Weck-Hannemann (1996) find a negative but weak relation between tax evasion and the likelihood of a tax audit. This finding supports Klepper and Nagin's (1989a, b) conclusion that the perception of detection and criminal prosecution deters tax evasion (also see Becker, 1968; Allingham and Sandmo, 1972; Sandmo, 2005). To avoid detection, however, evaders will move wealth from countries willing to share information with the evader's home country to countries that maintain discretion (Johannesen and Zucman, 2014).

Murphy (2008) also finds that tax evaders in Australia, who feel poorly treated by the tax authorities, develop resentment against paying taxes and are more likely to evade again. In contrast, evaders who felt treated respectfully are less likely to evade in the future. Hence, being shamed by authorities is not necessarily a deterrent but, on the contrary, can lower an evader's level of tax law compliance or tax morale.

28.3.4 Tax morale

An individual's attitude towards paying taxes is their tax morale; clearly, it is low in tax evaders. Factors that influence one's tax morale include age, religion, financial stress, support of government decisions, and education (Lago-Peñas and Lago-Peñas, 2010). Additional factors include moral rules, fairness, and the relationship between taxpayers and government (Torgler, 2001). In addition to measuring tax morale in individuals, we can also measure a country's level of tax morale (OECD, 2019). A country has low tax morale if citizens perceive evading taxes as acceptable (Kemme *et al.*, 2020). The more people participate in evasion, the lower the probability of detection by the tax authorities (Sandmo, 2005). The level of a country's tax morale can be ascertained via the World Value Survey (Kemme *et al.*, 2020; Norris and Inglehart, 2003). We see that tax morale is related to morality in general. Countries that rank high in morality view tax evasion as a moral cost and tend to evade less (Lee, 2016).

28.3.5 Trust in public institutions

In countries where the population generally trusts public government institutions and other individuals to pay their taxes, tax evasion is less prevalent (Wintrobe and Gërxhani, 2004). Using the World Values Survey and its question regarding if people can be trusted,[14] Kanagaretnam *et al.* (2018) developed a societal trust measure and found that countries with higher trust evade less. If taxes are perceived to be fair, people are more likely to pay their share and not try to evade it (Niesiobędzka, 2014). Hammar *et al.* (2009) show that distrust in politicians increases tax evasion. They also note that distrust in politicians is more critical than distrust in fellow citizens regarding tax evasion.

28.4 Characteristics of tax havens

The OECD (1998) bases its definition of a tax haven on four key indicators:

1. No or only nominal taxes (a place where non-residents escape from the taxation in their home country)
2. Lack of transparency (such as the absence of beneficial ownership information and bank secrecy)
3. Unwillingness to exchange information with the tax administrations of OECD member countries
4. Absence of a requirement that activity is substantial (transactions may be "booked" in the country with no or little real economic activity)

Most, but not all, researchers design their classifications around these criteria.

Hines and Rice (1994) classify 41 countries as tax havens. They note that there were seven tax haven countries during the 1990s with a population of above one million, which account for more than 80% of the total population and 89% of GDP for the sample of tax havens. The remaining 34 tax haven countries (population less than 200,000), commonly called "Dots," control about 60% of assets, net income, and equity in tax havens. Hines (2005) confirms that tax havens have a small population and high GDP per capita. Of course, low corporate tax rates also attract foreign companies to register in tax havens to avoid high home country tax rates.

Other characteristics may also be considered. For example, Dharmapala and Hines (2009) note that tax havens tend to be located near countries that are significant capital exporters.

In addition, most tax haven countries score high on governance quality measures like voice and accountability, political stability, government effectiveness, the rule of law, and control of corruption. Other common traits for tax haven countries are British Legal Origins, primarily English-speaking countries, a parliamentary legal system, a highly developed communication infrastructure, and scarce natural resources.

Hines (2005) notes that tax haven economies grew at an average annual real per capita rate of 3.3% compared to 1.4% for the rest of the world from 1982 to 1999. Mara's (2015) analysis shows that the percentage of services in GDP and the growth in the financial and legal services are essential factors for tax havens to be effective. The services and infrastructure of countries identified as tax havens vary significantly. Tax havens can be classified based on the financial and other services to both individuals and corporations. Hampton and Christensen (2002) divide tax havens into three fundamental categories, functional tax havens, notional tax havens, and hybrid tax havens.[15] Functional tax havens provide financial activities. They offer full bank branches and other financial services such as offshore fund management, trust companies, etc. (e.g., Bermuda, Jersey, Guernsey, and the Isle of Man). Notional tax havens house shell, "brass plate," or "cubicle" bank offices that make book entries of financial transactions (e.g., Anguilla, Vanuatu, the Cook Islands, and Seychelles). Hybrid tax havens host a mixture of functional and notional activities (e.g., The Bahamas and the Cayman Islands).

Alternatively, Palan *et al.* (2011) classify countries as corporate tax havens if they offer incorporation centers with low regulation or tax rates: registration centers (e.g., British Virgin Islands, Panama); secrecy locations (e.g., Liechtenstein); specialist service providers (e.g., Bermuda, Isle of Man); and market-entry conduits (e.g., the Netherlands).

28.5 Characteristics of source (tax-evading) countries

Previous research has found significant tax evasion via foreign portfolio flows, yet the magnitudes differ significantly from country to country. Thus, to understand the determinants of flows associated explicitly with tax evasion, we must first identify and control for other determinants of foreign portfolio investments (FPIs). These may be broadly categorized as (1) traditional determinants, (2) systemic and institutional determinants, including the role of government autocracy and SWFs, and (3) cultural differences, including tax morale and familiarity. Discussing them below, we explicitly note when and if these factors contribute to tax evasion, mainly through tax havens. We also describe the unique aspects of transition economies that may contribute to tax evasion. Here, we discuss each group of determinants. In Section 28.6, which follows, we look at economic policies and tax rate issues.

28.5.1 Traditional determinants

FPI is directly related to investment opportunities (Doukas, 1985), which is typically proxied by market size as measured by GDP or GDP per capita (Portes and Rey, 2005). Fewer domestic investment opportunities suggest that investors will look abroad for opportunities in larger economies. These measures are positively correlated with FPI inflows in general and are also more desirable locations for individuals that wish to evade taxes. In addition, the overall size of the domestic capital market matters. Larger capital markets provide greater liquidity and depth and are more efficient, highly desirable characteristics for investors. For example, Aggarawal *et al.* (2012) and Kemme *et al.* (2021) find the size of the capital market to be highly correlated with tax evasion via international portfolio flows. Furthermore, for a sample of 30 countries, Riahi-Belkaoui (2004) finds, *inter alia*, that the perceived importance of the equity market in providing financing opportunities for the production of private goods improves tax morale and lowers tax evasion. Information costs, information asymmetries, and transaction costs, as proxied by distance (Portes and Rey, 2005), are essential determinants of roundtripping (Kemme *et al.*, 2021).

28.5.2 Systemic and cultural determinants

While purely economic determinants of tax evasion are clearly important, early research suggests that non-economic determinants may be more important for domestic personal tax evasion. For example, Strielkowski and Čábelková (2015) analyze the impact of culture and religion on tax evasions in the Czech Republic. They find that religiosity for church-visiting attendees results in higher tax compliance. However, Jun and Yoon (2018) show a statistically insignificant relationship between religiosity and tax evasion in South Korea. Similarly, Khalil and Sidani (2020) find no linkage between Lebanon's tax evasion attitudes and religiosity levels.

In a review article, Jackson and Milliron (1986) identify several common demographic, economic, and behavioral variables contributing to domestic tax evasion. In a follow-on review and analysis, Richardson (2006), using a 45-country sample, found that the tax code complexity, level of education, source of income, perceived fairness, and tax morale are significantly related to domestic tax evasion.[16] However, there has been less research on the role of these factors for tax evasion via international routes. We contribute to the tax evasion literature by focusing more closely on factors indirectly associated with economic determinants of international tax evasion at the country level.

28.5.3 Income inequality

Unequal income distribution suggests that high-income individuals have higher savings to invest domestically and abroad. The recent rise in income inequality is most pronounced at the highest end of the income distribution in most countries (Jaumotte *et al.*, 2013). This observation suggests that a larger pool of wealthy individuals may evade taxes in some way. The role of income inequality as a determinant of FPI flows is complicated and also linked to other country characteristics. Kemme *et al.* (2021) find that OECD countries attract more FPI from countries with high-income inequality. If the country is autocratic, the FPI flows associated with income inequality are even greater, but the flows are less if the country has a SWF. Further, there are fewer FPI flows through tax havens from countries with higher income inequality. Finally, flows from autocratic countries and countries with SWFs through tax havens are not statistically significantly different than flows from other countries.

28.5.4 Autocracy

Autocratic countries typically do not have well-developed markets or democratic institutions (Olson, 1993). Economic agents behave differently (Adam *et al.*, 2011) and can mobilize domestic capital and direct it to specific foreign investments with less concern for public opinion. Therefore, autocratic countries may be an attractive source of funding for some foreign firms. Alstadsaeter *et al.* (2018) find that autocracies also have very high levels of wealth held abroad. Brada *et al.* (2011) argue that if these individuals are members of the "kleptocratic elite," they are better able to exploit society and move wealth abroad, the more autocratic the country is. Jensen (2003) finds that up to 70% more FDI flows into democratic host countries vis-à-vis autocratic host countries. Brada *et al.* (2011), Ghosh et al. (2020), and Asiedu and Lien (2004) all argue that autocratic countries are more likely to exhibit government repression, regulations, and capital controls that discourage FDI into autocracies.

All of these arguments suggest that there will be significant FPI flows from autocratic countries toward more desirable investment opportunities abroad but do not suggest that those flows will go through tax havens. In fact, Kemme *et al.* (2021) show that these characteristics (autocracy and SWF) may be as significant as traditional determinants of cross-border equity flows in the developed economies literature. However, they find no statistically significant relationship between autocracies and FPI flows through tax havens.

28.5.5 Sovereign wealth funds

SWFs are typically found in natural resource-based economies that enjoy large current foreign exchange inflows from resource export revenues. The funds usually invest the fees, royalties, and taxes associated with the exports abroad to limit the effects on the domestic economy and save for the use of future generations. Such investments result in large unidirectional cross-border equity flows. While the SWFs are not always transparent in their activities, they are seen as an attractive funding source because of their long-term investment horizon.[17] Megginson *et al.* (2013) find SWFs favor investing in countries with high levels of investor protection and developed capital markets.

Similarly, Ciarlone and Miceli (2016) find SWFs invest in more liquid financial markets, offering higher protection of legal rights and a stable macroeconomic environment. Aizenman and Glick (2007, 2009) find that these countries also tend to have lower scores on democracy and governance indices than developed countries (more autocratic) but higher than less developed countries. Most countries with SWF are relatively small (small non-oil GDP) with few wealthy individual investors. Thus, most outgoing FPI is from the SWF alone. Because the SWF itself faces no domestic tax challenges, they tend to be disinterested in tax avoidance or investing through tax havens. Nevertheless, they have democracy and governance scores more like autocratic countries that may support through tax havens, as found by Kemme *et al.* (2021).

28.5.6 Tax morale

Tax morale is the intrinsic motivation of individuals to pay taxes or feel guilt from failure to comply with tax laws and regulations. Tax morale itself is positively associated with direct democracy and negatively correlated with shadow economy activities.[18] These correlations may be explained by perceived fairness or tax administration, equity of fiscal exchange, attitude toward government (Cummings *et al.* 2004), differences in culture and demographics (Botelho *et al.* 2001), and trustworthiness (Ashraf *et al.*, 2006). While most research focuses on the link between tax morale and domestic tax evasion, Kemme *et al.* (2021) show that this link is so strong that it influences international FPI flows. Specifically, tax evasion via roundtripping through tax havens is higher for low tax morale countries.

28.5.7 Transition economy issues

There has been some research on domestic tax evasion in transition economies. However, research on international tax evasion is more limited and mainly focuses on capital flight. Interestingly, most of the non-economic determinants of tax evasion studied in developed economies are also crucial in the transition economies, except that the effects are greatly magnified for the earliest stages of transition. During the era of central planning, there was a high level of shadow, or black-market, economic activity, which completely evaded taxes, out of necessity – to overcome rigid planning bureaucracies or chronic shortages. With the dissolution of central planning and sometimes chaotic privatization, shadow market transactions and corruption were motivated more by pure economic self-interest. Corruption increased significantly as individuals tried to gain control of state-owned assets, government subsidies, or contracts. The introduction of a market economy tax system and appropriate institutions also lagged noticeably. For 26 out of 42 transition economies, the level of corruption was generally much higher than the world average, as measured by the World Bank's (2007) corruption perception index. Iwasaki and Suzuki (2012) find that for the transition economies, corruption and the associated tax evasion were directly related to progress toward transition and the existence of an egalitarian religious society in each country. The presence of a centralized administrative system (which did vary in the pre-transition period) and the institutional inertia of the communist regime were significant detriments to a rapid transition. However, as the transition proceeded, the level of corruption fell.

28.6 Economic impact and policy responses

Tax evasion is a hidden activity and is difficult to measure. As a result, estimates of tax evasion and international tax evasion, in particular, are wide ranging. The economic impact is also difficult to measure. Lost revenues deprive the government of resources for its normal functions and the various initiatives to aid society. Disentangling the effects of lost revenues due to tax evasion from generally low revenues, *per se*, is difficult. While direct taxes are lost due to tax evasion, the "saved" taxes are often spent on goods and services in the formal economy, thereby generating indirect tax revenues.

Tax evasion is a criminal offense in most countries under federal, state, and local statutes. Estimates of the actual amount of revenues forgone are wide ranging. Slemrod (2007) argued that the U.S.'s tax gap (uncollected taxes for a given year) in 2001 was $345 billion, amounting to 16.3% of the estimated actual tax liability for the year, and by 2019 it was over 400 billion (US GAO (2019)). Most of the individual reduction in tax payments using international avenues reflects tax evasion, and Guttentag and Avi-Yonah (2005) have estimated U.S. tax evasion to range between $40 and 70 billion for the year 2002. Di Nola *et al.* (2021) study how tax evasion in the self-employment sector affects overall outcomes and welfare. With 2016 OECD data and 2018 data from the Bank of International Settlements (BIS), Mansour (2020) notes that there is about $10 trillion in financial assets held abroad[19] and calculates that worldwide; countries are losing a total of $427 billion in tax revenue each year due to corporate and individual tax evasion. Individuals use foreign bank deposit accounts, and corporations establish subsidiaries in low-tax jurisdictions. Mansour (2020) also reports that tax evasion generates positive welfare effects for the self-employed at the expense of formally employed workers. Tax havens collectively cost governments $500 to $600 billion annually in lost corporate tax revenue, depending on the estimate (Crivelli *et al.*, 2015; Cobham and Janský, 2017), through both legal and illegal paths. Of that total lost revenue, low-income economies account for about $200 billion – a more significant loss as a percentage of GDP than advanced economies.

American Fortune 500 companies alone held an estimated $2.6 trillion offshore in 2017, though a small portion of that amount has been repatriated following U.S. tax reforms in 2018. Of course, corporations are not the only beneficiaries. Individuals have stashed $8.7 trillion of their wealth in tax havens, estimates Zucman (2017). Henry's (2012) more comprehensive assessments yield an astonishing total of up to $36 trillion. Assuming very different rates of return, both researchers put global individual income tax losses at around $200 billion a year.

There have been many studies of tax losses in developing countries as well. For example, in Pakistan, Aslam (1998) calculates tax evasion between 1960 and 1998 and finds it close to 4.7% of GDP. High tax evasion has complicated Pakistan's fiscal and monetary policies, notably increasing the budget deficit. Manasan (1988) estimates individual tax evasion using various methodologies for the years 1981–1985 for the Philippines. Based on different estimation methods of tax evasion (gap, tax elasticity, special amnesties, audit, and underground economy approach), he found that individual tax evasion varied from 8.8 billion (tax audit approach, 0.19% of GDP) to 17.3 billion pesos (gap approach, 0.38% of GDP). Passive income tax evaded was close to 711 million pesos for dividends and 18.5 billion pesos for interest income for 1981–1985. Between 1970 and 2010, African countries have likely lost up to $1.3 trillion (in 2010 dollars) through capital flight (Boyce and Ndikumana, 2012). Amoh and Adafula (2019) estimate the relationship between tax evasion and the size of the underground economy in Ghana. Their results confirm that a large underground economy causes a higher level of tax evasion in Ghana. Using data from the World Development Indicators and the Bank of Ghana for the time period of 1990–2015, the authors calculate that the underground economy has averaged about 20.87% of GDP. They conclude that a high tax burden and higher unemployment contribute to the ever-deteriorating problem of tax evasion in Ghana. Andersen *et al.* (2017) and Hebous and Lipatov (2013) estimate that at least 8% of the petroleum rents earned by oil-rich countries with weak institutions arrive in private accounts in offshore financial centers (OFC).

28.6.1 Methods of international evasion

28.6.1.1 Evasion of investment income via roundtripping

Measuring tax evasion is challenging since data from evading individuals is, naturally, not readily accessible. The wealthy elites do not simply underreport income on their income statements; instead, they frequently funnel capital out of the country and out of the reach of local tax authorities. Tax haven countries offer attractive options to host such capital. One commonly used vehicle is shell corporations in the tax haven, in which individuals hold their wealth in the name of a foreign individual or company. From there, the wealth can be redeployed into the capital markets of the owner's home country as well as other countries.

This process of roundtripping portfolio equity has three components:

1. Establish a shell corporation overseas in a name different from your own.
2. Send capital from your home country into the shell corporation in the foreign country.
3. Invest the capital from the shell corporation back into your home capital market under the guise of a foreign entity.[20]

Hanlon *et al.* (2015) and Kemme *et al.* (2017) show that when the taxes levied on domestic citizens increase relative to the taxes collected from foreign investors, this roundtripping scheme becomes more lucrative and enticing. Specifically, Hanlon *et al.* (2015) find more capital roundtrips into the U.S. when the tax gap between U.S. taxpayers and foreign investors increases. The issue is, of course, systematic and prevalent in many countries. For example, there is strong evidence of tax evasion in OECD countries, where roundtripping increases as the gap between tax rates for domestic and foreign investors widen (Kemme *et al.*, 2017).

In a follow-up study, Kemme *et al.* (2020) also show that the OECD countries with low tax morale primarily engage in tax evasion via roundtripping. Analogous roundtripping of foreign direct investment also has a sizeable economic impact, as it represents close to 30% of foreign direct investment flows (Aykut *et al.*, 2017). Karhunen *et al.* (2021) explore Russian FDI roundtripping from the perspective of institutional arbitrage. They find that FDI roundtripping does not reduce tax avoidance for Russian firms but enhances firm competitiveness in the home country by shifting their funds abroad to an offshore financial center. This shift will positively aid the firm in generating and protecting its funds from the unethical behavior of its home institutions. The Russian firms also tend to seek offshore financial centers that offer low taxes and strong property rights.

28.6.1.2 Bank deposits and tax evasion

Huizinga and Nicodéme (2004) study the extent to which international banking flows reflect tax policies, regulations, and enforcement efforts. Their empirical results suggest that interest income taxation has encouraged the international movement of bank deposits. Domestic bank interest reporting requirements to tax authorities also appear to contribute to international bank deposit placements. They find minimal evidence that interest withholding taxes discourage such deposits, perhaps because non-resident withholding taxes are relatively low and imposed by relatively few countries. Similarly, they find little evidence that international information exchange agreements impact bilateral or cross-country bank deposit flows. However, later research does suggest international information exchange agreements have had modest relocation effects on bank deposit flows from one tax haven to another.

During the 2008–2009 Financial Crisis, the fight against tax evasion became a political priority in developed countries, and the pressure on tax havens mounted. G20 countries urged each tax haven to sign at least 12 information exchange treaties. By the end of 2009, the world's tax havens signed a total of more than 300 treaties.[21] Johannesen and Zucman (2014) study the effectiveness of this crackdown on offshore tax evasion. They construct a rich dataset of cross-border bank deposits and find that treaties have had a statistically significant but relatively modest impact on bank deposits in tax havens. For example, the treaty between France and Switzerland caused an approximate 11% decline in the Swiss deposits held by French residents. More importantly, the treaties signed by tax havens have not triggered significant repatriations of funds but rather a relocation of deposits between tax havens.

Johannesen (2014) looks at the impact of the European Savings Directive and its impact on offshore bank accounts. The Savings Directive enforces offshore wealth taxation without compromising the cooperating offshore centers (Switzerland, Luxembourg, and Jersey). If a household decides to report their offshore interest income, they are exempted from the withholding taxes. In general, this directive only affects households who are unwilling to report their offshore interest income. In the case of Switzerland, he finds that the Savings Directive reduced EU-owned bank deposits in Switzerland by approximately 30–40%. The reduction occurred immediately before and after the implementation of this policy. More minor reductions of bank deposits occurred in other EU financial centers (Luxembourg, Isle of Man, Jersey, and Guernsey). There are two critical findings. First, a significant portion of offshore wealth is undeclared. Second, tax evaders are highly responsive to changes in the international tax regulatory environment. In addition, Johannesen (2014) found that when EU-owned bank deposits dropped in Switzerland, there was no repatriation of funds to other EU nations. Instead, there was an increase in EU-owned bank deposits in Macao and Panama.

Menkhoff and Miethe (2019) explore critical questions regarding non-bank deposits and information request agreements (IRAs). Using BIS data, they show that information exchange requests had an early impact, but tax evaders have adapted by disguising their bank deposits. Neither double taxation agreements nor tax information exchange agreements affect the volume of bank deposits in tax havens vis-à-vis non-tax havens.

Vo *et al.* (2020) constructed a new tax evasion index using the World Bank Enterprises Survey. The index includes tax and social security contribution burden, regulations, public sector services, quality of institutions, and tax compliance. Along with the index, they have looked at the contribution of information sharing and bank penetration to tax evasion practices of emerging markets. Their empirical results show that larger firms are less likely to evade taxes in countries with a robust financial sector. Firms located in smaller cities appear to evade more taxes than those located in medium to large cities with a high level of bank penetration and information sharing.

In 2014, the OECD implemented the Common Reporting Standard (CRS). The OECD calls on members to obtain information from financial institutions and automatically exchange information with other jurisdictions every year (OECD, 2015). It provides the minimum information requirements that financial institutions should collect and the due diligence processes that they should follow.[22] Casi *et al.* (2020) examine the effectiveness of the CRS. They first examine the effect of the CRS on cross-border deposits held in traditional tax havens and then investigate the relocation of cross-border deposits to the U.S., in particular, because it is the only major economy not committed to the CRS. Overall, Casi *et al.* (2020) find a short-term decrease of USD 45 billion in cross-border deposits held in the tax havens and a short-term increase of USD 55 billion in cross-border deposits held in the U.S. post-CRS.

Moreover, upon adopting the CRS in the deposit country, cross-border deposits held in tax havens decrease on average by 11.5% compared to non-tax havens. This decline is an immediate reaction to CRS. The authors find that post-CRS, cross-border deposits held in the U.S. were on average 10.0% higher than those in non-havens.

28.6.2 *Tax amnesty programs and their impact*

Tax authorities have offered many incentives to increase tax collections and lower evasion, including tax amnesty programs. In general, tax amnesties are government programs that allow a short period for tax evaders to voluntarily repay previously evaded taxes without being subject to prosecution and penalties that discovery of such tax evasion normally brings. Amnesty programs have been implemented in Europe, the United States, and developing countries with varying results. Amnesty programs are not without criticism. Keller (2004) notes that the general problem of tax amnesty is that it allows individuals/institutions to profit while they initially did not follow the law. Moreover, a tax amnesty program plays down the criminal meaning of tax evasion, and it may further provide incentives for others to evade taxes. We discuss a few examples below.

After the federal government in Germany increased capital gains taxes in the early 1990s, several thousand German citizens secretly transferred their wealth into tax havens such as Switzerland and Luxembourg. In 2005, German lawmakers enacted an amnesty for citizens who had evaded taxes between 1993 and 2002.

Leenders *et al.* (2020) present an overview of 27,000 participants in the Dutch amnesty program between 2002 and 2018. They find that the participants in the voluntary disclosure program are primarily older males. The median estimated hidden wealth was around €435,000. For most years, they find that Netherland's residents held their undeclared assets primarily in Switzerland, Belgium, and Luxembourg.

Argyropoulou (2018) looks at the tax amnesty program of 2010 in Greece. The program repatriated around €425 million and collected about €25 million in tax revenues. However, tax evasion had increased in 2011 compared to 2010.

Similar effects are found in developing countries. For example, the Indonesian government implemented a tax amnesty program from July 2016 to March 2017. For this program, tax amnesty was a tax write-off policy to be implemented with no administrative sanctions and criminal sanctions for tax regulations violations when revealing assets and paying penalties or fees.

28.7 Latest developments and conclusion

International personal tax evasion has taken on greater importance for tax and fiscal authorities across the globe. We describe various methods to evade personal taxes, focusing primarily on tax evasion using tax havens, the preferred method for the top 1% of income producers. There are several motivations for an individual to evade taxes, such as higher tax rates in their home country, lower detection of being caught by tax authorities, lack of trust in government institutions overall, and low tax morale.

Tax havens also have unique characteristics: relatively low population, lack of transparency, and unwillingness to share information with other nations. High tax evasion is typically due to traditional international portfolio flow determinants, cultural differences, poorly governed institutions, tax code complexity, and lack of enforcement policies.

The economic impact of tax evasion is difficult to measure. Estimates vary widely, but it has cost billions of dollars to many nations. The lost revenue can profoundly impact the fiscal balance and the resulting fiscal policies. As a result, many countries have introduced tax amnesty programs, but only with limited success. In addition, the OECD and other global bodies have developed bilateral and multilateral agreements (primarily information exchange) to curb tax evasion, again only with modest success (OECD, 2002). Overall, tax evasion continues to persist.

When blockchain and cryptocurrency were first introduced, many argued that Bitcoin's primary purpose was to conduct illicit transactions.[23] It is not considered legal tender in most countries (El Salvador is the notable exception as of 2021) but rather a volatile speculative asset. To the extent that transactions can remain anonymous, some claim that Bitcoin may serve as a vehicle for concealing and moving wealth across the world. However, with the introduction of know-your-customer (KYC), anti-money laundering laws, and other regulations on cryptocurrency exchanges and tokens, buying and selling cryptocurrencies may no longer be truly anonymous. The creation of widely used digital currencies which truly function as money may reduce cash and other electronic transactions but simultaneously increase the velocity of money due to its convenience. The extent to which this limits illicit transactions via cryptocurrencies is unknown, but greater regulatory oversight is being prepared and enacted. In the United States, the most recent regulations are embedded in the 2021 infrastructure bill. The U.S. Treasury is developing reporting standards for transactions above $10,000 in virtual currency,[24] and the SEC is further developing regulations for digital currency exchanges.

Marian (2013) notes that cryptocurrencies have similar tax haven traits where crypto earnings are not subject to taxes and taxpayer anonymity is maintained. One other advantage of cryptocurrencies is that their operation is not based on the existence of financial institutions. As a result, recent efforts by global regulators and governments to curb tax evasion could be thwarted. Cryptocurrency might gain momentum among expected tax evaders who generally use tax haven jurisdiction and operate via offshore accounts.

In addition, there are now more and louder calls from other organizations across the world to tackle tax evasion. For example, PIPSC (Professional Institute of the Public Service of Canada)[25] has provided the initial groundwork for legal methods to fight tax evasion. In particular, they recommend that the Canada Revenue Agency (CRA) should better enforce existing tax laws, prevent political interference, have better protection for whistleblowers, and invest more in technology to detect patterns in tax evasion. For Budget 2021, the Canadian parliament passed new wide-ranging legislation, including a digital service tax for companies like Netflix, Amazon, and other tech companies. Second, a publicly accessible ownership registry is being created to identify actual owners of shell companies. Similarly, a recent study by Reck *et al.* (2021) shows that American taxpayers in the top 1% now use sophisticated methods like a pass-through business for tax evasion. The authors argue that tax authorities should increase scrutiny for pass-through companies, encourage whistleblowing, perform more comprehensive audits, and increase litigation of tax disputes. The IRS already invests in many of these enforcement strategies, but recent budget cuts have curtailed the agency's ability to conduct them efficiently and effectively. China's increasing push for "common prosperity," reducing income inequality among its citizens, led the Chinese State Taxation Administration to create and strengthen existing tax supervision guidelines for high-income and high-net worth individuals.

Across the globe, higher income and wealth inequality and the perceived lack of fairness in current tax codes have captured the public's attention, and government authorities are responding. It remains to be seen if the Pandora Papers will result in better tools and resources for tax authorities and new international laws to help curb tax evasion.

Acknowledgments

We would like to thank the editors of this volume, Bruno Dallago and Sara Casagrande, and Wladimir Andreff for helpful comments on earlier drafts of this chapter.

Notes

1 Fitzgibbon and Hudson (2021).
2 https://www.cbc.ca/news/canada/british-columbia/sec-freezes-assets-british-columbians-investment-scheme-1.6148981
3 https://www.bbc.com/news/world-58780561
4 https://www.icij.org/investigations/pandora-papers/
5 https://www.oecd.org/g20/topics/international-taxation/
6 Dharmapala (2017, p. xv) defines tax avoidance as "the lawful reduction of tax obligations, while maintaining the same substantive economic outcome".
7 Follow this issue at European Commission Tax Fraud and Tax Evasion website: https://ec.europa.eu/taxation_customs/fight-against-tax-fraud-and-tax-evasion_en
8 Note that actual taxes evaded are difficult to measure and researchers often use proxies. Tsakumis et al. (2007) use the size of a country's shadow economy relative to total GDP. This is taken as a measure of tax evasion in general.

9 See Kieser (1994) for a popular summary of Hofstede's (1980) cultural dimensions.

10 Products and services produced legally or illegally and not reported so as to be included in GDP, hence, not subject to any taxation, constitute the shadow economy (Schneider and Enste, 2013). Lopez (2017) provides a theoretical model and the conditions under which establishments select into the informal economy, tax compliance, or tax evasion leading to quite different levels of tax collections and growth paths for the economy.

11 Some famously convicted U.S. tax evaders include Darryl Strawberry, Martha Stewart, Wesley Snipes, Willie Nelson, and Ty Warner (Kratsas, 2014).

12 https://stats.oecd.org/Index.aspx?DataSetCode=TABLE_I7 (last accessed June 22, 2021).

13 In comparison, the other mentioned high-tax countries contribute a combined 6.2%: Korea (0.2%), Denmark (0.4%), Canada (1.4%), France (2.3%), Chile (0.1%), Norway (0.3%), Belgium (1.0%), and Sweden (0.5%). Note the Tax Justice Network provides individual country estimates and a "corporate tax haven index" and "bank secrecy index" for cross-country comparisons. See Tax Justice Network (2020) for details.

14 The World Values Survey specifically asks: "Generally speaking, would you say that most people can be trusted or that you need to be very careful in dealing with people? 1. Most people can be trusted; 2. Need to be very careful; 9. Don't know".

15 Functional tax havens provide financial activities. Notional tax havens house shell, "brass plate," or "cubicle" bank offices that make book entries of financial transactions. Hybrid tax havens support offshore shell offices that might eventually become operational branches in the future.

16 In the "varieties of capitalism literature," Williams *et al.* (2012) characterize economies by the size of the informal economy. This is correlated with domestic tax evasion and suggests that the level of tax evasion may vary by "variety" of capitalist states. This linkage may be worth pursuing further.

17 See Kemme (2012)and Kemme (2013) for an overview and details relating to the National Fund of Kazakhstan.

18 Torgler and Schneider (2009) show the link between evasion and the size of the shadow economy, and Torgler (2003) finds that among transition economies, Central and Eastern European countries have higher tax morale than former Soviet Union countries.

19 Estimates of assets held abroad by corporations, individuals, and in total are wide ranging.

20 See Figure 1 in Kemme *et al.* (2020) for a visual depiction of roundtripping.

21 https://www.oecd.org/ctp/exchange-of-tax-information/taxinformationexchangeagreementsti eas.htm

22 For more information on CRS: https://www.oecd.org/tax/automatic-exchange/common-reporting-standard/

23 Now there are well over a thousand crypto, digital, and virtual currencies assets and tokens.

24 https://www.cnbc.com/2021/05/20/us-treasury-calls-for-stricter-cryptocurrency-compliance-with-irs.html

25 https://pipsc.ca/news-issues/tax-fairness/forefront-fight-against-tax-evasion

References

Adam, A., Delis, M.D. and Kammas, P. (2011). Are democratic governments more efficient? *European Journal of Political Economy*, 27(1), 75–86. https://doi.org/10.1016/j.ejpoleco.2010.04.004

Aggarwal, R., Kearney, C. and Lucey, B. (2012). Gravity and culture in foreign portfolio investment. *Journal of Banking & Finance*, 36(2), 525–538. https://doi.org/10.1016/j.jbankfin.2011.08.007

Aizenman, J. and Glick, R. (2007). Sovereign wealth funds: Stumbling blocks or stepping stones to financial globalization? *FRBSF Economic Letter*, 2007(38).

Aizenman, J. and Glick, R. (2009). Sovereign wealth funds: Stylized facts about their determinants and governance. *International Finance*, 12(3), 351–386. https://doi.org/10.1111/j.1468-2362.2009.01249.x

Allingham, M.G. and Sandmo, A. (1972). Income tax evasion: A theoretical analysis. *Journal of Public Economics*, 1(3–4), 323–338. https://doi.org/10.1016/0047-2727(72)90010-2

Alstadsæter, A., Johannesen, N. and Zucman, G. (2018). Who owns the wealth in tax havens? Macro evidence and implications for global inequality. *Journal of Public Economics*, 162, 89–100. https://doi.org/10.1016/j.jpubeco.2018.01.008

Alstadsæter, A., Johannesen, N. and Zucman, G. (2019). Tax evasion and inequality. *American Economic Review*, 109(6), 2073–2103. https://doi.org/10.1257/aer.20172043

Amoh, J.K. and Adafula, B. (2019). An estimation of the underground economy and tax evasion: Empirical analysis from an emerging economy. *Journal of Money Laundering Control*, 22(4), 626–645. https://doi.org/10.1108/jmlc-01-2019-0002

Andersen, J.J., Johannesen, N., Lassen, D.D. and Paltseva, E. (2017). Petro rents, political institutions, and hidden wealth: Evidence from offshore bank accounts. *Journal of the European Economic Association*. https://doi.org/10.1093/jeea/jvw019

Argyropoulou, V. (2018). "Coming in from the cold" The latest tax amnesty in Greece and lessons from the future. *Journal of International Law and Policy UC Davis School of Law*, 24(2), 125–34.

Ashraf, N., Bohnet, I. and Piankov, N. (2006). Decomposing trust and trustworthiness. *Experimental Economics*, 9(3), 193–208. https://doi.org/10.1007/s10683-006-9122-4

Aslam, S. (1998). The underground economy and tax evasion in Pakistan: Annual estimates (1960-1998) and the impact of dollarisation of the economy. *Pakistan Development Review*, 621–631. https://www.jstor.org/stable/41261074

Auerbach, A.J. and King, M.A. (1983). Taxation, portfolio choice, and debt-equity ratios: A general equilibrium model. *Quarterly Journal of Economics*, 98(4), 587–609. https://doi.org/10.2307/1881779

Austin, C.R. and Wilson, R.J. (2017). An examination of reputational costs and tax avoidance: Evidence from firms with valuable consumer brands. *Journal of the American Taxation Association*, 39(1), 67–93. https://doi.org/10.2308/atax-51634

Aykut, D., Sanghi, A. and Kosmidou, G. (2017). What to do when foreign direct investment is not direct or foreign: FDI round tripping. World Bank Policy Research Working Paper, No. 8046. https://doi.org/10.1596/1813-9450-8046

Becker, G.S. (1968). Crime and punishment: An economic approach. *Journal of Political Economy*, 76, 169–217.

Benedek, D. and Lelkes, O. (2011). The distributional implications of income under-reporting in Hungary. *Fiscal Studies*, 32(4), 539–560. https://doi.org/10.1111/j.1475-5890.2011.00150.x

Bernasconi, M., Corazzini, L. and Seri, R. (2014). Reference dependent preferences, hedonic adaptation and tax evasion: Does the tax burden matter? *Journal of Economic Psychology*, 40, 103–118. https://doi.org/10.1016/j.joep.2013.01.005

Botelho, A., Harrison, G.W., Hirsch, M. and Elisabet, R. (2001). Bargaining behavior, demographics and nationality: A reconsideration of the experimental evidence. *NIMA Working Papers 16*, Núcleo de Investigação em Microeconomia Aplicada (NIMA), Universidade do Minho.

Boyce, J.K. and Ndikumana, L. (2012). Capital flight from Sub-Saharan African countries: Updated estimates, 1970–2010. PERI Research Report. https://dx.doi.org/10.2139/ssrn.2202215

Brada, J.C., Kutan, A.M. and Vukšić, G. (2011). The costs of moving money across borders and the volume of capital flight: The case of Russia and other CIS countries. *Review of World Economics*, 147(4), 717–744. https://doi.org/10.1007/s10290-011-0100-3

Casi, E., Spengel, C. and Stage, B.M. (2020). Cross-border tax evasion after the common reporting standard: Game over? *Journal of Public Economics*, 190, 104240. https://doi.org/10.1016/j.jpubeco.2020.104240

Chen, K.P. and Chu, C.C. (2005). Internal control versus external manipulation: A model of corporate income tax evasion. *RAND Journal of Economics*, 36(1), 151–164. http://www.jstor.org/stable/1593759

Chiarini, B., Marzano, E. and Schneider, F. (2013). Tax rates and tax evasion: An empirical analysis of the long-run aspects in Italy. *European Journal of Law and Economics*, 35(2), 273–293. https://doi.org/10.1007/s10657-011-9247-6

Christensen, J. (2011). The looting continues: Tax havens and corruption. *Critical Perspectives on International Business*, 7(2), 177–196. https://doi.org/10.1108/17422041111128249

Ciarlone, A. and Miceli, V. (2016). Escaping financial crises? Macro evidence from sovereign wealth funds' investment behaviour. *Emerging Markets Review*, 27, 169–196. https://doi.org/10.1016/j.ememar.2016.05.004

Clotfelter, C.T. (1983). Tax evasion and tax rates: An analysis of individual returns. *Review of Economics and Statistics*, 65(3), 363–373. https://doi.org/10.2307/1924181

Cobham, A. (2005). Tax Evasion, Tax Avoidance and Development Finance. Queen Elizabeth House Working Paper No. 129, Queen Elizabeth House, University of Oxford.

Cobham, A. and Janský, P. (2017). "Measurement of Illicit Financial Flows," *UNODC-UNCTAD Expert consultation on the SDG Indicator on Illicit financial flows: Background paper prepared for UNCTAD*: https://www.unodc.org/documents/data-and-analysis/statistics/IFF/Background_paper_B_ Measurement_of_Illicit_Financial_Flows_UNCTAD_web.pdf. *Benefits and Costs of the IFF Targets, 187*, 2017.

Crivelli, E., De Mooij, R.A. and Keen, M.M. (2015). *Base Erosion, Profit Shifting and Developing Countries.* International Monetary Fund.

Crocker, K.J. and Slemrod, J. (2005). Corporate tax evasion with agency costs. *Journal of Public Economics,* 89(9–10), 1593–1610. https://doi.org/10.1016/j.jpubeco.2004.08.003

Cummings, R.C., Martinez-Vazquez, J., McKee, M. and Torgler, B. (2004). Effects of culture on tax compliance: A cross check of experimental and survey evidence, *CREMA Working Paper Series 2004-13,* Center for Research in Economics, Management and the Arts (CREMA).

DeBacker, J., Heim, B.T. and Tran, A. (2015). Importing corruption culture from overseas: Evidence from corporate tax evasion in the United States. *Journal of Financial Economics,* 117(1), 122–138. https://doi.org/10.1016/j.jfineco.2012.11.009

Desai, M.A. and Dharmapala, D. (2006). Corporate tax avoidance and high-powered incentives. *Journal of Financial Economics,* 79(1), 145–179. https://doi.org/10.1016/j.jfineco.2005.02.002

Desai, M.A. and Dharmapala, D. (2009). Corporate tax avoidance and firm value. *Review of Economics and Statistics,* 91(3), 537–546. http://www.jstor.org/stable/25651357

Dharmapala, D. (2017). The economics of tax avoidance and evasion. *The International Library of Critical Writings in Economics,* 334, Edward Elgar Publishing.

Dharmapala, D. and Hines Jr, J.R. (2009). Which countries become tax havens? *Journal of Public Economics,* 93(9–10), 1058–1068. https://doi.org/10.1016/j.jpubeco.2009.07.005

Di Nola, A., Kocharkov, G., Scholl, A. and Tkhir, A.M. (2021). The aggregate consequences of tax evasion. *Review of Economic Dynamics,* 40, 198–227. https://doi.org/10.1016/j.red.2020.09.009

Doukas, J. (1985). Determinants of foreign portfolio investment: Another approach. *Canadian Journal of Administrative Sciences/Revue Canadienne des Sciences de l'Administration,* 2(2), 264–277. https://doi.org/10.1111/j.1936-4490.1985.tb00406.x

Dyreng, S.D., Hanlon, M. and Maydew, E.L. (2008). Long-run corporate tax avoidance. *Accounting Review,* 83(1), 61–82. https://doi.org/10.2308/accr.2008.83.1.61

Fakhrutdinova, E.V., Fakhrutdinov, R.M., Kolesnikova, J.S. and Yagudin, R.H. (2015). Shadow economy in Russia. *Mediterranean Journal of Social Sciences,* 6(1 S3), 67. doi: 10.5901/mjss.2015. v6n1s3p67. Retrieved from https://www.mcser.org/journal/index.php/mjss/article/view/5672

Fisman, R. and Wei, S. (2004). Tax rates and tax evasion: Evidence from "Missing Imports" in China. *Journal of Political Economy,* 112(2), 471–496. https://doi.org/10.1086/381476

Fitzgibbon, W. and Hudson, M. (2021). "Five years later, Panama Papers still having big impact," International Consortium of Investigative Journalists. https://www.icij.org/investigations/ panama-papers/five-years-later-panama-papers-still-having-a-big-impact/

Friedland, N., Maital, S. and Rutenberg, A. (1978). A simulation study of income tax evasion. *Journal of Public Economics,* 10(1), 107–116. https://doi.org/10.1016/0047-2727(78)90008-7

Ghosh, A.R., Kim, J.I. and Qureshi, M.S. (2020). What's in a name? That which we call capital controls. *Economic Policy,* 35(101), 147–208. https://doi.org/10.1093/epolic/eiaa009

Gorodnichenko, Y., Martinez-Vazquez, J. and Sabirianova Peter, K. (2009). Myth and reality of flat tax reform: Micro estimates of tax evasion response and welfare effects in Russia. *Journal of Political economy,* 117(3), 504–554. https://doi.org/10.1086/599760

Graham, J.R. (2003). Taxes and corporate finance: A review. *Review of Financial Studies,* 16(4), 1075–1129. http://www.jstor.org/stable/1262738

Gravelle, J.G. (2009). Tax havens: International tax avoidance and evasion. *National Tax Journal,* 62(4), 727–753. https://doi.org/10.17310/ntj.2009.4.07

Guttentag, J. and Avi-Yonah, R.S. (2005). Closing the international tax gap. Reuven Avi-Yonah, co-author. In *Bridging the Tax Gap: Addressing the Crisis in Federal Tax Administration,* edited by M.B. Sawicky, 99–110. Washington, DC: Economic Policy Institute.

Hamilton, R. and Stekelberg, J. (2016). The effect of high-quality information technology on corporate tax avoidance and tax risk. *Journal of Information Systems,* 31(2), 83–106. https://doi.org/10.2308/ isys-51482

Hammar, H., Jagers, S.C. and Nordblom, K. (2009). Perceived tax evasion and the importance of trust. *Journal of Socio-Economics,* 38(2), 238–245. https://doi.org/10.1016/j.socec.2008.07.003

Hampton, M.P. and Christensen, J. (2002). Offshore pariahs? Small island economies, tax havens, and the re-configuration of global finance. *World Development*, 30(9), 1657–1673. https://doi.org/10.1016/s0305-750x(02)00054-2

Hanlon, M., Maydew, E.L. and Thornock, J.R. (2015). Taking the long way home: U.S. tax evasion and offshore investments in U.S. equity and debt markets. *Journal of Finance*, 70(1), 257–287. https://doi.org/10.1111/jofi.12120

Hanlon, M., Mills, L. and Slemrod, J. (2007). An Empirical Examination of Corporate Tax Noncompliance. In A. Auerbach, J. Hines, Jr. and J. Slemrod (Eds.), *Taxing Corporate Income in the 21st Century* (pp. 171–210), Cambridge: Cambridge University Press.

Hebous, S. and Lipatov, V. (2014). A journey from a corruption port to a tax haven. *Journal of Comparative Economics*, 42(3), 739–754. https://doi.org/10.1016/j.jce.2013.05.006

Henry, J.S. (2012). The price of offshore revisited. New Estimates for "Missing" Global Private Wealth, Income, Inequality, and Lost Taxes. *Tax Justice Network, 2012*. http://www.taxjustice.net/cms/upload/pdf/Price_of_Offshore_Revisited_120722.pdf

Hines, J.R. (2005). Do tax havens flourish? *Tax Policy and the Economy*, 19, 65–99. https://doi.org/10.1086/tpe.19.20061896

Hines, J.R. and Rice, E.M. (1994). Fiscal paradise: Foreign tax havens and American business. *Quarterly Journal of Economics*, 109(1), 149–182. https://doi.org/10.2307/2118431

Hofstede, G. (1980). Culture's consequences: International differences in work-related values. *Academy of Management Review*, 6(4), 681–683. https://doi.org/10.5465/amr.1981.4285738

Huizinga, H. and Nicodème, G. (2004). Are international deposits tax-driven. *Journal of Public Economics*, 88(6), 1093–1118. https://doi.org/10.1016/S0047-2727(03)00058-6

IMF. (2021). *The Global Informal Workforce: Priorities for Inclusive Growth*, Chpt. 2, Washington, DC: IMF.

Iwasaki, I. and Suzuki, T. (2012). The determinants of corruption in transition economies. *Economics Letters*, 114(1), 54–60. https://doi.org/10.1016/j.econlet.2011.08.016

Jackson, B. and Milliron, V. (1986). Tax compliance research: Findings, problems and prospects. *Journal of Accounting Literature*, 5, 125–165.

Jansky, P. and Prats, A. (2015). International profit-shifting out of developing countries and the role of tax havens. *Development Policy Review*, 33(3), 271–292. https://doi.org/10.1111/dpr.12113

Jaumotte, F., Lall, S. and Papageorgiou, C. (2013). Rising income inequality: Technology, or trade and financial globalization? *IMF Economic Review*, 61(2), 271–309. https://doi.org/10.1057/imfer.2013.7

Johannesen, N. (2014). Tax evasion and Swiss bank deposits. *Journal of Public Economics*, 111, 46–62. https://doi.org/10.1016/j.jpubeco.2013.12.003

Johannesen, N. and Zucman, G. (2014). The end of bank secrecy? An evaluation of the G20 tax haven crackdown. *American Economic Journal: Economic Policy*, 6(1), 65–91. https://doi.org/10.1257/pol.6.1.65

Joulfaian, D. (2000). Corporate income tax evasion and managerial preferences. *Review of Economics and Statistics*, 82(4), 698–701. https://doi.org/10.1162/rest.2000.82.4.698

Jun, B.W. and Yoon, S.M. (2018). Taxpayer's religiosity, religion, and the perceptions of tax equity: Case of South Korea. *Religions*, 9(333), 1–15.

Kanagaretnam, K., Lee, J., Lim, C.Y. and Lobo, G. (2018). Societal trust and corporate tax avoidance. *Review of Accounting Studies*, 23(4), 1588–1628.

Karhunen, P., Ledyaeva, S. and Brouthers, K.D. (2021). Capital round-tripping: Determinants of emerging market firm investments into offshore financial centers and their ethical implications. *Journal of Business Ethics*. https://doi.org/10.1007/s10551-021-04908-y

Keller, W. (2004). International Technology Diffusion. *Journal of Economic Literature*, 42, 752–782. DOI: 10.1257/0022051042177685

Kemme, D.M. (2012). Sovereign wealth fund issues and the national Fund(s) of Kazakhstan, William Davidson Institute Working Paper No. 1036, 2012. Available at SSRN: https://ssrn.com/abstract=2188391 or http://dx.doi.org/10.2139/ssrn.2188391

Kemme, D.M. (2013). Measuring disclosure and transparency for Kazakhstan firms. IREX, Scholar Research Brief.

Kemme, D.M., Parikh, B. and Steigner, T. (2017). Tax havens, tax evasion and tax information exchange agreements in the OECD. *European Financial Management*, 23(3), 519–543. https://doi.org/10.1111/eufm.12118

Kemme, D.M., Parikh, B. and Steigner, T. (2020). Tax morale and international tax evasion. *Journal of World Business*, 55(3). https://doi.org/10.1016/j.jwb.2019.101052

Kemme, D.M., Parikh, B. and Steigner, T. (2021). Inequality, autocracy and sovereign funds as determinants of foreign portfolio equity flows. *Journal of Financial Research*, 44(2), 249–278. https://doi.org/10.1111/jfir.12240

Khalil, S. and Sidani, Y. (2020). The influence of religiosity on tax evasion attitudes in Lebanon. *Journal of International Accounting, Auditing and Taxation*, 40, 100335. https://doi.org/10.1016/j.intaccaudtax.2020.100335

Khan, M., Srinivasan, S. and Tan, L. (2016). Institutional ownership and corporate tax avoidance: New evidence. *Accounting Review*, 92(2), 101–122. https://doi.org/10.2308/accr-51529

Khlif, H., Guidara, A. and Hussainey, K. (2016). Sustainability level, corruption and tax evasion: A cross-country analysis. *Journal of Financial Crime*, 23(2), 328–348. https://doi.org/10.1108/jfc-09-2014-0041

Kieser, A. (1994). Why organization theory needs historical analyses – And how this should be performed. *Organization Science*, 5(4), 608–620. https://doi.org/10.1287/orsc.5.4.608

Klepper, S. and Nagin, D. (1989a). The anatomy of tax evasion. *Journal of Law, Economics, & Organization*, 5, 1.

Klepper, S. and Nagin, D. (1989b). Tax compliance and perceptions of the risks of detection and criminal prosecution. *Law and Society Review*, 209–240. https://doi.org/10.2307/3053715

Kourdoumpalou, S. (2016). Do corporate governance best practices restrain tax evasion? Evidence from Greece. *Journal of Accounting and Taxation*, 8(1), 1–10. https://doi.org/10.5897/jat2015.0203

Kratsas, G. (2014). 13 infamous tax cheaters. *USA Today* [online]. Retrieved August 9, 2018, from https://www.usatoday.com/story/money/business/2014/02/28/famous-tax-cheats/5903143

Lago-Peñas, I. and Lago-Peñas, S. (2010). The determinants of tax morale in comparative perspective: Evidence from European countries. *European Journal of Political Economy*, 26(4), 441–453. https://doi.org/10.1016/j.ejpoleco.2010.06.003

Lee, K. (2016). Morality, tax evasion and equity. *Mathematical Social Sciences*, 82, 97–104. https://doi.org/10.1016/j.mathsocsci.2016.05.003

Leenders, W., Lejour, A., Rabaté, S. and Maarten, V.T.R. (2020). Offshore tax evasion and wealth inequality: Evidence from a tax amnesty in the Netherlands. CentER Discussion Paper Series No. 2020-031, http://dx.doi.org/10.2139/ssrn.3723731

Levin, M. and Satarov, G. (2000). Corruption and institutions in Russia. *European Journal of Political Economy*, 16(1), 113–132. https://doi.org/10.1016/s0176-2680(99)00050-6

Lopez, J.J. (2017). A quantitative theory of tax evasion. *Journal of Macroeconomics*, 53, 107–126. https://doi.org/10.1016/j.jmacro.2017.06.005

Manasan, R. (1988). Tax evasion in the Philippines. *Journal of Philippine Development*, 15(2), 167–190.

Mansour, M.B. (2020). $427 bn lost to tax havens every year: Landmark study reveals countries losses and worst offenders. Tax Justice Network, November 20, https://www.taxjustice.net/2020/11/20/427bn-lost-to-tax-havens-every-year-landmark-study-reveals-countries-losses-and-worst-offenders/

Mara, E.R. (2015). Determinants of tax havens. *Procedia Economics and Finance*, 32, 1638–1646. https://doi.org/10.1016/s2212-5671(15)01490-2

Marian, O. (2013). Are cryptocurrencies 'Super' tax havens? *Michigan Law Review First Impressions*, 38 (2013). https://repository.law.umich.edu/mlr_fi/vol112/iss1/2

Matsaganis, M. and Flevotomou, M. (2010). Distributional implications of tax evasion in Greece. Hellenic Observatory Papers on Greece and Southeast Europe (GreeSE Paper No. 31). Hellenic Observatory, London School of Economics and Political Science, London, UK.

Megginson, W.L., You, M. and Han, L. (2013). Determinants of sovereign wealth fund cross-border investments. *Financial Review*, 48(4), 539–572. https://doi.org/10.1111/fire.12015

Menkhoff, L. and Miethe, J. (2019). Tax evasion in new disguise? Examining tax havens' international bank deposits. *Journal of Public Economics*, 176, 53–78. https://doi.org/10.1016/j.jpubeco.2019.06.003

Murphy, K. (2008). Enforcing tax compliance: To punish or persuade? *Economic Analysis and Policy*, 38(1), 113–135. https://doi.org/10.1016/s0313-5926(08)50009-9

Niesiobędzka, M.A. (2014). Relations between procedural fairness, tax morale, institutional trust and tax evasion. *Journal of Social Research & Policy*, 5(1), 41–52.

Norris, P. and Inglehart, R. (2003). *Human Values and Social Change: Findings from the Values Surveys (Ser. International Studies in Sociology and Social Anthropology, v. 89)*. Leide, The Netherlands: Koninklijke Brill NV. ISBN 9004128107 Retrieved November 20, 2021.

O'Donovan, J., Wagner, H.F. and Zeume, S. (2019). The value of offshore secrets: Evidence from the panama papers. *Review of Financial Studies*, 32(11), 4117–4155. https://doi.org/10.1093/rfs/hhz017

OECD. (1998). *Harmful Tax Competition: An Emerging Global Issue*, Paris: OECD Publishing. https://doi.org/10.1787/9789264162945-en

OECD. (2002). *Agreement on the Exchange of Information on Tax Matters*. https://www.oecd.org/ctp/harmful/2082215.pdf. Accessed June 28.

OECD. (2015). *Tax Transparency 2015, Report on Progress*. http://www.oecd.org/tax/transparency/global-forum-annual-report-2015.pdf. Accessed June 28.

OECD. (2019). *Tax Morale: What Drives People and Businesses to Pay Tax?* Paris: OECD Publishing. https://doi.org/10.1787/f3d8ea10-en

Olson, M. (1993). Dictatorship, democracy, and development. *American Political Science Review*, 87(3), 567–576. https://doi.org/10.2307/2938736

Palan, R., Murphy, R. and Chavagneux, C. (2011). Tax Havens: How Globalization Really Works. *Journal of Economic Geography*, 11(4), 753–756. https://doi.org/10.1093/jeg/lbr008

Pommerehne, W.W. and Weck-Hannemann, H. (1996). Tax rates, tax administration and income tax evasion in Switzerland. *Public Choice*, 88(1–2), 161–170. https://doi.org/10.1007/bf00130416

Portes, R. and Rey, H. (2005). The determinants of cross-border equity flows. *Journal of International Economics*, 65(2), 269–296. https://doi.org/10.1016/j.jinteco.2004.05.002

Raczkowski, K. (2015). Measuring the tax gap in the European economy. *Journal of Economics and Management*, 21, 3.

Reck, D., Risch, M. and Zucman, G. (2021). Response to a Comment by Auten and Splinter on "Tax Evasion at the Top of the Income Distribution: Theory and Evidence". *University of California Berkeley*.

Riahi-Belkaoui, A. (2004). Relationship between tax compliance internationally and selected determinants of tax morale. *Journal of International Accounting, Auditing and Taxation*, 13(2), 135–143. https://doi.org/10.1016/j.intaccaudtax.2004.09.001

Richardson, G. (2006). Determinants of tax evasion: A cross-country investigation. *Journal of International Accounting, Auditing and Taxation*, 15(2), 150–169. https://doi.org/10.1016/j.intaccaudtax.2006.08.005

Sandmo, A. (2005). The theory of tax evasion: A retrospective view. *National Tax Journal*, 58(4), 643–663. https://doi.org/10.17310/ntj.2005.4.02

Schneider, F. and Enste, D.H. (2013). *The shadow economy: An international survey*. Cambridge University Press.

Shiel, F. (2021). About the Pandora Papers. *International Consortium of Investigative Journalists*. Retrieved October 8, 2021, from https://www.icij.org/investigations/pandora-papers/about-pandora-papers-investigation

Slemrod, J. (2007). Cheating ourselves: The economics of tax evasion. *Journal of Economic Perspectives*, 21(1), 25–48. https://doi.org/10.1257/jep.21.1.25

Strielkowski, W. and Čábelková, I. (2015). Religion, culture, and tax evasion: Evidence from the czech republic. *Religions*, 6, 657–669. doi:10.3390/rel6020657

Tax Justice Network. (2020). The State of Tax Justice 2020: Tax Justice in the Time of COVID-19, https://taxjustice.net/wp-content/uploads/2020/11/The_State_of_Tax_Justice_2020_ENGLISH.pdf

Thomsen, M. and Watrin, C. (2018). Tax avoidance over time: A comparison of European and U.S. firms. *Journal of International Accounting, Auditing and Taxation*, 33, 40–63. https://doi.org/10.1016/j.intaccaudtax.2028.11.002

Torgler, B. (2001). What do we know about tax morale and tax compliance? *International Review of Economics and Business (RISEC)*, 48, 395–419. https://doi.org/10.4337/9781847207203.00006

Torgler, B. (2003). Tax morale in transition Countries. *Post-communist Economies*, 15(3), 357–381.

Torgler, B. and Schneider, F. (2009). The impact of tax morale and institutional quality on the shadow economy. *Journal of Economic Psychology*, 30(2), 228–245.

Tsakumis, G.T., Curatola, A.P. and Porcano, T.M. (2007). The relation between national cultural dimensions and tax evasion. *Journal of International Accounting, Auditing and Taxation*, 16(2), 131–147. https://doi.org/10.1016/j.intaccaudtax.2007.06.004

US GAO. (2019). TAX GAP. Multiple Strategies Are Need to Reduce Noncompliance. Retrieved June 22, 2021, from https://www.gao.gov/assets/gao-19-558t.pdf

Vo, D.H., Nguyen, H.M., Vo, T.M. and McAleer, M. (2020). Information sharing, bank penetration and tax evasion in emerging markets. *Risks*, 8(2), 38. https://doi.org/10.3390/risks8020038

Williams, C.C., Kedir, A., Fethi, M. and Nadin, S. (2012). Evaluating 'Varieties of Capitalism' by the extent and nature of the informal economy: The case of South-Eastern Europe. *South Eastern Journal of Economics*, 2, 113–130.

Wintrobe, R. and Gërxhani, K. (2004). Tax evasion and trust: A comparative analysis. *Proceedings of the annual meeting of the European Public Choice Society, 2004.*

World Bank. (2007). The Worldwide Governance Indicators (WGI). Retrieved from http://info. worldbank.org/governance/wgi/index.aspx#home

Zucman, G. (2014). Taxing across borders: Tracking personal wealth and corporate profits. *Journal of Economic Perspectives*, 28(4), 121–48. https://doi.org/10.1257/jep.28.4.121

Zucman, G. (2017). How corporations and the wealthy avoid taxes (and how to stop them). *New York Times*. Retrieved November 11, 2017, from https://www.nytimes.com/interactive/2017/11/10/ opinion/gabriel-zucman-paradise-papers-tax-evasion.html

PART V

Looking back and forging ahead: Where are comparative economic studies heading?

29

HOW ECONOMIC SYSTEMS AND PERFORMANCE INFLUENCE REGIME CHANGE

Vilde Lunnan Djuve and Carl Henrik Knutsen

DEPARTMENT OF POLITICAL SCIENCE, UNIVERSITY OF OSLO, OSLO, NORWAY

29.1 Introduction

Economic and political systems are intertwined, and particular changes in one of them often spur certain types of changes in the other. Indeed, many economists, historians, political scientists, and sociologists share the notion that "political development" (often equated with democratization and state-building) and "economic development" (often equated with income growth, urbanization, and industrialization) are causally, and perhaps even conceptually, interlinked (e.g., Lipset, 1959; Sen, 1999).

Different mechanisms may contribute to covariation between particular features of the economic and political systems. Political institutions and regimes shape who are selected into positions of power and the incentives of politicians to choose economic and social policies in different areas – from investment policies to market regulation to education – which, in turn, shape the outlook of the economic system and economic performance. Conversely, the economic system shapes the outlook of the political system, for example, by affecting how different individuals and social groups accrue income and wealth, thus influencing the distribution of power resources that may be used to influence politics.

Both types of relationships have spurred large bodies of work, with contributions from scholars across the social sciences. Concerning the political system's influence on the economy, "institutionalist" explanations of economic development, which increased in prominence especially from the 1990s (e.g., North, 1990; Knack and Keefer, 1995; Acemoglu et al., 2001), highlight how a well-functioning institutional environment that guarantees well-defined, secure, and broad-based property rights is critical for investments and subsequent income growth. In the last decade or two, comparative social scientists have advanced this research program, for instance, by nuancing and specifying both the independent and dependent variables, asking which institutions (free and fair elections, electoral rules, Weberian bureaucracies, institutionalized political parties, etc.) matter and for what particular economic outcomes (GDP per capita growth, foreign direct investment, income inequality, inflation, etc.).[1]

A similar development has taken place in the broader research program that assesses the "reverse" causal relationship, namely the one running from economic systems and performance to political outcomes. Stability in and change to the political regime has been a

DOI: 10.4324/9781003144366-35

central point of focus for decades (e.g., Lipset, 1959; Moore, 1966, Huntington, 1968), and explanations pointing to the causal role of features of the economic system have been prominent (see e.g., Munck, 2019; Knutsen and Dahlum, 2022). As we will detail below, early studies from the 1950s and 60s – often subsumed under the broad heading of modernization theory – posited a general link between economic development and democratization. While modernization theory was quickly criticized as being too simplistic by scholars drawing on in-depth historical case studies from different regions (especially Europe and Latin America; see Moore, 1966; O'Donnell, 1973), the last two decades have also seen a growth in more nuanced large-n studies. Several studies have differentiated between regime changes to and from democracy, often finding that economic conditions matter differently for democratizing and autocratizing changes (e.g., Przeworski et al., 2000). Researchers also incorporate a greater variety of regime changes – for example, considering changes between different types of autocratic regimes (Geddes et al., 2014) – and study several processes through which regimes break down, such as coups (Powell and Thyne, 2011), revolutions (Knutsen, 2014), and incumbent-guided transitions (Djuve et al., 2020).

In this chapter, we will review literatures on how economic performance and different features of economic systems affect political regime stability and change, focusing on work from the last two decades. To illustrate how these relationships might play out "on the ground", we provide a few brief case studies of countries from different regions. In order to provide an updated overview of selected empirical patterns of relevance, we will also present some descriptive statistics on developments, globally and in certain major regions. To this end, we draw on data from the Varieties of Democracy dataset (Coppedge et al., 2018) and the Historical Regimes Data (HRD) (Djuve et al., 2020), which cover 202 polities from across the world and with time series extending all the way from the start of the French Revolution (1789) to the present (2020).

The remainder of the chapter is structured as follows: In the next section, we discuss how different features of the economic system and economic performance relate to the most widely studied type of regime change, namely democratization. When reviewing this extensive literature, we will further specify the "independent variable" and address, in sequence, the relevance of the level of economic development, the production structure of the economy, economic inequality, and, finally, short-term economic crises. In the following section, we address how above-listed economic factors relate to the "opposite" type of regime change, namely autocratization, characterized by the post-transition regime being substantially less democratic than the pre-transition regime. In the third section, we will consider a subset of these economic features – with a particular focus on short-term economic crises – that pertain to regime change more generally. In the fourth section, we will consider how economic features, again with a focus on economic crises, relate to particular processes leading to regime transition, notably military coups, revolutions, and incumbent-guided regime transitions. We complement our review in this section by presenting descriptive patterns and analyses based on the HRD. The fifth and final section concludes by summarizing some of the most important findings and distilling some overarching patterns and conclusions on how economic systems and performance matter (or not) for regime change. For example, we discuss how many economic factors relate very differently to different types of (and processes behind) regime changes. There is one pattern, however, that seems to apply more generally: short-term crises drive up the probability of several (and very different) types of regime changes.

Before we start our discussion, we should clarify the concept of a "political regime" and the related notion of "regime change". The very general definition of a political regime that we rely on considers a regime as the rules – both formal as written in constitutions and informal as established in unwritten practices and norms – through which political leaders are selected and deselected (Geddes et al., 2014). Accordingly, a regime change is simply a non-trivial change in these rules (for a discussion on different thresholds for considering a rule change substantial enough to count as a regime change, we refer to Djuve et al., 2020). There are numerous ways to categorize political regimes, for example, according to how many people are involved in selecting and retaining leaders in power (Bueno de Mesquita et al., 2003) or whether those leaders selected typically rule in the common interest (Aristotle, 2000). Yet, the most common way to categorize political regimes – both in the social sciences and in the wider public discourse – is according to their degree of democracy (where regimes that are characterized by a low degree of democracy are typically labelled "autocracies" or "dictatorships").[2] Definitions of what exactly democracy is vary, with some notions focusing squarely on the existence of competitive multi-party elections for selecting members of parliament and the chief executive (e.g., Przeworski et al., 2000), whereas others define democracy according to principles (rather than institutions) such as "popular control over political decision-making" or "political equality among all citizens" (e.g., Beetham, 1999). Yet, the existence of free and fair elections for core political offices and universal suffrage remain key components to most democracy concepts as well as democracy measures (see Coppedge et al. 2020), including most of the measures used in the studies reviewed below, even though exact definitions and operationalizations differ.[3] With this caveat in mind, we start our survey by reviewing studies considering democratization – i.e., regime changes bringing the regime in a more democratic direction – as an outcome.

29.2 Democratization

The natural point of departure for a discussion on how economic factors influence prospects is modernization theory, the presumably most widely discussed theory of democratization (Munck, 2019), which is still being hotly debated (Dahlum, 2018). In a nutshell, modernization theory, among other things, predicts that economic development should lead to more democratic regimes, inter alia, through enhancing prospects for democratization.

Modernization theory comes in different shapes and forms, but one widely cited early version is Lipset (1959). What Lipset shares with many other modernization theorists is thinking about economic and social development in systemic terms, in the sense that there are several processes of change that tend to correspond (and reinforce each other), and it is this systemic transformation of the economy that makes societies ripe and ready for democratization. Lipset highlighted how growth in productive capacity and income is related to industrialization and urbanization, but also to changing the composition of class structures and widespread norms in the population. More specifically, Lipset surmised that a developing economy should bring with it the growth of the urban middle class, and these citizens should also tend to hold values such as tolerance and a culture of compromise that make societies better fit for democracy as a system of government. In his empirical analysis of Latin American and European countries, Lipset found that more urbanized, better educated, and richer countries had higher levels of democracy. Several scholars subsequently replicated such correlations (e.g., Diamond, 1992), interpreting this as evidence that economic development, over time, enhanced the chances of democratization.

While the cross-country correlations between various measures of economic development and level of democracy are high, later work would either nuance the above interpretation or call it into question. First, concerning nuances, the correlations between, say, level of GDP per capita, education outcomes, and class composition are high, but far from perfect, and the question nevertheless remains if one or more of these distinct socio-economic features play a stronger causal role in engendering democratization than others. Income level could play a role by, e.g., enhancing job prospects in the private sector and thus give viable alternative options for autocratic regime elites, thereby making them less willing to resist demands for democratization (e.g., Boix and Stokes, 2003). Yet, a high level of education could be more important since it enhances the capacities and skills that citizens require to mobilize against an autocratic regime, but presumably also because it alters the norms and attitudes of citizens in a pro-democratic direction (e.g., Dahlum, 2017). Others contend that industrialization, urbanization, and related change in the class composition of the economy are more important, as the urban social groups that grow and are empowered by these processes have particularly strong incentives and capabilities to organize against the autocratic regime and work for democratization; several scholars have highlighted that the urban industrial working class fit this description well and may be especially important agents of democracy in many contexts (Rueschemeyer et al., 1992; Collier, 1999; Dahlum et al., 2019). Hence, economic growth and expanded education in a society that does not experience industrialization may not be fertile ground for democratization, after all, if the latter notion is correct.

When it comes to empirical analysis of GDP per capita and democratization, Przeworski and Limongi's (1997) seminal study highlighted that – despite the correlation between income and levels of democracy – there is at best a tenuous relationship between income and the probability of transitioning from an autocracy to a democracy. While subsequent studies highlighted that the correlation is strengthened once accounting for natural resource income or extending the sample back before World War II (Boix and Stokes, 2003; Boix, 2011), different sensitivity analyses have shown that the relationship is very sensitive also to other model specification, sample, and measurement choices, and that the relationship is far from robust (Gassebner et al., 2013; Rød et al., 2020). The lack of a clear relationship between a high-income level and democratization has also been explained well by recent studies disaggregating the democratization process. Kennedy (2010) finds evidence that a high-income level actually stabilizes autocratic (and all other) regimes; wealthy autocracies presumably have better capabilities for repressing opponents and more resources to spend on coopting yet other threats. However, when the autocratic regime first experiences a change, Kennedy finds, it is much more likely to be a democratizing one if the income level is high.[4] These two mechanisms pull in opposite directions on the aggregate relationship between income and democratization probability and may be the main reason behind the tenuous results from other studies.

29.2.1 Case in point: Income and democracy in Venezuela, 1960–1999

Before the authoritarian turn under Hugo Chavez, Venezuelan democracy was long considered unusually resilient in the South American context. In the region overall, the last decades of the 20th century were a time period marred by military strongmen and frequent regime changes. In Venezuela, however, a political agreement known as the Pact of Punto Fijo from 1958 ushered in a relatively inclusive democratic period, which – albeit not without its problems – was characterized by regular free elections and protection of civil liberties. One common explanation for this consolidation of democracy is the concurrent growth and stabilization of the Venezuelan economy. Having already become one of the largest oil exporters in the world, Venezuela's income from oil exports only grew for a couple of decades, with an extreme boom after the 1973 oil crisis leading to the quadrupling of export profits. This income was then invested in the rest of the economy, creating one of the largest middle classes in Latin America at the time. As described by Coppedge (2005), this middle class, along with the industrialized working class, provided popular support for a system with two large catch-all parties, who in turn emphasized a political culture of compromise and peaceful alternation of executive power. When the oil boom eventually turned to a bust, however, Venezuelan democracy proved to be less resilient.

We will deal with processes of autocratization in the next section, but let us here foreshadow some relevant insights from the Venezuelan case. Interestingly, some of the most significant challenges against the Venezuelan government came when President Carlos Andrés Pérez introduced neoliberal economic reforms in 1989, weakening the influence of those favored by the preceding domestically focused, natural resource-dependent, economic system (Crisp, 1998). As such, the lack of successful industrialization and diversification of the Venezuelan economy during these largely democratic years – pointed to as important mechanisms in modernization theory – might ultimately also play a role in explaining its vulnerability to the most recent authoritarian turn in Venezuelan politics.

As for other aspects of development and structural features of the economy, some studies have reported that higher levels of education are conducive to democratization, but also for this aspect of development, the results are mixed (for a review, see Dahlum, 2017). When it comes to the more specific type of production and asset structure of the economy, there is clearer evidence that this matters for democratization chances. For instance, wealthy and powerful land owners could have especially strong incentives to block democratization (see e.g., Ansell and Samuels, 2015; Albertus, 2017), due to the land being an immovable asset that may be taxed heavily after democratization (instead of shipped abroad, as elites may do with, e.g., financial assets). Accordingly, Boix (2003) and Ansell and Samuels (2015) find that concentration of land ownership hinders democratization, whereas Knutsen and Dahlum (2022) find that a high agricultural production share in the economy is negatively related to democratization. Similarly, several studies report that autocracies in oil-dependent economies – with oil being another immovable asset that elites can control and use for their own benefits under autocracy – are less likely to experience democratization (e.g., Ross, 2001; 2012; Gassebner et al., 2013; Rød et al., 2020).

Above we discussed the mixed findings on the national (average) income level and democratization. Could it be that the distribution of income within society is more important for democratization chances than the average level of income? Several theoretical models suggest that this may be the case, with income inequality playing a prominent role in explaining both the incentives of relatively poor citizens (Acemoglu and Robinson, 2000, 2006) and non-incumbent elite groups (Ansell and Samuels, 2015) to fight for democratization as well as the incentives of non-incumbent elites to resist or yield to demands for democratization (Boix, 2003; Acemoglu and Robinson, 2006). However, different theoretical models give different predictions on the sign of the income inequality – democratization relationship, and empirical studies do not find a robust relationship between measures of income inequality and democratization (e.g., Houle, 2009; Teorell, 2010; Knutsen, 2015; Knutsen and Dahlum, 2021). Still, recent studies have reported several more nuanced findings, linking income inequality to democratization in particular contexts or linking other types of economic inequalities to democratization. Regarding the latter, Ansell and Samuels (2010) report evidence suggesting that high inequality in land hurts democratization prospects. Regarding the former, Freeman and Quinn (2012) find that high-income inequality improves democratization chances in autocracies that are financially open and where the elites' assets are easier to move across borders.

29.2.2 Case in point: Land inequality in Prussia

Why did it take so long for democracy to be established in Germany while democratization occurred in many other European states? In answering this question, historians routinely look to the largest German state, Prussia, and its very high levels of land inequality. As a powerful political and military entity, Prussia won several wars in the 18th and 19th centuries, and eventually, under chancellor Otto von Bismarck, became a driving force in the unification of Germany. As for its political system, Prussia was notably undemocratic with a particular "three class" voting system based on the tax revenue from each class: those who paid the most taxes formed the first class, while those who paid the least formed the third. Each class still elected a third of the electors, so that the very few, rich, members of the first (and second) class had highly disproportionate control over state politics.

Now the origins and, importantly, sustainment of this voting system are very often linked to the very unequal distribution of land in Prussia. As pointed by Ansell and Samuels (2010), Albertus (2017), and others, landowners, in protection of their assets, are often the least likely group to support democracy. In a roll-call analysis of proposed Prussian electoral reforms in 1912, Ziblatt (2008) even finds robust evidence from inside the parliamentary decision-making process: representatives from those Prussian constituencies with the highest levels of landholding inequality were significantly more likely to vote against electoral reforms than those from more equal constituencies. By dismissing the 1912 reforms, the "three class" voting system persisted.

Finally, different empirical studies have found a tight relationship between short-term economic performance, often measured as GDP per capita growth in the preceding year or by using various operationalizations of economic crises, and democratization. For example, the seminal study by Przeworski and Limongi (1997) finds that slow growth increases the likelihood of transitioning from an autocratic to a democratic regime (especially in poor countries), whereas Teorell (2010: chapter 3) finds similar results when considering gradual increases in the level of democracy. The sensitivity analysis by Gassebner et al. (2013) also reports that short-term growth in GDP per capita is one of few robust determinants of democratizing regime transitions. When autocratic regimes face economic crises, a subsequent episode of democratization is more likely than if the economy is growing (see also, e.g., Kennedy, 2010; Knutsen and Dahlum, 2021). While the above-referenced studies rely on observational cross-country time series data, from which it is difficult to draw rock-solid causal inferences (especially absent valid instruments that satisfy the exclusion restriction, as is the case here), a causal interpretation of the robust relationship is still plausible, as these studies account for several plausible confounders and often measure crises prior to the dependent variable.

29.3 Autocratization

Sensitivity analyses assessing different determinants of democratization and the reverse process – sometimes referred to as democratic breakdown, democratic erosion, or autocratization – have tended to find fewer robust determinants of the latter than the former (Gassebner et al., 2013; Rød et al., 2020). The same is true when we only focus on the economic determinants of these two types of regime changes (see Knutsen and Dahlum, 2021). There may be several reasons for this. One is that processes of autocratization are inherently harder to explain than processes of democratization. A second is that the theoretical literature on democratization is still much larger, suggesting that comparative social scientists have yet to identify important candidate explanations for autocratization. A third is that there are less data on autocratization episodes – they have been less common than democratization episodes in recent decades (and centuries), which makes it statistically harder to obtain robust results.

Whatever the reason, researchers have identified fewer robust economic determinants of autocratization than democratization. For instance, while a natural resource-dependent economy seems to hinder transitions from autocracy to democracy, evidence is much less clear on transitions in the opposite direction (see e.g., Rød et al., 2020). Yet, there are a handful of economic factors that are very important for understanding which democracies are more likely to degrade, and even turn into autocracies.

First, income level, as operationalized by GDP per capita, is a robust covariate of autocratization (e.g., Przeworski and Limongi, 1997; Przeworski et al., 2000; Boix and Stokes, 2003; Gassebner et al., 2013; Rød et al., 2020).[5] This is a particularly noteworthy finding, given how many times it has been replicated across different datasets and model specifications (only with a few deviating findings; see e.g., Acemoglu et al., 2009), but also in light of the non-robust relationship between GDP per capita and democratization, discussed in the previous section. Whereas higher income levels are not clearly linked to transitions from more autocratic to more democratic regimes, they seem to vaccinate existing democracies from degrading and especially from breaking down and turning into a dictatorship. As we will discuss in the penultimate section, there are many processes that can drive regime change, but studies show that the two main processes through which democracies break down are military coups and self-coups conducted (often in a gradual manner) by elected incumbents (Svolik, 2015; Lührmann and Lindberg, 2019). A high-income level may mitigate the incentives and capabilities of military actors to intervene in and remove democratic governments (Schiel, 2019) but also reduce the incentives of incumbent leaders to cling to power as a well-functioning economy provides them with better alternative options if they are to step down after an election loss (Przeworski and Limongi, 1997). A high-income level and developed economy may also insulate democracies through other channels, such as altering the values and strengthening the normative commitments of citizens to democracy, thereby making it more costly for those who try to grab power and overthrow the democratic system (e.g., Inglehart and Welzel, 2005, but see Dahlum and Knutsen, 2017).

High economic inequality, for instance in wealth or income, is another structural feature of the economy that has been highlighted as dangerous to democracies. In inegalitarian societies, large differences in economic resources may translate into large differences in political resources, and elites may undermine the functioning of democracies through various channels of influence (such as lobbying or corruption) to alter both institutions and policies in a direction that they desire (e.g., Albertus and Menaldo, 2018). This could lead to democracies of lower quality. In certain instances, economic elites may even have strong incentives to organize (or at least condone) coups that replace the democracy with an autocratic regime that promises to lower taxes, pursue less redistribution, or implement other policies that elites prefer. Indeed, some empirical analysis (e.g., Houle, 2009) do find a clear relationship between measures of income inequality (and especially those measuring inequality between distinct groups, notably employers and employees) and democratic breakdown or autocratization.[6]

29.3.1 Case in point: Inequality and democratic breakdown in Guatemala, 1944–1954

The first successful democratic government of Guatemala was instated after the 1944 Revolution that ousted the oppressive president Jorge Ubico from power. For ten years, democratically elected presidents Arévalo and Árbenz pursued liberalizing policies and encouraged freedom of association, allowing for the formation of labor unions and different political parties. In 1954, however, Árbenz was removed in a CIA-backed coup supported by powerful financial elites, and democratic elections would not be held again in Guatemala for more than 30 years. Why was this democratic project so short-lived?

When considering potential structural causes in the Guatemalan case, the severity of economic inequality stands out. As previously mentioned, economic inequality can be present in many forms, through income inequality, land-holding inequality, and inequality between ethnic groups. In Guatemala, inequality was present in all these forms. In the 1960s, the middle class made up less than 20% of the population, while the middle and upper classes together received over two-thirds of the nation's income (Caumartin, 2005). Under Ubico, the United Fruit Company alone owned 42% of Guatemala's land (La Feber, 1997). And throughout Guatemalan political history, indigenous people, still making up over half the population in 1950, were systematically poorer and had less access to education, income, and land (Caumartin, 2005; Kistler, 2014). These economic inequities translated into several troubling political issues for the democratic government. While democratically elected, historians often argue that the indigenous part of the population was generally skeptical of the mainly Ladino (non-indigenous) politicians, meaning that the government did not have strong and broad popular support. And while disenfranchised agrarian workers participated widely in the overthrow of Ubico, political reform under the democratic regime did not manage to redistribute power sufficiently to thwart the influence of the upper class. Arguably, this is the crux of the democratic regime's downfall: the far-reaching attempts at agrarian reform by Arevalo and Ardenz became so threatening to the powerful business elites (United Fruit in particular) that they sought foreign support (from the United States) to oust the democratic government altogether. As such, the Guatemalan case serves as an illustration of the findings by both Houle (2009) and Albertus and Menaldo (2014) on how ethnic inequality and disgruntled elites, respectively, can contribute to the fragility of democracy.

However, when testing the various relationships on inequality and autocratization across larger samples, they do not seem to be robust to various specification changes (see e.g., Teorell, 2010; Rød et al., 2020). In particular, the choice of inequality measure and the data source is important for the results (Knutsen 2015). While the theoretical rationale for an adverse effect of economic inequality on the quality and duration of democracy seems plausible, as illustrated by the Guatemalan case, democracies continue to survive in many inegalitarian settings. Hence, the jury is still out on whether or not there exists a general and systematic relationship.

In contrast, there seems to be a much clearer relationship between economic performance in the short term and the resilience of democracies. Notably, various measures of economic crisis (based on rates of growth, inflation, or unemployment) seem to correlate quite strongly with autocratization and increased risk of democracies breaking down (e.g., Knutsen and Dahlum, 2021; Przeworski and Limongi, 1997; Teorell, 2010). Short-term crises may endanger democracies through various mechanisms. Steep economic crises that reduce incomes of various population segments often spur different types of political instability, including civil wars (Hegre and Sambanis, 2006) and riots and protests (Ponticelli and Voth, 2020). Increased popular grievances and a loss of legitimacy for the current government and wider system could further reduce the expected costs of conducting a coup d'état (Gasiorowski, 1995) – and coups are, in fact, much more likely after an economic crisis (Gassebner et al., 2016). Crisis may also spur the second main mode of democratic breakdown, namely a change to the system that is conducted mainly by elected incumbents themselves. Especially crises that are viewed as being caused by other actors than the regime – be it foreign governments, businesses or domestic non-incumbent elite groups – present incumbent leaders with a golden window of opportunity for enforcing changes to the current regime (Djuve and Knutsen, 2019). This could be done, for example, via a self-coup following a declaration of state of emergency (Lührmann and Rooney, 2021). Regardless of the mechanisms at play, democracies seem to be at increased risk when production and income levels tank.

29.4 Regime breakdown

Having discussed the literatures on democratization and autocratization – two very particular forms of regime change that have received a lot of scholarly attention – we now turn to a more general notion of regime change. Drawing on the definition of regime change laid out in the introduction, namely a substantial change in the informal or formal rules on how leaders are selected, we consider notable results on economic factors related to all such regime change (and not only those that draw the regime in a clearly more democratic or autocratic direction). This is a much smaller literature, which may in part be explained by the fact that cross-country datasets capturing different types of regime change have been missing until fairly recently.

One notable dataset that opened up for the study of a broader array of regime changes is the one developed by Barbara Geddes and colleagues (Geddes, 1999; Geddes et al., 2014). An important feature of this dataset is the classification of autocratic regimes into different subtypes – dominant party regimes, military regimes, personalist regimes, and autocratic monarchies – which opens up for studying regime transitions between these different subtypes, as well as between democracy and the different subtypes. The dataset has global coverage, and currently extends back to 1946. Recently, Anckar and Fredriksson (2019) have extended a similar coding scheme back to 1800. Other datasets differentiating between various autocracy types, following somewhat different classification schemes, exist (see e.g., Wahmann et al., 2013). Providing an even more inclusive operationalization of regime changes, Djuve et al.'s (2020) HRD incorporate more than 2000 distinct political regimes for 202 polities from 1789 to the present. These data also code substantial changes in the rules for selecting leaders also within relatively democratic regimes (such as major franchise expansions, e.g., to all women) as well as changes between autocracies of similar type (for example, the transition from one military regime led by a particular junta to another military regime led by a rivalling junta).

What do studies that draw on such more expansive operationalizations of regime change – the clear majority of recorded regime changes are, in fact, between different regimes that are both autocratic (Geddes et al., 2014, Djuve et al., 2020) – tell us about the stabilizing or destabilizing roles of economic factors? While not entirely robust (for example, to accounting for country-fixed effects, see Djuve et al. 2020), one finding is that regimes in countries with higher income levels seem to last longer. Kennedy (2010) finds this as a general pattern for both democracies and autocracies when relying on operationalization of regime change that counts even small changes on the Polity scale, whereas Djuve et al. (2020) find this pattern when using both the data and operationalization of regime breakdown from Geddes et al. (2014) and their own HRD data. One possible explanation is that the amount of resources available to governments, and which may be used both for effective repression and cooptation of potential threats, typically increases with income levels. This interpretation finds some support also by the correspondence between natural resource income – which is perhaps the easiest revenue source for governments to monopolize and use for repression and cooptation (e.g., Ross, 2012) – and regime duration. In particular, Wright et al. (2015) find that higher oil income is especially important for prolonging the life of autocratic regimes by mitigating risks of these regimes being replaced by other autocratic regimes.

An even clearer relationship seems to be the one between short-term macroeconomic performance, often measured as GDP per capita growth in the preceding year(s), and the probability of regime breakdowns, overall. Kennedy (2010), for example, finds evidence that poor short-term economic performance is conducive to changes on the Polity scale for both democratic and autocratic regimes, whereas Djuve et al. (2020) find that it enhances the likelihood of regime breakdown according to the Geddes et al. and HRD data in various statistical specifications. The main interpretation is that while strong performance may bolster incumbent regimes of various kinds, an economic crisis puts different regimes at risk. As our discussion below details, the robust overall relationship may be because economic crises tend to spur so many different types of processes that can lead regimes to break down.

29.4.1 Case in point: The consolidation of Fujimori's rule in Peru

On April 5, 1992, President Alberto Fujimori set in motion a self-coup in Peru. Elected in 1990 after four years of negative GDP pc growth, Fujimori was known as an economic reformer and ran on a platform of invigorating fiscal policies and increased prosperity. Fujimori's predecessor was Alan Garcia, from the center-left American Popular Revolutionary Alliance (APRA) (Crabtree, 1992), who's five-year term in office was characterized by a drastic and protracted economic downturn. With very different economic ideas, Garcia's lack of success might have enhanced popular support for Fujimori and his policy program. Yet the latter's measures for combating the economic crisis that he inherited remained controversial and exasperated the ongoing internal conflict in Peru. Hence, when the opposition reeled at a series of severe austerity measures, Fujimori eventually dissolved Congress in the autogolpe of April 5, 1992, with substantial support from the military.

After the self-coup, Fujimori promulgated a new version of the constitution and pushed through his reforms without curtailment from democratic institutions (Mauceri, 2006). As such, we can use this case to illustrate an indirect way in which an economic crisis can destabilize regimes. When facing economic grievances, popular support for institutions in the existing regime can erode, paving the way for aspiring autocrats wanting to override existing playing rules. In the Peruvian case, an ongoing internal military conflict with the insurgent group Sendero Luminoso was also exasperated by the economic situation and contributed to military support for Fujimori. Thus, the general strength of the relationship between crisis and regime breakdown is likely a result of crises' potential to influence political players in diverse ways.

29.5 Specific processes of breakdown

In the previous section, we addressed how economic factors affect regime durability and the likelihood of breaking down, using a comprehensive definition of regime change incorporating both transitions from autocracies to democracies, from democracies to autocracies, and transitions between two regimes that are both autocratic. While these regime changes are similar in that the formal and informal rules for selecting leaders in a country are substantially altered, it is obvious that these rules can be changed in a number of ways. Regime transitions differ in speed (one day vs. years), use of violence (a civil war vs. a non-violent revolution), whether or not the changes are in line with the existing constitution (a major suffrage extension approved by the parliament vs. a coup d'état), and who the main actors driving

Table 29.1 Relative frequency of 13 main modes of regime breakdown

Modes of breakdown	Relative frequency (%)	
	1789–2020	*1945–2020*
Military coup	15.5	23.1
Coup by other	7.7	2.8
Self-coup	6.5	9.1
Assassination of sitting leader	1.6	0.9
Natural death of sitting leader	0.9	0.9
Civil war	4.5	5.0
Inter-state war	11.8	1.6
Foreign intervention	7.9	5.0
Popular uprising	5.8	4.0
Directed democratization	13.5	18.1
Directed transition	19.9	26.6
Non-directed democratization	1.6	1.7
Other process	1.8	0.9
Total number	**1911**	**824**

Source: Based on updated HRD data included in V-Dem v.11.1.

the process are (incumbent leaders themselves vs. other regime elites vs. broader population segments vs. foreign actors).

Different categorization schemes exist. The one constructed by Djuve et al. (2020), for example, counts 13 separate categories of processes that lead to regime breakdown. Some of them are far more frequent than others, as shown in Table 29.1, which gives relative frequencies across 202 polities from 1789 to 2020 as well as the more recent period from 1946 to 2020. The most frequent categories are military coups and directed transitions (both democratizing and non-democratizing ones) that are partly or fully controlled by the incumbent regime's elites. In contrast, only a handful of regimes have ended through the assassination or natural death of sitting leaders throughout modern history. So how are these events distributed across different regions of the world? In the following, we will take a closer look at the two most frequent modes, military coups and directed transitions, in the post-WWII period.

Figure 29.1 is a map showing the total number of regime deaths due to military coups that have happened in each country since 1945. As the shading shows, military coups have been

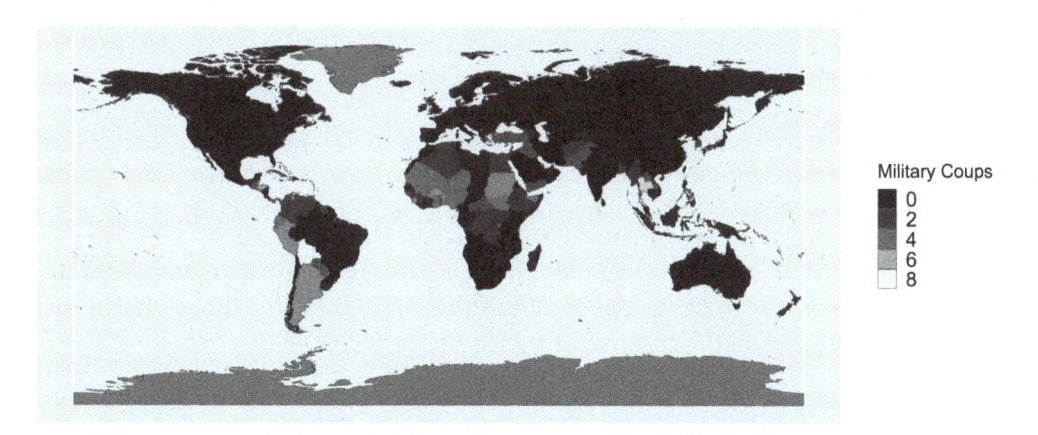

Figure 29.1 Regime changes due to military coups by country: 1945–2020. (According to HRD data.)

virtually non-existent in North America, Europe, and Northern Asia over this period, but rather frequent in South America, Western Africa, and the MENA (Middle East and North Africa) region. The countries that experienced the most regime-ending military coups – eight each – during this time period were Bolivia and Syria.

When it comes to the focus of the academic literature, coups and revolutions are the processes that have received by far most attention in the literature on regime change[7]. We will briefly review these literatures below, but then focusing even more narrowly on how income levels and economic crises are proposed to spur or deter these processes of regime change. After that, we will discuss how the two mentioned economic factors may affect the propensity of countries to experience the empirically frequent, but less studied, processes that involve incumbent leaders being the main actors behind the regime.

Concerning coups, Gassebner et al. (2016) highlight that there is disagreement on whether or not structural economic factors are conducive to such processes: "Londregan and Poole (1990) argue that being less economically developed is almost a necessary condition for coups. This position is echoed by many researchers, sometimes formulated in a more precise fashion…others again argue that economic conditions are rather unimportant as coup predictors" (p. 298). In their sensitivity analysis, Gassebner et al. find some indications that poor countries are more coup-prone, but income level is far from being a robust determinant. The recent empirical literature has largely relied on the coup dataset by Powell and Thyne (2011), which counts both coup attempts and successful coups. Utilizing this distinction, Olar (2019) finds that income level relates negatively to the probability of coups attempts, but only in some model specifications, and he finds no indications that income is related to successful coups. Analyzing only coups leading to regime breakdown, Djuve et al. (2020) also fail to find a clear relationship between income level and regime-ending coups. In contrast, economic crises and shocks seem to drive coups (e.g., Kim, 2016). This pattern is reflected in the same studies that found weak results for income levels, referenced above. Djuve et al. (2020) find that low short-term economic growth is related to regime-ending coups, whereas Olar (2019) finds a strong relationship with coup attempts, and Gassebner et al. (2016) also find fairly strong (though not entirely robust) evidence in their sensitivity analysis that coups are related to short-term growth.

Concerning revolutions, Djuve et al. (2020) find that mass uprisings leading to regime change are more likely to occur in poor countries than in rich ones. Using different data and separating between revolutionary attempts and whether revolutions where successful in removing the incumbent leader or not, Knutsen (2014: 920) finds "some evidence that higher income levels mitigate revolution attempts, but this is not robust and further analysis indicates that any association may stem from oil income more specifically". Further, he finds "no net effect of income level on successful revolution". Once again, the relationship with short-term economic performance turns out more robust across the studies. Djuve et al. (2020) find that regime-changing mass uprisings are more likely to take place when economic growth has been slow in the preceding year and Knutsen (2014) finds robust relationships between economic crises, on the one hand, and revolutionary attempts and successful revolutions on the other.

Figure 29.2 maps the total number of directed transitions in each country since 1945. In a nutshell, directed transitions are regime changes that are initiated by the sitting regime. They can be democratizing in nature, for example, by incumbent governments introducing free and fair elections, or they can be autocratizing, for example, by incumbent presidents removing their own term limits or severely repressing free media. Finally, incumbents sometimes initiate regime changes that move the regime in neither of these directions.[8] In contrast with military coups, directed transitions have been a global phenomenon, affecting all

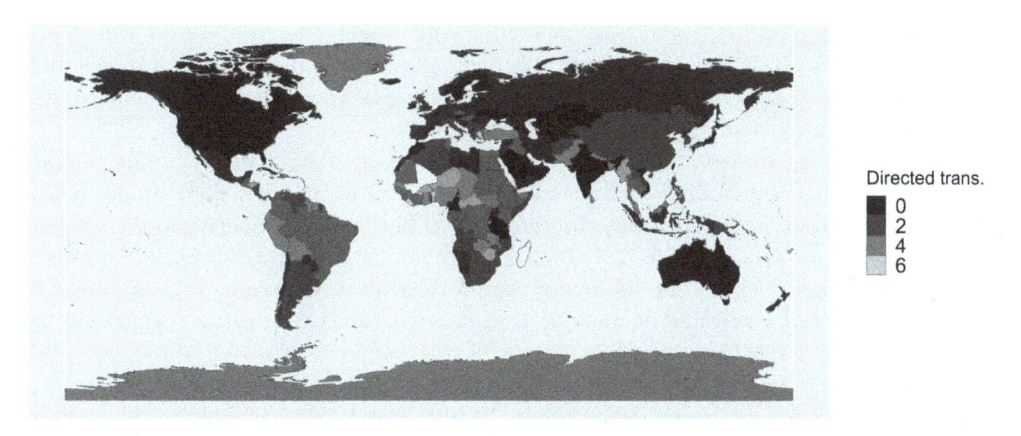

Figure 29.2   Regime changes due to directed (incumbent-guided) transitions by country: 1945–2020. (According to HRD data.)

regions except North America. The countries that have experienced the highest number of transitions emanating from within the incumbent government are Mali and Madagascar, with seven such transitions each. In Madagascar, these transitions are an important part of a particularly turbulent political history since WWII – the political regime has changed a total of 12 times after 1945. Having experienced five non-democratizing and two democratizing-directed transitions, regime changes stemming from within the regime have made up the majority of all regime changes.

As illustrated in Table 29.1 and Figure 29.2, the most frequent mode in which regimes break down is through incumbents altering the rules of the regime from within, either in a democratizing direction or not. These regime changes are relatively under-studied compared to regime changes induced by forces external to the regime elite such as revolutions or coups. One factor that correlates strongly with these incumbent-guided transitions, however, is a preceding economic crisis. Djuve and Knutsen (2019) find that overall, economic crisis is associated with incumbent-guided transitions as a whole, but that the relationship is particularly robust between crisis and incumbent-guided transitions that are *not* democratizing. These include events such as transitions from military juntas to personal dictatorship or from at least partially free semi-democracies to party-based autocracy. Crises may thereby be powerful general de-stabilizers of all types of regimes by increasing the likelihood of a breakdown in many ways.

29.6   Conclusion

In this chapter, we have reviewed the literatures connecting different features of economic systems or types of economic performance to different types or processes of regime change. We have emphasized the large theoretical and empirical literatures on economic determinants of democratization, especially related to modernization theory and its critics, but we also discussed several studies on the economic determinants of autocratization processes. Further, we discussed studies considering how economic factors, and economic crises in particular, influence overall regime durability (and the corresponding likelihood of regime breakdown). Finally, we considered studies on how economic factors relate to more specific processes of regime breakdown, focusing on coups, revolutions, and incumbent-guided regime transitions.

We will not sum up all the more specific findings and insights from this vast body of scholarly work in this conclusion. Instead, we will highlight a few of the most notable ones and draw some more general insights from patterns that pertain across different economic factors or different regime change outcomes.

First, for several features of the economic system, there seem to be asymmetric effects in the sense that they matter differently for different types of regime breakdown. For example, high-income levels clearly relate to democratic breakdown but not to democratization, whereas natural resource dependence stabilizes autocracies but not necessarily democracies. Likewise, there are asymmetric effects on different processes through which regimes break down: A high-income level, for example, seems to be more clearly related to mitigating regime-ending revolutions than coups (Djuve et al., 2020).

A second and related point is that some regime outcomes seem to be "better explained", overall, by the economic system than others. While diverse features such as oil dependence, foreign aid dependence, and an economy dominated by agricultural production seem to hinder democratizing regime transitions (and, correspondingly, diversification away from oil dependence, reduced foreign aid dependence, and a reduced share of production coming from agriculture enhances chances of democratization), the consistent and robust findings for democratic breakdowns are limited to income levels and short-term economic crises (e.g., Rød et al., 2020). Accordingly, scholars studying why democracies break down have highlighted alternative factors related to the political system as key causes. Notable explanations of democratic survival center on strong political parties and a vibrant civil society (Cornell et al., 2020), an autonomous parliament that can check executive transgressions on democracy (Fish, 2006), or the absence of political polarization (Svolik, 2019), to name a few.

A final general point that we want to highlight is the destabilizing role played by economic crises. Theoretical accounts have linked crises to several types of regime change and other forms of instability because they induce grievances against the incumbent regime (e.g., Davies, 1962; Gurr, 1970), because they drain the regime for resources required for repression or cooptation (e.g., Bratton and van de Walle, 1997), or because they serve as focal points for mobilizing regime opposition (e.g., Acemoglu and Robinson, 2006). In contrast to more structural factors and features of the economic system, short-term macroeconomic performance is then also consistently related to various processes behind and types of regime changes. Notably, measures of economic crises such as low short-term growth are related both to democratizing regime changes and democratic breakdowns (e.g., Przeworski and Limongi, 1997) as well as more encompassing measures of regime change (also) taking into account transitions between regimes that are at about similar levels of democracy (Djuve et al., 2020). Crises also relate to a host of processes that bring about, or at least are conducive, to regime change. These include civil wars (Hegre and Sambanis, 2006), coups (Gassebner, Gutmann and Voigt, 2016), irregular leadership changes (Campante and Chor, 2019), riots and mass protests (Ponticelli and Voth, 2020), revolutions (Knutsen, 2014), and self-coups and other incumbent guided transitions (Djuve et al., 2020). In other words, poor short-term economic performance induces political instability of different kinds, and both autocratic and democratic regimes are less safe in the presence or direct aftermath of an economic crisis.

Notes

1 We shall not review this enormous literature here, but for a recent overview of large-n comparative research conducted on the effects of democracy on around 20 economic and social outcomes, see Gerring et al. (2022).

2 There is a long-standing discussion on whether democracy is best conceptualized as a matter of degree or as a dichotomous variable (see e.g., Przeworski et al., 2000; Munck and Verkuilen, 2002; Skaaning et al., 2015; Coppedge et al., 2020). We will not review this debate here, but note that we review studies using both dichotomous and continuous measures of democracy (and notify what different studies are using whenever this is of relevance to interpreting the results). Personally, we favor continuous conceptualizations of democracy but often refer to "democracies" and "autocracies" as short-hand terms for regimes that, respectively, have relatively high and low levels of democracy, beyond or below some threshold level.

3 The most widely used measures are continuous indices from Polity (Marshall et al., 2019), Freedom House (Freedom House, 2020), and V-Dem's Polyarchy measure (Teorell et al., 2019) as well as the dichotomous measures from Cheibub et al. (2010) and Boix et al. (2013).

4 In a similar vein, Treisman (2015) finds that a high-income level is conducive to democratization only when the chief executive dies, thus opening up a window for regime change.

5 However, when disaggregating the democracy concept, the relationship seems much tighter with aspects of democracy related to the execution of free and fair elections than other aspects such as rule of law or protection of civil rights (Knutsen et al., 2019).

6 As for democratization, it may be that different types of economic inequality may have different effects on democratic survival. Houle (2015) finds that high-income inequality measured across different ethnic groups (e.g., some ethnic groups are much poorer than others) is harmful for the longevity of democracies.

7 There are vast literatures on the causes and consequences of civil war and interstate war, but only a fraction of these focus solely on how wars induce regime change.

8 For an elaborate discussion of the three forms of directed transitions, see Djuve et al (2020). Concerning autocratizing directed transitions, much focus has recently been placed on the relevance of "populist leaders" building down important elements of democracy while still appealing to the people and claiming popular support and legitimacy. Despite their concurrence in several high-profile empirical contexts, such as Turkey, Brazil, the Philippines, and Hungary, "populism" and "autocratization" are distinct concepts. Populism, in current political science, typically refers to a subset of anti-elite ideologies that invoke notions of the will of the "people" as the legitimate basis for decision-making (see e.g., Mudde, 2004). This is, theoretically, perfectly consistent with democratic processes. Yet, many incumbent leaders have used such "thin ideologies" to whip up support among core supporters and use it not only to win elections but also in processes of consolidating power and building down democratic institutions, especially liberal democratic checks and constrains from, e.g., the judiciary on the executive. Hence, while populism and autocratization are conceptually distinct, they may be causally related.

References

Acemoglu, D., Johnson, S. and Robinson, J.A. (2001). The Colonial Origins of Comparative Development. *American Economic Review* 91(5): 1369–1401.

Acemoglu, D., Johnson, S., Robinson, J.A. and Yared, P. (2009). Reevaluating the Modernization Hypothesis. *Journal of Monetary Economics* 56(8): 1043–1058.

Acemoglu, D. and Robinson, J.A. (2000). Why Did the West Extend the Franchise? Democracy, Inequality, and Growth in Historical Perspective. *Quarterly Journal of Economics* 115(4): 1167–1199.

Acemoglu, D. and Robinson, J.A. (2006). *Economic Origins of Dictatorship and Democracy.* New York, NY: Cambridge University Press.

Albertus, M. (2017). Landowners and Democracy: The Social Origins of Democracy Reconsidered. *World Politics* 69(2): 233–276.

Albertus, M. and Menaldo, V. (2014). Gaming Democracy: Elite Dominance during Transition and the Prospects for Redistribution. *British Journal of Political Science* 44(3): 575–603. doi:10.1017/S0007123413000124.

Albertus, M. and Menaldo, V. (2018). *Authoritarianism and the Elite Origins of Democracy.* Cambridge: Cambridge University Press.

Anckar, C. and Fredriksson, C. (2019). Classifying Political Regimes 1800–2016: A Typology and a New Dataset. *European Political Science* 18(1): 84–96.

Ansell, B.W. and Samuels, D.J. (2010). Inequality and Democratization: A Contractarian Approach. *Comparative Political Studies* 43(12): 1543–1574.

Ansell, B.W. and Samuels, D.J. (2015). *Inequality and Democratization*. Cambridge: Cambridge University Press.

Aristotle. (2000). *Politics*. New York, NY: Dover Publications.

Beetham, D. (1999). *Democracy and Human Rights*. Cambridge: Polity Press.

Boix, C. (2003). *Democracy and Redistribution*. Cambridge: Cambridge University Press.

Boix, C. (2011). Democracy, Development, and the International System. *American Political Science Review* 105(4): 809–828.

Boix, C. and Stokes, S.C. (2003). Endogenous Democratization. *World Politics* 55(4): 517–549.

Boix, C., Miller, M. and Rosato, S. (2013). A Complete Dataset of Political Regimes, 1800-2007. *Comparative Political Studies* 46(12): 1523–1554.

Bratton, M. and van de Walle, N. (1997). *Democratic Experiments in Africa: Regime Transitions in Comparative Perspective*. Cambridge: Cambridge University Press.

Bueno de Mesquita, B., Smith, A., Morrow, J.D. and Siverson, R.M. (2003). *The Logic of Political Survival*. Cambridge, MA: MIT Press.

Campante, F.R., Chor, D. and Li, B. (2019). The Political Economy Consequences of China's Export Slowdown. Working Paper No. w25925. National Bureau of Economic Research.

Caumartin, C. (2005). Racism, Violence, and Inequality: An Overview of the Guatemalan Case. *CRISE Working Paper NO. 11*. University of Oxford.

Cheibub, J.A., Gandhi, J. and Vreeland, J. (2010). Democracy and Dictatorship Revisited. *Public Choice* 143(1–2): 67–101.

Collier, R.B. (1999). *Paths Towards Democracy: The Working Class and Elites in Western Europe and South America*. Cambridge: Cambridge University Press.

Coppedge, M. (2005). Explaining Democratic Deterioration in Venezuela through Nested Inference. In F. Hagopian and S. Mainwaring (eds.), *The Third Wave of Democratization in Latin America: Advances and Setbacks*. Cambridge: Cambridge University Press, 289–316.

Coppedge, M., Gerring, J., Glynn, A., Knutsen, C.H., Lindberg, S.I., Pemstein, D., Seim, B., Skaaning, S.-E. and Teorell, J. (2020). *Varieties of Democracy: Measuring Two Centuries of Political Change*. Cambridge: Cambridge University Press.

Coppedge, M., Gerring, J., Knutsen, C.H., Lindberg, S.I., Skaaning, S.-E., Teorell, J., Altman, D., Bernhard, M., Fish, M.S., Cornell, A., Dahlum, S., Gjerløw, H., Glynn, A., Hicken, A., Krusell, J., Lührmann, A., Marquardt, K.L., McMann, K., Mechkova, V., Medzihorsky, J., Olin, M., Paxton, P., Pemstein, D., Pernes, J., von Römer, J., Seim, B., Sigman, R., Staton, J., Stepanova, N., Sundström, A., Tzelgov, E., Wang, Y.-T., Wig, T., Wilson, S. and Ziblatt, D. (2018). V-Dem Dataset v8.

Cornell, A., Møller, J. and Skaaning, S.-E. (2020). *Democratic Stability in an Age of Crisis: Reassessing the Interwar Period*. Oxford University Press.

Crabtree, J. (1992). *Peru under Garcia: An Opportunity Lost*. London: Palgrave Macmillan.

Crisp, B.F. (1998). Lessons From Economic Reform in the Venezuelan Democracy. *Latin American Research Review* 33(1): 7–41.

Dahlum, S. (2018). Modernization Theory – What Do We Know After 60 Years? *Annals of Comparative Democratization* 16(3): 4–6.

Dahlum, S., Knutsen, C.H. and Wig, T. (2019). Who Revolts Empirically Revisiting the Social Origins of Democracy. *Journal of Politics* 81(4): 1494–1499.

Dahlum, S. and Knutsen, C.H. (2017). Democracy by Demand? Reinvestigating the Effect of Self-expression Values on Political Regime Type. *British Journal of Political Science* 47(2): 437–461.

Dahlum, S. (2017). *Schooling for dissent? Education, autocratic regime instability and transitions to democracy*. Oslo: University of Oslo. PhD Thesis.

Davies, J.C. (1962). Towards a Theory of Revolution. *American Sociological Review* 27(1): 5–19.

Diamond, L. (1992). Economic Development and Democracy Reconsidered. *American Behavioral Scientist* 35(4): 450–499.

Djuve, V.L. and Knutsen, C.H. (2019). Economic Crisis and Regime Transitions from Within. *V-Dem Working Paper 92*.

Djuve, V.L., Knutsen, C.H. and Wig, T. (2020). Patterns of Regime Change Since the French Revolution. *Comparative Political Studies* 53(6): 923–958.

Fish, M.S. (2006). Stronger Legislatures, Stronger Democracies. *Journal of Democracy* 17(1): 5–20.

Freedom House. (2020). *Freedom in the World 2020*. https://freedomhouse.org.

Freeman, J.R. and Quinn, D.P. (2012). The Economic Origins of Democracy Reconsidered. *American Political Science Review* 106(1): 58–80.

Gasiorowski, M.J. (1995). Economic Crisis and Political Regime Change: An Event History Analysis. *American Political Science Review* 89(4): 882–897.

Gassebner, M., Gutmann, J. and Vogt, S. (2016). When to Expect a Coup d'état? An Extreme Bounds Analysis of Coup Determinants. *Public Choice* (409): 1–21.

Gassebner, M., Lamla, M.J. and Vreeland, J.R. (2013). Extreme Bounds of Democracy. *Journal of Conflict Resolution* 57(2): 171–195.

Geddes, B. (1999). What Do We Know about Democratization After Twenty Years? *Annual Review of Political Science* 2: 115–144.

Geddes, B., Wright, J. and Frantz, E. (2014). Autocratic Breakdown and Regime Transitions: A New Data Set. *Perspectives on Politics* 12(2): 313–331.

Gurr, T.R. (1970). *Why Men Rebel*. Princeton: Princeton University Press.

Hegre, H. and Sambanis, N. (2006). Sensitivity Analysis of Empirical Results on Civil War Onset. *Journal of Conflict Resolution* 50(4): 508–535.

Houle, C. (2009). Inequality and Democracy: Why Inequality Harms Consolidation but Does Not Affect Democratization. *World Politics* 61(4): 589–622.

Houle, C. (2015). Ethnic Inequality and the Dismantling of Democracy: A Global Analysis. *World Politics* 67(3): 469–505.

Inglehart, R. and Welzel, C. (2005). *Modernization, Cultural Change and Democracy – The Human Development Sequence*. Cambridge: Cambridge University Press.

Kennedy, R. (2010). The Contradiction of Modernization: A Conditional Model of Endogenous Democratization. *Journal of Politics* 72(3): 785–798.

Kim, N.K. (2016). Revisiting Economic Shocks and Coups. *Journal of Conflict Resolution* 60(1): 3–31.

Kistler, S.A. (2014). Murder, Memory, and the Maya. *Latin American Research Review* 49(1): 251–260.

Knack, S. and Keefer, P. (1995). Institutions and Economic Performance: Cross-Country Tests Using Alternative Institutional Measures. *Economics & Politics* 7(3): 203–227.

Knutsen, C.H. (2014). Income Growth and Revolutions. *Social Science Quarterly* 95(4): 920–937.

Knutsen, C.H. (2015). Reinvestigating the Reciprocal Relationship between Democracy and Income Inequality. *Review of Economics and Institutions* 6(2): Article 1.

Knutsen, C.H. and Dahlum, S. (2022). Economic Determinants. In M. Coppedge, A. Edgell, C.H. Knutsen and S.I. Lindberg (eds.), *Why Democracies Develop and Decline*. Cambridge: Cambridge University Press.

Knutsen, C.H., Gerring, J., Skaaning, S.-E., Teorell, J., Maguire, M., Lindberg, S.I. and Coppedge, M. (2019). Economic Development and Democracy: An Electoral Connection. *European Journal of Political Research* 58(1): 292–314.

La Feber, W. (1997). *America, Russia, and the Cold War, 1945–1996*. 8th ed. New York, NY: McGraw-Hill Humanities, Social Sciences & World Languages.

Lipset, S.M. (1959). Some Social Requisites of Democracy: Economic Development and Political Legitimacy. *American Political Science Review* 53(1): 69–105.

Londregan, J.B. and Poole, K.T. (1990). Poverty, the Coup Trap, and the Seizure of Executive Power. *World Politics* 42(2): 151–183.

Lührman, A. and Lindberg, S.I. (2019). A Third Wave of Autocratization Is Here: What Is New about It? *Democratization* 26(7): 1095–1113.

Lührmann, A. and Rooney, B. (2021). Autocratization by Decree: States of Emergency and Democratic Decline. *Comparative Politics* 53(4): 617–649.

Marshall, M.G., Gurr, T.R. and Jaggers, K. (2019). "Polity IV project: political regime characteristics and transitions, 1800–2018". Center for Systemic Peace.

Mauceri, P. (2006). An Authoritarian Presidency. In J. Carrion (ed.), *The Fujimori Legacy: The Rise of Electoral Authoritarianism in Peru*. University Park, PA: Pennsylvania State University Press.

Moore, B. (1966). *Social Origins of Democracy and Dictatorship: Lord and Peasant in the Making of the Modern World*. Boston, MA: Beacon Press.

Mudde, C. (2004). The Populist Zeitgeist. *Government and Opposition* 39(4): 541–563.

Munck, G.L. and Verkuilen, J. (2002). Conceptualizing and Measuring Democracy: Evaluating Alternative Indices. *Comparative Political Studies* 35(1): 5–34.

Munck, G.L. (2019). *The Quest for Knowledge about Societies: How Advances in the Social Sciences Have Been Made*, Book manuscript, University of Southern California.

North, D.C. (1990). *Institutions, Institutional Change and Economic Performance*. Cambridge: Cambridge University Press.

O'Donnell, G.A. (1973). *Modernization and Bureaucratic-Authoritarianism: Studies in South American Politics*. Berkeley, CA: UC Berkeley Press.

Olar, R.-G. (2019). Fait Accompli, or Live to Fight Another Day? Deterring and Surviving Coups in Authoritarian Regimes. *Research & Politics* 6(1): 1–7.

Ponticelli, J. and Voth, H.-J. (2020). Austerity and Anarchy: Budget Cuts and Social Unrest in Europe, 1919–2008. *Journal of Comparative Economics* 48(1): 1–19.

Powell, J.M. and Thyne, C.L. (2011). Global Instances of Coups from 1950 to 2010: A New Dataset. *Journal of Peace Research* 48(2): 249–259.

Przeworski, A., Alvarez, M.E., Cheibub, J.A. and Limongi, F. (2000). *Democracy and Development: Political Institutions and Well-Being in the World, 1950–1990*. Cambridge: Cambridge University Press.

Przeworski, A. and Limongi, F. (1997). Modernization: Theories and Facts. *World Politics* 49(1): 155–183.

Rød, E.G., Knutsen, C.H. and Hegre, H., et al. (2020). The Determinants of Democracy: A Sensitivity Analysis. *Public Choice* 185(1–2): 87–111.

Ross, M.L. (2001). Does Oil Hinder Democracy. *World Politics* 53(3): 325–361.

Ross, M.L. (2012). *The Oil Curse: How Petroleum Wealth Shapes the Development of Nations*. Princeton, NJ: Princeton University Press.

Rueschemeyer, D., Stephens, E.H. and Stephens, J.D. (1992). *Capitalist Development and Democracy*. Chicago, IL: University of Chicago Press.

Schiel, R.E. (2019). An Assessment of Democratic Vulnerability: Regime Type, Economic Development, and Coups d'état. *Democratization* 26(8): 1439–1457.

Sen, A. (1999). *Development as Freedom*. Oxford: Oxford University Press.

Skaaning, S.-E., Gerring, J. and Bartusevičius, H. (2015). A Lexical Index of Electoral Democracy. *Comparative Political Studies* 48(12): 1491–1525.

Svolik, M.W. (2015). Which Democracies Will Last? Coups, Incumbent Takeovers, and the Dynamic of Democratic Consolidation. *British Journal of Political Science* 45(4): 715–738.

Svolik, M.W. (2019). Polarization versus Democracy. *Journal of Democracy* 30(3): 20–32.

Teorell, J. (2010). *Determinants of Democratization: Explaining Regime Change in the World, 1972–2006*. Cambridge: Cambridge University Press.

Teorell, J., Coppedge, M., Lindberg, S. and Skaaning, S.-E. (2019). Measuring Polyarchy across the Globe, 1900–2017. *Studies in Comparative International Development* 54(1): 71–95.

Treisman, D. (2015). Income, Democracy, and Leader Turnover. *American Journal of Political Science* 59(4): 927–942.

Wahmann, M., Hadenius, A. and Teorell, J. (2013). Authoritarian Regime Types Revisited: Updated Data in Comparative Perspective. *Contemporary Politics* 19(1): 19–34.

Wright, J., Frantz, E. and Geddes, B. (2015). Oil and Autocratic Regime Survival. *British Journal of Political Science* 45(2): 287–306.

Ziblatt, D. (2008). Does Landholding Inequality Block Democratization? A Test of the Bread and Democracy Thesis and the Case of Prussia. *World Politics* 60(4): 610–641.

30

A SYSTEMIC APPROACH TO ECONOMIC RESILIENCE

William Hynes

OECD, PARIS, FRANCE

Alan Kirman

CAMS, EHESS, PARIS, FRANCE

NAEC, OECD, PARIS, FRANCE

Clara Latini

OECD, PARIS, FRANCE

Davide Luzzati

OECD, PARIS, FRANCE

SANT'ANNA SCHOOL OF ADVANCED STUDIES, PISA, ITALY

30.1 Introduction

Bill Gates, during his now well-known TED (Technology Entertainment Design) speech in 2015, stated that "we've actually invested very little in a system to stop an epidemic. We're not ready for the next epidemic." Gates rightfully suggested that the next epidemic would be dramatically more devastating than Ebola, reducing global wealth by trillions of dollars and causing millions of deaths. These fears materialized with the COVID-19 pandemic and its consequent economic and social disruption. According to the World Bank (2020), COVID-19 is estimated to have pushed between 88 and 115 million people into extreme poverty in 2020, which is predicted to rise to 150 million by 2021 and will have accounted for 1.9 million deaths (Ritchie et al., 2021).

In 2009, Andy Haldane, Chief Economist of the Bank of England, presented a speech on "Rethinking the financial network," urging financial risk experts to incorporate lessons from epidemiology to understand the Global Financial Crisis. Haldane (2009) stated how difficult it is to predict future crises from complex systems, and how crucial it is to prepare a systemic response for the future. Haldane compared previous epidemic diseases to the 2008–2009 Financial Crisis, drawing attention to various examples, for instance, when human flight led to contagion and contagion-fed human catastrophes such as with 20th-century influenza or yellow fever.

During the SARS epidemic, flights were prohibited, the contagion was contained, and the crisis did not scale up to the global level. During the Financial Crisis, the flight involved capital. Haldane believed that in order to avoid the spread of future financial epidemics, it is important

DOI: 10.4324/9781003144366-36

to remember the lessons from SARS and from other nonfinancial networks. However, this is not what we have experienced in 2020. The financial and COVID-19 crisis allow policymakers and experts to reflect on how critical it is to rethink the role of economic resilience not only to speed the post-COVID recovery but also to be better prepared for future crises.

30.2 Definitions of resilience

The word resilience comes from the Latin verb "resilio," i.e., to "jump back." Even though the term is generally intended to describe the capacity of a system to respond to a disturbance or a change, different definitions have been used in several contexts and fields. The first definition is linked with the physical properties of an entity that are subject to change: its plastic deformation and the ability to reconfigure into the initial shape. In line with the literature, we will define this as the engineering definition (Fraccascia et al., 2018). In a broader sense, this can be intended as the capacity of a system to return into its initial state after being subjected to a perturbation and the ability to recover from such shocks. For a more general meta-analysis on the different definitions of the term, see the work of Fraccascia et al. (2018) or Aligica and Iordache (in this Handbook) for the role of resilience in the Comparative Economic Systems literature.

However, the very notion of returning to the "initial state," or equilibrium, has been disputed and seen as not very realistic. Presenting the notion of resilience in ecological systems, Holling (1973) defines resilience as the "measure of the persistence of systems and their ability to absorb change and disturbance and maintain the same relationships between populations or state variables." This definition, which has been defined as the ecological one, moves away from the view of the system as displaced from its initial equilibrium, shifting the attention to a qualitative view of the system. The other interesting implication of such a definition is the premise of a different regime, one where previous relationships do not hold, and state variables take on different values from those before the perturbation. Apart from the lexical differences between the two, these two definitions encapsulate two very different approaches to studying and modeling systems. The first one is based on an "equilibrist" thinking: displacement around an equilibrium will eventually end up with the system returning to its previous steady state (Simmie and Martin, 2010). On the other hand, the second presupposes a more complex evolution landscape, one where shocks can lead the system, always moving in out-of-equilibria situations to entirely different paths, calling for an adaptive type of resilience (Martin and Sunley, 2015). As Holling (1973) already pointed out, "an equilibrium-centered view is essentially static and provides little insights into the transient behavior of systems that are not near the equilibrium."

In cases where the system is genuinely dynamic, and continuously adapting, it is characterized by self-organization which engenders continuous change without necessarily experiencing any external shock. Poincaré (1908) already pointed out that the evolution of systems of interacting components could depend heavily on initial conditions. Indeed, this is just what the complex systems approach to several disciplines has been calling for and has been developing ever since. While this approach had been developed in the physical sciences, it was extended to other disciplines such as evolutionary biology and neuroscience. More recently, the case for analyzing socio-economic systems as complex systems has been made and has gained traction (Farmer and Foley, 2009; Helbing and Kirman, 2013; Arthur, 2021). Moreover, it has also been shown analytically that complex systems, such as financial networks, are characterized by high degrees of instability so that when reaching critical points their state can undergo a rapid change. An important error in looking at such systems has been to think of these "tipping points" as being "rare" or unlikely. What Per Bak, a physicist, and his economist co-authors Bak et al. (1993) showed was that complex systems organize themselves in such a way as to reach these critical points. Therefore, they cannot be dismissed as "improbable." Small shocks can have disastrous consequences for the system as a whole. Ian Goldin explained this more qualitatively and intuitively in his book *The Butterfly Defect*.

30.2.1 Economic resilience

In the strictly economic context, the concept of resilience has mainly been used in two ways. The first one is that of "regional resilience," i.e., "the ability of a region … to recover successfully from shocks to its economy that either throw it off its growth path or have the potential to throw it off its growth path" (Hill et al. 2008, p. 4). The policy implication of such a definition goes with the principle that to prevent disruptions, on the whole, it is better to micromanage, i.e., to elaborate preventive checks (which are easier on a smaller scale) in order for shocks not to propagate further. Studies in these directions have been helpful in studying how different parts and regions react to different shocks in order to explain uneven regional development as responses (Simmie and Martin, 2010). However, most of the literature has focused on an equilibrist notion on resilience, i.e., the ability of the system to recover and return to the previous state (i.e., related to engineering type of resilience).

The second notion involves a broader, macro, perspective and is concerned mainly with the reaction of the entire economy after a disaster (natural or financial): quoting from the World Bank definition (Hallegatte, 2014), "The ability of an economy or a society to minimize welfare losses for a disaster of a given magnitude is often referred to as its resilience." In fact, welfare disturbances also depend on the ability of the economy to recover and to minimize the costs that such shocks may induce.

Thus, economic resilience should work on two levels: a macroeconomic one (of the aggregate consumption, for instance), in which the system should first be able to both absorb and recover, and a microeconomic one, for which the focus is instead on the impact on individuals (welfare loss). With such a framework, policies may be devised to mitigate the risks of the crises themselves and their consequences. For the former, this means developing adequate tools to detect the types of vulnerabilities that create the conditions for adverse shocks to turn into crises and to take actions to stem the build-up of such vulnerabilities before it is too late (OECD, 2020).

However, two points have to be made. First, most of the concepts of economic resilience have focused on regional or local shocks, for which the extension of general equilibrium theories has been used to study how the economy reacts in such situations and how to facilitate a smoother recovery. The presence of hysteresis, multiple equilibria, and a continuously changing environment often render such frameworks not very informative and/or too simplistic. For instance, an empirical report by the OECD (2017) found that after a negative economic shock, countries that can prop up the economy by shifting from domestic goods and foreign sectors toward domestic services are more resilient. In other words, the economy restructures differently. In light of structural change, equilibrist notions that make little sense when the system is continuously changing often fail to capture these phenomena. As already pointed out before, a more holistic, multifaceted approach is needed, one where resilience is a concept dealing with the way in which complex systems undergo, react, and evolve. Thus, we need a more multidisciplinary definition and implementation to assess how economies and financial systems can react to, and prepare for, such shocks.

30.3 The stability of the economy

We have presented several definitions of the term resilience, applicable in different contexts and fields. We now turn our attention to answering (partly) the questions which Carpenter et al. et al. (2001) posed in their seminal work "resilience of what to what?" with a digression on economic systems. In this work, we are interested in economic resilience: generally speaking, in how the economy can respond and recover from a shock. It is not easy to define what the economy is and is not: the economy and its interconnection with society is multifaceted, and it is often hard to distinguish between the two.

For the sake of the discussion, which will be on the stability of the economy, we will focus on the way in which it is generally treated in the literature: we will talk about business cycles, markets, financial networks, etc. Later, we will argue that this is just part of the picture and that economic resilience should also incorporate other aspects of society and should not be measured only by utilizing GDP gains/losses.

As outlined in the first section, the notion of resilience is coupled with that of stability. One of the critical questions that have puzzled economists for decades is whether the economy is inherently stable or unstable. This question, often posed in economic theory, has many interpretations. In General Equilibrium theory, the question means will a change in some parameter of the system meet a reaction within the system which will bring it back to equilibrium? In that context, the answer is provided by examining the mechanism which governs price adjustment. In macroeconomics, the question is less formal. As Beaudry et al. (2015) explain, advocates for considering the economy as stable are based on the empirical evidence of the relatively smooth growth path that the economy seemed to have experienced in the last hundred years. Moreover, the little volatility that OECD countries seemed to have undergone from the mid-80s onwards seemed to have called for an "end of economic history" (Portier, 2018). This has eventually led to theories based on the idea that the economy moves due to exogenous shocks around a stable path, which is dictated by technological, demographic, and societal changes.

The macromodels encapsulating this narrative are centered around a single (dynamic and/ or stochastic) equilibrium, to which the economy will eventually return after being subjected to an "exogenous" shock and rearranging itself. These "shock-based" business cycle theories can be traced back to the approach by Frisch (1933) and Slutzky (1937) who posited that random shocks were behind an economy's swings and cycles that move the latter out of its equilibrium path. Whether economic cycles arise naturally (or endogenously) or are the product of "random fluctuations" have clear implications on how crisis are perceived: in the first case, they are just unpredictable events, in the latter, they are somehow "endemic" and, to some extent, predictable.

Moreover, in the first case, there is no real need for stabilization policies, and the role of structural reform is then to smoothen out the return to the stable state determined by the "fundamentals" of the economy. The workhorse of monetary policy, DSGE models (the E stands for equilibrium), are based on this framework. Despite this, what Bernanke et al. (1996) has defined as the "small shock, large cycles puzzle" still relevant and much-debated.

Why is the economy subject to such high volatility if it is (supposedly) inherently stable? The importance of the issue can help in improving our understanding of crises which Guzman and Stiglitz (2020) define crises as substantial macroeconomic fluctuations, thus creating a link between the volatility of output and crises. Much research was done to answer this question, mainly following two lines. The first is based on the idea that microshocks propagate through the economy, leading to shocks on the macrolevel (Gabaix, 2011). The other is based on the idea that the economy is subject to endogenous dynamics, which would cause volatile outputs even without noise, or external shocks, in the system (Moran and Bouchaud, 2019).

Interestingly, work in the latter direction was already pursued around the 1990s, during the collaboration between economists and physicists at the Santa Fe Institute, while economic mainstream research was also focused on how economic fluctuations may arise naturally from a purely deterministic system (see Boldrin and Woodford (1990) and Scheinkman (1990) for surveys on the matter and Beaudry et al. (2020) for a short historical summary of these). It was also during these times that the financial system and market were analyzed through new lenses, through the emerging field of econophysics or the use of fractal theory to study the stock market (by Mandelbrot and Hudson (2007), for instance). It is of no surprise that these theories found a great revival in light of the crisis of 2007–2008.

One of the most fruitful ideas of the Santa Fe collaboration elaborated was to think of the economy as a self-organizing system: the economy can be thought of as a system continuously changing and correcting itself, but that could eventually reach a critical state, after which small perturbations could have disastrous consequences for the system, leading to cascade effects and making it vulnerable to shocks. This phenomenon is generally defined as "self-organized criticality," which was also discussed by the Nobel Laureate Paul Krugman (1996) in his book *The Self-Organizing Economy*.

These ideas were recently revived after the Financial Crisis, which was arguably also a crisis of the economic profession and its models (Colander et al., 2009). Critics of the models can be found in several places in the literature, but one of the main arguments is that the sudden collapse of the financial sector, and its repercussion on the economy, was an endogenous phenomenon, rather than an "exogenous shock" that could not be predicted because excluded a priori by the very own models that were being used to analyze the economy. This has led to a new revival of theories based on the idea that the economy experiences a much richer, complex behavior than the one specified by equilibrium theories and that it should rather be seen as a "complex evolving system," i.e., as an ecology populated by heterogeneous agents, acting in nonequilibrium situations, continuously adapting and changing the environment in which they are embedded (Dosi and Roventini, 2019). These theories often use concepts, ideas, and tools coming from sciences such as ecology, biology, and physics to model economic behavior and dynamics. The parallel of the socio-economic structure as akin to an ecological, complex system brings us back to the question of stability and resilience in systems, which was analyzed much more thoroughly in these disciplines than in economics. Perhaps the closest that economists have come to the sort of approach adopted in physics, for example, is the work of Portier and his co-authors (Portier, 2018).

In this view, the "shocks" are short term rather rapid phenomena which perturb the underlying cyclicity of the economy. So, rather than having a deterministic cycle the economy moves from one state to another but does so in a random and unpredictable manner. This is highly reminiscent of Parisi's (a 2021 Nobel laureate in physics) work in which he, with Benzi tried to untangle the patterns that could be found in climatic time series, and developed the theory of stochastic resonance. It is the stochastic nature of these shifts from one "climate" to another that makes it so difficult to devise measures which will diminish their impact. As Portier says,

"It is in a way the fate of prosperous economies to oscillate endogenously and be chronically in deficit of demand" Portier (2018, p. 232).

30.4 Resilience in systems

There are two opposing views on whether complexity and stability are positively or negatively correlated. On the one hand, complexity, heterogeneity, and diversification can help systems be more robust toward disruptions. Redundancies in supplies and geographical diversification can help the global supply chain adapt and survive shocks; thus, resilience increases as systems become more connected and integrated. For instance, in urban studies and megacities, Shutters et al. (2016) report that "highly integrated system…show high degrees of resilience." Higher connectedness should in fact better withstand shocks since replacement and continuous working should be easier to implement.

On the other side, where we find most complexity theorists, the claim is that complexity scales with instability due to the high nonlinearity and continuous feedback loops rendering the system subject to complex endogenous dynamics and vulnerable to collapses. For instance, Bob May (1972) famously showed how "a large complex system will be more unstable" after a critical point. Much work in this direction has been done in light of the financial crises for financial networks, where models were built to show that these were indeed subject to systemic instabilities (Haldane and May, 2011; Battiston et al., 2012; Helbing and Kirman 2013). This, of course, runs counter to the intuitive idea that the more connected financial markets are, the more risk is spread, and therefore the more stable the system is.

Similarly, Kauffman (1993) coined the expression "complexity catastrophes": an increase in a system's components will hinder the systems' ability to search for optimal configurations, so after a critical value, the complexity of the system imposes a bound on the eventual adaptive progression of itself. On a more general note, the complexity theorist James Crutchfield makes a similar point in his self-explanatory article "The Hidden Fragility of Complex Systems" (Crutchfield, 2009). He argued that one of complex systems' emergent phenomena is fragility itself and that the positivistic and constructive approaches, especially in economics, have shifted the narrative and made the case of precisely the opposite: the more, the bigger and intricate, the better posing several troubles for the stability of our system. Striving for maximum efficiency and optimization in such systems has neglected resilience against disruptions (Marchese et al., 2012). In a piece in the *Wall Street Journal*, William Galston (2020) also echoed this, asking: "What if the relentless pursuit of efficiency, which has dominated American business thinking for decades, has made the global economic system more vulnerable to shocks?" Similar points were raised by Helbing (2013). Drawing the parallel with the standard neoclassical framework in economics, it is not hard to see how the systemic risk endemic to complex systems fails to be captured by the neoclassical narrative since it is the "risk of having not just statistically independent failures, but interdependent, so-called 'cascading failures'" (Helbing, 2013).

To sum up, specific mechanisms at play make the economy self-adjust (as envisaged by Adam Smith's invisible hand): for instance, the agents that populate it manage to coordinate themselves even though their motives are selfish, giving rise to ordered macro structures such as institutions and organizations. On the other hand, its complexity makes the system highly uncertain, unpredictable, and with dynamics that often undergoes endogenous failures. So it is both stable (stabilizing would be a better term) and unstable.

Recently, Guzman and Stiglitz (2020) argue that "to understand deep downturns is to think of the economy experiencing a constant evolution, marked by uncertainty, in which there is continual learning about the economic system." From a policy perspective, this poses a rather tricky question: should we intervene to stabilize the system, or let the economy (or, often, the market) self-adjust? We can then ask ourselves: what would benefit from a notion of equilibrium in a system with i) continuous endogenous, complex dynamics, and ii) continuously changing? This is coupled with another policy-related question: how can structural policies be effective when the economy settles on a trajectory? How can we devise policies for a changing environment, do those policies have to be conditional on the innately unpredictable evolution of the economy?

30.5 Resilience vs. efficiency

In a way, the traditional way economics is taught is the world of efficiency: optimize under a budget constraint, optimize portfolio while minimizing risk, etc. In this sense, there is a clear trade-off between resilience and efficiency. They are both related to the heterogeneity, diversity, and connectivity of the system but work in opposite directions. Redundancy (typical of more resilient systems) and heterogeneity may help in preventing total collapse as they make it less likely that local disruptions will undermine the system as a whole. At the same time, high diversity can undermine efficiency, with parts of the system that will be inefficient or not used at all (Ulanowicz et al., 2009). Efficiency comes, in fact, from an optimal adaptation to an existing environment, while resilience requires the capacity to adapt to disruptive changes in the environment. Optimal adaptation to an existing environment and adaptation to disruptive changes in the environment are seen thus in contradiction to each other (Gölgeci and Kuivalainen, 2020).

However, from a complexity perspective, this trade-off is not straightforward. Trying to optimize a complex system may not be optimal (Taleb, 2007) in the longer run. For, if one thinks of resilience as the ultimate survival of the system, as it is often treated in ecology, where unpredictable "noise" can lead to disastrous ruptures myopic optimization may lead to long-term collapse. Clear evidence for this comes from the recent collapse of some global supply chains. The ontological unpredictability of complex systems also stems from the presence of Knightian uncertainty and/or the occurrence of a Black Swan-type of event, which can lead to the system's collapse. It is thus necessary for the system to not be full of optimized constraints to leave space for "noise." Resilient systems might be, from a technical point of view less efficient, but they can recover better from ruptures. So, aiming for resilience does not fully imply an abandonment of efficiency since one maximizes for long-term sustainability (Trump et al., 2020) rather than short-term optimization according to the (limited) amount of information available when the system is studied or devised.

For instance, Ulanowicz et al. (2009) argued that systems should find the optimal trade-off between resilience and efficiency in order to be optimal (although, again, one has to be careful as to the objective which is being maximized) since "[...] after a certain point, increasing a system's efficiency makes it more brittle even as it grows bigger and more directed. Conversely, while increasing diversity and connectivity makes the system technically more resilient beyond a certain point, the loss of efficiency also makes it more stagnant. The upshot is that systems become unsustainable whenever they have either too much or too little diversity/connectivity."

What is of fundamental relevance for the preservation of the system is how the absence of something can critically impact the former (Ulanowicz et al., 2009). In the policy-making context, this translates into managing and discounting future, possibly unforeseeable, shocks and it is generally known as the "precautionary principle." For instance, a recent manifesto for more honest models (Saltelli et al., 2020) called for a better acceptance of the "unknowns" from policymakers, stressing the importance of focusing on both what we know and what we do not know (similarly to what is described by the via Negativa in Taleb (2012)).

In other words, the critical question that we must ask ourselves relates to the number of resources we want to allocate to achieve more resilient and agile economic systems. It is also worth considering what shocks the system may face. Economics has typically dealt with exogenous shocks – those from outside the system, e.g., a climate or geopolitical shock, which knock the system off course but typically it, gravitates back to a steady state or equilibrium. However, crises can also exhibit endogenous dynamics, e.g., financial crises. As this chapter suggests, the economy is inherently intricate and interlinked with complex interactions on individual levels that give rise to emergent properties at the macro level and endogenous shocks. Even climate shocks and pandemics involving zoonosis emerge endogenously in the convergence of natural and economic systems. Understanding system dynamics equips us to withstand rare but dangerous events. However, the answer to these questions is not easy: these events are most likely not known a priori, nor them, nor their probability (Jenny, 2020). Jean Tirole recently argued in an article in Le Monde that the choice is between making reasoned choices for the future (to gain more control) or letting future events decide for us, with potentially catastrophic consequences.

A striking example of the issue is the case of leftover masks after the H1N1 virus in France: after the pandemic, the country was left with a significant provision of masks that were eventually thrown away, and that would surely have been of great help in recent times (OECD, 2020). In such cases, what should policymakers do? What would be the proper allocation of resources and investment for future risks? As Wildavsky (1988) writes: "real human situations usually involve a mixture of the known and unknown; hence, there is a trade-off – the most likely large dangers if they are known and can be countered without making things worse, can, and should be, prevented." What about those we do not know? When it comes to policy, the question in the presence of such high degrees of uncertainty is on how to discount for almost infinity, i.e., on how to account for possible future shocks with a potentially very high impact.

For instance, in the context of policies related to climate change, Hepburn and Farmer (2020) state that "One might complain that it is almost impossible to set appropriate precautionary buffers if we do not know where the thresholds [before a tipping point] lie." Climate change, arguably the most complex issue of our generation, is dictated by highly nonlinear dynamics, tipping points, and filled with both known and unknown unknowns. The question of how to act upon it is still highly debatable, despite the amount of work that has been done. In this context, Hepburn and Farmer (2020) explain how: "given that such systems are constantly evolving, policy must also continually evolve and adapt. Knowing this, the policy interventions can be designed to ensure the flexibility and optionality of responding in different ways in the future are preserved. [...] it is also useful to avoid needlessly locking policy into a regime that may subsequently turn out to be ill-suited to the system as it evolves and responds, including to policy announcements."

In what way can then a systemic approach to resilience help in studying if not addressing such phenomena? The first way is to acknowledge the complex relationship between scales, both in space and time, which work in two ways. The first is that the larger scale affects the small one (think of the education system or local government) and that the macro, aggregate, outcome results from the microlevel. Complex societal issues are in fact a result of concurrent interactions between different systems of events which do not necessarily tend toward stable outcomes but can respond dramatically to small changes in conditions. Challenges must be continuously re-evaluated since they cannot be resolved permanently and mutate dynamically. Thus, the assumption of linearity in policy is often fallacious even if common and tends to represent problems as solvable from a vertical unpacking of hierarchies and with a unique solution (Fuerth, 2009).

In the economic sphere, this often takes place by means of a regulated market that should nevertheless correct itself, given we take into account potential "negative externalities." From a complexity perspective, the precautionary principle transforms into the field of "anticipatory governance," according to which it is the sum of its components, but is also its own environment with its own set of characteristics (Fuerth, 2009). These would represent the interaction of subsystems for foresight, networking, and feedback systems, thus shifting our thinking from a component-oriented to an interaction- and network-oriented view (Helbing, 2013).

Anticipatory governance would be a process that works at all scales, with similar relationships displayed at every level of governance, from bureaucracy to politics. It is of no surprise that Fuerth (2009), who coined the term, used system thinking and complexity theory to construct the foundations of his principle.

We claim that a system-thinking approach is needed to move to a longer-term strategy to better integrate better risk factors; both in the way, we postulate economic issues and their related policy requirements. Such a mindset acknowledges that the vast number of future threats cannot be adequately predicted and measured, and they are certainly not amenable to complete prediction. Resilience acknowledges that massive disruptions can and will happen, and core systems must have the capacity for recovery and adaptation. Consideration must be given not just to hardening the healthcare system but to a range of critical systems connected to it. This involves examining how these systems absorb and mitigate risk and how they will recover, adapt, and preferably "bounce forward" (Ganin et al. 2016, 2017; Linkov et al. 2018a, 2018b).

If one uses the standard "resilience as the ability of the economy to withstand a shock," a portion of the literature has focused on what is the link between the policy and structure of an economy and its resilience, often using negative GDP losses as a proxy for sudden negative shock. For instance, Acemoglu et al. (2003) and Rodrik (1999) reported a positive role of institutions in managing volatility of output and on larger shocks. Others have looked into the impact of labor and market policies on resilience, with different results, especially since flexibility vs. rigidity is debated. For instance, Canova et al. (2012) found that a high level of product market regulation has a negative impact on resilience to adverse shock across European countries. Similarly, Duval and Vogel (2008) found that rigid labor and product markets lengthen the time it takes to recover from a shock. From a competitiveness perspective, Biroli et al. (2010) found that inflation differentials were more persistent in the face of excessive regulations, which in the European zone imply that there is no automatic smoothing of shocks.

In a further survey, Sondermann (2018) found robust evidence that flexible and robust institutions allow countries to increase resilience to adverse shocks and that flexible and adaptable institutions reduce the likelihood of crises. This runs counter to several papers in finance which argue that market flexibility may engender fragility, as facilitating capital movements can lead to large flows of capital from one place to another in search of a small increase in returns. This explains why, after years of negotiation, the OECD countries have agreed to put a floor on corporate tax rates. Introducing what some will call a "friction" may actually stabilize economies. It is worth noting that the figure of 15% agreed to is below the average corporate income tax rate (23.5%) in the OECD countries. Moreover, corporate income tax rates have been steadily dropping in recent years. Much stronger measures will be needed in the future to effectively slow international capital movements. The same can be said of regulating the labor market. Making hiring and firing easier has given rise to the "gig market" in which workers are no longer "employed" but can be taken on or released immediately. As a result, real wages have stagnated in many countries since 1974 as labor's bargaining power diminished (Weil, 2014). However, jobs play important role beyond their economic contribution in terms of individual identity and social stability and mobility.

30.6 Resilience in policy

One of the arguments behind the lack of resilience of our systems, mainly concerning value chains, is a lack of an effective antitrust policy, with too much concentration leaving competition weakened. As President Biden stated in a recent statement regarding competition: "competition has weakened in too many markets, denying Americans the benefits of an open economy and widening racial, income, and wealth inequality. Federal Government inaction has contributed to these problems, with workers, farmers, small businesses, and consumers paying the price. Consolidation has increased the power of corporate employers, making it harder for workers to bargain for higher wages and better work conditions. Powerful companies require workers to sign non-compete agreements that restrict their ability to change jobs. The American information technology sector has long been an engine of innovation and growth, but today a small number of dominant Internet platforms use their power to exclude market entrants, to extract monopoly profits, and to gather intimate personal information that they can exploit for their own advantage."

According to this view, devising a system of regulations and subsidization aimed at deconcentrating and redistributing the main industrial capacities would be key to strengthening the resilience of the international production system and global economic growth. For instance, by ensuring that no more than 25% of capacity for a good should be located within their own borders. This would avoid bottlenecks such as the striking case of the sudden economic slowdown after Japan's north coast earthquake and tsunami due to the shutdown of a single semiconductor factory.

A recent report from the Wealth Economy team at the University of Cambridge (Agarwala et al., 2020)) has also stressed how building back from the pandemic is not the real challenge but that the stress should be on Building Forward as we recover from the pandemic. The main point is that in order to generate a more prosperous and resilient future we should be looking at different dimensions of our socio-economic structure, such as health, environmental, economic, and social challenges, which are all deeply intertwined. The evidence on government intervention to execute an agenda for change has been limited, with most of the funds going to a rescue type of policy. Indeed, President Biden's ambitious infrastructure plan has faced opposition even from within his own party. There are, in fact, differences between immediate rescue and job preservation and strategies for growth and recovery with the former necessary to protect people (and has arguably, worked quite well), while the latter are the vital ones to move forward. These policies have not paid much attention to sustainability, but there is already evidence of support for lower emissions, more resilient service-oriented economy feeding policy objectives (Larsen et al., 2021). In this context, what is of key importance is targeted investments that can generate both short and long-term growth by increasing productive capacity and stimulating innovation. In times of crisis, in fact, fiscal spending can reach multipliers as high as 2.5 (Christiano et al., 2011; DeLong et al., 2012). If these are then pursued toward a longer and broader span of vision, they will support growth and will be able to service the debt accumulated.

Another important sector to invest in is human capital, through active labor market policies to secure the skills and jobs necessary for the new centuries to come. Robins et al. (2019) make a compelling case for providing new tools and reskilling the most affected workers to enhance their participation in the new economy. Thus, the need to invest in social and institutional capital. For instance, Sawhill (2020) suggests ways to do so: providing a universal national service, enhancing subsidies for charitable giving and providing further resources to local communities to innovate, and rebuild in ways more akin to their values and circumstances.

Another lesson from the pandemic on the importance of planning ahead for a resilient recovery can be taken by comparing the US and the EU policy responses and their difference with respect to automatic stabilizers and discretionary resources. The former allows governments to plan further for the green recovery. In fact, most of the funds from the EU came from automatic stabilizers which eventually allowed the European Commission to focus on a greener recovery than that envisaged in their original agenda. The US Congress, on the other hand, debated first emergency plans and immediate needs to minimize the economic cost of the pandemic, pushing green measures off the table. This was also due to a clearer and coordinated investment agenda for climate and innovation policy by the EU that was already completed at the beginning of 2020, showing a more proactive approach and propensity for green types of stimulus and a program for a more resilient recovery (Rhodium Group Report, 2021). One of the latest Rhodium Group report (2021), which monitors green stimulus spending across the globe, reports that: "we find that only the EU has committed to green a meaningful share of its stimulus—15%. The United States, India, and China have allocated a negligible share (around 1% or less) of COVID-specific spending toward green measures. Experience in the first full year of the pandemic reveals that relying on emergency measures alone is likely insufficient to adequately prioritize a green recovery."

30.6.1 Systemic resilience

Two systematic methodologies have been created so far to face sudden crises. The first approach consists in preventing a threat from happening in the first place or in mitigating the consequences of the threat. The second approach accepts the uncertain and unpredictable systemic threats and addresses them through building system resilience. The need for resilience acknowledges that massive disruptions can and will happen. It is essential that core systems have the capacity for recovery and adaptation to ensure their survival into the future, and even take advantage of new opportunities revealed by the crises to improve the system through broader systemic changes (Hynes et al., 2020).

A systems approach is fundamental to prepare the global interconnected socioeconomic systems to reduce the impact of future shocks. It promotes cross-sectoral and multidisciplinary collaboration between different specializations and scientific and institutional "silos." Systems thinking allows us to identify the key drivers, interactions, and dynamics of the economic, social, and environmental nexus that policy seeks to shape and to select points of intervention in a selective, adaptive way. This allows us to emphasize the importance of system resilience to a variety of shocks and stresses, allowing systems to recover from lost functionality and adapt to new realities regarding international economics, societal needs, and human behavior, as well as the risks of a more unpredictable climate.

In order to promote positive social and economic change, a range of policies has to be integrated, including educational, demographic, employment, well-being, and technology and innovation policies. Systems thinking provides a methodology to achieve a better understanding of the behavior of complex systems and to improve the assessment of the consequences of policy interventions (Hynes et al., 2020).

Resilience, or the ability to recover from and adapt to unexpected threats, has been a focus of specific parts of our system, for instance, military and public health authorities. However, the notions of viability and resilience can be in tension with short-term profitability and apparent efficiency (Aubin, 2010). Striving for maximum efficiency and optimization, such systems have neglected resilience against disruptions (Marchese et al., 2012), the shocks from which may leave governments, the public, and the environment in a weakened state. Moreover, the concentration of industrial capacities and economic activity into smaller and more efficient sectors, up to the international level, has produced highly lucrative yet fragile supply chains and economic exchanges whose disruptions could have sweeping effects in unexpected areas. The science of systems engineering teaches us that when you try to optimize one part of a complex system, you can end up destabilizing the system as a whole.

Moreover, resilience-based policymaking offers a number of advantages over policy informed only by risk assessment. First, resilience acknowledges the evolution of circumstances in the recovery period. Second, resilience requires a holistic understanding of the system and supports the identification of resilience management strategies across the whole system (Bostick et al., 2018).

Until now, we have surveyed some of the literature on resilience and economic recovery as it is generally presented in the literature, i.e., by defining a negative economic shock as a sudden break in volatility or level of GDP. In several other contexts, it has been argued that GDP is probably not the best measure of economic activity (we point to Wagener (in this Handbook) and Valli (in this Handbook) for a comparative economic system approach) and today's challenges such as those of climate and the environment, and inequality, cannot be monitored and solved by GDP growth alone (Wealth Economy Report, 2020). Moreover, most policy-oriented empirical work has focused on economic resilience only (OECD, 2014), despite the fairly large consensus that building resilience requires a broader perspective and a systemic view that incorporates the entire process of societal well-being production.

As Ulanowicz et al. (2009) put it, "measuring economies by their GDP comes back to measuring the whole volume of the system, but ignores the structure of the underlying network. As a result, it is a poor indicator of its ability to sustain itself in the long term." What we would want is for a society to be considered resilient if it retains the ability to deliver societal well-being in a sustainable way even in the face of shocks and persistent structural changes. This approach adopts an individual-centric perspective where the focus is on societal well-being and a disaggregated view of society based on "beyond-GDP" principle (Giovannini et al., 2020). Moreover, this interpretation of resilience offers a positive narrative that allows addressing societal challenges as windows of opportunity instead of just difficulties to overcome, reminding us of the antifragile concept developed by Taleb (2012).

Translating this into economic terms means that there might be social costs due to the hysteretic nature of systemic shocks such as COVID-19. The pandemic has, in fact, exposed people and communities to a complex array of stressors with worrying implications for mental health and a widening of economic and social inequalities. In general, the absorptive and adaptive capacity of resilience also means that despite some initial inevitable losses after a shock, a resilient society tends to restore its original well-being and even to improve on its previous functionality. As Giovannini et al. (2020) put it, "a resilient society is one where individuals are resilient." For instance, the Joint Research Centre has been working on related issues, compiling surveys, and dashboards for social and economic resilience.

Another common trait of the negative impact of systemic shock, such as pandemics and natural hazards, is that those who are more affected, vulnerable, and more likely to experience adverse outcomes are the economically disadvantaged (Van Bavel et al., 2020), increasing the level of socio-economic inequality which is already affecting our society. Students most impaired as a result of online learning are likely to have been those from lower socio-economic backgrounds (Engzell et al., 2021). Firms with more market power were more prone to be affected, but less likely to incur liquidity problems than smaller ones (Hyun et al., 2020; Bartik et al., 2020). Individuals working in more precarious conditions were those more likely to be affected by lockdown measures (Fana et al., 2020) and the lower paid, the young, women, and temporary workers among those hardest hit by the crisis (OECD, 2020). Moreover, differently than after the Great Financial Crisis (GFC) it has been reported that women were hit harder by the pandemic due to their overrepresentation in affected sectors and the fact that they disproportionately hold precarious jobs (OECD, 2020).

It is not easy to measure resilience at the societal level, capture the multidimensionality of a system, and assess its ability to undergo and recover from crises. We argue that multidisciplinary system thinking is necessary to resolve such issues. For instance, Wernli et al. (2021) elaborated on the notion of a "multisystemic approach for the societal resilience to COVID-19," defined as "the ability of societies to contain the pandemic while maintaining their core governance functions and minimizing any undesirable systemic effects." The idea being that societies are, in fact, complex adaptive systems composed of many interacting sectors which have to be studied and analyzed together.

They decomposed it into "environmental," "economic," "social," "health," and "governance," each with its own definitions and capacity for resilience in order to transform it into a genuinely effective policy tool that would no longer suffer the lack of agreement on its measurement (Martin and Sunley, 2015). Each one of these subsystems could then be divided into further scales: from individual, to family, to the community, to society. As they put it: "In other words, societal resilience is an emergent property of complex systems that results from interactions across different scales of social organization and levels of governance." In this light, what is emphasized are the interactions, feedbacks, and possible nonlinearities among the different entities and layers of the system. This "system view" can help understand how shocks spread among the different segments of the system, how they interact, and the complex relationship with the actors, at which point one can decide how to and where to intervene.

However, this approach should also run in the long term since a resilient society aims to sustain its level of individual and societal well-being in an intergenerationally fair distribution, i.e., ensuring current well-being without seriously compromising that of future generations. Societies that are more resilient to disturbances will also be able to ensure a higher level of well-being as the shock will impact them in a less severe way (Manca et al., 2017).

30.7 Systemic resilience related to COVID-19

COVID-19 is the latest instance of an unpredictable shock to interconnected systems, where international recovery will have vast implications for future economic, social, and governmental activity. According to Trump and Linkov (2020), building resilience is of crucial importance in overcoming the current pandemic.

COVID-19 is seen as a multisystem challenge. Where the threats, exposed vulnerabilities, and consequences of COVID-19 continue to manifest themselves around the globe, a great deal of attention must be paid not only to how risk is absorbed and mitigated, but how the systems affected will recover, adapt, and preferably "bounce forward" toward a more satisfactory system state (Hynes et al., 2020).

Beginning with a slow, yet unchecked spread of disease on a global scale, the pandemic quickly disrupted hospital systems and associated resource and labor requirements (Hynes et al., 2020). Simultaneously, as socioeconomic activity waned as the government issued orders for quarantine and shelter-in-place, systemic disruption spread beyond the public health domain and into economics and finance, and even the broader political systems of various states. The loss of functionality triggered by this single disruption origin is one that requires robust recovery to minimize extensive and even permanent multisystem losses.

The COVID-19 crisis is an illustration of how systems modify each other. The initial cause, as in previous coronavirus outbreaks, is thought to have been a transmission from animals to humans of a virus. When we look in more detail at how this happened, we will probably find that a range of social, economic, and environmental changes contributed to creating conditions where zoonosis could become so damaging – for example, changing land-use patterns and agricultural practices. However, we could also argue that the 2020 Health Crisis was made far worse by the 2008 Financial Crisis, or more precisely, the austerity measures that left many health systems without the basic resources such as protective clothing needed to cope with a sudden, unexpected upsurge in the number of patients (Hynes et al., 2020).

Complementing risk-based approaches with resilience-based approaches for the management of epidemics, as well as for other systemic threats, is a necessity. There is an awareness that the systemic threats modern societies face are increasingly difficult to model, and are often too complex to be solved for the "optimal response" using traditional approaches of risk assessment that focus primarily upon system hardness and ability to absorb threats before breaking. Hynes et al. (2020) suggest a new approach to resilience focusing on the ability of a system to anticipate, absorb, recover from, and adapt to a wide array of systemic threats.

Resilience must become a core philosophy within system management and operation to ensure that we are able to continue to function despite disruptions like COVID-19, and are able not only to adapt and improve in its aftermath but also to seize upon new or revealed opportunities. An emphasis upon developing resilience within the international economic system will be necessary for a post-COVID-19 world, where systems are designed to facilitate recovery and adaptation in the aftermath of disruption. OECD (OECD, 2020) suggests specific recommendations for building resilience to contain epidemics and other systemic threats:

1. Design systems, including infrastructure, supply chains, and economic, financial, and public health systems, to be resilient, i.e., recoverable and adaptable.
2. Develop methods for quantifying resilience so that trade-offs between a system's efficiency and resilience can be made explicit and guide investments.
3. Control system complexity to minimize cascading failures resulting from unexpected disruption by decoupling unnecessary connections across infrastructure and make necessary connections controllable and visible.
4. Manage system topology by designing appropriate connection and communications across the interconnected infrastructure.
5. Add resources and redundancies in system-crucial components to ensure functionality.
6. Develop real-time decision support tools integrating data and automating the selection of management alternatives based on explicit policy trade-offs in real time.

Andy Haldane (2020) proposes improving tools to weight trade-offs between health and wealth and further calls for the need for highly granular data embedded in high-dimensional models of various interacting agents. Agent-based models need to be applied in order to better understand our economies, predict crises, and increase resilience. New models need to be created with the collaboration between statisticians, physicists, epidemiologists, meteorologists, sociologists, and economists. Policymakers need to invest in new means of analysis as the use of new analytical tools and techniques to simulate the dynamics of crises using network and agent-based models will enable us to better understand how shocks emerge and spread (OECD, 2020).

30.8 Conclusion

What is now becoming increasingly clear is that the very notion of resilience is undergoing a shift. The world has moved on from defining resilience as "the capacity to bounce back to normal" in large part because "normal" is no longer as well defined as it seemed in the past. As the acceleration of the transition from one "state of the world" to another is happening, we now have to think about where the whole system will be in the future rather than how to deal with those aspects that have temporarily become unsatisfactory. Rather we should be orienting ourselves to work out how to achieve a soft landing on the new planet that is emerging. Too much of the debate is on how what is happening will prevent us from returning to the comfortable existence that we had before. That comfortable existence is a thing of the past for wealthy countries and did not exist for many poorer countries. So the task is twofold, to find a route for the developed countries to a better, even if less materially oriented future and to guarantee to poorer countries access to those things that can make life less unbearable than it currently seems to be.

References

Acemoglu, D., Johnson, S., Robinson, J. and Thaicharoen, Y. (2003). Institutional causes, macroeconomic symptoms: Volatility, crises and growth. *Journal of Monetary Economics*, 50(1), pp. 49–123.

Agarwala, M., Cinamon Nair, Y., Cordonier Segger, M.C., Coyle, D., Felici, M., Goodair, B., Leam, R., Lu, S., Manley, A., Wdowin, J. and Zenghelis, D. (2020). Building Forward: Investing in a Resilient Recovery. *Wealth Economy Report to Letterone*. Bennett Institute for Public Policy, University of Cambridge.

Arthur, W.B. (2021). Foundations of complexity economics. *Nature Reviews Physics*, 3(2), pp. 136–145.

Aubin, J.P. (2010). Une approche viabiliste du couplage des systèmes climatique et économique. *Natures Sciences Sociétés*, 18(3), pp. 277–286.

Bak, P., Chen, K., Scheinkman, J. and Woodford, M. (1993). Aggregate fluctuations from independent sectoral shocks: Self-organized criticality in a model of production and inventory dynamics. *Ricerche Economiche*, 47(1), pp. 3–30.

Bartik, A.W., Bertrand, M., Cullen, Z., Glaeser, E.L., Luca, M. and Stanton, C. (2020). The impact of COVID-19 on small business outcomes and expectations. *Proceedings of the National Academy of Sciences*, 117(30), pp. 17656–17666.

Battiston, S., Gatti, D.D., Gallegati, M., Greenwald, B. and Stiglitz, J.E. (2012). Liaisons dangereuses: Increasing connectivity, risk sharing, and systemic risk. *Journal of Economic Dynamics and Control*, 36(8), pp. 1121–1141.

Beaudry, P., Galizia, D. and Portier, F. (2015). Reviving the limit cycle view of macroeconomic fluctuations (No. w21241). National Bureau of Economic Research.

Beaudry, P., Galizia, D. and Portier, F. (2020). Putting the cycle back into business cycle analysis. *American Economic Review*, 110(1), pp. 1–47.

Bernanke, B., Gertler, M. and Gilchrist, S. (1996). The financial accelerator and the flight to quality. *Review of Economics and Statistics*, 78(1), pp. 1–15.

Biroli, P., Mourre, G. and Turrini, A. (2010). Adjustment in the Euro area and regulation of product and labour markets: An empirical assessment.

Boldrin, M. and Woodford, M. (1990). Equilibrium models displaying endogenous fluctuations and chaos: A survey. *Journal of Monetary Economics*, 25(2), pp. 189–222.

Bostick, T.P., Connelly, E.B., Lambert, J.H. and Linkov, I. (2018). Resilience science, policy and investment for civil infrastructure. *Reliability Engineering & System Safety*, 175, pp. 19–23.

Canova, F., Coutinho, L. and Kontolemis, Z.G. (2012). Measuring the macroeconomic resilience of industrial sectors in the EU and assessing the role of product market regulations (Vol. 112). Publications Office of the European Union.

Carpenter, S., Walker, B., Anderies, J.M. and Abel, N. (2001). From metaphor to measurement: Resilience of what to what? *Ecosystems*, 4(8), pp. 765–781.

Christiano, L., Eichenbaum, M. and Rebelo, S. (2011). When is the government spending multiplier large? *Journal of Political Economy*, 119(1), pp. 78–121.

Colander, D., Föllmer, H., Haas, A., Goldberg, M.D., Juselius, K., Kirman, A., Lux, T. and Sloth, B. (2009). The financial crisis and the systemic failure of academic economics. Univ. of Copenhagen Dept. of Economics Discussion Paper No. 09-03.

Cotis, J.-P. and Coppel, J. (2005). Business Cycle Dynamics in OECD Countries: Evidence, Causes and Policy Implications. In Kent, C. and Norman, D. (Eds.). *The Changing Nature of the Business Cycle*. Reserve Bank of Australia 2005 Conference Proceedings, Sydney, pp. 8–57.

Crutchfield, J.P. (2009). The Hidden Fragility of Complex Systems. *Cultures of Change: Changing Cultures*. Barcelona, Spain: ACTAR.

DeLong, J.B., Summers, L.H., Feldstein, M. and Ramey, V.A. (2012). Fiscal policy in a depressed economy [with comments and discussion]. Brookings Papers on Economic Activity, pp. 233–297.

Dosi, G. and Roventini, A. (2019). More is different… and complex! the case for agent-based macroeconomics. *Journal of Evolutionary Economics*, 29(1), pp. 1–37.

Duval, R. and Vogel, L. (2008). Economic resilience to shocks: The role of structural policies. *OECD Journal: Economic Studies*, 2008(1), pp. 1–38.

Engzell, P., Frey, A. and Verhagen, M.D. (2021). Learning loss due to school closures during the COVID-19 pandemic. *Proceedings of the National Academy of Sciences*, 118(17), pp. 1–7.

Fana, M., Pérez, S.T. and Fernández-Macías, E. (2020). Employment impact of COVID-19 crisis: From short term effects to long terms prospects. *Journal of Industrial and Business Economics*, 47(3), pp. 391–410.

Farmer, J.D. and Foley, D. (2009). The economy needs agent-based modelling. *Nature*, 460(7256), pp. 685–686.

Fraccascia, L., Giannoccaro, I. and Albino, V. (2018). Resilience of complex systems: State of the art and directions for future research. *Complexity*, 2018, pp. 1–44.

Frisch, R. (1933). *Propagation Problems and Impulse Problems in Dynamic Economics* (No. 3). G. Allen & Unwin, London.

Fuerth, L.S. (2009). Foresight and anticipatory governance. Foresight.

Gabaix, X. (2011). The granular origins of aggregate fluctuations. *Econometrica*, 79(3), pp. 733–772.

Galston, W.A. (2020). 'Efficiency isn't the Only Economic Virtue'. *Wall Street Journal*, March 10. https://www.wsj.com/articles/efficiency-isnt-the-only-economic-virtue-11583873155

Ganin, A.A., Kitsak, M., Marchese, D., Keisler, J.M., Seager, T. and Linkov, I. (2017). Resilience and efficiency in transportation networks. *Science Advances*, 3(12), p. e1701079.

Ganin, A.A., Massaro, E., Gutfraind, A., Steen, N., Keisler, J.M., Kott, A., … and Linkov, I. (2016). Operational resilience: Concepts, design and analysis. *Scientific Reports*, 6(1), pp. 1–12.

Gates, B. (2015). The next outbreak? We're not ready. TED. https://www.youtube.com/watch?v=6Af6b_wyiwI [30.10.2021]

Giovannini, E., Benczur, P., Campolongo, F., Cariboni, J. and Manca, A.R. (2020). Time for transformative resilience: The COVID-19 emergency (No. JRC120489). Joint Research Centre (Seville site).

Gölgeci, I. and Kuivalainen, O. (2020). Does social capital matter for supply chain resilience? The role of absorptive capacity and marketing-supply chain management alignment. *Industrial Marketing Management*, 84, pp. 63–74.

Guzman, M. and Stiglitz, J.E. (2020). Towards a dynamic disequilibrium theory with randomness. *Oxford Review of Economic Policy*, 36(3), pp. 621–674.

Haldane, A. (2020). To set coronavirus policy, model lives and livelihoods in lockstep. *Nature*, 581(7808), pp. 357–358.

Haldane, A.G. and May, R.M. (2011). Systemic risk in banking ecosystems. *Nature*, 469(7330), pp. 351–355.

Haldane, A.G. (2009). Rethinking the financial network. Speech at the Financial Student Association, Amsterdam.

Hallegatte, S. (2014). Economic resilience: definition and measurement. The World Bank.

Helbing, D. and Kirman, A. (2013, July). Rethinking economics using complexity theory. *Real-world Economics Review*, (64), pp. 23–52.

Helbing, D. (2013). Globally networked risks and how to respond. *Nature*, 497(7447), pp. 51–59.

Hepburn, C. and Farmer, J.D. (2020). Less Precision, More Truth: Uncertainty in Climate Economics and Macroprudential Policy. In Chichilnisky, G. and Rezai, A. (Eds.). *Handbook on the Economics of Climate Change*. Oxford: Edward Elgar Publishing.

Hill, E., Wial, H. and Wolman, H. (2008). Exploring regional economic resilience (No. 2008, 04). Working paper.

Holling, C.S. (1973). Resilience and stability of ecological systems. *Annual Review of Ecology and Systematics*, 4(1), pp. 1–23.

Hynes, W., Trump, B., Love, P. and Linkov, I. (2020). Bouncing forward: a resilience approach to dealing with COVID-19 and future systemic shocks. *Environment Systems and Decisions*, 40(2), pp. 174–184.

Hyun, J., Kim, D. and Shin, S.R. (2020). The role of global connectedness and market power in crises: Firm-level evidence from the COVID-19 pandemic. *COVID Economics: Vetted and Real-Time Papers*, 49, pp. 148–171.

Jenny, F. (2020). Economic resilience, globalization and market governance: Facing the COVID-19 test. Globalization and Market Governance: Facing the COVID-19 Test (March 28, 2020).

Kauffman, S.A. (1993). *The Origins of Order: Self-organization and Selection in Evolution.* Oxford University Press.

Krugman, P. (1996). *The Self Organizing Economy.* London: John Wiley & Sons.

Larsen, K., Larsen, J., Chaudhuri, P.P., Kirkegaard, J.F. and Wright, L. (2021). 2020 Green Stimulus Spending in the World's Major Economies. Rhodium Group. February, 4.

Linkov, I., Trump, B.D. and Keisler, J. (2018b). Risk and resilience must be independently managed. *Nature,* 555(7694): 30.

Linkov, I., Trump, B.D., Poinsatte-Jones, K., Love, P., Hynes, W. and Ramos, G. (2018a). Resilience at OECD: Current state and future directions. *IEEE Engineering Management Review,* 46(4), pp. 128–135.

Mandelbrot, B. and Hudson, R.L. (2007). *The Misbehavior of Markets: A Fractal View of Financial Turbulence.* New York: Basic Books.

Marchese, K., Paramasivan, S. and Held, M. (2012). Bouncing back: Supply chain risk management lessons from post-tsunami Japan. Industry Week, 1–3.

Martin, R. and Sunley, P. (2015). On the notion of regional economic resilience: Conceptualization and explanation. *Journal of Economic Geography,* 15(1), pp. 1–42.

May, R.M. (1972). Will a large complex system be stable? *Nature,* 238(5364), pp. 413–414.

Moran, J. and Bouchaud, J.P. (2019). May's instability in large economies. *Physical Review E,* 100(3).

OECD. (2020). New Approaches to Economic Challenges. 2020. A systemic resilience approach to dealing with COVID-19 and future shocks.

OECD. (2014). The Overview Paper on Resilient Economies and Societies. https://www.oecd.org/mcm/C-MIN(2014)7-ENG.pdf

OECD. (2017). Resilience in a Time of High Debt. In *OECD Economic Outlook,* Volume 2017, Issue 2. Paris: OECD Publishing. https://doi.org/10.1787/eco_outlook-v2017-2-3-en

Poincaré, H. (1908). *Science et méthode.* Paris: Flammarion.

Portier, F. (2018). The instability of market economies [1]. *Revue de l'OFCE,* 157(3), pp. 225–233.

Ritchie, H., Mathieu, E., Rodés-Guirao, L., Appel, C., Giattino, C., Ortiz-Ospina, E., Hasell, J., Macdonald, B., Beltekian, D., Roser, M. (2020). Coronavirus Pandemic (COVID-19). https://ourworldindata.org/coronavirus

Robins, N., Gouldson, A., Irwin, W. and Sudmant, A. (2019). Investing in a just transition in the UK How investors can integrate social impact and place-based financing into climate strategies. Lse. Ac. UK.

Rodrik, D. (1999). Where did all the growth go? External shocks, social conflict, and growth collapses. *Journal of Economic Growth,* 4(4), pp. 385–412.

Saltelli, A., Bammer, G., Bruno, I., Charters, E., Di Fiore, M., Didier, E., Espeland, W.N., Kay, J., Piano, S.L., Mayo, D. and Pielke Jr, R. (2020). Five ways to ensure that models serve society: A manifesto.

Sawhill, I.V. (2020). Social capital: Why we need it and how we can create more of it. Brookings Institution, Washington, DC.

Scheinkman, J.A. (1990). Nonlinearities in economic dynamics. *Economic Journal,* 100(400), pp. 33–48.

Shutters, S.T., Herche, W. and King, E. (2016). Anticipating megacity responses to shocks: using urban integration and connectedness to assess resilience. *Small Wars Journal,* 26, p. 21.

Simmie, J. and Martin, R. (2010). The economic resilience of regions: Towards an evolutionary approach. *Cambridge Journal of Regions, Economy and Society,* 3(1), pp. 27–43.

Slutzky, E. (1937). The summation of random causes as the source of cyclic processes. *Econometrica: Journal of the Econometric Society,* 5(2), pp. 105–146.

Sondermann, D. (2018). Towards more resilient economies: The role of well-functioning economic structures. *Journal of Policy Modelling,* 40(1), pp. 97–117.

Taleb, N.N. (2007). *The Black Swan: The Impact of the Highly Improbable* (Vol. 2). New York, NY: Random House.

Taleb, N.N. (2012). Antifragile: Things That Gain from Disorder (Vol. 3). New York, NY: Random House Incorporated.

Trump, B.D., Linkov, I. and Hynes, W. (2020). Combine resilience and efficiency in post-COVID societies. *Nature,* 588(7837), pp. 220–221.

Trump, B.D. and Linkov, I. (2020). Risk and resilience in the time of the COVID-19 crisis. *Environment Systems and Decisions,* 40, pp. 171–173.

Ulanowicz, R.E., Goerner, S.J., Lietaer, B. and Gomez, R. (2009). Quantifying sustainability: Resilience, efficiency and the return of information theory. *Ecological Complexity*, 6, pp. 27–36.

Van Bavel, J.J., Baicker, K., Boggio, P.S., Capraro, V., Cichocka, A., Cikara, M., Crockett, M.J., Crum, A.J., Douglas, K.M., Druckman, J.N. and Drury, J. (2020). Using social and behavioural science to support COVID-19 pandemic response. *Nature Human Behaviour*, 4(5), pp. 460–471.

Weil, D. (2014). *The Fissured Workplace*. Boston, MA: Harvard University Press.

Wernli, D., Clausin, M., Antulov-Fantulin, N., Berezowski, J., Biller, N., Blanchet, K., Böttcher, L., Burton-Jeangros, C., Escher, G., Flahault, A. and Fukuda, K. (2021). Building a multisystemic understanding of societal resilience to the COVID-19 pandemic. *BMJ Global Health*, 6(7), p. e006794.

Wildavsky, A.B. (1988). *Searching for Safety (Vol. 10)*. Transaction Publishers.

World Bank. (2020). COVID-19 to Add as Many as 150 Million Extreme Poor by 2021. https://www.worldbank.org/en/news/press-release/2020/10/07/COVID-19-to-add-as-many-as-150-million-extreme-poor-by-2021 [30.10.2021]

31

GLOBAL HEALTH CARE SYSTEM AFTER CORONAVIRUS

Who Has Responsibility to Protect

Vladimir Popov

CEMI RAN (CENTRAL ECONOMICS AND MATHEMATICS INSTITUTE OF
THE RUSSIAN ACADEMY OF SCIENCES), MOSCOW, RUSSIA

In early 2020, the United States and China were blaming each other for the spreading of the coronavirus. American politicians were seriously talking about taking China to court for the damage it did to the United States and/or imposing sanctions intended to punish China and influence its behavior. The United States withheld its contribution to the World Health Organization, accusing it of acting in Chinese interests. US President Donald Trump and Secretary of State Mike Pompeo have repeatedly blamed China for the damages caused by the COVID-19, and Missouri Attorney General Mr. Schmitt even filed a lawsuit against China.

"The Chinese government lied to the world about the danger and contagious nature of COVID-19, silenced whistleblowers, and did little to stop the spread of the disease," Mr. Schmitt said. "They must be held accountable for their actions". He believed that Missouri residents have suffered possibly tens of billions of dollars in economic damages[1].

Of course, there is no legal basis for US claims to get compensation, and there are no legal ways to force an unwanted policy on a country that is a permanent member of the UN Security Council and enjoys a veto power. The question is, however, whether the world order should be changed in the future, so that such measures become possible? It is argued that countries should be required to maintain the appropriate standards of public sanitation and health care, so that epidemics are controlled, do not spread to other countries and do not become pandemics. The higher the level of development of the country, the greater the responsibilities to maintain certain health care standards. From this point of view, the free health care system is a must for all countries, especially for rich countries, so that the outbursts of contagious diseases can be rapidly eliminated. Minimal vaccination levels for certain diseases, including corona virus infections, should be considered as the international responsibility of national governments. Where exactly, in what country or region, the virus emerges is an important research question[2], but what matters most for global security is the ability of the country to control the spread of the virus quickly at early stages.

If the responsibility to protect (*R2P*) concept is extended to public health domain, the performance of the United States that does not have universal health care insurance, spends more than other countries on health care as a percentage of GDP (17%), but lags in terms of

 DOI: 10.4324/9781003144366-37

life expectancy, would be considered substandard. The US record in fighting the 2020 coronavirus pandemic poses additional questions about the adequacy of the American health care system. On the contrary, Chinese performance is quite impressive on all these counts.

31.1 Costs of COVID pandemic

At the time of writing (2022), the coronavirus pandemic is not over; the analysis of the relative performance of countries is yet to be completed, lessons are yet to be derived, but as preliminary statistics suggests, death rates from COVID-19 differ between countries by two orders of magnitude – from several to several hundred per 1 million of inhabitants (Figure 31.1).

Partly, these differences are explained by statistical deficiencies: the higher the number of tests, the higher the number of infections and the higher the number of registered corona deaths – this may partly explain why developed countries, on average, have higher corona death rates than developing. The final analysis should be possible when the information on monthly death rates by countries would be available, so that monthly 2020–2021 rates could be compared with the rates for the same months of the previous years to compute excess deaths (EUROMOMO, 2020).

Some preliminary results on the excess mortality during the pandemic across the world are quite telling. Table 31.1 reports increases in age-adjusted mortality rate in 2020, and

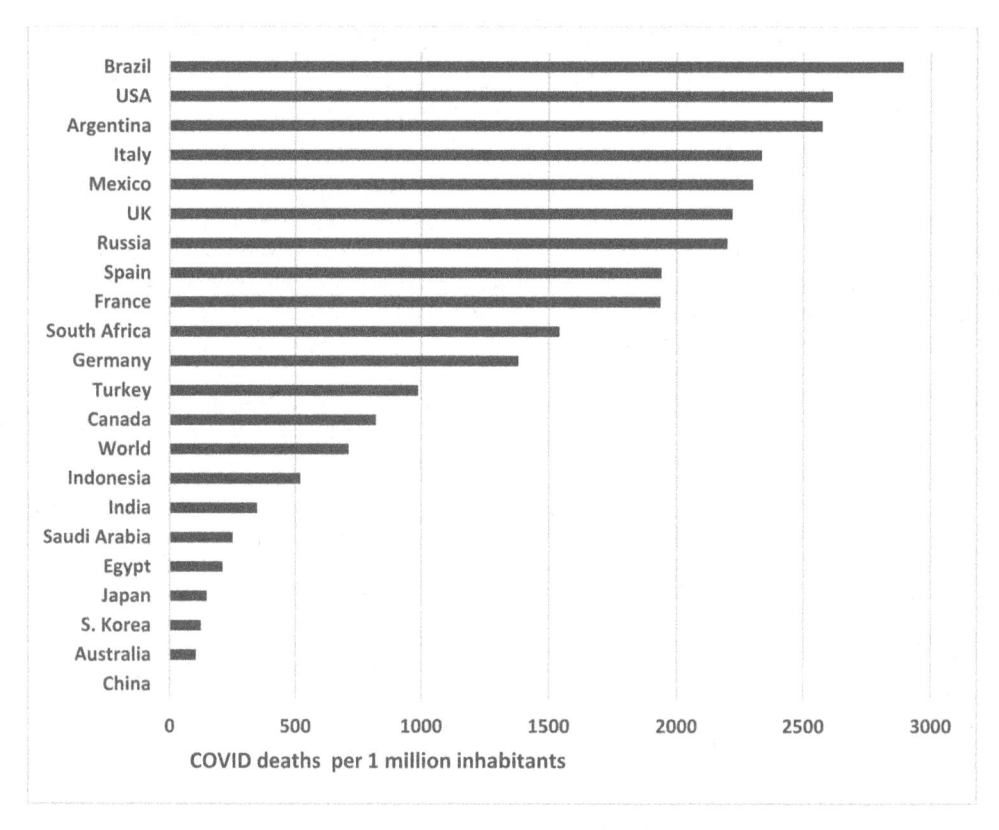

Figure 31.1 Death rate from COVID-19 in G20 countries, per 1 million inhabitants (by January 16, 2022).

Source: Worldometers. https://www.worldometers.info/coronavirus.

Table 31.1 Excess age–adjusted mortality[a] in 2020 as compared to the average of 2014–2019 (countries with less than 5% increase are highlighted in bold)

Country	*Expected age-standardized mortality 2020 (per 100,000)*	*Actual age-standardized total excess mortality per 100,000*	*Excess age-standardized mortality per 100,000*	*Percentage increase in mortality per age-adjusted 100,000*
Austria	938	1009	71	7.6%
Belgium	956	1072	116	12.2%
Bulgaria	1597	1788	191	12.0%
Canada	709	751	42	6.0%
Chile	1041	1184	143	13.8%
Czechia	1147	1258	111	9.7%
Denmark	**1016**	**972**	**−44**	**−4.3%**
England & Wales	960	1060	100	10.5%
Estonia	**1178**	**1178**	**0**	**0%**
Finland	**948**	**919**	**−29**	**−3.1%**
France	839	895	56	6.7%
Germany	**1016**	**1049**	**33**	**3.3%**
Greece	**912**	**957**	**45**	**4.9%**
Hungary	**1420**	**1473**	**53**	**3.7%**
Iceland	**755**	**724**	**−31**	**−4.1%**
Israel	864	920	56	6.5%
Italy	728	792	63	8.7
Latvia	**1446**	**1414**	**−32**	**−2.2%**
Lithuania	1393	1468	75	5.4%
Luxembourg	**842**	**852**	**9.5**	**1.1%**
Netherlands	971	1040	70	7.2%
Norway	**893**	**861**	**−32**	**−3.6%**
Poland	1216	1391	175	14.4%
Portugal	977	1043	66	6.8%
Scotland	1134	1219	85	7.5%
Slovakia	**1219**	**1236**	**17**	**1.4%**
Slovenia	996	1116	120	12.0%
South Korea	**779**	**757**	**−22**	**−2.9%**
Spain	838	946	108	12.9%
Sweden	**883**	**896**	**13**	**1.5%**
Switzerland	**783**	**817**	**34**	**4.3%**
USA	1020	1152	132	12.9%
Russia[b]	1230	1450	220	17.9%
China[b]	**714**	**740**	**26**	**3.6%**
Japan[b]	**1065**	**1090**	**25**	**2.3%**

Sources: Excess Mortality across Countries in 2020. Centre for Evidence-Based Medicine. March 3, 2021 (https://www.cebm.net/COVID-19/excess-mortality-across-countries-in-2020/); Statista (https://www.statista.com/statistics/); Смертность в РФ в 2020 году выросла на 17.9% по сравнению с 2019 годом (Interfax, Feb. 8, 2021, https://www.interfax.ru/russia/749931).

[a] To account for the age structure, normalized the excess mortality estimates were normalized by the annual baseline mortality, i.e. the expected number of deaths per year without a pandemic event. Absolute excess is the difference between the expected and total age-standardized mortality. The relative increase, also known as a P-score (Aron was by far the highest in Latin America: Peru (114%), Ecuador (63%), Bolivia (55%), and Mexico (52%). These Latin American countries have much younger populations compared to the European and North American countries, which is why the excess mortality per 100,000 inhabitants there was similar to some European countries, but the relative increase in mortality was much higher, suggesting much higher COVID-19 prevalence.

Canada only has data up to week 42, and Iceland and Italy up to week 44. **Slovakia** only has data up to week 48, and **Greece & South Korea** up to week 49. **Switzerland & Czech Republic** are based on data up to week 50, and **Hungary, Slovenia, and the USA** are based on data up to week 51.

[b] **China, Japan and Russia** – crude mortality rate (not adjusted for age structure) increase in 2020 as compared to 2019.

Table 31.2 Excess deaths since country's first 50 COVID deaths: Countries with highest and lowest (negative) excess deaths per capita. Last updated on January 10, 2022

Country/City	Time period	Excess deaths per 100,000
Bulgaria	Apr 20, 2020–Dec 26, 2021	872
Russia	Apr 1, 2020–Dec 31, 2021	742
Serbia	Apr 1, 2020–Nov 30, 2021	709
North Macedonia	Apr 1, 2020–Oct 31, 2021	660
Peru	Mar 23, 2020–Jan 2, 2022	622
Lithuania	May 25, 2020–Dec 19, 2021	615
Bosnia and Herzegovina	Apr 1, 2020–Sep 30, 2021	515
Romania	Mar 30, 2020–Oct 31, 2021	495
Mexico	Mar 30, 2020–Nov 14, 2021	465
Kazakhstan	Jun 1, 2020–Oct 31, 2021	416
Poland	Mar 30, 2020–Dec 12, 2021	411
Latvia	Oct 19, 2020–Dec 12, 2021	399
South Africa	Apr 13, 2020–Jan 2, 2022	398
Albania	Jun 1, 2020–Sep 30, 2021	391
Bolivia	Apr 1, 2020–Sep 30, 2021	390
Croatia	Apr 20, 2020–Nov 28, 2021	386
Slovakia	Sep 28, 2020–Nov 14, 2021	375
Ecuador	Mar 23, 2020–Dec 26, 2021	375
Hungary	Apr 6, 2020–Nov 28, 2021	373
Czech Republic	Mar 30, 2020–Nov 28, 2021	367
Belarus	Apr 1, 2020–Mar 31, 2021	357
Montenegro	Jul 27, 2020–May 23, 2021	348
Kosovo	Jul 1, 2020–Sep 30, 2021	330
Moldova	Apr 1, 2020–Sep 30, 2021	325
Ukraine	Apr 1, 2020–Oct 31, 2021	317
United States	Mar 8, 2020–Dec 18, 2021	316
South Korea	Mar 2, 2020–Oct 31, 2021	0
Cuba	Apr 1, 2020–Dec 31, 2020	−1
Dominican Republic	Mar 1, 2020–Sep 30, 2020	−1
Singapore	Feb 1, 2020–Sep 30, 2021	−3
Australia	Apr 6, 2020–Oct 31, 2021	−14
Iceland	Feb 3, 2020–Oct 31, 2021	−16
Taiwan	Feb 1, 2020–Nov 30, 2021	−18
Liechtenstein	Jan 1, 2021–Nov 30, 2021	−37
Mauritius	Feb 1, 2020–Jun 30, 2021	−43
New Zealand	Feb 3, 2020–Dec 5, 2021	−53

Source: Tracking COVID-19 excess deaths across countries. *Economist*, January 2022. Based on EuroMOMO; European Centre for Disease Prevention and Control (https://www.economist.com/graphic-detail/coronavirus-excess-deaths-tracker?utm_campaign=data-newsletter&utm_medium=newsletter&utm_source=salesforce-marketing-cloud&utm_term=2022-01-04&utm_content=data-nl-article-link-4&etear=data_nl_4).

Table 31.2 provides data for the increases in the number of deaths and in mortality rates from the beginning of the pandemic (first 50 COVID deaths reported) to January 2022[3]. The increases in age-adjusted mortality rates below 5% in Table 31.1 are highlighted in yellow – these are three East Asian countries (China, Japan, South Korea) and several European countries.

In fact, in 2020–2021 only several East Asian countries (South Korea, Singapore, Taiwan[4]), as well as Australia and New Zealand, Iceland, Mauritius, Lichtenstein, Cuba and Dominican Republic were able to avoid the increase in the mortality rates from the preceding years'

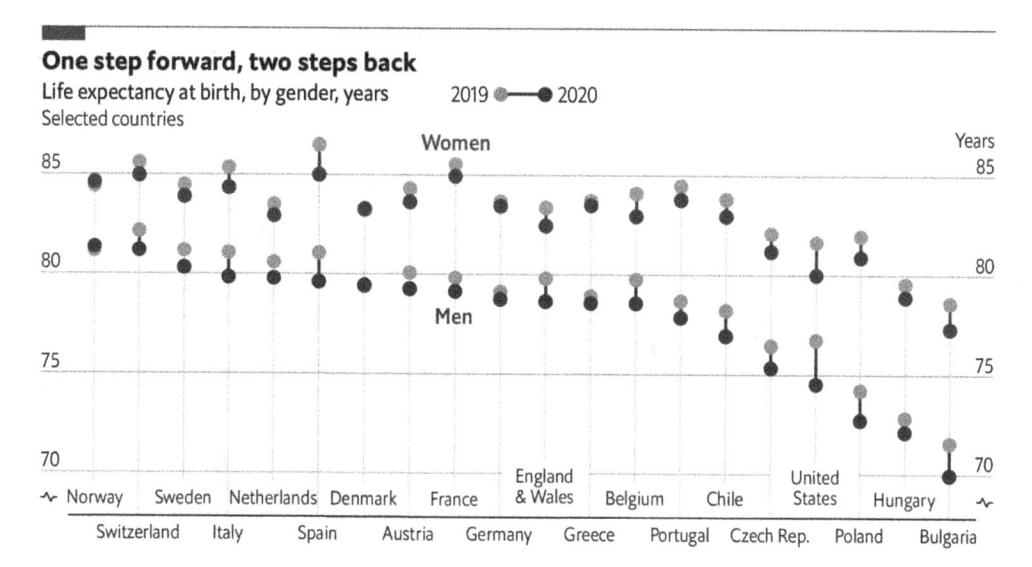

Figure 31.2   Life expectancy at birth in 2019 and 2020 for men and women in the United States and major European countries.

averages, whereas in some Latin American and East European countries, the increases were several pro mille (Table 31.2). Out of the first 25 countries leading in excess deaths per capita in 2020–2021 are 20 post-communist countries and 5 Latin American countries (Table 31.2). The average pre-pandemic mortality rate in the world is about 1% or 10 pro mille, so the increase by 1–2–3 pro mille is equivalent to the 10–20–30% increase in mortality rate.

Figure 31.2 shows changes in life expectancy in 2020 as compared to 2019 – life expectancy at birth dropped in all but two of the countries studied between 2019 and 2020. Only in Denmark and Norway, and for women in Finland, did it rise. America, which has reported the world's highest COVID-19 death toll, fared worst, with male life expectancy at birth falling by more than two years. But in many other countries, including Italy, Poland and Spain, more than one year was wiped off expected lifespans.

As the *Economist* (Sept. 29, 2021) put it, "demographers are used to seeing life expectancy rise steadily over time: in the 20th century lifespans in Britain rose by roughly three years every decade. The data from 2020 buck this trend. Life expectancy at birth last year fell below 2015 levels for women in more than half of the countries studied, and for men in more than a third. For many Western European countries, like Belgium and Spain, the drop was the largest in a single year since the second world war".

Besides, economic performance during the coronavirus pandemic was better in Asia than in most countries of the world. Only two G-20 countries – Turkey and China (shown in bold in Table 31.3) – were able to achieve positive growth rates in 2020; all the other G20 countries experienced a recession, sometimes as deep as 5 to 10% reduction of annual GDP (Table 31.3).

Obviously, there are questions why East Asian countries were able to cope better with the pandemics. One possible explanation is that the East Asian model with the primacy of the collective, societal interest over the interest of individuals and particular groups proved out to be more competitive in preventing the spread of the virus (Popov, 2020b, 2020c). The ability to carry out symptomatic tracking (even without testing) and isolation in East Asian countries was way better than in most developed countries, where strict tracing, isolation, and lock down quarantine measures were often regarded as a violation of human rights.

Table 31.3 GDP growth rates, % (2021: IMF economic forecast, April 2021)

Country	2019	2020	2021 (Estimate)	2022 (Forecast)	2023(Forecast)
Argentina	−2.1	−9.9	10.0	3.0	2.5
Australia	1.9	−2.2	4.2	4.1	2.5
Brazil	1.4	−3.9	4.7	0.3	1.6
Canada	1.9	−5.2	4.7	4.1	2.8
China	**5.8**	**2.3**	**8.1**	**4.8**	**5.2**
France	1.5	−8.0	6.7	3.5	1.8
Germany	0.6	−4.6	2.7	3.8	2.5
India	4.0	−7.3	9.0	9.0	7.1
Indonesia	5.0	−2.1	3.3	5.6	6.0
Italy	0.3	−8.9	6.2	3.8	2.2
Japan	0.3	−4.5	1.6	3.3	1.8
Korea	2.0	−0.9	4.0	3.0	2.9
Mexico	−0.1	−8.2	5.3	2.8	2.7
Russia	2.0	−2.7	4.5	2.8	2.1
Saudi Arabia	0.3	−4.1	2.9	4.8	2.8
South Africa	0.2	−6.4	4.6	1.9	1.4
Spain	2.0	−10.8	4.9	5.8	3.8
Turkey	**0.9**	**1.8**	**11.0**	**3.3**	**3.3**
United Kingdom	1.4	−9.4	7.2	4.7	2.3
United States	2.2	−3.4	5.6	4.0	2.6

Source: World Economic Outlook, January 2022 *Update*, IMF, 2022. World Economic Outlook, IMF, April 2021.

It is argued that Asian countries "accept certain degree of privacy violations if it is justi-fied by public interest. Related to this, in Asia civil society shows high level of conformity and norm compliance, which is an obvious precondition for successful social distancing and lockdowns. Such preconditions give them a head start in responding to epidemic. Common denominators of successful responses among Asian countries seemed to have been early travel restrictions, quarantine arrangements, effective social distancing, efficient healthcare system and knowledge-intensive approach" (Anttiroiko, 2021).

At the same time, East Asian countries, especially "communist" (or to be more precise, former communist – China and Vietnam), had a greater capacity to carry out industrial policies facilitating the transfer of resources to the crucially important for fighting the pan-demic industries – health care, hospital construction, production of individual protective suits, ventilators, other medical equipment, etc. The COVID recession was basically a supply-side recession (the need to transfer capital and labor quickly from hotels, travel and restaurant businesses to health care and quarantine-ensuring activities), so traditional Keynesian demand management policies (fiscal and monetary expansion) had, at best, only a limited effect (Popov, 2020d).

This paper, however, is not about the causes of varying social and economic performance of various countries, but rather about the consequences, in particular about the implications for the world economy, new world order and international relations. Jared Diamond (2021) argued that we are lucky to have this pandemic as a sort of rehearsal for the coming future greater cataclysms – global warming, resource depletion, rising inequality. "…Climate change, resource depletion, and inequality pose far more serious threats to our survival and quality of life than the current pandemic does. Even in the worst-case scenario, if every human on Earth is exposed to COVID-19 and 2% of us die as a result, that's 'only' 154 million deaths. That leaves 7,546,000,000 people still alive: far more than enough to ensure human survival.

COVID-19 is a bagatelle, compared with the dangers that climate change, resource depletion, and inequality imply for all of us" (Diamond, 2021).

Like the COVID pandemic, these future global crises require the cooperation of all countries and readiness to put the interests of humanity above the interests of particular countries, communities, companies and individuals, and readiness to make sacrifices for the global common good and the survival of humanity.

31.2 Responsibility to protect the concept and global health care system

The R2P concept refers to a global political commitment of sovereign countries to protect all populations from mass atrocities, crimes and human rights violations; it was endorsed by all member states of the United Nations at the 2005 World Summit. Should we extend this responsibility beyond cases of genocide, ethnic cleansing, war crimes and crimes against humanity, so that the R2P also includes the commitment to protect the population in case of pandemics and natural disasters? If a country does a poor job in protecting its own population from diseases, tsunamis and earthquakes, should the international community (on the decision of the UN Security Council) have the right and the obligation to intervene?

Consider the current coronavirus pandemic. It is extremely interesting from the scientific point of view to find out from where the virus originated initially, but for establishing a legal and moral responsibility, it does not really matter, whether it came from the wet market, from the bio laboratory in Wuhan, or from elsewhere, as long as the spread was not intentional and the sanitary and safety regulations were not violated. For the future though, it would be good to adopt additional regulations that prevent the uncontrollable spread of the viruses.

In particular, these regulations should be associated with the proper standards for sanitary conditions, for the national health care systems and for the capacity of countries to introduce proper quarantine measures in cases of pandemics. It is widely accepted by experts in public health economics that health care is an area with a lot of externalities – social returns from the investment into health care are greater than private returns, and hence this investment should be financed by the state. The same goes for the national spending on health care – global benefits from spending on health care are greater than the national benefits, whereas the costs of underinvestment into the national health care system are borne not only by the country in question but by the whole world.

Imagine unimaginable today – the world without borders with a democratically elected benevolent social planner fixing the global health care system so as to make it beneficial for all leaving no one behind. She will probably be following a strategy based on (but not limited to) several general principles.

31.3 Global health care system for all

First, countries have a responsibility to ensure a certain level of life expectancy for their citizens provided they have a certain level of economic development (per capita income). As Figure 31.3 suggests, there is a strong correlation between per capita income and life expectancy, but some countries are doing better than the trend line suggests. China, Japan and many EU countries have higher life expectancy than their income per capita suggests, whereas South Africa, Russia, Saudi Arabia and the United States have lower life expectancy than could be predicted given their purchasing power parity (PPP) per capita GDP.

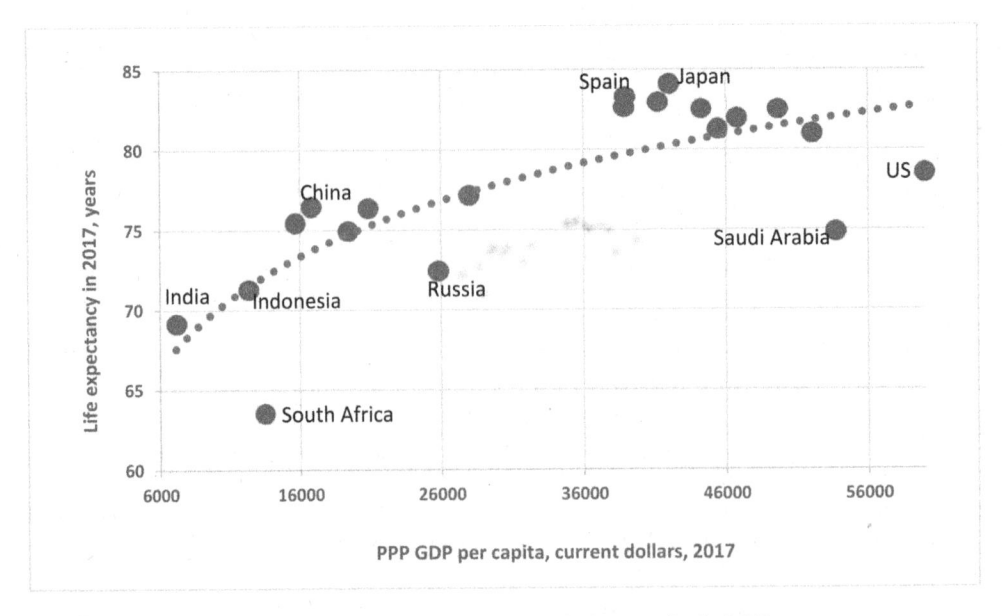

Figure 31.3 Life expectancy and PPP GDP per capita in G20 countries in 2017.

Source: WDI (2022).

Usually, this happens when the income of the countries is distributed unevenly and access to the healthcare system is not the same for rich and poor.

In general, in former communist countries, income inequalities were low and access to health care was free and rather universal. Even after the mortality crisis in the 1990s, life expectancy in former communist countries was on average 5 years higher than in other countries with the same level of development (Popov, 2018, Popov, 2020a). In China, universal access to health care that existed before the market liberalization 1979 reforms was weakened in 1980–1990s, but strengthened afterwards with the creation of the national health care insurance system and especially after the SARS 2003 epidemics. In the USSR in the 1960s, life expectancy reached 70 years – nearly the same as in much richer developed countries, but in the 1990s, there was a mortality crisis associated with the transition to the market and life expectancy fell by over 5 years (Popov, 2018, 2020).

As Figure 31.4 shows, there is an obvious negative relationship between life expectancy and income inequalities, as measured by Gini coefficient of the income distribution, even without control for the level of development.

In any case, it is the responsibility of the national governments to ensure that the life expectancy of the citizens is commensurate with the economic potential of the country.

Second, countries have a responsibility to ensure that the health care system is efficient, i.e. that a certain level of health care spending results in commensurate life expectancy. As Figure 31.5 shows, there is a correlation between total health care spending as a % of GDP and life expectancy, but South Africa, Saudi Arabia and the United States are below the regression line, i.e. their health care spending produces worse results in extending life expectancy than in other countries. The reason is usually the same – health care spending is not distributed evenly among the population, so that the rich have better access to health care than the poor.

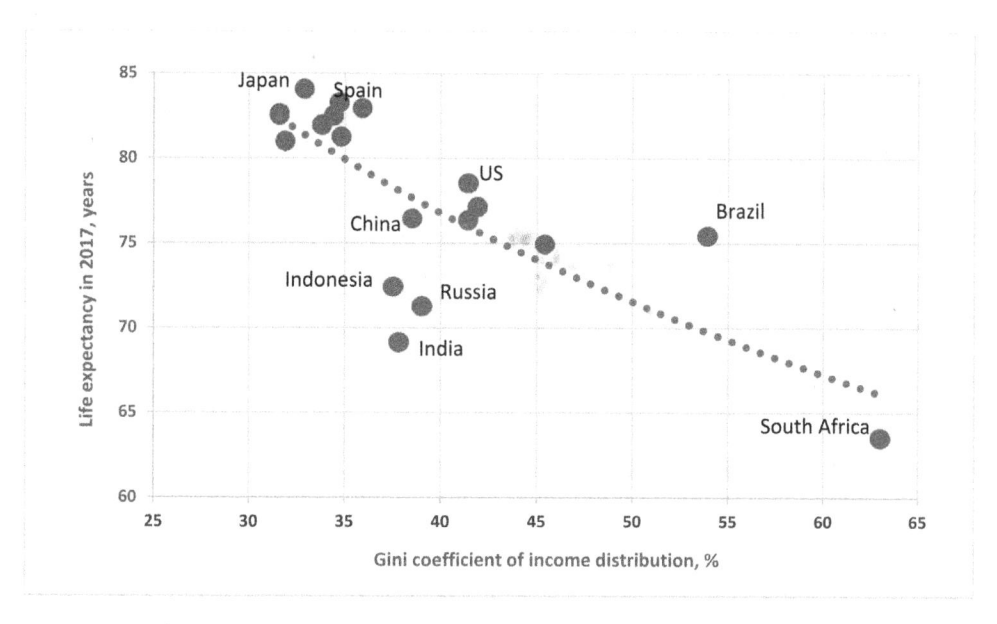

Figure 31.4 Life expectancy and Gini coefficient of income distribution in G20 countries in 2017.

Source: WDI.

Similar results could be observed in Figure 31.6. While there is an expected strong correlation between life expectancy and health care spending per person, the deviations from the regression line are quite telling. Countries with relatively low inequalities in the distribution of health care spending (i.e. countries with free universal health care and/or low-income inequalities) – Cuba, EU countries, China, Japan, South Korea – are above the regression

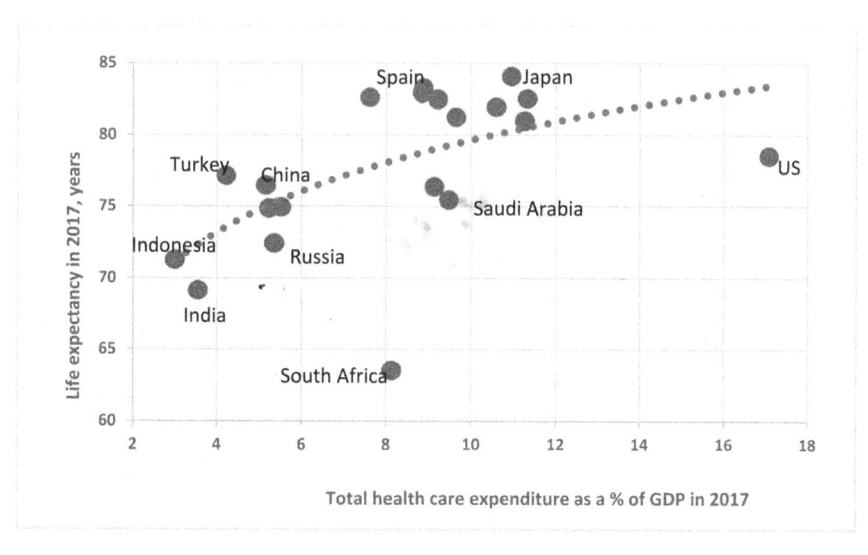

Figure 31.5 Life expectancy in years and total health care expenditure as a % of GDP in 2017 in G20 countries.

Source: WDI.

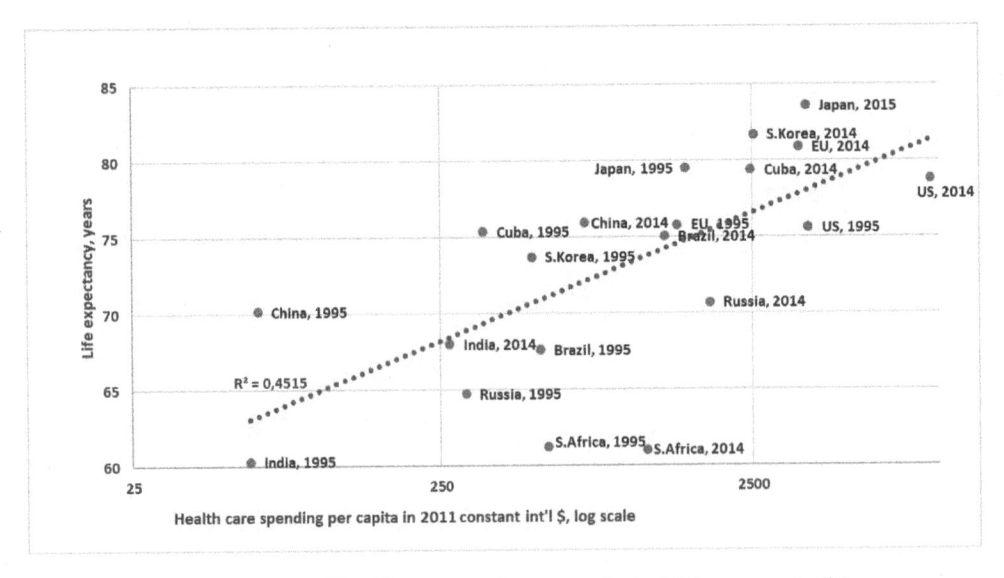

Figure 31.6 Life expectancy and health care spending per capita in 2011 constant int'l $.

Source: Our World in Data, https://ourworldindata.org/life-expectancy. Accessed on Dec 4, 2021.

line (higher life expectancy than could have been predicted based on information on per capita healthcare spending). On the contrary, countries with high inequalities and uneven distribution of health care spending –India, Russia, South Africa, United States – are below regression line (lower life expectancy than could have been predicted based on the information about per capita health care spending). Brazil that moved from below the regression line in 1995 to above the line position in 2014 is a case in point as well – it is the country that experiences a considerable decline in inequality in the period in question.

Third, national governments have a responsibility to guarantee a certain minimal level of access to the health care system for all citizens irrespective of their income. Figure 31.7 shows the relationship between the share of government in total (public and private) health care spending and per capita income – generally, the share of the government increases with the rise in per capita income. But there are some outliers – in India, Brazil, South Korea, Saudi Arabia and the United States, in which the share of private financing is higher than in countries with a similar level of economic development. For countries with a relatively even income distribution (South Korea, for instance), this pattern cannot push life expectancy below the trend (Figure 31.3), but for other countries, it decreases the efficiency of health care spending and lowers life expectancy. South Africa, with one of the most uneven income distributions in the world (Gini coefficient exceeding 60%), is a case in point: over half of its relatively high (8% of GDP and over $1000 in constant 2011 international dollars) health care spending comes from the government (Figures 31.5–31.7) – better indicator, that in countries with similar income levels, but this is not enough to raise its life expectancy (only 64 years) to the level of the similar income per capita countries, such as Indonesia with a life expectancy of 71 years (Figure 31.3).

Finally, fourth, national governments should be ready and able to introduce quarantine and isolation of the infected individuals in case of epidemics and to

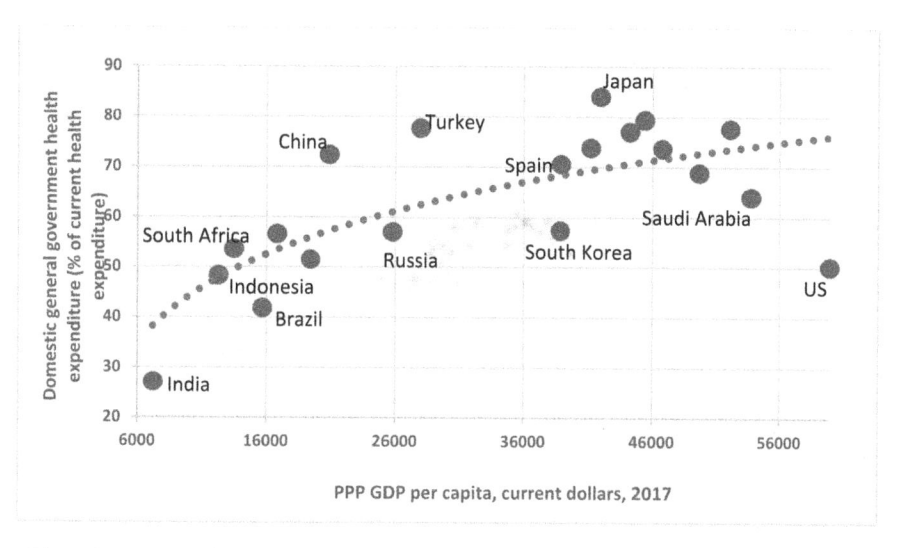

Figure 31.7 Government health expenditure (% of total health expenditure) and PPP GDP per capita in 2017 in G20 countries.

Source: WDI.

carry out quick and universal vaccination of the population. As compared to the first wave of pandemic (spring 2020) that affected mostly developed countries (Figures 31.1 and 31.2, Tables 31.1 and 31.2), the second wave (late 2020 to early 2021) and the third wave (summer 2021) caused greater loss of human lives in developing countries (with the notable exception of China[5]). The majority of the population in most developed countries by the end of 2021 was vaccinated, but in developing countries, especially in Africa, vaccination was lagging behind. China (and Cuba) once again was an exception: it was one of the leaders in vaccination, with nearly 90% of the population vaccinated (two shots) by the end of 2021 (Figure 31.8).

As was already mentioned, the greater effectiveness of the East Asian economic and social model in fighting the pandemic is likely based on what is often referred to as "Asian values" – the primacy of collectivist interests over individual interests. In particular, East Asian countries performed way better in carrying out symptomatic tracking (even without testing) and isolation than most developed countries, where strict tracing, isolation and lock down quarantine measures were often regarded as a violation of human rights. And the vaccination campaign in China was more successful than in most developing countries and even most developed countries.

31.4 Conclusion

On all four counts, China performed so far way better than the United States – its life expectancy is higher than in countries with similar per capita income and similar health care spending as a % of GDP; its government spending on health care is higher than in countries with the same level of development, and its ability to contain epidemics via symptomatic tracking, isolation and vaccination was really miraculous and surprised the whole world.

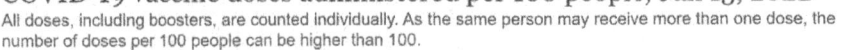

COVID-19 vaccine doses administered per 100 people, Jan 15, 2022

All doses, including boosters, are counted individually. As the same person may receive more than one dose, the number of doses per 100 people can be higher than 100.

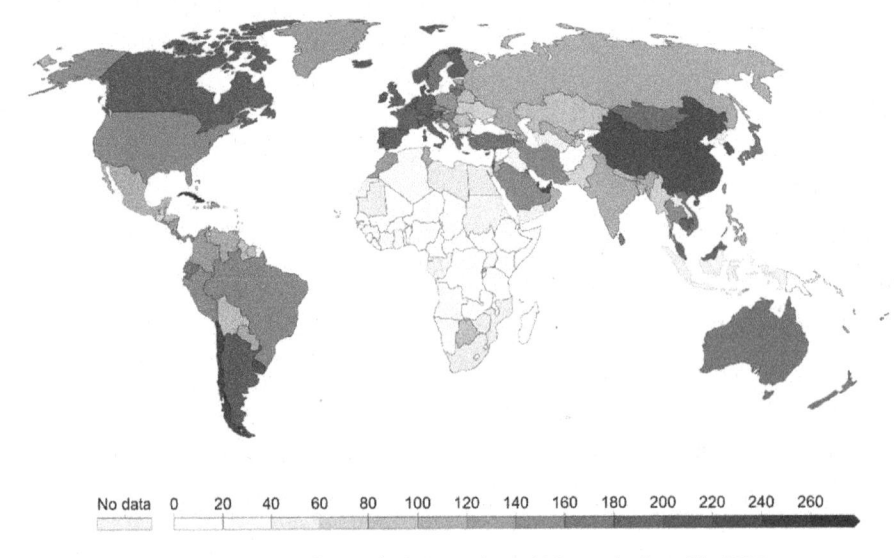

No data 0   20   40   60   80   100 120 140 160 180 200 220 240 260

Figure 31.8   COVID-19 vaccine doses administered per 100 people: Jan. 15, 2022.

If there is a global benevolent social planner or even if the international community (UN, WHO) adopts R2P principles with respect to health care systems, China would deserve a lot of praise and a bonus, whereas the US performance would be considered substandard. This kind of comparison of relative performance will not have any legal consequences unless there are new international treaties and new powers are given to the UN and WHO. But it would impose important moral obligations on respective countries.

Our potential to deal with future crises will depend on our ability to derive lessons from the current COVID pandemic. The optimistic scenario implies that countries will adopt free health care for all systems that will be financed by the national government (proportionally to the level of development) and assisted by international organizations. Same principles (national state financing + international assistance from rich to poor nations) would be used to address climate change, resource depletion and global inequality. The pessimistic scenario is national egoism and refusal of the rich nations to contribute the fair share of national resources to the solution of global problems. If the current pandemic was the general rehearsal of the behavior patterns for future crises, it definitely revealed that there is still room for improvement. Minimum national state financing + international assistance from rich to poor nations should be used to address the current pandemic, as well as future issues of climate change, resource depletion and global inequality.

Notes

1 Coronavirus: Missouri sues Chinese government over virus handling. BBC News, April 22, 2020. (https://www.bbc.com/news/business-52364797).
2 There is mounting evidence that the virus was circulating in Europe at the end of 2019 (Amendola, Bianchi, Gori et al. 2021; Apolone, Montomoli, Manenti et al. 2020; Deslandes, Berti, Tandjaoui-Lambotte et al. 2020; La Rosa, Mancini, Ferraro et al. 2021; Percivalle et al., 2020).

3 Excess deaths are computed as the number of people who die from any cause in a given region and period as compared with a historical baseline from recent years. The baseline is the predicted number of deaths each region would normally have recorded in 2020 and 2021.

4 Japan had a negligible increase of 15 deaths per 100,000 inhabitants. Data on China are not available, but it is obvious from other statistics that mortality rates in China fell in 2020–2021 as compared to the previous period.

5 Relatively few cases were registered in Sub-Saharan Africa – possibly due to less intensive testing and lower travel activity.

References

Amendola, A., Bianchi, S., Gori, M., et al. (2021). Evidence of SARS-CoV-2 RNA in anoropharyngeal swab specimen, Milan, Italy, early December 2019, *Emerging Infectious Diseases*, Vol. 27, No. 2, pp. 648–650 (https://doi.org/10.3201/eid2702.204632).

Anttiroiko, A.-V. (2021, April–June). Successful government responses to the pandemic: Contextualizing national and urban responses to the COVID-19 outbreak in East and West, *International Journal of E-Planning Research*, Vol. 10, No. 2, pp. 1–17.

Apolone, G., Montomoli, E., Manenti, A., et al. (2020). Unexpected detection of SARS-CoV-2 antibodies in the prepandemic period in Italy, *Tumori* (https://doi:10.1177/0300891620974755).

Deslandes, A., Berti, V., Tandjaoui-Lambotte, Y., et al. (2020). SARS-CoV-2 was already spreading in France in late December 2019, *International Journal of Antimicrobial Agents*, Vol. 55, No. 6, p. 106006 (https://doi.org/10.1016/j.ijantimicag.2020.106006).

Diamond, J. (2021). People around the world are being forced to acknowledge that we all face a shared threat that no country can overcome by itself. *Project Syndicate*. Last Updated: Jan. 12, 2021 at 9:24 a.m. ET, First Published: Jan. 12, 2021 at 9:12 a.m. ET (https://www.marketwatch.com/story/jared-diamond-explains-how-COVID-19-might-change-the-worldfor-the-better-11610460783).

EUROMOMO. (2020). Graphs and maps (https://www.euromomo.eu/graphs-and-maps).

Excess Mortality across Countries in 2020. Centre for Evidence-Based Medicine. March 3, 2021 (https://www.cebm.net/COVID-19/excess-mortality-across-countries-in-2020/); Statista (https://www.statista.com/statistics/).

La Rosa, G., Mancini, P., Ferraro, G.B., et al. (2021). SARS-CoV-2 has been circulating in northern Italy since December 2019: Evidence from environmental monitoring. *Science of the Total Environment*, Vol. 750, No. 1, p. 141711 (https://doi.org/10.1016/j.scitotenv.2020.141711).

Our World in Data. https://ourworldindata.org/life-expectancy. Accessed on Dec. 4, 2021.

Percivalle, E., Cambiè, G., Cassaniti, I., et al. (2020). Prevalence of SARS-CoV-2 specific neutralising antibodies in blood donors from the Lodi Red Zone in Lombardy, Italy, ASAT 06 April 2020, *Eurosurveillance*, Vol. 25, No. 24, p. 2001031 (https://doi.org/10.2807/1560-7917.ES.2020.25.24.2001031).

Popov, V. (2018). Mortality and life expectancy in postcommunist countries: What are the lessons for other countries? A concept note for a new DOC research project. *DOC-RI*, June 5, 2018.

Popov, V. (2020a). Mortality Crisis in Russia Revisited: Evidence from a Cross-Regional Comparison. In: When Life Expectancy Is Falling: Mortality Crises in Post-Communist Countries in a Global Context. Edited by V. Popov. Hauppauge, NY: Nova Publishers, p. 2.

Popov, V. (2020b). Which economic model is more competitive? The West and the South after the COVID-19 pandemic, *Seoul Journal of Economics*, Vol. 33, No. 4, pp. 505–538.

Popov, V. (2020c). COVID-19 pandemic and long-term development trajectories of East Asian and Western economic models, *Pathways to Peace and Security* (Пути к миру и безопасности), No. 2 (59), pp. 41–62.

Popov, V. (2020d). How to Deal with a Coronavirus Economic Recession? MPRA Paper No. 100485, May 2020.

WDI. (2022). World Development Indicators, World Bank (https://databank.worldbank.org/source/world-development-indicators).

World Economic Outlook. (2021). IMF. April. Worldometers (https://www.worldometers.info/coronavirus/).

32

ECONOMICS OF CLIMATE CHANGES WITH COMPARATIVE PERSPECTIVES

Gang Fan

PEKING UNIVERSITY AND NATIONAL ECONOMIC RESEARCH INSTITUTE, CHINA

Lailai Li

STOCKHOLM ENVIRONMENT INSTITUTE, STOCKHOLM, SWEDEN

Climate change is one of the most challenging issues for modern economics. Global warming is not only a public bads but also a **global** public bads, with the greatest externality for humankind. It also has inter-generational impacts, retrospectively and prospectively. But the future generations which will be affected are not yet present themselves in the current debate.

This chapter includes three sections: Section 32.1, Economics of climate change which provides a sketch of the general approach by the modern economics for analyses of the issues of climate change. Section 32.2, development economics, which looks at the different perspectives and positions between developed countries and developing countries when they are facing the same climate change. And then, Section 32.3, on variant policies and practices taken by different countries for carbon emission mitigation.

32.1 Economics: Uncertainty and cost-benefit analyses of preventive actions

32.1.1 Cost-benefit analyses

Climate change was noticed a long time ago by scientists, and the relationship between global warming and human activities has been widely discussed since the 60s of the last century. As evidences accumulating, more and more people accepted the fact that global warming is a human-caused climate change. In 1988, the **Intergovernmental Panel on Climate Change (IPCC)** was established by World Meteorological Organization (WMO) and UN Environment Program (UNEP) as an intergovernmental body to provide policymakers with regular scientific assessments on climate change, its implications, and potential future risks, as well as to put forward adaptation and mitigation options[1]. Since it was established, it has released a series of assessment reports with growing evidence of the causes of climate changes. In 2019, some polls showed that meteorology and climatology experts had reached 100% scientific consensus on human-caused global warming (Powell, 2019).

DOI: 10.4324/9781003144366-38

Nevertheless, the scientists acknowledged that there are many uncertainties in their predictions particularly regarding the timing, magnitude, and regional patterns of climate change, due to our incomplete understanding (IPCC, 1992). At the same time, there are still disagreements from various sources and even conspiracy theories due to misinformation and political lobby. The public awareness of climate change and its causes are still not as high as they should be.

Meanwhile, major actions have been taken globally to reduce carbon emissions and mitigate the damages of climate change. Among them are the United Nations Framework Convention on Climate Change (UNFCCC), adopted in 1992, that commits its state parties to reduce greenhouse gas (GHG) emissions, and the Kyoto Protocol, which set up bending targets of carbon emission reduction for developed countries, adopted in 1997 and affected in 2005. Of course, the most significant achievement is the Paris Agreement that has set up a clear global climate target of "holding the increase in the global average temperature to well below 2°C above pre-industrial levels and pursuing efforts to limit the temperature increase to 1.5°C above pre-industrial levels, recognizing that this would significantly reduce the risks and impacts of climate change".

Economists played positive roles in studying the impacts of global warming on economic well-being and policy options to combat it. Economics has been using probability statistics methodology for dealing with uncertainties that can easily be used in dealing with climate change. The establishment of the probability relationship between human activities and climate change allows us to have quantitative measurements of the costs it may cause and the benefits which may be resulted in from preventive actions.

Among many academic and empirical contributions, one was outstandingly influential and widely read and discussed, that is the *Stern Review: Economics of Climate Change*, written by a research team led by British economist Nicolas Stern. The *Stern Review* provides systematic cost-benefit analyses with emphasis that the benefits of strong, early action on climate change outweigh the costs. It suggested that from now on, we the world should spend 1% of global annual GDP to combat climate change. The benefit of that effort will be saving 5% and more global annual GDP for many years to come (Stern, 2007).

The academic discussions of the *Stern Review* by economists were mainly focused on the measurement issues, such as how to measure the costs needed to mitigate the damages (Helm, 2008), how to estimate future consumption/GDP (Dietz, Hope, Stern, & Zenghelis, 2007), how to measure the future gains of current efforts, what should be the discount rate and inherent discount rate (Nordhaus, 2007; Heal, April 2008) in measuring the opportunity costs of current investment, how to treat the uncertainty (Weitzman, 2007), how we need to take into consideration of the future technology progress, and how we can bring all social damages and damages to ecological system altogether into the estimation of the impacts of global warming (Spash, 2010), and so on. There must be controversies about such a complex issue. However, the significant contribution of the *Stern Review* was to send a clear and strong "economic message" that the price of inaction would be extraordinary and the cost of action modest, and we have to take action right now! Just like what Nobel prize winner Kenneth Arrow has commented on the *Stern Review* in the Economist's Voice (Arrow, Global Climate Change: a Challenge to Policy, 2007) "Critics of the *Stern Review* don't think serious action to limit CO_2 emissions is justified, because there remains substantial uncertainty about the extent of the costs of global climate change, and because these costs will be incurred far in the future. However, I believe that Stern's fundamental conclusion is justified: we are much better off reducing CO_2 emissions substantially than risking the consequences of failing to act, even if, unlike Stern, one heavily discounts uncertainty and the future".

32.1.2 *Other elements of economics of climate change*

Besides the cost-benefit analyses of the economics of climate change, the approaches of modern economics can also serve as a tool to understand and deal with other practical issues regarding climate change.

Different interest groups. Any public goods issue involves conflicting interests of different groups towards the same goods or bads. The externality may be very different for different groups. Global warming may cause the disappearance of a small island into the sea but may turn a vast frozen land into a farmable pasture on the northern continent. The demand for the development of renewable energies creates opportunities for many new technology companies to flourish, while the traditional fossil fuel technology industries have to deal with the declines of their market. The most important issue of conflicting interests exists between the developed countries and developing countries, which we will discuss in more detail later.

Because of the interest conflicts, ignorance, and lack of proper communications, there have been "climate change skepticism" or "global warming denial", and even conspiracy theories about climate change. Such things are undermining the efforts to act on climate change or adapting to the warming climate. Those who promote denial disinformation often use rhetorical tactics to give the appearance of a scientific controversy where there is actually none, as we mentioned above that meteorology and climatology experts had reached 100% scientific consensus on human-caused global warming (Powell, 2019). Such political divisions and oppositions could derail and delay the actions needed to combat the urgent real problems.

This is important for economists who want to not only develop the theory of climate change but also want to promote public policies in order to take real actions to deal with the problem with the support of public and government. The nature of the issue requires a political economy approach and good techniques to communicate with ordinary people. Economists should even think of the "sequencing" of policy introduction and adoption with the consideration of people acceptance. One way for doing so is to push out the "non-regret actions" as the start step.

32.1.3 *"Combined-benefits" and non-regret actions*

So-called "non-regret" action can be defined as the mitigation actions that you may not regret for taking even if one day it would be proved that, as said by some people, global warming is not caused by human activities (Kartha, Baer, Athanasiou, & Kemp-Benedict, 2009).

Compared to the local pollutions, global warming is a slow process; thus, its impacts are easily ignored and often seen as "far away" from local community and the contribution by the local community seems not to matter very much in such a global big picture. As a result, it could be difficult to reach policy consensus to take actions, and the "moral hazard" problems could be much easier to spread. In contrast, the local pollution can be aware of more directly by the local public and much easier to mobilize people to take actions battling it.

However, to a great extent, the local air pollution has the same sources of carbon emission that is the burning of fossil fuels. While it is difficult to sell a policy package against global warming, it might be easier to start to tackle local smog, which requires using less currently available fossil fuels and developing cleaner energy, so it will reduce the carbon emission anyway. The side benefits may serve as additional incentive for the policy pursuit.

There are many other situations in which we can achieve a win-win outcome. For example, improving the energy efficiency not only reduces the carbon intensity but also increases the welfare of people with respect to reducing local air pollution, and adds more profits to the companies due to the reduction of energy costs. And some time, the immediate benefits may be the first incentive people get to start to do something in the direction of carbon reduction.

This may also be helpful in dealing with political oppositions from interest groups, which deny the facts and scientific conclusions and spread misinformation on the causes of global warming. Their campaign sometimes makes people skeptical and reluctant to accept the truth and refuse to take actions. Even if people do believe the scientific conclusions, they may still be unwilling to take actions, hoping to be a free rider and letting other people bear the costs. In such cases, it would be better to form the policy package beginning with the emphasis on the "immediate benefits" such as cleaner local air condition or higher corporate revenues and more employment.

32.1.4 Government and market

The issue of government and market comes whenever the policies are considered and real actions are about to take place for public goods. A great part of literature on economics of climate change focuses on the discussion of policy options that involve the roles of government and market players. While we leave more detailed analyses of this matter until later when we go into the policy discussions, it may be useful to summarize the main differences of institutional arrangements with comparative perspectives as the following:

The first arrangement may be called "the minimum government role with market mechanism". This may refer to the "carbon trade" framework in which the government set up the distribution of "emission allowance "or "emission permit" and then let the market demand and supply determine carbon prices in the carbon emission (permit) trading. The most European countries adopted this mechanism.

The second arrangement may be called "direct government intervention of carbon price", where the government makes a decision for levying a certain "carbon tax". Some European countries use this approach to increase directly the costs of carbon emission. Some countries adopt both the first and second mechanisms.

The third arrangement may be called "government administrative enforcement" of emission reduction targets without a market pricing system. China is a typical example of this approach as the government sets up and enforces "(fossil) energy consumption quotas" for regions and industries without market pricing (e.g., the carbon emission trade) or taxation to play the roles.

32.2 Development economics: Different perspectives between developed countries and developing/emerging economies

32.2.1 The legacy differences

One of the major differences between the global warming issue and other "usual" public goods issues is that human-incurred emission of GHG concentrated and accumulated in the atmosphere causing the temperature rising can be traced back to over 200 years since Industrial Revolution in late 18th century. During that long period, early industrialized countries were the source of the problem. By 1980, CO_2 which has been accumulated in the atmosphere was emitted by the developed countries; 28 EU member countries and the United States was accounted for 77% of the CO_2 stock emitted in the atmosphere, while Asia including China and India had contributed less than 10% of the total[2]. This is the first difference between the developed and developing countries (see Figure 32.1).

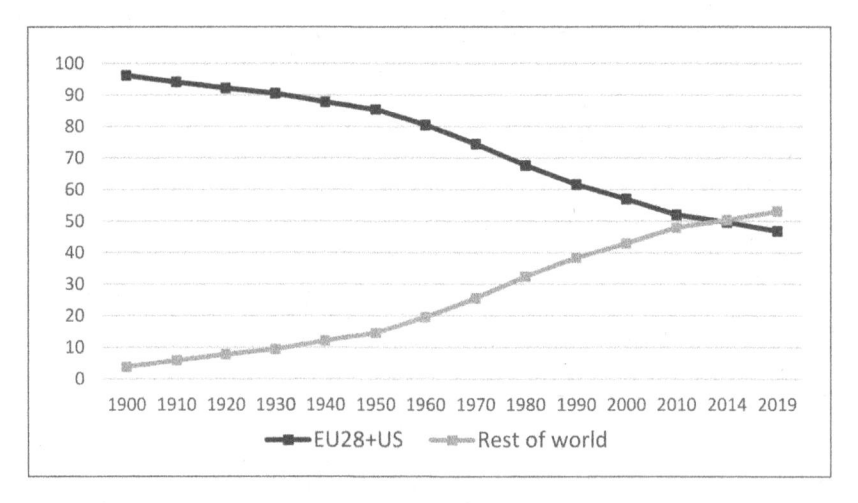

Figure 32.1   Share of global cumulative CO_2 emission (%): 1900–2019.

Source: Our World in Data, https://ourworldindata.org/co₂-and-other-greenhouse-gas-emissions.

This is not only about who are responsible for the carbon emission and consequently climate change, who should bear the costs for emission reduction, and who should be subject to the prevention restrictions; it is also about, more importantly, the issue of "Greenhouse Development Rights (GDR)" (Kartha, Baer, Athanasiou, & Kemp-Benedict, 2009). The underdeveloped countries were just about to start their industrialization process and increase their consumption of energy. Should they be stopped doing so? By definition, the developing countries are backward in technologies, including carbon-efficient technologies. The international arrangement of global mitigation should take these into consideration. In the discussion of climate change, we may call this the "**Legacy Difference**" to express the emission gap crossing countries with a historical perspective.

Although the legacy difference started decreasing since 2014 in terms of countries' "total" contribution to the CO_2 stock in the atmosphere, the gap is still significant between major countries when emission per capita is examined (Figure 32.2).

32.2.2 The structural difference

The second difference may be categorized as "**Structural Difference**". When the developing countries start industrialization and their production and income start to increase, their emissions start to increase as well. At the same time, due to globalization, more and more manufacturing industries moved to emerging markets from the developed countries which now more and more concentrate in service industries such as finance, trade, tourism, entertainment, etc., which consume much less energy. Meanwhile, consumption in developed countries continues to be at a high level and even increase further, but now they have to rely more and more on imported consumer goods made in the emerging economies. In such a structure of the global economy, the carbon emission rose in low-income countries rapidly, and developed countries appear achieving success in the direction of lower emission. Naturally, people may ask questions about who should be responsible for the carbon emission embodied in the "imported goods". In the market of global trade, supply is because of demand so it should be the consumers of the importing countries to be responsible for the emission,

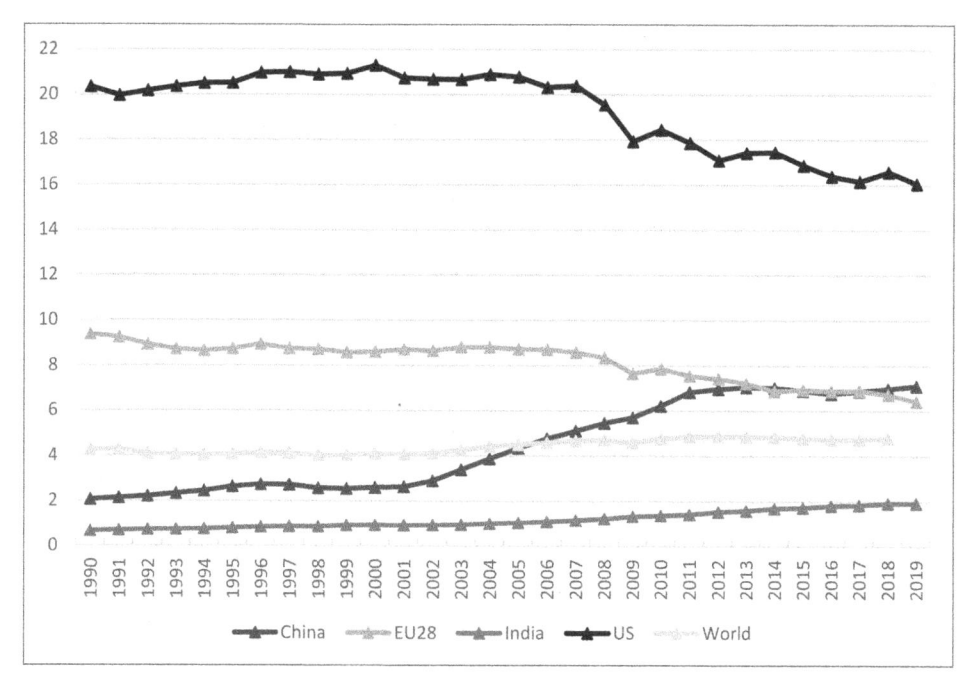

Figure 32.2 Emission of CO_2 per capita in selected countries/regions.

Source: Our World in Data, https://ourworldindata.org/co$_2$-and-other-greenhouse-gas-emissions.

not the producers. CO_2 emission embedded in trade has been discussed academically (Ackerman, 2011; Aichele & Felbermayr, 2012; Fernández-Amador, Francois, & Tomberger, 2016), focusing on the domestic and international policy agendas of, e.g., OECD and WTO.

This structural difference existed actually in history in the other way around. Germany and the United States possess the most advanced manufacturing industries and export a great deal of emission-intensive manufacturing and import much energy and resource. And they had traded surplus in a long period 1950–2005. In contrast, India and Brazil export a great number of primary products and resources (with lower carbon emissions) to exchange for foreign manufacturing in history (Kainuma, Matsuoka, & Morita, 2000; Munksgaard & Pedersen, 2001; Lenzen, 2001).

Therefore, Fan Gang and others argued that the fairway of counting responsibilities of emission is to attribute the carbon emission to the consumption, not the domestic production or GDP, in both total and per capita terms, in the past and today, under the assumptions of international trade (supply is caused by demand) and globalization of production (allocation of production is determined by comparative advantages of different nations) (Fan, Cao, & Su, 2010, 2011). This is the first proposition of the "Consumption Emission" theory. It means that part of the carbon emission that occurred in the production in one country may be responsible by another country which imported the products in concern and should be added this part to latter's total emission and emission per capita, while the producer country should be minus the same amount, in counting the contribution and responsibility (of mitigation) for different countries. The second proposition of the theory is that it is arguable that not only the carbon emission can be ultimately attributed to the consumption, but also it is important to understand the impacts of "high consumption lifestyle model" of the developed countries on the consumer behavior of the emerging economies with the "spill-over effect" of carbon-intensive consumption (Fan, Cao, & Su, 2010, 2011).

This issue of who is responsible for the emissions embodied in goods traded between countries is directly related to the practical matter of "border tax", which we will be analyzed in more details, when we discuss the policy issues in Section 3.2.3.

32.2.3 *The capability differences*

The third difference is so-called "**Capability Difference**", referring to the vulnerability and lack of means of developing countries in facing the global warming and energy transition, technically, financially, and even geographically, in comparison to the developed countries. In this regard, as the protection of our climate is global public goods, the more capable parties of the "global public" should contribute more in terms of their own efforts, and their financial aids and technical assistance to the parties with lower capabilities.

In the public goods provision, it is common practice that the more financially capable people, the rich, pay more (through the tax system) to the program. For the global public goods, i.e., the global climate, the same principle should apply too. Therefore, the "shared and differentiated responsibilities" should include the mechanism the rich countries provide financial and technical aids to the poor developing countries, in addition to the resources used in their own countries for the mitigation. At COP15 in Copenhagen in 2009, developed countries pledged to provide $100bn a year by 2020 to help developing countries cope with the challenge of climate change. But more than a decade later, developed countries are lagging far behind on this commitment.

32.2.4 *The common and differentiated responsibility*

The differences we listed above have been recognized by the international community in principle and had been taken into the international arrangement of global action strategies and distribution plan. The principle of "common but differentiated responsibility" had been adopted and established as the pillar of the framework of a global agreement on the battle against global warming since as early as 1972. The Kyoto Protocol of 1997 distinguished two groups of countries, refering to Appendix 1 for industrial countries and Appendix 2 for developing countries. The former agreed to take "binding target" of emission reduction (5.2% on average, United States 8%, EU 7%, Japan 6%, etc.) by 2012, while the latter were allowed to take voluntary actions toward the reduction of CO_2 emission in their course of economic and social development.

With the rapid economic development and the increase of income/consumption of emerging markets such as China and India, the "legacy share" of carbon emission by the developed countries has been falling and the current share of emission by the emerging economies has been rising. The differences are narrowing. By the end of 2017, the national emission of the two groups became almost 50–50% in the total (please see Figure 32.3). Although there are still large differences between the "national *per capita* emission" which is far from equal, this dynamism led to the new approach toward the target distribution. In the Paris Agreement 2015, under the global gross target of below 2 degree, all countries were asked to set "Nationally Determined Contributions" target, respectively, regarding CO_2 emission. Developed countries are still asked to consider more to contribute, including the provision of assistance to the developing countries, but no internationally set binding requirement for anyone.

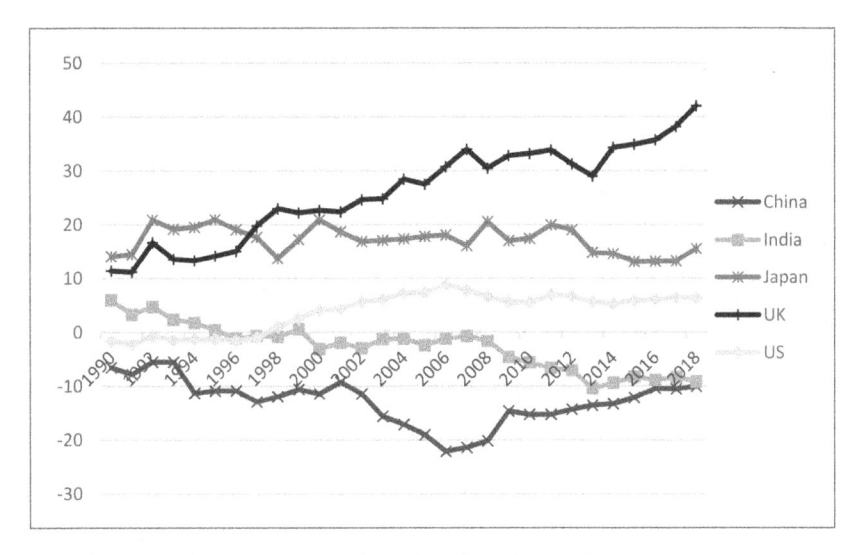

Figure 32.3 Share of trade CO_2 emissions from the selected countries.

Source: Ritchie (2020).

32.3 Policies and practices

The theories provide an academic foundation for the policy debates and policy implementation, which lead to real actions to combat climate change. Policy studies consist of the main part of the literature on the economics of climate change.

There are basically two kinds of mechanisms to implement the carbon reduction target: market approach and the administrative approach, which are well reflected in the national policies to mitigate carbon emissions adopted by the government of different countries. If putting these policies on a spectrum, we can easily see on the one end policies largely relying on market mechanism and, on the other end, the policies featuring mainly administrative enforcement in the command-and-control manner. In reality, hardly any country is located on either end, as both market and the government must play roles simultaneously or complementarily in dealing with the public goods' issues.

The market approach for emission mitigation is basically putting a price on the emission, i.e., to establish a "carbon price", in order to capture part of the external costs of GHG emissions, for which the current and future generations would have to pay. In other words, underlying policy instruments are the principle of "polluters pay".

Administrative enforcement is unlike the market approach which provides financial incentives for mitigation. Instead, it relies basically on non-financial arrangements to mobilize lower-level subsidiary parties to carry on mitigation plans.

32.3.1 The roles of government

For any public goods provision, there must be a public choice or public decision in order to mobilize resources and organize actions. The decision may come from a referendum, a congressional legislation, or pre-authorized administrative regulation. For dealing with global warming, we need an international governance body such as the UNFCCC. It actually serves as the formal global "congress" to assess progress in dealing with climate change and, beginning in the mid-1990s, to negotiate the Kyoto Protocol to establish legally binding obligations for developed countries to reduce their GHG emissions. From 2011, the UNFCCC has also been used to negotiate the Paris Agreement as part of the Durban platform activities until its conclusion in 2015 which set the legal framework for the governance of global actions on global warming. The signing parties (countries) of the Agreement, i.e., the national governments, will play their roles under their "National Determined Contributions".

In order to achieve the goal of climate change, government, central, or federal level or local level alike should play active roles in education, communication, scientific/technologic researches, and coordination of various policy/actions of various sectors/industries, in order to achieve the mitigation goals. We may call these as the roles of providing public service in mobilizing resources for public goods provision.

What is the fundamental role the government must play in order to get the market mechanism to function in dealing the climate change is nothing but to set up the quantitative target of reduction of GHG emission and distribute the total carbon budget among the lower-level parties under their authority.

The Kyoto Protocol set up a binding target for developed countries, and Paris Agreement makes every country to set up its own target. It first appears as the national total target up to 2050 or 2060; then, it can be an annual target for every year towards the final day. Then, the government's role is to distribute the national target to lower-level governments of regions, and industries and companies or other subsidiary units, as the "emission allowance" or carbon budgets, or the "cap" of the emission. (Hereafter, we use "subsidiary" to indicate all kinds of bodies, which receive allowances from the central public authority.)

All the targets, international, national, regional, or industrial, should be measurable and verifiable in order to avoid the "leakage".

There are four main mechanisms in order to reduce the carbon emission or turning energy consumption to non-fossil energies: the emission trading, carbon tax, subsidies on new energy, and administrative enforcement of implementation of GHG reduction. All these approaches require the government play the "goal-setting" role in the first place.

32.3.2 Emission trading: Pricing by supply and demand

The essential element of the market mechanism is to find a price to bring the supply and demand to equilibrium at that the carbon emission is approaching the targeted quantity. There are two ways to price carbon. The first is letting the supply meet the demand, i.e., emission trading; the second is setting a carbon tax.

Kyoto Protocol was adopted in 1997 at the Third Conference of the Parties to UNFCCC (COP3) and entered into force in 2005. It introduced three flexible mechanisms: emission trading scheme (ETS), clean development mechanism (CDM) and joint implementation (JI). European Union established ETS to trade the capped amount of CO_2 emission allowances allocated by EU to increase the efficiency and cost effectiveness of mitigation. CDM was performed between developed countries and developing countries so that the former could lower its mitigation costs through buying the certified emission reductions (CER) from the latter while transferring finance and/or technologies to developing countries as a practice of "common but differentiated responsibilities[3]". The emission trading and carbon tax, as well as CDM, are summarized as "carbon pricing initiative" in a report publicized in 2020 by the World Bank. There are now 61 carbon pricing initiatives in place or scheduled for implementation, consisting of 31 ETSs and 30 carbon taxes, covering 12 gigatons of carbon dioxide equivalent or about 22% of global GHG emissions (World Bank, 2020).

The reason why the government's role of target setting is so important and is a must for the mitigation lies in the fact that without an enforceable strictive target/allowance, the market mechanism will not be able to function in the battle against climate change. "No cap, no trade".

An emission trading system (ETS) – sometimes referred to as a **cap-and-trade** system – sets the total level of GHG emissions and allows those industries with actual lower emissions to sell their extra allowances to larger emitters. And allows those who are in deficit of allowance to buy additional emission permit. By creating supply and demand for emission allowances, an ETS establishes a market price for GHG emissions. The cap helps ensure that the required emission reductions will take place to keep the emitters (in aggregate) within their pre-allocated carbon budget. In the case of the cap is too large (supply) over the demand, the market may collapse, and price may go down towards zero. This really happened in 2007 in the EU market, as the EU distributed too generous emission allowances to everyone and only few market players had the need to buy more. If the situation is other way round, i.e., the demand is too much, the price may go too high. However, so far there have only been the cases of over-supply (of the cap) but no over-demand. This means that the government tendentiously gives out a quantity of carbon emission permits larger than actually needed. One of the possible reasons why the government had not done the opposite (i.e., creating over-demand) is that the current government, which set up the cap, is generally intend to be much nicer and looser to the current economic players than to the future generations which are not present yet in current market. The over-supply may be better avoided if using the **auction mechanism** for the distribution of permits, which was started in the third phase of EU ETS, together with measures of reducing the total quantity of emission allowance.

Different countries with different amounts of emission allowance may have different carbon prices because of the different relationship between supply and demand. The developing countries have been allowed to cut their emission on a voluntary base. This means that the emission permits could be unlimitedly supplied and the carbon price can be none in the countries without setting up the carbon reduction target, or the price could be lower if the supply of the permits is relatively larger.

The trade can take place internationally as well. The **CDM** was designed under the Kyoto Protocol to utilize the price difference to encourage companies of developed countries to buy carbon credits at a lower price from the developing country so the developing country can get more financial support for their development and mitigation. (Critics often point out that this may provide a channel for carbon leakage and the projects mostly produce no "additional emission reduction" (Schneider, 2007; Martin et al., 2016).

The reality just evidences that even with those highly market-based policy instruments as practiced in Europe, the role of the governments, including the regional authorities, e.g., EU, is crucial because they set the national/regional mitigation targets and control the supplies of emission allowances, which are directly shaping the carbon price. The distribution of public goal on public goods is the pre-condition for the market mechanism to work among private parties.

32.3.3 *Carbon tax*

Another form of pricing carbon is setting a carbon tax on the emissions. It is recognized as an effective tool for meeting domestic emission mitigation commitments, based on the estimation of the value of damage to future generations caused by past and current emissions. Because these taxes increase the prices of fossil fuels, electricity, and general consumer products and lower prices for (fossil) fuel producers (and their profits), the taxes promote

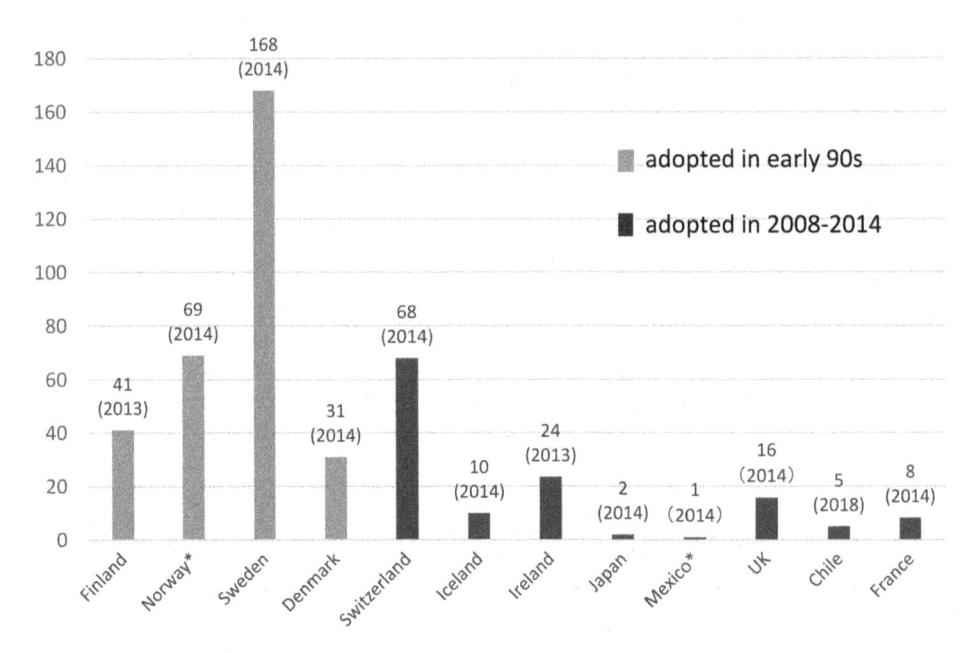

Figure 32.4 Carbon taxes practiced in selected countries (US$).

Sources: "Putting a Price on Carbon with a Tax", "World Bank Group", and Nadel, Steven (2016).

ᵃ The countries with ★ had carbon tax rates varying during the corresponding periods, with the highest rate reached in the year as indicated on top of the bars, respectively.

switching to lower-carbon fuels in power generation, conserving on energy use, and shifting to cleaner vehicles, among other things. The studies found, however, that the responsiveness of emissions to taxes is different for different countries and most responsive in countries consuming a great deal of coal, such as China, India, and South Africa (Parry, 2019).

Finland is the first country that introduced the carbon tax in 1990, followed by Sweden and Norway in 1991, one year before the establishment of UNFCCC, where combating climate change was made on the global agenda at the Earth Summit in Rio de Janeiro of Brazil.

Now *carbon tax* was adopted in about 30 countries. The tax rate globally averages US $36 per ton of CO_2e so far, ranging from US $137 per ton as the highest practiced in Sweden to US $0.08 as the lowest in Poland. Second to Sweden are Switzerland and Liechtenstein with the tax rate at $101 and Finland at $73.02 (see Figure 32.4 for details).

The most "successful" practice happened in Sweden, in terms of the strength of the pricing signal and the effectiveness. Carbon tax was officially implemented first in Sweden in 1991, as a result of the tax reform which was started in 1988. The government took an incremental approach, starting the tax rate in 1991 at $28, increasing to more than $40 in 2000, further beyond $100 in 2008, and reaching $137 in 2018. It also took the Swedish government nearly 30 years to equalize the tax level for industries, terminating all their favorite treatment, i.e., tax cut or exempt. In parallel with the change in carbon tax rate is the progress of the national mitigation targets. In 1993, the target was set to stabilize carbon emission at the level of 1990 by 2000 before bending it down (Swedish Ministry of Environment, 2001). In 2009, the commitment was made to reduce emission by 40% from the level of 1990. In 2017, the target was updated to reach net zero GHG emission by 2045 (Swedish Ministry of Environment, 2017). In 2005, many industries chose to join EU ETS and thus were exempt from carbon tax. The two policy instruments cover 95% of Sweden's carbon emissions from fossil fuels.

On the other hand, Sweden has its specific features which are helpful for implementing carbon tax. The country has no fossil fuel energy resources or producers, and carbon tax is largely levied on two sectors, transport and district heating made by individual consumers who are thus unable to join ETS.

Carbon tax seems simpler for implementation than the carbon trade. It will universally affect everyone in terms of carbon emissions. Therefore, it is less flexible than the carbon trade system, which allows individual companies to adjust with supply and demand individually.

32.3.4 *The "border tax" issue*

The so-called border tax has been proposed in order to tax imported goods from countries that produce the goods with higher carbon emissions. In European Union, this is formally named as "carbon border adjustment mechanism". It becomes a centerpiece of phase 4 program of EU ETS.

Although the border tax can be put on the imported goods from any of the countries, giving the current structure of global economy, it would mainly take place by developed countries levying taxes on the imports from developing countries. The statistics shows (see OECD, 2019) that with the current structure of the global economy, developed countries are mostly "net importer" of manufactured goods for their domestic consumption (demanded) and export less (supply). In contrast, developing countries produce and export more. Therefore, this is an issue about development and "structural difference" too.

The arguments for border tax mainly based on the different "carbon intensity" of the products in concern. The developing countries normally use less sophisticated carbon efficient technology in their production. So, the production of the same unit of goods emits more carbon dioxide in developing countries than that in developed countries. Under the principle of "polluters pay", the developing countries should put a tax on the production in order to mitigate the environment damages and discourage the production. If they do not put such taxes or not set the same level of carbon prices, there could be "leakage" of emission from one country to another and discourage the mitigation in general.

Actually, even for the countries which have the same carbon intensity of the production, the tax rate differences could be a reason for border tax in order to prevent leakage of emission from higher tax countries to lower restrictive countries.

The European Union puts the carbon border tax as a central piece in the EU's "Fit for 55" plan, which is to charge higher tariffs on imports of products made in ways that generate higher emissions than EU producers will be permitted to generate for the same goods. The scheme will begin by targeting four prominent carbon-intensive sectors: cement, steel, aluminum, and fertilizer.

There are a few problems for this tax/tariff arrangement. First, it will create trade disputes and significant impacts on the trade and global supply chain. And second, as the tax is levied on "other side" of the border, it will be part of the government revenues of the importing countries other than the exporting ones. This raises the question of how to use this additional revenue. It may be used for emission mitigation in general but may not be used in the mitigation of the countries on "this side" of the border with higher carbon intensity and therefore higher marginal returns to the mitigation investment. So it is a question if the revenue from this taxation could be most effectively and efficiently allocated in terms of battling the climate change?

More important issue here again is about the "Greenhouse Development Rights". The latecomer countries should not be punished simply because they do not have sophisticated production technologies for carbon efficiency like their developed counterparts do. And their industrialization process should be supported rather than limited by the same carbon standard of developed countries. More industrial supply chains should be encouraged to move to developing countries rather than from them. It is arguable that given the historical legacy difference and the capability difference, the "price for carbon" should be different in developing countries and developed countries. At least, we need to think about how much the differences would make the border tax eligible in regarding the balance between the development rights and the prevention of carbon leakage?

This is closely related to the discussion of a differentiated carbon price scheme which may serve as a standard for international practice (World Bank, 2020). It is arguable that the carbon price for developed countries should be higher, the developing countries be lower, given the historical "polluters' responsibility". If developed countries want to set up border tax on the imports from developing countries in order to prevent "leakages", the financial standard should be lower carbon prices for developing countries, not the higher ones for their own.

Apparently, all these issues are as highly controversial as the other versions of the same theme: the development rights of non-industrialized countries.

32.3.5 Carbon offsets in the United States

Further towards the market end of the policy spectrum is seen in the United States among other countries. Although there is no national trading scheme in the United States, the state cap-and-trade voluntary schemes, e.g., California cap-and-trade and offset programs, Chicago Climate Exchange (CCX) and Western Climate Initiative (WCI), etc., have contributed to emission reduction.

The national program of carbon mitigation in the United States is the so-called **Renewable Portfolio Standard (RPS)**, which is a regulation that places an obligation on electricity supply companies to produce a specified fraction of their electricity from renewable energy sources. Certified renewable energy generators earn certificates for every unit of electricity they produce and can sell these along with their electricity to supply companies. RPS programs have been adopted in 29 of 50 US states and the District of Columbia. Altogether, the obligations apply to 55% of total US retail electricity sales (Brown, 2017 Spring: Science and Law). States with RPS programs have often associated **Renewable Energy Certificate (REC)** trading programs because energy supply companies are required to redeem certificates equal to their obligation under the RPS program.

RECs provide a mechanism by which to track the amount of renewable power being sold and to financially reward eligible power producers. For each unit of power that an eligible producer generates, a certificate or credit is issued. These can then be sold either in conjunction with the underlying power or separately to energy supply companies.

A carbon offset represents a quantity of GHG emissions reductions that would not have naturally or otherwise occurred without an additional project or effort. These reductions can then be used to reduce or offset any GHG emissions for which the purchaser is responsible.

Carbon offsets and RECs are both environmental commodities used by businesses and individuals to reduce GHG emissions and support higher levels of renewable energy generation (Sappi Fine Paper North America, 2011). While the carbon market is global, RECs only address the GHG emissions from electricity use known as "Scope 2" emissions, i.e., indirect emissions from electricity purchased and used by the organization[4]. REC and offset markets do co-exist in the United States with one condition that is only renewable energy facilities that are additional can generate offsets. Additionality is checked via a series of instrument managed and approved by the California Air Resources Board.

As environment commodities, RECs and carbon offsets can be traded in compliance or voluntary market (CRS, 2012) (Sappi Fine Paper North America, 2011).

1. Compliance markets are created and regulated by mandatory regional, national, and international carbon reduction regimes.
2. Voluntary offset markets function outside of the compliance markets and enable companies, individuals, and other entities to purchase carbon offsets to mitigate their own GHG emissions from transportation, electricity use, and other sources.
3. Ownership of the carbon offsets must be clear, and the offsets must be retired from the carbon market so that they are not double counted.

All credible certification standards for offset projects should be designed to ensure what is called P.A.V.E.R. criteria. P.A.V.E.R. stands for Permanent, Additional, Verified, Enforceable, and Real (CRS, 2012). The retirement of offsets from the carbon market is the most outstanding condition for the linkage between the two commodities in the market.

32.3.6 *Administrative enforcement*

The non-market mechanism may be found where there are no direct and significant financial incentives involved in the policy enforcement and implementation. It is similar to the planning-administrative system in which financial incentives play secondary roles, if any. **China is an example of this kind of mechanism**.

32.3.6.1 *The "target"*

China did not have a national cap for carbon emissions per se in the past 20 years as a developing country. But China committed itself to voluntary mitigation of emission and started since 2005 to set up the cap on "energy consumption" and "energy intensity (of GDP)" as "binding targets" for localities (province or city), industries, and major energy consuming companies. The energy target may be translated into carbon targets, given the energy structure between fossil fuels and renewables. And the targets have been dynamically adjusted over time through Five-Year Plans and annual economic development plans. The energy consumption target has been still increasing (not "peak" yet), but the intensity has been falling even since.

The reasons why China did not adopt a direct carbon emission target might be as the followings. As a developing country, China could not be subject to binding obligations for emission reduction like the developed countries were under the Kyoto Protocol. Although the public awareness of climate change has been rising, the "sentiment of late comers" on the GHG emission issue has been strong that fueled the political resistance against carbon emission mitigation policies. So, for the government, selling a policy with the name of "carbon" to the domestic public is much more difficult than the policy with the name of energy which is apparently also related to local pollution and economic efficiency.

The shortcomings of the energy control, compared to direct carbon control, are apparent. As renewable carbon-free energies, such as solar, wind, tidal, are counted as part of total energy, indifferent to oil and coal, the energy control policy does not provide people with incentives for shifting to new energies, and people cannot pursue higher economic growth by using more new energies which would not be limited if the target is carbon itself. In order to promote carbon-free renewables, the government has to adopt other policies that we will discuss later in the section on "fit-in-tariff".

32.3.6.2 The enforcement

The main feature of the Chinese system is its way to implement the national target. There has been no carbon tax adopted, and no clear-cut restrictive and verifiable carbon permits were distributed so no carbon trade can take place. The government tried to imitate carbon trading by establishing carbon exchanges in Beijing and Shanghai, but in 10-year time since 2010, there were only very few nominal trading taking place with some "pilot" programs between state companies. By the end of 2016, only a cumulative 86 $MtCO_2e$ has been traded by all seven pilots, while total China's annual carbon emissions is roughly 10,642 $MtCO_2e$ in 2015 and pilots region cover 17.22% of the total emission, that is about 1,832 $MtCO_2e$ (Zhang, Zheng, & Li, 2019). Some companies traded their "energy consumption" allowances. This means that in China's mitigation efforts, there are basically no financial incentives or disincentives involved like market revenues or tax payment in past years. Then, the question is: How can the targets of carbon emission, or energy intensity of GDP, be achieved?

The Chinese way can be called as "administrative enforcement". In China's unitary political and administrative system, officials of lower-level governments are appointed, rewarded (or punished), and promoted by the upper-level government according to their performance of achieving the planned targets of the central government. The rewards of course may include some financial/material benefits, besides some moral rewards and the honor of promotion, but those benefits are never proportionate to the market value of the subjects in concerns. And the performance evaluation of officials is overall on multiple dimensions, not only on one target of energy efficiency. Such a system was working during the year of the planned economy (1950–1980), and still working within the government system and state enterprises system. There could be loopholes, "leakage", or even problems of corruptions, and the overall incentive stimulus may not be as strong as financial benefits, but basically speaking, it worked and can explain why China can achieve some voluntary emission reduction in past years without a market mechanism for the carbon mitigation. Looked at the issues from other perspectives, it should be noticed that because local governments and state companies are not exactly market players with "hard budget constraints" and not give much consideration to cost-benefit analyses like other market players do, the government has to rely more on "administrative forces" instead of "market forces".

The administrative enforcement also involves direct interferences by the central government. For example, the Ministry of Environment may directly order a province to reduce energy consumption in certain period of time, if the locality's energy consumption is approaching the ceiling target well before the target time. Sometimes such an interference may cause blackout of the cities and stop of production (as it happened in late 2020 and mid-2021).

Now China announced in late 2020 to enhance its National Determined Contribution as to peak the carbon emission in 2030 and realize carbon neutrality by 2060. It will still be going with the administrative enforcement, but it seems not enough. More financial incentives can be expected to include in the policy package, and more market instrument will be used. While this chapter is being drafted, RPS is officially adopted in China[5] after stakeholder consultations for a few years, increasing its RPS to 35% of electricity consumption by 2030. The Chinese government mandated six new entity categories that must meet the renewables obligation. Adoption of RPS will provide China with an opportunity of linking its green electricity certificates (GECs) with carbon offsets. If pricing is right, the interface of the two markets is an effective incentive for carbon mitigation as done in California of United States to be reviewed briefly above.

32.3.7 Feed-in-tariff: Subsidies for renewables

The government, in many countries, has had one financial incentive to provide financial subsidies for the development of carbon-free renewable energies and related consumer goods such as electricity automobiles. The typical way to do so worldwide is to cover the cost differences between new energy/product and the traditional ones, and phase it out when the technology advanced and market scale enlarged bringing down the costs.

Feed-in tariff (FiT) is one such policy adopted by over 50 countries as of 2019. The goal is to offer cost-based compensation to renewable energy producers, providing price certainty and long-term contracts that help finance renewable energy investments (Gagnon & Couture, 2010). In addition, FiT in some countries is also offered to micro distributed generation (e.g., solar, PV, wind), waste, co-generation and CHP generation from renewable resources. FiT as an incentive policy did play a positive role in stimulating development of renewable energy and RE technologies, although its implementation varied crossing countries.

China adopted a national FiT for wind power in 2009 and for solar power in 2011. According to the state of wind energy resources and project construction conditions, the country is divided into four types of wind energy resource areas, and the benchmark electricity price of wind power is formulated accordingly in a range of 0.51–0.61 yuan per kWh, respectively. These represent a significant premium on the average rate of 0.34 yuan per kWh paid to coal-fired electricity generators. The fit-in price scheme for solar power was similar too. Such a program tremendously speeded up the development of new technologies and production capabilities of related products of renewable energies. However, China's problem is that the percentage of renewable energy electricity usage is much lower compared to the installed capacity. In 2019, the renewable energy electricity generation capability counted for 24% of total power generation capacity, but the percentage of actual usage of renewable electricity only account for about 10% of total power consumption, less than India's 10.3% in the same year. As a result, a great deal of renewable energy capacity was left "abandoned" without being accepted by the grid. Two political economy causes are behind this. The first is about vested interests. The industrial groups of traditional fossil fuel power providers are so strong and so influential in the decisions making on how much non-fossil electricity can be fed into the state grid system. The second cause is the "target system" as we mentioned above. When the control target is total energy but not the carbon itself, the local governments are indifferent to the use of new energy, so they would not have strong interest in policy campaign, together with the new energy industrial groups, for the development of carbon-free energies for the sake of their own development.

To date, most countries have adopted supporting policies for the use of renewable energy. In the United States, in 1978, President Jimmy Carter signed the National Energy Act (NEA), consisting of five separate Acts. One was the Public Utility Regulatory Policies Act (PURPA) to encourage energy conservation and develop new energy resources, e.g., renewables. PURPA requires utilities to purchase electricity generated from such sources.

In 1990, Germany adopted its "Law on Feeding Electricity into the Grid", requiring utilities to purchase electricity generated from renewable energy suppliers at a percentage of the prevailing retail price of electricity. The percentage offered to solar and wind power was set at 90% of the residential electricity price, while other technologies such as hydropower and biomass sources were offered percentages ranging from 65% to 80%.

India established its latest solar power program to date in 2010, aiming to install 20 GW of solar power by 2022. The first phase of this program targeted 1,000 MW, by paying a tariff fixed by the Central Electricity Regulatory Commission (CERC) of India. And more and more developing countries have joined the global trend to adopt their own renewable energy programs.

32.3.8 *Green financing*

The general concept of green financing is the phenomenon that financial institutions add some "green" variables into their business equations so the allocation of financial resources can be more inclined to low-carbon or environmentally friendly projects, including the development of carbon-free energy (OECD, 2016). It can be a private voluntary initiative with government policy supports but also can be a mandated action by a governmental financial institution. Typically, green financial institutions use public funds to leverage private investment in clean energy and expedite the transition to a low-carbon economy.

In the United States, green banks have been created at the state and local levels. The United Kingdom, Australia, Japan, New Zealand, and Malaysia have all created national banks dedicated to leveraging private investment in clean energy technologies. Together, green banks around the world have driven approximately $30 billion of clean energy investment.

32.4 Conclusion remark

Comparing the countries/regions from the perspective of the effectiveness of policies and practice so far, the European Union seems most successful in emission reduction. China has been in advance of renewable energy development. The United States achieved some progress but not as it should be or can be, due to domestic political disputes. Most developing countries which have signed the Paris Agreement are yet to make more efforts to adopt more effective policies and mechanisms to make their contribution.

The battle against climate change is a great unprecedented course of humankind in order to preserve our planet. It is a mission underway far from accomplished. So the theories and policies would be undergoing changes, development, modifications, and new creation. This chapter is only a brief review of what we have so far. We are looking forward to revising it broadly in the near future when the new edition of the book becomes necessary.

Notes

1 https://www.ipcc.ch/
2 See note (1).
3 "United Nations Framework Convention on Climate Change" (PDF). UNFCCC. 1992. p. 4.
4 Organizations that endorse using RECs for Scope 2 carbon claims include the US Environmental Protection Agency (EPA), the World Resources Institute (WRI), the US Green Building Council's (USGBC's) Leadership in Energy and Environmental Design (LEED) program, the US Department of Energy (DOE), the Carbon Disclosure Project (CDP), Center for Resource Solutions (CRS), and others.
5 http://www.ndrc.gov.cn/zcfb/zcfbtz/201905/t20190515_936170.html?from=groupmessage&isapp installed=0

References

Ackerman, F. (2011). Carbon Embedded in China's Trade. In The Economics of Climate Change in China, Edited by Fan, G., Stern, N., Edenhofer, O., Xu, S., Eklund, K., Ackerman, F., Li, L. and Hallding, K. London: Earthscan, pp. 123–132.

Aichele, R. and Felbermayr, G. (2012). Kyoto and the Carbon Footprint of Nations. Journal of Environmental Economics and Management, 63 (3): 336–354.

Arrow, K. (2007, February). Global Climate Change: A Challenge to Policy. The Economists Voice, 4 (3): 2. doi:10.2202/1553-3832.1270

Brown, A. (2017, Spring). RPS Evolving: States Take on U.S. Climate Goals, American Bar Association's Natural Resources & Environment Spring 2017 Issue Science & the Law.

CRS. (2012). Renewable Energy Certificates, Carbon Offsets, and Carbon Claims. San Francisco, CA: Center for Resource Solution. Retrieved from www.resource-solutions.org

Dietz, S., Hope, C., Stern, N. and Zenghelis, D. (2007). Reflections on the Stern Review (1): A Robust Case for Strong Action to Reduce the Risks of Climate Change. World Economics, 8 (1): 121–168.

Fan, G., Jing, C. and Ming, S. (2010). Economic Analyses of Final Consumption and Emission Mitigation Responsibility. Jing Ji Yan Jiu (Economic Studies in Chinese), (1): 4–14.

Fan, G., Jing, C. and Ming, S. (2011). Fair Emissions: Rights, Responsibilities and Obligations. In The Economics of Climate Change in China, Edited by Fan, G., Stern, N., Edenhofer, O., Xu, S., Eklund, K., Ackerman, F., Li, L. and Hallding, K. London: Earthscan, pp. 69–88.

Fan, G., Stern, N., Edenhofer, O., Xu, S., Eklund, K., Ackerman, F., Li, L. and Hallding, K. (2011). The Economics of Climate Change in China. London: Earthscan, pp. 69–87.

Fernández-Amador, O., Francois, J.F. and Tomberger, P. (2016, May). Carbon Dioxide Emissions and International Trade at the Turn of the Millennium. Ecological Economics, 125: 14–26.

Gagnon, Y. and Couture, T. (2010). An Analysis of Feed-in Tariff Remuneration Models: Implications for Renewable Energy Investment. Energy Policy, 38 (2): 955–965.

Heal, G. (2008). Climate Economics: A Meta-Review and Some Suggestions. NBER Working Paper 13927 (PDF). The National Bureau of Economic Research. Archived from the original (PDF) on 15 May 2011.

Helm, D. (2008). Climate-change Policy: Why Has so Little Been Achieved? Oxford Review of Economic Policy, 24 (2): 211–238.

IPCC. (1992). Climate Change: The IPCC 1990 and 1992 Assessments. Canada: UNEP & WMO. Retrieved from https://www.ipcc.ch/report/climate-change-the-ipcc-1990-and-1992-assessments/

Kainuma, M., Matsuoka, Y. and Morita, T. (2000, April). Estimation of Embodied CO_2 Emissions by General Equilibrium Model. European Journal of Operational Research, 122 (2): 392–404.

Kartha, S., Baer, P., Athanasiou, T. and Kemp-Benedict, E. (2009). The Greenhouse Development Rights Framework. Climate and Development, 1 (2): 147–165.

Lenzen, M. (2001). The Importance of Goods and Services Consumption in Household Greenhouse Gas Calculators. Ambio: A Journal of the Human Environment, 30 (7): 439–442.

Martin, C., Harthan, R., Füssler, J., Lazarus, M., Lee, C., Erickson, P. and Spalding-Fecher, R. (2016). How additional is the Clean Development Mechanism? Technical report, Öko-Institut, INFRAS, Stockholm Environment Institute. Retrieved from https://www.oeko.de/publikationen/p-details/how-additional-is-the-clean-development-mechanism

Munksgaard, J. and Pedersen, K. (2001). CO_2 Accounts for Open Economies: Producer or Consumer Responsibility? Energy Policy, 29 (4): 327–334.

Nadel, S. (2016). Learning from 19 Carbon Taxes: What Does the Evidence Show? 2016 ACEEE Summer Study on Energy Efficiency in Buildings.

Nordhaus, W.D. (2007). A Review of the Stern Review on the Economics of Climate Change. Journal of Economic Literature, 45: 686–702. https://doi.org/10.1257/jel.45.3.686

OECD. (2016). "Green Investment Banks: Scaling up Private Investment in Low-carbon, Climate-resilient Infrastructure". Oecd.org. May 2016. Retrieved 2016-07-21.

OECD. (2019). OECD, Trade in Embodied CO Database (TECO), April 2019. https://www.oecd.org/

Powell, J. (2019). Scientists Reach 100% Consensus on Anthropogenic Global Warming. Bulletin of Science, Technology & Society, 37 (4): 183–184. https://doi.org/10.1177/0270467619886266

Ritchie, H., Rosser, M. and Rosado, P. (2020). CO_2 and Greenhouse Gas Emissions. OurWorldInData. org. Retrieved from https://ourworldindata.org/co$_2$-and-other-greenhouse-gas-emissions [online resource].

Sappi Fine Paper North America. (2011, November). Carbon Offsets and Renewable Energy Certificates (RECs). eQ Insight, 3.

Schneider, L. (2007). Is the CDM Fulfilling its Environmental and Sustainable Development Objectives? An Evaluation of the CDM and Options for Improvement. Berlin: Öko-Institut.

Spash, C. (2010). The Brave New World of Carbon Trading. New Political Economy, 15 (2): 169–195.

Stern, N. (2007). Stern Review on the Economics of Climate Change. New York, NY: Cambridge University Press.

Swedish Ministry of Environment. (2001). Sweden's Third National Communication on Climate Change. Stockholm: Swedish Ministry of Environment.

Swedish Ministry of Environment. (2017). Sweden's Seventh National Communication on Climate Change. Stockholm: Swedish Ministry of Environment.

Weitzman, M. (2007). A Review of the Stern Review on the Economics of Climate Change. Journal of Economic Literature, 45 (3): 703–724.

World Bank. (2020). State and Trends of Carbon Pricing 2020. Washington, DC: The World Bank. doi:10.1596/978-1-4648-1586-7

Zhang, L., Zheng, Y. and Li, D. (2019). China's Emissions Trading Scheme: First Evidence on Pilot Stage. Polish Journal of Environmental Studies, 28 (2): 543–551.

33

YOUTH LABOR MARKET PERFORMANCE AND BIG MACROECONOMIC SHOCKS

Misbah Tanveer Choudhry

LUMS UNIVERSITY

Enrico Marelli

UNIVERSITY OF BRESCIA

Marcello Signorelli

UNIVERSITY OF PERUGIA

33.1 Introduction

The 2020 pandemic shock caused an unprecedented fall in production and income in most countries in the world. The impact on labor markets has been dramatic, although not yet fully revealed (also because of the incompleteness of empirical data). However, we know also from the Global Financial Crisis of 2008, followed by the Great Recession of 2009, that the unemployment rates increase slowly in the following years after the crisis, but the increase tends to be – in many countries – persistent.

One thing is clear from the previous crisis (2008–2009). Young people, whose unemployment rate is normally much higher (double or even three times) than that of the total population, tend to be disproportionately affected by the crisis (Choudhry et al., 2012a; Bruno et al., 2017; Caroleo et al., 2018). This is because young workers constitute a large part of new hires (that are, of course, halted during the crisis) and are frequently hired through temporary or precarious working contracts (i.e., they are the first to be dismissed). Even worse, the Pandemic shock damaged to a greater extent young worker because they are over-represented in the most damaged sectors (tourism, hotels and restaurants, retail trade, some other services).

This chapter empirically analyzes the effects of big macroeconomic shocks on youth labor market performance. In particular, we investigate the existence of structural breaks in the dynamics of several youth labor market indicators and the impact of financial crises, including 2008 global crisis, and the pandemic shock. We will also extend our analysis by gender and by considering alternative indicators of labor market (labor force participation and NEET rates) as well. The main objective of this paper is to identify and quantify the implications of big shocks on young people and to suggest targeted policy interventions.

DOI: 10.4324/9781003144366-39

The structure of this paper is the following. In Section 33.2, there is a literature review, especially focusing on youth labor market performance. Section 33.3 provides some empirical evidence on the impact on young people of the two big economic shocks: the 2008 Global Financial Crisis and the 2020 pandemic shock. Section 33.4 includes the econometric investigations, both on structural breaks and on the determinants of the youth unemployment rate (YUR). Section 33.5 concludes and provides some policy implications.

33.2 Literature review

The impact of big shocks on young people is a specific but crucial topic of the general problem of the resilience of the economic systems in face of great economic shocks; as for a comparative approach, see Aligica and Iordache (in this Handbook).

The key importance and the huge difficulties of investigating the youth labor market performance are recognized by a growing and diversified theoretical and empirical literature. As for developed countries, the scientific debate started more than three decades ago mainly focusing on the role of institutions, the more or less flexible regulations of labor markets and the diffusion of temporary employment (e.g., Clark and Summers, 1982; Rice, 1986; Lindbeck and Snower, 1988; Lazear, 1990;Layard et al., 1991; O'Higgins, 1997; Booth et al., 2002; Liotti, 2021). The extension of research to less developed economies is more recent (e.g., O'Higgins, 2001; Choudhry et al., 2012a; Brada et al., 2014) also due to data availability and the higher difficulties in distinguishing formal and informal employment.

In general, as discussed by Brada et al. (2014), it should be recalled that theories concerning youth unemployment are often part of the broader theories explaining unemployment in general and at least three groups of determinants can be identified: (i) macroeconomic cyclical conditions, primarily GDP growth, i.e., the so-called Okun's law; (ii) demographic, individual, social, and structural conditions; and (iii) policies and institutions. For example, Boeri and Bruecker (2011) highlighted the importance of internal flexibility through working hour adjustments and short-time work during the Great Recession.

In particular, the empirical evidence and literature highlighted that: (i) young people generally exhibit worse labor market outcomes than adults worldwide and with remarkable country and regional differences (e.g., Pastore, 2018; Bruno et al., 2014) and (ii) macroeconomic shocks produce a much worse impact on the young part of the labor force (e.g., Choudhry et al., 2012a; Bruno et al., 2017; Bachmann and Felder, 2021).

Cross-country differences depend on many factors, including the quality of the educational systems; as for a comparative perspective on the relationship between higher education systems, transversal skills and labor market relevance, see Régent and Ecker (in this Handbook).

As for the impact of macroeconomic shocks on labor markets, a part of the literature follows the approach by Blanchard and Wolfers (2000) focusing on the role of the interaction with labor market institutions. For example, for periods including the 2009 Great Recession, Bachmann and Felder (2021) examine to what extent macro shocks were transmitted to national labor markets and found a significant influence of trade unions, while Bruno et al. (2014) focused on the regional differences for both youth unemployment and NEET indicators. Following a different approach, Choudhry et al. (2012b) and Bruno et al. (2017) estimated the impact of the macroeconomic shocks due to financial crises on the YUR, compared to the total unemployment rate (TUR), and found a higher short- and long-run impact jointly with a significant persistence over time.[1]

So, young people bore the brunt of the labor adjustment to macroeconomic shocks, like the 2009 Great Recession, and also the 2020 COVID-19 shock had partly similar effects;

International Labor Organization (ILO) (2021) highlighted that pandemic crisis has severely affected labor markets around the world, hurting young people more than other age groups.

Considering the existing literature, this paper contributes to the investigation of the dynamics of youth labor market performance according to several indicators, gender differences, and including countries of different development levels, especially focusing on the impact of big macroeconomic shocks, like the 2009 Great Recession and the 2020 pandemic.

33.3 Evidence of the impact on young people of the 2008 Financial Crisis and 2020 pandemic shock

The 2008 Global Financial Crisis – followed by the 2009 Great Recession – led to an unprecedented fall in GDP and to an increase in unemployment, large and quick in more flexible countries (e.g. the United States, the United Kingdom), more delayed but in some cases more persistent in some other countries (Italy and Spain in Europe, but also in most developing countries). Thanks to accommodating labor market institutions, the unemployment rate – as usually defined as unemployed people out of the labor force – did not increase in some other countries such as Germany (in fact, during the Great Recession, labor hoarding and working hour adjustments were the prevailing outcome). In 2019, in most countries, especially in the developed world, unemployment reached the lowest levels, thanks to the sizable new hires experienced in many countries in the second half of the decade, although it should be emphasized that such hires mostly referred – especially among young people – to temporary work and precarious jobs. Then, in 2020, the pandemic shock – that was both a supply-side and a demand-side shock – produced an even greater loss of GDP (compared to 2008–2009) see Coibion et al. (2020) and Andrews et al. (2020). Although in 2021 the economic recovery has been robust in many countries, few of them will reach at the end of this year the preceding production levels. The labor market impact has been huge: ILO (2021) has estimated that in 2020 working hours in the world had decreased by 8.8% (employment levels by a lower percentage because many workers shifted to part-time work).

Once more, job losses are concentrated among the young generations, whose unemployment rate is normally much higher (double or even three times) than that of the total population. The larger impact of the recent crisis on young people is caused by the fact that, first of all, they are over-represented in the most damaged sectors (tourism, hotels and restaurants, retail trade, some other services) and, secondarily, because they constitute a large part of new hires (that, of course, are halted during the crises) and are frequently engaged through temporary or precarious working contracts (Choudhry et al., 2012a; Caroleo et al., 2018).[2]

Thus, youth employment has decreased more intensively than in the case of remaining workers (by 8.7% vs. 3.7% in 2020, according to ILO, 2021). Even worse, not only unemployment has increased, but in many countries, youth labor force participation has fallen (this effect has been greater in developed countries); on the other hand, informal workers – particularly spread in developing countries – exhibited a job loss risk three times greater than formal workers. Thus, poverty levels have further leaped worldwide, affecting disproportionately young people. Even when the crisis ends and recovery becomes more substantial, they are not immediately engaged because of the "youth experience gap", thus making their joblessness more persistent and leading to a "lost generation". In the world, the young population (estimated by ILO, 2012 at 1.2 billion) is mostly engaged in education or training (42%), or also in working activities (36%), but a great part is to be considered NEET (22%).

Before presenting some initial empirical evidence, a few cautionary notes are helpful.

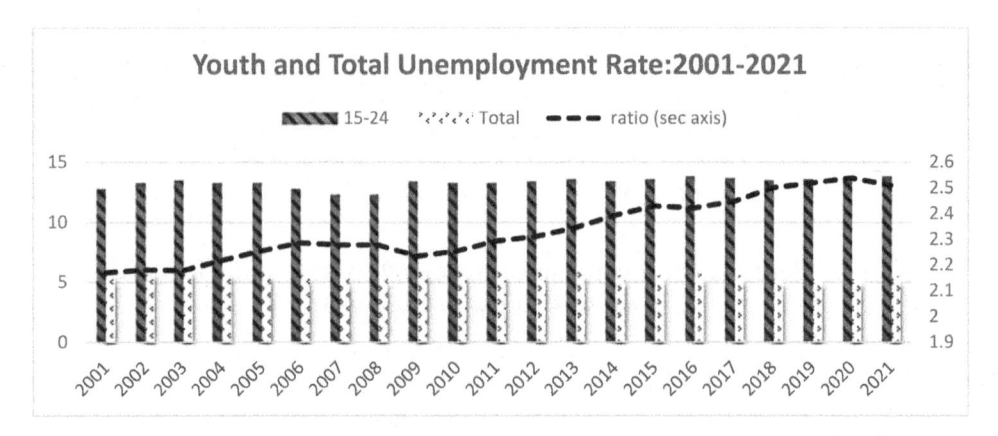

Figure 33.1   Total and youth unemployment rate and ratio: Global trend.

Source: Authors' calculations based on ILO wesodata.

The investigation of youth labor market performance is extremely complex, also due to higher or lower involvement in formal education and informal employment, and a single indicator (unemployment calculated on labor force) is surely not sufficient and often at least the NEET indicator (percent of young people who are neither employed nor in education or training) is added. Also, the age class to be considered (15–24 is usually adopted for youth unemployment) is under debate and more or less appropriate depending also on the development level, not to mention the difficulties to consider and measure the "irregular employment" and to distinguish, especially in less developed countries, formal and informal employment. However, this topic is also extremely important in terms of general and specific policy implications favoring a better future for young people and the whole society.

The trend of the unemployment rate is represented in Figure 33.1. As regards unemployment, according to the ILO, from which the YUR and TUR data were extracted, the unemployed comprise all persons above a specified age who, during the reference period, were (a) without work, (b) currently available for work, and (c) actively seeking work. So the unemployment rate is defined as the number of unemployed in an age group divided by the labor force for that group.[3] The youth to TUR ratio shows that globally, youth unemployment is more than double in all years see Figure 33.1.

The TUR reached a minimum value in 2007–2008, and then the Global Financial Crisis and the Great Recession caused a rise in 2009, followed by a slow but continuous decrease in the last decade. On the contrary, the YUR, after the 2008 minimum, continued to rise until 2016, thus exhibiting more persistence (and again in 2020–2021). It is worth to stress that, globally, the ratio between youth and the TUR reached a maximum of 2.5 in 2020. Of course, for a subset of countries, for instance, for developed countries, we would get a different picture.

33.4 Econometric investigation: Determinants of youth unemployment and structural breaks

33.4.1 Detecting structural break in youth unemployment rate

A structural break occurs when an event/incident affects the trend of a particular variable. It appears when there is a noticeable visual difference in the direction and movement of a variable before and after an incident. Examples of such incidents may be financial crises, oil price

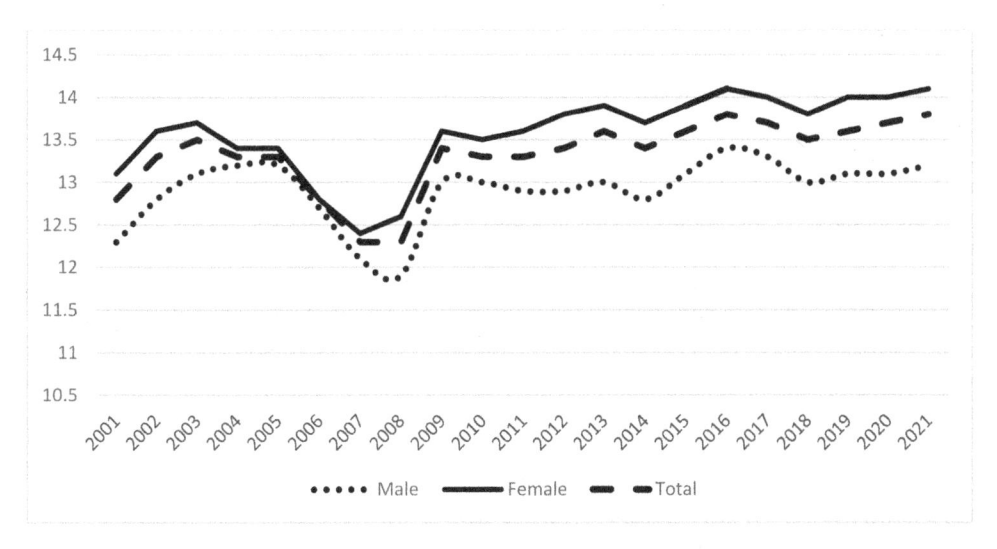

Figure 33.2   Global youth (15–24) unemployment rate: 2001–2021.

Source: International Labor Office, Trends Econometric Models (ilo.org/wesodata).

shocks, Brexit, and the COVID pandemic. Structural breaks can influence the interpretation and policy implications of the empirical findings. There is a need to test the potential structure break in labor market indicators after financial crises and the COVID pandemic. We have enough data points after the financial crises which help us to detect a structural break in labor market variables. However, for COVID, we still need more data points at the national and international levels. However, the adverse impact of COVID on different indicators of the youth labor market is quite evident as discussed in our previous section.

A visual analysis of the YUR (Figure 33.2) suggests that there seems a structural break in the year 2008, after a significant decline in the period 2003–2007. As for the last decade, a slightly increasing trend contains accelerations in the periods 2014–2016, with a partial reduction in the following two years, and in the period 2019–2021 especially due to pandemic shock.

A structural break[4] in various labor market indicators at the global level is tested, and the results are presented in Table 33.1. We can see from the results that we can reject the null hypothesis of no structural break in 2008–2009 for most cases, including the YUR and labor force participation rate. An interesting finding is that we cannot reject the null hypothesis of

Table 33.1 Structural break test in labor market indicators: Global level

Variables	Test for known SB point – 2008–2009			
	Test statistic –W(tau)	P-value (F)	P-value (chi)	Decision
Youth Unemployment Rate (YUR)	5.47	0.01	0.07	Reject H_0
YUR – Female	1.94	0.78	0.58	Accept H_0
YUR – Male	7.09	0	0.02	Reject H_0
Labor Force Participation Rate	40.55	0	0	Reject H_0
Total Unemployment Rate	0.28	0.76	0.87	Accept H_0
EU28	3.59	0.06	0.07	Reject H_0

Note: Structural break test is conducted by applying Bai and Parron structural break test, where the null hypothesis is there is no structural break.

no break for the TUR and unemployment rate among young females; however, it is evident in the YUR and other indicators of the labor market.

33.4.2 *Panel data structural break*

The structural break in panel data is checked by following Bai and Perron (1998) structural break test to detect multiple change points. We used this test by applying the xtbreak[5] program (latest version August 2021) developed by Ditzen et al. (2021). This program is still an Alpha version; results may change subject to modification or upgradation of the program. Period of analysis for panel data structural break was 1980–2018. Though these results (Tables 33.2–33.4) are not very reliable yet, they still give us a good idea about the structural break in YUR data after the financial crises in 2008 onward. We can see from the following results that in panel data structural break analysis, overall, and bifurcation by male and female, we can reject the null hypothesis of no structural break in all cases. As a test is conducted for

Table 33.2 Youth unemployment rate (15–24): Total

Test for multiple breaks at unknown breakdates
(Ditzen et al. 2021)
Ho: no break(s) vs. H1: 2 break(s)

		Bai and Perron critical values		
	Test statistics	*1% Critical value*	*5% Critical value*	*10% Critical Value*
SupW (tau)	11.93	9.36	7.22	6.28

Estimated break points: 1994, 2008.

Table 33.3 Youth unemployment rate (15–24): Male

Test for multiple breaks at unknown breakdates
(Ditzen et al. 2021)
Ho: no break(s) vs. H1: 2 break(s)

		Bai and Perron critical values		
	Test statistics	*1% Critical value*	*5% Critical value*	*10% Critical value*
SupW (tau)	32.1	9.36	7.22	6.28

Estimated break points: 2008, 2015.

Table 33.4 Youth unemployment rate (15–24): Female

Test for multiple breaks at unknown breakdates
(Ditzen et al. 2021)
Ho: no break(s) vs. H1: 2 break(s)

		Bai and Perron critical values		
	Test statistics	*1% Critical value*	*5% Critical value*	*10% Critical value*
SupW (tau)	17.18	9.36	7.22	6.28

Estimated break points: 1994, 2008.

unknown structural breaks, the year 2008 is detected in all three cases, reaffirming that structural breaks occur after financial crises.

33.4.3 Determinants of youth unemployment

This section presents the econometric analysis of our primary research question, i.e., the determinants of the YUR, specifically the impact of macroeconomic shocks like financial crises and the COVID. Moreover, how do these variables affect the TUR and different labor market indicators? As in the previous section, we have analyzed the structural break in the global time-series data of various labor market indicators and panel data series. We will analyze the effect of this structural break by including a financial crisis dummy in our regression.

33.4.3.1 Variables, data, and sample

To econometrically estimate the impact of various macroeconomic, structural, and institutional variables on the unemployment rate – especially YUR and TUR – we used the sample 127–135 countries from 2000 to 2019. The unbalanced panel of countries is used to get the maximum benefit of available data points.

We have included various explanatory variables to capture their impact on YUR and TUR. These control variables belong to different categories, i.e., macroeconomic situation, demographic condition, labor market indicators, and financial crises. The choice of control variables for econometric analysis was well motivated above in our literature review section and, in particular, we take guidance from previous literature (Booth et al., 2002; OECD, 2012; Caroleo et al., 2018; Choudhry et al., 2012a). Our control variables include lagged GDP growth rate, financial crisis, inflation rate, part-time employment, gross capital formation, and labor force participation rate. Data summary stats and correlation matrix of our dependent and explanatory variables are presented in the Appendix see Tables A1 and A2.

33.4.3.2 Model and econometric specification

The empirical investigation of the impact of potential determinants and macroeconomic shocks on YUR, TUR, and different labor market indicators is carried out for a panel of countries worldwide for 2000–2019. The empirical estimation is done with unbalanced panel data to utilize the available information for our variables of interest fully.

The baseline model for estimation is

$$YUR_{i,t} = \alpha_i + FC_{i,t}\lambda + X'_{i,t}\beta + \varepsilon_{i,t,}$$

where $YUR_{i,t}$ indicates the YUR in country $i = 1,...,N$ at time $t = 1,...,T_i$ and it is our dependent variable (alternatively, it is replaced by $TUR_{i,t}$ when we use TUR as our dependent variable). $FC_{i,t}$ indicates the financial crisis dummy. $X'_{i,t}$ is a row vector comprising the macroeconomic conditions prevailing in country i at time t.

33.4.3.3 Econometric results and discussion

Tables 33.5 and 33.6 present coefficient estimates for YUR and TUR, respectively. Models 1–3 just introduced the control variables one by one, which can play a role in determining the youth and TUR. In model 4, we introduced the financial crisis dummy as suggested by our structural

Table 33.5 Determinant of the youth unemployment rate: Impact of macroeconomic shocks

	Model 1 b/se	Model 2 b/se	Model 3 b/se	Model 4 b/se	Model 5 b/se	Model 6 b/se	Model 7 b/se	Model 8 b/se
GDPG (−1)	−0.127***	−0.155***	−0.153***	−0.152***	−0.146***	−0.147***	−0.308***	−0.154***
	0.014	0.018	0.018	0.018	0.018	0.018	0.038	0.019
Gross Capital formation		−0.180***	−0.180***	−0.184***	−0.191***	−0.188***	−0.420***	−0.184***
		0.015	0.015	0.015	0.015	0.015	0.038	0.015
Inflation			−0.002	−0.002	−0.002	−0.002	−0.089***	−0.002
			0.002	0.002	0.002	0.002	0.03	0.002
Financial Crisis				0.376**	0.359**	0.331**	0.825***	0.451***
				0.164	0.164	0.164	0.289	0.166
Urbanization					0.110***			
					0.027			
Labor force participation rate (LFPR; youth)						−0.100***		
						0.021		
Part-time Employment							0.027	
							0.028	
Labor Productivity								−0.000***
								0
Constant	17.200***	21.252***	21.252***	21.235***	14.987***	25.805***	28.209***	22.645***
	0.086	0.343	0.343	0.343	1.592	1.035	1.215	0.543
Observations	3626	3223	3222	3222	3222	3222	1353	3162
No of Countries	188	173	173	173	173	173	135	168
R-Square	0.024	0.082	0.081	0.083	0.088	0.089	0.194	0.087
Overall Sig of Model	84.044***	135.363***	89.849***	68.790***	58.536***	59.789***	58.238***	56.929***

Note: Standard errors are reported under the coefficient value. * Significant at 10%; ** Significant at 5%; and *** Significant at 1%.

Table 33.6 Total unemployment rate and impact of macroeconomic shocks

	Model 1 b/se	Model 2 b/se	Model 3 b/se	Model 4 b/se	Model 5 b/se	Model 6 b/se	Model 7 b/se	Model 8 b/se
GDPG (−1)	−0.058*** (0.007)	−0.067*** (0.009)	−0.066*** (0.009)	−0.066*** (0.009)	−0.068*** (0.009)	−0.065*** (0.009)	−0.145*** (0.019)	−0.062*** (0.01)
Gross Capital formation		−0.094*** (0.008)	−0.094*** (0.008)	−0.095*** (0.008)	−0.093*** (0.008)	−0.102*** (0.008)	−0.199*** (0.019)	−0.095*** (0.008)
Inflation			−0.001 (0.001)	−0.001 (0.001)	−0.001 (0.001)	−0.001 (0.001)	−0.028* (0.015)	−0.001 (0.001)
Financial Crisis				0.113 (0.085)	0.112 (0.085)	0.091 (0.084)	0.324** (0.146)	0.168** (0.086)
Urbanization					−0.035*** (0.014)			
LFPR (youth)						−0.110*** (0.018)		
Part-time Employment							0.007 (0.014)	
Labor Productivity								−0.000*** (0)
Constant	8.124*** (0.044)	10.184*** (0.175)	10.175*** (0.175)	10.171*** (0.175)	12.184*** (0.797)	17.791*** (1.23)	13.034*** (0.614)	11.750*** (0.27)
Observations	3805	3351	3350	3350	3350	3222	1356	3290
No of Countries	188	173	173	173	173	173	135	168
R–Square	0.018	0.073	0.072	0.073	0.074	0.089	0.166	0.09
Overall Sig of Model	64.832***	124.653***	82.108***	62.030***	51.055***	59.176***	48.331***	61.573***

Note: Standard errors are reported under the coefficient value. * Significant at 10%; ** Significant at 5%; and *** Significant at 1%.

break test results. Model 4 is the most economical, with *Lagged GDP growth*, gross capital formation and *Inflation* as additional explanatory variables. We also consider the following regressors:
urbanization, part-time employment, labor force participation rate, and labor *productivity in
models 5–8.*

Our main results can be summarized as follows:

1. As expected, *lagged GDP growth impact is negative and* is always statistically significant in
   all models for YUR and TUR.
2. Gross capital formation negatively impacts the YUR and overall unemployment rate and
   is significant in all specifications.
3. The impact of uncertainty, as mentioned by our structural break tests, is always positively
   significant in YUR and models 7–9 in TUR equations. The coefficient value is higher
   in the case of the YUR than the TUR. Moreover, the introduction of other control
   variables does not change the significance of this variable, which reflects the robustness
   of our findings.
4. Increase in labor force participation rate reduces the unemployment rate and increase in
   labor productivity will also have negative implications for YUR and TUR. However,
   the part-time employment impact is not statistically significant.
5. The sign of the coefficients on all regressors, when significant, are consistent with our
   theoretical priors.

As a sensitivity analysis, we changed our dependent variable by introducing various measures
of labor market performance. The result is presented in Table 33.7, and we can see that the
impact of macroeconomic shock remains positive and significant for YUR, TUR, NEET, and
YURM (youth unemployment rate male). Uncertainty impacts the labor force participation

Table 33.7 Various indicators of labor market and global crisis

Dependent variable	UR Total b/se	UR Youth b/se	LFPR b/se	NEET b/se	URYM b/se	URYF b/se
GDPG (−1)	−0.145***	−0.308***	−0.002	−0.078**	−0.342***	−0.226***
	0.019	0.038	0.016	0.03	0.04	0.041
Gross Capital formation	−0.199***	−0.420***	−0.017	−0.145***	−0.481***	−0.343***
	0.019	0.038	0.017	0.031	0.041	0.042
Inflation	−0.028*	−0.089***	−0.018	0.005	−0.092***	−0.095***
	0.015	0.03	0.013	0.024	0.032	0.033
Financial Crisis	0.324**	0.825***	−0.660***	0.466**	1.156***	0.48
	0.146	0.289	0.126	0.21	0.307	0.317
Part time Emp	0.007	0.027	0.129***	−0.059***	0.026	0.039
	0.014	0.028	0.012	0.022	0.03	0.031
Constant	13.034***	28.209***	66.372***	21.686***	29.001***	27.447***
	0.614	1.215	0.531	0.97	1.288	1.333
Observations	1356	1353	1353	1163	1353	1353
No of Countries	135	135	135	127	135	135
R–Square	0.166	0.194	0.104	0.046	0.217	0.113
Overall Sig of Model	48.331***	58.238***	28.260***	9.833***	67.042***	30.886***

Note: Standard errors are reported under the coefficient value. * Significant at 10%; ** Significant at 5%; and
*** Significant at 1%.

rates negatively and is significant as well. The financial crisis dummy impact on female youth unemployment is not statistically significant, and our structural break test result reflected it. Our results remain robust and consistent.

33.5 Conclusions

The first conclusion of our empirical analysis is that big economic shocks cause structural breaks in labor market indicators. This has been econometrically confirmed in the case of the big shock caused by the Global Financial Crisis: a structural break in 2008 concerns, in particular, the YUR and the labor force participation rate (although the break is less sure for the TUR and the female unemployment rate). It should be added that the economic shocks cause an increase in unemployment, persistence of high unemployment rates – especially among young people – is often caused by wrong economic policies, such as inadequate structural policies or erroneous macroeconomic policies (for example, the austerity approach followed in the EU in the initial years after the Great Recession and the sovereign debt crisis).

The second important conclusion refers to the key determinants of the YUR, in comparison to the TUR. A long list of explanatory variables has been considered. The key results are the following: (i) the lagged GDP growth negatively and significantly affects both YUR and TUR; (ii) big economic shocks, such as the Global Financial Crisis, affect more heavily the YUR, probably because they increase uncertainty; (iii) among all macroeconomic variables, the gross fixed capital formation is especially important in explaining the dynamics of YUR (but also TUR); and (iv) cyclical conditions are more important for young people, as confirmed by the size of the coefficients of YUR and also by the NEET specification (in fact also the NEET indicator depends negatively on the lagged GDP growth).

As for the impact of the pandemic shock, from the descriptive statistic, we have seen that young people have been, once more, the most affected. Although the econometric investigation concerns more than 100 countries in the world, there certainly are some differences among them, for example, while informal work prevails in developing countries, temporary and precarious jobs are frequently present in developed countries. However, increasing unemployment rates and decreasing participation rates, during the pandemic, seem smaller and generalized phenomena.

As for the policy implications, it is important to adopt not only macroeconomic policies that strengthen the economic recovery and improve the general labor market indicators but also specific structural policies oriented to the needs of young people, for example, by lessening the experience gap and supporting their reinstatement in the labor market, but also avoiding (whenever possible) their engagement in low-qualified, precarious or informal jobs.

Notes

1 As for the gender impact of financial crises, see Choudhry et al. (2012b).
2 In some sectors, a large part of seasonal contracts are precarious, notwithstanding that some legislation include the possibility to have "permanent vertical part-time".
3 In the case of our YUR, the labour force of that age group (15–24 years) is used as the denominator. Similarly, when we are using total unemployment rate as our dependent variable, it is calculated as total unemployed labour force divided by total labour force (in the age group 15–64).
4 *xtbreak test* implements the tests for structural breaks discussed in Bai and Perron (1998, 2003), Karavias et al. (2021), and Ditzen et al. (2021). *xtbreak test* can test the breakpoints. The F-Statistic

for the test with s breaks at known dates is: F(s,q) = dof_adj sigma' R' (R V R')$^{(-1)}$ R sigma *dof_adj* is a degree of freedom adjustment, *sigma* a matrix containing the coefficient estimates of *sigma*, R is the convential matrix of a Wald test, and *V* is a variance-covariance matrix. Under the null *F(s,q)* is F distributed.

5 xtbreak is stata module for testing and estimating structural breaks in time series and panel data models. The command is based on time series methods of Bai and Perron (1998) and the panel data methods of Ditzen et al. (2021).

References

Andrews, D., Deutscher, N., Hambur, J. and Hansell, D. (2020). The scarring effects of downturns on young workers. *CEPR Policy Portal*.

Bachmann, R. and Felder, R. (2021). Labour Market Transitions, Shocks and Institutions in Turbulent Times: A Cross-country Analysis. *Empirica*, 48, 329–352.

Bai, B.Y.J. and Perron, P. (1998). Estimating and Testing Linear Models with Multiple Structural Changes. *Econometrica*, 66, 1, 47–78.

Bai, J. and Perron, P. (2003). Computation and Analysis of Multiple Structural Change Models. *Journal of Applied Econometrics*, 18, 1, 1–22.

Blanchard, O. and Wolfers, J. (2000). The Role of Shocks and Institutions in the Rise of European Unemployment: The Aggregate Evidence. *Economic Journal*, 110, 1–33.

Boeri, T. and Bruecker, H. (2011). Short-Time Work Benefits Revisited: Some Lessons from the Great Recession. *Economic Policy*, 26, 68, 697–765.

Booth, A.L., Francesconi, M. and Frank, J. (2002). Temporary Jobs: Stepping Stones or Dead Ends? *Economic Journal*, 112, 480, F189–F213.

Brada, J., Marelli, E. and Signorelli, M. (2014). Young People and the Labor Market: Key Determinants and New Evidence. *Comparative Economic Studies*, 56, 4, 556–566.

Bruno, G., Choudhry, M.T., Marelli, E. and Signorelli, M. (2017). The Short- and Long-Run Impacts of Financial Crises on Youth Unemployment in OECD Countries. *Applied Economics*, 34.

Bruno, G., Marelli, E. and Signorelli, M. (2014). The Rise of NEET and Youth Unemployment in EU Regions After the Crisis. *Comparative Economic Studies*, 56, 592–615.

Caroleo, F.E., Demidova, O., Marelli, E. and Signorelli, M. (2018). (Eds.). *Young People and the Labour Market: A Comparative Perspective*. Routledge, Abindgon, UK.

Choudhry, M.T., Marelli, E. and Signorelli, M. (2012a). Youth Unemployment Rate and Impact of Financial Crises. *International Journal of Manpower*, 33, 1, 76–95.

Choudhry, M.T., Marelli, E. and Signorelli, M. (2012b). The Impact of Financial Crises on the Female Labour. *European Journal of Development Research*, 24, 3, 413–433.

Clark, K.B. and Summers, L.H. (1982). "The Dynamics of Youth Unemployment", NBER Working Paper Series No. 274.

Coibion, O., Gorodnichenko, Y. and Weber, M. (2020). "Labor Markets During the COVID-19 Crisis: A Preliminary View", NBER Working Paper No. 27017.

Ditzen, J., Karavias, Y. and Westerlund, J. (2021). Testing and Estimating Structural Breaks in Time Series and Panel Data in Stata.

ILO. (2012). *Global Employment Trends for Youth. Special Issue on the Impact of Global Economic Crisis on Youth*. Geneva, August.

ILO. (2021). An update on the youth labour market impact of the COVID-19 crisis. *Statistical Brief*, June.

Karavias, Y., Narayan, P.K. and Westerlund, J. (2022). Structural Breaks in Interactive Effects Panels and the Stock Market Reaction to COVID-19. *Journal of Business & Economic Statistics*, 1–14. DOI: 10.1080/07350015.2022.2053690

Layard, R., Nickell, S. and Jackman, R. (1991). *Unemployment: Macroeconomic Performance and the Labour Market*. Oxford University Press, Oxford.

Lazear, E.P. (1990). Job Security Provisions and Employment. *Quarterly Journal of Economics*, 105, 699–726.

Lindbeck, A. and Snower, D.J. (1988). Cooperation, Harassment, and Involuntary Unemployment: An Insider-outsider Approach. *American Economic Review*, 78, 167–188.

Liotti, G. (2021). Labour Market Regulation and Youth Unemployment in the EU-28. *Italian Economic Journal*, online June. https://doi.org/10.1007/s40797-021-00154-3

O'Higgins, N. (1997). The Challenge of Youth Unemployment. *International Social Security Review*, 50, 4, 63–93.

O'Higgins, N. (2001). *Youth Unemployment and Employment Policy: A Global Perspective*. ILO, Geneva.

OECD. (2012). *The Challenge of Promoting Youth Employment in the G20 Countries*. OECD Publishing, Paris.

Pastore, F. (2018). Why Is Youth Unemployment so High and Different across Countries? *IZA World of Labor*, 420. https://doi.org/10.15185/izawol.42

Rice, P. (1986). Juvenile Unemployment, Relative Wages and Social Security in Great Britain. *Economic Journal*, 96, 382, 352–374.

Appendix

Table A1 Summary statistics

Variable	Mean	Std. Dev.	Min	Max
YUR total	16.89	11.98	0.37	65.44
YUR male	15.86	11.19	0.19	64.82
YUR female	19.15	14.41	0.16	69.52
UR total	7.99	5.94	0.11	37.25
Gross Capital Formation	22.78	7.68	1.10	81.05
Part time	27.48	12.01	0.14	96.31
Urbanization	58.29	24.25	8.25	100.00
Not in Employment Education and Training	17.40	9.24	0.06	68.56
LFPR Youth	45.30	13.93	15.14	82.82
LFPR total	67.38	10.62	37.55	90.34

Table A2 Pairwise correlation matrix

	YURT	UR	GCF	Part	URB	NEET	YLFPR	LFPR
YURT	1.00							
UR	0.94	1.00						
GCF	−0.05	−0.07	1.00					
Part	−0.25	−0.24	−0.07	1.00				
URB	0.16	0.08	−0.02	0.21	1.00			
NEET	0.38	0.40	0.05	−0.34	−0.40	1.00		
Youth Labor Force Participation Rate	−0.48	−0.40	−0.03	0.54	−0.20	−0.30	1.00	
LFPR	−0.40	−0.38	0.01	0.42	0.02	−0.63	0.79	1.00

34

THE POLITICAL ECONOMY
OF ALTERNATIVE ECONOMIC
FUTURES[1]

Panagiotis E. Petrakis

NATIONAL AND KAPODISTRIAN UNIVERSITY OF ATHENS, ATHENS, GREECE

34.1 Introduction

This chapter describes the basic requirements for alternative future developments in the Western economy for the coming decade. It is beyond certain that the articulation of mere projections of the basic economic variables does not provide an adequate analytic framework for describing the future unless the essential parameters of the development of the political economy are pinpointed. Those parameters refer to sustainability, inclusivity, sustainable governance, cultural dynamics, and the dynamic aspects of economic growth.

The art of scenario planning originates from the postwar era and the work of K. Herman but it was developed and used by different organizations ranging from the White House to Big Corporations after the 1960s (Schwartz, 1991). Scenario construction was mainly developed prior to and during the Great Moderation period of the world economy (1980–2008) (Chermack et al., 2001; Bishop et al., 2007; Dator, 2009).

The Great Moderation period (1980–2008) was characterized by positive structural changes (Groshen & Potter, 2003), good fortune (Stock & Watson, 2002; Justiniano & Primiceri, 2006) and good policy (Bernanke, 2004), resulting in a continuous and steady rate of growth, low and steady inflation and rapid growth in developing countries. During this period, scenario planning was a mature and important tool for predicting output growth rate because the overall environment of stability and future predictability allowed and encouraged speculation for the prospects of the world economy.

At the present, scenario building of alternative futures is significantly more difficult mainly due to the conditions emerged during the three major crises (2010, 2020 and 2022). The conditions in reference are (a) high uncertainty, (b) major technological advancements due to the fourth industrial revolution, and (c) the fact that the world economy is at the lowest point of a conceivably long-term world economic cycle (50–60 years).[2]

The structure of the present chapter is as follows: Section 34.2 refers to scenarios as a visioning tool of the alternative futures. In Section 34.3, the consequences and certain features of the three recent crises (2010, 2020, 2022) are discussed provided that they operated as a trigger for future growth path. In Section 34.4, a comparison is undertaken of different forms of the capitalist system as well as the political phenomena that emerge in Western societies (populism,

DOI: 10.4324/9781003144366-40

neoliberalism). In Section 34.5, the motivating conditions (drivers) are examined of the future structuring of economic activity, particularly concerning to megatrends (social, financial, and political) and technological change. In Section 34.6, the future landscape is discussed influenced by the swinging factors that will affect the future. Finally, Section 34.7, is devoted to the conclusions.

34.2 Scenario planning as a visioning tool of alternative futures

Scenarios are effective foresight tools for predicting the future as they incorporate uncertainty. The creation of scenarios focuses on what could happen, allowing analysis of the problem and the determination of the consequences associated with new information and our own reactions to contingencies (Petrakis et al., 2016a).

Scenarios often define behaviors and events that could be considered expected. As a visioning tool, a scenario must state multiple versions of the future. The main reason for this is that even highly plausible scenarios that will eventually become fact still carry associated uncertainty and risk. The uncertainties surrounding the future are best met with numerous plausible scenarios, rather than traditional, quantitative predictions or a single scenario (Van der Merwe, 2008).

We usually distinguish different types of scenarios based on questions about the future such as *'What will happen?'* *'What could happen?'* and *'How can a specific target be reached?'* (Börjeson et al., 2006). In search for the answers to the above questions, we distinguish three types of scenarios: (a) forecast and 'what if' scenarios, (b) explorative scenarios, and (c) normative scenarios that should be chosen if the analysis requires scenarios that meet specific goals.

The goals for alternative scenario construction are to highlight preconditions for avoiding possible negative developments, to locate optimal patterns of action and policymaking, to understand the inherent possibilities of alternative futures, and to discover new possibilities (Rhisiart et al., 2015).

This chapter uses the explorative scenario approach as it incorporates a greater ability to include certain possibilities. Explorative scenario approach allows for an evolutionary approach of the trends that eventually will shape the future. Furthermore, these kinds of scenarios are based on scientific pluralism, contradicting forecasting positivism, including critical and cultural elements (Gidley, 2017).

Specifically, explorative scenarios have a significant duration and are created under the pressure of endogenous forces of the system, which are affected by exogenous factors. Thus, they require experts to be studied and to follow an evolutionary approach to current situations and trends. Because of their nature, internal cohesion is required for a scenario as well as utilization of the basic features of the corresponding organizational system.

Explorative scenario planning is chosen when the uncertainty of the future accommodates of several possible situations. This type of scenario building admits of several possible future pathways after locating the conditions under which these paths may become realities. Thus, explorative scenarios are of a long-term timescale which is shaped under endogenous and exogenous factors.

34.3 The triggering: Three crises at once: Theoretical and policy implications

The Great Moderation period was overturned by three large economic crises that can only be compared to the Great Depression of 1929: The Great Recession of 2008, the COVID-19 crisis of 2020, and the energy crisis of 2022. A major outcome of this coincidence was that the operation and regulation of policies and institutions were closely scrutinized in terms both of their moderating value and the upgrading of policies in the wake of a recessional disturbance.

These three back-to-back crises, almost simultaneous in the framework of human history, have profound, long-term implications for the ideological underpinnings of the political economy while also impacting the realm of politics and the production of new economic theory. Even though these three crises had major consequences to the economic activity, they were not followed by a production of new theory regarding their causes and consequences. For example, in the past, critical economic turning points – such as the Great Depression and Stagflation of the 1970s – led to new complete theoretical perceptions such as Keynesian economics and endogenous growth theory; this does not seem to happen today.

Nowadays, the prevailed economic theory views there are no more than ideological loans from the past. Although the invocation of past theories is a must, the question stands as to whether they alone are adequate. To this end, it is deemed necessary for a synthetic conception of economics and politics to include sustainability, inclusiveness, and the political and cultural aspects of growth and development (Petrakis et al., 2021).

The Great Recession bequeathed to the world economy very high and rising levels of uncertainty (Born et al., 2017), which, however, were accompanied by low levels of calculable risk (Altunbas et al., 2010; Gnabo & Moccero, 2015) due to the fiscal policies in place. Over time, different viewpoints emerged regarding what role[3] should the state have. This conversation is very relevant to the current circumstances when we are discussing the policies and measures followed to overcome the Great Recession and especially the COVID-19 crisis.

The role of the state was highlighted due to the unconventional policy tools (Gertler & Karadi, 2011) and the followed fiscal expansion. Thus, rethinking the role of the state in supporting a more political perception of public policies is a critical element for the following years (Mazzucato, 2021a). However, these policies may lead to crowding out private investment and draining creativity, at least in the short term, postponing creative destruction and leading to stagnation. Under these circumstances, envisioning a future for the capitalist economy may be more challenging but, also, a lot more interesting.

The subprime mortgage economic crisis of 2008 – that led to the following prolonged European debt crises – was linked to the financial system (Stiglitz, 2010; Petrakis et al., 2013). Thus, the Great Recession was an endogenous shock that was related to market risk as well as the availability of information. The Great Recession is compared to a '*storm over a warm sea*' (Danielsson et al., 2009).

The Financial Crisis arose and was subsequently reinforced by coordinated decisions within the market for the sale of assets [Minsky Moment (1985)]. Consequently, the financial system was at the center of the crisis, already numbered 151 systemic crises on its record (Laeven & Valencia, 2020). This fact directly implicates expectations and issues of asymmetries in information as well as broader issues related to externalities and incomplete contractualization. Asymmetries in the course of contractualization may lead to unjustifiable risk-taking in the economy and, hence, cause contractual externalities (Ozdenoren & Yuan, 2017).

Financial crises may conceivably change the perception of the role of banks as new utilities (Goodhart, 2011; Buch & Dages, 2018). This was the case for the Financial Crisis of 2008 and the subsequent crises in Europe as well. To stabilize the economy and consolidate the banking system, stricter boundaries were set in place (Buch & Dages, 2018). Better data collection and the macroprudential management of banks were at center stage (Arslan & Upper, 2018) with governments ensuring the smoothness of the process. The reforms concerned loan criteria, risk-taking, and deficits in payment balancing (Danielsson, 2015; Sironi, 2018). Furthermore, the governments focused on problems of asset quality (Alhassan et al., 2014) as it was the trigger for the crisis of nonperforming loans in the first place (Ratnovski, 2020; Kasinger et al., 2021).

Moreover, the economic crisis highlighted an important debate on macroeconomic policies and the conception of economic theory (Petrakis, 2020a). The root of this debate was the altered relationship between inflation and growth, which made apparent that policies that exclusively target inflation are not sufficient for the stabilization of the economic activity while, in parallel, expansionary policies lead to great state deficits (Akerlof et al., 2014). These processes resulted in a continuous rekindling of the crisis for Europe and considerable economic repercussions due to the structural aspects of the Eurozone (Petrakis et al., 2013).[4]

On the other hand, the COVID-19 crisis was exogenous, and its ramifications initially had to do with issues of life and safety but, as it persists in time, it raises critical matters of a macroeconomic nature (Baldwin & Weder di Mauro, 2020; Cadamuro & Papadia, 2020; Petrakis 2020a).[5] The technical sudden stop in the world economy disrupted supply chains (Bartholomeusz, 2021). Lockdown measures (König & Winkler, 2021) for public health protection held behind the economic activity, affecting the labor market's structure and prospects of recovery in the coming years (Khamis et al., 2021; Tyson and Lund, 2021).

The COVID-19 crisis emerged shortly after the aftermath of the Great Recession, and economies had not yet fully recovered. Many of the resulting concerns in the macroeconomic realm were associated with the instabilities caused by the Great Recession. Policy responses to COVID-19 were immediate to eliminate the risk of dispersion in the bank system, through the drop of values and nonperforming loans. Measures for facing the pandemic were based on immediate state intervention following an expansionary fiscal policy. Thus, nonconventional policies were adopted, which even took the form of 'helicopter' money (Bossone & Natarajan, 2020; Cukierman, 2020).

Meanwhile, it has been argued that among the negative consequences of the pandemic (and maybe to an extent due to them), there were positive shifts in the technologies that utilized the production processes (Kotz et al., 2021).

The Ukrainian war (2022) is a major rapid geopolitical conflict – which was in progress (2022) when this chapter was authored. Its consequences will be reflected on the mapping of the future (i.e. de-globalization, inflation, recession).

34.4 The political and cultural system

The analysis of the political and cultural system is required when we try to predict the future or the outcomes of a policy. The cultural background, salient institutions, and values influence the way an individual thinks and acts (Petrakis, 2020a). In this case, the political and cultural system is of great significance as it corresponds to the 'spine' of the societies. In other words, altered society priorities are translated to altered priorities for the individual actors.

Developments, particularly close to the end of the 20th century and the emergence of comparative political economy, have introduced the framework of the varieties of capitalism (VoC) that analyzes the role of the firms in comparative capitalism (Hall & Soskice, 2001). The forms of capitalism are related to coordination, to the extent that it determines the relationship of businesses with other actors. In liberal market economies (LMEs), businesses cooperate with other actors based on predetermined relationships. In coordinated mixed market economies (CMEs), businesses are in strategic interaction with other players.

Businesses process a range of transactions that depend both on their particular structural characteristics and on the structural characteristics and coordination issues of the market to which they belong. So, in practical terms, an exceedingly complex environment emerges, which receives feedback from imperfections in information that, in turn, create imperfections in contractualization and are affected overall by the prevailing conditions (Whitley, 1999; Hall & Soskice, 2001).

We assume that both businesses and individuals act rationally or, at least, under bounded rationality. Relaxing this assumption, we are led to expressions of human behavior that are not necessarily rational, with individuals motivated by incentives associated with their personality and identity. For example, individuals may not be egocentrically oriented but, rather, may exhibit altruistic tendencies and be interested in inter-generational utility, a fact that will shape social aims differently, which in turn affect political institutions.

There are extensive critiques related to the VoC theory (Bohle & Greskovits, 2009; Howell, 2003) arguing that the dichotomous typology of the VoC framework is overly narrow and parsimonious as it may not even capture the full range of political-economic systems (Feldmann, 2019). Regardless of its disadvantages, the VoC theoretical discussion is central to the analysis for the operation of businesses – as rational agents – since they constitute a fundamental and representative component of the economy.

Inglehart and Baker (2000) found that in almost all industrial societies, behavior has shifted from traditional values to secular and rational values. Hence, it appears that values within a society are the product of changes due to historical path-dependence (Inglehart, 2000). Once a society has been through the stage of industrial development, it leans on the new knowledge, emphasizing post-materialist values related to self-expression rather than survival values (Inglehart, 1999, 2000).

The orientation toward post-materialistic values shifts the cultural background (Norris & Inglehart, 2019). These shifts to the collective behavioral tendencies are of great significance when we try to predict the future because they operate as swinging factors for alternative scenarios. For example, societies that rely on self-expression are defined by different characteristics such as the main emphasis on the protection of the environment, tolerance of diversity (acceptance of marginal population groups), and trust in interpersonal relationships.

On the other hand, we could observe negative ramifications that also shift the cultural background. The theory of the cultural backlash might explain tendencies such as the rise of populist parties due to the insecurity hypothesis (Rodrik, 2018) and the economic have-not hypothesis (Norris & Inglehart, 2019) or with existential insecurity (Vail et al., 1999), which refers to life-threatening circumstances.

The observation of Norris and Inglehart is confirmed by the World Values Survey. For example, in the Western world between 2005 and 2014, we observe a hint of a tendency toward non-materialistic values, with a return to the existing state (economic have-not hypothesis) in recent years, from 2017 to 2020 (Petrakis et al., 2021). Although this period seems short for long-term cultural considerations (like societal values), it can provide us with useful hints for foresight because of the endogeneity and path dependence of the future to the past.

34.5 Forces for change: The megatrends

The trends that will shape the future relate to wider social changes, including urbanization (European Strategy and Policy Analysis System—ESPAS, 2019), demographic changes (Cravino et al., 2019; Kharas & Fengler, 2019) and population mobility (International Organization for Migration—IOM, 2019), the introduction of technologies by the fourth industrial revolution (Manyika et al., 2013; Petrakis, 2020b; Phillips, 2020), climate change (Aydinalp & Cresser, 2008; Intergovernmental Panel on Climate Change—IPCC, 2014;

Kahn et al., 2019), globalization (Cohen-Setton, 2015; Irwin, 2015), and de-globalization (Fitch Solutions, 2020) in the context of a multipolar world (O'Neill & Terzi, 2014; Tovar & Nor, 2018) where the geostrategic fence will constitute an important role.

In the economic field, we perceive six significant trends that will determine economic reality. The increase of the debt (public and private) (Blanchard, 2019; Mbaye et al., 2018) mainly due to the expansionary policies. The inherent financial instability of the credit system (Calomiris & Haber, 2014; Cerutti et al., 2018), as well as the increase of uncertainty (Petrakis 2020a; van Asselt & Rotmans, 2002; Walker et al., 2003). Other important aspects refer to the evolution of the rate of productivity, the deviations of which are manifesting features of divergence or convergence between countries (van Ark et al., 2015; Johnson & Papageorgiou, 2018; Organization for Economic Co-Operation and Development—OECD, 2019). Furthermore, Industrial 4.0 and the technological transformation (Wu, 2018) are rapidly changing the production structure requirements and the industrial organization model (Cravino et al., 2019).

In the political field, trends impact economic and social life as they cause significant and continuous changes to the social structure. These trends concern income and wealth inequality (Acemoglu et al., 2008; Hellebrandt & Mauro, 2015; Perotti, 1996), restricted social mobility (World Economic Forum—WEF, 2020), the strengthening of privacy (Argyris, 1998), the role of the middle class (Kharas, 2010), and the large changes in collective social behaviors due to the shift of the cultural values.

Even though all the above trends are characterized by different degrees of intensity, they take place simultaneously resulting in nonlinear coordinates and complex future alternative scenarios. In this case, the prevailed scenario will be determined by the swinging factors manifested by the megatrends.

34.6 The landscape of the alternative economic futures

Before discussing future alternative economic scenarios, capitalism's basic characteristics should be noted down. Capitalism is an established economical system around the world with only a very few exceptions. Its establishment across the board is founded on the remarkable change at the level of social prosperity and, also, in the belief that tomorrow will be different and probably better than yesterday (Reeves, 2009).

The decentralized economic production is based on the voluntary labor supply (individuals are not obligated to work, they choose to) and the main private possession of capital (with an antagonistic to the weak presence of the state). Significant drivers for capitalism's prevalence are the private and corporate incentives that motivate financial behavior. Those incentives are outcome-oriented and seek some kind of profit maximization (direct or through the financial markets), perhaps with an expanded sense of benefit and prosperity.

The contradictions that characterize capitalism are equally important. The system's dynamic raises the living standard of individuals causing, however, at the same time social inequalities. In general, contemporary capitalism displays lower social and intergenerational mobility (Davis & Mazumder, 2017).[6] Thus, over time, these contradictions result in critical periods of intense social and political dissent leading to political backlashes (Rodrik, 2018).

Capitalism is a central subject in the ongoing discussions about the role of the state and the markets for growth, income distribution and efficiency, and the relation between democracy and economic performance with the appearance of crony capitalism (Kang, 2002). Crony capitalism refers to a system where private corporate and powerful political agents create close internal relationships, to secure powerful benefits. Overall, the greater the participation of the state, the more are the opportunities for these kinds of divergence from the typical model of capitalism.

When the regulations, taxes, and grants are planned to encourage innovation, they promote competitiveness and ensure the spreading of knowledge. In this case, market capitalism promotes prosperity (Therborn, 1987). However, when the regulatory policy is widely practiced and the competition aims at supporting powerful special interests, market capitalism can also fail. The one fundamental difference to be born in the mind is that democratic processes continue to stand out as the most effective tools for repairing the problem (Dervis, 2019).

In its course, capitalism has evolved by adapting to the new circumstances of every era. Thus, in the aftermath of the first industrial revolution, mercantile capitalism changed into the free competitive capitalism of laissez-faire which, due in part to the Great Depression of 1929 and after the war, was reformed into a 'Keynesian form' of capitalism. In the seventies, because of the fatigue it manifested, it evolved into what we have recently come to know as globalized (financial) capitalism.

The big question is whether capitalism, independently of the form it will take in the near future, continues to be defined by those forces that prompt current and future generations to increase their prosperity as years pass. This question is imperative because, in the Western world and under the duration of the three crises, a greater skepticism is observable among millennials, along with lower expectations about the future, even though that in many respects (such as education) they are in a much better state.

34.6.1 *The exclusion of the growth scenario and the remaining unsustainable and transformed scenarios: The realms for policymaking*

An adequate description of the future of capitalism admits four generic scenarios that are shaped by the influence of the megatrends. Megatrends as mentioned before influence all aspects of social, economic, and political life because they take place globally. Some of them have been accelerated by the COVID-19 pandemic, while others are expected to be altered by the Ukrainian crisis. Regardless of the way they unravel historically, they exert effects independently of any general development due to inevitable path-dependency. The scenarios concerning the future are described below.

A *growth scenario* describes those elements that will ensure a significant rate of growth for the economy. An *unsustainable growth scenario* describes a state of affairs where the pursuit of steady growth is possible but is either undesirable or unsustainable, with high degrees of uncertainty (climate change and debt issues). A *transformation scenario* describes a state of drastic changes either through changes in technology with interdisciplinary character (biology, artificial intelligence, etc.) impacting important aspects of the society and economy, or through man-made decisions, or other forces and trends (economic policies). Lastly, a *collapse scenario* is characterized by catastrophic states of affairs, which radically change (for the worse) the economy and society.

The analysis of these four basic scenarios offers a good grasp of the possible alternatives for the future. In short, we could say that these four scenarios are grasping the most important possible interactions of the socioeconomic trends described earlier. The playing out of these scenarios concerns five complementary realms that comprise the Political Economy of Development and Growth. The realms are different and possible general states of the world where the megatrends exercise their influences, and they are constituted by a set of conditions produced by policies or path-dependent outcomes.

The five realms are the following: (a) The conditions of economic growth (secular stagnation, 2020 lower bound, divergence rather than convergence within and between economies);

(b) the conditions of sustainable development (climate change, health, and geostrategic risks); (c) sustainable governance (institutional revitalization and populism vs. liberalism); (d) the condition of inclusive growth (distribution and redistribution), and, finally, (e) human behaviors, pro-growth, and nudging policies (Petrakis & Kostis 2020).

In each realm, the megatrends conclude to different effects based on their different intensities and qualities. For example, debt (through fiscal expansion) supports growth but high levels of debt may also reach unsustainable levels, a situation reinforced as well by minor changes in productivity and higher uncertainty levels. Meanwhile, convergence will prove to be fundamental for inclusive growth as well as sustainable governance. Along with the megatrends, we need to always consider the possibility of the appearance of Black and White Swans (Taleb, 2010).

The emerging question is which of these scenarios seems most likely to prevail in the next one to two decades. For reasons of methodological principle, we will exclude the fourth scenario of collapse. Collapse may occur, surprisingly, based on exogenous effects (like the COVID-19 pandemic, a serious military conflict, or a collapse of the climate). However, these exogenous forces lay beyond the present scope of the present chapter. On the other hand, endogenous pressures (like political discontent) are most likely to move us toward the unsustainable scenario; thus, the possibilities of endogenous collapse are negligible, and the collapse scenarios should be analyzed separately based on multidisciplinary approaches (Intergovernmental Panel on Climate Change—IPCC, 2014). That being said, within the confines of this chapter, we will concentrate on the first three scenarios.

It is argued that the (first) growth scenario will not prevail as the first two years after the pandemic (2021–2022) are expected to be associated with low performances for capital in the context of a secular stagnation and high uncertainty (Hansen, 1939; Summers, 2014; Duprat, 2021), which will be especially felt in the Eurozone (Petrakis et al., 2013). Low returns in the developed Western economies (Blanchard, 2021; Petrakis 2020a) as well as the dominance of Big Tech companies (Petrakis, 2020b), which create barriers to entry by controlling inventive entrepreneurship, combined with the blow to economic activity from COVID-19, will bring about a reconsideration of investments in non-technological activities outside Western economies, in favor of large-scale infrastructure activities. Such activities, although they, too, have low returns, preserve the value of the investments made.

There is a range of factors that contribute to low, short-term returns:

1. Global demographics (fertility and longevity) will remain conducive to high saving rates (Zhang & Zhang, 2005).
2. The downward trend of labor productivity (Gordon, 2016) without accounting though for possible positive effects of the Industrial 4.0 (Petropoulos, 2019; Damioli et al., 2021).
3. The ongoing fiscal expansion (mainly due to the COVID-19 pandemic) will decrease safe asset shortage (Oxford Economics, 2021) although their levels will remain high, resulting in continued pressure on capital returns.
4. The increase in inequalities, exacerbated by the COVID-19 crisis, contributes to low returns (European Parliamentary Research Service—EPRS, 2020).
5. Stagnation may arise with the remobilization of inflation, manifesting to stagflation (Martin, 1985; Roubini, 2021).

Thus, an increase in low returns can derive only from generous fiscal raises. Not only fiscal expansion favors large public investments (big infrastructure in the United States, green and digital transformation in the EU) (Marmefelt, 2020) by strengthening the total factor of productivity – one of the basic sources of the economy's growth (Solow, 1957) – but also it leads to an increase of public debt and generates issues of intergenerational utility and fairness.

34.6.2 *The common characteristics of the unsustainable and transformed scenarios: What can we say about the prevailing scenario?*

Taking into consideration the above analysis, we thus conclude that we can speak about alternative futures of the economic system that are characterized by unsustainable growth and transformed growth (2nd and 3rd scenario). Both of these have six sets of circumstances in common.

34.6.2.1 *Low interest rates and returns, and secular conditions*

The following decade will be characterized by low rates and returns regardless of the case of the interests to rise higher than the zero-lower bound. In the short term, interest rates will be pressured (compared to the long term) by the slightly higher inflation as a result of the energy crisis.

Energy prices will remain in relatively high levels (World Energy Outlook, 2021) due to lag of green growth and development reforms that would assist the economy's adjustment to the green economy (especially in Europe). In addition, the geopolitical conflict in Eastern Europe leads to further increases in energy prices because it resulted in an energy crisis and rise in uncertainty. The emphasis on intellectual capital (Granstrand, 1999) and in the creative economy will not provide a satisfactoriness frame of growth dynamics (Thurow, 1996) as they do not lead to physical investments.

34.6.2.2 *Macroeconomic evolution*

Macroeconomic management involves the mass intervention of the Central Banks, toward shaping an economic framework backed by low capital returns. Thus, the allocation of resources is no longer susceptible to price fluctuations and hinges on quantitative allocative decisions contributing to low capital returns and, hence, to low differential returns for investors.

However, the allocation of resources according to quantitative criteria will amplify the problem of the unequal distribution of information between lenders and borrowers and between shareholders and management, mainly in the banking sector since it will decrease the value of allocative efficiency through the pricing system. Therefore, the financial system will be more susceptible to bailout and bail-in interventions. For that reason, it will intensify the processes of quantitative apportionment at the expense of price-efficient allocative methods. The weakening of the equality of information distribution increases due to the increase in complexity of the economy and of society. A part is played in this by social information systems that are growing but have not been constructed to provide information aiming at economic efficiency.

Economic vulnerabilities exposed by the three crises, geopolitical pressures, and lower economic activity (like falling productivity) will result in a shift in economic policy framework and a continuous state intervention.[7] The continuous use of monetary and fiscal policies, linked with the upgrading of the regulatory role of the public sector, came as a result of the three crises (2010, 2020, 2022). In general, the two economic crises weakened the market's efficiency by altering exogenously (compared to the natural functioning of the system) the investment and consumption incentives. Both consumers and investors had to deal with a 'Minsky moment' in 2010 and a 'technical recession' due to the COVID-19 pandemic.

The upshot of both crises is a disequilibrium path toward a new equilibrium during which the pricing mechanism is unable to stabilize the economy. Therefore, the competitive allocation of resources is disturbed. The regulation process is hard and of doubtful success. The intervention of the central banks to regulate the economy is of great significance as they increase the allocation of resources but with the maintenance of low-interest rates.

A quantitative asset allocation system (instead of a pricing mechanism) is more susceptible to interventions by centers of power,[8] which are the big beneficiaries (Beder, 2006). Thus, taking into account the increased roles of the state and central banks', there is a tendency toward a highly managed and hierarchically organized economy rather than a competitive one. In this type of economy, the mutually beneficial interactions between elites and power centers are easier to manifest, which is at the expense of free competition, efficiency, or/and fiscal deficits. That being, increases in the unequal distribution of income and wealth are more probable.

34.6.2.3 Rising geopolitical uncertainty

Rising Uncertainty due to mainly geopolitical reasons, attributable to the Thucydides trap (Allison, 2015), may result in economic distress. The Thucydides trap applies where a rising power (China) threatens to prevail over a preexisting one (USA). Uncertainty could also arise from the traditional conflict between the West and Russia that will further contribute to the de-globalization forces. Naturally, an additional contributing factor to uncertainly is regional conflicts (Israel, Iran) as well as the emergence of rising, regional powers. Thus, geopolitical conflicts with periods of high and low uncertainty will continue to exist due to the transition to a multipolar world (Easton, 2011).

34.6.2.4 The new role of the state

As mentioned before, the new role of the state is related to the presence of a regulating state that operates to diminish macroeconomic uncertainty. Thus, the role of the state was redefined after the two recent crises, especially during the COVID-19 pandemic. This fact is confirmed by the expansionary policies that were followed, including investments financed by common resources (Europe, Recovery and Resilience Facility) and the coordination of collective services provided (health, environment).

However, the state would not seem to act as an investor of the first resort but rather as a positive lender of the last resort in bailing-out society (Mazzucato, 2021b). In any case, this would result in a greater role for the state in the economy, although it opens the door wide to the creation of different variables of capitalism.

34.6.2.5 Climate change

Climate change is characterized by four discrete features (United States Environmental Protection Agency—USEPA, 2021): the rise in average temperature, the melting of ice in the Arctic, extreme weather phenomena, and the rise of the sea level. All of these features are of critical significance for the future. Immediate consequences will bear on the degradation of usable lands, water resources pollution, and air pollution, which are detrimental to prosperity as they lead to food shortages, migratory flows, and the destruction of infrastructures.

These developments lead to a decline of the conditions for human security related to human health, food, water, energy security, migratory flows, and the loss of natural resources. Thus, not only new policy opportunities emerge concerning energy, technological change, and environmental adaptation but also conflicts of interest emerge as well.

For example, considering CO_2 emissions, the greatest amounts originate in China, the United States, the EU, and India (International Energy Agency—IEA, 2020). Major conflict of interests will arise among the competing economic powers related to control of emissions and taking on the cost of the externalities, since no one will accept a reduction in production with an increase of costs. Essentially, then, the continuation of CO_2 emissions becomes the necessary condition for the redefinition of economic superiority and its transfer from the West to the East.

Thus, we are inevitably led to a state of increase in social costs that will, in turn, compress both the competitiveness of new products and public finances and, hence, also the future course of the economy and the position of economies relative to one another, a fact which is a central feature in both scenarios. A key point for regulating such conditions could be occurred by technological advancements and Industrial 4.0, but of course, it would require public and private investments in a long-term process.

34.6.2.6 Individual, social and political behaviors

Human behavior is not always consistent with the assumptions of economic theory. In the contrast, human behavior shows differences between different cultures. Behavioral analysis includes the placement of societies along the spectrum of behaviors and societal values (Hofstede, 1980; Schwartz, 1994). Where societies stand regarding societal values and collective behaviors could be enlightening for the application of efficient economic policies. Examples could be given by the debates concerning the support for privacy vs. collectivity, long-term orientation vs. indulgence, power distance, as well as identification concerning uncertainty and loss aversion (Kahneman & Tversky, 1979).

In short, we could sum up four changing features that affect future social and political behaviors. (a) Demographic changes include big waves of migrant movement and the consequent sociopolitical change, aging of the population, and the following turn of consumption patterns (Cravino et al., 2019) as well as burdens on public budgets, and urbanization (Davis, 2017). (b) Disruptive technological changes alter the production structure and require active education policies (Giouli et al. 2021; Petrakis, 2022). (c) Pollution mitigation and the sequential alteration of individual preferences and pro-environmental behavior. (d) Globalization and transition to a multipolar world (growing global trade and formation of socioeconomic blocks) and their effects on social behaviors.

It is clear that positive economic changes related to social and political behaviors – critical for the support of growth in the future – are followed by rising sociopolitical pressures. Thus, these circumstances are picturing precisely a dilemma between the unsustainable and the transformative path based on their common characteristics.

34.6.3 The swinging factors for the prevailing scenarios and the critical role of political and cultural behaviors

The big question in envisioning the future of the economic system relates to the factors that will come into play for either an unsustainable or a transformed future to prevail. An unsustainable future entails the continuous increase of (both public and private) debt (with an ongoing burdening of the next generations) to maintain effective demand at high levels. On the contrary, a transformed future will pay far greater attention to technological transformability, accelerating technological transformation through structural reforms. Such policies are close to supply-side economic policies (Fang, 2019).

Furthermore, the prevalence of one of the competing scenarios (unsustainable vs. transformed) depends on the mitigation of climate change and environmental degradation. The same applies to the remaining common features that have already been mentioned (secular stagnation, low returns, macroeconomic stability, geostrategic uncertainty, role of the state, and human behaviors and dynamics). The related policies will determine the extent of their influence and, thus, the degree to which they will enable the prevalence of one or the other scenario or, of course, a combination of the two.

How will conventional vs. unconventional monetary policies work and how much financial policies will be used to cover the gaps of potential outputs and effective demand are the keys to whether we are dealing with an unsustainable future with rising debts or a transformed future with structural reforms. Moreover, the observed post-COVID-19 reduction in uncertainty – which reached historically high levels in 2020 (Ahir et al., 2020) – will be succeeded by rising geopolitical uncertainty. The geopolitical tensions in Eastern Europe as well as the tensions between China and Taiwan dominate the overall scene resulting in de-globalization and pushing toward the unsustainable growth or collapse scenarios because of the rising existential and economic uncertainty. If the uncertainty trend reverses, the transformed scenario is more likely to prevail over the unsustainable scenario.

An issue common to both scenarios emerges from the analysis of cultural aspects of Western societies, which refers to the conflict generated between human behaviors, resulting from three different sets of choices: (a) post-materialistic values vs. economic have-not hypothesis; (b) insecurity and loss aversion hypothesis vs. certainty behaviors, and (c) individual utility maximization vs. group cooperation and common decision-making. The prevalence of one or the other of these behaviors will be decisive in which scenario will predominate.

Given that locating the alternative futures and determining alternative scenarios is a learning process (Rhisiart et al., 2015) insofar as new knowledge is produced, it is reasonable to expect that the way of thinking and the attitudes of the protagonists of the analysis, also change. This process, however, takes place based on a range of hypotheses concerning the organizational cultural background and especially those features that are adjusted for a mid-to-long-term horizon. A specific set of cultural aspects may exert positive or negative effects in the process of determining alternative future developments.

The appraisal of the role of the cultural background in the process of determining alternative scenarios for the future may involve two levels of analysis: individual and social. There are mutual influences between the levels, impacting decisively on knowledge and the different aspects of future developments. Thus, those national values (collective consciousness), organizational values, and, finally, individual values that prevail create the conditions for the development of socioeconomic systems. It has been observed, too, that the more internally oriented values are, the easier it is to accept a process of seeking alternative futures, and the reverse (Wiener & Boer 2019).

In economic terms, the inflated asymmetries in information may lead selfish policymakers to generate inefficiencies that are generally more harmful than market and government inefficiencies (Ciccarone, 2020). By weakening the political system's ability to monitor the economy, important questions are raised regarding the future of sustainable economic development.

In the political realm, the basic opposition is projected of liberal democracy vs. populism, which has nowadays replaced the traditional opposition of left vs. right. Liberal institutions can more effectively moderate the effects of economic crises by comparison to autarchic regimes that safeguard the interests of the elites and are more resistant to instability (Acemoglu et al., 2003; Cavallo & Cavallo, 2010). Of course, a certain version of populism may have beneficial effects in the sense that it favors the adoption of more people-friendly policies, rather than structural reforms that tend to change the people's present way of living. So, the degree of political intervention in economic activity and the planning of political institutions remains one of the most critical social issues (Aghion et al., 2004).

The above considerations and how the great political dilemmas will be resolved will have a decisive bearing on the role of the state as well. Thus, the new role of the state will be the outcome of the above major political considerations while also, being, in itself, a factor shaping the future. A more powerful (though not necessarily bigger) state will be more aligned with a transformed future, while a weak state is aligned with an unsustainable future. The political field plays an important part; it is hence the catalyst affecting alternative futures and the prevalence of either the unsustainable or the transformed scenario.

34.6.4 Capitalism alternatives

The above megatrends do not only shape future economic alternatives but pose fundamental questions related to the future of capitalism and the aims which it serves. Thus, for instance, if climate change is accentuated, it will lead to enormous externality costs that will cause serious turbulence to the pricing system and, ultimately, to the mechanics of capitalism. The growth in economic inequalities may work similarly, insofar as it can impact the vital human economic incentives for labor supply. Events such as the COVID-19 pandemic operate in the same way followed by the possibility of violent imbalances in the global recovery process.

Finally, the geopolitical tensions (USA vs. China, West vs. Russia) might affect the global organization of the economic system by distressing the trade affairs and creating a de-globalization process. Hence, such circumstances will affect the rate of growth pushing toward a weak stagnation phase of the economy.

One of the immediate effects of the above great changes will be the retreat at a political level of the liberal forces that underpinned for decades the thriving of the capitalist system and their replacement by a synergistic set of official commitments, economic models, emblematic policies, and new vernacular economics by which people understand and seek to improve their livelihood and future (Bowles & Carlin, 2021). Thus, a new paradigm of political economy could emerge, expressing a limited but, nevertheless, not fundamentally altered capitalism.

34.7 Conclusions and policy implications: The search for normative scenarios

This chapter used scenario building which recognizes four possible alternative futures: a growth scenario, an unsustainable one, a transformation scenario, and a collapse scenario. The future will be shaped under the features of the unsustainable and transformation scenarios.

The future reality will be the outcome of the megatrends that have a social, economic, and political character. The social trends determining the future include urbanization, demographic changes and the movement of populations, the introduction of technologies, climate change, and de-globalization in a multipolar world. In the field of economics, we are looking at the development of debt (public and private), the financial instability, the productivity trends, the global economies' convergence or divergence, the growth of uncertainty especially due to geopolitical tensions, and, finally, changes in the industrial model due to the fourth industrial revolution. In the political field, large-scale developments are noted regarding the unequal distribution of wealth and income, along with social mobility, the strengthening of privacy, and the role of the middle class in the Western world.

There are also five policy realms that will generate influences for various piecemeal policies that will determine the future. These realms concern (a) the conditions of economic growth, (b) the climate change and general health and geopolitical risks, (c) the revitalization of institutions and politics (populism vs. liberalism), (d) the inclusive requirements (distribution and redistribution), and, finally, (e) pro-growth human behaviors.

All scenarios will have six common characteristics: (a) low rates and reforms, (b) macroeconomic stability, (c) rising geostrategic uncertainty, (d) the new role of the state, (e) climate change, and (f) altered individual, social, and political behaviors.

Analysis has singled out the so-called swinging factors that play a great role in shaping the future, particularly in terms of the prevalence of an unsustainable or a transformed scenario. All the above trends are characterized by different degrees of intensity, and they take place simultaneously resulting in nonlinear coordinates and complex future alternative scenarios. Certain of these active forces conquer a leading role but over time they give precedence to other forces. Hence, when we make future projections we should consider and specify forces such as the aforementioned. Such forces exert the most serious influence on the development of particular issues and are important in order to accurately pinpoint the sources of future developments.

Closing this chapter, it is cardinal to mention that scenarios describe possibilities rather than certainties, meaning that they require a constant re-evaluation of their content, especially when the circumstances change. A great example for this statement regards the outbreak of the Ukrainian crisis which will reshape the future in many ways that have not discussed in the present chapter due to the recency of the event. However, as the consequences of the conflict will become more apparent and severe, scenario planning will require adjustments to reflect a realistic version of the future and how these consequences will impact economic and social activity, especially in terms of the rising uncertainty.

Nevertheless, scenario processes are, above all, learning processes (Rhisiart et al., 2015). One of the most important effects of formulating alternative future scenarios is the increase in the levels of knowledge and awareness about the future. Thus, accumulated knowledge facilitates the transition from explorative scenarios to normative scenarios which have specific scope and targets allowing a more organized and efficient mobilization of society's resources by setting specific goals and policymaking targets.

Notes

1 The present chapter draws from the paper *"On the Alternative Futures of Capitalism"* that was presented, in cooperation with Anna-Maria Kanzola, at the 33rd Annual Meeting of the Society for the Advancement of socio-Economics (July 2021). The final version benefitted from the comments of an anonymous referee.
2 Different types of crises lead to the creation of complex patterns within which cyclical components usually interweave in intricate ways (Grinin et al., 2016). During this process, long-term cycles appear mainly concerning the technological, political, and socio-economical advances of each era. The analysis of long-term economic cycles allows us to predict and understand the possible outcomes of the world economy.

Kondratiev's long-wave analysis is concentrated at the end of the previous cycle in line with the advancements of information and communications technology (ICT) (Scherrer, 2021) that could lead to technological maturity, but also disruptive features that have not been manifested. Thus, a new wave is expected to be initiated by the cyber-physical systems (Xu et al., 2018; Scherrer, 2021). Regarding the current state of the world economy, possible explanations involve the fact that the consequences of the Great Recession expanded like a 'snowball effect' followed by the COVID-19 crisis, which resembles entangled webs (Baldwin & Mauro 2020) in the presence of course of the Industry 4.0.

3 Historically, the role of the state is defined depending on the salient circumstances of each period. Classical analysis (Smith, 1776; Ricardo, 1817; Marx, 1867) focused on the idea that state intervention should be limited to functional responsibilities such as tax collection, the legislative framework, and the financing of high costs such as protection, and education. After the Great Depression and the rise of Keynesian economics, the state was perceived as the 'spender of the last resort' (Mazzucato, 2015). During the Great Moderation period, policies focused on the dilemma 'rules vs. discretion' (Kydland & Prescott, 1977). This debate was resurfaced with the Great Depression and the COVID-19 crisis. In general, however, the main goal of the state is to promote growth and innovation (Mazzucato, 2015).

4 Although the main causes of financial crises are in the realm of finances, a part was played by the breaching of the rule of law and property rights, investors' incentives, and the pace of technological change (Reinhart & Reinhart, 2015). Significant repercussions may also originate in microeconomic, idiosyncratic shocks due to important asymmetries between sectors of economic activity (Acemoglu et al., 2012).

5 The economic impact of COVID-19 was perceptible by the time this manuscript was authored.

6 One way to consider inequality in the capitalist system is, for example, the economic crises consequences to the labor market. A shock in the system affects labor demand trends and leads to shifts in the relative importance of occupations in the economy. In the same way, technological advancements are followed by a productivity effect and a displacement effect (Acemoglu & Restrepo, 2018). This is translated to skill mismatch and generated inequality that could mainly be addressed by public expenditure.

7 See current discussion of Green New Deal, Green Recovery, or the earlier discussion regarding quantitative easing.

8 Such centers of power could be oligopoly-style economic organizations such as mass media, big-corporations with political influence or affiliations with think tanks, as well as economic and political alliances between power centers.

References

Acemoglu, D., Johnson, S., Robinson, J. and Thaicharoen, Y. (2003). Institutional Causes, Macroeconomic Symptoms: Volatility, Crises and Growth, *Journal of Monetary Economics*, 50(1): 49–123.

Acemoglu, D. and Restrepo, P. (2018). Artificial Intelligence, Automation and Work. National Bureau of Economic Research. Working Paper No. 24196.

Acemoglu, D., Carvalho, V., Ozdaglar, A. and Tahbaz-Salehi, A. (2012). The Network Origins of Aggregate Fluctuations, *Econometrica*, 80(5): 1977–2016. http://www.jstor.org/stable/23271439

Acemoglu, D., Johnson, S., Robinson, S.J. and Yared, P. (2008). Income and Democracy, *American Economic Review*, 98(3): 808–842.

Aghion, P., Alesina, A. and Trebbi, F. (2004). Endogenous Political Institutions, *Quarterly Journal of Economics*, 119(2): 565–611. http://www.jstor.org/stable/25098694

Ahir, H., Bloom, N. and Furceri, D. (2020). Global Uncertainty Related to Coronavirus at Record High. IMF Blog. https://blogs.imf.org/2020/04/04/global-uncertainty-related-to-coronavirus-at-record-high/

Akerlof, G., Blanchard, O., Romer, D. and Stiglitz, J. (Eds.). (2014). What Have We Learned? Macroeconomic Policy after the Crisis. Cambridge, MA; London, England: MIT Press. http://www.jstor.org/stable/j.ctt9qf899

Alhassan, A.L., Kyereboah-Coleman, A. and Andoh, C. (2014). Asset Quality in a Crisis Period: An Empirical Examination of Ghanaian Banks, *Review of Development Finance*, 4(1): 50–62. https://doi.org/10.1016/j.rdf.2014.03.001

Allison, G. (2015). The Thucydides Trap. Are the U.S. and China Headed for War? *The Atlantic*. Accessed in website on December 20, 2021.

Altunbas, Y., Gambacorta, L. and Marques-Ibanez, D. (2010). Does Monetary Policy Affect Bank Risk-Taking? *ECB Working Paper Series, No. 1166*.

Argyris, C. (1998). Empowerment: The Emperor's New Clothes, *Harvard Business Review*, 76(3): 98–105.

Arslan, Y. and Upper, C. (2018). Macroprudential Frameworks: Implementation and Effectiveness, BIS Papers, No. 94.

Aydinalp, C. and Cresser, M. (2008). The Effects of Global Climate Change on Agriculture, *American-Eurasian Journal of Agricultural and Environmental Sciences*, 3(5): 672–676.

Baldwin, R. and Weder di Mauro, B. (2020). Mitigating the COVID Economic Crisis: Act Fast and Do Whatever It Takes, a VoxEU.org eBook, CEPR Press.

Bank of International Settlements-BIS. (2018). Structural Changes in Banking after Crisis. CGFS Papers, 60, ISBN 978-92-9259-131-1. https://www.bis.org/publ/cgfs60.pdf

Bartholomeusz, S. (2021, December 15). Supply chain blues: AdBlue crisis a symptom of larger problems in the world economy. The Sydney Morning Herald. https://www.smh.com.au/business/the-economy/supply-chain-blues-adblue-crisis-a-symptom-of-larger-problems-in-the-world-economy-20211215-p59ho6.html

Beder, S. (2006). Suiting Themselves: How Corporations Drive the Global Agenda. Routledge.

Bernanke, S.N. (2004). Gradualism. Speech 540, Board of Governors of the Federal Reserve System (U.S.). https://www.federalreserve.gov/boarddocs/speeches/2004/200405202/default.htm

Bishop, P., Hines, A. and Collins, T. (2007). The Current State of Scenario Development: An Overview of Techniques, *Foresight*, *9*(1): 5–25. http://dx.doi.org/10.1108/14636680710727516

Blanchard, O. (2019). Public Debt and Low Interest Rates, *American Economic Review*, *109*(4): 1197–1229.

Blanchard, O. (2021). Why low interest rates force us to revisit the scope and role of fiscal policy: 45 takeaways. Peterson Institute for International Economics. Realtime economics issues watch. https://www.piie.com/blogs/realtime-economic-issues-watch/why-low-interest-rates-force-us-revisit-scope-and-role-fiscal

Bohle, D. and Greskovits, B. (2009). Varieties of Capitalism and Capitalism 'tout court', *European Journal of Sociology*, *50*(3): 355–86. https://doi.org/10.1017/S0003975609990178

Börjeson, L., Höjer, M., Dreborg, K.H., Ekvall, T. and Finnveden, G. (2006). Scenario Types and Techniques: Towards a User's Guide, *Futures*, *38*(7): 723–739. https://doi.org/10.1016/j.futures.2005.12.002

Born, B., Breuer, S. and Elstner, S. (2017). Uncertainty and the Great Recession, *Oxford Bulletin of Economics and Statistics*, *80*(5): 951–971.

Bossone, B. and Natarajan, H. (2020). Getting funds to those in need and enabling access to money during COVID-19, part 3: Central bank digital currencies and other instruments, VoxEu.org, 15 July.

Bowles, S. and Carlin, W. (2021). Rethinking Economics – IMF F&D. https://www.imf.org/external/pubs/ft/fandd/2021/03/rethinking-economics-by-samuel-bowles-and-wendy-carlin.htm

Buch, C. and Dages, B.G. (2018). Structural Changes in Banking after the Crisis: The Nature of Regulatory Capital Requirements. Committee on the Global Financial System, Bank for International Statements. https://www.bis.org/publ/cgfs60.pdf

Cadamuro, L. and Papadia, F. (2020). Three macroeconomic issues and COVID-19. https://www.bruegel.org/2020/03/three-macroeconomic-issues-and-COVID-19/

Calomiris, C.W. and Haber, S.H. (2014). Fragile by Design: The Political Origins of Banking Crises and Scarce Credit. Princeton, NJ: Princeton University Press.

Cavallo, A.F. and Cavallo, E.A. (2010). Are Crises Good for Long-Term Growth? The Role of Political Institutions, *Journal of Macroeconomics*, *32*(3): 838–857.

Cerutti, E., Claessens, S. and Laeven, L. (2018). The increasing faith in macroprudential policies. Vox CEPR Policy Portal. https://voxeu.org/article/increasing-faith-macroprudential-policies

Chermack, T., Lynham, S.A. and Ruona, E.A. (2001). A Review of Scenario Planning Literature, *Futures Research Quarterly*, *17*(2): 7–31. https://scienceimpact.mit.edu/sites/default/files/documents/Scenario%20PlanningA%20Review%20of%20the%20Literature.PDF

Ciccarone, G. (2020). Market Versus Government Failures Under Risk and Under Uncertainty, *Journal of Public Finance and Public Choice*, *35*(1). https://doi.org/10.1332/251569120X15802174243174

Cohen-Setton, J. (2015). Why is global trade slowing down? World Economic Forum. https://www.weforum.org/agenda/2015/09/why-is-global-trade-slowing-down/

Cravino, J., Levchenko, A.A. and Rojas, M. (2019). Population Aging and Structural Transformation. *NBER Working Paper No. 26327*.

Cukierman, A. (2020). Quantitative easing and helicopter money: Not so distant cousins, VoxEu.org, 27 July.

Damioli, G., Van Roy, V. and Vertesy, D. (2021). The Impact of Artificial Intelligence on Labor Productivity, *Eurasian Business Review*, *11*, 1–25. https://doi.org/10.1007/s40821-020-00172-8

Danielsson, J. (Ed.). (2015). Post-Crisis Banking Regulation. Evolution of economic thinking as it happened on Vox, a VoxEU.org Book, CEPR Press.

Danielsson, J., Shin, H.S. and Zigrand, J.P. (2009). Risk Appetite and Endogenous Risk. FMG Discussion Papers dp647, Financial Markets Group. https://ideas.repec.org/p/fmg/fmgdps/dp647.html

Dator, J. (2009). Alternative Futures at the Manoa School, *Journal of Future Studies, 14*(2): 1–18. https://jfsdigital.org/wp-content/uploads/2014/01/142-A01.pdf

Davis, J. and Mazumder, B. (2017). The Decline in Intergenerational Mobility After 1980. In Working Paper Series (WP-2017-5; Working Paper Series). Federal Reserve Bank of Chicago. https://ideas.repec.org/p/fip/fedhwp/wp-2017-05.html

Davis, M. (2017). Planet of Slums (Reprint edition). Verso.

Dervis, K. (2019). Cronies Everywhere. Project Syndicate. https://www.project-syndicate.org/onpoint/cronies-everywhere-by-kemal-dervis-2019-12?barrier=accesspaylog

Duprat, M.H. (2021). Risk and Opportunities. COVID-19 and Secular Stagnation. Societe Generale Economics & Sector Studies 14. https://www.societegenerale.com/sites/default/files/documents/2021-01/COVID-19-and-Secular-Stagnation-EN.pdf

European Parliamentary Research Service—EPRS. (2020). Global Mega-Trends: Scanning Post-Coronavirus Horizon. Beyond the Coronavirus Pandemic: Global Foresight Perspectives. https://www.europarl.europa.eu/RegData/etudes/BRIE/2020/659344/EPRS_BRI(2020)659344_EN.pdf

European Strategy and Policy Analysis System—ESPAS. (2019). (Rep) Global Trends to 2030. Challenges and Choices for Europe. An Inter-Institutional EU Project. https://www.iss.europa.eu/sites/default/files/EUISSFiles/ESPAS_Report.pdf

Fang, M. (2019). Supply-Side Structural Reform from the Perspective of Political Economy, *China Political Economy, 2*(2).

Feldmann, M. (2019). Global Varieties of Capitalism, *World Politics, 71*(1): 162–196. https://doi.org/10.1017/S0043887118000230

Fitch Solutions. (2020). Towards 2050: Megatrends in Industry, Politics, and the Global Economy 2020 Edition. https://store.fitchsolutions.com/towards-2050-megatrends-in-industry-politics-and-the-global-economy-2020-edition

Gertler, M. and Karadi, P. (2011). A Model of Unconventional Monetary Policy, *Journal of Monetary Economics, 58*(1): 17–34. https://doi.org/10.1016/j.jmoneco.2010.10.004

Gidley, J.M. (2017). The Future: A Very Short Introduction. Oxford, UK: Oxford University Press.

Giouli, E., Pisinas, Y., Kanzola, A.-M. and Petrakis, P.E. (2021). Human Capital and Production Structure: Evidence from Greece, *European Journal of Economics and Business Studies, 7*(1): 42–56.

Gnabo, J.Y. and Moccero, D.N. (2015). The risk management approach to monetary policy, non-linearity and aggressiveness: the case of the US Fed, ECB Working Paper Series, No. 1792.

Goodhart, C. (2011). If banks should act as utilities, why not treat them as such? VoxEu.org. https://voxeu.org/article/if-banks-should-act-utilities-why-not-treat-them-such

Gordon, R.J. (2016). The Rise and Fall of American Growth: The U.S. Standard of Living Since the Civil War. Princeton, NJ: Princeton University Press.

Granstrand, O. (1999). Intellectual Capitalism – An Overview, *Nordic Journal of Political Economy, 25*: 115–127.

Grinin, L.E., Korotayev, A. and Tausch, A. (2016). Kondratieff Waves and Technological Revolutions. 10.1007/978-3-319-41262-7_5

Groshen, E.L. and Potter, S. (2003). Has Structural Change Contributed to a Jobless Recovery? *Current Issues in Economic and Finance, FED, 9*(8). https://www.newyorkfed.org/medialibrary/media/research/current_issues/ci9-8.pdf

Hall, P. and Soskice, D. (2001). Varieties of Capitalism: The Institutional Foundations of Comparative Advantage. Oxford: Oxford University Press.

Hansen, A. (1939). Economic Progress and Declining Population Growth, *American Economic Review, 29*(1): 1–15.

Hellebrandt, T. and Mauro, P. (2015). The Future of Worldwide Income Distribution. *Peterson Institute for International Economics,* Working Paper No. 15-7.

Hofstede, G. (1980). Culture's Consequences: International Differences in Work-related Values. Beverly Hills, CA: Sage Publications.

Howell, C. (2003). Review: Varieties of Capitalism: And Then There Was One? *Comparative Politics, 36*(1): 103–124. https://doi.org/10.2307/4150162

Inglehart, R. (1999). Modernization and Postmodernization: Cultural, Economic, and Political Change in 43 Societies, 1999. Princeton, NJ: Princeton University Press.

Inglehart, R. (2000). Globalization and Postmodern Values, *Washington Quarterly*, *23*(1): 215–228.

Inglehart, R. and Baker, W.E. (2000). Modernization, Culture Change, and the Persistence of Traditional Values, *American Sociological Review*, *65*: 19–51.

Intergovernmental Panel on Climate Change—IPCC. (2014). Climate Change 2014: Synthesis Report. Contribution of Working Groups I, II and III to the Fifth Assessment Report of the Intergovernmental Panel on Climate Change. IPCC, Geneva, Switzerland.

International Energy Agency—IEA. (2020). Global Energy Review: CO_2 Emissions in 2020.

International Organization for Migration—IOM. (2019). World Migration Report 2020. United Nations. https://www.iom.int/wmr/

Irwin, D. (2015). Free Trade Under Fire, Fourth Edition. Princeton, NJ; Woodstock, Oxfordshire: Princeton University Press. https://doi.org/10.2307/j.ctt9qh0ch

Johnson, P. and Papageorgiou, C. (2018). What Remains of Cross-Country Convergence? *Journal of Economic Literature*, *58*(1): 129–175.

Justiniano, A. and Primiceri, G. (2006). The Time-Varying Volatility of Macroeconomic Fluctuations, *NBER Working Paper No. 12022*.

Kahn, M.E., Mohaddes, K., Ng, R.N.C., Pesaran, M.H., Raissi, M. and Yang, J.-C. (2019). Long-Term Macroeconomic Effects of Climate Change: A Cross-Country Analysis. IMF Working Papers 19/215.

Kahneman, D. and Tversky, A. (1979). Prospect Theory: An Analysis of Decision under Risk, *Econometrica*, *47*(2): 263–291. https://doi.org/10.2307/1914185

Kang, D.C. (2002). Crony Capitalism: Corruption and Development in South Korea and the Philippines. Cambridge: Cambridge University Press. ISBN 978-0-521-00408-4.

Kasinger, J., Krahnen, J.P., Ongena, S., Pelizzon, L., Schmeling, M. and Wahrenburg, M. (2021). Preparing for a wave of non-performing loans: Empirical insights and important lessons, VoxEU, CEPR.

Khamis, M., Prinz, D., Newhouse, D., Palacios-Lopez, A., Pape, U. and Weber, M. (2021). The Early Labor Market Impacts of COVID-19 in Developing Countries: Evidence from High-Frequency Phone Surveys. Jobs Working Paper; No. 58. World Bank, Washington, DC. https://openknowledge.worldbank.org/handle/10986/35044 License: CC BY 3.0 IGO.

Kharas, H. (2010). The Emerging Middle Class in Developing Countries. OECD Development Centre Working Papers No. 285.

Kharas, H. and Fengler, F. (2019). Double tipping points in 2019: When the world became mostly rich and largely old. Brookings. https://www.brookings.edu/blog/future-development/2019/10/09/double-tipping-points-in-2019-when-the-world-became-mostly-rich-and-largely-old/

König, M. and Winkler, A. (2021). COVID-19: Lockdowns, Fatality Rates and GDP Growth, *Intereconomics*, *56*(1): 32–39. https://doi.org/10.1007/s10272-021-0948-y

Kotz, H., Mischke, J. and Smit, S. (2021). Pathways for productivity and growth after the COVID-19 crisis. https://voxeu.org/article/pathways-productivity-and-growth-after-COVID-19-crisis

Kydland, F. and Prescott, E. (1977). Rules Rather Than Discretion: The Inconsistency of Optimal Plans, *Journal of Political Economy*, *85*(3): 473–491. http://www.jstor.org/stable/1830193

Laeven, L. and Valencia, F. (2020). Systematic Banking Crises Database: A Timely Updated in COVID-19 Times. CEPR Discussion Papers 14569.

Manyika, J., Chui, M., Bughin, J., Dobbs, R., Bisson, P. and Marrs, M. (2013). Disruptive Technologies: Advances That Will Transform Life, Business, and the Global Economy. McKinsey Global Institute.

Marmefelt, T. (2020). COVID-19 and Economic Policy Toward the New Normal: A Monetary-Fiscal Nexus After the Crisis? Monetary Dialogue Papers, European Parliament. https://www.europarl.europa.eu/RegData/etudes/IDAN/2020/658193/IPOL_IDA(2020)658193_EN.pdf

Martin, L.W. (1985). 'Stagflation': A Condition Created by Accelerated Demand-Pull Inflation, *American Journal of Economics and Sociology*, *44*(4): 497–501.

Marx, K. (1867). Capital. A Critique of Political Economy.

Mazzucato, M. (2015). The Entrepreneurial State. Debunking Public vs. Private Sector Myths. *Public Affairs, New York*.

Mazzucato, M. (2021a). Mission Economy: A Moonshot Guide to Changing Capitalism. London: Harper Business.

Mazzucato, M. (2021b). The Mission-Oriented Government. Published by the Berggruen Institute. https://www.noemamag.com/the-mission-oriented-government/

Mbaye, S., Moreno-Badia, M. and Chae, K. (2018). Global Debt Database: Methodology and Sources. IMF Working Paper No. 18/111.

Minsky, H.P. (1985). The Financial Instability Hypothesis: A Restatement. In P. Arestis and T. Skouras (Eds.), Post Keynesian Economic Theory: A Challenge to Neoclassical Economics. Brighton: Wheatsheaf.

Norris, P. and Inglehart, R. (2019). Cultural Backlash: Trump, Brexit, and Authoritarian Populism. Cambridge: Cambridge University Press. https://doi.org/10.1017/9781108595841

O'Neill, J. and Terzi, A. (2014). Changing trade patterns, unchanging European and global governance. Bruegel Working Papers No. 817.

Organization for Economic Co-Operation and Development—OECD. (2019). Compendium of Productivity Indicators 2019. Paris: OECD Publishing. https://doi.org/10.1787/b2774f97-en

Ozdenoren, E. and Yuan, K. (2017). Contractual Externalities and Systematic Risk, *Review of Economic Studies, 84*(4(301)): 1789–1817. https://www.jstor.org/stable/26543872

Perotti, R. (1996). Growth, Income Distribution, and Democracy: What the Data Say, *Journal of Economic Growth, 1*(2): 149–187.

Petrakis, P.E. (2020a). Theoretical Approaches to Economic Growth and Development. An Interdisciplinary Perspective. Palgrave Macmillan. https://doi.org/10.1007/978-3-030-50068-9

Petrakis, P.E. (2020b). The New Political Economy of Greece up to 2030. London, UK: Palgrave Macmillan.

Petrakis, P.E. (2022). Human Capital and Production Structure: Knowledge, Abilities, Skills, Working Activities. Cham, Switzerland: Palgrave Macmillan.

Petrakis, P.E. and Kostis, P.C. (2020b). Policies for a Stronger Greek Economy: Actions for the Next Decade. Cham, Switzerland: Palgrave Macmillan.

Petrakis, P.E., Kostis, P.C. and Valsamis, D.G. (2013). European Economics and Politics in the Midst of the Crisis: From the Outbreak of the Crisis to the Fragmented European Federation. New York and Heidelberg: Springer, ISBN 978-3-642-41343-8, p. 274.

Petrakis, P.E., Kostis, P.C. and Kafka, K.I. (2016a). Secular Stagnation, Faltering Innovation, and High Uncertainty: New-era Entrepreneurship Appraisal Using Knowledge-based Thinking, *Journal of Business Research, 69*(5): 1909–1913. https://doi.org/10.1016/j.jbusres.2015.10.078

Petrakis, P.E., Kafka, K.I., Kostis, P.C. and Valsamis, D.G. (2021). Greek Culture after the Financial Crisis and COVID-19 Crisis. An Economic Analysis. Palgrave Macmillan, ISSN 2662-7248.

Petropoulos, G. (2019). AI and the Productivity Paradox, Bruegel. https://www.bruegel.org/2019/12/ai-and-the-productivity-paradox/

Phillips, T. (2020). A roadmap for digital-led economic development. Vox CEPR Policy Portal. https://voxeu.org/article/roadmap-digital-led-economic-development

Ratnovski, L. (2020). COVID-19 and Non-performing Loans: Lessons from Past Crises, *Research Bulletin, European Central Bank, 71.* https://www.ecb.europa.eu/pub/economic-research/resbull/2020/html/ecb.rb200527~3fe177d27d.en.pdf

Reeves, R. (2009). Capitalism used to promise a better future. Can it still do that? Broken Capitalism. The Guardian, International Edition. https://www.theguardian.com/commentisfree/2019/may/22/capitalism-broken-better-future-can-it-do-that

Reinhart, C.M. and Reinhart, V.R. (2015). Financial Crises, Development, and Growth: A Long-term Perspective, *World Bank Economic Review, 29*: 53–S76. https://www.jstor.org/stable/48566468

Rhisiart, M., Miller, R. and Brooks, S. (2015). Learning to Use the Future: Developing Foresight Capabilities through Scenario Processes, *Technological Forecasting and Social Change, 101*: 124–133. https://doi.org/10.1016/j.techfore.2014.10.015

Ricardo, D. (1817). The Principles of Political Economy and Taxation. Batoche Books, Kitchener. Kitchener, Ontario, Canada.

Rodrik, D. (2018). Populism and the Economics of Globalization, *Journal of International Business Policy, 1.* 10.1057/s42214-018-0001-4

Roubini, N. (2021). Why stagflation is a growing threat to the global economy, *Guardian*, 15 April.

Scherrer, W. (2021). Industry 4.0 as a 'Sudden Change': The Relevance of Long Waves of Economic Development for the Regional Level, *European Planning Studies, 29*(9): 1723–1737. https://doi.org/10.1080/09654313.2021.1963054

Schwartz, P. (1991). The Art of the Long View: Planning for the Future in an Uncertain World. New York, NY: Doubleday Business.

Schwartz, S.H. (1994). Beyond Individualism/collectivism: New Cultural Dimensions of Values. In U. Kim, H.C. Triantis, C. Kagitcibasi, S.C. Choi and G. Yoon, Individualism and Collectivism. Thousand Oaks, CA: Sage, 85–119.

Sironi, A. (2018). The Evolution of Banking Regulation Since the Financial Crisis: A Critical Assessment. BAFFI CAREFIN Centre Research Paper No. 2018-103. http://dx.doi.org/10.2139/ssrn.3304672

Smith, A. (1776). An Inquiry into the Nature and Causes of the Wealth of Nations.

Solow, R.M. (1957). Technical Change and the Aggregate Production Function, *Review of Economics and Statistics, 39*: 312–320.

Stiglitz, J.E. (2010). Lessons from the Global Financial Crisis of 2008, Columbia University Commons. https://doi.org/10.7916/D8DV1VQH

Stock, J. and Watson, M. (2002). Forecasting Using Principal Components from a Large Number of Predictors, *Journal of the American Statistical Association, 97*(460): 1167–1179. http://www.jstor.org/stable/3085839

Summers, L.H. (2014). U.S. Economic Prospects: Secular Stagnation, Hysteresis, and the Zero Lower Bound, *Business Economics, 49*(2): 65–73.

Taleb, N.N. (2010). The Black Swan: The Impact of the Highly Improbable. New York: Random House Trade Paperbacks.

Therborn, G. (1987). Welfare States and Capitalist Markets, *Acta Sociologica, 30*(3/4): 237–254. http://www.jstor.org/stable/4194686

Thurow, L.C. (1996). The Future of Capitalism: How Today's Economic Forces Shape Tomorrow's World. New York: William Morrow and Company, Inc.

Tovar, C.E. and Nor, M.T. (2018). Reserve Currency Blocs: A Changing International Monetary System? IMF Working Paper No. 18/20.

Tyson L. and Lund S. (2021). How COVID-19 will change the low-wage labor market permanently, McKinsey Global Institute. https://www.mckinsey.com/mgi/overview/in-the-news/how-COVID-19-will-change-the-low-wage-labor-market-permanently

United States Environmental Protection Agency—USEPA. (2021). Climate Change Indicators: Snow and Ice, United States Environmental Protection Agency.

Vail, J., Wheelock, J. and Hill, M. (Eds.). (1999). Insecure Times. Living with Security in Contemporary Society. London: Routledge Publications.

van Ark, B., Ozyildirim, A., Bhide, P., Crofoot, E., Erumban, A. and Levanon, G. (2015). Prioritizing Productivity to Drive Growth, Profitability, and Competitiveness. The Conference Board, June. https://www.conference-board.org/topics/productivity-competitiveness

van Asselt, M.B.A. and Rotmans, J. (2002). Uncertainty in Integrated Assessment Modelling, *Climatic Change, 54*(1): 75–105.

Van der Merwe, L. (2008). Scenario Based Strategy in Practice: A Framework, *Advances in Developing Human Resources, 10*(2): 216–239. https://doi.org/10.1177/1523422307313321

Walker, W.E., Harremoës, P., Rotmans, J., van der Sluijs, J.P., van Asselt, M.B.A., Janssen, P. and von Krauss, M.P.K. (2003). Defining Uncertainty: A Conceptual Basis for Uncertainty Management in Model-Based Decision Support, *Integrated Assessment, 4*(1): 5–17.

Whitley, R. (1999). Divergent Capitalisms: The Social Structuring and Change of Business Systems. Oxford: Oxford University Press.

Wiener, M. and Boer, H. (2019). Cultural Prerequisites for Participating in Open Foresight, *R&D Management, 49*(5): 703–715. https://doi.org/10.1111/radm.12363

World Economic Forum—WEF. (2020). The Global Social Mobility Report 2020. Equality, Opportunity and a New Economic Imperative.

World Energy Outlook. (2021). International Energy Agency. www.iea.org/weo

Wu, T. (2018). The Curse of Bigness: Antitrust in the New Gilded Age. New York: Columbia Global Reports.

Xu, L.D., Xu, E.L. and Li, L. (2018). Industry 4.0: State of the Art and Future Trends, *International Journal of Production Research, 56*(8): 2941–2962. https://doi.org/10.1080/00207543.2018.1444806

Zhang J. and Zhang J. (2005). The Effect of Life Expectancy on Fertility, Saving, Schooling and Economic Growth: Theory and Evidence, *Scandinavian Journal of Economics, 107*(1): 45–66.

35

THE INTERACTION AMONG FINANCIAL DEVELOPMENT, MACROPRUDENTIAL POLICY AND ECONOMIC GROWTH

A Cross-Country Perspective

Mikhail Stolbov

DEPARTMENT OF APPLIED ECONOMICS, MOSCOW STATE INSTITUTE OF
INTERNATIONAL RELATIONS (MGIMO–UNIVERSITY), MOSCOW, RUSSIA

Maria Shchepeleva

DEPARTMENT OF THEORETICAL ECONOMICS, NATIONAL RESEARCH UNIVERSITY
HIGHER SCHOOL OF ECONOMICS (NRU HSE), MOSCOW, RUSSIA

35.1 Introduction

In the wake of the 2007–2009 Global Financial Crisis, the question of safeguarding financial stability along with maintaining price stability has come to the forefront of academic research. Macroprudential policy is aimed at decreasing systemic risk in the financial sector, thereby stabilizing the situation in the face of an upcoming crisis. Advanced economies and emerging markets have intensified the use of macroprudential policy instruments since 2010, though the question of their effectiveness still remains largely open.

On the one hand, there is a strand of research that provides evidence for the pro-growth effect of macroprudential regulation. The mechanics of the stimulating effect on GDP is described as follows: macroprudential regulation contributes to financial stability in the long run; in its turn, a well-functioning financial sector being effective in transforming savings into investments positively impacts the country's GDP growth. On the other hand, macroprudential regulation as any kind of prudential regulation is associated with curbing financial depth and constraining innovations. This hampers financial development (FD) and potentially can slow down economic growth.

Thus, the impact of macroprudential regulation on GDP is linked to a country's FD. According to the IMF, there are different dimensions of the country's FD: financial depth, access and efficiency. Based on the literature, we conjecture that macroprudential policy first and foremost decreases the depth component, while increasing stability.

DOI: 10.4324/9781003144366-41

This chapter aims to study lead–lag relationships in the following tangle of variables: GDP growth (GDP), FD and macroprudential regulation (IMAPP) for a sample of 126 countries. To conduct this research, we build a Bayesian panel vector autoregression (VAR) (BPVAR) model. Then, we extend the baseline methodology by introducing different components of FD instead of the aggregate index and also split macroprudential policy index into two sub-indices, thereby capturing measures targeted at borrowers and financial institutions.

Our results provide evidence for the bidirectional linkages between macroprudential policy and FD, mainly its components capturing depth and access to finance. We find that an increase in financial depth or access leads to tougher macroprudential restrictions. Meanwhile, stricter macroprudential policy leads to a decrease of depth and access components.

However, the results for advanced economies, emerging markets and low-income countries exhibit certain differences. In advanced economies, there is no evidence of macroprudential policy affecting FD, though there is a direct linkage from macroprudential policy to GDP growth. In low-income countries, the only relationship identified runs from FD to macroprudential policy. For the group of emerging markets, the results are the same as for the whole sample.

Our study contributes to the literature in two ways. First, we identify the linkage between macroprudential policy and growth conditional not only on the overall level of a country's FD but also on its components of depth, access and efficiency. Second, we examine the difference in the relationship between growth and macroprudential sub-indices. Thus, our study provides a more granular view on how growth, macroprudential policy and FD interact and could help policymakers develop more targeted measures to manage financial and business cycles.

This chapter proceeds as follows: in Section 35.3, we describe the data, while Section 35.4 covers the methodology used. We discuss the results in Section 35.5 and provide robustness checks in Section 35.6. Section 35.8 concludes.

35.2 Literature review

Before exploring the relationship among FD, economic growth and macroprudential policy, we review the literature on bivariate linkages between these variables.

35.2.1 *Financial development and economic growth*

Does FD contribute to a country's economic growth? Historically, we can identify four streams of thought in the literature related to the question.

The first one is represented by research that dates back to the 1980s (Lucas and Robert, 1988). It argues that the role of finance as a determinant of growth is very much exaggerated. The second group of theories supports the idea that FD is an important driver of economic development (Bagehot, 1873; Schumpeter, 1911; Bencivenga and Smith,1991; King and Levine, 1993; Levine et al., 2000; Calderon and Liu, 2003). The positive impact on growth is related to a more efficient resource allocation, reduction of agency costs, better risk-sharing and enhanced conditions for innovations facilitated by the financial system. The third strand of research promotes the idea that FD simply follows economic development (Robinson, 1952). Finally, there are theories that emphasize the risks stemming from FD, i.e. the possibility of financial crises and resource misallocation in favor of the fast-developing financial sector (Kindleberger, 1978; Andersen and Tarp, 2003; Allen and Carletti, 2006; Philippon, 2010).

Thus, we can identify two channels through which financial sector affects economic activity. The positive effect comes from intermediary functions performed by the financial sector: decrease in transaction costs, better capital and risk allocation and, as a result, increased investment. The negative effect arises from competition between the financial sector and other industries for capital and labor, which leads to an unbalanced growth and higher odds of financial crises.

Recent empirical findings support the view that there is an optimal level of FD. There is a consensus that the relationship is mainly nonlinear and time-varying and takes on the form of an inverted U-shape curve (time-varying relationship is described in Loayza and Ranciere, 2006; Rousseau and Wachtel, 2011; Beck et al., 2014; nonlinear dependence[1] – Deidda and Fattouh, 2002; Cecchetti and Kharroubi, 2012, Manganelli and Popov, 2013). Thus, at low levels of FD, increased finance is good for growth. But at some point, a larger financial system starts to hamper economic development. The challenge is to identify a country-specific threshold after which the financial system becomes excessively complex, less efficient, and starts to undermine growth in the non-financial sector.

35.2.2 Financial development and macroprudential policy

In contrast to the research on finance–growth nexus, there are a limited number of studies examining the relationship between a country's level of FD and the effectiveness of macroprudential policies. Researchers mainly focus on the impact of macroprudential measures on growth, while FD itself serves as a control variable.

Lim et al. (2011) were the first to highlight the importance of FD for the choice of macroprudential policy instruments.

Başkaya (2016) wrote about the difference in the effectiveness of price-based and quantity-based macroprudential tools, taking into account the level of a country's FD. While the quantity-based tools are effective irrespective of the level of FD, the price-based tools turn out to be successful only in terms of advanced economies that have deeper financial systems. Thus, in an economy where the financial sector is less developed, borrowers are insensitive to changes in loan interest rates, because the availability of loanable funds matters more in this economy than their price. Naceur et al. (2019) confirm this evidence.

Most of the macroprudential tools target the banking sector. There is scarce evidence that instruments are efficient in a bank-based or market-based financial system. Still, Neuberger and Rissi (2012) show that market-based financial systems benefit more not from capital or liquidity regulations (strictly speaking, the main instruments of macroprudential policy), but from a ban on proprietary trading (Volcker rule). Given the shift from bank loans to a more active use of market-based finance around the globe, it seems that the broad set of conventional macroprudential instruments may be soon limited, while policymakers will have to develop new tools capturing risks beyond the banking sector.

Agénor et al. (2018) analyze the relationship among prudential regulation, FD, financial openness and economic growth and conclude that regulation can contribute to growth only if it is aimed at promoting FD.

Bernier and Plouffe (2019) examine financial innovation–economic growth nexus and test how macroprudential policy can affect this relationship. The research provides evidence of the positive linkage between innovations and gross capital formation, while macroprudential policy is found to have little impact on the former.

Thus, different studies concur that the effectiveness of macroprudential tools depends on the level of FD. In our study, we also assume that the relationship may equally run in the opposite direction, i.e. the level of FD (in particular, the indicators of depth and access) depends on how restrictive macroprudential policy is.

35.2.3 Economic growth and macroprudential policy

The relationship between macroprudential policy and GDP growth is still an open question in the literature.

On the one hand, macroprudential policy can bring benefits for the economy. The main advantage stems from the reduction of systemic risk and a lower probability of financial crises. On the other hand, macroprudential restrictions can increase the costs of intermediation and curb credit supply, eventually hindering economic growth. The adverse impact of macroprudential policy is translated into the real activity through the decline in financial depth and inclusion.

The empirical literature partially supports both parties of the debate.

Boar et al. (2017) document a positive impact of macroprudential policy on growth. They find that the countries that are more active in applying macroprudential measures experience higher GDP per capita growth rates and reduced economic volatility. Still, these effects are sensitive to a country's financial openness and its level of FD.

Behn et al. (2016) emphasize the importance of banks' reaction to introduced macroprudential measures. They study the effect of additional capital requirements on GDP growth and conclude that if the requirements are met through raising equity, it will not hinder economic growth. Andries and Melnic (2019) show that the type of macroprudential measures used also matters: instruments which target financial institutions have greater impact on real economic activity than borrower-based measures. Moreover, macroprudential policy tends to be less effective in contributing to economic growth in the countries that are very financially open or financially developed.

Kawata et al. (2013) build a theoretical model, showing that macroprudential instruments can negatively impact growth in normal times, but this effect is rather small. The increase in growth due to a lower likelihood of financial crises is higher, so that macroprudential policy in the end creates net benefits for the economy.

In contrast, Sanchez and Rohn (2016) conclude that the use of additional macroprudential instruments is associated with a reduction in the quarterly GDP growth by 0.1% points. Slovik and Cournede (2011) demonstrate that if capital requirements are met through rising lending spreads, GDP growth will decline in the range between -0.05 and -0.15% per annum. The results are confirmed by Angelini et al. (2015).

To sum up, the effect of macroprudential policy on the real economy is ambiguous. The result is conditional on the type of macroprudential instruments used and such structural characteristics of the economy as the level of FD and openness.

Taking all the evidence into account, we propose the following scheme (Figure 35.1) capturing possible relationship among economic growth, FD and macroprudential policy.

35.3 Data

We use three variables in our empirical analysis: FD index from the IMF database by Svirydzenka (2016), GDP growth rate (GDP) borrowed from the World Development Indicators and the macroprudential policy index (IMAPP) coming from Alam et al. (2019). Descriptive statistics of the data are presented in Table 35.1.

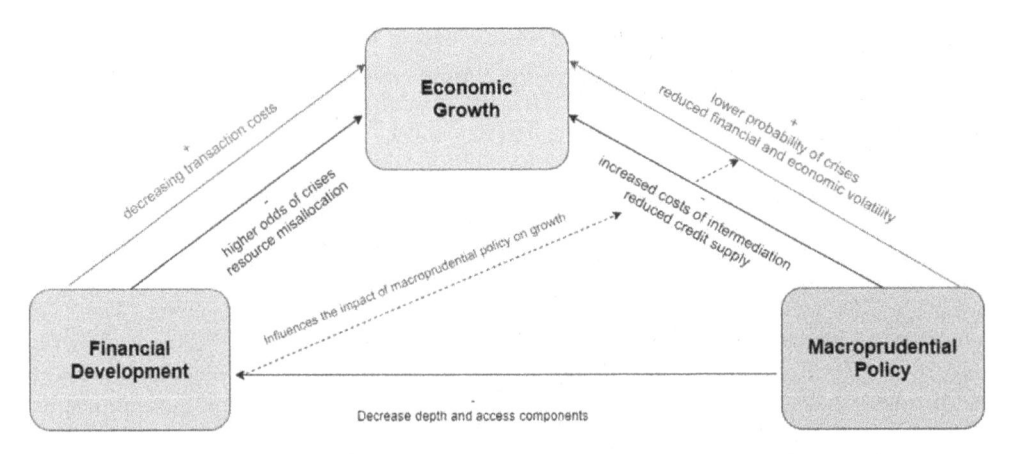

Figure 35.1 Theoretical relationships among economic growth, financial development and macroprudential policy.

Table 35.1 Descriptive statistics

Variable	Variable definition	Obs	Mean	Std. Dev.	Min	Max
GDP	GDP growth rate	3402	3.47	5.09	−44.90	88.96
IMAPP	Macroprudential policy index	3402	0.21	1.03	−9.00	13.00
IMAPP_BOR	Macroprudential policy sub-index responsible for borrow-targeted measures	3402	0.04	0.30	−2.00	4.00
IMAPP_FI	Macroprudential policy sub-index encompassing the instruments targeted at financial institutions	3402	0.18	0.92	−8.00	12.00
FD	Financial development index	3402	0.33	0.23	0.00	1.00
FI	Index of financial institutions' sub-index	3402	0.42	0.23	0.00	1.00
FM	Index of financial markets' sub-index	3402	0.24	0.25	0.00	1.00
FID	Financial institutions' depth index	3402	0.24	0.25	0.00	1.00
FIA	Financial institutions' access index	3402	0.34	0.29	0.00	1.00
FIE	Financial institutions' efficiency index	3402	0.62	0.19	0.00	0.94
FMD	Financial markets' depth index	3402	0.23	0.27	0.00	1.00
FMA	Financial markets' access index	3402	0.24	0.28	0.00	1.00
FME	Financial markets' efficiency index	3402	0.25	0.33	0.00	1.00

Furthermore, to investigate how different components of FD, namely financial depth, access to finance, the efficiency of financial intermediaries, are linked to economic growth, we consider the FD index alongside its sub-indices. The data on individual components of FD is also taken from the IMF database. Besides, we split the macroprudential policy index into two parts: the sub-index responsible for borrower-targeted macroprudential instruments (captures the changes in Loan-to-Value (LTV) and Debt Service-to-Income (DSTI) ratios together in a particular country) and the second sub-index encompassing the instruments targeted at financial institutions. The latter summarizes the dynamics of the remaining 15 macroprudential instruments represented in the database by Alam et el. (2019).

35.4 Methodology

Our methodology consists in specifying a BPVAR model and then validating the results we get from its impulse-responses by running the Dumitrescu-Hurlin panel causality test.

Bayesian panel vector autoregression' models allow considering the interaction between different variables as conventional VARs do, but they also impose a cross-sub-sectional structure on the model. The approach owes to Canova and Ciccarelli (2013).

A standard panel VAR model describes the evolution of y_{it} – the vector of G dependent variables for each country $i \in (1, ..., N)$ at time $t = 1, 2, ..., T$ with p lags.

The unrestricted PVAR is defined as:

$$Y_t = AY_{t-1} + u_t, \tag{35.1}$$

where $Y_t = (y'_{1t}, ..., y'_{Nt})'$ is a $NG \times 1$ vector of endogenous variables, $u_t \sim (0, \Sigma)$ with Σ a full $NG \times NG$ matrix. It is assumed that $cov(u_{it}, u_{jt}) = \Sigma_{ij} \neq 0$, where Σ_{ij} denotes the covariance matrix between the errors of country i and country j.

The unrestricted panel VARs very often suffer from computational problems due to a large number of parameters that should be estimated ($p*(NG^2)$ autoregression coefficients and $NG*(NG+1)/2$ parameters in the error covariance matrix). Koop and Korobilis (2016) describe three possible categories of restrictions that can be imposed on the unrestricted panel VAR:

- $N(N-1)$ dynamic interdependencies that occur when the dynamics of one country's variables affect another country's lagged variables, i.e. $A_{i,j} \neq 0$ for $i, j = 1, 2, ..., N; i \neq j$.
- $N(N-1)/2$ static interdependencies, i.e. the innovations $u_{t,i}$ can be correlated across units, i.e. $\Sigma_{i,j} \neq 0$ for $i, j = 1, 2, ..., N; i \neq j$.
- cross-unit (sub-sectional) heterogeneity – the two countries have VARs with different coefficients, i.e. $A_{ii} \neq A_{jj}$ for $i, j = 1, 2, ..., N; i \neq j$.

In this chapter, we employ an unrestricted panel VAR and rely on a Bayesian inference to deal with the "curse of dimensionality": for a limited number of observations, we have to estimate a large number of coefficients. Thus, we need to specify the priors on the parameter space. We opt for a standard normal-Wishart prior with default hyperparameter values.[2] This prior assumes that the model parameters (both panel VAR coefficients and the residual covariance matrix) are unknown, and in this respect, it is superior to the Minnesota (Litterman) prior, which assumes that the residual covariance matrix is known. As the objective of our empirical exercise is to infer average dynamic responses to the shocks of interest, we use a pooled estimator, which is a Bayesian counterpart of the mean-group estimator for a simple panel regression and implies that the coefficients are homogeneous across countries.

35.5 Results

Based on the impulse-response functions derived from the Bayesian VAR (Figure 35.2) built for the sample of 126 countries, we observe that in general increased FD (and its sub-indices reflecting financial market depth and financial market access components – FMD and FMA) leads to tougher macroprudential restrictions (higher value of the IMAPP index) and decreases GDP growth, which is in line with Ductor and Grechyna (2015) as well as Loayza and Ranciere (2006). This holds for both measures of macroprudential policy: targeted at financial institutions and at borrowers.[3] In terms of FD sub-indices, we not only find similar links for financial markets' depth and access components but also observe the inverse linkage running from the IMAPP index to the FMD and FMA, testifying to the effectiveness of macroprudential policy.

We also consider whether there are any nuances in our results for different country sub-groups: advanced economies, emerging markets and low-income countries. The sub-groups are compiled based on the IMF country classification.

First, for the group of advanced countries, the baseline relationship – higher FD (and its depth and access components measured both for financial institutions and markets) leading to a stricter macroprudential regulation – still holds. However, we do not observe the inverse linkage running from macroprudential policy to FD sub-indices as for the whole sample. At the same time, the IMAPP index directly contributes to GDP growth, which accords with the results derived by Boar et al. (2017), Stolbov et al. (2021) and Bonciani et al. (2021). Thus, we conclude that macroprudential measures in advanced economies impact the business cycle in the first place leaving financial indicators mainly unaffected (Table 35.2). This relationship pattern is true for the aggregate IMAPP index and for the IMAPP sub-index targeted at

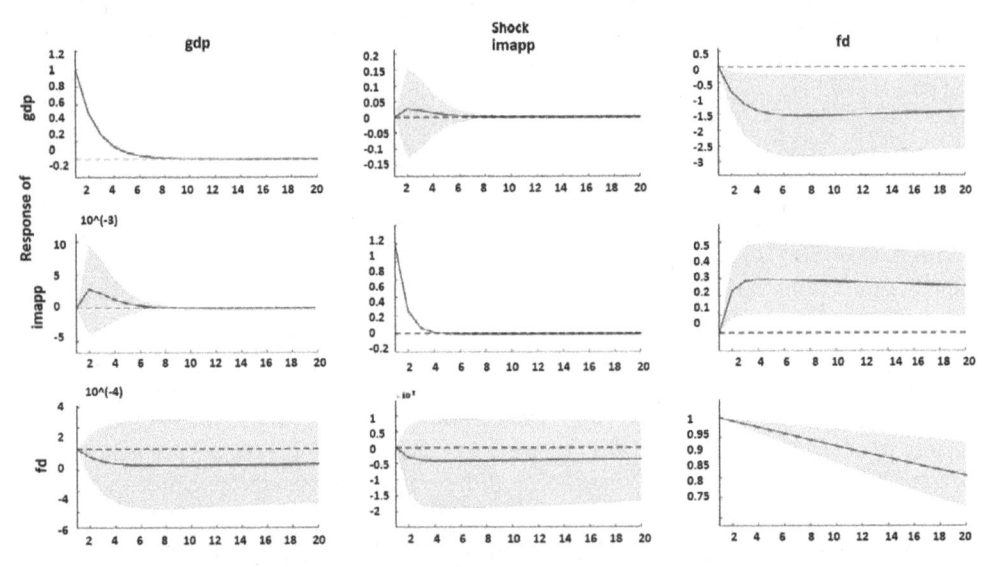

Figure 35.2 Impulse responses from Bayesian panel VAR with three variables: GDP growth, the financial development index and the IMAPP index.

Table 35.2 Linkages among GDP, IMAPP and FD and their sub-indices in a Bayesian panel VAR for advanced countries

Aggregate IMAPP index	*IMAPP_FI*	*IMAPP_BORROWER*
↑IMAPP →↑GDP	↑IMAPP_FI →↑GDP	↑FIA →↓GDP
↑FD →↑IMAPP	↑FD →↑IMAPP_FI	↑GDP →↑FIA
↑FID →↑IMAPP	↑FID →↑IMAPP_FI	↑GDP →↑FIE
↑FIA →↓GDP	↑FIA →↓GDP	↑FME →↓GDP
↑GDP →↑FIA	↑FM →↑IMAPP_FI	
↑GDP →↑FIE	↑FMD →↑IMAPP_FI	
↑FM →↑IMAPP	↑FMA →↑IMAPP_FI	
↑FMD →↑IMAPP	↑FME →↓GDP	
↑FMA →↑IMAPP		

financial institutions, while the IMAPP capturing borrower-based measures appears neutral to GDP and FD, as no linkages between them are found.

As for the emerging markets, the results are analogous to those for the whole sample (Table 35.3): we observe the linkages running from the FD index to the IMAPP index and from the IMAPP index to FMD and FMA sub-indices. However, we do not find evidence of the IMAPP directly impacting GDP growth in contrast to the group of advanced countries. Thus, we conclude that macroprudential policy in emerging markets turns out to be more targeted, impacting the financial sector without transmitting its influence on the real economy. We also note that the number of linkages in the group of emerging markets is biased toward the IMAPP sub-index comprising measures targeted at financial institutions. Thus, our analysis indicates that in both groups of countries measures impacting institutions turn out to be more effective than borrower-based instruments, which is corroborated by Andrieș and Melnic (2019).

Table 35.3 Linkages among GDP, IMAPP and FD and their sub-indices in a Bayesian panel VAR for emerging markets

Aggregate IMAPP index	*IMAPP_FI*	*IMAPP_BORROWER*
↑FD →↑IMAPP	↑FD →↑IMAPP_FI	↑GDP →↑FD
↑GDP →↑FD	↑GDP →↑FD	↑GDP →↑FID
↑FID →↑IMAPP	↑GDP →↑FID	↑FIA →↓GDP
↑GDP →↓FID	↑FIA →↓GDP	↑FIE →↑GDP
↑FIA →↓GDP	↑IMAPP_FI →↑FIA	↑GDP →↑FM
↑IMAPP →↑FIA	↑FIE →↑GDP	↑IMAPP_BOR →↓FM
↑FIE →↑GDP	↑GDP →↑FM	↑FMD →↑GDP
↑GDP →↑FM	↑FMD →↑GDP	↑GDP →↑FMA
↑GDP →↑FMD	↑FMD →↑IMAPP_FI	↑FME →↑IMAPP_BOR
↑IMAPP →↓FMD	↑IMAPP_FI →↓FMD	↑GDP →↑FME
↑GDP →↑FMA	↑GDP →↑FMA	
↑IMAPP →↓FMA	↑IMAPP_FI →↓FMA	
↑GDP →↑FME	↑GDP →↑FME	

Table 35.4 Linkages among GDP, IMAPP and FD and their sub-indices in a Bayesian panel VAR for low-income countries

Aggregate IMAPP index	*IMAPP_FI*	*IMAPP_BORROWER*
↑ IMAPP →↑ FIA	↑ IMAPP_FI →↑ FIA	↑ FD →↑ IMAPP_BOR
↑ FIE →↑ GDP	↑ FIE →↑ GDP	↑ FI →↑ IMAPP_BOR
↑ FM →↑ IMAPP		↑ FID →↑ IMAPP_BOR
		↑ FIA →↑ IMAPP_BOR
		↑ FIE →↑ GDP
		↑ FM →↑ IMAPP_BOR
		↑ FMD →↑ IMAPP_BOR
		↑ FMA →↑ IMAPP_BOR
		↑ FME →↑ IMAPP_BOR

Finally, in low-income countries, the largest number of relationships is associated with borrower-based macroprudential instruments (Table 35.4). Therefore, higher values of the FD index, together with the markets and institutions sub-indices, lead to a more tightened borrower-based macroprudential measures. The inverse relationship is not found.

To sum it up, our main finding boils down to the fact that macroprudential policy in all country group accounts for the level of a country's FD, especially those indicators that capture financial depth and access to finance. In advanced countries, macroprudential policy exerts a direct impact on GDP growth, while in emerging markets, it primarily influences financial sector. There is no evidence of the effect of macroprudential regulation either on the financial sector or the real economy in low-income countries.

35.6 Robustness checks

We apply the Dumitrescu-Hurlin panel causality test with individual coefficients to check the robustness of our results. Under the null hypothesis in this test, we assume that there is no causal relationship for any of the units of the panel. The alternative hypothesis is that there is a causality relationship from X to Y for at least one cross-sectional unit. The results are provided in Table 35.5 for the whole sample.

Table 35.5 Dumitrescu-Hurlin panel causality test results

Null hypothesis	*W-Stat.*	*Zbar-Stat.*	*Prob.*
IMAPP does not homogeneously cause FD	**1.45**	**−3.48**	**0.00**
FD does not homogeneously cause IMAPP	2.54	1.43	0.15
GDP does not homogeneously cause FD	**3.02**	**3.62**	**0.00**
FD does not homogeneously cause GDP	**4.05**	**8.25**	**0.00**
GDP does not homogeneously cause IMAPP	2.15	−0.32	0.75
IMAPP does not homogeneously cause GDP	2.39	0.75	0.45

Note: If the p-value is less than 0.05, we reject the Null hypothesis and consider the alternative hypothesis to be true. In the table we indicate in bold the cases, where we reject the Null hypothesis and, thus, accept the statement about one variable granger causing another one.

The test statistics indicate that the IMAPP index granger causes the FD index and there is a bidirectional relationship between GDP growth and FD. Qualitatively, this supports the results based on the BPVAR.

35.7 Policy implications

Our findings have some implications for policymakers.

First, we conclude that the effect of macroprudential policy on growth is conditional on how developed the financial sector is. Thus, when discussing the implementation of new policy measures and their effects on growth, policymakers should take into account the country's level of FD. In advanced countries with well-developed financial markets, the effect of macroprudential policy on economic growth will be direct and presumably faster. In emerging markets, where the relationship between the three variables is more consistent with the theory, i.e. macroprudential policy affects in the first place financial system and then contributes to economic growth, the effect of newly introduced restrictions will manifest itself with some lag. In low-income countries, macroprudential policy, based on the findings, will not affect growth at all.

Second, for the whole sample of countries, we find that higher FD is associated with lower GDP growth. We hypothesize that this result can be impacted by the composition of our sample: there are a sufficiently large number of advanced economies, which may have already passed the threshold after which further FD is regarded as the increase in system's complexity and has a negative effect on real activity. In terms of sub-indices, this effect is due to the increase in depth and access components. For the country groups, there are some differences. In advanced economies, the decrease in GDP comes from the shock of access to services provided by financial institutions, in the emerging markets – also from the Financial Institutions Access (FIA) sub-index. But at the same time in the emerging markets, an increase in financial depth contributes to GDP growth. This calls for special macroprudential measures in emerging markets, which constrain access from less reliable borrowers to financial institutions, while keeping depth indicators unaffected.

Finally, we find that in advanced and emerging market economies the largest number of linkages comprises the IMAPP sub-index targeted at financial institutions, while in the low-income countries – the sub-index capturing borrow-based measures. This suggests that in rich and middle-income countries policymakers should rely more on instruments impacting excess loan supply, while in low-income countries, measures curbing excess demand will be more effective in curtailing an unbalanced credit growth.

35.8 Conclusions

Our research deals with the linkages between three variables capturing the stance of macroprudential policy, FD and economic growth. By estimating BPVAR for a panel of 126 countries, we demonstrate that tighter macroprudential policy on average is observed in the countries with higher levels of FD. In its turn, a more restrictive policy leads to the decrease in financial depth and inclusion indicators, whose increased levels are usually associated with credit and asset price bubbles.

We find certain differences in the results for country sub-groups. In case of advanced countries, we additionally observe that macroprudential policy tightening contributes to economic growth, presumably through a more stable and efficient financial system in the long run. In emerging markets, there is no impact of macroprudential policy on real activity. In both sub-groups, the number of statistically significant linkages between the variables is biased toward macroprudential policy sub-indices targeting financial institutions. Finally, there are very few significant relationships found for low-income countries.

Notes

1 Nonlinear dependence is a term used in statistics to describe the relationship between the variables when there is no direct correlation between them; in other words, the change in the independent variable does not provide an obvious corresponding change in the dependent variable. A linear relationship, when plotted on the graph, represents a straight line, while nonlinear relationship is characterized by a curvy line.

2 We estimate the Bayesian panel VAR using the BEAR-toolbox devised by Alistair Dieppe and Bjorn van Roye (2016) for MATLAB. The standard hyperparameter values used by default for the normal Wishart prior are as follows: autoregressive coefficient equal to 0.8; overall tightness equal to 0.1; cross-variable weighting – 0.5; lag decay – 1.

3 For brevity, we do not present all the impulse-response plots. Additional plots for the financial development and the IMAPP sub-indices can be provided upon request.

References

Agénor, P.-R., Gambacorta, L., Kharroubi, E. and Pereira da Silva, L. (2018). The effects of prudential regulation, financial development, and financial openness on economic growth. BIS Working Papers No. 752.

Alam, Z., Alter, A., Eiseman, J., Gelos, G., Kang, H., Narita, M., Nier, E. and Wang, N. (2019). Digging deeper – evidence on the effects of macroprudential policies from a new database. IMF Working Papers No. 66.

Allen, F. and Carletti, E. (2006). Credit risk transfer and contagion. *Journal of Monetary Economics*, 53(1), 89–111.

Andersen, T.B. and Tarp, F. (2003). Financial liberalization, financial development and economic growth in LDCs. *Journal of International Development*, 15(2), 189–209.

Andries, A. and Melnic, F. (2019). Macroprudential policies and economic growth. *Review of Economic and Business Studies*, 23, 95–112.

Angelini, P., Clerc, L., Curdia, V., Gambarcorta, L., Gerali, A., Locarno, A., Motto, R., Roeger, W., Van den Heuvel, S. and Vlček, J. (2015). Basel III: long-term impact on economic performance and fluctuations. *Manchester School*, 83(2), 217–251.

Bagehot, W. (1873). *Lombard Street: A Description of the Money Market*. New York: Charles Scribner's Sons.

Baskaya, Y. (2016). Financial development and the effectiveness of macroprudential measures. In *Macroprudential policy*, vol. 86. Bank for International Settlements, pp. 103–116.

Beck, T., Degryse, H. and Kneer, C. (2014). Is more finance better? Disentangling intermediation and size effects of financial systems. *Journal of Financial Stability*, 10, 50–64.

Behn, M., Gross, M. and Peltonen, T.A. (2016). Assessing the costs and benefits of capital-based macroprudential policy. ESRB Working Paper Series 17, European Systemic Risk Board.

Bencivenga, R. and Smith, D. (1991). Financial intermediation and endogenous growth. *Review of Economic Studies*, 58(2), 195–209.

Bernier, M. and Plouffe, M. (2019). Financial innovation, economic growth, and the consequences of macroprudential policies. *Research in Economics*, 73(2), 162–173.

Boar, C., Gambacorta, L., Lombardo, G. and Pereira da Silva, L. (2017). What are the effects of macroprudential policies on macroeconomic performance? BIS Quarterly Review, Bank for International Settlements, September.

Bonciani, D., Gauthier, D. and Kanngiesser, D. (2021). Slow recoveries, endogenous growth and macroprudential policy. Bank of England Working Papers 917, Bank of England.

Calderon, C. and Liu, L. (2003). The direction of causality between financial development and economic growth. *Journal of Development Economics*, 72(1), 321–334.

Canova, F. and Ciccarelli, M. (2013). Panel vector autoregressive models: a survey. Working Paper Series 1507, European Central Bank.

Cecchetti, S. and Kharroubi, E. (2012). Reassessing the impact of finance on growth. Bank for International Settlements Working Paper No. 381.

Deidda, L. and Fattouh, B. (2002). Non-linearity between finance and growth. *Economics Letters*, 74(3), 339–345.

Dieppe, A., Legrand, R. and van Roye, B. (2016). The BEAR toolbox. ECB Working Paper No. 1934.

Ductor, L. and Grechyna, D. (2015). Financial development, real sector, and economic growth. *International Review of Economics and Finance*, 37, 393–405.

Kawata, H., Kurachi, Y., Nakamura, K. and Teranishi, Y. (2013). Impact of macroprudential policy measures on economic dynamics: simulation using a financial macro-econometric model. Bank of Japan Working Paper Series No. 13-E-3.

Kindleberger, C. (1978). *Manias, Panics and Crashes. A History of Financial Crises.* Hoboken, NJ: Wiley (fourth edition).

King, G. and Levine, R. (1993). Finance and growth: Schumpeter might be right. *Quarterly Journal of Economics*, 108(3), 717–737.

Koop, G. and Korobilis, D. (2016). Model uncertainty in panel vector autoregressive models. *European Economic Review*, 81, 115–131.

Levine, R., Loayza, N. and Beck, T. (2000). Financial intermediation and growth: causality and causes. *Journal of Monetary Economics*, 46(1), 31–77.

Lim, C., Columba, F., Costa, A., Kongsamut, P., Otani, A., Saiyid, M., Wezel, T. and Wu, X. (2011). Macroprudential policy: what instruments and how to use them? Lessons from country experiences. IMF Working Paper 11/238.

Loayza, N. and Ranciere, R. (2006). Financial development, financial fragility, and growth. *Journal of Money, Credit and Banking*, 38(4), 1051–1076.

Lucas, R. and Robert, E. (1988). On the mechanics of economic development. *Journal of Monetary Economics*, 22(1), 3–42.

Manganelli, S. and Popov, A. (2013). Financial dependence, global growth opportunities, and growth revisited. *Economics Letters*, 120(1), 123–125.

Naceur, B., Candelon, B. and Quentin, L. (2019). Taming financial development to reduce crises. *Emerging Markets Review*, 40(C), 100618.

Neuberger, D. and Rissi, R. (2012). Macroprudential banking regulation: does one size fit all? Thünen-Series of Applied Economic Theory Working Paper 124.

Philippon, T. (2010). Financiers versus engineers: should the financial sector be taxed or subsidized? *American Economic Journal: Macroeconomics*, 2(3), 158–182.

Robinson, J. (1952). *The Rate of Interest and Other Essays.* London: Macmillan.

Rousseau, P.L. and Wachtel, P. (2011). What is happening to the impact of financial deepening on economic growth? *Economic Inquiry*, 49(1), 276–288.

Sanchez, A. and Rohn, O. (2016). How do policies influence GDP tail risks? OECD Economics Department Working Paper No. 1339.

Schumpeter, J.A. (1911). *The Theory of Economic Development.* Cambridge, MA: Harvard University Press.

Slovik, P. and Cournede, B. (2011). Macroeconomic impact of Basel III. OECD Working Papers No. 844.

Stolbov, M., Shchepeleva, M. and Karminsky, A. (2021). A global perspective on macroprudential policy interaction with systemic risk, real economic activity, and monetary intervention. *Financial Innovation*, 7(1), 1–25.

Svirydzenka, K. (2016). Introducing a new broad-based index of financial development. IMF Working Papers 2016/005.

36

CHINA'S BELT AND ROAD INITIATIVE

New Research Agenda of Global Infrastructure Initiatives[1]

Euston Quah

ALBERT WINSEMIUS CHAIR PROFESSOR, DIVISION OF ECONOMICS, NANYANG TECHNOLOGICAL UNIVERSITY, SINGAPORE

HENGYI VISITING CHAIR PROFESSOR, ZHEJIANG UNIVERSITY, CHINA

Iuldashov Nursultan

RESEARCH ASSOCIATE, SCHOOL OF SOCIAL SCIENCES, NANYANG TECHNOLOGICAL UNIVERSITY, SINGAPORE

36.1 Introduction

More than 80 countries have already participated in China's Belt and Road Initiative (BRI) since 2013. China seeks to increase trade and commerce through increased connectivity, promoting economic growth and development through massive investments in infrastructure in these countries. From hydroelectric power plants, and transmission stations, to oil pipelines, and highways to port developments, the scale is unprecedented in historical and contemporary times. All of these efforts have their historical roots in the old or Ancient Silk Road (ASR) where the impacts were primarily on trade and cultural exchange without a coordinated strategy in providing loans, infrastructure development and more as in today's reincarnation of the Silk Road. We discuss some of these historical dynamics and parallels in Section 36.2.

Much has been written on the political economy of the BRI by political scientists and on the economic benefits and trade impacts by economists and business commentators. Many have criticized the BRI for the potential of corruption, debt inundation, political influence and external intervention into domestic affairs, and the like. Some of these projects also have drawn criticisms in the host countries given possible environmental impacts and local dissent towards untransparent loan provision practices. This was spotlighted, for example, in the extensive report by World Bank published in 2018 (World Bank, 2019). Our chapter, however, attempts to discuss a new research agenda on BRI that was not given sufficient attention in the literature. In this chapter, we identify three areas as new research agenda for BRI.

The first challenge is concerned with the challenge of facility siting, that is where should a proposed infrastructure be located in such a way so as to maximize acceptance by the local residents hosting the facility and minimizing social costs. Such facilities aptly labelled, NIMBY (Not-In-My-Backyard), have been the subject of much discussion in Europe and North America, and more recently in Asian countries as the latter expands their infrastructure in the pursuit of economic growth. There has been only limited research and analysis of the Asian experience with regard to the siting issue of the NIMBY facilities but no doubt increasing in importance. Since the BRI involves a number of megaprojects, this issue of NIMBYs would take greater importance and urgency. In this chapter, we will highlight some conflict-resolution instruments as to what works and what do not. We will also discuss the use of sealed bid auctions in resolving this issue. This area of research is discussed in Section 36.3.

The second challenge concerns the question of whether conventional cost-benefit analysis (CBA) and its framework are applicable to BRI countries. Since many BRI countries are poor and developing countries, the issue is whether the methodologies used in CBA are valid for these countries compared with the developed countries. Because of differences in labour, goods and financial markets, we argue that conventional CBA needs to be modified and adapted to suit the differences between poor and developing countries with developed countries. What these differences are and why they affect CBA are explained. We suggest some potentially useful ways to address these issues for CBA. This is discussed in Section 36.4.

The third challenge has to do with the arrival of new competing initiatives from the European Union and the United States, and even Japan. Starting from Japan's Partnership for Quality Infrastructure (PQI), Blue Dot Network (BDN) led by the United States and emerging Global Gateway of EU, there are many initiatives overlapping with BRI both in the scope and scale. Given these new competing and alternative initiatives, what does this mean and how will they impact the BRI? We discuss the implications and speculate on the BRI's future in Section 36.5 while also providing the concluding remarks.

36.2 Dynamics of the Silk Road from historical to contemporary

36.2.1 Ancient Silk Road

The ASR had served merchants and traders from different kingdoms and spanned centuries, living to see the rise and fall of dynasties and overturn of the ancient powers. Once a series of networks connecting the Eastern Mediterranean, Central Asia and China, today, it is a metaphor for the huge global network to which China exports its economic influence.

The ASR had played an instrumental role in facilitating trade between China and its regional neighbours. Expeditions by merchants and the desire to trade have resulted in the rise of trading colonies that eventually ultimately led to the creation of trading cities, such as those in Northern China (Vaissiere, 2014). During the Tang Dynasty, at opposite ends of the Silk Road, Chang'an (present-day Xi'an) and Baghdad rose to importance as cosmopolitan cities (Zou, 2018a). Chang'an was a melting pot of merchants who came from different backgrounds both in terms of ethnicity and social class (Pingshuan, 2006). The importance of trade and the central location of Chang'an made the city prosperous and population-dense.

Silk, the commodity that had given the route its name, was one of the many goods that had been passed along the road. Its creation and production in China were kept secret through the 6th-century CE, giving China monopoly power on its production (Friedland and Rheinstrom, n.d.). Trade dynamics for silk was hence driven by comparative advantage, and silk trade became significant for both China and the Mediterranean, reaching Rome as well, where it was so popular that there were attempts to implement price ceilings (Wood, 2003). The sheer demand for Chinese silk from distant lands resultantly involved many people who often with the price inflating every time it swapped hands. Just like our modern economy, the lucrative silk trade with the West enticed many Chinese to join the trade. While the middle class and peasant Chinese could not afford silk, the burgeoning demand meant many devoted themselves to its production. Silk also served strategic purposes as well, such as being used as a currency in western regions of China under the Tang administration. They were also used as diplomatic gifts on embassy trips to the nomadic people whose cities and depots served as vital stopovers for merchant caravans on their long journey both ways.

Besides goods, intangibles travelled along the ASR as well. Buddhism made its way to China from India through the Silk Road, such as the road that connects Bactria and Taxila to the Bengal Coast. Monasteries were established along the route, and the symbiotic relationship between merchants and monks helped spread the teachings of Buddhism further to the East where it contacted Thailand, Korea, Japan and Indonesia, and took a form which resonated with the locals. Knowledge of techniques such as the production of refined cane sugar from India travelled the Silk Road too. More importantly, in medical history, the outbreak of smallpox and the threat it posed to Central Eurasian nomads who did not have a strong immunity to diseases due to their sparsely spread population made the disease a challenging and feared one. Mongolian and Tibetan allies of China were afraid of contracting the disease and were hence unwilling to visit the capital when the Manchus sought to cultivate alliances with them. This led to experimentation with inoculation which originated from Manchu and was later advocated by the wife of the British ambassador in the Ottoman Empire for use in Britain following her learning of the technique (Millward, 2013, p. 81). The Silk Road had hence spread novel ideas throughout the region and brought about development and progress.

Following its decline in the early 10th century due to the collapse of the Tang dynasty, the Silk Road trade flourished again under "Pax Mongolica" under the Mongolian administration (UNESCO, n.d.). Favourable trade policies of the Mongols resulted in the rebirth of trade and revival of the Silk Road. Unlike the Chinese administration, the Mongols did not harass travelling merchants for confiscatory taxation. Under Kublai Khan, foreign traders were given privileges from which even his subjects were excluded from. In Persia, merchants were granted higher tax breaks and benefits in order to promote commerce. The national postal station system allowed merchants to obtain the supplies they needed and early forms of capital formation and accumulation were seen in the establishment of merchant associations called *Ortogh*. These associations served as a form of risk pooling fund for merchants given that travelling across the road was risky and expensive. The Mongols encouraged *Ortogh* membership by offering lower interest rates for loans to merchants as long as they belonged to an association (Asia for Educators, C. U., n.d.).

Geographical labour mobility under Mongol rule was flexible for a certain trade, the Mongols appreciated culture, crafts and arts and moved and allocated people from such trades around their territory, and the employment of these workers in new areas resulted in cultural immersion and technological diffusion throughout the Silk Road. Examples of artistic and cultural exchange were said to include the migration of three distinct weaving communities from Central Asia and Persia to China due to their production of a unique textile – a cloth of gold (Asia for Educators, C. U., n.d.).

36.2.2 Belt and Road Initiative

The BRI mainly comprises two parts: the belt and the road. The belt, denoting the Silk Road Economic Belt, refers to a number of land routes which connect China all the way to Europe through Central Asia and the Middle East. The "road" on the other hand refers to the Maritime Silk Road which links the southern coast of China with Africa, Europe and parts of Asia especially Southeast Asia. This link connects China via the South China Sea, Indian Ocean, Arabian Sea and the Straits of Hormuz. In all, this Modern Silk Road will stretch across 3 major continents and over 80 countries.

The Belt Road Initiative seeks to usher in a new era of regional interconnectivity by facilitating the movement of goods, people and information through the construction and expansion of communication and transport infrastructure as well as export of Chinese technology to BRI participating countries. The initiative is expected to increase the inflow of trade and foreign direct investment to BRI countries through cross-border economic cooperation zones where the construction and expansion of cross-border infrastructure projects for transport and energy will take place. The China-Kazakhstan International Border Cooperation Centre which is situated at the fringes of both countries serves as a hub for the New Eurasian Land Bridge and China-Central Asia-West Asia Economic Corridor (Hyun, 2018). These zones are also expected to boost employment as Chinese companies seek to utilize the cheaper labour of Southeast Asia to reduce production costs (Pitakdumrongkit, 2019).

Some ongoing and completed projects under this BRI include Longyangxia gravity dam on the Yellow River in Qinghai province in China, the Quaid-e-Azam solar park in Pakistan, the Dawood Wind Power project, the world's largest wind farm, the Digital BRI International Centre of Excellence in Bangkok, Thailand, the Pakistan-China Economic Corridor which is a 46 billion dollar project terminating at the Arabian seaport of Gwadar, the China-Laos railway project, the new Yalu Bridge in North Korea, Turkey's third nuclear power station and Kiev's fourth metro line in Russia. These projects are expected to improve connectivity, stimulate regional growth and economic development and ultimately, improve the lives of the millions of people living in BRI countries.

While the mix of countries which have accepted BRI projects span from low income to high, a good proportion falls under low- or low-middle income (Nedopil, 2021). China's infrastructure projects may help narrow the global infrastructure gap and infrastructure investment deficit that impedes global trade and connectivity. These infrastructure investment projects will also benefit China's manufacturing sectors, especially the steel and cement industry, which have been facing overcapacity (Bruce-Lockhart, 2017). China's demand for raw materials such as fossil fuels, metals and minerals for its investment-led infrastructure projects has led to strong export-led economic growth in these countries too. For instance, ASEAN countries saw a rise of 37% in their collective exports to China from January to July of 2021 (Savic and Shira, 2021).

36.2.3 Similarities and differences between ASR and BRI

There are some fundamental parallels between the ASR and the factors that led to its prosperity as well as the terms and components of BRI. These include the span, type of exchanges, need for infrastructure and institutions and international treaties (see Table 36.1).

While the area covered by BRI (have BRI projects) far exceed those by ASR, there is an overlap between the two. The ASR was a series of routes that connected China to South Asia, Persia, Arabian Peninsula, East Africa and Rome. It also included a maritime route which carried goods from the East to Europe through the Mediterranean Sea. Under BRI,

Table 36.1 ASR and BRI similarities and differences

	ASR	BRI
Similarities		
Geographical coverage	Both span from China to Central Asia and onwards to Europe	
Types of exchanges	Goods (raw materials, finished), tech-transfer (military, health, inventions), information (culturally Buddhism, knowledge – sea navigation techniques), people exchange (travelling merchants, artists – under Mongols)	Goods (raw materials, finished), tech-transfer (digital, energy, infrastructure), services, information sharing/ training, people exchange (rural to urban to meet labour demands, skilled experts for planning and execution of projects)
Presence of financial institutions and supporting infrastructures	Merchant associations, Pigeonhole postal system for merchants	Exim, China Development Bank, New Development Bank, supporting boards and ministries
Differences		
Capital inflow	Little capital inflow from foreigners, capital accumulation and investment were not practiced	Foreign direct investment from China in BRI countries
Origin	Emerged spontaneously, maintained collectively and by different ruling power	Initiated and endorsed by China
Scope	Knowledge and technology spread but was not the main use of the Silk Road	Information exchange, technology sharing are key aspects of BRI, equally important as trade

the Silk Road Economic Belt comprises roads, railways and high-speed rails that will connect China to Central and South Asia and ultimately to Europe and the New Maritime Silk Road, through its ports will connect China to Southeast Asia, North Africa, the Gulf states and onwards to Europe. Much like the ASR of the past, the final destination of these routes ends in Europe and serves to bridge East and West.

The ASR helped goods such as silk and horses, information such as sea navigation techniques and technology such as gunpowder and inoculation reach different domains, integrating different regions while the openness of countries to trade and exchanges helped the ASR thrive. Today, the Modern Silk Road will likewise increase the flow of goods, services, foreign direct investments, technology and information exchange. Through technical training, foreign trade is expanded and trade volume has grown as closer ties are forged between China and its partners. China's General Administration of Customs has reported increases in China's exports to BRI countries, increasing by 25.3% annually as of 2021 (*Global Times*, 2021). In total, trade volume between China and BRI countries have reached about $1.46 trillion in October 2021. China has also adapted BRI to the times such as the proposal of Health Silk Road (HSR) that has been revived during the COVID-19 pandemic to promote health cooperation. In sum, the high trade volume, favourable trade zones and open border policies will further integrate the economies of China and BRI countries, similar to how the progress and prosperity brought about by trade had spread along the ASR.

As mentioned, a primitive form of financial infrastructure came in the form of merchant associations known as *Ortogh* under the Mongol Empire. These state-merchant relationships provided credit to merchants for trade and gave them the platform to pool risk and promote long-distance trade. The importance of financial institutions that support development and expansion is vital to industrialization and modernization. China has in place sources of funding for its BRI projects which include state-owned commercial banks, multilateral institutions and a state-owned investment fund – Silk Road Fund. The Export Import (Exim) Bank of China finances trade, China Development Bank supports infrastructure, energy and transport projects which contributes to 45% of BRI funding, while the four leading commercial banks support 51% of funding. The Asian Infrastructure Investment Bank is a multilateral international financial institution that has been launched by China for development financing which funds BRI projects as well. China's Ministry of Finance, since 2015, had accelerated the improvement and development of foreign trade policies and consolidated both AIIB and the New Development Bank, increasing financial exchanges and participating in other multilateral bodies such as G20 and BRICS. All of these infrastructures and coordination efforts by the respective bodies of China with BRI countries will lead to further financial integration and internationalization of the Renminbi (Zou, 2018b).

It is worth noting that not all regions have benefitted equally from trade, much like how the strategic location of Xi'an and Constantinople gave them a central role in trade along the Silk Road, regions closer to the border benefit more than their rural counterparts due to accessibility. This would require better domestic transportation networks, flexible labour policies that could facilitate labour migration and mobility to distribute benefits and economic activity across the different regions and mitigate widening spatial inequality (Gill et al., 2019). Additionally, some BRI countries face a trade deficit with China due to weaker domestic manufacturing capabilities. India faces a trade deficit with China of around USD30 billion (Press Trust of India, 2021), fuelling fears of increasing debt burdens to China. Additionally, while the ASR was more of a common good used by different kingdoms and managed by different ruling powers over the centuries, BRI was initiated and endorsed by China.

36.2.4 Belt and Road Initiative 2.0

By far, the main difference between ASR and BRI is the coordinated and controlled nature of the cultural and technological impacts that were characteristic of the Silk Road historically. Aside from the cultural aspect[2] of BRI, there are Green Silk Road (GSR), HSR and Digital Silk Road (DSR). All these "dimensions" of BRI existed since the inception of BRI in its conceptual framework but received more prominence and spotlight in recent years due to the COVID-19 pandemic. Hence, we are still in the midst of a formation of modern Silk Road. Partial shift of focus from improving transport, energy and technology infrastructure to increasing digital and health infrastructure spending is expected. Climate-related projects are also likely to come into focus. This ushers the new era of BRI that we coin as BRI 2.0.

36.2.4.1 Green Silk Road (GSR)

Apart from major infrastructure projects, China has also invested heavily in green energy, public health, new technologies and digital cities. There are clearly benefits and costs to this BRI. Such costs as investments worth trillions of dollars, economic and social costs through increased income inequity, trafficking of drugs, corruption and environmental damages, including pollution of all types, increased carbon emissions, impact on ecotourism and accelerated depletion of resources and raw materials. There are also economic and social benefits through global trade, tourism, reduced production costs, employment, connectivity of otherwise isolated human settlements, resource security such as reduced crop losses and increased access to markets for both inputs and outputs. Not many would appreciate nor understand that there are also environmental benefits, and that comes mainly from China's long experience with environmental degradation as it grows economically.

In 2015, the GSR Fund was founded by Chinese private companies specializing in green technologies such as ecological restoration by Elion Group (Meng, 2015). Elion Group is recognized by the United Nations Environment Programme and United Nations Convention to Combat Desertification for its contributions to the development of anti-desertification and ecological restoration technologies in China (PR Newswire, 2015). In addition, the initial fund of USD4.8 billion was supported by several big investment conglomerates from China which are eager to invest in anti-desertification industry globally. This is a good example of public-private partnership that could bring about the advancement of green technologies world-wide where they are most needed. In fact, desertification and land degradation is a common problem along the economic corridors. This problem is especially bad in Kyrgyzstan, Mongolia, Pakistan and Egypt. If regular infrastructure projects of energy, mining, oil pipelines and railways advance without ecological considerations, this will exacerbate existing land erosion further and create transboundary environmental security risks (Qin, 2016). China is aware of these risks as it deals with them domestically and stands to lose directly from environmental degradation in BRI countries.

During Second BRI Forum in April 2019, China pledged to reform the BRI, including placing emphasis on "high quality" green and clean projects that would be inclusive, market-driven and sustainable. The BRI allows China to showcase its efforts and methods in handling and overcoming many of these environmental episodes in time and promotes and strengthens its environmental legislation, and national and regional policies. With good management, the BRI can act as a catalyst to spur China's sustainability efforts and develop a framework for responsible development, environmental and social assessments domestically and globally. The BRI provides ample opportunities for environmental stewardship by China and thus sets a good example to create an impetus and assist other countries to achieve their sustainable goals, achieving economic growth alongside environmental management. Essentially the BRI countries could gain much from consulting, learning and working with China. Overall, BRI potentially provides a coordinated environmental and economic development, achieving green transformation of the regional economies.

36.2.4.2 Health Silk Road (HSR)

The HSR was conceived in 2016 alongside the establishment of the Healthy China 2030 programme, though its concept can be traced back to 2015, under the "people-to-people exchanges" component of BRI which called for international health cooperation. In the BRI policy document, eight areas of priority for health cooperation were outlined. These include the creation of information exchange mechanisms for coordinated pandemic responses, the built-up of capacities in the form of hospitals, education programmes and exchange of expertise and the provision of medical aid to lacking BRI countries among others.

The definition of HSR activities and its scope of activities and aid are not clearly defined. It should also be noted that many developments and initiatives launched under the banner of HSR are actually a continuation of China's health diplomacy, which has been established even prior to HSR.

During the outbreak of COVID-19, some of the transport networks and infrastructure that has been laid by BRI were utilised to deliver medical aid and supplies to countries in need. Despite its messy handling of the outbreak at the start, Beijing has mobilized impressive amounts of Chinese aid, in the form of medical items and antivirus experience, to other hotspots and the vulnerable regions in the health crisis (Alizila, 2020). For many countries, the overwhelming surge in cases exposed the vulnerabilities of their healthcare system and public health infrastructure. China's investments in healthcare could potentially bridge this gap while introducing health-tech that could increase efficiency.

There is a symbiotic relationship between HSR and BRI, with the physical infrastructure and enhanced connectivity granted by BRI providing the infrastructure network for efficient delivery of aid and enhancing working relationship on the healthcare front intergovernmentally. Rather than a new geopolitical agenda, the HSR is an emerging diplomatic initiative for promoting health cooperation in a world increasingly threatened by new and resurgent infectious diseases and which needs a coordinated build-up of healthcare capacities.

36.2.4.3 Digital Silk Road (DSR)

Digital infrastructure is becoming increasingly crucial to modern economies. The arrival of faster networks, cheaper sensors, and the proliferation of connected devices bring about new complexities, risks to address and business opportunities. The potential for growth in the developing world is vast. Asia and Africa, where demand for international telecommunication bandwidth is growing fastest, are expected to account for 90% of global population growth through 2050 (Hillman, 2021).

It is no coincidence that many BRI projects have been launched in collaboration with giant Chinese tech companies. While BRI focuses on industrial development and expansion, beyond physical infrastructure, there is the DSR. Technical and industrial development go hand-in-hand to achieve China's interrelated goals of industrial capacity cooperation and Internet-enabled "inclusive globalization" (Shen, 2018). The use of big data, artificial intelligence and the creation of smart cities which can connect the landlocked and developing countries to the global economic is thought to be achieved via DSR (Wang, 2016).

However, tracking the progress of DSR is difficult as the effects are not always observable and have to be tracked using official government announcements and those of states and corporations. Additionally, the broad concepts of BRI can be interpreted as ambiguous or flexible as while there are guiding principles, there is no clear-cut blueprint.

The outbreak of a contagious virus has not only boosted the digital economy (through the implementation of safe-distancing measures and cross-border e-commerce) but also increased demand for digital solutions such as health-monitoring apps and movement, mobility tracking and tracing, with the increase in demand for such tools come the demand for telecommunication and digital infrastructure.

There are opportunities aplenty for the emergence of full digital value chains under DSR Starting from ICT companies to e-commerce platforms, including high-tech firms that are well established throughout the BRI geography such as Huawei, Alibaba and Tencent. It is a natural fit for Chinese tech companies, e.g., Alibaba's DingTalk, Tencent's WeChat Work and Huawei's WeLink to bid for market share outside of China.

Moving forward, the DSR will be the main priority for China's BRI cooperation with some of the announced initiatives, including the Global Initiative on Data Security.[3]

36.3 The NIMBY challenge

36.3.1 Characteristics of NIMBY facilities, NIMBY syndrome and its occurrence in BRI

Industrial and development projects are necessary for development and growth; however, their construction could also burden the local communities where they are not only situated with varying negative externalities, energy plants, transport infrastructure and facilities but also associated with infrastructure arising from labour influx in places of construction. While the general public enjoys the benefits brought about by the project, the local residents and immediate neighbourhood must face the dis-amenities of these NIMBY facilities. The situation of NIMBY facilities hence results in an asymmetric distribution of the costs and benefits involved. A NIMBY project could easily be approved of using CBA by manipulating the accounting stance (whether local, regional or national), which results in the locals having to sacrifice their welfare for the benefit of the greater population. Those who live in NIMBY neighbourhoods and suffer these negative externalities directly are also unlikely to be compensated as evaluated by the Kaldor-Hicks criterion or undercompensated by the federal government.

Unlike in the past, affected residents in developing countries are no longer indifferent and are finding it difficult to be heard amongst exchanges between large corporations and governments. Greater education levels, higher literacy rates and more platforms for widespread information dissemination have allowed NIMBY Syndrome to grow stronger in communities, and digital media has allowed individuals to share their criticisms online, sparking more social contention. Public distrust in the government and private corporations are common, especially in countries that lack transparency or with corruption. Individuals might be sceptical of the efficiency of the project and whether touted benefits will truly accrue to locals, others may take reference to previous projects and question the management and operation of the proposed facility by the local government. An example of such a project would be the Myitkyina Economic Development Zone (MEDZ), between China and the Kachin State Government. Part of the land used for the project overlaps with an area used by locals to plant crops, locals were uninformed of the project and their concerns on the ownership of their land went unanswered. The president of the Kachin Democratic Party, Gumgrawng Awng Hkam, said that an alliance of Kachin parties will oppose the MEDZ if there is a lack of transparency and opposed by local residents (Nan, 2019).

36.3.2 Relevance, importance to BRI countries

BRI countries are estimated to include 60% of the world's population, 40% of total land area, 30% of global GDP and 55% of total carbon emissions. The impact that BRI projects will have is significant and extensive with possible long-term effects impacting both the environment and human development alike. In the worst case, the constructed infrastructure could be unsustainable, pollutive and damaging with long-lasting effects on both the environment and communities in the area and transboundary negative externalities. As such, it is necessary to make informed decisions and have social and environmental safeguards.

The majority of BRI projects fit the criteria to be classified as NIMBYs. They involve the public sector, generate non-exclusive externalities and are located in remote areas. There are also conflicts between outside resident's demands for quicker responses for project siting approval and local resident's opposition. This is especially true for pollutive energy projects, such as coal-fired power plants. Much of the promised green reform of BRI has yet to be seen; most past and ongoing projects do not adhere to sustainable development goals. BRI mostly caters to needs of developing countries and will therefore continue to favour conventional energy sources.

For example, while the world turns to greener, renewable energy, Balkan states rely on coal-powered energy production which has grown out of favour with institutions such as the World Bank and European Union. Its pollutive energy projects are financed by China, one of which is the Ugljevik III, a coal-fired power station in Bosnia that is expected to emit fumes that would degrade the already poor health of the residents there. Local backlash is strong as the existing high levels of SO_2 emissions are already driving higher respiratory cancer incidence. High health and environmental costs also mean these projects are scrutinised by locals and watchdogs alike who expect accountability for the potential hazards through well-defined safety standards and assessments and clear waste management protocol. However, the lack of transparency and the red flags raised by independent investigators have not helped these projects gain favour with the locals. This illustrates a conflict in the countries' desire for facility expansion fuelled growth and local demands for better quality of life or at the very least, mitigation of health costs.

36.3.3 Conflict-resolution instruments

Often, governments adopt a decide-announce-defend (dad) approach in three stages. In stage one, the proposer makes a series of technological choices using engineering analyses, suitability of geographical terrain and geological structures. At this stage, an objective and scientific report is the focus, with little discussion of potential local sentiments. In stage two, the proposer announces the site and type of NIMBY facility to be constructed, and in stage three, the proposer defends the choice of site, often resulting in local disgruntlement and opposition.

The economics literature suggests that active public involvement together with mitigation and compensation actions during a siting decision process would be the most effective strategy overall. Socially efficient compensation systems could also be achieved through different forms of auction mechanism which would site a NIMBY facility in a community which bears the lowest social costs. There are six commonly suggested conflict-resolution instruments used to address the siting problem of NIMBY facilities. They are (1) local regulations such as bylaws and zoning requirements, (2) licenses and permits, (3) compulsory acquisition of land, with market compensation, (4) public hearings and environmental impact assessments (EIA), (5) mitigation policies and (6) general compensation for immediate local residents (Quah and Tan, 1999).

36.3.3.1 Local regulations, zoning and bylaws

Local governments have the authority to impose certain bylaws and regulations pertaining to environment and land use. Zoning involves the division of land into districts with different regulations. These regulations are usually based on a master plan designed to protect and promote the health and safety of the local population.

While it is seen as an effective regulatory measure in the public sector to promote efficient land use, zoning requirements in the form of legal constraints of land use, rights and entitlements are not very practical to deal with NIMBYs in BRI countries. This is due to the lack of institutional expertise and capacity in these developing countries to design or implement complex master plans, let alone the political stability needed for continuous enforcement of them. It has been criticized for dilettantism and bureaucracy as zoning planners are unable to account fully for the entire complex array of land use conflict. There is hence a need for flexibility for rezoning but a balance is necessary as over-flexibility defeats the purpose of regulations. Additionally, zoning does not eliminate the negative externalities generated by the facility on the surroundings and ultimately and does not protect nor compensate residents of less favourably zoned areas.

When megaprojects involve several states and authorities, local government regulations may become ineffective. Land could end up rezoned and special permits are given when political pressure is applied. Infrastructure projects affecting several countries require more extensive strategies and would necessitate the developmental goals of participating countries to converge.

36.3.3.2 Licenses and permits

Licensing and obtainment of permits require considerable documentation and at times comprehensive surveys and evaluation lists which could delay the project. Even though it presents the opportunity for public hearing and involvement, it has a similar issue as zoning, being difficult to implement in countries with weaker legal institutions and corruption in tendering processes.

36.3.3.3 Compulsory acquisition of land with market compensation

Compulsory acquisition of land where private owners are compensated with market values for their land is another widely used conflict-resolution instrument, but may, however, result in welfare losses to private landowners. Compulsory acquisition recognises the need for the legal-state machinery to compel reluctant landowners to dispose of their land for a public purpose. It is also used to prevent unjust enrichment on the part of private landowners who are only prepared to give up their land for a price several times higher than the market value.

It must be emphasised that compulsory land acquisition can only be justified if the public benefits outweigh the private costs inclusive of the losses to dispossessed landowners. The rationale of paying market compensation is that the monetary sum awarded to the expropriated landowners would enable them to purchase a similar property and, consequently, be made no worse off. Society can then make use of the land resource for whatever public purpose it has in mind that would confer a positive net benefit, thereby increasing social welfare.

However, in most compulsory acquisitions, property owners feel real losses as their preferred price often exceeds the law-appointed price, making them worse off. Also, it is well-known that land, unlike most goods and services traded in the market, is not identical. Hence, the implicit assumption behind market compensation, the availability of near or perfect substitutes, is unrealistic. The psychological costs of a relocation to a different community are uncompensated by disturbance damage awards. Insufficient compensation payments may also result in the over-implementation of public projects and market compensation may result in undervaluation of the land.

This conflict-resolution mechanism can be highly efficient if a method can be devised to compensate dispossessed landowners for their actual losses incurred. Negative externalities imposed by an environmentally noxious facility can be internalised by also compulsorily purchasing adjacent land from its owners and paying actual loss compensation. A buffer zone could hence be established. More conscious efforts should be made to obtain property with compensation payments that are agreeable to both sides: bid pricing from alternative locations may be made known to landowners so that unreasonableness and unwarranted enrichment can be minimised. A value-to-owner compensation standard based on compensating or equivalent variation may also be applied (Knetsch and Borcherding, 1979).

Some governments in BRI countries have already used similar methods with mixed success. For example, series of dam projects in Cambodia, such as Lower Se San 2 Dam, which is a completed hydropower dam project under BRI, was inherently beneficial for Cambodia's energy grid but involved a forced relocation of local residents to specially built settlements and adverse environmental impacts locally. Despite the relocation of removed settlers, the dissent remained due to inadequate compensation.

36.3.3.4 Public hearings and environmental impact assessments (EIA)

International lending agencies such as the Asian Development Bank and World Bank increasingly require explicit attention be given to the environmental impact of proposed projects and be included in loan applications (especially after 1992 Earth Summit). During the process of accounting, measuring and valuing environmental impacts of projects, opportunities are provided for informal public hearings, review and comments from professionals and various interest groups. Assessments can be improved further by infusing them with information on public attitudes and the use of more generally applied CBA techniques to aspects beyond the environment (e.g., more local public opinion surveys and forums). These environmental impact statements would allow potential environmental damage to be assessed and flagged out early, so that mitigation of the damages, modification, relocation or rescale of the proposed project may be considered). Coupled with mitigation measures and/or compensation schemes, EIA may lead to better acceptance of a facility by the local residents.

China vowed to implement its own environmental standards in April 2019 for future BRI projects. The practical realization of this is yet to be seen while current and planned projects will continue to operate under environmentally sub-optimal standards. The main limitation of EIA is that it is time-consuming and requires money due to the large preparatory work required, often needing a handful of professionals. The report is intended to be comprehensive and hence multi-disciplinary necessitating the participation of economists, geologists and so on which could result in delays. This method is also harder to implement in developing countries with weak institutional quality and civil rights as any evaluation would be affected by political interests rather than independent inquiries and public hearings.

36.3.3.5 Mitigation policy

Measures to mitigate environmental degradation and negative externalities are commonly seen as a useful conflict-resolution instrument in facility siting. These mitigation measures usually involve some redesigning of the facility or improved monitoring and decision procedures to reduce actual or perceived risks arising from the facility. Such measures may include the provision of a sealed covering for a sewage treatment facility (to reduce unpleasant odours and air pollution), placing of reinforced materials around chemical storage tanks (to reduce chances of a leakage) or installation of monitoring devices within and around the facility.

Apart from those above which involve some kind of engineering or technological options, there are also mitigation measures which aim to regulate the operation of the facility through local residents' participation by way of their representation on the facility's governing board. This type of institutional mitigation measure is useful if the facility is primarily of the hazardous kind, as in the case of nuclear power stations and toxic chemical plants, for they represent efforts to reduce the level of mistrust between the facility operator and the host community. These measures also aim to raise the level of comprehension among local residents as to the actual statistical risks of accidents and the measures that are being taken to prevent them (Gregory and Kunreuther, 1990).

Mitigation measures do more for the acceptability of a NIMBY facility than using compensation alone in some cases. Many economists see mitigation measures as being more effective than compensation as they seek to redress the real problems posed by the facility. Risk mitigating factors also clarify and change the unfavourable risk perceptions of local residents. Feedback from host residents can hence be seen as internalised by project planners, increasing confidence and support for the facility.

Still, mitigation measures are limited as they cannot deal with all impacts effectively such as health risks in the longer term, loss of property values and damage to the natural landscape. Mitigation measures are more suited towards problems such as traffic congestion, pollution, crime containment and reduction in renewable resources. Compensation measures should be paired with mitigation measures to resolve the issues caused by NIMBY facilities.

36.3.3.6 General compensation

Compensation measures emphasize cost sharing and apportion of benefits from the output of a NIMBY facility to those who are directly affected by its construction or operation. Compensation measures can be monetary or in kind or both and may involve several mechanisms such as estimated social costs, auctions and tenders. Payment vehicles include subsidies, lump-sum transfers, reduction in property taxes, tax rebates and/or user fees from the NIMBY facility proposed. In-kind compensation includes free disposal services, replacement of affected habitat and provision of emergency vehicles.

However, for compensation to be effective, the risks associated with the facility must be mitigated early in the process, otherwise, monetary compensation may come across as bribery. It is tough to determine the appropriate magnitude and manner of compensation for local communities. For hazardous facilities, communities would perceive compensation as a form of bribe to accept health-threatening dis-amenities and as a result lead to stronger resistance and disapproval (called the "bribe effect").

There is an issue of equity: in which attempts to address siting problems result in a biased concentration of such facilities in impoverished neighbourhoods. People may view health and safety as inherent inalienable rights and would refuse to trade them for money. Monetary compensation would also be inequitable as it is likely that in more affluent countries, meanwhile those who are lower income are disadvantaged when it comes to spillover effects as the rich have better legal protection over their property, wider choice of neighbourhoods to live in and more resources to form an opposition (Mishan, 1981a, 1981b, 1993). There is also an intra-equity problem where compensation may not be based on proximity to the facility. While a community may accept a facility given the appropriate compensation, it is those who reside in the immediate vicinity of the facility that bear the greatest magnitude of the negative externalities that arise from its situation and operation. These immediate residents may hence be undercompensated as not all parties in the community are equally affected by the facility. Similarly, for fringe communities who reside downstream of the host community when the generated externality is air or water pollution. These fringe residents bear the impact of these externalities generated, yet they neither have a say in the negotiation process nor receive the compensation for it. In the case of environmental degradation, the impact the facility and infrastructures have on the wildlife there may be of value to the larger community as well.

Compensation schemes and economic incentives are plausible in garnering support and acceptance for low-risk NIMBY facilities but less so for hazardous ones. It is impossible to compensate an individual for safety, rather, a reduction in perceived risks would be the best way to increase acceptability and ease the worries of local residents. Some BRI projects such as copper minefield in Las Bambas (Peru) in 2016–2021 and gold mine in Solton-Sary (Kyrgyzstan) in 2019 failed to reconcile as local communities continuously denied monetary compensations from Chinese mining companies.

36.3.3.7 Compensation auction, auction mechanisms with sealed bids

A "compensation auction" is used to assess and address the actual and perceived asymmetry brought by the siting of the facility where it is assumed that all bidders; valuations are independently and identically distributed. Given that the assumptions of compensation auctions are met, and conducted efficiently, the transaction costs in terms of delays and local opposition would be significantly reduced. Instead of hiring policy consultants and using a compensation formula crafted by bureaucrats, auction schemes will instead draw from communities' own valuation of their own intangible and tangible costs.

One simple compensation scheme (called scheme I for reference) calls for local governments to submit sealed bids indicating the minimum compensation sum that they would be willing to accept from a higher level government or quasi-government body to locate an environmentally noxious facility within their vicinity. The bids are then compared, and the facility will be built in that jurisdiction which has submitted the lowest bid. This is consistent with the idea that efficiency is attained with the least cost host provider. Each community's optimal bid will always be greater than the absolute valuation of siting the facility and hence the winning bidder will always receive a net gain from hosting the facility, a result that corroborates with that of Kunreuther and Kleindorfer (1986). In the event that bids for facility are too high, the plans should be shelved, reduced in scale or rebid in a new proposed site.

As the number of communities involved in the bidding increases, the optimum bid of each community approaches its true social cost. However, it is highly likely that the community specifying the smallest benefit-sharing package will be relatively poor, and since poorer communities normally require a smaller package to improve their welfare over the status quo, this may be perceived as unfair by some, even if volunteering communities view it as eminently fair.

Another compensation scheme (scheme II), might call for all municipalities to submit sealed bids, similar to scheme I. However, the compensation is to be paid by all the remaining non-host communities. Hence if a community is not selected to host the facility, they will have to pay a tax to the hosting community as compensation. As the willingness-to-pay value is independent from willingness-to-accept value, this auction mechanism is free of coalition. The reasoning is that the imposed negative externalities on the host community should be shouldered by all communities since the output of said facility is enjoyed by all. Like in scheme I, the selected host community would be the one that offers to accept the facility the least compensation sum. Such a "compensation auction" method would allow one to assess the actual and perceived external diseconomy brought about by the siting of the facility on the local residents to ensure that social costs were minimised in the selection for the optimal location, and if conducted systematically, transaction costs are reduced that arise from project delay due to local opposition.

An assumption made by these "compensation auctions" is that the local government knows how to estimate the actual and perceived welfare loss on behalf of their residents and their own municipalities. Valuation of certain non-market goods, aspects such as social pollution, aesthetic nuisance and other social costs might be difficult to price. This hence would require the establishment of an agreed-upon structure and methodology for environment impact assessments and CBA between the locals and state government. An arbitration compensation board may be set up to resolve disputes, whose decisions are final.

The potential downside of schemes I and II is that they may induce strategic bidding on part of municipalities. In order to avoid hosting the proposed noxious facility, they may place high bids. Likewise, there may be municipalities bidding more than their social costs in hopes of gaining from the compensation in the event they are selected as the host community. However, at least in scheme II, there is some element of restraint as a high bid is less likely to be selected and the municipality would have to pay for the social costs on the selected host.

Schemes I and II can take on different bidding formats as well such as first price sealed bid and second price sealed bid. Even though scheme II is able to restrain strategically higher bids. Nonetheless, experimental findings suggest that scheme II is not efficient in the siting of NIMBY facilities because winning bidders are often not the ones with the lowest social costs.

Even though there was no exact application of "compensation auctions" in practice, its transparency and sound basis compels it to be listed among other conflict-resolution methods as an option or in combination when the situation allows. Such as when there are many potential spots for a NIMBY facility across region or within a country. Benefits from key infrastructure like railroads or energy grid go well beyond one country's interests. If China could build up a unified transparent framework to resolve NIMBY conflicts on such scale, auctions might one day become a way to resolve these conflicts. The big number of projects and myriad of affected communities urge BRI to form a structured approach to conflict resolutions.

36.4 Cost-benefit analysis and BRI

36.4.1 Adapting CBA to developing countries and evaluation of suitability of valuation techniques

CBA provides a comprehensive framework that could be used by policymakers to evaluate the relative contributions of projects by accounting for tangible and intangible benefits and costs in order to maximize social welfare. Its framework for systematic evaluation based on economic principles would allow one to consider the standing from China and the whole region. A comprehensive analysis would allow environmental, social and economic concerns to be addressed from the start and mitigation and management manoeuvres to be established from the initial stages of BRI forward.

It is necessary to be cognizant of the differences between developing and developed countries which might require adaptation of the conventional CBA framework. This is important because most BRI participants are from developing countries dealing with the evolving financing framework of BRI financial institutions. The fundamentals of CBA are the same across: CBA must be complete, valuations must reflect the true social costs and benefits, time, uncertainty, and equity must be considered, double counting must be avoided and transfer payments should be ignored. However, differences in financial, labour and goods market and income inequality must be addressed and adapted. These differences are elaborated below.

The financial markets of developing countries are underdeveloped and less transparent than those of developed countries. Private banks hold greater market power resulting in higher interest rate and risk premium. Market power is shared amongst the big banks resulting in oligopolistic banks. Profiteering by private banks in developing countries result in interest rates being higher than the true opportunity costs of capital. Should the social discount rate for developing countries be calculated using the market interest rate as the opportunity cost of capital, the result is a higher social discount rate than is appropriate for measurement leading to bias in favour of projects that yield short-term benefit and long-term costs (Quah, 2017). An example would be coal plants that boost economic growth but are costly in the long run in the form of higher disease incidence and burden on the healthcare. It is hence necessary to make a downward adjustment to both the opportunity cost rate and the social time preference rate used in cost-benefit studies in developing countries. Additionally, populations in developing countries have shorter lifespans and lower incomes, possibly resulting in higher preference for current consumption as compared to future. These shorter time preferences would translate to higher social discount rate, ceteris paribus.

CBA requires items to be valued at their opportunity costs, for labour, its associated cost is the wage rate. Unlike in developed countries, the labour markets in developing countries differ since a large proportion of the workforce are employed in agriculture and/or employed in name and given a token wage despite making no marginal contributions to the production process, a practice known as a disguised unemployment. In this case, when the worker is moved to a government project, the cost associated is his wage, however, in his previous employment where he does not produce output, there is no opportunity cost as his previous employer does not lose anything from his departure, resulting in an overestimation of costs. For example, family farming businesses often employ their own family members who, while receiving a salary, may not be contributing to the production. A similar case happens if government hires more workers than needed to tackle unemployment in a country. There are also labour costs that are unaccounted for in the form of household production of those who are homemakers or contribute to production in terms of household chores, as there is no wage associated with household production, the opportunity costs for this group are calculated as zero. As a result, wages in developing countries might not be true reflections of the opportunity costs of labour and the calculation of the Value of Statistical Life (VoSL) based on wage differentials may not be accurate. Minimum wages might not be useful in estimating labour costs due to the lower labour market regulations in developing countries which result in informal markets where wages might be lower.

Likewise, the goods markets in developing countries are less efficient due to larger information asymmetry, and there could be higher instances of "lemon" markets in which buyers have to pick from a poor selection of sellers. Prices of goods and services might not truly reflect the value of the goods due to price distortions from taxes, subsidies, protectionism policies and other government market interventions. At the front end of the supply chain, this results in distorted prices of direct inputs. For non-market goods, a revealed preference approach might be used to determine the valuation of the good. In developed countries where the goods markets are considered efficient, intangibles and externalities are valued relatives in relation to consumption through a revealed preference approach. However, for developing countries, this approach is not as credible as the goods market does not produce prices that match the quality characteristics of the good and hence might result in incomplete values of externalities and non-market costs. For example, rations create price distortions and the demand curve obtained through typical techniques would not be accurate. To correct this, shadow prices might be necessary (though for tradeable goods fluctuations in currency would make it difficult to determine shadow prices).

These differing conditions confer the need to adapt the conventional valuation techniques of CBA. We evaluate the broad categories of techniques, including the (1) revealed preference approach, (2) stated preference approach, (3) benefit-transfer method and a novel approach and (4) paired comparison method or damaged schedules approach.

36.4.1.1 Revealed preference approach

Revealed preferences seek to estimate the willingness to pay (WTP) of an individual on non-market goods based on implicit trades of the good. Some techniques that fall under this approach include hedonic pricing method and travel cost method. The former is usually used for real estate prices, in which there are implicit variables such as environmental characteristics that are included in the price. However, developing countries may not have the efficient and responsive property market that is necessary for this method to be employed effectively and barriers to mobility may be greater in developing countries where ancestral land is passed down or income tied to a plot of land. The travel cost method allows one to obtain an approximate demand function for amenities that do not have a direct cost associated with them, from there, one can estimate the benefit of the site through a calculation of consumer surplus. However, these approaches require strong assumptions such as rationality and perfect information and mobility which are unlikely to hold in developing countries. Markets of developing countries are largely incomplete and imperfect and suffer from data insufficiency and distorted data. Lack of communication networks and platforms prevent agents from having perfect information.

36.4.1.2 Stated preference approach

The stated preference approach directly asks individuals for their WTP, a method that falls under this category is the Contingent Valuation Method (CVM). However, they are often subject to behavioural bias such as framing effects, status quo bias, loss aversion and sunk cost fallacy.

Loss aversion is shown through the difference in the median WTP and the willingness to accept which arise from people valuing losses much more than gains. Where there are losses (such as environmental damage or degradation from a neutral standpoint), willingness to accept (WTA) would be more acceptable. The usual practice globally would be to use an amount lesser than what people would pay to preserve it (WTP) but this could lead to an understatement of values and can lead to bad choices that compromise public welfare and unwarranted deterioration of the environment. A different method would call for the clustering of goods and conduct a literature review on the magnitude of WTP and WTA for these groups to adjust WTP for each cluster of goods using a reference discrepancy table.

While behavioural economics reveal that individuals consider sunk costs in their decision-making, CBA does not. However, sunk costs would have implications for infrastructure expansion (or demolition and replacement of infrastructure).

These biases are likely to be greater in developing countries where survey experiences are limited and awareness of these fallacies is low. Methodological biases such as the confusion between WTP and the ability to pay may affect the responses as well. Both of these biases are also likely to be exacerbated by a lack of trained interviewers.

36.4.1.3 Benefit-transfer method

In developing countries, a lack of indigenous studies (e.g., VoSL) and poor data availability hampers good CBA. The benefit-transfer method transfers values from foreign studies to the local contexts and is advantageous as it relatively inexpensive and less time-consuming than conducting a new primary study. This is conducted through a review of existing studies for quality and applicability (e.g., similarities of health effects, in population demographics and whether the differences in contexts can be adjusted for). When estimates are transferred, necessary adjustments should be made, transfers may be based on the results of a single study or multiple studies and uncertainty needs to be addressed through sensitivity or probabilistic analysis and the implication of uncertainty needs to be discussed. Even so, this method has its disadvantages as well, such as the fact that it hinges on good judgement of analyst and the need to account for cultural differences and are likely to be less accurate than well-designed and implemented studies. Between developed and developing countries, one needs to account for differences in resource endowments, facilities and amenities such as the availability of medical care which may affect the valuation of health and life.

36.4.1.4 *Paired comparison method/damaged schedules approach*

The paired comparison method does not require the strong assumptions of the revealed preference approaches and can be combined with CVM to provide monetary valuations. It directly addresses the population and effects of concern, unlike benefit-transfer method and comparisons could be between market goods and non-market goods (environmental goods). The procedure of the paired comparison method is as follows, participants make discrete binary choices between pairs in a survey and the preference score of a good is then derived and its rank is obtained from variance stable rank method, this method allows for the measurement of intensity of preferences by calculating the proportion of times an item is preferred.

To sum, the primary weakness of CBA is that it is efficiency-oriented and may neglect accounting for equity, which will need to be considered separately which may be a greater problem for developing countries where income inequity may be more severe. While weights have been applied in other areas, they may not be the ideal solution due to the technical issue of weight determination and its possibility of manipulation and abuse. A qualitative checklist of how the rich or poor are affected by each benefit and cost item should be used.

While the fundamentals of CBA do not vary between developed and developing countries, the technique required might differ. These adaptions of techniques are due to constraints in market efficiency, education literacy and time preferences of developing countries which necessitate a different approach. Every CBA valuation technique has its relative advantages and disadvantages hence care and caution must be exercised when choosing the appropriate valuation technique. CBA remains a useful framework for guiding developing countries to allocate their resources optimally.

36.5 New competing initiatives and future of BRI

In 2015, Japan announced PQI which was designed to address quality-control and governance risks associated with BRI. Its conceptual scope went beyond normal infrastructure and included hospitals and energy security frameworks similarly to multifaceted platform of BRI. PQI emerged as a response to BRI and compelled BRI to improve.

Likewise, BDN formed by the United States, Japan and Australia in 2019 is mainly focused on financial transparency, sustainable development and equity. It is conceptualized as a primarily assessing, evaluating, and coordinating institution while funding is drawn from public-private partnership. OECD had committed to supporting BDN in 2021 (OECD, 2021).

European Union announced its own upcoming global infrastructure bill as recent as in 2021. Many EU members are participating in BRI which probably compelled EU to embark on its own global infrastructure initiative. EU very recently announced the name of its connectivity initiative – Global Gateway. It focuses on climate change, development of democratic institutions, and human rights in the context of infrastructure investments. Otherwise, as a younger transboundary infrastructure plan, it is still shaping its framework.

The Asian Development Bank (ADB, 2017) estimated an investment need of around USD26 trillion until 2030 globally, and those existing investment efforts will not be able to meet this need. China's infrastructure projects will hence bolster the financing of Asia's infrastructure needs (Organisation for Economic Co-operation and Development [OECD], 2018). Countries in economic transition, such as those in Eastern Europe require modern infrastructure which China offers as part of its investment projects. For example, Serbia's needs for good railways and modern transport infrastructure that have cargo potential (DW Documentary, 2019), which is vital to a landlocked country, will be met by China's megaprojects in the region and in the country. The new EU's initiative is likely to be a competitive alternative for BRI in the Eastern Europe since it is a strategically important region for EU.

The infrastructure needs of the emerging and transitioning economies are here to stay and this competition as well as cooperation between global initiatives will only bolster and transform future economy. These fundamental shifts will go far beyond the physical infrastructure and economic growth and will include built up of digital security, export of technologies as well as climate change-focused cooperation. The US–China trade war and COVID-19 incentivize China to adopt a more collaborative approach in dealing with partners and other stakeholders.

The new era of global infrastructure plans is coming. The many challenges of growing NIMBY Syndrome, difficulties with project evaluation and application of CBA in developing countries are all the same for BRI, BDN and Global Gateway. Perhaps, the mutual competition and cooperation will promote structurization and innovation in the use of conflict-resolution instruments as well as in valuation techniques. The emerging literature on Comparative Economics of Transboundary Infrastructure Initiatives is yet to enrich and intellectualize this New Research Agenda.

The Silk Road is still very much alive from ancient times to contemporary and it continues to facilitate and motivate the grand exchange of goods, technologies and cultures. It is only that we are now living in a much more complex world with digitalization, climate change and public health risks caused by globalization. BRI was already evolving to address criticisms by giving a greater emphasis on sustainable technologies, creating framework for digital risks and more. The COVID-19 pandemic will only accelerate this evolution of BRI into BRI 2.0. The advent of competing initiative is only welcomed since it will bolster improvements and quality controls as well as provision of viable alternatives for participating countries with differing needs.

Notes

1 The authors thank Ms Dara Ng for her research assistance in this chapter.
2 It should be noted that while cultural projects under BRI do not attract as much attention as the large-scale infrastructure construction, these cultural cooperation are also integral to the concept of BRI and important for BRI researchers. Examples include collaboration in movie-production, building of museums and schools and student exchange and scholarships which are proliferating alongside roads, factories and digital networks in a holistic fashion (Winter, 2016).
3 https://www.fmprc.gov.cn/mfa_eng/zxxx_662805/t1841513.shtml

References

ADB. (2017). *Meeting Asia's Infrastructure Needs.* Asian Development Bank, Japan. Retrieved from https://www.adb.org/sites/default/files/publication/227496/special-report-infrastructure.pdf

Alizila. (2020, April 15). Factsheet: Jack Ma Foundation and Alibaba Foundation's Global Donations and Efforts to Combat COVID-19. *Alizila News from Alibaba.* https://www.alizila.com/factsheet-jack-ma-foundation-alibaba-foundations-coronavirus-donations-and-efforts/

Asia for Educators, C. U. (n.d.). *Mongols in World History: Asia for Educators.* Mongols in World History. Retrieved December 3, 2021, from http://afe.easia.columbia.edu/mongols/history/history6_a.htm

Bruce-Lockhart, A. (2017, June 26). *China's $900 Billion New Silk Road. What You Need to Know.* World Economic Forum. Retrieved December 4, 2021, from https://www.weforum.org/agenda/2017/06/china-new-silk-road-explainer/

DW Documentary. (2019). *The New Silk Road, Part 1: From China to Pakistan* [Video file]. Retrieved from https://www.youtube.com/watch?v=cUxw9Re-Z-E

Friedland, R. and Rheinstrom, D. (n.d.). *The Silk Road.* Khan Academy. Retrieved December 3, 2021, from https://www.khanacademy.org/humanities/world-history/ancient-medieval/silk-road/a/the-silk-road

Gill, I., Lall, S.V. and Lebrand, M. (2019, June 21). *Winners and Losers Along China's Belt and Road.* Brookings. Retrieved from https://www.brookings.edu/blog/future-development/2019/06/21/winners-and-losers-along-chinas-belt-and-road/

Global Times. (2021, August 9). China's Exports to B&R Countries Show Robust Growth Despite COVID-19 Challenge by Xie Jun and Shen Weiduo. *Global Times*, China. Retrieved from https://www.globaltimes.cn/page/202108/1230967.shtml

Gregory, R. and Kunreuther, H. (1990). Successful Siting Incentives. *Journal of Civil Engineering, 60*, 73–75.

Hillman, J.E. (2021, February 9). Competing with China's Digital Silk Road. *Centre for Strategic and International Studies.* https://www.csis.org/analysis/competing-chinas-digital-silk-road

Hyun, S.B. (2018). *China's BRI and Cross-Border Economic Cooperation: Status and Implications for Korea.* Sejong-si, Korea: Korea Institute for International Economic Policy Opinions. Republic of Korea. http://hdl.handle.net/11540/9409

Knetsch, J. and Borcherding, T. (1979). *Expropriation of Private Property and the Basis for Compensation.* University of Toronto Law J. 39, 237–252.

Kunreuther, H. and Kleindorfer, P.R. (1986). A Sealed-Bid Auction Mechanism for Siting Noxious Facilities. *American Economic Review, 76*, 2, 295–299. https://EconPapers.repec.org/RePEc:aea:aecrev:v:76:y:1986:i:2:p:295-99

Meng, J. (2015, March 9). *First PE Fund for Green Silk Road Launched in Beijing.* China.org.cn. Retrieved from http://www.china.org.cn/environment/2015-03/09/content_34997671.htm

Millward, J.A. (2013). *The Silk Road: A Very Short Introduction.* New York, NY: Oxford University Press.

Mishan, E.J. (1981a). *Economic Efficiency and Social Welfare: Selected Essays on Fundamental Aspects of the Economic Theory of Social Welfare.* London and Boston, MA: Allen & Unwin.

Mishan, E.J. (1981b). *Introduction to Normative Economics.* New York: Oxford University Press.

Mishan, E.J. (1993). *The Costs of Economic Growth.* London: Weidenfeld & Nicolson.

Nan, L. (2019, April 9). *Kachin Locals in the Dark Over China-Backed Industrial Zone Plan.* The Irrawaddy. https://www.irrawaddy.com/news/burma/kachin-locals-dark-china-backed-industrial-zone-plan.html

Nedopil, C. (2021). *Countries of the Belt and Road Initiative.* Shanghai, Green Finance and Development Center. FISF Fudan University. www.greenfdc.org

OECD. (2018). China's Belt and Road Initiative in the Global Trade, Investment and Finance Landscape. OECD Business and Finance Outlook.

OECD. (2021). *Towards a Global Certification Framework for Quality Infrastructure Investment: Private Sector and Civil Society Perspectives on the Blue Dot Network – Highlights.* OECD.

Pingshuan, X. (2006). The Merchants of Chang'an in the Sui and Tang Dynasties (Abstract). Frontiers of History in China, *1*(2), 254–275. https://doi.org/10.1007/s11462-006-0005-1

Pitakdumrongkit, K. (2019). *Economics and Trade Impact of the Silk Road Economic Belt Initiative.* Panorama: Insights into Asian and European Affairs, 47–58.

PR Newswire. (2015, March 23). *Elion Joining in RE100.* Retrieved from https://www.prnasia.com/story/86519-1.shtml

Press Trust of India. (2021, December 1). India-China Trade Deficit Stands at $30 Billion during Apr-Sept. *Business Standard*. Retrieved from https://www.business-standard.com/article/economy-policy/india-china-trade-deficit-stands-at-30-billion-during-apr-sept-121120101327_1.html

Qin, L. (2016, September 10). *China's New Silk Road Could Expand Asia's Deserts*. The Diplomat. Retrieved from https://thediplomat.com/2016/09/chinas-new-silk-road-could-expand-asias-deserts/

Quah, E. (2017). Using Cost-Benefit Analysis in Developed and Developing Countries: Is It the Same? *Annual Macroeconomic Review.*

Quah, E. and Tan, K.C. (1999). Economics of NIMBY Syndrome: Siting Decisions. *Environment and Planning C: Government and Policy, 16*, 255–264.

Savic, B. and Shira, D. (2021). BRI Countries' Exports to China Surge as Global Producer Prices Boom. *Silk Road Briefing*. Retrieved from https://www.silkroadbriefing.com/news/2021/09/16/bri-countries-exports-to-china-surge-as-global-producer-prices-boom/

Shen, H. (2018). Building a Digital Silk Road? Situating the Internet in China's Belt and Road Initiative. *International Journal of Communication*, 12, 19. Retrieved from https://ijoc.org/index.php/ijoc/article/view/8405

UNESCO The Silk Roads Programme. (n.d.). *Did You Know? The Silk Routes of the Mongols.* Retrieved December 3, 2021, from https://en.unesco.org/silkroad/content/did-you-know-silk-routes-mongols

Vaissiere, E.D.L. (2014). Trans-Asian trade, or the silk road: Deconstructed (antiquity, middle ages). In L. Neal (Ed.), *The Rise of Capitalism*, Vol. 1, The Cambridge History of Capitalism. Cambridge: Cambridge University Press, 100–126.

Wang, Y. (2016). Yidaiyilu: Chongsu jingji quanqiuhua huayuquan [The Belt and Road Initiative: Restructuring the Economic Globalization]. *Red Flag Manuscript*, 21.

Winter, T. (2016, March 29). One Belt, One Road, One Heritage: Cultural Diplomacy and the Silk Road. *The Diplomat*. Retrieved from https://thediplomat.com/2016/03/one-belt-one-road-one-heritage-cultural-diplomacy-and-the-silk-road/

Wood, F. (2003). *The Silk Road: Two Thousand Years in the Heart of Asia*. Berkeley: University of California Press.

World Bank. (2019). *Belt and Road Economics: Opportunities and Risks of Transport Corridors*. Washington: World Bank. License: Creative Commons Attribution CC BY 3.0 IGO.

Zou, L. (2018a). Reflections on the Ancient Silk Road. In *The political economy of China's Belt and Road Initiative*. World Scientific, Singapore.

Zou, L. (2018b). *The Political Economy of China's Belt and Road Initiative*. World Scientific, Singapore.

37

FROM ECONOMIC COMPETITION TO THE "ALLIANCE OF VALUES"

Reconstructing a "New World Order" or a "New Cold War"?

Kumiko Haba

AOYAMA GAKUIN UNIVERSITY, SHIBUYA CITY, TOKYO, JAPAN

37.1 Prologue: "Democracy" and authoritarianism: A New Cold War by the "Alliance of Values"?

The United States and Europe currently face the greatest postwar challenges in domestic affairs, diplomacy, universal values, and interests. First, domestic and international forces are urgently recommending updating the universal scheme of freedom, democracy, market economy, and prosperity in Europe and the United States, particularly during the COVID-19 pandemic. Trump's swinging health policy ended with more than 400,000 deaths from COVID-19. However, one year later, in February 2022, during the first year of the Biden government, that numbered more than doubled, with 980,000 deaths and 80 million infections.[1] The situation was not better in the European Union, where 150 million people were infected and nearly 1.7 million died of COVID-19. The political situation continued to be hesitant and demonstrating the merits of regional integration was not possible until now.

Second, East Asia's power – China – has successfully contained the coronavirus and recovered its economy by providing masks, medical devices, and vaccines to developing countries and southeastern Europe to expand its influence.[2] The initial outburst of the COVID-19 pandemic in Wuhan, China, infected nearly 80,000 people and 4,000 people died. However, China prevented the spread of COVID-19 by rapidly implementing a set of measures, including among others blockading cities with infections and using IT and AI technologies to trace infections. In contrast, in the United States and Europe, infections exploded and spread from March 2020 and initially accounted for 80–90% of global infections and deaths (see *Financial Times*, 2021).

The third fundamental issue is the reorganization of the international system. At the June 2021 G7 held in the United Kingdom, President Biden aimed at introducing the post-COVID-19 world order by pursuing the Alliance of Values. Biden considered a complex world

 DOI: 10.4324/9781003144366-43

simply, compared with Wilson and Roosevelt who created the League of Nations and United Nations, including Russia and Asia, but Biden only insisted "Alliance of Values," and it divided the world into two: "Democracy" and Autocracy. He could not integrate the world; he divided the world between their own camp and "enemy camp," and that is why the war happened. But real global world is more complex; therefore, China, India, and African countries do not accept Biden's "Alliance of Value" and China and India form the group of Non-Allied Powers.

Under the banner of the "Alliance," Biden announced the withdrawal from Afghanistan and aimed at containing China and Russia by militarily and economic means. This strategy seems to conflict with the interests of the EU, ASEAN, and Japan, which have many features in common. Decoupling economic relations with China could bring strong economic disadvantages in Europe and Japan, after the COVID-19 damage. Both economies are more dependent on China than on the United States. In particular, economic and technological cooperation with China and other Asian countries is indispensable for the regeneration and future development of the European and Japanese economies. Particularly important cases are the rapid development of IT/AI technology, 5G, and others, all fields in which Europe and Japan are behind the United States and China.

The EU is facing the urgent goal of increasing its resilience to COVID-19 pandemic and recovering economically. The initially soft EU attitude to the Alliance of Values has been evolving following the Russian invasion of Ukraine. The EU is trying to keep its political and military engagement with both the United States and Japan and continuing its economic cooperation with China. Both positions are indispensable for political and economic recovery from COVID-19 in Europe and Japan. A review of America's reckless withdrawal from Afghanistan shows that the country faces difficulty winning the world's universal support with respect to its sole international order.

As COVID-19's Delta and Omicron mutants ravaged the world one after another, the important and tough question remains of how the post-Brexit and post-Merkel EU and Japan will find an accommodation between the anti-China–US Alliance of Values and the continuing economic engagement with an authoritarian China. The issue of the following analysis is the relationship among Europe, the United States, and Asia with respect to constructing a New World Order[3] after the COVID-19 pandemic.

37.2 Economic growth in developed countries peaks during COVID-19

The most important question is the peak of economic growth in developed countries and the new problems related to liberalism and capitalism. The 20 years from the end of the Cold War in 1989 to the turn of the century and the enlargement of the EU can be called the pinnacle of European politics. The division of Europe for 45 years after World War II was finally overcome, and former Eastern European countries abandoned the Soviet socialist system and "returned to Europe" under the name of Central Europe on the basis of liberal democracy and marketization. There was euphoria in both Western and Eastern Europe.

However, the collapse of the Soviet Union in 1991, the victory of democracy, liberalism, and the market economy, and the expansion of the EU and the North Atlantic Treaty Organization (NATO) eventually led to unilateralism by the United States. However, in reality, the regime change after the Cold War expanded regional conflicts, especially in Islamic countries, and led to the 9/11 attacks on the World Trade Center in New York in 2001. The "Clash of Civilizations" (Huntington, 2002) began.

The eastern half of Europe joined the EU/NATO from 2004 to 2013, except for the Balkans. The EU GDP became the largest in the world before the Euro Crisis, from 2007 to 2011. It was declared a victory of freedom, democracy, and the market economy. However, the situation did not last long, and former Eastern Europe, especially Hungary and Poland, became dissatisfied with their situation and with ideas like "Two Speed and Two Dimension EU" and took a critical position against the EU (see Haba, 2021c).

After the terrorist attacks on the New York World Trade Center building on September 11, 2001, "the era of terrorism" and the war against terrorism began with the war against Afghanistan and Iraq in 2003. The Lehman shock in 2008, the ensuing International Financial Crisis, and the Euro Crisis in 2010–2012 jeopardized the economic situation. As a result of the Financial Crisis, the widening East-West and North-South disparities, the political and economic effects of the expansion of the EU and NATO, the widening of globalization, the dominance of neoliberal policies and competition, and the increase of migration flows, societies came to face numerous and significant threats to their stability and well-being. Social polarization, the increase of poverty, and the growing gap between the ultra-rich and the middle class have widened rapidly since 2010, as the so-called elephant curve[4] shows (Lakner and Milanovic, 2016).

During the years of the International Financial Crisis and the Euro Crisis, the economic growth of developed countries such as the United States, Europe, and Japan has been modest, whereas China and India experienced sustained annual economic growth rates. China overtook Japan's GDP in 2010 (see Table 37.1) and overtook the US PPP-based GDP in 2014 (see also Table 37.2). The 2012–2020 economic recovery, including the positive effects of the so-called Abenomics and the "Three-Arrows" by the Abe administration in Japan, further promoted the polarization of the gap between the rich and the poor in developed countries.[5] At international level, due to the sluggish performance of Japan's GDP and China's rapid GDP growth, the latter has almost tripled Japan's GDP in just six years (see Tables 37.1–37.4). For additional long-term comparative studies, see Maddison (2001, 2008) and Kawai (2018).

In 2060, GDP of India and China will account for 20–25% each of the world economy, and the sum of the OECD countries' combined GDP is predicted to account for approximately 40% of the world GDP (OECD, 2018). Therefore, GDP of India and China will surpass the sum of the OECD GDP in 2060. It is calculated by OECD itself.

Table 37.1 World GDP (2010 and 2019)

	Country/Region	2010	2019
	World	62,909	87,552
	EU	16,282	18,700
1	United States	14,582	21,433
2	China	5,879	14,731
3	Japan	5,498	5,079
4	Germany	3,310	3,861
5	India	1,729	2,868
6	United Kingdom	2,246	2,830
7	France	2,560	2,715
8	Italy	2,051	2,001
9	Brazil	2,088	1,839
10	Canada	1,574	1,738
11	Russia	1,480	1,702
12	Korea	1,155	1,646

Source data: World Bank.

Table 37.2 PPP-based GDP (2019: billion dollars)

	Country/Region	2019
	World	134,556
	EU	16,220
1	China	23,393
2	United States	21,433
3	India	9,542
4	Japan	5,450
5	Germany	4,672
6	Russia	4,135
7	Indonesia	3,331
8	United Kingdom	3,254
9	France	3,228
10	Brazil	3,222
11	Italy	2,665
12	Mexico	2,625

Source data: IMF.

Table 37.3 World economic growth development (190 countries)

1	Nauru	10.3%	128	United Kingdom	1.8%
2	Iraq	10.0%	129	Germany	1.8%
3	Ethiopia	8.0%	131	America	1.6%
4	Uzbekistan	7.8%	148	France	1.23%
5	Cote d'Ivoire	7.5%	155	Japan	0.99%
6	Iceland	7.2%	169	Russia	−0.225%
7	Cambodia	7.0%	189	South Sudan	−13.8%
8	Laos	6.9%	190	Venezuela	−18%
9	Bangladesh	6.9%			
10	Tajikistan	6.9%			
11	Philippines	6.8%			
12	India	6.8%			
13	China	6.7%			

Source data: IMF April 2017.

Table 37.4 Economic growth ranking (2019)

Rank	Country/Region	Real GDP growth rate (%)	Rank	Country/Region	Real GDP growth rate (%)
1	South Sudan	11.3	100	United States	2.3
2	Rwanda	10.1	133	Zambia	1.5
3	Libya	9.9	134	United Kingdom	1.4
4	Dominica	9.2	135	Belgium	1.4
5	Ethiopia	9.0	136	Russia	1.3
6	Bangladesh	8.2	137	France	1.3
7	Armenia	7.6	138	São Tomé e Príncipe	1.3
8	Tajikistan	7.5	139	United Arab Emirates	1.3
9	Djibouti	7.5	140	Solomon Island	1.2
10	Nepal	7.1	141	Sweden	1.2
11	Cambodia	7.0	159	Japan	0.7
12	Vietnam	7.0			

Source data: IMF.

Table 37.5 Reported cases and deaths by country

#	Country	Total cases	New cases	Total deaths	New deaths
	World	391,682,865	2,963,068	5,743,514	11,631
1	United States	77,861,660	303,273	924,604	2,693
2	India	42,080,660	127,952	501,143	1,056
3	Brazil	26,319,030	219,298	631,069	1,068
4	France	20,388,390	241,049	132,207	355
5	United Kingdom	17,689,420	83,898	157,984	254
6	Russia	12,452,760	168,202	334,039	682
7	Turkey	12,051,850	111,152	88,312	248
8	Italy	11,449,630	99,557	148,167	433
9	Germany	10,778,820	235,517	119,234	165
10	Spain	10,274,650	74,937	942,345	195

Source data: Worldometer, February 2022.

Meanwhile, the US–China trade war began to increase tariffs on mutual trade to 20–25%. As a result, the trade war hit American companies that produce semiconductors and electronic devices in China. The Trump administration proposed the exclusion of Huawei and TikTok from the United States and other Western countries, the procurement of parts from Chinese companies in the 5G race, and the exclusion of the purchase of IT-related products from China.

The COVID-19 pandemic found a partial solution in the fast development of vaccines; their effect started to be felt in May and June 2021. However, even in 2022, the United States and Europe have the highest number of infections and deaths, in spite of their high-level medical technology and science (see Table 37.5). In contrast, the number of infections in Asia and Africa and particularly in China was relatively low, a fact that raised concerns about the United States and its allies' actual success in their intent to contain China.

37.3 "Containment of China" by the United States and the concept of "New World Order"

The start of the Biden administration on January 20, 2021, was welcomed around the world as it resumed efforts to tackle global issues, such as improving medical systems, tackling the expansion of COVID-19, restoring alliances with Europe and Asia, and addressing climate change.

However, subsequent policies not only strengthened a sense of caution against China but also recruited allies in Europe, Asia, and Oceania to promote China's isolation and oppose the strengthening of its military power in East Asia. The Biden administration did not follow the Trump administration's economic policies and attempted to compromise and collaborate with the Chinese regarding the economy. However, it pursued a containment policy against China through its security and military strategy, including by sending arms to the US basis in Okinawa and to Taiwan and strengthening its military power in the South and East China Seas.

The Trump administration opposed North Korea's nuclear missile development and ordered the destruction of its intercontinental ballistic missiles that could reach Washington, DC, or New York. Conversely, the United States unblocked the freezing of intermediate-range missile weapons with Russia. In other words, long-range nuclear missiles threatening the United States had to be removed, but intermediate-range nuclear missiles were tolerated. This foresees a strategy accepting that a regional conflict in northeast Asia would be acceptable. This also means that the United States does not protect Japan: it is Japan protecting the United States by avoiding those long-range missiles that will not reach US territory.

37.3.1 Tension caused by the containment policy against China

The containment policy against China and the increase of US troops dispatched to Okinawa and Taiwan created extreme tensions in East Asia. If war or conflict had broken out in East Asia, the Japanese archipelago would have been at the forefront. When the Japanese archipelago is viewed from the Asian continent, Japan is a natural fortress covering 3,000 km and blocking the access to the Pacific Ocean by Russia, China, and North Korea. It should be reminded that Japan still has territorial conflicts with neighboring countries: Russia (North Islands), Korea (Takeshima), and China (Senkaku/Diaoyu/Diaoyutai Islands) (Bukh, 2020).

37.3.2 United States Indo-Pacific strategy, the QUAD, and the EU's role

The Four-Countries Alliance (QUAD) was devised as a wide-ranging alliance organization to contain China; it was originally proposed by the Abe administration from early 2007 to 2017. The QUAD includes the United States, Australia, India, and Japan and its aim, similar to NATO's, is the containment of China. However, India, traditionally a non-allied country, was reluctant to join the American military alliance.

At the G7 meeting in June 2021, the United States approached Europe and Japan, proactively called for stronger relations with its allies, and insisted on countering China and maintaining the value of liberal democracy. Furthermore, through the QUAD Plus concept, they sought cooperation with South Korea, Vietnam, New Zealand, and Taiwan to isolate China.

However, India and Japan were not willing to actively contain China within QUAD. India's position is that of a non-allied country, and Japan adopts an economic-trade perspective. Therefore, the United States started to organize AUKUS (for additional information, see Wilkins, 2021). AUKUS is a Security Partnership between Australia, the United Kingdom, the United States, all Anglo-Saxon countries, which does not include Asian countries. Although AUKUS does not use the term alliance, it is military-security cooperation. AUKUS, together with the Anglo-Saxon intelligence network called Five Eyes (United States, United Kingdom, Australia, New Zealand, Canada), is a system that jointly takes responsibility for world security, especially for Asia and Europe, complementing the role and activity of the United States. Noteworthy is the conflict with France following Australia's unilateral decision to buy an American nuclear-powered submarine instead of the French diesel submarine, as was originally arranged. Although the United States did not notify France, it included France in the military expansion to the South and East Asia Seas by also deploying French warships (Haba, 2022b).[6]

The United States is attempting to contain China through international cooperation, in response to the perspective that the country will be overtaken by China in terms of economic power and technology in approximately ten years. However, Europe and Japan are not always in tune with this view. Even during the Abe administration, which promoted militarization, Japanese economic policy was trying to maintain trade with China at the request of the country's main trade associations (Keidanren or Japan Business Federation, Keizai Doyukai or Japan Association of Corporate Executives, SME Chamber of Commerce). Japanese trade with China is directly affecting the development of Japan and Japanese companies. Large Japanese companies have the view that "political and security interests are with the United States, but economic interests are with China and Asian countries". In fact, in December 2021, Keidanren declared that it would continue its "economic partnership with China"[7] in coincidence with the US military deployment to Taiwan and Okinawa.

The same situation is observed in Europe. As the European economy declined significantly during 2020–2021 because of COVID-19, many countries continued economic relations with China in contrast with US pressures. In particular, Central, South, and Eastern European countries, especially Hungary, Serbia, Greece, and Italy, are linked to China's Belt and Road Initiative (BRI) strategy and investments, IT/infrastructure, and medical technology (vaccines). This relation also took a more formalized nature through 16 + 1 cooperation (including Central and Eastern European countries) and 17 + 1 cooperation (also including Greece). In these countries, where a large number of deaths have occurred from COVID-19, Chinese investments, infrastructure developments, and provision of medical technology and vaccines were fundamentally important. A telling event was also the establishment in Hungary of Fudan University's overseas branch in 2021, the first European branch, while the Hungarian government expelled the Central European University to Vienna in 2018. The widespread criticism that Hungary is the "Trojan horse" of Chinese universities in the EU and NATO countries (AFP BB News, 2021) was opposed by the Orban administration's aim to develop education and the economy with the support of China.[8]

37.3.3 Is it the New Cold War? US–China nuclear war scenario

The United States and Europe are nervous about China's expansion into southern and Eastern Europe and its growing influence in Asia and Africa. The presence of the US Navy in the South China Sea is formally based on the need to protect "free navigation". However, these are waters close to the cost of China and 10,000 km away from the United States. At the same time, the United States condemns China's expansion for creating international tension. It is a curious situation.

Five points can be cited to avoid a US–China war (cf. Stavridis 2021).[9] First, in maintaining and expanding the military power of the United States, it is necessary to avoid any miscalculation that China will be able to beat the United States. Second, regarding alliances, China can only count on Russia and North Korea. The United States has a strong relationship with Japan, Australia, New Zealand, the Philippines, Thailand, Singapore, Malaysia, and India. However, all these countries, including Australia and New Zealand, attach great importance to economic relations with China, and they are unlikely to form a military alliance against China as easily as during the Cold War. Third, if China attacks the United States, the latter will impose large-scale economic sanctions. Fourth is communication strategy, which calls for international cooperation considering the importance of climate change and pandemics. The fifth is technical cooperation between Japan and the United States and cooperation in cyber and artificial intelligence (see also Stavridis, 2021). From the viewpoint of Asian countries, these points are not very persuasive.

37.3.4 Who will start the war? China or the United States? No, Russia

While writing this chapter, Russia invaded Ukraine and started a war on February 24, 2022. The war by Russia is hasty, violent, and poorly prepared; so far it was almost impossible to reach an international consensus on how to end it (Haba, 2022c). The international community around the world is blaming Russia's actions. However, Russia could not overlook the fact that Ukrainian troops were fighting with US and Turkish weapons in the Eastern Ukraine region near the Russian border and strengthening their military power through US military support, even if Ukraine is not a NATO member.

Europe must have understood Russian fear and was cautious about NATO expansion, but it was overwhelmed by the US request to expand NATO. Europe has intended to create its own European army (see The Week 2022 and Braw, 2022) independent from the influence of the United States. However, Europeans preferred improving their social welfare than paying the high costs of a European army. Moreover, an independent European command will not be approved by the United States.

We need to consider that the weakening economic influence of the United States leaves only military power to expand its international influence in a most powerful and aggressive manner. This creates a risky situation not only at the Russian border, but also at the Chinese and Taiwanese borders.

China has no interest to start a war. If China's economic growth continues and will overtake the United States and so will India ten years later, why would China dare to wage war against the United States? The United States has an overwhelming military advantage in the world: if China starts a war, it may be easily defeated as was the Soviet Union. China may take military action, but it is hard to believe it will.

The United States has already begun preparations by sending large amounts of weapons to Taiwan and Okinawa. China may take a provocation and participate in an accidental war. Any scenario in which Japan undertakes the role of repelling China's attacks at the forefront should be strategically avoided. The risks and disadvantages are significant. The United States appears to be hoping for an advanced war strategy, similar to the Munich Agreement strategy in 1938, when Britain and France wanted their enemy Germany be forced to fight against the Soviet Union, thus weakening both countries, without fighting Western Europe and the United States. The United States apparently has more interests in provoking a war.

Conceivably, Japan and Taiwan may be forced to start a war or a conflict with China as a proxy war for the United States, or Japan may become a breakwater when the war begins. This position is of no benefit to Japan and will undermine the long-term economic growth and prosperity of East Asia. Therefore, this scenario should be avoided. If war begins in East Asia, it will not benefit any country or region, including Japan, China, South Korea, Taiwan, and Okinawa. War only benefits the United States. At the beginning of any small conflict, building trust in neighboring countries and resolving the conflict by maintaining peace and stability in Asia is essential.

37.4 US withdrawal from Afghanistan and European choice

Thirty years after the end of the Cold War, the Alliance of Values that promotes the democratization of the world has caused tragedy in various parts, including Afghan War, Iraqi War, Arab Spring, Ukraine conflict, Hong Kong repression, and at last the withdrawal of US troops from Afghanistan.

Since Wilson stated the Fourteen Points at the end of World War I, the United States has promoted democracy and liberalism against the USSR socialist regime. The United States has also upheld the Alliance of Values through the idea of universal values. Roosevelt attempted to reorganize the postwar world order by four policemen: the United States, the United Kingdom, the Soviet Union, and China. However, the subsequent start of the Cold War by the Truman administration and Stalin once again led to bipolarism by means of ideology and military force.

After the end of the Cold War, Central and Eastern Europe and then Russia wished to "return to Europe" under the banner of liberalism, democracy, and market economy. However, after 9/11, the "clash of civilizations" started under the name of "war against terrorism". A democratization movement occurred in various countries, including Arab countries, Ukraine, and Hong Kong, all unified by Western values. However, democratization from outside didn't take root.

However, Europe has always been skeptical. The Kosovo Conflict and Serbian bombing in 1999 and the use of depleted uranium ammunition split the United States and the EU. Germany and France strongly opposed the Iraq War as a war without cause. Germany and Central and Eastern Europe were also economically and politically cautious about "democratization" of Ukraine and elsewhere through the overwhelming military power of the United States. In this frame, the EU–China Investment Partnership Agreement was signed in 2020 in the frame of the EU–China Comprehensive Agreement on Investment.[10]

However, pressure from the United States in conjunction with the Hong Kong protests and the human rights violations of the Xinjiang Uighur forced the EU to retreat. Lithuania left from 17 + 1 cooperation created by China in collaboration with the former Central and Eastern Europe and Greece. Hungarian citizens opposed the establishment of a European branch of Fudan University in the middle of the Hungarian capital. At present, cooperation with China has begun to collapse (Kunio, 2021) in Eastern Europe as well.

The disastrous experience of the war against Iraq and the US withdrawal from Afghanistan was on the basis of the disappointment in the attitude of the Biden administration. In spite of this, in February and March 2022, because of the threat of Russia's invasion of Ukraine, the United States sent an army to the Polish and Romanian border, with Chancellor Schultz of Germany reluctantly accepting them. Germany also sent anti-aircraft missiles to Ukraine for the first time (see Herszenhorn et al 2022; NDTV, 2022; DW, 2022).

Unlike the United States, Europe emphasizes "norms" and can continue to cooperate with the world. It should consider multiethnic coexistence and meditate on US mistakes and its own colonial past and whether the protection of human rights of minorities has been realized. Also fundamental is the proper appraisal of the COVID-19 pandemic and the high death toll in Europe and North America, corresponding to half of the world's coronavirus deaths. The appraisal should be done particularly in terms of citizens' equal access to public health and welfare, and the strong inequalities between rich and poor.

The question of the deep nature of "democracy" and how "democratization" can take place are extremely difficult and complex.[11] These recent dramatic experiences show that democracy cannot be simply imported, let alone implemented or imposed from abroad. Normal people, officials, and scholars started to realize this reality.

37.5 Epilogue: Instead of a conclusion

When Wilson and Roosevelt advocated the League of Nations and the United Nations to institutionalize "universal values" after the two world wars of the 20th century, the world praised America's world order concept and has attempted to rely on it.

After the Trump administration from 2017 to 2020, we welcomed and trusted the Biden administration. However, the Biden administration lacked universalistic values like Wilson and Roosevelt, and its Alliance of Values is only a strategy that has been going to contain China on the ground of "human rights". The US aim is to remain on the world's top with the help of military power.

The Alliance is necessary to the United States since the country is no longer self-sufficient in the 21st century and needs to include its allies in Asia and Europe and other countries. This approach does not reflect the "universal values" that Wilson and Roosevelt sought to pursue and replaces them with a short-circuit strategy similar to Trump's advocating "Make America Great Again".

As Odd Arne Westad of Yale University responded to Asahi Shimbun's question, "Is the US–China conflict a 'new Cold War'?" – the conflict between the two countries is not an ideological conflict in the polarized Cold War sense. It is a conflict of a multilateral era that requires coexistence. "The United States is no longer a superpower that maintains an international system. Also, China is not like the Soviet Union's superpower during the Cold War" (Westad, 2021).

The G7 countries also showed different positions. Japan and some European countries were pulled into the alliance with the United States, but they kept their differences, and this prevented the construction of a unified alliance. The United States prepared for a military conflict in East Asia but collaborating in that effort is not in the interest of Asian countries. In Europe as well, the gains that can be obtained by forming an alliance with the United States by excluding China are limited. In fact, China has a comprehensive BRI policy, including investment and infrastructure, the support to the introduction of IT and AI, medical care, and wide trade networks.

Japan's and Europe's role is to act as a bridge or buffer between the United States and China, not to cause wasteful wars and regional conflicts. Nothing is more useless to Japan than to stand in front of China as a vanguard to defend the US supremacy. Japan and Europe should play a role in supporting Asia's economic development while connecting with China, India, and ASEAN countries. Moreover, in the event that the United States, Japan, and Europe decline as dominant powers, cooperating with growing China, India, and ASEAN countries makes it possible to take advantage of the growth and stability of Asia and thus attenuate or stop their decline.

Although Japan does not have the strong political will of the European Union, economically Japan had become the world's second and then third largest economy 75 years after the war from which it emerged as a defeated nation. Contributing to and utilizing its economic power and the diligence of its people to combine with Asia, the United States, and Europe by fostering trust would be desirable for Japan's future.

Instead of fighting the neighboring power of China as an ally of the United States, Japan should utilize its knowledge as an economically and technologically highly developed nation thanks to the skills and diligence of its population. Japan, together with Europe, should be prepared for the latter half of the 21st century, when the international order of the three big powers – the United States, Europe, and Asia – will be established, contributing technologically and economically to the common progress (Haba, 2021a, 2022a).

Europe's leading values include postwar recovery from the scorched soil, collaboration in energy, and achieving the ultimate nonwar community through reconciliation with war enemies and recovery from the Spanish flu and COVID-19. Such an achievement would represent resilience as a universal value, strengthening the historical lesson of the recovery from the pandemic plague during the Renaissance, from which the world can still learn.

The invasion of Russian troops into Ukraine since February 2022 is a new, fundamentally epoch-making issue that shakes the post-COVID-19 International Order. It is to be established whether it also puts a brake on or conversely accelerates the militarization of East Asia and the containment of China.

Notes

1 For additional details on these topics, see Haba (2021b, 2021c, 2020a, 2020b).
2 It is already investigated even before the COVID-19 pandemic by the Japan Association for Comparative Politics (2020).
3 In the 20th century, after World War I, the US President Wilson proposed the New World Order and formed the League of Nations. At the end of World War II, the US President Roosevelt envisioned the New World Order by the four victorious powers (United States, United Kingdom,

Soviet Union, and China) and formed the United Nations. In the 33rd year of the end of the Cold War, the question is who will reconstruct what kind of New World Order, taking into account the post-COVID-19 and rising China?

4 The "Elephant Curve" is a well-known graph showing the growing gap between the ultra-rich and the middle class. The curve is called the "elephant curve" because it resembles an elephant lifting its nose. The horizontal axis is the world's richest to poorest, showing how much each class has increased its income over a period of time. The inventors (see Lakner and Milanovic, 2016) analyzed the data for 20 years from 1988. From the right side of the graph, the tip of the nose, which indicates the wealthy class, grows high and drops sharply, mainly in the middle class of developed countries.

5 "Abenomics and 'Three Arrows' are economic policies announced by Prime Minister Abe during the second Abe administration that began in December 2012. Positioning the biggest goal as economic recovery, (1) bold monetary policy (breaking out of deflation), (2) flexible fiscal stimulus (large-scale budgeting), and (3) growth strategy to stimulate private investment (growth industries, job creation, deregulation, attracting investment), the plan is to rebuild the Japanese economy. See the article published in Toyo Keizai (2020).

6 About these conflicts between the United States and Europe, Fumio Banno (2021) wrote that it is the starting point from Anglo-Saxon era to global multinational era. On the other hand, Ian Bremmer (2018) wrote it is the new era of conflicts, and the end of globalism. John Dower (2017) also wrote that it is an American Violence era.

7 On December 21, 2021, the Japan Business Federation (Keidanren) and the China International Economic Exchange Center (CCIEE) held the seventh Japan–China Entrepreneurs and Former Government Officials Dialogue Online for Regional Comprehensive Economic Partnership. A joint statement was issued in support of the Agreement (RCEP) and jointly developing the economy. *Policy and Action*, Keidanren, December 21, 2021.

8 See the full text of Viktor Orban's speech at Baile Tusnad (Tusnadfurdo) of July 26 and 29, 2014. By Csaba Toth, Budapest Beacon, October 13, 2013 and April 13, 2018.

9 In 2021, a novel about the US–China War became a hot topic. The writer is James Stavridis, former commander-in-chief of the US-European Army and the NATO Army. He described a nuclear war scenario between the United States and China in a nonfiction novel on the theme of the US–China War, 2034. See also Ackerman and Stavridis (2021).

10 See "EU-China Comprehensive Agreement on Investment: Milestones and documents" https://trade.ec.europa.eu/doclib/press/index.cfm?id=2115.

11 In Iraq in early 2003, Mr. Jabouri, who believed in democratization, pulled down the statue of Saddam Hussein during the fall of Baghdad. In 2021, 18 years later, he said the following words to journalists at Asahi Shimbun: "America is an enemy who killed people while shouting 'democracy' in my country... America has killed our children, mothers, and women, shouting 'democracy.' America has been and will always be an enemy in the future". (See the articles "After the reverence of that dictator, the image of Iraq again, and the joy" (9.11–20) "The United States is the enemy who killed people while shouting democracy" August 25, 2021). At a lecture in Japan, former ASEAN Secretary-General Surin Pitsuwan was asked, "Is there a 'democratization' problem in Asia and Arab countries?" He answered, "Democracy must not bring from outside, but it needs to construct from inside" (see Pitsuwan, 2017, the former Secretary-General of ASEAN and former Minister of Foreign Affairs). This response can be characterized as profound and essential. Andrew Bacevich, Professor Emeritus at Boston University, also said, "The United States has relied on military force to promote 'democratization,' arguing that it originated in McArthur's democratization of Japan and the success of Germany occupied and ruled by the Allied Forces after WWII. The United States attempted to do the same in Afghanistan and Iraq, but it was a ridiculous idea. ... And the responsibility for this foolish idea of 'democratizing the world with military power' lies not only with the 'democratic' Biden administration, but also with the people who support it" (Bacevich, 2021).

References

Ackerman, E. and Stavridis, A.J. (2021). *2034: US-China War, A Novel of the Next World War*, Penguin Press, March 9.

AFP BB News. (May 7, 2021). "Building a prestigious Chinese campus in Hungary 'Nobody agrees.'"

Bacevich, A. (2021). "Afghanistan, Lost Decades: The Illusion of Rice, a Country Building Relying on Military Forces," *Asahi Shimbun*, August 25.

Banno, F. (2021). *2050, Choice of Future Order: From the Age of Anglo-Saxon "to" Global Cooperative*, NHK Publisher, Tokyo.

Braw, E. (March 20, 2022). "Is an EU Army Coming? Russia's war in Ukraine is turning the European Union into a serious military player," Foreign Policy. Interview. https://foreignpolicy.com/2022/03/20/is-an-eu-army-coming/

Bremmer, I. (2018). *Us vs. Them: The Failure of Globalism.*

Bukh, A. (2020). *These Islands Are Ours: The Social Construction of Territorial Disputes in Northeast Asia.* Stanford University Press, Stanford, CA.

Dower, J.W. (2017). *The Violent American Century: War and Terror Since World War II* (Dispatch Books), Haymarket Books, Chicago, IL.

DW. (March 4, 2022). "Germany to ship anti-aircraft missiles to Ukraine," reports of DW.com dj/nm (AFP, dpa, Reuters) https://www.dw.com/en/germany-to-ship-anti-aircraft-missiles-to-ukraine-reports/a-60995325

Financial Times. (December 20, 2021). "Coronavirus tracker: the latest figures as countries fight the COVID-19 resurgence," https://www.ft.com/content/a2901ce8-5eb7-4633-b89c-cbdf5b386938

Haba, K. (2020a). "'The End of Developed Countries', which will decline significantly due to the COVID-19 Crisis," *Kodansha, Gendai Ismedia*, April 29. https://gendai.ismedia.jp/articles/-/72177

Haba, K. (2020b). "Does Coronavirus Change the World? From the perspective of international politics, lectures were delivered at *the World Peace Research Institute*" on June 8.

Haba, K. (2021a). Final Lecture, "Where Leads the New World Order? The US, China, and the EU in the 21st century? Europe's Historical and Global Significance and Its Resilience," *Journal of Aoyama International Politics and Economics*, Vol. 106, May, 81–91.

Haba, K. (2021b). "International Politics and COVID-19," *Journal of Kanagawa University*, Vol. 98, July 30, 95–106.

Haba, K. (2021c). "Post Brexit and Post Corona: The UK, the EU and Central East Europe; 'Illiberal Democracy' and the Influence of China," *Brexit and After: Perspectives on European Crises and Reconstruction from Asia and Europe*, in K. Haba and M. Holland (Eds.), Springer Nature, Singapore, pp. 17–40.

Haba, K. (2022a). "Strategy that Japan should take before China overtakes America to become the world's number One in economy – economy with Asia, politics with America," *Kodansha Gendai Ismedia*, January 24. https://gendai.ismedia.jp/articles/-/91690

Haba, K. (2022b). "Why is France expanding its arms to Asia Pacific?" *Kodansha Gendai Ismedia*, February 20, 2022. https://gendai.ismedia.jp/articles/-/92522

Haba, K. (2022c). "Russian invasion to Ukraine and its effect," *Kodansha, Ismedia*, April 2022. Online Article.

Herszenhorn, D.M., Bayer, L. and von der Burchard, H. (February 26, 2022). "Germany to send Ukraine weapons in historic shift on military aid," *Politico.* https://www.politico.eu/article/ukraine-war-russia-germany-still-blocking-arms-supplies/

Huntington, S. (2002). *The Clash of Civilizations: The Remaking of World Order*, Simon & Schuster, Re-issue.

Japan Association for Comparative Politics. (Ed.). (2020). *The Vulnerability of Democracy and the Resilience of Authoritarianism*, Annual Report No. 22, Minerva Shobo, 2020.

Kawai, M. (2018). *Economic Growth in Northeast Asia-Structural Reform and Regional Cooperation*, Economic Research Institute for Northeast Asia, Nihon Hyoronsha.

Kunio, T. (2021). "Modulated China-Europe Relations," Vice President of International Institute for Strategic Studies, Japan Research Institute, International Institute for Strategic Studies, *Monthly Report on China Situation*, No. 2021-03, June 30.

Lakner, C. and Milanovic, B. (2016). "Global Income Distribution: From the Fall of the Berlin Wall to the Great Recession Get Access Arrow," *World Bank Economic Review*, Vol. 30, No. 2, 203–232.

Maddison, A. (2001). *The World Economy: A Millennial Perspective, Development Centre of the Organisation for Economic Co-Operation and Development*, OECD, Paris.

Maddison, A. (2008). *The West and the Rest in the World Economy: 1000–2030*, Maddisonian and Malthusian Interpretations, Economic and Financial Publication, London.

NDTV. (March 24, 2022). "Germany to Send 2,000 More Anti-Tank Weapons to Ukraine: Report," https://www.ndtv.com/world-news/russia-ukraine-war-germany-to-send-2-000-more-anti-tank-weapons-to-ukraine-report-2839664

OECD. (2018). *Economic Scenarios to 2060 Reveal Long-Term Benefits of Structural Reform*. OECD, Paris, July 12.

Pitsuwan, Surin H.E. (2017). "The 50th Anniversary of ASEAN Special Lecture Series," ASEAN – Japan Centre, May 19, Online Jun 2, 2017. https://www.mfa.go.th/en/content/5d5bd0c615e39c3060021361?cate=5d5bcb4e15e39c306000683e

Stavridis, J. (2021). "Warning of the 2034 US-China War," *Asahi Shimbun*, May 20.

The Week. (March 29, 2022). "The arguments for and against an EU army: President Macron wants self-determination for the bloc but some fear operational headaches," https://www.theweek.co.uk/news/world-news/956217/the-arguments-for-and-against-an-eu-army

Toyo Keizai. (August 28, 2020). "What was the eight years of Abenomics? Even if the stock price temporarily tripled, there is no sense of exhilaration in the real economy."

Westad, O.A. (2021). "Is the US-China conflict a 'New Cold War?'" *Asahi Shimbun*, April 20.

Wilkins, T. (2021). Senior Lecturer, University of Sydney "AUKUS (US, UK, Australia Security Collaboration) and its significance for Australia," *International Information Network Analysis*, Sasagawa Peace Foundation, November 15.

38

CONCLUSIONS

Bruno Dallago and Sara Casagrande

UNIVERSITY OF TRENTO, TRENTO, ITALY

Horst Brezinski

TU BERGAKADEMIE FREIBERG, FREIBERG, GERMANY, AND POZNAN UNIVERSITY
OF ECONOMICS AND BUSINESS, POZNAN, POLAND

Elodie Douarin

SCHOOL OF SLAVONIC AND EAST EUROPEAN STUDIES – SSEES, UCL, LONDON, UK

Paul Roderick Gregory

UNIVERSITY OF HOUSTON, HOOVER INSTITUTION AND GERMAN INSTITUTE
FOR ECONOMIC RESEARCH

Justin Yifu Lin

PEKING UNIVERSITY, BEIJING, CHINA

Martin Myant

EUROPEAN TRADE UNION INSTITUTE, BRUSSELS, BELGIUM

Vito Tanzi

INTERNATIONAL INSTITUTE OF PUBLIC FINANCE, MUNICH, GERMANY

Andrei Yakovlev

HIGHER SCHOOL OF ECONOMICS, MOSCOW, RUSSIA

A series of important shocks during recent years complemented evolutionary processes and initiated a long wave of changes that challenged old economic and social features and structures and routines of policy making. Some of these events were of endogenous nature, while others were exogenous black swans. The first event was the end of the world socialist system and the process of economic, political and social transformation that followed. The International Financial Crisis of 2008 was a major endogenous effect that ended the "Great

Moderation" and subverted the interaction between markets and the state. Policy making became more interventionist. This was considered an extraordinary answer to extraordinary problems in extraordinary times. Yet the recovery of many economies was ailing for years, policies were seldom really effective and there were concerns for their side effects, particularly for long-term financial stability. Other threats were smoldering under the surface though. Processes that the crisis at least facilitated were the rise and spread of populism and sovereign movements and policies in quite a substantial number of countries in different parts of the world and at different levels of economic development.

Parallelly with these developments, the environmental crisis and climate change were and are certainly among the most important and the most durable events. It is clear that to solve this challenge economies should deeply and extensively transform technology and production and consumption habits. To make things worse, the COVID-19 pandemic broke out abruptly. Linked to the environmental crisis, the pandemic represented the most important black swan of the post-war era. It costed millions of human lives, it disrupted production particularly via the interruption of global value chains, it dramatically jeopardized the mobility of people and normal life and consumption habits. Perhaps this was not enough: while closing this Handbook, the Russian army invaded Ukraine causing a major humanitarian, geopolitical, military and economic crisis.

This dramatic event is the tipping point of progressively deteriorating international political and economic relations. Their relevance for comparative economic systems is manifold: from the different management, performance and adaptation to the consequences of these events in different countries to the appearance of a potentially permanent fault line between different parts of the world, particularly the West and the largest emerging economies. Are different systems and countries drifting away again?

These events open a host of questions for comparative economic systems. To close the Handbook and look at the future, the editors asked a group of prominent experts some of the most important questions for outlining problems and possible answers. The scholars who accepted the challenge represent a broad span of expertise, approaches, interests, country of origin and age. This contributes to have a broad brain storming and ideas. Some of them are well-known scholars in the CES field, others are prominent personalities in other fields of economics. The common trait is their interests for the daunting problems humanity is affording and their willingness to contribute to their much-needed solutions.

In alphabetic order, the participants to the virtual panel are: Horst Brezinski (TU Bergakademie Freiberg and Poznan University of Economics and Business), Elodie Douarin (School of Slavonic and East European Studies – SSEES, UCL), Paul Roderick Gregory (University of Houston, Hoover Institution and German Institute for Economic Research), Justin Yifu Lin (Peking University), Martin Myant (European Trade Union Institute), Vito Tanzi (International Institute of Public Finance, Munich), Andrei Yakovlev[1] (Higher School of Economics, Moscow).

Question 1. *Various events in the last three decades – from the actual outcome of the transition process in Central-Eastern Europe through the rise of China and other emerging economies to the international crisis and the COVID-19 pandemic – have revealed that the standard approach to economic analysis and policy making is insufficient to understand and govern economies in an age of rapid and deep changes. What could the study of Comparative Economic Systems offer to a better understanding and governance of the world economies and the advancement of economic analysis?*

Brezinski: The traditional approach of Comparative Economic Systems (CES) started out from ideal models which made the distinction the capitalist market-based system and the socialist centrally planned system which led then to the economic systems in practice giving rise to variants of capitalism and of socialism and especially looking and comparing the performance of the systems existing. Thus, the world was divided into two major models and their variations in practice. The transition processes during the past 30 years have shown that there is no simple path toward a capitalist market-based system. Moreover, it has turned out that the transitional processes did not only lead toward capitalist structures and institutions but also to new autocratic systems with partially market-type institutions. The concept of present Comparative Economic Systems (CES) which is based on the analysis of institutions has especially led to the distinction between formal and informal institutions. Moreover, it has enlarged the analysis by the integration of historical, political, social as well as cultural determinants. The advancement of economic analysis has been driven by interdisciplinarity taking among others into account evolutionary and behavioral aspects. Consequently, the comparative economic systems approach has got a broader perspective and has offered better explanations for the development of the variety of economic systems. In addition, the present approach analyses also developing and emerging economies which had been neglected in the past. Since several of the present economic problems which have been addressed by the catalog of sustainable development goals are originating from this group of countries Comparative Economic Systems offers a tool to a better understanding of the difficulties in achieving these goals in this large group of countries in which most of the world population is living.

Douarin: The standard approach to providing policy-advice is to narrow down the analysis to a small number of potential drivers and to, as much as possible, evaluate their independent causal effects on a given outcome of interest. While this approach can be highly effective especially for small-scale targeted policies, it is generally difficult to assess the external validity of the findings and it is not well suited to address broader issues which are typically embedded in complex endogenous processes (see Smith 2021). COVID-19 is a case in point: as the appropriate policy response in a given country will critically depend on the extend of governmental trust, social trust, information available on the disease, communication infrastructure, trust in and understanding of that information, pre-existing social safety net (both as governmental aid and social capital or social network support) etc. (e.g. Bentkowska 2021). Many of these factors cannot be externally modified or manipulated, and they are also not independent from one another. In such a context, credible policy recommendations should be based on a detailed understanding of the role of diverse but intertwined factors, making a "comparative system" approach desirable. This does not mean that more disaggregated causal analyses are not desirable or informative, but it does mean that the broader picture derived from a system-based analysis can provide complementary insights, with potentially broader implications (Douarin and Havrylyshyn 2021b).

In addition, because the CES focus on systems implies a context-dense analysis, researchers engaging with this type of approach are also more typically engaged in pluri-disciplinary discussions, hopefully in a way that supports greater learning across disciplines. This is *per se* an important contribution to better policy advice.

Overall, the key is thus to recognize the relative contributions different approaches can make, as well as their limitations, so that policy-makers can build a broader picture of what works where and why.

Gregory: "Comparative economic systems" combines a challenging mix of disciplines – transition, comparative economics, political economy, institutional economics and Marxist economics. Although comparative systems incorporate the most modern and challenging fields of economic study, it retains the stodgy image of the shopworn study of "isms" from the Cold War; namely, capitalism versus socialism. Given the challenges of incorporating a complex mix of disciplines into one college course or textbook, the teaching of comparative systems is still done largely by purveyors of the "isms" approach or by "newcomers" attracted by the challenge of transition. Lacking a consensus paradigm, comparative economic systems is not thriving among university course offerings just as its relevance is becoming plain for all to see.

Comparative economic systems is much more than the study of transition and reform. The process of transition has been largely completed. Its common outcome in the former Soviet Union has spawned a new expression – kleptocracy – in which an elite from the planned system gain oligarchic control of valuable resources, like energy, telecommunications and transportation. They then capture the state, so that weak state institutions dominate political life.

Transition of the former Soviet Union and Eastern Europe proved to be a humbling experience for overconfident specialists. To economic advisors from international organizations, "transition" and "reform" meant the move to freer trade and sound money rather than a wholesale move from plan to market. On the other side, specialists on the Soviet economy understood its working arrangements, but they did not know how to dismantle its pillars, whether one by one or all at once. Western advisors were also confronted with new behavioral assumptions. They did not initially realize that kleptocratic resource-holders of the planned economy era were "better off" securing those resources for themselves rather than for shareholders, stake holders or society at large.

The distinctive geographical distribution of transition success added the complexity of non-economic variables to the study of transition. No former Soviet republic, other than the three Baltic states, registered clear transition successes, suggesting that non-economic factors – culture, history, religion, etc. – needed to be added to the mix. In response to this challenge, international organizations and NGOs made a significant contribution in the form of an array of institutional measures, such as economic freedom, corruption and the like. These indexes have given us the ability to incorporate "non-economic" variables as both right and left side variables in comparative analysis. Another methodological development – natural experiments – has offered a new approach to the study of non-economic factors. Natural experiments require identifying two settings that are identical in all but one aspect (such as religion or geography) and trying to extract the effect of that one factor, largely by econometric methods.

China's remarkable economic growth starting in the late 1970s gave a new impulse to the study of economic systems. The emergence of China shifted attention from the "failed" Soviet model to the industrial policy story of China. China, because it adopted Soviet institutions after the communist victory in 1949, must also be regarded as a transition success, but one quite different from the European and Eurasian models. Delayed for more than a generation by the excesses of Mao, China began its transition as a rural country with surplus labor in the countryside. Once China's communist leaders opted for openness to world markets, China became a quasi-market economy, fast growing despite the absence of secure property rights and domination by the state sector. China's combination of rapid growth and weak property rights can be likened to defying gravity and raises serious questions about its durability. In fact, China's "institutional ranking" places it alongside Sub-Saharan Africa. The big question about China is whether its industrial-policy model will fail it before it escapes the middle-income trap.

Lin: Economic research is for the purpose of understanding the nature and causes of the researched subject so as to guide people's actions related to the subject for social betterment. Comparative Economic Systems (CES) as a subfield of modern economics, emerging from the research on comparing socialism and capitalism, contributed greatly to the understanding of poor performance of socialist planning system and gave supports to the capitalist triumph (Wiles 1995). The big-bang transition to market economy was influenced by the neoliberalism and following the Washington Consensus recommended by mainstream macro-economists, in Central and Eastern Europe and Former Soviet Union in 1990s, resulting in economic collapse and prolonged stagnation (Easterly 2001; Lin 2014). The socialist planning economies in East Asia, including China, Vietnam and Cambodia, did not follow the prevailing Washington Consensus in their transition, instead they adopted a piecemeal, gradual approach. Such a half-hearted approach was considered a worst transition strategy, destined to worsen the economic performance (Murphy, Schleifer and Vishny 1992). Unexpectedly they achieved stability and dynamic growth during the transition. The contrast of performance between these two transition strategies highlights the incapability of mainstream economics as a discipline for system reform advice (Murrell 1991).

The studies of CES, following the convention of neoclassical economics, take the socialist planning system and its constituent institutions, such as financial repressions, administrative allocation and soft budget constraint, as exogenous and analyzed primarily their impacts on economic performance. The institutions in the socialist planning system appeared to be distortions compared to ideal market institutions in neoclassical economics. However, they were adopted for the purpose of supporting nonviable firms in the priority sectors for building up advanced capital-intensive industries in an economy relatively scarce in capital (Lin 2009; Lin, Fang and Li 1994). Those institutions were interrelated and endogenous to the state's development strategy and thus second best in nature. Without addressing the causes of those "distortions", the attempt to eliminate them in the transition is bound to deteriorate economic performance (Lipsey and Lancaster 1956).

Countries at different stages of development have many institutions that appear to be distortions from the perspective of neoclassical economics and even new institutional economics, however, they exist for good reasons. If economists of New Comparative Economics (Djankov et al. 2003; Douarin and Havrylyshyn 2021a) hope to do well and do good as well, their studies should focus on not only the impacts but also the causes of those "distorted" institutions and how to accomplish Pareto-improvement reforms in a second-best environment (Rodrik 2008).

Myant: The approach to economic theory building from an abstract model of a market in equilibrium has never been happy confronting crises or systemic transformations. That is not to say that the analytical tools of "standard" economics are not useful for investigating elements in the functioning of a market economy, particularly where quantitative methods can be used, but they are not enough for understanding many of the big economic questions of the day or for giving good policy guidance. They would give a very incomplete explanation of the economic effects of the COVID pandemic. That has depended on decisions of political leaders influenced by scientific advice, business interests and voter opinions, all based on varying levels of ignorance. For understanding the relative economic performance of countries, we would do better starting with Porter's (1990) comparative approach, eclectically combining historical and societal influences with management theory. Remarkably, non-economists – historians, sociologists, political scientists and others – have seemed more enthusiastic investigators of the 2008 Financial Crisis which, perhaps according to "standard" economic theory, should not have taken place and certainly seems not have troubled established modes of thought.

A comparative approach is valuable for interpreting economic phenomena both before formulating precise theories and as a means of testing those theories. Even there, excessive abstraction can lead to over-simplification when specifying a small number of precisely defined economic systems, as was once fashionable. Economic performance differed between socialist and capitalist economies before 1990 and also within each category. Comparative analyses help to show, for example, how Poland's economic difficulties related to specificities in its history, politics and society. A key lesson from comparative analysis is that there is no discrete economic system in which economic consequences are determined by identifiably economic factors alone. An economic system is part of a broader society and economic outcomes are determined in large part by forces ignored by "standard" economics.

Tanzi: At the beginning of the 17th century, an economist from the Kingdom of Naples, Antonio Serra, wrote a book that Schumpeter considered the first technical book in economics. Serra advised countries to follow autarchic (mercantilist) policies to become rich, at a time when balance of payment outcomes were settled in gold and silver. After World War II, the influential Argentine economist Raul Prebisch recommended similar policies to Latin American countries. These policies, followed by many of them, were not successful to make them rich.

In the 19th century, the UK and the USA forced some Asian countries (China and Japan) to open their economies to free trade. Free trade would be promoted in combination with domestic laissez faire policies, policies that paid little attention to the income distribution but much attention to national economic growth. Policies were expected to promote national objectives and national public goods. In the 20th century, there was the experiment by many countries with Central Planning, following the Russian example. These policies in turn were followed, in the 1980s and later, by market fundamentalism. All the above experiments land themselves to comparative economic studies.

The globalization of the world economy, in the past 40–50 years, in several countries, accompanied by "market fundamentalism" has not changed the basic objectives of policies. Policies continue to be chosen and promoted by *national* governments and they continue to pursue *national* objectives and public goods.

However, public goods and public "bads" have become increasingly global, requiring policies that aim at global goods, including pandemics and global warming. However, there are yet no global institutions capable of promoting such global goods in an adequate way. Perhaps, comparative economic systems should begin to focus on the theoretical possibility of creating a World Federal System, one that would include a "World Government" responsible exclusively for global public goods. What power should such a government have? How would it be financed? How would it relate to national governments? (Tanzi 2021).

Yakovlev: The emergence of Comparative Economic Studies (CES) as a separate discipline in economics was closely linked to competition between economic systems represented by the planned and market economies. The deep crisis of the planned economy that led to the collapse of the USSR and socialist block in Eastern Europe in the late 1980s created a feeling of the "end of history" – in terms of the absolute victory of liberal democracy and the end of the competition of ideas (Fukuyama 1989). At the same time, there was a dominant conviction among Western intellectuals that to ensure successful development of the former socialist countries and the Third World it would be sufficient to simply introduce the "right" norms and institutions established in most developed countries. The illusory nature of these ideas has become apparent already by the end of the 1990s (Stiglitz 1999). However, market reforms, the removal of barriers to international trade and active inclusion of former socialist countries (with the exception of Cuba and North Korea) in the global market were one of the key factors of accelerating the new wave of globalization that began in the West in the 1970s.

Globalization has resulted in greater efficiency of firms operating in global value chains and brought current gains for end consumers in terms of value for money of the goods and services they buy. Globalization has also opened new opportunities, above all for entrepreneurs and for more educated and mobile social groups. At the same time, however, globalization has engendered acute negative externalities. These include inequalities depressing consumption and social mobility, environmental degradation (due to companies moving their production facilities from developed countries to countries without environmental laws), corporate tax evasion (due to tax competition and the spread of offshoring), growing social tensions associated with rising religious fundamentalism and terrorism (resulting from the increasing national inequalities and loss of opportunities for many social groups).

Under conditions of integration of national economies into the global market and their interdependence on each other, all these acute problems cannot be tackled without global governance. However, in order to build efficient mechanisms of global governance, it is not enough to take into account standard set of political, social and cultural factors, it is necessary to understand the interests and incentives that guide the key stakeholders of this coordination process in different countries. A comparative analysis of the economic models and social orders in different countries can provide such understanding. In this sense, the need to resolve the contradictions created by globalization opens up new opportunities for CES.

Question 2. *Institutions, both formal and informal, differ through countries. Their change through reforms is complex and often difficult. One important issue in explaining such difficulties and surprises of reforms and policy making is that institutions come in bundles and are under the influence of non-economic factors. How can the study of Comparative Economic Systems and the use of a systemic perspective contribute to better understanding the complexity of reforms and ease reform and policy making at national level in a strongly interdependent world? Or can surprises and difficulties be disentangled by better considering non-economic factors?*

Brezinski: Institutional arrangements were at first developed at the national level and their impact was seen through the eye of the capitalist or socialist perspective. Thus, the adaptation of the models to changing situations was rather limited by the dominating respective value system. Performance was predominantly measured by monetary values putting the focus on private goods and services. However, our present situation copes with finding solutions to stop pandemic diseases, such as COVID-19, to protect biodiversity, to internationally promote and give access to knowledge, to regulate international migration and to protect climate. All these issues relate to the category of global public goods and demand solutions on a global level. Given the present crises originating from the existence of global public goods, we must ask whether efficiency is still correctly measured by either the traditional Gross Domestic Product, either the Human Development Index or the Multidimensional Poverty Index. The recent crises have put forward a proposal which was recently made popular by Markus K. Brunnermeier (2021), the concept of resilience. This concept originating from psychology relates to the idea that a crisis will not destroy you. On the contrary, when you will recognize the determinants for the crisis, you can by adaptation to the new situation and appropriate resources for resilience dynamically overcome the crisis. The concept of resilience was used in the past, e.g., by the OECD to make macroeconomic institutions more resilient, however, it should also be used for offering solutions overcoming the various present crises we can observe such as corona pandemics, rising inequality within as well between countries, and climate change. CES must focus on the study of appropriate institutional arrangements how to solve the problem of organizing the production and distribution of global public goods.

Douarin: To me, this is probably one of the most exciting area of research for the coming years – improving our understanding of informal institutions, and their interplay with formal institutions. This is particularly relevant to the questions of why the general public might support or oppose specific policies and relatedly why similar policies can have very different impacts in different societies (as support for, implementation of and adherence to these reforms will differ). To me, this is interesting, not necessarily as a way to design policies that can change informal institutions (even though this is also an interesting question), but foremost as a way to progress toward designing policies that are mindful of informal institutions and relevant non-economic factors (this was also a point I made in my chapter in the Palgrave Handbook of Comparative Economics – Douarin 2021). In other words, I strongly believe that we need to strengthen our understanding of informal institutions especially, and that doing so would support more effective policy design. Then, formal and informal institutions are shaped by external shocks and slower endogenous change, and we also need to strengthen our understanding of these factors (i.e. external shocks and endogenous change), and especially when and how they can be transformative.

This can be illustrated through the example of transition: in this context of wholesale policy and institutional change, discussions are still quite intense even 30 years down the line on the role of historical legacies and cultural norms or values on the degree to which change was possible, and the factors that might have facilitated sudden change. Examples (not an exhaustive list!) of these include past experience with democracy or civil liberties (e.g. Bruszt et al., 2012), strength of the communist/authoritarian experience (e.g. Pop-Eleches and Tucker 2017) or longer historical legacies (e.g. Djankov 2021) among others. However, as the interest in informal institutions, values, norms, identity has increased, we are increasingly better placed to study them, as better terminologies and measurements are being developed through time. There is still a lot of scope for harmonization, but beyond the disagreements, it is important that these issues are investigated further. So, are institutions better seen as an equilibrium in which formal and informal institutions come in bundles and cannot be separated, or is it more useful to see institutions as rules, which can be either formal or informal – in which case the separation makes more sense? The answer is likely to depend on the specific research question at hand, and there is most likely space to recognize the advantages and drawbacks of both approaches and to try and learn from both. Accordingly (and more broadly), different conceptualizations of systems are similarly likely to contribute to enlighten these issues, but transparency on concepts and operationalizations is needed to facilitate academic dialogue among proponents of different approaches.

Gregory: The challenge of comparative economic systems is to organize the world's economies into clusters that share enough common features to be classified as an "economic system". Most of the world's economies find themselves in something approaching an equilibrium where change is incremental and political-economy debate proceeds at the margins, such as political debates between Republicans and Democrats in the United States. If transition and reform are the sole focus of comparative economic systems, we will capture only a small percentage of world GDP.

In my own work, I have found it useful to divide economies into Anglo-Saxon, European, Asian, Soviet, Islamic and transition models. In this regard, I follow the "cluster analysis" approach proposed by Frederic Pryor (2005). Specifically, it can be demonstrated that these clusters differ with respect to capital markets, labor markets, legal systems, state enterprise, tax burden, relational versus legal contracting and constitutional foundations. The division of the world's economies into "systems" (or clusters) may allow us to address the question of economic performance. If we are prepared to set performance standards, we can venture which economic systems perform better than others. Once we address the performance issues, we must study trade-offs, such as the European welfare state versus the Anglo-Saxon model of individual responsibility.

Back when comparative economic systems was the study of capitalism versus socialism, we were vitally interested in the question of performance. Was capitalism in some sense superior to socialism, or vice versa? We now can look back on the capitalism versus socialism debate and see that, by most measures, including viability, planned socialism in the USSR and Eastern Europe failed. A remarkable feature of what came to be called the USSR's "period of stagnation" is that prominent economists were reluctant to state that capitalism was outperforming the planned variant of socialism. Paul Samuelson's Economics into the mid-1980s was still asserting that East Germany was performing on par with West Germany. By the 13th edition, Samuelson and co-author Nordhaus declared, "the Soviet economy is proof that, contrary to what many skeptics had earlier believed, a socialist command economy can function and even thrive" (Samuelson and Nordhaus 1989, p. 837). Remarkably, this assessment was delivered the year of the fall of the Berlin Wall.

If we resort to clusters to ask which economic system type is outperforming another, we can scarcely avoid value judgments. The Anglo-Saxon model has maintained personal incentives, economic freedom and venture capital markets. The European model has greater state intervention, lacks venture capital markets and has strong guarantees against poverty and unemployment. The Asian model manages to generate high rates of capital formation and uses relational contracting.

Although we can't derive from this assortment judgments as to which type is "better", we can have strong opinions on this matter.

Lin: Based on the new structural economics (NSE), which reflects the spirit of Marxism's historical materialism and uses the neoclassical approach as its tool for analysis, the economic system in an economy consists of a set of interrelated structures, including endowments structure, production (industries and technologies) structure, infrastructure and superstructure, or alternatively, in new institutional economics' terminology, institutions including formal ones such as laws, rules and economic, social and political institutions, and informal ones such as behavior patterns, traditions, beliefs, values and ideology; the production structure in an economy is endogenous to the economy's endowments structure, which is given at any specific time and changeable over time, because the endowments structure determines the economy's comparative advantages and thus the appropriate technologies and industries; and different technology and industry have different technical features, such as requirements for specific capital, skill and infrastructure, and economies of scale and risk, and thus to unleash the productivity of technologies and industries in a production structure, proper infrastructure and superstructure are required, therefore, the appropriate infrastructure and superstructure are endogenous to the production structure and indirectly to the endowments structure of the economy (Lin 2011a).

For an economic system to function well in a country, two fundamental institutions are essential, a competitive market and a facilitating state. The former is needed for providing incentives and relative prices information to guide entrepreneurs' production (industry and technology) choices according to the economy's comparative advantages and the latter, which is the only institution with a legitimate power to use coercion in the country, is needed to overcome inevitable market failures arising from externalities of innovation and coordination for the needed improvements in infrastructure and superstructure in the process of development, characterized by structural transformation (Lin 2011a).

There are two main sources of structural disequilibrium in an economic system in the modern world with cross-border flows of ideas, information and trade. The first is that the constituent structures in an economic system have different rigidities. The endowments structure will change quickly, if the economy has appropriate production structure, infrastructure and superstructure in view of endowment structure because with such ideal structures in the system, the growth of the economy and the accumulation of capital will be fast, triggering the change of relative weight of capital in the endowments structure and comparative advantages of the economy, calling for subsequent changes in production structure, infrastructure and superstructure. The change in superstructure, especially informal institutions such as behavior patterns, traditions, beliefs, values and ideology, is most sluggish. When the change in endowments structure happens, owing to the accumulation of capital as discussed above or other sources such as population growth, education, migration, foreign capital inflow or new discovery of natural resources, structural disequilibrium will arise if the changes in the upper-level structures do not synchronize with the change in the lower level structures. The second source of structural disequilibrium may arise from the state's interventions in the production structure such as the adoption of structuralist comparative-advantage-defying import substitution strategy in the socialist as well as many other developing countries after the World War II (Lin 2009) or from the inheritance of, or model after, the political, legal and other formal institutions of advanced countries in the developing countries when obtaining political independence or after some social/political turmoil often with educated elites' aspiration, advice from multilateral development institutions or influence of global powers. Those first-order interventions from the state, like throwing a pebble in a pool, will lead to the emergence of other second-order ripple-like institutions. Both types of structural disequilibrium will result in poor economic performance and even social, political instability.

The restoration of structural equilibrium will be somewhat straightforward for the disequilibrium from the first source because the condition for change is ready as long as the state or some business/political/institutional entrepreneurs provide leadership and coordination for the change (Lin 1989). For the transition to restore structural equilibrium arising from the second source of state intervention, it is crucial to recognize that many seemingly distorted second-order institutions in the economic system, originating endogenously from the state's first-order interventions in production structure or superstructure, are second best in nature as discussed in my response to *Question 1*, and thus it is desirable to adopt a pragmatic approach to avoid systemic upheaval and prepare conditions in the low-level structures before reforming those institutions in the upper level structures so that a Pareto improvement may be achieved in the process of transition. For example, the removals of financial repression and soft budget constraint, which resulted from the need to protect nonviable firms in the structuralist import-substitution strategy's priority sectors, should wait until the nonviable firms become viable from the accumulation of capital and change of comparative advantages made possible by fast growth of comparative-advantaging-conforming new sectors in a gradual, dual-track transition (Lin 2009, 2014). For developing countries with imposed formal institutions of advanced countries, they may overcome this type of structural disequilibrium if they happen to have enlightened political leaders as those in the catching up stage of East Asian economies after the World War II, with the wisdom of exercising their discretionary powers to maintain political stability in their countries on the one hand and using the window of opportunity from political stability on the other hand to develop their economies dynamically so as to upgrade their economic base to meet the required conditions for the well-functioning of imposed institutions and for elimination of institutional conflicts with old informal institutions such as nepotism and second-order distortions such as patronage (Lin 1989, 2009).

Myant: The post-1989 transformations show that private ownership and free prices were not enough to create successful market economies. By the end of the 1990s, international agencies were recognizing the importance of "institutions", although this often seemed only to mean copying legal frameworks from advanced market economies. The approach needs to be broader, recognizing the roles of informal as well as formal institutions and how they influence the working of an economic system. Even among so-called institutional economists, as surveyed by Chavance (2009), institutions have varying definitions – sometimes spanning habits, customs and modes of thought, sometimes including organizations – and their precise effects are difficult to assess.

Understanding how an economic system behaves needs an analysis of multiple relationships that have developed together over decades. Every unit in a market economy depends on an environment providing inputs, services and constraints – including physical infrastructure, financial and advisory services, habits and laws to create good corporate governance, support policies from governments – that have developed together over time. A historical view on how economic systems have developed shows that they were not, and cannot be, created quickly and that they cannot be understood on the basis of "standard" economic theory alone.

Tanzi: In most countries, policies changes that become necessary, because of fast changing technologies and developments face the impediments that the existing institutions pose to the changes. Some institutions do not pose major obstacles because they are sustained by only current laws that can be changed by simple majority rules. Other institutions are very strong because they are backed by Constitutions, which are very difficult to change. For example, in the United States, a president who wins the popular vote in the general elections by seven million votes, because of constitutional rules, could have lost the elections if only about 40,000 electors, in a few, key states had voted differently, as happened in the 2020 election.

Often, Constitutions can only be changed by very difficult procedures, by civil wars (as with the war between the states, in the United States, that abolished slavery), or by major wars or revolutions. Constitutions were often created a long time ago when the world was different. Constitutions can become major obstacles to needed changes in a fast-changing world. Adherence to a Constitution had been strongly defended by some economists, such as the late James Buchanan, and by the followers of the School of Public Choice that he created.

The study of Comparative Economic Systems can cast some useful light on the role that difficulties to change Constitutions have played in impeding needed reforms. It can show the specific ways in which Constitutions impede needed reforms, for example reforms that could make the popular vote determine the winner of a US election.

Perhaps a world in which Constitutions could be more easily amended or modernized might be a more desirable world, as long as it did not make it easier for majorities to suppress basic rights of minorities. In countries where there are strong informal rules or institutions that protect the fundamental rights of minorities, more facility in changing Constitutions would be less of a problem.

Yakovlev: A systemic view of economic processes has in fact for a long time been an advantage of Comparative Economics. However, it should be acknowledged that over the past two decades scholars from other fields have also started considering economic and social development comprehensively. This concerns political scientists comparing different types of a market economy within the Varieties of Capitalism framework, as well as economists using the New Institutional Economics approaches. The "limited access orders" (LAO) framework elaborated in the late works of Douglass North (North et al. 2009, 2013) deserve special mention. In addition to the role of non-economic factors (and violence in particular), an important strength of the LAO framework is its understanding of the evolution of social orders resulting from changes in their institutions. North and his co-authors acknowledge the possibility of both progress and regress of the LAO. However, despite all its broadness, the LAO framework is a very general theoretical concept. Its empirical testing and further substantive development would require an analysis of historical cases of individual countries. And this is where the rich experience of Comparative Economics can be applied, with detailed studies of transition in Eastern Europe and the former Soviet Union and an analysis of the possibilities of transition from one model of the economy and society to another.

It is also important to understand that each economic system is characterized by its own institutions, both formal and informal ones. But the effectiveness of these institutions changes over time. What used to be effective in the USSR in the 1950s was no longer working in the 1960s and 1970s as the economy and society became more complex and complicated. Experience of transition in the 1990s showed that mere transfer of different institutions from another economic system is not a solution. To ensure successful transition from one model to another requires a search for institutions that would be compatible with the institutions of the old model, while simultaneously being able to ensure economic and social development as part of the movement toward the new model. In this regard, CES should also take into consideration the concept of "second best institutions" proposed by scholars of development economics (Rodrik 2008) when elaborating economic policy ideas.

Question 3. *Innovation and technical progress are perhaps more important than in the past for the competitiveness of enterprises and economies. This is due, among others, to the integration of economies and the consequent need to better coordinate macro-policies. As a consequence, the importance of the context for innovation – including particularly technological innovations, organizational innovation and social innovation – is increasingly important and this highlights the critical significance of the economic system and its features. Incremental innovation and path-breaking innovation are apparently the preferred domain of different countries, as much as labor mobility and investment of human capital are. In which sense and how can the economic system support the innovation in enterprises and of countries and how can the study of Comparative Economic Systems highlight and explain the different working of markets, the performance of enterprises and countries in innovation?*

Brezinski: The various economic systems have different approaches to the handling and embeddedness of innovation in their respective systems. In market-type systems, innovations are driven on the enterprise level by incentives given to the entrepreneurs and investors. Private property rights especially concerning intellectual capital must be secured for a certain fixed period thus allowing for pioneer profits. However, these temporary monopoly profits should just attract investors and entrepreneurs to look for innovative solutions to overcome the monopolistic barriers of entry into markets. Research for basic technical innovations regarded as public goods on the other side must be promoted and financed by the society. In socialist planned economies, technology-driven innovation is regarded as a top-down process, decided by central planning authorities.

This used to be the standard approach of Comparative Economic Systems. Modern Comparative Economic Systems looks at the coevolution between private and public institutions. History has shown us plenty of different cases where this coevolution in democratic market-type economies took place. Almudi and Fatas-Villafranca mention numerous examples in their recent study on "Coevolution in Economic systems" (2021) such as coevolution in industries like civil engineering and construction, nanotechnology and medical devices and the case of radical innovations in computer software such as the specific case of the development of COBOL which emerged from joint activities by Grace B. Hopper, the US Navy and private corporations closely connected with universities. Pyrgidis on the other hand shows the case of high-speed train technology in present China which can be characterized by an autocratic and socialist regime (2018). The previously mentioned examples demonstrate that CES will benefit from the integration of the evolutionary approach. A major part of innovations is driven by a dialog between various disciplines which is also demonstrated when looking at the experiences in smart specialization where, e.g., a cooperation of the traditional textile industry with material science has led to a structural change and led to the transformation toward the production of technical textiles leading to a rebirth of textile industry at the traditional locations such as in the region of Lyon or in Saxony. Moreover, the challenges ahead force us to consider also organizational and social innovation. CES will have to analyze the various solutions in organizational innovation to improve economic efficiency. One new example for such an organizational innovation is the gig economy described by Mankiw et al. (2019) which can be characterized as a labor market in which workers, more akin to being self-employed than employed, have short-term, freelance or zero hours contracts with employers. CES must also look at social innovations leading to less consumption of resources such as car sharing, renting of E-scooters in city centers, reuse of computers, public book shelves or food sharing. Thus, CES by looking at these cases and analyzing the institutional arrangements which are favorable for an implementation of these innovations can offer a better understanding for the development of economic systems.

Douarin: As highlighted in the question itself, innovation is a social product. The ways problems are identified, ideas emerged and can be translated in solutions to societal problems are all socially embedded processes, which depends on education, values, infrastructure, the economic system, etc. Thus, the extent to which the overall innovation process is based on interdependences and spillovers means that a methodology focusing on individuals and their personal incentives does not seem particularly well suited. Building on my previous answers, small-scale interventions where it is possible to "keep constant" many of the parameters that are likely relevant to innovation – depending on the economic system? – can be useful, but external validity, and thus broader lessons for comparative development are maybe more likely to come from a broader understanding of systems and their relevant components. This is recognizing that different policies are likely to be needed in different contexts and different policies have different effects in different economic systems (see Amable 2000). In a globalized economy, it may be more important to stress that different objectives might be pursued in different places, among other things, as a way to emphasize complementarities rather than competition, to recognize that different societies might also pursue different objectives when it comes to identifying "progress" or development; or that there are different ways of getting to the same outcomes (e.g. Bruno and Estrin 2021).

Gregory: The early studies of innovation and technical progress used a residual approach to measure the pace of innovation and technical progress. Technological progress was measured by what was left over after we had calculated the contribution of labor and capital. Yes, innovation and technological progress still cannot be measured directly, although we tend to have good intuition as to the innovations that have changed our lives. Hence, we were left with compilations of important innovations, in what economic system they occurred, and we can seek for explanations of why. Despite this crude approach, we recognize that the economic system matters as far as innovation is concerned. The Soviet economic system, for example, shunned innovation because the complexity of planning required a form of planning based on incremental change – planning from the achieved level. We know that rewards to innovators matter. Why undertake entrepreneurial risk, if the rewards go elsewhere? Also, we know that financial systems based on current-day bank lending cannot create venture capital markets. We also understand that granting property rights to innovators, say, in the form of patents, should spur the competitiveness of enterprises and economies.

An under-researched issue has been the dominant role of US innovation in the world economy (joined to a lesser degree by Israel and Switzerland) that has allowed the rest of the world to piggyback from US innovation, and, in the case of China, to acquire innovation by theft. We must ask whether such a model of the distribution of innovation among economic systems is viable?

Lin: Innovation embodied in swift technological progress and industrial upgrading is the foundation to trigger sweeping structural changes and make an economy transformed from a stagnant traditional agrarian economy to a dynamic modern economy (Kuznets 1966).

For a developed country, the innovation means implementation of new invention and sometimes path breaking because its technologies and industries have already been in the global frontiers. Historical evidence shows that the advanced countries achieve on average 2 percent growth in per capita GDP annually since the mid-19th century (Maddison 2006). Developing countries with different economic systems may have different performances in terms of allocative efficiency, equity, health and other dimensions of development. However, a developing country, no matter with what type of economic system, has the potential to grow faster than advanced countries due to the existence of both advantages of backwardness, which refers to the lower opportunity cost of adopting a new vintage of technology directly in its upgrading to a new industry, while the advanced countries need to retire the old vintage before adopting the new vintage (Gerschenkron 1962), and the latecomer advantages, which refers to the possibility for a developing country to borrow better, often mature and not necessary new, technologies from advanced countries at a cost lower than reinventing it (Lin 2016).

No matter with what type of economic system for a developing country to tap into the above two potential sources of rapid growth, the country's enterprises must carry out their innovations according to changes in the economy's comparative advantages so that they have production costs advantage in domestic and international markets and the state needs to play a facilitating role for compensating the first mover's externality and overcoming bottlenecks in infrastructure and related institutions in the superstructure so as to reduce transaction costs and turn the comparative advantages from "latent" to "actual" (Lin and Monga 2012). Due to the constraints of available resources and implementation capacity, the state in a developing country with overall poor infrastructure and business environment in the economy needs to play its facilitating function pragmatically (Lin 2011b, 2017). One feasible strategy is to target industries of the country's latent comparative advantages in its investment promotions and building special economic zones to provide adequate infrastructure and business environment in the enclaves for the targeted industries so as to jumpstart a dynamic growth and pave the economic foundation to expand the infrastructure improvements to other parts of the economy and trigger transformations in upper structures. With this pragmatic approach, there is a hope that any country with whatsoever economic system can grow dynamically (Lin and Monga 2017).

In view of the advancement of artificial intelligence in the Fourth Industrial Revolution and the coming of automation age with robots replacing labor in most industries, the developing countries should strive to grow as fast and accumulate capital, both financial and human, as much as possible by improving their infrastructure and reforming their institutions to turn their existing comparative advantages from latent to actual so that they will have suffi-cient capital and conducive environment to employ robots in industries of their comparative advantages, generate sufficient decent jobs in other activities for the labor replaced by robots and maintain competitiveness in the globalized world when the era arrives, just like what happened in the previous generations of industrial revolution, also featured by labor-saving and/or labor-replacement technological changes.

Myant: Innovation has always been important for economic and social development and for the competitiveness of firms and countries. The distinction between incremental and "path breaking" innovations is valid at a general level, but not the most helpful for understanding the innovation process. A more fruitful observation is the extent to which innovations require involvement of multiple actors, from a range of organizations and with diverse incentives, including often a massive role for state-funded research. "Standard" economic theory is out of its depths here, its advocates often pointing only to increasing financial incentives through tax concessions, a factor found from comparative analyses to be of limited importance. There is no alternative to setting innovation within the context of a broader economic system and adopting a comparative approach, as used over many years in studies by the OECD, putting together the diverse causal factors in the concept of national innovation systems.

Studies of socialist economies before 1989 showed that substantial innovation activity took place, despite the apparent weakness of financial incentives, but that it was inferior to that in the most advanced capitalist economies. Studies also showed the diversity of systemic factors determining this lag, including incentives at various levels, organizational barriers and rigidities, limited international contacts and restrictions on the free flow of information. Creating the basic frameworks of open market economies eliminated some of these barriers but also failed to create, or even maintain, elements of the necessary support system for successful innovation.

It is noteworthy that among the few successful innovation areas in East–Central Europe have been those that require neither public backing nor complex networks of contacts, such as some areas of computer software. Among the biggest failures were firms that could not even afford incremental innovations as new owners extracted wealth for their personal enrichment. Thus, the comparative approach, between countries and time periods, is essential for showing the innovation potential of different economic systems.

Tanzi: In the distant past innovation and technological progress played very limited roles in the countries' economies. However, starting with the industrial revolution, technological change became very important and slowly changed the way people looked at technology. It changed the productivity of many workers; it created large concentration of workers and output in a few places; and, because of that, it made it possible for governments to increase the level of taxes and public spending in their economies (Tanzi 2018a). The Industrial Revolution was in many ways the most radical of all revolutions in its long-run impact on countries and economies.

Such a revolution changed the policies that were possible and needed by countries. It also created greater needs for coordinating some global policies, including the mobility of able individuals and the sharing of innovations. While in the distant past all countries had been, to some extent, "developing countries", the industrial revolution created a sharper distinction between rich and poor countries.

The distinction depended largely on the countries' ability to create human capital and the conditions for the promotion of innovations and their exploitation for improving productivity and incomes. Some countries were better able to create good schools and, especially, to create the social conditions that could attract rare talent from the rest of the world. The USA, more than others, benefited from its ability to attract talented innovators from the rest of the world. Many of the US Nobel Prize Winners and innovators have been individuals born in other countries. Their talent might not have been recognized and used in their countries of origin. The attraction of this talent was partly due to abundant resources, partly to flexible institutions, and partly to laws that, with some exceptions, reduced obstacles to the newly arrived.

The study of comparative economic systems should in part focus on the institutions that have made some countries better able than others to change and adapt the institutions and the conditions that have facilitated the developments of innovations and that have promoted their welfare. For example, why it is easier for Italian scholars to get academic positions in some foreign universities than it is for foreigners to get comparable positions in Italian Universities?

Yakovlev: The USSR's defeat in the Cold War was largely predetermined by a lack of incentives for innovation and introduction of new technologies at enterprise level (Kornai 1980). The USSR succeeded in achieving a military-strategic parity with the USA by creating the necessary technology through concentration of enormous resources in priority sectors and tight administrative pressure on the heads of research centers and enterprise directors. However, the Soviet planned economy proved incapable of leveraging new technologies to increase productivity in civilian industries. Under these circumstances, the economics was dominated by the idea that the necessary incentives for innovation were generated by competition between firms within a liberal market economy.

Nevertheless, China's impressive technological leap over the past 15–20 years raises new questions for comparative studies of economic systems. As in the case of the USSR in the 1930s, this leap was initially triggered by active borrowing of technology. But afterwards Chinese firms began offering their own technological solutions and today they openly compete with companies from developed countries.

This result was achieved due to the export orientation of the Chinese economy – in the logic of the catch-up development models in Japan and South Korea (Johnson 1982; Amsden 1989). However, the banking, energy and infrastructure sectors in China remain under state control. The authorities also exert a strong influence on the actions of the owners of private firms. The COVID-19 pandemic has created a new dimension for competition of different economic models, raising questions about the effectiveness of national health systems and their ability to respond adequately to such crises. In this context, the experience of Comparative Economics in analyzing innovation processes and incentives for innovation in economies and societies with a high stake of the state is likely to be in demand in the coming years.

Question 4. *In recent years, inequalities within countries have been significantly increasing, although inequalities among countries decreased in various significant cases. At the same time, social and intergenerational mobility slowed down. Within enterprises and in the economy at large, efforts were concentrated on the attempt to attract highly mobile capital to the disadvantage of labor. At the same time, the increasing importance of knowledge and specialized skills created a growing split among employees to the disadvantage of low-skill workers. How far can the lack of a systemic alternative, such as the Soviet Union and socialist countries in the past, explain the greater cohesion of societies and the lack of governance of globalization that generated some of these effects? Can the revival of external threats in the form of the pandemic, the climate and environmental emergency and (for Western countries) the emergence of China (and vice versa for China) help move governments to better manage and ease those effects? Should the study of Comparative Economic Systems deal more with these issues?*

Brezinski: The study of CES has for a long time concentrated especially on capitalist economies and socialist economies. The collapse of the socialist countries after 1989 and the systemic change of most of these countries were especially analyzed by CES neglecting to a large extent the developing economies. CES has focused on the study of economic institutions by dividing them into inclusive and extractive economic institutions. Inclusive economic institutions offer secure property rights, create a legal system allowing for reliable private contracts and financial transactions as well as for a relatively open access to markets and education. Extractive economic institutions on the contrary create insecure property rights, partial judicial systems and entry barriers which protect a small segment of the society at the expense of the rest. A vacuum of appropriate inclusive economic institutions and the return of old extractive economic institutions gave rise to enormous inequalities in income and wealth within these countries. CES must analyze in the future more than ever, how appropriate inclusive economic institutions can be created because they do not emerge by itself. This relates specially to developing economies. Foreign aid does not automatically wipe out poverty. CES must pay attention to the institutional roots as well to geographical and cultural aspects to contribute in a positive way to the debate of sustainable development.

In the recent past, the development of information and communication technologies has given additional rise to the emergence of higher inequalities within developed industrialized nations but also between developing and industrialized nations. Digitalization has contributed to a faster shift toward the service sector and led to increasing differences in income in favor of the modern service sector and to the disadvantage of the traditional manufacturing sector. Moreover, the fast rise of digitalization led to the emergence of global tycoons such as Google, Amazon and Facebook endowing them with de facto monopolistic positions and getting taxed their profits in states with favorable tax conditions. The less developing countries not being able to build up a digital infrastructure will suffer from being reduced to the role of delivering raw materials and being at best producers of manufacture which in turn will have dramatic consequences for environment and climate. Those who will seize the opportunities provided by information and communication technologies may become dominant powers and thus change geopolitics as is witnessed in the case of China. Rising inequalities do manifest themselves not only in income but also in a more difficult access to better living conditions and genuine human rights. One of the consequences will be rising migration. CES consequently will have to put the focus on the impact of digitalization and the rise of artificial intelligence on the chances to achieve the Sustainable Development Goals. The changing geopolitical situation will be a challenge for the present democratic market-typed economies toward autocratic regimes. The study of CES may provide us by starting out in an interdisciplinary way with innovative institutional arrangements. By comparisons, you do not start out from the scratch. However, you will get ideas how to restructure your inclusive economic institutions. Moreover, modern CES has turned out in the past by being open for new economic theories such as especially new institutional economics, evolutionary economics, behavioral economics and able to integrate geopolitics by the new field of geoeconomics being the study of the spatial, temporal and political aspects of economies and resources.

Douarin: In recent years, issues around inequality and social mobility have attracted more interest. One characteristic of both is that there is little scope to set objective targets of what inequality or social mobility should be. The alternative is thus instead to focus on (context-specific) desirable benchmarks, and this can only mean exploring the realities of these phenomena through a comparative lens, and in an integrated fashion – in line with what I would identify as the key "comparative advantage" of comparative economic systems (as also argued in my responses above).

Now, can the existence of systemic alternative incentivize this comparative approach? Yes, but to me there are enough "alternative systems" already, and polarization might not help. The polarization of economic systems into socialist versus capitalist systems has always been an oversimplified way of characterizing systems, even at odd with the reality of the work done within the field of Comparative Economic Systems. Within the "socialist bloc", differences existed in the organization of decision-making and its degree of centralization, the provision and coordination of information (i.e. the extent of planning, as opposed to reliance on market mechanisms), the extend of private property or the scope to engage in private economic activities, the incentive structure (to paraphrase the "features of Economic Systems", as defined in Gregory and Stuart 1985, p. 22). Systems are indeed defined along different dimensions and more often than not, data points do not exclusively congregate at opposite ends of the spectrum on all of them to form a small number of neatly defined clusters with strongly contrasted characteristics. Thirty years after, the fall of the Berlin Wall, discussions of systems sometimes continue to over-emphasize simplified characterization that can blur the policy debate. As an example of this, the operationalization of specific concepts in the empirical literature is not systematically consistent: is there a commonly accepted definition and operationalization of "neo-liberalism" or even "socialism" in the 21st century? With this in mind, narratives around threat by encouraging simplified, and highly contrasted, characterization of systems might actually be detrimental to the relevant academic debate itself, but more importantly to how it is translated in the public debate. There is no doubt that there is a lot to learn from a comparative analysis of systems, but learning is more likely when engaging in a detailed and nuanced characterization of these systems.

External threats, such as the current pandemic, or climate emergencies are possibly more interesting, as they can be seen as "system-stressors" (see my answers to *Questions 1 and 2* above) and offer an opportunity to gain more knowledge about the fragilities and areas of resilience of different systems and thus better understand their distinctive features and their relevance.

Gregory: Comparative economists have devoted considerable research to income inequality. We are interested in "fairness" and in the trade-offs between the distribution of income and economic performance. We still lack answers as to this relationship. How income is distributed is often pigeonholed under value judgments. Often the presumption is that the more equal the distribution of income, the "better" the distribution.

Counter to the presumption that more equal automatically equals "better" is the fact that innovation is stimulated if the innovators can keep the rents from their innovation. A sophisticated property right system may allow the innovator to maintain ownership of the innovation through patents. Finally, there is the matter of differential wages to foster greater effort and the incentive to move up the pay ladder.

We have valuable case studies of the effects of income distribution on performance of centrally planned economies. In the command socialist economy, only charges for depreciation captured capital costs, and gains to innovation were practically non-existent insofar as the gains to innovation did not go to innovators but were passed on as lower prices. Wages were differentiated largely on the basis of labor-market forces in which enterprise had to pay a quasi-market price for labor.

In sum, there was practically no "capital income" in planned economies. So, the planned economies gave us case studies of economies lacking in non-wage income.

Income distribution studies from the Cold War era yielded some surprising results. If we compare the two prototypes of planned and market economies (the USA and USSR), we do indeed find a more unequal distribution of income under the capitalist variant. But if we compare the European welfare states with the planned economies of Eastern Europe, we cannot find any real difference in the after-tax distribution of income.

The lesson from these studies is that capitalist countries can maintain after-tax income distributions that are nearly identical to those of planned socialist countries. A capitalist society that chooses a welfare state can match the level of equality of centrally planned economies. This was a surprising result at the time. It suggested that, if income equality is a major objective, the European welfare state could produce this result and achieve higher levels of income and efficiency.

Lin: To achieve dynamic economic development with continuous improvement in income distribution, that is the common prosperity advocated by President Xi Jinping of China, is a dream for any nation.

Countries with different economic systems may put different policy weights on efficiency and equity due to their value or ideological reasons. From the perspective of new structural economics, the best way to achieve a dynamic, sustainable and inclusive growth in a country is to follow the following principles: (1) to develop a country's production structure according to the country's comparative advantages in a market economy with a facilitating state to ensure market competition and overcome hard and soft infrastructure bottlenecks for technological innovation and industrial upgrading so that the equity and efficiency can be achieved simultaneously in the primary distribution: (2) the state uses funds from tax revenues to carry out secondary distribution, with a strength determined by the country's value and ideological orientation, to further narrow the gap of income distribution arising from inequalities in inherited wealth, social networks and innate talents and use inheritance tax to reduce the intergenerational transmission of wealth gap; and (3) values of mutual cares are encouraged and tax incentives are provided to encourage philanthropic donations to help the under privileged and support other social goods such as research and innovation as a means for the tertiary distribution.

The source of income for the poor is primarily the wage earnings from their labor employment, while the rich have a large share of income from capital earnings. The first principle will lead to efficiency and rapid growth in a country, which is elaborated in my response to *Question 3*. The rapid growth will narrow the country's income gap with advanced countries, contributing to the equity across countries. More importantly, the principle will also result in equity within the country because not only largest possible amount of jobs will be generated so the poor will have more opportunities to be employed than otherwise but also capital will be accumulated fast, causing relative prices of labor to capital to rise rapidly in favor of the poor wage earners over the rich capital owners (Lin and Liu 2008; Kuo, Fei and Ranis 1979). In addition, in such an economy, the enterprises will be viable in open, competitive market and the state does not oblige to give them protection and subsidies (Lin and Tang 1999). Therefore, the state will have more resources for secondary distribution than otherwise from both the tax revenues of dynamic economic growth and no needs of subsidizing nonviable enterprises. The income distribution will be further improved if the state uses its available resources to incentivize and facilitate entrepreneurs' technological innovation and industrial upgrading according to the change in comparative advantages so as to generate more higher income jobs, to invest in the poor's human capital to make them employable in higher skill works and to provide direct transfer through social benefits for the underprivileged to mitigate the adverse distributional effects of personal endowments in wealth and talents. The third principle is also desirable in the modern world. Due to rapid technological innovations and structural transformation, some technology and business geniuses will become super rich quickly. Tax incentives should be provided to encourage philanthropic donations, which should also receive social recognitions, for their own self-satisfaction and for social harmony and a better society.

Due to the differences in the endowment structure and cultural heritage for countries at different levels of development, their economic systems will be different in many aspects. Moreover, due to the fact that an institutional service can be provided by different institutional arrangements and institutional change proceeds in a path-dependence manner, for countries at a similar level of development, their economic systems are also likely to have many different institutional features. So just like no two apples look exactly the same, the economic system in each country will be somewhat different. The system plurality in the world, just like biodiversity, should be appreciated. No matter with what economic systems, people in all nation in the world share the same dream of growth with equity. Hope the humanity's internal drive for betterment and the competition among different economic systems will bring the impetus for institutional reforms and innovation to achieve growth with equity and the study of Comparative Economic Systems will enhance our understanding about how an economic system functions and contributes to the ideas, policies and institutional reforms for realizing the dream in every country in the world.

Myant: This question ranges over problems that cannot be resolved without big political and social changes and international coordination. That said, inequalities in income and wealth within countries, although accentuated by international pressures, can be addressed, at least in part, within individual countries. They cannot be understood from a narrowly economic perspective. Causes of trends are diverse including the effects of globalization, which has hit particular social groups in different parts of the world, and specific policy choices that have increased inequalities both before and after taxes. The comparative historical approach used by Piketty (2014) also shows the importance of countervailing policy measures and events that in certain periods temporarily reversed the tendency for inequalities to increase as inherited wealth increases privilege through the generations. To these factors can be added a positive feedback loop such that the more high-income people there are, the more political influence they can wield to defend and enhance their privileged position.

A comparative approach, as much comparing time periods as countries, has been crucial to understanding this. Remedies proposed by Atkinson (2015) – giving a universal endowment to young adults to break the advantage conferred to others from inherited wealth – and by Piketty – a progressive global tax on capital – might not appear to require fundamental changes to the economic system. However, they have been widely criticized as unrealistic which is a fair assessment of current political realities and hence of the extent to which economic changes depend on wider changes in society.

Tanzi: Different economic systems have given more importance in their policies either to efficiency or to equity.

The laissez faire systems generally favored efficiency and paid little attention to equity. The centrally planned systems generally favored equity and paid a price in efficiency. The welfare states, which came into existence after World War II, tried to accommodate both growth and equity. There continues to be debate among economists as to the extent that they have succeeded. The "market fundamentalism" or "supply-side economics", which became fashionable (especially in Anglo-Saxon countries), in the 1980s and later years, gave preference to efficiency and paid a high price in equity. One of the most prominent supporters of "supply-side economics", the Nobel Prize Winner, Robert Lucas, was reported to have declared that: "Of all the tendency that are harmful to sound economics, the most seductive, and ... the most poisonous is to focus on questions of distribution" (Tanzi 2018b, p. 38).

In recent decades, most of the countries that had been "centrally-planned", including China, made a transition toward a market economy. In the process, they became more economically efficient, but their income distributions became less equal. Especially Anglo-Saxon countries became more "supply-side oriented" and saw their Gini coefficients go up significantly. It is less evident that they became more efficient.

On the other hand, several "welfare states", and especially the Scandinavian countries and a few others, have managed to remain more equitable, without paying high prices in terms of efficiency and economic liberty. These countries continue to do well in comparative indices of income distribution, labor force participation, economic liberty, economic performance and other relevant indices.

There should be a wide scope for analyzing in more details and analytically the differences in efficiency and equity among these groups of countries. Some differences are obvious. Others less so. Analysis should replace a priori conclusions and should also consider, to the extent possible, non-economic factors such as culture, legal systems, social relations and, perhaps, even history.

Yakovlev: To ensure further development of Comparative Economics, it is important to understand that norms and values are an essential element of economic systems (or social orders). As Dani Rodrik pointed some years ago, "new ideas about policy ... can exert an independent effect on equilibrium outcomes even in the absence of changes in the configuration of political power" (Rodrik 2014. p. 190). Just as technological innovations relax the conventional resource constraint, political innovation relaxes the political transformation frontier and open up opportunities for a new level of development. However, these opportunities can materialize only if the relevant ideas are confirmed in real life. Otherwise, systematic discrepancy between declared values and reality can generate deep disappointment and cynicism in society, which will undermine incentives for development (as has been the case in the USSR since the late 1960s).

In this context, part of the agenda for the CES is to analyze the competition of ideas that underlie different models of economic and social organization and which are (or are not) confirmed in practice over the long term. To carry out such an analysis, it is important to take a political economy perspective on how new ideas are formed and implemented in the field of economic policy. In particular: the interests of what social groups do they represent? To what extent do the new ideas correlate with the interests of the political and business elites? Who benefits and who loses from their implementation? It is equally important to understand that while economic systems compete, they also learn from each other. And the ability to borrow an alternative economic model's effective elements is a sign of sustainability of that model.

From this point of view, the disappearance of the systemic alternative represented by the USSR and the socialist countries led in the 1990s and 2000s to an easing of pressure on the elites and to the elites' lesser willingness to self-restrict for the sake of broader public interests. The growing social tensions in the developed world (which became evident in the mid-2010s) and the emergence of the Chinese alternative certainly require new solutions and open up possibilities for comparative economics.

Note

1 Andrei Yakovlev's contribution reflects the results of research prepared within the framework of the Basic Research Program at the HSE University.

References

Almudi, I. and Fatas-Villlafranca, F. (2021). *Coevolution in Economic Systems*, Cambridge: Cambridge University Press.

Amable, B. (2000). "Institutional Complementarity and Diversity of Social Systems of Innovation and Production," *Review of International Political Economy*, 7 (4): 645–687.

Amsden, A.H. (1989). *Asia's Next Giant: South Korea and Late Industrialization*, New York, NY: Oxford University Press.

Atkinson, A.B. (2015). *Inequality What Can Be Done?* Cambridge, MA: Harvard University Press.

Bentkowska, K. (2021). "Response to Governmental COVID-19 Restrictions: The Role of Informal Institutions," *Journal of Institutional Economics*, 17 (5): 729–745.

Brunnermeier, M.K. (2021). *The Resilient Society*, Washington, DC: Endeavor Litbury Press LLC.

Bruno, R. and Estrin, S. (2021). "Taxonomies and Typologies: Starting to Reframe Economic Systems," in E. Douarin and O. Havrylyshyn, eds. *The Palgrave Handbook of Comparative Economics*, Cham: Palgrave Macmillan.

Bruszt, L., Campos, N., Fidrmuc, J. and Roland, G. (2012). "Civil Society, Institutional Change and the Politics of Reform: The Great Transition," in G. Roland, ed. *Economies of Transition the Long-Run View, Studies in Development Economics and Policy*, Cham: Palgrave Macmillan, pp. 194–221.

Chavance, B. (2009). *Institutional Economics*, London and New York: Routledge.

Djankov, S. (2021). "Effect of Historical Forces on Liberalization and Democratization in Transition," in E. Douarin and O. Havrylyshyn, eds. *The Palgrave Handbook of Comparative Economics*, Cham: Palgrave Macmillan.

Djankov, S., Glaeser, E., La Porta, R., Lopez-de-Silanes, F. and Shleifer, A. (2003). "The New Comparative Economics," *Journal of Comparative Economics*, 31 (4): 595–619.

Douarin, E. (2021). "Institutional Change in Transition: An Evolving Research Agenda," in E. Douarin and O. Havrylyshyn, eds. *The Palgrave Handbook of Comparative Economics*, Cham: Palgrave Macmillan.

Douarin, E. and Havrylyshyn, O. (2021a). "Introduction to the Palgrave Handbook of Comparative Economics," in E. Douarin and O. Havrylyshyn, eds. *The Palgrave Handbook of Comparative Economics*, Cham: Palgrave Macmillan, pp. 1–15.

Douarin, E. and Havrylyshyn, O. (2021b). "Conclusions: So, What Is Comparative Economics Now?" in E. Douarin and O. Havrylyshyn, eds. *The Palgrave Handbook of Comparative Economics*, Cham: Palgrave Macmillan.

Easterly, W. (2001). "The Lost Decades: Developing Countries' Stagnation in Spite of Policy Reform 1980-1998," *Journal of Economic Growth*, 6: 135–157.

Fukuyama, F. (1989). "The End of History?" *National Interest*, 16 (Summer 1989): 3–18.

Gerschenkron, A. (1962). *Economic Backwardness in Historical Perspective, a Book of Essays*, Cambridge, MA: Belknap Press of Harvard University Press.

Gregory, P. and Stuart, R. (1985). *Comparative Economic Systems*, 2nd ed., Boston, MA: Houghton Mifflin Company.

Johnson, C. (1982). *MITI and the Japanese Miracle: The Growth of Industrial Policy, 1925–1975*, Stanford: Stanford University Press.

Kornai, J. (1980). *Economics of Shortage*, Vol. *A–B*, Amsterdam: North Holland Press.

Kuo, S.W., Fei, J. and Ranis, G. (1979). *Growth with Equity: The Taiwan Case*, London: Oxford University Press.

Kuznets, S. (1966). *Modern Economic Growth: Rate, Structure and Speed*, New Haven, CT: Yale University Press; Oxford, UK: Oxford University Press.

Lin, J.Y. (1989). "An Economic Theory of Institutional Change: Induced and Imposed Change," *Cato Journal*, 9, Sep 1989: 1–33.

Lin, J.Y. (2009). *Economic Development and Transition: Thought, Strategy and Viability*, Cambridge, UK: Cambridge University Press.

Lin, J.Y. (2011a). "New Structural Economics: A Framework for Rethinking Economic Development," *World Bank Observer, 26*: 193–221.

Lin, J.Y. (2011b). "Growth Identification and Facilitation: The Role of State in the Process of Dynamic Growth," *Development Policy Review, 29* (3): 264–290; "Rejoinder": 304–309.

Lin, J.Y. (2014). "The Washington Consensus Revisited: A New Structural Economics Perspective," *Journal of Economic Policy Reform, 18* (2): 96–113.

Lin, J.Y. (2016). "The Latecomer Advantages and Disadvantages: A New Structural Economics Perspective," in M. Andersson and T. Axelsson, eds. *Diverse Development Paths and Structural Transformation in Escape from Poverty,* Cambridge: Cambridge University Press, pp. 43–67.

Lin, J.Y. (2017). "Industrial Policies for Avoiding the Middle-Income Trap: A New Structural Economics Perspective," *Journal of Chinese Economic and Business Studies, 15* (1): 5–18.

Lin, J.Y., Fang, C. and Li, Z. (1994). *The China Miracle: Development Strategy and Economic Reform,* Shanghai People's Publishing House and Shanghai Sanlian Sudian (for Mainland China); The Chinese University of Hong Kong Press, 1995 (for overseas), 1996 (English edition), Tokyo: Nihon Hyo Ron Sha, 1996 (Japanese edition); and Seoul: Baeksan Press, 1996 (Korean edition); Ho Chi Minh City: Saigon Times, 1999 (Vietnamese edition); Paris: Economica, 2000 (French edition); Shanghai People's Publishing House and Shanghai Sanlian Shudian, 1999 (revised version, for Mainland China).

Lin, J.Y. and Liu, P. (2008). "Achieving Equity and Efficiency Simultaneously in the Primary Distribution Stage in the People's Republic of China," *Asian Development Review, 25* (1–2), 34–57.

Lin, J.Y. and Monga, C. (2012). "The Growth Report and New Structural Economics," in J.Y. Lin, ed. *New Structural Economics: A Framework for Rethinking Development and Policy,* Washington, DC: The World Bank Press, pp. 83–112.

Lin, J.Y. and Monga, C. (2017). *Beating the Odds: Jump-starting Developing Countries,* Princeton, NJ: Princeton University Press.

Lin, J.Y. and Tang, G. (1999). "Policy Burdens, Accountability, and the Soft Budget Constraint," *American Economic Review: Papers and Proceedings, 89* (2), May 1999: 426–431.

Lipsey, R.G. and Lancaster, K. (1956). "The General Theory of Second Best," *Review of Economic Studies, 24* (1): 11–32.

Maddison, A. (2006). *The World Economy,* Paris: Organisation for Economic Cooperation and Development.

Mankiw, N.G., Taylor, M.P. and Ashwin, A. (2019). *Business Economics,* 3rd ed., Andover, MA: Cengage Learning, EMEA.

Murphy, K., Schleifer, A. and Vishny, R. (1992). "The Transition to a Market Economy: Pitfall of Partial Reform," *Quarterly Journal of Economics, 107*: 889–906.

Murrell, P. (1991). "Can Neoclassical Economics Underpin the Reform of Centrally Planned Economies?" *Journal of Economic Perspectives, 5* (4): 59–76.

North, D., Wallis, J.J. and Weingast, B.R. (2009). *Violence and Social Orders: A Conceptual Framework for Interpreting Recorded Human History,* Cambridge and New York: Cambridge University Press.

North, D., Wallis, J.J. and Weingast, B.R. eds. (2013). *In the Shadow of Violence: Politics, Economics, and the Problems of Development,* Cambridge: Cambridge University Press.

Piketty, T. (2014). *Capital in the Twenty-First Century,* Cambridge, MA: Belknap Press.

Pop-Eleches, G. and Tucker, J.A. (2017). *Communism's Shadow: Historical Legacies and Contemporary Political Attitudes,* Princeton, NJ: Princeton University Press.

Porter, M. (1990). *The Competitive Advantage of Nations,* New York, NY: The Free Press.

Pryor, F.L.P. (2005). "Market Economic Systems," *Journal of Comparative Economics, 33*, 25–46.

Pyrgidis, C.N. (2018). *Railway Transportation Systems: Design, Construction and Operation,* London: Taylor & Francis.

Rodrik, D. (2008). "Second-Best Institutions," *American Economic Review, 98* (2): 100–104.

Rodrik, D. (2014). "When Ideas Trump Interests: Preferences, Worldviews, and Policy Innovations," *Journal of Economic Perspectives, 28* (1): 189–208.

Samuelson, P. and Nordhaus, W. (1989). *Economics,* 13th ed., New York, NY: Richard D. Irwin.

Smith, R. (2021). "The Challenge of Identification and the Value of Descriptive Evidence," in E. Douarin and O. Havrylyshyn, eds. *The Palgrave Handbook of Comparative Economics,* Cham: Palgrave Macmillan.

Stiglitz, J. (1999). Whither Reform? Ten Years of the Transition. World Bank. Annual Bank Conference on Development Economics, Washington, DC, April 28–30, 1999.

Tanzi, V. (2018a). *The Ecology of Tax Systems: Factors That Shape the Demand and Supply of Taxes*, Cheltenham: E.E. Elgar.

Tanzi, V. (2018b). *Termites of the State: Why Complexity Leads to Inequality*, Cambridge: Cambridge University Press.

Tanzi, V. (2021). "Economic Theory Versus Economic Reality: Dealing With Global Public Goods and Bads," Chapter 1, in M. Mustafa Erdogdu, E. Alaverdov, A. Concepcion Garcia and K. Tryma, eds. *Impact of COVID-19 on Societies and Economies*, London: IJOPEC Publications. No. 2021/08.

Wiles, P. (1995). "Capitalist Triumphalism in the Eastern European Transition," in H. Chang and P. Nolan, eds. *The Transformation of the Communist Economies*, London: Macmillan Press, pp. 46–77.

INDEX